THE AMERICAN CITY

LITERARY SOURCES & DOCUMENTS

Edited and with an Introduction by
Graham Clarke

Volume III
The American City: The Individual Context

HELM INFORMATION

Selection and editorial matter

The Banks,
Mountfield,
near Robertsbridge,
East Sussex TN32 5JY
U.K.

ISBN: 1-873403-20-8

A CIP catalogue record for this book is available from the British Library.

Frontispiece: Photograph of Times Square, New York, 1992 by Don Hunstein

Printed on neutral-sized ('acid-free') paper and bound by Hartnolls Ltd, Bodmin, Cornwall

Contents

VOLUME III
The American City: The Individual Context

New York

Chicago

Los Angeles and San Francisco

Washington D. C.

Boston

New Orleans

Into the Desert: A Footnote on Las Vegas

List of Illustrations

Volume III:
The American City:
The Individual Context

Plate 21: Central Park, New York, 1864. Lithograph by Martel and H. Geissler

New York

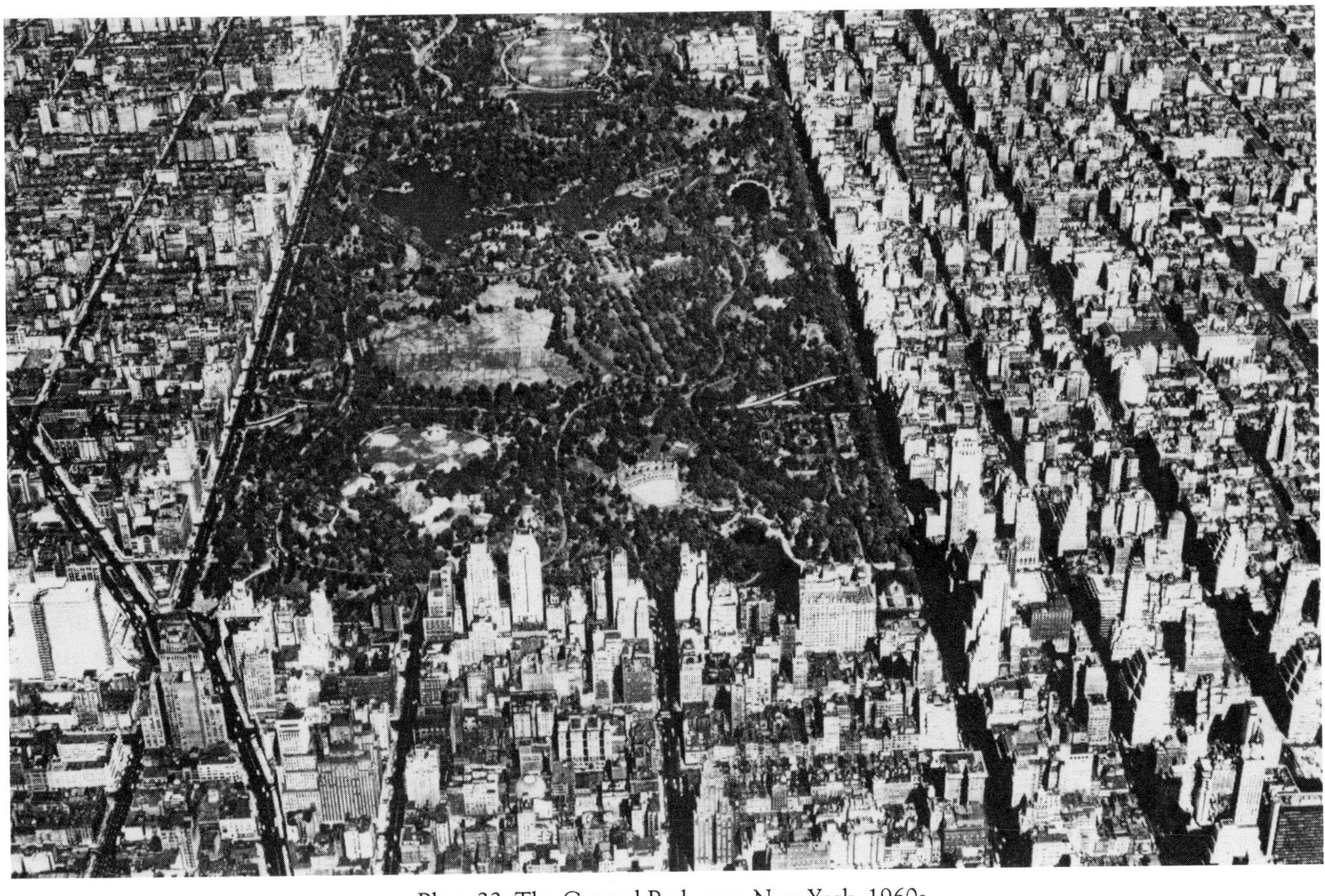

Plate 22: The Central Park area, New York, 1960s

93

A 'Sublime and Atrocious' Spectacle: New York and the Iconography of Manhattan Island

GRAHAM CLARKE

> "Please sir what's that?"
> "That's New York ... You see New York is on Manhattan Island."
> "Is it really on an island?"
> "Well what do you think of a boy who don't know that his own home town is on an island."
>
> John Dos Passos, *Manhattan Transfer*[1]

Two of the most memorable responses to New York City in the nineteenth century must surely be Walt Whitman's poem "Mannahatta" (1860) and Herman Melville's short story "Bartleby the Scrivener" (1853). Although seven years separates their publication part of their significance is that they not only offer very different experiences of the city, they suggest two of the fundamental, but contradictory poles between which the literary and pictorial responses to New York City have developed.

In Whitman's poem the city is a tangle of images alive with transcendent presence. In "Manhattan", "an/island sixteen miles long, solid founded" the poet sees

> *Numberless crowded streets, high growths of iron, slender, strong,*
> *light, splendidly uprising toward clear skies,*
> *Tides swift and ample, well-loved by me, toward sundown,*
> *The flowing sea—currents, the little islands, larger adjoining islands,*
> *the heights, the villas,*
> *The countless masts, the white shore-steamers, the lighters, the*
> *ferry-boats, the black sea-steamers well model'd.*[2]

The progression of Whitman's eye, as in "A Broadway Pageant", is undaunted. Manhattan is, to use Ben Lubeschz's phrase, a "magical island"[3]—imminent with

Source: Graham Clarke, "A 'Sublime and Atrocious' Spectacle: New York and the Iconography of Manhattan Island." (Look at New York, 1988). This is a specially revised version of an essay which originally appeared in *The American City: Literary and Cultural Perspectives*, ed. Graham Clarke, pp. 36–61.

spiritual meaning as it is also a city in the making. The details of the city (and its history) are seen as part of a larger unity: the transcendent destiny to which the city moves. It is "a city of spires and masts", a "city of hurried and sparkling waters". Energy, both natural and man-made, is seen as part of a single process on which the eye of the poet looks: a spectacle of wonder in which the *vertical* growth of the city is redolent of its promise. The "spires", "masts", "high growths" move upwards "towards clear skies"—the ultimate point of rest for a celestial city characteristic of American promise.

But "Bartleby" has nothing of this élan. If Whitman's New York is a city of light and energy, so Melville's is an anti-city redolent of Edgar Allan Poe and William Burroughs. "Bartleby the Scrivener" is the antithesis of Whitman's urban rhetoric. Indeed Bartleby is a character who neither speaks nor moves: seemingly the apex of urban alienation and meaninglessness. Just as Whitman's eye is liberated by what it sees in Manhattan, so Bartleby's is paralysed. "Bartleby" is thus a story of closure and enclosure. In its "view" of the city New York prohibits the movement of the eye just as it exhausts the spirit. Indeed Whitman's dynamic is displaced by a developing commercialism, for the setting of the story is Wall Street and Bartleby's office has only "an unobstructed view of a lofty brick wall" which, just ten feet from the window, has been made black by "age".[4] As the "wasted" Bartleby deteriorates within this environment, so he moves to the Tombs (a nineteenth-century city prison) in which he can only "stand at his window in his dead-wall reverie". Finally, unable to move or speak, he dies. "Bartleby the Scrivener", then, reverses Whitman's urban metaphysic and establishes a wholly different sense of the city. The *vertical* growth so basic to Whitman's image of "Mannahatta's" spiritual destiny is given its opposite image in the daunting and empty vacuum of Melville's New York: a *horizontal* axis which rarely leaves a street-level in which movement, such as it is, is into a dark and inner nothingness where the spirit is literally paralysed.

In Melville's *Pierre* (1852) we had moved deeper into this darkness, so that there the journey into New York City becomes an almost unconscious patterning of Bartleby's world writ large. The sense is of a *descent* into the environs of the city, as the characters ride over "the buried hearts" of "dead citizens" which have "come to the surface". To enter the city by night is thus to experience a verbal darkness which denies escape and meaning. As the novel moves deeper into this environment, so we hear "a strange shuffling and clattering", a "locking, and bolting, and barring of windows and doors; [for] the town's people are going to their Crane's city of "entrancing vistas"; it is, rather, a city of alleys: "long, narrow, dismal side-glooms" which emerge "from under dark beetling secrecies of mortar and stone".[5] An anti-city in which metropolis has become necropolis.

Melville's New York City, thus, reverses the image of the city found in Whitman's "Mannahatta". It is, as it were, its dark other. And yet their differences are not simply aspects of alternative ways of seeing the city. Rather, what they suggest are the extreme limits through which a sense of New York City has been viewed, and continues to be viewed, as a symbol of modern American urban life. And this symbolic significance is most obviously, held within the *visual* experience which the city offers. Thus Melville and Whitman are extremes because they suggest, in very direct ways, the opposing poles of New York's significance *as* (and perhaps *the*) American city.

Whitman's New York is essentially that of Manhattan: a visual experience in which the eye seeks the *upward* movement of the city's construction as redolent of other iconic codes. Melville's, in contrast, is downward and outwards. His New York is an experience of the street, not the sky; of the enclosed, not the open. Whitman's eye seeks the buildings of the city as images of construction and symbols of a larger process. Melville looks upon the individuals who live *within* those structures. Where Whitman seeks myth, so Melville implies history. As Whitman celebrates process, so Melville notes stasis. Just as Nick Carraway was both "simultaneously enchanted and repelled"[6] by his New York experience, so Whitman and Melville offer images of the city as both a "sublime" and "atrocious" spectacle. As such, Whitman looks upon Manhattan. Melville, in contrast, experiences New York City.

If I have laboured the distinctions, I do so precisely because they remain so fundamental to the way in which New York City has been "read" by writers and artists since the 1850s. Indeed, New York remains a double city. As Manhattan it retains its mythic promise and remains an image at once familiar and inviting. As New York City it becomes part of a different *urban* process: denied its mythic energy, its transcendent base, it moves into an historical reality in which social, political and economic questions are prominent. It becomes, in other words, a city of people rather than images—of social contingencies rather than mythic projections.

Even though Whitman's poem is from 1856, before any *distinctive* landmarks of the kind we would recognize today, it speaks to a sense of modern Manhattan to a high degree. For in its stress on the vertical, and its awareness of the sky, it suggests the fundamental sense of New York (as Manhattan) which every visitor to the city would recognize—that of the island's skyline. It thus speaks to a *modern* city: a city which, in the latter half of the nineteenth century, emerged as *the* city of modernism. Thus 1887 sees the construction of Brooklyn Bridge, 1909 of the Queensboro Bridge, in 1901 of the Flat Iron Building, in 1911 of the Woolworth Building, and in 1931 of the Empire State Building. All icons of a new (and commercial) urban city and yet, *as* icons, all part of a mythic Whitmanian process: the skyline which, even in its most clichéd response, still retains a sense of wonder. In part this fed upon the rapid growth of the city's immigrant population in the same period. As a major gateway, for millions of immigrants from Europe—Jews, Italians, Irish, Germans and Russians, for example—so Manhattan seemed the very image of radical promise: a new kind of city appropriate to the twentieth century. By 1900 fifty per cent of the city's population was foreign born, and in this the plurality of language and culture became part of its mythic energy: equivalent to the skyscrapers as part of the city's especial significance.

Melville's New York speaks to this *human* experience, to an awareness of what happens in a city which grows from a population of some 60,000 in 1800, to one of 3,400,000 in 1900 and 5,600,000 in 1920. The *density* of Melville's urban setting was actual, rather than symbolic. Indeed in parts of the Lower East Side, the density of population reached the equivalent of some 640,000 inhabitants per square mile.[7] If ethnic and religious diversity was to be celebrated, the immigrant areas also signified poverty on a massive scale. As the city grew commercially—evincing its image in the skyscraper office—so it grew also on the new pockets of immigrant settlement—on the Lower East Side, as Little Italy and SoHo added their presence to the Five Points Area, the Bowery, and to the west, Hell's Kitchen: a density of population which spreads out from the borough of Manhattan into the four other boroughs of New York City—Brooklyn, the Bronx, Queens and Richmond (Staten Island). An urban cityscape of tenement and brownstone, street and alley rather than skyscraper and bridge, avenue and park.

And yet Manhattan remains magical: a city in which

> steel, glass, tile, concrete will be the material of the skyscrapers. Crammed on the narrow island the million-windowed buildings will jut glittering, pyramid on pyramid like the white cloudhead above a thunderstorm.[8]

A city which promises "the centre of things" and into which the characters of *Manhattan Transfer* (1925) move—to Broadway (what Mayakovsky recognized as the "Great White Way" alive with "brightness, brightness, brightness")[9] to Lincoln Square and Columbus Circle. Onwards, as it were, in search of substance—to ground the spectacle of a city in the making. Thus the city's status—as I. N. Phelps Stokes called Manhattan in 1915, it is *the* "American Metropolis".[10]

This is, perhaps, the especial importance of *Manhattan Transfer*, a novel not so much concerned to *judge* the city as to admit to its design on inhabitant and spectator alike. Thus the sense, in the novel, of an endless energy and imagery always in the making. The effect is of an interplay between individuals and the city which denies, so to speak, interpretation in favour of a realized sense of process. Like the novel's title the city becomes an endless *transference* of meaning and energy held in a succession of images which promise significance but render only partial admittance. Thus the double nature of the novel—aware of what the city does (to its inhabitants) but, equally, spellbound by its activity and energy as both image and experience. The city is both image and event.[11]

Manhattan Transfer, then, is a significant novel of the city as a modern phenomenon. As I have suggested, it moves between extreme iconographies within a dynamic energy *seen* as fundamental to the way Manhattan has been read. In this sense the human (historical) index—its dense texture and detail—has always been an experience of the street. The myth, in contrast, is sustained by the long view: the city as a single image in which what Roland Barthes called the city's "great commonplace" (the skyscraper) is dominant. Indeed Barthes sees the response to the city (*Manhattan*) as "a mythic combat ... between the base and the summit" of the skyscraper. In other words, the city's extreme points of reference: street and sky. A vertical symbolic code which changes as the eye moves *from* the base (the street) *to* the summit (the sky). History, as it were, gives way to myth as the eye moves upwards into the assumed dynamic of Manhattan's ultimate energy: the natural habitat of Whitman's Mannahatta. To view the city thus, for Barthes, is to "direct history into metaphysics." History, in this view, belongs to the street. "It is not up, toward the sky, that you must look in New York; it is down, toward men and merchandise. ..."[12]

To move the eye downward to "men and merchandise" is to confront the city as a history rather than as a myth—an *atrocious* New York—the New York of Stephen Crane and Theodore Dreiser, for example, where the focus is upon the tenement areas of Manhattan: the Lower East Side and the Bowery, in which the city is a dense and dark amalgam of human deprivation redolent of Melville's city of the dead. Thus in *Maggie* (1892):

> The girl went into the gloomy districts near the river, where the tall black factories shut in the street and only occasional broad beams of light fell across the pavements from saloons.[13]

And again, "further on in the darkness she met a ragged being with shifting, bloodshot eyes and grimy hands." In the "blackness of the final block" the "shutters of the tall buildings were closed like grim lips" while "At the feet of the tall buildings appeared the deathly black hue of the river."[14] This is more akin to Charles Dickens and James Thomson than Whitman. The experience of the street is at once grotesque and nightmarish—a blackness redolent of Maggie's inner condition. But this is also the *base* of a scale in which the human presence is so *dense* as to suggest a blackness from which it is impossible to escape. The density, as it were, *grounds* the eye, as it encloses it within an experience of the street as an endless nightmare: "a dark region" where doorways expel "loads of babies to the street and gutter" and buildings "quivered and creaked from the weight of humanity" in their "bowels".[15]

Maggie, of course, offers a view of the city characteristic of the naturalists. But it also suggests the way in which different *areas* of New York become part of an imagery in which the street functions as essentially threatening and dreamlike. Even while, for example, the New York of *Sister Carrie* moves between the Bowery and Broadway, the inference is of different aspects of the same condition. Broadway is a manufactured light—not the natural light of the sky beyond the skyscraper. The world at the *base* of the summit is garish as it is strange. Broadway and Times Square become part of a spectacle in which the street is "full of juggled colored lights" and "criss-crossed corrugations of glare".[16] A sense of Times Square echoed by John Rechy as "an electric island floating on a larger island of lonesome parks and lonesome apartment houses ...".[17]

Indeed these two scales of meaning—of natural and manufactured light, of street and sky—are basic to the way in which the camera is used to picture the city in the 1890s and 1900s. Maggie's world, for example, is most obviously that of Jacob Riis in *How the Other Half Lives* (1890), a series of photographs (and a text) dealing with appalling social and human poverty in the Lower East Side. Part of their significance is precisely the way *light* is brought into the areas photographed; to expose the poverty but also to literally *see* what is hidden by the darkness. In picture after picture there is a sense of private space lit up by the glare of the camera—a dark Manhattan of alley and slum where the human figures exist as roaches pushed together in small and enclosed spaces.

Lewis Hine's photographs of New York are quite different and yet they too are invariably committed to the street and to the human: the immigrant figures Hine photographed on Ellis Island or in the Lower East Side, for example. Once again there is a density of detail so that the figure is always viewed through its surroundings. Even when in the 1930s Hine photographs the construction of the Empire State Building, the figure is made central. We tend to look *down* upon the city below, not *up* toward the sky, with a human figure always present. Manhattan emerges as a human construction in which the figure is foregrounded in relation to historical and social contexts. Hine, as it were, displaces Whitman's mythic dynamic and gives the city over to its human basis.[18]

Hine, however, is distinctive for precisely how much he remains outside the myth of Manhattan: a position made more extreme by the extent to which Alfred Stieglitz—and the central group of New York artists and writers associated with him—remain *inside* it. In this sense Stieglitz seeks a visual equivalent to Whitman's rhetoric of "Mannahatta": a sense of the city as both transcendent spectacle and cultural milieu appropriate to a modernist metropolitan aesthetic.[19]

Stieglitz's photographs of the 1890s and 1900s, for example, image a city of Whitmanian energies. Whether the focus is upon a street or avenue, or of the city from a distance, the environment is invariably referred to an assumed ideal and abstract (natural) form. The photograph of the Flat Iron Building)1902), for example, suggests precisely this response. An image of the modern American city "still in the making",[20] it freezes the activity of construction so basic to *Manhattan Transfer*. And where Whitman's poems of Manhattan chant and chart an urban metaphysic, so Stieglitz's make *still* that which is radiant. As such Stieglitz's make *still* that which is radiant. As such Stieglitz effaces the human from his photographs and gives the city over to the play and presence of light and water: elements which "bathe" the city and expunge human marks from its text. The photographs seek a white city of radiant light—not a dark city of human evidence.

Rarely, for example, do we meet a human face in Stieglitz's photographs of New York. Rather, streets are emptied and erased of figures as they become part of a formal geometry. The dominant presence is water—the ideal medium of a radiant and transcendental America. The water which falls upon and surrounds the island of Manhattan in these photographs is not the black water of *Maggie*; it is the sacred water of *Walden*. And thus it *reigns* in the photographs: as mist, vapour, river, rain and snow; just as the presence of white (light) plays against dark. All are aspects of the Whitmanian rhetoric through which the images are sustained. In the 1930s, as Stieglitz moves higher and higher above the city—photographing it from the thirtieth floor of the mid-town Shelton Hotel—so his images of the city are literally emptied of the human. The Waldorf Astoria, the

General Electric Building and the Rockefeller Center have only a ghost-like presence: imaging back the shell of that transcendent base of the 1900s. Manhattan has been emptied of its energy as Stieglitz reaches the summit. From his position in the sky the street has all but disappeared. We are left with what Lewis Mumford called the "cold exhalations of a depopulated world".[21]

And yet Manhattan as the image of a radiant and mythic energy is clearly the belief of those artists and writers associated with Stieglitz. Indeed, it is basic to Paul Rosenfeld's *Port of New York* (1924) where if the city is the terminal for a European heritage (and aesthetic) brought to bear on the liberating energy of the American city, it is also a port given credence precisely by its spiritual presence—a dynamic, once again, held in the spectacle of a sublime iconography: its skyscrapers and bridges and the waters which surround it. For Rosenfeld (and the aesthetic for which he speaks) New York is the "ultimate edge of life". American artists, then, need no London, Paris or Venice. They "are content to remain in New York. In the *very middle* of the city, one can feel the *fluid of life* to be *present*" (my italics). Like Whitman, "One can see [the city's] mystic aspiration above the skyscrapers ..."[22]

Rosenfeld, like the Stieglitz group, reinforces Whitman's rhetoric with a visual vocabulary akin to its abstract principles. The *energy* it seeks to make *still* is part of a larger dynamic underpinning America as modernist text. As such it seeks the myth of Manhattan—not the history of New York. Manhattan exists as a liberating hieroglyph: an island in which change and process are part of a sacred energy. As Dreiser stated in *The Color of a Great City* (1930) Manhattan is a "new dynamic, new world metropolis" into which immigrants "from all parts of the world ... are pouring ..."[23]. But the dynamic is abstracted—part of a larger unity (and myth) in which the city takes its place.

In the work of John Marin, for example, an artist seen by Sheldon Reich as a precursor to the Abstract Expressionism, the city is dissolved into a geometry of sublime energies redolent of this assumed dynamic and magic élan. Similarly in the painting of Max Weber, Abraham Walkowitz as much as in Georgia O'Keeffe and the etchings of Joseph Pennell[24] the city is viewed as essentially an image of imminence: frenzied movement caught as key to a sublime condition. In their work the skyscraper remains pre-eminent as *the* image of Manhattan, a sense echoed by E. B. White's response to it as "the visible symbol of aspiration and faith" in a city "unique, cosmopolitan, mighty, and unparalleled".[25] The skyscraper, as iconic presence, is part of "a spectacle that is continuing", a "riddle in steel and stone". In the paintings of Georgia O'Keeffe it becomes an image of presentiment: a sublime geometry in which the energy of Marin, Walkowitz and Feininger's Manhattan has found its mystical symbol. Again, in Glenn Coleman's *Manhattan, the Old and the New*,[26] for example, the details and thick textures of the Lower East Side and South Street (the old) are displaced by the insistent image of a skyscraper and dirigible (the new): double axis of height and upward movement.

Essentially, of course, this sense of Manhattan has much to do with the tourist's eye-view. It is, for example, the view of Manhattan basic to Nick

Carraway's experience in *The Great Gatsby* (1925):

> Over the great bridge, with the sunlight through the girders making a constant flicker upon the moving cars, with the city rising up across the river in white heaps and sugar lumps and built with a wish out of non-olfactory money. The city seen from the Queensboro Bridge is always the city seen for the first time, in its first wild promise of all the mystery and the beauty in the world.[27]

Once again, New York city (as *Manhattan*) "rises up" as a white city devoid of history. Nothing here interferes with the eye's engagement with the spectacle and the spectacular: a mythic continuous present of the stranger's (i.e. Carraway's) *gusto*. Like a character in Janet Flanner's New York novel *The Cubical City* (1926) Carraway responds with "provincial emotional enthusiasm" seeing Manhattan as "the only glamorous city that compensated the western American eye".[28] A view found equally in Paul Strand's and Charles Sheeler's 1925 Whitmanesque celebratory film of New York: *Mannahatta*.[29]

And yet Carraway's view of the city rapidly succumbs to a very different experience. The "white chasms" and "enchanted metropolitan twilight", the view of Fifth Avenue as "warm and soft, almost pastoral" is displaced by fractured images of violence and the surreal. Carraway comes to see a different city. The romanticism of his first response is emptied of credence. Whitman's radiant city which Carraway sees from the Queensboro Bridge gives way to a human text in which New York exists as flawed environment rather than as majesterial projection. It *falls* from grace for Carraway as it did also for Fitzgerald. In *My Lost City*, for example, from the top of the Empire State Building, Fitzgerald tells us how he saw

> that the city was not the endless succession of canyons he had supposed but that *it had limits* ... [with] the awful realization that New York was a city after all and not a universe. The whole shining edifice that he had reared in his imagination came crashing to the ground.[30]

As it "crashes" for Carraway so it remains as a series of images without unity or promise. Carraway, like Fitzgerald, falls, so to speak, *into* history.

The tension between such extremes is the basis also on which Hart Crane develops his monumental poem of New York *The Bridge* (1930). In this Brooklyn Bridge is, of itself, symbol of an engineering impulse given a spiritual dimension as key to the city's wider energies of construction. Like the skyscraper for Crane the bridge is an equivalent unifying presence pulling disparate images into a single unity, paralleled by the way the Bridge holds its "endless" cables in a single act of suspension over the East River. An image found also in Dorothy Landers Beall's *The Bridge* (1913). Thus against a crystalline skyline:

> *The mist cleared off, the buildings gleamed and shone,*
> *The river leaped on bravely—and the bridge*
> *Like a pure dominating presence, bound*
> *It all—and made a way for men to meet!*[31]

A "pure presence" given specific pictorial shape and equal symbolic significance in paintings of Brooklyn Bridge by Peter Blume, Albert Gleizer, Peter Knoll,

John Marin and, of course, Joseph Stella.[32]

Indeed Stella's views of Brooklyn Bridge have an important place in relation to Crane's poem. His memoir, *The Brooklyn Bridge (A Page in my Life)* (1929), not only parallels Crane's response but, like Crane, takes the figures of Poe and Whitman as extreme precursors underpinning his aesthetic. Poe is here akin to Melville, for opposite Stella's Brooklyn studio is "a huge factory" of Poe's dark "drama" as it reveals "the swirling horrors of the maelstrom". Against this "the verse of Walt Whitman" soars "above as a white aeroplane of Help". Thus Stella's eye, like his metaphysic, escapes the maelstrom and enters a rhetoric which feeds from the myth he seeks to paint: the image of Brooklyn bridge:

> Seen for the first time, as a weird metallic apparition under a metallic sky, out of proportion with the winged lightness of its arch, traced for the conjunction of worlds, supported by the massive dark towers dominating the surrounding tumult of the surging skyscrapers with their gothic majesty sealed in the purity of their arches, the cables, like divine messages from above, transmitted to the vibrating coils, cutting and dividing into innumerable musical spaces the wide immensity of sky, it impressed me as the shrine containing all the efforts of the new civilization of AMERICA—the eloquent meeting point of all forces arising in a superb assertion of their powers, in APOTHEOSIS.

Standing on the bridge Stella feels "deeply moved, as if on the threshold of a new religion or in the presence of a new DIVINITY". The sentence swirls around its subject. The bridge here is not only, like the "surging skyscrapers", part of a dynamic new world, it is also given an overwhelming spiritual resonance in which an ideal *urban* condition is figured.[33] It is, once again, a divine apotheosis—for Stella (and Crane) *the* image of Whitman's city.

Crane's *The Bridge* establishes its energies from a similar "logic of metaphor". The poem, as an "epic of the modern consciousness", seeks a verbal alacrity which has the force of sublime meaning. In "Proem" Brooklyn Bridge is thus invoked as a divine object amidst the waters of the East River and the Atlantic, the Statue of Liberty and the "multitudes" of Manhattan itself (in offices, cinemas and subways). *The Bridge* as both artifact and poem is thus the unifying symbol which gathers into itself the surrounding environment. As both "harp" and "altar" of this condition, so Crane's rhetoric seeks an equivalent "curveship" that will "lend a myth to God" and, by implication, sanctify the city as a single (and transcendent) condition.

The Bridge, then, invokes a divinity centred *in* Manhattan but figured in the very structure of the bridge itself: the "hundreds of strands" (of the suspension) which constitute Crane's myth of America. The poem seeks a "synergy" and Manhattan becomes the *gate* to this Atlantis of potential energy. The poem, *as* a bridge, is "one arc synoptic" which absorbs the "labyrinthine mouths of history" as "translating time" it infers the ultimate unity of its vision:

> *Into what multitudinous Verb the suns*
> *And synergy of waters ever fuse, recast*
> *In myriad syllables,—Psalm of Cathay!*
> *O Love, thy white, pervasive Paradigm. ...*[34]

This is the hope and, of course, the parallel to Whitman's rhetoric of Manhattan. And yet Crane's poem falters not because of its outrageous claims to this vision but, rather, because of the compelling presence of its own negation—the "ghost" of Edgar Allan Poe which, this time, Whitman's Chant of Manhattan cannot transcend. If *The Bridge* seeks to answer back *The Waste Land* (1922) offering an American urban scene to counteract Eliot's sense of a modern London and Paris, ultimately the image of New York it achieves is the city *of* Poe and Melville as it extends into the twentieth century; paradoxically a city closer to Eliot than Whitman. The poem, in other words, is sucked into an underground New York which, in "The Tunnel" becomes the sight of the text's anti-vision; the very opposite to the light, radiance, and dynamism of Crane's myth and wish.[35]

This, then, is a New York of the subway—redolent of Allen Tate's experience in his own poem "The Subway" (1927),[36] just as it suggests George Tooker's painting of 1950: *The Subway*. In Crane's poem we go *under* Times Square and Columbus Circle—an alternative "geometry" of the city in which what is heard is the echo of "multitudes" whose text *is* the street (and subway map) of a historicized urban experience. In the subway we meet the *body* rather than the spirit of the city: the "retching flesh" of Poe's vision. An unconscious picturing, as it were, of a Manhattan as the repository of a different myth: Hades and Hell rather than Atlantis and Heaven.

Crane's myth, is heavily dependent upon Whitman and seeks to maintain his vision into the 1930s. But equally there is a body of literature which actively denies the mythology and radiance of a magical Manhattan. In this the energies so basic to Whitman and Stieglitz are *seen* as destructive and anonymous, just as the spectacle of the city is emptied of connotative resonance and given over to a material rather than spiritual reading of the city's meaning.

This is, of course, a fundamental characteristic of the immigrant experience. Manhattan as *the* port of New York is, thus, devoid of its magic. Entry is not through a gate of possibility—it is through the customs authorities of Ellis Island. In *The Rise of David Levinsky* (1917), for example, Abraham Cahan's hero sees Manhattan from the sea as an image which "unfolded itself like a divine revelation"[37]; a naïve view rapidly dispelled once he walks through the streets of the Lower East Side. In *Manhattan Transfer* the Statue of Liberty, as symbol of this "entrance" to the city, is reduced to "A tall green woman in a dressing gown standing on an island holding up her hand",[38] just as in William Carlos Williams's "Sicilian Emigrant's Song" the statue is "the big woman there with the candle" in a "grey" and "cold" land. Wholly distinctive from the compulsive energy of another Williams New York poem: "The Great Figure".[39] In *Call it Sleep* (1934) the statue's significance as part of the rhetoric of promise is measured against the immigrants" "delivery" from "the stench and throb of the steerage to the stench and throb of New York tenements":

> The spinning disk of the late afternoon sun slated behind her, and to those on board who gazed, her features were charred with shadow, her depths exhausted,

> her masses ironed to one single plane. Against the luminous sky the rays of her halo were spikes of darkness roweling the air; shadow flattened the torch she bore to a black cross against flawless light—the blackened mist of a broken sword. Liberty. The child and his mother stared again at the massive figure in wonder.[40]

As the bearer of myth Liberty has, here, been emptied of significance. The statue's symbolic resonance is undercut to the extent that it presages a different *kind* of city—and urban history. For Roth sets this "vision" in 1907, "the year that was destined to bring the greatest number of immigrants to the shores of the United States",[41] and offers the perspective (like Hine and Dos Passos) of a thick *human* density amassing in the city. Just as O'Henry felt that the Flat Iron building was not so much an image of a "new America" but a symbol which "might well have stood for the tower of Babel", so Roth sees Manhattan as a spectacle emptied of the spectacular. The word "wonder" in the passage is no more than a synonym for naïvité and innocence.

If 1907 was auspicious for Roth, 1908 was the date of James's "The Jolly Corner", concerned with another entry (or re-entry) to Manhattan and, again, a response quite antagonistic to any sense of the city as sublime spectacle. The main character, Spencer Brydon, sees a New York which "assaulted his vision" and offered an image of "dreadful multiplied numberings which seemed to him to reduce the whole place to some vast ledger-page, overgrown, fantastic, of ruled and criss-crossed lines and figures ..." This is the "long, shrill city" heard in *Washington Square* (1880) and the thunderous energy James reports upon in *The American Scene* (1907). Unlike Hart Crane's vision, Manhattan here is the embodiment of a raucous and destructive energy, the image of which finds its apotheosis in *The Education of Henry Adams* (1907). There Adams, as the historian, gazes upon an "outline of the city" which had become "frantic in its effort to explain something that defied meaning". Manhattan is now seen as the product of an amorphous "power". The dynamic, as a dynamo, has "exploded and thrown great masses of stone and steam against the sky. The city had the air and movement of hysteria. ..." From his club on Fifth Avenue Adams witnesses not a sublime Manhattan but its direct reverse: a nightmare akin to Yeats's vision in "The Second Coming". In Manhattan, says Adams, "the failure of Christianity" could be heard as it "roared up Broadway". The Great White Way of Whitman and Mayakovsky had become, for Adams, the depository of a daemonic and anarchic presence unredeemable except as an image of chaos.

Waldo Frank also looked for a mythic Manhattan on his return to the city and, like James and Adams, finds only its opposite. *In the American Jungle* (1925—the year of *Gatsby* and *Manhattan Transfer* and the founding of *The New Yorker*) speaks of "A savage isle" even though Frank's eyes were "shiningly ready" to gaze upon a magic skyline. But, says Frank,

> I saw no scintillating city rising like an army of arrows toward the sun, its father. What I saw was a conglomerate of buildings, formless with haphazard shapes, a phalanx of skyscrapers as formidable from the distance as an old comb lacking half its teeth. A sprawling and grimy town above the noble Hudson.[44]

Emptied of its myth-making presence, the city Frank finds is only a city of "empty lots", of faces "sullen" and "dehumanized": a city akin to the paintings of Edward Hopper rather than of John Marin. In this sense Whitman's "Mannahatta" gives way, once again, to a brutal opposite in which the eye is held to and by the street: an area of activity which denies escape to the skyline above or to a view of the island from afar. This, rather, is a sense of the city *as* a hell made-up from a closely plotted imagery of the street itself: a human presence which is both anonymous and scatological rather than "divine" and celebratory. It is, indeed, the New York of Federico Garcia Lorca who, in his *Poeta En Nueva York* (1940), feels "adrift/in the vomiting multitudes" and finds himself in a city which is "not hell, but a street". This is a "filthy New York" where "dawn" brings "four pillars of slime/ and a storm of black pigeons/that dabble dead water".[45]

Once the spectacle of New York is emptied of myth the eye of writer and artist roams through streets noting an iconography of the surreal and strange; an endless series of images and figures which, like the photographs of Weegee, create an alternative but compulsive Manhattan as a city of fragments and detritus. This, in part, is the Manhattan of dispelling realism and outsiders—once again the *body* of the city that Crane met in the subway. It is the New York of Hubert Selby's *Last Exit to Brooklyn* (1964), John Rechy's *City of Night* (1964), of Jack Kerouac, Kathy Acker,[46] and William Burroughs: an underground and dark city of sidewalk and alley with its centre at Times Square and Forty-second Street. It is, as it were, the nightmare Manhattan of Norman Mailer's *An American Dream* (1965).

And this is also the Manhattan of Saul Bellow's *Mr. Sammler's Planet* (1970) which views the city from the perspectives of its central character's failing Jewish heritage, Bellow's Chicago, and the twin poles of Sammler's concentration camp experience and his earlier life in 1920s' London spent amidst Bloomsbury and the Bloomsbury Group. In the novel Sammler's single remaining eye roams Manhattan at street level noting the general tawdriness and confusion as signs of imminent breakdown and collapse. In contrast to this, Sammler recalls a London based upon traditional civil and civic codes in which restraint, discipline and high culture made for a civilized life. Sammler's New York is a "barbarous world" full of extreme and excessive violence, decay and filth: all part of a "state of singular dirty misery". Appropriately the subway is "an abomination"—sink-hole of a city which "makes one think about the collapse of civilization".[47] While he yearns for Bloomsbury and the British Museum, he faces a squalid and shabby Forty-second Street on his way to a brief area of respite: the New York Public Library.

Bellow's novel is very much of its time and draws heavily on a sense of the 1960s as apocalyptic rather than radical. Equally there is, in the imagery of breakdown and collapse, a parallel with New York's own fiscal crises and the wider sense of collapse exemplified in, for example, the rapid deterioration of the Bronx area. But *Mr. Sammler's Planet* is also a novel of retreat—the reverse of *Seize the Day* (1956).[48] It views Manhattan very much from the perspectives of Henry James and T. S. Eliot, and there is neither celebration nor energy, nor any sense of saving human presence. All is decay, much in the way the city is emptied and reduced to a wasteland of falling tenements in Malamud's *The Tenants* (1971). The final effect is of individuals locked in the private spaces of apartments and rooms which offer only a limited and partial rest from the chaos outside. Public space, as it were, no longer exists.

In contrast to Bellow, Donald Barthelme offers suggestive and enigmatic stories of "city life" in which the response to Manhattan is neither ambivalent nor celebratory but rather one of inevitable and repeated *paradox*. New York thus emerges as *endlessly* sublime and atrocious—a text which changes from the ideal to the real as the inhabitants of the city constantly reconstruct an image of the city. The stories offer parables not so much of city life, as the way in which cities are seen, imagined and projected *as* texts.

I want to consider briefly three stories from *City Life* (1970), two related directly to New York, which develop this ambivalence and parody the ways in which the imagination shapes the city as an image. New York becomes the site (and the sight) of contrary impulses. In "The Glass Mountain", for example, we are told of a "glass mountain" which "stands at the corner of Thirteenth Street and Eighth Avenue". It "towers" over the avenue "like some splendid, immense office building" and has "sparkling blue-white depths" suggestive of a significance far beyond its practical function. As such it stands, to the protagonist who sets out to climb it, as "a beautiful enchanted symbol". As he begins his ascent up the outside of the building, so he leaves behind the *street*: an area of "many people with disturbed eyes" amidst a "heap of corpses". But once he reaches the summit so his "symbol" turns into a "beautiful princess" who he throws down onto the street below. In "The Balloon" a balloon appears over Fourteenth Street and continues to expand in size until it reaches Central Park. The inhabitants respond to its overwhelming presence, seeing it as an anti-city of the reality below. As a balloon—malleable and responsive to touch—it yields to what they wish it to be: what they seek to make it into.

Both these stories are parables of the way we read cities and, in particular, of the way in which Manhattan has been imaginatively seen. Essentially they suggest states of desire—ideal projections which, in their fabulous contexts, evince endless possibilities for "city life" and the spectacle of architecture while admitting to the "reality" of the street. As such in Barthelme the imagination is suspended between contrary states: between the sky and the street, the ethereal and substantial. It is a state which, in "City Life" is given a quintessential Barthelmian ambiguity:

> I have to admit we are locked in the most exquisite mysterious muck. This muck heaves and palpitates. It is multi-directional and has a mayor. To describe it takes many hundreds of thousands of words.[49]

This offers a condition rather than a judgement—a tantalizingly complex image of the city held within the paradox of a reality at once attractive and repellent. It is, indeed, wholly appropriate to Manhattan as both urban environment and ideal image. Indeed it recalls Le Corbusier's response to New York as "a vertical city, under the sign of the new times", a "city of the Incredible Towers", a "beautiful and worthy catastrophe" simultaneously "sublime and atrocious".[50]

It seems wholly appropriate, then that Manhattan was the locale of America's most significant art movement this century: Abstract Expressionism. In the 1940s and 1950s New York City not only became the "first" city of art—supplanting Paris as the centre of post-modernism and building upon its artistic development in the 1920s—it developed an aesthetic in Abstract Expressionism which was both fundamentally American and urban and, significantly, echoed the way Manhattan had been viewed by earlier writers and artists. The painters, once again, hovered between extremes as they situated an art which moved between sky and street. If they established their studios in Lower Manhattan, around Eighth Street on the Lower East Side, their paintings sought the main chance of the city's energy as suggested by the spectacle of mid-town Manhattan. Indeed, the very *size* of their canvasses evoked an art at once public and monumental: equivalent texts of the city's continuing presence as, to use Peter Berger's phrase, "a city of transcendence".[51]

Collectively the gesture and colour-field painters replay, as it were, the city *as* a condition, and their paintings express at once possibility and entrapment: the dual perspectives of Whitman's and Melville's New York.[52] In the work of Franz Kline, for example, the textured black and white patterns suggest the structures of Manhattan's bridges and highways: geometries of metal and space which Barbara Rose has described as a celebration of the "special dynamism of the urban environment".[53] They extend the singular ambiguities of Aaron Siskind's found textures: abstract patterns photographed, literally, from the surfaces of Manhattan walls and doors—the "exquisite muck" of the city's habitat. Equally, Willem De Kooning's almost tortured and brash semi-figural paintings evoke a "raw and violent" world: portraits, as it were, of the human form "intimately shaped by urban living".[54]

It is, however, in the work of Jackson Pollock and Mark Rothko that the most sustained (and most extreme) response to Manhattan is to be found. Both relate their painting to a vocabulary of energy basic to Manhattan's meaning *as* an American city. The "action painting" of Pollock becomes part of a continuing *test* of the self amidst the existential possibilities of the city as an endless play of energies. Each canvas is, thus, a recasting of identity amidst a daunting dynamic as Pollock seeks a unity of being: the *one* of a painting's title. The paintings exist as the trace of the self through the city in space and time: a signature of artist and environment in a mutual state of tension. In a similar response Mark Rothko's spectacular colour planes seek an energy of the city given over to a sublime arena of transcendence. His paintings suggest a pure moment: a presence held within the city as an ultimate and ideal myth. They are, in the end, as much images of supreme contemplation as Pollock's are of frenzied action (and possible destruction).[55]

In this sense both Pollock and Rothko take the myth of Manhattan to its furthest point. Their art, in the act of defining the indefinable, *exhausts* itself as it tests the city amidst its rhetoric of becoming. The painters always face emptiness: the canvas is as much absence as presence; as much myth and history as the *act* of identity (of self and city) is given over to the *act* of painting. Abstract Expressionism is thus wholly appropriate to Manhattan and deeply embedded (for all its European aspects) in the mythology and iconography of the island. An art which, in seeking the possibility of the city as a fundamental presence, always faces the city as existential vacuum. Myth, as it were, faces its moment in history.

Indeed Pollock and Rothko return us to Whitman and Melville. Pollock's canvasses infer precisely that metaphysic so insisted upon by Whitman's "Mannahatta" (and, for example, "Crossing Brooklyn Ferry") just as Rothko's edge towards the emptiness and stasis of "Bartleby". Rothko's art moves closer *to* becoming a wall as its transcendent centre fades away into a frightening emptiness. As the floating blues and deep reds give way to overwhelming blacks, so the later paintings evince not so much the spectacle of Whitman's radiant Manhattan as the "dead wall reverie" of Bartleby's and *Pierre's* dark city.

The "transcendent" possibility of Manhattan, as found in Abstract Expressionism, was equally evident in the so-called "New York School" of poets, especially in the writing of Frank O'Hara. Indeed, O'Hara's position as a curator in the Museum of Modern Art made him at once centrally *placed* in the mid-town Manhattan he celebrates but also placed *amongst* the work of the painters he so admired, wrote about, and knew: Pollock, Rothko, Kline and De Kooning,[56] His poetry is rightly associated with them. Thus his poems give the sense of moving between these two worlds—the one informing the other in a continuing play of possibility and reference. The paintings *in* the Museum seemingly open out *into* Manhattan itself: a sense of the city suggested in one of O'Hara's most optimistic of poems, "A Step Away From Them":

> *It's my lunch hour, so I go*
> *for a walk among the hum-colored*
> *cabs. First, down the sidewalk*
> *where laborers feed their dirty*
> *glistening torsos sandwiches*
> *and Coca-Cola, with yellow helmets*
> *on*

And again:

> *on*
> *to Times Square, where the sign*
> *blows smoke over my head, and higher*
> *the waterfall pours lightly. A*
> *Negro stands in a doorway with a*
> *toothpick, languorously agitating.*
> *A blonde chorus girl clicks: he*
> *smiles and rubs his chin. Everything*
> *suddenly honks: it is 12.40 of*
> *a Thursday.*[57]

Like the title of an O'Hara poem this is an aesthetic "in favour of one's time" and of one's city. The "city" here is a series of images with their own assured significance. Like James Schuyler, O'Hara often looks upon Manhattan as an image in which he "can't get over/how it all works together"[58] O'Hara's poems, thus, *use* Manhattan as a canvas akin to Pollock's painting. The city becomes a "limitless space of air and light in which the spirit can act freely and with unpremeditated knowledge"[59] and where "things exist in a sort of miraculous emulsion."[60] O'Hara's Manhattan is, thus, very much a transcendent urban world framed by the Museum of Modern Art: an urban iconography read through the painting. As such, it is always a "step away" because, ultimately, it is always alive with *potential* meaning: an imminence underpinned by the promise of transcendence and the experience of an especial New York aesthetic.

And yet despite O'Hara's response (given added significance in this poem by Sammler's own "movement" in the same area), New York art, certainly after Abstract Expressionism, moved more and more into an examination of the "exquisite muck" which made itself so basic to Manhattan street experience. Indeed, much of this art is an art of the minimal and the found: the refuge *of* the street emptied of any significance other than its presence *as* rubbish. Manhattan thus is figured not so much as an environment of disorder and chaos but as an experience of multiple orderings: signs, objects, images which, at street level, are themselves the urban text. The city becomes a *collage* of disparate elements unbound to any larger unity except the momentary condition of which they are a part. Rauschenberg's collages, for example, like the photographs of Joel Meyerowitz, are collections and *found* assemblages of the multiple and unrelated. The artist here collects details—he no longer attempts unity. The details remain just that, "the expendable detritus of a concrete, steel and glass leviathan".[61] How significant, then, that that most Whitmanian of American poets, Allen Ginsberg, should feel quite alien to New York city. In "Waking in New York" he can only speak of his isolation: "Oh fathers, how I am alive in this/vast human wilderness." New York is a city "too vast to know", and yet asks the poet "Am I not breathing here frightened/and amazed?[62] Fear and amazement—the two poles, as it were, that this essay has plotted. Two different "New Yorks" held together within a continuing dialectic. How appropriate, perhaps, that in a recent "New York" novel *Bright Lights, Big City* 1984) the story ends on a characteristic reference to the lure and presence of the Manhattan Skyline as "The first light of the morning outlines the towers of the World Trade Center at the tip of the island."[63] These towers have supplanted other icons of earlier periods but, as the tallest buildings in Manhattan, they also fulfil Whitman's sense of the city as a vertical growth. And yet, at the same time, as a trade *centre* of offices and walls they also complete Bartleby's sense of the city. Once again they signify the paradox of New York—its seemingly endless play, as spectacle, between myth and history. As Michel De Certeau has said, "the person who ascends to the top of these towers" leaves behind "the mass"—of people, of the city. The city exists as a myth. To descend to the street is not only to "redescend into the sombre space through which crowds of people move about", it is to be reminded that "History begins at ground level, with footsteps.[64] Sounds on the streets of New York, not eyes on the sights of Manhattan. No wonder

Ginsberg was both frightened and amazed.

Notes

1. John Dos Passos, *Manhattan Transfer* (Boston: Houghton Mifflin, 1953), p. 68.
2. Walt Whitman, *Leaves of Grass* (Reader's Edition, New York and London, 1965), p. 474.
3. See the introduction to Ben Lubeschz's *Manhattan The Magical Island* (New York, 1927).
4. Herman Melville, "Bartleby the Scrivener" in *Billy Budd and Other Tales* (New American Library edition, 1961).
5. Herman Melville, *Pierre* (New American Library edition, 1964). See pp. 264–79. "First Night of their Arrival in the City" (Book XVI).
6. F. Scott Fitzgerald, *The Great Gatsby* (Harmondsworth: Penguin 1950), p. 42.
7. The figure comes from Peter Hall's *The World Cities* (New York, 1966), p. 192. He reminds us that by 1900 half of the city's population was "foreign born". See also Irving Howe *The Immigrant Jews of New York: 1881 to the Present* (London, 1976) published in America as *The World of our Fathers*, and Alfred Kazin, *A Walker in the City* (New York, 1951).
8. *Manhattan Transfer*, p. 12.
9. Wiktur Woroszylski, *The Life of Mayakovsky* (New York, 1970), p. 372.
10. I. N. Phelps Stokes, *The Iconography of Manhattan Island 1498–1909* (6 vols.), vol. I (New York, 1915), p. xxxi. The study remains central to an understanding of the city. Of more recent studies see Peter Conrad, *The Art of the City Views and Versions of New York* (Oxford and New York, 1984) and Jan Morris *Manhattan '45* (New York and London, 1983). See also Alfred Kazin's essay "New York from Melville to Mailer" in *Literature and the American Urban Experience*, ed. Michael C. Jaye and Ann Chalmers Watts (Manchester, 1981), pp. 81-92.
11. Significantly, Sinclair Lewis felt that *Manhattan Transfer* was "the first book to catch Manhattan. What have we had before, what have we had? Whitman? That is not our Manhattan; it is a provincial city, near the frontier. Howells, Wharton, James? A provincial city near to Bath and the vicar's tea-cups." See his *Introduction* to the novel (1926, Fulcroft Library Editions, 1977).
12. Roland Barthes, "Buffet Finishes off New York" (1959) in *Selected Writings*, intro. Susan Sontag (Oxford, 1983), pp. 158–61.
13. Stephen Crane, *Maggie a Girl of the Streets* (First Novel Library Edition, London, 1966), p. 5.
14. Ibid., p. 74.
15. Ibid., p. 5.
16. *Manhattan Transfer*, p. 244.
17. John Rechy, *City of Night* (London, 1964; 1965 edition), p. 25.
18. In relation to Hine's work, see *America and Lewis Hine: Photographs 1904–1940* (New York, 1977), with forward by Walter Rosenblum. See also Hank O'Neal, *Berenice Abbott: Sixty Years of Photography* (London, 1982).
19. See, for example, *America and Alfred Stieglitz*, ed. Waldo Frank, Lewis Mumford, *et al.* (New York, 1934). See also Bram Dijkstra, *The Hieroglyphics of a New Speech: Cubism, Stieglitz, and the Poetry of William Carlos Williams* (Princeton, New Jersey, 1969); Dickran Tashjian, *Skyscraper Primitives Dada and the American Avant-Garde 1910–1925* (Middleton, Conn., 1975): and William Innes Homer, *Alfred Stieglitz and the American Avant-Garde* (Boston, 1977).
20. Stieglitz said this of his response to the Flat Iron. See Homer, p. 20.
21. Lewis Mumford, *America and Alfred Stieglitz*, p. 34.
22. Paul Rosenfeld, *Port of New York: Essays on Fourteen American Moderns*, intro. by Sherman Paul (University of Illinois Press, Indiana, 1961), pp. 285–92. See the sections on Marin, Stieglitz and the "Epilogue".
23. Theodore Dreiser, *The Color of a Great City* (London, 1930), pp. vii and 7.
24. See, for example, Sheldon Rach, *John Marin: A Stylistic Analysis and Catalogue Raisonné* (2 vols.), (Tuscon, 1970); Lloyd Goodrich, *American Art of our Century* (New York, 1961); and Barbara Rose (ed.), *Readings in American Art 1900–1975* (New York, 1975).
25. E. B. White, "Here is New York" in *Perspectives*, No. 4 (Summer, 1953), 26–45. The essay remains a central response to New York.
26. See *American Art of the '20s and '30s*, forward by Alfred H. Barr, Jr., Museum of Modern Art (New York, 1932). The volume also contains an illustration of Thurman Rotan's *Skyscrapers*.
27. *The Great Gatsby*, p. 69.

28. Janet Flanner, *The Cubical City* (1926, reprint edition 1974, Southern Illinois University Press), p. 45.
29. See Dickran Tashjian, *William Carlos Williams and the American Scene, 1920–1940* (New York, 1978), p. 74.
30. F. Scott Fitzgerald *The Crack-Up* (Harmondsworth, Penguin edition, 1965), p. 30.
31. Dorothy Landers Beall, *The Bridge and Other Poems* (New York, 1913), p. 37.
32. The major study of the relationship between Crane's poem and Brooklyn Bridge remains Allen Trachtenberg's *Brooklyn Bridge Fact and Symbol* (Chicago and London, 1965).
33. Quoted by George Knox in "Crane and Stella: Conjunction of Painterly and Poetic Worlds" in *Texas Studies in Literature and Language*, vol. xii (1970–71), pp. 689–707. See also B. Jaffe "Joseph Stella and Hart Crane: The Brooklyn Bridge" in *The American Art Journal*, vol. 1 (Fall 1969), 98–107.
34. Hart Crane, *The Complete Poems and Selected Letters and Prose*, ed. and intro. by Brom Weber (London, 1968), p. 115. See, in particular, "To Brooklyn Bridge" and "Atlantis".
35. See "The Tunnel" section.
36. Allen Tate, *Collected Poems 1919–1976* (New York, 1977), p. 19.
37. Abraham Cahan, *The Rise of David Levinsky* (Harper Torchbook edition, 1960), p. 87.
38. *Manhattan Transfer*, p. 69.
39. See *The Collected Earlier Poems* (Norfolk, Conn. 1951), pp. 35 and 230.
40. Henry Roth, *Call it Sleep* (Harmondsworth, Penguin edition, 1983), p. 14.
41. Ibid., p. 9.
42. O'Henry (William Sydney Porter), *The Complete Works of O'Henry* (Kingsward, Surrey, 1928), p. 1175. See "The Making of a New Yorker" and "A Little Local Color".
43. Henry Adams, *The Education of Henry Adams*, ed. Ernest Samuels (Boston, Houghton Mifflin edn., 1973), p. 499.
44. Waldo Frank, *In the American Jungle (1925–1936)* (Freeport, New York, 1937), pp. 17–18.
45. Federico Garcia Lorca, *Poet in New York*, trans. Ben Belitt, intro. by Angel Del Rio (New York, 1955), p. 63.
46. See, for example, Kathy Acker's "Slums in New York City" in *Blood and Guts in High School Plus Two* (London, 1984), pp. 56–8.
47. Saul Bellow, *Mr. Sammler's Planet* (Harmondsworth, Penguin edition, 1977), p. 277.
48. In *Seize the Day* (Harmondsworth, Penguin edition, 1966) we read, for example, of a Broadway which "quaked and gleamed" with the "great, great crowd, the inexhaustible current of millions", p. 122. The ethos goes back directly to Whitman. *Mr. Sammler's Planet* has none of this.
49. David Barthelme, *Sixty Stories* (New York, 1981), p. 158.
50. See Le Corbusier, *When the Cathedrals were White*, trans. by T. E. Hyslop (1947; Paperback edition McGraw Hill, New York, 1968).
51. Peter Berger, "New York City 1976: A Signal of Transcendence" in *Facing Up to Modernity* (1977, New York; Harmondsworth, Penguin edition, 1979), pp. 258–68.
52. There is, of course, a large number of texts on this subject. See, amongst others, Gregory Battock (ed.) *The New Art* (New York, 1973), especially G. C. Goosen "The Big Canvas" 57–65, and Thomas B. Hess "A Tale of Two Cities", pp. 84–102. See also: Harold Rosenberg, *Discovering the Present* (Chicago and London, 1973); Bernard Rosenberg and Norris Fliegel (eds.), *The Vanguard Artist* (New York, 1979); and "Notes on Modernism in New York" in Marshall Berman's *All That is Solid Melts into Air* (New York, 1982), pp. 287–348. Specific studies include Dore Ashton *The New York School of Cultural Reckoning* (New York, 1973) and Irving Sandler *The Triumph of American Painting: A History of Abstract Expressionism* (New York, 1970).
53. Barbara Rose, *American Art Since 1900: A Critical History* (New York, 1967), p. 203.
54. Irving Sandler, *The New York School: The Painters and Sculptors of the Fifties* (New York, 1978), p. 2.
55. See, for example, Peter Selz, *Mark Rothko* (Museum of Modern Art, New York, 1961) and Diane Waldman, *Mark Rothko* (London and New York, 1978). For Jackson Pollock, see Bryan Robertson, *Jackson Pollock* (London, 1960) and "The Radical Vision of Whitman and Pollock" by Edwin Havilland Miller in *Artistic Legacy of Walt Whitman*, ed. Edwin Havilland Miller (New York, 1970), pp. 55–72.
56. See Marjorie Perloff, *O'Hara, Poet Among Painters* (New York, 1977) and *An Anthology of New York Poets*, ed. Ron Padgett and David Shapiro (New York, 1970). See also O'Hara's *Standing Still and Walking in New York*, ed. Donald Allen (Berkeley, 1975).
57. Frank O'Hara, *Collected poems*, ed. Donald Allen (New York, 1971), p. 257. On page 198 O'Hara announces: "I love this hairy city."

58. *An Anthology of New York Poets*, pp. 5–6.
59. Frank O'Hara, *Art Chronicles 1954–66* (New York, 1975), p. 26.
60. John Ashbery in *Homage to Frank O'Hara*, ed. Bill Berkson and Joe Lesuew (Bolinas, 1978), p. 142.
61. Irving Sandler, *The New York School* (1978), p. 143.
62. Allen Ginsberg, *Collected Poems 1947–1980* (New York, 1985), p. 341. In *Homage to Frank O'Hara*, Ginsberg said that O'Hara taught him "to really see New York for the first time".
63. Jay McInerney, *Bright Lights, Big City* (1984; Fontana edition, 1986), p. 180.
64. Michel de Certeau, "Practices of Space" in *On Signs a Semiotics Reader*, ed. Marshall Blonsky (Oxford, 1985), p. 129.

94

Notions of the Americans: New York

JAMES FENIMORE COOPER

James Fenimore Cooper (1789–1851) is perhaps the most significant American novelist of the early nineteenth century. Born in Burlington, New Jersey, he spent his early years in Cooperstown, a frontier settlement in upstate New York. He is most well-known for his cycle of novels which constitute *The Leatherstocking Tales*. Beginning with *The Pioneers* (1823), these feature the character of Natty Bumppo, the archetypal frontier pioneer figure who increasingly comes into conflict with the inevitable expansion of settlement westwards across the continent. *The Last of the Mohicans* (1826), *The Prairie* (1827), *The Pathfinder* (1840) and *The Deerslayer* (1841) complete the cycle. As a whole, the novels chart the "inevitable" settlement of the continent by European pioneers. They offer a complex and subtle picture of America at a crucial point in its history—as much in relation to its cultural perspectives as to its ecological future. Although influenced by the British writing of Jane Austen and Sir Walter Scott, Cooper is very much an indigenous American writer. *Notions of the Americans* (1828) is a central example of the range of his interests, and his concerns with the social and economic development of the new Republic. He was acutely aware of the significance of urban development, and of the place cities played within a society. See George Dekker, *James Fenimore Cooper the Novelist,* (1969) and Kay S. House, *Cooper's Americans* (1965).

To the Baron Von Kemperfelt, &c. &c.

New-York, 1824.

I feel that a description of this ancient city of the United Provinces is due to you. In dwelling on its admirable position, its growing prosperity, and its

Source: James Fenimore Cooper *From Notions of the Americans* "New York". (1828, London), Vol. 1.

probable grandeur, I wish to excite neither your hopes, nor your regrets. I have seen enough of this country already, to know, that in losing the New-Netherlands in their infancy, you only escaped the increased misfortune of having them wrested from your power by their own efforts at a more advanced period, when the struggle might have cost you, like that which England has borne, and Spain still suffers—an incalculable expenditure of men and money. You are thrice happy that your dominion in this quarter of America did not endure long enough to leave, in its train, any mortifying and exasperating recollections. The Dutch are still remembered here with a feeling strongly allied to affinity, by thousands of their descendants, who if, among their more restless and bustling compatriots of the east, they are not distinguished for the great enterprise which is peculiar to that energetic population, have ever maintained the highest character for thrift, undeniable courage, and inflexible probity. These are qualities which never fail to create respect, and which, by some unfortunate construction of the human mind, as rarely excite envy as emulation.

The name of the town, itself, is far from being happy. The place stands on a long narrow island, called Manhattan, a native appellation which should have been perpetuated through that of the city. There was a precedent for innovation which might have been followed to advantage. It is a little surprising that these republicans, who are not guiltless of sundry absurd changes in their nomenclature of street, squares, counties, and towns, should have neglected the opportunity of the Revolution, not only to deprive the royal family of England of the honour of giving a name to both their principal State and principal town, but to restore a word so sonorous, and which admits of so many happy variations as the appellation of this island. A "Manhattanese" has certainly a more poetical sound than a "New Yorker"; and there is an euphony in the phrase of "Men of Manhattan" that the lovers of alliteration many long sigh in vain to hear equalled by any transposition of the present unmusical and complex term. Nor would the adoption of a new name be attended with half of the evils in the case of a city or a county, as in that of a street or a market, since the very notoriety and importance of the alteration would serve to apprise all men of the circumstance. But a century and a half have confirmed the present title; and while the city of the white rose has been mouldering in provincial quiet, her western god-child has been growing into an importance that is likely to carry the name to that distant period when the struggles of the adverse factions shall be lost in the obscurity of time, or be matter of vague and remote history.

A nation as commercial and active as this, has only fairly to elect the position of its favourite mart to put it on a level with the chief places of the earth. London and Paris, Vienna, Rome, Carthage, and, for any thing we know, Pekin and Nankin, can refer the causes of their greatness to little beside accident or caprice. The same might be said of hundreds more of the principal places of antiquity, or of our own times. But it is only necessary to sit down with a minute map of the country before you, to perceive, at a glance, that Nature herself has intended the island of Manhattan for the site of one of the greatest commercial towns in the world. The spirit of its possessors is not likely to balk this intention; and it may be truly said, that the agents, both physical and moral, are in the happiest possible unison to accomplish the mighty plan. Although all description must fail to give a clear idea of the advantages of such a position, yet, as your imagination may be somewhat aided by one as imperfect as that must necessarily be which comes from my pen, it shall be attempted after my own desultory and irregular manner.

You must have obtained, through my letters, some general impression concerning the two great bays which lie between New-York and the ocean. The former, you will recollect, is known by the name of "Raritan", and the latter forms what is properly called the "Harbour". Raritan Bay is an extensive roadstead, abounding with situations where vessels may be partially protected from every wind that blows. It is, in fact, only open to the sea on the east; but, by the aid of the low sandy cape I have mentioned, shelter can be had in it against the heaviest gales from that quarter, as it may also be found in some one of its many anchoring grounds, against the wind from every other point of the compass. The harbour is still more secure; a vessel being entirely land-locked, when anchored a mile or two within the Narrows. Here then are space and security united to an extraordinary degree; for, with the exception of a few well-defined reefs, there is scarcely a rock in the whole port to endanger a ship, or even to injure a cable. But the true basins for the loading and unloading of freights, and for the repairs and construction of vessels, are in the Hudson river, and in that narrow arm of the sea which connects the waters of the bay with those of the sound. The latter is most occupied at present by the ships engaged in foreign commerce. This strait is near half-a-mile in width, has abundance of water for any thing that floats, and possesses a moderately swift, and a sufficiently accurate current. From the point of its junction with the bay, to an island, which, by narrowing its boundaries, increases the velocity of its tides too much for the convenience of handling ships at wharfs, the distance cannot be a great deal less than five miles. The wharfs on Manhattan Island already extend more than three of these miles. On the opposite shore (Long Island) there is also a long range of quays. In the Hudson, it is impossible to fix limits to the facilities for commerce. As the river is a mile in width, and possesses great depth, it is plain that docks or wharfs may be extended as far as the necessities of the place shall ever require. The river is navigable for a heavy draught of water about a hundred miles, and for sloops and lighter craft some fifty or sixty more.

The time has not yet come for the formation of massive, permanent quays in the harbour of New-York. Wood is still too cheap, and labour too dear, for so heavy an investment of capital. All the wharfs of New-York are of very simple construction. A frame-work of hewn logs is filled with loose stone, and covered with a surface of trodden earth. This species of quay, if durability be put out of the question, is perhaps the best in the world. The theory that wood subject to the action of tides in salt water may become the origin of disease, is, like a thousand other theories, much easier advanced than supported. It is very true that the yellow fever has often existed in the immediate vicinity of some of these wharfs; but it is quite as true that there are miles of similarly constructed quays, in precisely the same climate, where it has never existed at all. The Americans appear to trouble themselves very little on this point, for they are daily constructing great ranges of these wooden piers, in order to meet the increasing demands of their trade, while the whole of the seven miles of water which fronts the city, is lined with similar constructions, if we except the public mall, called "the Battery", which is protected from the waves of the bay by a wall of stone.

The yellow fever is certainly the only drawback on the otherwise unrivalled commercial position of New-York; but the hazard of this disease is greatly magnified in Europe. The inhabitants of the place appear to have but little dread on the subject, and past experience would seem, in a great measure, to justify their indifference. So far as I can learn, there never have been but three of four summers when that fatal malady has committed any very serious ravages in this latitude. These seasons occurred at the close of the last, and at the commencement of the present century. Since the year 1804, there have been but two autumns when the yellow fever has existed to any dangerous degree in New-York, and neither of them proved very fatal, though it is certain that the arrangements of the city were excessively inconvenienced by its appearance. I believe it is admitted by scientific men, that this dangerous malady, though it is always characterized by certain infallible symptoms, often exhibits itself under forms so very much modified as to render different treatments necessary different seasons. The wharfs of New-York form a succession of little basins, which are sometimes large enough to admit thirty or forty sail, though often much smaller. These irregular docks have obtained the name of "slips". One of the former was shown me that was particularly foul and offensive. Around this slip, at the close of the hot weather in 1819, the yellow fever made its appearance. A few individuals became its victims before the existence of the danger was fully established. The city authorities took prompt and happy measures for its suppression. The question of contagion or of non-contagion had long been hotly contested among the medical men, and a sort of middle course, between the precautions inculcated by the two theories, had begun to be practised. So soon as it was found how far the disease extended, (and its limits were inconceivable small), the inhabitants were all removed, and the streets were fenced, in order to prevent access to what was proclaimed by authority to be "the infected district". The sick were conveyed into other quarters of the town, or to the country, some dying and others recovering. When the removal was made in time, or when the disease did not make its appearance until after the patient had experienced the benefit of pure air, the malady was generally more mild, though still often fatal. No one took the disease by contagion, it being affirmed that every case that occurred could be distinctly traced to "the infected district". The taint, corruption, or animalculæ in the air, whichever the cause of the malady might be, gradually spread, until it was found necessary to extend the limits of "the infected district" in every direction. I am told that thousands remained in their dwellings, within musket-shot of this spot dedicated to death, perfectly satisfied that the enemy could make no inroads on their security without giving notice of his approach through some of those who dwelt nearest to the proscribed region. As the latter, however, acted as a sort of forlorn hope, a very respectable space was left around the fences, and, in one or two instances, especially in 1822, the disease, for want of nearer subjects, surprised a few who believed themselves sufficiently removed from its ravages. In neither year, however, did a case occur that could not be distinctly traced to "the infected district", or to a space that does not exceed one thirtieth part of the surface of the whole city. The progress of the disease was exceedingly slow, extending in a circle around the point whence it appeared to emanate. I heard several curious and well authenticated circumstances, that serve to confirm these facts, one of which I will relate.

A lady of fortune had retired to the country on the first appearance of the fever. The house she left, stood a few hundred feet beyond the limits of the "infected district". Her son had occasion to visit this dwelling, which he did without scruple, since the guardians of the city were thought to be on the alert, and hundreds were still residing between the house and the known limits of the disease. On the return of the young gentleman to the country he was seized with the fever, but happily recovered. The fortune and connexions of the youth gave notoriety to his case, and the fences were removed under the impression that the danger was spreading. After his recovery, however, Mr. — acknowledged that, led by his curiosity, he had gone to the fence the day he was in town, where he stood for some time contemplating the solitude of the deserted streets. My informant, who could be a little waggish even on this grave subject, added, that some pretended that the curiosity of the young gentleman was so strong as to induce him to thrust his head *though* an opening in the fence. He, however, gave credit to the story in its substance.

The malady rarely appears before the last of August, and has invariably disappeared with the first frosts, which are commonly felt here in October. The fever of 1822 caused much less alarm than that of 1819, though the infected district was far more extensive, and occupied a part of the city that was supposed to be more healthy. But experience had shown that the disorder has its limits, and that its march is slow and easily avoided. The merchants estimate the danger of the fever in this climate at a very low rate; and, perhaps, like the plague, or those fatal diseases which have ravaged London, and other towns in the centre of Europe, it will soon cease to create uneasiness at all.

I have endeavoured to glean all the interesting facts in my power concerning this disease, from men of intelligence, who have not, like the physicians, enlisted themselves in favour of one or the other of the conflicting theories of contagion or non-contagion, importation or non-importation. It appears to be admitted all round, that the disorder cannot be contracted in a pure atmosphere. If the circumstances I have heard be true, and from the authority I cannot doubt their being so, it seems also to be a nearly inevitable conclusion, that the disease is never generated in this climate. This, however, is a knotty point, and one that covers much of the grounds of disagreement. That a certain degree and concentration of heat is necessary for the appearance of the yellow fever, is a fact very generally admitted. There is a common opinion that it has never been known in New-York, except in summers when the thermometer has stood something above 80 for a given number of days in succession. And yet the temperature is often as high, and for similar periods, without the appearance of the fever. The seeds of the disease are undoubtedly imported, whether it is ever generated here or not; for it has often happened that labourers who have been employed in vessels from the West Indies, after the crews had left them, have sickened and died. These cases must have arisen from a contaminated air, and not from strict contagion. Indeed there is scarce a summer in which some case of the fever does not occur at the Lazaretto, through vessels from the West Indies, or the more southern points of the United States. That the disorder does not extend itself is imputed to the pureness of the atmosphere at the time being. In a question in which important facts are liable to so much qualification, it is necessary, however, to admit their inferences with great caution. So much must depend, for instance, on the particular state of the system of the individual, that each case seems to require a close examination before any very conclusive reasoning can be grounded on its circumstances. One of the theories of the disorder, as you probably know, assumes that it is no more than a high bilious fever exhibited under a peculiarly malignant form. All this may be very true, and yet the agent to produce that malignity, may exist in the atmosphere in such a condition as to render it capable of transportation, and if I may so express it, of expansion. There is a vulgar opinion that certain vicious animalculæ are generated in the warmer climates, and when conveyed to this latitude, if they meet with a genial temperature, they thrive and propagate their species like other people, until growing bold with their numbers they wander abroad, are inhaled, and continue to poison the springs of human existence, until a day of retribution arrives in the destroying influence of a sharp frost. It is certain that the inhabitants of New-York, who would have considered their lives in jeopardy by entering their dwellings one day, take peaceable possession of them the morning after a wholesome frost, with entire impunity. I have no doubt that much of the embarrassment under which this subject labours, is produced by the near resemblance between the fever which is certainly imported, and that which sometimes originates in the climate; though the latter, perhaps, is limited to those cases in which the patient has a strong predisposition to the malady. After all, the most exaggerated notions prevail in Europe concerning the danger of the disease in this latitude. Nine-tenths of the space covered by this city never had an original case of yellow fever in it, and its appearance at all is of rare occurrence. Indeed, I am led to believe that New-York, owing to its fine situation, is on the whole more healthy than most large towns. It has also been told to me, that the deaths by consumption, as reported, are probably greatly magnified beyond the truth, since the family physician or friend of one who has died, for instance, by excessive use of ardent liquors, would not be apt to tell the disreputable truth, especially as it is not exacted under the obligations of an oath. Though I have as yet seen no reason be believe that intemperance, particularly among the native Americans, abounds here more than in other countries, yet I can readily believe it is very fatal in its consequences in a latitude where the temperature is so high in summer. There are certainly disorders that are more or less incidental to the climate, but there are many others of a pernicious character, that are either relatively innocent, or utterly unknown. When it is remembered that, compared with the amount of the whole population, a far greater number than usual of the inhabitants of this city are of that reckless and adventurous class that regard indulgence more than life, and how easy it is to procure indulgence here, I think it will be found by the official reports, that the city of New-York may claim a high place among the most salubrious ports of the world. This impression will be increased, when one recalls how little has as yet been done towards obtaining wholesome water, or to carry off the impurities of the place by means of drains. Still, as it is, New-York is far from being a dirty town. It has certainly degenerated from that wholesome and untiring cleanliness which it may be supposed to have inherited from its first possessors. The houses are no longer scrubbed externally, nor is it required to leave one's slippers at its gates, lest the dust of the roads should sully the brightness of glazed tiles and glaring bricks. But Paris is foul indeed, and London, in its more crowded parts, far from being cleanly, compared to New-York. And yet the commercial emporium of this nation bears no goodly reputation in this particular, among the Americans themselves. Her sister cities are said to be far more lovely, and the filth of the town is a subject of daily moanings in its own journals.

But admitting the civil in its fullest extent, it is but a trifling blot on the otherwise high pretensions of the place. Time, and a better regulated police, will serve to remedy much greater evils than this. In order to view the city in its proper light, it must be considered in connexion with those circumstances which are fast giving to it the character of the great mart of the western hemisphere.

By referring to the description already given, you will find that New-York possesses the advantages of capacious and excellent roadstead, a vast harbour, an unusually extensive natural basin, with two outlets to the sea, and a river that, in itself, might contain all the shipping of the earth. By means of the Sound, and its tributary waters, it has the closest connexion with the adjoining State of Connecticut; and, through the adjacent bays, small vessels penetrate in almost every direction into that of New-Jersey. These are the channels by which the town receives its ordinary daily supplies. Cadwallader pointed out on the map seven considerable navigable rivers, exclusive of the noble Hudson, and a vast number of inlets, creeks, and bays, all of which were within a hundred miles of this place, and with which daily an hourly intercourse is held by means of sloops, or steam-boats. Still these are no more than the minor and more familiar advantages of New-York, which, however they may contribute to her convenience, become insignificant when compared to the more important sources of her prosperity. It is true that in these little conveniences, Nature has done the work that man would probably have to perform a century hence, and thereby is the growth of the town greatly facilitated, but the true springs of its future grandeur must be described on a far more magnificent scale.

New-York stands central between the commerce of the north and that of the south. It is the first practicable port, at all seasons of the year, after you quit the mouth of the Chesapeake, going northward. It lies in the angle formed by the coast, and where the courses to Europe, to the West Indies, or to the Southern Atlantic, can be made direct. The ship from Virginia, or Louisiana, commonly passes within a day's sail of New-York, on its way to Europe, and the coaster from Boston frequently stops at the wharfs of this city to deposit part of its freight before proceeding further south.

Now, one so conversant with the world as yourself, need not be reminded that in every great commercial community there is a tendency to create a common mart, where exchanges can be regulated, loans effected, cargoes vended in gross, and all other things connected with trade, transacted on a scale commensurate to the magnitude of the interests involved in its pursuits. The natural advantages of New-York had indicated this port to the Americans for that spot, immediately after the restoration of the peace in 1783. Previously to that period, the whole proceedings of the colonies were more or less influenced by the policy of the mother country. But for a long time after the independence of the States was acknowledged, the possessors of the island of Manhattan had to contend for supremacy against a powerful rivalry. Philadelphia, distant less than a hundred miles, was not only more wealthy and more populous, but for many years it enjoyed the *éclat* and advantage of being the capital of the Union. Boston and Baltimore are both seaports of extensive connexions, and of great and enlightened enterprise. Against this serious competition, however, New-York struggled with success; gradually obtaining the superiority in tonnage and inhabitants, until within a few years, when opposition silently yielded to the force of circumstances, and those towns which had so long been rivals became auxiliaries to her aggrandizement. All this is perfectly in the natural course of things, though I find that a lingering of the ancient jealousy still tempts many of the merchants of the other towns to ascribe the ascendancy of New-York to any cause but the right one. Among other things, the establishment of those numerous lines of packets, to which I have alluded in a previous letter, is thought to have had an influence on her progress. It appears to me that this is mistaking the effect for the cause. If I am rightly informed, the merchant of Boston already sends his ship here for freight; frequently sells his cargo under the hammer of the New-York auctioneer to his own neighbour, and buys a new one to send to some distant part of the world, without seeing, from the commencement of the year to its close, the vessel which is the instrument of transporting his wealth to the various quarters of the world. Philadelphians have been pointed out to me who are said to be employed in pursuits of the same nature. The whole mystery of these transactions rests on a principle that is within the compass of any man's understanding. Though articles can be and are sometimes vended by itinerants in its streets, the material wants of every great town are supplied in the common market-place. It is easier to find a purchaser where much than where little is sold, and it is precisely for the reason that prices take a wider range in an extensive than in a limited market, that men congregate there to feed their wants or to glut their avarice. That New-York must, in the absence of any counteracting moral causes, at some day have become this chosen mart of American commerce, is sufficiently evident by its natural advantages; and that the hour of this supremacy has arrived is, I think, apparent by the facts which I have mentioned, supported as they are by the strong corroborating circumstance, that hundreds are now daily quitting the other towns to resort to this.

The consequences of its rapid growth, and the extraordinary medley of which its population is composed, serve to give something of a peculiar character to New-York. Cadwallader tells me that, with perhaps the exception of New-Orleans, it is the only city in the Union that has not the air of a provincial town. For my own part, I have found in it such a *mélange* to customs, nations, society, and manners, all tempered, without being destroyed, by the institutions and opinions of the country, that I despair of conveying a correct idea of either by description. We shall have more definite data in speaking of its unprecedented growth.

In 1756, the city of New-York contained 13,000 souls; in 1790, 33,000; in 1800, 60,000; in 1810, 96,000; in 1820, 123,000; and, in 1825, 166,000.[1] The latter enumeration is exclusive of Brooklyn, a flourishing village which has arisen within the last half dozen years from next to nothing; which, from its position and connexion with the city, is in truth no more than a suburb differently governed; and which in itself contains about 10,000 souls.

By the foregoing statement, you will see that, while the growth of New-York has been rather regular than otherwise, its population has doubled within the last thirty-five years nearly at the rate of once in fifteen years. Between 1790 and 1800, the comparative increase was the greatest. This was probably owing to the fact that it was the moment when the peculiar situation of the world gave an extraordinary impulse to the American commerce. Between 1800 and 1820, were felt the effects of a highly thriving trade, the re-action of embargoes, non-intercourse and ware, and the relative stagnation attendant on the return of business to its more natural channels. The extraordinary increase in the last five years, during a period of ordinary commerce, is, I think, to be imputed to the accessions obtained by the silent acquiescence of her rivals in the future supremacy of this town as the great mart of the nation. To what height, or how long this latter cause may serve to push the accumulation of New-York beyond what would be its natural growth, exceeds my ability to estimate. Though it may receive checks from the variety of causes which affect all prosperity, it will probably be some years before the influence of this revolution in opinion shall entirely cease; after which period, the growth of the city must be more regular, though always in proportion to the infant vigour of the whole country.

It is a curious calculation, and one in which the Americans very naturally love to indulge, to estimate the importance of this place at no very distant day. If the rate of increase for the last thirty-five years (or the whole period when the present institutions of the country have had an influence on its advancement) is to be taken as a guide for the future, the city of New-York will contain about 900,000 souls in the year 1860. Prodigious as this estimate may at first seem, it can be supported by arguments of a weight and truth of which you are most probably ignorant. Notwithstanding the buoyant character of this nation's prosperity, and the well-known fact that the growth of towns is by no means subject to the same general laws as that of countries, were it not for one circumstance, I should scarcely presume to hazard a calculation which wears the air of extravagance by its very amount, since, by merely adding another fifteen yeas, you have the largest town in Christendom as the reward of your addition. But, in point of fact, in order to keep pace with the progress of things in this extraordinary country, something like that which elsewhere might be termed extravagance of anticipation becomes absolutely necessary. Although the ideas of my companion are reasonably regulated by an extensive acquaintance with the eastern hemisphere, I confess I have been startled with the entire gravity with which he sometimes speaks of the power of the United States; not as an event to affect the fortunes of future ages, but as a thing that would be operative in the time of our own children, dear Baron, had not our egotistical habits left us without the hope of living in those who come after us. But when he paused this morning in our promenade through the Broadway, a noble street that runs for two miles through the heart of the place, and pointed out the limits of the city, as he himself had known them in his boyhood, and then desired me to look along the fine vista in front, which I knew was supported by vast masses of buildings on each of its sides, I felt the force of the reasons he had for entertaining opinions, that to me had just before seemed visionary.

The circumstances to which this town is to be indebted for most of its future greatness, is the immense and unprecedented range of interior which, by a bold and noble effort of policy, has recently been made tributary to its interest. By examining the map of the United States, you can easily make yourself master of all the facts necessary to a perfect understanding of what I mean. The river Hudson runs northward from New-York for the distance of about two hundred miles. It is navigable for large sloops to Waterford, a place that is situated near the junction of the Mohawk with the former river, and at a distance a little exceeding one hundred and fifty miles from this city. Sixty miles further north brings one to the head of Lake Champlain, which separates Vermont from New-York, and communicates with the St. Lawrence by means of a navigable outlet. By following the route of the Mohawk westward, you pass directly through the heart of this flourishing state, until you reach a place called Rome, whence the country to Lake Erie was found to be perfectly practicable for water communication. Once in Lake Erie, it is possible to extend a domestic trade, by means of those little inland, fresh-water seas, through a fertile and rapidly growing country, for a distance of near or quite fifteen hundred miles further. As if this were not enough, Nature has placed the head waters of the Mississippi so near the navigable tributaries of the lakes Michigan, Superior, and Erie, that there is nothing visionary in predicting that artificial communication will soon bring them into absolute contact.

It is a matter of dispute with whom the bold idea of connecting the waters of the lakes with those of the Hudson originated. The fact will probably never be known, since the thoughts of one may have been quickened by those of another, the speculations of each successor enlarging on those of him who went before, until the plaint of some Indian that nature had denied a passage to his canoe from the Mohawk into a stream of the lesser lakes, has probably given birth to them all. But there can be no question as to the individual, who, in a government so particularly cautious of its expenditures, has dared to stake his political fortunes on the success of the hazardous undertaking. Mr. Clinton, the present Governor of this State, is the only highly responsible political man who can justly lay claim to be the parent of the project. For many years, I am told, he was persecuted as a visionary projector, and it was clear that his downfall was to be the penalty of failure; though now that success is certain, or rather realized, there are hundreds ready to depreciate his merits, and not a few willing to share in all his honours. But these are no more than the detractions which are known every where to sully the brightness of a new reputation. Time will remove them all, since posterity never fails to restore with interest that portion of fame which is temporarily abstracted by the envy or the hostility of contemporaries.

The plan has been to reject the use of all the rivers, except as feeders, and to make two canals, one from the Lake Champlain, and the other from the Lake Erie, which were to meet at the junction of the Mohawk and the Hudson, whence they are to proceed to Albany, and issue into the latter river. The former of these canals is about sixty miles in length, and the other three hundred and fifty. The work was commenced in the year 1817, and is already nearly completed.

Really, reflection on this subject is likely to derange the ideas of the gravest man. Imagine, for instance, that Africa were a populous and civilized region; that Spain were peopled by an active and enlightened population; that their habits were highly commercial; and then assume that Gibraltar was not only one of the most noble, convenient and safe havens of the world, but that, from its central position, it had secured an ascendancy in European trade. Remove all serious rivals which chance or industry had raised in the other parts of Europe, to the prosperity of this unrivalled mart, placing it already foremost among the cities of our hemisphere. Then, suppose the Mediterranean, with all its tributaries, a narrow, convenient river, having direct communication with vast lakes, whose banks were peopled by men of similar educations and opinions, wants and wishes, governed by the same policy, and subject to the same general laws, and I commit you to your own imaginative powers to fancy what the place would become in the space of a century.

With these views unavoidably before the eye, it is difficult to descend to the sober reality of existing things. I can now easily understand the perspective of American character. It is absolutely necessary to destroy thought, to repress it. I fear we owe a good deal of our exemption from the quality we laugh at, to the same penetrating faculty of the mind. A state of things may easily exist, in which it is quite as pleasant to look back as forward; but here, though the brief retrospect be so creditable, it absolutely sinks into insignificance compared with the mighty future. These people have clearly only to continue discreet, to be foremost among the nations of the earth, and that too, most probably, before the discussion as to their future fate shall be forgotten.

While a subject so great is intensely pressing itself on the mind, as it unavoidably must on that of every intelligent stranger who has sufficient philanthropy to regard with steadiness the prosperity of a people who may so soon be a formidable rival, it is difficult to descent to those more immaterial and evanescent customs and appearances that mark the condition of the present hour. Still they are of importance as they may influence the future, and are not without interest by their peculiarities and national characteristics.

In construction, New-York embraces every variety of house, between that of the second-rate English town-residence, and those temporary wooden tenements that are seen in the skirts of most large cities. I do not think, however, that those absolutely miserable, filthy abodes which are often seen in Europe, abound here. The houses of the poor are not indeed large, like those in which families on the continent are piled on one another for six or seven stories, but they are rarely old and tottering; for the growth of the place, which, by its insular situation, is confined to one direction, forces them out of existence before they have had time to decay. I have been told, and I think it probable, that there are not five hundred buildings in New-York, that can date further back than the peace of '83. A few old Dutch dwellings yet remain, and can easily be distinguished by their little bricks, their gables to the street, and those steps on their battlement walls, which your countrymen are said to have invented, in order to ascend to regulate the iron weathercocks at every variation of the fickle-winds.

Although poverty has no permanent abode, yet New-York has its distinct quarters. I think they are sufficiently known and understood. Commerce is gradually taking possession of the whole of the lower extremity of the island, though the bay, the battery, and the charming Broadway, still cause many of the affluent to depart with reluctance. The fashion of the place is gradually collecting on the highest and healthiest point of land, where its votaries may be equally removed from the bustle of the two rivers (for the strait is strangely enough called a river), while other portions are devoted to the labouring classes, manufacturers, and the thousand pursuits of a seaport.

In outward appearance, New-York, but for two things, would resemble a part of London that should include fair proportions of Westminster (without the great houses and recent improvements), the city, and Wapping. The points of difference are owing to the fact that, probably without an exception, the exterior of all the houses are painted, and that there is scarce a street in the place which I was a long time puzzled to account. At first I imputed it to the brightness of the atmosphere, which differs but little from that of Italy; and then I thought it might be owing to the general animation and life that pervaded all the principal streets. Cadwallader explained the causes, and added, that the custom was nearly peculiar (with the exception of wooden buildings) to the towns in the ancient colony of the United Provinces. The common practice is to deepen the colour of the bricks by a red paint, and then to interline them with white; a fashion, that scarcely alters their original appearance, except by imparting a neatness and freshness that are exceedingly pleasant. But, in many instances, I saw dwellings of a lively cream colour; and there are also several varieties of stone that seem to be getting much in use latterly.

The principal edifice is the City Hall, a building in which the courts are held, the city authorities assemble, and the public offices are kept. This building is oddly enough composed of two sorts of stone, which impairs its simplicity, and gives it a patched and party-coloured appearance. Neither is its *façade* in good taste, being too much in detail, a fault the ancients were not fond of committing. Notwithstanding these glaring defects, by aid of its material, a clear white marble, and the admirable atmosphere, it at first strikes one more agreeably than many a better edifice. Its rear is of a deep red, dullish freestone, and in a far better taste. It is not unlike the *façade* of the *Hotel de Monnaies* at Paris; though not quite so large, more wrought, and I think something handsomer.

The moment the rear of the City Hall was seen, I was struck with an impression of the magnificent effect which might be produced by the use of its material in Gothic architecture. It seems to me to be the precise colour that good taste would select for the style, and the stone possesses the advantage of being easily worked, and is far less fragile than the common building materials of the vicinity of Paris. While the modern Gothic is much condemned, everybody appears willing that it is the most imposing style for churches. I can see no reason why that which everybody likes should not be done; and nothing is easier than to omit those horrible images and excrescences which we should not tolerate in the finest cathedrals of Europe, if they did not furnish unequivocal evidences of the humours of the age in which they were carved.

New-York is rich in churches, if number alone be considered. I saw more than a dozen in the process of construction, and there is scarce a street of any magnitude that does not possess one. There must be at least a hundred, and there may be many more. But in a country where the state does not meddle with religion, one is not to look for much splendour in its religious edifices. Private munificence cannot equal the expenditures of a community. Besides, I am told it is a laudable practice of the rich in this country, instead of concentrating their efforts to rear up one magnificent monument of their liberality, to bestow sufficient to meet the wants of a particular parish in a style suited to its character, and then to give, freely, aid to some other congregation of their faith that may be struggling into existence, perhaps, in a distant part of the country. Indeed, instances are said to be frequent, in which affluent men contribute cheerfully and liberally to assist in the erection of churches of a persuasion different from their own. You are to recollect that a territory large as a third of Europe, has to be furnished with places of worship by a population which does not exceed that of Prussia, and that too by voluntary contributions. In estimating what has been done in America in all things, it is absolutely necessary to do justice, and for a right understanding of the case, to remember the time, the means, and the amount that was to be executed. An honest consideration of these material points can alone show the true character of the country. For my own part, when I reflect on the extended division of the inhabitants, and on the absolute necessity of so much of their efforts being expended in meeting the first wants of civilized life, I am astonished to find how much they have done to embellish and improve it. Under this view of the subject, though certainly under no other, even their works of art become highly respectable. There is not much pretension to good taste in a great majority of their public edifices, nor is there much more ground to claim it in any other country, so far as modern architecture is concerned. Most of the churches in New-York are of brick, and constructed, internally, with direct reference to the comfort of the congregations, who, as you know, in most Protestant countries, remain when they once enter the temple. There are, however, some churches in this city that would make a creditable appearance any where among similar modern constructions; but it is in the number, rather than in the elegance of these buildings, that the Americans have reason to pride themselves.

Whatever you may have heard concerning neglect of religion on this side of the water, so far as the portion of the country I have seen is concerned, disbelieve. It is the language of malice and not of truth. So far as the human eye can judge, there is *at least* as much respect paid to religion in the northern and middle States, as in any part of the world I have ever visited. Were the religion of Europe to be stripped of its externals, and to lose that deference which the influence of the state and of the clergy produces, among a poor who are so dependant; in short, were man left to himself, or subject only to the impulses of public opinion, and the influence of voluntary instruction, as here, I am persuaded it would be found that there is vastly more. There is much cant, and much abuse of cant, in America, just as elsewhere; but I have been in numberless churches here; watched the people in their ingress and egress; have examined the crowd of *men* no less than of women, that followed the summons of the parish bell; and, in fine, have studied all their habits on those points which the conscience may be supposed to influence, and, taking town and country together, I should not know where to turn to find a population more uniform in their devotions, more guarded in their discourse, or more consistent in all their practices. No stronger proof can be given of the tone of the country in respect to religion than the fact, that men who wish to stand well in popular favour are compelled to feign it at least; public opinion producing, in this way, a far more manifest effect here than does state policy in our hemisphere. These remarks are of course only made in reference to what I have yet seen, but they may serve as a standard to compare by, when we shall come to speak of the other portions of the republic.

My paper is exhausted, and I shall refer you to the colonel, whom I known you are to meet at Palermo, for a continuation of the subject on some of those branches in which his nicer tact may find peculiar sources of interest.—Adieu.

To the Count Jules De Béthizy, Colonel En Retraite of the Imperial Guard.

New York, —

A man who has revelled so often on the delicacies of Very and Robert; who has so long flourished with éclat in the saloons of the modern queen of cities, who has sickened his taste under the arches of the Coliseum, or on the heights of the Acropolis, and who must have often cast a glance at that jewel of architecture, the Bourse of Paris, as he has hurried into its din to learn the fate of his last investment in the three per cents of M. de Villele, may possibly turn with disdain from a description of the inartificial beauties of nature, a republican drawing-room, or a mall in a commercial town of North America. But you will remember how often I have passed the bridge of Lodi in your company, (methinks I hear the whizzing of the bullets now!) how patiently I have listened to your sonnets on the mien and mind of Sophie, and how meekly I have seen you discussing the fragments of a *pâté de foie gras*, without so much as begrudging you a mouthful of the unctuous morsel, though it were even the last. Presuming on this often tried, and seemingly inexhaustible patience, I shall proceed to trespass on your more elevated pursuits in the shape of one of my desultory accounts of the manners and mode of life of the grave burghers of New-York.

I may say openly to you, what consideration for the national pride of Kemperfelt may have suppressed in my letters to him, that very little of its former usages can now be traced in the ancient capital of the New-Netherlands. One hears certain sonorous names in the streets to remind him of the original colony, it is true, but with these rare memorials of the fact, and a few angular, sidelong edifices, that resemble broken fragments of prismatic ice, there is no other passing evidence of its former existence. I have elsewhere said that the city of New-York is composed of inhabitants from all the countries of Christendom. Beyond a doubt, a very large majority, perhaps nine-tenths, are natives of the United States; but it is not probable that one-third who live here first saw the light on the island of Manhattan. It is computed that one in three are either natives of New-England, or are descendants of those who have emigrated from that portion of the country. To these must be added the successors of the Dutch, the English, the French, the Scotch and the Irish, and not a few who came in their proper persons from the countries occupied by these several nations. In the midst of such a mélange of customs and people it is exceedingly difficult to extract any thing like a definite general character. Perhaps there is none that can be given, without great allowance, to this community. Though somewhat softened, a good deal of that which is distinctive between the puritans and their brethren of the other States, is said to continue to exist for a long period after their emigration. As the former generally go to those points where they are tempted by interest, in great numbers, it is probable that they communicate quite as much, or, considering their active habits, perhaps more, of character than they receive. With these warnings, to take all I say with due allowance, I shall proceed to my task.

To commence *ab origine*, I shall speak of the products of nature, which,, if endowed with suitable capabilities, rarely fail of favour in your eyes. I know no spot of the habitable world to which the culinary sceptre is so likely to be transferred, when the art shall begin to decline in your own renowned capital, as this city. It is difficult to name fish, fowl, or beast that is not, either in its proper person, or in some species nearly allied to it, to be obtained in the markets of New-York. The exceptions that do certainly occur, are more than balanced by the animals that are peculiar to the country. Of fish alone, a gentleman here, of a spirit not uncongenial to your own, has named between seventy and eighty varieties, all of which are edible; most of which are excellent; and some of which it would be the pride of my heart to see placed within the control of your scientific skill. Of fowls there is a rare and admirable collection! I have had a list nearly, or quite as long as the catalogue of fishes placed before me, and it would do your digestive powers good to hear some of the semi-barbarous epicures of this provincial town expatiate on the merits of grouse, canvas-backs, brants, plover, wild turkeys, and all the *et cœteras* of the collection. In respect to the more vulgar products of regular agriculture I shall say nothing. They are to be found here, as elsewhere, with the exception, that, as a great deal is still left to nature, perfection and variety in vegetables is not as much attended to as in the vicinity of older and larger places. But of the game I may speak with confidence; for, little as I have yet seen of it, at this particular season, one mouthful is sufficient to prove that there is a difference between a partridge and a hen, greater than what is demonstrated by the simple fact that one sleeps on a roost, and the other in a tree. That delicious, wild, and peculiar flavour, that we learned to prize on the frontiers of Poland, and in the woods of Norway, exists in every thing that ranges the American forest. They tell me that so very dependent is the animal on the food it eats for its flavour, that the canvas-back of the Hudson, which, in the eyes of M. de Buffon, would be precisely the same bird as that of the Chesapeake, is in truth endowed with another nature; that is to say, in all those useful purposes for which a canvas-back was beyond a doubt created. But these are still matters of faith with me, though the delicacy of the plover, the black-fish, the sheep's-head, the woodcock, and numberless other delightful inhabitants of these regions, disposes me to believe all I hear.

Of the fruits I can speak of my own knowledge. The situation of New-York is singularly felicitous in this respect. In consequence of the great range of the thermometer, there is scarce a fruit which will endure the frost that is not found in a state nearly approaching to perfection. Indeed either owing to the freshness of the soil, or the genial influence of the sun, or to both, there is an extraordinary flavour imparted to most of the animal and vegetable food which I have tasted. Cadwallader reasons on the subject in this manner, assuming, what I believe to be true, that most of the meats, no less than the fruits, possess this peculiar richness and delicacy of taste. He says, that in Europe the value of land is commonly so great, that the cattle are obliged to crop *all* the herbage, whereas, in America, the animal is usually allowed to make its choice, and that, too, often amid such a delicious odour of the white or natural clover of the country, as might cause even a miserable victim of the anger of Djezzar Pacha momentarily to forget his nasal dilapidation. I wish now to be understood as speaking literally, and not in those terms of exaggeration which are perhaps appropriate to the glories of a well-ordered banquet. I scarce remember any fragrance equal to that I have scented in the midst of a field of this clover. My companion tells me he was first made sensible of this peculiarity in the herbage of his native country, by remarking how comparatively devoid of scent was a field of buckwheat, by the side of which he was once walking in the centre of France. Now, buckwheat in this climate is a plant that exhales a delicious odour that is often to be scented at the distance of a quarter of a mile. In short, so far as my own observation has extended, the sun imparts a flavour to every grass, plant, or fruit here, that must be tasted, and tasted with discrimination, in order to be appreciated. Yet man has done but little to improve these inestimable advantages. There is no extraordinary show of fruits in the public market-places. Peaches, cherries, melons, and a few others of the common sorts, it is true, abound; but the Americans appear not to be disposed to make much sacrifice of time, or money, to the cultivation of the rarer sorts.

I cannot close this subject, however, without making one remark on the nature of a peculiar difference that I have noticed between the fruits of this country, and those of your own capital in particular. A French peach is juicy, and, when you first bring it in contact with your palate, sweet, but it leaves behind it a cold, water, and almost sour taste. It is for this reason so often eaten with sugar. An American is exceedingly apt to laugh if he sees ripe fruit of any sort eaten with any thing sweet. The peaches here leave behind a warm, rich, and delicious taste, that I can only liken in its effects to that which you call the *bouquet* of a glass of *Romanée*. You who, as a Parisian, say so much for, and think so much of, your *goût*, may be disposed to be incredulous when I tell you these people would positively reject the best melon that ever appears on your table. There is a little one to be picked up in the markets here for a few sous, say twelve at the utmost, that exceeds any thing, of its kind, that I have ever admitted into the sanctuary of my mouth. I want terms to describe it. It is firm, and yet tender; juicy, without a particle of the cold, watery taste we know, and of an incomparable flavour and sweetness. Its equal can only be found in the Crimea, or the adjacent parts of Turkey, and perhaps of Persia. The Americans admit that it is the only melon that can appear on the table of one who understands the difference between eating and tasting, and to me it seems to have been especially created for an epicure. In the gardens of the gentlemen you find not only a greater variety, but, a few common fruits excepted, a far better quality than in the markets. I have tasted a great many old acquaintances, transplanted from the eastern to the western hemisphere, and I declare I do not remember one that has not been benefited by the change, in flavour, though not always in appearance. It is a standing joke of Cadwallader to say his countrymen consult the substance much more than the shadow, when I venture to qualify my praises by some remark on externals. I remember, however, one day he effectually silenced my criticism, by leading me to a peach-tree that grew in the shade of an adjacent building. The fruit was beautiful, exceedingly large, and without a blemish. Culling one of the finest, I bit it, and involuntarily rejected what I had so incautiously admitted to my mouth. Then placing a peach which had grown in the open air, in my hands, my companion pointed significantly to the sun, and walked on, leaving me to reflect on an argument that was more potent than a thousand words.

And yet I have met, during my short residence in America, Europeans who have affected to rail at, or even to deny the existence of her fruits! I have always wished, on such occasions, that I could transport the products of one of the laboured gardens of our hemisphere into this, and set them to culling without a knowledge of the transfer. My life on it, their own palates would contradict their assertions in the first five minutes.

Indeed, one has only to remember that the United States extend from forty-five to twenty-five degrees of latitude, to see that Nature has placed their dominions in the very centre of her most favoured regions. There is, too, a peculiarity of climate here, which is unknown to similar parallels of latitude in Europe. The apple and the peach are found in perfection, side by side; and in such a perfection too, as, believe me, dear colonel, you must seek for the equal of the one in Italy, and that of the other, I scarcely know where.

Owing to the facility and constancy of intercourse with the Southern States, the fruits of the tropics are found here, not quite as fresh, certainly, as when first culled from the plant itself, but well flavoured, and in absolute context with the products of the temperate zones. Pine-apples, large, rich, golden, and good, are sold from twelve to twenty-five sous; delicious oranges are hawked in the streets much cheaper than a tolerable apple can be bought in the ships of Paris, and bannanas, yams, water-melons, &c., are as common as need be in the markets. It is this extraordinary combination of the effects of different climates, the union of heat and cold, and of commercial facilities, added to the rare bounties of Nature, that incline me to think the empire of gastronomy will, sooner or later, be transferred to this spot. At present it must be confessed that the science is lamentably defective, and, after all, perhaps, it is in those places where Nature has been most liberal that man is apt to content himself, without exerting those efforts of his own, without which no perfect enjoyment in any branch of human indulgence can exist.

Passing from the means of gratification possessed by these people, we will turn our attention, for a moment, to the manner in which they are improved. The style of living of all the Americans, in the Northern States, is essentially English. As might be expected in a country where labour is comparatively high, and the fortunes, though great, still not often so princely as in the mother country, the upper classes live in a more simple form, wanting some of the most refined improvements of high English life, and yet indulging, under favour of their climate, situation and great commercial freedom, in perhaps a greater combination of luxury and comfort than any other people in the world. In respect of comfort itself, there is scarce any known in England, that is not to be found here; the point of difference is in its frequency. You are, therefore, to deduct rather in the amount of English comfort, than in its quality, and you are not to descend far below the refinements at all, since all the substantials of that comfort which makes England so remarkable in Europe, are to be found equally in America. There are points, perhaps, even in the latter, in which the Englishman (rarely very much disposed to complacency) would complain in America; and there are, certainly, others, on which the American (who has a cast of the family likeness) would boldly vent his spleen in England. I am of opinion the two nations might benefit a good deal by a critical examination of each other. Indeed, I think the American has, and does, daily profit by his observation, though I scarce know whether his kinsman is yet disposed to admit that he can learn by the study of a people so new, so remote, and so little known, as those of the United States.

After you descend below the middle classes in society, there is no comparison to be drawn between the condition of the American and that of the native of England, or of any other place. I have seen misery here, it is true, and filth, and squalid, abject poverty, always in the cities, however; but it is rare; that is, rare indeed to what I have been accustomed to see in Europe. At first, I confess there was a feeling of disappointment came over me at seeing it at all; but reflection convinced me of the impossibility of literally bringing all men to a state in which they might profit by the advantages of their condition. Cadwallader, also, who has a silent, significant manner of conveying truths, has undeceived me more than once when I have been on the very threshold of an error. I remember that one day, while I stood contemplating, in the suburbs of this city, a scene of misery that one might not have expected to witness out of Europe, he advanced to the door of the dreary hovel I gazed at, and asked the inhabitants how long they had resided in America. The answer proved that he had not deceived himself as to the birth-place of its luckless tenants. In this manner, in more than a dozen instances, he has proved that his own country has not given birth to the vice and idleness which here could alone entail such want. In perhaps as many more instances he has passed on, shaking his head at my request that he would examine the causes, admitting frankly that he saw the subjects were natives. It is astonishing how accurate his eye is in making this distinction. I do not know that he has been deceived in a solitary instance. Where misery is so rare, it is a vast deal to admit, that perhaps half of its objects are the victims of a different system than that under which it is exhibited.

There is something exceedingly attractive in the exhibition of neatness and domestic comfort which one sees throughout this country. I think the brilliancy of the climate, the freshness of the paint, and the exterior ornaments of the houses, contribute to the charm. There is a species of second-rate, genteel houses, that abound in New-York, into which I have looked when passing, with the utmost pleasure. They have, as usual, a story that is half sunk in the earth receiving light from an area, and two floors above. The tenants of these buildings are chiefly merchants, or professional men, in moderate circumstances, who pay rents of from 300 to 500 dollars a year. You know that no American, who is at all comfortable in life, will share his dwelling with another. Each has his own roof, and his own little yard. These buildings are finished, and exceedingly well finished too, to the attics; containing, on the average, six rooms, besides offices, and servants' apartments. The furniture of these houses is often elegant, and always neat. Mahogany abounds here, and is commonly used for all the principal articles, and very frequently for doors, railings of stairs, &c. &c. Indeed, the whole world contributes to their luxury. French clocks, English and Brussels carpets, curtains from Lyons, and the Indies, alabaster from France and Italy, marble of their own, and from Italy, and, in short, every ornament below the rarest that is known in every other country in Christendom, and frequently out of it, is put within the reach of the American of moderate means, by the facilities of their trade. In that classical taste which has been so happily communicated to your French artisans, their own are, without doubt, miserably deficient; but they are good imitators, and there is no scarcity of models. While, in consequence of want of taste or want of wealth, the Americans possess, in very few instances, any one of the articles that contribute to the grace of life in the same perfection as they are known in some one other country, they enjoy, by means of their unfettered trade, a combination of the same species of luxuries, in a less advanced state, that is found nowhere else. They often, nay, almost always, fail in the particular excellence, but they possess an aggregate of approximate perfection that is unrivalled, perhaps, even in England; certainly if we descend below the very highest classes in the latter country.

But there are hundreds, I believe I might almost say a thousand, houses in New-York of pretensions altogether superior to those just named. A particular description of one belonging to a friend of Cadwallader, by whose favour I was permitted to examine it, may serve to give you an idea of the whole of its class. The proprietor is a gentleman of the first society of the country, and of what is here called an easy fortune, though hundreds of his neighbours enjoy the goods of this world in a far greater degree than himself.

The dwelling of Mr. — is on the Broadway, one of the principal streets, that runs on the height of land along the centre of the island, for the distance of about two miles. It is the fashionable mall of the city, and certainly, for gaiety, the beauty and grace of the beings who throng it, and, above all, the glorious sun that seems to reign here three days out of four, it may safely challenge competition with most if not any of the promenades of the old world. The house in question occupies, I should think, a front of about thirty-four feet on the Broadway, and extends into the rear between sixty and seventy more. There are no additions, the building ascending from the ground to its attics in the same proportions. The exterior necessarily presents a narrow, ill-arranged facade, that puts architectural beauty a good deal at defiance. The most that can be done with such a front is to abstain from inappropriate ornament, and to aim at such an effect as shall convey a proper idea of the more substantial comforts, and of the neatness that predominate within. The building is of bricks, painted and lined, as already described, and modestly ornamented, in a very good taste, with caps, sills, cornices, &c. &c. in the dark red freestone of the country. The house is of four stories; the lower, or *rez de chaussée*, being half sunk, as is very usual, below the surface of the ground, and the three upper possessing elevations well proportioned to the height of the edifice. The door is at one of the corners of the front, and is nearly on a level with the windows of the first floor, which may commence at the distance of about a dozen feet above the pavement of the street. To reach this door, it is necessary to mount a flight of steep, inconvenient steps, also in freestone, which compensate, in a slight degree, for the pain of the ascent, (neither of us, colonel, is as young now as the day you crossed the bridge of Lodi), by their admirable neatness, and the perfect order of their iron rails and glittering brass ornaments. The entrance is into a little vestibule, which may be some twelve feet long, by eight in width. This apartment is entirely unfurnished, and appears only constructed to shelter visitors while the servant is approaching to admit them through the inner door. The general excellence of the climate, and, perhaps, the customs of the country, have, as yet, prevented the Americans from providing a proper place for the reception of the servants of their guests: they rarely wait, unless during the short calls, and then it is always in the street. As visitors are never announced, and as but one family occupies the same building, there is little occasion, unless to assist in unrobing, for a servant to attend his master, or mistress, within the outer door. From the vestibule the entrance is into a long, narrow, high, and handsome corridor, at the farther extremity of which are the principal stairs. This corridor, or passage, as it is called here, is carpeted, lighted with a handsome lamp, has a table, and a few chairs; and, in short, is just as unlike a French corridor as any thing of the sort can very well be. From this passage you enter the rooms on the first floor; you ascend to the upper, and descend to the lower story, and you have egress from and ingress to the house by its front and rear. The first floor is occupied by two rooms that communicate by double doors. These apartments are of nearly equal size, and, subtracting the space occupied by the passage, and two little china closets, that partially separate them, they cover the whole are of the house. Each room is lighted by two windows; is sufficiently high; has stuccoed ceiling, and cornices in white; hangings of light, airy, French paper; curtains in silk and in muslin; mantel-pieces of carved figures in white marble (Italian in manufacture, I should think); Brussels carpets; large mirrors; chairs, sofas, and tables, in mahogany; chandeliers; beautiful, neat, and highly wrought grates in the fire-places of home work; candelabras, lustres, &c. &c., much as one sees them all over Europe. In one of the rooms, however, is a spacious, heavy, ill-looking side-board, in mahogany, groaning with plate, knife and spoon cases, all handsome enough, I allow, but sadly out of place where they are seen. Here is the first great defect that I find in the ordering of American domestic economy. The eating, or dining-room, is almost invariably one of the best in the house. The custom is certainly of English origin, and takes it rise in the habit of sitting an hour or two after the cloth is removed, picking nuts, drinking wine, chatting, yawning, and gazing about the apartment. The first great improvement to be made in the household of these people is to substitute taste for prodigality in their tables; and the second, I think, will be to choose an apartment for their meals, that shall be convenient to the offices, suited to the habits of the family, plain in its ornaments, and removed from the ordinary occupations of those who are to enjoy it. In some houses this is already partially effected; but, as a rule, I am persuaded that the American guest, who should find himself introduced into a *salle à manger* as plain as that in which a French duke usually takes his repast would not think his host a man who sufficiently understood the fitness of things. I have heard it said, that the occupant of the White House gives his dinners in one of these plain rooms, and that the meanness of Congress is much laughed at because they do not order one better furnished for him. Certes if Congress never showed a worse taste than this, they might safely challenge criticism. As the President, or his wife, directs these matters, I suppose, however, the great national council is altogether innocent of the innovation.

You ascend, by means of the stairs at the end of the passage, into what is here called the second story, but which, from the equivocal character of the basement, it is difficult to name correctly. This ascent is necessarily narrow, crowded, and inconvenient. The beautiful railings in mahogany and brass, and the admirable neatness of every part of an American house of any pretension, would serve to reconcile one to a thousand defects. As respects this cardinal point, I think there is little difference between the English and the Americans, at least, so far as I have yet seen the latter; but the glorious sun of this climate illumines every thing to such a degree, as to lend a quality of brightness that is rarely known in Britain. You know that a diamond will hardly glitter in London. It must also be remembered that an American house is kept in this order by the aid of perhaps one third of the domestics that would be employed in the mother country.

On the second floor (or perhaps you will get a better idea if I call it the first) of the house of Mr. —, there is a spacious saloon, which occupies the whole width of the building, and possesses a corresponding breadth. This apartment, being exclusively that of the mistress of the mansion, is furnished with rather more delicacy than those below. The curtains are in blue India damask, the chairs and sofa of the same coloured silk, and other things are made to correspond. The library of the husband is on the same floor, and between the two there is a room used as a bed-chamber. The third story is appropriated to the sleeping-rooms of the family; the attic to the same purpose for the servants, and the basement contains a nursery and the usual offices. The whole building is finished with great neatness, and with a solidity and accuracy of workmanship that it is rare to meet in Europe, out of England. The doors of the better rooms are of massive mahogany, and wherever wood is employed, it is used with great taste and skill. All the mantel-pieces are marble, all the floors are carpeted, and all the walls are finished in a firm, smooth cement.

I have been thus minute in my account, because in describing the house of Mr. —, I am persuaded that I convey a general idea of those of all of the upper classes in the northern section of this country. There are, certainly, much larger and more pretending buildings than his in New-York, and many far richer and more highly wrought; but this is the habitation of an American in the very best society, who is in easy circumstances, of extensive and high connexions, and who receives a fair proportion of his acquaintances. By extending the building a little, adding something to the richness of the furniture, and now and then going as far as two or three cabinet pictures, you will embrace the establishments of the most affluent; and by curtailing the whole, perhaps, to the same degree, you will include an immense majority of all that part of the community who can lay claim to belong to the class of *les gens comme il faut*. It is here, as elsewhere, a fact that the parvenus are commonly the most lavish in their expenditures, either because money is a novelty, or, what is more probably the case, because they find it necessary to purchase consideration by its liberal use. We will now quit this dwelling, in which I am fond of acknowledging that I have been received with the most kind and polished hospitality, by its execrable flight of steps, and descend into the street.

The New-Yorkers (how much better is the word Manhattanese!) cherish the clumsy inconvenient entrances, I believe, as heir-looms of their Dutch progenitors. They are called "stoops", a word of whose derivation I am ignorant, though that may be of Holland too, and they are found disfiguring the architecture, cumbering the side-walks, and endangering the human neck, attached to the front doors of more than two thirds of the dwellings of this city. A better taste is, however, gradually making its way, and houses with regular basements are seen, in which the occupants can ascend to their apartments without encountering the dangers that in winter must frequently equal those of an ascent to the summit of Mont Blanc.

You will see, by the foregoing description, that the family of an American gentleman in town, though not always so conveniently, is on the whole about as well lodged as the great majority of the similar class in your own country. The house of Mr. — contains, including three capacious saloons, ten considerable rooms, besides offices, and servants' chambers. The deficiency is in the dining-room, in the inconvenience of the narrow stairs, and in the bad division of the principal apartments on the different floors; a fault that arises from the original construction of the building. Though the ornaments are in general more simple, the Americans have in very many things a great advantage. Profiting by their nearly unshackled commerce, they import any thing they choose, and adopt, or reject its use, as fancy dictates. Almost every article of foreign industry can be purchased here at a very small advance on the original cost, and in many instances even cheaper. Competition is so active, and information so universal, and so rapidly imparted, that a monopoly can hardly exist for a week, and a glut is far more common than a scarcity.

You will also see by what I have written, that the Americans have not yet adopted a style of architecture of their own. Their houses are still essentially English, though neither the winters nor the summers of their climate would seem to recommend them. There is, however, something in the opposite characters of the two seasons, to render a choice difficult. A people in whose country the heats of Florence and the colds of St. Petersburg periodically prevail, may well hesitate between a marble fountain and a Russian stove. I am not certain that, considering their pursuits, and the peculiarity of climate, they are very wrong in their present habits. But I shall for ever protest against the use of carpets, while the thermometer is at 90°, nor shall I soon cease to declaim against those hideous excrescences called "stoops". Beautiful, fragrant, and cool India mats, are, notwithstanding, much in use in midsummer, in the better houses. Still, with all my efforts, I have not been able to find a room to sleep in, that it is not fortified with a Brussels, or a double English ingrain. The perspiration stands on my forehead while I write of them! Another defect in the American establishments is the want of *cabinets de toilette.* They are certainly to be found in a few houses, but I have occupied a bed-room five and twenty feet square, in a house, otherwise convenient, that had not under its roof a single apartment of the sort. This is truly a sad prodigality of room, though space be unquestionably so very desirable in a warm climate.

I should think about the same proportion of the inhabitants keep carriages here as in France. But the ordinary coaches of the stands in New-York are quite as good, and often far better than those *voitures de remise* that one usually gets by the day in Paris. There is even a still better class of coaches to be ordered by the day, or hour, from the stables, which are much used by the inhabitants. The equipages of this city, with the exception of liveries, and heraldic blazonries, are very much like those of your own mighty capital. When I first landed, coming as I did from England, I thought the coaches so exceedingly light as to be mean; but, too experienced a traveller to be precipitate, I waited for the old impressions to lose a little of their influence before an opinion was formed, and in a short time I came to see their beauties. Cadwallader told me that when he first arrived in England, he was amazed at the clumsiness of the English vehicles, but that time, by rendering them familiar, soon changed his opinion. We went together lately to examine a coach from London, which its owner had abandoned, either in distaste, or because he found it unsuited to the country, and really it was calculated to renew all the original opinions of my friend. I have heard of an American who carried to England one of the light vehicles of his country, and after it had arrived, he was positively ashamed to exhibit it among its ponderous rivals. In this manner do we all become the subjects of a capricious and varying taste that is miserably dependent on habit; a fact, simple as it is, which might teach moderation and modesty to all young travellers, and rather less dogmatism than is commonly found among some that are older.—Adieu.

Note

1. It is supposed to contain about 200,000 at the present moment.

95

Five Poems

WALT WHITMAN

Walt Whitman (1819–1892) remains, apart from Emily Dickinson, the greatest American poet of the nineteenth century. He spent virtually all of his life in the New York area, especially Brooklyn and (after crossing on the Fulton Ferry) meandering along his beloved Broadway area. His work depicts an acutely observed sense of the city undergoing an almost mythic image of change and development. His poetry attempts to celebrate what he saw as a new dynamic urban energy and process which reflected an ideal image of a new culture based on democratic and modern principles. His ideal vision, much influenced by transcendentalism and the philosophy of Emerson, was first extolled in *Leaves of Grass* (1855), which he published in several editions until his death. In spite of his negative experiences in the Civil War period, Whitman made New York a central icon of his radical vision. The free-form of his verse is at once a reflection of physical and sexual freedom as it is a response to the rhythms of a new urban experience. *Specimen Days* (1882–83) offers a prose account of his response, especially his "jaunts" in the West. There is, however, a dark side to Whitman and the examples which follow reflect the extremes of his response. See Paul Zweig, *Walt Whitman the Poet* (1987), Gay Wilson Allen, *The Solitary Singer—A Critical Biography* (1955), and Graham Clarke, *Walt Whitman: The Poem as Private History* (1991).

Crossing Brooklyn Ferry

1

Flood-tide below me! I see you face to face!
Clouds of the west—sun there half an hour high—I see you also face to face.

Crowds of men and women attired in the usual costumes, how curious you are to me!

Source: Walt Whitman, "Crossing Brooklyn Ferry" (1856), "Mannahatta" (1860), "A Broadway Pageant" (1860), "The City Dead-House" (1867), "Broadway" (1888).

On the ferry-boats the hundreds and hundreds that cross, returning home, are more curious to me than you suppose,
And you that shall cross from shore to shore years hence are more to me, and more in my meditations, than you might suppose.

2

The impalpable sustenance of me from all things at all hours of the day,
The simple, compact, well-join'd scheme, myself disintegrated, every one disintegrated yet part of the scheme,
The similitudes of the past and those of the future,
The glories strung like beads on my smallest sights and hearings, on the walk in the street and the passage over the river,
The current rushing so swiftly and swimming with me far away,
The others that are to follow me, the ties between me and them,
The certainty of others, the life, love, sight, hearing of others.

Others will enter the gates of the ferry and cross from shore to shore,
Others will watch the run of the flood-tide,
Others will see the shipping of Manhattan north and west, and the heights of Brooklyn to the south and east,
Others will see the islands large and small;
Fifty years hence, others will see them as they cross, the sun half an hour high,
A hundred years hence, or ever so many hundred years hence, others will see them,
Will enjoy the sunset, the pouring-in of the flood-tide, the falling-back to the sea of the ebb-tide.

3

It avails not, time nor place—distance avails not,
I am with you, you men and women of a generation, or ever so many generations hence,
Just as you feel when you look on the river and sky, so I felt,
Just as any of you is one of a living crowd, I was one of a crowd,
Just as you are refresh'd by the gladness of the river and the bright flow, I was refresh'd.
Just as you stand and lean on the rail, yet hurry with the swift current, I stood yet was hurried,
Just as you look on the numberless masts of ships and the thick-stemm'd pipes of steamboats, I look'd.

I too many and many a time cross'd the river of old,
Watched the Twelfth-month sea-gulls, saw them high in the air floating with motionless wings, oscillating their bodies,
Saw how the glistening yellow lit up part of their bodies and left the rest in strong shadow,
Saw the slow-wheeling circles and the gradual edging toward the south,

Saw the reflection of the summer sky in the water,
Had my eyes dazzled by the shimmering track of beams,
Look'd at the fine centrifugal spokes of light round the shape of my head in the sunlit water,
Look'd on the haze on the hills southward and south-westward,
Look'd on the vapor as it flew in fleeces tinged with violet,
Look'd toward the lower bay to notice the vessels arriving,
Saw their approach, saw aboard those that were near me,
Saw the white sails of schooners and sloops, saw the ships at anchor,
The sailors at work in the rigging or out astride the spars,
The round masts, the swinging motion of the hulls, the slender serpentine pennants.
The large and small streamers in motion, the pilots in their pilot-houses,
The white wake left by the passage, the quick tremulous whirl of the wheels,
The flags of all nations, the falling of them at sunset,
The scallop-edged waves in the twilight, the ladled cups, the frolicsome crests and glistening,
The stretch afar growing dimmer and dimmer, the gray walls of the granite storehouses by the docks,
On the river the shadowy group, the big steam-tug closely flank'd on each side by the barges, the hay-boat, the belated lighter,
On the neighboring shore the fires from the foundry chimneys burning high and glaringly into the night,
Casting their flicker of black contrasted with wild red and yellow light over the tops of houses, and down into the clefts of streets.

4

These and all else were to me the same as they are to you,
I loved well those cities, loved well the stately and rapid river,
The men and women I saw were all near to me,
Others the same—others who look back on me because I look'd forward to them,
(The time will come, though I stop here to-day and to-night.)

5

What is it then between us?
What is the count of the scores or hundreds of years between us?

Whatever it is, it avails not—distance avails not, and place avails not,
I too lived, Brooklyn of ample hills was mine,
I too walk'd the streets of Manhattan island, and bathed in the waters around it,
I too felt the curious abrupt questionings stir within me,
In the day among crowds of people sometimes they came upon me,
In my walks home late at night or as I lay in my bed they came upon me,
I too had been struck from the float forever held in solution,

I too had receiv'd identity by my body,
That I was I knew was of my body, and what I should be I knew I should be of my body.

6

It is not upon you alone the dark patches fall,
The dark threw its patches down upon me also,
The best I had done seem'd to me blank and suspicious,
My great thoughts as I supposed them, were they not in reality meagre?
Nor is it you alone who know what it is to be evil,
I am he who knew what it was to be evil,
I too knitted the old knot of contrariety,
Blabb'd, blush'd, resented, lied, stole, grudg'd,
Had guile, anger, lust, hot wishes I dared not speak,
Was wayward, vain, greedy, shallow, sly, cowardly, malignant,
The wolf, the snake, the hog, not wanting in me,
The cheating look, the frivolous word, the adulterous wish, not wanting,
Refusals, hates, postponements, meanness, laziness, none of these wanting,
Was one with the rest, the days and haps of the rest,
Was call'd by my nighest name by clear loud voices of young men as they saw me approaching or passing,
Felt their arms on my neck as I stood, or the negligent leaning of their flesh against me as I sat,
Saw many I loved in the street or ferry-boat or public assembly, yet never told them a word,
Lived the same life with the rest, the same old laughing, gnawing, sleeping,
Play'd the part that still looks back on the actor or actress,
The same old role, the role that is what we make it, as great as we like,
Or as small as we like, or both great and small.

7

Closer yet I approach you,
What thought you have of me now, I had as much of you—I laid in my stores in advance,
I consider'd long and seriously of you before you were born.

Who was to know what should come home to me?
Who knows but I am enjoying this?
Who knows, for all the distance, but I am as good as looking at you now, for all you cannot see me?

8

Ah, what can ever be more stately and admirable to me than mast-hemm'd Manhattan?
River and sunset and scallop-edg'd waves of flood-tide?
The sea-gulls oscillating their bodies, the hay-boat in the twilight, and the

belated lighter?
What goods can exceed these that clasp me by the hand, and with voices I love call me promptly and loudly by my nighest name as I approach?
What is more subtle than this which ties me to the woman or man that looks in my face?
Which fuses me into you now, and pours my meaning into you?

We understand then do we not?
What I promis'd without mentioning it, have you not accepted?
What the study could not teach—what the preaching could not accomplish is accomplish'd, is it not?

9

Flow on, river! flow with the flood-tide, and ebb with the ebb-tide!
Frolic on, crested and scallop-edg'd waves!
Gorgeous clouds of the sunset! drench with your splendor me, or the men and women generations after me!
Cross from shore to shore, countless crowds of passengers!
Stand up, tall masts of Mannahatta! stand up, beautiful hills of Brooklyn!
Throb, baffled and curious brain! throw out questions and answers!
Suspend here and everywhere, eternal float of solution!
Gaze, loving and thirsting eyes, in the house or street or public assembly!
Sound out, voices of young men! loudly and musically call me by my nighest name!
Live, old life! play the part that looks back on the actor or actress!
Play the old role, the role that is great or small according as one makes it!
Consider, you who peruse me, whether I may not in unknown ways be looking upon you;
Be firm, rail over the river, to support those who lean idly, yet haste with the hasting current;
Fly on, sea-birds! fly sideways, or wheel in large circles high in the air;
Receive the summer sky, you water, and faithfully hold it till all downcast eyes have time to take it from you!
Diverge, fine spokes of light, from the shape of my head, or any one's head, in the sunlit water!
Come on, ships from the lower bay! pass up or down, white-sail'd schooners, sloops, lighters!
Flaunt away, flags of all nations! be duly lower'd at sunset!
Burn high your fires, foundry chimneys! cast black shadows at nightfall! cast red and yellow light over the tops of the houses!
Appearances, now or henceforth, indicate what you are,
You necessary film, continue to envelop the soul,
About my body for me, and your body for you, be hung our divinest aromas,
Thrive, cities—bring your freight, bring your shows, ample and sufficient rivers,
Expand, being than which none else is perhaps more spiritual,

Keep your places, objects than which none else is more lasting.

You have waited, you always wait, you dumb, beautiful ministers,
We receive you with free sense at last, and are insatiate hence-forward,
Not you any more shall be able to foil us, or withhold yourselves from us,
We use you, and do not cast you aside—we plant you permanently within us,
We fathom you not—we love you—there is perfection in you also,
You furnish your parts toward eternity,
Great or small, you furnish your parts toward the soul.

1856

Mannahatta

I was asking for something specific and perfect for my city,
Whereupon lo! upsprang the aboriginal name.

Now I see what there is in a name, a word, liquid, sane, unruly, musical, self-sufficient,
I see that the word of my city is that word from of old,
Because I see that word nested in nests of water-bays, superb,
Rich, hemm'd thick all around with sailships and steamships, an island sixteen miles long, solid-founded,
Numberless crowded streets, high growths of iron, slender, strong, light, splendidly uprising toward clear skies,
Tides swift and ample, well-loved by me, toward sundown,
The flowing sea-currents, the little islands, larger adjoining islands, the heights, the villas,
The countless masts, the white shore-steamers, the lighters, the ferry-boats, the black sea-steamers well-model'd,
The down-town street, the jobbers' houses of business, the houses of business of the ship-merchants and money-brokers, the river-streets,
Immigrants arriving, fifteen or twenty thousand in a week,
The carts hauling goods, the manly race of drivers of horses, the brown-faced sailors,
The summer air, the bright sun shining, and the sailing clouds aloft,
The winter snows, the sleigh-bells, the broken ice in the river, passing along up or down with the flood-tide or ebb-tide,
The mechanics of the city, the masters, well-form'd, beautiful-faced, looking you straight in the eyes,
Trottoirs throng'd, vehicles, Broadway, the women, the ships and shows,
A million people—manners free and superb—open voices—hospitality—the most courageous and friendly young men,
City of hurried and sparkling waters! city of spires and masts!
City nested in bays! my city!

1860

A Broadway Pageant

1

Over the Western sea hither from Niphon come,
Courteous, the swart-cheek'd two-sworded envoys,
Leaning back in their open barouches, bare-headed, impassive,
Ride to-day through Manhattan.

Libertad! I do not know whether others behold what I behold,
In the procession along with the nobles of Niphon, the errand-bearers,
Bringing up the rear, hovering above, around, or in the ranks marching,
But I will sing you a song of what I behold Libertad.

When million-footed Manhattan unpent descends to her pavements,
When the thunder-cracking guns arouse me with the proud roar I love,
When the round-mouth'd guns out of the smoke and smell I love spit their salutes,
When the fire-flashing guns have fully alerted me, and heaven-clouds canopy my city with a delicate thin haze,
When gorgeous the countless straight stems, the forests at the wharves, thicken with colors,
When every ship richly drest carries her flag at the peak,
When pennants trail and street-festoons hang from the windows,
When Broadway is entirely given up to foot-passengers and foot-standers, when the mass is densest,
When the façades of the houses are alive with people, when eyes gaze riveted tens of thousands at a time,
When the guests from the islands advance, when the pageant moves forward visible,
When the summons is made, when the answer that waited thousands of years answers,
I too arising, answering, descend to the pavements, merge with the crowd, and gaze with them.

2

Superb-faced Manhattan!
Comrade Americanos! to us, then at last the Orient comes.

To us, my city,
Where our tall-topt marble and iron beauties range on opposite sides, to walk in the space between,
To-day our Antipodes comes.

The Originatress comes,
The nest of languages, the bequeather of poems, the race of eld,
Florid with blood, pensive, rapt with musings, hot with passion,

Sultry with perfume, with ample and flowing garments,
With sunburnt visage, with intense soul and glittering eyes,
The race of Brahma comes.

See my cantabile! these and more are flashing to us from the procession,
As it moves changing, a kaleidoscope divine it moves changing before us.
For not the envoys nor the tann'd Japanee from his island only,
Lithe and silent the Hindoo appears, the Asiatic continent itself appears, the past, the dead,
The murky night-morning of wonder and fable inscrutable,
The envelop'd mysteries, the old and unknown hive-bees,
The north, the sweltering south, eastern Assyria, the Hebrews, the ancient of ancients,
Vast desolated cities, the gliding present, all of these and more are in the pageant-procession.

Geography, the world, is in it,
The Great Sea, the brood of islands, Polynesia, the coast beyond,
The coast you henceforth are facing—you Libertad! from your Western golden shores,
The countries there with their populations, the millions en-masse are curiously here,
The swarming market-places, the temples with idols ranged along the sides or at the end, bonze, brahmin, and llama,
Mandarin, farmer, merchant, mechanic, and fisherman,
The singing-girl and the dancing-girl, the ecstatic persons, the secluded emperors,
Confucius himself, the great poets and heroes, the warriors, the castes, all,
Trooping up, crowding from all directions, from the Altay mountains,
From Thibet, from the four winding and far-flowing rivers of China,
From the southern peninsulas and the demi-continental islands, from Malaysia,
These and whatever belongs to them palpable show forth to me, and are seiz'd by me,
And I am seiz'd by them, and friendlily held by them,
Till as here them all I chant, Libertad! for themselves and for you.

For I too raising my voice join the ranks of this pageant,
I am the chanter, I chant aloud over the pageant,
I chant the world on my Western sea,
I chant copious the islands beyond, thick as stars in the sky,
I chant the new empire grander than any before, as in a vision it comes to me,
I chant America the mistress, I chant a greater supremacy,
I chant projected a thousand blooming cities yet in time on those groups of sea-islands,
My sail-ships and steam-ships threading the archipelagoes,
My stars and stripes fluttering in the wind,

Commerce opening, the sleep of ages having done its work, races reborn, refresh'd,
Lives, works resumed—the object I know not—but the old, the Asiatic renew'd as it must be,
Commencing from this day surrounded by the world.

3

And you Libertad of the world!
You shall sit in the middle well-pois'd thousands and thousands of years,
As to-day from one side the nobles of Asia come to you,
As to-morrow from the other side the queen of England sends her eldest son to you.

The sign is reversing, the orb is enclosed,
The ring is circled, the journey is done,
The box-lid is but perceptibly open'd, nevertheless the perfume pours copiously out of the whole box.

Young Libertad! with the venerable Asia, the all-mother,
Be considerate with her now and ever hot Libertad, for you are all,
Bend your proud neck to the long-off mother now sending messages over the archipelagoes to you,
Bend your proud neck low for once, young Libertad.

Were the children straying westward so long? so wide the tramping?
Were the precedent dim ages debouching westward from Paradise so long?
Were the centuries steadily footing it that way, all the while unknown, for you, for reasons?
They are justified, they are accomplish'd, they shall now be turn'd the other way also, to travel toward you thence,
They shall now also march obediently eastward for your sake Libertad.

1860

The City Dead-House

By the city dead-house by the gate,
As idly sauntering wending my way from the clangor,
I curious pause, for lo, an outcast form, a poor dead prostitute brought,
Her corpse they deposit unclaim'd, it lies on the damp brick pavement,
The divine woman, her body, I see the body, I look on it alone,
That house once full of passion and beauty, all else I notice not,
Nor stillness so cold, nor running water from faucet, nor odors morbific impress me,
But the house alone—that wondrous house—that delicate fair house—that ruin!
That immortal house more than all the rows of dwellings ever built!
Or white-domed capitol with majestic figure surmounted, or all the old high-

spired cathedrals,
That little house alone more than them all—poor, desperate house!
Fair, fearful wreck—tenement of a soul—itself a soul,
Unclaim'd, avoided house—take one breath from my tremulous lips,
Take one tear dropt aside as I go for thought of you,
Dead house of love—house of madness and sin, crumbled, crush'd,
House of life, erewhile talking and laughing—but ah, poor house, dead even then,
Months, years, an echoing, garnish'd house—but dead, dead, dead.

1867

Broadway

What hurrying human tides, or day or night!
What passions, winnings, losses, ardors, swim thy waters!
What whirls of evil, bliss and sorrow, stem thee!
What curious questioning glances—glints of love!
Leer, envy, scorn, contempt, hope, aspiration!
Thou portal—thou arena—thou of the myriad long-drawn lines and groups!
(Could but thy flagstones, curbs, façades, tell their inimitable tales;
Thy windows rich, and huge hotels—thy side-walks wide;)
Thou of the endless sliding, mincing, shuffling feet!
Thou, like the parti-colored world itself—like infinite, teeming, mocking life!
Thou visor'd, vast, unspeakable show and lesson!

1888

96

New York Revisited

HENRY JAMES

Henry James (1843-1916), one of the most prolific and distinguished of American writers, had an ambivalent relationship with the United States. A novelist, short story writer, and critic, he produced a series of novels which compare and contrast American and Europe; what became known as the "international theme". *The Portrait of a Lady* (1881) remains his central work—a wonderfully realised dramatic rendition of a young woman's sensibility and moral awareness reflected through the different claims of her New England heritage and European expectations.

His response to the American city, most notably to New York and Boston, was characteristically ambivalent. Born in New York City (Washington Square), he viewed both the culture and the environment of America as the apogee of an increasingly rampant materialism. From his adopted European perspectives, he viewed Paris, London, and Rome, as arbiters of an historical urban tradition dense in its resonance and capacity for cultural enlightenment and moral education. *The American Scene (1907)* records his overwhelmingly negative response to his native country after an absence of twenty-one years. He notes a New York undergoing fundamental change—both visual and social—aspects he considered in "The Jolly Corner" and *Washington Square.* His negative attitude is given an ambivalent context in *The Bostonians* (1886). See F. O. Matthiesson, *Henry James the Major Phase* (1946); Tony Tanner (ed), *Henry James: Modern Judgements* (1968); and Graham Clarke (ed), *Henry James: Critical Assessments* (4 vols. 1991).

The single impression or particular vision most answering to the greatness of the subject would have been, I think, a certain hour of large circumnavigation that I found prescribed, in the fulness of the spring, as the almost immediate crown of a return from the Far West. I had arrived at one of the transpontine stations of the Pennsylvania railroad; the question was of proceeding to Boston, for the occasion, without pushing through the terrible town—why "terrible," to

Source: Henry James, *The American Scene*, New York, 1907, Ch. II:"New York Revisited."

my sense, in many ways, I shall presently explain—and the easy and agreeable attainment of this great advantage was to embark on one of the mightiest (as appeared to me) of train-bearing barges and, descending the western wastes, pass round the bottom of the city and remount the other current to Harlem; all without "losing touch" of the Pullman that had brought me from Washington. This absence of the need of losing touch, this breadth of effect, as to the whole process, involved in the prompt floating of the huge concatenated cars not only without arrest or confusion, but as for positive prodigal beguilement of the artless traveller, had doubtless much to say to the ensuring state of mind, the happily-excited and amused view of the great face of New York. The extent, the ease, the energy, the quantity and number, all notes scattered about as if, in the whole business and in the splendid light, nature and science were joyously romping together, might have been taking on again, for their symbol, some collective presence of great circling and plunging, hovering and perching seabirds, white-winged images of the spirit, of the restless freedom of the Bay. The Bay had always, on other opportunities, seemed to blow its immense character straight into one's face—coming "at" you, so to speak, bearing down on you, with the full force of a thousand prows of steamers seen exactly on the line of their longitudinal axis; but I had never before been so conscious of its boundless cool assurance or seemed to see its genius so grandly at play. This was presumably indeed because I had never before enjoyed the remarkable adventure of taking in so much of the vast bristling promontory from the water, of ascending the East River, in especial, to its upper diminishing expanses.

Something of the air of the occasion and of the mood of the moment caused the whole picture to speak with its largest suggestion; which suggestion is irresistible when once it is sounded clear. It is all, absolutely, an expression of things lately and currently *done*, done on a large impersonal stage and on the basis of inordinate gain—it is not an expression of any other matters whatever; and yet the sense of the scene (which had at several previous junctures, as well, put forth to my imagination its power) was commanding and thrilling, was in certain lights almost charming. So it befell, exactly, that an element of mystery and wonder entered into the impression—the interest of trying to make out, in the absence of features of the sort usually supposed indispensable, the reason of the beauty and the joy. It is indubitably a "great" bay, a great harbour, but no one item of the romantic, or even of the picturesque, as commonly understood, contributes to its effect. The shores are low and for the most part depressingly furnished and prosaically peopled; the islands, though numerous, have not a grace to exhibit, and one thinks of the other, the real flowers of geography in this order, of Naples, of Capetown, of Sydney, of Seattle, of San Francisco, of Rio, asking how if *they* justify a reputation, New York should seem to justify one. Then, after all, we remember that there are reputations and reputations; we remember above all that the imaginative response to the conditions here presented may just happen to proceed from the intellectual extravagance of the given observer. When this personage is open to corruption by almost any large view of an intensity of life, his vibrations tend to become a matter difficult even for *him* to explain. He may have to confess that the group of evident facts fails to account by itself for the complacency of his appreciation. Therefore it is that I find myself rather backward with a perceived sanction, of an at all proportionate kind, for the fine exhilaration with which, in this free wayfaring relation to them, the wide waters of New York inspire me. There is the beauty of light and air, the great scale of space, and, seen far away to the west, the open gates of the Hudson, majestic in their degree, even at a distance, and announcing still nobler things. But the real appeal, unmistakably, is in that note of vehemence in the local life of which I have spoken, for it is the appeal of a particular type of dauntless power.

The aspect the power wears then is indescribable; it is the power of the most extravagant of cities, rejoicing, as with the voice of the morning, in its might, its fortune, its unsurpassable conditions, and imparting to every object and element, to the motion and expression of every floating, hurrying, panting thing, to the throb of ferries and tugs, to the plash of waves and the play of winds and the glint of lights and the shrill of whistles and the quality and authority of breeze-born cries—all, practically, a diffused, wasted clamour of *detonations*—something of its sharp free accent and, above all, of its sovereign sense of being "backed" and able to back. The universal *applied* passion struck me as shining unprecedentedly out of the composition; in the bigness and bravery and insolence, especially, of everything that rushed and shrieked; in the air as of a great intricate frenzied dance, half merry, half desperate, or at least half defiant, performed on the huge water floor. This appearance of the bold lacing-together, across the waters, of the scattered members of the monstrous organism—lacing as by the ceaseless play of an enormous system of steam-shuttles or electric bobbins (I scarce know what to call them), commensurate in form with their infinite work—does perhaps more than anything else to give the pitch of the vision of energy. One has the sense that the monster grows and grows, flinging abroad its loose limbs even as some unmannered young giant at his "larks," and that the binding stitches must for ever fly further and faster and draw harder; the future complexity of the web, all under the sky and over the sea, becoming thus that of some colossal set of clockworks, some steel-souled machine-room of brandished arms and hammering fists and opening and closing jaws. The immeasurable bridges are but as the horizontal sheaths of pistons working at high pressure, day and night, and subject, one apprehends with perhaps inconsistent gloom, to certain, to fantastic, to merciless multiplication. In the light of this apprehension indeed the breezy brightness of the Bay puts on the semblance of the vast white page that awaits beyond any other perhaps the black overscoring of science.

Let me hasten to add that its present whiteness is precisely its charming note, the frankest of the signs you recognize and remember it by. That is the distinction I was just feeling my way to name as the main ground of its doing so well, for effect, without technical scenery. There are great imposing ports—Glasgow and Liverpool and London—that have already their page blackened almost beyond redemption from any such light of the picturesque as can hope to irradiate fog and grime, and there are others, Marseilles and Constantinople say, or, for all I know to the contrary, New Orleans, that contrive to abound before everything else in colour, and so to make a rich and instant and obvious show. But memory and the actual impression keep investing New York with the tone, predominantly, of summer dawns and winter frosts, of sea-foam, of bleached sails and stretched awnings, of blanched hulls, of scoured decks, of new ropes, of polished brasses, of streamers clear in the blue air; and it is by this harmony, doubtless, that the projection of the individual character of the place, of the candour of its avidity and the freshness of its audacity, is most conveyed. The "tall buildings," which have so promptly usurped a glory that affects you as rather surprised, as yet, at itself, the multitudinous sky-scrapers standing up to the view, from the water, like extravagant pins in a cushion already overplanted, and stuck in as in the dark, anywhere and anyhow, have at least the felicity of carrying out the fairness of tone, of taking the sun and the shade in the manner of towers of marble. They are not all of marble, I believe, by any means, even if some may be, but they are impudently new and still more impudently "novel"—this in common with so many other terrible things in America—and they are triumphant payers of dividends; all of which uncontested and unabashed pride, with flash of innumerable windows and flicker of subordinate gilt attributions, is like the flare, up and down their long, narrow faces, of the lamps of some general permanent "celebration."

You see the pin-cushion in profile, so to speak, on passing between Jersey City and Twenty-third Street, but you get it broadside on, this loose nosegay of architectural flowers, if you skirt the Battery, well out, and embrace the whole plantation. Then the "American beauty," the rose of interminable stem, becomes the token of the cluster at large—to that degree that, positively, this is all that is wanted for emphasis of your final impression. Such growths, you feel, have confessedly arisen but to be "picked," in time, with a shears; nipped short off, by waiting fate, as soon as "science," applied to gain, has put upon the table, from far up its sleeve, some more winning card. Crowned not only with no history, but with no credible possibility of time for history, and consecrated by no uses save the commercial at any cost, they are simply the most piercing notes in that concert of the expensively provisional into which your supreme sense of New York resolves itself. They never begin to speak to you, in the manner of the builded majesties of the world as we have heretofore known such—towers or temples or fortresses or palaces—with the authority of things of permanence or even of things of long duration. One story is good only till another is told, and sky-scrapers are the last word of economic ingenuity only till another word be written. This shall be possibly a word of still uglier meaning, but the vocabulary of thrift at any price shows boundless resources, and the consciousness of that truth, the consciousness of the finite, the menaced, the essentially *invented* state, twinkles ever, to my perception, in the thousand glassy eyes of these giants of the mere market. Such a structure as the comparatively windowless bell-tower of Giotto, in Florence, looks supremely serene in its beauty. You don't feel it to have risen by the breath of an interested passion that, restless beyond all passions, is for ever seeking more pliable forms. Beauty has been the object of its creator's idea, and, having found beauty, it has found the form in which it splendidly rests.

Beauty indeed was the aim of the creator of the spire of Trinity Church, so cruelly overtopped and so barely distinguishable, from your train-bearing barge, as you stand off, in its abject helpless humility; and it may of course be asked how much of this superstition finds voice in the actual shrunken presence of that laudable effort. Where, for the eye, is the felicity of simplified Gothic, of noble pre-eminence, that once made of this highly-pleasing edifice the pride of the town and the feature of Broadway? The answer is, as obviously, that these charming elements are still there, just where they ever were, but that they have been mercilessly deprived of their visibility. It aches and throbs, this smothered visibility, we easily feel, in its caged and dishonoured condition, supported only by the consciousness that the dishonour is no fault of its own. We commune with it, in tenderness and pity, through the encumbered air; our eyes, made, however unwillingly, at home in strange vertiginous upper atmospheres, look down on it as on a poor ineffectual thing, an architectural object addressed, even in its prime aspiration, the patient pedestrian sense and permitting thereby a relation of intimacy. It was to speak to me audibly enough on two or three other occasions—even through the thick of that frenzy of Broadway just where Broadway receives from Wall Street the fiercest application of the maddening lash; it was to put its tragic case there with irresistible lucidity. "Yes, the wretched figure I am making is as little as you see my fault—it is the fault of the buildings whose very first care is to deprive churches of their visibility. There are but two or three—two or three outward and visible churches—left in New York 'anyway', as you must have noticed, and even they are hideously threatened: a fact at which no one, indeed, appears to be shocked, from which no one draws the least of the inferences that stick straight out of it, which every one seems in short to take for granted either with remarkable stupidity or with remarkable cynicism." So, at any rate, they may still effectively communicate, ruddy-brown (where not browny-black) old Trinity and any pausing, any attending survivor of the clearer age—and there is yet more of the bitterness of history to be tasted in such a tacit passage, as I shall presently show.

Was it not the bitterness of history, meanwhile, that on that day of circumnavigation, that day of highest intensity of impression, of which I began by speaking, the ancient rotunda of Castle Garden, viewed from just opposite, should have lurked there as a vague nonentity? One had known it from far, far back and with the indelibility of the childish vision—from the time when it was the commodious concert-hall of New York, the firmament of long-extinguished stars; in spite of which extinction there outlives for me the image of the infant phenomenon Adelina Patti, whom (another large-eyed infant) I had been benevolently taken to hear: Adelina Patti, in a fan-like little white frock and "pantalettes" and a hussar-like red jacket, mounted on an armchair, its back supporting her, wheeled to the front of the stage and warbling like a tiny thrush even in the nest. Shabby, shrunken, barely discernible today, the ancient rotunda, adjusted to other uses, had afterwards, for many decades, carried on a conspicuous life—and it was the present remoteness, the repudiated barbarism of all this, foreshortened by one's own experience, that dropped the acid into the cup. The sky-scrapers and the league-long bridges, present and to come, marked the point where the age—the age for which Castle Garden could have been, in its day, a "value"—had come out. That in itself was nothing—ages do come out, as a matter of course, so far from where they have gone in. But it had done so, the latter half of the nineteenth century, one's own more or less immediate presence; the difference, from pole to pole, was so vivid and concrete that no single shade of any one of its aspects was lost. This impact of the whole condensed past at once produced a horrible, hateful sense of personal antiquity.

Yet was it after all that those monsters of the mere market, as I have called them, had more to say, on the question of "effect," than I had at first allowed?—since they are the element that looms largest for me through a particular impression, with remembered parts and pieces melting together rather richly now, of "down-town" seen and felt from the inside. "Felt"—I use that word, I dare say, all presumptuously, for a relation to matters of magnitude and mystery that I could begin neither to measure nor to penetrate, hovering about them only in magnanimous wonder, staring at them as at a world of immovably-closed doors behind which immense "material" lurked, material for the artist, the painter of life, as we say, who shouldn't have begun so early and so fatally to fall away from possible initiations. This sense of a baffled curiosity, an intellectual adventure forever renounced, was surely enough a state of feeling, and indeed in presence of the different half-hours, as memory presents them, at which I gave myself up both to the thrill of Wall Street (by which I mean that of the whole wide edge of the whirlpool), and the too accepted, too irredeemable ignorance, I am at a loss to see what intensity of response was wanting. The imagination might have responded more if there had been a slightly less settled inability to understand what every one, what any one, was really doing; but the picture, as it comes back to me, is, for all this foolish subjective poverty, so crowded with its features that I rejoice, I confess, in not having more of them to handle. No open apprehension, even if it be as open as a public vehicle plying for hire, can carry more than a certain amount of life, of a kind; and there was nothing at play in the outer air, at least, of the scene, during these glimpses, that didn't scramble for admission into mine very much as I had seen the mob seeking entrance to an up-town or a down-town electric car fight for life at one of the apertures. If it had been the final function of the Bay to make one feel one's age, so, assuredly, the mouth of Wall Street proclaimed it, for one's private ear, distinctly enough; the breath of existence being taken, wherever one turned, as that of youth on the run and with the prize of the race in sight, and the new landmarks crushing the old quite as violent children stamp on snails and caterpillars.

The hour I first recall was a morning of winter drizzle and mist, of dense fog in the Bay, one of the strangest sights of which I was on my way to enjoy; and I had stopped in the heart of the business quarter to pick up a friend who was to be my companion. The weather, such as it was, worked wonders for the upper reaches of the buildings, round which it drifted and hung very much as about the flanks and summits of emergent mountain-masses—for, to be just all round, there *was* some evidence of their having a message for the eyes. Let me parenthesize, once for all, that there are other glimpses of this message, up and down the city, frequently to be caught; lights and shades of winter and summer air, of the literally "finishing" afternoon in particular, when refinement of modelling descends from the skies and lends the white towers, all new and crude and commercial and over-windowed as they are, a fleeting distinction. The morning I speak of offered me my first chance of seeing one of them from the inside—which was an opportunity I sought again, repeatedly, in respect to others; and I became conscious of the force with which this vision of their prodigious working, and of the multitudinous life, as if each were a swarming city in itself, that they are capable of housing, may beget, on the part of the free observer, in other words of the restless analyst, the impulse to describe and present the facts and express the sense of them. Each of these huge constructed and compressed communities, throbbing, through its myriad arteries and pores, with a single passion, even as a complicated watch throbs with the one purpose of telling you the hour and the minute, testified overwhelmingly to the *character* of New York—and the passion of the restless analyst, on his side, is for the extraction of character. But there would be to much to say, just here, were this incurable eccentric to let himself go; the impression in question, fed by however brief an experience, kept overflowing the cup and spreading in a wide waste of speculation. I must dip into these depths, if it prove possible, later on; let me content myself for the moment with remembering how from the first, on all such ground, my thought went straight to poor great wonder-working Émile Zola and *his* love of the human aggregation, the artificial microcosm, which had to spend itself on great shops, great businesses, great "apartment-houses," of inferior, of mere Parisian scale. His image, it seemed to me, really asked for compassion—in the presence of this material that his energy of evocation, his alone, would have been of a stature to meddle with. What if *Le Ventre de Paris*, what if *Au Bonheur des Dames*, what if *Pot-Bouille* and *L'Argent*, could but have come into being under the New York inspiration?

The answer to that, however, for the hour, was that, in all probability, New York was not going (as it turns such remarks) to produce both the maximum of "business" spectacle and the maximum of ironic reflection of it. Zola's huge reflector got itself formed, after all, in a far other air; it had hung there, in essence, awaiting the scene that was to play over it, long before the scene really approached it in scale. The reflecting surfaces, of the ironic, of the epic order, suspended in the New York atmosphere, have yet to show symptoms of shining out, and the monstrous phenomena themselves, meanwhile, strike me as having, with their immense momentum, got the start, got ahead of, in proper parlance, any possibility of poetic, of dramatic capture. That conviction came to me most perhaps while I gazed across at the special sky-scraper that overhangs poor old Trinity to the north—a south face as high and wide as the mountain-wall that drops the Alpine avalanche, from time to time, upon the village, and the village spire, at its foot; the interest of this case being above all, as I learned, to my stupefaction, in the fact that the very creators of the extinguisher are the churchwardens themselves, or at least the trustees of the church property. What was the case but magnificent for pitiless ferocity?—that inexorable law of the growing invisibility of churches, their everywhere reduced or abolished *presence*, which is nine-tenths of their virtue, receiving thus, at such hands, its supreme consecration. This consecration was positively the greater that just then, as I have said, the vast money-making structure quite horribly, quite romantically justified itself, looming through the weather with an insolent cliff-like sublimity. The weather, for all that experience, mixes intimately with the fulness of my impression; speaking not least, for instance, of the way "the state of the streets" and the assault of the turbid air seemed all one with the look, the tramp, the whole quality and *allure*, the consummate monotonous commonness, of the pushing male crowd, moving in its dense mass—with the confusion carried to chaos for any intelligence, any perception; a welter of objects and sounds in which relief, detachment, dignity, meaning, perished utterly and lost all rights. It appeared, the muddy medium, all one with every other element and note as well, all the signs of the heaped industrial battlefield, all the sounds and silences, grim, pushing, trudging silences too, of the universal will to move—to move, move, move, as an end in itself, an appetite at any price.

In the Bay, the rest of the morning, the dense raw fog that delayed the big boat, allowing sight but of the immediate ice-masses through which it thumped its way, was not less of the essence. Anything blander, as a medium, would have seemed a mockery of the facts of the terrible little Ellis Island, the first harbour of refuge and stage of patience for the million or so of immigrants annually knocking at our official door. Before this door, which opens to them there only with a hundred forms and ceremonies, grindings and grumblings of the key, they stand appealing and waiting, marshalled, herded, divided, subdivided, sorted, sifted, searched, fumigated, for longer or shorter periods—the effect of all which prodigious process, an intendedly "scientific" feeding of the mill, is again to give the earnest observer a thousand more things to think of than he can pretend to retail. The impression of Ellis Island, in fine, would be—as I was to find throughout that so many of my impressions would be—a chapter by itself; and with a particular page for recognition of the degree in which the liberal hospitality of the eminent Commissioner of this wonderful service, to whom I had been introduced, helped to make the interest of the whole watched drama poignant and unforgettable. It is a drama that goes on, without a pause, day by day and year by year, this visible act of ingurgitation on the part of our body politic and social, and constituting really an appeal to amazement beyond that of any sword-swallowing or fire-swallowing of the circus. The wonder that one couldn't keep down was the thought that these two or three hours of one's own chance vision of the business were but as a tick or two of the mighty clock, the clock that never, never stops—least of all when it strikes, for a sign of so much winding-up, some louder hour of our national fate than usual. I think indeed that the simplest account of the action of Ellis Island on the spirit of any sensitive citizen who may have happened to "look in" is that he comes back from his visit not at all the same person that he went. He has eaten of the tree of knowledge, and the taste will be for ever in his mouth. He had thought he knew before, thought he had the sense of the degree in which it is his American fate to share the sanctity of his American consciousness, the intimacy of his American patriotism, with the inconceivable alien; but the truth had never come home to him with any such force. In the lurid light projected upon it by those courts of dismay it shakes him—or I like at least to imagine it shakes him—to the depths of his being; I like to think of him, I *positively* have to think of him, as going about ever afterwards with a new look, for those who can see it, in his face, the outward sign of the new chill in his heart. So is stamped, for detection, the questionably privileged person who has had an apparition, seen a ghost in his supposedly safe old house. Let not the unwary, therefore, visit Ellis Island.

The after-sense of that acute experience, however, I myself found, was by no means to be brushed away; I felt it grow and grow, on the contrary, wherever I turned: other impressions might come and go, but this affirmed claim of the alien, however immeasurably alien, to share in one's supreme relation was everywhere the fixed element, the reminder not to be dodged. One's supreme relation, as one had always put it, was one's countrymen and one's countrywomen. Thus it was as if, all the while, with such a fond tradition of what these products predominantly were, the idea of the country itself underwent something of that profane overhauling through which it appears to suffer the indignity of change. Is not our instinct in this matter, in general, essentially the safe one—that of keeping the idea simple and strong and continuous, so that it shall be perfectly sound? To touch it overmuch, to pull it about, is to put it in peril of weakening; yet on this free assault upon it, this readjustment of it in *their* monstrous, presumptuous interest, the aliens, in New York, seemed perpetually to insist. The combination there of their quantity and their quality—that loud primary stage of alienism which New York most offers to sight—operates, for the native, as their note of settled possession, something they have nobody to thank for; so that *un*settled possession is what we, on our side, seem reduced to—the implication of which, in its turn, is that, to recover confidence and regain lost ground, we, not they, must make the surrender and accept the orientation. We must go, in other words, *more* than half-way to meet them; which is all the difference, for us, between possession and dispossession. This sense of dispossession, to be brief about it, haunted me so, I was to feel, in the New York street and in the packed trajectiles to which one clingingly appeals from the streets, just as one tumbles back into the streets in appalled reaction from *them*, that the art of beguiling or duping it became an art to be cultivated—though the fond alternative vision was never long to be obscured, the imagination, exasperated to envy, of the ideal, in the order in question; of the luxury of some such close and sweet and *whole* national consciousness as that of the Switzer and the Scot.

II

My recovery of impressions, after a short interval, yet with their flush a little faded, may have been judged to involve itself with excursions of memory—memory directed to the antecedent time—reckless almost to extravagance. But I recall them today, none the less, for that value in them which ministered, at happy moments, to an artful evasion of the actual. There was not escape from the ubiquitous alien into the future, or even into the present; there was an escape but into the past. I count as quite a triumph in this interest an unbroken ease of frequentation of that ancient end of Fifth Avenue to the whole neighbourhood of which one's earlier vibrations, a very far-away matter now, were attuned. The precious stretch of space between Washington Square and Fourteenth Street had a value, had even charm, for the revisiting spirit—a mild and melancholy glamour which I am conscious of the difficulty of "rendering" for new and heedless generations. Here again the assault of suggestion is too great; too large, I mean, the number of hares started, before the pursuing imagination, the quickened memory, by this fact of the felt moral and social value of this comparatively unimpaired morsel of the Fifth Avenue heritage. Its reference to a pleasanter, easier, hazier past is absolutely comparative, just as the past in question itself enjoys as such the merest courtesy-title. It is all recent history enough, by the measure of the whole, and there are flaws and defacements enough, surely, even in its appearance of decency of duration. The tall building, grossly tall and grossly ugly, has failed of an admirable chance of distinguished consideration for it, and the dignity of many of its peaceful fronts has succumbed to the presence of those industries whose foremost need is to make "a good thing" of them. The good thing is doubtless being made, and yet this lower end of the once agreeable street, still just escapes being a wholly bad thing. What held the fancy in thrall, however, as I say, was the admonition, proceeding from all the facts, that values of this romantic order are at best, anywhere, strangely relative. It was an extraordinary statement of the subject of New York that the space between Fourteenth Street and Washington Square *should* count for "tone," figure as the old ivory of an overscored tablet.

True wisdom, I found, was to let it, to make it, so count and figure as much as it would, and charming assistance came for this, I also found, from the young good-nature of May and June. There had been neither assistance nor good-nature during the grim weeks of mid-winter; there had been but the meagre fact of a discomfort and an ugliness less formidable here than elsewhere. When, toward the top of the town, circulation, alimentation, recreation, every art of existence, gave way before the full onset of winter, when the upper avenues had become as so many congested bottle-necks, through which the wine of life simply refused to be decanted, getting back to these latitudes resembled really a return from the North Pole to the Temperate Zone: it was as if the wine of life had been poured for you, in advance, into some pleasant old punch-bowl that would support you through the temporary stress. Your condition was not reduced to the endless vista of a clogged tube, of a thoroughfare occupied as to the narrow central ridge with trolley-cars stuffed to suffocation, and as to the mere margin, on either side, with snow-banks resulting from the cleared rails and offering themselves as a field for all remaining action. Free existence and good manners, in New York, are too much brought down to a bare rigour of marginal relation to the endless electric coil, the monstrous chain that winds round the general neck and body, the general middle and legs, very much as the boa-constrictor winds round the group of the Laöcoon. It struck me that when these folds are tightened in the terrible stricture of the snow-smothered months of the year, the New York predicament leaves far behind the anguish represented in the Vatican figures. To come and go where East Eleventh Street, where West Tenth, opened their kind short arms was at least to keep clear of the awful hug of the serpent. And this was a grace that grew large, as I have hinted, with the approach of summer, and that made in the afternoons of May and of the first half of June, above all, an insidious appeal. There, I repeat, was the delicacy, there the mystery, there the wonder, in especial, of the unquenchable intensity of the impressions received in childhood. They are made then once for all, be their intrinsic beauty, interest, importance, small or great; the stamp is indelible and never wholly fades. This in fact gives it an importance when a lifetime has intervened. I found myself intimately recognizing every house my officious tenth year had, in the way of imagined adventure, introduced to me—incomparable master of ceremonies after all; the privilege had been offered since to millions of other objects that had made nothing of it, that had gone as they came; so that here were Fifth Avenue corners with which one's connection was fairly exquisite. The lowered light of the days' ends of early summer became them, moreover, exceedingly, and they fell, for the quiet northward perspective, into a dozen delicacies of composition and tone.

One could talk of "quietness" now, for the shrinkage of life so marked, in the higher latitudes of the town, after Easter, the visible early flight of that "society" which, by the old custom, used never to budge before June or July, had almost the effect of clearing some of the streets, and indeed of suggesting that a truly clear New York might have an unsuspected charm or two to put forth. An approach to peace and harmony might have been, in a manner, promised, and the sense of other days took advantage of it to steal abroad with a ghostly tread. It kept meeting, half the time, to its discomfiture, the lamentable little Arch of Triumph which bestrides these beginnings of Washington Square—lamentable because of its poor and lonely and unsupported and unaffiliated state. With this melancholy monument it could make no terms at all, but turned its back to the strange sight as often as possible, helping itself thereby, moreover, to do a little of the pretending required, no doubt, by the fond theory that nothing hereabouts was changed. Nothing *was*, it could occasionally appear to me—there was no new note in the picture, not one, for instance, when I paused before a low house in a small row on the south side of Waverley Place and lived again into the queer mediæval costume (preserved by the daguerreotypist's art) of the very little boy for whom the scene had once embodied the pangs and pleasures of a dame's small school. The dame must have been Irish, by her name, and the Irish tradition, only intensified and coarsened, seemed still to possess the place, the fact of the survival, the sturdy sameness, of which arrested me, again and again, to fascination. The shabby red house, with its mere two storeys, its lowly "stoop," its dislocated ironwork of the forties, the early fifties, the record, in its face, of blistering summers and of the log stages of the loss of self-respect, made it as consummate a morsel of the old liquor-scented, heated-looking city, the city of no pavements but of such a plenty of politics, as I could have desired. And neighbouring Sixth Avenue, overstraddled though it might be with feats of engineering unknown to the primitive age that otherwise so persisted, wanted only, to carry off the illusion, the warm smell of the bakery on the corner of Eighth Street, a blessed repository of doughnuts, cookies, cream-cakes and pies, the slow passing by which, on returns from school, must have had much in common with the experience of the shipmen of old who came, in long voyages, while they tacked and hung back, upon those belts of ocean that are haunted with the balm and spice of tropic islands.

These were the felicities of the backward reach, which, however, had also its melancholy checks and snubs; nowhere quite so sharp as in presence, so to speak, of the rudely, the ruthlessly suppressed birthhouse on the other side of the Square. That was where the pretence that nearly nothing was changed had most to come in; for a high, square, impersonal structure, proclaiming its lack of interest with a crudity all its own, so blocks, at the right moment for its own success, the view of the past, that the effect for me, in Washington Place, was of having been amputated of half my history. The grey and more or less "hallowed" University building—wasn't it somehow, with a desperate bravery, both castellated and gabled?—has vanished from the earth, and vanished with it the two or three adjacent houses, of which the birthplace was one. This was the snub, for the complacency of retrospect, that, whereas the inner sense had positively erected there for its private contemplation a commemorative mural tablet, the very wall that should have borne this inscription had been smashed as for demonstration that tablets, in New York, are unthinkable. And I have had indeed to permit myself this free fantasy of the hypothetic rescued identity of a given house—taking the vanished number in Washington Place as most pertinent—in order to invite the reader to gasp properly with me before the fact that we not only fail to remember, in the whole length of the city, one of these frontal records of birth, sojourn, or death, under a celebrated name, but that we have only to reflect an instant to see any such form of civic piety inevitably and for ever absent. The form is cultivated, to the greatly quickened interest of street-scenery, in many of the cities of Europe; and is it not verily bitter, for those who feel a poetry in the noted passage, longer or shorter, here and there, of great lost spirits, that the institution, the profit, the glory of any such association is denied in advance to communities tending, as the phrase is, to "run" preponderantly to the sky-scraper? Where, in fact, is the point of inserting a mural table, at any legible height, in a building certain to be destroyed to make room for a sky-scraper? And from where, on the other hand, in a façade of fifty floors, does one "see" the pious plate recording the honour attached to one of the apartments look down on a responsive people? We have but to ask the question to recognize our necessary failure to answer it as a supremely characteristic local note—a note in the light of which the great city is projected into its future as, practically, a huge, continuous fifty-floored conspiracy against the very idea of the ancient graces, those that strike us as having flourished just in proportion as the parts of life and the signs of character have *not* been lumped together, not been indistinguishable sunk on the common fund of mere economic convenience. So interesting, as object-lessons, may the developments of the American gregarious ideal become; so traceable, at every turn, to the restless analyst at least, are the heavy footprints, in the finer texture of life, of a great commercial democracy seeking to abound supremely in its own sense and having none to gainsay it.

Let me not, however, forget, amid such contemplations, what may serve here as a much more relevant instance of the operation of values, the price of the as yet undiminished dignity of the two most southward of the Fifth Avenue churches. Half the charm of the prospect, at that extremity, is in their still being there, and being as they are; this charm, this serenity of escape and survival positively works as a blind on the side of the question of their architectural importance. The last shade of pedantry or priggishness drops from your view of that element; they illustrate again supremely your grasped truth of the *comparative* character, in such conditions, of beauty and of interest. The special standard they may or may not square with signifies, you feel, not a jot: all you know, and want to know, is that they are probably menaced—some horrible voice of the air has murmured it—and that with them will go, if fate overtakes them, the last cases worth mentioning (with a single exception), of the modest felicity that sometimes used to be. Remarkably certainly the state of things in which mere exemption from the "squashed" condition can shed such a glamour; but we may accept the state of things if only we can keep the glamour undispelled. It reached its maximum for me, I hasten to add, on my penetrating into the Ascension, at chosen noon, and standing for the first time in presence of that noble work of John La Farge, the representation, on the west wall, in the grand manner, of the theological event from which the church takes its title. Wonderful enough, in New York, to find one's self, in a charming and considerably dim "old" church, hushed to admiration before a great religious picture; the sensation, for the moment, upset so all the facts. The hot light, outside, might have been that of an Italian *piazetta*, the cool shade, within, with the important work of art shining through it, seemed part of some other-world pilgrimage—all the more that the important work of art itself, a thing of the highest distinction, spoke, as soon as one had taken it, with that authority which makes the difference, ever afterwards, between the remembered and the forgotten quest. A rich note of interference came, I admit, through the splendid window-glass, the finest of which, unsurpassably fine, to my sense, is the work of the same artist; so that the church, as it stands, is very nearly as commemorative a monument as a great reputation need wish. The deeply pictorial windows, in which clearness of picture and fulness of expression consort so successfully with a tone as of magnified gems, did not strike one as looking into a yellow little square of the south—they put forth a different implication; but the flaw in the harmony was, more than anything else, that sinister voice of the air of which I have spoken, the fact that one *could* stand there, vibrating to such impressions, only to remember the suspended danger, the possibility of the doom. Here was the loveliest cluster of images, begotten on the spot, that the preoccupied city had ever taken thought to offer itself; and here, to match them, like some black shadow they had been condemned to cast, was this particular prepared honour of "removal" that appeared to hover about them.

One's fear, I repeat, was perhaps misplaced—but what an air to live in, the shuddering pilgrim mused, the air in which such fears are not misplaced only when we are conscious of very special reassurances! The vision of the doom that does descend, that had descended all round, was at all events, for the half-hour, all that was wanted to charge with the last tenderness one's memory of the transfigured interior. Afterwards, outside, again and again, the powers of removal struck me as looming, awfully, in the newest mass of multiplied floors and windows visible at this point. *They*, ranged in this terrible recent erection, were going to bring in money—and was not money the only thing a self-respecting structure could be thought of as bringing in? Hadn't one heard, just before, in Boston, that the security, that the sweet serenity of the Park Street Church, charmingest, there, of aboriginal notes, the very light, with its perfect position and its dear old delightful Wren-like spire, of the starved city's eyes, had been artfully practised against, and that the question of saving it might become, in the near future, acute? Nothing, fortunately, I think, is so much the "making" of New York, at its central point, for the visual, almost for the romantic, sense, as the Park Street Church is the making, by its happy coming-in, of Boston; and, therefore, if it were thinkable that the peculiar rectitude of Boston might be laid in the dust, what mightn't easily come about for the reputedly less austere conscience of New York? Once such questions had obtained lodgement, to take one's walks was verily to look at almost everything in their light; and to commune with the sky-scraper under this influence was really to feel worsted, more and more, in any magnanimous attempt to adopt the æsthetic view is invariably blighted sooner or later by their most salient characteristic, *the* feature that speaks loudest for the economic idea. Window upon window, at any cost, is a condition never to be reconciled with any grace of building, and the logic of the matter here happens to put on a particularly fatal front. If quiet interspaces, always half the architectural battle, exist no more in such a structural scheme than quiet tones, blest breathing-spaces, occur, for the most part, in New York conversation, so the reason is, demonstrably, that the building can't afford them. (It is by very much the same law, one supposes, that New York conversation cannot afford stops.) The building can only afford lights, each light having a superlative value as an aid to the transaction of business and the conclusion of sharp bargains. Doesn't it take in fact acres of window-glass to help even an expert New Yorker to get the better of another expert one, or to see that the other expert one doesn't get the better of *him*? It is easy to conceive that, after all, with this origin and nature stamped upon their foreheads, the last word of the mercenary monsters should not be their address to our sense of formal beauty.

Still, as I have already hinted, there was always the case of the one other rescued identity and preserved felicity, the happy accident of the elder day still ungrudged and finally legitimated. When I say ungrudged, indeed, I seem to remember how I had heard that the divine little City Hall had *been* grudged, at a critical moment, to within an inch of its life; had but just escaped, in the event, the extremity of grudging. It lives on securely, by the mercy of fate—lives on in the delicacy of its beauty, speaking volumes again (more volumes, distinctly, than are anywhere else spoken) for the exquisite truth of the *conferred* value of interesting objects, the value derived from the social, the civilizing function for which they have happened to find their opportunity. It is the opportunity that gives them their price, and the luck of there being, round about them, nothing greater than themselves to steal it away from them. They strike thus, virtually, the supreme note, and—such is the mysterious play of our finer sensibility!—one takes this note, one is glad to work it, as the phrase goes, for all it is worth. I so work the note of the city Hall, no doubt, in speaking of the spectacle there constituted as "divine"; but I do it precisely by reason of the spectacle taken *with* the delightful small facts of the building: largely by reason, in other words, of the elegant, the gallant little structure's situation and history, the way it has played, artistically, ornamentally, its part, has held out for the good cause, through the long years, alone and unprotected. The fact is it has been the very centre of that assault of vulgarity of which the innumerable mementos rise within view of it and tower, at a certain distance, over it; and yet it has never parted with a square inch of its character, it has forced them, in a manner, to stand off. I hasten to add that in expressing thus its uncompromised state I speak of its outward, its æsthetic character only. So, at all events, it has discharged the civilizing function I just named as inherent in such cases—that of representing, to the community possessed of it, all the Style the community is likely to get, and of making itself responsible for the same.

The consistency of this effort, under difficulties, has been the story that brings tears to the eyes of the hovering kindly critic, and it is through his tears, no doubt, that such a personage reads the best passages of the tale and makes out the proportions of the object. Mine, recognize, didn't prevent my seeing that the pale yellow marble (or whatever it may be) of the City Hall has lost, by some late excoriation, the remembered charm of its old surface, the pleasant promiscuous patina of time; but the perfect taste and finish, the reduced yet ample scale, the harmony of parts, the just proportions, the modest classic grace, the living look of the type aimed at, these things, with gaiety of detail undiminished and "quaintness" of effect augmented, are all there; and I see them, as I write, in that glow of appreciation which made it necessary, of a fine June morning, that I should somehow pay the whole place my respects. The simplest, in fact the only way, was, obviously, to pass under the charming portico and brave the consequences: this impunity of such audacities being, in America, one of the last of the lessons the repatriated absentee finds himself learning. The crushed spirit he brings back from European discipline never quite rises to the height of the native argument, the brave sense that the public, the civic building is his very own, for any honest use, so that he may tread even its most expensive pavements and staircases (and very expensive, for the American citizen, these have lately become,) without a question asked. This further and further unchallenged penetration begets in the perverted person I speak of a really romantic thrill: it is like some assault of the dim seraglio, with the guards bribed, the eunuchs drugged and one's life varied in one's hand. The only drawback to such freedom is that penetralia it is so easy to penetrate fail a little of a due impressiveness, and that if stationed sentinels are bad for the temper of the freeman they are good for the "prestige" of the building.

Never, in any case, it seemed to me, had any freeman made so free with the majesty of things as I was to make on this occasion with the mysteries of the City Hall—even to the point of coming out into the presence of the Representative of the highest office with which City Halls are associated, and whose thoroughly gracious condonation of my act sets the seal of success upon the whole adventure. Its dizziest intensity in fact sprang precisely from the unexpected view opened into the old official, the old so thick-peopled local, municipal world: upper chambers of council and state, delightfully of their nineteenth-century time, as to design and ornament, in spite of rank restoration; but replete, above all, with portraits of past worthies, past celebrities and city fathers, Mayors, Bosses, Presidents, Governors, Statesmen at large, Generals and Commodores at large, florid ghosts, looking so unsophisticated now, of years not remarkable, municipally, for the absence of sophistication. Here were types, running mainly to ugliness and all bristling with the taste of their day and the quite touching provincialism of their conditions, as to many of which nothing would be more interesting than a study of New York annals in the light of their personal look, their very noses and mouths and complexions and heads of hair—to say nothing of their waistcoats and neckties; with such colour, such sound and movement would the thick stream of local history then be interfused. Wouldn't its thickness fairly become transparent? since to walk through the collection was not only to see and feel so much that had happened, but to understand, with the truth again and again inimitably pointed, why nothing could have happened otherwise; the whole array thus presenting itself as an unsurpassed demonstration of the real reasons of things. The florid ghosts look out from their exceedingly gilded frames—all that *that* can do is bravely done for them—with the frankest responsibility for everything; their collective presence becomes a kind of copious tell-tale document signed with a hundred names. There are few of these that at this hour, I think, we particularly desire to repeat; but the place where they may be read is, all the way from river to river and from the Battery to Harlem, the place in which there is most of the terrible town.

III

If the Bay had seemed to me, as I have noted, most to help the fond observer of New York aspects to a sense, through the eyes, of embracing possession, so the part played there for the outward view found its match for the inward in the portentous impression of one of the great caravansaries administered to me of a winter afternoon. I say with intention "administered": on so assiduous a guide, through the endless labyrinth of the Waldorf-Astoria was I happily to chance after turning out of the early dusk and the January sleet and slosh into permitted, into enlightened contemplation of a pandemonium not less admirably ordered, to all appearance, than rarely intermitted. The seer of great cities is liable to easy error, I know, when he finds this, that or the other caught glimpse the supremely significant one—and I am willing to preface with that remark my confession that New York told me more of her story at once, then and there, than she was again and elsewhere to tell. With this apprehension that she was in fact fairly shrieking it into one's ears came a curiosity, corresponding, as to its kind and its degree of interest; so that there was nought to do, as we picked our tortuous way, but to stare with all our eyes and miss as little as possible of the revelation. That harshness of the essential conditions, the outward, which almost any large attempt at the amenities, in New York, has to take account of and make the best of, has at least the effect of projecting the visitor with force upon the spectacle prepared for him at this particular point and of marking the more its sudden high pitch, the character of violence which all its warmth, its colour and glitter so completely muffle. There is violence outside, mitigating sadly the frontal majesty of the monument, leaving it exposed to the vulgar assault of the street by the operation of those dire facts of absence of margin, of meagreness of site, of the brevity of the block, of the inveteracy of the near thoroughfare, which leave "style," in construction, at the mercy of the impertinent cross-streets, make detachment and independence, save in the rarest cases, an insoluble problem, preclude without pity any element of court or garden, and open to the builder in quest of distinction the one alternative, and the great adventure, of seeking his reward in the sky.

Of their licence to pursue it there to any extent whatever New Yorkers are, I think, a trifle too assertively proud; no court of approach, no interspace worth mention, ever forming meanwhile part of the ground-plan or helping to receive the force of the breaking public wave. New York pays at this rate the penalty of her primal topographic curse, her old inconceivable bourgeois scheme of composition and distribution, the uncorrected labour of minds with no imagination of the future and blind before the opportunity given them by their two magnificent water-fronts. This original sin of the longitudinal avenues perpetually, yet meanly intersected, and of the organized sacrifice of the indicated alternative, the great perspectives from East to West, might still have earned forgiveness by some occasional departure from its pettifogging consistency. But, thanks to this consistency, the city is, of all great cities, the least endowed with any blest item of stately square or goodly garden, with any happy accident or surprise, any fortunate nook or casual corner, any deviation, in fine, into the liberal or the charming. That way, however, for the regenerate filial mind, madness may be said to lie—the way of imagining what might have been the putting it all together in the light of what so helplessly is. One of the things that helplessly are, for instance, is just this assault of the street, as I have called it, upon any direct dealings with our caravansary. The electric cars, with their double track, are everywhere almost as tight a fit in the narrow channel of the roadway as the projectile in the bore of a gun; so that the Waldorf-Astoria, sitting by this absent margin for life with her open lap and arms, is reduced to confessing, with a strained smile, across the traffic and the danger, how little, outside her mere swing-door, she can do for you. She seems to admit that the attempt to get at her may cost you your safety, but reminds you at the same time that any good American, and even any good inquiring stranger, is supposed willing to risk that boon for her. "*Un bon mouvement*, therefore: you must make a dash for it, but you'll see I'm worth it." If such a claim as this last be ever justified, it would indubitably be justified here; the survivor scrambling out of the current and up the bank finds in the amplitude of the entertainment awaiting him an instant sense as of applied restoratives. The amazing hotel-world quickly closes round him; with the process of transition reduced to its minimum he is transported to conditions of extraordinary complexity and brilliancy, operating—and with proportionate perfection—by laws of their own and expressing after their fashion a complete scheme of life. The air swarms, to intensity, with the *characteristic*, the characteristic condensed and accumulated as he rarely elsewhere has had the luck to find it. It jumps out to meet his every glance, and this unanimity of its spring, of all its aspects and voices, is what I just now referred to as the essence of the loud New York story. That effect of violence in the whole communication, at which I thus hint, results from the inordinate mass, the quantity of presence, as it were, of the testimony heaped together for emphasis of the wondrous moral.

The moral in question, the high interest of the tale, is that you are in presence of a revelation of the possibilities of the hotel—for which the American spirit has found so unprecedented a use and a value; leading it on to express so a social, indeed positively an æsthetic ideal, and making it so, at this supreme pitch, a synonym for civilization, for the capture of conceived manners themselves, that one is verily tempted to ask if the hotel-spirit may not just *be* the American spirit most seeking and most finding itself. That truth—the truth that the present is more and more the day of the hotel—had not waited to burst on the mind at the view of this particular establishment; we have all more or less been educated to it, the world over, by the fruit-bearing action of the American example: in consequence of which it has been opened to us, to see still other societies moved by the same irresistible spring and trying, with whatever grace and ease they may bring to the business, to unlearn as many as possible of their old social canons, and in especial their old discrimination in favour of the private life. The business for them—for communities to which the American ease in such matters is not native—goes much less of itself and produces as yet a scantier show; the great difference with the American show being that in the United States every one is, for the lubrication of the general machinery, practically in everything, whereas in Europe, mostly, it is only certain people who are in anything; so that the machinery, so much less generalized, works in a smaller, stiffer way. This one caravansary makes the American case vivid, gives it, you feel, that quantity of illustration which renders the place a new thing under the sun. It is an expression of the gregarious state breaking down every barrier but two—one of which, the barrier consisting of the high pecuniary tax, is the immediately obvious. The other, the rather more subtle, is the condition, for any member of the flock, that he or she—in other words especially she—be presumably "respectable," be, that is, not discoverably anything else. The rigour with which any appearance of pursued or desired adventure is kept down—adventure in the florid sense of the word, the sense in which it remains an euphemism—is not the least interesting note of the whole immense promiscuity. Protected at those two points the promiscuity carries, through the rest of the range, everything before it.

It sat there, it walked and talked, and ate and drank, and listened and danced to music, and otherwise revelled and roamed, and bought and sold, and came and went there, all on its own splendid terms and with an encompassing material splendour, a wealth and variety of constituted picture and background, that might well feed it with the finest illusions about itself. It paraded through halls and saloons in which art and history, in masquerading dress, muffled almost to suffocation as in the gold brocade of their pretended majesties and their conciliatory graces, stood smirking on its passage with the last cynicism of hypocrisy. The exhibition is wonderful for that, for the suggested sense of a promiscuity which manages to be at the same time an inordinate untempered monotony; manages to be so, on such ground as this, by an extraordinary trick of its own, wherever one finds it. The combination forms, I think, largely, the very interest, such as it is, of these phases of the human scene in the United States—if only for the pleasant puzzle of our wondering how, when types, aspects, conditions, have so much in common, they should seem at all to make up a conscious miscellany. That question, however, the question of the play and range, the practical elasticity, of the social sameness, in America, will meet us elsewhere on our path, and I confess that all questions gave way, in my mind, to a single irresistible obsession. This was just the ache of envy of the spirit of a society which had found there, in its prodigious public setting, so exactly what it wanted. One was in presence, as never before, of a realized ideal and of that childlike rush of surrender to it and clutch at it which one was so repeatedly to recognize, in America, as the note of the supremely gregarious state. It made the whole vision unforgettable, and I am now carried back to it, I confess, in musing hours, as to one of my few glimpses of perfect human felicity. It had the admirable sign that it was, for a "mixed" social manifestation, blissfully exempt from any principle or possibility of disaccord with itself. It was absolutely a fit to its conditions, those conditions which were both its earth and its heaven, and every part of the picture, every item of the immense sum, every wheel of the wondrous complexity, was on the best terms with all the rest.

The sense of these things became for the hour as the golden glow in which one's envy burned, and through which, while the sleet and the slosh, and the clangorous charge of cars, and the hustling, hustled crowds held the outer world, one carried one's charmed attention from one chamber of the temple to another. For that is how the place speaks, as great constructed and achieved harmonies mostly speak—as a temple builded, with clustering chapels and shrines, to an idea. The hundreds and hundreds of people in circulation, the innumerable huge-hatted ladies in especial, with their air of finding in the gilded and storied labyrinth the very firesides and pathways of home, became thus the serene faithful, whose rites one would no more have sceptically brushed than one would doff one's disguise in a Mohammedan mosque. The question of who they all might be, seated under palms and by fountains, or communing, to some inimitable New York tune, with the shade of Marie Antoinette in the queer recaptured actuality of an easy Versailles or an intimate Trianon—such questions as that, interesting in other societies and at other times, insisted on yielding here to the mere eloquence of the general truth. Here was a social order in positively stable equilibrium. Here was a world whose relation to its form and medium was practically imperturbable; here was a conception of publicity *as* the vital medium organized with the authority with which the American genius for organization, put on its mettle, alone could organize it. The whole thing remains for me, however, I repeat, a gorgeous golden blur, a paradise peopled with unmistakable American shapes, yet in which, the general and the particular, the organized and the extemporized, the element of ingenuous joy below and of consummate management above, melted together and left one uncertain which of them one was, at a given turn of the maze, most admiring. When I reflect indeed that without my clue I should not have even known the maze—should not have known, at the given turn, whether I was engulfed, for instance, in the *vente de charité* of the theatrical profession and the onset of persuasive peddling actresses, or in the annual tea-party of German lady-patronesses (of I know not what) filling with their Oriental opulence and their strange idiom a play-house of the richest rococo, where some other expensive anniversary, the ball of a guild or the carouse of a club, was to tread on their heels and instantly mobilize away their paraphernalia—when I so reflect I see the sharpest dazzle of the eyes as precisely the play of the genius for organization.

There are a thousand forms of this ubiquitous American force, the most ubiquitous of all, I was in no position to measure; but there was often no resisting a vivid view of the form it may take, on occasion, under pressure of the native conception of the hotel. Encountered embodiments of the gift, in this connection, master-spirits of management whose influence was as the very air, the very expensive air, one breathed, abide with me as the intensest examples of American character; indeed as the very interesting supreme examples of a type which has even on the American ground, doubtless, not said its last word, but which has at least treated itself there to a luxury of development. It gives the impression, when at all directly met, of having at its service something of that fine flame that makes up personal greatness; so that, again and again, as I found, one would have liked to see it more intimately at work. Such failures of opportunity and of penetration, however, are but the daily bread of the visionary tourist. Whenever I dip back, in fond memory, none the less, into the vision I have here attempted once more to call up, I see the whole thing overswept as by the colossal extended arms, waving the magical bâton, of some high-stationed orchestral leader, the absolute presiding power, conscious of every note of every instrument, controlling and commanding the whole volume of sound, keeping the whole effect together and making it what it is. What may one say of such a spirit if not that he understands, so to speak, the forces he sways, understands his boundless American material and plays with it like a master indeed? One sees it thus, in its crude plasticity, almost in the likeness of an army of puppets whose strings the wealth of his technical imagination teaches him innumerable ways of pulling, and yet whose innocent, whose always ingenuous agitation of their members he has found means to make them think of themselves as delightfully free and easy. Such was my impression of the perfection of the concert that, for fear of its being spoiled by some chance false note, I never went into the place again.

It might meanwhile seem no great adventure merely to walk the streets; but (beside the fact that there is, in general, never a better way of taking in life), this pursuit irresistibly solicited, on the least pretext, the observer whose impressions I note—accustomed as he had ever been conscientiously to yield to it: more particularly with the relenting year, when the breath of spring, mildness being really installed, appeared the one vague and disinterested presence in the place, the one presence not vociferous and clamorous. Any definite presence that doesn't bellow and bang takes on in New York by that simple fact a distinction practically exquisite; so that one goes forth to meet it as a guest of honour, and that, for my own experience, I remember certain aimless strolls as snatches of intimate communion with the spirit of May and June—as abounding, almost to enchantment, in the comparatively *still* condition. Two secrets, at this time, seemed to profit by that influence to tremble out; one of these to the effect that New York would really have been "meant" to be charming, and the other to the effect that the restless analyst, willing at the lightest persuasion to let so much of its ugliness edge away unscathed from his analysis, must have had for it, from far back, one of those loyalties that are beyond any reason.

"It's all very well," the voice of the air seemed to say, if I may so take it up; "it's all very well to 'criticize,' but you distinctly take an interest and are the victim of your interest, be the grounds of your perversity what they will. You can't escape from it, and don't you see that this, precisely, is what *makes* an adventure for you (an adventure, I admit, as with some strident, battered, questionable beauty, truly some 'bold bad' charmer), of almost any odd stroll, or waste half-hour, or other promiscuous passage, that results for you in an impression? There is always your bad habit of receiving through almost any accident of vision more impressions than you know what to do with; but that, for common convenience, is your eternal handicap and may not be allowed to plead here against your special responsibility. You *care* for the terrible town, yea even for the 'horrible,' as I have overheard you call it, or at least think it, when you supposed no one would know; and you see now how, if you fly such fancies as that it was conceivably meant to be charming, you are tangled by that weakness in some underhand imagination of its possibly, one of these days, as a riper fruit of time, becoming so. To do that, you indeed sneakingly provide, it must get away from itself; but you are ready to follow its hypothetic dance even to the mainland and to the very end of its tether. What makes the general relation of our adventure with it is that, at bottom, you are all the while wondering, in presence of the aspects of its genius and its shame, what elements or parts, if any, would be worth its saving, worth carrying off for the fresh embodiment and the better life, and which of them would have, on the other hand, to face the notoriety of going *first* by the board. I have literally heard you qualify the monster as "shameless"—though that was wrung from you, I admit, by the worst of the winter conditions, when circulation, in any fashion consistent with personal decency or dignity, was merely mocked at, when the stoney-hearted 'trolleys,' cars of Juggernaut in their power to squash, triumphed all along the line, when the February blasts became as cyclones in the darkened gorges of masonry (which downtown, in particular, put on, at their mouths, the semblance of black rat-holes, holes of gigantic rats, inhabited by whirlwinds;) when all the pretences and impunities and infirmities, in fine, had massed themselves to be hurled at you in the fury of the elements, in the character of the traffic, in the unadapted state of the place to almost *any* dense movement, and, beyond everything, in that pitch of all the noises which acted on your nerves as so much wanton provocation, so much conscious cynicism. The fury of sound took the form of derision of the rest of your woe, and thus it *might*, I admit, have struck you as brazen that the horrible place should, in such confessed collapse, still be swaggering and shouting. It might have struck you that great cities, with the eyes of the world on them, as the phrase it, should be capable either of a proper form or (failing this) of a proper compunction; which tributes to propriety were, on the part of New York, equally wanting. This made you remark, precisely, that nothing was wanting, on the other hand, to that analogy with the character of the bad bold beauty, the creature the most blatant of whose pretensions is that she is one of those to whom everything is always forgiven. On what ground 'forgiven'? of course you ask; but note that you ask it while you're in the very act of forgiving. Oh yes, you are; you've as much as said so yourself. So there it all is; arrange it as you can. Poor dead bad bold beauty; there must indeed be something about her——!"

Let me grant then, to get on, that there *was* doubtless, in the better time, something about her; there was enough about her, at all events, to conduce to that distinct cultivation of her company for which the contemplative stroll, when there was time for it, was but another name. The analogy was in truth complete; since the repetition of such walks, and the admission of the beguiled state contained in them, resembled nothing so much as the visits so often still incorrigibly made to compromised charmers. I defy even a master of morbid observation to perambulate New York unless he be interested; so that in a case of memories so gathered the interest must be taken as a final fact. Let me figure it, to this end, as lively in every connection–and so indeed no more lively at one mild crisis than at another. The crisis–even of observation at the morbid pitch–is inevitably mild in cities intensely new; and it was with the quite peculiarly insistent newness of the upper reaches of the town that the spirit of romantic inquiry had always, at the best, to reckon. There are new cities enough about the world, goodness knows, and there are new parts enough of old cities–for examples of which we need go no farther than London, Paris and Rome, all of late so mercilessly renovated. But the newness of New York–unlike even that of Boston, I seemed to discern–had this mark of its very own, that it affects one, in every case, as having treated itself as still more provincial, if possible, than any poor dear little interest of antiquity it may have annihilated. The very sign of its energy is that it doesn't believe in itself; it fails to succeed, even at a cost of millions, in persuading you that it does. Its mission would appear to be, exactly, go gild the temporary, with its gold, as many inches thick as may be, and then, with a fresh shrug, a shrug of its splendid cynicism for its freshly detected inability to convince, give up its actual work, however exorbitant, as the merest of stop-gaps. The difficulty with the compromised charmer is just this constant inability to convince; to convince ever, I mean, that she is serious, serious about any form whatever, or about anything but that perpetual passionate pecuniary purpose which plays with all forms, which derides and devours them, though it may pile up the cost of them in order to rest a while, spent and haggard, in the illusion of their finality.

The perception of this truth grows for you by your simply walking up Fifth Avenue and pausing a little in presence of certain forms, certain exorbitant structures, in other words, the elegant domiciliary, as to which the illusion of finality was within one's memory magnificent and complete, but as to which one feels today that their life wouldn't be, as against any whisper of a higher interest, worth an hour's purchase. They sit there in the florid majesty of the taste of their time–a light now, alas, generally clouded; and I pretend of course to speak, in alluding to them, of no individual case of danger or doom. It is only a question of that unintending and unconvincing expression of New York everywhere, as yet, on the matter of the *maintenance* of a given effect–which comes back to the general insincerity of effects, and truly even (as I have already noted) to the insincerity of the effect of the sky-scrapers themselves. There results from all this–and as much where the place most smells of its millions as elsewhere–that unmistakable New York admission of unattempted, impossible maturity. The new Paris and the new Rome do at least propose, I think, to be old–one of these days; the new London even, erect as she is on leaseholds destitute of dignity, yet does, for the period, appear to believe in herself. The vice I glance at is, however, when showing, in our flagrant example, on the forehead of its victims, much more a cause for pitying than for decrying them. Again and again, in the upper reaches, you pause with that pity; you learn, on the occasion of a kindly glance up and down a quiet cross-street (there being objects and aspects in many of them appealing to kindness), that such and such a house, or a row, is "coming down"; and you gasp, in presence of the elements involved, at the strangeness of the moral so pointed. It rings out like the crack of that lash in the sky, the play of some mighty teamster's whip, which ends by affecting you as the poor New Yorker's one association with the idea of "powers above." "No"—this is the tune to which the whip seems flourished—"there's no step at which you shall rest, no form, as I'm constantly showing you, to which, consistently with my interests, you *can*. I build you up but to tear you down, for it I were to let any tenderness of association once accumulate, or any 'love of the old' once pass unsnubbed, what would become of *us*, who have our hands on the whipstock, please? Fortunately we've learned the secret for keeping association at bay. We've learned that the great thing is not to suffer it to so much as begin. Wherever it does begin we find we're lost; but as that takes you some time we get in ahead. It's the reason, if you must know, why you shall "run," all, without exception, to the fifty floors. We defy you even to aspire to venerate shapes so grossly constructed as the arrangement in fifty floors. You may have a feeling for keeping on with an old staircase, consecrated by the tread of generations—especially when it's 'good,' and old staircases are often so lovely; but how can you have a feeling for keeping on with an old elevator, how can you have it any more than for keeping on with an old omnibus? You'd be ashamed to venerate the arrangement in fifty floors, accordingly, even if you could; whereby, saving you any moral trouble or struggle, they are conceived and constructed—and you must do us the justice of this care for your sensibility—in a manner to put the thing out of the question. In such a manner, moreover, as that there shall be immeasurably more of them, in quantity, to tear down than of the actual past that we are now sweeping away. Wherefore we shall be kept in precious practice. The word will perhaps be then—who knows?—for building from the earth-surface downwards; in which case it will be a question of tearing, so to speak, 'up.' It little matters, so long as we blight the superstition of rest."

Yet even in the midst of this vision of eternal waste, of conscious, sentient-looking houses and rows, full sections of streets, to which the rich taste of history is forbidden even while their fresh young lips are just touching the cup, something charmingly done, here and there, some bid for the ampler permanence, seems to say to you that the particular place only asks, as a human home, to lead the life it has begun, only asks to enfold generations and gather in traditions, to show itself capable of growing up to character and authority. Houses of the best taste are like clothes of the best tailors—it takes their age to show us how good they are; and I frequently recognized, in the region of the upper reaches, this direct appeal of the individual case of happy construction. Construction at large abounds in the upper reaches, construction indescribably precipitate and elaborate—the latter fact about it always so oddly hand in hand with the former; and we should exceed in saying that felicity is always its mark. But some highly liberal, some extravagant intention almost always is, and we meet here even that happy accident, already encountered and acclaimed, in its few examples, down-town, of the object shining almost absurdly in the light of its merely comparative distinction. All but lost in the welter of instances of sham refinement, the shy little case of real refinement detaches itself ridiculously, as being (like the saved City Hall, or like the pleasant old garden-walled house on the north-west corner of Washington Square and Fifth Avenue) of so beneficent an admonition as to show, relatively speaking, for priceless. These things, which I may not take time to pick out, are the salt that saves, and it is enough to say for their delicacy that they are the direct counterpart of those other dreadful presences, looming round them, which embody the imagination of new kinds and new clustered, emphasized quantities of vulgarity. To recall these fine notes and these loud ones, the whole play of wealth and energy and untutored liberty, of the movement of a breathless civilization reflected, as brick and stone and marble may reflect, through all the contrasts of prodigious flight and portentous stumble, is to acknowledge, positively, that one's rambles were delightful, and that the direct abutting on the east side of the Park, in particular, never engaged my attention without, by the same stroke, making the social question dance before it in a hundred interesting forms.

The social question quite fills the air, in New York, for any spectator whose impressions at all follow themselves up; it wears, at any rate, in what I have called the upper reaches, the perpetual strange appearance as of Property perched high aloft and yet itself looking about, all ruefully, in the wonder of what it is exactly doing there. We see it perched, assuredly, in other and older cities, other and older social orders; but it strikes us in those situations as knowing a little more where it is. It strikes us as knowing how it has got up and why it must, infallibly, stay up; it has not the frightened look, measuring the spaces around, of a small child set on a mantleshelf and about to cry out. If old societies are interesting, however, I am far from thinking that young ones may not be more so—with their collective countenance so much more presented, precisely, to observation, as by their artless need to get themselves explained. The American world produces almost everywhere the impression of appealing to any attested interest for the word, the *fin mot*, of what it may mean; but I somehow see those parts of it most at a loss that are already explained not a little by the ample possession of money. This is the amiable side there of the large developments of private ease in general—the amiable side of those numerous groups that are rich enough and, in the happy vulgar phrase, bloated enough, to be candidates for the classic imputation of haughtiness. The amiability proceeds from an essential vagueness; whereas real haughtiness is never vague about itself—it is only vague about others. That is the human note in the huge American rattle of gold—so far as the "social" field is the scene of the rattle. The "business" field is a different matter—as to which the determination of the audibility in it of the human note (so interesting to try for if one had but the warrant) is a line of research closed to me, alas, by my fatally uninitiated state. My point is, at all events, that you cannot be "hard," really, with any society that affects you as ready to learn from you, and from this resource for it of your detachment combining with your proximity, what in the name of all its possessions and all its destitutions it would honestly be "at."

⊱ 97 ⊰

The Color of a Great City

THEODORE DREISER

Theodore Dreiser (1871–1945) was born in Terre Haute, Indiana. Although primarily a novelist, Dreiser also worked for newspapers in Chicago, St. Louis, and Pittsburgh. He arrived in New York in 1894. His major novel (written very much in the naturalist mode) *Sister Carrie* (1900) concerns the rise and fall of characters fundamentally altered by their respective and very different experiences and expectations of the city. *Sister Carrie* observes its main characters almost at the mercy of chance and coincidence in Chicago and New York. Vividly alert to the rhythms and processes of the city, he is much taken by the way the *look* of the American city suggested a new series of social or economic relationships based on its consumer imagery. *The Color of a Great City* (1923) is his *paean* to New York. See W. A. Swanberg, *Dreiser* (1965) and Rachel Boulby, *Just Looking* (1987).

Foreword

My only excuse for offering these very brief pictures of the city of New York as it was between 1900 and 1914 or '15, or thereabout, is that they are of the very substance of the city I knew in my early adventurings in it. Also, and more particularly, they represent in part, at least, certain phases which at that time most arrested and appealed to me, and which now are fast vanishing or are no more. I refer more particularly to such studies as *The Bread-line, The Push-cart Man, The Toilers of the Tenements, Christmas in the Tenements, Whence the Song,* and *The Love Affairs of Little Italy.*

For, to begin with, the city, as I see it, was more varied and arresting and, after its fashion, poetic and even idealistic then than it is now. It offered, if I may venture the opinion, greater social and financial contrasts than it does now: the splendor of the purely social Fifth Avenue of the last decade of the last century and the first decade of this, for instance, as opposed to the purely commercial area that now bears that name; the sparklingly personality-dotted Wall Street of 1890–

Source: Theodore Dreiser, from *The Color of a Great City*, London, 1923.

1910 as contrasted with the commonplace and almost bread and butter world that it is to-day. (There were argonauts then.) The astounding area of poverty and of beggary even,—I refer to the east side and the Bowery of that period—unrelieved as they were by civic betterment and social service ventures of all kinds, as contrasted with the beschooled and beserviced east side of to-day. Who recalls Steve Brodies, McGurks, Doyers Street and "Chuck" Connors?

The city is larger. It has, if you will, more amazing architectural features. But has it as vivid and moving social contrasts,—as hectic and poignant and disturbing mental and social aspirations as it had then? I cannot see that it has. Rather, as it seems to me, it is duller because less differentiated. There are millions and millions but what do they do? Tramp aimlessly, for the most part, here and there in shoals, to see a ball game, a football game, a parade, a prize-fight, a civic betterment or automobile exhibition or to dance or dine in a hall that holds a thousand. But of that old zest that seemed to find something secret and thrilling in a thousand nooks and corners of the old city, its Bowery, its waterfront, its rialto, its outlying resorts, not a trace. One cannot even persuade the younger generation, that never even knew the old city, to admit that they feel a tang of living equivalent to what they imagined once was. The truth is that it is not here. It has vanished—along with the generation that felt it.

The pictures that I offer here, however, are not, I am compelled to admit, of that more distinguished and vibrant crust, which my introduction so far would imply. Indeed they are the very antithesis, I think, of all that glitter and glister that made the social life of that day so superior. Its shadow, if you will, its reverse face. For being very much alone at the time, and having of necessity, as the situation stood, ample hours in which to wander here and there, without, however, sufficient financial means to divert myself in any other way, I was given for the most part to rambling in what to me were the strangest and most peculiar and most interesting areas I could find as contrasted with those of great wealth and to speculating at length upon the phases and the forces of life I then found so lavishly spread before me. The splendor of the, to me, new dynamic, new-world metropolis! Its romance, its enthusiasm, its illusions, its difficulties! The immense crowds everywhere—upon Manhattan Island, at least. The beautiful rivers and the bay with its world of shipping that washed its shores. Indeed, I was never weary of walking and contemplating the great streets, not only Fifth Avenue and Broadway, but the meaner ones also, such as the Bowery, Third Avenue, Second Avenue, Elizabeth Street in the lower Italian section and East Broadway. And at that time even (1894) that every different and most radically foreign plexus, known as the East Side, already stretched from Chatham Square and even farther south—Brooklyn Bridge—north to Fourteenth Street. For want of bridges and subways the city was not, as yet, so far-flung but for that reason more concentrated and almost as congested.

Yet before I was fifteen years in the city, all of the additional bridges, other than Brooklyn Bridge which was here when I came and which so completely served to change New York from the thing it was then to what it is now, were already in place—Manhattan, Williamsburg, Queens Borough Bridges. And the subways had been built, at least in part. But before then, if anything, the great island, as I have said, was even more compact of varied and foreign groups, and one had only to wander casually and not at any great length to come upon the Irish in the lower East and West Sides; the Syrians in Washington Street—a great mass of them; the Greeks around 26th, 27th and 28th Streets on the West Side; the Italians around Mulberry Bend; the Bohemians in East 67th Street, and the Sicilians in East 116th Street and thereabouts. The Jews were still chiefly on the East Side.

Being fascinated by these varying nationalities, and their neighborhoods, I was given for the first year or two of my stay here to wandering among them, as well as along and through the various parks, the waterfronts and the Bowery, and thinking, thinking, thinking on this welter of life and the difficulties and the strangeness of it. The veritable tides of people that were forever moving here—so different to the Middle-West cities I had known. And the odd, or at least different, devices and trades by which they made their way—the small shops, trades, tricks even. For one thing, I was often given to wondering how so many people could manage to subsist in New York by grinding hand organs alone, or shining shoes or selling newspapers or peanuts, or fruits or vegetables from a small stand or cart.

And the veritable shoals and worlds, even, of beggars and bums and idlers and crooks in the Bowery and elsewhere. Indeed I was more or less dumbfounded by the numerical force of these and the far cry it was from them to the mansions in Fifth Avenue, the great shops in Sixth Avenue and Twenty-third Street, the world famous banking houses and personalities in Wall Street, the comfortable cliff-dwellers who occupied the hotels and apartment houses of the upper West side and along Broadway. For being young and inexperienced and penniless, these economic differences had more significance for me then than they have since been able to maintain. Yet always and primarily fascinated by the problem of life itself, the riddle of its origin, the difficulties seemingly attending its maintenance everywhere, such a polyglot city as this was, not only an economic problem, but a strange and mysterious picture, and I was never weary of spying out how the other fellow lived and how he made his way. And yet how many years it was, really, after I arrived here, quite all of ten, before it ever occurred to me that apart from the novel or short story, these particular scenes and my own cogitations in connection might possess merit as pictures.

And so it was that not before 1904—ten years later, really—that I was so much as troubled to sketch a single impression of all that I had seen and then only at the request of a Sunday editor of a New York newspaper who was short of "small local stuff" to fill in between his more lurid features. And even at that, not more than seven or eight of all that are here assembled were at that time even roughly sketched,—*The Bowery Mission, The Waterfront, The Cradle of Tears, The Track Walker, The Realization of an Ideal, The Log of a Harbor Pilot*. Later, however, in 1908 and '09, finding space in a magazine of my own—*The Bohemian*—as well as one conducted by Senator Watson of Georgia, and bethinking me of all I had seen and how truly wonderful and colorful it really was, I began to try to do more of them, and at that time wrote at least seven or eight more—*The Flight of Pigeons, Six O'clock, The Wonder of Water, The Men in the Storm,* and *The Men in the Dark.* The exact titles of all, apart from these, I have forgotten.

Still later, after the opening of the World War, and because I was noting how swiftly and steadily the city was changing and old landmarks and conditions were together, not only all the scenes I had previously published or sketched, but to add some others which from time to time I had begun but never finished. Among these at that time were *The Fire, Hell's Kitchen, A Way-place of the Fallen, The Man on the Bench.* And then, several years ago, having in the meanwhile once more laid aside the material to the advantage of other matters, I decided that it was still worth while. And getting them all out and casting aside those I no longer cared for, and rewriting others of which I approved, together with new pictures of old things I had seen, i.e., *Bums, The Michael J. Powers Association, A Vanished Summer Resort, The Push-cart Man, The Sandwich Man, Characters, The Men in the Snow, The City Awakes*—I finally evolved the present volume. But throughout all these latest additions I sought only to recapture the flavor and the color of that older day—nothing more. If they are anything, they are mere representations of the moods that governed me at the time that I had observed this material at first hand—not as I know the city to be now.

In certain of these pictures, as will be seen, reference is made to wages, hours and working and living conditions not now holding, or at least not to the same severe degree. This is especially true of such presentations as *The Men in the Dark, The Men in the Storm, The Men in the Snow, Six O'clock, The Bread-line,* (long since abolished), *The Toilers of the Tenements,* and *Christmas in the Tenements.* Yet since they were decidedly true of that particular period, I prefer to leave them as originally written. They bear, I believe, the stamp of their hour.

The City of My Dreams

It was silent, the city of my dreams, marble and serene, due perhaps to the fact that in reality I knew nothing of crowds, poverty, the winds and storms of the inadequate that blow like dust along the paths of life. It was an amazing city, so far-flung, so beautiful, so dead. There were tracks of iron stalking through the air, and streets that were as cañons, and stairways that mounted in vast flights to noble plazas, and steps that led down into deep places where were, strangely enough, underworld silences. And then, after twenty years, here it stood, as amazing almost as my dream, save that in the waking the flush of life was over it. It possessed the tang of contests and dreams and enthusiasms and delights and terrors and despairs. Through its ways and cañons and open spaces and underground passages were running, seething, sparkling, darkling, a mass of beings such as my dream-city never knew.

The thing that interested me then as now about New York—as indeed about any great city, but more definitely New York because it was and is so preponderantly large—was the sharp, and at the same time immense, contrast it showed between the dull and the shrewd, the strong and the weak, the rich and the poor, the wise and the ignorant. This, perhaps, was more by reason of numbers and opportunity than anything else, for of course humanity is much the same everywhere. But the number from which to choose was so great here that the strong, or those who ultimately dominated, were so very strong, and the weak so very, very weak—and so very, very many.

I once knew a poor, half-demented, and very much shriveled little seamstress who occupied a tiny hall-bedroom in a side-street rooming-house, cooked her meals on a small alcohol stove set on a bureau, and who had about space enough outside of this to take three good steps either way.

"I would rather live in my hall-bedroom in New York than in any fifteen-room house in the country that I ever saw," she commented once, and her poor little colorless eyes held more of sparkle and snap in them than I ever saw there, before or after. She was wont to add to her sewing income by reading fortunes in cards and tea-leaves and coffee-grounds, telling of love and prosperity to scores as lowly as herself, who would never see either. The color and noise and splendor of the city as a spectacle was sufficient to pay her for all her ills.

And have I not felt the glamour of it myself? And do I not still? Broadway, at Forty-second Street, on those selfsame spring evenings when the city is crowded with an idle, sightseeing crowd of Westerners; when the doors of all shops are open, the windows of nearly all restaurants wide to the gaze of the idles passer-by. Here is the great city, and it is lush and dreamy. A May or June moon will be hanging like a burnished silver disc between the high walls aloft. A hundred, a thousand electric signs will blink and wink. And the floods of citizens and visitors in summer clothes and with gay hats; the street cars jouncing their endless carloads on indifferent errands; the taxis and private cars fluttering about like jeweled flies. The very gasoline contributes a distinct perfume. Life bubbles, sparkles; chatters gay, incoherent stuff. Such is Broadway.

And then Fifth Avenue, that singing, crystal street, on a shopping afternoon, winter, summer, spring or fall. What tells you as sharply of spring when, its windows crowded with delicate effronteries of silks and gay nothings of all description, it greets you in January, February and March? And how as early as November again, it sings of Palm Beach and Newport and the lesser or greater joys of the tropics and the warmer seas. And in September, how the haughty display of furs and rugs, in this same avenue, and costumes de luxe for ball and dinner, cry out of snows and blizzards, when you are scarcely ten days back from mountain or seaside. One might think, from the picture presented and the residences which line the upper section, that all the world was inordinately prosperous and exclusive and happy. And yet, if you but knew the tawdry underbrush of society, the tangle and mat of futile growth between the tall trees of success, the shabby chambers crowded with aspirants and climbers, the immense mansions barren of a single social affair, perfect and silent!

I often think of the vast mass of underlings, boys and girls, who, with nothing but their youth and their ambitions to commend them, are daily and hourly setting their faces New Yorkward reconnoitring the city for what it may hold in the shape of wealth or fame, or, if not that, position and comfort in the future; and what, if anything, they will reap. Ah, their young eyes drinking in its promise! And then, again, I think of all the powerful or semi-powerful men and women throughout the world, toiling at one task or another—a store, a mine, a bank, a profession—somewhere outside of New York, whose one ambition is to reach the place where their wealth will permit them to enter and remain in New York, dominant above the mass, luxuriating in what they consider luxury.

The illusion of it, the hypnosis deep and moving that it is! How the strong and the weak, the wise and the fools, the greedy of heart and of eye, seek the nepenthe, the Lethe, of its something hugeness. I always marvel at those who are willing, seemingly, to pay any price—*the* price, whatever it may be—for one sip of this poison cup. What a stinging, quivering zest they display. How beauty is willing to sell its bloom, virtue its last rag, strength an almost usurious portion of that which it controls, youth its very best years, its hope or dream of fame, fame and power their dignity and presence, age its weary hours, to secure but a minor part of all this, a taste of its vibrating presence and the picture that it makes. Can you not hear them almost, singing its praises?

The City Awakes

Have you ever arisen at dawn or earlier in New York and watched the outpouring in the meaner side-streets or avenue? It is a wondrous thing. It seems to have so little to do with the later, showier, brisker life of the day, and yet it has so very much. It is in the main so drab or shabby-smart at best, poor copies of what you see done more efficiently later in the day. Typewriter girls in almost stage or society costumes entering shabby offices; boys and men made up to look like actors and millionaires turning into the humblest institutions, where they are clerks or managers. These might be called the machinery of the city, after the elevators and street cars and wagons are excluded, the implements by which things are made to go.

Take your place on Williamsburg Bridge some morning, for instance, at say three or four o'clock, and watch the long, the quite unbroken line of Jews trundling pushcarts eastward to the great Wallabout Market over the bridge. A procession out of Assyria or Egypt or Chaldea, you might suppose, Biblical in quality; or, better yet, a huge chorus in some operatic dawn scene laid in Paris or Petrograd or here. A vast silent mass it is, marching to the music of necessity. They are so grimy, so mechanistic, so elemental in their movements and needs. And later on you will find them seated or standing, with their little charcoal buckets or braziers to warm their hands and feet, in those gusty, icy streets of the East Side in winter, or coatless and almost shirtless in hot weather, open-mouthed for want of air. And they are New York, too—Bucharest and Lemberg and Odessa come to the Bowery, and adding rich, dark, colorful threads to the rug or tapestry which is New York.

Since these are but a portion, think of those other masses that come from the surrounding territory, north, south, east and west. The ferries—have you ever observed them in the morning? Or the bridges, railway terminals, and every elevated and subway exit?

Already at six and six-thirty in the morning they have begun to trickle small streams of human beings Manhattan or cityward, and by seven and seven-fifteen these streams have become sizable affairs. By seven-thirty and eight they have changed into heavy, turbulent rivers, and by eight-fifteen and eight-thirty and nine they are raging torrents, no less. They overflow all the streets and avenues and every available means of conveyance. They are pouring into all available doorways, shops, factories, office-buildings—those huge affairs towering so significantly above them. Here they stay all day long, causing those great hives and their adjacent streets to flush with a softness of color not indigenous to them, and then at night, between five and six, they are going again, pouring forth over the bridges and through the subways and across the ferries and out on the trains, until the last drop of them appears to have been exuded, and they are pocketed in some outlying side-street or village or metropolitan hall-room—and the great, turbulent night of the city is on once more.

And yet they continue to stream cityward,—this cityward. From all parts of the world they are pouring into New York: Greeks from Athens and the realms of Sparta and Macedonia, living six seven, eight, nine, ten, eleven, twelve, in one room, sleeping on the floors and dressing and eating and entertaining themselves God knows how; Jews from Russia, Poland, Hungary, the Balkans, crowding the East Side and the inlying sections of Brooklyn, and huddling together in thick, gummy streets, singing in street crowds around ballad-mongers of the woes of their native land, seeking with a kind of divine, poetic flare a modicum of that material comfort which their natures so greatly crave, which their previous condition for at least fifteen hundred years has scarcely warranted; Italians from Sicily and the warmer vales of the South, crowding into great sections of their own, all hungry for a taste of New York; Germans, Hungarians, French, Polish, Swedish, Armenians, all with sections of their own and all alive to the joys of the city, and how eager to live—great gold and scarlet streets throbbing with the thoughts of them!

And last but not least, the illusioned American from the Middle West and the South and the Northwest and the Far West, crowding in and eyeing it all so eagerly, so yearningly, like the others. Ah, the little, shabby, blue light restaurants! The boarding houses in silent streets! The moral, hungry "homes"—how full they are of them and how hopeless! How the city sings and sings for them, and in spite of them, flaunting ever afresh its lures and beauties—a city as wonderful and fateful and ironic as life itself.

The Car Yard

If I were a painter one of the first things I would paint would be one or another of the great railroad yards that abound in every city, those in New York and Chicago being as interesting as any. Only I fear that my brush would never rest with one portrait. There would be pictures of it in sunshine and cloud, in rain and snow, in light and dark, and when heat caused the rails and the cars to bake and shimmer, and the bitter cold the mixture of smoke and steam to ascend in tall, graceful, rhythmic plumes that appear to be composed of superimposed circles and spirals of smoke and mist.

The variety of the cars. The variety of their contents. The long distances and differing climates and countries from which they have come—the Canadian snows, the Mexican uplands, Florida, California, Texas and Maine. As a boy, in the different cities and towns in which our family dwelt, I was forever arrested by the spectacle of those great freight trains, yellow, white, red, blue, green, toiling through or dissipating themselves in some terminal maze of tracks. I was always interested to note how certain cars, having reached their destination, would be sidetracked and left, and then presently the consignee or his agent or expressman would appear and the car be opened. Ice, potatoes, beef, furniture, machinery, boxed shipments of all kinds, would be taken out by some lone worker who, having come with a wagon, would back it up to the opened door and remove the contents. Most interesting of all to me were the immense shipments of live stock, the pigs, sheep, steers, on their last fatal journey and looking so non-understandingly out upon the strange world in which they found themselves, and baa-ing or moo-ing or squealing in tones that gave evidence of the uncertainty, the distress and the wonder that was theirs.

For a time in Chicago, between my eighteenth and nineteenth years, I was employed as a car-tracer in one of the great freight terminals of a railroad entering Chicago, a huge, windy, forsaken realm far out on the great prairie west of the city and harboring literally a thousand or more cars. And into it and from it would move such long freight trains, heavy with snow occasionally, or drenched with rain, and presenting such a variety of things in cars: coal, iron, cattle, beef, which would here be separated and entangled with or disentangled from many others and then moved on again in the form of other long trains. The clanging engine bells, the puffing stacks, the arresting, colorful brakemen and trainmen in their caps, short, thick coats, dirty gloves, and with their indispensable lanterns over their arms. In December and January, when the days were short and the nights fell early, I found my self with long lists of car numbers, covering cars in transit and concerning which or their contents owners or shippers were no doubt anxious, hurrying here and there, now up and down long tracks, or under or between the somber cars that lined them, studying by the aid of my lantern the tags and car numbers, seeing if the original labels or addresses were still intact, whether the seals had remained unbroken, on what track the car was, and about where, and checking these various items on the slip given me, and, all being correct, writing O.K. across the face of it all. Betimes I would find a consigned car already in place on some far sidetrack, the consignee having already been notified, and some lone worker with a wagon busily removing the contents. Sometimes, being in doubt, I would demand to see the authorization, and then report. But except for occasional cars, that however accurately billed never seemed to appear, no other thing went wrong.

Subsequent to that time I have always been interested by these great tangles. Seeing them as in New York facing river banks where ships await their cargoes, or surrounded by the tall coal pockets and grain elevators of a crowded commercial section, I have often thought how typical of the shift and change of life they are, how peculiarly of this day and no other. Imagine a Roman, a Greek, an Egyptian or an Assyrian being shown one of these immense freight yards with their confusing mass of cars, their engines, bells, spirals of smoke and steam, their interesting variety of color, form and movement. How impossible to explain to such an one the mechanism if not the meaning of it all. How impossible it would be for him to identify what he saw with anything that he knew. The mysterious engines, the tireless switching, the lights, the bells, the vehicles, the trainmen and officials. And as far as some future age that yet may be is concerned, all that one sees here or that relates to this form of transportation may even in the course of a few hundred years have vanished as completely as have the old caravansaries of the Orient—rails, cars, engines, coal and smoke and steam, even the intricate processes by which present freight exchange is effected. And something entirely different may have come in its place, transportation by air, for instance, the very mechanism of flight and carriage directed by wireless from given centers.

And yet, as far as life itself is concerned, its strife and change, how typical of it are these present great yards with their unending evidences of movement and change. These cars that come and go, how heavy now with freight, or import; how empty now of anything suggesting service or use even, standing like idle, unneeded persons upon some desolate track, while the thunder of life and exchange passes far to one side. And anon, as in life, each and every one of them finds itself in the very thick of life, thundering along iron rails from city to city, themselves, or rather their contents, eagerly awaited and welcomed and sought after, and again left, as before. And then the old cars, battered and sway-backed by time and the elements and long service, standing here and there unused and useless, their chassis bent and sometimes cracked by undue strain or rust, their sides bulging, their roofs and doors decayed and warped or broken, quite ready for that limbo of old cars, the junk yard rather than the repair shop.

And yet they have been so useful, have seen and done so much, been in such varied and interesting places—the cities, the towns, the country stations, the lone sidings where they have waited or rolled in sun and rain. Here in this particular New York yard over which I am now brooding, upon a great viaduct which commands it all, is one old car, recently emptied of its load of grain, about which on this winter's day a flock of colorful pigeons are rising and falling, odd companions for such a lumbering and cumbersome thing, yet so friendly to and companionable with it, some of them walking peacefully upon its roof, others picking up remaining grains within its open door, others on the snowy ground before it picking still other fallen grains, and not at all disturbed by the puffing engines elsewhere. It might as well be a great boat accompanied by a cloud of gulls. And that other car there, that dusty, yellow one, labelled Central of Georgia, yet from which now a great wagonful of Christmas trees is being taken from Georgia, or where? Has it been to Maine or Labrabor or the Canadian north for these, and where will it go, from here, and how soon? Leaning upon this great viaduct that crosses this maze of tracks and commands so many of the, a great and interesting spectacle, I am curious as to the history or the lives of these cars, each and every one, the character of the places and lives among which each and every one of them has passed its days. They appear so wooden, so lumpish, so inert and cumbersome and yet the place they have been, the things they have seen!

I am told by the physicists that each and every atom of all of this wealth of timber and steel before me is as alive as life; that it consists, each and every particle, of a central spicule of positive energy about which revolve at great speed lesser spicules of negative energy. And so these same continue to revolve until each particular atom, for some chemic or electronic reason, shall have been dissolved, when forthwith these spicules re-arrange themselves into new forms, to revolve as industriously and as unceasingly as before. Springs the thought then: Is anything inert, lacking in response, perception, mood? And if not, what may each of these individual cars with their wealth of experience and observation think if this life, their place in it, their journeys and their strange and equally restless and unknowing companion, man?

The Toilers of the Tenements

New York City has one hundred thousand people who, under unfavorable conditions, work with their fingers for so little money that they are understood, even by the uninitiated general public, to form a class by themselves. These are by some called sewing-machine workers, by others tenement toilers, and by still others sweatshop employees; but, in a general sense, the term, tenement workers, includes them all. They form a great section in one place, and in others little patches, ministered to by storekeepers and trade agents who are as much underpaid and nearly as hard-working as they themselves.

Go into any one of these areas and you will encounter a civilization that is as strange and un-American as if it were not included in this land at all. Pushcarts and market-stalls are among the most distinctive features. Little stores and grimy windows are also characteristic of these sections. There is an atmosphere of crowdedness and poverty which goes with both. Any one can see that these people are living energetically. There is something about the hurry and enthusiasm of their life that reminds you of ants.

If you stay and turn your attention from the traffic proper, the houses begin to attract your attention. They are nearly all four-story or five-story buildings, with here and there one of six, and still another of seven stories; all without elevators, and all, with the exception of the last, exceedingly old. There are narrow entrance-ways, dingy and unlighted, which lead up dark and often rickety stairs. There are other alley-ways, which lead, like narrow tunnels, to rear tenements and back shops. Iron fire escapes descend from the roof to the first floor, in every instance, because the law compels it. Iron stairways sometimes ascend, where no other means of entrance is to be had. There are old pipes which lead upward and carry water. No such thing as sanitary plumbing exists. You will not often see a gas-light in a hall in as many as two blocks of houses. You will not see one flat in ten with hot and cold water arrangement. Other districts have refrigerators and stationary washstands, and bath tubs as a matter of course, but these people do not know what modern conveniences mean. Steam heat and hot and cold water tubs and sinks have never been installed in this area.

The houses are nearly all painted a dull red, and nearly all are divided in the most unsanitary manner. Originally they were built five rooms deep, with two flats on a floor, but now the single flats have been subdivided and two or three, occasionally four or five, families live and toil in the space which was originally intended for one. There are families so poor, or so saving and unclean, that they huddle with other families, seven or eight persons in two rooms. Iron stands covered by plain boards make a bed which can be enlarged or reduced at will. When night comes, four, five, six, sometimes seven such people stretch out on these beds. When morning comes the bedclothes, if such they may be called, are cleared away and the board basis is used as a table. One room holds the stove, the cooking utensils, the chairs, and the sewing machine. The other contains the bed, the bed-clothing, and various kinds of stored material. Eating, sleeping, and usually some washing are done there.

I am giving the extreme instances, unfortunately common to the point of being numerous. In the better instances three or four people are housed in two rooms. How many families there are that live less closely quartered than this would not be very easy to say. On the average, five people live in two rooms. A peddler or a pushcart man who can get to where he can occupy two rooms, by having his wife and children work, is certain that he is doing well. Fathers and mothers, sons and daughters, go out to work. If the father cannot get work and the mother can, then that is the order of procedure. If the daughter cannot get work and the mother and father can, it is the daughter's duty to take care of the house and take in sewing. If any of the boys and girls are too young to go out and enter the shops, duty compels them to help on the piecework that is taken into the rooms. Everything is work, in one form or another, from morning until night.

As for the people themselves, they are a strange mixture of all races and all creeds. Day after day you will see express wagons and trucks leaving the immigration station at the Battery, loaded to crowding with the latest arrivals, who are being taken as residents to one or another colony of this crowded section. There are Greeks, Italians, Russians, Poles, Syrians, Armenians and Hungarians. Jews are so numerous that they have to be classified with the various nations whose language they speak. All are poverty-stricken, all venturing into this new world to make their living. The vast majority have absolutely nothing more than the ten dollars which the immigration inspectors are compelled to see that they have when they arrive. These people recruit the territory in question.

In the same hundred thousand, and under the same tenement conditions, are many who are not foreign-born. I know personally of American fathers who have got down to where it is necessary to work as these foreigners work. There are home-grown American mothers who have never been able to lift themselves above the conditions in which they find themselves to-day. Thousands of children born and reared in New York City are growing up under conditions which would better become a slum section of Constantinople. I know a chamber in this section where, at a plain wooden bench or table, sits a middle-aged Hungarian and his wife, with a fifteen-year-old daughter, sewing. The Hungarian is perhaps not honestly Gentile, for he looks as if he might have Hebrew blood in his veins. The mother and the daughter partake of a dark olive tinge, more characteristic of the Italian than of anything else. It must be a coincidence, however, for these races rarely mix. Between them and upon a nearby chair are piled many pairs of trousers, all awaiting their labor. Two buckles and a button must be sewed on every one. The rough edges at the bottom must be turned up and blasted, and the inside about the top must be lined with a kind of striped cotton which is already set loosely in place. It is their duty to sew closely with their hands what is already basted. No machine worker can do this work, and so it is sent out to such as these, under the practice of tenement distribution. Their duty is to finish it.

There would be no need to call attention to these people except that in this instance they have unwittingly violated the law. Tenement workers, under the new dispensation, cannot do exactly as they please. It is not sufficient for them to have an innate and necessitous desire to work. They must work under special conditions. Thus, it is now written that the floors must be clean and the ceilings whitewashed. There must not be any dirt on the walls. No room in which they work must have such a thing as a bed in it, and no three people may ever work together in one room. Law and order prescribe that one is sufficient. These others—father and daughter, or mother and daughter, or mother and father—should go out into the shops, leaving just one here to work. Such is the law.

These three people, who have only these two trades, have complied with scarcely any of these provisions. The room is not exactly as clean as it should be. The floor is dirty. Overhead is a smoky ceiling, and in one corner is a bed. The two small windows before which they labor do not give sufficient ventilation, and so the air in the chamber is stale. Worst of all, they are working three in a chamber, and have no license.

"How now," asks an inspector, opening the door—for there is very little civility of manner observed by these agents of the law who constantly regulate these people—"any pants being finished here?"

"How?" says the Hungarian, looking purblindly up. It is nothing new to him to have his privacy thus invaded. Unless he has been forewarned and has his door locked, police and detectives, to say nothing of health inspectors and other officials, will frequently stick their heads in or walk in and inquire after one thing or another. Sometimes they go leisurely through his belongings and threaten him for concealing something. There is a general tendency to lord it over and browbeat him, for what reason he has no conception. Other officials do it in the old country; perhaps it is the rule here.

"So," says the inspector, stepping authoritatively forward, "finishing pants, eh? All three of you? Got a license?"

"Vot?" inquires the pale Hungarian, ceasing his labor.

"Where is your license—your paper? Haven't you got a paper?"

The Hungarian, who has not been in this form of work long enough to know the rules, puts his elbows on the table and gazes nervously into the newcomer's face. What is this now that the gentleman wants? His wife looks her own inquiry and speaks of it to her daughter.

"What is it he wants?" says the father to the child.

"It is a paper," returns the daughter in Hungarian. "He says we must have a license."

"Paper?" repeats the Hungarian, looking up and shaking his head in the negative. "No."

"Oh, so you haven't got a license then? I thought so. Who are you working for?"

The father stares at the child. Seeing that he does not understand, the inspector goes on: "The boss, the boss! What boss gave you these pants to finish?"

"Oh," returns the little girl, who understands somewhat better than the rest, "the boss, yes. He wants to know what boss gave us these pants." This last in a foreign tongue to her father.

"Tell him," says the mother in Hungarian, "that the name is Strakow."

"Strakow," repeats the daughter.

"Strakow, eh?" says the inspector. "Well, I'll see Mr. Strakow. You must not work on these any more. Do you hear? Listen, you," and he turns the little girl's face up to him, "you tell your father that he can't do any more of this work until he gets a license. He must go up to No. 1 Madison Avenue and get a paper. I don't know whether they'll give it to him or not, but he can go and ask. Then he must clean this floor. The ceiling must be whitewashed—see?"

The little girl nods her head.

"You can't keep this bed in here, either," he adds. "You must move the bed out into the other room if you can. You mustn't work here. Only one can work here. Two of you must go out into the shop."

All the time the careworn parents are leaning forward eagerly, trying to catch the drift of what they cannot possibly understand. Both interrupt now and then with a "What is it?" in Hungarian, which the daughter has no time to heed. She is so busy trying to understand half of it herself that there is no time for explanation. Finally she says to her parents:

"He says we cannot all work here."

"Vot?" says the father. "No vork?"

"No." replies the daughter. "Three of us can't work in one room. It's against the law. Only one. He says that only one can work in this room."

"How!" he exclaims, as the little girl goes on making vaguely apparent what these orders are. As she proceeds the old fellow's face changes. His wife leans forward, her whole attitude expressive of keen, sympathetic anxiety.

"No vork?" he repeats. "I do no more vork?"

"No," insists the inspector, "not with three in one room."

The Hungarian puts out his right leg, and it becomes apparent that an injury has befallen him. Words he pours upon his daughter, who explains that he has been a pushcart peddler but has received a severe injury to his leg and cannot walk. Helping to sew is all that he can do.

"Well," says the inspector when he hears of this, "that's too bad, but I can't help it. It's the law. You'll have to see the department about it. I can't help it."

Astonished and distressed, the daughter explains, and then they sit in silence. Five cents a pair is all they have been able to earn since the time the father became expert, and all they can do, working from five in the morning until eleven at night, is two dozen pairs a day—in other words, to earn seven dollars and twenty cents a week. If they delay for anything, as they often must, the income drops to six, and quite often to five, dollars. Two dollars a week is their tax for rent.

"So!" says the father, his mouth open. He is too deeply stricken and nonplussed to know what to do. The mother nervously turns her hands.

"You hear now," says the inspector, taking out a tag and fastening it upon the goods—"no more work. Go and see the department."

"How?" asks the father, staring at his helpless family after the door has closed.

How indeed!

In the same round the inspector will come a little later to the shop from which the old Hungarian secured the trousers for finishing. He is armed with full authority over all of these places. In his pocket lie the tags, one of which he puts on a lot of clothing just ordered halted. If that tag is removed it is a penal offence. If it stays on no one can touch the goods until the contractor explains to the factory inspector how he has come to be giving garments for finishing to dwellers in tenements who have not a license. This is a criminal offence on his part. Now he must not touch the clothes he sent over there. If the old Hungarian returns them he must not accept them or pay him any money. This contractor and his clients offer a study in themselves.

His shop is on the third floor of a rear building, which was once used for dwelling purposes but is now given over entirely to clothing manufactories or sweatshops. A flight of dark, ill-odored, rickety stairs gives access to it. There is noise and chatter audible, a thick mixture of sounds from whirring sewing machines and muttering human beings. When you open the door a gray-haired Hebrew, whose long beard rests patriarchally upon his bosom, looks over his shoulders at you from a brick furnace, where he is picking up a reheated iron. Others glance up from their bent positions over machines and ironing-boards. It is a shadowy, hot-odored, floor littered room.

"Have you a finisher doing work for you by the name of Koslovsky?" inquiries the inspector of a thin, bright-eyed Syrian Jew, who is evidently the proprietor of this establishment.

"Koslovsky?" he says after him, in a nervous, fawning, conciliatory manner. "Koslovsky? What is he? No."

"Finisher, I said."

"Yes, finisher—finisher, that's it. He does no work for me—only a little—a pair of pants now and then."

"You knew that he didn't have a license, didn't you?"

"No, no. I did not. No license? Did he not have a license?"

"You're supposed to know that. I've told you that before. You'll have to answer at the office for this. I've tagged his goods. Don't you receive them now. Do you hear?"

"Yes," says the proprietor excitedly. "I would not receive them. He will get no more work from me. When did you do that?"

"Just this morning. Your goods will go up to headquarters."

"So," he replied weakly. "That is right. It is just so. Come over here."

The inspector follows him to a desk in the corner.

"Could you not help me out of this?" he asks, using a queer Jewish accent. "I did not know this once. You are a nice man. Here is a present for you. It is funny I make this mistake."

"No," returns the inspector, shaking his head. "Keep your money. I can't do anything. These goods are tagged. You must learn not to give out finishing to people without a license."

"That is right," he exclaims. "You are a nice man, anyhow. Keep the money."

"Why should I keep the money? You'll have to explain anyhow. I can't do anything for you."

"That is all right," persists the other. "Keep it, anyhow. Don't bother me in the future. There!"

"No, we can't do that. Money won't help you. Just observe the law—that's all I want."

"The law, the law," repeats the other curiously. "That is right. I will observe him."

Such is one story—almost the whole story. This employer, so nervous in his wrongdoings, so anxious to bribe, is but a little better off than those who work for him.

In other tenements and rear buildings are other shops and factories, but they all come under the same general description. Men, women and children are daily making coats, vests, knee-pants and trousers. There are side branches of overalls, cloaks, hats, caps, suspenders, jerseys and blouses. Some make dresses and waists, underwear and neckwear, waist bands, skirts, shirts and purses; still others, fur, or fur trimmings, feathers and artificial flowers, umbrellas, and even collars. It is all a great allied labor of needlework, needlework done by machine and finishing work done by hand. The hundred thousand that follow it are only those who are actually employed as supporters. All those who are supported—the infants, school children, aged parents, and physically disabled relatives—are left out. You may go throughout New York and Brooklyn, and wherever you find a neighbourhood poor enough you will find these workers. They occupy the very worst of tumbledown dwellings. Shrewd Italians, and others called padrones, sometimes lease whole blocks from such men as William Waldorf Astor, and divide up each natural apartment into two or three. Then these cubbyholes are leased to the toilers, and the tenement crowding begins.

You will see by peculiar evidences that things have been pretty bad with these tenements in the past. For instance, between every front and back room you will find a small window, and between every back room and the hall, another. The construction of these was compelled by law, because the cutting up of a single apartment into two or three involved the sealing up of the connecting door and the shutting off of natural circulation. Hence the state decided that a window opening into the hall would be some improvement, anyhow, and so this window-cutting began. It has proved of no value, however. Nearly every such window is most certainly sealed up by the tenants themselves.

In regard to some other matters, this cold enforcement of the present law is, in most cases, a blessing, oppressive as it seems at times. Men should not crowd and stifle and die in chambers where seven occupy the natural space of one. Landlords should not compel them to, and poverty ought to be stopped from driving them. Unless the law says that the floor must be clean and the ceiling white, the occupants will never find time to make them so. Unless the beds are removed from the workroom and only one person allowed to work in one room, the struggling "sweater" will never have less than five or six suffering with him. Enforce such a law, and these workers, if they cannot work unless they comply with these conditions, will comply with them, and charge more for their labor, of course. Sweatshop manufacturers cannot get even these to work for nothing, and landlords cannot get tenants to rent their rooms unless they are clean enough for the law to allow them to work in them. Hence the burden falls in a small measure on the landlord, but not always.

The employer or boss of a little shop, who is so nervous in wrongdoing, so anxious to bribe, is but a helpless agent in the hands of a greater boss. He is no foul oppressor of his fellow man. The great clothing concerns in Broadway and elsewhere are his superiors. What they give, he pays, barring a small profit to himself. If these people are compelled by law to work less or under more expensive conditions, they must receive more or starve, and the great manufactories cannot let them actually starve. They come as near to it now as ever, but they will pay what is absolutely essential to keep them alive; hence we see the value of the law.

To grow and succeed here, though, is something very different. Working, as these people do, they have very little time for education. The great struggle is for bread, and unless the families are closely watched, children are constantly sent to work before they are twelve. I was present in one necktie factory once where five of its employees were ordered out for being without proof that they were fourteen years of age. I have personally seen shops, up to a dozen, inspected in one morning, and some struggling little underling ordered out from each.

"For why you come home?" is the puzzled inquiry of the parents at night.

"Da police maka me."

Down here, and all through this peculiar world, the police are everything. They regulate the conduct, adjudicate for quarrels, interfere with the evil-doers. The terror of them keeps many a child studying in the school-room where otherwise it would be toiling in the chamber at home or the shop outside. Still the struggle is against them, and most of them grow up without any of those advantages so common to others.

At the same time, there are many institutions established to reach these people. One sees Hebrew and Legal Aid Societies in large and imposing buildings. Outdoor recreation leagues, city playgrounds, schools, and university settlements—all are here; and yet the percentage of opportunity is not large. Parents have to struggle too hard. Their ignorant influence upon the lives of the young ones is too great.

I know a lawyer, though, of considerable local prestige, who has worked his way out of these conditions; and Broadway from Thirty-fourth Street south, to say nothing of many other streets, is lined with the signs of those who have overcome the money difficulty of lives begun under these conditions. Unfortunately the money problem, once solved, is not the only thing in the world. Their lives, although they reach to the place where they have gold signs, automobiles and considerable private pleasures, are none the more beautiful. Too often, because of these early conditions, they remain warped, oppressive, greedy and distorted in every worthy mental sense by the great fight they have made to get their money.

Nearly the only ideal that is set before these strugglers still toiling in the area, is the one of getting money. A hundred thousand children, the sons and daughters of working parents whose lives are as difficult as that of the Hungarian portrayed and whose homes are as unlovely, are inoculated in infancy with the doctrine that wealth is all,—the shabbiest and most degrading doctrine that can be impressed upon anyone.

"And how much does your father make a day?" I finally asked, after some other questions.

This is a lawless question anywhere. It earned its own reward. The son inquired of the father in Italian. The latter tactfully shrugged his shoulders and held out his hands. His wife laughed and shrugged her shoulders.

"'One, two dollars,' he says," said the boy.

There was no going back of that. He might have made more. Why should he tell anybody—the police or any one else?

And so I came away.

But the case of this one seemed to me to be so typical of the lot of many in our great cities. All of us are so pushed by ambition as well as necessity. Yet all the feelings and intuitions of the average American-born citizen are more or less at variance with so shrewd an acceptance of difficulties. We hurry more, fret and strain more, and yet on the whole pretend to greater independence. But have we it? I am sure not. When one looks at the vast army of clerks and underlings, pushing, scheming, straining at their social leashes so hopelessly and wearing out their hearts and brains in a fruitless effort to be what they cannot, one knows that they are really no better off and one wishes for them a measure of this individual's enduring patience.

98

Epilogue: Port of New York

PAUL ROSENFELD

Paul Rosenfeld's *Port of New York* (1924) is one of the central cultural documents relating to New York City in the period. It is both a celebration of the city's possibility and of its symbolic status as an alternative to Paris. Thus it responds to the ways in which American painters, poets and photographers were beginning to celebrate the city as a dynamic and vibrant possibility of the "new". Its terms of reference are directly opposed to the response we find in T. S. Eliot, Henry James and Henry Adams. With chapters on such figures as Van Wyck Brooks, Sandberg, William Carlos Williams, John Marin, Georgia O'Keeffe, Arthur Dove and, above all, Alfred Stieglitz, it constitutes a veritable celebration of one kind of native American modernism. Its leading light is Alfred Stieglitz, and the often inflated and romantic idealism of its prose parallels his own search for a spiritual America in an urban context. See *Port of New York*, Introduction Sherman Paul (1961). The "epilogue" is an exemplary statement on the part of New York's symbolic meaning in relation to a rhetoric of hope and possibility.

The liners emerge from the lower bay. Up through the Narrows they heave their sharp prows. In sleety, in blue, in sullen weather, throughout the lighted hours, mouse-colored shapes are stretched off Quarantine. Between cheesebox fort and fume of nondescript South Brooklyn waterfront, metal abdomens which were not seated there yesterday are submitted to rising concrete sides, masts, red iron, ferryslips. In New York harbor, always, new-come bodies foreign to it; issued from Southampton and Bergen, Gibraltar and Bremen, Naples and Antwerp; now engirdled by sullen shorelines and lapped by tired crisscrossed wavelets.

The lean voyagers steer under the tower-jumbled point of Manhattan. Flanks are lashed to the town; holds thrown open to the cobbled street. Decks are annexes of the littoral, portion of New York no less than the leagues of "L" sweeping past dismal brick over caverned thoroughfares. And through periods of

Source: Paul Rosenfeld, "Epilogue: Port of New York", *Port of New York*, 1924, New York.

many days, for weeks, even, the liners lie roped to their piersides, rows of captives handcuffed to policemen. The plated sides list obediently toward bald sheds. Only feeble brownish wisps of smoke adrift from silent smokestacks betray the incorporation incomplete. Then, one day, a pierside is found stripped. Next day, another; two. The vigilantes stand stupid. In the open quadrangle between docks, merely a dingy freighter, and small lighter-fry. By sea-coated piles, the muckerish North River water shrugs its shoulders. The liners have evaded; fled again through the straits. Beyond where eye can reach iron rumps dwindle down the ocean.

And has it really faded from the port, the painful glamour? Has it really gone off them, the fiction that was always on the movements of the liners in and out the upper bay? Or has it merely retreated for a while behind the bluffs of the Jersey shore, to return on us again tomorrow and draw the breast away once more into the distance beneath Staten Island hill? It was on a day just like this one, year before last or last year even—and outside the window the sun fell much as it does now across asphalt grimy with a little last snow, and people came about the corner house and walked past brick walls, and motors ticked and drays banged—that the harbor of New York was somehow the inexplicable scene of a mysterious cruel translation. And nothing in the traffic of the port and in the city streets has changed. Below Battery point the liners stand off Quarantine all through the lighted hours; and here inside the town the solid gazing house and shadowed walls have not gone. Steel hooves ring brilliant in the lightening air. Coal roars as it slides down iron into the neighbors' cellars. The truckmen stand like Pharaohs behind their horses and yell at the chickens. From a block away the elevated train comes up like a thunderstorm. These and the bells and the fire-escapes are where they were last year and the year before. How is it that the strange dream light should have gone off the port, and left us in another New York City?

It seemed the liners did not come across the Atlantic on a single plane. Somewhere, in the course of their voyage from the European coasts, they left one plane and descended to another. True, they were stream-packets plying in a huge oceanic ferryboat business, moving in well-known lanes through fog with smell of boilers and pounding of machines. Nevertheless, a mysterious translation took place before they reached their American terminus. If indeed they did plow over the regular surface of the globe, they also came out of delicious unknown qualities of light, and out of wafts of air lighter and fierier than any aplay this side the water. In coming, they had descended as one descends from a heaven-near plateau under blue skylands into a dank and shadowy vale. Going to Europe, coming from Europe, might abolish the illusion; at a touch of the new world earth it was upon one again, not to be rationalized and not to be expelled. But a few hours before their entrance into Ambrose channel, the mighty voyagers now ringed about with smoky land and the sullen objects of the rawly furnished shores had experienced, it seemed, not alone the fishy white Atlantic, but the clear, free, ineffable space which does not know the port. Against steel plates and salt-soaked yellow, white, and pitch-black paint; about funnels and masts erect against the stars, there had lain the otherwhere than New York, the hidden side of the city moon; the unknown aspect of the flower of the moment. Rock lighter than sea-water, the visitor had swum in the space relieved of all the depressure of new world objects; the space that the gas-tuns, chimney pennons of coal-fume, smoky length of Staten Island hill would not let be seen, and stood upon like gravestones upon graves. About it with the sky and salt and ocean was the place that labors in man's behalf, and calls forth and lets bloom in beauty the stuff the new world sites repress and force back and will not let grow. Warming suns and long mild days had poured on it.

But here, in the workman bay, the mysterious waterworld it seemed was wrenched from the liners, wrenched as eelskins are drawn. A bad change had been worked. Upon the very sides which had known the free untrammelled space and moved through rich elastic stuff, another vulgarer world had imposed itself. Brightness was no longer about the ship. The city horizon was the one horizon. And when once more the cables were thrown off, the departed liners seemed marine expresses less than they had ever seemed. They were exiled princes gone to regain their thrones. They had shaken from them the situation of frustrating objects and mediocre unsatisfying forms quite as they had shaken from the tired choppy waters and rims of murky brown. Experienced once again was the spirit morning. The liners had left New York.

There was a sun overhead here in New York, blazing cruelly enough in the Yankee summer. But the sun which makes life fragrant and rich did not stand overhead. That sun shone far away across the Atlantic, upon the coasts of Europe. High up, one saw the European coast-line gleaming a fertile yellow and green, shining with a soft gold like Alp pinnacles saluted by the first liquor of daylight. But the sun which shone direct upon the eastern margent of the ocean struck the western slantingly and faint. New York lay in blue twilight as in a valley which the sun never comes to bake with heat. One lived, here in New York, upon ultimate edge of life, a kind of hyperborean edge midmost the temperate zone; the border of a perpetual shadow. For behind us, to the west, a continent lay submerged in chaotic pre-creation darkness. Movement, noise, rise and fall of perpetually displaced matter, all these seeming products of sun-power, were unsubstantial quite, dusty mirages of all the senses. For the very heat was not here. Or merely faintly enough to let us know what it was we wanted. Nothing moved indeed. Nothing came into relation.

The seed inside did not take root. It was a curious thing to know that one had been born here; to know that in precisely this dull red house on the avenue corner, with the precise number, say of 1186, one had undergone the experience which the Englishman underwent in his little island, or the Frenchman in his pleasant land of France, or the German in deep Germany. For, when the European was born, did he not begin the process of coming into relationship with the people and the things which stood about him? Did not something in him, the free-moving particle, cleave to the sites, the walls, the trees, the waters amid which he found himself, so that forever after the sight and memory of these objects had power to bring him nourishment comparable to the nourishment the tree draws from out its rock and loam? But here one did not come into blood relation. Oh, yes, here it was very formally inscribed in the records that on a certain day in a certain month of a certain year, a child had been born a certain citizen and his wife, with the sex male; which meant that one could, legally, become President; and, failing that, vote, sit on a jury, and have consular protection when traveling. But they only said one belonged to these things here, and they to one. In truth, a red spired village seen from railway windows over German cornfields; a prim Holland garden descending from a glass-enclosed verandah; the vision of an avenue with iron balconies in Paris; these foreign things were more life-giving, more feeding and familiar to one for all their strangeness, than the corner of New York rounded regularly each morning and evening. For in the city, things were very definitely outside you, apart from you; you were very definitely over here, they very definitely over there. You were alien to them, it seemed, and for your part you could not move closer to them, no more than to the people who moved amongst them; even to those of the people you were supposed to know the best of all and with whom you had spent years. It was as useless trying to feel yourself through the crowding towers of the lower town, and feel a whole, as it was trying to feel yourself through the forbidding people in the streets. The towers were not a whit less hard, less mutually exclusive, less eager to crowd each other out, than the people who had made them. They snatched the light from each other; rough-shouldered each other; were loud, anarchical, showy, ... unfriendly; flaunting money; calling for money. Edges stood, knife against knife. Nothing ever came with the warmth of heaven to do the work of the sun and melt the many antagonistic particles. The breast entire strained out toward the place of fruitful suns. With sad wonder, one was aware of the movements of liners. For these were things which through the power of motion threw off like an old coat the hyperborean state which held them awhile, and regained climates fertilized by spirit pours.

Nevertheless, one could not break with New York. If one floated aimlessly about inside its walls, within them one nevertheless remained. The suction which drew the psyche out of New York harbor was exerted upon one only in the city. The voyage to Europe once actually undertaken, the pumping force relaxed and dwindled down under the horizon. Two weeks of the green and gold of the Parisian boulevards; and a counter-magnet began exerting its attractive rays. The free, low-arching skies and Louvre flanks and chestnut avenues, what had their beauty really to do with us? This beauty was in its way as remote from us as the awful meaninglessness of the ways and granites of New York. It had its roots in a past which was not ours, and which we might never adopt. To feel it was to squander the best stuff of the bosom not on the true wife, but on the indifferent courtesan. It was beauty in America one wanted, not in France or Switzerland. It was the towers of Manhattan one wanted to see suddenly garlanded with loveliness. One wanted life for them and for oneself together. Somewhere in one always there had been the will to take root in New York; to come into relation with the things and the people, not in the insane self-abnegation of current patriotism and nationalism, but in the form of one's utmost self; in the form of realizing all the possibilities for life shut inside one, and simultaneously finding one-self one with the people. Somewhere within, perhaps in obedience to some outer voice trusted in childhood, there was a voice which promised one day the consummation. One day a miracle should happen over the magnificent harbor, and set life thrilling and rhythming through the place of New York. How it was to happen, one did not know. And sometimes, one supposed that where the immigrant ships had come in, a supernatural and winged visitor would have to appear, fall into the port as a meteorite might fall from the sky, before the new state which had not been reached when the immigrant feet had touched earth at Castle Garden would declare itself. But it was to happen, that one knew; and within, slumbrous power patiently awaited the divine event. And in Europe, one heard, distinct again, the promise. One knew the secret allegiance to the unfriendly new world; and it if did not take the form of a red, white, and blue rosette in the buttonhole, nevertheless something like a precious promissory letter was carried underneath the heart through all the monuments and treasure houses.

So one went back over the sea, eyes peeled for the moment when the arms of the port would open up and receive one, and the sense of home be written large over every crevice and electric sign. But the welcome proved cold, and the day after landing the buildings recommenced their languid snubbing. The restlessness came back. The water world beyond Sandy hook began to draw again. There was scarcely a place, two or three at the very utmost, which did anything for you, and urged you out into life and adventure and experiment. The city would not give and stood defiant. There were moments: the river at sundown, West Street with its purple blotches on walls, one pile against another. But one became sore so easily. One could accomplish only a little at a time; one became sore and shrank away, and found it impossible to press further. It was impossible as ever to sit before a table and work for long. One gave a little; here was a little trickle of beauty, a moment of absorption. Then something gave out, and one wanted to run off, to hide, to forget, to go out of doors, anything rather than sit before the table and press further. And, in dreams; in the dreams of many, in the dreams of a whole city and country perhaps, steamers departed for Europe, steamers silently discharged from New York harbor, great iron liners headed and predestined for the opposite coasts of the North Atlantic.

It may be that it was yesteryear they still went forth. It was not long ago. And yet, this year, it is certain they have ceased to move. The line has passed away. If any dream-voyagers stir in dreams, their bows are presented to us. The steamers, small, dogged, shoulderful, come headed America-ward. Merely a fistful of months may separate us from the time they still moved out; and sometimes it seems the time cannot indeed be gone. But it is gone. The enormous spaces that divide world from world separate us from it. The impossible thing has indeed come to pass on us. What seemed a miracle alone could accomplish has taken place. There is no one not aware something has happened in New York. What, it is possible, may not be clearly seen. But that an event has taken place is universally sure. No supernatural and winged flyer has descended into the bay. No enchanter has touched the buildings and made them change their forms. The town still stands the same; no littoral has rearranged itself about the bay. Morning upon morning mouse-colored new-come shapes are stretched off Quarantine; and in the North River tug-boats drag the departers into midstream. Nevertheless, we could go from the world to-day and still feel that life had been wonderfully good.

The steamers no longer descend from one plane onto another when they come into New York harbor. The port is not the inferior situation, depressive to every spiritual excellence and every impulse to life, which once it was. Glamour lies upon it still; but not the painful dreamlight of yesteryear. A kind of strong, hearty daylight has come upon the port. Once, thought of it filled us with nostalgia and wander-dreams. To-day, it brings a wash of strength and power over us. Sudden, at the foot of a street, the vague wandering eye perceives with a joyous shock a loading steamer carrying high its mast as a child carries a cross in an all-saints procession. The port-nights loom blue and enormous over the leagues of massy masonries. Out of the purpling evening above office piles there comes a breeze, and in that breath there are, like two delicious positive words in an evasive letter, the fishy hoarse Atlantic. The tall street lamps in brown-stone gulches on winter nights press back a soft fog that has in it the gray rims and biting wind and tramps of all nations steering. Or, some afternoon, from a bridge train, the salt tide unrolls before our eyes; the sun casts a little orange onto the tide off Battery, and illuminates Bayonne beyond with the cadences of daylight; and the clay giants of the lower city fuse into a bluish mass. Then it is almost beauty that comes to dress the slipshod harbor of New York.

For what we once could feel only by quitting New York: the fundamental oneness we have with the place and the people in it, that is sensible to us to-day in the very jostling, abstracted streets of the city. We know it here, our relationship with this place in which we live. The buildings cannot deprive us of it. For they and we have suddenly commenced—between the objects, and between the objects and ourselves. The form is still very vague. One is still alone; among people who are alone, scattered like seed or pebbles thrown. And perhaps the form is still most like the faint scum-like build first taken by the embryo in the womb. It seems a misty architectural shape taking up into itself like individual building stones the skyscraper, tenements, thoroughfares, and people; and with the mass of them erecting a tower higher than any of them, even the highest, toward the sky. But if it is faint, still, it is none the less evident. Day after day in gray and desperate weather even, one can see its mystic aspiration above the skyscrapers of New York. Over our melancholy it rises high. It seems that we have taken root. The place has gotten a gravity that holds us. The suction outward has abated. No longer do we yearn to quit New York. We are not drawn away. We are content to remain in New York. In the very middle of the city, we can feel the fluid of life to be present. We know the space beyond Staten Island hill is no more filled with the elixir than the air about the buildings. Other places may have it no whit less than New York; but New York has it no whit less than they; the stuff of the breast can make its way into the world here too. Something outside works with it. The city is a center like every other point upon the circumference of the globe. The circle of the globe commences here, too. The port of New York lies on a single plane with all the world to-day. A single plane unites it with every other port and seacoast and point of the whole world. Out of the American hinterland, out of the depths of the inarticulate American unconsciousness, a spring has come, a push and a resilience; and here where Europe meets America we have come to sit at the focal point where two upspringing forces balance. The sun is rising overhead, the sun which once shone brightly on Europe alone and threw slanting rays merely upon New York. The sun has moved across the Atlantic. The far coasts of Europe still shine with his light. But they shine mildly, softly, like eastern coasts in late summer afternoon when the sun commences to slope toward the western sea. And behind us, over the American hinterland, morning rays slant where deep, impenetrable murkiness lay, and begin to unveil the face of a continent. But over New York the dayspring commences to flood his fruity warmth.

It is that the values have come to stand among us. It is they that out-top the heaven-storming piles, and make the sun to float aloft and the steam to shoot like flags. It was their absence that made the buildings stand like tombstones, and life to lie inert. We never knew them here. They may have stood before, in earlier American days. But in our time they were gone. What bore their name and aped their style were the conventions of middle-class trading society giving themselves out for the worth of civilization. We had the smug safe bourgeois values of the "humanists," the pontifical allies of the anarchistic business men. But the principles which lift men out of themselves and lead them to human growth and human beauty were gone from the scene; and unrelation of all things and all people filled the land with black. For values and religion and relation rise together. So it stood until the second decade of the new century when the new orientation began. What gave it to a dozen or more of artists to find the values again here on the soil, to restate ideas of work and growth and love, and run the flag of mature developed life once more to the masthead, we do not know. It may be that conditions were favorable to the new erection. Life has perhaps commenced to stabilize itself on the new continent, and men begun to cease excluding one another. Perhaps the new world of new expression of life which should have been reached when the feet first stepped from off the boats on American soil has faintly begun. Perhaps the tradition of life imported over the Atlantic has commenced expressing itself in terms of the new environment, giving the Port of New York a sense at last, and the entire land the sense of the Port of New York. It seems possible the European war helped the values to the masthead. We had been sponging on Europe for direction instead of developing our own, and Europe had been handing out nice little packages of spiritual direction to us. But then Europe fell into disorder and lost her way, and we were thrown back on ourselves to find inside ourselves sustaining faith. Yet, whether there was indeed a general movement anterior to the work of the worth-givers or whether the movement which we feel today merely flows from the songs they sang and the cries they uttered, we cannot know for sure. We saw it only after they had spoken. But what we do know, whatever the cause, is that we have to thank them for a wondrous gift. For, if to-day, the values stand aloft; if to-day the commencement of a religious sense is here; if to-day men on American land are commencing to come into relationship with one another and with the places in which they dwell, it is through the labor of some dozens of artist hands. Through words, lights, colors, the new world has been reached at last. We have to thank a few people—for the gift that is likest the gift of life.

99

The Subway

ALLEN TATE

Allen Tate (1899–1979) was a major poet and critic who was born in Kentucky. Very much a "Southerner", he graduated from Vanderbilt University (Tennessee) where, along with John Crowe Ransom, Donald Davidson, and Cleanth Brooks, he became a member of the *Fugitive Group* which, in 1930, published *I'll Take My Stand*—a polemic against Northern standards, especially in their industrial and urban influence on the American South. Tate wrote much significant criticism for example, *Reason in Madness*, (1941) and *The Forlorn Demon* (1953). "The Subway" is a distinctive response to the relatively recent phenomenon of travelling underground, and may be compared with Hart Crane's depiction of the subway in "The Tunnel" section of *The Bridge*. For Tate's poems see: *Mr. Pope and Other Poems* (1928), and see also *Collected Essays* (1959), *Poems* (1960), and J. C. Stewart, *The Burden of Time* (1965).

The Subway

Dark accurate plunger down the successive knell
Of arch on arch, where ogives burst a red
Reverberance of hail upon the dead
Thunder like an exploding crucible!
Harshly articulate, musical steel shell
Of angry worship, hurled religiously
Upon your business of humility
Into the iron forestries of hell:

Till broken in the shift of quieter
Dense altitudes tangential of your steel,
I am become geometries, and glut
Expansions like a blind astronomer
Dazed, while the worldless heavens bulge and reel
In the cold revery of an idiot.

Source: Allen Tate, "The Subway" 1927.

100

A Savage Isle

WALDO FRANK

For an introductory note to Waldo Frank, see Volume II, Chapter 76.

a.

I've been away from home for almost a year. In France, in Germany, in Lithuania and Poland, in Egypt and Palestine and Tunis, I've talked with eager men about my own fabulous country. Everywhere people knew about America. They told me all about it. I learned a lot.

I'm a peaceful fellow, not given to argument. And I'm impressionable, delighted to agree with what is told me. This I find particularly easy when what I hear is pleasant; when I am taken, for instance, in my capacity of American, for a citizen of Eldorado or of Ophir. So gradually, as the months of my absence grew, I found myself accepting what I heard, in Europe, Africa and Asia, about my native land.

By the time I took ship from Boulogne, this—more or less—is the portrait of America which the industrialist of Essen, the rabbi of Posen, the Vilna medical professor, the Tunisian judge, the merchant of Damascus, the Parisian dentist, the nationalist of Egypt, had impressed upon me:

America ... meaning above all New York ... is the most modern, the most civilized, the most genteel, the most efficient, the most expeditious, the most comfortable spot on earth. In America, there are no low or humble classes. In America, everywhere, the families dwell on the twentieth floors of palaces equipped with electric ice and radiant heat; and when they descend to the street it is to roll away in private autos. In America, everybody has a hand in the state; everybody has a heart for public welfare; everybody reads; everybody considers everybody's right to peace and comfort. In America, the rich lavish their money upon scientific progress for its own sake; and of course, in America, everyone is rich.

... In America, the women are beautiful, free and pure. They are comrades to men. The American man is as pure as his mother. Vice is not tolerated, drink is unknown.

Source: Waldo Frank, "A Savage Isle" [1928], *In the American Jungle*, New York, 1937.

... It is true that this American folk is overconcerned with material well-being. But at least it has uplifted material well-being to the rank of an art. The American people have perhaps too great a care for money. But, at least, they spend it with splendor, and get for what they spend their heart's desire. For here are gleaming cities, marvelously fed with sun and air; here are farmlands ribboned with smooth roads and labored by miraculous machines.

... In America, to sum up, are men and women elegant, cheerful, leisured, powerful, serene. The rest of the backward world is jealous of America, of course. The world, in places, quite sincerely thinks that there are spiritual values which shining America may have missed. But America is the apogee of material refinement. Beside American towns, Paris must seem an unkempt village, Warsaw a dumpheap....

b.

Finally my boat put into the great American harbor. I came up on deck, my eyes shiningly ready to enjoy the America of the talkers of Europe, Africa and Asia.

I saw no scintillant city rising like an army of arrows toward the Sun, its father. What I saw was a conglomerate of buildings, formless with haphazard shapes, a phalanx of skyscrapers as formidable from the distance as an old comb lacking half its teeth. A sprawling and grimy town above the noble Hudson. And the famous buildings, if they were at all the symbol of power, made me think of a baby giant, in weak control of his muscles, who had heaped this tilting mess of blocks upon the floor of his playroom.

The river-front streets had a brash rottenness that hurt, after the mellow rottenness of Fez. The houses were cheap and dirty. They revealed no imagination: a dull obsession seemed the architect of these innumerable banks of brick. A folk had dumped these houses where they stood, with its mind elsewhere or totally absent, with its heart cold or altogether lacking. As the taxi shunted me along, going slower than a rickshaw in Pekin (a taxi dirtier than any in Madrid, and driven by a man who needed but a soiled burnoose and a turban to brother him with the sword-eater in the Tangier Sacco), I thought of the improvised squalor in certain modern sections of Egyptian towns and of the far sweeter and swifter rhythm of the Saharan camel. And as the traffic crawled under the marshaling terror of the cop, I remembered the ease and speed with which one flies through the intricate network of Paris. Fifth Avenue has a splendor; Park Avenue (when at last I reached it) flaunted the elegance of a Brobdingnagian refrigerator, electrically cooled. But I'd gone through an hour of back yard and alley to get there. ...

I went uptown. I discovered empty lots throughout the heart of the city, and unpaved stretches of street where my car bumped precisely as I had been bumped on the winter-logged roads of Poland. Indeed, more and more, this iridescent city of men's dreams—in its disorder, in its dirt, in its noise, in its lack of form and style—brought to my mind the towns I had seen in Eastern Europe: towns where for ten unceasing years armies, rebellions, insurrections, pogroms, have spewed their havoc.

I dismounted at last from my taxi, and began to look into the faces of this most pampered, ultracivilized and genteel people. Since they are having a good time, enjoying the "top of the world," why are they so gloomy about it? Since they are at ease in their Zion of physical comfort, why are they so uncomfortable, so nervous, so harassed? Since they have been polished off by all the polishing machines of the Modernist Machine Age, why do their brutal faces make me quake? I am no dauntless Galahad. But I have roamed the water front of Antwerp, searched the night kasbah of Algiers, tramped the lightless wastes of London's Wapping, tempted the traps of Cádiz and of Jaffa. I have never seen faces more sullen, more dehumanized, than these of New Yorkers. I forgot all about my conversations with the informed gentlemen of Europe, Africa and Asia. I recalled certain statistics and knew that I was in a town where thieving is a soft profession and where holdups and assassinations hugely outnumber the totals in populous European countries.

Also, I was forced to remember that alcohol intoxicates. In my first ten hours I saw more drunkenness in my native village than I had observed in as many months in Spain.

c.

At last I was safely in bed in a room the price of which for the night was a little over the cost of a week's rental of a furnished farm in France. There came to my blasted ears, beneath the zephyrous purr of a million motors emitting carbon gas and of a thousand radios drenching the air with the still more noxious fumes of ballyhoo, fragments of flattering talks about my native land in Paris, Berlin, Warsaw, Jerusalem and Cairo.

"Comfort" ... I heard: "speed ... efficiency" ... "mechanical perfection" ... "civilization too easy, too happy, too refined." ... On the fields of France they had once built great Gothic myths; and Egypt has her Sphinx; and Palestine wove the legends of Jehovah. Now, the sons of these mythmakers croon fables of an America where houses sing with gladness, and men move noiselessly and swift from pleasure to pleasure.

Please do not mistake me. I have no grouch; I am not pessimistic. I live in the land of my birth through choice; I deem myself fortunate in being a New Yorker. But the notion that our country is at an apex of perfection is the most inept falsehood. We are barbarians in a savage jungle, we are at the sultriest beginning.

That, precisely, is the fun of living here. Everything, however primitive and basic, still must be accomplished: the present generation of Americans are more profoundly pioneers than Daniel Boone, more original adventurers than Columbus. The myth consists of supposing that we are, to date, more than a lot of babies rising from the womb of Europe.

Of course, the European and African and Asiatic supporters of this myth have been helped by ourselves. They have got their "information" and their "facts" from the News. That modern Wonder, compact of cable, print, radio, and motion picture—has it not "linked the whole world close together," making each man know all about his brothers? And could I expect the American myth to fail to carry in Morocco, when it succeeds right here?

Grab your paper and plunge into the subway. The steel corridors have an infernal beauty and the subway stinks. The noise deafens you and you are jammed for forty minutes between strap-hanging troglodytes all reading the same paper. That paper shrieks an incessant alternation of Lust and Death, fulfilling the portrait of a savage jungle. No matter. On the editorial page you will be sweetly informed that your land is the Pinnacle of Progress, your town the culmination of man's seeking ages. And you, too, will be convinced of the American—the modern—myth.

d.

I know a way out, if you want one. Let the conduits of "information" and "news" be placed in the hands of philosophers and men of science. For instance, give the dailies to the metaphysicians; the weeklies to the psychologists, the radio and movies to experts in social science. And let it be stipulated that no edition and no story be released, until the *entire Board agree upon the truth.* This would at once diminish the output of press, radio and cinema to precisely what that output was in the year 1200 B.C., and thereby enhance our accurate knowledge of the world—and of America—to what that knowledge was in those more illumined days.

1928

101

Mayakovsky

MICHAEL GOLD, SHAKHNO EPSTEIN and VLADIMIR MAYAKOVSKY

Vladimir Vladimirovich Mayakowski (1893–1930) was one of the leading Russian poets of the revolutionary period. Influenced by the European Futurists, his work reflected an underlying concern with the radical and the new, as expressed in *A Cloud in Trousers* (1914–15), and *Ode to the Revolution* (1918). A supporter of the Revolution, Mayakovsky undertook a tour of Europe and America in 1925 and stayed in the United States for three months. His mixed response to Brooklyn Bridge needs to be compared with Hart Crane's *The Bridge*. Like Crane, Mayakowsky committed suicide in 1930. The "interview" which follows is of interest in the way it depicts a Russian revolutionary confronted by the exemplary image of American capitalism.

Interview with Michael Gold, *New York World*, Aug. 9, 1925:

Russia's Dynamic Poet Finds New York Tame; We're Old-Fashioned, Unorganized, to Mayakovsky; "Manhattan is an Accident Stumbled On By Children," He Declares

Mayakovsky is in New York; Vladimir Mayakovsky! Boom, bang, boom!

Tear the subway out of the ground. Wrap it around the neck of the Woolworth Tower, and let it wave like a modern scarf in the wind.

Sharpshoot the meaningless sun out of the sky and turn it to modern uses. Paint it with futurist advertisements for culture and release it back into the vacant heavens.

Source: "Interview with Michael Gold, *New York World*", Aug. 9, 1925 from Vladimir Mayakovsky, "My Discovery of America"; and Shakhno Epstein, "With Vladimir Mayakovsky through Fifth Avenue", (in the New York Yiddish communist newspaper *Freiheit*, 14 August, 1925) in Wiktor Woroszylski, *The Life of Mayakovsky*, New York, 1970, pp. 368–75.

Church bells for cymbals, huge cannons for drums, and a thousand wild brass cornets and trombones and tubas to serenade Mayakovsky!

Let the elevated roar twice as loud as ever, the street cars clang, the taxis rattle and squeal and honk, the riveters spatter and punch, the city is too quiet for Mayakovsky! Get up a parade to impress him; with floats holding derricks, steam-shovels, garment factory dynamos, and sewing machines and a procession of giant proletarians juggling skyscrapers and steel foundries coming last in triumph ...

The Industrial Age, this is what Mayakovsky arrived in New York a few days ago to see, Mayakovsky, who for the past ten years has been the best-known poet in Soviet Russia, the voice of its new storm and chaos and construction, the laureate of its new machinery, the apostle of industrialism to a nation still half Asiatic and medieval ...

"No, New York, is not modern," he said, in his room near Washington Square, as he restlessly paced the floor. "New York is unorganized. Mere machinery, subways, skyscrapers and the like to not make a real industrial civilization. These are only the externals.

"America has gone through a tremendous material development which has changed the face of the world. But the people have not yet caught up to their new world ... Intellectually, New Yorkers are still provincials. Their minds have not accepted the full implications of the industrial age.

"That is why I say New York is unorganized—it is a gigantic accident stumbled upon by children, not the full-grown, mature product of men who understood what they wanted and planned it like artists. When our industrial age comes in Russia it will be different—it will be planned—it will be conscious ...

"Or take these self-same skyscrapers of yours. They are glorious achievements of the modern engineer. The past knew nothing like them. The plodding hand-workers of the Renaissance never dreamed of these great structures that sway in the wind and defy the laws of gravity. Fifty stories upward they march into the sky; and they should be clean, swift, complete, and modern as a dynamo. But the American builder, only half aware of the miracle he has produced, scatters obsolete and silly Gothic and Byzantine ornaments over the skyscrapers. It is like tying pink ribbons on a steam dredge, or like putting Kewpie figures on a locomotive ...

I interrupted the torrent of futurist energy and asked him a question which he did not like: "These liberal intellectual mystics you mentioned run away, in America, from the machine. They think it is destroying the soul of man. Don't you Russians have the same fear of becoming too mechanical?"

"No," said the poet positively. "We are the masters of the machine and therefore do not fear it. The old mystic, emotional life is dying, yet, but a new one will take its place. Why should one fear history? Or fear that men will become machines? It is impossible."

... he was raging up and down, puffing cigarettes like a smokestack. But he wanted to say these things to the Russians, on paper, in a futurist poem. And so the interview closed abruptly and he was left to himself, to stand by the window and contemplate lower Fifth Avenue.

The modern Russians have a great respect for this young giant ... Not an insignificant achievement for a young man of thirty, living in a nation of 150 million. And now the young man is living near Washington Square and at night he goes to Negro cabarets in Harlem or shoots pool on Fourteenth Street. Occasionally he talks to a friend and complains about the peculiar provincialism and smalltownishness of New York.

"My Discovery of America" by Vladimir Mayakovsky

I like New York in the fall, on ordinary working days.

Six in the morning. Stormy and rainy. It is dark and will be dark till noon.

A man gets dressed by electric light, in the streets electric lights, houses with electric lights, evenly cut by windows like the pattern of a publicity poster. Houses, spread endlessly, traffic lights flash with colored signals, movements double, triple, multiply on the asphalt, on the rain-licked mirror. In the narrow groves of buildings some adventurous wind roars, tears, rattles the signboards, tries to sweep people off their feet and escapes unpunished, unarrested by anyone, down the many miles of dozens of avenues cutting through Manhattan Island—from the ocean to the Hudson. On both sides the storm is accompanied by the countless little voices of narrow streets, also even, to measure, cutting across Manhattan, water to water. Under cover—or on fine days just on the pavement—big bunches of newspapers are lying, brought earlier by trucks and thrown down here by newsboys ...

Down below, a mass of human flesh is flowing: first the black mass of Negroes, who do the hardest and least pleasant work. Then—at about seven—a sea of whites. They go in one direction, hundreds of thousands of them, to their places of work. Only the yellow impregnated raincoats are shining in the electric light, wet through but unextinguished even under that rain.

There are almost no cars or taxis yet.

The crowd flows, filling the entrance holes to the subway and the covered passages of the elevated railway, going up in the air on two levels and three parallel tracks in fast trains, seldom stopping, and local trains stopping every five blocks ...

I like New York best in the mornings and in the storm: there are no gaping passers-by, not one superfluous person, only members of the huge working army of a city of 10 million inhabitants.

Masses of workers disappear into clothing factories, into the new, not yet completed subway tunnels, go to the innumerable occupations in the port. At eight the streets are filled with slender, cleaner, and more cultivated young ladies, most of them with short hair, bare knees, rolled stockings—they work in banks, offices, and shops. This crowd will disperse throughout the many stories of the downtown skyscrapers, on both sides of the corridors reached by the main entrance with dozens of elevators ...

If you need an office, you do not have to think about how you are going to arrange for one.

You just telephone someone on the thirtieth floor: "Hallo! Get a six-room office ready for tomorrow. Twelve typists. Signpost: 'The Great and Reputable Business for the Provision of Provision of Pressed Air for Pacific Submarines.' Two office boys in brown livery—caps with star ribbons and 12,000 letterheads, headlined as above. Goodbye."

On the next day you can just go to your office and will be greeted by your enthralled messengers: "How do you do, Mr. Mayakovsky."

At one—a break: an hour for the office staff and fifteen minutes for the workers.

Lunch.

Everyone consumes lunch according to the weekly pay he gets. The fifteen-dollar earners buy a packed lunch for a nickel and munch it with youthful diligence.

The thirty-five dollar earners go to a large automat, deposit 5 cents, press a button, and an exact measure of coffee pours into a cup; two or three more coins open a glass compartment with sandwiches on large, food-filled shelves.

The sixty-dollar earners eat pancakes with syrup and scrambled eggs in bathroom-white Childs' Rockefeller restaurants.

Those who earn more than a hundred dollars go to restaurants of all nationalities—Chinese, Russian, Assyrian, French, Indian—all but American, because those serve bad food and guarantee indigestion caused by Armour's canned meat, which almost reminds one of the War of Independence ...

You would try in vain in New York to find grotesque organizational methods, speed, cold bloodedness—all those qualities made famous through literature.

You will find many people walking about without any particular purpose. Everyone will stop and talk to you on any subject. If you raise your eyes and stop for a while, you will soon be surrounded by a crowd, controlled with difficulty by a policeman. I am, for the most part, reconciled to the New York crowd thanks to their ability to find other entertainment besides the stock exchange.

Work again till five, six, seven in the evening.

The hours from five to seven are the noisiest and most crowded.

Those who are on their way home from work are joined by shoppers and people just talking a walk.

On the very crowded Fifth Avenue, which divides the city in two, from the heights of the upper decks of hundreds of buses, you will see, washed down by a recent rain and now shining, tens of thousands of cars, rushing in both directions in rows of six to eight ...

At six or seven, Broadway lights are up. This is my favorite street, which, among streets and avenues that are as straight as prison bars, is the only one that cuts, capriciously and insolently, across the others. To lose one's way in New York is more difficult than in Tula. Avenues run from south to north; streets, from east to west. That is all. I am at the corner of Eighth Street and Fifth Avenue, and I am looking for the corner of Fifty-third Street and Second Avenue; that means I have to walk uptown, pass forty-five side streets, and turn right to the corner of Second Avenue.

Lights do not go on all along the entire, twenty-five-mile-long Broadway (here a man is not going to say, "Please drop in; we're neighbors; we both live on Broadway") but only from Twenty-fifth to Fiftieth Street, particularly at Times Square—this is, as the Americans say, the Great White Way.

It really is white and one really has the impression that it is brighter there at night than in the daytime, because there is light everywhere in the daytime, but this White Way, against the background of the black night, is bright as day. The lights of street lamps, the jumping lights of advertisements, the glow of shop windows and windows of the never-closing shops, the lights illuminating huge posters, lights from the opening doors of cinemas and theaters, the rushing lights of automobiles and trolley cars, the lights of the subway trains glittering under one's feet through the glass pavements, the lights of inscriptions in the sky.

Brightness, brightness, brightness.

One can read a newspaper, the newspaper of the person next to one and in foreign language.

There is light in the restaurants and in the theater district.

The main streets, where owners and those who are grooming themselves for the part live, are clean.

But in the poor Jewish, Negro, Italian quarters—where most of the workers and office staff live—on Second and Third Avenues, between First and Thirtieth Streets, it is dirtier than in Minsk. And it is very dirty in Minsk.

Garbage cans stand there with all kinds of refuse, from which beggars pick out bones and other scraps. Stinking pools of yesterday's and the day before yesterday's rain, are still around.

One walks ankle-deep in all kinds of rubbish, not metaphorically but literally ankle-deep.

All this at a distance of only fifteen minutes' walk, or five minutes by car, from the dazzling Fifth Avenue and Broadway.

The closer to the port, the darker, dirtier, and more dangerous it is.

In the daytime it is a most interesting quarter. There is a constant roar here—work, shots, shouts. The ground is shaken by cranes which unload ships, and are almost capable of lifting up a whole house at once.

When there is a strike, picket lines are set up and no strikebreakers are allowed to pass through.

The avenues next to the port, are called the "Avenues of Death," because of the freight trains, which drive right onto the street, and because of the little bars full of gangsters.

They provide bandits for the whole of New York ...

A bandit who gets caught risks the electric chair in Sing Sing. But he can get out of it, too. When setting out on a robbery, he goes to his solicitor and declares, "Give me a ring, sir, at such and such a time, such and such a number. If I am not there, it means you have to stand bail for me and get me out of the jug."

Bail is always large, but bandits are not poor and they are well organized ...

Newspapers have written about a certain bandit who left the prison forty-two times on bail. The Irish are active here on the Avenue of Death; in other quarters there are other nationalities.

Negroes, Chinese, Germans, Jews, Russians—all have their own quarters, with their own customs and languages, keeping their identity intact through the decades.

In New York, not counting the suburbs, there are approximately:

1,700,000 Jews
1,000,000 Italians
500,000 Germans
300,000 Irishmen
300,000 Russians
250,000 Negroes
150,000 Poles
300,000 Spaniards, Chinese, Finns

A puzzling picture: who are the Americans, and who among them is 100 percent American? ...

At midnight those who come out of the theaters drink one last soda, eat one last ice-cream cone, and are at home by one or by three, if they have spent about two hours rubbing against each other in a foxtrot, or in the latest fashion—the Charleston. But life does not end even then. Shops of all kinds are open as usual, elevated and subway trains run as usual, one can find an all-might movie house and sleep there to one's heart's content for the 25 cents he has paid for admission.

Having come home, if this is spring or summer, shut the windows to keep out the mosquitoes; wash your ears and nose and cough out the coal dust ... If you have scratched yourself, put iodine on it: the New York air is full of all kinds of bacteria, from which you can get sties (all scratches are apt to swell), and which millions who have nothing and cannot get away anywhere, have to breathe ...

"With Vladimir Mayakovsky through Fifth Avenue" by Shakhno Epstein

"Well, Vladimir Vladimirovich, how do you like America?"

Mayakovsky throws away the stub of a Russian cigarette, lights another cigarette, and begins to walk across the big furnished room on Fifth Avenue. His tall, strong figure, with energetic suntanned face and strong muscles is as deft as if he had been marching ... It is very difficult to recognize the Russian in him. He looks more like a Mexican cowboy. He stops, glances through the window at Fifth Avenue and says in his deep, thundering voice, which fills the entire room with its reverberation, "Eh, it's boring here ..."

We walked down into the street ... Around us a merry-go-round of cars, a deafening noise of advertisers ... The poet says, "So we are supposed to be a 'backward,' 'barbarian' nation. We are only just starting. Every new tractor is an event for us. Every new threshing machine, a very important thing. And if a new power plant is opened, this is something sensational. We still come here for these things. But, in spite of everything, it is dull here, while in our parts it is gay. Here everything smells of decay, is dying, rotting, while our life is boiling over, the future is ours ...

"We are walking now through one of the richest streets in the world—skyscrapers, palaces, hotels, shops, and crowds. But I have a feeling I am walking among ruins, and I am depressed. Why am I not depressed in Moscow, where the pavements are really dilapidated and still not repaired, where there are many ruined houses, where streetcars are over-crowded and worn out past repair? The answer is simple: because there is life there, thriving, seething; the energy of an entire nation-collective has been liberated and is overflowing.

"Let us take our films and yours. Our technical equipment (lights etc.) is still very bad. You have all the latest technical inventions, a sea of lights. But with us, all the old trash is being swept away, everything reaches for the light. And here? You don't have those aspirations; you have only dirty little "moralizing," sentimental sniveling, as if one suddenly found oneself in the deepest provinces, in the Middle Ages. How can this kind of "moralizing" coexist with the highest technical achievement—I mean radio?"

We had been so engrossed in our conversation that we hardly noticed that we had arrived at Central Park. We sat down on a bench in a path leading to Fifth Avenue. It was dusk. A mad whirlpool of cars, buses, streetcars, ever-growing crowds of people, never beginning, never ending. All this rattles and roars, rings and crackles. Mayakovsky withdrew into himself. I could see what an effect the peculiar language of the street had on him. It was as if he were taking in all those sounds. He took out a black, leather notebook and began to write something in it, very fast, as if to the rhythm of the din surrounding us. His figure gradually attracted general attention. Some people began to gape at him with a surprised look. But he did not notice anyone, not even me sitting next to him.

Suddenly Mayakovsky got up and said, "Let's go."

When we were back in his room, Mayakovsky said, "I have caught the tempo of New York, the dull, suppressed tempo. It will be a new poem: "Mayakovsky on Fifth Avenue" ...

101
New York

O'HENRY

O'Henry (or Oliver Henry) was the pseudonym of William Sydney Porter (1862–1910). Born in North Carolina, he became one of the major short story writers of the late nineteenth century. He had an uneven private life. He founded *The Rolling Stone* (1894), but also spent a period of time in prison. His major literary achievement was the way his short stories reflected a very particular ambience of New York City at a very particular moment in its history. Although limited in their effect, (their predictable conclusions became known as "the O'Henry ending"), they remain one of the most significant reflections of New York life—to be placed alongside the works of Stephen Crane and the painting of the Ash-Can School. *The Collected Works* (1953) confirmed New York as the "Bag-dad-on-the-subway". See G. Langford, *Alias O'Henry: A Biography of William Sydney Porter*, (1957).

The Making of a New Yorker

Besides many things, Raggles was a poet. He was called a tramp; but that was only an elliptical way of saying that he was a philosopher, an artist, a traveller, a naturalist, and a discoverer. But most of all he was a poet. In all his life he never wrote a line of verse; he lived his poetry. His Odyssey would have been a Limerick, had it been written. But, to linger with the primary proposition, Raggles was a poet.

Raggles's specialty, had he been driven to ink and paper, would have been sonnets to the cities. He studied cities as women study their reflections in mirrors; as children study the glue and sawdust of a dislocated doll; as the men who write about wild animals study the cages in the zoo. A city to Raggles was not merely a pile of bricks and mortar, peopled by a certain number of inhabitants; it was a thing with soul characteristic and distinct; an individual conglomeration of life, with its own peculiar essence, flavor, and feeling. Two thousand miles to the north

Source: O'Henry, "The Making of a New Yorker"; "A Little Local Color"; and "The Voice of the City", *The Complete Works of O'Henry*, New York, 1928.

and south, east and west, Raggles wandered in poetic fervor, taking the cities to his breast. He footed it on dusty roads, or sped magnificently in freight cars, counting time as of no account. And when he had found the heart of a city and listened to its secret confession, he strayed on, restless, to another. Fickle Raggles!—but perhaps he had not met the civic corporation that could engage and hold his critical fancy.

Through the ancient poets we have learned that the cities are feminine. So they were to poet Raggles; and his mind carried a concrete and clear conception of the figure that symbolized and typified each one that he had wooed.

Chicago seemed to swoop down upon him with a breezy suggestion of Mrs. Partington, plumes and patchouli, and to disturb his rest with a soaring and beautiful song of future promise. But Raggles would awake to a sense of shivering cold and a haunting impression of ideals lost in a depressing aura of potato salad and fish.

Thus Chicago affected him. Perhaps there is a vagueness and inaccuracy in the description; but that is Raggles's fault. He should have recorded his sensations in magazine poems.

Pittsburg impressed him as the play of *Othello* performed in the Russian language in a railroad station by Dockstader's minstrels. A royal and generous lady this Pittsburg, though—homely, hearty, with flushed face, washing the dishes in a silk dress and white kid slippers, and bidding Raggles sit before the roaring fireplace and drink champagne with his pigs' feet and fried potatoes.

New Orleans had simply gazed down upon him from a balcony. He could see her pensive, starry eyes and catch the flutter of her fan, and that was all. Only once he came face to face with her. It was at dawn, when she was flushing the red bricks of the banquette with a pail of water. She laughed and hummed a chansonette and filled Raggles's shoes with ice-cold water. Allons!

Boston construed herself to the poetic Raggles in an erratic and singular way. It seemed to him that he had drunk cold tea and that the city was a white, cold cloth that had been bound tightly around his brow to spur him to some unknown but tremendous mental effort. And, after all, he came to shovel snow for a livelihood; and the cloth, becoming wet, tightened its knots and could not be removed.

Indefinite and unintelligible ideas, you will say; but your disapprobation should be tempered with gratitude, for these are poets' fancies—and suppose you had come upon them in verse!

One day Raggles came and laid siege to the heart of the great city of Manhattan. She was the greatest of all; and he wanted to learn her note in the scale; to taste and appraise and classify and solve and label her and arrange her with the other cities that had given him up the secret of their individuality. And here we cease to be Raggles's translator and become his chronicler.

Raggles landed from a ferry-boat one morning and walked into the core of the town with the blasé air of a cosmopolite. He was dressed with care to play the role of an "unidentified man." No country, race, class, clique, union, party clan, or bowling association could have claimed him. His clothing, which had been donated to him piece-meal by citizens of different height, but same number of inches around the heart, was not yet as uncomfortable to his figure as those specimens of raiment, self-measured, that are railroaded to you by trans-continental tailors with a suit case, suspenders, silk handkerchief and pearl studs as a bonus. Without money—as a poet should be—but with the ardor of an astronomer discovering flow from his fountain pen, Raggles wandered into the great city.

Late in the afternoon he drew out of the roar and commotion with a look of dumb terror on his countenance. He was defeated, puzzled, discomfited, frightened. Other cities had been to him as long primer to read; as country maidens quickly to fathom; as send-price-of-subscription-with-answer rebuses to solve; as oyster cocktails to swallow; but here was one as cold, glittering, serene, impossible as a four-carat diamond in a window to a lover outside fingering damply in his pocket his ribbon-counter salary.

The greetings of the other cities he had known—their homespun kindliness, their human gamut of rough charity, friendly curses, garrulous curiosity, and easily estimated credulity or indifference. This city of Manhattan gave him no clue; it was walled against him. Like a river of adamant it flowed past him in the streets. Never an eye was turned upon him; no voice spoke to him. His heart yearned for the clap of Pittsburg's sooty hand on his shoulder; for Chicago's menacing but social yawp in his ear; for the pale and eleemosynary stare through the Bostonian eyeglass—even for the precipitate but unmalicious boot-toe of Louisville or St. Louis.

On Broadway Raggles, successful suitor of many cities, stood, bashful, like any country swain. For the first time he experienced the poignant humiliation of being ignored. And when he tried to reduce this brilliant, swiftly changing, ice-cold city to a formula he failed utterly. Poet though he was, it offered him no color similes, no points of comparison, no flaw in its polished facets, no handle by which he could hold it up and view its shape and structure, as he familiarly and often contemptuously had done with other towns. The houses were interminable ramparts loopholed for defense; the people were bright but bloodless spectres passing in sinister and selfish array.

The thing that weighted heaviest on Raggles's soul and clogged his poet's fancy was the spirit of absolute egotism that seemed to saturate the people as toys are saturated with paint. Each one that he considered appeared a monster of abominable and insolent conceit. Humanity was gone from them; they were toddling idols of stone and varnish, worshipping themselves and greedy for though oblivious of worship from their fellow graven images. Frozen, cruel, implacable, impervious, cut to a identical pattern, they hurried on their ways like statues brought by some miracle to motion, while soul and feeling lay unaroused in the reluctant marble.

Gradually Raggles became conscious of certain types. One was an elderly gentleman with a snow-white, short beard, pink, unwrinkled face, and stoney, sharp blue eyes, attired in the fashion of a gilded youth, who seemed to personify the city's wealth, ripeness and frigid unconcern. Another type was a woman, tall, beautiful, clear as a steel engraving, goddess-like, calm, clothed like the princesses of old, with eyes as coldly blue as the reflection of sunlight on a glacier. And another was a by-product of this town of marionettes—a broad, swaggering, grim, threateningly sedate fellow, with a jowl as large as a harvested wheat field, the complexion of a baptized infant, and the knuckles of a prize-fighter. This type leaned against cigar signs and viewed the world with frappéd contumely.

A poet is a sensitive creature, and Raggles soon shriveled in the bleak embrace of the indecipherable. The chill, sphinx-like, ironical, illegible, unnatural, ruthless expression of the city left him downcast and bewildered. Had it no heart? Better the woodpile, the scolding of vinegar-faced housewives at back doors, the kindly spleen of bartenders behind provincial free-lunch counters, the amiable truculence of rural constables, the kicks, arrests, and happy-go-lucky chances of the other vulgar, loud, crude cities than this freezing heartlessness.

Raggles summoned his courage and sought alms from the populace. Unheeding, regardless, they passed on without the wink of an eyelash to testify that they were conscious of his existence. And then he said to himself that this fair but pitiless city of Manhattan was without a soul; that its inhabitants were mannikins moved by wires and springs, and that he was alone in a great wilderness.

Raggles started to cross the street. There was a blast, a roar, a hissing and a crash as something struck him and hurled him over and over six yards from where he had been. As he was coming down like the stick of a rocket the earth and all the cities thereof turned to a fractured dream.

Raggles opened his eyes. First an odor made itself known to him—an odor of the earliest spring flowers of Paradise. And then a hand soft as a falling petal touched his brow. Bending over him was the woman clothed like the princess of old, with blue eyes, now soft and humid with human sympathy. Under his head on the pavement were silks and furs. With Raggles's hat in his hand and with his face pinker than ever from a vehement outburst of oratory against reckless driving, stood the elderly gentleman who personified the city's wealth and ripeness. From a near-by café hurried the by-product with the vast jowl and baby complexion, bearing a glass full of crimson fluid that suggested delightful possibilities.

"Drink dis, sport," said the by-product, holding the glass to Raggles's lips.

Hundreds of people huddled around in a moment, their faces wearing the deepest concern. Two flattering and gorgeous policemen got into the circle and pressed back the overplus of Samaritans. An old lady in a black shawl spoke loudly of camphor; a newsboy slipped one of his papers beneath Raggles's elbow, where it lay on the muddy pavement. A brisk young man with a note-book was asking for names.

A bell clanged importantly, and the ambulance cleaned a lane through the crowd. A cool surgeon slipped into the midst of affairs.

"How do you feel, old man?" asked the surgeon, stooping easily to his task. The princess of silks and satins wiped a red drop or two from Raggles's brow with a fragrant cobweb.

"Me?" said Raggles, with a seraphic smile, "I feel fine."

He had found the heart of his new city.

In three days they let him leave his cot for the convalescent ward in the hospital. He had been in there an hour when the attendants heard sounds of conflict. Upon investigation they found that Raggles had assaulted and damaged a brother convalescent—a glowering transient whom a freight train collision had sent in to be patched up.

"What's all this about?" inquired the head nurse.

"He was runnin' down me town," said Raggles.

"What town?" asked the nurse.

"Noo York," said Raggles.

A Little Local Color

I mentioned to Rivington that I was in search of characteristic New York scenes and incidents—something typical, I told him, without necessarily having to spell the first syllable with an "i".

"Oh, for your writing business," said Rivington; "you couldn't have applied to a better shop. What I don't know about little old New York wouldn't make a bonnet to a sunbonnet. It'll put you right in the middle of so much local color that you won't know whether you are a magazine cover or in the erysipelas ward. When do you want to begin?"

Rivington is a young-man-about-town and a new Yorker by birth, preference, and incommutability.

I told him that I would be glad to accept his escort and guardianship so that I might take notes of Manhattan's grand, gloomy, and peculiar idiosyncrasies, and that the time of so doing would be at his own convenience.

"We'll begin this very evening," said Rivington, himself interested, like a good fellow. "Dine with me at seven, and then I'll steer you up against metropolitan places so thick you'll have to have a kinetoscope to record 'em."

So I dined with Rivington pleasantly at his club, in Forty-eleventh Street, and then we set forth in pursuit of the elusive tincture of affairs.

As we came out of the club there stood two men on the sidewalk near the steps in earnest conversation.

"And by what process of ratiocination," said one of them, "do you arrive at the conclusion that the division of society into producing and non-possessing classes predicates failure when compared with competitive systems that are monopolizing in tendency and result inimically to industrial evolution?"

"Oh, come off your perch!" said the other man, who wore glasses. "Your premises won't come out in the wash. You wind-jammers who apply bandy-legged theories to concrete categorical syllogisms and logical conclusions skally-bootin' into the infinitesimal ragbag. You can't pull my leg with an old sophism with whiskers on it. You quote Marx and Hyndman and Kautsky—what are they?—shines! Tolstoi?—his garret is full of rats. I put it to you over the home-plate that the idea of a coöperative commonwealth and an abolishment of competitive systems simply takes the rag off the bush and gives me hyperesticula of the roopteetoop! The skookum house for yours!"

I stopped a few yards away and took out my little notebook.

"Oh, come ahead," said Rivington, somewhat nervously; "you don't want to listen to that."

"Why man," I whispered, "this is just what I do want to hear. These slang types are among your city's most distinguishing features. Is this the Bowery variety? I really must hear more of it."

"If I follow you," said the man who had spoken first, "you do not believe it possible to reorganize society on the basis of common interest?"

"Shinny on your own side!" said the man with glasses. "You never heard say such music from my foghorn. What I said was that I did not believe it practicable just now. The guys with wads are not in the frame of mind to slack upon the mazuma, and the man with the portable tin banqueting canister isn't exactly ready to join the Bible class. You can bet your variegated socks that the situation is all spiflicated up from the Battery to breakfast! What the country needs is for some bully old bloke like Cobden or some wise guy like old Ben Franklin to sashay up to the front and biff the nigger's head with the baseball. Do you catch my smoke? What?"

Rivington pulled me by the arm impatiently.

"Please come on," he said. "Let's go see something. This isn't what you want."

"Indeed, it is," I said resisting. "This tough talk is the very stuff that counts. There is a picturesqueness about the speech of the lower order of people that is quite unique. Did you say that this is the Bowery variety of slang!"

"Oh, well," said Rivington, giving it up, "I'll tell you straight. That's one of our college professors talking. He ran down for a day or two at the club. It's a sort of fad with him lately to use slang in his conversation. He thinks it improves language. The man he is talking to is one of New York's famous social economists. Now will you come on? You can't use that, you know."

"No," I agreed; "I can't use that. Would you call that typical of New York?"

"Of course not," said Rivington, with a sigh of relief. "I'm glad you see the difference. But if you want to hear the real old tough Bowery slang I'll take you down where you'll get your fill of it."

"I would like it," I said; "that is, if it's the real thing. I've often read it in books, but I never heard it. Do you think it will be dangerous to go unprotected among those characters?"

"Oh, no," said Rivington; "not at this time of night. To tell the truth, I haven't been along the Bowery in a long time, but I know it as well as I do Broadway. We'll look up some of the typical Bowery boys and get them to talk. It'll be worth your while. They talk a peculiar dialect that you won't hear anywhere else on earth."

Rivington and I went east in a Forty-second Street car and then south on the Third Avenue line.

At Houston Street we got off and walked.

"We are now on the famous Bowery," said Rivington; "the Bowery celebrated in song and story."

We passed block after block of "gents'" furnishing stores—the windows full of shirts with prices attached and cuffs inside. In other windows were neckties and no shirts. People walked up and down the sidewalks.

"In some ways," said I, "this reminds me of Kokomono, Ind., during the peach-crating season."

Rivington was nettled.

"Step into one of these saloons or vaudeville shows," said he, "with a large roll of money, and see how quickly the Bowery will sustain its reputation."

"You make impossible conditions," said I, coldly.

By and by Rivington stopped and said we were in the heart of the Bowery. There was a policeman on the corner whom Rivington knew.

"Hallo Donahue!" said my guide. "How goes it? My friend and I are down this way looking up a bit of local color. He's anxious to meet one of the Bowery types. Can't you put us on to something genuine in that line—something that's got the color, you know?"

Policeman Donahue turned himself about ponderously, his florid face full of good-nature. He pointed with his club down the street.

"Sure!" he said, huskily. "Here comes a lad now that was born on the Bowery and knows every inch of it. If he's ever been above Bleecker Street he's kept it to himself."

A man about twenty-eight or twenty-nine, with a smooth face, was sauntering toward us with his hands in his coat pockets. Policeman Donahue stopped him with a courteous wave of his club.

"Evening, Kerry," he said. "Here's a couple of gents, friends of mine, that want to hear you spiel something about the Bowery. Can you reel 'em off a few yards?"

"Certainly, Donahue," said the young man, pleasantly. "Good evening, gentlemen," he said to us, with a pleasant smile. Donahue walked off on his beat.

"This is the goods," whispered Rivington, nudging me with his elbow. "Look at his jaw!"

"Say, cull," said Rivington, pushing back his hat, "wot's doin'? Me and my friend's taking a look down de old line—see? De copper tipped us off dat you was wise to de Bowery. Is dat right?"

I could not help admiring Rivington's power of adapting himself to his surroundings.

"Donahue was right," said the young man, frankly; "I was brought up on the Bowery. I have been newsboy, teamster, pugilist, member of an organized band of 'toughs,' bartender, and a 'sport' in various meanings of the word. The experience certainly warrants the supposition that I have at least a passing acquaintance with a few phases of Bowery life. I will be pleased to place whatever knowledge and experience I have at the service of my friend Donahue's friends."

Rivington seemed ill at ease.

"I say," he said—somewhat entreatingly, "I thought—you're not stringing us, are you? It isn't just the kind of talk we expected. You haven't even said 'Hully gee!' once. Do you really belong on the Bowery?"

"I am afraid," said the Bowery boy, smilingly, "that at some time you have been enticed into one of the dives of literature and had the counterfeit coin of the Bowery passed upon you. The 'argot' to which you doubtless refer was the invention of certain of your literary 'discoverers' who invaded the unknown wilds below Third Avenue and put strange sounds into the mouths of the inhabitants. Safe in their homes far to the north and west, the credulous readers who were beguiled by this new 'dialect' perused and believed. Like Marco Polo and Mungo Park—pioneers indeed, but ambitious souls who could not draw the line of demarcation between discovery and invention—the literary bones of these explorers are dotting the trackless wastes of the subway. While it is true that after the publication of the mythical language attributed to the dwellers along the Bowery certain of its pat phrases and apt metaphors were adopted and, to a limited extent, used in this locality, it was because our people are prompt in assimilating whatever is to their commercial advantage. To the tourists who visited our newly discovered clime, and who expressed a realization of their literary guide books, they applied the demands of the market.

"But perhaps I am wandering from the question. In what way can I assist you, gentlemen? I beg you will believe that the hospitality of the streets is extended to all. There are, I regret to say, many catchpenny places of entertainment, but I cannot conceive that they would entice you."

I felt Rivington lean somewhat heavily against me.

"Say!" he remarked, with uncertain utterance; "come and have a drink with us."

"Thank you, but I never drink. I find that alcohol, even in the smallest quantities, alters the perspective. And I must preserve my perspective, for I am studying the Bowery. I have lived in it nearly thirty years, and I am just beginning to understand its heartbeats. It is like a great river fed by a hundred alien streams. Each influx brings strange seeds on its flood, strange silt and weeds, and now and then a flower of rare promise. To construe this river requires a man who can build dykes against the overflow, who is a naturalist, a geologist, a humanitarian, a diver, and a strong swimmer. I love my Bowery, it was my cradle and is my inspiration. I have published one book. The critics have been kind. I put my heart in it. I am writing another, into which I hope to put both heart and brain. Consider me your guide, gentleman. Is there anything I can take you to see, any place to which I can conduct you?"

I was afraid to look at Rivington except with one eye.

The Voice of the City

Twenty-five years ago the school children used to chant their lessons. The manner of their delivery was a singsong recitative between the utterance of an Episcopal minister and the drone of a tired sawmill. I mean no disrespect. We must have lumber and sawdust.

I remember one beautiful and instructive little lyric that emanated from the physiology class. The most striking line of it was this:

"The shin-bone is the long-est bone in the human bod-y."

What an inestimable boon it would have been if all the corporeal and spiritual facts pertaining to man had thus been tunefully and logically inculcated in your youthful minds! But what we gained in anatomy, music, and philosophy was meagre.

The other day I became confused. I needed a ray of light. I turned back to those school days for aid. But in all the nasal harmonies we whined forth from those hard benches I could not recall one that treated of the voice of agglomerated mankind.

In other words, of the composite vocal message of massed humanity.

In other words, of the Voice of a Big City.

Now, the individual voice is not lacking. We can understand the song of the poet, the ripple of the brook, the meaning of the man who wants $5 until next Monday, the inscriptions on the tombs of the Pharaohs, the language of flowers, the "step lively" of the conductor, and the prelude of the milk cans at 4 A.M. Certain large-eared ones even assert that they are wise to the vibrations of the tympanum produced by concussion of the air emanating from Mr. H. James. But who can comprehend the meaning of the voice of the city?

I went out for to see.

First, I asked Aurelia. She wore white Swiss and a hat with flowers on it, and ribbons and ends of things fluttered here and there.

"Tell me," I said, stammeringly, for I have no voice of my own, "what does this big—er—enormous—er—whopping city say? It must have a voice of some kind. Does it ever speak to you? How do you interpret its meaning? It is a tremendous mass, but it must have a key."

"Like a Saratoga trunk?" asked Aurelia.

"No," said I. "Please do not refer to the lid. I have a fancy that every city has a voice. Each one has something to say to the one who can hear it. What does the big one say to you?"

"All cities," said Aurelia, judicially, "say the same thing. When they get through saying it there is an echo from Philadelphia. So, they are unanimous."

"Here are 4,000,000 people," said I, scholastically, "compressed upon an island, which is mostly lamb surrounded by Wall Street water. The conjunction of so many units into so small a space must result in an identity—or, or rather a homogeneity—that finds its oral expression through a common channel. It is as you might say, a consensus of translation, concentrating in a crystallized, general idea which reveals itself in what may be termed the Voice of the City. Can you tell me what it is?"

Aurelia smiled wonderfully. She sat on the high stoop. A spray of insolent ivy bobbed against her right ear. A ray of impudent moonlight flickered upon her nose. But I was adamant, nickel-plated.

"I must go and find out," I said, "what is the Voice of this City. Other cities have voices. It is an assignment. I must have it. New York," I continued, in a rising tone, "had better not hand me a cigar and say: 'Old man, I can't talk for publication.' No other city acts in that way. Chicago says, unhesitatingly, 'I will'; Philadelphia says, 'I should'; New Orleans says, 'I used to'; Louisville says, 'Don't care if I do'; St. Louis says, 'Excuse me'; Pittsburg says, 'Smoke up.' Now, New York—"

Aurelia smiled.

"Very well," said I, "I must go elsewhere and find out."

I went into a palace, tile-floored, cherub-ceilinged, and square with the cop. I put my foot on the brass rail and said to Billy Magnus, the best bartender in the diocese:

"Billy, you've lived in New York a long time—what kind of a song-and-dance does this old town give you? What I mean is, doesn't the gab of it seem to kind of bunch up and slide over the bar to you in a sort of a amalgamated tip that hits off the burg in a kind of an epigram with a dash of bitters and a slice of —"

"Excuse me a minute," said Billy, "somebody's punching the button at the side door."

He went away; came back with an empty tin bucket; again vanished with it full; returned and said to me:

"That was Mame. She rings twice. She likes a glass of beer for supper. Her and the kid. If you ever saw that little skeesicks of mine brace up in his high chair and take his beer and— But, say, what was yours? I get kind of excited when I hear them two rings—was it the baseball score or gin fizz you asked for?"

"Ginger ale," I answered.

I walked up to Broadway. I saw a cop on the corner. The cops take kids up, women across, and men in. I went up to him.

"If I'm not exceeding the spiel limit," I said, "let me ask you. You see New York during its vocative hours. It is the function of you and your brother cops to preserve the acoustics of the city. There must be a civic voice that is intelligible to you. At night during your lonely rounds you must have heard it. What is the epitome of its turmoil and shouting? What does the city say to you?

"Friend," said the policeman, spinning his club, "it don't say nothing. I get my orders from the man higher up. Say, I guess you're all right. Stand here for a few minutes and keep an eye open for the roundsman."

The cop melted into the darkness of the side street. In ten minutes he had returned.

"Married last Tuesday," he said, half gruffly. "You know how they are. She comes to that corner at nine every night for a—comes to say 'hello!' I generally manage to be there. Say, what was it you asked me a bit ago—what's doing in the city? Oh, there's a roof-garden or two just opened, twelve blocks up."

I crossed a crow's-foot of street-car tracks, and skirted the edge of an umbrageous park. An artificial Diana, gilded, heroic, poised, wind-ruled, on the tower, shimmered in the clear light of her namesake in the sky. Along came my poet, hurrying, hatted, haired, emitting dactyls, spondees and dactylis. I seized him.

"Bill," said I (in the magazine he is Cleon), "give me a lift. I am on an assignment to find out the Voice of the City. You see, it's a special order.

Ordinarily a symposium comprising the views of Henry Clews, John L. Sullivan, Edwin Markham, May Irwin and Charles Schwab would be about all. But this is a different matter. We want a broad, poetic, mystic vocalization of the city's soul and meaning. You are the very chap to give me a hint. Some years ago a man got at the Niagara Falls and gave us its pitch. The note was about two feet below the lowest G on the piano. Now, you can't put New York into a note unless it's better indorsed than that. But give me an idea of what it would say if it should speak. It is bound to be a mighty and far-reaching utterance. To arrive at it we must take the tremendous crash of the chords of the day's traffic, the laughter and music of the night, the solemn tones of Dr. Parkhurst, the rat-time, the weeping, the stealthy hum of cab-wheels, the shout of the press agent, the tinkle of fountains on the roof-gardens, the hullabaloo of the strawberry vender and the covers of *Everybody's Magazine*, the whispers of the lovers in the parks—all these sounds must go into your Voice—not combined, but mixed, and of the mixture an essence made; and of the essence an extract—an audible extract, of which one drop shall form the thing we seek."

"Do you remember," asked the poet, with a chuckle, "that California girl we met at Stiver's studio last week? Well, I'm on my way to see her. She repeated that poem of mine, 'The Tribute of Spring,' word for word. She's the smartest proposition in this town just at present. Say, how does this confounded tie look? I spoiled four before I got one to set right."

"And the Voice that I asked you about?" I inquired.

"Oh, she doesn't sing," said Cleon. "But you ought to hear her recite my 'Angel of the Inshore Wind.'"

I passed on. I cornered a newsboy and he flashed at me prophetic pink papers that outstripped the news by two revolutions of the clock's longest hand.

"Son," I said, while I pretended to chase coins in my penny pocket, "doesn't it sometimes seem to you as if the city ought to be able to talk? All these ups and downs and funny business and queer things happening every day—what would it say, do you think, if it could speak?"

"Quit yer kidding'," said the boy. "Wot paper yer want? I got no time to waste. It's Mag's birthday, and I want thirty cents to git her a present."

Here was no interpreter of the city's mouth-piece. I bought a paper, and consigned its undeclared treaties, its premeditated murders and unfought battles to an ash can.

Again I repaired to the park and sat in the moon shade. I thought and thought, and wondered why none could tell me what I asked for.

And then, as swift as light from a fixed star, the answer came to me. I arose and hurried—hurried as so many reasoners must, back around my circle. I knew the answer and I hugged it in my breast as I flew, fearing lest some one would stop me and demand my secret.

Aurelia was still on the stoop. The moon was higher and the ivy shadows were deeper. I sat at her side and we watched a little cloud tilt at the drifting moon and go asunder quite pale and discomfited.

And then, wonder of wonders and delight of delights! our hands somehow touched, and our fingers closed together and did not part.

After half an hour Aurelia said, with that smile of hers:

"Do you know, you haven't spoken a word since you came back!"

"That," said I, nodding wisely, "is the Voice of the City."

103

My Lost City

F. SCOTT FITZGERALD

Francis Scott Fitzgerald (1896–1940) is one of the major American writers of the twentieth century. Born in St. Paul, Minnesota, he established himself as a writer central to the so-called "Jazz Age" of the 1920s, and especially in relation to New York City. *The Beautiful and the Damned* (1922) set the terms of his exhaustive and self-destructive mythology ending in his alcoholism and the breakdown of his wife, Zelda. *Tender is the Night* (1934) is the flawed novel of his European experience, whilst *The Crack-Up* (1936) records his breakdown as a symbol of the culture he sought to record. "My Lost City", in this context, is especially poignant. However, it is *The Great Gatsby* (1925) which achieved exemplary status as an *ur*-text of the period. A brilliant analysis of 1920s America, this also focuses on New York City and is a central text for any understanding of the city in the context of the period. See Andrew Turnbull, *Scott Fitzgerald* (1962), H. D.. Piper, *F. Scott Fitzgerald: A Critical Portrait*, (1967), and Henry Claridge (ed), *F. Scott Fitzgerald: Critical Assessments*, (4 vols. 1992).

There was first the ferry boat moving softly from the Jersey shore at dawn—the moment crystallized into my first symbol of New York. Five years later when I was fifteen I went into the city from school to see Ina Claire in *The Quaker Girl* and Gertrude Bryan in *Little Boy Blue*. Confused by my hopeless and melancholy love for them both, I was unable to choose between them—so they blurred into one lovely entity, the girl. She was my second symbol of New York. The ferry boat stood for triumph, the girl for romance. In time I was to achieve some of both, but there was a third symbol that I have lost somewhere, and lost for ever.

I found it on a dark April afternoon after five more years.

"Oh, Bunny," I yelled. "*Bunny!*"

He did not hear me—my taxi lost him, picked him up again half a block down the street. There were black spots of rain on the sidewalk and I saw him walking briskly through the crowd wearing a tan raincoat over his inevitable brown get-up;

Source: F. Scott Fitzgerald, "My Lost City", *The Crack-Up*, New York, 1936.

I noted with a shock that he was carrying a light cane.

"Bunny!" I called again, and stopped. I was still an undergraduate at Princeton while he had become a New Yorker. This was his afternoon walk, this hurry along with his stick through the gathering rain, and as I was not to meet him for an hour it seemed an intrusion to happen upon him engrossed in his private life. But the taxi kept pace with him and as I continued to watch I was impressed: he was no longer the shy little scholar of Holder Court—he walked with confidence, wrapped in his thoughts and looking straight ahead, and it was obvious that his new background was entirely sufficient to him. I knew that he had an apartment where he lived with three other men, released now from all undergraduate taboos, but there was something else that was nourishing him and I got my first impression of that new thing—the Metropolitan spirit.

Up to this time I had seen only the New York that offered itself for inspection—I was Dick Whittington up from the country gaping at the trained bears, or a youth of the Midi dazzled by the boulevards of Paris. I had come only to stare at the show, though the designers of the Woolworth Building and the Chariot Race Sign, the producers of musical comedies and problem plays, could ask for no more appreciative spectator, for I took the style and glitter of New York even above its own valuation. But I had never accepted any of the practically anonymous invitations to debutante balls that turned up in an undergraduate's mail, perhaps because I felt that no actuality could live up to my conception of New York's splendour. Moreover, she to whom I fatuously referred as "my girl" was a Middle Westerner, a fact which kept the warm centre of the world out there, so I thought of New York as essentially cynical and heartless—save for one night when she made luminous the Ritz Roof on a brief passage through.

Lately, however, I had definitely lost her and I wanted a man's world, and this sight of Bunny made me see New York as just that. A week before, Monsignor Fay had taken me to the Lafayette where there was spread before us a brilliant flag of food, called an *hors d'oeuvre*, and with it we drank claret that was as brave as Bunny's confident cane—but after all it was a restaurant, and afterwards we would drive back over a bridge into the hinterland. The New York of undergraduate dissipation, of Bustanoby's, Shanley's, Jack's, had become a horror, and though I returned to it, alas, through many an alcoholic mist, I felt each time a betrayal of a persistent idealism. My participance was prurient rather than licentious and scarcely one pleasant memory of it remains from those days; as Ernest Hemingway once remarked, the sole purpose of the cabaret is for unattached men to find complaisant women. All the rest is a wasting of time in bad air.

But that night, in bunny's apartment, life was mellow and safe, a finer distillation of all that I had come to love at Princeton. The gentle playing of an oboe mingled with city noises from the street outside, which penetrated into the room with difficulty through great barricades of books; only the crisp tearing open of invitations by one man was a discordant note. I had found a third symbol of New York and I began wondering about the rent of such apartments and casting about for the appropriate friends to share one with me.

Fat chance—for the next two years I had as much control over my own destiny as a convict over the cut of his clothes. When I got back to New York in 1919 I was so entangled in life that a period of mellow monasticism in Washington Square was not to be dreamed of. The thing was to make enough money in the advertising business to rent a stuffy apartment for two in the Bronx. The girl concerned had never seen New York but she was wise enough to be rather reluctant. And in a haze of anxiety and unhappiness I passed the four most impressionable months of my life. New York had all the iridescence of the beginning of the world. The returning troops marched up Fifth Avenue and girls were instinctively drawn east and north towards them—this was the greatest nation and there was gala in the air. As I hovered ghost-like in the Plaza Red Room of a Saturday afternoon, or went to lush and liquid garden parties in the East Sixties or tippled with Princetonians in the Biltmore Bar, I was haunted always by my other life—my drab room in the Bronx, my square foot of the subway, my fixation upon the day's letter from Alabama—would it come and what would it say?—my shabby suits, my poverty, and love. While my friends were launching decently into life I had muscled my inadequate bark into midstream. The gilded youth circling around young Constance Bennett in the Club de Vingt, the classmates in the Yale-Princeton Club whooping up our first after-the-war reunion, the atmosphere of the millionaires' houses that I sometimes frequented—these things were empty for me, though I recognized them as impressive scenery and regretted that I was committed to other romance. The most hilarious luncheon table or the most moony cabaret—it was all the same; from them I returned eagerly to my home on Claremont Avenue—home because there might be a letter waiting outside the door. One by one my great dreams of New York became tainted. The remembered charm of Bunny's apartment faded with the rest when I interviewed a blowsy landlady in Greenwich Village. She told me I could bring girls to the room, and the idea filled me with dismay—why should I want to bring girls to my room?—I had a girl. I wandered through the town of 127th Street, resenting its vibrant life; or else I bought cheap theatre seats at Gray's drugstore and tried to lose myself for a few hours in my old passion for Broadway. I was a failure—mediocre at advertising work and unable to get started as a writer. Hating the city, I got roaring, weeping drunk on my last penny and went home. ...

... Incalculable city. What ensued was only one of a thousand success stories of those gaudy days, but it plays a part in my own movie of New York. When I returned six months later the offices of editors and publishers were open to me, impresarios begged plays, the movies panted for screen material. To my bewilderment, I was adopted, not as a Middle Westerner, not even as a detached observer, but as the archetype of what New York wanted. This statement requires some account of the metropolis in 1920.

There was already the tall white city of today, already the feverish activity of the boom, but there was a general inarticulateness. As much as anyone the columnist F.P.A. guessed the pulse of the individual crowd, but shyly, as one watching from a window. Society and the native arts had not mingled.—Ellen Mackay was not yet married to Irving Berlin. Many of Peter Arno's people would have been meaningless to the citizen of 1920, and save for F.P.A.'s column there was no forum for metropolitan urbanity.

Then, for just a moment, the "younger generation" idea became a fusion of many elements in New York life. People of fifty might pretend there was still a four hundred, or Maxwell Bodenheim might pretend there was a Bohemia worth its paint and pencils—but the blending of the bright, gay, vigorous elements began then, and for the first time there appeared a society a little livelier than the solid-mahogany dinner parties of Emily Price Post. If this society produced the cocktail party, it also evolved Park Avenue wit, and for the first time an educated European could envisage a trip to New York as something more amusing than a gold-trek into a formalized Australian Bush.

For just a moment, before it was demonstrated that I was unable to play the role, I, who knew less of New York than any reporter of six months' standing and less of its society than any hall-room boy in a Ritz stag line, was pushed into the position not only of spokesman for the time but of the typical product of that same moment. I, or rather it was "we" now, did not know exactly what New York expected of us and found it rather confusing. Within a few months after our embarkation on the Metropolitan venture we scarcely knew any more who we were and we hadn't a notion what we were. A dive into a civic fountain, a casual brush with the law, was enough to get us into the gossip columns, and we were quoted on a variety of subjects we knew nothing about. Actually our "contacts" included half a dozen unmarried college friends and a few new literary acquaintances—I remember a lonesome Christmas when we had not one friend in the city, nor one house we could go to. Finding no nucleus to which we could cling, we became a small nucleus ourselves and gradually we fitted our disruptive personalities into the contemporary scene of New York. Or rather New York forgot us and let us stay.

This is not an account of the city's changes but of the changes in this writer's feeling for the city. From the confusion of the year 1920 I remember riding on top of a taxicab along deserted Fifth Avenue on a hot Sunday night, and a luncheon in the cool Japanese gardens at the Ritz with the wistful Kay Laurel and George Jean Nathan, and writing all night again and again, and paying too much for minute apartments, and buying magnificent but broken-down cars. The first speak-easies had arrived, the toddle was *passé*, the Montmartre was the smart place to dance and Lillian Tashman's fair hair weaved around the floor among the enliquored college boys. The plays were *Declassée* and *Sacred and Profane Love*, and at the Midnight Frolic you danced elbow to elbow with Marion Davies and perhaps picked out the vivacious Mary Hay in the pony chorus. We thought we were apart from all that; perhaps everyone thinks they are apart from their milieu. We felt like small children in a great bright unexplored barn. Summoned out to Griffith's studio on Long Island, we trembled in the presence of the familiar face of the *Birth of a Nation*; later I realized that behind much of the entertainment that the city poured forth into the nation there were only a lot of rather lost and lonely people. The world of the picture actors was like our own in that it was in New York and not of it. It had little sense of itself and no centre: when I first met Dorothy Gish I had the feeling that we were both standing on the North Pole and it was snowing. Since then they have found a home but it was not destined to be New York.

When bored we took our city with a Huysmans-like perversity. An afternoon alone in our "apartment" eating olive sandwiches and drinking a quart of Bushmill's whisky presented by Zoë Atkins, then out into the freshly bewitched city, through strange doors into strange apartments with intermittent swings along in taxis through the soft nights. At last we were one with New York, pulling it after us through every portal. Even now I go into many flats with the sense that I have been there before or in the one above or below—was it the night I tried to disrobe in the *Scandals*, or the night when (as I read with astonishment in the paper next morning) "Fitzgerald Knocks Officer This Side of Paradise"? Successful scrapping not being among my accomplishments, I tried in vain to reconstruct the sequence of events which led up to this dénouement in Webster Hall. And lastly from that period I remember riding in a taxi one afternoon between very tall buildings under a mauve and rosy sky; I began to bawl because I had everything I wanted and knew I would never be so happy again.

It was typical of our precarious position in New York that when our child was to be born we played safe and went home to St Paul—it seemed inappropriate to bring a baby into all that glamour and loneliness. But in a year we were back and we began doing the same things over again and not liking them so much. We had run through a lot, though we had retained an almost theatrical innocence by preferring the role of the observed to that of the observer. But innocence is no end in itself and as our minds unwillingly matured we began to see New York whole and try to save some of it for the selves we would inevitably become.

It was too late—or too soon. For us the city was inevitably linked up with Bacchic diversions, mild or fantastic. We could organize ourselves only on our return to Long Island and not always there. We had no incentive to meet the city half way. My first symbol was now a memory, for I knew that triumph is in oneself; my second one had grown commonplace—two of the actresses whom I had worshipped from afar in 1913 had dined in our house. But it filled me with certain fear that even the third symbol had grown dim—the tranquillity of Bunny's apartment was not to be found in the ever-quickening city. Bunny himself was married, and about to become a father, other friends had gone to Europe, and the bachelors had become cadets of houses larger and more social than ours. By this time we "knew everybody"—which is to say most of those whom Ralph Barton would draw as in the orchestra on an opening night.

But we were no longer important. The flapper, upon whose activities the popularity of my first books was based, had become *passé* by 1923—anyhow in the East. I decided to crash Broadway with a play, but Broadway sent its scouts to Atlantic City and quashed the idea in advance, so I felt that, for the moment, the city and I had little to offer each other. I would take the Long Island atmosphere that I had familiarly breathed and materialize it beneath unfamiliar skies.

It was three years before we saw New York again. As the ship glided up the river, the city burst thunderously upon us in the early dusk—the white glacier of lower New York swooping down like a strand of a bridge to rise into uptown New York, a miracle of foamy light suspended by the stars. A band started to play on deck, but the majesty of the city made the march trivial and tinkling. From that moment I knew that New York, however often I might leave it, was home.

The tempo of the city had changed sharply. The uncertainties of 1920 were drowned in a steady golden roar and many of our friends had grown wealthy. But the restlessness of New York in 1927 approached hysteria. The parties were bigger—those of Condé Nast, for example, rivalled in their way the fabled balls of the nineties; the pace was faster—the catering to dissipation set an example to Paris; the shows were broader, the buildings were higher, the morals were looser and the liquor was cheaper; but all these benefits did not really minister to much delight. Young people wore out early—they were hard and languid at twenty-one, and save for Peter Arno none of them contributed anything new; perhaps Peter Arno and his collaborators said everything there was to say about the boom days in New York that couldn't be said by a jazz band. Many people who were not alcoholics were lit up four days out of seven, and frayed nerves were strewn everywhere; groups were held together by a generic nervousness and the hangover became a part of the day as well allowed-for as the Spanish siesta. Most of my friends drank too much—the more they were in tune to the times the more they drank. And so effort *per se* had no dignity against the mere bounty of those days in New York, a depreciatory word was found for it: a successful programme became a racket—I was in the literary racket.

We settled a few hours from New York and I found that every time I came to the city I was caught into a complication of events that deposited me a few days later in a somewhat exhausted state on the train for Delaware. Whole sections of the city had grown rather poisonous, but invariably I found a moment of utter peace in riding south through Central Park at dark towards where the façade of 59th Street thrusts its lights through the trees. There again was my lost city, wrapped cool in its mystery and promise. But that detachment never lasted long—as the toiler must live in the city's belly, so I was compelled to live in its disordered mind.

Instead there were the speak-easies—the moving from luxurious bars, which advertised in the campus publications of Yale and Princeton, to the beer gardens where the snarling face of the underworld peered through the German good nature of the entertainment, then on to strange and even more sinister localities where one was eyed by granite-faced boys and there was nothing left of joviality but only a brutishness that corrupted the new day into which one presently went out. Back in 1920 I shocked a rising young business man by suggesting a cocktail before lunch. In 1929 there was liquor in half the downtown offices, and a speak-easy in half the large buildings.

One was increasingly conscious of the speak-easy and of Park Avenue. In the past decade Greenwich Village, Washington Square, Murray Hill, the chateaux of Fifth Avenue had somehow disappeared, or become unexpressive of anything. The city was bloated, gutted, stupid with cake and circuses, and a new expression "Oh yeah?" summed up all the enthusiasm evoked by the announcement of the last super-skyscrapers. My barber retired on a half million bet in the market and I was conscious that the head waiters who bowed me, or failed to bow me, to my table were far, far wealthier than I. This was no fun—once again I had enough of New York and it was good to be safe on shipboard where the ceaseless revelry remained in the bar in transport to the fleecing rooms of France.

"What news from New York?"

"Stocks go up. A baby murdered a gangster."

"Nothing more?"

"Nothing. Radios blare in the street."

I once thought that there were no second acts in American lives, but there was certainly to be a second act to New York's boom days. We were somewhere in North Africa when we heard a dull distant crash which echoed to the farthest wastes of the desert.

"What was that?"

"Did you hear it?"

"It was nothing."

"Do you think we ought to go home and see?"

"No—it was nothing."

In the dark autumn of two years later we saw New York again. We passed through curiously polite customs agents, and then with bowed head and hat in hand I walked reverently through the echoing tomb. Among the ruins a few childish wraiths still played to keep up the pretence that they were alive, betraying by their feverish voices and hectic cheeks the thinness of the masquerade. Cocktail parties, a last hollow survival from the days of carnival, echoed to the plaints of the wounded: "Shoot me, for the love of God, someone shoot me!", and the groans and wails of the dying: "Did you see that United States Steel is down three more points?" My barber was back at work in his shop; again the head waiters bowed people to their tables, if there were people to be bowed. From the ruins, lonely and inexplicable as the sphinx, rose the Empire State Building and, just as it had been a tradition of mine to climb to the Plaza Roof to take leave of the beautiful city, extending as far as eyes could reach, so now I went to the roof of the last and most magnificent of towers. Then I understood—everything was explained: I had discovered the crowning error of the city, its Pandora's box. Full of vaunting pride the New Yorker had climbed here and seen with dismay what he had never suspected, that the city was not the endless succession of canyons that he had supposed but that *it had limits*—from the tallest structure he saw for the first time that it faded out into the country on all sides, into an expanse of green and blue that alone was limitless. And with the awful realization that New York was a city after all and not a universe, the whole shining edifice that he had reared in his imagination came crashing to the ground. That was the rash gift of Alfred W.

Smith to the citizens of New York.

Thus I take leave of my lost city. Seen from the ferry boat in the early morning, it no longer whispers of fantastic success and eternal youth. The whoopee mamas who prance before its empty parquets do not suggest to me the ineffable beauty of my dream girls of 1914. And Bunny, swinging along confidently with his cane towards his cloister in a carnival, has gone over to communism and frets about the wrongs of southern mill workers and western farmers whose voices, fifteen years ago, would not have penetrated his study walls.

All is lost save memory, yet sometimes I imagine myself reading, with curious interest, a *Daily News* of the issue of 1945:

MAN OF FIFTY RUNS AMUCK IN NEW YORK
Fitzgerald Feathered Many Love Nests Cutie Avers
Bumped Off By Outraged Gunman

So perhaps I am destined to return some day and find in the city new experiences that so far I have only read about. For the moment I can only cry out that I have lost my splendid mirage. Come back, come back, O glittering and white!

104

A Vision of the City

THOMAS WOLFE

Thomas Wolfe (1900–1978), American novelist, was born in Asheville, North Carolina. A "Southern" writer, he played his cultural background against a sense of New York City as at once intense, symbolic and idealized. He lived in New York City between 1924 and 1930. *Look Homeward Angel* (1921), *Of Time and the River* (1925), *The Web and the Rock* (1937), and *You Can't Go Home Again* (1940), remain his major works. Much undervalued as a writer, his response to the city reflects a distinctive dynamic attuned to an energy redolent of Walt Whitman. See Andrew Turnbull, *Thomas Wolfe* (1968) and *Modern Fiction Studies* (1965), a special Wolfe issue.

It was a cruel city, but it was a lovely one;
A savage city, yet it had such tenderness;
A bitter, harsh, and violent catacomb of stone and steel and tunneled rock,
Slashed savagely with light,
And roaring, fighting a constant ceaseless warfare of men and of machinery;
And yet it was so sweetly and so delicately pulsed,
As full of warmth, of passion, and of love,
As it was full of hate.

And even the very skies that framed New York,
The texture of the night itself,
Seemed to have the architecture and the weather
Of the city's special quality.

It was, he saw, a Northern city:
The bases of its form were vertical.
Even the night here, the quality of darkness,
Had a structural framework, and architecture of its own.
Here, compared with qualities of night
In London or in Paris,

Source: Thomas Wolfe, "A Vision of the City", New York, 1935.

Which were rounder, softer, of more drowsy hue,
The night was vertical, lean, immensely clifflike, steep and clear.
Here everything was sharp.
It burned so brightly, yet it burned sweetly, too.

For what was so incredible and so lovely
About this high, cool night
Was that it could be so harsh and clear,
So arrogantly formidable, and yet so tender, too.

There were always in these nights, somehow,
Even in nights of clear and bitter cold,
Not only the structure of lean steel,
But a touch of April, too:
They could be insolent and cruel,
And yet there was always in them
The suggestion of light feet, of lilac darkness,
Of something swift and fleeting,
Almost captured, ever gone,
A maiden virginal as April.

Here in this sky-hung faëry of the night,
The lights were sown like flung stars.
Suddenly he got a vision of the city
That was overwhelming in its loveliness.
It seemed to him all at once that there was nothing there
But the enchanted architecture of the dark,
Star-sown with a million lights.
He forgot the buildings:
All of a sudden, the buildings did not seem to exist,
To be there at all.
Darkness itself seemed to provide the structure
For the star-dust of those million lights,
They were flung there against the robe of night
Like jewels spangled on the gown of the dark Helen
That is burning in man's blood forevermore.

And the magic of it was incredible.
Light blazed before him, soared above him, mounted in linkless chains,
Was sown there upon a viewless wall, soared to the very pinnacles of night,
Inwrought into the robe of dark itself,
Unbodied, unsustained,
Yet fixed and moveless as a changeless masonry,
A world of darkness, the invisible,
Lighted for some immortal feast.

105

New York: Sketch of Megaloplis with a Word on Wall Street

JOHN GUNTHER

John Gunther's article is an interesting, if somewhat obvious, response to New York and, like *Inside USA*, remains very much on the surface of the experience it seeks to reflect. However, in terms of the 1930s, its perspective is significant, reflecting as it does an almost touristic view of Manhattan as a visual phenomenon based on an individual and distinct energy and cultural process. If it is clichéd, it underlines the significance of the cliché in the way we continue view and represent the city.

Submit to no models but your own O city!
—Walt Whitman

New York is all the cities.
—W. L. George

So now we come to New York City, the incomparable, the brilliant star city of cities, the forty-ninth state, a law unto itself, the Cyclopean paradox, the inferno with no out-of-bounds, the supreme expression of both the miseries and the splendors of contemporary civilization, the Macedonia of the United States. It meets the most severe test that may be applied to definition of a metropolis—it stays up all night. But also it becomes a small town when it rains.

Paradox? New York is at once the climactic synthesis of America, and yet the negation of America in that it has so many characteristics called un-American. One friend of mine, indignant that it seems impossible for any American city to develop on the pattern of Paris or Vienna, always says that Manhattan is like Constantinople—not the Istanbul of old Stamboul but of the Pera or Levantine side. He meant not merely the trite fact that New York is polyglot, but that it is full of people, like the Levantines, who are interested basically in only two things,

Source: John Gunther, "New York—Sketch of Megalopolis, with a Word on Wall Street", *Inside USA*, London, 1930s, Ch. 33.

living well and making money. I would prefer a different analogy—that only Istanbul, of all cities in the world, has as enchanting and stimulating a profile.

Also I have heard New York characterized as nothing but "a cluster of small islets in the North Atlantic." These at any rate fling their luster far. The most important single thing to say about Manhattan in relation to the rest of the United States is that it dominates what, for want of a better phrase, may be called American culture. New York is the publishing center of the nation; it is the art, theater, musical, ballet, operatic center; it is the opinion center; it is the radio center; it is the style center. Hollywood? But Hollywood is nothing more than a suburb of the Bronx, both financially and from the point of view of talent. Politically, socially, in the world of ideas and in the whole world of entertainment, which is a great American industry needless to say, New York sets the tone and pace of the entire nation. What books 140 million Americans will read is largely determined by New York reviewers. Most of the serious newspaper columns originate in or near New York; so do most of the gossip columns, which condition Americans from Mobile to Puget Sound to the same patterns of social behavior. In a broad variety of fields, from serious drama to what you will hear on a jukebox, it is what New York says that counts; New York opinion is the hallmark of both intellectual and material success; to be accepted in this nation, New York acceptance must come first. I do not assert that this is necessarily a good thing. I say merely that it is true. One reason for all this is that New York, with its richly cosmopolitan population, provides such an appreciative audience. It admires artistic quality. It has a fine inward gleam for talent. Also New York is a wonderfully opulent center for bogus culture. One of its chief industries might be said to be the manufacture of reputations, many of them fraudulent.

The field of culture or quasi culture aside, New York City's tremendous importance has traditionally been based on four factors:

(1) It was by far the greatest point of entry for European immigrants. Karl Marx, writing in the New York *Tribune* a good many years ago, predicted not only that these would come, but that the great bulk of them, having arrived, would tend to remain in the New York area.

(2) It was by far the greatest American port for exports, primarily of wheat. New York was the city where people came in, and goods went out.

(3) It was the financial and credit capital of the United States.

(4) It was a great place for residents of other American cities to visit, shop in, and throw money at.

New York has to come extent lost ground in all these categories. First, immigration was largely cut off. Second, wheat and other exports turned to other ports (though New York is still the biggest ocean port in the country). Third, Washington replaced it as the financial capital, as we shall see. Fourth (though still the Number One American tourist attraction),[1] New York has lost something of its inevitableness as the place that all Americans want to see before they die.

This situation makes it clear incidentally why New York made such a fight to get the UN. The city is not exactly what you would call moribund, and actually the

UN will serve to further its transformation from merely a national into a world metropolis. Nevertheless, most of New York was glad to have the UN safely tucked in between the East River and shabby old Turtle Bay.

Little Old New York

More than anywhere else in this book, the author must now steer tightly between Scylla and Charybdis, between saying too much and too little. How can we talk about the Statue of Liberty without seeming ridiculously supererogatory? But how can we omit Brooklyn Bridge and still give a fair, comprehensive picture? One must either take the space to mention something that everybody knows everything about, or else risk omission of things that everybody will think ought certainly to be included.

Park Avenue in summer near Grand Central, a thin quivering asphalt shelf, and the asphalt soft, a thin quivering layer of street separating the automobiles above from the trains below; avenues as homespun with small exquisite shops as Madison, and streets as magnificent as 57th; the fat black automobiles doubleparked on Fifth Avenue on sleety afternoons; kibitzers watching strenuously to see if the man running will really catch the bus; bridges soaring and slim as needles like the George Washington; the incomparable moment at dusk when the edges of tall buildings melt invisibly into the sky, so that nothing of them can be seen except the lighted windows; the way the pace of everything accelerates near Christmas; how the avenues will be cleared of snow and actually dry a day after a six-inch fall, while the side streets are still banked solid with sticky drifts; how the noon sun makes luminous spots on the rounded tops of automobiles, crowded together on the slope of Park Avenue so that they look like seashells; the shop that delivers chocolates by horse—all this is too familiar to bear mention.

That Manhattan was discovered by Henry Hudson in 1609, and bought from the Indians for $24 in 1626 I refuse to enlarge upon. Not so well known are such details as that the city's flag still bears the Dutch royal colors (orange, white, and blue), and that, in 1811, it was decided that only three sides of the City Hall need be finished, since surely there would be no more movement of the city northward. Of course New York has been pushing outward like a swarm of bees ever since, and not merely to the north. It covers 365.4 square miles today; it has upwards of five thousand miles of streets.

As of 1940 the population of New York City within city limits was 7,454,995; as of early 1947, it is estimated at 7,768,000. Only two states, Pennsylvania, and California (aside from New York state itself) contain more people; of the seventy-five nations in the world, it has a greater population than forty-one. By 1970, according to census estimates, the population will have risen to 8,500,000; after 1980, along with that of the rest of the country, it is expected to decline. These figures refer to city limits only. As of 1940 the New York "metropolitan district" actually held 11,690,520 people and an estimate today is that 12,500,000 people live within a radius of thirty-five miles, making the area by all odds the greatest urban concentration the world has ever known. Newark and Jersey City are, to all intents and purposes except politically, subdivisions of Manhattan; I have heard a Pennsylvanian say that even Scranton was "part of New York"; speaking in the broadest way, "New York" includes the whole region from Bridgeport to Trenton and beyond.

Turn now to racial fusions. The best remark I know in this field is from Bryce, that New York "is a European city, but of no particular country." He might of course have said, "but of many countries." Details are well known. For instance two hundred newspapers not in English are published in New York. We have talked about enclaves like Hamtramck in Detroit. New York is full of Hamtramcks. More than two million New Yorkers are foreign born; more than two and a half million others are of foreign or mixed parentage. Of the foreign-born the largest group is Italian (more than 400,000), followed closely by Russian (395,000), and with Germany (225,000), Eire (160,000) and Poland (195,000) next. Those of mixed parentage follow the same order. There are 26,884 foreign-born Czechs, 28,593 Greeks, and 12,000 Chinese. All told there are representatives of at least seventy nationalities in New York, from Bulgarians to Yemenites. Cutting across national categories are the Jews, of whom the city has about two million; New York is, as everybody knows, overwhelmingly the first Jewish city in the world.

A grave and estimable Bourbon of my acquaintance put it to me a few days ago, with internal frothings but probably with tongue in cheek as well, that the most powerful single influence in the United State today is that of Minsk, the provincial capital of Byelo-Russia. His train of thought went like this. Minsk is the birthplace of Max Lerner, the well-known editorial writer and political scientist. Lerner runs *PM*. *PM* runs the American Labor party. The American Labor party runs New York City. New York City runs New York state. And New York state of course runs the nation.[2]

Hamilton Fish Armstrong, writing in Foreign Affairs, once had some illuminating things to say about the New York potpourri. One is that, in spite of all that has been added, the basic Anglo-Dutch stock still gives marked coloration to the city. Another is that New York's conglomerateness dates from the very beginning, and has given it a tolerance unmatched by any other American city except one much smaller, San Francisco. From the early Du Ponts to Otto Habsburg, from Leon Trotsky to Haya de la Torre, Manhattan has been traditionally generous to refugees. It has a cosmopolitanism of the mind as well as pocket. It may be built on islands, but it is not insular.

New York of course has religions in profusion too. It is a very strong Roman Catholic and Episcopalian as well as Jewish city. It is the headquarters of the Collegiate Reformed Protestant Dutch church, and it has a powerful upper sprinkling of Christian Scientist. The best indication of the importance of religion in New York is real estate. Stroll down Fifth Avenue. In block after patrician block are churches of various denominations occupying sites of the most prodigious value. Or—as an instance of the influence of religion in another secular field—consider Christmas shopping.

It is a proud boast of New York that, what with its enormous pools of foreign-born, any article or object known in the world may be found there. You can buy anything from Malabar spices to stamps from Mauritius to Shakespeare folios. A stall on Seventh Avenue sells about a hundred different varieties of razor blades. Also it is incomparably the greatest manufacturing town on earth; in an average year it produces goods valued at more than four billion dollars. It houses no fewer than 36,000 different industrial concerns, representing more than 312 different manufactures—even if, as noted in the chapter preceding, you can see deer in Westchester a few miles away. Also it is by far the first city in the nation in the service industries. Manhattan alone employs more wage earners than Detroit and Cleveland put together; Brooklyn more than Boston and Baltimore put together; Queens more than Washington and Pittsburgh put together.[3] The two most important New York industries are printing and the garment trade. To attempt to describe Manhattan, without at least one mention of the Garment Center, is impossible. Everybody knows how, on the one hand, mammoth trucks choke the streets between 34th and 38th, and how, on the other, men on foot push through the crowds with their movable racks hung with clothes. The Garment Center means also that New York has two of the most powerful unions in the country, the Amalgamated Clothing Workers which was Sidney Hillman's union, and the International Ladies Garment Workers Union run by as able a man as American labor knows, David Dubinsky. This union has elaborate extracurricular activities, like its famous summer camps. Once it produced a musical comedy, *Pins and Needles*, that became a great Broadway hit.[4]

In *Inside Asia* I had a small passage describing the variety of strange occupations in India, like grasshopper selling. I have just thumbed through the classified New York telephone directory, a volume 1,600 solid pages long. Among occupations in New York are cinders, chenille dotting, bullet-proof protective equipment, breast pumps, bungs, boiler baffles, glue room equipment, abattoirs, flow meters, eschatology, mildew-proofing, pompons, potato chip machinery, rennet, spangles, solenoids, and spats. Also this book contains literally twenty-two columns of associations of one kind or another.

Items in Physiognomy

> No king, no clown, to rule this town!
>
> —William O. Bartlett

> Well, little old Noisyville-on-the-Subway is good enough for me.
>
> —O. Henry

As almost everybody knows, New York is divided into five counties called boroughs. The extraordinary tongue of Manhattan is only 12½ miles long and 2½ miles wide, but by 1947 estimates it contains 1,906,000 people. It has twenty bridges, roughly 100,000 out-of-town visitors a day, 915 night-clubs, Columbia University, and Central Park, which many people think is the most satisfactory park in the world, with its 840 acres spread out like a carpet for the skyscrapers to tiptoe up to. It has subdivisions as divergent as Kips Bay, the Gas House District, Hell's Kitchen and Greenwich Village. BROOKLYN (estimated population 2,798,000) is of course a world in itself, with local bosses like Peter J. McGuinness, a fierce local nationalism, the Dodgers, the Bush Terminal, Coney Island, and the *Tablet*, one of the most reactionary Catholic papers in the country. Geographically Brooklyn, which was once spelled Bruekelen, is the huge, bumpy, watery "head and shoulders" of Long Island. It covers 88.8 square miles; merely to list its street names takes 192 pages in a pocket guide. It delivers the biggest Democratic vote in the nation, and is a famous haunt of Christian Fronters; the viceroy of this formidable province, who died in 1946, was Frank V. Kelly. The BRONX, which borders on Westchester County and is the only borough on the mainland, covers 54.4 square miles and has 1,489,000 people. It is heavily Jewish like Brooklyn, and likewise a great community for baseball, having the Yankee Stadium; it contains sub-Bronxes like Throg's Neck, Morrisania, Clason's Point, and Mott Haven. It has its own flag, a well-known zoo, the Hall of Fame of New York University, and seven hundred miles of streets; for a proud interval it called itself the capital of the world, when the UN sat at Hunter College.

In the Bronx, one might say in parenthesis, live two notable New York politicians, Edward J. Flynn and Michael J. Quill. Mr. Flynn, its boss for many years, has craggy importance on the national level too; he is a former chairman of the Democratic National Committee, and FDR once named him ambassador to Australia. He was rejected by the Senate, however, because some Belgian paving blocks got found in the wrong place. Of all the great American municipal bosses, Flynn is the most superior, the most civilized and cultivated man. Mr. Quill is on the left-wing side of the political fence. He was born in County Kerry in 1905, and was a soldier in the Irish Republican Army; he came to New York, and got a job as a subway worker. Quill is two things today: head of the powerful Transport Workers Union, which threatened a serious strike in 1946, and a city councilman.

Queens, the biggest borough in area (126.6 square miles), has 1,456,000 people; it is the most diffuse of the boroughs, the least distinctive.[5] It has La Guardia Field and Forest Hills, the tennis capital of America; it has 196 miles of waterfront, and relentlessly unending rows of ugly small houses; in Queens, as well as anywhere in the country, you may see how a great city frays at the periphery; no community has more untidy edges. Finally, Richmond (population 186,000) which is another world in itself, Staten Island. A curious community, half an hour away by boat, Richmond has only one vote out of sixteen in the Board of Estimate (the governing body of New York City); this it resents, and occasionally it threatens to secede.

One should, at this point, at least mention the other New York islands; they are untidily picturesque—Governor's Island, North Brother Island, Randall's Island, Riker's Island—to say nothing of Ellis, Welfare, and South Brother. Then too there are the great and vital rivers, the Hudson, "like a state highway" as a writer in the Times[6] said aptly, and the East, "synonymous with poverty and ugliness," "churlish and oil-pocked," "treated with no more reverence than ... a subway excavation, and traditionally New York's watery main street."

Finally, the Port. Here, once more, we reach what Hollywood (or New York) would call the supercolossal. "This is at once the front door of the nation and its service entrance."[7] The Port of New York, run and run well by its unique authority, is the biggest natural harbor in the world; it comprises "seven bays, four river mouths, four estuaries"; it covers 431 square miles of water, has 307 miles of shore line, and 1,800 docks. Out of it, in a normal year, travel some 60 million tons of goods on 13,000 ships, to carry 41.7 per cent of the entire foreign trade of the United States.

New York, Neighborhoods & Spectacle

> The city like a ragged purple dream, the wonderful, cruel, enchanting, bewildering, fatal, great city.
>
> —O. Henry

> *Vulgar of manner, overfed,*
> *Overdressed and underbred.*
>
> —Byron R. Newton

A point to make now is New York's extreme brittleness, its vulnerability. As fascinating as any story in America is how it gets its water; the supply system represents an investment of two billion dollars, and some water comes from points at least a hundred miles away. What might a small bomb or two, at any of several strategic points, do to this enterprise? Also the city's life depends on water in another direction, that is, on the bridges and tunnels by which water is traversed. New York learned grimly about its vulnerability in this respect during a tug-boat strike early in 1946. A handful of 3,500 workers, manning three hundred tugboats, paralyzed the city from stem to stern; the entire Atlantean metropolis was forced to shut down for 16 hours. Most neutral observers thought that the operators had as grave, if not a graver, responsibility for this strike than the AF or L workers who struck; but this is beside the point. What counted (and could count again) is that the city, without these tugboats, cannot live. New York uses about 34,500,000 pounds of food a day, 98,000 tons of coal, and 4,000,000 gallons of oil, which help provide its gas, steam, and electricity. Seventy per cent of all this is moved by tugs and barges. Consider too elevator strikes; a brief one occurred in September, 1945. New York City has more than 43,000 elevators (about 20 per cent of all in the country), which carry about 17,500,000 passengers daily. Their shafts, put end to end, would stretch 1,600 miles; they go halfway to the moon, 125,000 miles, every day. When the elevators stop, New York stops too.[8]

At the Manhattan skyscrapers, every name in the book has been thrown. They have been called "the inconceivable spires of Manhattan, composed, repeating the upthrust torch of Liberty," "gypsum crystals," "a mass of stalagmites," "a ship of living stone," "an irregular tableland intersected by shadowy canyons," "dividends in the sky," "a giant cromlech," and, best of all, "a pincushion."[9] A more utilitarian-minded description is one by H. G. Wells; the skyscrapers reminded him irresistibly of the commercial nature of our civilization, being like "piled-up packing cases outside a warehouse."

Last Christmas I sent a lady a book. She lives in the Waldorf-Astoria Towers but the bookstore didn't understand me on the telephone, and, remarkable as it may seem, the book was dispatched not across the street but a distance of some 2,500 miles, to Mrs. So-and-So, Waldorf-Astoria, Taos (New Mexico). When it was retrieved I could not but reflect that, after all, American history is little more than the record of progress from Taos to Towers. Progress? New Yorkers, cliff dwellers still, have simply moved into a new type of pueblo.

No city changes so quickly as New York; none has so short a memory or is so heartless to itself; it has an inhuman quality. Very few New Yorkers pay the slightest attention to the historical monuments that fill the city. Most know very little about its wonders. How many realize that, by a simple mathematical trick, anybody can calculate where house numbers on the avenues are? How many ever recall that Theodore Roosevelt was born at 26 East 20th Street,[10] or that the oldest building in the city is on Peck Slip, or even that a three-million dollar treasure ship is supposed to be lying in the East River near 53rd Street? My publisher lives in the east 30's. I had been in his delightful house fifty times before I learned that James Monroe had once lived in it.

Glance at Baedeker's *United States* of 1893. To what sights does this worthy guide give its severely rationed stars? What was the 1893 equivalent of Rockefeller Center? Let the reader go to the public library and find out. But as to other details the midtown hotels starred are the Everett House, the Westminster, and the Windsor. ("Fees to waiters and bellboys are unfortunately becoming more and more customary in New York hotels.") The first uptown restaurant starred is the Café Brunswick; the chief "oyster saloon" is Dorlon's; the first theater mentioned is Daly's ("Shakespearean and modern comedy—Miss Ada Rehan"). As to shops, Baedeker says, "Many of the New York shops are very large and handsome, easily bearing comparison with those of Europe." As to baths it mentions that "hot and cold baths may be obtained at all the hotels (25c–75c) and large barber shops."[11]

One extraordinary phenomenon all over New York is its unequal rate of growth. On one side of a courtyard in the east 60's is a glittering modern apartment house where, I doubt not, you could find a tolerable small place to live for a rental of $5,000 a year, if apartments were available at all. On the other side, not fifty feet away, is a dirty balcony hung with laundry, part of a frowsy tenement built over squalid shops.

I live in midtown Manhattan; I have just walked around the block to see concretely what illimitable variety this neighborhood affords. Within a hundred yards I can go to church, have my hair cut, admire flowers, visit two banks (both low Georgian buildings in red brick), and dine in one of the supreme restaurants of the world or a Hamburg Heaven. Within a slightly greater radius I can buy a Cézanne ($55,000), a chukar partridge ($7.50), a pound of Persian caviar ($38), or a copy of the Civil Service Leader (10c). Within two hundred yards are three competing pharmacies comfortably busy, a shop for religious goods and missals, a delicatessen squeezed into a four-foot frontage, windows full of the most ornately superior English saddlery, a podiatrist, a good French bookstore, a Speed Hosiery repair shop, and, of course, the inevitable small stationery shop with its broad red band across the window advertising a variety of cigar.

New York is so volatile, so diffuse, that it has no more recognizable social frontiers; it is too big a community to be a community. As *Fortune* once observed, even the greater millionaires no longer live in houses for the most part, but in apartments; the *Social Register* contains upward of 30,000 names. Fifty years ago the "400" constituted a genuine enough inner nucleus. Today practically anybody who can buy a drink at "Twenty-One" or be seen in the Cub Room of the Stork Club is a member of society, because the criterion is no longer merely wealth or lineage. It is not Mrs. Vanderbilt who draws attention at the opera; it is a visiting movie star. Nor does it matter much nowadays where people live; anybody who has the money can buy a house in the east 70's (if he can find the house). People shoot up; people shoot down. Ask any New Yorker to list the dozen leading citizens of the town. The variety of names you will get is astonishing.

Finally, what are the chief New York issues today, political, semi-political, and otherwise? First, traffic. The violent snarled congestion in bursting streets costs the city at least a million dollars a day. Second, housing. Mayor O'Dwyer estimates that the city has an "absolute shortage" of 150,000 apartments, which means that about 500,000 people are living "under the crudest and most difficult conditions." Another estimate is that 450,000 families, or roughly one-fifth of the total population, live in "subhuman" tenements or houses. Third, a complex internecine struggle over airport development and the future of the great airport now being built, Idlewild. Fourth, the subway fare. It costs the city about 70 million dollars a year to maintain this ("Biggest Ride in the World," about twenty-five miles) at a nickel.

"Go East, Young Man"

New York City sucks in humanity from all over the world, as it sucks in New Orleans prawn and Idaho potatoes. This city, a parasite, would die without new blood. New Yorkers born in New York City are, as is notorious, rare. Consider some distinguished citizens in various fields and where they came from. John J. McCloy, presumptive president of the world bank, was born in Philadelphia, James A. Farley in Grassy Point (New York), Judge Sam Rosenman in San Antonio, Herbert Bayard Swope in St. Louis, and Gustav Metzman, president of the New York Central, in Baltimore. Henry R. Luce was born in China, Elsa Maxwell in Iowa, and Judge Learned Hand in Albany. Harold Ross, editor of the *New Yorker*, comes from Aspen, Colorado, and Lewis W. Douglas from Bisbee, Arizona. H. V. Kaltenborn was born in Wisconsin, George Jean Nathan in Indiana, Bruce Bliven of the *New Republic* in Iowa, and Winthrop W. Aldrich, probably the most important banker in the city, in Rhode Island. Among great churchmen John Haynes Holmes was born in Philadelphia and Harry Emerson Fosdick in buffalo. The Van Doren literary family derives from Illinois, Mary Simkhovitch from Massachusetts, and Mrs. Ogden Reid of the *Herald Tribune* from Wisconsin. Walter S. Gifford, president of AT&T, was born in Massachusetts, former governor Charles Poletti in Vermont, Sherman Billingsley in Oklahoma, John W. Davis in West Virginia, and Arturo Toscanini in Parma, Italy. There are, of course, a few exceptions. Robert I. Gannon, president of Fordham University, was born on Staten Island, and former comptroller Joseph D. McGoldrick in Brooklyn. Born actually in Manhattan are Gilbert Miller, the theatrical producer, Arthur H. Sulzberger, publisher of the New York Times, Hamilton Fish Armstrong, and Charles G. Bolté, the brilliant young chairman of the American Veterans' Committee.

Mayor Bill O'Dwyer and City Politics

Countless times in this book we have mentioned people with a great variety of experience, but I know none who quite matches O'Dwyer for abundance in this respect. He was born in 1890 in Bohola, County Mayo, Ireland, one of eleven children; both his parents were schoolteachers.[12] He ran off to Spain when a boy, and studied for two years with the Jesuits at the University of Salamanca; he planned to be a priest. But he changed his mind, took ship for New York, and arrived here in 1910, twenty years old, with $23.35 in his pocket. In the next few years he held every possible sort of job. First he became a handyman in a Bronx grocery at $9 a week; then he worked as a deckhand on a freighter in the South American trade, as a stoker, and later as a fireman on the river boats between New York and Albany. Meantime, he studied stenography at night school. He had a turn as a hod carrier and pasterer's apprentice, working on a building near Maiden Lane; he can look out from the City Hall today and see where the scaffolding was, and he still holds his membership in the Plasterers Helpers Union, AF of L. Also—it pleases him to recall this now—he was a bartender for a brief elegant period in the Hotel Plaza.

Then came a great decision. O'Dwyer decided to become a cop. He had been granted United States citizenship in 1916, and he joined the New York police department a year later. Also he kept on studying at night, now at Fordham Law School; it was a long grind, but he was graduated in 1923. Finally, in 1925, after great ardors and sacrifices, he was admitted to the New York bar.

The fact that Mayor O'Dwyer, who has the nice numerical luck to be the one-hundredth elected mayor in New York City history, was a policeman has considerable importance. It means, first of all, that he knows cops. One can talk about issues and involvements like housing, subways, or what you will, but basically the mayor of any great American city stands or falls by his police department. Any time a police department, through horrible circumstance, chooses to embarrass a mayor by lying down on the job, the mayor is beaten.

There are 19,000 policemen in New York City, and it is no easy thing to keep that many men, who may be continuously exposed to temptation, honest all the time. The average New York cop gets $3,420 a year. Twice a week, in the old days anyway, he may have had to turn down a hundred-dollar bill. The police have nice distinctions in graft. Gambling money, so the legend goes, is "clean"; vice money is, however, dirty. The terrific difficulty of dealing with gambling may be illustrated by one small point, that at Mr. La Guardia's request the Stock and Curb exchanges for a brief time published no daily sales totals except in round numbers, so that the tens of thousands of people in the "policy" racket couldn't use the last digits as the basis for their calculations.

But to resume. Mr. O'Dwyer knows cops and understands them and likes to deal with them. He was an honest cop himself and he has an honest police force now. He took over the commissioner appointed by Mr. La Guardia, Arthur W. Wallender, gave him a free hand to do a good job, and backed him up.

O'Dwyer's political career may be outlined briefly. In 1932 he was appointed a city magistrate, which meant that he was politically "right." Governor Lehman promoted him to the county court in 1938; later he won an election to a fourteen-year term on this bench. This was a well-paid job, and he could have looked forward to security and a pleasant routine existence for years and years. He dropped it the next year, however, to run for the district attorneyship of Kings County (Brooklyn), and won. His record in this post—though a subsequent investigation accused him of mild inefficiencies—made him famous. The job he did as a prosecutor is fully as remarkable as Dewey's, though he never sensationalized it as Dewey did. Brooklyn had, in those years, a gang nicknamed Murder Incorporated, led by a notable killer named Louis Lepke and including some fancy folk like Abe "Kid Twist" Reles; that O'Dwyer got first-degree murder indictments against Lepke who was later duly electrocuted, and several of his lieutenants, is as unprecedented in its field as Dewey's conviction of Jimmy Hines. Altogether, O'Dwyer's friends say that he solved eighty-seven murders. His opponent in the 1945 mayoralty race, however, charged widely that his record was spurious in several important respects, that most of the real work was done by an assistant prosecutor, and that wily folk behind the scenes, who were the masters of the actual front-line killers, were never touched. However, the fact remains that Murder Incorporated was broken up.

In 1941, O'Dwyer ran for mayor; La Guardia beat him. Came the war. O'Dwyer volunteered for service the day after Pearl Harbor, and was presently commissioned as a major; the Army put him to work investigating contract frauds, and by 1944 he was a brigadier general. Then Roosevelt sent him as his personal representative to the Allied Control Commission in Italy, and later he was appointed executive director of the War Refugee Board. he ran for re-election as Kings County district attorney in absentia while still in the Army; Democratic, Republican and American Labor parties all endorsed him. Then came the mayoralty race of 1945. (New York, like most American cities, has its mayoralty election in off-years.) O'Dwyer won—there were some highly special circumstances connected with this election as we shall see—with an absolute majority of 285,000, and the biggest plurality in the history of the city.

His first year in office, at what is generally considered the third biggest and most difficult job in the United States, was certainly trying enough. He had the tugboat strike to deal with, and then the threat of a subway strike. His wife, who had been a telephone operator at the Hotel Vanderbilt when he met her in 1916, died after a long and exhausting illness. His appointments were excellent on the whole; he kept some of the best La Guardia men, like Bob Moses; he got William H. Davis, former head of the War Labor Board, to work with him on transportation. He fired two of his cabinet members, one following a scandal in professional football, the other after a tenement collapsed with the loss of thirty-seven lives. He worked hard to bring the UN to New York; it might not have come, however, had not John D. Rockefeller Jr. made possible the purchase of the site through an $8,500,000 gift. He did what he could on taxes, sought to bring a showdown on subway fare, and raised the pay of city employees to meet the advancing cost of living. In a city like New York, however, very little of this really matters. What does matter is the relation of a mayor to what is behind him. O'Dwyer is, after all, a Democrat. What everybody wanted to know was what he was going to do with Tammany. "A vast, corrupt organization, starved through twelve long years, is panting for its revenge," wrote the New York *Herald Tribune* when he assumed office. During the La Guardia years, Tammany was of course frozen out. Was Mr. O'Dwyer going to let it in again, and if so in what form? The answer to this came in early 1947, after prolonged sub-surface struggles. The mayor pushed out the old Tammany leaders, shook the organization up from top to bottom, removed some of its more adhesive members, and became in effect, Tammany chieftain himself with the slate washed clean.

I went down to the City Hall the other day and had an hour with O'Dwyer after not having seen him for several years. He is a shade grayer, a shade stockier, and still a grand man to talk to—easy-going, bluff, friendly, and informal. He wore a light brown sports jacket; he was as relaxed—working a fourteen-hour day—as a character in the *Crock of Gold*. O'Dwyer has heavy, very short, blunt fingers, a decisive nose, and expressive, eloquent blue eyes. He is full of Irish wit and bounce. Also he is very modest. Mostly we talked about things personal. But occasionally there were remarks like, "How the hell does democracy work, anyhow?" This was not, I hasten to add, said with any lack of faith. The mayor is a very gregarious man, and he loves people; especially he loves those who have fought their way out of a bad environment. What he hates most are stuffy people. ("I am sorry for the selfish ones; they only see one side.") I asked him how he took the load off. "A thousand ways!" One is music and another books. Then suddenly Mr. O'Dwyer was reminiscing about his childhood. "It was all a series of breaks ... you know how rebellious Irish kids are ... and everybody yearning for a piece of poetry." He wanted to be a doctor. Medicine, the mysterious agencies of disease, the world of pain, fascinated him, and he was bursting with humanity for the sick, though "healthy as a trout" himself. To contribute to that field, he thought, would be something. "What is it that makes people happy? To contribute!" He couldn't afford the long years of schooling that medicine entailed; he chose the law as the next best thing. "When a guy gets along in his twenties he begins to get uneasy; people stare at themselves, and know that they'll be sore as hell at life at sixty if they don't do something to improve themselves." He asked himself, while a cop on a beat, "Is life just a process of eating and destroying food?" The urge to get ahead stirred him, as he put it, "like a bug on an elephant's tail." And to do something for the little fellow. As a magistrate he had the power to be a tough guy, "to swing a hatchet." When youngsters and old men came into his court he tried to "soothe 'em down." Then suddenly O'Dwyer was talking about what is, as he knows and everybody knows, the dominant problem of our time, the relationship of government to the people. I asked him what he was proudest of in his record as mayor so far. He hesitated. "The guy who follows me will find a million things wrong, of course." Again he paused. "One thing I kinda like—it might be a contribution." This is a system he has worked out for dealing with potential labor troubles before they reach a climax; a body called the division of labor relations goes to work a month before the expiration date of any collective agreement so that, if there is the possibility of a strike, early discussions may avert it.

A word now on the 1945 mayoralty election that brought O'Dwyer in. Of all crazy elections in the history of New York City, this was certainly the craziest. He was the candidate of both the Democratic and American Labor parties, which was interpreted by anti-O'Dwyer folk as meaning that he was the candidate of (*a*) Tammany and (*b*) the Communists, unnatural as this coalition may seem. Of course O'Dwyer is about as Communistic as Saint Peter or Monsignor Sheen. In the old Brooklyn days the Christian Front boys vociferously sided with him for the most part. Nevertheless, he was bracketed with Vito Marcantonio, the industrious leader of the ALP. O'Dwyer, a good vote-getter with a good record, was obviously going to be a hard man to beat. After ponderous deliberations (in which Governor Dewey of course shared) the Republicans chose a judge of the general sessions court, Jonah J. Goldstein, to run against him.[13] This was in part a device to catch the Jewish vote which is roughly 30 per cent of the total city vote as a rule. The only trouble with Judge Goldstein was that he was a Democrat! This fact may not be believed by the man from Mars, but it is true. Judge Goldstein, the Republican candidate to beat O'Dwyer, was a member of the Democratic party until the night before the nomination.[14]

Meantime, of course, much finagling had been going on in higher reaches of the Democratic party too—Roosevelt, Hannegan, Flynn, Kelly, all played a role. O'Dwyer would not consent to run until after a stiff fight with both Kelly and Flynn, who wanted to put people on the slate he wouldn't have. Finally O'Dwyer (Democrat-ALP) and Goldstein (Republican but a Democrat) squared off against one another. Also behind Goldstein were the Fusion and the Liberal parties—which, however, were not at the time parties! All seemed simple. Then entered a new and disruptive factor—the Little Flower. Previously Mr. La Guardia had announced the names of a dozen people who he thought would make good mayors and whom he would support, among them Adolf A. Berle Jr., Lewis W. Douglas, Robert Moses, Gordon S. Rentschler, chairman of the board of the National City Bank, General Brehon Somervell, and Newbold Morris, then president of the City Council. Now Mr. Morris (an able and amiable man, about whom the crude witticism was spread that he had been born with a silver foot in his mouth) decided to enter the race himself. This made the struggle triangular. La Guardia vigorously supported Morris, who ran as a "No Deal" candidate. He knew of course that this would split the opposition, and help elect O'Dwyer; the only explanation is that (though in theory a Republican himself and a mortal foe of Tammany) La Guardia disliked the Dewey-Goldstein brand of Republicanism so much that he was willing to see a Tammany Democrat elected. O'Dwyer would have won anyway. Nevertheless, Morris's candidacy did what Mr. La Guardia hoped it would do, and the New York *Herald Tribune* was soon writing, "The fundamental reason why William O'Dwyer is mayor today is that Mr. La Guardia willed it."[15]

> Tiger Tamed; Wigwam Sublet
> *They have such refined and delicate palates*
> *That they can discover no one worthy of their ballots,*
> *And then when someone terrible gets elected*
> *They say, There, that's just what I expected.*
> —Ogden Nash

> A reformer is a guy who rides through a sewer in a glass-bottomed boat.
> —The late James J. Walker

> Voters of the laboring class in the cities are very emotional ...
> In the lower wards [of New York City] where there is a large vicious population, the condition of politics is often fairly appalling, and the local boss is generally a man of grossly immoral public and private character.
> —Theodore Roosevelt in 1886

Of various puppets and ephemeral riffraff in New York City politics this book tells nothing. Nor have we the space to mention here how proportional representation makes a goulash of elections to the city council, how New York (just like a village) has big red signs near the polls telling people not to loiter, how Fusion is not something that you can call up on the telephone, how the Greater New York City Charter was first set up and how the city has a triple central government the inter-relations of which can only be calculated by a slide rule, how the well-known entrepreneur of slot machines, Mr. Costello, lost $27,200 in a taxi and finally got about $150 back, and how the Liberal party broke off from the American Labor party (the father of which was Mr. La Guardia) after a vicious left-right split.

But about the institution known as Tammany and its camorra we must, if only for the record, have a brief line. Actually Tammany goes back into American history as far as the federal government itself. One of its founders was Aaron Burr, and it was a quite worthy organization in older days. Bob Wagner and Al Smith both came out of Tammany. It was the first classic example of the American political machine, and its role was the orthodox one of being a bridge between the newly arrived immigrant and citizenship. It taught him how to vote and for whom. Also it really rendered service. If Sally Snooks of West 98th Street got measles, the district leader saw to it that she was taken care of. Tammany purveyed help, if not justice. Whether or not the corner cop would let your youngster play under the water hydrant on a hot day depended on Tammany. It could do anything for a man from granting a bus franchise to a suspension of sentence for a serious crime; whether or not you could build a skyscraper—and how cheaply or expensively—or a chicken coop, depended on the Tiger. The Seabury investigation told much about the sale of judgeships. Then, after a long period of satiety and deliquescence, came the crushing blows of fifteen years ago. Judge Seabury demonstrated that it was extremely unwise for politicians to maintain safety deposit boxes with big amounts of cash in New York City. Jimmy Walker resigned rather than be forced out of office by Mr. Roosevelt, and the great days of Tammany were over.

Aside from scandals and witless leadership three major factors have contributed to the collapse of Tammany:

(1) The movement of people out of Manhattan itself into Brooklyn and the Bronx. Tammany is, of course, the Democratic machine in Manhattan only.

(2) Mr. La Guardia, who was beaten by Tammany in 1929, beat it in 1933, 1937, and 1941—which drove it into the wilderness.

(3) Above all, the New Deal. Tammany favors were small stuff compared to public works through the WPA. These latter, moreover, were administered honestly.

Wall Street, the Solar Plexus

I must atone for my wealth.

—Otto Kahn

There was a time, I am told on good authority, when John D. Rockefeller was getting one million dollars a day; and still, I have reason to believe, they buried him in a pair of pants.

—Milton Mayer

A bank is the thing that will always lend you money if you can prove you don't need it.

—Joe E. Lewis

The main thing to say about Wall Street today is that it is not what it once was. Much of the brutal golden power, the sheen, is gone. Consider as typical of a whole great evolution what has happened to the "Corner," i.e., the House of Morgan. J. P. Morgan himself, the Younger, died in 1943, and his will was made public in 1947. After deduction of tax, debts, and expenses, his net estate amounted to the bagatelle of $4,642,791. Nothing could more dramatically illustrate how times have irremediably changed.[16]

About American finance and business in general, monopoly, profits and the like, I hope to write in another place. Here is room only for the briefest highlights on Wall Street itself. The United States is the last stronghold of the capitalist system left in the world. We cannot but inspect its liver and solar plexus.

Wall Street is, strange as it may seem, so called because Peter Stuyvesant, in 1653, built a wall roughly where it lies today. It is a narrow, noisy, trenchlike little chasm, scarcely six hundred yards long. Here, or in the immediate neighbourhood, are banks like Chase ("the most influential bank in the United States"),[17] the National City, and the Guaranty. (Mr. Bell's essay tells much about who owns these banks, for instance of the Giannini holdings in National City, and which are "Morgan banks" and which are not.) Here are potent underwriting houses like Halsey Stuart and Morgan Stanley; here is the Stock Exchange, on which are listed 200 billion dollars' worth of securities and which transacted business worth 15 billion dollars in 1945. But another index of the way things have been going is that in 1929 the price of an Exchange seat was $625,000, and today is about $68,000. At the depth of the depression a seat cost $17,000. Details like these are as familiar to most Americans as the trademark of a brand of cigarettes, but let us point out once more than outlanders may not be so well informed.

In the vivid, fragrant days before 1929 Wall Street was, though disliked and distrusted by many people, an object of profound veneration to the business world. To become a Morgan partner, or even a Kuhn Loeb partner was for most rising young men of the East practically like becoming a cardinal, only more so. The path was well beaten for any really bright and ambitious youngster, and it was often a golden path—St. Paul's or Lawrenceville, Yale or Princeton, and then the Street. Bankers were really looked up to in those days. Now of course they have to spend most of their time explaining themselves. Morgan and Kuhn Loeb had the juiciest parts of the investment business almost without competition, with Morgan concentrating on British and domestic industrial issues mostly, Kuhn Loeb on German and Scandinavian issues and some railroads. Another pregnant point is that in this era bankers played a very definite role in international political affairs. The House of Morgan was like the Board of Trade in England; to all intents and purposes it was a silently functioning agency of the American government itself. A Morgan partner could have much more influence than, say, an assistant secretary of state. Mr. Bell, if I may allude to his essay once more, makes mention of the way Wall Street kept in close touch with Washington, and told it, bluntly if necessary, what it was to do. Now as to the domestic side we must mention railroads in particular. The railway empires of the country were also more or less divided between Kuhn Loeb and Morgan, though other firms in time pushed their way in. The railroads could not promote their massive issues without money, and it was Wall Street which gave them money. Finally—and this is of course still true today—the bankers, through interlocking directorates and otherwise, had germinal influence on the affairs of almost all the great American manufacturing corporations.

Where do the bright youngsters turn today? A good many, if they hope to become millionaires some day by a conservative route, go into law. (Many, not exclusively interested in making money, more interested in making *things* or public policy, go into small businesses or government service, after a period at law.) The great law firms of Wall Street still pick the best brains in the nation.

They have consummate power, ability, and intelligence. Their profits may still be enormous; since the SEC, a great deal more legal work attends financial issues than heretofore.[18] One point to reflect on, though, is their inhospitality to Jews. Many big law firms—and to a certain extent banks—rigidly exclude Jews; even Jewish underlings and clerks are uncommon. In no American milieu is this more conspicuous. For a Jew to get into a good legal firm below Chambers Street is almost as difficult as to get into the Ku-Klux Klan. The upper reaches of the law in Wall Street are the last frigid citadel of Anglo-Saxon Protestantism.

To proceed. In 1930 James W. Gerard, formerly ambassador to Germany, made a national sensation—it will seem very tame now—by listing the sixty-four men who "ruled the United States." He included only one politician (Mellon); he did not include the president, Mr. Hoover. These shoguns, he said, were the real powers behind the throne, too busy to run for office themselves but decisive in determining who did run, and in utter control of the nation's purse strings. Perhaps the list has relevance today:

John D. Rockefeller Jr.
Andrew W. Mellon
J. P. Morgan
George F. Baker, banker
John D. Ryan, copper magnate
Walter C. Teagle, president of Standard Oil of New Jersey
Henry Ford
Frederick E. Weyerhaeuser, lumber
Myron C. Taylor
James A. Farrell, U.S. Steel
Arthur Curtiss James, large holder of railway securities
Charles Hayden, financier
Daniel O. Jackling, president of the Utah Copper Co.
Arthur V. Davis, president of Alcoa
P. M. Gossler, president of the Columbia Gas & Electric Corp.
R. C. Holmes, president of the Texas Corp.
John J. Raskob
Seven members of the Du pont family
Edward J. Berwind, financier
Daniel Willard, Baltimore & Ohio
Sosthenes Behn, IT&T
Walter S. Gifford, AT&T
Owen D. Young, General Electric
Gerard Swope, General Electric
Thomas W. Lamont
Albert H. Wiggin, banker
Charles E. Mitchell, banker
Charles M. Schwab, Bethleham Steel
Eugene G. Grace, Bethlehem Steel
Harry M. Warner, movies
Adolph Zukor, movies
William H. Crocker, San Francisco banker
O. P. and M. J. Van Sweringen, railway magnates

W. W. Atterbury, president of the Pennsylvania R.R.
Samuel Insull
The seven Fisher brothers
Daniel Guggenheim and William Loeb, mining magnates
George Washington Hill, American Tobacco Co.
Adolph S. Ochs
William Randolph Hearst
Robert R. McCormick
Joseph M. Patterson
Julius S. Rosenwald, merchant
Cyrus H. Curtis
Roy W. Howard
Sidney Z. Mitchell, chairman of the board, Electric Bond & Share
Walter Edwin Few, Corn Exchange Bank
A. P. Giannini
William Green and Matthew Woll, labor[19]

What are the main reasons why Wall Street has declined so notably in prestige, authority, and influence? Following are a few. They are not listed chronologically or in order of importance:

(*a*) First, of course, the crash and the depression, which not only obliterated a great proportion of the national wealth, but drastically lowered confidence in bankers.

(*b*) Scandals. It was a severe blow to Wall Street that men like Richard Whitney, a former president of the Stock Exchange, and in a different category Charles E. Mitchell, the president of the National City Bank, no less, went on public trial. Something was wrong. When Whitney first got into trouble people said, "Oh, the Morgans will never let him go to jail." But he went.

(*c*) Income tax. It is, after all, almost insuperably difficult nowadays to accumulate a fortune. It may not be impossible to make big money; to hold on to it is a different matter. What does it profit a man to spend thirty years trying to make money in large amounts, and have his major earnings go to taxes?

(*d*) More pertinent than any of these items so far, the transfer of much of the control of credit from Wall Street to the government. "Freedom to speculate" became severely limited. Moreover the government extended its direct financial power through such agencies as the RFC (created by Mr. Hoover). Many corporations didn't have to go to Wall Street any more. They went to Washington.

(*e*) The growth of corporations themselves. Plenty of companies, especially new companies (like Kaiser) do of course still come to Wall Street for underwriting. But the colossi like AT&T are big enough to be their own bankers for the most part. In the old days a middle western railway could be as dependent on Morgan as a cripple on a crutch. Nowadays even small corporations do their banking locally. Financial power has become much more diffused. Also Ford (a special case of course) financed himself in an emergency through his own dealers.

(*f*) Various regulatory devices, initiated by the New Deal for the public interest. We accept these today, it has been said, almost as automatically as we accept—and welcome—the strictures of the Pure Food and Drug Act. But think back to 1929!

A private bank did not even have to make public its condition. There was no federal regulation whatever of the issue of securities except of certain minor types.

(g) Among specific acts, the Banking Act of 1933, which enforced a separation of banks of deposit from investment banking ("and so took all the gravy out of Wall Street") and the Securities Act of 1934 which set up the SEC. Today—something so obviously correct that it seems barbarous that it did not exist fifteen years ago—every underwriter is under strict legal compulsion to declare in the most minute detail every relevant fact about an impending issue. "It is the underwriters themselves," notes *Life*, "not the corporation, that are legally liable for false or misleading statements in such a prospectus." Every material fact bearing on an issue must be made known.

(*h*) One might also mention the Investment Trust Act and similar acts, regulating the operation of investment trusts and councilors, and forbidding the latter to act as brokers, and also, in another and wider field, the Johnson Act, which cut off loans to foreign nations in default on obligations to the United States.

(*i*) Competitive bidding. Except in isolated cases the railroads and utilities are no longer able to negotiate their financing with banking houses of their own choice. Instead they must offer their securities publicly to the highest bidder. This, as much as anything, has served to upset old banking ties, lower the morale of the Street, and cut profits to the bone.

(*j*) During the hearings of a subcommittee of the United States Senate investigating the banking business and the stock market, a lively press agent managed to put a midget on J. P. Morgan's knee.

Perhaps this last item marked the turning point. With that midget, an impregnability was shattered, a myth was broken, an era ended. The Pecora hearings were the Great Divide, Wall Street has never been quite the same since.

Some testimony by Mr. Morgan and his associates during this astonishing investigation shows nicely what a Divine-Right-of-Kings world we lived in then:

> Q. Should not private banks be examined and forced to publish statements of their condition?
> A. Possibly.
> Q. What assurance has a depositor of the solvency of Morgan & Company?
> A. Faith.
> Q. Are not depositors entitled to statements of Morgan & Company's condition?
> A. They can have them if they want them; no one has ever asked.
> Q. Has any public statement ever been made ... since the Elder Morgan testified before the Pujo committee twenty years ago?
> A. No. That was the only public statement we have ever made about anything.

It was at this hearing, incidentally, that the country learned with a burning incredulous shock that neither Morgan nor any of his great partners, men like George Whitney and Thomas W. Lamont, had paid any income tax during the depression years 1931 and 1932, and that in 1930 their payments had totaled only $48,000. This was, of course, because the partnership had taken advantage of the capital gains and losses provision in income tax regulations. The late

Senator Glass of Virginia snapped in icy disgust, "The fault is with the law." (It should also be noted that few among those outraged by this nonpayment of taxes for two years paid much attention to the fact that from 1917 to 1927 members of the firm had paid taxes of more than 50 million dollars.)

Also in this investigation it became known that the Morgan partners followed the practice of offering certain stocks to a group of selected friends at prices considerably below market, before issuing them. The question was asked, "Was not the offer of such shares at wholesale prices a kind of bribe?" The answer was, "No. The shares were only offered to clients and friends who could afford to take a risk ... regarded as too speculative for the general public."[20] Among Morgan acquaintances–who got Standard Brands at bargain rates–were Calvin Coolidge (3,000 shares), John J. Raskob (2,000), General Pershing (500), Colonel Lindbergh (500), Bernard M. Baruch (4,000), Norman H. Davis (500), Cornelius S. Kelley of Anaconda (2,000), Charles E. Mitchell) 10,000), Alfred P. Sloan (7,500), Clarence H. Mackay (2,000). Similar bargains in Allegheny Corporation stock went to Charles Francis Adams (1,000), Newton D. Baker (2,000), and Owen D. Young (5,000).[21]

Morgan partners in 1933 held 167 directorships in 89 corporations, it was revealed, with aggregate assets of about 20 billion dollars. Among the 89 were 15 banks and trust companies, 7 miscellaneous holding companies, 10 railroads, 5 public utility holding corporations, 8 public utility operating companies, 38 industrial companies and 6 insurance companies. Asked about this, Mr. Morgan himself said that he disliked having his partners serve as directors; they did so "only by the earnest request of companies which wanted them as financial advisers." But, according to *Time*, "The Morgan-First National influence in 1935 was estimated by a National Resources Committee report as still reaching into $30,210,000 worth of U.S. railroads, utilities, industries, banks. Yet some of the proudest Morgan nurslings, like General Electric, had long since outgrown their Morgan link."[22]

Meantime the 1933 Banking Act was passed. "J. P. Morgan & Co.," wrote the New York *Times* in its obituary of Mr. Morgan, "had to choose between its security underwriting business, the leading business of its kind in the world, and its private deposit banking." It decided to remain a private commercial bank, and therefore had to drop its investment business. Morgan's son Henry and two other partners resigned from the parent house to form a new investment firm, totally independent, Morgan Stanley & Company, Inc. Morgan's other son, Junius, stayed on with the parent bank, which was still "the largest private bank in the world."

In 1940 came another bruising and revolutionary stop. The financial writers cried, "*Götterdämmerung!*" What happened was that the Morgan bank decided to incorporate itself. This was as if Carry Nation had done a midnight strip tease at Leon & Eddie's. Morgan no longer a private bank! It applied to the authorities for a charter of incorporation and then moved into the sphere of "government supervision and growing accountability to the public." The *ancien régime* was no more. This was Louis XVI's head bouncing into the cart. "It was understood," wrote the New York *Times*, that "the firm was incorporated because death and inheritance taxes raised difficulties of keeping the bank's capital intact as partners died or withdrew. The firm had deposits of more than $600 million at the time of this change from a purely private bank to a state-chartered institution." Some time after this—another shock to the old-fashioned—J. P. Morgan & Company, Inc., offered stock to the public for the first time, and in 1942 it was admitted to membership in the Federal Reserve system.

Now to conclude. No one should think from the above that Wall Street is powerless these days. By no means! It is still incontestably the most powerful financial center in the world. It still has an influence on America pervasive, tenacious, and articulate. All that has happened is that it can no longer play its game exclusively its own way. it must obey house rules.

As to the place in the national economy of some great corporations not so directly in the Wall Street arc, though most are based in or near New York, the most interesting presentation I have seen is that in a pamphlet prepared by Senator O'Mahoney's Temporary National Economic Committee. Some of this material also appeared in the *Congressional Record.*[23] There were, as of that date, forty-one American corporations with total assets of a billion dollars or more. In the year preceding there had been thirty-eight; in 1941, thirty-two. There are, of course, other and perhaps better ways of measuring the size of a corporation than by its assets. But considered strictly from the point of view of assets, the biggest—and the largest enterprise in the United States—is the Metropolitan Life Insurance Company, with almost six and a half billion dollars in assets; next comes Bell Telephone, with more than six billion; next comes the Prudential Insurance Company with more than five. A fingerful of banks are runners-up, with more than three and a half billion each; then come two more insurance companies, with more than three billion. The first railway on the list is the Pennsylvania, with assets of $2,800,000,000 plus. The first industrial corporation is Standard Oil of New Jersey, with $2,300,000,000 plus. General Motors is thirteenth on the list; U.S. Steel fourteenth; the New York Central fifteenth; the Santa Fe twenty-third; the Union Pacific twenty-fifth; Consolidated Edison twenty-seventh; Du Pont thirty-eighth; and Ford forty-first. Senate statisticians made much play with this list. They showed, for instance, that only six American states (New York, Pennsylvania, Ohio, California, Michigan, Massachusetts) have a total assessed valuation of property greater than the assets of Metropolitan Life. Both AT&T and the Prudential Insurance Company have greater assets than all but thirteen states. Assets of Chase National run nip and tuck with those of Kentucky, and Standard Oil (New Jersey) is richer than Virginia. The Northwestern Mutual Life Insurance Company of Milwaukee has assets almost equivalent to those of the state of Georgia; similarly the Chemical Bank & Trust Company of New York runs neck and neck with Florida; the Baltimore & Ohio Railway with Washington; and Commonwealth & Southern with Colorado. As of 1942 there were thirty-two American corporations with considerably greater wealth than eighteen states. Mr.

Berle, the former American ambassador to Brazil and assistant secretary of state, said once that two hundred companies owned half the wealth of the United States. Probably he was not far wrong.[24]

What happened to Wall Street and the nation during 1946 is hardly part of our story here. The long bull market finally collapsed. Pages might be written about the reasons for this. One striking fact is that the market did not climb, but actually sagged, after the Republican victory in 1946. What will happen next? This country has at hand at least some of the techniques that might prevent a new crash or a new depression. It remains to be seen, however, if it will use them. Plenty of people still hate the idea of government controls so much that they would rather ruin themselves—and everybody else to boot—than make use of them.

The Harlems

> Harlem has a black belt where darkies dwell in a heaven and where white men seek a little hell.
>
> —Alfred Kreymborg

There are several. One is Puerto Rican, one Haitian, and another, verging into what might be called the Marcantonio territory on the east side, Italian. I drove through this area before the 1946 election; loud speakers brought campaign speeches—in warm whole-toned Italian—out into the dreary, chilly streets. (It was in this neighborhood that a Republican election official, Joseph Scottoriggio, was killed in mysterious circumstances.) Also there are Russians in Harlem, Spaniards, Mexicans, a considerable salting of Chinese, some Japanese Nisei who do not want to return to California, and, of all things, the largest Finnish community in the United States. Take the Benjamin Franklin High School on the East River Drive. It may be doubted if any school in the country has such a bizarrely commingled student body.

Next to the Negroes, the biggest group in Harlem is that from Puerto Rico, which numbers about 100,000. Negroes and Puerto Ricans get on well together by and large. One Puerto Rican told me that this was natural because his people want to get Americanized as quickly as possible, and the Negroes represent Anglo-Saxon culture! Another item in this general field is probably apocryphal. Harlem had a small angry upsurge in 1943 which, but for instant sharp work by Mr. La Guardia and the police, might have become a serious riot. The Negro community seemed to feel so secure and confident of adequate protection, however, that a Chinese laundryman is supposed to have hung a sign on his shop, *Me Colored Too!* Still another point in Harlem mixedupness is the fact that a well-known small community exists of Negro Jews.

Though not necessarily the biggest, Harlem is by all odds the most important concentration of Negroes in America. Roughly from 110th Street to 155th on the east side, and from Madison Avenue to St. Nicholas, live some 310,000 Negroes. This is more than the population of whole cities like Atlanta, Dallas, or Portland, Oregon. Yet Harlem holds only about half the total number of Negroes (600,000) in New York City as a whole; there are approximately 150,000 in Brooklyn, about 30,000 in the Bronx, and about 30,000 in Queens. Years ago New York Negroes lived in a few scattered and isolated enclaves: Minetta Lane in Greenwich Village, "San Juan Hill" on West 63rd Street near the river, and some areas in German Yorkville (especially on East 88th near Third). Now, as everybody knows, they have spread all over the city. Harlem itself is expanding all the time. It has no fixed frontiers.

Since "Harlem" has become a kind of abstraction (like "Hollywood"), it is extremely difficult to describe. The easiest thing to say is that it is a profoundly complex cross section of the whole of New York in black miniature. People are tempted to think of Harlem as exclusively a slum; it is also talked about as if it were a cave full of night clubs. Many Harlemites have of course never seen a night club. Some parts of it are indeed slums, and one block, near Lenox and 143rd Street, is commonly said to be the most crowded in the world. A recent commissioner of housing and building visited a sixty-four-year-old tenement in the neighborhood of Fifth and 117th not long ago, and found it "infested, scaly, shabby," a menace to health, a disgrace otherwise, and a fire trap. Rats were so much in evidence that the remark was reported, "They not only come here to eat, but I think they cook their own food, too."

But Harlem as a whole is by no means a slum. This is not the Bowery. A good many apartment blocks, built long before the district became Negro, are still in good shape; the trouble is that they are viciously overcrowded and badly maintained. For instance there will be only one superintendent for six buildings, jammed with sublet flats, and containing literally hundreds of families. Also Harlem has several handsome, modern, and well-maintained apartment buildings. One, at 409 Edgecombe, is in the area known locally as "Sugar Hill"; here lives, as I heard it put, "the glamor set of Black America."[25] But this description makes Sugar Hill sound frivolous, which it is not. A great number of eminent Negroes live there—Walter White, the competent discerning secretary of the National Association for the Advancement of Colored People, Municipal Judge Charles E. Toney, Roy Wilkins the editor of Crisis, one of the best-known Negro lawyers in the country Thurgood Marshall, William T. Andrews who is one of the senior members of the state assembly, and W. E. B. Du Bois. The rents on Sugar Hill are perhaps $85.00 a month, for something very much like apartments on Park Avenue, and which on Park Avenue would cost $300.

I went up to Harlem with two Negro friends a few evenings ago, and tried to learn a little. It is a community constantly in motion. Like New Rochelle, it is a kind of bedroom for the rest of New York; people live here, and work downtown. It has several Negro newspapers, including the conservative *Amsterdam News* and the radical *People's Voice*. There is no Negro department store; most of the shopkeepers on the main street (125th) are Jews. Almost all real estate is white absentee owned, though one Negro businessman, A. A. Austin, is a substantial owner; there is no Negro bank (but local branches of the great white banks employ Negro personnel); about seventy-five saloons and one movie house are Negro owned, but no more; the chief hotel is a remarkable establishment called the Theresa, almost exclusively Negro, but it is white owned, and several whites live in it. The chief Negro business in Harlem on a broad level is insurance (unless you want to count religion as a business), and on a narrower level hairdressing.

The whole community is, of course, strongly labor conscious. At least 50,000 Negroes in New York City are members of unions, including laundry workers, garment workers, hod carriers, longshoremen, painters, maritime workers, and members of the United Office and Professional Workers, CIO. Probably some single streets in Harlem have more Negro trade unionists than the entire state of Georgia. In New York as a whole there is probably less discrimination against Negroes, in employment and otherwise, than in any other city in America. In fact many familiar forms of anti-Negro discriminations, illegal or not, do continue to exist.

Harlem has no single political boss, any more than New York City itself has a single boss. You can find every shade of opinion on any question. Some Harlemites are "handkerchief-heads"; some frankly call themselves "antiwhite." Once the community had a picturesque creature, Abdul Hamid Sufi, who was called the Black Hitler, and who, despite this name, operated a "Temple of Peace and Tranquillity." There are extremely conservative Negroes, like Dr. Clilan B. Powell, editor of the *Amsterdam News*, a member of the State Boxing Commission, and assistant publicity director of the Republican National Commission, and there are equally some extreme radicals, as well as many who defy classification. The president of the New York City Civil Service Commission, Ferdinand Q. Morton, is a Negro, and so is a member of the state Committee Against Discrimination set up by the Ives Bill, Elmer Carter (who also lives on Sugar Hill incidentally). The only Communist on the New York City council is a competent and accomplished Negro, Benjamin J. Davis Jr. Also Davis, who played football at Williams and is a graduate of the Harvard Law School, is publisher of the *Daily Worker*. His father interestingly enough, an Atlanta publisher, is an important Republican politician. In a recent council manic election, under proportional representation, Davis's vote was only topped by that of Stanley M. Isaacs, an able Republican who has been entrenched in New York politics for many years.

On a street corner near the Theresa we listened to a campaign speech by Congressman Adam Clayton Powell Jr.[26] Many Negroes dislike Powell, and call him a spellbinder. He has a blistering hot voice; he never pauses a second between sentences; he gestures like a piston. This evening, with his words reverberating up and down the street, he denied with ringing animosity that his wife, Hazel Scott, a well-known Negro pianist, was white (as some silly people had alleged); he excused some absences from Congress by saying that, after all, his constituents ought not mind that he had taken a brief honeymoon—how the crowd roared!—and, anyway, his mother was very ill. "Any Negro born of a Negro," Powell cried out, "must be a Negro, must be a radical, must be a fighter, all the time!" Powell has fire and courage. By profession he is a preacher, as was his father before him. His Abyssinian Baptist church has, in fact, what is believed to be the largest

Protestant congregation in the world, numbering at least ten thousand. Like almost all Negroes running for office in 1946, Powell was vulnerable on the score that the Democratic party was also the party of Mr. Bilbo, an embarrassing paradox indeed. But he squeezed through, and is now serving his second term in the House of Representatives. He was the first Negro councilman in New York City, and is one of two Negroes in the Congress.

To sum up: the chief characteristic of Harlem is that, by and large, its Negroes (and others in New York) have greater opportunities in more fields than in any comparable city; they have better chances in education, jobs, social evolution, and civil service; they are the nearest to full citizenship of any in the nation.

New York Olla Podrida

New York City has more trees (2,400,000) than houses, and it makes 18,200,000 telephone calls a day, of which about 125,000 are wrong numbers. Its rate of divorces is the lowest of any big American city, less than a tenth of that of Baltimore for instance, and even less than that in the surrounding countryside. One of its hotels, built largely over railway tracks, has an assessed valuation of $22,500,00 (there are 124 buildings valued at more than a million dollars in Manhattan alone), and it is probably the only city in the world that still maintains sheriff's juries and has five district attorneys.

New York City has such admirable institutions as the New School for Social Research, the Council on Foreign Relations, Cooper Union, the Museum of Modern Art, and the Century Association. It has 17 billion dollars' worth of real estate, and a black market in illegitimate babies. It has 492 playgrounds, more than 11,000 restaurants, 2,800 churches, and the largest store in the world, Macy's, which wrote 40,328,836 sales checks in 1944, and serves more than 150,000 customers a day. It has the Great White Way, bad manners, 33,000 schoolteachers (average pay $3,803), and 500 boy gangs.

New York makes three-quarters of all the fur coats in the country, and its slang and mode of speech can change hour by hour. It has New York University, a wholly private institution which is the second largest university in the country, 13,800 Jews in its student body, 12,000 Protestants, and 7,200 Catholics, and a great municipal institution, the City College of the College of the City of New York, one of four famous city colleges. In New York people drink 14 million gallons of hard liquor a year, and smoke about 20 billion cigarettes. It has 301,850 dogs, and one of its unsolved murders is the political assassination of Carlo Tresca.

New York has 9,371 taxis and more than 700 parks. Its budget runs to $175,000,000 for education alone, and it drinks 3,500,000 quarts of milk a day. The average New York family (in normal times) moves once every eighteen months, and more than 2,200,000 New Yorkers belong to the Associated Hospital Service. New York has a birth every five minutes, and a marriage every seven. It has "more Norwegian-born citizens than Tromsoe and Narvik put together," and only one railroad, the New York Central, has the perpetual right to enter it by land. It has 22,000 soda fountains, and 112 tons of soot fall per square mile every month, which is why your face is dirty.

Notes

1. "New York is a bigger summer resort than Atlantic City and a bigger winter resort than Miami." Simeon Strunsky, *No Mean City*, p. 52.

2. David Sarnoff, one of the most enlightened capitalists in the United States and president of the Radio Corporation of America, was also born in Minsk.

3. New York *Herald Tribune*, June 21, 1945, quoting *A Survey of the New York Market* published by the Consolidated Edison Company.

4. A *New Yorker* cartoon of the time presented two girls sweating at their sewing machines. One says to the other, "Now what's my cue line after your song in Act II?"

5. Four subdivisions of New York City are, it will be seen, greater in population than any American cities except Chicago, Philadelphia, Detroit, and Los Angeles.

6. Article by Murray Schumach, January 19, 1947.

7. *New York City*, in the American Guide Series, Random House, p. 410.

8. These figures and details are all from the New York *Times*, September 30, 1945, and February 10, 1946. A remarkable point is the safety record of the New York elevators. The ratio is one person killed to 196,000,000 carried.

9. These phrases are from a brilliant essay on New York by Vincent McHugh. It was originally published in the New York City volume of the WPA series, and was later reprinted by Clifton Fadiman in his anthology, *Reading I've Liked*.

10. Strunsky, *op. cit.*

11. Another item is that the average Englishman will find offensive the American habit of spitting on the floor, but that the Americans are now keenly alive to this "weak point" and are "doing their best" to remove it.

12. Two of his brothers, who also emigrated to America, met violent deaths; one, John, was killed by gunmen in a Brooklyn holdup some years ago; another, James, a New York City fireman, lost his life while answering a false alarm.

13. Not to be confused with Attorney General Goldstein mentioned in the last chapter.

14. *Time*, September 24, 1945.

15. A minor but illuminating item is the way the New York newspapers lined up during this campaign. The *Times* backed Morris; so did the *Post*. *PM* supported O'Dwyer until a day or two before the election, and then switched to Morris. The Brooklyn *Eagle* supported O'Dwyer and so did the *Daily Worker*. Supporting Goldstein were the *Herald Tribune* and the *Sun*. What line the *News*, *Mirror*, *World-Telegram*, and *Journal-American* took was difficult to figure out.

16. The best single thing on Wall Street in short space I have ever read is an essay by Elliot V. Bell in an anthology called *We Saw It Happen*. Mr. Bell was a financial reporter for the New York *Times* when he wrote it. He is now a leading member of Governor Dewey's brain trust and the head of the New York State Banking Department.

17. See *Life* in a useful pictorial essay, January 7, 1946.

18. *Life op. cit.*, says that the charge for preparing a prospectus may be $100,000.

19. It is not uninteresting that while making out this list, Mr. Gerard was the guest of General Cornelius Vanderbilt at Newport, Rhode Island. One singular point is that none of the great insurance companies are represented.

20. One of Morgan's own statements about this was the following: "Our lists of private subscribers naturally were composed of men of affairs and position; but they were selected because of established business and personal relations and not because of any actual or potential political relations. We never had any occasion to ask favors from legislators or persons in public office, nor have we ever done so." From the obituary of Mr. Morgan in the New York *Times*, March 4, 1943.

21. This list has been printed often. Here I am following *Time*, June 5, 1933.

22. February 26, 1940.

23. February 12, 1945.

24. As to concentration of ownership the *New Republic* states (September 2, 1946) that of the two

hundred largest nonfinancial corporations in the country, 6 per cent of the common stock is owned by the upper 1 per cent of registered stockholders. Three family groups—Du Ponts, Mellons and Rockefellers—still control fifteen of these two hundred biggest corporations, with assets of eight billion dollars. In 1935 nearly a third of the directorships of the two hundred largest nonfinancial corporations and the fifty largest financial corporations were held by only four hundred men.

25. For much detail on this and similar matters see Roi Ottley's *New World A-Coming.*

26. No relation to the Powell named above, I believe.

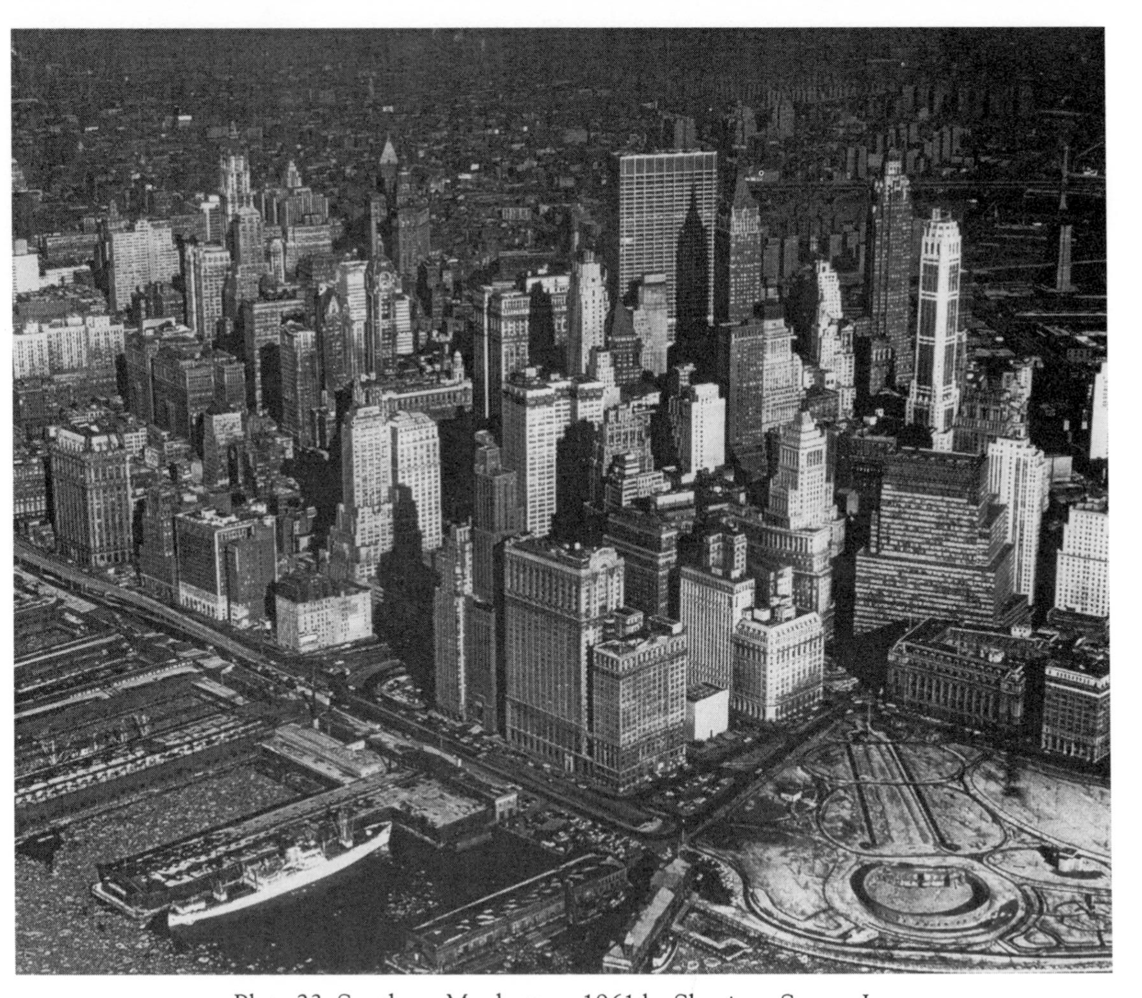

Plate 23: Southern Manhattan, 1961 by Skyviews Survey Inc.

Plate 24: The Rockefeller Center, New York City, 1930s

106

New York, A Vertical but Incomplete City

LE CORBUSIER

Le Courbusier (Charles Edouard Jeanneret; 1887–1965) was a Swiss architect and artist. A major influence on design in the twentieth century, his work is characterised by what was termed "functionalism", although it is equally associated with "brutalism". An overtly "modern" style, both in design, concept and materials (he was an advocate of ferroconcrete), his work made its central mark in France. In many senses, New York (as Manhattan) *was* his city.

New York is a vertical city, under the sign of the new times. It is a catastrophe with which a too hasty destiny has overwhelmed courageous and confident people, though a beautiful and worthy catastrophe. Nothing is lost. Faced with difficulties, New York falters. Still streaming with sweat from its exertions, wiping off its forehead, it sees what it has done and suddenly realizes: "Well, we didn't get it done properly. Let's start over again!" New York has such courage and enthusiasm that everything can be begun again, sent back to the building yard and made into something still greater, something mastered! These people are not on the point of going to sleep. In reality, the city is hardly more than twenty years old, that is the city which I am talking about, the city which is vertical and on the scale of the new times. ...

It is the first time that men have projected all their strength and labor into the sky—a whole city in the free air of the sky. Good God, what disorder, what impetuosity! What perfection already, what promises! What unity in a molecular state, gridiron street plan, office on top of office, clear crystallization. It is sublime and atrocious, and nothing succeeds any longer. There is nothing to do except to see clearly, think, conceive, begin over again. Of course New York is ready to begin over again. Those people have courage!

Source: Le Corbusier, from "New York, A Vertical but Incomplete City", *When the Cathedrals Were White*, 1947, New York, Trans. T. E. Hyslop.

That afternoon I had gone through the Holland Tunnel to the other side of the Hudson and over the Skyway, an elevated road so named because it rises on piles or arches high above industrial areas, arms of the sea, railways and roads, over an immense expanse. A road without art because no thought was given to it, but a wonderful tool. The "Skyway" rises up over the plain and leads to the "skyscrapers." Coming from the flat meadows of New Jersey, suddenly it reveals the City of the Incredible Towers....

107

Here is New York

E. B. WHITE

Elwyn Brooks White (1899–1985) is best known as a humorist writer and critic. His forte was as an essayist and he was especially associated with the *New Yorker* magazine. *Here is New York* is very much in the spirit of the *New Yorker*—a celebration of the city in relation to its variety and sense of difference from other urban habitats. See *The Wild Flag* (1946) and *The Points of My Compass* (1962).

A look into the soul
of an international capital

On any person who desires such queer prizes, New York will bestow the gift of loneliness and the gift of privacy. It is this largess that accounts for the presence within the city's walls of a considerable section of the population; for the residents of Manhattan are to a large extent strangers who have pulled up stakes somewhere and come to town, seeking sanctuary or fulfillment or some greater or lesser grail. The capacity to make such dubious gifts is a mysterious quality of New York. It can destroy an individual, or it can fulfill him, depending a good deal on luck. No one should come to New York to live unless he is willing to be lucky.

New York is the concentrate of art and commerce and sport and religion and entertainment and finance, bringing to a single compact area the gladiator, the evangelist, the promoter, the actor, the trader, and the merchant. It carries on its lapel the unexpungeable odor of the long past, so that no matter where you sit in New York you feel the vibrations of great times and tall deeds, of queer people and events and undertakings. I am sitting at the moment in a stifling hotel room in 90-degree heat, halfway down an air shaft, in mid-town. No air moves in or out of the room, yet I am curiously affected by emanations from the immediate surroundings. I am twenty-two blocks from where Rudolph Valentino lay in state, eight blocks from where Nathan Hale was executed, five blocks from the publisher's office

Source: E. B. White "Here is New York", *Perspectives*, No 4, Summer, 1953.

where Ernest Hemingway hit Max Eastman on the nose, four miles from where Walt Whitman sat sweating out editorials for the *Brooklyn Eagle*, thirty-four blocks from the street Willa Cather lived in when she came to New York to write books about Nebraska, one block from where Marceline used to clown on the boards of the Hippodrome, thirty-six blocks from the spot where the historian Joe Gould kicked a radio to pieces in full view of the public, thirteen blocks from where Harry Thaw shot Stanford White, five blocks from where I used to usher at the Metropolitan Opera, and only a hundred and twelve blocks from the spot where Clarence Day the Elder[1] was washed of his sins in the Church of the Epiphany (I could continue this list indefinitely); and for that matter I am probably occupying the very room that any number of exalted and some wise memorable characters sat in, some of them on hot, breathless afternoons, lonely and private and full of their own sense of emanations from without.

When I went down to lunch a few minutes ago I noticed that the man sitting next to me (about eighteen inches away along the wall) was Fred Stone, the actor. The eighteen inches were both the connection and the separation that New York provides for its inhabitants. My only connection with Fred Stone was that I saw him in *The Wizard of Oz*[2] around the beginning of the century. But our waiter felt the same stimulus from being close to a man from Oz, and after Mr. Stone left the room the waiter told me that when he (the waiter) was a young man just arrived in this country and before he could understand a world of English, he had taken his girl for their first theater date to *The Wizard of Oz*. It was a wonderful show, the waiter recalled—a man of straw, a man of tin. Wonderful! (And still only eighteen inches away.) "Mr. Stone is a very hearty eater," said the waiter thoughtfully, content with this fragile participation in destiny, this link with Oz.

New York blends the gift of privacy with the excitement of participation; and better than most dense communities it succeeds in insulating the individual (if he wants it, and almost everybody wants or needs it) against all enormous and violent and wonderful events that are taking place every minute. Since I have been sitting in this miasmic air shaft, a good many rather splashy events have occurred in town. A man shot and killed his wife in a fit of jealousy. It caused no stir outside his block and got only small mention in the papers. I did not attend. Since my arrival, the greatest air show ever staged in all the world took place in town. I didn't attend and neither did most of the eight million other inhabitants, although they say there was quite a crowd. I didn't even hear any planes except a couple of west-bound commercial airliners that habitually use this air shaft to fly over. The biggest ocean-going ships on the North Atlantic arrived and departed. I didn't notice them and neither did most other New Yorkers. I am told this is the greatest seaport in the world, with six hundred and fifty miles of water front, and ships calling here from many exotic lands, but the only boat I've happened to notice since my arrival was a small sloop tacking out of the East River night before last on the ebb tide when I was walking across the Brooklyn Bridge. I heard the liner *Queen Mary* blow one midnight, though, and the sound carried the whole history of departure and longing and loss. The Lions[3] have been in convention. I've seen not one Lion. A friend of mine saw one and told me about him. (He was lame, and was wearing a bolero.) At the ballgrounds and horse parks the greatest sporting spectacles have been enacted. I saw no ball-players, no race horse. The governor came to town. I heard the siren scream of his motorcycle police escort, but that was all there was to that—an eighteen-inch margin again. A man was killed by a falling cornice. I was not a party to the tragedy, and again the inches counted heavily.

I mention these merely to show that New York is peculiarly constructed to absorb almost anything that comes along (whether a thousand-foot liner out of the East or a twenty-thousand-man convention out of the West) without inflicting the event on its inhabitants; so that every event is, in a sense, optional, and the inhabitant is in the happy position of being able to choose his spectacle and so conserve his soul. In most metropolises, small and large, the choice is often not with the individual at all. He is thrown to the Lions. The Lions are overwhelming; the event is unavoidable. A cornice falls, and it hits every citizen on the head, every last man in town. I sometimes think that the only event that hits every New Yorker on the head is the annual St. Patrick's Day parade, which is fairly penetrating—the Irish are a hard race to tune out, there are 500,000 of them in residence, and they have the police force right in the family.

The quality in New York that insulates its inhabitants from life may simple weaken them as individuals. Perhaps it is healthier to live in a community where, when a cornice falls, you feel the blow; where, when the governor passes, you see at any rate his hat.

I am not defending New York in this regard. Many of its settlers are probably here merely to escape, not face, reality. But whatever it means, it is a rather rare gift, and I believe it has a positive effect on the creative capacities of New Yorkers—for creation is in part merely the business of forgoing the great and small distractions.

Although New York often imparts a feeling of great forlornness or forsakenness, it seldom seems dead or unresourceful; and you always feel that either by shifting your location ten blocks or by reducing your fortune by five dollars you can experience rejuvenation. Many people who have no real independence of spirit depend on the city's tremendous variety and sources of excitement for spiritual sustenance and maintenance of morale. In the country there are a few chances of sudden rejuvenation—a shift in weather, perhaps, or something arriving in the mail. But in New York the chances are endless. I think that although many persons are here from some excess of spirit (which caused them to break away from their small town), some, too, are here from a deficiency of spirit, who find in New York a protection, or an easy substitution.

There are roughly three New Yorks. There is first, the New York of the man or woman who was born here, who takes the city for granted and accepts its size and its turbulence as natural and inevitable. Second, there is the New York of the commuter—the city that is devoured by locusts each day and spat out each night. Third, there is the New York of the person who was born somewhere else and came to New York in quest of something. Of these three trembling cities the greatest is the last—the city of final destination, the city that is a goal. It is this third city that accounts for New York's high-strung disposition, its poetical deportment, its dedication to the arts, and its incomparable achievements. Commuters give the city its tidal restlessness; natives give it solidity and continuity; but the settlers give it passion. And whether it is a farmer arriving from Italy to set up a small grocery store in a slum, or a young girl arriving from a small town in Mississippi to escape the indignity of being observed by here neighbors, or a boy arriving from the Corn Belt with a manuscript in his suitcase and a pain in his heart, it makes no difference: each embraces New York with the intense excitement of first love, each absorbs New York with the fresh eyes of an adventurer, each generates heat and light to dwarf the Consolidated Edison Company.[4]

The commuter is the queerest bird of all. The suburb he inhabits has no essential vitality of its own and is a mere roost where he comes at day's end to go to sleep. Except in rare cases, the man who lives in Mamaroneck or Little Neck or Teaneck, and works in New York, discovers nothing much about the city except the time of arrival and departure of trains and buses, and the path to a quick lunch. He is desk-bound, and has never, idly roaming in the gloaming, stumbled suddenly on Belvedere Tower in the Park, seen the ramparts rise sheer from the water of the pond, and the boys along the shore fishing for minnows, girls stretched out negligently on the shelves of the rocks; he has never come suddenly on anything at all in new York as a loiterer, because he has had no time between trains. He has fished in Manhattan's wallet and dug out coins, but has never listened to Manhattan's breathing, never awakened to its morning, never dropped off to sleep in its night. About 400,000 men and women come charging onto the Island each week-day morning, out of the mouths of tubes and tunnels. Not many among them have ever spent a drowsy afternoon in the great rustling oaken silence of the reading room of the Public Library, with the book elevator (like an old water wheel) spewing out books onto the trays. They tend their furnaces in Westchester and in Jersey, but have never seen the furnaces of the Bowery, the fires that burn in oil drums on zero winter nights. They may work in the financial district downtown and never see the extravagant plantings of Rockefeller Center—the daffodils and grape hyacinths and birches and the flags trimmed to the wind on a fine morning in spring. Or they may work in a midtown office and may let a whole year swing round without sighting Governors Island from the sea wall. The commuter dies with tremendous mileage to his credit, but he is no rover. His entrances and exits are more devious than those in a prairie-dog village; and he calmly plays bridge while his train is buried in the mud at the bottom of the East River. The Long Island Rail Road alone carried forty million commuters last year; but many of them were the same fellow retracing his steps.

The terrain of New York is such that a resident sometimes travels farther, in the end, than a commuter. The journey of the composer Irving Berlin from Cherry Street in the lower East Side to an apartment uptown was through an alley and was only three or four miles in length; but it was like going three times around the world.

A poem compresses much in a small space and adds music, thus heightening its meaning. The city is like poetry: it compresses all life, all races and breeds, into a small island and adds music and the accompaniment of internal engines. The island of Manhattan is without any doubt the greatest human concentrate on earth, the poem whose magic is comprehensible to millions of permanent residents but whose full meaning will always remain illusive. At the feet of the tallest and plushiest offices lie the crummiest slums. The genteel mysteries housed in the Riverside Church are only a few blocks from the voodoo charms of Harlem. The merchant princes, riding to Wall Street in their limousines down the East River Drive, pass within a few hundred yards of the gypsy kings; but the princes do not know they are passing kings, and the kings are not up yet anyway—they live a more leisurely life than the princes and get drunk more consistently.

New York is nothing like Paris; it is nothing like London; and it is not Spokane multiplied by sixty, or Detroit multiplied by four. It is by all odds the loftiest of cities. It even managed to reach the highest point in the sky at the lowest moment of the depression. The Empire State Building shot twelve hundred and fifty feet into the air when it was madness to put out as much as six inches of new growth. (The building has a mooring mast that no dirigible has ever tied to; it employs a man to flush toilets in slack times; it has been hit by an airplane in a fog, struck countless times by lighting, and been jumped off of by so many unhappy people that pedestrians instinctively quicken step when passing Fifth Avenue and 34th Street.)

Manhattan has been compelled to expand skyward because of the absence of any other direction in which to grow. This, more than any other thing, is responsible for its physical majesty. It is to the nation what the white church spire is to the village—the visible symbol of aspiration and faith, the white plume saying that the way is up. The summer traveler swings in over Hell Gate Bridge and from the window of his sleeping car as it glides above the pigeon lofts and back yards of Queens looks southwest to where the morning light first strikes the steel peaks of mid-town, and he sees its upward thrust unmistakable: the great walls and towers rising, the smoke rising, the heat not yet rising, the hopes and ferments of so many awakening millions rising—this vigorous spear that presses heaven hard.

It is a miracle that New York works at all. The whole thing is implausible. Every time the residents brush their teeth, millions of gallons of water must be drawn from the Catskill mountains and the hills of Westchester. When a young man in Manhattan writes a letter to his girl in Brooklyn, the love message gets blown to her through a pneumatic tube—*pfft*—just like that. The subterranean system of telephone cables, power lines, stream pipes, gas mains, and sewer pipes is reason enough to abandon the island to the gods and the weevils. Every time an incision is made in the pavement, the noisy surgeons expose ganglia that are tangled beyond belief. By rights New York should have destroyed itself long ago, from panic or fire or rioting or failure of some vital supply line in its circulatory system or from some deep labyrinthine short circuit. Long ago the city should have experienced an insoluble traffic snarl at some impossible bottleneck. It should have been wiped out by a plague staring in its slums or carried in by ships' rats. It should have been overwhelmed by the sea that licks at it on every side. The workers in its myriad cells should have succumbed to nerves, from the fearful pail of smoke-fog that drifts over every few days from Jersey, blotting out all light at noon and leaving the high offices suspended, men groping and depressed, and the sense of world's end. It should have been touched in the head by the August heat and gone off its rocker.

Mass hysteria is a terrible force, yet New Yorkers seem always to escape it by some tiny margin: they sit in stalled subways without claustrophobia, they extricate themselves from panic situations by some lucky wisecrack, they meet confusion and congestion with patience and grit—a sort of perpetual muddling through. Every facility is inadequate—the hospitals and schools and playgrounds are overcrowded, the express highways are feverish, the unimproved highways and bridges are bottlenecks; there is not enough air and not enough light, and there is usually either too much heat or too little. But the cry makes up for its hazards and its deficiencies by supplying its citizens with massive doses of a supplementary vitamin—the sense of belonging to something unique, cosmopolitan, mighty, and unparalleled.

To an outlander a stay in New York can be and often is a series of small embarrassments and discomforts and disappointments: not understanding the waiter, not being able to distinguish between a sucker joint and a friendly saloon, riding the wrong subway, being slapped down by a bus driver for asking an innocent question, enduring sleepless nights when the street noises fill the bedroom. Tourists make for New York, particularly in summertime—they swarm all over the Statue of Liberty (where many a resident of the town has never set foot), they invade the Automat,[5] visit radio studios, St. Patrick's Cathedral, and they window shop. Mostly they have a pretty good time. But sometimes in New York you run across the disillusioned—a young couple who are obviously visitors, newlyweds perhaps, for whom the bright dream has vanished. The place has been too much for them; they sit languishing in a cheap restaurant over a speechless meal.

The oft-quoted thumbnail sketch of New York is, of course: "It's a wonderful place, but I'd hate to live there." I have an idea that people from villages and small towns, people accustomed to the convenience and the friendliness of neighborhood over-the-fence living, are unaware that life in New York follows the neighborhood pattern. The city is literally a composite of tens of thousands of tiny neighborhood units. There are, of course, the big districts and big units: Chelsea and Murray Hill and Gramercy (which are residential units), Harlem (a racial unit), Greenwich Village (a unit dedicated to the arts and other matters), and there is Radio City (a commercial development), Peter Cooper Village (a housing unit), the Medical

Center (a sickness unit) and many other sections each of which has some distinguishing characteristic. But the curious thing about New York is that each large geographical unit is composed of countless small neighborhoods. Each neighborhood is virtually self-sufficient. Usually it is no more than two or three blocks long and a couple of blocks wide. Each area is a city within a city within a city. Thus, no matter where you live in New York, you will find within a block or two a grocery store, a barbershop, a newsstand and shoeshine shack, an ice-coal-and-wood cellar (where you write your order on a pad outside as you walk by), a dry cleaner, a laundry, a delicatessen (beer and sandwiches delivered at any hour to your door), a flower shop, an undertaker's parlor, a movie house, a radio-repair shop, a stationer, a haberdasher, a tailor, a drugstore, a garage,, a tearoom, a saloon, a hardware store, a liquor store, a shoe-repair shop. Every block or two, in most residential sections of New York, is a little main street. A man starts for work in the morning and before he has gone two hundred yards he has completed half a dozen missions: bought a paper, left a pair of shoes to be soled, picked up a pack of cigarettes, ordered a bottle of whisky to be dispatched in the opposite direction against his home-coming, written a message to the unseen forces of the wood cellar, and notified the dry cleaner that a pair of trousers awaits call. Homeward bound eight hours later, he buys a bunch of pussy willows, a Mazda bulb, a drink, a shine—all between the corner where he stops off the bus and his apartment. So complete is each neighborhood, and so strong the sense of neighborhood, that many a New Yorker spends a lifetime within the confines of an area smaller than a country village. Let him walk two blocks from his corner and he is in a strange land and will feel uneasy till he gets back.

Storekeepers are particularly conscious of neighborhood boundary lines. A woman friend of mine moved recently from one apartment to another, a distance of three blocks. When she turned up, the day after the move, at the same grocer's that she had patronized for years, the proprietor was in ecstasy—almost in tears—at seeing her. "I was afraid," he said, "now that you've moved away I wouldn't be seeing you any more." To him *away* was three blocks, or about seven hundred and fifty feet.

I am, at the moment of writing this, living not as a neighborhood man in New York but as a transient, or vagrant, in from the country for a few days. Summertime is a good time to re-examine New York and to receive again the gift of privacy, the jewel of loneliness. In summer the city contains (except for tourists) only die-hards and authentic characters. No casual, spotty dwellers are around, only the real article. And the town has a somewhat relaxed air, and one can lie in a loincloth, gasping and remembering things.

I've been remembering what it felt like as a young man to live in the same town with giants. When I first arrived in New York my personal giants were a dozen or so columnists and critics and poets whose names appeared regularly in the papers. I burned with a low steady fever just because I was on the same island with Don Marquis, Heywood Broun, Christopher Morley, Franklin P. Adams, Robert C. Benchley, Frank Sullivan, Dorothy Parker, Alexander Woollcott, Ring Lardner, and Stephen Vincent Benét.[6] I would hang around the corner of Chambers Street and Broadway, thinking: "Somewhere in that building is the typewriter that archy the cockroach[7] jumps on at night." New York hardly gave me a living at that period, but it sustained me. I used to walk quickly past the house in West 13th Street between Sixth and Seventh where Franklin P. Adams lived, and the block seemed to tremble under my feet—the way Park Avenue trembles when a train leaves Grand Central. This excitation (nearness of giants) is a continuing thing. The city is always full of young worshipful beginners—young actors, young aspiring poets, ballerinas, painters, reporters, singers—each depending on his own brand of tonic to stay alive, each with his own stable of giants.

New York provides not only a continuing excitation but also a spectacle that is continuing. I wander around, re-examining this spectacle, hoping that I can put it on paper. It is Saturday, toward the end of the afternoon. I turn through West 48th Street. From the open windows of the drum and saxophone parlors come the listless sounds of musical instruction, monstrous insect noises in the brooding field of summer. The Cort Theater is disgorging its matinee audience. Suddenly the whole block is filled with the mighty voice of a street singer. He approaches, looking for an audience, a large, cheerful Negro with grand-opera contours, strolling with head thrown back, filling the canyon with uninhibited song. He carries a long cane as his sole prop, and is tidily but casually dressed—slacks, seersucker jacket, a book showing in his pocket.

This is perfect artistic timing; the audience from the Cort, where Sartre's *The Respectful Prostitute* is playing,[8] has just received a lesson in race relations and is in a mood to improve the condition of the black race as speedily as possible. Coins (most quarters) rattle to the street, and a few minutes of minstrelsy improves the conditions of one Negro by about eight dollars. If he does as well as this at every performance, he has a living right there. New York is the city of opportunity, they say. Even the mounted cop, clumping along on his nag a few minutes late, scans the gutter carefully for dropped silver, like a bird watching for split grain.

It is seven o'clock and I re-examine an ex-speakeasy in East 53rd Street, with dinner in mind. A thin crowd, a summer-night buzz of fans interrupted by an occasional drink being shaken at the small bar. It is dark in here (the proprietor sees no reason for boosting his light bill just because liquor laws have changed). How dark, how pleasing; and how miraculously beautiful the murals showing Italian lake scenes—probably executed by a cousin of the owner. The owner himself mixes. The fans intone the prayer for cool salvation. From the next booth drifts the conversation of radio executives; from the green salad comes the little taste of garlic. Behind me (eighteen inches again) a young intellectual is trying to persuade a girl to come live with him and be his love. She has her guard up, but he is extremely reasonable, careful not to overplay his hand. A combination of intellectual companionship and sexuality is what they have to offer each other, he feels. In the mirror over the bar I can see the ritual of the second drink. Then he has to go the men's room and she has to go to the ladies' room, and when they return, the argument has lost its tone. And the fan takes over again, and the heat and the relaxed air and the memory of so many good little dinners in so many good little illegal places, with the theme of love, the sound of ventilation, the brief medicinal illusion of gin.

Another hot night I stop off at the Goldman Band concert in the Mall in Central Park. The people seated on the benches fanned out in front of the band shell are attentive, appreciative. In the trees the night wind stirs, bringing the leaves to life, endowing them with speech; the electric lights illuminate the green branches from the under side, translating them into a new language. Overhead a plane passes dreamily, its running lights winking. On the bench directly in front of me, a boy sits with his arm around his girl; they are proud of each other and are swathed in music. The cornetist steps forward for a solo, begins, "Drink to me only with thine eyes ..." In the wide, warm night the horn is startlingly pure and magical. Then from the North River another horn solo begins—the *Queen Mary* announcing her intentions. She is not on key; she is a half tone off. The trumpeter in the bandstand never flinches. The horns quarrel savagely, but no one minds having the intimation of travel injected into the pledge of love. "I leave," sobs Mary. "And I will pledge with mine," sighs the trumpeter. Along the asphalt paths strollers pass to and fro; they behave considerately, respecting the musical atmosphere. Popsicles[9] are moving well. In the warm grass beyond the fence, forms wriggle in the shadows, and the skirts of the girls approaching on the Mall are ballooned by the breeze, and their bare shoulders catch the lamplight. "Drink to me only with thine eyes." It is a magical occasion, and it's all free.

On week ends in summer the town empties. I visit my office on a Saturday afternoon. No phone rings, no one feeds the hungry IN-baskets, no one disturbs the papers; it is a building of the dead, a time of awesome suspension. The whole city is honeycombed with abandoned cells—a jail that has been effectively broken. Occasionally from somewhere in the building a night bell rings, summoning the elevator—a special fire alarm ring. This is the pit of loneliness, in an office on a summer Saturday. I stand at the window and look down at the batteries and batteries of offices across the way, recalling how the thing looks in winter twilight when everything is going full blast, every cell lighted, and how you can see in pantomime the puppets fumbling with their slips of paper (but you don't hear the rustle), see them pick up their phone (but you don't hear the ring), see the noiseless, ceaseless moving about of so many passers of pieces of paper: New York, the capital of memoranda, in touch with Calcutta, in touch with Reykjavik, and always fooling with something.

In the café of the Lafayette, the regulars sit and talk. It is busy yet peaceful. Nursing a drink, I stare through the west windows at the Manufacturers Trust Company and at the red brick fronts on the north side of Ninth Street, watching the red turning slowly to purple as the light dwindles. Brick buildings have a way of turning color at the end of the day, the way a red rose turns bluish as it wilts. The café is a sanctuary. The waiters are ageless and they change not. Nothing has been modernized. Notre Dame stands guard in its travel poster. The coffee is strong and full of chicory, and good.

Walk the Bowery under the elevated railway at night and all you feel is a sort of cold guilt. Touched for a dime, you try to drop the coin and not touch the hand, because the hand is dirty; you try to avoid the glance, because the glance accuses. This is not so much personal menace as universal—the cold menace of unresolved human suffering and poverty and the advanced stages of the disease alcoholism. On a summer night the drunks sleep in the open. The sidewalk is a free bed, and there are no lice. Pedestrians step along and over and around the still forms as though walking on a battlefield among the dead. In doorways, on the steps of the savings bank, the bums lie sleeping it off. Standing sentinel at each sleeper's head is the empty bottle from which he drained his release. Wedged in the crook of his arm is the paper bag containing his things. The glib barker on the sight-seeing bus tells his passengers that this is the "street of lost souls," but the Bowery does not think of itself as lost; it meets its peculiar problem in its own way—plenty of gin mills, plenty of flophouses, plenty of indifference, and always, at the end of the line, Bellevue Hospital.

A block or two east and the atmosphere changes sharply. In the slums are poverty and bad housing, but with them the reassuring sobriety and safety of family life. I head east along Rivington. All is cheerful and filthy and crowded. Small shops overflow onto the sidewalk, leaving only half the normal width for passers-by. In the candid light from unshaded bulbs gleam watermelons and lingerie. Families have fled the hot rooms upstairs and have found relief on the pavement. They sit on orange crates, smoking, relaxed, congenial. This is the nightly garden party of the vast Lower East Side—and on the whole they are more agreeable-looking hot-weather groups than some you see in bright canvas deck chairs on green lawns in country circumstances. It is folksy here with the smell of warm flesh and squashed fruit and fly-bitten filth in the gutter, and cooking.

At the corner of Lewis, in the playground behind the wire fence, an open-air dance is going on—some sort of neighborhood affair, probably designed to combat delinquency. Women push baby carriages in and out among the dancers, as though to exhibit what dancing leads to at last. Overhead, like banners decorating a cotillion hall, stream the pants and bras from the pulley lines. The music stops, and a beautiful Italian girl takes a brush from her handbag and stands under the street lamp brushing her long blue-black hair till it shines. The cop in the patrol car watches sullenly.

The Consolidated Edison Company says there are eight million people in the five boroughs of New York, and the company is in a position to know. As in every dense community, virtually all races, all religions, all nationalities are represented. Population figures are shifty—they change almost as fast as one can break them down. It is safe to say that about two million of New York's eight million are Jews—roughly one in four. Among this two million who are Jewish are, of course, a great many nationalities—Russian, German, Polish, Rumanian, Austrian, a long list. The Urban League of Greater New York estimates that the number of Negroes in New York is about 700,000. Of these, about 500,000 live in Harlem, a district that extends northward from 110th Street. The Negro population has increased rapidly in the last few years. There are half again as many Negroes in New York today as there were in 1940. There are about 230,000 Puerto Ricans living in New York. There are half a million Irish, half a million Germans. There are 900,000 Russians, 150,000 English, 400,000 Poles, and there are quantities of Finns and Czechs and Swedes and Danes and Norwegians and Latvians and Belgians and Welsh and Greeks, and even Dutch, who have been here from away back. It is very hard to say how many Chinese there are. Officially there are 12,000 but there are many Chinese who are in New York illegally and who don't like census takers[10]

The collision and the intermingling of these millions of foreign-born people representing so many races and creeds make New York a permanent exhibit of the phenomenon of one world. The citizens of New York are tolerant not only from disposition but from necessity. The city has to be tolerant, otherwise it would explode in a radio-active cloud of hate and rancor and bigotry. If the people were to depart even briefly from the peace of cosmopolitan intercourse, the town would blow up higher than a kite. In New York smoulders every race problem there is, but the noticeable thing is not the problem but the inviolate truce. Harlem is a city in itself, and being a city Harlem symbolizes segregation; yet Negro life in New York lacks the more conspicuous elements of Jim Crowism. Negroes ride subways and buses on terms of equality with whites, but they have not yet found that same equality in hotels and restaurants. Professionally, Negroes get on well in the theater, in music, in art, and in literature; but in many fields of employment the going is tough. The Jim Crow principle lives chiefly in the housing rules and customs. Private owners of dwellings legally can, and do, exclude Negroes. Under a recent city ordinance, however, apartment buildings that are financed with public moneys or that receive any tax exemption must accept tenants without regard to race, color, or religion.

To a New Yorker the city is both changeless and changing. In many respects it neither looks nor feels the way it did twenty-five years ago. The elevated railways have been pulled down, all but the Third Avenue. An old-timer walking up Sixth past the Jefferson Market jail misses the railroad, misses its sound, its spotted shade, its little aerial stations, and the tremor of the thing. Broadway has changed in aspect. It used to have a discernible bony structure beneath its loud bright surface; but the signs are so enormous now, the buildings and shops and hotels have largely disappeared under the neon lights and letters and the frozen-custard façade. Broadway is a custard street with no frame supporting it. In Greenwich Village the light is thinning: big apartments have come in, bordering Washington Square, and the bars are mirrored and chromed. But there are still in the Village the lingering traces of poesy, Mexican glass, hammered brass, batik, lamps made of whisky bottles, first novels made of fresh memories—the old Village with its alleys and ratty one-room rents catering to the erratic needs of those whose hearts are young and gay.

Grand Central Terminal has became honky-tonk, with its extra-dimensional advertising displays and its tendency to adopt the tactics of a travel broker. I practically lived in Grand Central at one period (it has all the conveniences and I had no other place to stay) and the great hall seemed to me one of the more inspiring interiors in New York, until advertisements for Lastex and Coca-Cola got into the temple.

All over town the great mansions are in decline. Schwab's house facing the Hudson on Riverside is gone. Morgan's house on Madison Avenue is a church administration office. What was once the Fahnestock house is now Random House. Rich men nowadays don't live in houses; they live in the attics of big apartment buildings and plant trees on the setbacks, hundreds of feet above the street.

There are fewer newspapers than there used to be, thanks somewhat to the late Frank Munsey.[11] One misses the *Globe*, the *Mail*, the *Herald*; and to many a New Yorker life has never seemed the same since the *World* took the count.

Police now ride in radio prowl cars instead of gumshoeing around the block swinging their sticks. A ride in the subway costs ten cents, and the seats are apt to be dark green instead of straw yellow. Men go to saloons to gaze at televised events instead of to think long thoughts. It is all very disconcerting. Even parades have changed some. The last triumphal military procession in Manhattan simply filled the city with an ominous and terrible rumble of heavy tanks.

The slums are gradually giving way to the lofty housing projects—high in stature, high in purpose, low in rent. There are a couple of dozens of these new developments scattered around; each is a city in itself (one of them in the Bronx accommodates twelve thousand families), sky acreage hitherto untilled, lifting people far above the street, standardizing the sanitary life, giving them some place to sit other than an orange crate. Federal money, state money, city money, and private money have flowed into these projects. Banks and insurance companies are in back of some of them. Architects have turned the buildings slightly on their bases, to catch more light. In some of them, rents are as low as eight dollars a month a room. Thousands of new units are still needed and will eventually be built, but New York never quite catches up with itself, is never in equilibrium. In flush times the population mushrooms and the new dwellings sprout from the rock. Come bad times and the population scatters and the lofts are abandoned and the landlord withers and dies.

New York has changed in tempo and in temper during the years I have known it. There is greater tension, increased irritability. You encounter it in many places, in many faces. The normal frustrations of modern life are here multiplied and amplified—a single run of a crosstown bus contains, for the driver, enough frustration and annoyance to carry him over the edge of sanity: the traffic light that changes always an instant too soon, the passenger that bangs on the shut door, the truck that blocks the only opening, the coin that slips to the floor, the question asked at the wrong moment. There is greater tension and there is greater speed. Taxis roll faster than they rolled ten years ago—and they were rolling fast then.

Hackmen used to drive with verve; now they sometimes seem to drive with desperation, toward the ultimate tip. On the West Side Highway, approaching the city, the motorist is swept along in a trance—a sort of fever of inescapable motion, goaded from behind, hemmed in on either side, a mere chip in a millrace.

The city has never been so uncomfortable, so crowded, so tense. Money has been plentiful and New York has responded. Restaurants are hard to get into; businessmen stand in line for a Schrafft's luncheon as meekly as idle men used to stand in soup lines. (Prosperity creates its bread lines, the same as depression.) The lunch hour in Manhattan has been shoved ahead half an hour, to 12:00 or 12:30, in the hopes of beating the crowd to a table. Everyone is a little emptier at quitting time than he used to be. Apartments are festooned with No Vacancy signs. There is standing-room-only in Fifth Avenue buses, which once reserved a seat for every paying guest. The old double-deckers are disappearing—people don't ride just for the fun of it any more.

At certain hours on certain days it is almost impossible to find an empty taxi and there is a great deal of chasing around after them. You grab a handle and open the door, and find that some other citizen is entering from the other side. Doormen grow rich blowing their whistles for cabs; and some doormen belong to no door at all—merely wander about through the streets, opening cabs for people as they happen to find them. By comparison with other less hectic days, the city is uncomfortable and inconvenient; but New Yorkers temperamentally do not crave comfort and convenience—if they did they would live elsewhere.

The subtlest change in New York is something people don't speak much about but that is in everyone's mind. The city, for the first time in its long history, is destructible. A single flight of planes not bigger than a wedge of geese can quickly end this island fantasy, burn the towers, crumble the bridges, turn the underground passages into lethal chambers, cremate the millions. The intimation of mortality is part of New York now: in the sound of jets overhead, in the black headlines of the latest edition.

All dwellers in cities must live with the stubborn fact of annihilation; in New York the fact is somewhat more concentrated because of the concentration of the city itself, and because, of all targets, New York has a certain clear priority. In the mind of whatever perverted dreamer might loose the lightning, New York must hold a steady, irresistible charm.

It used to be that the Statue of Liberty was the signpost that proclaimed New York and translated it for all the world. Today Liberty shares the role with Death. Along the East River, from the razed slaughterhouses of Turtle Bay, as though in a race with the spectral flight of planes, men are carving out the permanent headquarters of the United Nations—the greatest housing project of them all. In its stride, New York takes on one more interior city, to shelter, this time, all governments, and to clear the slum called war. New York is not a capital city—it is not a national capital or a state capital. But it is by way of becoming the capital of the world. The Secretariat Building, a marble and glass cigar box set on end, is already a familiar landmark. Forty-seventh street has been widened and traffic will soon flow in a new tunnel under First Avenue. Once again the city will absorb, almost without showing any sign of it, a congress of visitors. It has already shown itself capable of stashing away the United Nations—a great many of the delegates have been around town during the past couple of years, and the citizenry has hardly caught a glimpse of their coattails or their black Homburgs.

This race—this race between the destroying planes and the struggling Parliament of Man—it sticks in all our heads. The city at last perfectly illustrates both the universal dilemma and the general solution, this riddle in steel and stone is at once the perfect target and the perfect demonstration of nonviolence, of racial brotherhood, this lofty target scraping the skies and meeting the destroying planes halfway, home of all people and all nations, capital of everything, housing the deliberations by which the planes are to be stayed and their errand forestalled.

A block or two west of the new City of Man in Turtle Bay there is an old willow tree that presides over an interior garden. It is a battered tree, long suffering and much climbed, held together by strands of wire but beloved of those who know it. In a way it symbolizes the city: life under difficulties, growth against odds, sap-rise in the midst of concrete, and the steady reaching for the sun. Whenever I look at it nowadays, and feel the cold shadow of the planes, I think: "This must be saved, this particular thing, this very tree." If it were to go, all would go—this city, this mischievous and marvelous monument which not to look upon would be like death.

Notes

1. Rudolf Valentino, who died in 1925, was a popular star in the early days of films. Nathan Hale was an American patriot executed by the British as a spy in the American Revolution. Hemingway had a critical and personal difference of opinion with the writer and poet Max Eastman. Walt Whitman, the poet, was for a time on the staff of the newspaper *The Brooklyn Eagle*. Willa Cather was one of America's most important and popular novelists. The Hippodrome, where the clown and impersonator Marceline appeared, has since been torn down. Joe Gould is a famous Greenwich Village literary character. Harry Thaw, in 1906, killed the architect Stanford White, who, Thaw believed, had succeeded in winning the affections of Thaw's wife. Clarence Day was a distinguished New York citizen who was made the hero of the book *God and My Father*, and later of the successful play *Life with Father*, by his son Clarence Day, Jr. The delayed baptism of the elder Day was a central episode of the play.

2. A play based on a well-known American book of fantasy for children.

3. The International Association of Lions Clubs, a fraternal order with branches in most American towns.

4. The Consolidated Edison Company supplies electric power for New York City.

5. One of a chain of low-priced, self-service restaurants where food is obtained by inserting coins in slots.

6. American writers prominent in the 1920's and 30's.

7. The hero of books by Don Marquis. (The cockroach was unable to type capital letters.)

8. In 1948, when this essay first appeared.

9. Sherbet frozen on a stick.

10. All these figures are as of 1948. There are now approximately 750,000 Negroes and 376,000 Puerto Ricans in the city.

11. An American publisher who successfully set the pattern for combining newspapers.

108

Buffet Finishes Off New York

ROLAND BARTHES

Roland Barthes (1915–1980) is a major figure in the French school of criticism associated with semiotics. *Mythologies*, *Writing Degree Zero*, and *Elements of Semiology* are amongst his most significant critical writings. Barthes was instrumental in establishing a concern with the "sign" as a cultural integer—part of a complex visual language by which the social and psychological meanings and values of the culture were charted and defined. In characteristic Barthian terms, the essay which follows reflects his radical, even idiosyncratic, response to New York. It is a wonderful example of his way with the world, and needs to be placed alongside the response to the United States by such French critics as Jean Baudrillard.

Bernard Buffet's New York will not unsettle many prejudices: it is a city of geometric heights, a petrified desert of grids and lattices, an inferno of greenish abstraction under a flat sky, a real Metropolis from which man is absent by his very accumulation; the implicit morality of our new Greuze is that we are distinctly happier in Belleville than in Manhattan. This is a folklore New York rather like Bizet's Spain or the Italy of the Théâtre Mogador: an exoticism which confirms the Frenchman in the excellence of his habitat.

According to Buffet, the architecture of this city is uniformly longiform and quadrangular. Here the grid reigns under its most ill-favored aspect: the contour, this black line which encloses everything obviously intends to expel man from the city. By obsessively multiplying the window, by inlaying it with black, Buffet empties it, destroys it, makes the living edifice into a dead surface, as if number, unless it is swarming, must fatally establish an abstract order; Buffet geometrizes New York the better to depopulate it: everyone knows that abstraction is "sterile." Now, to my sense of it, one of the lessons of this marvelous city is that abstraction is alive, and it must paradoxically be a painter who denies us this truth. But no doubt only an "abstract" painter could do justice to New York, could understand

Source: Roland Barthes, "Buffet Finishes off New York", *The Eiffel Tower and Other Mythologies*, (written 1959), trans. Richard Howard, New York, 1979.

that planes and lines form and meaning are as intensely alive here as in one of Mondrian's compositions: here figuration cunningly serves to destroy: to paint is to deceive. Buffet has "figured" New York in order to get rid of it.

The same aggression is to be noted with regard to the city's great commonplace, the skyscraper. What is astonishing about the skyscraper is that it does not astonish. When we actually see one (but do we ever see one, actually?) the feeling it inspires is: *why not?* For Buffet, on the contrary, the skyscraper always seems to remain in an anthological state, and this is always what he presents, refining on the needle, that obsessive shape of his thin and angular style. As if his very canvas, in its material proportions, *makes* the skyscraper; for him the skyscraper is a Being, and a prejudged one. Of course Buffet is sometimes sensitive to the city's magnificent *breadth*, to the scope of its *base* (for New York is a splendidly *set* city, like all fabulous metropolises); hence he paints a veritable façade of structures, he sees New York full-face, which is a good way of freeing himself from it, or he suspends the great scroll of a bridge in his foreground; but even in these efforts at enlargement, height surreptitiously reappears: the panorama spreads out the skyscrapers only to profile them in a jerky succession, the bridge dominates them only to manifest their aggressive vigor in the distance. Three is a mythic combat here between the *Base and the Summit*, as Char says; but instead of altitude being absorbed in the foreground mass (for New York is in fact a deep city, not a high one), Buffet bequeaths it his absurd solitude; he paints the skyscrapers as if they were empty cathedrals: he flattens the "landscape."

Buffet finishes off New York by depopulating the streets. I am not saying that the truth of New York is a swarm, which is a Neapolitan, a European notion. Urbanism itself, this checkerboard of nameless streets, is the price that has to be paid in order that the streets be useful and no longer picturesque, in order that men and objects circulate, adapt themselves to the distances, rule effectively over this enormous urban nature: the biggest city in the world (with Tokyo) is also the one we possess in an afternoon, by the most exciting of operations, since here *to possess is to understand*: New York exposes itself to intellection, and our familiarity with it comes very quickly. This is the purpose of these numbered streets, inflexibly distributed according to regular distances: not to make the city into a huge machine and man into an automaton, as we are repeatedly and stupidly told by those for whom tortuosity and dirt are the gauges of spirituality, but on the contrary to master the distances and orientations by the mind, to put at one man's disposal the space of these twelve million, this fabulous reservoir, this world emporium in which *all* goods exist except the metaphysical variety. This is the purpose of New York's geometry: that each individual should be *poetically* the owner of the capital of the world. It is not up, toward the sky, that you must look in New York; it is down, toward men and merchandise: by an admirable static paradox, the skyscraper establishes the block, the block creates the street, the street offers itself to man. Buffet of course proceeds in the opposite direction: he empties the street, climbs up the façades, grazes the surfaces, he rarefies: his New York is an anti-city.

To paint New York from above, at the top, is to rely once again on the first spiritualist myth, i.e., that geometry kills man. In his way, Buffet follows in the wake of our venerable moralists, for whom the refrigerator is antipathetic to the soul. The intentional desolation of his New York–what can it mean except that it is bad for man to live in groups, that number kills the spirit, that too many bathrooms are harmful to the spiritual health of a nation, that a world that is too "modern" is a sinister world, that we are bored when we are comfortable, in short, according to the most reactionary remark of human history, the alibi of all exploitations, that "money doesn't make happiness"? Myself, I can readily imagine that working in New York is a terrible thing, but it is not New York which is terrible, it is work. By making this city into a petrified, infantile necropolis looming up out of an "abstract" age (but not, alas! out of an abstract art), Buffet once again diverts history into metaphysics. Black looks at America always begin with the skyscrapers, and stick there. Yet what the Pilgrims unloaded from the Mayflower was not only empiricism, the spirit of enterprise, in short the seed which has doubtless produced the most stupendous city in the world, but also Puritanism and profit, money and metaphysics. What is good, Buffet discredits. And what is bad, he passes over in silence.

109
Two Poems

FRANK O'HARA

Frank O'Hara (1920–1966) was born in Baltimore but is associated with New York City. Indeed, he is one of the major exponents of what was known as the "New York School" of poetry. From 1951 he worked for the New York Museum of Modern Art (MOMA) and this reflects his concern with an interest in Abstract Expressionism—notably Jackson Pollock and Robert Motherwell. His poetry is very much a literary reflection of his visual interests, and speaks to the extraordinary vibrancy of the visual arts in New York at the time.

He defined his philosophy as "personism"—a somewhat dismissive attitude suggestive of the moment's potential which, in an academic context, looks to the photography of Meyerowitz. However, his own writing (both poetry and essays) reveals an aesthetic informed by a rich and wide range of influences—most notably Abstract Expressionism and French Surrealism. O'Hara's New York is a Whitmanian Manhattan, transposed to the context of a museum culture—a privileged aesthetic eye, the very opposite of, for example, *Last Exit to Brooklyn. Lunch Poems* (1964) reflects his urban ambience and élan at its best, whilst *Second Avenue* suggests painterly parallels with the work of Jackson Pollock. As Eric Mottram noted, "his sense of New York is unique". See Marjorie Perloff, *Poet Amongst Painters* (1978).

A Step Away from Them

It's my lunch hour, so I go
for a walk among the hum-colored
cabs. First, down the sidewalk
where laborers feed their dirty
glistening torsos sandwiches
and Coca-Cola, with yellow helmets

Source: Frank O'Hara, "A Step Away from Them", "The Day Lady Died', *Lunch Poems*, New York, 1956.

on. They protect them from falling
bricks, I guess. Then onto the
avenue where skirts are flipping
above heels and blow up over
grates. The sun is hot, but the
cabs stir up the air. I look
at bargains in wristwatches. There
are cats playing in sawdust.
On
to Times Square, where the sign
blows smoke over my head, and higher
the waterfall pours lightly. A
Negro stands in a doorway with a
toothpick, languorously agitating.
A blonde chorus girl clicks: he
smiles and rubs his chin. Everything
suddenly honks: it is 12:40 of
a Thursday.
Neon in daylight is a
great pleasure, as Edwin Denby would
write, as are light bulbs in daylight.
I stop for a cheeseburger at JULIET'S
CORNER. *Giulietta Masina, wife of*
Federico Fellini, é bell' attrice.
And chocolate malted. A lady in
foxes on such a day puts her poodle
in a cab.
There are several Puerto
Ricans on the avenue today, which
makes it beautiful and warm. First
Bunny died, then John Latouche,
then Jackson Pollock. But is the
earth as full as life was full, of them?
And one has eaten and one walks,
past the magazines with nudes
and the posters for BULLFIGHT *and*
the Manhattan Storage Warehouse,
which they'll soon tear down. I
used to think they had the Armory
Show there.
A glass of papaya juice
and back to work. My heart is in my
pocket, it is Poems by Pierre Reverdy.

1956

The Day Lady Died

It is 12:20 in New York a Friday
three days after Bastille day, yes
it is 1959 and I go get a shoeshine
because I will get off the 4:19 in Easthampton
at 7:15 and then go straight to dinner
and I don't know the people who will feed me

I walk up the muggy street beginning to sun
and have a hamburger and a malted and buy
an ugly NEW WORLD WRITING to see what the poets
in Ghana are doing these days
I go on to the bank
and Miss Stillwagon (first name Linda I once heard)
doesn't even look up my balance for once in her life
and in the GOLDEN GRIFFIN I get a little Verlaine
for Patsy with drawings by Bonnard although I do

think of Hesiod, trans. Richmond Lattimore or
Brendan Behan's new play or Le Balcon or Les Nègres
of Genet, but I don't, I stick with Verlaine
after practically going to sleep with quandariness

and for Mike I just stroll into the PARK LANE
Liquor Store and ask for a bottle of Strega and
then I go back where I came from to 6th Avenue
and the tobacconist in the Ziegfeld Theatre and
casually ask for a carton of Gauloises and a carton
of Picayunes, and a NEW YORK POST with her face on it

and I am sweating a lot by now and thinking of
leaning on the john door in the 5 SPOT
while she whispered a song along the keyboard
to Mal Waldron and everyone and I stopped breathing

1959

110

New York Scenes

JACK KEROUAC

Jack Kerouac (1922–1969) was born in Lowell, Massachusetts—a relatively small New England town. His significance rests in the way his writing reflects the philosophy of the Beats—a group of writers including Allen Ginsberg and William Burroughs which fundamentally challenged the attitudes of 1950s white America.

Kerouac's "novels" invoke a free-wheeling existentialism which speaks to the moment and an almost anarchic concern with intense experience. In this, the road and the city (especially New York and San Francisco) become central terms of reference and play upon the incantatory terms by which Walt Whitman (very much the nineteenth century precursor) saw them as part of a larger dynamic of personal experience and possibility. *On the Road* (1957) remains one of the definitive statements of a self "on the move"—free (supposedly) from social and cultural constraints. The reality, of course, was very different.

Other texts which continued his personal journey are *The Dharma Bums* (1959) and *Doctor Sax* (1959). *Lonesome Traveller* (1960) is a collection of travel sketches. The inference of the title is significant. Throughout Beat writing, "freedom" is often a euphemism for loneliness, especially in cities. See Thomas Parkinson (ed), *A Casebook on the Beats* (1961), Ann Charters, *Kerouac—A Biography* (1974) and Dennis McNally, *Desolate Angel* (1979).

At this time my mother was living alone in a little apartment in Jamaica Long Island, working in the shoe factory, waiting for me to come home so I could keep her company and escort her to Radio City once a month. She had a tiny bedroom waiting for me, clean linen in the dresser, clean sheets in the bed. It was a relief after all the sleepingbags and bunks and railroad earth. It was another of the many opportunities she's given me all he life to just stay home and write.

I always give her all my leftover pay. I settled down to long sweet sleeps, day-long

Source: Jack Kerouac, "New York Scenes", *Lonesome Traveller* Ch. 5, New York, 1960.

meditations in the house, writing, and long walks around beloved old Manhattan a half hour subway ride away. I roamed the streets, the bridges, Times Square, cafeterias, the waterfront, I looked up all my poet beatnik friends and roamed with them, I had love affairs with girls in the Village, I did everything with that great mad joy you get when you return to New York City.

I've heard great singing Negroes call it "The Apple!"

"There now is your insular city of the Manhattoes, belted round by wharves," sang Herman Melville.

"Bound round by flashing tides," sang Thomas Wolfe.

Whole panoramas of New York everywhere, from New Jersey, from skyscrapers.—

Even from bars, like a Third Avenue bar—4 p.m. the men are all roaring in clink bonk glass brassfoot barrail "where ya going" excitement—October's in the air, in the Indian Summer sun of door.—Two Madison Avenue salesmen who been working all day long come in young, well dressed, just-suits, puffing cigars, glad to have the day done and the drink comin in, side by side march in smiling but there's no room at the roaring (Shit!) crowded bar so they stand two deep from it waiting and smiling and talking.—Men do love bars and good bars should be loved.—It's full of businessmen, workmen, Finn MacCools of Time.—Be-overalled old gray topers dirty and beerswiggin glad.—Nameless truck busdrivers with flashlites slung from hips—old beatfaced beerswallers sadly upraising purple lips to happy drinking ceilings.—Bartenders are fast, courteous, interested in their work as well as clientele.—Like Dublin at 4:30 p.m. when the work is done, but this is great New York Third Avenue, free lunch, smells of Moody street exhaust river lunch in road of grime by smashing the door, guitarplaying long sideburned heroes smell out there on wood doorsteps of afternoon drowse.—But it's New York towers rise beyond, voices crash mangle to talk and chew the gossip till Earwicker drops his load—Ah Jack Fitzgerald Mighty Murphy where are you?—Semi bald blue shirt tattered shovellers in broken end dungarees fisting glasses of glistenglass foam top brown afternoon beer.—The subway rumbles underneath as man in homburg in vest but coatless executive changes from right to left foot on ye brass rail.—Colored man in hat, dignified, young, paper underarm, says goodbye at bar warm and paternal leaning over men—elevator operator around the corner.—And wasnt this where they say Novak the real estator who used to stay up late a-nights line-faced to become right and rich in his little white worm cellule of the night typing up reports and letters wife and kids go mad at home at eleven p.m.—ambitious, worried, in a little office of the Island, right on the street undignified but open to all business and in infancy any business can be small as ambition's big—pushing how many daisies now? and never made his million, never had a drink with So Long Gee Gee and I Love You Too in this late afternoon beer room of men excited shifting stools and footbottom rail scuffle heel soles in New York?—Never called Old Glasses over and offered his rim red nose a drink—never laughed and let the fly his nose use as a landing-mark—but ulcerated in the middle of the night to be rich and get his family the best.—So the best American sod's his blanket now, made in upper mills of Hudson Bay Moonface Sassenach and carted down by housepainter in white coveralls (silent) to rim the roam of his once formed flesh, and let worms ram—Rim! So have another beer, topers—Bloody mugglers! Lovers!

My friends and I in New York city have our own special way of having fun without having to spend much money and most important of all without having to be importuned by formalistic bores, such as, say, a swell evening at the mayor's ball.—We dont have to shake hands and we dont have to make appointments and we feel all right.—We sorta wander around like children.—We walk into parties and tell everybody what we've been doing and people think we're showing off.—They say: "Oh look at the beatniks!"

Take, for example, this typical evening you can have:—

Emerging from the Seventh Avenue subway on 42nd Street, you pass the john, which is the beatest john in New York—you never can tell if it's open or not, usually there's a big chain in front of it saying it's out of order, or else it's got some white-haired decaying monster slinking outside, a john which all seven million people in New York City have at one time passed and taken strange notice of—past the new charcoal-fried-hamburger stand, Bible booths, operatic jukeboxes, and a seedy underground used-magazine store next to a peanut-brittle store smelling of subway arcades—here and there a used copy of that old bard Plotinus sneaked in with the remainders of collections of German highschool textbooks—where they sell long ratty-looking hotdogs (no, actually they're quite beautiful, particularly if you havent got 15 cents and are looking for someone in Bickford's Cafeteria who can lay some smash on you) (lend you some change).—

Coming up that stairway, people stand there for hours and hours drooling in the rain, with soaking wet umbrellas—lots of boys in dungarees scared to go into the Army standing halfway up the stairway on the iron steps waiting for God Who knows what, certainly among them some romantic heroes just in from Oklahoma with ambitions to end up yearning in the arms of some unpredictable sexy young blonde in a penthouse on the Empire State Building—some of them probably stand there dreaming of owning the Empire State Building by virtue of a magic spell which they've dreamed up by a creek in the backwoods of a ratty old house on the outskirts of Texarkana.—Ashamed of being seen going into the dirty movie (what's its name?) across the street from the New York *Times*—The lion and the tiger passing, as Tom Wolfe used to say about certain types passing that corner.—

Leaning against that cigar store with a lot of telephone booths on the corner of 42nd and Seventh where you make beautiful telephone calls looking out into the street and it gets real cozy in there when it's raining outside and you like to prolong the conversation, who do you find? Basketball teams? Basketball coaches? All those guys from the roller-skating rink go there? Cats from the Bronx again, looking for some action, really looking for romance? Strange duos of girls coming out of dirty movies? Did you ever seen them? Or bemused drunken businessmen with their hats tipped awry on their graying heads staring catatonically upward at the signs floating by on the Times Building, huge sentences about Khrushchev reeling by, the populations of Asia enumerated in flashing lightbulbs, always five hundred periods after each sentence.—Suddenly a psychopathically worried policeman appears on the corner and tells everybody to go away.—This is the center of the greatest city the world has ever known and this is what beatniks do here.—"Standing on the street corner waiting for no one is Power," sayeth poet Gregory Corso.

Instead of going to night clubs—if you're in a position to make the nightclub scene (most beatniks rattle empty pockets passing Birdland)—how strange to stand on the sidewalk and just watch that weird eccentric from Second Avenue looking like Napoleon going by feeling cooky crumbs in his pocket, or a young 15-year-old kid with a bratty face, or suddenly somebody swishing by in a baseball hat (because that's what you see), and finally an old lady dressed in seven hats and a long ratty fur coat in the middle of the July night carrying a huge Russian woolen purse filled with scribbled bits of paper which say "Festival Foundation Inc., 70,000 Germs" and moths flying out of her sleeve—she rushes up and importunes Shriners. And dufflebag soldiers without a war—harmonica players off freight trains.—Of course there are the normal New Yorkers, looking ridiculously out of place and as odd as their own neat oddity, carrying pizzas and *Daily Newses* and headed for brown basements or Pennsylvania trains—W. H. Auden himself may be seen fumbling by in the rain—Paul Bowles, natty in a Dacron suit, passing through on a trip from Morocco, the ghost of Herman Melville himself followed by Bartleby the Wall Street Scrivener and Pierre the ambiguous hipster of 1848 out on a walk—to see what's up in the news flashes of the *Times*—Let's go back to the corner newsstand.—SPACE BLAST ... POPE WASHES FEET OF POOR ...

Let's go across the street to Grant's, our favored dining place. For 65 cents you get a huge plate of fried clams, a lot of French fried potatoes, a little portion of cole slaw, some tartar sauce, a little cup of red sauce for fish, a slice of lemon, two slices of fresh rye bread, a pat of butter, another ten cents brings a glass of rare birch beer.—What a ball it is to eat here! Migrations of Spaniards chewing on hotdogs, standing up, leaning against big pots of mustard.—Ten different counters with different specialities.—Ten-cent cheese sandwiches, two liquor bars for the Apocalypse, oh yeah and great indifferent bartenders.—And cops that stand in the back getting free meals—drunken saxophone players on the nod—lonely dignified ragpickers from Hudson Street supping soup without a word to anybody, with black fingers, woe.—Twenty thousand customers a day—fifty thousand on rainy days—one hundred thousand on snowy days.—Operation twenty-four hours a night. Privacy—supreme under a glary red light full of conversation.—Toulouse-Lautrec, with his deformity and cane, sketching in the corner.—You can stay there for five minutes and gobble up your food, or else stay there for hours having insane philosophical conversation with your buddy and wondering about the people.—"Let's have a hotdog before we go to the movie!" and you get so high in there you never get to the movies because it's better than a show about Doris Day on a holiday in the Caribbean.

"But what are we gonna do tonight? Marty would go to a movie but we're going to connect for some junk.—Let's go down to the Automat."

"Just a minute, I've got to shine my shoes on top of a fire hydrant."

"You wanta see yourself in the fun mirror?"

"Wanta take four pictures for a quarter? Because we're on the eternal scene. We can look at the picture and remember it when we're wise old white-haired Thoreaus in cabins."

"Ah, the fun mirrors are gone, they used to have fun mirrors here."

"How about the Laff Movie?"

"That's gone too."

"They got the flea circus."

"They still got donzinggerls?"

"The burlesque is gone millions and millions of years ago."

"Shall we go down by the Automat and watch the old ladies eating beans, or the deaf-mutes that stand in front of the window there and you watch 'em and try to figure the invisible language as it flees across the window from face to face and finger to finger ... ? Why does Times Square feel like a big room?"

Across the street is Bickford's, right in the middle of the block under the Apollo Theater marquee and right next door to a little bookshop that specializes in Havelock Ellis and Rabelais with thousands of sex fiends leafing at the bins.—Bickford's is the greatest stage on Times Square—many people have hung around there for years man and boy searching God alone knows for what, maybe some angel of Times Square who would make the whole big room home, the old homestead—civilization needs it.—What's Times Square doing there anyway? Might as well enjoy it.—Greatest city the world has ever seen.—Have they got a Times Square on Mars? What would the Blob do on Times Square? Or St. Francis?

A girl gets off a bus in the Port Authority Terminal and goes into Bickford's, Chinese girl, red shoes, sits down with coffee, looking for daddy.

There's a whole floating population around Times Square that has always made Bickford's their headquarters day and night. In the old days of the beat generation some poets used to go in there to meet the famous character "Hunkey" who used to come in and out in an oversized black raincoat and a cigarette holder looking for somebody to lay a pawnticket on—Remington typewriter, portable radio, black raincoat—to score for some toast, (get some money) so he can go uptown and get in trouble with the cops or any of his boys. Also a lot of stupid gangsters from 8th Avenue used to cut in—maybe they still do—the ones from the early days are all in jail or dead. Now the poets just go there and smoke a peace pipe, looking for the ghost of Hunkey or his boys, and dream over the fading cups of tea.

The beatniks make the point that if you went there every night and stayed there you could start a whole Dostoevski season on Times Square by yourself and meet all the midnight newspaper peddlers and their involvements and families and woes—religious fanatics who would take you home and give you long sermons over the kitchen table about the "new apocalypse" and similar ideas:—"My Baptist minister back in Winston-Salem told me the reason that God invented television was that when Christ comes back to earth again they shall crucify Him right on the streets of this here Babylon and they gonna have television cameras pointin' down on that spot and the streets shall run with blood and every eye shall see."

Still hungry, go out down to the Oriental Cafeteria—"favored dining spot" also—some night life—cheap—down in the basement across the street from the Port Authority monolith bus terminal on 40th Street and eat big oily lambs' heads with Greek rice for 90c.—Oriental zig-zag tunes on the juke-box.

Depends how high you are by now—assuming you've picked up on one of the corners—say 42nd Street and 8th Avenue, near the great Whelan's drug store, another lonely haunt spot where you can meet people—Negro whores, ladies limping in a Benzedrine psychosis.—Across the street you can see the ruins of New York already started—the Globe Hotel being torn down there, an empty tooth hole right on 44th Street—and the green McGraw-Hill building gaping up in the sky, higher than you'd believe—lonely all by itself down towards the Hudson River where freighters wait in the rain for their Montevideo limestone.—

Might as well go on home. It's getting old.—Or: "Let's make the Village or go to the Lower East Side and play Symphony Sid on the radio—or play our Indian records—and eat big dead Puerto Rican steaks—or lung stew—see if Bruno has slashed any more car roofs in Brooklyn—though Bruno's gentled now, maybe he's written a new poem."

Or look at Television. Night life—Oscar Levant talking about his melancholia on the Jack Paar show.

The Five Spot on 5th Street and Bowery sometimes features Thelonious Monk on the piano and you go on there. If you know the proprietor you sit down at the table free with a beer, but if you dont know him you can sneak in and stand by the ventilator and listen. Always crowded weekends. Monk cogitates with deadly abstraction, clonk, and makes a statement, huge foot beating delicately on the floor, head turned to one side listening, entering the piano.

Lester Young played there just before he died and used to sit in the back kitchen between sets. My buddy poet Allen Ginsberg went back and got on his knees and asked him what he would do if an atom bomb fell on New York. Lester said he would break the window in Tiffany's and get some jewels anyway. He also said, "What you doin' on your knees?" not realizing he is a great hero of the beat generation and now enshrined. The Five Spot is darkly lit, has weird waiters, good music always, sometimes John "Train" Coltrane showers his rough notes from his big tenor horn all over the place. On weekends parties of well-dressed uptowners jam-pack the place talking continuously—nobody minds.

O for a couple of hours, though, in the Egyptian Gardens in the lower West Side Chelsea district of Greek restaurants.—Glasses of ouzo, Greek liqueur, and beautiful girls dancing the belly dance in spangles and beaded bras, the incomparable Zara on the floor and weaving like mystery to the flutes and tingtang beats of Greece—when she's not dancing she sits in the orchestra with the men plapping a drum against her belly, dreams in her eyes.—Huge crowds of what appear to be Suburbia couples sit at the tables clapping to the swaying Oriental idea.—If you're late you have to stand along the wall.

Wanta dance? The Garden Bar on Third Avenue where you can do fantastic sprawling dances in the dim back room to a jukebox, cheap, the waiter doesnt care.

Wanta just talk? The Cedar Bar on University Place where all the painters hang out and a 16-year-old kid who was there one afternoon squirting red wine out of a Spanish wine skin into his friends' mouths and kept missing. ...

The night clubs of Greenwich Village known as the Half Note, the Village Vanguard, the Café Bohemia, the Village Gate also feature jazz (Lee Konitz, J. J. Johnson, Miles Davis), but you've got to have mucho money but the sad commercial atmosphere is killing jazz and jazz *is* killing itself there, because jazz belongs to open joyful ten-cent beer joints, as in the beginning.

There's a big party at some painter's loft, wild loud flamenco on the phonograph, the girls suddenly become all hips and heels and people try to dance between their flying hair.—Men go mad and start tackling people, flying wedges hurtle across the room, men grab men around the knees and lift them nine feet from the floor and lose their balance and nobody gets hurt, blonk.—Girls are balanced hands on men's knees, their skirts falling and revealing frills on their thighs.—Finally everybody dresses to go home and the host says dazedly.—"You all look so *respectable.*"

Or somebody just had an opening, or there's a poetry reading at the Living Theater, or at the Gaslight Café, or at the Seven Arts Coffee Gallery, up around Times Square (9th Avenue and 43rd Street, amazing spot) (begins at midnight Fridays), where afterward everybody rushes out to the old wild bar.—Or else a huge party at Leroi Jones's—he's got a new issue of Yugen Magazine which he printed himself on a little cranky machine and everybody's poems are in it, from San Francisco to Gloucester Mass., and costs only 50 cents.—Historic publisher, secret hipster of the trade.—Leroi's getting sick of parties, everyone's always taking off his shirt and dancing, three sentimental girls are crooning over poet Raymond Bremser, my buddy Gregory Corso is arguing with a New York *Post* reporter saying., "But you don't understand Kangaroonian weep! Forsake thy trade! Flee to the Enchenedian Islands!"

Let's get out of here, it's too literary.—Let's go get drunk on the Bowery or eat those long noodles and tea in glasses at Hong Pat's in Chinatown.—What are we always eating for? Let's walk over the Brooklyn Bridge and build up another appetite.—How about some okra on Sands Street?

Shades of Hart Crane!

"Let's go see if we can find Don Joseph!"

"Who's Don Joseph?"

Don Joseph is a terrific cornet player who wanders around the Village with his little mustache and his arms hangin at the sides with the cornet, which creaks when he plays softly, any whispers, the greatest sweetest cornet since Bix and more.—He stands at the jukebox in the bar and plays with the music for a beer.—He looks like a handsome movie actor.—He's the great super glamorous secret Bobby Hackett of the jazz world.

What about that guy Tony Fruscella who sits crosslegged on the rug and plays Bach on his trumpet, by ear, and later on at night there he is blowing with the guys at a session, modern jazz—

Or George Jones the secret Bowery shroud who plays great tenor in parks at dawn with Charley Mariano, for kicks, because they love jazz, and that time on the waterfront at dawn they played a whole session as the guy beat on the dock with a stick for the beat.

Talkin of Bowery shrouds, what about Charley Mills walkin down the street with bums drinkin his bottle of wine singing in twelve tone scale.

"Let's go see the strange great secret painters of America and discuss their paintings and their visions with them—Iris Brodie with her delicate fawn Byzantine filigree of Virgins—"

"Or Miles Forst and his black bull in the orange cave."

"Or Franz Klein and his spiderwebs."

"His bloody spiderwebs!"

"Or Willem de Kooning and his White."

"Or Robert De Niro."

"Or Dody Muller and her Annunciations in seven feet all flowers."

"Or Al Leslie and his giant feet canvases."

"Al Leslie's giant is sleeping in the Paramount building."

There's another great painter, his name is Bill Heine, he's a really secret subterranean painter who sits with all those weird new cats in the East Tenth street coffeeshops that dont look coffeeshops at all but like sorta Henry Street basement second-hand clothes stores except you see an African sculpture or maybe a Mary Frank sculpture over the door and inside they play Frescobaldi on the hi fi.

Ah, let's go back to the village and stand on the corner of Eighth Street and Sixth Avenue and watch the intellectuals go by.—AP reporters lurching home to their basement apartments on Washington Square, lady editorialists with huge German police dogs breaking their chains, lonely dikes melting by, unknown experts on Sherlock Holmes with blue fingernails going up to their rooms to take scopolamine, a muscle-bound young man in a cheap gray German suit explaining something weird to his fat girl friend, great editors leaning politely at the newsstand buying the early edition of the Times, great fat furniture movers out of 1910 Charlie Chaplin films coming home with great bags full of chop suey (feeding everybody), Picasso's melancholy harlequin now owner of a print and frame shop musing on his wife and newborn child lifting up his finger for a taxi, rolypoly recording engineers rush in fur hats, girls artists down from Columbia with D. H. Lawrence problems picking up 50-year-old men, old men in the Kettle of Fish, and the melancholy spectre of New York Women's prison that looms high and is folded in silence as the night itself—at sunset their windows look like oranges—poet e. e. cummings buying a package of cough drops in the shade of that monstrosity.—If it's raining you can stand under the awning in front of Howard Johnson's and watch the street from the other side.

Beatnik Angel Peter Orlovsky in the supermarket five doors away buying Uneeda Biscuits (late Friday night), ice cream, caviar, bacon, pretzels, sodapop, *TV Guide*, Vaseline, three toothbrushes, chocolate milk (dreaming of roast sucking pig), buying whole Idaho potatoes, raisin bread, wormy cabbage by mistake, and fresh-felt tomatoes and collecting purple stamps.—Then he goes home broke and dumps it all on the table, takes out a big book of Mayakovsky poems, turns on the 1949 television set to the horror movie, and goes to sleep.

And this is the beat night life of New York.

111

New York City 1976: A Signal of Transcendence

PETER BERGER

The following essay originally appeared in *Commentary* (February, 1977) and was subsequently published as the final chapter of *Facing Up to Modernity* (1977). Its interest lies in the way Berger propounds a dynamic sense of New York as a great symbol of modernity, both as an image and a condition. At a time when many commentators viewed the city as in rapid decline and morally bankrupt (e.g. Bellow's *Mr. Sammler's Planet*), so Berger offers a sparkling view of New York as a continuing city of possibility—not only "the prototypical cosmopolis of our age" but a continuing "signal of transcendence".

Different cities acquire great symbolic significance at different moments in human history. Paris was significant in this way in the eighteenth and nineteenth centuries, as was London (though perhaps to a lesser degree), and Rome, over and beyond anything that was actually going on there, has retained its powerful symbolic character over many centuries. New York City undoubtedly has a comparable symbolic significance today. It is perceived as a symbol of modernity, of Western civilization and (despite the often-repeated statement that "New York is not America") of the civilization of the United States. The curious thing is that it is widely perceived as a negative symbol, that is, as a metaphor of everything that has gone wrong with our society.

Much of the rest of the country sees New York City as one gigantic agglomeration of social ills: crime, poverty, racial hatred, mismanaged and corrupt government—not to mention dirt, pollution, and traffic congestion of virtually metaphysical dimensions. The same perceptions have been widely diffused abroad, and foreign tourists come to the city with the piquant ambivalence of apprehension and fascination that used to go with dangerous expeditions into the jungles of central

Source: Peter Berger, "New York City 1976: A Signal of Transcendence", from *Facing Up to Modernity*, Harmondsworth, 1977. © Peter Berger
[This Chapter appeared as "In Praise of New York" in *Commentary* Feb., 1977.]

Africa. (Such an attitude can be quite profitable to the tourist industry. I know of a German tourist, a middle-aged women, who went for solitary walks in Central Park every evening, in thrilled anticipation of being sexually assaulted. She was, alas, disappointed. The worst—or best—result of her effort was that an inept mugger tried unsuccessfully to snatch her purse.) Interestingly, New York has negative symbolic value right across the political spectrum: As seen from the right, New York is the habitat of an anti-American intellectual and media establishment, bent on converting the entire nation into the decadent welfare state that the city, supposedly, has already become. Seen from the left, New York is, above all, Wall Street—the heart of the beast, headquarters of capitalist imperialism, cosmic cancer *par excellence*; Madison Avenue has a slightly lesser place in this particular demonological vision.

And yet, despite all this, New York City continues to be a magnet and even an object of love, sometimes fierce love. People, especially the young, continue to come in large numbers, irresistibly drawn to the city by expectations of success and excitement. And New Yorkers themselves, although they too frequently share the negative views of their own city (indeed, they relish topping each other's horror stories—'You think *you* had a parking problem today, well, let me tell you what happened to *me* this morning'), nevertheless continue to be inexplicably, perhaps dementedly, attached to the cesspool of perdition in which they reside. Such ambivalence suggests that the reality of New York is more complicated than its symbolic imagery. And so, of course, it is. From a sociological viewpoint, I could now proceed to delve into the welter of empirical facts that underlie the various perceptions of this city. My purpose here, though, is not sociological but theological.

Specifically, I propose to talk about New York City as a signal of transcendence—*not* New York in some romanticized past, *nor* New York in some utopian future, but New York *today*, a time of disillusion and of many fears, but also a time of promise and of hope. To speak of a signal of transcendence is neither to deny nor to idealize the often harsh empirical facts that make up our lives in the world. It is rather to try for a glimpse of the grace that is to be found 'in, with, and under' the empirical reality of our lives. In other words, to speak of a signal of transcendence is to make an assertion about the presence of redemptive power in this world. Let me begin by telling you the most New York joke that I know. It comes, of course, from the pen of Woody Allen, and it concerns the hereafter. There are really only two questions about the hereafter, Woody Allen suggests: *How long does it stay open? And can you get there by cab from midtown Manhattan?* In a quite non-jocular way, the rest of this chapter may be taken as a *mid-rash* on this text.

New York is no longer the world's most potent symbol of urbanism and urbanity (two related but distinct matters). It seems to me that an exploration into its possibilities as a signal of transcendence must begin with this root fact: Here is not only a vast and vastly important city, but *the* city *par excellence*, the prototypical cosmopolis of our age. I think this is why visitors and new arrivals feel at home there so quickly. Every urban experience that they have had before has been, in a way, an anticipation of New York, and the encounter with the real thing thus has a strong note of familiarity, of déjà vu (apart from the fact that the major landmarks of New York are known everywhere and serve as instant orientations for the newcomer). Wherever skyscrapers reach up towards the clouds, wherever masses of cars stream back and forth over steel-girded bridges, wherever heterogeneous crowds pour through subways, underground concourses, or cavernous lobbies encased in glass, there is a bit of New York. Conversely, the New Yorker visiting other cities finds everywhere the sights and sounds, even the smells, that remind him of home. The mystique of New York City is, above all, the mystique of modern urban life, concentrated more massively than anywhere else.

It is not accidental, I think, that the biblical imagery of redemptive fulfilment is so persistently urban. Jerusalem became the focus of religious devotion from an early period of the spiritual history of ancient Israel, and it has remained the holy city in both Jewish and Christian religious imagination ever since. And this same Jerusalem, of course, came to be transformed into an image of eschatological expectation—the Jerusalem that is to come, the heavenly city, 'its radiance like a most rare jewel, like a jasper, clear as crystal'. Biblical scholars disagree on the precise origins and status of the Zion tradition in the Old Testament, on the religious significance of Jerusalem at, say, the time of David and Solomon, and on the significance of the various images in the Apocalypse. Yet there is, I believe, far-reaching consensus on one simple point: The city as a sociopolitical formation marks a transition in human history from bonds based exclusively on kinship to more comprehensive human relationships. Perhaps this was not the case everywhere, but it was clearly so in the ancient Mediterranean world. Here cities—as markets, centres of political or military administration, and amphictyonic sanctuaries—served to weaken and eventually to liquidate the archaic bonds of blood, of clan and tribe. Max Weber has argued that, in this, cities are incipiently 'rationalizing', that is, they constitute a social and political order based on reason, as against an older order based on magical taboos. This development reached a dramatic climax in the emergence of the Greek *polis*, but it is not fanciful to suggest that the biblical imagery of the city served as a religious legitimation of the same underlying liberation from the magic of the blood. Whatever else the city is, it is a place where *different* people come together and find a new unity with each other—and, in the context of the ancient world, that is a revolutionary event. But let me not get entangled here in historical controversies. Instead, let me make this proposition: *The city is a signal of transcendence inasmuch as it embodies universalism and freedom.*

If universalism is a root urban characteristic, then surely New York is the most universalistic of cities. And, of course, it is this quality of universalism that most impresses the newcomer and that is so often bragged about by the native. In this small space are pressed together all the races and all the nations of the world. A short subway ride separates worlds of mind-boggling human diversity—black Harlem borders on the Upper West Side, the *barrio* on the territory of East Side swingers, the Village on Little Italy, Chinatown on the financial district. And that is only in Manhattan, beyond which lie the mysterious expanses of the boroughs—places like Greenpoint, Bay Ridge, or Boro Park, each one a world of meaning and belonging almost unpenetrated by outsiders. In this city you can enter a phone booth shaped like a pagoda and make a reservation in a Czechoslovak restaurant (or more precisely, in one of *several* Czechoslavak restaurants). You can spend weeks doing nothing else, if you have the leisure, than savouring the world's greatest concentration of museums, art galleries, musical and theatrical performances, and other cultural happenings of every conceivable kind, from the sublime to the unspeakable. When I first lived in New York as a student, I had a job as a receptionist in a now-defunct dispensary on the Lower East Side. I still recall with pleasure my lunch hours: I would buy a bialy with lox in the old Essex Street Market, munch it while strolling through the teeming street life at the foot of the Williamsburg Bridge, and then have a quiet coffee with baklava in one of several Turkish cafes on Allen Street, surrounded by old men smoking waterpipes and playing checkers (apparently their only occupation). What I recall most of all is the exhilarating sense that here I was, in New York City, where all these things were going on and where, in principle, everything was possible.

Are these sentimental trivialities, fit only as copy for tourist promotion? I think not. For the mundane facts contain a mighty promise—the promise that God loves the human race in *all* its incredible variety, that His redemptive grace embraces *all* of humanity without any exception, and that His Kingdom will mean not the end but the glorious transfiguration of every truly human expression. The heavenly city, too, will contain every human type and condition, and in this it will necessarily resemble New York; needless to add, it will *not* resemble New York in that it will be without the degradations and deprivations that afflict human life in this aeon. Also, God's promise is one of perfect freedom. There is no such freedom short of the Kingdom of God; in this aeon, every liberty is bought at a price (often an ugly one), every liberation is incomplete, and some liberations are illusory. It is important to remember this. Nevertheless, wherever human beings are liberated from oppression or narrowness to wider horizons of life, thought, and imagination, there is a foreshadowing of the final liberation that is to come. Thus, I believe, New York City is a signal of transcendence also in the exhilaration of its freedom—and let me assure you that, in saying this, I do not forget for a moment the sordidness that may also be found here.

To some extent, the characteristics of universalism and freedom are endemic to urban life nearly everywhere, in varying degrees. The distinctiveness of New York comes from the enormous magnitude of these features. The same may be said of another characteristic which, I propose, may be taken as a signal of transcendence: *The city is a place of hope.*

If there is any New York legend that is generally known, it is that of the immigrant, and the legend, of course, has its most famous physical representation in the Statue of Liberty. This legend is, above all, a story of hope. I arrived in America a short time after World War II, very poor and very young, after a long ocean voyage that sticks in my memory as an endless bout with seasickness. The ship sailed into New York Bay in the early morning, in a dense fog, so that very little could be seen at first. Then, dramatically, the fog was pierced, and we saw first the Statue, which seemed perilously close to the ship, and then the skyline of lower Manhattan. All the passengers were assembled on the deck, and there was a hushed silence. But, curiously, what impressed me most at the time was not these majestic sights; I had, after all, expected to see them. There was something else. As the ship sailed up the Hudson towards its pier, I was fascinated by the traffic on what I later learned was the West Side Highway. All these cars seemed enormous to me. But, more than their size, it was their colours that impressed me. This was before New York taxis all came to be painted yellow; then, they came in all the colours of the rainbow, though yellow was predominant. I didn't know that these garish cars were taxis. The exuberance of colour, I thought, was characteristic of ordinary American automobiles. This, then, was my first unexpected sight in New York, and it pleased me greatly. I don't think I put it quite this way to myself, but implicity in my visual pleasure was the notion that someday I, too, might be driving past the skyscrapers in a bright yellow car of surrealistic proportions, engaged (no doubt) in some business of great importance and enjoying the company of the most beautiful woman imaginable.

As immigrant stories go, mine has been lucky although I've never driven a yellow cab. Indeed, I could say that New York has kept all its promises to me. I know full well that this has not been so for all newcomers to this city. If New York has been a place of hope, it has also been a place of disappointed hope, of shattered expectations, of bitterness and despair. It has been fashionable of late to stress this negative aspect of the American dream—mistakenly so, I believe, because America has fulfilled far more expectations than it has frustrated. I would go even farther than that: The currently fashionable intellectuals, who decry the hopefulness of America, are far more in a state of 'false consciousness' than the millions of immigrants who came and who continue to come to America full of hope. Nevertheless, just as it would be false to speak of the universalism and the freedom of this city without also speaking of the sordid underside of these facts, so would it be dishonest to pretend that the hopeful message emblazoned on the Statue of Liberty is an accurate description of empirical reality. Of course it is not. And yet the proclamation of hope to all those who came here across the ocean is a signal of transcendent portent. For all of us, men and women of this aeon, are on a long journey, across vast and dangerous seas, towards a city of hope.

There is more: *This is a place of useless labour*. Just compare New York with an honest-to-goodness industrial city like Detroit or Pittsburg, or even Chicago. In these cities most people are engaged in labour that has at least an indirect relation to economic utility. Certainly there are such people in New York. The peculiarity of New York, however, is the large portion of its labour force employed in activities which only the most ingenious economic theory can interpret as a contribution to the gross national product. Leave aside the enormous number of people working in municipal government and other public services (and leave aside the timely question of how long the city will be able to afford this); you are still left with legions of people making their livelihood, or at least trying to do so, through activities which, economically speaking, are bizarre. Look at them: promoters of Renaissance music, producers of non-verbal theatre, translators of Swahili literature, purveyors of esoteric erotica, agents of non-existent governments, revolutionaries in exile, Egyptologists, numismatic experts, scream therapists, guidance counsellors for geriatric recreation, Indonesian chefs, belly dancers and teachers of belly dancing (and, for all I know, belly dancing therapists)—not to mention individuals who are on university payrolls to provide instruction in phenomenological sociology (I have frequently thought that a society that can afford *me* must somehow be heading for a economic crisis). Let me make a practical suggestion in this matter: Go for lunch someday to one of my favourite restaurants in New York, the Russian Tea Room on West 57th Street, in the heart of the music and ballet district. Study the customers. A few will be easy to place; these, most likely, are tourists from the Bronx. An attempt to guess the occupations of the rest should be enough to induce a nervous breakdown in any labour economist, especially if he also tries to figure out how such occupations can generate enough income to pay the price of a beef Stroganoff preceded by blinis with caviar.

A Chicagoan will know what to say to all of this: These people can't be serious. Precisely! The opposite of being serious is being playful; the invincible playfulness of New York City is, I believe, in itself a signal of transcendence. *Homo ludens* is closer to redemption than *homo faber*; the clown is more of a sacramental figure than the engineer. In the heavenly Jerusalem there will be no need for psychotherapy and geriatrics, but I confidently expect that there will be an unbelievable variety of restaurants—metaphysically transfigured restaurants, to be sure, but restaurants nonetheless— and, if so, there is certain to be the Platonic prototype of the Indonesian *rijstafel*, its pure ideal, its *Urform*, its ultimate culmination. May I also confess to the (perhaps crypto-Muslim) expectation that there will be *something* like belly dancers? Anyway, I think it is good theology to expect the Kingdom of God to be a very playful affair—and in *that*, at the very least, it will resemble New York more than Chicago!

New Yorkers, like the inhabitants of other large cities, are supposed to be sophisticated. The word, of course, is related to sophistry—the ability to be clever with words, to be quick, to be surprised at nothing. This notion of sophistication is closely related to that of urbanity, and it is as much a source of pride for the urbanite as it is a provocation to others. Somebody once defined a true metropolis as a place where an individual can march down the street wearing a purple robe and a hat with bells on it, beating a drum and leading an elephant by the leash, and only get casual glances from passers-by. If so, then surely New York is the truest metropolis there is. To some extent, of course, this is but another expression of the aforementioned universalism. But there is more: *The city is a place of magic.* And in that, too, I would contend, it offers us a signal of transcendence. I don't mean occultism, though there is enough of that around as well. I mean magic in a more ample sense, namely, the quality of the surreal, the intuition that reality is manipulable, unpredictable, subject to the strangest metamorphoses at any moment. If you will, I mean what Rudolf Otto called the *mysterium fascinans.* The British author Jonathan Raban, in his curious book *Soft City*, argues that modern urban life is characterized by magic, and *not* (as it is more customarily thought to be) by rationality. I think that there is much to be said for this view; Raban also maintains that New York has this magic in a particularly potent form. The magic of the city can be summed up in a sentence that sums up a recurring experience: *Anything can happen here—and it could happen right now.*

Magic always has its dark side, and it is hardly necessary to spell out the sinister possibilities of the insight that anything can happen. But it would be a mistake to limit the experience to its negative aspect. The city is a place of strangers and of strangeness, and this very fact implies a fascination of a special kind. Ordinary-looking houses contain unimaginable mysteries within. Casual encounters are transformed into revelations of shocking impact. Passions explode in the most unexpected occasions. All of this helps to account for the excitement of the city, but it also makes for a general vision of the world: Reality is not what it seems; there are realities behind the reality of everyday life; the routine fabric of our ordinary lives is not self-contained, it has holes in it, and there is no telling what wondrous things may at any moment rush in through these holes. This vision of the world is perhaps not itself religious, but it is in close proximity to the root insights of the religious attitude. The magic of the city should not, then, be identified with religious experience, but it may be said to be an antechamber of the latter. Thus, when people say that New York City is a surrealistic place, they are saying more than they intend. They are making an ontological statement about the reality of human life. Behind the empirical city lurks *another city*, a city of dreams and wonders. They are also making a soteriological statement, for redemption always comes into the world as a big surprise—I would even say, as a cosmic joke. Anything at all can come through the holes in the fabric of ordinary reality—a man leading an elephant by the leash, or a man riding on a donkey to inaugurate the mystery of our salvation.

Some of the above may sound as if I have become a latter-day convert to some version of secular theology (maybe a sort of North American centrist adaptation of the theology of liberation?). Let me say as strongly as I can that this is not at all the case. Indeed, the theological considerations in this chapter are directly opposite to the procedure that has been characteristic of the various expressions of secular theology. That procedure, in the final analysis, is always the same: The symbols of transcendence in the Christian tradition are reinterpreted to become symbols of the human condition, the divine becomes a metaphor of the human, the meta-empirical of ordinary empirical reality. I'm suggesting here the precisely opposite procedure: The human condition itself is to be seen as the penumbra of the transcendent, the human points to the divine, the empirical is a metaphor of the meta-empirical. Whatever have been the shifting contents of secular theology—philosophical, psychological, most recently political—they have served as the substratum to which the traditional symbols are reduced. I strongly reject this reductionist procedure. I suggest the precise opposite of reduction, namely, a hesitantly inductive procedure which begins with the empirical realities of human life, but which intends from the start to transcend these realities.

Nor am I proposing that these or any other signals of transcendence be taken as the substance of our faith. Rather, they are particular experiences which, for some of us, may serve as auxiliaries of faith. Contrary to what some may think, I'm not suggesting that my particular vision of New York City be incorporated in the *kerygma* of the church. And I'm definitely willing to remain in full Christian communion with all those who fail to understand the deeper significance of this city. If there is a polemical edge to what I have written here, it is against those who would provide a theological rationale for the anti-urbanism that is rampant today in the radical wing of the ecology movement—but this was certainly not foremost in my mind.

There is a route I drive regularly, between Rutgers University in New Jersey, where I teach, and Brooklyn, where I live. It crosses from Staten Island over the Verrazano-Narrows Bridge. It has often occurred to me, especially in the evening when the light is soft and the contours of visual reality seem to lack firmness, that the entrance to heaven may well look something like this wonderful bridge, with its majestic arcs and its breathtaking vistas on both sides. I wish for all of us that we will be part of this traffic in the evening of our lives, that we will be forgiven the toll at the gate, and that we will know that, in the city on the other side of the bridge, what awaits us is home. I, for one, will not be overly surprised if the gatekeeper addresses me in a Brooklyn accent.

112

Modernism in New York

MARSHALL BERMAN

Marshall Berman is Professor of Political Science at City University of New York. He lives on the City's Upper West Side and writes very much as an inhabitant of New York rather than as a commentator. *All That Is Solid Melts Into Air* (1982) is a wide-ranging discussion of "the experience of modernity", a condition full "of paradox and contradiction" in which "immense bureaucratic organizations ... have the power to control and often to destroy all communities". The section which follows applies these "modern" terms of reference to New York and takes the work of Robert Moses as a primary icon of the age.

1. Robert Moses: The Expressway World

When you operate in an overbuilt metropolis, you have to hack your way with a meat ax.

I'm just going to keep right on building. You do the best you can to stop it.

Maxims of Robert Moses

... She it was put me straight
about the city when I said, it
makes me ill to see them run up
a new bridge like that in a few months
and I can't find time even to get
a book written. They have the power,
that's all, she replied. That's what you all
want. If you can't get it, acknowledge
at least what it is. And they're not
going to give it to you.

William Carlos Williams, "The Flower"

What sphinx of cement and aluminum hacked open their skulls
and ate up their brains and imagination? ...
Moloch whose buildings are judgment!

Allen Ginsberg, "Howl"

Source: Marshall Berman, "Robert Moses: The Expressway World", *All That is Solid Melts into Air*, New York, 1982.

Among the many images and symbols that New York has contributed to modern culture, one of the most striking in recent years has been an image of modern ruin and devastation. The Bronx, where I grew up, has even become an international code word for our epoch's accumulated urban nightmares: drugs, gangs, arson, murder, terror, thousands of buildings abandoned, neighborhoods transformed into garbage- and brick-strewn wilderness. The Bronx's dreadful fate is experienced, though probably not understood, by hundreds of thousands of motorists every day, as they negotiate the Cross-Bronx Expressway, which cuts through the borough's center. This road, although jammed with heavy traffic day and night, is fast, deadly fast; speed limits are routinely transgressed, even at the dangerously curved and graded entrance and exit ramps; constant convoys of huge trucks, with grimly aggressive drivers, dominate the sight lines; cars weave wildly in and out among the trucks: it is as if everyone on this road is seized with a desperate, uncontrollable urge to get out of the Bronx as fast as wheels can take him. A glance at the cityscape to the north and south—it is hard to get more than quick glances, because much of the road is below ground level and bounded by brick walls ten feet high—will suggest why: hundreds of boarded-up abandoned buildings and charred and burnt-out hulks of buildings; dozens of blocks covered with nothing at all but shattered bricks and waste.

Ten minutes on this road, an ordeal for anyone, is especially dreadful for people who remember the Bronx as it used to be: who remember these neighborhoods as they once lived and thrived, until this road itself cut through their heart and made the Bronx, above all, a place to get out of. For children of the Bronx like myself, this road bears a load of special irony: as we race through our childhood world, rushing to get out, relieved to see the end in sight, we are not merely spectators but active participants in the process of destruction that tears our hearts. We fight back the tears, and step on the gas.

Robert Moses is the man who made all this possible. When I heard Allen Ginsberg ask at the end of the 1950s, "Who was that sphinx of cement and aluminum," I felt sure at once that, even if the poet didn't know it, Moses was his man. Like Ginsberg's "Moloch, who entered my soul early," Robert Moses and his public works had come into my life just before my Bar Mitzvah, and helped bring my childhood to an end. He had been present all along, in a vague subliminal way. Everything big that got built in or around New York seemed somehow to be his work: the Triborough Bridge, the West Side Highway, dozens of parkways in Westchester and Long Island, Jones and Orchard beaches, innumerable parks, housing developments, Idlewild (now Kennedy) Airport, a network of enormous dams and power plants near Niagara Falls; the list seemed to go on forever. He had generated an event that had special magic for me: the 1939–40 World's Fair, which I had attended in my mother's womb, and whose elegant logo, the trylon and perisphere, adorned our apartment in many forms—programs, banners, postcards, ashtrays—and symbolized human adventure, progress, faith in the future, all the heroic ideals of the age into which I was born.

But then, in the spring and fall of 1953, Moses began to loom over my life in a new way: he proclaimed that he was about to ram an immense expressway, unprecedented in scale, expense and difficulty of construction, through our neighborhood's heart. At first we couldn't believe it; it seemed to come from another world. First of all, hardly any of us owned cars: the neighborhood itself, and the subways leading downtown, defined the flow of our lives. Besides, even if the city needed the road—or was it the state that needed the road? (in Moses' operations, the location of power and authority was never clear, except for Moses himself)—they surely couldn't mean what the stories seemed to say: that the road would be blasted directly through a dozen solid, settled, densely populated neighborhoods like our own; that something like 60,000 working- and lower-middle-class people, mostly Jews, but with many Italians, Irish and blacks thrown in, would be thrown out of their homes. The Jews of the Bronx were nonplussed: could a fellow-Jew really want to do this to us? (We had little idea of what kind of Jew he was, or of how much we were all an obstruction in his path.) And even if he did want to do it, we were sure it couldn't happen here, not in America. We were still basking in the afterglow of the New Deal: the government was *our* government, and it would come through to protect us in the end. And yet, before we knew it, steam shovels and bulldozers were there, and people were getting notice that they had better clear out fast. They looked numbly at the wreckers, at the disappearing streets, at each other, and they went. Moses was coming through, and no temporal or spiritual power could block his way.

For ten years, through the late 1950s and early 1960s, the center of the Bronx was pounded and blasted and smashed. My friends and I would stand on the parapet of the Grand Concourse, where 174th Street had been, and survey the work's progress—the immense stream shovels and bulldozers and timber and steel beams, the hundreds of workers in their variously colored hard hats, the giant cranes reaching far above the Bronx's tallest roofs, the dynamite blasts and tremors, the wild, jagged crags of rock newly torn, the vistas of devastation stretching for miles to the east and west as far as the eye could see—and marvel to see our ordinary nice neighborhood transformed into sublime, spectacular ruins.

In college, when I discovered Piranesi, I felt instantly at home. Or I would return from the Columbia library to the construction site and feel myself in the midst of the last act of Goethe's Faust. (You had to hand it to Moses: his works gave you ideas.) Only there was no humanistic triumph here to offset the destruction. Indeed, when the construction was done, the real ruin of the Bronx had just begun. Miles of streets alongside the road were choked with dust and fumes and deafening noise—most strikingly, the roar of trucks of a size and power that the Bronx had never seen, hauling heavy cargoes through the city, bound for Long Island or New England, for New Jersey and all points south, all through the day and night. Apartment houses that had been settled and stable for twenty years emptied out, often virtually overnight; large and impoverished black and Hispanic families, fleeing even worse slums, were moved in wholesale, often under the auspices of the Welfare Department, which even paid inflated rents, spreading panic and accelerating flight. At the same time, the construction had destroyed many commercial blocks, cut others off from most of their customers and left the storekeepers not only close to bankruptcy but, in their enforced isolation, increasingly vulnerable to crime. The borough's great open market, along Bathgate Avenue, still flourishing in the late 1950s, was decimated; a year after the road came through, what was left went up in smoke. Thus depopulated, economically depleted, emotionally shattered—as bad as the physical damage had been the inner wounds were worse—the Bronx was ripe for all the dreaded spirals of urban blight.

Moses seemed to glory in the devastation. When he was asked, shortly after the Cross-Bronx road's completion, if urban expressways like this didn't pose special human problems, he replied impatiently that "there's very little hardship in the thing. There's a little discomfort and even that is exaggerated." Compared with his earlier, rural and suburban highways, the only difference here was that "There are more houses in the way ... more people in the way—that's all." He boasted that "When you operate in an overbuilt metropolis, you have to hack your way with a meat ax.[1]" The subconscious equation here—animals' corpses to be chopped up and eaten, and "people in the way"—is enough to take one's breath away. Had Allen Ginsberg put such metaphors into his Moloch's mouth, he would have never been allowed to get away with it: it would have seemed, simply, too much. Moses' flair for extravagant cruelty, along with his visionary brilliance, obsessive energy and megalomaniac ambition, enabled him to build, over the years, a quasi-mythological reputation. He appeared as the latest in a long line of titanic builders and destroyers, in history and in cultural mythology: Louis XIV, Peter the Great, Baron Haussmann, Joseph Stalin (although fanatically anti-communist, Moses loved to quote the Stalinist maxim "You can't make an omelette without breaking eggs"), Bugsy Siegel (master builder of the mob, creator of Las Vegas), "Kingfish" Huey Long; Marlowe's Tamburlaine, Goethe's Faust, Captain Ahab, Mr. Kurtz, Citizen Kane. Moses did his best to raise himself to gigantic stature, and even came to enjoy his increasing reputation as a monster, which he believed would intimidate the public and keep potential opponents out of the way.

In the end, however—after forty years—the legend he cultivated helped to do him in: it brought him thousands of personal enemies, some eventually as resolute and resourceful as Moses himself, obsessed with him, passionately dedicated to bringing the man and his machines to a stop. In the late 1960s they finally succeeded, and he was stopped and deprived of his power to build. But his works still surround us, and his spirit continues to haunt our public and private lives.

It is easy to dwell endlessly on Moses' personal power and style. But this emphasis tends to obscure one of the primary sources of his vast authority: his ability to convince a mass public that he was the vehicle of impersonal world-historical forces, the moving spirit of modernity. For forty years, he was able to pre-empt the vision of the modern. To oppose his bridges, tunnels, expressways, housing developments, power dams, stadia, cultural centers, was—or so it seemed—to oppose history, progress, modernity itself. And few people, especially in New

York, were prepared to do that. "There are people who like things as they are. I can't hold out any hope to them. They have to keep moving further away. this is a great big state, and there are other states. Let them go to the Rockies.[2]" Moses struck a chord that for more than a century has been vital to the sensibility of New Yorkers: our identification with progress, with renewal and reform, with the perpetual transformation of our world and ourselves—Harold Rosenberg called it "the tradition of the New." How many of the Jews of the Bronx, hotbed of every form of radicalism, were willing to fight for the sanctity of "things as they are"? Moses was destroying our world, yet he seemed to be working in the name of values that we ourselves embraced.

I can remember standing above the construction site for the Cross-Bronx Expressway, weeping for my neighborhood (whose fate I foresaw with nightmarish precision), vowing remembrance and revenge, but also wrestling with some of the troubling ambiguities and contradictions that Moses' work expressed. The Grand Concourse, from whose heights I watched and thought, was our borough's closest thing to a Parisian boulevard. Among its most striking features were rows of large, splendid 1930s apartment houses: simple and clear in their architectural forms, whether geometrically sharp or biomorphically curved; brightly colored in contrasting brick, offset with chrome, beautifully interplayed with large areas of glass; open to light and air, as if to proclaim a good life that was open not just to the elite residents but to us all. The style of these buildings, known as Art Deco today, was called "modern" in their prime. For my parents, who described our family proudly as a "modern" family, the Concourse buildings represented a pinnacle of modernity. We couldn't afford to live in them—though we did live in a small, modest, but still proudly "modern" building, far down the hill—but they could be admired for free, like the rows of glamorous ocean liners in port downtown. (The buildings look like shell-shocked battleships in drydock today, while the ocean liners themselves are all but extinct.)

As I saw one of the loveliest of these buildings being wrecked for the road, I felt a grief that, I can see now, is endemic to modern life. So often the price of ongoing and expanding modernity is the destruction not merely of "traditional" and "pre-modern" institutions and environments but—and here is the real tragedy—of everything most vital and beautiful in the modern world itself. Here in the Bronx, thanks to Robert Moses, the modernity of the urban boulevard was being condemned as obsolete, and blown to pieces, by the modernity of the interstate highway. *Sic transit!* To be modern turned out to be far more problematical, and more perilous, than I had been taught.

What were the roads that led to the Cross-Bronx Expressway? The public works that Moses organized from the 1920s onward expressed a vision—or rather a series of visions—of what modern life could and should be. I want to articulate the distinctive forms of modernism that Moses defined and realized, to suggest their inner contradictions, their ominous undercurrents—which burst to the surface in the Bronx—and their lasting meaning and value for modern mankind.

Moses' first great achievement, at the end of the 1920s, was the creation of a public space radically different from anything that had existed anywhere before: Jones Beach State Park on Long Island, just beyond the bounds of New York City along the Atlantic. This beach, which opened in the summer of 1929, and recently celebrated its fiftieth anniversary, is so immense that it can easily hold a half million people on a hot Sunday in July without any sense of congestion. Its most striking feature as a landscape is its amazing clarity of space and form: absolutely flat, blindingly white expanses of sand, stretching forth to the horizon in a straight wide band, cut on one side by the clear, pure, endless blue of the sea, and on the other by the boardwalk's sharp unbroken line of brown. The great horizontal sweep of the whole is punctuated by two elegant Art Deco bathhouses of wood, brick and stone, and half-way between them at the park's dead center by a monumental columnar water tower, visible from everywhere, rising up like a skyscraper, evoking the grandeur of the twentieth-century urban forms that this park at once complements and denies. Jones Beach offers a spectacular display of the primary forms of nature—earth, sun, water, sky—but nature here appears with an abstract horizontal purity and a luminous clarity that only culture can create.

We can appreciate Moses' creation even more when we realize (as Caro explains vividly) how much of this space had been swamp and wasteland, inaccessible and unmapped, until Moses got there, and what a spectacular metamorphosis he brought about in barely two years. There is another kind of purity that is crucial to Jones Beach. There is no intrusion of modern business or commerce here: no hotels, casinos, ferris wheels, roller coasters, parachute jumps, pinball machines, honky-tonks, loudspeakers, hot-dog stands, neon signs; no dirt, random noise or disarray.[3] Hence, even when Jones Beach is filled with a crowd the size of Pittsburgh, its ambience manages to be remarkably serene. It contrasts radically with Coney Island, only a few miles to the west, whose middle-class constituency it immediately captured on its opening. All the density and intensity, the anarchic noise and motion, the seedy vitality that is expressed in Weegee's photographs and Reginald Marsh's etchings, and celebrated symbolically in Lawrence Ferlinghetti's "A Coney Island of the Mind," is wiped off the map in the visionary landscape of Jones Beach.[4]

What would a Jones Beach of the mind be like? It would be hard to convey in poetry, or in any sort of symbolic language that depends on dramatic movement and contrast for its impact. But we can see its forms in the diagrammatic paintings of Mondrian, and later in the minimalism of the 1960s, while its color tonalities belong in the great tradition of neoclassical landscape, from Poussin to the young Matisse to Milton Avery. On a sunny day, Jones Beach transports us into the great romance of the Mediterranean, of Apollonian clarity, of perfect light without shadows, cosmic geometry, unbroken perspectives stretching onward toward an infinite horizon. This romance is at least as old as Plato. Its most passionate and influential modern devotee is Le Corbusier. Here, in the same year that Jones Beach opened, just before the Great Crash, he delineates his classic modern dream:

If we compare New York with Istanbul, we may say that the one is a cataclysm, and the other a terrestrial paradise.

New York is exciting and upsetting. So are the Alps; so is a tempest; so is a battle. New York is not beautiful, and if it stimulates our practical activities, it wounds our sense of happiness. ...

A city can overwhelm us with its broken lines; the sky is torn by its ragged outline. Where shall we find repose? ...

As you go North, the crocketed spires of the cathedrals reflect the agony of the flesh, the poignant dreams of the spirit, hell and purgatory, and forests of pines seen through pale light and cold mist.

Our bodies demand sunshine.

There are certain shapes that cast shadows.[5]

Le Corbusier wants structures that will bring the fantasy of a serene, horizontal South against the shadowed, turbulent realities of the North. Jones Beach, just beyond the horizon of New York's skyscrapers, is an ideal realization of this romance. It is ironic that, although Moses thrived on perpetual conflict, struggle, *Sturm und Drang*, his first triumph, and the one of which he seems to be proudest half a century later, was a triumph of *luxe, calme et volupté*. Jones Beach is the giant Rosebud of this Citizen Cohen.

Moses' Northern and Southern State parkways, leading from Queens out to Jones Beach and beyond, opened up another dimensions of modern pastoral. These gently flowing, artfully landscaped roads, although a little frayed after half a century, are still among the world's most beautiful. But their beauty does not (like that of, say, California's Coast Highway or the Appalachian Train) emanate from the natural environment around the roads: it springs from the artificially created environment of the roads themselves. Even if these parkways adjoined nothing and led nowhere, they would still constitute an adventure in their own right. This is especially true of the Northern State Parkway, which ran through the country of palatial estates that Scott Fitzgerald had just immortalized in *The Great Gatsby*[6] (1925). Moses' first Long Island roadscapes represent a modern attempt to recreate what Fitzgerald's narrator, on the novel's last page, described as "the old island here that flowered once for Dutch sailors' eyes—a fresh, green breast of the new world." But Moses made this breast available only through the mediation of that other symbol so dear to Gatsby: the green light. His parkways could be experienced only in cars: their underpasses were purposely built too low for buses to clear them, so that public transit could not bring masses of people out from the city to the beach. This was a distinctively techno-pastoral garden, open only to those who possessed the latest modern machines—this was, remember, the age of the Model T—and a uniquely privatized form of public space. Moses used physical design as a means of social screening, screening out all those without wheels of their own. Moses, who never learned to drive, was becoming Detroit's man in New York. For the great majority of New Yorkers, however, his green new world offered only a red light.

Jones Beach and Moses' first Long Island parkways should be seen in the context of the spectacular growth of leisure activities and industries during the economic boom of the 1920s. These Long Island projects were meant to open up a pastoral world just beyond the city limits, a world made for holidays and play and fun—for those who had the time and the means to step out. The metamorphoses of Moses in the 1930s need to be seen in the light of great transformation in the meaning of construction itself. During the Great Depression, as private business and industry collapsed, and mass unemployment and desperation increased, construction was transformed from a private into a public enterprise, and into a serious and urgent public imperative. Virtually everything serious that was built in the 1930s—bridges, parks, roads, tunnels, dams—was built with federal money, under the auspices of the great New Deal agencies, the CWA, PWA, CCC, FSA, TVA. These projects were planned around complex and well-articulated social goals. First, they were meant to create business, increase consumption and stimulate the private sector. Second, they would put millions of unemployed people back to work, and help to purchase social peace. Third, they would speed up, concentrate and modernize the economies of the regions in which they were built, from Long Island to Oklahoma. Fourth, they would enlarge the meaning of "the public," and give symbolic demonstrations of how American life could be enriched both materially and spiritually through the medium of public works. Finally, in their use of exciting new technologies, the great New Deal projects dramatized the promise of a glorious future just emerging over the horizon, a new day not merely for a privileged few but for the people as a whole.

Moses was perhaps the first person in America to grasp the immense possibilities of the Roosevelt administration's commitment to public works; he grasped, too, the extent to which the destiny of American cities was going to be worked out in Washington from this point on. Now holding a joint appointment as City and State Parks Commissioner, he established close and lasting ties with the most energetic and innovative planners of the new Deal bureaucracy. He learned how to free millions of dollars in federal funds in a remarkably short time. Then, hiring a staff of first-rate planners and engineers (mostly from off the unemployment lines), he mobilized a labor army of 80,000 men and went to work with a great crash program to regenerate the city's 1700 parks (even more rundown at the nadir of the Depression than they are today) and create hundreds of new ones, plus hundreds of playgrounds and several zoos. Moses got the job done by the end of 1934. Not only did he display a gift for brilliant administration and execution, he also understood the value of ongoing public work as public spectacle. He carried on the overhauling of Central Park, and the construction of its reservoir and zoo, twenty-four hours a day, seven days a week: floodlights shined and jackhammers reverberated all through the night, not only speeding up the work but creating a new showplace that kept the public enthralled.

The workers themselves seem to have been caught up in the enthusiasm: they not only kept up with the relentless pace that Moses and his straw bosses imposed but actually outpaced the bosses, and took initiative, and came up with new ideas, and worked ahead of plans, so that the engineers were repeatedly forced to run back to their desks and redesign the plans to take account of the progress the workers had made on their own.[7] This is the modern romance of construction at its best—the romance celebrated by Goethe's Faust, by Carlyle and Marx, by the constructivists of the 1920s, by the Soviet construction films of the Five-Year Plan period, and the TVA and FSA documentaries and WPA murals of the later 1930s. What gave the romance a special reality and authenticity here is the fact that it inspired the men who were actually doing the work. They seem to have been able to find meaning and excitement in work that was physically gruelling and ill-paying, because they had some vision of the work as a whole, and believed in its value to the community of which they were a part.

The tremendous public acclaim that Moses received for his work on the city's parks served him as a springboard for something that meant far more to him than parks. This was a system of highways, parkways and bridges that would weave the whole metropolitan area together: the elevated West Side Highway, extending the length of Manhattan, and across Moses' new Henry Hudson Bridge, into and through the Bronx, and into Westchester; the Belt Parkway, sweeping around the periphery of Brooklyn, from the East River to the Atlantic, connected to Manhattan through the Brooklyn-Battery Tunnel (Moses would have preferred a bridge), and to the Southern State; and—here was the heart of the system—the Triborough Project, an enormously complex network of bridges and approaches and parkways that would link Manhattan, the Bronx and Westchester with Queens and Long Island.

These projects were incredibly expensive, yet Moses managed to talk Washington into paying for most of them. They were technically brilliant: the Triborough engineering is still a classic text today. They helped, as Moses said, to "weave together the loose strands and frayed edges of the New York metropolitan arterial tapestry," and to give this enormously complex region a unity and coherence it has never had. They created a series of spectacular new visual approaches to the city, displaying the grandeur of Manhattan from many new angles—from the Belt Parkway, the Grand Central, the upper West Side—and nourishing a whole new generation of urban fantasies.[8] The uptown Hudson riverfront, one of Moses' finest urban landscapes, is especially striking when we realize that (as Caro shows, in pictures) it was a wasteland of hoboes' shacks and garbage dumps before he got there. You cross the George Washington Bridge and dip down and around and slide into the gentle curve of the West Side Highway, and the lights and towers of Manhattan flash and glow before you, rising above the lush greenness of Riverside park, and even the most embittered enemy of Robert Moses—or, for that matter, of New York—will be touched: you know you have come home again, and the city is there for you, and you can thank Moses for that.

At the every end of the 1930s, when Moses was at the height of his creativity, he was canonized in the book that, more than any other, established the canon of the modern movement in architecture, planning and design: Siegfried Giedion's *Space, Time and Architecture*. Giedion's work, first delivered in lecture form at Harvard in 1938–39, unfolded the history of three centuries of modern design and planning—and presented Moses' work as its climax. Giedion presented large photos of the recently completed West Side Highway, the Randall's Island cloverleaf, and the "pretzel" interchange of the Grand Central Parkway. These works, he said, "proved that possibilities of a great scale are inherent in our period." Giedion compared Moses' parkways to cubist paintings, to abstract sculptures and mobiles, and to the movies. "As with many of the creations born out of the spirit of this age, the meaning and beauty of the parkway cannot be grasped from a single point of observation, as was possible from a window of the château at Versailles. It can be revealed only by movement, by going along in a steady flow, as the rules of traffic prescribe. The space-time feeling of our period can seldom be felt so keenly as when driving."[9]

Thus Moses' projects marked not only a new phase in the modernization of urban space but a new breakthrough in modernist vision and thought. For Giedion, and for the whole generation of the 1930s—Corbusierian or Bauhaus formalists and technocrats, Marxists, even agrarian neopopulists—these parkways opened up a magical realm, a kind of romantic bower in which modernism and pastoralism could intertwine. Moses seemed to be the one public figure in the world who understood "the space-time conception of our period"; in addition, he had "the energy and enthusiasm of a Haussmann." This made him "uniquely equal, as Haussmann himself had been equal, to the opportunities and needs of the period," and uniquely qualified to build "the city of the future" in our time. Hegel in 1806 had conceived of Napoleon as "the *Weltseele* on horse"; for Giedion in 1939, Moses looked like the *Weltgeist* on wheels.

Moses received a further apotheosis at the 1939–40 New York World's Fair, an immense celebration of modern technology and industry: "Building the World of Tomorrow." Two of the fair's most popular exhibits—the commercially oriented General Motors Futurama and the utopian Democracity—both envisioned elevated urban expressways and arterial parkways connecting city and country, in precisely the forms that Moses had just built. Spectators on their way to and from the fair, as they flowed along Moses' roads and across his bridges, could directly experience something of this visionary future, and see that it seemed to work.[10]

Moses, in his capacity as Parks Commissioner, had put together the parcel of land on which the fair was being held. With lightning speed, at minimal cost, with his typical fusion of menace and finesse, he had seized from hundreds of owners a piece of land the size of downtown Manhattan. His proudest accomplishment in this affair was to have destroyed the notorious Flushing ash heaps and mounds of garbage that Scott Fitzgerald had immortalized as one of the great modern symbols of industrial and human waste:

> a valley of ashes—a fantastic farm where ashes grow like wheat into ridges and hills and grotesque gardens; where ashes take the forms of houses and chimneys and rising smoke and, finally, with a transcendent effort, of men who move dimly and already crumbling through the powdery air. Occasionally a line of gray cars crawls along an invisible track, gives out a ghastly creak, and comes to rest, and immediately the ash-gray men swarm up with leaden spades and stir up an impenetrable cloud, which screens their obscure operations from your sight. [*The Great Gatsby*, Chapter 2]

Moses obliterated this dreadful scene and transformed the site into the nucleus of the fairgrounds, and later of Flushing Meadow Park. This action moved him to a rare effusion of Biblical lyricism: he invoked that beautiful passage from Isaiah (61:1–4) in which "the Lord has anointed me to bring good tidings to the afflicted; he has sent me to bind up the brokenhearted, to proclaim liberty to the captives, and the opening of the prison to those that are bound; ... to give unto them beauty for ashes ... [so that] they shall repair the ruined cities, the devastations of many generations." Forty years later, in his last interviews, he still pointed to this with special pride: I am the man who destroyed the Valley of Ashes and put beauty in its place. It is on this note—with the fervent faith that modern technology and social organization could create a world without ashes—that the modernism of the 1930s came to an end.

Where did it all go wrong? How did the modern visions of the 1930s turn sour in the process of their realization? The whole story would require far more time to unravel, and far more space to tell, than I have here and now. But we can rephrase these questions in a more limited way that will fit into the orbit of this book: How did Moses—and New York and America—move from the destruction of a Valley of Ashes in 1939 to the development of far more dreadful and intractable modern wastelands a generation later only a few miles away? We need to seek out the shadows within the luminous visions of the 1930s themselves.

The dark side was always there in Moses himself. Here is the testimony of Frances Perkins, America's first Secretary of Labor under FDR, who worked closely with Moses for many years and admired him all her life. She recalls the people's heartfelt love for Moses in the early years of the New Deal, when he was building playgrounds in Harlem and on the Lower East Side; however, she was disturbed to discover, "he doesn't love the people" in return:

> It used to shock me because he was doing all these things for the welfare of the people. ... To him, they were lousy, dirty people, throwing bottles all over Jones Beach. "I'll get them! I'll teach them!" He loves the public, but not as people. The public is ... a great amorphous mass to him; it needs to be bathed, it needs to be aired, it needs recreation, but not for personal reasons—just to make it a better public.[11]

"He loves the public, but not as people": Dostoevsky warned us repeatedly that the combination of love for "humanity" with hatred for actual people was one of the fatal hazards of modern politics. During the New Deal period, Moses managed to maintain a precarious balance between the poles and to bring real happiness not only to "the public" he loved but also to the people he loathed. But no one could keep up this balancing act forever. "I'll get them! I'll teach them!" The voice here is unmistakably that of Mr. Kurtz: "It was very simple," Conrad's narrator says, "and at the end of every idealistic sentiment it blazed at you, luminous and terrifying, like a flash of lightning in a serene sky: 'Exterminate all the brutes!'" We need to know what was Moses' equivalent for Mr. Kurtz's African ivory trade, what historical chances and institutional forces opened up the floodgates of his most dangerous drives: What was the road that led him from the radiance of "give unto them beauty for ashes" to "you have to hack your way with a meat ax" and the darkness that cleft the Bronx?

Part of Moses' tragedy is that he was not only corrupted but in the end undermined by one of his greatest achievements. This was a triumph that, unlike Moses' public works, was for the most part invisible: it was only in the late 1950s that investigative reporters began to perceive it. It was the creation of a network of enormous, interlocking "public authorities," capable of raising virtually unlimited sums of money to build with, and accountable to no executive, legislative or judicial power.[12]

The English institution of a "public authority" had been grafted onto American public administration early in the twentieth century. It was empowered to sell bonds to construct particular public works—e.g., bridges, harbors, railroads. When its project was completed, it would charge tolls for use until its bonds were paid off; at that point it would ordinarily go out of existence and turn its public work over to the state. Moses, however, saw that there was no reason for an authority to limit itself in time or space: so long as money was coming in—say, from tolls on the Triborough Bridge—and so long as the bond market was encouraging, an authority could trade in its old bonds for new ones, to raise more money, to build more works; so long as money (all of it tax-exempt) kept coming in, the banks and institutional investors would be only too glad to underwrite new bond issues, and the authority could go on building forever. Once the initial bonds were paid off, there would be no need to go to the city, state or federal governments, or to the people, for money to build. Moses proved in court that no government had any legal right even to look into an authority's books. Between the late 1930s and the late 1950s, Moses created or took over a dozen of these authorities—for parks, bridges, highways, tunnels, electric power, urban renewal and more—and integrated them into an immensely powerful machine, a machine with innumerable wheels within wheels, transforming its cogs into millionaires, incorporating thousands of businessmen and politicians into its production line, drawing millions of New Yorkers inexorably into its widening gyre.

Kenneth Burke suggested in the 1930s that whatever we might think of the social value of Standard Oil and U.S. Steel, Rockefeller's and Carnegie's work in creating these giant complexes had to be rated as triumphs of modern art. Moses' network of public authorities clearly belongs in this company. It fulfils one of the earliest dreams of modern science, a dream renewed in many forms of twentieth-century art: to create a system in perpetual motion. But Moses' system, even as it constitutes a triumph of modern art, shares in some of that art's deepest ambiguities. It carries the contradiction between "the public" and the people so far that in the end not even the people at the system's center—not even Moses himself—had the authority to shape the system and control its ever-expanding moves.

If we go back to Giedion's "bible," we will see some of the deeper meanings of Moses' work which Moses himself never really grasped. Giedion saw the Triborough Bridge, the Grand Central Parkway, the West Side Highway, as expressions of "the new form of the city." This form demanded "a different scale from that of the existing city, with its *rues corridors* and rigid divisions into small blocks." The new urban forms could not function freely within the framework of the nineteenth-century city: hence, "It is the actual structure of the city that most be changed." The first imperative was this: "There is no longer any place for the city street; it cannot be permitted to persist." Giedion took on an imperial voice here that was strongly reminiscent of Moses' own. But the destruction of the city streets was, for Giedion, only a beginning: Moses' highways "look ahead to the time when, after the necessary surgery has been performed, the artificially swollen city will be reduced to its natural size."

Leaving aside the quirks in Giedion's own vision (What makes any urban size more "natural" than any other?), we see here how modernism makes a dramatic new departure: the development of modernity has made the modern city itself old-fashioned, obsolete. True, the people, visions and institutions of the city have created the highway—"To New York ... must go the credit for the creation of the parkway."[13] Now, however, by a fateful dialectic, because the city and the highway don't go together, the city must go. Ebenezer Howard and his "Garden City" disciples had been suggesting something like this since the turn of the century (see above, Chapter IV). Moses' historical mission, from the standpoint of this vision, is to have created a new superurban reality that makes the city's obsolescence clear. To cross the Triborough Bridge, for Giedion, is to enter a new "space-time continuum," one that leaves the modern metropolis forever behind. Moses has shown that it is unnecessary to wait for some distant future: we have the technology and the origanizational tools to bury the city here and now.

Moses never meant to do this: unlike the "Garden City" thinkers, he genuinely loved New York—in his blind way—and never meant it any harm. His public works, whatever we may think of them, were meant to add something to city life, not to subtract the city itself. He would surely have recoiled at the thought that his 1939 World's Fair, one of the great moments in New York's history, would be the vehicle of a vision which, taken at face value, would spell the city's ruin. But when have world-historical figures ever understood the long-range meaning of their acts and works? In fact, however, Moses' great construction in and around New York in the 1920s and 30s served as a rehearsal for the infinitely greater reconstruction of the whole fabric of America after World War Two. The motive forces in this reconstruction were the multibillion-dollar Federal Highway Program and the vast suburban housing initiatives of the Federal Housing Administration. This new order integrated the whole nation into a unified flow whose lifeblood was the automobile. It conceived of cities principally as obstructions to the flow of traffic, and as junkyards of substandard housing and decaying neighborhoods from which Americans should be given every chance to escape. Thousands of urban neighborhoods were obliterated by this new order; what happened to my Bronx was only the largest and most dramatic instance of something that was happening all over. Three decades of massively capitalized highway construction and FHA suburbanization would serve to draw millions of people and jobs, and billions of dollars in investment capital, out of America's cities, and plunge these cities into the chronic crisis and chaos that plague their inhabitants today. This wasn't what Moses meant at all; but it was what he inadvertently helped to bring about.[14]

Moses' projects of the 1950s and 60s had virtually none of the beauty of design and human sensitivity that had distinguished his early works. Drive twenty miles or so on the Northern State Parkway (1920s), then turn around and cover those same twenty miles on the parallel Long Island Expressway (1950s/60s), and wonder and weep. Nearly all he built after the war was built in an indifferently brutal style, made to overawe and overwhelm: monoliths of steel and cement, devoid of vision or muance or play, sealed off from the surrounding city by great moats of stark empty space, stamped on the landscape with a ferocious contempt for all natural and human life. Now Moses seemed scornfully indifferent to the human quality of what he did: sheer quantity—of moving vehicles, tons of cement, dollars received and spent—seemed to be all that drove him now. There are sad ironies in this, Moses' last, worst phase.

The cruel works that cracked open the Bronx ("more people in the way—that's all") were part of a social process whose dimensions dwarfed even Moses' own megalomaniac will to power. By the 1950s he was no longer building in accord with his own visions; rather, he was fitting enormous blocks into a pre-existing pattern of national reconstruction and social integration that he had not made and could not have substantially changed. Moses at his best had been a true creator of new material and social possibilities. At his worst, he would become not so much a destroyer—though he destroyed plenty—as an executioner of directives and imperatives not his own. He had gained power and glory to institutionalize modernity into a system of grim, inexorable necessities and crushing routines. Ironically, he became a focus for mass personal obsession and hatred, including my own, just when he had lost personal vision and initiative and become an Organization Man; we came to know him as New York's Captain Ahab at a point when, although still at the wheel, he had lost control of the ship.

The evolution of Moses and his works in the 1950s underscores another important fact about the postwar evolution of culture and society: the radical splitting-off of modernism from modernization. Throughout this book I have tried to show a dialectical interplay between unfolding modernization of the environment—particularly the urban environment—and the development of modernist art and thought. This dialectic, crucial all through the nineteenth century, remained vital to the modernism of the 1920s and 1930s: it is central in Joyce's *Ulysses* and Eliot's *Waste Land* and Doblin's *Berlin, Alexanderplatz* and Mandelstam's *Egyptian Stamp*, in Lêger and Tatlin and Eisenstein, in William Carlos Williams and Hart Crane, in the art of John Marin and Joseph Stella and Stuart Davis and Edward Hopper, in the fiction of Henry Roth and Nathanael West. By the 1950s, however, in the wake of Auschwitz and Hiroshima, this process of dialogue had stopped dead.

It is not that culture itself stagnated or regressed: there were plenty of brilliant artists and writers around, working at or near the peak of their powers. The difference is that the modernists of the 1950s drew no energy or inspiration from the modern environment around them. from the triumphs of the abstract expressionists to the radical initiatives of Davis, Mingus and Monk in jazz, to Camus' *The Fall*, Beckett's *Waiting for Godot*, Malamud's *The Magic Barrel*, Laing's *The Divided Self*, the most exciting work of this era is marked by radical distance from any shared environment. The environment is not attacked, as it was in so many previous modernisms: it is simply not there.

This absence is dramatized obliquely in what are probably the two richest and deepest novels of the 1950s, Ralph Ellison's *Invisible Man* (1952) and Günter Grass's *The Tin Drum* (1959): both these books contained brilliant realizations of spiritual and political life as it had been lived in the cities of the recent past—Harlem and Danzig in the 1930s—but although both writers moved chronologically forward, neither one was able to imagine or engage the present, the life of the postwar cities and societies in which their books came out. This absence itself may be the most striking proof of the spiritual poverty of the new postwar environment. Ironically, that poverty may have actually nourished the development of modernism by forcing artists and thinkers to fall back on their own resources and open up new depths of inner space. At the same time, it subtly ate away at the roots of modernism by sealing off its imaginative life from the everyday modern world in which actual men and women had to move and live.[15]

The split between the modern spirit and the modernized environment was a primary source of anguish and reflection in the later 1950s. As the decade dragged on, imaginative people became increasingly determined not only to understand this great gulf but also, through art and thought and action, to leap across it. This was the desire that animated books as diverse as Hannah Arendt's *The Human Condition*, Norman Mailer's *Advertisements for Myself*, Norman O'Brown's *Life Against Death*, and Paul Goodman's *Growing Up Absurd*. It was a consuming but unconsummated obsession shared by two of the most vivid protagonists in the fiction of the late 1950s: Doris Lessing's Anna Wolf, whose notebooks overflowed with unfinished confessions and unpublished manifestos for liberation, and Saul Bellow's Moses Herzog, whose medium was unfinished, unmailed letters to all the great powers of this world.

Eventually, however, the letters did get finished, signed and delivered; new modes of modernist language gradually emerged, at once more personal and more political than the language of the 1950s, in which modern men and women could confront the new physical and social structures that had grown up around them. In this new modernism, the gigantic engines and systems of postwar construction played a central symbolic role. Thus, in Allen Ginsberg's "Howl":

> *What sphinx of cement and aluminum hacked open their skulls and ate up their brains and imagination? ...*
> *Moloch the incomprehensible prison! Moloch the crossbone soulless jailhouse and Congress of sorrows! Moloch whose buildings are judgment! ...*
> *Moloch whose eyes are a thousand blind windows! Moloch whose skyscrapers stand in the long streets like endless Jehovahs! Moloch whose factories dream and*

croak in the fog! Moloch whose smokestacks and antennae crown the cities!
Moloch! Moloch! Robot apartments! invisible suburbs! skeleton treasuries! blind capitals! demonic industries! spectral nations! invincible madhouses! granite cocks!
They broke their backs lifting Moloch to Heaven! Pavements, trees, radios, tons! lifting the city to Heaven which exists and is everywhere about us! ...
Moloch who entered my soul early! Moloch in whom I am a consciousness without a body! Moloch who frightened me out of my natural ecstasy! Moloch whom I abandon! Wake up in Moloch! Light streaming out of the sky!

There are many remarkable things happening here. Ginsberg is urging us to experience modern life not as a hollow wasteland but as an epic and tragic battle of giants. This vision endows the modern environment and its makers with a demonic energy and a world-historical stature that probably exceed even what the Robert Moseses of this world would claim for themselves. At the same time, the vision is meant to arouse us, the readers, to make ourselves equally great, to enlarge our desire and moral imagination to the point where we will dare to take on the giants. But we cannot do this until we recognize their desires and powers in ourselves—"Moloch who entered my soul early." Hence Ginsberg develops structures and processes of poetic language—an interplay between luminous flashes and bursts of desperate imagery and a solemn, repetitive, incantatory piling up of line upon line—that recall and rival the skyscrapers, factories and expressways he hates. Ironically, although the poet portrays the expressway world as the death of brains and imagination, his poetic vision brings its underlying intelligence and imaginative force of life—indeed, brings it more fully to life than the builders were ever able to do on their own.

When my friends and I discovered Ginsberg's Moloch and thought at once of Moses, we were not only crystallizing and mobilizing our hate; we were also giving our enemy the world-historical stature, the dreadful grandeur, that he had always deserved but never received from those who loved him most. They could not bear to look into the nihilistic abyss that his steam shovels and pile drivers opened up; hence they missed his depths. Thus it was only when modernists began to confront the shapes and shadows of the expressways world that it became possible to see that world for all it was.[16]

Did Moses understand any of this symbolism? It is hard to know. In the rare interviews he gave during the years between his enforced retirement[17] and his death at ninety-two, he could still explode with fury at his detractors, overflow with wit and energy and tremendous schemes, refuse, like Mr. Kurtz, to be counted out ("I'll carry out my ideas yet. ... I'll show you what can be done. ... I will return ... I ..."). Driven restlessly up and down his Long Island roads in his limousine (one of the few perquisites he had kept from his years of power), he dreamt of a glorious hundred-mile ocean drive to whip the waves, or of the world's longest bridge connecting Long Island with Rhode Island across the Sound.

This old man possessed an undeniable tragic grandeur; but it is not so clear that he ever achieved the self-awareness that is supposed to go with that grandeur. Replying to *The Power Broker,* Moses appealed plaintively to us all: Am I not the man who blotted out the Valley of Ashes and gave mankind beauty in its place? It is true, and we owe him homage for it. And yet, he did not really wipe out the ashes, only moved them to another site. For the ashes are part of us, no matter how straight and smooth we make our beaches and freeways, no matter how fast we drive—or are driven—no matter how far out on Long Island we go.

Notes

1. These statements are quoted by Robert Caro in his monumental study, *The Power Broker: Robert Moses and the Fall of New York* (Knopf, 1974), 849, 876. The "meat ax" passage is from Moses' memoir, *Public Works: A Dangerous Trade* (McGraw-Hill, 1970). Moses' appraisal of the Cross-Bronx Expressway occurs in an interview with Caro. *The Power Broker* is the main source for my narrative of Moses' career. See also my article on Caro and Moses, "Buildings Are Judgment: Robert Moses and the Romance of Construction," *Ramparts*, March 1975, and a further symposium in the June issue.

2. Speech to the Long Island Real Estate Board, 1927, quoted in Caro, 275.

3. But American enterprise never gives up. On weekends a continuous procession of small planes cruise just above the shoreline, skywriting or bearing banners to proclaim the glories of various brands of soda or vodka, or roller discos and sex clubs, of local politicians and propositions. Not even Moses has devised ways to zone business and politics out of the sky.

4. Coney Island epitomizes what the Dutch architect Rem Koolhaas calls "the culture of congestion." *Delirious New York: A Retrospective Manifesto for Manhattan*, especially 21-65. Koolhaas sees Coney Island as a prototype, a kind of rehearsal, for Manhattan's intensely vertical "city of towers"; compare the radically horizontal sweep of Jones Beach, which is only accentuated by the water tower, the one vertical structure allowed.

5. *The City of Tomorrow*, 64-66. See Koolhass, 199-223, on Le Corbusier and New York.

6. This generated bitter conflict with the estate owners, and enabled Moses to win a reputation as a champion of the people's right to fresh air, open space and the freedom to move. "It was exciting working for Moses," one of his engineers reminisced half a century later. "He made you feel you were a part of something big. It was you fighting for the people against these rich estate owners and reactionary legislators. ... It was almost like a war." (Caro, 228, 273) In fact, however, as Caro shows, virtually all the land Moses appropriated consisted of small homes and family farms.

7. For details of this episode, Caro, 368-72.

8. On the other hand, these projects made a series of drastic and near-fatal incursions into Manhattan's grid. Koolhaas, *Delirious New York*, 15, explains incisively the importance of this system to the New York environment: "The Grid's two-dimensional discipline creates undreamt-of freedom for three-dimensional anarchy. The Grid defines a new balance between control and decontrol. ... With its imposition, Manhattan is forever immunized against any [further] totalitarian intervention. In the single block—the largest possible area that can fall under architectural control—it develops a maximum unit of urbanistic Ego." It is precisely these urban ego-boundaries that Moses' own ego sought to sweep away.

9. *Space, Time and Architecture*, 823-32.

10. Walter Lippmann seems to have been one of the few who saw the long-range implications and hidden costs of this future. "General Motors has spent a small fortune to convince the American public," he wrote, "that if it wishes to enjoy the full benefit of private enterprise in motor manufacturing, it will have to rebuild its cities and its highways by public enterprise." This apt prophecy is quoted by Warren Susman in his fine essay "The People's Fair: Cultural Contradictions of a Consumer Society," included in the Queens Museum's catalogue volume, *Dawn of a New Day: The New York World's Fair*, 1939/40 (NYU, 1980), 25. This volume, which includes interesting essays by several hands, and splendid photographs, is the best book on the fair.

11. Frances Perkins, Oral History Reminiscences (Columbia University Collection), quoted in Caro, 318.

12. A definitive analysis of public authorities in America can be found in Anne-Marie Walsh, *The Public's Business: The Politics and Practices of Government Corporations* (MIT, 1978), especially Chapters 1, 2, 8, 11, 12. Walsh's book contains much fascinating material on Moses, but she places his work in a broad institutional and social context that Caro tends to leave out. Robert Fitch, in a perceptive 1976 essay, "Planning New York," tries to deduce all Moses' activities from the fifty-year

agenda that was established by the financiers and officials of the Regional Plan Association; it appears in Roger Alcaly and David Mermelstein, editors, *The Fiscal Crisis of American Cities* (Random House, 1977), 247–84.

13. Space, Time and Architecture, 831–32.

14. Moses at least was honest enough to call a meat ax by its real name, to recognize the violence and devastation at the heart of his works. Far more typical of postwar planning is a sensibility like Giedion's, for whom, "after the necessary surgery has been performed, the artificially swollen city will be reduced to its natural size." This genial self-delusion, which assumes that cities can be hacked to pieces without blood or wounds or shrieks of pain, points the way forward to the "surgical precision" bombing of Germany, Japan, and, later, Vietnam.

15. On the problems and paradoxes of that period, the best recent discussion is Morris Dickstein's essay "The Cold War Blues," which appears as Chapter 2 in his *Gates of Eden*. For interesting polemic on the 1950s, see Hilton Kramer's attack on Dickstein, "Trashing the Fifties," in the *New York Times Book Review*, 10 April 1977, and Dickstein's reply in the issue of 12 June.

16. For a slightly later version of this confrontation, very different in sensibility but equal in intellectual and visionary power, compare Robert Lowell's "For the Union Dead," published in 1964.

Chicago

113

Chicago: 'The Classical Center of American Materialism'

HENRY CLARIDGE

> Chicago asked in 1893 for the first time the question whether the American people knew where they were driving. Adams answered, for one, that he did not know, but would try to find out. On reflecting sufficiently deeply, under the shadow of Richard Hunt's architecture, he decided that the American people probably knew no more than he did; but that they might still be driving or drifting unconsciously to some point in thought, as their solar system was said to be drifting towards some point in space; and that, possibly, if relations enough could be observed, this point might be fixed. Chicago was the first expression of American thought as a unity; one must start there.
>
> —Henry Adams, *The Education of Henry Adams*, 1918.

I

Henry Adams visited Chicago in May and October of 1893, drawn there by the World's Fair (known also as the Columbian Exposition) with its grandiose displays of scientific and technological progress housed in buildings of an exaggerated classical and baroque splendour. Beyond the fair, however, the city that greeted Adams reflected the nascent triumphalism of what Adams characterized as a 'capitalistic system with all its necessary machinery'.[1] Chicago was substantially a product of the rebuilding that had followed the great fire of 1871; the fire had devastated a city in which some two-thirds of the buildings were entirely of wood, so much so that the reconstruction of the city presented the architects of Chicago with a *tabula rasa* on which to write their architectural innovations. The response was such that by the time Adams visited Chicago over $300,000,000 worth of building had been completed, most of it incorporating technological and design features that were unknown before the Civil War.[2] In 1893 Chicago boasted the tallest building in the world, the twenty-two storeys of the Masonic Temple, and a host of buildings between twelve and sixteen storeys high, notably the Monadnock Building and the Pontiac Building,

Source: Henry Claridge, "Chicago: 'The Classical Center of American Materialism'", *The American City: Literacy and Cultural Perspectives*. ed. Graham Clarke, London and New York, 1988, Ch. 4, pp. 86–104 © Henry Claridge.

buildings which have survived the devastation wrought by subsequent developers.

The city Adams saw was, in other words, unambiguously a product of the late nineteenth century; indeed, the city as a whole was exclusively a phenomenon of the nineteenth century: founded as a frontier post in 1803 with the establishment of Fort Dearborn on the south bank of the Chicago river, incorporated as a city in 1833, Chicago had, by 1893, become America's second most populous city, the census of 1890 giving a population in excess of 1,100,000, three-quarters of whom were foreign-born or their children. Chicago's rapid development was the result of geographical, economic, and technological conditions: it was at the head of a navigable river and even before the completion of the St. Lawrence Seaway was the largest inland port in the United States; the agricultural expansion of the Great Plains and of the South and South-West put Chicago at the centre of a network of distribution for farm produce; and the development of the railroad system gave Chicago unique economic and financial advantages which greatly facilitated the industrial growth of the city. By the time of the great fire of 1871 Chicago was the railroad hub of the United States and was simultaneously at the centre of the largest network of inland waterways in the world; with these came the commercial wealth that (on which) built the city Henry Adams saw in 1893.

2

Adams's observation that Chicago offers an image of "American thought as a unity" can be understood by contrasting the city with those other, older, American cities with which Adams was more than familiar. Unlike Boston or Washington, Chicago possessed no relics, physical or otherwise, of a republican or colonial past; indeed, its rapid development made it, virtually, a city without a history. Politics, society, history, religion, culture: all these things impress themselves upon Henry Adams as he recalls a childhood in Quincy or life as a political journalist in Washington and for him they have a rich particularity. Chicago, however, seems little more than an embodiment of forces, whether those of Darwinian evolution, the dynamo, the steam engine, or money. In many ways these forces are more real than the certainties of Adams's upbringing, but they are the precipitants of an unknown future rather than the memories of a known past. Thus in his writing about Chicago Adams is always looking forward, impressed by the possibilities of what the city may hold but distrustful of the culture (or its absence) that sustains it; so much so that he becomes one of the first commentators to register the Eastern seaboard's somewhat disdainful attitude to this provincial, midwestern upstart:

> If the people of the Northwest actually knew what was good when they saw it, they would some day talk about Hunt and Richardson, La Farge and St. Gaudens, Burnham and McKim, and Stanford White when their politicians and millionaires were otherwise forgotten. The artists and architects who had done the work offered little encouragement to hope it; they talked freely enough, but not in terms that one

> cared to quote; and to them the Northwest refused to look artistic. They talked as though they worked only for themselves; as though art, to the Western people, was a stage decoration; a diamond shirt-stud; a paper collar; but possibly the architects of Paestum and Girgenti had talked in the same way, and the Greek had said the same thing of Semitic Carthage two thousand years ago.[3]

This was, and is, a common question: does Chicago have a culture (and a cultural life), and if it does do its people take any interest in it? The difficulty Adams has in answering the question turns on an issue that runs as a kind of motif in the writing on Chicago: the belief that materialism, or commercial life, and artistic culture are mutually exclusive conditions. It is there in the writings of the early Chicago realists, notably Henry Blake Fuller and Theodore Dreiser, in the writers of the second phase of what has been called the "Chicago Renaissance" such as Sherwood Anderson and Carl Sandburg, and in the recent writings of Saul Bellow. That the issue is, in some senses, an illusory one is apparent when one remembers that it was a material, commercial society which paid for the very buildings Adams took as problematic evidence of Chicago's cultural life and which sustained, directly or indirectly, the writers of the Chicago Renaissance; and where would Saul Bellow be as a novelist without the Chicago backcloth that informs much of his fiction? The belief that the city is inimical to culture and the arts is an unavoidable consequence of our Romantic heritage which carries with it a complex set of assumptions about the moral superiority of the natural landscape.[4] But it is an illusion, nonetheless, and the paradox has been (and continues to be) that those writers on the city who argue its animosity to cultural and aesthetic life are, themselves, often the best evidence we have for maintaining the opposite viewpoint.

The view that the Chicago of the 1890s was uncivilized was not exclusive to American observers. Rudyard Kipling visited Chicago in 1891; he conceded it was "a real city" but found it "inhabited by savages" and displayed a barbarism of which a "Hottentot would not have been guilty ..."[5] He dwells at some length on the slaughterhouses of the Union Stockyards and on the people who work there, but there is no mention of the Art Institute, of the Auditorium Building of Dankmar Adler and Louis Sullivan, or of the Chicago Opera House; one sees, perhaps, what one wants to see. Yet the account of the city Kipling offers retains its interest, in part because it presents, in common with those accounts of so many other observers, past and present, the idea of Chicago as the realization of material ambitions and gives a strong sense of its restless physicality.

As Alfred Kazin has remarked, Chicago was, for the writers of the early years of American realism, "the symbolic city of the nineties".[6] Those who knew Chicago intimately, as did Henry Blake Fuller, Theodore Dreiser, Robert Herrick and Frank Norris, found that it offered them the richest of resources for their fiction: a density of social activity encompassing ambition, corruption, wealth, poverty, tragedy and comedy that seemed almost inexhaustible. In Fuller's *The Cliff-Dwellers* (1893), the first important novel about Chicago and the first novel set in a skyscraper, the novelist's civilized disdain of material, metropolitan civilization (something Fuller shared with Kipling) is oddly commingled with an obsessive interest in the vagaries of city life and the sense that in Chicago the new (imminent) century is made manifest, that the city is a transitional symbol in both American history and American geography. Fuller's real estate salesman, Eugene H. McDowell, is the voice which articulates this:

> You've got to have a big new country behind you. How much do you suppose people in Iowa and Kansas and Minnesota think about Down East? Not a great deal. It's Chicago they're looking to. This town looms up before them and shuts out Boston and New York and the whole seaboard from the sight and the thoughts of the West and the Northwest and the new Northwest and the Far West and all the other Wests yet to be invented. They read our papers, they come here to buy and to enjoy themselves. ... And what kind of a town is it that's wanted ... to take up a big national enterprise and pull it through with a rush? A big town, of course, but one that has grown big so fast that it hasn't had time to grow up. ...[7]

One hears here the "boosterism" for which Chicago got its reputation as "The Windy City". What upsets Fuller is the kind of future men like McDowell augur. In his next novel *With the Procession* (1895) Fuller explores the next stage of the money-making saga—once made what does one do with it? Here, in a variation on the Christian injunction "to store ye not up treasures on earth", the antiphonal relationship between commercial wealth and art is played out as a major theme. The dying capitalist, David Marshall, having lived a life circumscribed by the pursuit of money and profit, is now prevailed upon to use some of that wealth in the service of what the historian William E. Leuchtenburg calls "a benevolent materialism".[8] Mrs. Bates, who represents the solid backbone of Chicago wealth and whose husband has endowed a girls' dormitory at the new University of Chicago, is the voice of philantropic materialism:

> "You have made a good deal of money, they tell me, and you are getting ready to make a good deal more—*that* I see for myself. But doesn't it seem to you", she proceeded, carefully, "that things are beginning to be different?—that the man who enjoys the best position and the most consideration is not the man who is making money, but the man who is giving it away—not the man who is benefiting himself, but the man who is benefiting the community. *There* is an art to cultivate, David—the art of giving. Give liberally and rightly, and nothing can bring you more credit."[9]

Mrs. Bates is not an attractive figure, but she articulates Fuller's recognition that the Chicago of the 1890s sought to purchase the very culture that it had failed to produce, that, like other cities of the mid-west, it would assume something of a custodial rôle in the cultural affairs of the world, cultivating an orchestra to play European classics, an art gallery to house European paintings, and a university to disseminate European science and learning. Fuller had travelled widely, and he constantly compared the Chicago in which he lived with the older cities of Europe where he had been a visitor; the comparison was never particularly favourable to Chicago, but, we might say, the dice were always heavily loaded against his home town. Like Henry Adams, Fuller could see that Chicago stood, symbolically, for a transitional moment in the American experience; unlike

Adams he was not prepared to reserve his judgement with respect to the inherent properties of the symbol.

Chicago, like a number of American cities, sought what Umberto Eco has called "reassurance through imitation"[10]—where the iconic frame of reference serves as confirmation of the city's arrival as a metropolitan centre. The Columbian Exposition, the Opera House, the University of Chicago, all housed in buildings which mimicked a baroque and gothic architectural past, exemplified a city which was sharing, vicariously, in the heritage of a civilization and was guided, in turn, by what Thorstein Veblen has called "the canons of conspicuous waste and predatory exploit".[11] To a later generation of American intellectuals this sense of America living vicariously through a culture it had purchased, where conspicuous leisure was one of the by-products of a culture of industrialism, was used to bemoan the absence of an "organic culture", the argument presupposing that culture and industrialism are mutually exclusive conditions. One finds this theme, most saliently, in the writings of Van Wyck Brooks, particularly *Letters and Leadership* (1918), and it is tempting to see it as a further instance of that Eastern disdain of the mid-west noted in Henry Adams. Chicago was, in one sense, a frontier town, and the frontier thesis (appropriately articulated by Frederick Jackson Turner at the University of Chicago in 1893) with its implicit notions of restlessness and instability was a convenient instrument of explanation for the (supposed) absence of a durable culture; industrialists were merely the pioneers of the business age and, like any other pioneers (the Puritans were, for Brooks and his contemporaries, a particularly nasty example), they merely made their claims and moved on. The Chicago beyond the Exposition, however, gave (and continues to give) the lie to this kind of argument. It was Lewis Mumford who first noted the centrality of Louis Sullivan's buildings in the broader pattern of American cultural achievement, and in "rediscovering" Sullivan for his readers of the inter-war years he was implicitly rejecting the claims to architectural significance of Exposition architects such as Daniel Burnham and Richard Hunt. His summing-up of Sullivan's significance as an architect can be read as a more general statement of those conditions of American society at the turn of the century of which Chicago was, in many ways, a tangible expression:

> Sullivan saw that the business of the architect was to organize the forces of modern society, discipline them for humane ends, express them in the plastic-utilitarian form of building. To achieve this purpose the architect must abandon the tedious and unmeaning symbolism of older cultural forms: a modern building could no more wear the dress of the classic than the architect could wear a peruke and sword. The whole problem of building, Sullivan saw, must be thought out afresh, and the solution must be of such a nature that it would apply to every manner of structure, from the home to the factory, from the office to the tomb: no activity was too mean to escape the ministrations of the architect. While Sullivan manfully faced the problem of the tall building, he saw that the spirit that produced such congestion was "profoundly antisocial ... these buildings are not architecture but outlawry, and their authors criminals in the true sense of the word". So, though

> Sullivan respected the positive forces of his age, democracy, science, industry, he was not a go-getter, and he refused to accept an architecture which showed a "cynical contempt for all those qualities that real humans value".[12]

Sullivan was the architect of the new age, openly rejecting the decorative ostentation of a French-inspired, Beaux Arts pseudo-classicism; if the rejection involved accepting the felicific calculus of the age of industrial capitalism, then so be it, assuming, that is, that the culture of industrialism could be sufficiently humanized. This is what Sullivan and the architects who followed him, notably Frank Lloyd Wright, set out to do, and their buildings are the visible measurements of their success.

3

In the years following the turn of the century Chicago continued to expand at quite unprecedented rates. The population of the city, which had been growing at roughly the rate of 500,000 each decade since 1880, continued to do so in the years between 1900 and 1930, yielding an overall figure in 1930 of 3,376,438[13]; the composition of the population reflected Chicago's continuing attraction to those of foreign birth with an increase of over 194,000 as a result of immigration in the years between 1900 and 1910. The expanding economic base of the city also brought a dramatic increase in the number of black Americans who migrated to Chicago in search of jobs: between 1900 and 1920 the black population of Chicago increased by 79,000, while between 1920 and 1930 it expanded by a further 146,000. The economy itself grew and diversified in the years after 1900 creating a balance of industry and commerce that made (and continues to make) Chicago less vulnerable than many other American cities to the effects of economic recession.

As the population and the economy grew, so Chicago expanded outwards and upwards. The suburban area of the city stretched north, west, south and even south-east into north-western Indiana; communities which before the turn of the century had all the hallmarks of frontier villages were speedily and inexorably absorbed into the standard metropolitan area and found their populations growing with the migration of people from the inner city areas. In turn, the inner city changed its physical face: buildings grew higher and the high-rise itself, which began as a construction for commercial use, was increasingly adapted to meet the demands for housing, particularly along the Lake Front and the North Shore (between 1905 and 1930 some 360,000 apartment units were constructed in the city). The depression brought apartment construction to a stop, but not before the property developers and their architects had made a mark on the city as dramatic as that made by the commercial buildings erected between the great fire (1871) and the turn of the century. The best buildings of the post-war property boom reflected the emergence of what has been called "the International Style": flat surfaces, elongated windows, and a conspicuous absence of decorative features. Developments in building technology ensured that high-rise buildings got higher: apartment buildings in the "Gold Coast" area of the city reached thirty storeys while the Civic Opera buildings (now Kemper Insurance) possessed a main shaft of forty-five storeys and vied with the Tribune Tower for the reputation of being Chicago's most imposing structure. By 1930, effectively Chicago's 100th birthday, a flat, barren space at the foot of Lake Michigan had become the second city of the United States, its commercial and industrial heartland, and boasted a modern architectural heritage second to none.

As the population of Chicago grew, as its economy developed and diversified, as its physical face changed, so also life in the city grew more complex and prosperity brought in its wake that darker, more unpalatable side of city living that we have come to associate with urban existence. As Edward C. Banfield has argued, the growth and spread of affluence have inevitably carried in their train conditions which are undesirable: poverty, squalor, ignorance, and brutality.[14] As early as 1889 Jane Addams had established in the city a settlement home, Hull House, devoted to the amelioration of the conditions of the poor, to education, and to a form of political action close to that advocated by Christian socialists. Jane Addams reflected that part of late nineteenth-century thought which saw cities as arenas for social and moral reform. She read and admired the writings of English "reform" novelists such as Walter Besant and Mrs. Humphrey Ward, and she was instrumental in introducing the ideas of the Swiss educationalist Johann Pestalozzi to the United States. More significantly, for our purposes here, she embodies that combination of reform idealism and moral realism which sought to direct the city's energies towards humanizing its environment; she advocated ethnic pluralism, stressed the importance of the neighbourhood, and campaigned for political reforms which exploited, to beneficial ends, the ward politics that other commentators had seen as inherently corrupt. Like John Dewey she advocated a philosophy in the service of society, and like Dewey she sought to balance the city's tendency towards concentration, alienation and anonymity with a variation of Jeffersonian localism.[15]

The desire for reform had been prompted, in part, by the signs of civil disorder that had accompanied the negative side of Chicago's rise to affluence and prosperity. In 1877 a railroad strike had resulted in violence between protesting strikers and federal troops and the state militia; twelve workers were killed and many more injured and arrested. In 1866 a labour dispute at the McCormick Harvester factory in Chicago led to a series of disturbances culminating in a bomb explosion in Haymarket Square in which one policeman was killed and seventy others wounded; the police opened fire on the crowd, killing one person and wounding some fifty others. Five anarchists were subsequently executed. The complexities of Chicago's ethnic composition led many commentators to conclude that "anarchist" and "communist" agitation was an importation from East European, Slavic, countries, though Jews (who often came from the same areas) were seen equally as the culprits. No matter where the blame was apportioned and no matter how good the evidence of political agitation, grievances were legitimate and there were demands that they be rectified. The activities of reformers like Jane Addams did much to alert public attention to the conditions of deprivation and destitution that existed in Chicago and, by extension, all great cities, but political and social reform was, in turn, complemented by developments in literature, and the Chicago School of writing, to which we now turn our attention, was, in part, a response to the new conditions prevailing in American society and to the political and philosophical response these conditions had elicited.

In the years after 1900 Chicago became a literary mecca rivalling New York. The causes of this are various, but two, in particular, stand out: the economic and commercial development of Chicago brought with it the emergence of new publishing houses and new printing houses, and the changes in social conditions consequent upon economic growth created a demand for journalists who, through their "muckraking" endeavours, would bring to light the injustices and deprivations which reformers would then seek to remedy; similarly, Chicago's rise brought with it educational and intellectual advantages—libraries, a university, concert halls, lecture rooms, societies, and the rich, flourishing sub-culture of the salons, bohemian haunts and little magazines that live, symbiotically, alongside the "official" culture. For those writers of the mid-west disinclined, or simply not prosperous enough, to travel to London, Chicago offered similar, if not exactly comparable, attractions. Thus a wave of writers, some major, some minor, converged on Chicago and, effectively, created a literary culture for the city: Sherwood Anderson from Clyde, Ohio; Floyd Dell from Davenport, Iowa; Theodore Dreiser from Terre Haute, Indiana; Ben Hecht from New York; Robert Herrick from Boston; Vachel Lindsay from Springfield, Illinois; Edgar Lee Masters from Lewiston, Illinois; Carl Sandburg from Galesburg, Illinois.[16] As is evident, many of these writers came from small, rural communities where moral values were simple and unambiguous and life was circumscribed by the discipline and regularity imposed by nature. Paradoxically, these villages and small towns had once been at the western edge of the frontier, but the frontier passed them by and they retreated into a kind of prelapsarian innocence and ignorance. To many observers these mid-western communities remain an image of the "real America" (an observation that, in itself, measures the complexity and plurality of modern American society) but to the writers of the early 1900s they embodied an absence of culture and civilization so complete that an escape to the new, urban frontier with its concomitant attractions of liberality and glamour was an almost automatic response. In Chicago these young writers found work (often with newspapers), a responsive environment of like-minded individuals, and little magazines to publish their poetry and short stories. Two, in particular, are noteworthy, Harriet Monroe's Poetry: *A Magazine of Verse* and Margaret Anderson's *Little Review*, for through them, and through Ezra Pound's activities among the expatriate circle in London, Chicago was connected to broader developments in the arts in Europe, especially modernism in poetry and the novel.

Commentators—critics and literary historians—have tended to under-estimate the degree to which modern American literature was born out of an opposition of values; the very writers who "liberated" American literature (in the eyes of the historian) were themselves the products of the propriety and small-mindedness of the philistine society they sought to escape. The effectiveness of the opening scenes of *Sister Carrie* (1900) comes not from the wordly-wise, ironic stance of a detached author but from our sense of Dreiser re-enacting experiences and emotions that he had known, through his protagonist. He knows what Carrie feels, can see her story through the dramatic contrast of values and environments that the journey from the (fictional) Columbia City, Wisconsin, to Chicago entails,[17] and thus, through her responses, Dreiser registers the sense of the great city as it would look to the eyes of an innocent child. Dreiser recalled that "as a boy ... I had invested Chicago with immense color and force, and it was there, ignorant, American, semi-conscious, seeking, inspiring."[18] Although his background was not rural (the Terre Haute he left in 1887 already had the makings of an industrial town), an immigrant and impoverished family life determined that he would shape a response to the city which would dwell upon a dialectical pattern of circumstances (success and failure, wealth and poverty, venality and integrity) quite alien to his experiences as a small boy in a small town. There is in Dreiser's account of the city something comparable to that which one finds in the paintings of the New York artist John Sloan: the city as place of "mystery and terror and wonder" where the dense and complex patterns of human life seek their metaphorical realization in art (what George Santayana has called "a lyric cry in the midst of business"). Dreiser's non-fictional prose writings (especially *A Book About Myself* and *The Color of a Great City*) are a striking testimony to the degree to which the city "liberated" him from his background, and, in turn, his response to the city, notably in *Sister Carrie*, was responsible, in part, for that liberation of American Literature from the genteel tradition of the late nineteenth century; but the paradox is that the liberation was possibly only to the degree that Dreiser's upbringing and family circumstances created the opposition of values that, in the first place, enabled the response.

With Robert Herrick, Dreiser shares a common theme, one not unique to American literature but virtually ubiquitous in the realistic novel where the opposition between town and country, urban and rural, city and village, is played out: the story of a search for material rewards which, inevitably, leads to disintegration or corruption or both; the search may be realized but the achieved desires bring little succour. The treatment of the theme may be comic or tragic; Dreiser, like Balzac, was temperamentally inclined to the tragic and lacked comic gifts. In the American context, however, the theme as it is elaborated in the writings of the early twentieth-century realists had deeper implications. In Dreiser, as in Frank Norris and Stephen Crane, the treatment of the city carried populist and agrarian overtones: the city "crushes, enslaves, and ruins"[19] and it is a nursery for those very vices that undermine democratic values and thus, by extension, American society. These realists do not express or validate such sentiments, but the assumptions from which such observations arise are, in the American context it seems, simply unavoidable. The American novelist records the victory of industrial America over rural America simply by using the city as part of his deterministic background (novels, Harry Levin has reminded us, are "peculiarly urban products"),[20] but his vocabulary, especially in Dreiser, exudes as much agrarian myth as it does commodified language and reified character.

The writers of the Chicago renaissance whose work appeared during and after World War I were the inheritors of the struggle on behalf of realism and against the invocation of morality as a weapon against art that had been won by Dreiser, Norris, Crane and others. They were city writers, Chicago writers, but their work did not take the city as its essential and defining subject; in Edgar Lee Master's *Spoon River Anthology* (1915) and Sherwood Anderson's *Winesburg, Ohio* (1919) the city figures largely through its absence; they deal with the city by recalling what it has displaced. Both works are implicitly nostalgic, rather than regressive; both works were written in Chicago by writers remembering the narrowness and insularity of village America; both works confirm Alfred Kazin's observation that for the new realists to "know the truth of American life was to rise in some fashion above its prohibitions".[21] In many respects, for writers such as Masters and Anderson the escape to the city involved a process of transformation and metamorphosis (Dreiser had written of Frank Cowperwood's journey in *The Titan* (1914) to the "new city" of Chicago as the realization that "the old life he had lived in that city [Philadelphia] since boyhood was ended. ... He must begin again"[22]). So radical a break with the past, with traditional values and a traditional society, necessitated new responsibilities, intellectual and expressive; thus the tendency to invest realism with moral attributes (perhaps as an ironic inversion of the middle-class attack, at the turn of the century, on realism for its immorality) and the inclination to see dissension and revolt as a measurement of artistic fidelity and truthfulness. Equally, of course, the Chicago writers sought to shock: one of the important freedoms life in the city afforded for these writers was sexual freedom and the use of sexual themes and sexual reference as an instrument of protest in the writing of this period is not to be under-estimated.

The writers of the Chicago renaissance thus draw together two strands which, so far, we have been exploring separately: one, the tradition of urban reform, exemplified by Jane Addams and drawing much of its intellectual force from those teaching at the University of Chicago (notably John Dewey and Thorstein Veblen), which saw the city as a set of problems to be solved by the application of pragmatic social philosophy, and which was complemented, in part, by the first great wave of American realist writing; the other, that newly emergent tradition (or counter-tradition) characterized by a "revolt against the village" which sought both personal and expressive freedom and a displacement of the ethical precepts of a traditional society. Curiously, the two traditions while complementary and intertwined, invoke contradictory images: in Dreiser the city can suffocate and stifle, in Anderson the small town restrains and represses.

But in the coalescing of the two traditions Chicago achieved its double victory on behalf of the new America, the victory of the urban over the rural and the victory of unbridled realism over cautious gentility in the arts. One might see this double victory as marking, in Santayana's terms, the disappearance of Calvinism and transcendentalism, the chief sources of the genteel tradition,[23] and the pre-eminent repositories of values in nineteenth-century America.

Despite the close contact that many of the writers of the Chicago renaissance had with modernism in the arts, the dominant mode of writing about the city is, broadly speaking, within the realistic tradition and the four fiction writers most closely associated with the city in the period since the decline and dispersal of the writers of the 1910s and 1920s, James T. Farrell, Nelson Algren, Richard Wright, and Saul Bellow, give ample witness to the continuation of this tradition. Obviously, the modes and strategies of mimetic representation have undergone a sea-change and one finds less of that substantive grasp of material reality associated with Dreiser in the work of the younger realists. But the defining assumptions about realism remain. In Farrell's trilogy, *Studs Lonigan* (1932–35), perhaps the most detailed imaginative record of life in the city since *Sister Carrie*, the city is treated simply as brutalizing and degrading, the eponymous hero dying at age 29. The trilogy is, in many respects, a deliberate inversion of Dreiser's novel, and Farrell's indebtedness to a Dreiserian model is apparent from an article on Dreiser published in the *Chicago Review* in 1947:

> It was in Chicago, principally, that Dreiser saw the spectacle of grandeur and misery which he was later to describe so movingly; it was there that he attended popular lectures which were of great educative value to him; it was there that he read Eugene Field, and was inspired to want to write, to become a newspaper man. The conviction that in Chicago there was a great future was widespread among all sections of the population. Briefly, Chicago was conceived as a future metropolis, a world city in the making. Chicago was the center of gravity of the American Success Dream. The idea of the future was one of endless progress. The hope of insatiable progress produced its psychological correspondent of insatiable dreams. And central in the rosy vision of the future was the hope of and the desire to make money.[24]

Farrell presses these claims on us as if they applied to no other American city, as if Chicago uniquely determined such a response. "Grandeur and Misery" were to be found elsewhere (Dreiser was especially drawn to Balzac's evocation of Paris during the July Monarchy), but the hope of insatiable progress (echoes of a frontier philosophy) and the concomitant expectation of wealth and prosperity are, for Farrell, uniquely Chicagoan and presume an almost libidinal investment.

In the fiction of Nelson Algren and Richard Wright the concentration on detail, of a documentary kind, that we find in Farrell and Dreiser gives way to a kind of atmospheric realism and the world of the city becomes increasingly nightmarish and impalpable. Equally, the terms of reference are narrowed and the street becomes the symbolic focus for the city; in Wright's *Lawd Today* (published posthumously in 1963), his first novel, and its successor, *Native Son* (1940), the dramatized action moves through a world circumscribed by poverty and brutality where the apartment buildings ("tall buildings holding black life"), pool halls, cheap diners, and street corners function as determinants of character. Wright's Chicago is the South Side; in Algren the life of the street, especially in *The Neon Wilderness* (1947) and *The Man with the Golden Arm* (1949), is that of the Near-North Side, particularly the area around Division Street that Algren knew intimately. This world is white, ethnically complex, but brutalized in much the same way as Wright's black South Side; it is a world inhabited by derelicts, drug-addicts, vagrants, prostitutes, hoodlums and boxers; these characters cannot escape the street and thus, by extension, the city, but there are redemptive and sentimental aspects to Algren's treatment of them. Algren writes in a style that owes much to the proletarian realism advocated by Marxist writers and critics in the 1930s, and the deflation of mythological assumptions about Chicago as the city of opportunity (see, especially, *Chicago: City on the Make*, 1951) is a persistent theme in much of his work, but the city sustains him as a writer and the energy without purpose of its inhabitants is a rich repository of material for him.

The limitations of writers such as Wright and Algren are all too apparent and it would be hard to make a convincing case for a profound realization of the life of the city in the fiction of either. Despite Dreiser's stylistic weaknesses, his grasp of the contingent realities of the city, the fortuitous interplay of circumstance and context, and his refusal to preach through his material make him the greater novelist. Saul Bellow's admiration of Dreiser is well known, but his response to Chicago (a city where he has lived and worked for virtually all of his life) is more metonymic than realistic. He has written about Chicago in five novels, *Dangling Man* (1944), *The Adventures of Augie March* (1951), *Herzog* (1964), *Humboldt's Gift* (1975) and *The Dean's December* (1982), spanning the life of the city over five decades. Bellow's background (he was born of Russian Jews in Canada, the family moving to Chicago in 1924) and his adolescent years among the Slavic and Jewish communities of the Northwest Side have given him a grasp of the complexities of life in Chicago that speaks eloquently through his best fiction. More acutely than most American writers, Bellow is aware of the city as the most palpable manifestation of a mass society. As a novelist with an upbringing in a traditional society and possessing a strong affinity for novelists like Dostoevsky, whose works are metaphysical and religious, he is drawn to the city as an arena in which traditional and spiritual values confront the multiplication of interests and the dissolution of hierarchical codes of order. In many respects Bellow is a deeply conservative novelist: struck by the heterogeneity and plurality of life in the American city he has construed this as evidence of the decline of community and the onset of apocalypse. In *The Dean's December* these ruminations on the life (and death) of a great city strike, for Bellow, characteristically philosophical notes:

> ... Among other discoveries, I found that Chicago wasn't Chicago anymore. Hundreds of thousands of people lived there who had no conception of a place. People *used* to be able to say. ...
>
> "Ah, yes", said Spangler. "I'm with you there. It's no longer a location, it's

only a condition. South Bronx, Cleveland, Detroit, St. Louis, from Newark to Watts—all the same noplace."[25]

This conversation, towards the end of the novel, between Spangler and Bellow's protagonist, Albert Corde, is rich in the nostalgic recall of

> ... the good old days when Chicago was a city of immigrants who had found work, food and freedom and a kind of friendly ugliness around them, and they practised their Old World trades—cabinetmakers, tinsmiths, locksmiths, wurst-stuffers from Cracow, confectioners from Sparta.[26]

and the explicit contrast between this and the decaying, excremental city of the present day.

In a recent interview in *TriQuarterly* Bellow has elaborated upon the largely negative and pessimistic view of the city that emerges from his fiction. For him "Chicago has earned the right to be considered the center of American materialism—the classical center."[27] He disabuses those who think that Chicago's culture is anything more than a pretence, and the new city that has grown up around the old is, for him, simply "proud, synthetic Chicago ..."[28] But, most interestingly of all, Bellow's observations complete an historical irony:

> Dreiser's old Chicago, the Chicago of 1900, is gone; few traces of it remain. The old materialistic innocence has disappeared—florid bars, good carriage horses, substantial Victorian virtues, substantial carnality; German, Irish, Polish, Italian Chicago bursting with energy—the Protestant businessmen, bankers and empire builders. The crass, dirty, sinful, vulgar, rich town of politicians, merchant princes and land speculators, the Chicago of Yerkes and Samuel Insull, has vanished.[29]

The Chicago nostalgically recalled by Bellow (it comes from Dreiser and not from memory) is that problematic city Henry Adams saw and from which Rudyard Kipling retreated in horror; the city striking for its *absence* of history (to turn of the century witnesses) is here measured *by* its history; the nineteenth-century materialism that many saw as signalling the death of culture is here asserted as its source. But eclipsing all these paradoxes is our realization that the city Bellow rejects is the corner-stone of his art.

Notes

1. Henry Adams, *The Education of Henry Adams* (Boston: Houghton Mifflin Company, 1973), p. 343.
2. See Carl W. Condit, *The Chicago School of Architecture: A History of Commercial and Public Buildings in the Chicago Area, 1875–1925* (Chicago: University of Chicago Press, 1964).
3. Henry Adams, op. city., p. 341.
4. See, particularly, Raymond Williams, *The Country and the City* (London: Chatto & Windus, 1973) and Morton and Lucia White, *The Intellectual versus the City: From Thomas Jefferson to Frank Lloyd Wright* (Cambridge, Mass.: Harvard University Press, 1962).
5. Rudyard Kipling, *From Sea to Sea*, Vol. 2 (London: Macmillan & Co., 1900), p. 153.
6. Alfred Kazin, *On Native Grounds: An Interpretation of Modern American Prose Literature* (New York: Harcourt, Brace & Co., 1942), p. 25.
7. Henry Blake Fuller, *The Cliff-Dwellers* (New York: Holt, Rinehart and Winston, Inc., 1973), p. 41.
8. William E. Leuchtenburg, *The Perils of Prosperity*, 1914–32 (Chicago: University of Chicago Press, 1958), p. 9.

9. Henry Blake Fuller, *With the Procession* (Chicago: University of Chicago Press, 1965), p. 95.
10. See Umberto Eco, *Faith in Fakes* (London: Secker and Warburg, 1986).
11. Thorstein Veblen, *The Theory of the Leisure Class* (New York: New American Library, 1953), p. 226. Veblen taught at the University of Chicago between 1892 and 1906.
12. Lewis Mumford, *The Brown Decades: A Study of the Arts in America, 1865–1895* (New York: Dover Books, 1971), p. 74. Mumford's quotations are from Louis Sullivan, *The Autobiography of an Idea.*
13. Sources: United States Census; Carl W. Condit, op. cit.
14. See Edward C. Banfield, *The Unheavenly City: The Nature and Future of Our Urban Crisis* (Boston: Little Brown & Co., 1970).
15. See, especially, Jane Addams, *Twenty Years at Hull House* (New York: Macmillan, 1910). There is a very good discussion of Jane Addams's work in Christopher Lasch, *The New Radicalism in America: The Intellectual as a Social Type* (New York: Alfred A. Knopf, 1965), pp. 3–37.
16. Two general studies of Chicago's literary culture are recommended: Bernard Duffey, *The Chicago Renaissance in American Letters* (Westport, Connecticut: Greenwood Press, 1977) and Carl S. Smith, *Chicago and the American Literary Imagination, 1880–1920* (Chicago Press, 1984).
17. Interestingly, Columbia City, Wisconsin, is the only fictional place in the novel.
18. Theodore Dreiser, *A Book About Myself* (New York: Boni & Liveright, 1922), p. 451.
19. See Richard Hofstadter, *The Age of Reform: From Bryan to F.D.R.* (London: Jonathan Cape, 1962), p. 33.
20. Harry Levin, *The Gates of Horn: A Study of Five French Realists* (New York: Oxford University Press, 1966), p. 131.
21. Alfred Kazin, *On Native Grounds: An Interpretation of Modern American Prose Literature* (New York: Harcourt, Brace & Company, 1942), p. 209.
22. Theodore Dreiser, *The Titan* (New York: New American Library, 1965), p. 9.
23. See George Santayana, "The Genteel Tradition in American Philosophy" in Norman Henfrey (ed.) *Selected Critical Writings of George Santayana*, Vol. 2 (Cambridge: Cambridge University Press, 1968), pp. 85–107.
24. Luna Wolf (ed.), *James T. Farrell: Selected Essays* (New York: McGraw-Hill Book Company, 1964), p. 153.
25. Saul Bellow, *The Dean's December* (Harmondsworth: Penguin Books, 1982), p. 234.
26. *Ibid.*, p. 236.
27. "Interview with Saul Bellow", *TriQuarterly*, 60 (Spring/Summer 1984), 12.
28. *Ibid.*
29. *Ibid.*

114

Chicago and its Suburbs

EVERETT CHAMBERLAIN

Although the "suburb" is often considered as a twentieth-century phenomenon of American cities, especially in relation to Chicago, the extracts which follow underline the complex development of both the city *per se* and individual urban centres. The language of the extracts is of obvious interest, and posits a hierarchy of inhabitants quite different from the Chicago described by Jane Addams and, of course, Richard Wright.

Parkside

This suburb includes a subdivision consisting of twenty acres, lying between Seventieth and Seventy-first streets, and Stony Island boulevard and Madison avenue. In the neighborhood of the depot of the Illinois Central railroad, it is already well settled, with a fair class of residents.

Property does not range so high in this suburb as in some of its neighbors, but it is scarcely less available. The place has good school and church facilities.

Lake Forest

In 1856, the Lake Forest Association was formed by the members of the Presbyterian churches of Chicago. This Company was organized for the purchase of lands at Lake Forest, with a view to erection of a university, and other institutions of learning. About 2,000 acres of land were purchased by the Association, 1,400 of which went into Lake Forest, 39 acres were given to the university for building ground, 10 acres to the female seminary, and 10 acres were set aside for a park. Alternate lots were retained for the benefit of the university, and the others sold; and so rapidly did prices advance, and the suburb take a leading position as the favorite resort of the better class of Chicago's inhabitants, that the scheme proved an undoubted financial success. The Association still holds about 600 acres of land, at prices varying from $300

Source: Everett Chamberlain, *Chicago and its Suburbs*, Chicago, 1874, pp. 357, 396–97, 411, 415–16, 451–2.

to $1,000 per acre. ... The Company have built an elegant hotel overlooking the lake, and carried on different improvements all with admirable results. The hotel has been filled with visitors during the summer, and constitutes a resort which "is becoming [in the language of a Forester] as great a favorite with Chicago people as Newport or Long Branch is to the heated and worn out denizens of New York and other eastern cities."

The universities has not yet been built, but excellent educational establishments are found in the village. There is a young ladies' seminary, under the direction of Professor Weston, and an academy for young men under the care of Professor Allen. ... There are some funds in hand for the erection of the university, but the prosecution of the matter rests with a Board. It is expected that work will not be much longer delayed. There is a fine Presbyterian church in town, of which the Rev. Mr. Taylor is pastor.

Apart from public improvements, Lake Forest boasts of more elegant private residences than almost any other suburb. During the past year three estimable citizens have permanently located themselves in the village. ... Perhaps the most beautiful place in Lake Forest is that of Mrs. Alexander White, which was purchased by her late husband from H. M. Thompson, Esq. Possessed of a large fortune, as well as refined and luxurious taste, the late proprietor was able to make his estate very beautiful in all respects. The price put upon the place is not less than $100,000. Then the Farwells, dry goods merchants, own lovely palaces in the center of town. Mr. John V. Farwell lives in a turreted baronial castle, built of the concrete made in the town, and presenting a quaint and picturesque appearance. The interior is elegantly finished in black-walnut and cherry. His brother, Hon. C. B. Farwell, has a place on a commanding elevation overlooking the lake. The residence of Mr. Charles Bradley, one of Chicago's leading merchants, is very elaborate and costly. It is a large English cottage, which he has christened "Carlsruhe" and not without reason, for the grounds are as beautiful as that famed German retreat. ...

Riverside

No suburb of Chicago possesses greater interest, whether from a historical point of view or from its picturesque surroundings, than the suburb known of late years as Riverside. It is unfortunately the fact that much of the attention of the public which has been directed to it is owing to the continued litigation in which the Improvement Company, having charge of the fortunes of the place, have since the fire been involved. But apart from this, Riverside is worthy of some note. Some five or six years ago, the suburb had no existence on the charts of Cook county. The late city-treasurer, Mr. David A. Gage, owned a beautiful farm, lying on the banks of the Desplaines river, well wooded, with many charming points of scenery, and only some four miles from the city limits. Had this city been any other than Chicago, Mr. Gage might to-day be owning his pleasant retreat. But the eye of the far-seeing speculator alighted upon the spot, and the inevitable Company having been organized, the car of progress was speedily set in motion. The locality, in its natural condition, was beautiful; and the opportunity presented for the artist to elaborate upon, and improve the work of nature, was unquestionable. The Company had wealthy and responsible men upon its directorate, whose spirits were speedily aglow with the vision of the bright things before them if they could ever realize their dream of planting on the banks of the Desplaines the model suburb of America. Eastern architects came and surveyed the ground, and shortly afterwards presented a report to the Executive Board of the Association. Their plan was found to be exhaustive and expensive; it brought out with success the leading idea desired, of so laying out the suburb that it should practically be a public park for the benefit of private residents; and, after much debate, it was adopted.

The Company at once raised the funds necessary to proceed with the work. An army of workmen was engaged, and a considerable progress was soon perceptible, in the heavy task before them. The tract of land owned by the Company comprised about 1,600 acres, and of these it was proposed to devote 700 acres for roads, borders, walks, recreative grounds, and parks. The New York landscape artists (Messrs. Olmsted & Vaux) pressed very urgently the necessity of the construction of a carriage road or driveway from the city to the suburb; and, meeting assistance from the town of Cicero and the city of Chicago, the road running from Twelfth street directly to Riverside, 150 feet wide, was constructed. Among the other improvements suggested, and carried into effect, was a complete system of sewerage, the supply of water and gas, the adoption of the curved line for streets, and the planting of innumerable trees. Riverside, before it passed into the hands of the Company, possessed many beautiful groves of trees—elm, maple, and oak; but it was left for the standing wooded land to be utilized to its utmost extent by the skill of the artist. Everything likely to give the place the appearance of a resident park was done. Nor were opportunities offered by the curving course of the Desplaines river neglected. At one place, the river encircles a strip of land, of the shape of a peninsula, and of about one and a quarter square miles in extent, which, together with a neighboring island, has been improved so as to form public parks, access being had to one of them by means of rustic bridges. ...

Among the other enterprise undertaken and carried to a successful conclusion by the Company, was the erection of a grand hotel. Pleasantly situated, with excellent accommodation, containing a large number of rooms, and all the conveniences of a city establishment, it is a very agreeable place for summer resort. ...

During the last two years the suburb has made little progress. Litigation, financial embarrassments, and the reports widely circulated, and having some foundation in fact, of the unhealthy character of the location, have continued to retard its growth. The prospects of the place are better than they formerly were, and the persons having charge of Riverside are energetic and persevering, and, their present difficulties removed, will doubtless succeed in restoring the suburb to a more favorable position in public confidence. There is no doubt that both the Desplaines and Fox rivers, lying to the west of Chicago and affording great numbers of very beautiful sites, will soon be bordered with handsome improvements, and be relieved, sooner or later, of the incubus that now rests upon them, viz., a reputation for ague. The most obvious mode of remedying the summer defluxion of these streams is by dredging the channels and docking the shores, when flat, with the product of this operation; also turning into the stream the currents of numerous artesian wells along their banks. We look to see the Desplaines, within fifteen years, an exceptionally choice residence district.

Park Ridge

This eligible suburb is on the Wisconsin Division of the Chicago & Northwestern railroad, about thirteen miles from the Court-house. It is situated on the dividing ridge between the waters of Lake Michigan and the Mississippi river, and has an altitude of one hundred and thirty feet above the lake. Owing to this altitude, it is especially noted for the salubrity of its atmosphere. It is especially exempt from malarious diseases, and, in the seasons most remarkable in ague history, it wholly escaped the attacks of the shaking demon. In common with most of the suburbs of Chicago, the land was, in the first place, pre-empted and occupied as farms. ...

Away back in 1855, when the railroad was located, a brick manufactory was started on the present location of Park Ridge, and the unpoetical founders contented themselves with the dull, practical name of Brickton. But the manufacture of bricks proceeded equally well in a hamlet of that name, and, until the occurrence of the great fire, Brickton supplied a large quantity of the red bricks which were sold in the Chicago market. With the fire there came a change—not that the demand for bricks was less, but that the call for good, healthy suburban residence property was more. Brickton shook itself up, and merged into a new name—Park Ridge—one of the best located, as also one of the most promising of the city's suburbs.

The original plat of Brickton comprised only one hundred and sixty acres; but since the name was changed, large additions have been made, chiefly by Leonard Hodges, Esq., J. H. Burns, and J. H. Butler. The village was recently organized, with corporate powers and privileges, and now includes some twelve hundred acres of choice lands. The sentiment of the people being decidedly adverse, there has not, since the settlement of the village, been a single saloon or tippling-house tolerated within its borders. Following this, perhaps almost necessarily, the society of Park Ridge is first class, and its members all reputable, religious and law-loving people. They appreciate so well their pleasant country retreat, that they are decidedly adverse to allowing any objectionable element to obtrude therein. Hitherto they have succeeded, and the future is not likely to see any change in this respect.

The town possesses excellent school facilities, a prosperous Methodist church, a Congregational society, and two well attended Sabbath-schools. There are two or three stores; blacksmith's and carpenter's shops; a lumber, wood and coal yard; and a planing mill. A large and extensive manufactory of brick, drain tiles and pottery is in operation; and excellent supplies of building material are to be obtained on the ground.

Among the chief improvements which have been recently completed, must be mentioned the elegant suburban hotel structure, erected, at a cost of $15,000. ...

The residents of Park Ridge include many business men of Chicago who have generally chosen to erect pleasant, substantial residences, and to adorn the grounds in which the houses stand with all the talent and ingenuity that the landscape artist or lover of esthetics could desire. ...

115

With the Procession

HENRY B. FULLER

Henry Blake Fuller (1857–1929) was born in Chicago and remains one of its major (if underrated) novelists and was associated with the city throughout his career. He was a significant figure on *Poetry* magazine, a leading contemporary literary journal published in Chicago. His novels take the city very much as their subject. *The Cliff-Dwellers* (1893) concerns a skyscraper—an early response to the symbolic and cultural implications of a new form of architecture which saw its first examples in Chicago. *With the Procession* (1895), of which Chapter One follows, is a mix of the realism associated with the city and a response to the dynamic suggested by the energy and growth of cities like Chicago in the 1890s and 1900s.

When old Mr. Marshall finally took to his bed, the household viewed this action with more surprise than sympathy, and with more impatience than surprise. It seemed like the breaking down of a machine whose trustworthiness had been hitherto infallible; his family were almost forced to the acknowledgement that he was but a mere human being after all. They had enjoyed a certain intimacy with him, in lengths varying with their respective ages, but they had never made a full avowal that his being rested on any tangible physical basis. Rather had they fallen into the way of considering him as a disembodied intelligence, whose sole function was to direct the transmutation of values and credits and resources and opportunities into the creature comforts demanded by the state of life unto which it had please Providence to call them; and their dismay was now such as might occur at the Mint if the great stamp were suddenly and of its own accord to cease its coinage of double-eagles and to sink into a silence of supine idleness. His wife and children acknowledged, indeed, his head and his hands—those it were impossible to overlook; but his head stopped with the rim of his collar, while his hands—those long, lean hands, freckled, tufted goldishly between joints and knuckles—they never followed

Source: Henry B. Fuller, *With the Procession*, New York, 1895, pp. 3–12.

beyond the plain gilt sleeve-buttons (marked with a Roman M) which secured the overlapping of his cuffs. No, poor old David Marshall was like one of the early Tuscan arch-angels, whose scattered members are connected by draperies merely, with no acknowledged organism within; nor were his shining qualities fully recognized until the resolutions passed by the Association of Wholesale Grocers reached the hands of his bereaved—

But this is no way to begin.

The grimy lattice-work of the drawbridge swung to slowly, the stream-tug blackened the dull air and roiled the turbid water as it dragged its schooner on towards the lumber-yards of the South Branch, and a long line of waiting vehicles took up their interrupted course through the smoke and the stench as they filed across the stream into the thick of business beyond: first a yellow street-car; then a robust truck laden with rattling sheet-iron, or piled high with fresh wooden pails and willow baskets; then a junk-cart bearing a pair of dwarfed and bearded Poles, who bumped in unison with the jars of its clattering springs; then, perhaps, a bespattered buggy, with reins jerked by a pair of sinewy and impatient hands. Then more street-cars; then a butcher's cart loaded with the carcasses of calves—red, black, piebald—or an express wagon with a yellow cur yelping from its rear; then, it may be, an insolently venturesome landau, with created panel and top-booted coachman. Then drays and omnibuses and more street-cars; then, presently, somewhere in the line, between the tail end of one truck and the menacing tongue of another, a family carry-all—a carry-all loaded with its family, driven by a man of all work, drawn by a slight and amiable old mare, and encumbered with luggage which shows the labels of half the hotels of Europe.

It is a very capable and comprehensive vehicle, as conveyances of that kind go. It is not new, it is not precisely in the mode; but it shows material and workmanship of the best grade, and it is washed, oiled, polished with scrupulous care. It advances with some deliberation, and one might fancy hearing in the rattle of its tires, or in the suppressed flapping of its rear curtain, a word of plaintive protest. "I am not of the great world," it seems to say; "I make no pretence to fashion. We are steady and solid, but we are not precisely in society, and we are far, very far indeed, from any attempt to cut a great figure. However, do not misunderstand our position; it is not that we are under, nor that we are exactly aside; perhaps we have been left just a little behind. Yes, that might express it—just a little behind."

How are they to catch up again—how rejoin the great caravan whose fast and furious pace never ceases, never slackens? Not, assuredly, by the help of the little sorrel mare, whose white mane swings so mildly, and whose pale eyelashes droop so diffidently when some official hand at a crowded crossing brings her to a temporary stand-still. Not by the help of the coachman, who wears a sack-coat and a derby hat, and whose frank, good-natured face turns about occasionally for a friendly participation in the talk that is going on behind. Can it be, then, that any hopes for an accelerated movement are packed away in the bulging portmanteau which rests squeezed in between the coachman's legs? Two stout straps keep it from bursting, and the crinkled brown leather of its sides is completely pasted over with the mementoes used by the hosts of the Old World to speed the parting guest. "London" and "Paris" shine in the lustre of the last fortnight; "Tangier" is distinctly visible; "Buda-Pest" may be readily inferred despite the overlapping labels of "Wien" and "Bâle"; while away off to one corner a crumpled and lingering shred points back, though uncertainly, to the Parthenon and the Acropolis. And in the midst of this flowery field is planted a large M after the best style of the White Star Line.

Who has come home bearing all these sheaves?

Is it, to begin with, the young girl who shares the front seat with the driver, and who faces with an innocent unconcern all the clamor and evil of a great city? There is a half-smile on her red lips, and her black eyes sparkle with a girlish gayety—for she does not know how bad the world is. At the same time her chin advances confidently, and her dark eyebrows contract with a certain soft imperiousness—for she does not know how hard the world is nor how unyielding. Sometimes she withdraws her glance from the jostling throng to study the untidy and overlapping labels on the big portmanteau; she betrays a certain curiosity, but she shows at the same time a full determination not to seem over-impressed. No, the returned traveller is not Rosy Marshall; all that *she* knows of life she has learned from the broadcast cheapness of English story-tellers and from a short year's schooling in New York.

Is it, then, the older girl who fills half of the rear seat and who, as the cruel phrase goes, will never see thirty again? She seems to be tall and lean, and one divines, somehow, that here back is narrow and of a slab-like flatness. Her forehead is high and full, and its bulging outlines are but slightly softened by a thin and dishevelled bang. Her eyes are of a light and faded blue, and have the peculiar stare which results from over-full eyeballs when completely bordered by white. Her long fingers show knotted joints and nails that seem hopelessly plebeian; sometimes she draws on open-work lace mitts, and then her hands appear to be embroiling each other in a mutual tragedy. No, poor Jane is thoroughly, incorruptibly indigenous; she is the best and dearest girl in half the world, as you shall see; but all her experiences have lain between Sandusky and Omaha.

Perhaps, then, the returned traveller is the elderly woman seated by her side. Perhaps—and perhaps not. For she seems a bit too dry and sapless and self-contained—as little susceptible, in fact, to the gentle dews of travel as an umbrella in a waterproof case. Moreover, it is doubtful if her bonnet would pass current beyond the national confines. One surmises that she became years ago the victim of arrested development; that she is a kind of antiquated villager—a geologic survival from an earlier age; that she is a house-keeper cumbered and encompassed by minute cares largely of her own making. It is an easy guess that, for Eliza Marshall, London is in another world, that Tangier is but a remote and impracticable abstraction, and that all her strength and fortitude might be necessary merely to make the trip to Peoria.

There is but one other occupant of the carriage remaining—the only one, after all, who can or could be the owner of the baggage. He is a young man of twenty-three, and he sits with his back to the horse on a little seat which has been let down for the occasion between the usual two; his knees crowd one of the girls and his elbows the other. He seems uncommonly alert and genial; he focusses brilliantly the entire attention of the party. His little black mustache flaunts with a picturesque upward flourish, and it is supplemented by a small tuft at the edge of his underlip—an embellishment which overlays any slight trace of lingering juvenility with an effect which is most knowing, experienced, caprine, if you like, and which makes fair amends for the blanched cheeks, wrinkled brows and haggard eyes that the years have yet to accomplish for him. A navy-blue tie sprinkled with white interlacing circles spreads loosely and carelessly over the lapels of his coat; and while his clever eyes dart intelligently from one side to the other of the crowded thoroughfare, his admiring family make their own shy observations upon his altered physiognomy and his novel apparel—upon his shoes and his hat particularly; they become acquainted thus with the Florentine ideal of foot-wear, and the latest thing evolved by Paris in the way of head-gear.

This young man has passed back through London quite unscathed. Deduce from his costume the independence of his character and the precise slant of his propensities.

The carriage moves on, with a halt here, a spurt there, and many a jar and jolt between; and Truesdale Marshall throws over the shifting and resounding panorama an eye freshened by a four years' absence and informed by the contemplation of many strange and diverse spectacles. Presently a hundred yards of unimpeded travel ends in a blockade of trucks and street-cars and a smart fusillade of invective. During this enforced stoppage the young man becomes conscious of a vast unfinished structure that towers gauntly overhead through the darkening and thickening air, and for which a litter of iron beams in the roadway itself seems to promise an indefinite continuation skyward.

"Two, three, four—six, seven—nine," he says, craning his neck and casting up his eye. Then, turning with a jocular air to the elder lady opposite, "I don't suppose that Marshall & Belden, for instance, have got up to nine stories yet!"

"Marshall & Belden!" she repeated. Her enunciation was strikingly ejaculatory, and she laid an impatient and unforgiving emphasis upon the latter name. "I don't know what will happen if your father doesn't assert himself pretty soon."

"I should think as much!" observed the elder girl, explosively; "or they will never get up even to seven. The idea of Mr. Belden's proposing to enlarge by taking that ground adjoining! But of course poor pa didn't put up the building himself, nor anything; oh no! So *he* doesn't know whether the walls will stand a couple of extra stories or not. Upon my word," she went on with increased warmth, "I don't feel quite sure whether pa was the one to start the business in the first place and to keep it going along ever since, or whether he's just a new errand-boy, who began there a week ago! August, are we stuck here to stay forever?"

The little sorrel mare started up again and entered upon another stage of her journey. The first lights began to appear in the store-fronts; the newsboys were shrieking the last editions of the evening papers; the frenzied comedy of belated shopping commenced to manifest itself upon the pavements.

The throng of jostling women was especially thick and eager before a vast and vulgar front whose base was heaped with cheap truck cheaply ticketed, and whose long row of third-story windows was obscured by a great reach of cotton cloth tacked to a flimsy wooden frame. Unprecedented bargains were offered in gigantic letters by the new proprietors, "Eisendrath & Heide ..."—the rest of the name flapped loosely in the wind.

"Alas, poor Wethersby, I knew him well," observed Marshall, absently. He cast a pensive eye upon the still-remaining name of the former proprietor, and took off his hat to weight it in his hands with a pretence of deep speculation. "Well, the Philistines haven't got hold of *us* yet, have they?" he remarked, genially; he had not spent six months in Vienna for nothing. "I suppose we are still worth twenty sous in the franc, eh?"

"I suppose," replied his mother, with a grim brevity. She rather groped for his meaning, but she was perfectly certain of her own.

"I guess pa's all right," declared his sister, "as long as he is left alone and not interfered with."

The evening lights doubled and trebled—long rows of them appeared overhead at incalculable altitudes. The gongs of the cable cars clanged more and more imperiously as the crowds surged in great numbers round grip and trailer. The night life of the town began to bestir itself, and little Rosy, from her conspicuous place, beamed with a bright intentness upon its motley spectacle, careless of where her smiles might fall. For her the immodest theatrical poster drooped in the windows of saloons, or caught a transient hold upon the hoardings of uncompleted buildings; brazen blare and gaudy placards (disgusting rather than indecent) invited the passer-by into cheap museums and music-halls; all the unclassifiable riff-raff that is spawned by a great city leered from corners, or slouched along the edge of the gutters, or stood in dark doorways, or sold impossible rubbish in impossible dialects wherever the public indulgence permitted a foothold.

To Rosy's mother all this involved no impropriety. Eliza Marshall's Chicago was the Chicago of 1860, an Arcadia which, in some dim and inexplicable way, had remained for her an Arcadia still—bigger, noisier, richer, yet different only in degree, and not essentially in kind. She herself had traversed these same streets in the days when they were the streets of a mere town. Jane, accompanying her mother's courses as a child, had seen the town develop into a city. And now Rosy followed in her turn, though the *urbs in horto* of the earlier time existed

preliminary to building in Chicago, where, for one thing, the men who owned the land have not been those with the money for building. Where very great and costly buildings are concerned, the long leases often go to corporations or syndicates, who put up the houses. It seems to many strangers who visit Chicago that it is reasonable to prophesy a speedy end to the feverish impulse to swell the number of these giant piles, either through legislative ordinance or by the fever running its course. Many prophesy that it must soon end. ... So it seems, but not to a thoroughbred Chicagoan. One of the foremost business men in the city asserts that he can perceive no reason why the entire business heart of the town—that square half-mile of which I have spoken—should not soon be all builded up of cloud-capped towers. There will be a need for them, he says, and the money to defray the cost of them will accompany the demand. The only trouble he foresees will be in the solution of the problem what to do with the people who will then crowd the streets as never streets were clogged before.

This prophecy relates to a little block in the city, but the city itself contains 181½ square miles. It has been said of the many annexations by which her present size was attained that Chicago reached out and took to herself farms, prairie land, and villages, and that of such material the great city now in part consists. This is true. In suburban trips, such as those I took to Fort Sheridan and Fernwood, for instance, I passed the great cabbage farms, groves, houseless but plotted tracts, and long reaches of the former prairie. Even yet Hyde Park is a separated settlement, and a dozen or more villages stand out as distinctly by themselves as ever they did. If it were true, as her rivals insist, that Chicago added all this tract merely to get a high rank in the census reports of population, the folly of the action would be either ludricous or pitiful, according to the standpoint from which it was viewed. But the true reason for her enormous extension of municipal jurisdiction is quite as peculiar. The enlargement was urged and accomplished in order to anticipate the growth and needs of the city. It was a consequence of extraordinary foresight, which recognized the necessity for a uniform system of boulevards, parks, drainage, and water provision when the city should reach limits that it was even then seen must bound a compact aggregation of stores, offices, factories, and dwellings. To us of the East this is surprising. It might seem incredible were there not many other evidences of the same spirit and sagacity not only in Chicago, but in the other cities of the West, especially of the Northwest. What Minneapolis, St. Paul, and Duluth are doing towards a future park system reveals the same enterprise and habit of looking far ahead. And Chicago, in her park system, makes evident her intentions. In all these cities and in a hundred ways the observant traveller notes the same forehandedness, and prepares himself to understand the temper in which the greatest of the Western capitals leaned forth and absorbed the prairie. Chicago expects to become the largest city in America—a city which, in fifty years, shall be larger than the consolidated cities that may form New York at that time.

It seems to have ever been, as it is now, a city of young men. One Chicagoan accounts for its low death rate on the ground that not even its leading men are yet old enough to die. The young men who drifted there from the Eastern States after the close of the war all agree that the thing which most astonished them was the youthfulness of the most active business men. Marshall Field, Potter Palmer, and the rest, heading very large mercantile establishments, were young fellows. Those who came to Chicago from England fancied, as it is said that Englishmen do, that a man may not be trusted with affairs until he has lost half his hair and all his teeth. Our own Eastern men were apt to place wealth and success at the middle of the scale of life. But in Chicago men under thirty were leading in commerce and industry. The sight was a spur to all the young men who came, and they also pitched in to swell the size and successes of the young men's capital. The easy making of money by the loaning of it and by handling city realty—sources which never failed with shrewd men—not only whetted the general appetite for big and quick money-making, but they provided the means for the establishment and extension of trade in other ways and with the West at large.

It is one of the peculiarities of Chicago that one finds not only the capitalists but the storekeepers discussing the whole country with a familiarity as strange to a man from the Atlantic coast as Nebraska is strange to most Philadelphians or New Yorkers. But the well-informed and "hustling" Chicagoan is familiar with the differing districts of the entire West, North, and South, with their crops, industries, wants, financial status, and means of intercommunication. As in London we find men whose business field is the world, so in Chicago we find the business men talking not of one section or of Europe, as is largely the case in New York, but discussing the affairs of the entire country. The figures which garnish their conversation are bewildering, but if they are analyzed, or even comprehended, they will reveal to the listener how vast and how wealthy a region acknowledges Chicago as its market and its financial and trading centre. ... Chicago, then, is the centre of a circle of 1000 miles diameter. If you draw a line northward 500 miles, you find everywhere arable land and timber. The same is true with respect to a line drawn 500 miles in a northwesterly course. For 650 miles westward there is no change in the rich and alluring prospect, and so all around the circle, except where Lake Michigan interrupts it, the same conditions are found. Moreover, the lake itself is a valuable element in commerce. The rays or spokes in all these directions become materialized in the form of the tracks of 35 railways which enter the city. Twenty-two of these are great companies, and at a short distance sub-radials made by other railroads raise the number to 50 roads. As said above, in Chicago one-twenty-fifth of the railway mileage of the world terminates, and serves 30 millions of persons, who find Chicago the largest city easily accessible to them. Thus is found a vast population connected easily and directly with a common centre, to which everything they produce can be brought, and from which all that contributes to the material progress and comfort of man may be economically distributed.

A financier who is equally well known and respected in New York and Chicago put the case somewhat differently as to what he called Chicago's territory. He considered it as being 1000 miles square, and spoke of it as "the land west of the Alleghanies and south of Mason and Dixon's line." This region, the richest agricultural territory in the world, does its financiering in Chicago. The rapid increase in wealth to both the city and the tributary region is due to the fact that every year both produce more, and have more to sell and less to buy. ... Chicago has become the third manufacturing city in the Union, and she is drawing manufacturers away from the East faster than most persons in the East imagine. To-day it is a great Troy stove-making establishment that has moved to Chicago; the week before it was a Massachusetts shoe-factory that went there. Many great establishments have gone there, but more must follow, because Chicago is not only the centre of the midland region in respect of the distribution of made-up wares, but also for the concentration of raw materials. Chicago must lead in the manufacture of all goods of which wood, leather, and iron are the bases. ...

"Chicago is yet so young and busy," said he who is perhaps the leading banker there, "she has not time for anything beyond each citizen's private affairs. It is hard to get men to serve on a committee. The only thing that saves us from being boors is our civic pride. We are fond, proud, enthusiastic in that respect. But we know that Chicago is not rich, like New York. She has no bulk of capital lying ready for investment and reinvestment; yet she is not longer poor. She has just got over her poverty, and the next stage, bringing accumulated wealth, will quickly follow. Her growth in this respect is more than paralleled by her development into an industrial centre."

So much, then, for Chicago's reasons for existence. The explanation forms not merely the history of an American town, and a town of young men, it points an old moral. It demonstrates anew the active truth that energy is a greater force than money. It commands money. The young founders of Chicago were backed in the East by capitalists who discounted the energy they saw them display. And now Chicago capitalists own the best street railway in St. Louis, the surface railway system of Toledo, a thousand enterprises in hundreds of Western towns.

And here one is brought to reflect that Chicago is distinctly American. I know that the Chicagoans boast that theirs is the most mixed population in the country, but the makers and movers of Chicago are Americans. The streets of the city are full of strange faces of a type to which we are not used to in the East—a dish-faced, soft-eyed, light-haired people. They are Scandinavians; but they are malleable as lead, and quickly and easily follow and adopt every Americanism. In return, they ask only to be permitted to attend a host of Lutheran churches in flocks, to work hard, live temperately, save thriftily, and to pronounce every *j* as if it were a *y*. But the dominating class is of that pure and broad American type which is not controlled by New England or any other tenets, but is somewhat loosely made up of the overflow of the New England, the Middle, and the Southern States. It is as mixed and comprehensive as the West Point School of cadets. It calls its city "She-caw-ger." It inclines to soft hats, and only once in a great while does a visitor see a Chicagoan who has the leisure or patience to carry a cane.

But the visitor's heart warms to the town when he sees its parks and its homes. In them is ample assurance that not every breath is "business," and not every thought commercial. Once out of the thicket of the business and semi-business district, the dwellings of the people reach mile upon mile away along pleasant boulevards and avenues, or facing noble parks and parkways, or in a succession of villages green and gay with foliage and flowers. They are not cliff dwellings like our flats and tenements; there are no brownstone cañons like our up-town streets; there are only occasional hesitating hints there of those Philadelphian and Baltimorean mills that grind out dwellings all alike, as nature makes pease and man makes pins. There are more miles of detached villas in Chicago than a stranger can easily account for. As they are not only found on Prairie Avenue and the boulevards, but in the populous wards and semi-suburbs, where the middle folk are congregated, it is evident that the prosperous moiety of the population enjoys living better (or better living) than the same fraction in the Atlantic cities.

It is said, and I have no reason to doubt it, that the clerks and small tradesmen who live in thousands of these pretty little boxes are the owners of their homes; also that the tenements of the rich display evidence of a tasteful and costly garnering of the globe for articles of luxury and *virtu*. A sneering critic, who wounded Chicago deeply, intimated that theirs must be a primitive society where the rich sit on their door-steps of an evening. That really is a habit there, and in the finer districts of all the Western cities. To enjoy themselves the more completely, the people bring out rugs and carpets, always of gay colors, and fling them on the steps—or stoops, as we Dutch legatees should say—that the ladies' dresses may not be soiled. As these step clothing are as bright as the maidens' eyes and as gay as their cheeks, the effect may be imagined. For my part, I think it argues well for any society that indulges in the trick, and proves existence in such a city to be more human and hearty and far less artificial than where there is too much false pride to permit of it. ...

Chicago's park system is so truly her crown, or its diadem, that its fame may lead to the thought that enough has been said about it. That is not the case, however, for the parks change and improve so constantly that the average Chicagoan finds some of them outgrowing his knowledge, unless he goes to them as he ought to go to his prayers. It is not in extent that the city's parks are extraordinary, for, all told, they comprise less than two thousand acres. It is the energy that has given rise to them, and the taste and enthusiasm which have been expended upon them, that cause our wonder. Sand and swamp were at the bottom of them, and if their surfaces now roll in gentle undulations, it is because the earth that was dug out for the making of ponds has been subsequently applied to the forming of hills and knolls. The people go to some of them upon the boulevards of which I have spoken, beneath trees and beside lawns and gorgeous flower-beds, having their senses sharpened in anticipation of the pleasure-grounds beyond, as the heralds in some old plays prepare us for the action that is to follow. Once the parks are reached, they are found to be literally for the use of the people who own them. I have a fancy that a people who are so largely American would not suffer them to be otherwise. There are no signs warning the public off the grass, or announcing that they "may look, but mustn't touch" whatever there is to see. The people swarm all over the grass, and yet it continues beautiful day after day and year after year. The floral displays seem unharmed; at any rate, we have none to compare with them in any Atlantic coast parks. The people even picnic on the sward, and those who can appreciate such license find, ready at hand, baskets in which to hide the litter which follows. And, O ye who manage other parks we wot of, know that these Chicago playgrounds seem as free from harm and eyesore as any in the land.

The best parks face the great lake, and get wondrous charms of dignity and beauty from it. At the North Side the Lincoln Park commissioners, at great expense, are building out into the lake, making a handsome paved beach, sea-wall, esplanade, and drive to enclose a long, broad body of the lake-water. Although the great blue lake is at the city's edge, there is little or no sailing or pleasure-boating upon it. It is too rude and treacherous. Therefore these commissioners of the Lincoln Park are enclosing, behind their new-made land, a watercourse for sailing and rowing, for racing, and for more indolent aquatic sport.

I have an idea that all this is very American; but what is to be said of the Chicago Sunday, with its drinking shops all wide open, and its multitudes swarming out on pleasure bent? And what of the theatres opening to the best night's business of the week at the hour of Sunday evening service in the churches? I suspect that this also is American—that sort of American that develops under Southern and Western influences not dominated by the New England spirit. And yet the Puritan traditions are not without honor and respect in Chicago, witness the fact that the city spent seventeen and a quarter millions of dollars during the past five years upon her public schools.

117

Sister Carrie

THEODORE DREISER

For an introductory note, see Chapter 87, Volume II.

Chapter One
The Magnet Attracting: A Waif Amid Forces

When Caroline Meeber boarded the afternoon train for Chicago, her total outfit consisted of a small trunk, a cheap imitation alligator-skin satchel, a small lunch in a paper box, and a yellow leather snap purse, containing her ticket, a scrap of paper with her sister's address in Van Buren Street, and four dollars in money. It was in August, 1889. She was eighteen years of age, bright, timid, and full of the illusions of ignorance and youth. Whatever touch of regret at parting characterised her thoughts, it was certainly not for advantages now being given up. A gush of tears at her mother's farewell kiss, a touch in her throat when the cars clacked by the flour mill where her father worked by the day, a pathetic sigh as the familiar green environs of the village passed in review, and the threads which bound her so lightly to girlhood and home were irretrievably broken.

To be sure there was always the next station, where one might descend and return. There was the great city, bound more closely by these very trains which came up daily. Columbia City was not so very far away, even once she was in Chicago. What, pray, is a few hours—a few hundred miles? She looked at the little slip bearing her sister's address and wondered. She gazed at the green landscape, now passing in swift review, until her swifter thoughts replaced its impression with vague conjectures of what Chicago might be.

When a girl leaves her home at eighteen, she does one of two things. Either she falls into saving hands and becomes better, or she rapidly assumes the cosmopolitan standard of virtue and becomes worse. Of an intermediate balance, under the circumstances, there is no possibility. The city has its cunning wiles, no less than the infinitely smaller and more human tempter. There are large

Source: Theodore Dreiser, *Sister Carrie*, New York, 1900, Chs. 1–4, 30.

forces which allure with all the soulfulness of expression possible in the most cultured human. The gleam of a thousand lights is often as effective as the persuasive light in a wooing and fascinating eye. Half the undoing of the unsophisticated and natural mind is accomplished by forces wholly superhuman. A blare of sound, a roar of life, a vast array of human hives, appeal to the astonished senses in equivocal terms. Without a counsellor at hand to whisper cautious interpretations, what falsehoods may not these things breathe into the unguarded ear? Unrecognised for what they are, their beauty, like music, too often relaxes, then weakens, then perverts the simpler human perceptions.

Caroline, or Sister Carrie, as she had been half affectionately termed by the family, was possessed of a mind rudimentary in its power of observation and analysis. Self-interest with her was high, but not strong. It was, nevertheless, her guiding characteristic. Warm with the fancies of youth, pretty with the insipid prettiness of the formative period, possessed of a figure promising eventual shapeliness and an eye alight with certain native intelligence, she was a fair example of the middle American class—two generations removed from the emigrant. Books were beyond her interest—knowledge a sealed book. In the intuitive graces she was still crude. She could scarcely toss her head gracefully. Her hands were almost ineffectual. The feet, though small, were set flatly. And yet she was interested in her charms, quick to understand the keener pleasures of life, ambitious to gain in material things. A half-equipped little knight she was, venturing to reconnoitre the mysterious city and dreaming wild dreams of some vague, far-off supremacy, which should make it prey and subject—the proper penitent, grovelling at a woman's slipper.

"That," said a voice in her ear, "is one of the prettiest little resorts in Wisconsin."

"Is it?" she answered nervously.

The train was just pulling out of Waukesha. For some time she had been conscious of a man behind. She felt him observing her mass of hair. He had been fidgeting, and with natural intuition she felt a certain interest growing in that quarter. Her maidenly reserve, and a certain sense of what was conventional under the circumstances, called her to forestall and deny this familiarity, but the daring and magnetism of the individual, born of past experiences and triumphs, prevailed. She answered.

He leaned forward to put his elbows upon the back of her seat and proceeded to make himself volubly agreeable.

"Yes, that is a great resort for Chicago people. The hotels are swell. You are not familiar with this part of the country, are you?

"Oh, yes, I am," answered Carrie. "That is, I live at Columbia City. I have never been through here, though."

"And so this is your first visit to Chicago," he observed.

All the time she was conscious of certain features out of the side of her eye. Flush, colourful cheeks, a light moustache, a grey fedora hat. She now turned and looked upon him in full, the instincts of self-protection and coquetry mingling confusedly in her brain.

"I didn't say that," she said.

"Oh," he answered, in a very pleasing way and with an assumed air of mistake, "I thought you did."

Here was a type of the travelling canvasser for a manufacturing house—a class which at that time was first being dubbed by the slang of the day "drummers." He came within the meaning of a still newer term, which had sprung into general use among Americans in 1880, and which concisely expressed the thought of one whose dress or manners are calculated to elicit the admiration of susceptible young women—a "masher." His suit was of a striped and crossed pattern of brown wool, new at that time, but since become familiar as a business suit. The low crotch of the vest revealed a stiff shirt bosom of white and pink stripes. From his coat sleeves protruded a pair of linen cuffs of the same pattern, fastened with large, gold plate buttons, set with the common yellow agates known as "cat's eyes." His fingers bore several rings—one, the ever-enduring heavy seal—and from his vest dangled a neat gold watch chain, from which was suspended the secret insignia of the Order of Elks. The whole suit was rather tight-fitting, and was finished off with heavy-soled tan shoes, highly polished, and the grey fedora hat. He was, for the order of intellect represented, attractive, and whatever he had to recommend him, you may be sure was not lost upon Carrie, in this, her first glance.

Lest this order of individual should permanently pass, let me put down some of the most striking characteristics of his most successful manner and method. Good clothes, of course, were the first essential, the things without which he was nothing. A strong physical nature, actuated by a keen desire for the feminine, was the next. A mind free of any consideration of the problems or forces of the world and actuated not by greed, but an insatiable love of variable pleasure. His method was always simple. Its principal element was daring, backed, of course, by an intense desire and admiration for the sex. Let him meet with a young woman once and he would approach her with an air of kindly familiarity, not unmixed with pleading, which would result in most cases in a tolerant acceptance. If she showed any tendency to coquetry he would be apt to straighten her tie, or if she "took up" with him at all, to call her by her first name. If he visited a department store it was to lounge familiarly over the counter and ask some leading questions. In more exclusive circles, on the train or in waiting stations, he went slower. If some seemingly vulnerable object appeared he was all attention—to pass the compliments of the day, to lead the way to the parlor car, carrying her grip, or, failing that, to take a seat next to her with the hope of being able to court her to her destination. Pillows, books, a footstool, the shade lowered; all these figured in the things which he could do. If, when she reached her destination he did not alight and attend her baggage for her, it was because, in his own estimation, he had signally failed.

A woman should some day write the complete philosophy of clothes. No matter how young, it is one of the things she wholly comprehends. There is an indescribably faint line in the matter of a man's apparel which somehow divides for her those who are worth glancing at and those who are not. Once an individual has passed this faint line on the way downward he will get no glance from her. There is another line at which the dress of a man will cause her to study her own. This line the individual at her elbow now marked for Carrie. She became conscious of an inequality. Her own plain blue dress, with its black cotton tape trimmings, now seemed to her shabby. She felt the worn state of her shoes.

"Let's see," he went on, "I know quite a number of people in your town. Morgenroth the clothier and Gibson the dry goods man."

"Oh, do you?" she interrupted, aroused by memories of longings their show windows had cost her.

At last he had a clew to her interest, and followed it deftly. In a few minutes he had come about into her seat. He talked of sales of clothing, his travels, Chicago, and the amusements of that city.

"If you are going there, you will enjoy it immensely. Have you relatives?"

"I am going to visit my sister," she explained.

"You want to see Lincoln Park," he said, "and Michigan Boulevard. They are putting up great buildings there. It's a second New York—great. So much to see—theatres, crowds, fine houses—oh, you'll like that."

There was a little ache in her fancy of all he described. Her insignificance in the presence of so much magnificence faintly affected her. She realised that hers was not to be a round of pleasure, and yet there was something promising in all the material prospect he set forth. There was something satisfactory in the attention of this individual with his good clothes. She could not help smiling as he told her of some popular actress of whom she reminded him. She was not silly, and yet attention of this sort had its weight.

"You will be in Chicago some little time, won't you?" he observed at one turn of the now easy conversation.

"I don't know," said Carrie vaguely—a flash vision of the possibility of her not securing employment rising in her mind.

"Several weeks, anyhow," he said, looking steadily into her eyes.

There was much more passing now than the mere words indicated. He recognised the indescribable thing that made up for fascination and beauty in her. She realised that she was of interest to him from the one standpoint which a woman both delights in and fears. Her manner was simple, though for the very reason that she had not yet learned the many little affectations with which women conceal their true feelings. Some things she did appeared bold. A clever companion—had she ever had one—would have warned her never to look a man in the eyes so steadily.

"Why do you ask?" she said.

"Well, I'm going to be there several weeks. I'm going to study stock at our place and get new samples. I might show you 'round."

"I don't know whether you can or not. I mean I don't know whether I can. I shall be living with my sister, and—"

"Well, if she minds, we'll fix that." He took out his pencil and a little pocket note-book as if it were all settled. "What is your address there?"

She fumbled her purse which contained the address slip.

He reached down in his hip pocket and took out a fat purse. It was filled with slips of paper, some mileage books, a roll of greenbacks. It impressed her deeply. Such a purse had never been carried by any one attentive to her. Indeed, an experienced traveller, a brisk man of the world, had never come within such close range before. The purse, the shiny tan shoes, the smart new suit, and the *air* with which he did things, built up for her a dim world of fortune, of which he was the centre. It disposed her pleasantly toward all he might do.

He took out a neat business card, on which was engraved Bartlett, Caryoe & Company, and down in the left-hand corner, Chas. H. Drouet.

"That's me," he said, putting the card in her hand and touching his name. "It's pronounced Drew-eh. Our family was French, on my father's side."

She looked at it while he put up his purse. Then he got out a letter from a bunch in his coat pocket. "This is the house I travel for," he went on, pointing to a picture on it, "corner of State and Lake." There was pride in his voice. He felt that it was something to be connected with such a place, and he made her feel that way.

"What is your address?" he began again, fixing his pencil to write.

She looked at his hand.

"Carrie Meeber," she said slowly. "Three hundred and fifty-four West Van Buren Street, care S. C. Hanson."

He wrote it carefully down and got out the purse again. "You'll be at home if I come around Monday night?" he said.

"I think so," she answered.

How true it is that words are but the vague shadows of the volumes we mean. Little audible links, they are, chaining together great inaudible feelings and purposes. Here were these two, bandying little phrases, drawing purses, looking at cards, and both unconscious of how inarticulate all their real feelings were. Neither was wise enough to be sure of the working of the mind of the other. He could not tell how his luring succeeded. She could not realise that she was drifting, until he secured her address. Now she felt that she had yielded something—he, that he had gained a victory. Already they felt that they were somehow associated. Already he took control in directing the conversation. His words were easy. Her manner was relaxed.

They were nearing Chicago. Signs were everywhere numerous. Trains flashed by them. Across wide stretches of flat, open prairie they could see lines of telegraph poles stalking across the fields toward the great city. Far away were indications of suburban towns, some big smoke-stacks towering high in the air.

Frequently there were two-story frame houses standing out in the open fields, without fence or trees, lone outposts of the approaching army of homes.

To the child, the genius with imagination, or the wholly untravelled, the approach to a great city for the first time is a wonderful thing. Particularly if it be evening—that mystic period between the glare and gloom of the world when life is changing from one sphere or condition to another. Ah, the promise of the night. What does it not hold for the weary! What old illusion of hope is not here forever repeated! Says the soul of the toiler to itself, "I shall soon be free. I shall be in the ways and the hosts of the merry. The streets, the lamps, the lighted chamber set for dining, are for me. The theatre, the halls, the parties, the ways of rest and the paths of song—these are mine in the night." Though all humanity be still enclosed in the shops, the thrill runs abroad. It is in the air. The dullest feel something which they may not always express or describe. it is the lifting of the burden of toil.

Sister Carrie gazed out of the window. Her companion, affected by her wonder, so contagious are all things, felt anew some interest in the city and pointed out its marvels.

"This is Northwest Chicago," said Drouet. "This is the Chicago River," and he pointed to a little muddy creek, crowded with the huge masted wanderers from far-off water nosing the black-posted banks. With a puff, a clang, and a clatter of rails it was gone. "Chicago is getting to be a great town," he went on. "It's a wonder. You'll find lots to see here."

She did not hear this very well. Her heart was troubled by a kind of terror. The fact that she was alone, away from home, rushing into a great sea of life and endeavour, began to tell. She could not help but feel a little choked for breath—a little sick as her heart beat so fast. She half closed her eyes and tried to think it was nothing, that Columbia City was only a little way off.

"Chicago! Chicago!" called the brakeman, slamming open the door. They were rushing into a more crowded yard, alive with the clatter and clang of life. She began to gather up her poor little grip and closed her hand firmly upon her purse. Drouet arose, kicked his legs to straighten his trousers, and seized his clean yellow grip.

"I suppose your people will be here to meet you?" he said. "Let me carry your grip."

"Oh, no," she said. "I'd rather you wouldn't. I'd rather you wouldn't be with me when I meet my sister."

"All right," he said in all kindness. "I'll be near, though, in case she isn't here, and take you out there safely."

"You're so kind," said Carrie, feeling the goodness of such attention in her strange situation.

"Chicago!" called the brakeman, drawing the word out long. They were under a great shadowy train shed, where the lamps were already beginning to shine out, with passenger cars all about and the train moving at a snail's pace. The people in the car were all up and crowding about the door.

"Well, here we are," said Drouet, leading the way to the door. "Good-bye, till I see you Monday."

"Good-bye," she answered, taking his proffered hand.

"Remember, I'll be looking till you find your sister."

She smiled into his eyes.

They filed out, and he affected to take no notice of her. A lean-faced, rather commonplace woman recognised Carrie on the platform and hurried forward.

"Why, Sister Carrie!" she began, and there was a perfunctory embrace of welcome.

Carrie realised the change of affectional atmosphere at once. Amid all the maze, uproar, and novelty she felt cold reality taking her by the hand. No world of light and merriment. No round of amusement. Her sister carried with her most of the grimness of shift and toil.

"Why, how are all the folks at home?" she began; "how is father, and mother?"

Carrie answered, but was looking away. Down the aisle, toward the gate leading into the waiting-room and the street, stood Drouet. He was looking back. When he saw that she saw him and was safe with her sister he turned to go, sending back the shadow of a smile. Only Carrie saw it. She felt something lost to her when he moved away. When he disappeared she felt his absence thoroughly. With her sister she was much alone, a lone figure in a tossing, thoughtless sea.

Chapter Two
What Poverty Threatened: Of Granite and Brass

Minnie's flat, as the one-floor resident apartments were then being called, was in a part of West Van Buren Street inhabited by families of labourers and clerks, men who had come, and were still coming, with the rush of population pouring in at the rate of 50,000 a year. It was on the third floor, the front windows looking down into the street, where, at night, the lights of grocery stores were shining and children were playing. To Carrie, the sound of the little bells upon the horse-cars, as they tinkled in and out of hearing, was as pleasing as it was novel. She gazed into the lighted street when Minnie brought her into the front room, and wondered at the sounds, the movement, the murmur of the vast city which stretched for miles and miles in every direction.

Mrs. Hanson, after the first greetings were over, gave Carrie the baby and proceeded to get supper. Her husband asked a few questions and sat down to read the evening paper. He was a silent man, American born, of a Swede father, and now employed as a cleaner of refrigerator cars at the stockyards. To him the presence or absence of his wife's sister was a matter of indifference. Her personal appearance did not affect him one way or the other. His one observation to the point was concerning the chances of work in Chicago.

"It's a big place," he said. "You can get in somewhere in a few days. Everybody does."

It had been tacitly understood beforehand that she was to get work and pay her board. He was of a clean, saving disposition, and had already paid a number of monthly instalments on two lots far out on the West Side. His ambition was some day to build a house on them.

In the interval which marked the preparation of the meal Carrie found time to study the flat. She had some slight gift of observation and that sense, so rich in every woman—intuition.

She felt the drag of a lean and narrow life. The walls of the rooms were discordantly papered. The floors were covered with matting and the hall laid with a thin rag carpet. One could see that the furniture was of that poor, hurriedly patched together quality sold by the instalment houses.

She sat with Minnie, in the kitchen, holding the baby until it began to cry. Then she walked and sang to it, until Hanson, disturbed in his reading, came and took it. A pleasant side to his nature came out here. He was patient. One could see that he was very much wrapped up in his offspring.

"Now, now," he said, walking. "There, there," and there was a certain Swedish accent noticeable in his voice.

"You'll want to see the city first, won't you?" said Minnie, when they were eating. "Well, we'll go out Sunday and see Lincoln Park."

Carrie noticed that Hanson had said nothing to this. He seemed to be thinking of something else.

"Well," she said, "I think I'll look around to-morrow. I've got Friday and Saturday, and it won't be any trouble. Which way is the business part?"

Minnie began to explain, but her husband took this part of the conversation to himself.

"It's that way," he said, pointing east. "That's east." Then he went off into the longest speech he had yet indulged in, concerning the lay of Chicago. "You'd better look in those big manufacturing houses along Franklin Street and just the other side of the river," he concluded. "Lots of girls work there. You could get home easy, too. It isn't very far."

Carrie nodded and asked her sister about the neighbourhood. The latter talked in a subdued tone, telling the little she knew about it, while Hanson concerned himself with the baby. Finally he jumped up and handed the child to his wife.

"I've got to get up early in the morning, so I'll go to bed," and off he went, disappearing into the dark little bedroom off the hall, for the night.

"He works way down at the stock-yards," explained Minnie, "so he's got to get up at half-past five."

"What time do you get up to get breakfast?" asked Carrie.

"At about twenty minutes of five."

Together they finished the labour of the day, Carrie washing the dishes while Minnie undressed the baby and put it to bed. Minnie's manner was one of trained industry, and Carrie could see that it was a steady round of toil with her.

She began to see that her relations with Drouet would have to be abandoned. he could not come here. She read from the manner of Hanson, in the subdued air of Minnie, and, indeed, the whole atmosphere of the flat, a settled opposition to anything save a conservative round of toil. If Hanson sat every evening in the front room and read his paper, if he went to bed at nine, and Minnie a little later, what would they expect of her? She saw that she would first need to get work and establish herself on a paying basis before she could think of having company of any sort. Her little flirtation with Drouet seemed now an extraordinary thing.

"No," she said to herself, "he can't come here."

She asked Minnie for ink and paper, which were upon the mantel in the dining-room, and when the latter had gone to bed at ten, got out Drouet's card and wrote him.

"I cannot have you call on me here. You will have to wait until you hear from me again. My sister's place is so small."

She troubled herself over what else to put in the letter. She wanted to make some reference to their relations upon the train, but was too timid. She concluded by thanking him for his kindness in a crude way, then puzzled over the formality of signing her name, and finally decided upon the severe, winding up with a "Very truly," which she subsequently changed to "Sincerely." She sealed and addressed the letter, and going in the front room, the alcove of which contained her bed, drew the one small rocking-chair up to the open window, and sat looking out upon the night and streets in silent wonder. Finally, wearied by her own reflections, she began to grow dull in her chair, and feeling the need of sleep, arranged her clothing for the night and went to bed.

When she awoke at eight the next morning, Hanson had gone. Her sister was busy in the dining-room, which was also the sitting-room, sewing. She worked, after dressing, to arrange a little breakfast for herself, and then advised with Minnie as to which way to look. The latter had changed considerably since Carrie had seen her. She was now a thin, though rugged, woman of twenty-seven, with ideas of life coloured by her husband's, and fast hardening into narrower conceptions of pleasure and duty than had ever been hers in a thoroughly circumscribed youth. She had invited Carrie, not because she longed for her presence, but because the latter was dissatisfied at home, and could probably get work and pay her board here. She was pleased to see her in a way but reflected her husband's point of view in the matter of work. Anything was good enough so long as it paid—say, five dollars a week to begin with. A shop girl was the destiny prefigured for the newcomer. She would get in one of the great shops and do well enough until—well, until something happened. Neither of them knew exactly what. They did not figure on promotion. They did not exactly count on marriage. Things would go on, though, in a dim kind of way until the better thing would eventuate, and Carrie would be rewarded for coming and toiling in the city. It was under such auspicious circumstances that she started out this morning to look for work.

Before following her in her round of seeking, let us look at the sphere in which her future was to lie. In 1889 Chicago had the peculiar qualifications of growth which made such adventuresome pilgrimages even on the part of young girls plausible. Its many and growing commercial opportunities gave it widespread fame, which made of it a giant magnet, drawing to itself, from all quarters, the hopeful and the hopeless—those who had their fortune yet to make and those whose fortunes and affairs had reached a disastrous climax elsewhere. It was a city of over 500,000, with the ambition, the daring, the activity of a metropolis of a million. Its streets and houses were already scattered over an area of seventy-five square miles. Its population was not so much thriving upon established commerce as upon the industries which prepared for the arrival of others. The sound of the hammer engaged upon the erection of new structures was everywhere heard. Great industries were moving in. The huge railroad corporations which had long before recognised the prospects of the place had seized upon vast tracts of land for transfer and shipping purposes. Street-car lines had been extended far out into the open country in anticipation of rapid growth. The city had laid miles and miles of streets and sewers through regions where, perhaps, one solitary house stood out alone—a pioneer of the populous ways to be. There were regions open to the sweeping winds and rain, which were yet lighted throughout the night with long, blinking lines of gas-lamps, fluttering in the wind. Narrow board walks extended out, passing here a house, and there a store, at far intervals, eventually ending on the open prairie.

In the central portion was the vast wholesale and shopping district, to which the uniformed seeker for work usually drifted. It was a characteristic of Chicago then, and one not generally shared by other cities, that individual firms of any pretension occupied individual buildings. The presence of ample ground made this possible. It gave an imposing appearance to most of the wholesale houses, whose offices were upon the ground floor and in plain view of the street. The large plate of window glass, now so common, were then rapidly coming into use, and gave to the ground floor offices a distinguished and prosperous look. The casual wanderer could see as he passed a polished array of office fixtures, much frosted glass, clerks hard at work, and genteel business men in "nobby" suits and clean line lounging about or sitting in groups. Polished brass or nickel signs at the square stone entrances announced the firm and the nature of the business in rather neat and reserved terms. The entire metropolitan centre possessed a high and mighty air calculated to overawe and abash the common applicant, and to make the gulf between poverty and success seem both wide and deep.

Into this important commercial region the timid Carrie went. She walked east along Van Buren Street through a region of lessening importance, until it deteriorated into a mass of shanties and coal-yards, and finally verged upon the river. She walked bravely forward, led by an honest desire to find employment and delayed at every step by the interest of the unfolding scene, and a sense of helplessness amid so much evidence of power and force which she did not understand. These vast buildings, what were they? These strange energies and huge interests, for what purposes were they there? She could have understood the meaning of a little stone-cutter's yard at Columbia City, carving little pieces of marble for individual use, but when the yards of some huge stone corporation came into view, filled with spur tracks and flat cars, transpierced by docks from the river, and traversed overhead by immense trundling cranes of wood and steel, it lost all significance in her little world.

It was so with the vast railroad yards, with the crowded array of vessels she saw at the river, and the huge factories over the way, lining the water's edge. Through the open windows she could see the figures of men and women in working aprons, moving busily about. The great streets were wall-lined mysteries to her; the vast offices, strange mazes which concerned far-off individuals of importance. She could only think of people connected with them as counting money, dressing magnificently, and riding in carriages. What they dealt in, how they laboured, to what end it all came, she had only the vaguest conception. It was all wonderful, all vast, all far removed, and she sank in spirit inwardly and fluttered feebly at the heart as she thought of entering any one of these mighty concerns and asking for something to do—something that she could do—anything.

Chapter Three
We Question of Fortune: four-fifty a Week

Once across the river and into the wholesale district, she glanced about her for some likely door at which to apply. As she contemplated the wide windows and imposing signs, she became conscious of being gazed upon and understood for what she was—a wage-seeker. She had never done this thing before, and lacked courage. To avoid a certain indefinable shame she felt at being caught spying about for a position, she quickened her steps and assumed an air of indifference supposedly common to one upon an errand. In this way she passed many manufacturing and wholesale houses without once glancing in. At last, after several blocks of walking, she felt that this would not do, and began to look about again, though without relaxing her pace. A little way on she saw a great door which, for some reason, attracted her attention. It was ornamented by a small brass sign, and seemed to be the entrance to a vast hive of six or seven floors. "Perhaps," she thought, "they may want some one," and crossed over to enter. When she came within a score of feet of the desired goal, she saw through the window a young man in a grey checked suit. That he had anything to do with the concern, she could not tell, but because he happened to be looking in her direction her weakening heart misgave her and she hurried by, too overcome with shame to enter. Over the way stood a great six-story structure, labelled Storm and King, which she viewed with rising hope. It was a wholesale dry goods concern and employed women. She could see them moving about now and then upon the upper floors. This place she decided to enter, no matter what. She crossed over and walked directly toward the entrance. As she did so, two men came out and paused in the door. A telegraph messenger in blue dashed past her and up the few steps that led to the entrance and disappeared. Several pedestrians out of the hurrying throng which filled the sidewalks passed about her as she paused, hesitating. She looked helplessly around, and then, seeing herself observed, retreated. It was too difficult a task. She could not go past them.

So severe a defeat told sadly upon her nerves. Her feet carried her mechanically forward, every foot of her progress being a satisfactory portion of a flight which she gladly made. Block after block passed by. Upon street-lamps at the various corners she read names such as Madison, Monroe, La Salle, Clark, Dearborn, State, and still she went, her feet beginning to tire upon the broad stone flagging. She was pleased in part that the streets were bright and clean. The morning sun, shining down with steadily increasing warmth, made the shady side of the streets pleasantly cool. She looked at the blue sky overhead with more realisation of its charm than had ever come to her before.

Her cowardice began to trouble her in a way. She turned back, resolving to hunt up Storm and King and enter. On the way she encountered a great wholesale shoe company, through the broad plate windows of which she saw an enclosed executive department, hidden by frosted glass. Without this enclosure, but just within the street entrance, sat a grey-haired gentleman at a small table, with a large open ledger before him. She walked by this institution several times hesitating, but, finding herself unobserved, faltered past the screen door and stood humbly waiting.

"Well, young lady," observed the old gentleman, looking at her somewhat kindly, "what is it you wish?"

"I am, that is, do you—I mean, do you need any help?" she stammered.

"Not just at present," he answered smiling. "Not just at present. Come in some time next week. Occasionally we need some one."

She received the answer in silence and backed awkwardly out. The pleasant nature of her reception rather astonished her. She had expected that it would be more difficult, that something cold and harsh would be said—she knew not what. That she had not been put to shame and made to feel her unfortunate position, seemed remarkable.

Somewhat encouraged, she ventured into another large structure. It was a clothing company, and more people were in evidence—well-dressed men of forty and more, surrounded by brass railings.

An office boy approached her.

"Who is it you wish to see?" he asked.

"I want to see the manager," she said.

He ran away and spoke to one of a group of three men who were conferring together. One of these came towards her.

"Well?" he said coldly. The greeting drove all courage from her at once.

"Do you need any help?" she stammered.

"No," he replied abruptly, and turned upon his heel.

She went foolishly out, the office boy deferentially swinging the door for her, and gladly sank into the obscuring crowd. It was a severe setback to her recently pleased mental state.

Now she waked quite aimlessly for a time, turning here and there, seeing one great company after another, but finding no courage to prosecute her single inquiry. High noon came, and with it hunger. She hunted out an unassuming restaurant and entered, but was disturbed to find that the prices were exorbitant for the size of her purse. A bowl of soup was all that she could afford, and, with this quickly eaten, she went out again. It restored her strength somewhat and made her moderately bold to pursue the search.

In walking a few blocks to fix upon some probable place, she again encountered the firm of Storm and King, and this time managed to get in. Some gentlemen were conferring close at hand, but took no notice of her. She was left standing, gazing nervously upon the floor. When the limit of her distress had been nearly reached, she was beckoned to by a man at one of the many desks within the near-by railing.

"Who is it you wish to see?" he inquired.

"Why, any one, if you please," she answered. "I am looking for something to do."

"Oh, you want to see Mr. McManus," he returned. "Sit down," and he pointed to a chair against the neighbouring wall. He went on leisurely writing, until after a time a short, stout gentleman came in from the street.

"Mr. McManus," called the man at the desk, "this young woman wants to see you."

The short gentleman turned about towards Carrie, and she arose and came forward.

"What can I do for you, miss?" he inquired, surveying her curiously.

"I want to know if I can get a position," she inquired.

"As what?" he asked.

"Not as anything in particular," she faltered.

"Have you ever had any experience in the wholesale dry goods business?" he questioned.

"No, sir," she replied.

"Are you a stenographer or typewriter?"

"No, sir."

"Well, we haven't anything here," he said. "We employ only experienced help."

She began to step backward toward the door, when something about her plaintive face attracted him.

"Have you ever worked at anything before?" he inquired.

"No, sir," she said.

"Well, now, it's hardly possible that you would get anything to do in a wholesale house of this kind. Have you tried the department stores?"

She acknowledged that she had not.

"Well, if I were you," he said, looking at her rather genially, "I would try the department stores. They often need young women as clerks."

"Thank you," she said, her whole nature relieved by this spark of friendly interest.

"Yes," he said, as she moved toward the door, "you try the department stores," and off he went.

At that time the department store was in its earliest form of successful operation, and there were not many. The first three in the United States, established about 1884, were in Chicago. Carrie was familiar with the names of several through the advertisements in the "Daily News," and now proceeded to seek them. The words of Mr. McManus had somehow managed to restore her courage, which had fallen low, and she dared to hope that this new line would offer her something. Some time she spent in wandering up and down, thinking to encounter the buildings by chance, so readily is the mind, bent upon prosecuting a hard but needful errand, eased by that self-deception which the semblance of search, without the reality, gives. At last she inquired of a police officer, and was directed to proceed "two blocks up," where she would find "The Fair."

The nature of these vast retail combinations, should they ever permanently disappear, will form an interesting chapter in the commercial history of our nation. Such a flowering out of a modest trade principle the world had never witnessed up to that time. They were along the line of the most effective retail organisation, with hundreds of stores coördinated into one and laid out upon the most imposing and economic basis. They were handsome, bustling, successful affairs, with a host of clerks and a swarm of patrons. Carrie passed along the busy aisles, much affected by the remarkable displays of trinkets, dress goods, stationery, and jewelry. Each separate counter was a show place of dazzling interest and attraction. She could not help feeling the claim of each trinket and valuable upon her personally, and yet she did not stop. There was nothing there which she could not have used—nothing which she did not long to own. The dainty slippers and stockings, the delicately frilled skirts and petticoats, the laces, ribbons, hair-combs, purses, all touched her with individual desire, and she felt keenly the fact that not any of these things were in a range of her purchase. She was a work-seeker, an outcast without employment, one whom the average employee could tell at a glance was poor and in need of a situation.

It must not be thought that any one could have mistaken her for a nervous, sensitive, high-strung nature, cast unduly upon a cold, calculating, and unpoetic world. Such certainly she was not. But women are peculiarly sensitive to their adornment.

Not only did Carrie feel the drag of desire for all which was new and pleasing in apparel for women, but she noticed too, with a touch at the heart, the fine ladies who elbowed and ignored her, brushing past in utter disregard of her presence, themselves eagerly enlisted in the materials which the store contained. Carrie was not familiar with the appearance of her more fortunate sisters of the city. Neither had she before known the nature and appearance of the shop girls with whom she now compared poorly. They were pretty in the main, some even handsome, with an air of independence and indifference which added, in the case of the more favoured, a certain piquancy. Their clothes were neat, in many instances fine, and wherever she encountered the eye of one it was only to recognise in it a keen analysis of her own position—her individual shortcomings of dress and that shadow of manner which she thought must hang about her and make clear to all who and what she was. A flame of envy lighted in her heart. She realised in a dim way how much the city held—wealth, fashion, ease—every adornment for women, and she longed for dress and beauty with a whole heart.

On the second floor were the managerial offices, to which, after some inquiry, she was now directed. There she found other girls ahead of her, applicants like herself, but with more of that self-satisfied and independent air which experience of the city lends; girls who scrutinised her in a painful manner. After a wait of perhaps three-quarters of an hour, she was called in turn.

"Now," said a sharp, quick-mannered Jew, who was sitting at a roll-top desk near the window, "have you ever worked in any other store?"

"No, sir," said Carrie.

"Oh, you haven't," he said, eyeing her keenly.

"No, sir," she replied.

"Well, we prefer young women just now with some experience. I guess we can't use you."

Carrie stood waiting a moment, hardly certain whether the interview had terminated.

"Don't wait!" he exclaimed. "Remember we are very busy here."

Carrie began to move quickly to the door.

"Hold on," he said, calling her back. "Give me your name and address. We want girls occasionally."

When she had gotten safely into the street, she could scarcely restrain the tears. It was not so much the particular rebuff which she had just experienced, but the whole abashing trend of the day. She was tired and nervous. She abandoned the thought of appealing to the other department stores and now wandered on, feeling a certain safety and relief in mingling with the crowd.

In her indifferent wandering she turned into Jackson Street, not far from the river, and was keeping her way along the south side of that imposing thoroughfare, when a piece of wrapping paper, written on with marking ink and tacked up on the door, attracted her attention. It read, "Girls wanted—wrappers & stitchers." She hesitated a moment, then entered.

The firm of Speigelheim & Co., makers of boys' caps, occupied one floor of the building, fifty feet in width and some eighty feet in depth. It was a place rather dingily lighted, the darkest portions having incandescent lights, filled with machines and work benches. At the latter laboured quite a company of girls and some men. The former were drabby-looking creatures, stained in face with oil and dust, clad in thin, shapeless, cotton dresses and shod with more or less worn shoes. Many of them had their sleeves rolled up, revealing b are arms, and in some cases, owing to the heat, their dresses were open at the neck. They were a fair type of nearly the lowest order of shop-girls—careless, slouchy, and more or less pale from confinement. They were not timid, however; were rich in curiosity, and strong in daring and slang.

Carrie looked about her, very much disturbed and quite sure that she did not want to work here. Aside from making her uncomfortable by sidelong glances, no one paid her the least attention. She waited until the whole department was aware of her presence. Then some word was sent around, and a foreman, in an apron and shirt sleeves, the latter rolled up to his shoulders, approached.

"Do you want to see me?" he asked.

"Do you need any help?" said Carrie, already learning directness of address.

"Do you know how to stitch caps?" he returned.

"No, sir," she replied.

"Have you ever had any experience at this kind of work?" he inquired.

She answered that she had not.

"Well," said the foreman, scratching his ear meditatively, "we do need a stitcher. We like experienced help, though. We've hardly got time to break people in." He paused and looked away out of the window. "We might, though, put you at finishing," he concluded reflectively.

"How much do you pay a week?" ventured Carrie, emboldened by a certain softness in the man's manner and his simplicity of address.

"Three and a half," he answered.

"Oh," she was about to exclaim, but checked herself and allowed her thoughts to die without expression.

"We're not exactly in need of anybody," he went on vaguely, looking her over as one would a package. "You can come on Monday morning, though," he added, "and I'll put you to work."

"Thank you," said Carrie weakly.

"If you come, bring an apron," he added.

He walked away and left her standing by the elevator, never so much as inquiring her name.

While the appearance of the shop and the announcement of the price paid per week operated very much as a blow to Carrie's fancy, the fact that work of any kind was offered after so rude a round of experience was gratifying. She could not begin to believe that she would take the place, modest as her aspirations were. She had been used to better than that. Her mere experience and the free out-of-door life of the country caused her nature to revolt at such confinement. Dirt had never been her share. Her sister's flat was clean. This place was grimy and low, the girls were careless and hardened. They must be bad-minded and hearted, she imagined. Still, a place had been offered her. Surely Chicago was not so bad if she could find one place in one day. She might find another and better later.

Her subsequent experiences were not of a reassuring nature, however. From all the more pleasing or imposing places she was turned away abruptly with the most chilling formality. In others where she applied only the experienced were required. She met with painful rebuffs, the most trying of which had been in a manufacturing cloak house, where she had gone to the fourth floor to inquire.

"No, no," said the foreman, a rough, heavily built individual, who looked after a miserably lighted workshop, "we don't want any one. Don't come here."

With the wane of the afternoon went her hopes, her courage, and her strength. She had been astonishingly persistent. So earnest an effort was well deserving of a better reward. On every hand, to her fatigued senses, the great business portion grew larger, harder, more stolid in its indifference. It seemed as if it was all closed to her, that the struggle was too fierce for her to hope to do anything at all. Men and women hurried by in long, shifting lines. She felt the flow of the tide of effort and interest—felt her own helplessness without quite realising the wisp on the tide that she was. She cast about vainly for some possible place to apply, but found no door which she had the courage to enter. It would be the same thing all over. The old humiliation of her plea, rewarded by curt denial. Sick at heart and in body, she turned to the west, the direction of Minnie's flat, which she had now fixed in mind, and began that wearisome, baffled retreat which the seeker for employment at nightfall too often makes. In passing through Fifth Avenue, south towards Van Buren Street, where she intended to take a car, she passed the door of a large wholesale shoe house, through the plate-glass window of which she could see a middle-aged gentleman sitting at a small desk. One of those forlorn impulses which often grow out of a fixed sense of defeat, the last sprouting of a baffled and uprooted growth of ideas, seized upon her. She walked deliberately through the door and up to the gentleman, who looked at her weary face with partially awakened interest.

"What is it?" he said.

"Can you give me something to do?" said Carrie.

"Now, I really don't know," he said kindly. "What kind of work is it you want—you're not a typewriter, are you?"

"Oh, no," answered Carrie.

"Well, we only employ book-keepers and typewriters here. You might go around to the side and inquire upstairs. They did want some help upstairs a few days ago. Ask for Mr. Brown."

She hastened around to the side entrance and was taken up by the elevator to the fourth floor.

"Call Mr. Brown, Willie," said the elevator man to a boy near by.

Willie went off and presently returned with the information that Mr. Brown said she should sit down and that he would be around in a little while.

It was a portion of the stock room which gave no idea of the general character of the place, and Carrie could form no opinion of the nature of the work.

"So you want something to do," said Mr. Brown, after he inquired concerning the nature of her errand. "Have you ever been employed in a shoe factory before?"

"No, sir," said Carrie.

"What is your name?" he inquired, and being informed, "Well, I don't know as I have anything for you. Would you work for four and a half a week?"

Carrie was too worn by defeat not to feel that it was considerable. She had not expected that he would offer her less than six. She acquiesced, however, and he took her name and address.

"Well," he said, finally, "you report here at eight o'clock Monday morning. I think I can find something for you to do."

He left her revived by the possibilities, sure that she had found something at last. Instantly the blood crept warmly over her body. Her nervous tension relaxed. She walked out into the busy street and discovered a new atmosphere. Behold, the throng was moving with a lightsome step. She noticed that men and women were smiling. Scraps of conversation and notes of laughter floated to her. The air was light. People were already pouring out of the buildings, their labour ended for the day. She noticed that they were pleased, and thoughts of her sister's home and the meal that would be awaiting her quickened her steps. She hurried on, tired perhaps, but no longer weary of foot. What would not Minnie say! Ah, the long winter in Chicago—the lights, the crowd, the amusement! This was a great, pleasing metropolis after all, Her new firm was a goodly institution. Its windows were of huge plate glass. She could probably do well there. Thoughts of Drouet returned—of the things he had told her. She now felt that life was better, that it was livelier, sprightlier. She boarded a car in the best of spirits, feeling her blood still flowing pleasantly. She would live in Chicago, her mind kept saying to itself. She would have a better time than she had ever had before—she would be happy.

Chapter Four
The Spendings of Fancy: Facts Answer with Sneers

For the next two days Carrie indulged in the most high-flown speculations.

Her fancy plunged recklessly into privileges and amusements which would have been much more becoming had she been cradled a child of fortune. With ready will and quick mental selection she scattered her meagre four-fifty per week with a swift and graceful hand. Indeed, as she sat in her rocking-chair these several evenings before going to bed and looked out upon the pleasantly lighted street, this money cleared for its prospective possessor the way to every joy and every bauble which the heart of woman may desire. "I will have a fine time," she thought.

Her sister Minnie knew nothing of these rather wild cerebrations, though they exhausted the markets of delight. She was too busy scrubbing the kitchen woodwork and calculating the purchasing power of eighty cents for Sunday's dinner. When Carrie had returned home, flushed with her first success and ready, for all her weariness, to discuss the now interesting events which led up to her achievement, the former had merely smiled approvingly and inquired whether she would have to spend any of it for car fare. This consideration had not entered in before, and it did not now for long affect the glow of Carrie's enthusiasm. Disposed as she then was to calculate upon that vague basis which allows the subtraction of one sum from another without any perceptible diminution, she was happy.

When Hanson came home at seven o'clock, he was inclined to be a little crusty—his usual demeanour before supper. This never showed so much in anything he said as in a certain solemnity of countenance and the silent manner in which he slopped about. He had a pair of yellow carpet slippers which he enjoyed wearing, and these he would immediately substitute for his solid pair of shoes. This, and washing his face with the aid of common washing soap until it glowed a shiny red, constituted his only preparation for his evening meal. He would then get his evening paper and read in silence.

For a young man, this was rather a morbid turn of character, and so affected Carrie. Indeed, it affected the entire atmosphere of the flat, as such things are inclined to do, and gave to his wife's mind its subdued and tactful turn, anxious to avoid taciturn replies. Under the influence of Carrie's announcement he brightened up somewhat.

"You didn't lose any time, did you?" he remarked, smiling a little.

"No," returned Carrie with a touch of pride.

He asked her one or two more questions and then turned to play with the baby, leaving the subject until it was brought up again by Minnie at the table.

Carrie, however, was not to be reduced to the common level of observation which prevailed in the flat.

"It seems to be such a large company," she said, at one place. "Great big plate-glass windows and lots of clerks. The man I saw said they hired ever so many people."

"It's not very hard to get work now," put in Hanson, "if you look right."

Minnie, under the warming influence of Carrie's good spirits and her husband's somewhat conversational mood, began to tell Carrie of some of the well-known things to see—things the enjoyment of which cost nothing.

"You'd like to see Michigan Avenue. There are such fine houses. It is such a fine street."

"Where is 'H. R. Jacob's'?" interrupted Carrie, mentioning one of the theatres devoted to melodrama which went by that name at the time.

"Oh, it's not very far from here," answered Minnie. "It's in Halstead Street, right up here."

"How I'd like to go there. I crossed Halstead Street to-day, didn't I?"

At this there was a slight halt in the natural reply. Thoughts are a strangely permeating factor. At her suggestion of going to the theatre, the unspoken shade of disapproval to the doing of those things which involved the expenditure of money—shades of feeling which arose in the mind of Hanson and then in Minnie—slightly affected the atmosphere of the table. Minnie answered "yes," but Carrie could feel that going to the theatre was poorly advocated here. The subject was put off for a little while until Hanson, through with his meal, took his paper and went into the front room.

When they were alone, the two sisters began a somewhat freer conversation. Carrie interrupting it to hum a little, as they worked at the dishes.

"I should like to walk up and see Halstead Street, if it isn't too far," said Carrie, after a time. "Why don't we go to the theatre to-night?"

"Oh, I don't think Sven would want to go to-night," returned Minnie. "He has to get up so early."

"He wouldn't mind—he'd enjoy it," said Carrie.

"No, he doesn't go very often," returned Minnie.

"Well, I'd like to go," rejoined Carrie. "Let's you and me go."

Minnie pondered a while, not upon whether she could or would go—for that point was already negatively settled with her—but upon some means of diverting the thoughts of her sister to some other topic.

"We'll go some other time," she said at last, finding no ready means of escape.

Carrie sensed the root of the opposition at once.

"I have some money," she said. "You go with me."

Minnie shook her head.

"He could go along," said Carrie.

"No," returned Minnie softly, and rattling the dishes to drown the conversation. "He wouldn't."

It had been several years since Minnie had seen Carrie, and in that time the latter's character had developed a few shades. Naturally timid in all things that related to her own advancement, and especially so when without power or resource, her craving for pleasure was so strong that it was the one stay of her nature. She would speak for that when silent on all else.

"Ask him," she pleaded softly.

Minnie was thinking of the resource which Carrie's board would add. It would pay the rent and would make the subject of expenditure a little less difficult to talk about with her husband. But if Carrie was going to think of running around in the beginning there would be a hitch somewhere. Unless Carrie submitted to a solemn round of industry and saw the need of hard work without long for play, how was her coming to the city to profit them? These thoughts were not those of a cold, hard nature at all. They were the serious reflections of a mind which invariably adjusted itself, without much complaining, to such surroundings as its industry could make for it.

At last she yielded enough to ask Hanson. It was a half-hearted procedure without a shade of desire on her part.

"Carrie wants us to go to the theatre," she said, looking in upon her husband. Hanson looked up from his paper, and they exchanged a mild look, which said as plainly as anything: "This isn't what we expected."

"I don't care to go," he returned. "What does she want to see?"

"H. R. Jacob's," said Minnie.

He looked down at his paper and shook his head negatively.

When Carrie saw how they looked upon her proposition, she gained a still clearer feeling of their way of life. It weighted on her, but took no definite form of opposition.

"I think I'll go down and stand at the foot of the stairs," she said, after a time.

Minnie made no objection to this, and Carrie put on her hat and went below.

"Where has Carrie gone?" asked Hanson, coming back into the dining-room when he heard the door close.

"She said she was going down to the foot of the stairs," answered Minnie. "I guess she just wants to look out a while."

"She oughtn't to be thinking about spending her money on theatres already, do you think?" he said.

"She just feels a little curious, I guess," ventured Minnie. "Everything is so new."

"I don't know," said Hanson, and went over to the baby, his forehead slightly wrinkled.

He was thinking of a full career of vanity and wastefulness which a young girl might indulge in, and wondering how Carrie could contemplate such a course when she had so little, as yet, with which to do.

On Saturday Carrie went out by herself—first toward the river, which interested her, and then back along Jackson Street, which was then lined by the pretty houses and fine lawns which subsequently caused it to be made into a boulevard. She was struck with the evidences of wealth, although there was, perhaps, not a person on the street worth more than a hundred thousand dollars. She was glad to be out of the flat, because already she felt that it was a narrow, humdrum place, and that interest and joy lay elsewhere. Her thoughts now were of a more liberal character, and she punctuated them with speculations as to the whereabouts of Drouet. She was not sure but that he might call anyhow Monday night, and, while she felt a little disturbed at the possibility, there was, nevertheless, just the shade of a wish that he would.

On Monday she arose early and prepared to go to work. She dressed herself in a worn shirt-waist of dotted blue percale, a skirt of light-brown serge rather faded, and a small straw hat which she had worn all summer at Columbia City. Her shoes were old, and her necktie was in that crumpled, flattened state which time and much wearing impart. She made a very average looking shop-girl with the exception of her features. These were slightly more even than common, and gave her a sweet, reserved, and pleasing appearance.

It is no easy thing to get up early in the morning when one is used to sleeping until seven and eight, as Carrie had been at home. She gained some inkling of the character of Hanson's life when, half asleep, she looked out into the dining-room at six o'clock and saw him silently finishing his breakfast. By the time she was dressed he was gone, and she, Minnie, and the baby ate together, the latter being just old enough to sit in a high chair and disturb the dishes with a spoon. Her spirits were greatly subdued now when the fact of entering upon strange and untried duties confronted her. Only the ashes of all her fine fancies were remaining—ashes still concealing, nevertheless, a few red embers of hope. So subdued was she by her weakening nerves, that she ate quite in silence, going over imaginary conceptions of the character of the shoe company, the nature of the work, her employer's attitude. She was vaguely feeling that she would come in contact with the great owners, that her work would be where grave, stylishly dressed men occasionally look on.

"Well, good luck," said Minnie, when she was ready to go. They had agreed it was best to walk, that morning at least, to see if she could do it every day—sixty cents a week for car fare being quite an item under the circumstances.

"I'll tell you how it goes to-night," said Carrie.

Once in the sunlit street, with labourers tramping by in either direction, the horse-cars passing crowded to the rails with the small clerks and floor help in the great wholesale houses, and men and women generally coming out of doors and passing about the neighbourhood, Carrie felt slightly reassured. In the sunshine of the morning, beneath the wide, blue heavens, with a fresh wind astir, what fears, except the most desperate, can find a harbourage? In the night, or the gloomy chambers of the day, fears and misgivings wax strong, but out in the sunlight there is, for a time, cessation even of the terror of death.

Carrie went straight forward until she crossed the river, and then turned into Fifth Avenue. The thoroughfare, in this part, was like a walled cañon of brown stone and dark red brick. The big windows looked shiny and clean. Trucks were rumbling in increasing numbers; men and women, girls and boys were moving onward in all directions. She met girls of her own age, who looked at her as if with contempt for her diffidence. She wondered at the magnitude of this life and at the importance of knowing much in order to do anything in it at all. Dread at her own inefficiency crept upon her. She would not know how, she would not be quick enough. Had not all the other places refused her because she did not know something or other? She would be scolded, abused, ignominiously discharged.

It was with weak knees and a slight catch in her breathing that she came up to the great shoe company at Adams and Fifth Avenue and entered the elevator. When she stepped out on the fourth floor there was no one at hand, only great aisles of boxes piled to the ceiling. She stood, very much frightened, awaiting some one.

Presently Mr. Brown came up. He did not seem to recognise her.

"What is it you want?" he inquired.

Carrie's heart sank.

"You said I should come this morning to see about work—"

"Oh," he interrupted. "Um—yes. What is your name?"

"Carrie Meeber."

"Yes," said he. "You come with me."

He led the way through dark, box-lined aisles which had the smell of new shoes, until they came to an iron door which opened into the factory proper. There was a large, low-ceiled room, with clacking, rattling machines at which men in white shirt sleeves and blue gingham aprons were working. She followed him diffidently through the clattering automatons, keeping her eyes straight before her, and flushing slightly. They crossed to a far corner and took an elevator to the sixth floor. Out of the array of machines and benches, Mr. Brown signalled a foreman.

"This is the girl," he said, and turning to Carrie. "You go with him." He then returned, and Carrie followed her new superior to a little desk in a corner, which he used as a kind of official centre.

"You've never worked at anything like this before, have you?" he questioned, rather sternly.

"No, sir," she answered.

He seemed rather annoyed at having to bother with such help, but put down her name and then led her across to where a line of girls occupied stools in front of clacking machines. On the shoulder of one of the girls who was punching eye-holes in one piece of the upper, by the aid of the machine, he put his hand.

"You," he said, "show this girl how to do what you're doing. When you get through, come to me."

The girl so addressed rose promptly and gave Carrie her place.

"It isn't hard to do," she said, bending over. "You just take this so, fasten it with this clamp, and start the machine."

She suited action to word, fastened the piece of leather, which was eventually to form the right half of the upper of a man's shoe, by little adjustable clamps, and pushed a small steel rod at the side of the machine. The latter jumped to the task of punching, with sharp, snapping clicks, cutting circular bits of leather out of the side of the upper, leaving the holes which were to hold the laces. After observing a few times, the girl let her work at it alone. Seeing that it was fairly well done, she went away.

The pieces of leather came from the girl at the machine to her right, and were passed on to the girl at her left. Carrie saw at once that an average speed was necessary or the work would pile up on her and all those below would be delayed. She had no time to look about, and bent anxiously to her task. The girls at her left and right realised her predicament and feelings, and, in a way, tried to aid her, as much as they dared, by working slower.

At this task she laboured incessantly for some time, finding relief from her own nervous fears and imaginings in the humdrum, mechanical movement of the machine. She felt, as the minutes passed, that the room was not very light. It had a thick odour of fresh leather, but that did not worry her. She felt the eyes of the other help upon her, and troubled lest she was not working fast enough.

Once, when she was fumbling at the little clamp, having made a slight error in setting in the leather, a great hand appeared before her eyes and fastened the clamp for her. It was the foreman. Her heart thumped so that she could scarcely see to go on.

"Start your machine," he said, "start your machine. Don't keep the line waiting."

This recovered her sufficiently and she went excitedly on, hardly breathing until the shadow moved away from behind her. Then she heaved a great breath.

As the morning wore on the room became hotter. She felt the need of a breath of fresh air and a drink of water but did not venture to stir. The stool she sat on was without a back or foot-rest, and she began to feel uncomfortable. She found, after a time, that her back was beginning to ache. She twisted and turned from one position to another slightly different, but it did not ease her for long. She was beginning to weary.

"Stand up, why don't you?" said the girl at her right, without any form of introduction. "They won't care."

Carrie looked at her gratefully. "I guess I will," she said.

She stood up from her stool and worked that way for a while, but it was a more difficult position. Her neck and shoulders ached in bending over.

The spirit of the place impressed itself on her in a rough way. She did not venture to look around, but above the clack of the machine she could hear an occasional remark. She could also note a thing or two out of the side of her eye.

"Did you see Harry last night?" said the girl at her left, addressing her neighbour.

"No."

"You ought to have seen the tie he had on. Gee, but he was a mark."

"S-s-t," said the other girl, bending over her work. The first, silenced, instantly assumed a solemn face. The foreman passed slowly along, eyeing each worker distinctly. The moment he was gone, the conversation was resumed again.

"Say," began the girl at her left, "what jeh think he said?"

"I don't know."

"He said he saw us with Eddie Harris at Martin's last night."

"No!" They both giggled.

A youth with tan-coloured hair, that needed clipping very badly, came shuffling along between the machines, bearing a basket of leather findings under his left arm, and pressed against his stomach. When near Carrie, he stretched out his right hand and gripped one girl under the arm.

"Aw, let me go," she exclaimed angrily. "Duffer."

He only grinned broadly in return.

"Rubber!" he called back as she looked after him. There was nothing of the gallant in him.

Carrie at last could scarcely sit still. Her legs began to tire and she wanted to get up and stretch. Would noon never come? It seemed as if she had worked an entire day. She was not hungry at all, but weak, and her eyes were tired, straining at the one point where the eye-punch came down. The girl at the right noticed here squirmings and felt sorry for her. She was concentrating herself too thoroughly—what she did really required less mental and physical strain. There was nothing to be done, however. The halves of the uppers came piling steadily down. Her hands began to ache at the wrists and then in the fingers, and towards the last she seemed one mass of dull, complaining muscles, fixed in an eternal position and performing a single mechanical movement which became more and more distasteful, until at last it was absolutely nauseating. When she was wondering whether the strain would ever cease, a dull-sounding bell clanged somewhere down an elevator shaft, and the end came. In an instant there was a buzz of action and conversation. All the girls instantly left their stools and hurried away in an adjoining room, men passed through, coming from some department which opened on the right. The whirling wheels began to sing in a steadily modifying key, until at last they died away in a low buzz. There was an audible stillness, in which the common voice sounded strange.

Carrie got up and sought her lunch box. She was stiff, a little dizzy, and very thirsty. On the way to the small space portioned off by wood, where all the wraps and lunches were kept, she encountered the foreman, who stared at her hard.

"Well," he said, "did you get along all right?"

"I think so," she replied, for want of something better, and walked on.

Under better material conditions, this kind of work would not have been so bad, but the new socialism which involves pleasant working conditions for employees had not then taken hold upon manufacturing companies.

The place smelled of the oil of the machines and the new leather—a combination which, added to the stale odours of the building, was not pleasant even in cold weather. The floor, though regularly swept every evening, presented a littered surface. Not the slightest provision had been made for the comfort of the employees, the idea being that something was gained by giving them as little and making the work as hard and unremunerative as possible. What we know of foot-rests, swivel-back chair, dining-rooms for the girls, clean aprons and curling irons supplied free, and a decent cloak room, were unthought of. The washrooms were disagreeable, crude, if not foul places, and the whole atmosphere was sordid.

Carrie looked about her, after she had drunk a tinful of water from a bucket in one corner, for a place to sit and eat. The other girls had ranged themselves about the windows or the work-benches of those of the men who had gone out. She saw no place which did not hold a couple or a group of girls, and being too timid to think of intruding herself, she sought out her machine and, seated upon her stool, opened her lunch on her lap. There she sat listening to the chatter and comment about her. It was, for the most part, silly and graced by the current slang. Several of the men in the room exchanged compliments with the girls at long range.

"Say, Kitty," called one to a girl who was doing a waltz step in a few feet of space near one of the windows, "are you going to the ball with me?"

"Look out, Kitty," called another, "you'll jar your back hair."

"Go on, Rubber," was her only comment.

As Carrie listened to this and much more of similar familiar badinage among the men and girls, she instinctively withdrew into herself. She was not used to this type, and felt that there was something hard and low about it all. She feared that the young boys about would address such remarks to her—boys who, beside Drouet, seemed uncouth and ridiculous. She made the average feminine distinction between clothes, putting worth, goodness, and distinction in a dress suit, and leaving all the unlovely qualities and those beneath notice in overalls and jumper.

She was glad when the short half hour was over and the wheels began to whirr again. Though wearied, she would be inconspicuous. This illusion ended when another young man passed along the aisle and poked her indifferently in the ribs with his thumb. She turned about, indignation leaping to her eyes, but he had gone on and only once turned to grin. She found it difficult to conquer an inclination to cry.

The girl next to her noticed her state of mind. "Don't you mind," she said. "He's too fresh."

Carrie said nothing, but bent over her work. She felt as though she could hardly endure such a life. Her idea of work had been so entirely different. All during the long afternoon she thought of the city outside and its imposing show, crowds, and fine buildings. Columbia City and the better side of her home life came back. By three o'clock she was sure it must be six, and by four it seemed as if they had forgotten to note the hour and were letting all work overtime. The foreman became a true ogre, prowling constantly about, keeping her tied down to her miserable task. What she heard of the conversation about her only made her feel sure that she did not want to make friends with any of these. When six o'clock came she hurried eagerly away, her arms aching and her limbs stiff from sitting in one position.

As she passed out along the hall after getting her hat, a young machine hand, attracted by her looks, made bold to jest with her.

"Say, Maggie," he called, "if you wait, I'll walk with you."

It was thrown so straight in her direction that she knew who was meant, but never turned to look.

In the crowded elevator, another dusty, toil-stained youth tried to make an impression on her by leering in her face.

One young man, waiting on the walk outside for the appearance of another, grinned at her as she passed.

"Ain't going my way, are you?" he called jocosely.

Carried turned her face to the west with a subdued heart. As she turned the corner, she saw through the great shiny windows the small desk at which she had applied. There were the crowds, hurrying with the same buzz and energy-yielding enthusiasm. She felt a slight relief, but it was only at her escape. She felt ashamed in the face of better dressed girls who went by. She felt as though she should be better served, and her heart revolted....

Chapter Thirty
The Kingdom of Greatness: The Pilgrim Adream

Whatever a man like Hurstwood could be in Chicago, it is very evident that he would be but an inconspicuous drop in an ocean like New York. In Chicago, whose population still ranged about 500,000, millionaires were not numerous. The rich had not become so conspicuously rich as to drown all moderate incomes in obscurity. The attention of the inhabitants was not so distracted by local celebrities in the dramatic, artistic, social, and religious fields as to shut the well-positioned man from view. In Chicago the two roads to distinction were politics and trade. In New York the roads were any one of a half-hundred, and each had been diligently pursued by hundreds, so that celebrities were numerous. The sea was already full of whales. A common fish must needs disappear wholly from view—remain unseen. In other words, Hurstwood was nothing.

There is a more subtle result of such a situation as this, which, though not always taken into account, produces the tragedies of the world. The great create an atmosphere which reacts badly upon the small. This atmosphere is easily and quickly felt. Walk among the magnificent residences, the splendid equipages, the gilded shops, restaurants, resorts of all kinds; scent the flowers, the silks, the wines; drink of the laughter springing from the soul of luxurious content, of the glances which gleam like light from defiant spears; feel the quality of the smiles which cut like glistening swords and of strides born of place, and you shall know of what is the atmosphere of the high and mighty. Little use to argue that of such is not the kingdom of greatness, but so long as the world is attracted by this and the human heart views this as the one desirable realm which it must attain, so long, to that heart, will this remain the realm of greatness. So long, also, will the atmosphere of this realm work its desperate results in the soul of man. It is like a chemical reagent. One day of it, like one drop of the other, will so affect and discolour the views, the aims, the desire of the mind, that it will thereafter remain forever dyed. A day of it to the untried mind is like opium to the untried body. A craving is set up which, if gratified, shall eternally result in dreams and death. Aye! dreams unfulfilled—gnawing, luring, idle phantoms which beckon and lead, beckon and lead, until death and dissolution dissolve their power and restore us blind to nature's heart.

A man of Hurstwood's age and temperament is not subject to the illusions and burning desires of youth, but neither has he the strength of hope which gushes as a fountain in the heart of youth. Such an atmosphere could not incite in him the cravings of a boy of eighteen, but in so far as they were excited, the lack of hope made them proportionately bitter. He could not fail to notice the signs of affluence and luxury on every hand. He had been to New York before and knew the resources of its folly. In part it was an awesome place to him, for here gathered all that he most respected on this earth—wealth, place, and fame. The majority of the celebrities with whom he had tipped glasses in his day as manager hailed from this self-centred and populous spot. The most inviting stories of pleasure and luxury had been told of places and individuals here. He knew it to be true that unconsciously he was brushing elbows with fortune the livelong day; that a hundred or five hundred thousand gave no one the privilege of living more than comfortably in so wealthy a place. Fashion and pomp required more ample sums, so that the poor man was nowhere. All this he realised, now quite sharply, as he faced the city, cut off from his friends, despoiled of his modest fortune, and even his name, and forced to begin the battle for place and comfort all over again. He was not old, but he was not so dull but that he could feel he soon would be. Of a sudden, then, this show of fine clothes, place, and power took on peculiar significance. It was emphasised by contrast with his own distressing state.

And it was distressing. He soon found that freedom from fear of arrest was not the *sine qua non* of his existence. That danger dissolved, the sum of thirteen hundred and some odd dollars set against the need of rent, clothing, food, and pleasure for years to come was a spectacle little calculated to induce peace of mind in one who had been accustomed to spend five times that sum in the course of a year. He thought upon the subject rather actively the first few days he was in New York, and decided that he must act quickly. As a consequence, he consulted the business opportunities advertised in the morning papers and began investigations on his own account.

That was not before he had become settled, however. Carrie and he went looking for a flat, as arranged, and found one in Seventy-eighth Street near Amsterdam Avenue. It was a five-story building, and their flat was on the third floor. Owing to the fact that the street was not yet built up solidly, it was possible to see east to the green tops of the trees in Central Park and west to the broad waters of the Hudson, a glimpse of which was to be had out of the west windows. For the privilege of six rooms and a bath, running in a straight line, they were compelled to pay thirty-five dollars a month—an average, and yet exorbitant, rent for a home at the time. Carrie noticed the difference between the size of the rooms here and in Chicago and mentioned it.

"You'll not find anything better, dear," said Hurstwood, "unless you go into one of the old-fashioned houses, and then you won't have any of these conveniences."

Carrie picked out the new abode because of its newness and bright woodwork. It was one of the very new ones supplied with steam heat, which was a great advantage. The stationary range, hot and cold water, dumb-waiter, speaking tubes, and call-bell for the janitor pleased her very much. She had enough of the instincts of a housewife to take great satisfaction in these things.

Hurstwood made arrangement with one of the instalment houses whereby they furnished the flat complete and accepted fifty dollars down and ten dollars a month. He then had a little plate, bearing the name G. W. Wheeler, made, which he placed on his letter-box in the hall. It sounded exceedingly odd to Carrie to be called Mrs. Wheeler by the janitor, but in time she became used to it and looked upon the name as her own.

These house details settled, Hurstwood visited some of the advertised opportunities to purchase an interest in some flourishing down-town bar. After the palatial resort in Adams Street, he could not stomach the commonplace saloons which he found advertised. He lost a number of days looking up three and finding them disagreeable. He did, however, gain considerable knowledge by talking, for he discovered the influence of Tammany Hall and the value of standing in with the police. The most profitable and flourishing places he found to be those which conducted anything but a legitimate business, such as that controlled by Fitzgerald and Moy. Elegant back rooms and private drinking booths on the second floor were usually adjuncts of very profitable places. He saw by portly keepers, whose shirt fronts shone with large diamonds, and whose clothes were properly cut, that the liquor business here, as elsewhere, yielded the same golden profit.

At last he found an individual who had a resort in Warren Street, which seemed an excellent venture. It was fairly well-appearing and susceptible of improvement. The owner claimed the business to be excellent, and it certainly looked so.

"We deal with a very good class of people," he told Hurstwood. "Merchants, salesmen, and professionals. It's a well-dressed class. No bums. We don't allow 'em in the place."

Hurstwood listened to the cash-register ring, and watched the trade for a while.

"It's profitable enough for two, is it?" he asked.

"You can see for yourself if you're any judge of the liquor trade," said the owner. "This is only one of the two places I have. The other is down in Nassau Street. I can't tend to them both alone. If I had some one who knew the business thoroughly I wouldn't mind sharing with him in this one and letting him manage it."

"I've had experience enough," said Hurstwood blandly, but he felt a little diffident about referring to Fitzgerald and Moy.

"Well, you can suit yourself, Mr. Wheeler," said the proprietor.

He only offered a third interest in the stock, fixtures, and good-will, and this in return for a thousand dollars and managerial ability on the part of the one who should come in. There was no property involved, because the owner of the saloon merely rented from an estate.

The offer was genuine enough, but it was a question with Hurstwood whether a third interest in that locality could be made to yield one hundred and fifty dollars a month, which he figured he must have in order to meet the ordinary family expenses and be comfortable. It was not the time, however, after many failures to find what he wanted, to hesitate. It looked as though a third would pay a hundred a month now. By judicious management and improvement, it might be made to pay more. Accordingly he agreed to enter into partnership, and made over his thousand dollars, preparing to enter the next day.

His first inclination was to be elated, and he confided to Carrie that he thought he had made an excellent arrangement. Time, however, introduced food for reflection. He found his partner to be very disagreeable. Frequently he was the worse for liquor, which made him surly. This was the last thing which Hurstwood was used to in business. Besides, the business varied. It was nothing like the class of patronage which he had enjoyed in Chicago. He found that it would take a long time to make friends. These people hurried in and out without seeking the pleasures of friendship. It was no gathering or lounging place. Whole days and weeks passed without one such hearty greeting as he had been wont to enjoy every day in Chicago.

For another thing, Hurstwood missed the celebrities–those well-dressed, *élite* individuals who lend grace to the average bars and bring news from far-off and exclusive circles. He did not see one such in a month. Evenings, when still at his post, he would occasionally read in the evening papers incidents concerning celebrities whom he knew–whom he had drunk a glass with many a time. They would visit a bar like Fitzgerald and Moy's in Chicago, or the Hoffman House, uptown, but he knew that he would never see them down here.

Again, the business did not pay as well as he thought. It increased a little, but he found he would have to watch his household expenses, which was humiliating.

In the very beginning it was a delight to go home late at night, as he did, and find Carrie. He managed to run up and take dinner with her between six and seven, and to remain home until nine o'clock in the morning, but the novelty of this waned after a time, and he began to feel the drag of his duties.

The first month had scarcely passed before Carrie said in a very natural way: "I think I'll go down this week and buy a dress."

"What kind?" said Hurstwood.

"Oh, something for street wear."

"All right," he answered, smiling, although he noted mentally that it would be more agreeable to his finances if she didn't. Nothing was said about it the next day but the following morning he asked:

"Have you done anything about your dress?"

"Not yet," said Carrie.

He paused a few moments, as if in thought, and then said:

"Would you mind putting it off a few days?"

"No," replied Carrie, who did not catch the drift of his remarks. She had never thought of him in connection with money troubles before. "Why?"

"Well, I'll tell you," said Hurstwood. "This investment of mine is taking a lot of money just now. I expect to get it all back shortly, but just at present I am running close."

"Oh!" answered Carrie, "Why, certainly, dear. Why didn't you tell me before?" "It wasn't necessary," said Hurstwood.

For all her acquiescence, there was something about the way Hurstwood spoke which reminded Carrie of Drouet and his little deal which he was always about to put through. It was only the thought of a second, but it was a beginning. It was something new in her thinking of Hurstwood.

Other things followed from time to time, little things of the same sort, which in their cumulative effect were eventually equal to a full revelation. Carrie was not dull by any means. Two persons cannot long dwell together without coming to an understanding of one another. The mental difficulties of an individual reveal themselves whether he voluntarily confesses them or not. Trouble gets in the air and contributes gloom, which speaks for itself. Hurstwood dressed as nicely as usual, but they were the same clothes he had in Canada. Carrie noticed that he did not install a large wardrobe, though his own was anything but large. She noticed, also, that he did not suggest many amusements, said nothing about the food, seemed concerned about his business. This was not the easy Hurstwood of Chicago—not the liberal, opulent Hurstwood she had known. The change was too obvious to escape detection.

In time she began to feel that a change had come about, and that she was not in his confidence. He was evidently secretive and kept his own counsel. She found herself asking him questions about little things. This is a disagreeable state to a woman. Great love makes it seem reasonable, sometimes plausible, but never satisfactory. Where great love is not, a more definite and less satisfactory conclusion is reached.

As for Hurstwood, he was making a great fight against the difficulties of a changed condition. He was too shrewd not to realise the tremendous mistake he had made, and appreciate that he had done well in getting where he was, and yet he could not help contrasting his present state with his former, hour after hour, and day after day.

Besides, he had the disagreeable fear of meeting old-time friends, ever since one such encounter which he made shortly after his arrival in the city. It was in Broadway that he saw a man approaching him whom he knew. There was no time for simulating non-recognition. The exchange of glances had been too sharp, the knowledge of each other too apparent. So the friend, a buyer for one of the Chicago wholesale houses, felt, perforce, the necessity of stopping.

"How are you?" he said, extending his hand with an evident mixture of feeling and a lack of plausible interest.

"Very well," said Hurstwood, equally embarrassed. "How is it with you?"

"All right; I'm down here doing a little buying. Are you located here now?"

"Yes," said Hurstwood, "I have a place down in Warren Street."

"Is that so?" said the friend. "Glad to hear it. I'll come down and see you."

"Do," said Hurstwood.

"So long," said the other, smiling affably and going on.

"He never asked for my number," thought Hurstwood; "he wouldn't think of coming." He wiped his forehead, which had grown damp, and hoped sincerely he would meet no one else.

These things told upon his good-nature, such as it was. His one hope was that things would change for the better in a money way. He had Carrie. His furniture was being paid for. He was maintaining his position. As for Carrie, the amusements he could give her would have to do for the present. He could probably keep up his pretensions sufficiently long without exposure to make good, and then all would be well. He failed therein to take account of the frailties of human nature—the difficulties of matrimonial life. Carrie was young. With him and with her varying mental states were common. At any moment the extremes of feeling might be anti-polarised at the dinner table. This often happens in the best regulated families. Little things brought out on such occasions need great love to obliterate them afterward. Where that is not, both parties count two and two and make a problem after a while.

118

The Jungle

UPTON SINCLAIR

Upton Sinclair (1878–1968) was born in Baltimore, Maryland, although his writing is most obviously concerned with Chicago. Although primarily a novelist, he was also involved in a number of political undertakings, including standing for the Governorship of California. Always a radical figure, his writing embodies a polemical and invariably "left-wing" response to the industrial and social conditions of the city in relation to the burgeoning influence of capital and business corporations. *The Jungle* (1906) is an extraordinary account of the Chicago stock-yards and the "packing-town" where the meat was processed for a growing mass-market. American workers are seen as little more than as part of a continuous production line—be it in terms of food or cars. Other texts include *The Moneychangers* (1908), *King Coal* (1917), and *Boston* (1928), based on the trial of Sacho and Vanzetti. He wrote over eighty works. See Floyd Dell, *Upton Sinclair: A Study in Social Protest*, (1927).

Chapter Three

In this capacity as delicatessen vender, Jokubas Szedvilas had many acquaintances. Among these was one of the special policemen employed by Durham, whose duty it frequently was to pick out men for employment. Jokubas had never tried it, but he expressed a certainty that he could get some of his friends a job through this man. It was agreed, after consultation, that he should make the effort with old Antanas and with Jonas. Jurgis was confident of his ability to get work for himself, unassisted by any one.

As we have said before, he was not mistaken in this. He had gone to Brown's and stood there not more than half an hour before one of the bosses noticed his form towering above the rest, and signalled to him. The colloquy which followed was brief and to the point:

"Speak English?"

Source: Upton Sinclair, *The Jungle*, 1906, Chs. 3, 13, 21.

"No; Lit-uanian." (Jurgis had studied this word carefully.)

"Job?"

"Je." (A nod.)

"Worked here before?"

"No 'stand."

(Signals and gesticulations on the part of the boss. Vigorous shakes of the head by Jurgis.)

"Shovel guts?"

"No 'stand." (More shakes of the head.)

"Zarnos. Pagaiksztis. Szluota!" (Imitative motions.)

"Je."

"See door. Durys?" (Pointing.)

"Je."

"To-morrow, seven o'clock. Understand? Rytoj! Prieszpietys! Septyni!"

"Dekui, tamistai!" (Thank you, sir.) And that was all. Jurgis turned away, and then in a sudden rush the full realization of his triumph swept over him, and he gave a yell and a jump, and started off on a run. He had a job! He had a job! And he went all the way home as if upon wings, and burst into the house like a cyclone, to the rage of the numerous lodgers who had just turned in for their daily sleep.

Meantime Jokubas had been to see his friend the policeman, and received encouragement, so it was a happy party. There being no more to be done that day, the shop was left under the care of Lucija, and her husband sallied forth to show his friends the sights of Packingtown. Jokubas did this with the air of a country gentleman escorting a party of visitors over his estate; he was an old-time resident, and all these wonders had grown up under his eyes, and he had a personal pride in them. The packers might own the land, but he claimed the landscape, and there was no one to say nay to this.

They passed down the busy street that led to the yards. It was still early morning, and everything was at its high tide of activity. A steady steam of employees was pouring through the gate—employees of the higher sort, at this hour, clerks and stenographers and such. For the women there were waiting big two-horse wagons, which set off at a gallop as fast as they were filled. In the distance there was heard again the lowing of the cattle, a sound as of a far-off ocean calling. They followed it this time, as eager as children in sight of a circus menagerie—which, indeed, the scene a good deal resembled. They crossed the railroad tracks, and then on each side of the street were the pens full of cattle; they would have stopped to look, but Jokubas hurried them on, to where there was a stairway and a raised gallery, from which everything could be seen. Here they stood, staring, breathless with wonder.

There is over a square mile of space in the yards, and more than half of it is occupied by cattle pens; north and south as far as the eye can reach there stretches a sea of pens. And they were all filled—so many cattle no one had ever dreamed existed in the world. Red cattle, black, white, and yellow cattle; old cattle and young cattle; great bellowing bulls and little calves not an hour born; meek-eyed milch cows and fierce, long-horned Texas steers. The sound of them here was as of all the barnyards of the universe; and as for counting them—it would have taken all day simply to count the pens. Here and there ran long alleys, blocked at intervals by gates; and Jokubas told them that the number of these gates was twenty-five thousand. Jokubas had recently been reading a newspaper article which was full of statistics such as that, and he was very proud as he repeated them and made his guests cry out with wonder. Jurgis too had a little of this sense of pride. Had he not just gotten a job, and become a sharer in all this activity, a cog in this marvelous machine?

Here and there about the alleys galloped men upon horseback, booted, and carrying long whips; they were very busy, calling to each other, and to those who were driving the cattle. They were drovers and stock-raisers, who had come from far states, and brokers and commission-merchants, and buyers for all the big packing houses. Here and there they would stop to inspect a bunch of cattle, and there would be a parley, brief and businesslike. The buyer would nod or drop his whip, and that would mean a bargain; and he would note it in his little book, along with hundreds of others he had made that morning. Then Jokubas pointed out the place where the cattle were driven to be weighed upon a great scale that would weight a hundred thousand pounds at once and record it automatically. It was near to the east entrance that they stood, and all along this east side of the yards ran the railroad tracks, into which the cars were run, loaded with cattle. All night long this had been going on, and now the pens were full; by tonight they would all be empty, and the same thing would be done again.

"All what will become of all these creatures?" cried Teta Elzbieta.

"By tonight," Jokubas answered, "they will all be killed and cut up; and over there on the other side of the packing houses are more railroad tracks, where the cars come to take them away."

There were two hundred and fifty miles of track within the yards, their guide went on to tell them. They brought about ten thousand head of cattle every day, and as many hogs, and half as many sheep—which meant some eight or ten million live creatures turned into food every year. One stood and watched, and little by little caught the drift of the tide, as it set in the direction of the packing houses. There were groups of cattle being driven to the chutes, which were roadways about fifteen feet wide, raised high above the pens. In these chutes the stream of animals was continuous; it was quite uncanny to watch them, pressing on to their fate, all unsuspicious—a very river of death. Our friends were not poetical, and the sight suggested to them no metaphors of human destiny; they thought only of the wonderful efficiency of it all. The chutes into which the hogs went climbed high up—to the very top of the distant buildings, and Jokubas explained that the hogs went up by the power of their own legs, and then their weight carried them back through all the processes necessary to make them into pork.

"They don't waste anything here," said the guide, and then he laughed and added a witticism, which he was pleased that his unsophisticated friends should take to be his own: "They use everything about the hog except the squeal." In front of Brown's General Office building there grows a tiny plot of grass, and this, you may learn, is the only bit of green thing in Packingtown; likewise this jest about the hog and his squeal, the stock in trade of all the guides, is the one gleam of humor that you will find there.

After they had seen enough of the pens, the party went up the street, to the mass of buildings which occupy the centre of the yards. These buildings, made of brick and stained with innumerable layers of Packingtown smoke, were painted all over with advertising signs, from which the visitor realized suddenly that he had come to the home of many of the torments of his life. It was here they made those products with the wonders of which they pestered him so—by placards that defaced the landscape when he traveled, and by staring advertisements in the newspapers and magazines—by silly little jingles that he could not get out of his mind, and gaudy pictures that lurked for him around every street corner. Here was where they made Brown's Imperial Hams and Bacon, Brown's Dressed Beef, Brown's Excelsior Sausages! Here was the headquarters of Durham's Pure Leaf Lard, of Durham's Breakfast Bacon, Durham's Canned Beef, Potted Ham, Deviled Chicken, Peerless Fertilizer!

Entering one of the Durham buildings, they found a number of other visitors waiting, and before long there came a guide, to escort them through the place. They make a great feature of showing strangers through the packing plants, for it is a good advertisement. But Ponas Jokubas whispered maliciously that the visitors did not see any more than the packers wanted them to.

They climbed a long series of stairways outside of the building, to the top of its five or six stories. Here were the chute, with its river of hogs, all patiently toiling upward; there was a place for them to rest to cool off, and then through another passageway they went into a room from which there is no returning for hogs.

It was a long, narrow room, with a gallery along it for visitors. At the head there was a great iron wheel, about twenty feet in circumference, with rings here and there along its edge. Upon both sides of this wheel there was a narrow space, into which came the hogs at the end of their journey; in the midst of them stood a great burly Negro, bare-armed and bare-chested. He was resting for the moment, for the wheel had stopped while men were cleaning up. In a minute or two, however, it began slowly to revolve, and then the men upon each side of it sprang to work. They had chains which they fastened about the leg of the nearest hog, and the other end of the chain they hooked into one of the rings upon the wheel. So, as the wheel turned, a hog was suddenly jerked off his feet and borne aloft.

At the same instant the ear was assailed by a most terrifying shriek; the visitors started in alarm, the women turned pale and shrank back. The shriek was followed by another, louder and yet more agonizing—for once started upon that journey, the hog never came back; at the top of the wheel he was shunted off upon a trolley, and went sailing down the room. And meantime another was swung up, and then another, and another, until there was a double line of them, each dangling by a foot and kicking in frenzy—and squealing. The uproar was appalling, perilous to the eardrums; one feared there was too much sound for the room to hold—that the walls must give way or the ceiling crack. There were high squeals and low squeals, grunts, and wails of agony; there would come a momentary lull, and then a fresh outburst, louder than ever, surging up to a deafening climax. It was too much for some of the visitors—the men would look at each other, laughing nervously, and the women would stand with hands clenched, and the blood rushing to their faces, and the tears starting in their eyes.

Meantime, heedless of all these things, the men upon the floor were going about their work. Neither squeals of hogs nor tears of visitors made any difference to them; one by one they hooked up the hogs, and one by one with a swift stroke they slit their throats. There was a long line of hogs, with squeals and life-blood ebbing away together, until at last each started again, and vanished with a splash into a huge vat of boiling water.

It was all so very businesslike that one watched it fascinated. It was pork-making by machinery, pork-making by applied mathematics. And yet somehow the most matter-of-fact person could not help thinking of the hogs; they were so innocent, they came so very trustingly; and they were so very human in their protests—and so perfectly within their rights! They had done nothing to deserve it, and it was adding insult to injury, as the thing was done here, swinging them up in this cold-blooded, impersonal way, without a pretence at apology, without the homage of a tear. Now and then a visitor wept, to be sure; but this slaughtering machine ran on, visitors or no visitors. It was like some horrible crime committed in a dungeon, all unseen and unheeded, buried out of sight and of memory.

One could not stand and watch very long without becoming philosophical, without beginning to deal in symbols and similes, and to hear the hog-squeal of the universe. Was it permitted to believe that there was nowhere upon the earth, or above the earth, a heaven for hogs, where they were requited for all this suffering? Each one of these hogs was a separate creature. Some were white hogs, some were black; some were brown, some were spotted; some were old, some were young; some were long and lean, some were monstrous. And each of them had a individuality of his own, a will of his own, a hope and a heart's desire; each was a full of self-confidence, of self-importance, and a sense of dignity. And trusting and strong in faith he had gone about his business, the while a black shadow hung over him and a horrid Fate waited in his pathway. Now suddenly it had swooped upon him, and had seized him by the leg. Relentless, remorseless, it was; all his protests, his screams, were nothing to it—it did its cruel will with him, as if his wishes, his feelings, had simply no existence at all; it cut his throat and watched him gasp out his life. And now was one to believe that there was nowhere a god of hogs, to whom this hog-personality was precious, to whom these hog-squeals and agonies had a meaning? Who would take this hog into his arm and comfort him, reward him for his work well done, and show him the meaning of his sacrifice? Perhaps some glimpse of all this was in the thoughts of our humble-minded Jurgis, as he turned to go on with the rest of the party, and muttered: "*Dieve*—but I'm glad I'm not a hog!"

The carcass hog was scooped out of the vat by machinery, and then it fell to the second floor, passing on the way through a wonderful machine with numerous scrapers, which adjusted themselves to the size and shape of the animal, and sent it out at the other end with nearly all of its bristles removed. It was then again strung up by machinery, and sent upon another trolley ride; this time passing between two lines of men, who sat upon a raised platform, each doing a certain single thing to the carcass as it came to him. One scraped the outside of a leg; another scraped the inside of the same leg. One with a swift stroke cut the throat; another with two swift strokes severed the head, which fell to the floor and vanished through a hole. Another made a slit down the body; a second opened the body wider; a third with a saw cut the breastbone; a fourth loosened the entrails; a fifth pulled them out—and they also slid through a hole in the floor. There were men to scrape each side and men to scrape the back; there were men to clean the carcass inside, to trim it and wash it. Looking down this room, one saw, creeping slowly, a line of dangling hogs a hundred yards in length; and for every yard there was a man, working as if a demon were after him. At the end of this hog's progress every inch of the carcass had been gone over several times, and then it was rolled into the chilling room, where it stayed for twenty-four hours, and where a stranger might lose himself in a forest of freezing hogs.

Before the carcass was admitted here, however, it had to pass a government inspector, who sat in the doorway and felt of the glands in the neck for tuberculosis. This government inspector did not have the manner of a man who was worked to death; he was apparently not haunted by a fear that the hog might get by him before he had finished his testing. If you were a sociable person, he was quite willing to enter into conversation with you, and to explain to you the deadly nature of the ptomaines which are found in tubercular pork; and while he was talking with you you could hardly be so ungrateful as to notice that a dozen carcasses were passing him untouched. This inspector wore an imposing silver badge, and he gave an atmosphere of authority to the scene, and, as it were, put the stamp of official approval upon the things which were done in Durham's.

Jurgis went down the line with the rest of the visitors, staring open-mouthed, lost in wonder. He had dressed hogs himself in the forest of Lithuania; but he had never expected to live to see one hog dressed by several hundred men. It was like a wonderful poem to him, and he took it all in guilelessly—even to the conspicuous signs of demanding immaculate cleanliness of the employees. Jurgis was vexed when the cynical Jokubas translated these signs with sarcastic comments, offering to take them to the secret rooms where the spoiled meats went to be doctored.

The party descended to the next floor, where the various waste materials were treated. Here came the entrails, to be scraped and washed clean for sausage casings; men and women worked here in the midst of a sickening stench, which caused the visitors to hasten by, gasping. To another room came all the scraps to be "tanked," which meant boiling and pumping off the grease to make soap and lard; below they took out the refuse, and this, too, was a region in which the visitors did not linger. In still other places men were engaged in cutting up the carcasses that had been through the chilling rooms. First there were the "splitters," the most expert workmen in the plant, who earned as high as fifty cents an hour, and did not a thing all day except chop hogs down the middle. Then there were "cleaver men," great giants with muscles of iron; each had two men to attend him—to slide the half carcass in front of him on the table, and hold it while he chopped it, and then turn each piece so that he might chop it once more. His cleaver had a blade about two feet long, and he never made but one cut; he made it so neatly, too, that his implement did not smite through and dull itself—there was just enough force for a perfect cut, and no more. So through various yawning holes there slipped to the floor below—to one room hams, to another forequarters, to another sides of pork. One might go down to this floor and see the pickling rooms, where the hams were put into vats, and the great smoke rooms, with their airtight iron doors. In other rooms they prepared salt pork—there were whole cellars full of it, built up in great towers to ceiling. In yet other rooms they were putting up meat in boxes and barrels, and wrapping hams and bacon in oiled paper, sealing and labeling and sewing them. From the doors of these rooms went men with loaded trucks, to the platform where freight cars were waiting to be filled; and one went out there and realized with a start that he had come at last to the ground floor of this enormous building.

Then the party went across the street to where they did the killing of beef—where every hour they turned four or five hundred cattle into meat. Unlike the place they had left, all this work was done on one floor, and instead of there being one line of carcasses which moved to the workmen, there were fifteen or twenty lines, and the men moved from one to another of these. This made a scene of intense activity, a picture of human power wonderful to watch. It was all in one great room, like a circus amphitheater, with a gallery for visitors running over the center.

Along one side of the room ran a narrow gallery, a few feet from the floor, into which gallery the cattle were driven by men with goads which gave them electric shocks. Once crowded in here, the creatures were prisoned, each in a separate pen, by gates that shut, leaving them no room to turn around, and while they stood bellowing and plunging, over the top of the pen there leaned one of the "knockers," armed with a sledge hammer, and watching for a chance to deal a blow. The room echoed with the thuds in quick succession, and the stamping and kicking of the steers. The instant the animal had fallen, the "knocker" passed on to another, while a second man raised a lever, and the side of the pen was raised, and the animal, still kicking and struggling, slid out to the "killing bed." Here a man put shackles about one leg, and pressed another lever, and the body was jerked up into the air. There were fifteen or twenty such pens, and it was a matter of only a couple of minutes to knock fifteen or twenty cattle and roll them out. Then once more the gates were opened, and another lot rushed in; and so out of each pen there rolled a steady stream of carcasses, which the men upon the killing beds had to get out of the way.

The manner in which they did this was something to be seen and never forgotten. They worked with furious intensity, literally upon the run—at a pace with which there is nothing to be compared except a football game. It was all highly specialized labor, each man having his task to do; generally this would consist of only two or three specific cuts, and he would pass down the line of fifteen or twenty carcasses, making these cuts upon each. First there came the "butcher," to bleed them; this meant one swift stroke, so swift that you could not see it—only the flash of the knife; and before you could realize it, the man had darted on to the next line, and a stream of bright red was pouring out upon the floor. This floor was half an inch deep with blood, in spite of the best efforts of men who kept shoveling it through holes; it must have made the floor slippery, but no one could have guessed this by watching the men at work.

The carcass hung for a few minutes to bleed; there was not time lost, however, for there were several hanging in each line, and one was always ready. It was let down to the ground, and there came the "headsman," whose task it was to sever the head, with two or three swift strokes. Then came the "floorsman," to make the first cut in the skin; and then another to finish ripping the skin down the center; and then half a dozen more in swift succession, to finish the skinning. After they were through, the carcass was again swung up, and while a man with a stock examined the skin, to make sure that it had not been cut, and another rolled it up and tumbled it through one of the inevitable holes in the floor, the beef proceeded on its journey. There were men to cut it, and men to split it, and men to gut it and scrape it clean inside. There were some with hoses which threw jets of boiling water upon it, and others who removed the feet and added the final touches. In the end, as was with the hogs, the finished beef was run into the chilling room, to hang its appointed time.

The visitors were taken there and shown them, all neatly hung in rows, labelled conspicuously with the tags of the government inspectors—and some, which had been killed by a special process, marked with the sign of the "kosher" rabbi, certifying that it was fit for sale to the orthodox. And then the visitors were taken to the other parts of the building, to see what became of each particle of the waste material that had vanished through the floor; and to the pickling rooms, and the salting rooms, the canning rooms, and the packing rooms, where choice meat was prepared for shipping in refrigerator cars, destined to be eaten in all the four corners of civilization. Afterward they went outside, wandering about among the mazes of buildings in which was done the work auxiliary to this great industry. There was scarcely a thing needed in the business that Durham and Company did not make for themselves. There was a great steam power plant and an electricity plant. There was a barrel factory, and a boiler repair shop. There was a building to which the grease was piped, and made into soap and lard, and then there was a factory for making lard cans, and another for making soap boxes. There was a building in which the bristles were cleaned and dried, for the making of hair cushions and such things; there was a building where the skins were dried and tanned, there was another where heads and feet were made into glue, and another where bones were made into fertilizer. No tiniest particle of organic matter was wasted in Durham's. Out of the horns of the cattle they made combs, buttons, hairpins, and imitation ivory; out of the shin bones and other big bones they cut knife and tooth brush handles, and mouthpieces for pipes; out of the hoofs they cut hairpins and buttons, before they made the rest into glue. From such things as feet, knuckles, hide clippings, and sinews came such strange and unlikely products as gelatin, isinglass, and phosphorus, bone black, shoe blacking, and bone oil. They had curled-hair works for the cattle tails, and a "wool pullery" for the sheep skins; they made pepsin from the stomachs of the pigs, and albumen from the blood, and violin strings from the ill-smelling entrails. When there was nothing else to be done with a thing, they first put it into a tank and got out of it all the tallow and grease, and then they made it into fertilizer. All these industries were gathered into buildings near by, connected by galleries and railroads with the main establishment, and it was estimated that they had handled nearly a quarter of a billion of animals since the founding of the plant by the elder Durham a generation and more ago. It you counted with it the other big plants—and they were now really all one—it was, so Jokubas informed them, the greatest aggregation of labor and capital ever gathered in one place. It employed thirty thousand men; it supported directly two hundred and fifty thousand people in its neighborhood, and indirectly it supported half a million. It sent its products to every country in the civilized world, and it furnished the food for no less than thirty million people!

To all of these things our friends would listen open-mouthed—it seemed to them impossible of belief that anything so stupendous could have been devised by mortal man. That was why to Jurgis it seemed almost profanity to speak about the place as did Jokubas, sceptically; it was a thing as tremendous as the universe—the laws and ways of its working no more than the universe to be questioned or understood. All that a mere man could do, it seemed to Jurgis, was to take a thing like this as he found it, and do as he was told; to be given a place in it and a share in its wonderful activities was a blessing to be grateful for, as one was grateful for the sunshine and the rain. Jurgis was even glad that he had not seen the place before meeting with his triumph, for he felt that the size of it would have overwhelmed him. But now he had been admitted—he was a part of it all! He had the feeling that this whole huge establishment had taken him under its protection, and had become responsible for his welfare. So guileless was he, and ignorant of the nature of business, that he did not even realize that he had become an employee of Brown's, and that Brown and Durham were supposed by all the world to be deadly rivals—were even required to be deadly rivals by the law of the land, and ordered to try to ruin each other under penalty of fine and imprisonment!...

Chapter Thirteen

During this time that Jurgis was looking for work occurred the death of little Kristoforas, one of the children of Teta Elzbieta. Both Kristoforas and his brother, Juozapas, were cripples, the latter having lost one leg by having it run over, and Kristoforas having congenital dislocation of the hip, which made it impossible for him ever to walk. He was the last of Teta Elzbieta's children, and perhaps he had been intended by nature to let her know that she had had enough. At any rate he was wretchedly sick and undersized; he had the rickets, and though he was over three years old, he was no bigger than an ordinary child of one. All day long he would crawl around the floor in a filthy little dress, whining and fretting; because the floor was full of draughts he was always catching cold, and snuffling because his nose ran. This made him a nuisance, and a source of endless trouble in the family. For his mother, with unnatural perversity, loved him best of all her children, and made a perpetual fuss over him—would let him do anything undisturbed, and would burst into tears when his fretting drove Jurgis wild.

And now he died. Perhaps it was the smoked sausage he had eaten that morning—which may have been made out of some of the tubercular pork that was condemned as unfit for export. At any rate, an hour after eating it, the child had begun to cry with pain, and in another hour he was rolling about on the floor in convulsions. Little Kotrina, who was all alone with him, ran out screaming for help, and after a while a doctor came, but not until Kristoforas had howled his last howl. No one was really sorry about this except poor Elzbieta, who was inconsolable. Jurgis announced that so far as he was concerned the child would have to be buried by the city, since they had no money for a funeral; and at this the poor woman almost went out of her senses, wringing her hands and screaming with grief and despair. Her child to be buried in a pauper's grave! And her stepdaughter to stand by and hear it said without protesting! It was enough to make Ona's father rise up out of his grave to rebuke her! If it had come to this, they might as well give up at once, and be buried all of them together! ... In the end Marija said that she would help with ten dollars; and Jurgis being still obdurate, Elzbieta went in tears and begged the money from the neighbors, and so little Kristoforas had a mass and a hearse with white plumes on it, and a tiny plot in a graveyard with a wooden cross to mark the place. The poor mother was not the same for months after that; the mere sight of the floor where little Kristoforas had crawled about would make her weep. He had never had a fair chance, poor little fellow, she would say. He had been handicapped from his birth. If only she had heard about it in time, so that she might have had that great doctor to cure him of his lameness! ... Some time ago, Elzbieta was told, a Chicago billionaire had paid a fortune to bring a great European surgeon over to cure his little daughter of the same disease from which Kristoforas had suffered. And because this surgeon had to have bodies to demonstrate upon, he announced that he would treat the children of the poor, a piece of magnanimity over which the papers became quite eloquent. Elzbieta, alas, did not read the papers, and no one had told her; but perhaps it was as well, for just then they would not have had the carfare to spare to go every day to wait upon the surgeon, nor for that matter anybody with the time to take the child.

All this while that he was seeking for work, there was a dark shadow hanging over Jurgis; as if a savage beast were lurking somewhere in the pathway of his life, and he knew it, and yet could not help approaching the place. There are all stages of being out of work in Packingtown, and he faced in dread the prospect of reaching the lowest. There is a place that waits for the lowest man—the fertilizer plant!

The men would talk about it in awe-stricken whispers. Not more than one in ten had ever really tried it; the other nine had contented themselves with hearsay evidence and a peep through the door. There were some things worse than even starving to death. They would ask Jurgis if he had worked there yet, and if he meant to; and Jurgis would debate the matter with himself. As poor as they were, and making all the sacrifices that they were, would he dare to refuse any sort of work that was offered to him, be it as horrible as ever it could? Would he dare to go home and eat bread that had been earned by Ona, weak and complaining as she was, knowing that he had been given a chance, and had not had the nerve to take it?—And yet he might argue that way with himself all day, and one glimpse into the fertilizer works would send him away again shuddering. He was a man, and he would do his duty; he went and made application—but surely he was not also required to hope for success!

The fertilizer works of Durham's lay away from the rest of the plant. Few visitors ever saw them, and the few who did would come out looking like Dante, of whom the peasants declared that he had been into hell. To this part of the yards came all the "tankage," and the waste products of all sorts; here they dried out the bones—and in suffocating cellars where the daylight never came you might see men and women and children bending over whirling machines and sawing bits of bone into all sorts of shapes, breathing their lungs full of the fine dust, and doomed to die, every one of them, within a certain definite time. Here they made the blood into albumen, and made other foul-smelling things into things still more foul-smelling. In the corridors and caverns where it was done you might lose yourself as in the great caves of Kentucky. In the dust and the steam the electric lights would shine like far-off twinkling stars—red and blue, green and purple stars, according to the color of the mist and the brew from which it came. For the odors in these ghastly charnel houses there may be words in Lithuanian, but there are none in English. The person entering would have to summon his courage as for a cold-water plunge. He would go on like a man swimming under water; he would put his handkerchief over his face, and begin to cough and choke; and then, if he were still obstinate, he would find his head beginning to ring, and the veins in his forehead to throb, until finally he would be assailed by an overpowering blast of ammonia fumes, and would turn and run for this life, and come out half-dazed.

On top of this were the rooms where they dried the "tankage," the mass of brown stringy stuff that was left after the waste portions of the carcasses had had the lard and tallow dried out of them. This dried material they would then grind to a fine powder, and after they had mixed it up well with a mysterious but inoffensive brown rock which they brought in and ground up by the hundreds of carloads for that purpose, the substance was ready to be put into bags and sent out to the world as any one of a hundred different brands of standard bone phosphate. And then the farmer in Maine or California or Texas would buy this, at say twenty-five dollars a tonne, and plant it with his corn; and for several days after the operation the fields would have a strong odor, and the farmer and his wagon and the very horses that had hauled it would all have it too. In Packingtown the fertilizer is pure, instead of being a flavoring, and instead of a tonne or so spread out on several acres under the open sky, there are hundreds and thousands of tonnes of it in one building, heaped here and there in haystack piles, covering the floor several inches deep, and filling the air with a choking dust that becomes a blinding sand storm when the wind stirs.

It was to this building that Jurgis came daily, as if dragged by an unseen hand. The month of May was an exceptionally cool one, and his secret prayers were granted; but early in June there came a record-breaking hot spell, and after that there were men wanted in the fertilizer mill.

The boss of the grinding room had come to know Jurgis by this time, and had marked him for a likely man; and so when he came to the door about two o'clock this breathless hot day, he felt a sudden spasm of pain shoot through him—the boss beckoned to him! In ten minutes more Jurgis had pulled off his coat and overshirt, and set his teeth together and gone to work. Here was one more difficulty for him to meet and conquer!

His labor took him about one minute to learn. Before him was one of the vents of the mill in which the fertilizer was being ground—rushing forth in a great brown river, with a spray of the finest dust flung forth in clouds. Jurgis was given a shovel, and along with half a dozen others it was his task to shovel this fertilizer into carts. That others were at work he knew by the sound, and by the fact that he sometimes collided with them; otherwise they might as well not have been there, for in the blinding dust storm a man could not see six feet in front of his face. When he had filled one cart he had to grope around him until another came, and if there was none on hand he continued to grope till one arrived. In five minutes he was, of course, a mass of fertilizer from head to feet; they gave him a sponge to tie over his mouth, so that he could breathe, but the sponge did not prevent his lips and eyelids from caking up with it and his ears from filling solid. He looked like a brown ghost at twilight–from hair to shoes he became the color of the building and of everything in it, and for that matter a hundred yards outside it. The building had to be left open, and when the wind blew Durham and Company lost a great deal of fertilizer.

Working in his shirtsleeves, and with the thermometer at over a hundred, the phosphates soaked in through every pore of Jurgis's skin, and in five minutes he had a headache, and in fifteen was almost dazed. The blood was pounding in his brain like an engine's throbbing; there was a frightful pain in the top of his skull, and he could hardly control his hands. Still, with the memory of his four months' siege behind him, he fought on, in a frenzy of determination; and half an hour later he began to vomit–he vomited until it seemed as if his innards must be torn into shreds. A man could get used to the fertilizer mill, the boss had said, if he would only make up his mind to it; but Jurgis now began to see that it was a question of making up his stomach.

At the end of that day of horror, he could scarcely stand. He had to catch himself now and then, and lean against a building and get his bearings. Most of the men, when they came out, made straight for a saloon–they seemed to place fertilizer and rattlesnake poison in one class. But Jurgis was too ill to think of drinking–he could only make his way to the street and stagger on to a car. He had a sense of humor, and later on, when he became an old hand, he used to think it fun to board a street car and see what happened. Now, however, he was too ill to notice it–how the people in the car began to gasp and sputter, to put their handkerchiefs to their noses, and transfix him with furious glances. Jurgis only knew that a man in front of him immediately got up and gave him a seat; and that half a minute later the two people on each side of him got up; and that in a full minute the crowded car was nearly empty–those passengers who could not get room on the platform having gotten out to walk.

Of course Jurgis had made his home a miniature fertilizer mill a minute after entering. The stuff was a half an inch deep in his skin–his whole system was full of it, and it would have taken a week not merely of scrubbing, but of vigorous exercise, to get it out of him. At it was, he could be compared with nothing known to men, save that newest discovery of the savants, a substance which emits energy for an unlimited time, without being itself in the least diminished in power. He smelt so that he made all the food at the table taste, and set the whole family to vomiting; for himself it was three days before he could keep anything upon his stomach–he might wash his hands, and use a knife and fork, but were not his mouth and throat filled with the poison?

And still Jurtgis stuck it out! In spite of splitting headaches he would stagger down to the plant and take up his stand once more, and begin to shovel in the blinding clouds of dust. And so at the end of the week he was a fertilizer man for life–he was able to eat again, and though his head never stopped aching, it ceased to be so bad that he could not work.

So there passed another summer. It was a summer of prosperity, all over the country, and the country ate generously of packing-house products, and there was plenty of work for all the family, in spite of the packers' efforts to keep a superfluity of labor. They were again able to pay their debts and to begin to save a little sum; but there were one or two sacrifices they considered too heavy to be made for long—it was too bad that the boys should have to sell papers at their age. It was utterly useless to caution them and plead with them; quite without knowing it, they were taking on the tone of their new environment. They were learning to swear in voluble English; they were learning to pick up cigar-stumps and smoke them, to pass hours of their time gambling with pennies and dice and cigarette cards; they were learning the location of all the houses of prostitution on the "Lêvée," and the names of the "madames" who kept them, and the days when they gave their state banquets, which the police captains and the big politicians all attended. If a visiting "country customer" were to ask them, they could show him which was "Hinkydink's" famous saloon, and could even point out to him by name the different gamblers and thugs and "hold-up men" who made the place their headquarters. And worse yet, the boys were getting out of the habit of coming home at night. What was the use, they would ask, of wasting time and energy and a possible carfare riding out to the stockyards every night when the weather was pleasant and they could crawl under a truck or into an empty doorway and sleep exactly as well? So long as they brought home a half dollar for each day, what mattered it when they brought it? But Jurgis declared that from this to ceasing to come at all would not be a very long step, and so it was decided that Viliman and Nikalojus should return to school in the fall, and that instead Elzbieta should go out and get some work, her place at home being taken by her younger daughter.

Little Kotrina was like most children of the poor, prematurely made old; she had to take care of her little brother, who was a cripple, and also of the baby; she had to cook the meals and wash the dishes and clean house, and have supper ready when the workers came home in the evening. She was only thirteen, and small for her age, but she did all this without a murmur; and her mother went out, and after trudging a couple of days about the yards, settled down as a servant of a "sausage machine."

Elzbieta was used to working, but she found this change a hard one, for the reason that she had to stand motionless upon her feet from seven o'clock in the morning till half-past twelve, and again from one till half-past five. For the first few days it seemed to her that she could not stand it—she suffered almost as much as Jurgis had from the fertilizer, and would come out at sundown with her head fairly reeling. Besides this, she was working in one of the dark holes, by electric light, and the dampness, too, was deadly—there were always puddles of water on the floor, and a sickening odor of moist flesh in the room. The people who worked here followed the ancient custom of nature, whereby the ptarmigan is the color of dead leaves in the fall and of snow in the winter, and the chameleon, who is black when he lies upon a stump and turns green when he moves to a leaf. The men and women who worked in this department were precisely the color of the "fresh country sausage" they made.

The sausage room was an interesting place to visit, for two or three minutes, and provided that you did not look at the people; the machines were perhaps the most wonderful things in the entire plant. Presumably sausages were once chopped and stuffed by hand, and if so it would be interesting to know how many workers had been displaced by these inventions. On one side of the room were the hoppers, into which men shovelled loads of meat and wheelbarrows full of spices; in these great bowls were whirling knives that made two thousand revolutions a minute, and when the meat was ground fine and adulterated with potato flour, and well mixed with water, it was forced to the stuffing machines on the other side of the room. The latter were tended by women; there was a sort of spout, like the nozzle of a hose, and one of the women would take a long string of "casing" and put the end over the nozzle and then work the whole thing on, as one works on the finger of a tight glove. This string would be twenty or thirty feet long, but the woman would have it all on in a jiffy; and when she had several on, she would press a lever, and a stream of sausage meat would be shot out, taking the casing with it as it came. Thus one might stand and see appear, miraculously born from the machine, a wriggling snake of sausage of incredible length. In front was a big pan which caught these creatures, and two more women who seized them as fast as they appeared and twisted them into links. This was for the uninitiated the most perplexing work of all, for all that the woman had to give was a single centre. It was quite like the feat of a prestidigitator—for the woman worked so fast that the eye could literally not follow her, and there was only a mist of motion, and tangle after tangle of sausages appearing. In the midst of the mist, however, the visitor would suddenly notice the tense set face, with the two wrinkles graven in the forehead, and the ghastly pallor of the cheeks; and then he would suddenly recollect that it was time he was going on. The woman did not go on; she stayed right there—hour after hour, day after day, year after year, twisting sausage links and racing with death. It was piece work, and she was apt to have a family to keep alive; and stern and ruthless economic laws had arranged it that she could only do this by working just as she did, with all her soul upon her work, and with never an instant for a glance at the well-dressed ladies and gentlemen who came to stare at her, as at some wild beast in a menagerie....

Chapter Twenty-one

That was the way they did it! There was not half an hour's warning—the works were closed! it had happened that way before, said the men, and it would happen that way forever. They had made all the harvesting machines that the world needed, and now they had to wait till some wore out! It was nobody's fault—that was the way of it; and thousands of men and women were turned out in the dead of winter, to live upon their savings if they had any, and otherwise to die. So many tens of thousands already in the city, homeless and begging for work, and now several thousand more added to them!

Jurgis walked home with his pittance of pay in his pocket, heartbroken, overwhelmed. One more bandage had been torn from his eyes, one more pitfall was revealed to him! Of what help was kindness and decency on the part of employers—when they could not keep a job for him, when there were more harvesting machines made than the world was able to buy! What a hellish mockery it was, anyway, that a man should slave to make harvesting machines for the country, only to be turned out to starve for doing his duty too well!

It took him two days to get over this heart-sickening disappointment. He did not drink anything, because Elzbieta got his money for safekeeping, and knew him too well to be in the least frightened by his angry demands. He stayed up in the garret, however, and sulked—what was the use of a man's hunting a job when it was taken from him before he had time to learn the work? But then their money was going again, and little Antanas was hungry, and crying with the bitter cold of the garret. Also Madame Haupt, the midwife, was after him for some money. So he went out once more.

For another ten days he roamed the streets and alleys of the huge city, sick and hungry, begging for any work. He tried in stores and offices, in restaurants and hotels, along the docks an in the railroad yards, in warehouses and mills and factories where they made products that went to every corner of the world. There were often one or two chances—but there were always a hundred men for every chance, and his turn would not come. At night he crept into sheds and cellars and doorways—until there came a spell of belated winter weather, with a raging gale, and the thermometer five degrees below zero at sundown and falling all night. Then Jurgis fought like a wild beast to get into the big Harrison Street police station, and slept down in a corridor, crowded with two other men upon a single step.

He had to fight often in these days—to fight for a place near the factory gates, and now and again with gangs on the street. He found, for instance, that the business of carrying satchels for railroad passengers was a preempted one—whenever he essayed it, eight or ten men and boys would fall upon him and force him to run for his life. They always had the policeman "squared," and so there was no use in expecting protection.

That Jurgis did not starve to death was due solely to the pittance the children brought him. And even this was never certain. For one thing the cold was almost more than the children could bear; and then they, too, were in perpetual peril from rivals who plundered and beat them. The law was against them, too—little Vilimas, who was really eleven, but did not look to be eight, was stopped on the streets by a severe old lady in spectacles, who told him that he was too young to be working and that if he did not stop selling papers she would send a truant officer after him. Also one night a strange man caught little Kotrina by the arm and tried to persuade her into a dark cellarway, an experience which filled her with such terror that she was hardly to be kept at work.

At last, on a Sunday, as there was no use looking for work, Jurgis went home by stealing rides on the car He found that they had been waiting for him for three days—there was a chance of a job for him.

It was quite a story. Little Juozapas, who was near crazy with hunger these days, had gone out on the street to beg for himself. Juozapas had only one leg, having been run over by a wagon when a little child, but he had got himself a broomstick, which he put under his arm for a crutch. He had fallen in with some other children and found the way to Mike Scully's dump, which lay three or four blocks away. To this place there came every day many hundreds of wagon-loads of garbage and trash from the lake-front, where the rich people lived; and in the heaps the children raked for food—there were hunks of bread and potato peelings and apple cores and meat bones, all of it half frozen and quite unspoiled. Little Juozapas gorged himself, and came home with a newspaper full, which he was feeding to Antanas when his mother came in. Elzbieta was horrified, for she did not believe that the food out of the dumps was fit to eat. The next day, however, when no harm came of it and Juozapas began to cry with hunger, she gave in and said that he might go again. And that afternoon he came home with a story of how while he had been digging away with a stick, a lady upon the street had called him. A real fine lady, the little boy explained, a beautiful lady; and she wanted to know all about him, and whether he got the garbage for chickens, and why he walked with a broomstick, and why Ona had died, and how Jurgis had come to go to jail, and what was the matter with Marija, and everything. In the end she had asked where he lived, and said that she was coming to see him, and bring him a new crutch to walk with. She had on a hat with a bird upon it, Juozapas added, and along fur snake around her neck.

She really came, the very next morning, and climbed the ladder to the garret, and stood and stared about her, turning pale at the sight of the blood stains on the floor where Ona had died. She was a "settlement worker," she explained to Elzbieta—she lived around on Ashland Avenue. Elzbieta knew the place, over a feed store; somebody had wanted her to go there, but she had not cared to, for she thought that it must have something to do with religion, and the priest did not like her to have anything to do with strange religions. They were rich people who came to live there to find out about the poor people; but what good they expected it would do them to know, one could not imagine. So spoke Elzbieta, naïvely, and the young lady laughed and was rather at a loss for an answer—she stood and gazed about her, and thought of a cynical remark that had been made to her, that she was standing upon the brink of the pit of hell and throwing in snowballs to lower the temperature.

Elzbieta was glad to have somebody listen, and she told all their woes—what had happened to Ona, and the jail, and the loss of their home, and Marija's accident, and how Ona had died, and how Jurgis could get no work. As she listened the pretty young lady's eyes filled with tears, and in the midst of it she burst into weeping and hid her face on Elzbieta's shoulder, quite regardless of the fact that the woman had on a dirty old wrapper and that the garret was full of fleas. Poor Elzbieta was ashamed of herself for having told so woeful a tale, and the other had to beg and plead with her to get her to go on. The end of it was that the young lady sent them a basket of things to eat, and left a letter that Jurgis was to take to a gentleman who was superintendent in one of the mills of the great steel-works in South Chicago. "He will get Jurgis something to do," the young lady had said, and added, smiling through her tears—"If he doesn't, he will never marry me."

The steelworks were fifteen miles away, and as usual it was so contrived that one had to pay two fares to get there. Far and wide the sky was flaring with the red glare that leaped from rows of towering chimneys—for it was pitch dark when Jurgis arrived. The vast works, a city in themselves, were surrounded by a stockade; and already a full hundred men were waiting at the gate where new hands were taken on. Soon after daybreak whistles began to blow, and then suddenly thousands of men appeared, streaming from saloons and boarding-houses across the way, leaping from trolley cars that passed—it seemed as if they rose out of the ground, in the dim gray light. A river of them poured in through the gate—and then gradually ebbed away again, until there were only a few late ones running, and the watchman pacing up and down, and the hungry strangers stamping and shivering.

Jurgis presented his precious letter. The gatekeeper was surly, and put him through a catechism, but he insisted that he knew nothing, and as he had taken the precaution to seal his letter, there was nothing for the gatekeeper to do but send it to the person to whom it was addressed. A messenger came back to say that Jurgis should wait, and so he came inside of the gate, perhaps not sorry enough that there were other less fortunate watching him with greedy eyes.

The great mills were getting under way—one could hear a vast stirring, a rolling and rumbling and hammering. Little by little the scene grew plain: towering, black buildings here and there, long rows of shops and sheds, little railways branching everywhere, bare gray cinders under foot and oceans of billowing black smoke above. On one side of the grounds ran a railroad with a dozen tracks, and on the other side lay the lake, where steamers came to load.

Jurgis had time enough to stare and speculate, for it was two hours before he was summoned. He went into the office building, where a company time-keeper interviewed him. The superintendent was busy, he said, but he (the time-keeper) would try to find Jurgis a job. He had never worked in a steel mill before? But he was ready for anything? Well, then, they would go and see.

So they began a tour, among sights that made Jurgis stare amazed. He wondered if ever he could get used to working in a place like this, where the air shook with deafening thunder, and whistles shrieked warnings on all sides of him at once; where miniature steam engines came rushing upon him, and sizzling, quivering, white-hot masses of metal sped past him, and explosions of fire and flaming sparks dazzled him and scorched his face. The men in these mills were all black with soot, and hollow-eyed and gaunt; they worked with fierce intensity, rushing here and there, and never lifting their eyes from their tasks. Jurgis clung to his guide like a scared child to its nurse, and while the latter hailed one foreman after another to ask if they could use another unskilled man, he stared about him and marvelled.

He was taken to the Bessemer furnace, where they made billets of steel—a dome-like building the size of a big theater. Jurgis stood where the balcony of the theater would have been, and opposite, by the stage, he saw three giant caldrons, big enough for all the devils of hell to brew their broth in, full of something white and blinding, bubbling and splashing, roaring as if volcanoes were blowing through it—one had to shout to be heard in the place. Liquid fire would leap from these caldrons and scatter like bombs below—and men were working there, seeming careless, so that Jurgis caught his breath with fright. Then a whistle would toot, and across the curtain of the theater would come a little engine with a car-load of something to be dumped into one of the receptacles; and then another whistle would toot, down by the stage, and another train would back up—and suddenly, without an instant's warning, one of the giant kettles began to tilt and topple, flinging out a jet of hissing, roaring flame. Jurgis shrank back appalled, for he thought it was an accident; there fell a pillar of white flame, dazzling as the sun, swishing like a huge tree falling in the forest. A torrent of sparks swept all the way across the building, overwhelming everything, hiding it from sight; and then Jurgis looked through the fingers of his hands, and saw pouring out of the caldron a cascade of living, leaping fire, white with a whiteness not of earth, scorching the eyeballs. Incandescent rainbows shone above it, blue, red, and golden lights played about it; but the stream itself was white, ineffable. Out of regions of wonder it streamed, the very river of life; and the soul leaped up at the sight of it, fled back upon it, swift and resistless, back into far-off lands, where beauty and terror dwell.—Then the great caldron tilted back again, empty, and Jurgis saw to his relief that no one was hurt, and turned and followed his guide out into the sunlight.

They went through the blast furnaces, through rolling mills where bars of steel were tossed about and chopped like bits of cheese. All around and above giant machine-arms were flying, giant wheels were turning, giant hammers crashing; travelling cranes creaked and groaned overhead, reaching down iron hands and seizing iron prey—it was like standing in the center of the earth, where the machinery of time was revolving.

By and by they came to the place where steel rails were made; and Jurgis heard a toot behind him, and jumped out of the way of a car with a white-hot ingot upon it, the size of a man's body. There was a sudden crash and the car came to a halt, and the ingot toppled out upon a moving platform, where steel fingers and arms seized hold of it, punching it and prodding it into place, and hurrying it into the grip of huge rollers. Then it came out upon the other side, and there were more crashings and clatterings, and over it was flopped, like a pancake on a gridiron, and seized again and rushed back at you through another squeezer. So amid deafening uproar it clattered to and fro, growing thinner and flatter and longer. The ingot seemed almost a living thing; it did not want to run this mad course, but it was in the grip of fate, it was tumbled on, screeching and clanking and shivering in protest. By and by it was long and thin, a great red snake escaped from purgatory; and then, as it slid through the rollers, you would have sworn that it was alive—it writhed and squirmed, and wriggles and shudders passed out through its tail, all but flinging it off by their violence. There was no rest for it until it was cold and black—and then it needed only to be cut and straightened to be ready for a railroad.

It was at the end of this rail's progress that Jurgis got his chance. They had to be moved by men with crowbars, and the boss here could use another man. So he took off his coat and set to work on the spot.

It took him two hours to get to this place every day and cost him a dollar and twenty cents a week. As this was out of the question, he wrapped his bedding in a bundle and took it with him, and one of his fellow workingmen introduced him to a Polish lodging house, where he might have the privilege of sleeping upon the floor for ten cents a night. He got his meals at free-lunch counters, and every Saturday night he went home—bedding and all—and took the greater part of his money to the family. Elzbieta was sorry for this arrangement, for she feared that it would get him into the habit of living without them, and once a week was not every often for him to see his baby; but there was not other way of arranging it. There was no chance for a woman at the steelworks, and Marija was now ready for work again, and lured on from day to day by the hope of finding it at the yards.

In a week Jurgis got over his sense of helplessness and bewilderment in the rail mill. He learned to find his way about and to take all the miracles and terrors for granted, to work without hearing the rumbling and crashing. From blind fear he went to the other extreme; he became reckless and indifferent, like all the rest of the men, who took but little thought of themselves in the ardor of their work. It was wonderful, when one came to think of it, that these men should have taken an interest in the work they did; they had no share in it—they were paid by the hour, and paid no more for being interested. Also they knew that if they were hurt they would hurry to their task by dangerous short-cuts, would use methods that were quicker and more effective in spite of the fact that they were also risky. His fourth day at his work Jurgis saw a man stumble while running in front of a car, and have his foot mashed off; and before he had been there three weeks he was witness of a yet more dreadful accident. There was a row of brick furnaces, shining white through every crack with the molten steel inside. Some of these were bulging dangerously, yet men worked before them, wearing blue glasses when they opened and shut the doors. One morning as Jurgis was passing, a furnace blew out, spraying two men with a shower of liquid fire. As they lay screaming and rolling upon the ground in agony, Jurgis rushed to help them, and as a result he lost a good part of the skin from the inside of one of his hands. The company doctor bandaged it up, but he got no other thanks from anyone, and was laid up for eight working days without any pay.

Most fortunately, at this juncture, Elzbieta got the long-awaited chance to go at five o'clock in the morning and help scrub the office floors of one of the packers. Jurgis came home and covered himself with blankets to keep warm, and divided his time between sleeping and playing with little Antanas. Juozapas was away raking in the dump a good part of the time, and Elzbieta and Marija were hunting for more work.

Antanas was now over a year and half old, and was a perfect talking machine. He learned so fast that every week when Jurgis came home it seemed to him as if he had a new child. He would sit down and listen and stare at him, and give vent to delighted exclamations—"*Palauk! Muma! Tu mano szirdele!*" The little fellow was now really the one delight that Jurgis had in the world—his one hope, his one victory. Thank God, Antanas was a boy! And he was as tough as a pine-knot, and with the appetite of a wolf. Nothing had hurt him, and nothing could hurt him; he had come through all the suffering and deprivation unscathed—only shriller-voiced and more determined in his grip upon life. He was a terrible child to manage, was Antanas, but his father did not mind that—he would watch him and smile to himself with satisfaction. The more of a fighter he was the better—he would need to fight before he got through.

Jurgis had got the habit of buying the Sunday paper whenever he had the money; a most wonderful paper could be had for only five cents, a whole armful, with all the news of the world set forth in big headlines, that Jurgis could spell out slowly, with the children to help him at the long words. There was battle and murder and sudden death—it was marvelous how they ever heard about so many entertaining and thrilling happenings; the stories must be all true, for surely no man could have made such things up, and besides, there were pictures of them all, as real as life. One of these papers was as good as a circus, and nearly as good as a spree—certainly a most wonderful treat for a working-man, who was tired out and stupefied, and had never had any education, and whose work was one dull, sordid grind, day after day, and year after year, with never a sight of a green field nor an hour's entertainment, nor anything but liquor to stimulate his imagination. Among other things, these papers had pages full of comical pictures, and these were the main joy in life to little Antanas. He treasured them up, and would drag them out and make his father tell him about them; there were all sorts of animals among them, and Antanas could tell the names of all of them, lying upon the floor for hours and pointing them out with his chubby little fingers. Whenever the story was plain enough for Jurgis to make out, Antanas would have it repeated to him, and then he would remember it, prattling funny little sentences and mixing it up with other stories in an irresistible fashion. Also his quaint pronunciation of words was such a delight—and the phrases he would pick up and remember, the most outlandish and impossible things! The first time that the little rascal burst out with "Goddamn," his father nearly rolled off the chair with glee; but in the end he was sorry for this, for Antanas was soon "Godamning" everything and everybody.

And then, when he was able to use his hands, Jurgis took his bedding again and went back to his task of shifting rails. It was now April, and the snow had given place to cold rains, and the unpaved street in front of Aniele's house was turned into a canal. Jurgis would have to wade through it to get home, and if it was late he might easily get stuck to his waist in the mire. But he did not mind this much—it was a promise that summer was coming. Marija had now gotten a place as beef trimmer in one of the smaller packing plants; and he told himself that he had learned his lesson now, and would meet with no more accidents—so that at last there was prospect of an end to their long agony. They could save money again, and when another winter came they would have a comfortable place; and the children would be off the streets and in school again, and they might set to work to nurse back into life their habits of decency and kindness. So once more Jurgis began to make plans and dream dreams.

And then one Saturday night he jumped off the car and started home, with the sun shining low under the edge of a bank of clouds that had been pouring floods of water into the mud-soaked street. There was a rainbow in the sky, and another in his breast—for he had thirty-six hours' rest before him, and a chance to see his family. Then suddenly he came in sight of the house, and noticed that there was a crowd before the door. He ran up the steps and pushed his way in, and saw Aniele's kitchen crowded with excited women. It reminded him so vividly of the time when he had come home from jail and found Ona dying, that his heart almost stood still. "What's the matter?" he cried.

A dead silence had fallen in the room, and he saw that every one was staring at him. "What's the matter?" he exclaimed again.

And then, up in the garret, he heard sounds of wailing, in Marija's voice. He started for the ladder—and Aniele seized him by the arm. "No, no!" she exclaimed. "Don't go up there!"

"What is it?" he shouted.

And old woman answered him weakly: "It's Antanas. He's dead. He was drowned out in the street!"

119

Plan of Chicago

DANIEL H. BURNHAM and EDWARD H. BENNETT

For a discussion of Burnham and Bennett's "Plan of Chicago", see the Introduction in Volume I.

Origin of the Plan of Chicago

The tendency of mankind to congregate in cities is a marked characteristic of modern times. This movement is confined to no one country, but is world-wide. Each year Rome, and the cities of the Orient, as well as Berlin, New York, and Chicago, are adding to their population at an unprecedented rate. Coincident with this urban development there has been a widespread increase in wealth, and also an enlarged participation on the part of the people in the work of government. As a natural result of these causes has come the desire to better the conditions of living. Men are becoming convinced that the formless growth of the city is neither economical nor satisfactory; and that over-crowding and congestion of traffic paralyze the vital functions of the city. The complicated problems which the great city develops are now seen not to be beyond the control of aroused public sentiment; and practical men of affairs are turning their attention to working out the means whereby the city may be made an efficient instrument for providing all its people with the best possible conditions of living.

Chicago, in common with other great cities, realizes that the time has come to bring order out of the chaos incident to rapid growth, and especially to the influx of people of many nationalities without common traditions or habits of life. Among the various instrumentalities designed to accomplish this result, a plan for a well-ordered and convenient city is seen to be indispensable; and to the task of producing such a plan the Commercial club has devoted its energies for the past three years.

It is not to be expected that any plan devised while as yet few civic problems

Source: Daniel H. Burnham and Edward H. Bennett, *Plan of Chicago*, ed. Charles Moore, Chicago, Commercial Club, 1909.

have received final solution will be perfect in all its details. It is claimed for the plan herein presented, that it is the result of extended and careful study of the needs of Chicago, made by disinterested men of wide experience, amid the very conditions which it is sought to remedy; and that during the years devoted to its preparation the plan has had the benefit of varied and competent criticism. The real test of this plan will be found in its application; for, such is the determination of the people to secure more perfect conditions, it is certain that if the plan is really good it will commend itself to the progressive spirit of the times, and sooner or later it will be carried out. ...

To many who have given little consideration to the subject, a plan seems to call for large expenditures and a consequent increase in taxation. The reverse is the case. It is certain that civic improvement will go on at an accelerated rate; and if those improvements shall be marshaled according to a well-ordered plan great saving must result. Good order and convenience are not expensive; but haphazard and ill-considered projects invariably result in extravagance and wastefulness. A plan insures that whenever any public or semi-public work shall be undertaken, it will fall into its proper and predetermined place in the general scheme, and thus contribute to the unity and dignity of the city.

The plan frankly takes into consideration the fact that the American city, and Chicago pre-eminently, is a center of industry and traffic. Therefore attention is given to the betterment of commercial facilities; to methods of transportation for persons and for goods; to removing the obstacles which prevent or obstruct circulation; and to the increase of convenience. It is realized, also, that good workmanship requires a large degree of comfort on the part of the workers in their homes and their surroundings, and ample opportunity for that rest and recreation without which all work becomes drudgery. Then, too, the city has a dignity to be maintained; and good order is essential to material advancement. Consequently, the plan provides for impressive groupings of public buildings, and reciprocal relations among such groups. Moreover, consideration is given to the fact that in all probability Chicago, within the lifetime of persons now living, will become a greater city than any existing at the present time; and that therefore the most comprehensive plans of to-day will need to be supplemented in a not remote future. Opportunity for such expansion is provided for.

The origin of the plan of Chicago can be traced directly to the World's Columbian Exposition. The World's Fair of 1893 was the beginning, in our day and in this country, of the orderly arrangement of extensive public grounds and buildings. ...

In creating the ideal arrangement, every one who lives here is better accommodated in his business and his social activities. In bringing about better freight and passenger facilities, every merchant and manufacturer is helped. In establishing a complete park and parkway system, the life of the wage-earner and of his family is made healthier and pleasanter; while the greater attractiveness thus produced keeps at home the people of means and taste, and acts as a magnet to draw those who seek to live amid pleasing surroundings. The very beauty that attracts him who has money makes pleasant the life of those among whom he lives, while anchoring him and his wealth to the city. The prosperity aimed at is for all Chicago. ...

City Planning in Ancient and Modern Times

City planning, in the sense of regarding the city as an organic whole and of developing its various units with reference to their relations one to another, had its origin in Paris during the Bourbon period. Among great cities, Paris has reached the highest stage of development; and the method of this attainment affords lessons for all other cities. Paris owes its origin and its growth to the convenience of its location in view of increasing commercial conditions. Its beginnings go back to the century before the Christian era, when it was but a straggling village called Lutetia, occupying one of the islands in the Seine. On the vast level plain adjoining the town, houses could be erected indefinitely, while the numerous watercourses extending into the surrounding regions gave easy access to the trader. Fertile lands furnished an abundance of provisions; and brick-clay, lime, and sand, with timber from the neighboring forests, provided materials for building. The surroundings of Paris, so rich in all the requisites for the creation of a great city, are similar to those of London and Berlin and Chicago; and in each instance there is the same breadth in the landscape.

The architects to whom Louis XIV. entrusted his planning went far beyond the compact walled city of their day. In the open fields which the growth of Paris must sooner or later transform into streets and avenues they drew the central axis of the city. Straight, vast in width, and without limit of length, this avenue passed entirely through open country, with scarcely a dozen buildings throughout its great extent. To the noted city-builders of the seventeenth and eighteenth centuries,—Louis XIV., Colbert, Le Nôtre, Blondel, and the Academy of Architects,—Paris owes those vast reaches of avenue and boulevard which to-day are the crowning features of the most beautiful of cities. The Paris of their day was indeed a crowded, congested city; but the Paris which they conceived and laid out in the deserts and waste places was the wide spreading, well-adorned, and convenient city in which to-day all the world takes delight. The Madeleine, the Place de la Concorde, the Invalides, and the great axial avenue from the garden of the Tuileries to the Place de l'Etoile,—all existed on paper decades before they were finally realized in the progress of city building. The point of interest to us is, that as Paris increased in population, the city grew according to a well-devised, symmetrical, highly-developed plan; and that the greater portion of the beauty and convenience recognized to-day was attained at no money cost whatever. Artistic sense and foresight were the only price paid. It is unnecessary to do more than point out the fact that a similar opportunity is open to Chicago.

Old Paris remained, with its dirty, crowded, ill-smelling, narrow, winding streets, the hotbeds of vice and crime. Napoleon Bonaparte was quick to see that while the Paris of the future might indeed grow in attractiveness and convenience, the Paris of the present demanded his attention. Napoleon was disturbed over the condition of his capital. He realized that the city, then numbering some seven hundred thousand people, was destined to become the home of two, three, or even four millions; and he proposed to give it a splendor never before realized by any city in the world. He began to open the Rue de Rivoli, north of the Tuileries gardens; he created the Rue Napoleon (now the Rue de la Paix) in the axis of the Place Vendôme; from the mediæval bridges he swept the superstructures, adding three superb new crossings of the Seine; he built the first sidewalks in Paris, and lighted the streets at night; and he transformed the banks of the river by the construction of three thousand meters of new quays. He also gave to Paris her great commemorative monuments, the Arc de Triomphe de l'Étoile, which was finished by Louis Philippe, the Arc du Carrousel, and the Column Vendôme, all of which were foreshadowed in the designs of Louis XIV.

It remained for the third Napoleon, however, to accomplish the great work of breaking through the old city, of opening it to light and air, and of making it fit to sustain the army of merchants and manufacturers which makes Paris to-day the center of a commerce as wide as civilization itself. In 1853, Georges Eugène Haussmann became prefect of the Seine, the appointment being in the nature of a promotion due to the successful administration of the office of prefect in other French cities. Immediately Haussmann began a career which has established for all time his place among the city-builders of the world. As if by intuition he grasped the entire problem. Taking counsel neither of expediency nor of compromise, he ever sought the true and proper solution. To him Paris appeared as a highly organized unit, and he strove to create ideal conditions throughout the entire city. The world gives him credit for the highest success. The people of Paris have always supported those who aimed to make their city grand and beautiful. Proud, ambitious, endowed with good taste and an artistic sense, the Parisians have ever been zealous to make their city the capital not only of the state, but also of civilization.

Haussmann never overlooked the great and broad lines laid down by his predecessors; so that to a considerable extent his work was but the continuation of the plans prepared by Louis XIV. in the later years of the seventeenth century. His peculiar task, however, was to provide adequate means of circulation within the old city, by cutting new streets and widening old ones, by sweeping away unwholesome rookeries, and by opening up great spaces in order to disengage monuments of beauty and historic interest. He placed the great railway stations of Paris in a circle about the old center of the city, and opened up fine avenues of approach to them. At times he found it less expensive, and also less disturbing, to build a new street through the blocks, rather than to widen old streets; and it was his special care to create diagonal thoroughfares in order to shorten distances, and also to give picturesqueness to the street system by the creation of those corner lots which the architects of Paris have learned so well how to improve.

The task which Haussmann accomplished for Paris corresponds with the work which must be done for Chicago, in order to overcome the intolerable conditions which invariably arise from a rapid growth of population. ...

With the Germans the cutting through of new streets was undertaken for the twofold reason of facilitating traffic and of admitting light and air into a too congested and unwholesome city quarter. In Frankfort-on-the-Main, in Hamburg, in Berlin, and in Dresden it became necessary to abolish with firm hand evil conditions that had become intolerable, no matter at what sacrifice of buildings enveloped with historical associations. But the Germans have come to modify the French theory of the unconditional superiority of the rectilinear avenue; and now they seek to maintain the essential character of the city, as in the case of Darmstadt, by admitting strong curves, and, wherever desirable, by narrowing or widening the thoroughfare, making compensations by creating open spaces. They have found, also, that a too extensive clearing away of the old buildings which cluster about a great minster or cathedral results in an enhancement of effectiveness only at a sacrifice of scale and a loss of picturesqueness. As a consequence, the Germans have sought a golden mean by creating about a monumental structure free room for the beholder to see the essential parts of the building from a sufficiently remote point of view, while leaving undisturbed single structures small in scale, in order that the main building may appear to have grown out of its surroundings.

In general, then, it may be said that while the French or classical theory results in monumental effects for a city and establishes unity, the German or individualistic treatment preserves for an old city a homelike feeling and a pleasing variety. It is worthy of note, however, that where city planning has been undertaken by masters, whether in France or Germany, the two theories have been used as circumstances warranted. It is only where designers are not able to handle their subject in its entirety, but have become slaves to a system, that results have been attained at great money cost and with a loss of charm and picturesqueness that by intelligent study might have been saved. ...

We have found that those cities which retain their domination over the imaginations of mankind achieve that result through the harmony and beauty of their civic works; that these artistic creations were made possible largely by the gains of commerce promoted by years of peace; and that intense loyalty on the part of the great body of the citizens was the chief impulse which led them to strive to enhance the prestige and dignity of their city. We have found, also, that in modern times the cities of Europe are everywhere making those changes which a rapid increase in trade and population requires, and which the awakened artistic sense of the people demands. We turn now to our own country, to note the conditions which have controlled the development of the American city, and to recount briefly some of the more noteworthy attempts that are being made in the United States to give form and comeliness to our great towns.

Washington was planned and founded as the capital of a nation. The architects of Louis XIV. drew the lines of the new Paris beyond the walls of the existing town, and mapped avenues converging at central points where only gardens and farms then existed; and their plans were a wise provision for a not distant future.

Under the direction of President Washington, and with the aid and encouragement of Secretary Jefferson, Peter Charles L'Enfant, a young French engineer, deliberately drew the map of an entirely new capital city designed to accommodate a population one-third greater than was comprised in Paris at that date. In that plan no element of civic convenience, beauty, or adornment was lacking. The entire city was regarded as a unit, and that unit was to be developed in a form not surpassed by any existing city. Upon a rectilinear system of streets L'Enfant imposed diagonal avenues of stately width, converging upon focal points designed to be the location of important public buildings, statues, or monuments commemorating historic events. The Capitol and the President's House were connected by a spacious park, and axial relations between the two structures were developed; every other building necessary for national uses was provided for; and canals, cascades, and fountains were located with reference to existing springs and watercourses. This comprehensive and magnificent plan, designed for an area which then consisted of wide swamps and wooded hills, became the laughing-stock alike of foreign traveler and American citizen. But fortunately the foundations were laid broad and deep by means of the donation of the lands necessary for streets, avenues, and parks. Fortunately the plan was adopted and the streets, avenues, public squares, and circles were fixed; and although the development of the city during three-quarters of a century was slow, yet the rapid increase in wealth and power that followed the ending of the Civil War found Washington ready and waiting for the improvements which have lifted it from a straggling, ill-kept town, into one of the beautiful and stately capitals of the world.

Before the opening of the twentieth century, Washington had begun to expand over the surrounding country; and there unfortunately the L'Enfant plan stopped short. Moreover, within the city there had been perversions of the plan; and there had also been additions to the park area awaiting development. Congress dealt in part with the difficulties by extending the L'Enfant plan of streets and avenues over the entire District of Columbia; and in 1901 the task of preparing a report on the development of the park system of the Federal territory and the placing of public buildings was committed to an expert commission. As Haussmann aimed in large part to carry out the work that had been planned by the architects of Louis XIV., so the Senate Park Commission sought to re-establish and reanimate the plans of L'Enfant, which had the sanction of Washington and Jefferson. In spite of much opposition on the part of those who regard only the present, and take no thought for future advancement, the new plans have been carried to such a point that their general lines are well established, and already works to cost nearly $50,000,000 are in progress, each one of which strengthens the hold of the general scheme.

The plans for the improvement of Washington were prepared by the same hands that guided the artistic development of the World's Columbian Exposition in Chicago. The dream city on Lake Michigan, people said, should take on enduring form in the capital of the nation. Then as the Washington plans fired the imagination of the American people, the cities throughout the country began to ask why they too should not achieve whatever of beauty and convenience their situation and their civic pride would allow. ...

Each city differs from every other city in its physical characteristics and in the nature of its opportunities, so that the development of every city must be along individual lines. This very fact allows full scope for the development of that peculiar charm which, wherever discovered and developed irresistibly draws to that city people of discrimination and taste, and at the same time begets a spirit of loyalty and satisfaction on the part of the citizens. ...

The experience of other cities both ancient and modern, both abroad and at home, teaches Chicago that the way to true greatness and continued prosperity lies in making the city convenient and healthful for the ever-increasing numbers of its citizens; that civic beauty satisfies a craving of human nature so deep and so compelling that people will travel far to find and enjoy it; that the orderly arrangement of fine buildings and monuments brings fame and wealth to the city; and that the cities which truly exercise dominion rule by reason of their appeal to the higher emotions of the human mind. The problem for Chicago, therefore, resolves itself into making the best use of a situation, the central location and resources of which have already drawn together millions of people, and are clearly destined to assemble many times that number; and planning for that civic development which promotes present content and insures permanence....

Chicago, the Metropolis of the Middle West

The growth of the city has been so rapid that it has been impossible to plan for the economical disposition of the great influx of people, surging like a human tide to spread itself wherever opportunity for profitable labor offered place. Thoughtful people are appalled at the results of progress; at the waste in time, strength, and money which congestion in city streets begets; at the toll of lives taken by disease when sanitary precautions are neglected; and at the frequent outbreaks against law and order which result from narrow and pleasureless lives. So that while the keynote of the nineteenth century was expansion, we of the twentieth century find that our dominant idea is conservation. The people of Chicago have ceased to be impressed by rapid growth or the great size of the city. What they insist asking now is, How are we living? Are we in reality prosperous? Is the city a convenient place for business? Is it a good labor market in the sense that labor is sufficiently comfortable to be efficient and content? Will the coming generation be able to stand the nervous strain of city life? When a competence has been accumulated, must we go elsewhere to enjoy the fruits of independence? If the city does not become better as it becomes bigger, shall not the defect be remedied? These are questions that will not be brushed aside. They are the most pressing questions of our day, and everywhere men are anxiously seeking the answers. ...

City life has attractions that make a strong appeal to human nature. Opportunities for large success, for wealth and power and social consideration, for amusement and instruction, for the increase of knowledge and the cultivation of taste, are greater for the average person in the city than in the country. The city, therefore, is constantly drawing from the country the young men and women of ambition and self-reliance, who are lured thither by the great prizes which in a democracy are open to the competition of all.

When Chicago is adverted to as the metropolis of the Middle West, the meaning is that throughout this area Chicago newspapers circulate, and Chicago banks hold the banking reserves; that in Chicago are the chief offices of the large industrial enterprises, and the market for their products. New ideas in government, in civic improvement, in the creation and maintenance of parks, and pleasure grounds are apt to appear first in the metropolis, spreading thence to the surrounding country. On high-days and holidays the great city allures the people from the neighboring parts, and sends its own people on the water or into the country for rest and refreshment, so that there is a constant interchange of comers and goers. In the art schools of Chicago more than four thousand students are gathered; the theaters draw audiences from long distances, and in music Chicago is attaining a worthy position. In Chicago great political conventions are held, party policies are determined, and from the party headquarters here national campaigns are conducted.

It is not in the spirit of boasting that these facts are stated, but rather to show the responsibility which the very pre-eminence of the city imposes, and the necessity for establishing and maintaining those standards of commercial integrity, of taste, and of knowledge which are the prerequisites of lasting success, and the only real satisfaction of the human mind. The constant struggle of civilization is to know and to attain the highest good; and the city which brings about the best conditions of life becomes the most prosperous.

While the influence of Chicago extends throughout a domain larger than any European country except Russia, there exist between this city and outlying towns within a certain radius vital and almost organic relations. The steam and the trolley railways and the automobile have opened to the city workers all varieties of life, and have made possible to a large proportion of the people a habitation amid what might be healthful and attractive surroundings. Unfortunately, however, conditions near any rapidly growing city are apt to be both squalid and ugly.

Occasionally a suburb grows up at some sightly point on the Lake shore, or gathers about some educational institution; or a group of people engaged in a common enterprise select a picturesque spot on river banks and there build homes which, by their very relations one to another, indicate neighborliness. In each of these instances a community of feeling pervades the place and finds expression in well-shaded streets, broad lawns, and homelike architecture. Too often, however, the suburb is laid out by the speculative real estate agent who exerts himself to make every dollar invested turn into as many dollars as possible. Human ingenuity contrives to crowd the maximum number of building lots into the minimum space; if native trees exist on the land they are ruthlessly sacrificed. Then the speculative builder takes matters in hand and in a few months the narrow, grassless streets are lined with rows of cheaply constructed dwellings, and with ugly apartment houses occupying the more desirable sites. In ten years or less the dwellings are dropping to pieces; and the apartment houses, having lost their newness, become rookeries.

This manner of things is as true of London or of Rome as of Chicago; it is the rule wherever population increases rapidly, because human nature is alike the world over. England, however, is remedying this evil by means of town-planning laws executed by a central board; and is endeavoring to regulate the width and direction of streets, and to provide for sufficient open spaces for the health and convenience of the people. After the English manner, a commission should be appointed to lay out all that territory adjacent to the city of Chicago which is likely to become incorporated in the city at least during the next decade. ...

While good highways are of great value to the terminal cities, they are of even greater value to the outlying towns, and of greatest value to the farming communities through which they pass. Good roads add an element of better living to an agricultural community; they afford ready communication with the city and reduce materially the cost of handling farm products of all kinds; and also they promote communication between farms. These state highways should invariably include a work-road for heavy loads, and also a pleasure drive. The two should be separated by a grassway and there should be grass plots at the sides, and not less than three rows of trees should be planted. The country schools should be on these highways. ...

A satisfactory method of running highways is to parallel the railroads. The work-road should be next to the right-of-way; then should come the carriage driveway. Where electric railways exist, or are projected on thoroughfares, the most agreeable treatment if found in setting apart for the tracks a space which may be grassed over and well shaded. Besides adding to the comfort of the passengers, the uninterrupted use of the tracks permits high speed and thereby saves time. The improvement of the three roadways as a unit, with the appropriate planting, would give a charm to suburban travel where now there is none, while at the same time expenses of maintenance would be lessened. As a rule, the creation of highways along railroads involves only the bare cost of inexpensive land and the building of the road. The railroads are in themselves great diagonals; and by following them the shortest lines between important points are secured. Then, too, the right-of-way traversed by the tracks should be improved. The drainage should be perfect, so that pools of stagnant water shall not be an offense to the eye and a menace to health. The unsightly billboard should be replaced by shrubbery or by a wall; and the entire space should be free from the litter of papers or the accumulations of dirt and ashes.

The suburban resident is vitally interested in the means of communication between his home and his place of business. If his morning and his evening ride are made on the steam railway, he is interested not only in passing through pleasant scenes on his way to and from Chicago, but he is concerned also in having the railway station in his suburban town conveniently located, constructed simply but artistically, and placed amid surroundings which in themselves are harmonious and appropriate. A well-kept lawn, with shrubbery shutting out the necessarily unpleasant feature of a steam railway station; a sheltered platform well lighted at night, and a commodious station, architecturally in good taste—these accessories go a long way towards mitigating the nerve strain which every business man feels and from which too many suffer.

The electric railroads, with their frequent cars passing one's very door, have done a vast deal to bind the outlying towns firmly to the central city. More than this, they have promoted neighborliness among people of adjoining towns, and have broken up the isolation of farm life. These roads now strive to obtain private rights-of-way, excepting where for the convenience of passengers they pass through city streets; and the same observations as to good order along the routes and at the terminals that appertain to steam roads apply equally to trolley lines.

The rapidly increasing use of the automobile promises to carry on the good work begun by the bicycle in the days of its popularity in promoting good roads and reviving the roadside inn as a place of rest and refreshment. With the perfection of this machine, and the extension of its use, out-of-door life is promoted, and the pleasures of suburban life are brought within the reach of multitudes of people who formerly were condemned to pass their entire time in the city.

The Chicago Park System

Chicago, on becoming a city, choose for its motto *Urbs in horto*—a city set in a garden. Such indeed it then was, with the opalescent waters of the Lake at its front, and on its three sides the boundless prairie carpeted with waving grass bedecked with brilliant wild flowers. The quick advance of commerce and manufacturers, the rapid building of railroads and factories, and the hastily constructed homes of operatives crowded out nature's parterres of flowers. Still the motto lingered in the minds of men, and in 1839 the struggle began to secure for the fast-growing population park spaces which should at least recall the gardens that of necessity had been sacrificed. ...

Next in the importance to the development of the Lake shore possibilities is the acquisition and improvement of forest spaces. Both the water front and the near-by woodlands should be brought within easy reach of all the people, and especially of the wage-earners. Natural scenery furnishes the contrasting element to the artificiality of the city. All of us should often run away from the works of men's hands and back into the wilds, where mind and body are restored to a normal condition, and we are enabled to take up the burden of life in our crowded streets and endless stretches of buildings with renewed vigor and hopefulness. Those who have the means and are so placed in their daily employments that they can do so constantly seek the refreshment of the country. Should not the public see to it that every one may enjoy this change of scene, this restorer of bodily and mental vigor, and will not citizenship be better thereby? He who habitually comes in close contact with nature develops saner methods of thought than can be the case when one is habitually shut up within the walls of a city. If a census of the purposes and acts of all of the people of Chicago as they affect the general good could be made for this year of grace 1909, and again in 1933, after the creation of extensive forests in the suburbs, the percentage of improvement affecting the whole community would probably be quite surprising. The existing public parks go far in this direction, but not far enough. The spaces to be acquired should be wild forests, filled with such trees, vines, flowers, and shrubs as will grow in this climate, and all should be developed in a natural condition. Country roads and a few paths should run through these forests, but they should not be cut into small divisions. There should be open glades here and there, and other natural features, and the people should be allowed to use them freely. ...

Transportation

This report does not go into details of the roadways and stations, either trunk or intramural. Routes are suggested which seem to be the natural and logical ones. The expert engineers will find the best solutions of the constructive and mechanical problems as they arise. But all citizens are interested to see that the best and most comprehensive general schemes shall be adopted, and that in carrying out of any one of them, every detail shall be designed and executed with regard to its effect on the senses as well as on the basis of mere mechanical or constructive excellence. A million Chicago people who habitually use railway facilities will possess a higher average of good citizenship when the irritation of nerves is reduced to the minimum, and within a few years most of the waking hours of a million Americans will be spent in the business center of Chicago, where unpleasant sights and sounds should be abolished. The community will get far more out of its million workers when their nerves cease to be wracked by irritating conditions.

Again, the noise of surface and elevated road cars is often excruciating. It is not denied that this evil can be largely mitigated. These conditions actually cause misery to a large majority of people who are subjected to the constant strain, and in addition they undoubtedly cause a heavy aggregate loss of money to the business community. For the sake of the state, the citizen should be at his best, and it is the business of the state to maintain conditions conducive to his bodily welfare. Noises, ugly sights, ill smells, as well as dirty streets and workshops or offices, tend to lower average efficiency. It does not pay the state to allow them to continue. Moreover, citizens have pride in and loyalty to a city that is quiet, clean, and generally beautiful. It is not believed that "business" demands that our present annoying conditions be continued. In a state of good order all business must be done better and more profitably. With things as they should be, every business man in Chicago would make more money than he does now....

Streets Within the City

...Paris is the international capital because in its planning the universal mind recognizes that complete articulation which satisfies the craving for good order and symmetry in every part.

If Chicago were to be relocated to-day, it would still be placed at the spot where it now is; and if the streets were again to be mapped, the same general system would be adopted, because the present rectilinear street system best comports with the line of the Lake front which nature has unalterably fixed. The rectilinear system certainly accords with the ideas of rightness inherent in the human mind; and also it involvs a minimum waste of ground space. Moreover, the River, for the most part, allows the use of the right-angled system without playing havoc with the orderly arrangement of the streets. It is only when and as the city increases in population that diagonals become necessary in order to save considerable amounts of time and to prevent congestion by dividing and segregating the traffic. Thus it happens that no rectilinear city is perfect without the diagonal streets; and conversely, having the rectilinear system, the creation of diagonals produces the greatest convenience.

Now, while it happens that the planning of a new city imposes straightness as a duty, and diagonals as a necessity, it is equally true that a virtue should be made of these hard-and-fast conditions. There is a true glory in mere length, in vistas longer than the eye can reach, in roads of arrow-like purpose that speed unswerving in their flight; and when and where the opportunity of level ground permits, this glory should be sought after. Older cities may indeed bend and curve their new streets to preserve what is picturesque or historic; but new cities, built on level country, should see to it that as subdivisions are platted, the streets and avenues shall be adequate to bear the traffic which will come to them from the city itself, and that such thoroughfares shall form an integral part of the entire system of circulation.

At the same time the elliptical avenue may be used to introduce variety, and especially to serve as a link to connect parks. Chicago had no encircling fortifications to turn into boulevards such as those which beautify and distinguish the cities of Vienna, Brussels, Rouen, Milan, and especially Paris; but such avenues may well be created in order to relieve the monotony of the straight streets....

120

Twenty Years at Hull-House

JANE ADDAMS

Jane Addams (1860–1935) was one of the leading American figures in social concerns and women's rights. Her central achievement remains the establishment of Hull House (1889) in Chicago (which is still standing). Hull House was a settlement establishment and achieved an international reputation, especially in relation to Addams's consistent fight against poverty and urban deprivation. In 1931 she was awarded the Nobel Peace Prize. *Twenty Years at Hull House* (1910) is a remarkable record of both a continuing commitment to change urban conditions for the better, and an intimate portrait of life (especially immigrant) in a city undergoing rapid change. It was followed by the much less lively *The Second Twenty Years at Hull House* (1931). What follows are extracts only.

. . . Halsted Street has grown so familiar during twenty years of residence that it is difficult to recall its gradual changes—the withdrawal of the more prosperous Irish and Germans, and the slow substitution of Russian Jews, Italians, and Greeks. A description of the street such as I gave in those early addresses still stands in my mind as sympathetic and correct.

> Halsted Street is thirty-two miles long, and one of the great thoroughfares of Chicago; Polk Street crosses it midway between the stockyards to the south and the shipbuilding yards on the north branch of the Chicago River. For the six miles between these two industries the street is lined with shops of butchers and grocers, with dingy and gorgeous saloons, and pretentious establishments for the sale of ready-made clothing. Polk Street, running west from Halsted Street, grows rapidly more prosperous; running a mile east to State Street, it grows steadily worse, and crosses a network of vice on the corners of Clark Street and Fifth Avenue. Hull-House once stood in the suburbs, but the city has steadily grown up around it and its site now has corners on three or four foreign colonies. Between Halsted Street and the river live about ten thousand Italians—Neapolitans, Sicilians, and Calabrians, with an occasional Lombard or Venetion. To the south on Twelfth Street are many Germans, and side streets are given over almost entirely to Polish and Russian Jews. Still farther

Source: Jane Addams, *Twenty Years at Hull-House*, 1910, New York, pp. 81–98, 125–31, 144–7, 169–85.

south, these Jewish colonies merge into a huge Bohemian colony, so vast that Chicago ranks as the third Bohemian city in the world. To the northwest are many Canadian-French, clannish in spite of their long residence in America, and to the north are Irish and first-generation Americans. On the streets directly west and farther north are well-to-do English-speaking families, many of whom own their houses and have lived in the neighborhood for years; one man is still living in his old farmhouse.

The policy of the public authorities of never taking an initiative and always waiting to be urged to do their duty, is obviously fatal in a neighborhood where there is little initiative among the citizens. The idea underlying our self-government breaks down in such a ward. The streets are inexpressibly dirty, the number of schools inadequate, sanitary legislation unenforced, the street lighting bad, the paving miserable and altogether lacking in the alleys and smaller streets, and the stables foul beyond description. Hundreds of houses are unconnected with the street sewer. The older and richer inhabitants seem anxious to move away as rapidly as they can afford it. They make room for newly arrived immigrants who are densely ignorant of civic duties. This substitution of the older inhabitants is accomplished industrially also, in the south and east quarters of the ward. The Jews and Italians for the finishing for the great clothing manufacturers, formerly done by Americans, Irish, and Germans, who refused to submit to the extremely low prices to which the sweating system has reduced their successors. As the design of the sweating system is the elimination of rent from the manufacture of clothing, the "outside work" is begun after the clothing leaves the cutter. An unscrupulous contractor regards no basement as too dark, no stable loft too foul, no rear shanty too provisional, no tenement room too small for his workroom, as these conditions imply low rental. Hence these shops abound in the worst of the foreign districts where the sweater easily finds his cheap basement and his home finishers.

The houses of the ward, for the most part wooden, were originally built for the one family and are now occupied by several. They are after the type of the inconvenient frame cottages found in the poorer suburbs twenty years ago. Many of them were built where they now stand; others were brought thither on rollers, because their previous sites had been taken for factories. The fewer brick tenement buildings which are three or four stories high are comparatively new, and there are few large tenements. The little wooden houses have a temporary aspect, and for this reason, perhaps, the tenement-house legislation in Chicago is totally inadequate. Rear tenements flourish; many houses have no water supply save the faucet in the back yard, there are no fire escapes, the garbage and ashes are placed in wooden boxes which are fastened to the street pavements. One of the most discouraging features about the present system of tenement houses is that many are owned by sordid and ignorant immigrants. The theory that wealth brings responsibility, that possession entails at length education and refinement, in these cases fails utterly. The children of an Italian immigrant owner may "shine" shoes in the streets, and his wife may pick rags from the street gutter, laboriously sorting them in a dingy court. Wealth may do something for her self-complacency and feeling of consequence; it certainly does nothing for her comfort or her children's improvement nor for the cleanliness of anyone concerned. Another thing that prevents better houses in Chicago is the tentative attitude of the real estate men. Many unsavory conditions are allowed to continue which would be regarded with horror if they were considered permanent. Meanwhile, the wretched conditions persist until at least two generations of children have been born and reared in them.

In every neighborhood where poorer people live, because rents are supposed to be cheaper there, is an element which, although uncertain in the individual, in the aggregate can be counted upon. It is composed of people of former education and

> opportunity who have cherished ambitions and prospects, but who are caricatures of what they meant to be—"hollow ghosts which blame the living men." There are times in many lives when there is a cessation of energy and loss of power. Men and women of education and refinement come to live in a cheaper neighborhood because they lack the ability to make money, because of ill health, because of an unfortunate marriage, or for other reasons which do not imply criminality or stupidity. Among them are those who, in spite of untoward circumstances, keep up some sort of an intellectual life; those who are "great for books," as their neighbors say. To such the Settlement may be a genuine refuge.

In the very first weeks of our residence Miss Starr started a reading party in George Eliot's *Romola*, which was attended by a group of young women who followed the wonderful tale with unflagging interest. The weekly reading was held in our little upstairs dining room, and two members of the club came to dinner each week, not only that they might be received as guests, but that they might help us wash the dishes afterward and so make the table ready for the stacks of Florentine photographs.

Our "first resident," as she gaily designated herself, was a charming old lady who gave five consecutive readings from Hawthorne to a most appreciative audience, interspersing the magic tales most delightfully with recollections of the elusive and fascinating author. Years before she had lived at Brook Farm as a pupil of the Ripleys, and she came to us for ten days because she wished to live once more in an atmosphere where "idealism ran high." We thus early found the type of class which through all the years has remained most popular—a combination of a social atmosphere with serious study....

As these clubs have been continued during the twenty years they have developed classes in the many forms of handicraft which the newer education is so rapidly adapting for the delight of children; but they still keep their essentially social character and still minister to that large number of children who leave school the very week they are fourteen years old, only too eager to close the schoolroom door forever on a tiresome task that is at last well over. It seems to us important that these children shall find themselves permanently attached to a House that offers them evening clubs and classes with their old companions, that merges as easily as possible the school life into the working life and does what it can to find places for the bewildered young things looking for work. A large proportion of the delinquent boys brought into the juvenile court in Chicago are the oldest sons in large families whose wages are needed at home. The grades from which many of them leave school, as the records show, are piteously far from the seventh and eighth where the very first instruction in manual training is given, nor have they been caught by any other abiding interest.

In spite of these flourishing clubs for children early established at Hull-House, and the fact that our first organized undertaking was a kindergarten, we were very insistent that the Settlement should not be primarily for the children, and that it was absurd to suppose that grown people would not respond to opportunities for education and social life. Our enthusiastic kindergartner herself demonstrated this with an old woman of ninety, who, because she was left alone all day while her daughter cooked in a restaurant, had formed such a persistent habit of picking the plaster off the walls that one landlord after another refused to have her for a tenant. It required but a few weeks' time to teach her to make large paper chains, and gradually she was content to do it all day long, and in the end took quite as much pleasure in adorning the walls as she had formerly taken in demolishing them. Fortunately the landlord had never heard the æsthetic principle that the exposure of basic construction is more desirable than gaudy decoration. In course of time it was discovered that the old woman could speak Gælic, and when one or two grave professors came to see her, the neighborhood was filled with pride that such a wonder lived in their midst. To mitigate life for a woman of ninety was an unfailing refutation of the statement that the Settlement was designed for the young.

On our first New Year's Day at Hull-House we invited the older people in the vicinity, sending a carriage for the most feeble and announcing to all of them that we were going to organize an Old Settlers' Party.

Every New Year's Day since, older people in varying numbers have come together at Hull-House to relate early hardships and to take for the moment the place in the community to which their pioneer life entitles them. Many people who were formerly residents of the vicinity, but whom prosperity has carried into more desirable neighborhoods, come back to these meetings and often confess to each other that they have never since found such kindness as in early Chicago when all its citizens came together in mutual enterprises. Many of these pioneers, so like the men and women of my earliest childhood that I always felt comforted by their presence in the house, were very much opposed to "foreigners," whom they held responsible for a depreciation of property and a general lowering of the tone of the neighborhood. Sometimes we had a chance for championship; I recall one old man, fiercely American, who had reproached me because we had so many "foreign views" on our walls, to whom I endeavored to set forth our hope that the pictures might afford a familiar island to the immigrants in a sea of new and strange impressions. The old settler guest, taken off his guard, replied, "I see; they feel as we did when we saw a Yankee notion from down East"—thereby formulating the dim kinship between the pioneer and the immigrant, both "buffeting the waves of a new development." The older settlers as well as their children throughout the years have given genuine help to our various enterprises for neighborhood improvement, and from their own memories of earlier hardships have made many shrewd suggestions for alleviating the difficulties of that first sharp struggle with untoward conditions....

...I remember one family in which the father had been out of work for this same winter, most of the furniture had been pawned, and as the worn-out shoes could not be replaced the children could not go to school. The mother was ill and barely able to come for the supplies and medicines. Two years later she invited me to supper one Sunday evening in the little home which had been completely restored, and she gave as a reason for the invitation that she couldn't bear to have me remember them as they had been during that one winter, which she insisted, had been unique in her twelve years of married life. She said that it was as she had met me, not as I am ordinarily, but as I should appear misshapen with rheumatism or with a face distorted by neuralgic pain; that it was not fair to judge poor people that way. She perhaps unconsciously illustrated the difference between the relief-station relation to the poor and the Settlement relation to its neighbors, the latter wishing to know them through all the varying conditions of life, to stand by when they are in distress, but by no means to drop intercourse with them when normal prosperity has returned, enabling the relation to become more social and free from economic disturbance.

Possibly something of the same effort has to be made within the Settlement itself to keep its own sense of proportion in regard to the relation of the crowded city quarter to the rest of the country. It was in the spring following this terrible winter, during a journey to meet lecture engagements in California, that I found myself amazed at the large stretches of open country and prosperous towns through which we passed day by day, whose existence I had quite forgotten.

In the latter part of the summer of 1895, I served as a member on a commission appointed by the mayor of Chicago to investigate conditions in the county poorhouse, public attention having become centered on it through one of those distressing stories, which exaggerates the wrong in a public institution while at the same time it reveals conditions which need to be rectified. However necessary publicity is for securing reformed administration, however useful such exposures may be for political purposes, the whole is attended by such a waste of the most precious human emotions, by such a tearing of living tissue, that it can scarcely be endured. Everytime I entered Hull-House during the days of the investigation, I would find waiting for me from twenty to thirty people whose friends and relatives were in the suspected institution, all in such acute distress of mind that to see them was to look upon the victims of deliberate torture. In most cases my visitor would state that it seemed impossible to put their invalids in any other place, but if these stories were true, something must be done. Many of the patients were taken out only to be returned after a few days or weeks to meet the sullen hostility of their attendants and with their own attitude changed from confidence to timidity and alarm.

This piteous dependence of the poor upon the good will of public officials was made clear to us in an early experience with a peasant woman straight from the fields of Germany, whom we met during our first six months at Hull-House. Her four years in America had been spent in patiently carrying water up and down two flights of stairs, and in washing the heavy flannel suits of iron foundry workers. For this her pay had averaged thirty-five cents a day. Three of her daughters had fallen victims to the vice of the city. The mother was bewildered and distressed, but understood nothing. We were able to induce the betrayer of one daughter to marry her; the second, after a tedious lawsuit, supported his child; with the third we were able to do nothing. This woman is now living with her family in a little house seventeen miles from the city. She has made two payments on her land and is a lesson to all beholders as she pastures her cow up and down the railroad tracks and makes money from her ten acres. She did not need charity for she had an immense capacity for hard work, but she sadly needed the service of the State's attorney office, enforcing the laws designed for the protection of such girls as her daughters.

We early found ourselves spending many hours in efforts to secure support for deserted women, insurance for bewildered widows, damages for injured operators, furniture from the clutches of the instalment store. The Settlement is valuable as an information and interpretation bureau. It constantly acts between the various institutions of the city and the people for whose benefit these institutions were erected. The hospitals, the county agencies, and State asylums are often but vague rumors to the people who need them most. Another function of the Settlement to its neighborhood resembles that of the big brother whose mere presence on the playground protects the little one from bullies.

We early learned to know the children of hard-driven mothers who went out to work all day, sometimes leaving the little things in the casual care of a neighbor, but often locking them into their tenement rooms. The first three crippled children we encountered in the neighborhood had all been injured while their mothers were at work: one had fallen out of a third-story window, another had been burned, and the third had a curved spine due to the fact that for three years he had been tied all day long to the leg of the kitchen table, only released at noon by his older brother who hastily ran in from a neighboring factory to share his lunch with him. When the hot weather came the restless children could not brook the confinement of the stuffy rooms, and, as it was not considered safe to leave the doors open because of sneak thieves, many of the children were locked out. During our first summer an increasing number of these poor little mites would wander into the cool hallway of Hull-House. We kept them there and fed them at noon, in return for which we were sometimes offered a hot penny which had been held in a tight little fist "ever since mother left this morning, to buy something to eat with." Out of kindergarten hours our little guests noisily enjoyed the hospitality of our bedrooms under the so-called care of any resident who volunteered to keep an eye on them, but later they were moved into a neighboring apartment under more systematic supervision.

Hull-House was thus committed to a day nursery which we sustained for sixteen years first in a little cottage on a side street and then in a building designed for its use called the Children's House. It is now carried on by the United Charities of Chicago in a finely equipped building on our block, where the immigrant mothers are cared for as well as the children, and where they are taught the things which will make life in America more possible. Our early day nursery brought us into natural relations with the poorest women of the neighborhood, many of whom were bearing the bearing the burden of dissolute and incompetent husbands in addition to the support of their children. Some of them presented an impressive manifestation of that miracle of affection which outlives abuse, neglect, and crime,—the affection which cannot be plucked from the heart where it has lived, although it may serve only to torture and torment. "Has your husband come back?" you inquire of Mrs. S., whom you have known for eight years as an overworked woman bringing her three delicate children every morning to the nursery; she is bent under the double burden of earning the money which supports them and giving them the tender care which alone keeps them alive. The oldest two children have at last gone to work, and Mrs. S. has allowed herself the luxury of staying at home two days a week. And now the worthless husband is back again—the "gentlemanly gambler" type who, through all vicissitudes, manages to present a white shirtfront and a gold watch to the world, but who is dissolute, idle and extravagant. You dread to think how much his presence will increase the drain upon the family exchequer, and you know that he stayed away until he was certain that the children were old enough to earn money for his luxuries. Mrs. S. does not pretend to take his return lightly, but she replies in all seriousness and simplicity, "You know my feeling for him has never changed. You may think me foolish, but I was always proud of his good looks and educated appearance. I was lonely and homesick during those eight years when the children were little and needed so much doctoring, but I could never bring myself to feel hard toward him, and I used to pray the good Lord to keep him from harm and bring him back to us; so, of course, I'm thankful now." She passes on with a dignity which gives one a new sense of the security of affection.

I recall a similar case of a woman who had supported her three children for five years, during which time her dissolute husband constantly demanded money for drink and kept her perpetually worried and intimidated. One Saturday, before the "blessed Easter," he came back from a long debauch, ragged and filthy, but in a state of lachrymose repentance. The poor wife received him as a returned prodigal, believed that his remorse would prove lasting, and felt sure that if she and the children went to church with him on Easter Sunday and he could be induced to take the pledge before the priest, all their troubles would be ended. After hours of vigorous effort and the expenditure of all her savings, he finally sat on the front doorstep the morning of Easter Sunday, bathed, shaved and arrayed in a fine new suit of clothes. She left him sitting there in the reluctant spring sunshine while she finished washing and dressing the children. When she finally opened the front door with the three shining children that they might all set forth together, the returned prodigal had disappeared, and was not seen again until midnight, when he came back in a glorious state of intoxication from the proceeds of his pawned clothes and clad once more in the dingiest attire. She took him in without comment, only to begin again the wretched cycle. There were of course instances of the criminal husband as well as of the merely vicious. I recall one woman who, during seven years, never missed a visiting day at the penitentiary when she might see her husband, and whose little children in the nursery proudly reported the messages from father with no notion that he was in disgrace, so absolutely did they reflect the gallant spirit of their mother.

While one was filled with admiration for these heroic women, something was also to be said for some of the husbands, for the sorry men who, for one reason or another, had failed in the struggle of life. Sometimes this failure was purely economic and the men were competent to give the children, whom they were not able to support, the care and guidance and even education which were of the highest value. Only a few months ago I met upon the street one of the early nursery mothers who for five years had been living in another part of the city, and in response to my query as to the welfare of her five children, she bitterly replied, "All of them except Mary have been arrested at one time or another, thank you." In reply to my remark that I thought her husband had always had such admirable control over them, she burst out, "That has been the whole trouble. I got tired taking care of him and didn't believe that his laziness was all due to his health, as he said, so I left him and said that I would support the children, but not him. From that minute the trouble with the four boys began. I never knew what they were doing, and after every sort of a scrape I finally put Jack and the twins into institutions where I pay for them. Joe has gone to work at last, but with a disgraceful record behind him. I tell you I ain't so sure that because a woman can make big money that she can be both father and mother to her children."

As I walked on, I could but wonder in which particular we are most stupid—to judge a man's worth so solely by his wage-earning capacity that a good wife feels justified in leaving him, or in holding fast to that wretched delusion that a woman can both support and nurture her children.

One of the most piteous revelations of the futility of the latter attempt came to me through the mother of "Goosie," as the children for years called a little boy who, because he was brought to the nursery wrapped up in his mother's shawl, always had his hair filled with the down and small feathers from the feathers brush factory where she worked. One March morning, Goosie's mother was hanging out the washing on a shed roof before she left for the factory. Five-year-old Goosie was trotting at her heels handing her clothespins, when he was suddenly blown off the roof by the high wind into the alley below. His neck was broken by the fall, and as he lay piteous and limp on a pile of frozen refuse, his mother cheerily called him to "climb up again," so confident do overworked mothers become that their children cannot get hurt. After the funeral, as the poor mother sat in the nursery postponing the moment when she must go back to her empty rooms, I asked her, in a futile effort to be of comfort, if there was anything more we could do for her. The overworked, sorrow-stricken woman looked up and replied, "If you could give me my wages for tomorrow, I would not go to work in the factory at all. I would like to stay at home all day and hold the baby. Goosie was always asking me to take him and I never had any time." This statement revealed the condition of many nursery mothers who are obliged to forego the joys and solaces which belong to even the most poverty-stricken. The long hours of factory labor necessary for earning the support of a child leave no time for the tender care and caressing which may enrich the life of the most piteous baby.

With all of the efforts made by modern society to nurture and educate the young, how stupid it is to permit the mothers of young children to spend themselves in the coarser work of the world! It is curiously inconsistent that with the emphasis which this generation has placed upon the mother and upon the prolongation of infancy, we constantly allow the waste of this most precious material. I cannot recall without indignation a recent experience. I was detained late one evening in an office building by a prolonged committee meeting of the Board of Education. As I came out at eleven o'clock, I met in the corridor of the fourteenth floor a woman whom I knew, on her knees scrubbing the marble tiling. As she straightened up to greet me, she seemed so wet from her feet up to her chin, that I hastily inquired the cause. Her reply was that she left home at five o'clock every night and had no opportunity for six hours to nurse her baby. Her mother's milk mingled with the very water with which she scrubbed the floors until she should return at midnight, heated and exhausted, to feed her screaming child with what remained within her breasts.

These are only a few of the problems connected with the lives of the poorest people with whom the residents in a Settlement are constantly brought in contact....

At any rate the residents at Hull-House discovered that while their first impact with city poverty allied them to groups given over to discussion of social theories, their sober efforts to heal neighborhood ills allied them to general public movements which were without challenging creeds. But while we discovered that we most easily secured the smallest of much-needed improvements by attaching our efforts to those of organized bodies, nevertheless these very organizations would have been impossible, had not the public conscience been aroused and the community sensibility quickened by these same ardent theorists.

As I review these very first impressions of the workers in unskilled industries, living in a depressed quarter of the city, I realize how easy it was for us to see exceptional cases of hardship as typical of the average lot, and yet, in spite of alleviating phalanthropy and labor legislation, the indictment of Tolstoy applied to Moscow thirty years ago still fits every American city: "Wherever we may live, if we draw a circle around us of a hundred thousand, or a thousand, or even of ten miles circumference, and look at the lives of those men and women who are inside our circle, we shall find half-starved children, old people, pregnant women, sick and weak persons, working beyond their strength, who have neither food nor rest enough to support them, and who, for this reason, die before their time; we shall see others, full-grown, who are injured and needlessly killed by dangerous and hurtful tasks."

As the American city is awakening to self-consciousness, it slowly perceives the civic significance of these industrial conditions, and perhaps Chicago has been foremost in the effort to connect the unregulated overgrowth of the huge centers of population, with the astonishingly rapid development of industrial enterprises; quite as Chicago was foremost to carry on the preliminary discussion through which a basis was laid for like-mindedness and the coördination of diverse wills. I remember an astute English visitor, who had been a guest in a score of American cities, observed that it was hard to understand the local pride he constantly encountered; for in spite of the boasting on the part of leading citizens in the western, eastern, and southern towns, all American cities seemed to him essentially alike and all equally the results of an industry totally unregulated by well-considered legislation.

I am inclined to think that perhaps all this general discussion was inevitable in connection with the early Settlements, as they in turn were the inevitable result of theories of social reform, which in their full enthusiasm reached America by way of England, only in the last decade of the century. There must have been tough fiber somewhere; for, although the residents of Hull-House were often baffled by the radicalism within the Social Science Club and harassed by the criticism from outside, we still continued to believe that such discussion should be carried on, for if the Settlement seeks its expression through social activity, it must learn the difference between mere social unrest and spiritual impulse.

The group of Hull-House residents, which by the end of the decade comprised twenty-five, differed widely in social beliefs, from the girl direct from the country who looked upon all social unrest as mere anarchy, to the resident, who had become a socialist when a student in Zurich, and who had long before translated from the German Engel's *Conditions of the Working Class in England*, although at this time she had been read out of the Socialist Party because the Russian and German Impossibilists suspected her fluent English, as she always lightly explained. Although thus diversified in social beliefs, the residents became solidly united through our mutual experience in an industrial quarter, and we became not only convinced of the need for social control and protective legislation but also of the value of this preliminary argument.

This decade of discussion between 1890 and 1900 already seems remote from the spirit of Chicago of today. So far as I have been able to reproduce this earlier period, it must reflect the essential provisionality of everything; "the perpetual moving on to something future which shall supersede the present," that paramount impression of life itself, which affords us at one and the same time, ground for despair and for endless and varied anticipation....

Immigrants and Their Children

From our very first months at Hull-House we found it much easier to deal with the first generation of crowded city life than with the second or third, because it is more natural and cast in a simpler mold. The Italian and Bohemian peasants who live in Chicago still put on their bright holiday clothes on a Sunday and go to visit their cousins. They tramp along with at least a suggestion of having once walked over plowed fields and breathed country air. The second generation of city poor too often have no holiday clothes and consider their relations a "bad lot." I have heard a drunken man in a maudlin stage babble of his good country mother and imagine he was driving the cows home, and I knew that his little son who laughed loud at him would be drunk earlier in life and would have no pastoral interlude to his ravings. Hospitality still survives among foreigners, although it is buried under false pride among the poorest Americans. One thing seemed clear in regard to entertaining immigrants; to preserve and keep whatever of value their past life contained and to bring them in contact with a better type of Americans. For several years, every Saturday evening the entire families of our Italian neighbors were our guests. These evenings were very popular during our first winters at Hull-House. Many educated Italians helped us, and the house became known as a place where Italians were welcome and where national holidays were observed. They come to us with their petty lawsuits, sad relics of the vendetta, with their incorrigible boys, with their hospital cases, with their aspirations for American clothes, and with their needs for an interpreter.

An editor of an Italian paper made a genuine connection between us and the Italian colony, not only with the Neapolitans and the Sicilians of the immediate neighborhood, but with the educated *connazionali* throughout the city, until he went south to start an agricultural colony in Alabama, in the establishment of which Hull-House heartily coöperated.

Possibly the South Italians more than any other immigrants represent the pathetic stupidity of agricultural people crowded into city tenements, and we were much gratified when thirty peasant families were induced to move upon the land which they knew so well how to cultivate. The starting of this colony, however, was a very expensive affair in spite of the fact that the colonists purchased the land at two dollars an acre; they needed much more than raw land, and although it was possible to collect the small sums necessary to sustain them during the hard time of the first two years, we were fully convinced that undertaking of this sort could be conducted properly only by colonization societies such as England has established, or, better still, by enlarging the functions of the Federal Department of Immigration.

An evening similar in purpose to the one devoted to the Italians was organized for the Germans, in our first year. Owing to the superior education of our Teutonic guests and the clever leading of a cultivated German woman, these evenings reflected something of that cozy social intercourse which is found in its perfection in the fatherland. Our guests sang a great deal in the tender minor of the German folksong or in the rousing spirit of the Rhine, and they slowly but persistently pursued a course in German history and literature, recovering something of that poetry and romance which they had long since resigned with other good things. We found strong family affection between them and their English-speaking children, but their pleasures were not in common, and they seldom went out together. Perhaps the greatest value of the Settlement to them was in placing large and pleasant rooms with musical facilities at their disposal, and in reviving their almost forgotten enthusiasms. I have seen sons and daughters stand in complete surprise as their mother's knitting needles softly beat time to the song she was singing, or her worn face turned rosy under the hand-clapping as she made an old-fashioned curtsy at the end of a German poem. It was easy to fancy a growing touch of respect in her children's manner to her, and a rising enthusiasm for German literature and reminiscence on the part of all the family, an effort to bring together the old life and the new, a respect for the older cultivation, and not quite so much assurance that the new was the best.

This tendency upon the part of the older immigrants to lose the amenities of European life without sharing those of America has often been deplored by keen observers from the home countries. When Professor Masurek of Prague gave a course of lectures in the University of Chicago, he was much distressed over the materialism into which the Bohemians of Chicago had fallen. The early immigrants had been so stirred by the opportunity to own real estate, an appeal perhaps to the Slavic land hunger, and their energies had become so completely absorbed in money-making that all other interests had apparently dropped away. And yet I recall a very touching incident in connection with a lecture Professor Masurek gave at Hull-House, in which he had appealed to his countrymen to arouse themselves from this tendency to fall below their home civilization and to forget the great enthusiasm which had united them into the Pan-Slavic Movement. A Bohemian widow who supported herself and her two children by scrubbing, hastily sent her youngest child to purchase, with the twenty-five cents which was to have supplied them with food the next day, a bunch of red roses which she presented to the lecturer in appreciation of his testimony to the reality of the things of the spirit.

An overmastering desire to reveal the humbler immigrant parents to their own children lay at the base of what has come to be called the Hull-House Labor Museum. This was first suggested to my mind one early spring day when I saw an old Italian woman, her distaff against her homesick face, patiently spinning a thread by the simple stick spindle so reminiscent of all southern Europe. I was walking down Polk Street, perturbed in spirit, because it seemed so difficult to come into genuine relations with the Italian women and because they themselves so often lost their hold upon their Americanized children. It seemed to me that Hull-House ought to be able to devise some educational enterprise which should build a bridge between European and American experiences in such wise as to give them both more meaning and a sense of relation. I meditated that perhaps the power to see life as a whole is more needed in the immigrant quarter of a large city than anywhere else, and that the lack of this power is the most fruitful source of misunderstanding between European immigrants and their children, as it is between them and their American neighbors; and why should that chasm between fathers and sons, yawning at the feet of each generation, be made so unnecessarily cruel and impassable to these bewildered immigrants? Suddenly I looked up and saw the old woman with her distaff, sitting in the sun on the steps of a tenement house. She might have served as a model for one of Michelangelo's Fates, but her face brightened as I passed and, holding up her spindle for me to see, she called out that when she had spun a little more yarn, she would knit a pair of stockings for her goddaughter. The occupation of the old woman gave me the clue that was needed. Could we not interest the young people working in the neighborhood factories in these older forms of industry, so that, through their own parents and grandparents, they would find a dramatic representation of the inherited resources of their daily occupation. If these young people could actually see that the complicated machinery of the factory had been evolved from simple tools, they might at least make a beginning toward that education which Dr. Dewey defines as "a continuing reconstruction of experience." They might also lay a foundation for reverence of the past which Goethe declares to be the basis of all sound progress.

My exciting walk on Polk Street was followed by many talks with Dr. Dewey and with one of the teachers in his school who was a resident at Hull-House. Within a month a room was fitted up to which we might invite those of our neighbors who were possessed of old crafts and who were eager to use them.

We found in the immediate neighborhood at least four varieties of these most primitive methods of spinning and three distinct variations of the same spindle in connection with wheels. It was possible to put these seven into historic sequence and order and to connect the whole with the present method of factory spinning. The same thing was done for weaving, and on every Saturday evening a little exhibit was made of these various forms of labor in the textile industry. Within one room a Syrian woman, a Greek, an Italian, a Russian, and an Irishwoman enabled even the most casual observer to see that there is no break in orderly evolution if we look at history from the industrial standpoint; that industry develops similarly and peacefully year by year among the workers of each nation, heedless of differences in language, religion, and political experiences.

And then we grew ambitious and arranged lectures upon industrial history. I remember that after an interesting lecture upon the industrial revolution in England and a portrayal of the appalling conditions throughout the weaving districts of the north, which resulted from the hasty gathering of the weavers into the new towns, a Russian tailor in the audience was moved to make a speech. He suggested that whereas time had done much to alleviate the first difficulties in the transition of weaving from hand work to steam power, that in the application of steam to sewing we are still in our first stages, illustrated by the isolated woman who tries to support herself by hand needlework at home until driven out by starvation, as many of the hand weavers had been.

The historical analogy seemed to being a certain comfort to the tailor, as did a chart upon the wall showing the infinitesimal amount of time that steam had been applied to manufacturing processes compared to the centuries of hand labor. Human progress is slow and perhaps never more cruel than in the advance of industry, but is not the worker comforted by knowing that other historical periods have existed similar to the one in which he finds himself, and that the readjustment may be shortened and alleviated by judicious action; and is he not entitled to the solace which an artistic portrayal of the situation might give him? I remember the evening of the tailor's speech that I felt reproached because no poet or artist has endeared the sweaters' victim to us as George Eliot has made us love the belated weaver, Silas Marner. The textile museum is connected directly with the basket weaving, sewing, millinery, embroidery, and dressmaking constantly being taught at Hull-House, and so far as possible with the other educational departments; we have also been able to make a collection of products, of early implements, and of photographs which are full of suggestion. Yet far beyond its direct educational value, we prize it because it so often puts the immigrants into the position of teachers, and we imagine that it affords them a pleasant change from the tutelage in which all Americans, including their own children, are so apt to hold them. I recall a number of Russian women working in a sewing room near Hull-House, who heard one Christmas week that the House was going to give a party to which they might come. They arrived one afternoon, when, unfortunately, there was no party on hand and, although the residents did their best to entertain them with impromptu music and refreshments, it was quite evident that they were greatly disappointed. Finally it was suggested that they be shown the Labor Museum—where gradually the thirty sodden, tired women were transformed. They knew how to use the spindles and were delighted to find the Russian spinning frame. Many of them had never seen the spinning wheel, which has not penetrated to certain parts of Russian, and they regarded it as a new and wonderful invention. They turned up their dressed to show their homespun petticoats; they tried the looms; they explained the difficulty of the old patterns; in short, from having been stupidly entertained, they themselves did the entertaining. Because of a direct appeal to former experiences, the immigrant visitors were able for the moment to instruct their American hostesses in an old and honored craft, as was indeed becoming to their age and experience.

In some such ways as these have the Labor Museum and the shops pointed out the possibilities which Hull-House has scarcely begun to develop, of demonstrating that culture is an understanding of the long-established occupations and thoughts of men, of the arts with which they have solaced their toil. A yearning to recover for the household arts something of their early sanctity and meaning arose strongly within me one evening when I was attending a Passover Feast to which I had been invited by a Jewish family in the neighborhood, where the traditional and religious significance of the woman's daily activity was still retained. The kosher food the Jewish mother spread before her family had been prepared according to traditional knowledge and with constant care in the use of utensils; upon her had fallen the responsibility to make all ready according to Mosaic instructions that the great crisis in a religious history might be fittingly set forth by her husband and son. Aside from the grave religious significance in the ceremony, my mind was filled with shifting pictures of woman's labor with which travel makes one familiar; the Indian women grinding grain outside of their huts as they sing praises to the sun and rain; a file of white-clad Moorish women whom I had once seen waiting their turn at a well in Tangiers; south Italian women kneeling in a row along the stream and beating their wet clothes against the smooth white stones; the milking, the gardening, the marketing in thousands of hamlets, which are such direct expressions of the solicitude and affection at the basis of all family life.

There has been some testimony that the Labor Museum has revealed the charm of woman's primitive activities. I recall a certain Italian girl who came every Saturday evening to a cooking class in the same building in which her mother spun in the Labor Museum exhibit; and yet Angelina always left her mother at the front door while she herself went around to a side door because she did not wish to be too closely identified in the eyes of the rest of the cooking class with an Italian woman who wore a kerchief over her head, uncouth boots, and short petticoats. One evening, however, Angelina saw her mother surrounded by a group of visitors from the School of Education who much admired the spinning, and she concluded from their conversation that her mother was "the best stick-spindle spinner in America." When she inquired from me as to the truth of this deduction, I took occasion to describe the Italian village in which her mother had lived, something of her free life, and how, because of the opportunity she and the other women of the village had to drop their spindles over the edge of a precipice, they had developed a skill in spinning beyond that of the neighboring town. I dilated somewhat on the freedom and beauty of that life—how hard it must be to exchange it all for a two-room tenement, and to give up a beautiful homespun kerchief for an ugly department store hat. I intimated it was most unfair to judge her by these things alone, and that while she must depend on her daughter to learn the new ways, she also had a right to expect her daughter to know something of the old ways.

That which I could not convey to the child, but upon which my own mind persistently dwelt, was that her mother's whole life had been spent in a secluded spot under the rule of traditional and narrowly localized observances, until her very religion clung to local sanctities—to the shrine before which she had always prayed, to the pavement and walls of the low vaulted church—and then suddenly she was torn from it all and literally put out to sea, straight away from the solid habits of her religious and domestic life, and she now walked timidly but with poignant sensibility upon a new and strange shore.

It was easy to see that the thought of her mother with any other background than that of the tenement was new to Angelina, and at least two things resulted; she allowed her mother to pull out of the big box under the bed the beautiful homespun garments which had been previously hidden away as uncouth; and she openly came into the Labor Museum by the same door as did her mother, proud at least of the mastery of the craft which had been so much admired.

A club of necktie workers formerly meeting at Hull-House persistently resented any attempt on the part of their director to improve their minds. The president once said that she "wouldn't be caught dead at a lecture," that she came to the club "to get some fun out of it," and indeed it was most natural that she should crave recreation after a hard day's work. One evening I saw the entire club listening to quite a stiff lecture in the Labor Museum and to my rather wicked remark to the president that I was surprised to see her enjoying a lecture, she replied that she did not call this a lecture, she called this "getting next to the stuff you work with all the time." It was perhaps the sincerest tribute we have ever received as to the success of the undertaking.

The Labor Museum continually demanded more space as it was enriched by a fine textile exhibit lent by the Field Museum, and later by carefully selected specimens of basketry from the Philippines. The shops have finally included a group of three or four women, Irish, Italian, Danish, who have become a permanent working force in the textile department which has developed into a self-supporting industry through the sale of its homespun products.

These women and a few men, who come to the museum to utilize their European skill in pottery, metal, and wood, demonstrate that immigrant colonies might yield to our American life something very valuable, if their resources were intelligently studied and developed. I recall an Italian, who had decorated the doorposts of his tenement with a beautiful pattern he had previously used in carving the reredos of a Neapolitan church, who was "fired" by his landlord on the ground of destroying property. His feelings were hurt, not so much that he had been put out of his house, as that his work had been so disregarded; and he said that when people traveled in Italy they liked to look at wood carvings but that in America "they only made money out of you."

Sometimes the suppression of the instinct of workmanship is followed by more disastrous results. A Bohemian whose little girl attended classes at Hull-House, in one of his periodic drunken spells had literally almost choked her to death, and later had committed suicide when in delirium tremens. His poor wife, who stayed a week at Hull-House after the disaster until a new tenement could be arranged for her, one day showed me a gold ring which her husband had made for their betrothal. It exhibited the most exquisite workmanship, and she said that although in the old country he had been a goldsmith, in America he had for twenty years shoveled coal in a furnace room of a large manufacturing plant; that whenever she saw one of his "restless fits," which preceded his drunken periods, "coming on," if she could provide him with a bit of metal and persuade him to stay at home and work at it, he was all right and the time passed without disaster, but that "nothing else would do it." This story threw a flood of light upon the dead man's struggle and on the stupid maladjustment which had broken him down. Why had we never been told? Why had our interest in the remarkable musical ability of his child blinded us to the hidden artistic ability of the father? We had forgotten that a long-established occupation may form the very foundations of the moral life, that the art with which a man has solaced his toil may be the salvation of his uncertain temperament.

There are many examples of touching fidelity to immigrant parents on the part of their grown children; a young man who day after day attends ceremonies which n o longer express his religious convictions and who makes his vain effort to interest his Russian Jewish father in social problems; a daughter who might earn much more money as a stenographer could she work from Monday morning till Saturday night, but who quietly and docilely makes neckties for low wages because she can thus abstain from work Saturdays to please her father; these young people, like poor Maggie Tulliver, through many painful experiences have reached the conclusion that pity, memory, and faithfulness are natural ties with paramount claims.

This faithfulness, however, is sometimes ruthlessly imposed upon by immigrant parents who, eager for money and accustomed to the patriarchal authority of peasant households, hold their children in a stern bondage which requires a surrender of all their wages and concedes no time or money for pleasures.

There are many convincing illustrations that this parental harshness often results in juvenile delinquency. A Polish boy of seventeen came to Hull-House one day to ask a contribution of fifty cents "towards a flower piece for the funeral of an old Hull-House club boy." A few questions made it clear that the object was fictitious, whereupon the boy broke down and half-defiantly stated that he wanted to buy two twenty-five cent tickets, one for his girl and one for himself, to a dance of the Benevolent Social Twos; that he hadn't a penny of his own although he had worked in a brass foundry for three years and had been advanced twice, because he always had to give his pay envelope unopened to his father; "just look at the clothes he buys me" was his concluding remark.

Perhaps the girls are held even more rigidly. In a recent investigation of two hundred working girls it was found that only five per cent had the use of their own money and that sixty-two per cent turned in all they earned, literally every penny, to their mothers. It was through this little investigation that we first knew Marcella, a pretty young German girl who helped her widowed mother year after year to care for a large family of younger children. She was content for the most part although her mother's old-country notions of dress gave her but an infinitesimal amount of her own wages to spend on her clothes, and she was quite sophisticated as to proper dressing because she sold silk in a neighbourhood department store. Her mother approved of the young man who was showing her various attentions and agreed that Marcella should accept his invitation to a ball, but would allow her not a penny toward a new gown to replace one impossibly plain and shabby. Marcella spent a sleepless night and wept bitterly, although she well knew that the doctor's bill for the children's scarlet fever was not yet paid. The next day as she was cutting off three yards of shining pink silk, the thought came to her that it would make her a fine new waist to wear to the ball. She wistfully saw it wrapped in paper and carelessly stuffed into the muff of the purchaser, when suddenly the parcel fell upon the floor. No one was looking and quick as a flash the girl picked it up and pushed it into her blouse. The theft was discovered by the relentless department store detective who, for "the sake of the example," insisted upon taking the case into court. The poor mother wept bitter tears over this downfall of her "frommes Mädchen" and no one had the heart to tell her of her own blindness.

I know a Polish boy whose earnings were all given to his father who gruffly refused all requests for pocket money. One Christmas his little sisters, having been told by their mother that they were too poor to have any Christmas presents, appealed to the big brother as to one who was earning money of his own. Flattered by the implication, but at the same time quite impecunious, the night before Christmas he nonchalantly walked through a neighboring department store and stole a manicure set for one little sister and string of beads for the other. He was caught at the door by the house detective as one of those children whom each local department store arrests in the weeks before Christmas at the daily rate of eight to twenty. The youngest of these offenders are seldom taken into court but are either sent home with a warning or turned over to the officers of the Juvenile Protective Association. Most of these premature law breakers are in search of Americanized clothing and others are only looking for playthings. They are all distracted by the profusion and variety of the display, and their moral sense is confused by the general air of openhandedness.

These disastrous efforts are not unlike those of many younger children who are constantly arrested for petty thieving because they are too eager to take home food or fuel which will relieve the distress and need they so constantly hear discussed. The coal on the wagons, the vegetables displayed in front of the grocery shops, the very wooden blocks in the loosened street paving are a challenge to their powers to help out at home. A Bohemian boy who was out on parole from the old detention home of the Juvenile Court itself brought back five stolen chickens to the matron for Sunday dinner, saying that he knew the Committee were "having a hard time to fill up so many kids and perhaps these fowl would help out." The honest immigrant parents, totally ignorant of American laws and municipal regulations, often send a child to pick up coal on the railroad tracks or to stand at three o'clock in the morning before the side door of a restaurant which gives away broken food, or to collect grain for the chickens at the base of elevators and standing cars. The latter custom accounts for the large number of boys arrested for breaking the seals on grain freight cars. It is easy for a child thus trained to accept the proportion of a junk dealer to bring him bars of iron stored in freight yards. Four boys quite recently had thus carried away and sold to one man two tons of iron.

Four fifths of the children brought into the Juvenile Court in Chicago are the children of foreigners. The Germans are the greatest offenders, Polish next. Do their children suffer from the excess of virtue in those parents so eager to own a house and lot? One often sees a grasping parent in the court, utterly broken down when the Americanized youth who has been brought to grief clings as piteously to his peasant father as if he were still a frightened little boy in the steerage.

Many of these children have come to grief through their premature fling into city life, having thrown off parental control as they have impatiently discarded foreign ways. Boys of ten and twelve will refuse to sleep at home, preferring the freedom of an old brewery vault or an empty warehouse to the obedience required by their parents, and for days these boys will live on the milk and bread which they steal from the back porches after the early morning delivery. Such children complain that there is "no fun" at home. One little chap who was given a vacant lot to cultivate by the City Garden Association insisted upon raising only popcorn and tried to present the entire crop to Hull-House "to be used for the parties," with the stipulation that he would have "to be invited every single time." Then there are little groups of dissipated young men who pride themselves upon their ability to live without working and who despise all the honest and sober ways of their immigrant parents. They are at once a menace and a center of demoralization. Certainly the bewildered parents, unable to speak English and ignorant of the city, whose children have disappeared for days or weeks, have often come to Hull-House, evincing that agony which fairly separates the marrow from the bone, as if they had discovered a new type of suffering, devoid of the healing in familiar sorrows. It is as if they did not know how to search for the children without the assistance of the children themselves. Perhaps the most pathetic aspect of such cases is their revelation of the premature dependence of the older and wiser upon the young and foolish, which is in itself often responsible for the situation because it has given the children an undue sense of their own importance and a false security that they can take care of themselves.

On the other hand, an Italian girl who has had lessons in cooking at the public school will help her mother to connect the entire family with American food and household habits. That the mother has never baked bread in Italy—only mixed it in her own house and then taken it out to the village oven—makes all the more valuable her daughter's understanding of the complicated cooking stove. The same thing is true of the girl who learns to sew in the public school, and more than anything else, perhaps, of the girl who receives the first simple instruction in the care of little children—that skillful care which every tenement-house baby requires if he is to be pulled through his second summer. As a result of this teaching I recall a young girl who carefully explained to her Italian mother that the reason the babies in Italy were so healthy and the babies in Chicago were so sickly, was not, as her mother had firmly insisted, because her babies in Italy had goat's milk and her babies in America had cow's milk, but because the milk in Italy was clean and the milk in Chicago was dirty. She said that when you milked your own goat before the door, you knew that the milk was clean, but when you bought milk from the grocery store after it had been carried for many miles in the country, you couldn't tell whether it was fit for the baby to drink until the men from the City Hall who had watched it all the way said that it was all right.

Thus through civic instruction in the public schools, the Italian woman slowly became urbanized in the sense in which the word was used by her own Latin ancestors, and thus the habits of her entire family were modified. The public schools in the immigrant colonies deserve all the praise as Americanizing agencies which can be bestowed upon them, and there is little doubt that the fast-changing curriculum in the direction of the vacation-school experiments will react more directly upon such households.

It is difficult to write of the relation of the older and most foreign-looking immigrants to the children of other people—the Italians whose fruitcarts are upset simply because they are "dagoes" or the Russian peddlers who are stoned and sometimes badly injured because it has became a code of honor in a gang of boys to thus express their derision. The members of a Protective Association of Jewish Peddlers organized at Hull-House related daily experiences in which old age had been treated with such irreverence, cherished dignity with such disrespect, that a listener caught the passion of Lear in the old texts, as a platitude enunciated by the man who discovers in it his own experience thrills us as no unfamiliar phrases can possibly do. The Greeks are filled with amazed rage when their very name is flung at them as an opprobrious epithet. Doubtless these difficulties would be much minimized in America, if we faced our own race problem with courage and intelligence, and these very Mediterranean immigrants might give us valuable help. Certainly they are less conscious than the Anglo-Saxon of color distinctions, perhaps because of their traditional familiarity with Carthage and Egypt. They listened with respect and enthusiasm to a scholarly address delivered by Professor Du Bois at Hull-House on Lincoln's birthday, with apparently no consciousness of that race difference which color seems to accentuate so absurdly, and upon my return from various conferences held in the interest of "the advancement of colored people," I have had many illuminating conversations with my cosmopolitan neighbors.

The celebration of national events has always been a source of new understanding and companionship with the members of the contiguous foreign colonies not only between them and their American neighbors but between them and their own children. One of our earliest Italian events was a rousing commemoration of Garibaldi's birthday, and his imposing bust, presented to Hull-House that evening, was long the chief ornament of our front hall. It called forth great enthusiasm from the *connazionali* whom Ruskin calls, not the "common people" of Italy, but the "companion people" because of their power for swift sympathy.

A huge Hellenic meeting held at Hull-House, in which the achievements of the classic period were set forth both in Greek and English by scholars of well-known repute, brought us into a new sense of fellowship with all our Greek neighbors. As the mayor of Chicago was seated upon the right hand of the dignified senior priest of the Greek Church and they were greeted alternately in the national hymns of America and Greece, one felt a curious sense of the possibility of transplanting to new and crude Chicago some of the traditions of Athens itself, so deeply cherished in the hearts of this group of citizens.

The Greeks indeed gravely consider their traditions as their most precious possession and more than once in meetings of protest held by the Greek colony against the aggressions of the Bulgarians in Macedonia, I have heard it urged that the Bulgarians are trying to establish a protectorate, not only for their immediate advantage, but that they may claim a glorious history for the "barbarous country." It is said that on the basis of this protectorate, they are already teaching in their schools that Alexander the Great was a Bulgarian and that it will be but a short time before they claim Aristotle himself, an indignity the Greeks will never suffer!

To me personally the celebration of the hundredth anniversary of Mazzini's birth was a matter of great interest. Throughout the world that day Italians who believed in a United Italy came together. They recalled the hopes of this man who, with all his devotion to his country was still more devoted to humanity and who dedicated to the workingmen of Italy an appeal so philosophical, so filled with a yearning for righteousness, that it transcended all national boundaries and became a bugle call for "The Duties of Man." A copy of this document was given to every school child in the public schools of Italy on this one hundredth anniversary, and as the Chicago branch of the Society of Young Italy marched into our largest hall and presented to Hull-House an heroic bust of Mazzini, I found myself devoutly hoping that the Italian youth, who have committed their future to America, might indeed become "the Apostle of the fraternity of nations" and that our American citizenship might be built without disturbing these foundations which were laid of old time.

⁂121⁂

The Titan

THEODORE DREISER

For an introductory note on Theodore Dreiser, see Chapter 87, in Volume II. *The Titan* (1914) extends *The Financier* (1912) and is the second novel in the trilogy featuring Frank Cowperwood. The setting is Chicago. The final volume of the trilogy, *The Stoic* (1947), brings the "trilogy of desire" to a close.

Chapter I: The New City

When Frank Algernon Cowperwood emerged from the Eastern District Penitentiary in Philadelphia he realized that the old life he had lived in that city since boyhood was ended. His youth was gone, and with it had been lost the great business prospects of his earlier manhood. He must begin again.

It would be useless to repeat how a second panic following upon a tremendous failure—that of Jay Cooke & Co.—had placed a second fortune in his hands. This restored wealth softened him in some degree. Fate seemed to have his personal welfare in charge. He was sick of the stock-exchange, anyhow, as a means of livelihood, and now decided that he would leave it once and for all. He would get in something else—street-railways, land deals, some of the boundless opportunities of the far West. Philadelphia was no longer pleasing to him. Though now free and rich, he was still a scandal to the pretenders, and the financial and social world was not prepared to accept him. He must go his way alone, unaided, or only secretly so, while his quondam friends watched his career from afar. So, thinking of this, he took the train one day, his charming mistress, now only twenty-six, coming to the station to see him off. He looked at her quite tenderly, for she was the quintessence of a certain type of feminine beauty.

"By-by, dearie," he smiled, as the train-bell signaled the approaching departure. "You and I will get out of this shortly. Don't grieve. I'll be back in two or three weeks, or I'll send for you. I'd take you now, only I don't know how that country

Source: Theodore Dreiser, *The Titan*, 1914, New York, Chs. 1–4, 21.

is out there. We'll fix on some place, and then you watch me settle this fortune question. We'll not live under a cloud always. I'll get a divorce, and we'll marry, and things will come right with a bang. Money will do that."

He looked at her with his large, cool, penetrating eyes, and she clasped his cheeks between her hands.

"Oh, Frank," she exclaimed, "I'll miss you so! You're all I have."

"In two weeks," he smiled, as the train began to move, "I'll wire or be back. Be good, sweet."

She followed him with adoring eyes—a fool of love, a spoiled child, a family pet, amorous, eager, affectionate, the type so strong a man would naturally like—she tossed her pretty red gold head and waved him a kiss. Then she walked away with rich, sinuous, healthy strides—the type that men turn to look after.

"That's her—that's that Butler girl," observed one railroad clerk to another. "Gee! a man wouldn't want anything better than that, would he?"

It was the spontaneous tribute that passion and envy invariably pay to health and beauty. On that pivot swings the world.

Never in all his life until this trip had Cowperwood been farther west than Pittsburg. His amazing commercial adventures, brilliant as they were, had been almost exclusively confined to the dull, staid world of Philadelphia, with its sweet refinement in sections, its pretensions to American social supremacy, its cool arrogation of traditional leadership in commercial life, its history, conservative wealth, unctuous respectability, and all the tastes and avocations which these imply. He had, as he recalled, almost mastered that pretty world and made its sacred precincts his own when the crash came. Practically he had been admitted. Now he was an Ishmael, an ex-convict, albeit a millionaire. But wait! The race is to the swift, he said to himself over and over. Yes, and the battle is to the strong. He would test whether the world would trample him under foot or no.

Chicago, when it finally dawned on him, came with a rush on the second morning. He had spent two nights in the gaudy Pullman then provided—a car intended to make up for some of the inconveniences of its arrangements by an over-elaboration of plush and tortured glass—when the first lone outposts of the prairie metropolis began to appear. The side-tracks along the road-bed over which he was speeding became more and more numerous, the telegraph-poles more and more hung with arms and strung smoky-thick with wires. In the far distance, cityward, was, here and there, a lone working-man's cottage, the home of some adventurous soul who had planted his bare hut thus far out in order to reap the small but certain advantage which the growth of the city would bring.

The land was flat—as flat as a table—with a waning growth of brown grass left over from the previous year, and stirring faintly in the morning breeze. Underneath were signs of the new green—the New Year's flag of its disposition. For some reason a crystalline atmosphere enfolded the distant hazy outlines of the city, holding the latter like a fly in amber and giving it an artistic subtlety which touched him. Already a devotee of art, ambitious for connoisseurship, who had had his joy, training, and sorrow out of the collection he had made and lost in Philadelphia, he appreciated almost every suggestion of a delightful picture in nature.

The tracks, side by side, were becoming more and more numerous. Freight-cars were assembled here by thousands from all parts of the country—yellow, red, blue, green, white. (Chicago, he recalled, already had thirty railroads terminating here, as though it were the end of the world.) The little low one and two story houses, quite new as to wood, were frequently unpainted and already smoky—in places grimy. At grade-crossings, where ambling street-cars and wagons and muddy-wheeled buggies waited, he noted how flat the streets were, how unpaved, how sidewalks went up and down rhythmically—here a flight of steps, a veritable platform before a house, there a long stretch of boards laid flat on the mud of the prairie itself. What a city! Presently a branch of the filthy, arrogant, self-sufficient little Chicago River came into view, with its mass of sputtering tugs, its black, oily water, its tall, red, brown, and green grain-elevators, its immense black coal-pockets and yellowish-brown lumber-yards.

Here was life; he saw it at a flash. Here was a seething city in the making. There was something dynamic in the very air which appealed to his fancy. How different, for some reason, from Philadelphia! That was a stirring city, too. He had thought it wonderful at one time, quite a world; but this thing, while obviously infinitely worse, was better. It was more youthful, more hopeful. In a flare of morning sunlight pouring between two coal-pockets, and because the train had stopped to let a bridge swing and half a dozen in either direction—he saw a group of Irish stevedores idling on the bank of a lumber-yard whose wall skirted the water. Healthy men they were, in blue or red shirt-sleeves, stout straps about their waists, short pipes in their mouths, fine, hardy, nutty-brown specimens of humanity. Why were they so appealing, he asked himself. This raw, dirty town seemed naturally to compose itself into stirring artistic pictures. Why, it fairly sang! The world was young here. Life was doing something new. Perhaps he had better not go on to the Northwest at all; he would decide that question later.

In the mean time he had letters of introduction to distinguished Chicagoans, and these he would present. He wanted to talk to some bankers and grain and commission men. The stock-exchange of Chicago interested him, for the intricacies of that business he knew backward and forward, and some great grain transactions had been made here.

The train finally rolled past the shabby backs of houses into a long, shabbily covered series of platforms—sheds having only roofs—and amidst a clatter of trucks hauling trunks, and engines belching steam, and passengers hurrying to and fro he made his way out into Canal Street and hailed a waiting cab—one of a long line of vehicles that bespoke a metropolitan spirit. He had fixed on the Grand Pacific as the most important hotel—the one with the most social significance—and thither he asked to be driven. On the way he studied these streets as in the matter of art he would have studied a picture. The little yellow, blue, green, white, and brown street-cars which he saw trundling here and there, and tired, bony horses, jingling bells at their throats, touched him. They were flimsy affairs, these cars, merely highly varnished kindling-wood with bits of polished brass and glass stuck about them, but he realized what fortunes they portended if the city grew. Street-cars, he knew, were his natural vocation. Even more than stock-brokerage, even more than banking, even more than stock-organization he loved the thought of street-cars and the vast manipulative life it suggested.

Chapter II: A Reconnoiter

The city of Chicago, with whose development the personality of Frank Algernon Cowperwood was soon to be definitely linked! To whom may the laurels as laureate of this Florence of the West yet fall? This singing flame of a city, this all America, this poet in chaps and buckskin, this rude, raw Titan, this Burns of a city! By its shimmering lake it lay, a king of shreds and patches, a maundering yokel with an epic in its mouth, a tramp, a hobo among cities, with the grip of Cæsar in its mind, the dramatic force of Euripides in its soul. A very bard of a city this, singing of high deeds and high hopes, its heavy brogans buried deep in the mire of circumstance. Take Athens, oh, Greece! Italy, do you keep Rome! This was the Babylon, the Troy, the Nineveh of a younger day. Here came the gaping West and the hopeful East to see. Here hungry men, raw from the shops and fields, idyls and romances in their minds, builded them an empire crying glory in the mud.

From New York, Vermont, New Hampshire, Maine had come a strange company, earnest, patient, determined, unschooled in even the primer of refinement, hungry for something the significance of which, when they had it, they could not even guess, anxious to be called great, determined so to be without ever knowing how. Here came the dreamy gentleman of the South, robbed of his patrimony; the hopeful student of Yale and Harvard and Princeton; the enfranchised miner of California and the Rockies, his bags of gold and silver in his hands. Here was already the bewildered foreigner, an alien speech confounding him—the Hun, the Pole, the Swede, the German, the Russian—seeking his homely colonies, fearing his neighbor of another race.

Here was the negro, the prostitute, the blackleg, the gambler, the romantic adventurer *par excellence*. A city with but a handful of the native-born; a city packed to the doors with all the riff raff of a thousand towns. Flaring were the lights of the bagnio; tinkling the banjos, zithers, mandolins of the so-called gin-mill; all the dreams and the brutality of the day seemed gathered to rejoice (and rejoice they did) in this new-found wonder of a metropolitan life in the West.

The first prominent Chicagoan whom Cowperwood sought out was the president of the Lake City National Bank, the largest financial organization in the city, with deposits of over fourteen million dollars. It was located in Dearborn Street,

his direction vast railroad lines which penetrated this region, was confident of the future of it. Cowperwood gathered it all, almost by instinct. Gas, street-railways, land speculations, banks, wherever located, were his chief thoughts.

Finally he left the club to keep his other appointments, but something of his personality remained behind him. Mr. Addison and Mr. Rambaud, among others, were sincerely convinced that he was one of the most interesting men they had met in years. And he scarcely had said anything at all—just listened.

Chapter III: A Chicago Evening

After his first visit to the bank over which Addison presided, and an informal dinner at the latter's home, Cowperwood had decided that he did not care to sail under any false colors so far as Addison was concerned. He was too influential and well connected. Besides, Cowperwood liked him too much. Seeing that the man's leaning toward him was strong, in reality a fascination, he made an early morning call a day or two after he had returned from Fargo, whither he had gone at Mr. Rambaud's suggestion, on his way back to Philadelphia, determined to volunteer a smooth presentation of his earlier misfortunes, and trust to Addison's interest to make him view the matter in a kindly light. He told him the whole story of how he had been convicted of technical embezzlement in Philadelphia and had served out his term in the Eastern Penitentiary. He also mentioned his divorce and his intention of marrying again.

Addison, who was the weaker man of the two and yet forceful in his own way, admired this courageous stand on Cowperwood's part. It was a braver thing than he himself could or would have achieved. It appealed to his sense of the dramatic. Here was a man who apparently had been dragged down to the very bottom of things, his face forced in the mire, and now he was coming up again strong, hopeful, urgent. The banker knew many highly respected men in Chicago whose early careers, as he was well aware, would not bear too close an inspection, but nothing was thought of that. Some of them were in society, some not, but all of them were powerful. Why should not Cowperwood be allowed to begin all over? He looked at him steadily, at his eyes, at his stocky body, at his smooth, handsome, mustached face. Then he held out his hand.

"Mr. Cowperwood," he said, finally, trying to shape his words appropriately, "I needn't say that I am pleased with this interesting confession. It appeals to me. I'm glad you have made it to me. You needn't say any more at any time. I decided the day I saw you walking into that vestibule that you were an exceptional man; now I know it. You needn't apologize to me. I haven't lived in this world fifty years and more without having my eye-teeth cut. You're welcome to the courtesies of this bank and of my house as long as you care to avail yourself of them. We'll cut our cloth as circumstances dictate in the future. I'd like to see you come to Chicago, solely because I like you personally. If you decide to settle here I'm sure I can be of service to you and you to me. Don't think anything more about it; I sha'n't ever say anything one way or another. You have your own battle to fight, and I wish you luck. You'll get all the aid from me I can honestly give you. Just forget that you told me, and when you get your matrimonial affairs straightened out bring your wife out to see us."

With these things completed Cowperwood took the train back to Philadelphia.

"Aileen," he said, when these two met again—she had come to the train to meet him—"I think the West is the answer for us. I went up to Fargo and looked around up there, but I don't believe we want to go that far. There's nothing but prairie-grass and Indians out in that country. How'd you like to live in a board shanty, Aileen," he asked, banteringly, "with nothing but fried rattlesnakes and prairie-dogs for breakfast? Do you think you could stand that?"

"Yes," she replied, gaily, hugging his arm, for they had entered a closed carriage; "I could stand it if you could. I'd go anywhere with you, Frank. I'd get me a nice Indian dress with leather and beads all over it and a feather hat like they wear, and—"

"There you go! Certainly! Pretty clothes first of all in a miner's shack. That's the way."

"You wouldn't love me long if I didn't put pretty clothes first," she replied, spiritedly. "Oh, I'm so glad to get you back!"

"The trouble is," he went on, "that that country up there isn't as promising as Chicago. I think we're destined to live in Chicago. I made an investment in Fargo, and we'll have to go up there from time to time, but we'll eventually locate in Chicago. I don't want to go out there alone again. It isn't pleasant for me." He squeezed her hand. "If we can't arrange this thing at once I'll just have to introduce you as my wife for the present."

"You haven't heard anything more from Mr. Steger?" she put in. She was thinking of Steger's efforts to get Mrs. Cowperwood to grant him a divorce.

"Not a word."

"Isn't it too bad?" she sighed.

"Well, don't grieve. Things might be worse."

He was thinking of his days in the penitentiary, and so was she. After commenting on the character of Chicago he decided with her that so soon as conditions permitted they would remove themselves to the Western city.

It would be pointless to do more than roughly sketch the period of three years during which the various changes which saw the complete elimination of Cowperwood from Philadelphia and his introduction into Chicago took place. For a time there were merely journeys to and fro, at first more especially to Chicago, then to Fargo, where his transported secretary, Walter Whelpley, was managing under his direction the construction of Fargo business blocks, a short street-car line, and a fair-ground. This interesting venture bore the title of the Fargo Construction and Transportation Company, of which Frank A. Cowperwood was president. His Philadelphia lawyer, Mr. Harper Steger, was for the time being general master of contracts.

For another short period he might have been found living at the Tremont in

Chicago, avoiding for the time being, because of Aileen's company, anything more than a nodding contact with the important men he had first met, while he looked quietly into the matter of a Chicago brokerage arrangement—a partnership with some established broker who, without too much personal ambition, would bring him a knowledge of Chicago Stock Exchange affairs, personages, and Chicago ventures. On one occasion he took Aileen with him to Fargo, where with a haughty, bored insouciance she surveyed the state of the growing city.

"Oh, Frank!" she exclaimed, when she saw the plain, wooden, four-story hotel, the long, unpleasing business street, with its motley collection of frame and brick stores, the gaping stretches of houses, facing in most directions unpaved streets. Aileen in her tailored spick-and-spanness, her self-conscious vigor, vanity, and tendency to over-ornament, was a strange contrast to the rugged self-effacement and indifference to personal charm which characterized most of the men and women of this new metropolis. "You didn't seriously think of coming out here to live, did you?"

She was wondering where her chance for social exchange would come in—her opportunity to shine. Suppose her Frank were to be very rich; suppose he did make very much money—much more than he had ever had even in the past—what good would it do her here? In Philadelphia, before his failure, before she had been suspected of the secret liaison with him, he had been beginning (at least) to entertain in a very pretentious way. If she had been his wife then she might have stepped smartly into Philadelphia society. Out here, good gracious! She turned up her pretty nose in disgust. "What an awful place!" was her one comment at this most stirring of Western boom towns.

When it came to Chicago, however, and its swirling, increasing life, Aileen was much interested. Between attending to many financial matters Cowperwood saw to it that she was not left alone. He asked her to shop in the local stores and tell him about them; and this she did, driving around in an open carriage, attractively arrayed, a great brown hat emphasizing her pink-and-white complexion and red-gold hair. On different afternoons of their stay he took her to drive over the principal streets. When Aileen was permitted for the first time to see the spacious beauty and richness of Prairie Avenue, the North Shore Drive, Michigan Avenue, and the new mansions on Ashland Boulevard, set in their grassy spaces, the spirit, aspirations, hope, tang of the future Chicago began to work in her blood as it had in Cowperwood's. All of these rich homes were so very new. The great people of Chicago were all newly rich like themselves. She forgot that as yet she was not Cowperwood's wife; she felt herself truly to be so. The streets, set in most instances with a pleasing creamish-brown flagging, lined with young, newly planted trees, the lawns sown to smooth green grass, the windows of the houses trimmed with bright awnings and hung with intricate lace, blowing in a June breeze, the roadways a gray, gritty macadam—all these things touched her fancy. On one drive they skirted the lake on the North Shore, and Aileen, contemplating the chalky, bluish-green waters, the distant sails, the gulls, and then the new bright homes, reflected that in all certitude she would some day be the mistress of one of these splendid mansions. How haughtily she would carry herself; how she would dress! They would have a splendid house, much finer, no doubt, than Frank's old one in Philadelphia, with a great ball-room and dining-room where she could give dances and dinners, and where Frank and she would receive as the peers of these Chicago rich people.

"So you suppose we will ever have a house as fine as one of these, Frank?" she asked him, longingly.

"I'll tell you what my plan is," he said. "If you like this Michigan Avenue section we'll buy a piece of property out here now and hold it. Just as soon as I make the right connections here and see what I am going to do we'll build a house—something really nice—don't worry. I want to get this divorce matter settled, and then we'll begin. Meanwhile, if we have to come here, we'd better live rather quietly. Don't you think so?"

It was now between five and six, that richest portion of a summer day. It had been very warm, but was now cooling, the shade of the western building-line shadowing the roadway, a moted, wine-like air filling the street. As far as the eye could see were carriages, the one great social diversion of Chicago, because there was otherwise so little opportunity for many to show that they had means. The social forces were not as yet clear or harmonious. Jingling harnesses of nickel, silver, and even plated gold were the sign manual of social hope, if not of achievement. Here sped homeward from the city—from office and manufactory—along this one exceptional southern highway, the Via Appia of the South Side, all the urgent aspirants to notable fortunes. Men of wealth who had met only casually in trade here nodded to each other. Smart daughters, society-bred sons, handsome wives came down-town in traps, Victorias, carriages, and vehicles of the latest design to drive home their trade-weary fathers or brothers, relatives or friends. The air was gay with a social hope, a promise of youth and affection, and that fine flush of material life that recreates itself in delight. Lithe, handsome, well-bred animals, singly and in jingling pairs, paced each other down the long, wide, grass-lined street, its fine homes agleam with a rich, complaisant materiality.

"Oh!" exclaimed Aileen, all at once, seeing the vigorous, forceful men, the handsome matrons, and young women and boys, the nodding and the bowing, feeling a touch of the romance and wonder of it all. "I should like to live in Chicago. I believe it's nicer than Philadelphia."

Cowperwood, who had fallen so low there, despite his immense capacity, set his teeth in two even rows. His handsome mustache seemed at this moment to have an especially defiant curl. The pair he was driving was physically perfect, lean and nervous, with spoiled, petted faces. He could not endure poor horse-flesh. He drove as only a horse-lover can, his body bolt upright, his own energy and temperament animating his animals. Aileen sat beside him, very proud, consciously erect.

"Isn't she beautiful?" some of the women observed, as they passed, going north. "What a stunning young woman!" thought or said the men.

"Did you see her?" asked a young brother of his sister.

"Never mind, Aileen," commented Cowperwood, with that iron determination that brooks no defeat. "We will be a part of this. Don't fret. You will have everything you want in Chicago, and more besides."

There was tingling over his fingers, into the reins, into the horse, a mysterious vibrating current that was his chemical product, the off-giving of his spirit battery that made his hired horses prance like children. They chafed and tossed their heads and snorted.

Aileen was fairly bursting with hope and vanity and longing. Oh, to be Mrs. Frank Algernon Cowperwood here in Chicago, to have a splendid mansion, to have her cards of invitation practically commands which might not be ignored!

"Oh, dear!" she sighed to herself, mentally. "If only it were all true—now."

It is thus that life at its topmost toss irks and pains. Beyond is ever the unattainable, the lure of the infinite with its infinite ache.

Oh, life! oh, youth! oh, hope! oh, years!
Oh pain-winged fancy, beating forth with fears.

Chapter IV: Peter Laughlin & Co.

The partnership which Cowperwood eventually made with an old-time Board of Trade operator, Peter Laughlin, was eminently to his satisfaction. Laughlin was a tall, gaunt speculator who had spent most of his living days in Chicago, having come there as a boy from western Missouri. He was a typical Chicago Board of Trade operator of the old school, having an Andrew Jacksonish countenance, and a Henry Clay—Davy Crockett—"Long John" Wentworth build of body.

Cowperwood from his youth up had had a curious interest in quaint characters, and he was interesting to them; they "took" to him. He could, if he chose to take the trouble, fit himself in with the odd psychology of almost any individual. In his early peregrinations in La Salle Street he inquired after clever-traders on 'change, and then gave them one small commission after another in order to get acquainted. Thus he stumbled one morning on old Peter Laughlin, wheat and corn trader, who had an office in La Salle Street near Madison, and who did a modest business gambling for himself and others in grain and Eastern railway shares. Laughlin was a shrewd, canny American, originally, perhaps, of Scotch extraction, who had all the traditional American blemishes of uncouthness, tobacco-chewing, profanity, and other small vices. Cowperwood could tell from looking at him that he must have a fund of information concerning every current Chicagoan of importance, and this fact alone was certain to be of value. Then the old man was direct, plain-spoken, simple-appearing, and wholly unpretentious—qualities which Cowperwood deemed invaluable.

Once or twice in the last three years Laughlin had lost heavily on private "corners" that he had attempted to engineer, and the general feeling was that he was now becoming cautious, or, in other words, afraid. "Just the man," Cowperwood thought. So one morning he called upon Laughlin, intending to open a small account with him.

"Henry," he heard the old man say, as he entered Laughlin's fair-sized but rather dusty office to a young, preternaturally solemn-looking clerk, a fit assistant for Peter Laughlin, "git me them there Pittsburg and Lake Erie sheers, will you?" Seeing Cowperwood waiting, he added, "What kin I do for ye?"

Cowperwood smiled. "So he calls them 'sheers,' does he?" he thought. "Good! I think I'll like him."

He introduced himself as coming from Philadelphia, and went on to say that he was interested in various Chicago ventures, inclined to invest in any good stock which would rise, and particularly desirous to buy into some corporation—public utility preferred—which would be certain to grow with the expansion of the city.

Old Laughlin, who was now all of sixty yeas of age, owned a seat on the Board, and was worth in the neighborhood of two hundred thousand dollars, looked at Cowperwood quizzically.

"Well, now, if you'd 'a' come along here ten or fifteen years ago you might 'a' got in on the ground floor of a lot of things," he observed. "There was these here gas companies, now, that them Otway and Apperson boys got in on, and then all these here street-railways. Why, I'm the feller that told Eddie Parkinson what a fine thing he could make out of it if he would go and organize that North State Street line. He promised me a bunch of sheers if he ever worked it out, but he never give 'em to me. I didn't expect him to, though," he added, wisely, and with a glint. "I'm too old a trader for that. He's out of it now, anyway. That Michaels-Kennelly crowd skinned him. Yep, if you'd 'a' been here ten or fifteen years ago you might 'a' got in on that. 'Tain't no use a-thinkin' about that, though, any more. Them sheers is sellin' fer clost onto a hundred and sixty."

Cowperwood smiled. "Well, Mr. Laughlin," he observed, "you must have been on 'change a long time here. You seem to know a good deal of what has gone on in the past."

"Yep, ever since 1852," replied the old man. He had a thick growth of upstanding hair looking not unlike a rooster's comb, a long and what threatened eventually to become a Punch-and-Judy chin, a slightly aquiline nose, high cheek-bones, and hollow, brown-skinned cheeks. His eyes were as clear and sharp as those of a lynx.

"To tell you the truth, Mr. Laughlin," went on Cowperwood, "what I'm really out here in Chicago for is to find a man with whom I can go into partnership in the brokerage business. Now I'm in a banking and brokerage business myself in the East. I have a firm in Philadelphia and a seat on both the New York and Philadelphia exchanges. I have some affairs in Fargo also. Any trade agency can tell you about me. You have a Board of Trade seat here, and no doubt you do some New York and Philadelphia exchange business. The new firm, if you would go in with me, could handle it all direct. I'm a rather strong outside man myself. I'm thinking of locating permanently in Chicago. What would you say now to going into business with me? Do you think we could get along in the same office space?"

Cowperwood had a way, when he wanted to be pleasant, of beating the finger of his two hands together, finger for finger, tip for tip. He also smiled at the same time—or, rather, beamed—his eyes glowing with a warm, magnetic, seemingly affectionate light.

As it happened, old Peter Laughlin had arrived at that psychological moment when he was wishing that some such opportunity as this might appear and be available. He was a lonely man, never having been able to bring himself to trust his peculiar temperament in the hands of any woman. As a matter of fact, he had never understood women at all, his relations being confined to those sad immoralies of the cheapest character which only money—grudgingly given, at that—could buy. He lived in three small rooms in West Harrison Street, near Throup, where he cooked his own meals at times. His one companion was a small spaniel, simple and affectionate, a she dog, Jennie by name, with whom he slept. Jennie was a docile, loving companion, waiting for him patiently by day in his office until he was ready to go home at night. He talked to this spaniel quite as he would to a human being (even more intimately, perhaps), taking the dog's glances, tail-waggings, and general movements for answer. In the morning when he arose, which was often as early as half past four, or even four—he was a brief sleeper—he would begin by pulling on his trousers (he seldom bathed any more except at a down-town barber shop) and talking to Jennie.

"Git up, now, Jinnie," he would say. "It's time to git up. We've got to make our coffee now and git some breakfast. I can see yuh, lyin' there, pertendin' to be asleep. Come on, now! You've had sleep enough. You've been sleepin' as long as I have."

Jennie would be watching him out of the corner of one loving eye, her tail tap-tapping on the bed, her free ear going up and down.

When he was fully dressed, his face and hands washed, his old string tie pulled around into a loose and convenient knot, his hair brushed upward, Jennie would get up and jump demonstratively about, as much as to say, "You see how prompt I am."

"That's the way," old Laughlin would comment. "Allers last. Yuh never git up first, do yuh, Jinnie? Allers let yer old man do that, don't you?"

On bitter days, when the car-wheels squeaked and one's ears and fingers seemed to be in danger of freezing, old Laughlin, arrayed in a heavy, dusty greatcoat of ancient vintage and a square hat, would carry Jennie down-town in a greenish-black bag along with some of his beloved "sheers" which he was meditating on. Only then could he take Jennie in the cars. On other days they would walk, for he liked exercise. He would get to his office as early as seven-thirty or eight, though business did not usually begin until after nine, and remain until four-thirty or five, reading the papers or calculating during the hours when there were no customers. Then he would take Jennie and go for a walk or to call on some business acquaintance. His home room, the newspapers, the floor of the exchange, his officers, and the streets were his only resources. He cared nothing for plays, books, pictures, music—and for women only in his one-angled, mentally impoverished way. His limitations were so marked that to a lover of character like Cowperwood he was fascinating—but Cowperwood only used character. He never idled over it long artistically.

As Cowperwood suspected, what old Laughlin did not know about Chicago financial conditions, deals, opportunities, and individuals was scarcely worth knowing. Being only a trader by instinct, neither an organizer nor an executive, he had never been able to make any great constructive use of his knowledge. His gains and his losses he took with reasonable equanimity, exclaiming over and over, when he lost: "Shucks! I hadn't orter have done that," and snapping his fingers. When he won heavily or was winning he munched tobacco with a seraphic smile and occasionally in the midst of trading would exclaim: "You fellers better come in. It's a-gonta rain some more." He was not easy to trap in any small gambling game, and only lost or won when there was a free, open struggle in the market, or when he was engineering some little scheme of his own.

The matter of this partnership was not arranged at once, although it did not take long. Old Peter Laughlin wanted to think it over, although he had immediately developed a personal fancy for Cowperwood. In a way he was the latter's victim and servant from the start. They met day after day to discuss various details and terms; finally, true to his instincts, old Peter demanded a full half interest.

"Now you don't want that much, Laughlin," Cowperwood suggested, quite blandly. They were sitting in Laughlin's private office between four and five in the afternoon, and Laughlin was chewing tobacco with the sense of having a fine, interesting problem before him. "I have a seat on the New York Stock Exchange," he went on, "and that's worth forty thousand dollars. My seat on the Philadelphia exchange is worth more than yours here. They will naturally figure as the principal assets of the firm. It's to be in your name. I'll be liberal with you, though. Instead of a third, which would be fair, I'll make it forty-nine per cent., and we'll call the firm Peter Laughlin & Co. I like you, and I think you can be of a lot of use to me. I know you will make more money through me than you have alone. I could go in with a lot of these silk-stocking fellows around here, but I don't want to. You'd better decide right now, and let's get to work."

Old Laughlin was pleased beyond measure that young Cowperwood should want to go in with him. He had become aware of late that all of the young, smug newcomers on 'change considered him an old fogy. Here was a strong, brave young Easterner, twenty years his junior, evidently as shrewd as himself—more so, he feared—who actually proposed a business alliance. Besides, Cowperwood, in his young, healthy, aggressive way, was like a breath of spring.

"I ain't keerin' so much about the name," rejoined Laughlin. "You can fix it that-a-way if you want to. Givin' you fifty-one per cent. gives you charge of this here shebang. All right, though; I ain't a-kickin'. I guess I can manage allus to git what's a-comin' to me."

"It's a bargain, then," said Cowperwood. "We'll want new offices, Laughlin, don't you think? This one's a little dark."

"Fix it up any way you like, Mr. Cowperwood. It's all the same to me. I'll be glad to see how yer do it."

In a week the details were completed, and two weeks later the sign of Peter Laughlin & Co., grain and commission merchants, appeared over the door of a handsome suite of rooms on the ground floor of a corner at La Salle and Madison, in the heart of the Chicago financial district.

"Get onto old Laughlin, will you?" one broker observed to another, as they passed the new, pretentious commission-house with its splendid plate-glass windows, and observed the heavy, ornate bronze sign placed on either side of the door, which was located exactly on the corner. "What's struck him? I thought he was almost all through. Who's the Company?"

"I don't know. Some fellow from the East, I think."

"Well, he's certainly moving up. Look at the plate glass, will you?"

It was thus that Frank Algernon Cowperwood's Chicago financial career was definitely launched.

Chapter XXI: A Matter of Tunnels

The question of Sohlberg adjusted thus simply, if brutally, Cowperwood turned his attention to Mrs. Sohlberg. But there was nothing much to be done. He explained that he had now completely subdued Aileen and Sohlberg, that the latter would make no more trouble, that he was going to pension him, that Aileen would remain permanently quiescent. He expressed the greatest solicitude for her, but Rita was now sickened of this tangle. She had loved him, as she thought, but through the rage of Aileen she saw him in a different light, and she wanted to get away. His money, plentiful as it was, did not mean as much to her as it might have meant to some women; it simply spelled luxuries, without which she could exist if she must. His charm for her had, perhaps, consisted mostly in the atmosphere of flawless security, which seemed to surround him—a glittering bubble of romance. That, by one fell attack, was now burst. He was seen to be quite as other men, subject to the same storms, the same danger of shipwreck. Only he was a better sailor than most. She recuperated gradually; left for home; left for Europe; details too long to be narrated. Sohlberg, after much meditating and fuming, finally accepted the offer of Cowperwood and returned to Denmark. Aileen, after a few days of quarreling, in which he agreed to dispense with Antoinette Nowak, returned home.

Cowperwood was in no wise pleased by this rough dénouement. Aileen had not raised her own attractions in his estimation, and yet, strange to relate, he was not unsympathetic with her. He had no desire to desert her as yet, though for some time he had been growing in the feeling that Rita would have been a much better type of wife for him. But what he could not have, he could not have. He turned his attention with renewed force to his business; but it was with many a backward glance at those radiant hours when, with Rita in his presence or enfolded by his arms, he had seen life from a new and poetic angle. She was so charming, so naïve—but what could he do?

For several years thereafter Cowperwood was busy following the Chicago street-railway situation with increasing interest. He knew it was useless to brood over Rita Sohlberg—she would not return—and yet he could not help it; but he could work hard, and that was something. His natural aptitude and affection for street-railway work had long since been demonstrated, and it was now making him restless. One might have said of him quite truly that the tinkle of car-bells and the plop of plodding horses' feet was in his blood. He surveyed these extending lines, with their jingling cars, as he went about the city, with an almost hungry eye. Chicago was growing fast, and these little horse-cars on certain streets were crowded night and morning—fairly bulging with people at the rush-hours. If he could only secure an octopus-grip on one or all of them; if he could combine and control them all! What a fortune! That, if nothing else, might salve him for some of his woes—a tremendous fortune—nothing less. He forever busied himself with various aspects of the scene quite as a poet might have concerned himself with rocks and rills. To own these street-railways! To own these street-railways! So rang, the song of his mind.

Like the gas situation, the Chicago street-railway situation was divided into three parts—three companies representing and corresponding with the three different sides or divisions of the city. The Chicago City Railway Company, occupying the South Side and extending as far south as Thirty-ninth Street, had been organized in 1859, and represented in itself a mine of wealth. Already it controlled some seventy miles of track, and was annually being added to on Indiana Avenue, or Wabash Avenue, on State Street, and on Archer Avenue. It owned over one hundred and fifty cars of the old-fashioned, straw-strewn, no-stove type, and over one thousand horses; it employed one hundred and seventy conductors, one hundred and sixty drivers, a hundred stablemen, and blacksmiths, harness-makers, and repairers in interesting numbers. Its snow-plows were busy on the street in winter, its sprinkling-cars in summer. Cowperwood calculated its shares, bonds, rolling-stock, and other physical properties as totalling in the vicinity of over two million dollars. The trouble with this company was that its outstanding stock was principally controlled by Norman Schryhart, who was now decidedly inimical to Cowperwood, or anything he might wish to do, and by Anson Merrill, who had never manifested any signs of friendship. He did not see how he was to get control of this property. Its shares were selling around two hundred and fifty dollars.

The North Chicago City Railway was a corporation which had been organized at the same time as the South Side company, but by a different group of men. Its management was old, indifferent, and incompetent, its equipment about the same. The Chicago West Division Railway had originally been owned by the Chicago City or South Side Railway, but was now a separate corporation. It was not yet so profitable as the other divisions of the city, but all sections of the city were growing. The horsebell was heard everywhere tinkling gaily.

Standing on the outside of this scene, contemplating its promise, Cowperwood much more than any one else connected financially with the future of these railways at this time was impressed with their enormous possibilities—their enormous future if Chicago continued to grow, and was concerned with the various factors which might further or impeded their progress.

Not long before he had discovered that one of the chief handicaps to street-railway development, on the North and West Sides, lay in the congestion of traffic at the bridges spanning the Chicago River. Between the street ends that abutted on it and connected the two sides of the city ran this amazing stream—dirty, odorous, picturesque, compact of a heavy, delightful, constantly crowding and moving boat traffic, which kept the various bridges momentarily turning, and tied up the street traffic on either side of the river until it seemed at times as though the tangle of teams and boats would never any more be straightened out. It was lovely, human, natural, Dickensesque—a fit subject for a Daumier, a Turner, or a Whistler. The idlest of bridge-tenders judged for himself when the boats and when the teams should be made to wait, and how long, while in addition to the regular pedestrians a group of idlers stood at gaze fascinated by the crows of masts, the crush of wagons, and the picturesque tugs in the foreground below. Cowperwood, as he sat in his light runabout, annoyed by a delay, or dashed swiftly forward to get over before a bridge turned, had long since noted that the street-car service in the North and West Sides was badly hampered. The unbroken South Side, unthreaded by a river, had no such problem, and was growing rapidly.

Because of this he was naturally interested to observe one day, in the course of his peregrinations, that there existed in two places under the Chicago River—in the first place at La Salle Street, running north and south, and in the second at Washington Street, running east and west—two now soggy and rat-infested tunnels which were never used by anybody—dark, dank, dripping affairs only a vaguely lighted with oil-lamp, and oozing with water. Upon investigation he learned that they had been built years before to accommodate this same tide of wagon traffic, which now congested at the bridges, and which even then had been rapidly rising. Being forced to pay a toll in time to which a slight toll in cash, exacted for the privilege of using a tunnel, had seemed to the investors and public infinitely to be preferred, this traffic had been offered this opportunity of avoiding the delay. However, like many another handsome commercial scheme on paper or bubbling in the human brain, the plan did not work exactly. These tunnels might have proved profitable if they had been properly built with long, low-per-cent. grades, wide roadways, and a sufficiency of light and air; but, as a matter of fact, they had not been judiciously adapted to public convenience. Norman Schryhart's father had been an investor in these tunnels, and Anson Merrill. When they had proved unprofitable, after a long period of pointless manipulation—cost, one million dollars—they had been sold to the city for exactly that sum each, it being poetically deemed that a growing city could better afford to lose so disturbing an amount than any of its humble, ambitious, and respectable citizens. That was a little affair by which members of council had profited years before; but that also is another story.

After discovering these tunnels Cowperwood walked through them several times—for though they were now boarded up, there was still an uninterrupted footpath—and wondered why they could not be utilized. It seemed to him that if the street-car traffic were heavy enough, profitable enough, and these tunnels, for a reasonable sum, could be made into a lower grade, one of the problems which now hampered the growth of the North and West Sides would be obviated. But how? He did not own the tunnels. He did not own the street-railways. The cost of leasing and rebuilding the tunnels would be enormous. Helpers and horses and extra drivers on any grade, however slight, would have to be used, and that meant an extra expense. With street-car horses as the only means of traction, and with the long, expensive grades, he was not so sure that this venture would be a profitable one.

However, in the fall of 1880, or a little earlier (when he was still very much entangled with the preliminary sex affairs that led eventually to Rita Sohlberg), he became aware of a new system of traction relating to street-cars which, together with the arrival of the arc-light, the telephone, and other inventions, seemed destined to change the character of city life entirely.

Recently in San Francisco, where the presence of hills made the movement of crowded street-railway cars exceedingly difficult, a new type of traction has been introduced—that of the *cable*, which was nothing more than a traveling rope of wire running over guttered wheels in a conduit, and driven by immense engines, conveniently located in adjacent stations or "power-houses." The cars carried a readily manipulated "grip-lever," or steel hand, which reached down through a slot into a conduit and "gripped" the moving cable. This invention solved the problem of hauling heavily laden street-cars up and down steep grades. About the same time he also heard, in a roundabout way, that the Chicago City Railway, of which Schryhart and Merrill were the principal owners, was about to introduce this mode of traction on its lines—to *cable* State Street, and attach the cars of other lines running farther out into unprofitable districts as "trailers." At once the solution of the North and West Side problems flashed upon him—cables.

Outside of the bridge crush and the tunnels above mentioned, there was one other special condition which had been for some time past attracting Cowperwood's attention. This was the waning energy of the North Chicago City Railway Company—the lack of foresight on the part of its directors which prevented them from perceiving the proper solution of their difficulties. The road was in a rather unsatisfactory state financially—really open to a coup of some sort. In the beginning it had been considered unprofitable, so thinly populated was the territory they served, and so short the distance from the business heart. Later, however, as the territory filled up, they did better; only then the long waits at the bridges occurred. The management, feeling that the lines were likely to be poorly patronized, had put down poor, little, light-weight rails, and run slimpsy cars which were as cold as ice in winter and as hot as stove-ovens in summer. No attempt had been made to extend the down-town terminus of the several lines into the business center—they stopped just over the river which bordered it at the north. (On the South Side Mr. Schryhart had done much better for his patrons. He had already installed a loop for his cable about Merrill's store.) As on the West Side, straw was strewn in the bottom of all the cars in winter to keep the feet of the passengers warm, and but few open cars were used in summer. The directors were adverse to introducing them because of the expense. So they had gone on and on, adding lines only where they were sure they would make a good profit from the start, putting down the same style of cheap rail that had been used in the beginning, and employing the same antique type of car which rattled and trembled as it ran, until the patrons were enraged to the point of anarchy. Only recently, because of various suits and complaints inaugurated, the company had been greatly annoyed, but they scarcely knew what to do, how to meet the onslaught. Though there was here and there a man of sense—such as Terrence Mulgannon, the general superintendent; Edwin Kaffrath, a director; William Johnson, the constructing engineer of the company—yet such other men as Onias C. Skinner, the president, and Walter Parker, the vice-president, were reactionaries of an elderly character, conservative, meditative, stingy, and, worst of all, fearful or without courage for great adventure. It is a sad commentary that age almost invariably takes away the incentive to new achievement and makes "Let well enough alone" the most appealing motto.

Mindful of this, Cowperwood, with a now splendid scheme in mind, one day invited John J. McKenty over to his house to dinner on a social pretext. When the latter, accompanied by his wife, had arrived, and Aileen had smiled on them both sweetly, and was doing her best to be nice to Mrs. McKenty, Cowperwood remarked:

"McKenty, do you know anything about these two tunnels that the city owns under the river at Washington and La Salle streets?"

"I know that the city took them over when it didn't need them, and that they're no good for anything. That was before my time, though," explained McKenty, cautiously. "I think the city paid a million for them. Why?"

"Oh, nothing much," replied Cowperwood, evading the matter for the present. "I was wondering whether they were in such condition that they couldn't be used for anything. I see occasional references in the papers to their uselessness."

"They're in pretty bad shape, I'm afraid," replied McKenty. "I haven't been through either of them in years and years. The idea was originally to let the wagons go through them and break up the crowding at the bridges. But it didn't work. They made the grade too steep and the tolls too high, and so the drivers preferred to wait for the bridges. They were pretty hard on horses. I can testify to that myself. I've driven a wagon-load through them more than once. The city should never have taken them over at all by rights. It was a deal. I don't know who all was in it. Carmody was mayor then, and Aldrich was in charge of public works."

He relapsed into silence, and Cowperwood allowed the matter of the tunnels to rest until after dinner when they had adjourned to the library. There he placed a friendly hand on McKenty's arm, an act of familiarity which the politician rather liked.

"You felt pretty well satisfied with the way that gas business came out last year, didn't you?" he inquired.

"I did," replied McKenty, warmly. "Never more so. I told you that at the time." The Irishman liked Cowperwood, and was grateful for the swift manner in which he had been made richer by the sum of several hundred thousand dollars.

"Well, now, McKenty," continued Cowperwood, abruptly, and with a seeming lack of connection, "has it ever occurred to you that things are shaping up for a big change in the street-railway situation here? I can see it coming. There's going to be a new motor power introduced on the South Side within a year or two. You've heard of it?"

"I read something of it," replied McKenty, surprised and a little questioning. He took a cigar and prepared to listen. Cowperwood, never smoking, drew up a chair.

"Well, I'll tell you what that means," he explained. "It means that eventually every mile of street-railway track in this city—to say nothing of all the additional miles that will be built before this change takes place—will have to be done over on an entirely new basis. I mean this cable-conduit system. These old companies that are hobbling along now with an old equipment will have to make the change. They'll have to spend millions and millions before they can bring their equipment up to date. If you've paid any attention to the matter you must have seen what a condition these North and West Side lines are in."

"It's pretty bad; I know that," commented McKenty.

"Just so," replied Cowperwood, emphatically. "Well, now, if I know anything about these old managements from studying them, they're going to have a hard time bringing themselves to do this. Two to three million are two to three million, and it isn't going to be an easy matter for them to raise the money—not as easy, perhaps, as it would be for some of the rest of us, supposing we wanted to go into the street-railway business."

"Yes, supposing," replied McKenty, jovially. "But how are you to get in it? There's no stock for sale that I know of."

"Just the same," said Cowperwood, "we can if we want to, and I'll show you how. But at present there's just one thing in particular I'd like you to do for me. I want to know if there is any way that we can get control of either of those two old tunnels that I was talking to you about a little while ago. I'd like both if I might. Do you suppose that is possible?"

"Why, yes," replied McKenty, wondering; "but what have they got to do with it? They're not worth anything. Some of the boys were talking about filling them in some time ago—blowing them up. The police think crooks hide in them."

"Just the same, don't let any one touch them—don't lease them or anything," replied Cowperwood, forcefully. "I'll tell you frankly what I want to do. I want to get control, just as soon as possible, of all the street-railway lines I can on the North and West Sides—new or old franchises. Then you'll see where the tunnels come in."

He paused to see whether McKenty caught the point of all he meant, but the latter failed.

"You don't want much, do you?" he said, cheerfully. "But I don't see how you can use the tunnels. However, that's no reason why I shouldn't take care of them for you, if you think that's important."

"It's this way, " said Cowperwood, thoughtfully. "I'll make you a preferred partner in all the ventures that I control if you do as I suggest. The street-railways, as they stand now, will have to be taken up lock, stock, and barrel, and thrown into the scrap heap within eight or nine years at the latest. You see what the South Side company is beginning to do now. When it comes to the West and North Side companies they won't find it so easy. They aren't earning as much as the South Side, and besides they have those bridges to cross. That means a severe inconvenience to a cable line. In the first place, the bridges will have to be rebuilt to stand the extra weight and strain. Now the question arises at once—at whose expense? The city's?"

"That depends on who's asking for it," replied Mr. McKenty, amiably.

"Quite so," assented Cowperwood. "In the next place, this river traffic is becoming impossible from the point of view of a decent street-car service. There are waits now of from eight to fifteen minutes while these tows and vessels get through. Chicago has five hundred thousand population to-day. How much will it have in 1890? In 1900? How will it be when it has eight hundred thousand or a million?"

"You're quite right," interpolated McKenty. "It will be pretty bad."

"Exactly. But what is worse, the cable lines will carry trailers, or single cars, from feeder lines. There won't be single cars waiting at these draws—there will be trains, crowded trains. It won't be advisable to delay a cable-train from eight to fifteen minutes while boats are making their way through a draw. The public won't stand for that very long, will it, do you think?"

"Not without making a row, probably," replied McKenty.

"Well, that means what, then?" asked Cowperwood. "Is the traffic going to get any lighter? Is the river going to dry up?"

Mr. McKenty stared. Suddenly his face lighted. "Oh, I see," he said, shrewdly. "It's those tunnels you're thinking about. Are they in any shape to be used?"

"They can be made over cheaper than new ones can be built."

"True for you," replied McKenty, "and if they're in any sort of repair they'd be just what you'd want." He was emphatic, almost triumphant. "They belong to the city. They cost pretty near a million apiece, those things."

"I know it," said Cowperwood. "Now, do you see what I'm driving at?"

"Do I see!" smiled McKenty. "That's a real idea you have, Cowperwood. I take off my hat to you. Say what you want."

"Well, then, in the first place," replied Cowperwood, genially, "it is agreed that the city won't part with those two tunnels under any circumstances until we can see what can be done about this other matter?"

"It will not."

"In the next place, it is understood, is it, that you won't make it any easier than you can possibly help for the North and West Side companies to get ordinances extending their lines, or anything else, from now on? I shall want to introduce some franchises for feeders and outlying lines myself."

"Bring in your ordinances," replied McKenty, "and I'll do whatever you say. I've worked with you before. I know that you keep your word."

"Thanks," said Cowperwood, warmly. "I know the value of keeping it. In the mean while I'll go ahead and see what can be done about the other matter. I don't know just how many men I will need to let in on this, or just what form the organization will take. But you may depend upon it that your interests will be properly taken care of, and that whatever is done will be done with your full knowledge and consent."

"All very good," answered McKenty, thinking of the new field of activity before them. A combination between himself and Cowperwood in a matter like this must prove very beneficial to both. And he was satisfied, because of their previous relations, that his own interests would not be neglected.

"Shall we go and see if we can find the ladies?" asked Cowperwood, jauntily, laying hold of the politician's arm.

"To be sure," assented McKenty, gaily. "It's a fine house you have here—beautiful. And your wife is as pretty a woman as I ever saw, if you'll pardon the familiarity."

"I have always thought she was rather attractive myself," replied Cowperwood, innocently.

122

'How I Struck Chicago, and How Chicago Struck Me'

RUDYARD KIPLING

Rudyard Kipling (1865–1936), an English writer of novels, stories and poems, is associated more with British India and Empire than Chicago. However, *From Sea to Sea* (1899) is an account of his travels to Japan and America—and reveals a sense of the United States influenced by an increasingly negative view of its social and cultural values. He is akin to Henry James in the way he brings an 'English' (or European) perspective to modern urban life. An enormously prolific writer, he was the first British writer to be awarded the Nobel Prize for Literature (1907). His major stories include *The Jungle Book* (1894), *Captains Courageous* (1897) and *Puck of Pook's Hill* (1906).

I have struck a city—a real city—and they call it Chicago. The other places do not count. San Francisco was a pleasure-resort as well as a city, and Salt Lake was a phenomenon. This place is the first American city I have encountered. It holds rather more than a million people with bodies, and stands on the same sort of soil as Calcutta. Having seen it, I urgently desire never to see it again. It is inhabited by savages. Its water is the water of the Hughli, and its air is dirt. Also it says that it is the "boss" town of America.

I do not believe that it has anything to do with this country. They told me to go to the Palmer House which is a gilded and mirrored rabbit-warren, and there I found a huge hall of tessellated marble, crammed with people talking about money and spitting about everywhere. Other barbarians charged in and out of this inferno with letters and telegrams in their hands, and yet others shouted at each other. A man who had drunk quite as much as was good for him told me that this was "the finest hotel in the finest city on God Almighty's earth." ...

... *Then* I went out into the streets, which are long and flat and without end.

Source: Rudyard Kipling, "How I Struck Chicago, and How Chicago Struck Me", *From Sea to Sea*, Part II, Garden City, NY, 1914, pp. 230–48.

And verily it is not a good thing to live in our East for any length of time. Your ideas grow to clash with those held by every right-thinking white man. I looked down interminable vistas flanked with nine, ten, and fifteen storied houses, and crowded with men and women, and the show impressed me with a great horror. Except in London—and I have forgotten what London is like—I had never seen so many white people together, and never such a collection of miserables. There was no colour in the street and no beauty—only a maze of wire-ropes overhead and dirty stone flagging underfoot. A cab-driver volunteered to show me the glory of the town for so much an hour, and with him I wandered far. He conceived that all this turmoil and squash was a thing to be reverently admired; that it was good to huddle men together in fifteen layers, one atop of the other, and to dig holes in the ground for offices. He said that Chicago was a live town, and that all the creatures hurrying by me were engaged in business. That is to say, they were trying to make some money, that they might not die through lack of food to put into their bellies. He took me to canals, black as ink, and filled with untold abominations, and bade me watch the stream of traffic across the bridges. He then took me into a saloon, and, while I drank, made me note that the floor was covered with coins sunk into cement. A Hottentot would not have been guilty of this sort of barbarism. The coins made an effect pretty enough, but the man who put them there had no thought to beauty, and therefore he was a savage. Then my cab-driver showed me business blocks, gay with signs and studded with fantastic and absurd advertisements of goods, and looking down the long street so adorned it was as though each vender stood at his door howling: "For the sake of money, employ, or buy of, *me* and me only!" Have you ever seen a crowd at our famine-relief distributions? You know then how men leap into the air, stretching out their arms above the crowd in the hope of being seen; while the women dolorously slap the stomachs of their children and whimper. I had sooner watch famine relief than the white man engaged in what he calls legitimate competition. The one I understand. The other makes me ill. And the cab-man said that these things were the proof of progress; and by that I knew he had been reading his newspaper, as every intelligent American should. The papers tell their readers in language fitted to their comprehension that the snarling together of telegraph wires, the heaving up of houses, and the making of money is progress.

I spent ten hours in that huge wilderness, wandering through scores of miles of these terrible streets, and jostling some few hundred thousand of these terrible people who talked money through their noses. The cabman left me: but after a while I picked up another man who was full of figures, and into my ears he poured them as occasion required or the big blank factories suggested. Here they turned out so many hundred thousand dollars' worth of such and such an article; there so many million other things; this house was worth so many million dollars; that one so many million more or less. It was like listening to a child babbling of its hoard of shells. It was like watching a fool playing with buttons. But I was expected to do more than listen or watch. He demanded that

I should admire; and the utmost that I could say was: "Are these things so? Then I am very sorry for you." That made him angry, and he said that insular envy made me unresponsive. So you see I could not make him understand.

Sunday brought me the queerest experience of all—a revelation of barbarism complete. I found a place that was officially described as a church. It was a circus really, but that the worshippers did not know. There were flowers all about the building, which was fitted up with plush and stained oak and much luxury, including twisted brass candlesticks of severest Gothic design. To these things, and a congregation of savages, entered suddenly a wonderful man completely in the confidence of their God, whom he treated colloquially and exploited very much as a newspaper reporter would exploit a foreign potentate. But, unlike the newspaper reporter, he never allowed his listeners to forget that he and not He was the centre of attraction. With a voice of silver and with imagery borrowed from the auction-room, he built up for his hearers a heaven on the lines of the Palmer House (but with all the gilding real gold and all the plate-glass diamond) and set in the centre of it a loud-voiced, argumentative, and very shrewd creation that he called God. One sentence at this point caught my delighted ear. It was *apropos* of some question of the Judgment Day and ran: "No! I tell you God don't do business that way." He was giving them a deity whom they could comprehend, in a gold and jewel heaven in which they could take a natural interest. He interlarded his performance with the slang of the streets, the counter, and the Exchange, and he said that religion ought to enter into daily life. Consequently I presume he introduced it *as* daily life—his own and the life of his friends.

Then I escaped before the blessing, desiring no benediction at such hands. But the persons who listened seemed to enjoy themselves, and I understand that I had met with a popular preacher. Later on, when I had perused the sermons of a gentleman called Talmage and some others, I perceived that I had been listening to a very mild specimen. ... All that Sunday I listened to people who said that the mere fact of spiking down strips of iron to wood and getting a steam and iron thing to run along them was progress. That the telephone was progress, and the network of wires overhead was progress. They repeated their statements again and again. One of them took me to their city hall and board of trade works and pointed it out with pride. It was very ugly, but very big, and the streets in front of it were narrow and unclean. When I saw the faces of the men who did business in that building I felt that there had been a mistake in their billeting. ...

... But I don't think it was the blind hurry of the people, their argot, and their grand ignorance of things beyond their immediate interests that displeased me so much as a study of the daily papers of Chicago. Imprimis, there was some sort of dispute between New York and Chicago as to which town should give an exhibition of products to be hereafter holden, and through the medium of their more dignified journals the two cities were ya-hooing and hi-yi-ing at each other like opposition newsboys. They called it humour, but it sounded like something quite different. That was only the first trouble. The second lay in the tone of the productions. Leading articles which indulge gems such as: "Back of such and such a place," or "We noticed, Tuesday, such an event," or "don't" for "does not" are things to be accepted with thankfulness. All that made me weep was that, in these papers, were faithfully reproduced all the war-cries and "back-talk" of the Palmer House bar, the slang of the barbers' shops, the mental elevation and integrity of the Pullman-car porter, the dignity of the Dime Museum, and the accuracy of the excited fishwife. I am sternly forbidden to believe that the paper educates the public. Then I am compelled to believe that the public educate the paper?

Just when the sense of unreality and oppression was strongest upon me, and when I most wanted help, a man sat at my side and began to talk what he called politics. I had chanced to pay about six shillings for a traveling-cap worth eighteen pence, and he made of the fact a text for a sermon. He said that this was a rich country and that the people liked to pay two hundred per cent on the value of a thing. They could afford it. He said that the Government imposed a protective duty of from ten to seventy per cent on foreign-made articles, and that the American manufacturer consequently could sell his goods for a healthy sum. Thus an imported hat would, with duty, cost two guineas. The American manufacturer would make a hat for seventeen shillings and sell it for one pound fifteen. In these things, he said, lay the greatness of America and the effeteness of England. Competition between factory and factory kept the prices down to decent limits, but I was never to forget that this people were rich people, not like the pauper Continentals, and that they enjoyed paying duties. To my weak intellect this seemed rather like juggling with counters. Everything that I have yet purchased costs about twice as much as it would in England, and, when native-made is of inferior quality ...I am an alien, and for the life of me cannot see why six shillings should be paid for eighteen-penny caps, or eight shillings for half-crown cigar-cases. When the country fills up to a decently populated level a few million people who are not aliens will be smitten with the same sort of blindness.

But my friend's assertion somehow thoroughly suited the grotesque ferocity of Chicago. ... Chicago husks and winnows her wheat by the million bushels, a hundred banks lend hundreds of millions of dollars in the year, and scores of factories turn out plow gear and machinery by steam. Scores of daily papers do work which Hukm Chund and the barber and the midwife perform, with due regard for public opinion, in the village of Isser Jang. So far as manufactures go, the difference between Chicago on the lake and Isser Jang on the Montgomery road [in India] is one of degree only, and not of kind. So far as the understanding of the uses of life goes Isser Jang, for all its seasonal cholera, has the advantage over Chicago. Jowala Singh knows and takes care to avoid the three or four ghoul-haunted fields on the outskirts of the village; but he is not urged by millions of devils to run about all day in the sun and swear that his plowshares are the best in the Punjab; nor does Puran Dass fly forth in a cart more than once or twice a year, and he knows, on a pinch, how to use the railway and the telegraph as well as any son of Israel in Chicago. But this is absurd. The East is not the West, and these men must continue to deal with the machinery of life, and to call it progress. Their very preachers dare not rebuke them. They gloss over the hunting for money and the twice-sharpened bitterness of Adam's curse by saying that such things dower a man with a larger range of thoughts and higher aspiration. They do not say: "Free yourself from your own slavery," but rather, "If you can possibly manage it, do not set quite so much store on the things of this world." And they do not know what the things of this world are.

I went off to see cattle killed by way of clearing my head, which, as you will perceive, was getting muddled. They say every Englishman goes to the Chicago stock-yards. You shall find them about six miles from the city; and once having seen them you will never forget the sight. As far as the eye can reach stretches a township of cattle-pens, cunningly divided into blocks so that the animals of any pen can be speedily driven out close to an inclined timber path which leads to an elevated covered way straddling high above the pens. These viaducts are two-stored. On the upper storey tramp the doomed cattle, stolidly for the most part. On the lower, with a scuffling of sharp hoofs and multitudinous yells, run the pigs. The same end is appointed for each. Thus you will see the gangs of cattle waiting their turn—as they wait sometimes for days; and they need not be distressed by the sight of their fellows running about in the fear of death. All they know is that a man on horseback causes their next-door neighbors to move by means of a whip. Certain bars and fences are unshipped, and, behold, that crowd have gone up the mouth of a sloping tunnel and return no more. It is different with the pigs. They shriek back the news of the exodus to their friends, and a hundred pens skirl responsive. It was to the pigs I first addressed myself. Selecting a viaduct which was full of them, as I could hear though I could not see, I marked a sombre building whereto it ran, and went there, not unalarmed by stray cattle who had managed to escape from their proper quarters. A pleasant smell of brine warned me of what was coming. I entered the factory and found it full of pork in barrels, and on another storey more pork unbarrelled, and in a huge room the halves of swine, for whose use great lumps of ice were being pitched in at the window. That room was the mortuary chamber where the pigs lie for a little while in state ere they being their progress through such passages as kings may sometimes travel. Turning a corner and not noting an overhead arrangement of greased rail, wheel, and pulley, I ran into the arms of four eviscerated carcasses, all pure white and of a human aspect, being pushed by a man clad in vehement red. When I leaped aside, the floor was slippery under me. There was a flavour of farmyard in my nostrils and the shouting of a multitude in my ears. But there was no joy in that shouting. Twelve men stood in two lines—six a side. Between them and overhead ran the railway of death that had nearly shunted me through the window. Each man carried a knife, the sleeves of his shirt were cut off at the elbows, and from bosom to heel he was blood-red. The atmosphere was stifling as a night in the Rains, by reason of the steam and the crowd. I climbed to the beginning of things and, perched upon a narrow beam, overlooked very nearly all the pigs ever bred in Wisconsin. They had just been shot out of the mouth of the viaduct and huddled together in a large pen. Thence they were flicked persuasively, a few at a time, into a smaller chamber, and there a man fixed tackle on their hinder legs so that they rose in the air suspended from the railway of death. Oh! it was then they shrieked and called on their mothers and made promises of amendment, till the tackleman punted them in their backs, and they slid head down into a brick-floored passage, very like a big kitchen sink that was blood-red. There awaited them a red man with a knife which he passed jauntily through their throats, and the full-voiced shriek became a sputter, and then a fall as of heavy tropical rain. The red man who was backed against the passage wall stood clear of the wildly kicking hoofs and passed his hand over his eyes, not from any feeling of compassion, but because the spurted blood was in his eyes, and he had barely time to stick the next arrival. Then that first stuck swine dropped, still kicking, into a great vat of boiling water, and spoke no more words, but wallowed in obedience to some unseen machinery, and presently came forth at the lower end of the vat and was heaved on the blades of a blunt paddle-wheel-thing which said, "Hough! Hough! Hough!" and skelped all the hair off him except what little couple of men with knives could remove. Then he was again hitched by the heels to that said railway and passed down the line of the twelve men—each man with a knife—leaving with each man a certain amount of his individuality which was taken away in a wheelbarrow, and when he reached the last man he was very beautiful to behold, but immensely unstuffed and limp. ...

The dissecting part impressed me not so much as the slaying. They were so excessively alive, these pigs. And then they were so excessively dead, and the man in the dripping, clammy, hot passage did not seem to care, and ere the blood of such an one had ceased to foam on the floor, such another, and four friends with him, had shrieked and died. But a pig is only the Unclean animal—forbidden by the Prophet.

I was destined to make rather a queer discovery when I went over to the cattle-slaughter. All the buildings were on a much larger scale, and there was no sound of trouble, but I could smell the salt reek of blood before I set foot in the place. The cattle did not come directly through the viaduct as the pigs had done. They debouched into a yard by the hundred, and they were big red brutes carrying much flesh. In the centre of that yard stood a red Texan steer with a head-stall on his wicked head. No man controlled him. He was, so to speak, picking his teeth and whistling in an open byre of his own when the cattle arrived. As soon as the first one had fearfully quitted the viaduct, this red devil put his hands in his pockets and slouched across the yard, no man guiding him. Then he lowed something to the effect that he was the regularly appointed guide of the establishment and would show them round. They were country folk, but they knew how to behave; and so followed Judas some hundred strong, patiently, and with a look of bland wonder in their faces. I saw his broad back jogging in advance of them, up a lime-washed incline where I was forbidden to follow. Then a door-shut, and in a minute back came Judas with the air of a virtuous plough-bullock and took up his place in his byre. Somebody laughed across the yard, but I heard no sound of cattle from the big brick building into which the mob had disappeared. Only Judas chewed the cud with a malignant satisfaction, and so I knew there was trouble, and ran round to the front of the factory and so entered and stood aghast.

Who takes count of the prejudices which we absorb through the skin by way of our surroundings? It was not the spectacle that impressed me. The first thought that almost spoke itself aloud was: "They are killing kine"; and it was a shock. The pigs were nobody's concern, but cattle—the brothers of the Cow, the Sacred Cow—were quite otherwise. The next time an M.P. tells me that India either Sultanises or Brahminises a man, I shall believe about half what he says. It is unpleasant to watch the slaughter of cattle when one has laughed at the notion for a few years. I could not see actually what was done in the first instance, because the row of stalls in which they lay was separated from me by fifty impassable feet of butchers and slung carcasses. All I know is that men swung open the doors of a stall as occasion required, and there lay two steers already stunned, and breathing heavily. These two they pole-axed, and half raising them by tackle they cut their throats. Two men skinned each carcass, somebody cut off the head, and in half a minute more the overhead rail carried two sides of beef to their appointed place. There was clamour enough in the operating-room, but from the waiting cattle, invisible on the other side of the line of pens, never a sound. They went to their death, trusting Judas, without a word. They were slain at the rate of five a minute, and if the pig men were splattered with blood, the cow butchers were bathed in it. The blood ran in muttering gutters. There was no place for hand or foot that was not coated with thicknesses of dried blood, and the stench of it in the nostrils bred fear.

And then the same merciful Providence that has showered good things on my path throughout sent me an embodiment of the City of Chicago, so that I might remember it for ever. Women come sometimes to see the slaughter, as they would come to see the slaughter of men. And there entered that vermilion hall a young woman of large mould, with brilliantly scarlet lips, and heavy eyebrows, and dark hair that came in a "widow's peak" on the forehead. She was well and healthy and alive, and she was dressed in flaming red and black, and her feet (know you that the feet of American women are like unto the feet of fairies?)—her feet, I say, were cased in red leather shoes. She stood in a patch of sunlight, the red blood under her shoes, the vivid carcasses tacked round her, a bullock bleeding its life away not six feet away from her, and the death factory roaring all round her. She looked curiously, with hard, bold eyes, and was not ashamed.

Then said I: "This is a special Sending. I have seen the City of Chicago!" And I went away to get peace and rest.

123

Chicago Poems

CARL SANDBURG

Carl Sandburg (1878–1967) was one of the central poets that formed the Chicago Renaissance. The son of Swedish immigrants who settled in Illinois, Sandburg's cultural perspectives are underpinned by a fierce sense of the mid-West and of its democratic and populist basis as symbolic of the American process. He is very much in the tradition of Walt Whitman and (like Whitman) saw the city, especially Chicago, as endemic of a new, raw, and potential energy reflecting the experience of a new age and new values.

After leaving school at the age of thirteen, he was involved in a series of different jobs. He published his first pamphlet of poems, *Reckless Energy,* in 1904, but it was *Chicago Poems* (1916) which established his poetry as speaking to a sense of the city as brash as it was vivid. His Whitmanian perspectives continue in *Smoke and Steel* (1920), *Good Morning America* (1928), and *The People, Yes* (1936). His populist roots are equally reflected in his "biography" of Abraham Lincoln (1926–31). See H. W. Wells, *The American Way of Poetry* (1964).

Chicago

Hog Butcher for the World,
Tool Maker, Stacker of Wheat,
Player with Railroads and the Nation's Freight Handler;
Stormy, husky, brawling,
City of the Big Shoulders:

They tell me you are wicked and I believe them, for I have seen your painted women under the gas lamps luring the farm boys.
And they tell me you are crooked and I answer: Yes, it is true I have seen the gunman kill and go free to kill again.
And they tell me you are brutal and my reply is: On the faces of women and children I have seen the marks of wanton hunger.

Source: Carl Sandburg, "Chicago" (1916). "Prayers of Steel" (1918), "The Windy City" (1922).

And having answered so I turn once more to those who sneer at this my city, and I give them back the sneer and say to them:
Come and show me another city with lifted head singing so proud to be alive and coarse and strong and cunning.
Flinging magnetic curses amid the toil of piling job on job, here is a tall bold slugger set vivid against the little soft cities;
Fierce as a dog with tongue lapping for action, cunning as a savage pitted against the wilderness,
Bareheaded,
Shoveling,
Wrecking,
Planning,
Building, breaking, rebuilding,
Under the smoke, dust all over his mouth, laughing with white teeth,
Under the terrible burden of destiny laughing as a young man laughs,
Laughing even as an ignorant fighter laughs who has never lost a battle,
Bragging and laughing that under his wrist is the pulse, and under his ribs the heart of the people,
Laughing!
Laughing the stormy, husky, brawling laughter of Youth, half-naked, sweating, proud to be Hog Butcher, Tool Maker, Stacker of Wheat, Player with Railroads and Freight Handler to the Nation.

Prayers of Steel

Lay me an the anvil, O God.
Beat me and hammer me into a crowbar.
Let me pry loose old walls.
Let me lift and loosen old foundations.

Lay me on an anvil, O God.
Beat me and hammer me into a steel spike.
Drive me into the girders that hold a skyscraper together.
Take red-hot rivets and fasten me into the central girders.
Let me be the great nail holding a skyscraper through blue nights into white stars.

From 'The Windy City'

The lean hands of wagon men
put out pointing fingers here,
picked this crossway, put it on a map,
set up their sawbucks, fixed their shotguns,
found a hitching place for the pony express,
made a hitching place for the iron horse,

the one-eyed horse with the fire-spit head,
found a homelike spot and said, "Make a home,"
saw this corner with a mesh of rails, shuttling
people, shunting cars, shaping the junk of
the earth to a new city.

The hands of men took hold and tugged
And the breaths of men went into the junk
And the junk stood up into skyscrapers and asked:
Who am I? Am I a city? And if I am what is my name?
And once while the time whistles blew and blew again
The men answered: Long ago we gave you a name,
Long ago we laughed and said: You? Your name is Chicago.

Early the red men gave a name to a river,
the place of the skunk,
the river of the wild onion smell,
She-caw-go.

Out of the payday songs of steam shovels,
Out of the wages of structural iron rivets,
The living lighted skyscrapers tell it now as a name,
Tell it across miles of sea blue water, gray blue land:
I am Chicago, I am a name given out by the breaths of working
men, laughing men, a child, a belonging.

So between the Great Lakes,
The Grand De Tour, and the Grand Prairie,
The living lighted skyscrapers stand,
Spotting the blue dusk with checkers of yellow,
streamers of smoke and silver,
parallelograms of night gray watchmen,
Singing a soft moaning song: I am a child, a belonging.

Put the city up; tear the city down;
put it up again; let us find a city.
Let us remember the little violet-eyed
man who gave all, praying, "Dig and
dream, dream and hammer, till your
city comes."
Every day the people sleep and the city dies;
every day the people shake loose, awake and
build the city again.
The city is a tool chest opened every day,
a time clock punched every morning,
a shop door, bunkers and overalls
counting every day.

CHICAGO

The city is a balloon and a bubble plaything
shot to the sky every evening, whistled in
a ragtime jig down the sunset.

The city is made, forgotten, and made again,
trucks hauling it away haul it back
steered by drivers whistling ragtime
against the sunsets.

Every day the people get up and carry the city,
carry the bunkers and balloons of the city,
lift it and put it down.

. . . .

Winds of the Windy City, come out of the prairie,
all the way from Medicine Hat.
Come out of the inland sea blue water, come where
they nickname a city for you.

Corn wind in the fall, come off the black lands,
come off the whisper of the silk hangers,
the lap of the flat spear leaves.

Blue water wind in summer, come off the blue miles
of lake, carry your inland sea blue fingers,
carry us cool, carry your blue to our homes.

White spring winds, come off the bag wool clouds,
come off the running melted snow, come white
as the arms of snow-born children.

Gray fighting winter winds, come along on the tearing
blizzard tails, the snouts of the hungry
hunting storms, come fighting gray in winter.

Winds of the Windy City,
Winds of corn and sea blue,
Spring wind white and fighting winter gray,
Come home here—they nickname a city for you.

The wind of the lake shore waits and wanders.
The heave of the shore wind hunches the sand piles.
The winkers of the morning stars count out cities
And forget the numbers.

124

Towertown

HARVEY ZORBAUGH

Harvey Zorbaugh's *The Gold Coast and the Slum* was published in Chicago in 1929 and, in its depiction of Towertown, reflected a sense of the city much in evidence in the literature of the period. Here the city is an agent of change and individual possibility; an alternative to the cloying restrictions and narrow mores of small town American life. It is the city as much anticipated by Carrie Meeber in Dreiser's *Sister Carrie* (1900), as it is the Chicago alternative to Winesburg imagined by George Willard in Anderson's *Winesburg, Ohio* (1919). In the 1920s especially, the city was seen as the nexus of Bohemian life. If Chicago offered some of this, it was New York's Greenwich Village which many saw as its apogee. Others, of course, abandoned America altogether and chose the then capital of modernism and the "new"—Paris.

The Towertown of today ... is largely made up of individuals who have sought in its unconventionality and anonymity—sometimes under the guise of art, sometimes not—escape from the conventions and repressions of the small town or the outlying and more stable communities of the city. Some of these individuals have a genuine hunger for new experience, a desire to experiment with life. They run the tearooms and art shops and book stalls of the "village," or work in the Loop by day and frequent its studios and restaurants by night. Perhaps, like Collie, they keep a little red notebook with a list of the things they have always wanted to do, and strike them off as one experiment in living after another is completed. Most of these experimenters are young women. For Towertown, like Greenwich Village, is predominantly a woman's bohemia. ... It is the young women who open most of the studios, run most of the tearooms and restaurants, most of the little art shops and book stalls, manage the exhibits and little theatres, dominate the life of the bohemians of American cities. And in Towertown the women are, on the whole, noticeably superior to the men.

Source: Harvey Zorbaugh, "Towertown", *The Gold Coast and the Slum*, Chicago, 1929, pp. 91–2, 96–101.

But these genuine experimenters with life are few. Most of Towertown's present population are egocentric poseurs, neurotics, rebels against the conventions of Main Street or the gossip of the foreign community, seekers of atmosphere, dabblers in the occult, dilettantes in the arts, or parties to drab lapses from a moral code which the city has not yet destroyed. ... "Self-expression" is the avowed goal of "village" life. And where talent is lacking, self-expression runs to the playing of roles and the wearing of masques, sometimes of the most bizarre sort. ...

The villager is usually content with assuming an eccentricity in dress or manner, an indifference to opinion that is far from real, a contempt for Rodin, Debussy, or Shakespeare, or a pose as the prophet of some new movement in drama, poetry, music, or painting. Once the role is adopted, or perchance thrust upon one, the whole "village" plays up to it, and a personality is crystallized.

> The Neo Arlimusc recently held an exhibit for "Chicago's primitive artist." This primitive artist is P——, a conventional, small business man of sixty-two, who a year ago suddenly began to paint. He had been a clothing peddler in the ghetto, had earned a very mediocre living, but had managed to save a little and had retired. One day the old man dropped some papers from his pocket on which a friend saw some sketches. The old man was much embarrassed, but the friend insisted on taking them to W——, who exclaimed, "This man is a genius, a primitive artist!" P—— had never had a lesson in his life, and paints very crudely. With this encouragement P—— began to paint more crudely than ever. Then it was arranged to give P—— an exhibit. Only his own things were hung. They had an art critic from the University who came and discussed P——'s primitive unconscious for the explanation of his turning to painting at so late an age. De K—— got up, and pointing to some Jewish sweatshop scenes painted on old cardboard, exclaimed: "See that? The artist's expression will out! Poverty stricken, he seizes on the only medium available." The P—— was sent off to New York, where Greenwich Village hailed him as the exponent of a new art form. Under this definition by the group, P—— has ceased to be the timid clothing peddler, sketching and secreting his sketches, having constantly to be reassured he is an artist and has a place in the world, and has accepted the role created for him as the creator of a new and primitive art, and continues to paint more and more crudely.

Behind these masques which the "villagers" present to one another and to the world one usually discovers the egocentric, the poseur, the neurotic, or the "originality" of an unimaginative nature. Occasionally, however, one finds behind these masques young persons who are struggling to live out their own lives, to remake the world a bit more after the fashion of their dreams—young persons who have come from north and west and south, from farm and village and suburb, to this mobile, isolated, anonymous area of a great city where they imagine they may live their dreams. It is these occasional dreams behind the masque, and the enthusiasms, intimacies, disillusionments that are a part of the living out of these dreams, that lend the "village," despite its tawdry tinsel, a certain charm. ...

Transient but intense personal contacts are characteristic of this "bohemian" life of "studio" and "tearoom." Combined with the unconventional tradition of the "village," its philosophy of individualism, and the anonymity which its streets afford, these contacts give rise to unconventional types of sex relationship. Moreover, Towertown's debates on free love and its reputation for promiscuity, coupled with its unconventionality and anonymity, attract to its studios many individuals who are not bohemians, but who seek in Towertown escape from the repressive conventions of the larger community. Many of them become hangers-on of bohemia, but others isolate themselves in its midst.

The anonymity and unconventionality of "village" streets attracts to them many who merely want to be "let alone." I was talking one night, near "Bughouse Square," about life in the "village." Afterwards a girl came up to me and said: "Why can't social agencies let us alone? There's at least a year in everybody's life when he wants to do just as he damn pleases. The "village" is the only place where he can do it without sneaking off in a hole by himself."

Plenty of individuals do use the anonymity of "village" life, however, to sneak off into holes by themselves. Business and professional men use its studio apartments to keep their mistresses. B—— and her mother live in a beautiful apartment, with Japanese servants and every luxury. B—— is supported by a wealthy business man, married with a wife and family, who spends occasional week-ends with her. Intervening nights she entertains an army officer, a penniless adventurer, to whom she even gives money. G—— is a well-to-do lawyer, and bachelor and keeps his mistress in the village. There are many such cases, especially of young men, "philistines" through and through, who nevertheless like the laissez faire of bohemia. R—— is a wealthy dilettante in the arts whose elaborate studio parties are celebrated for the fact that all the women present are his mistresses—past, present, and prospective.

Distorted forms of sex behaviour also find a harbor in the "village." Many homosexuals are among the frequenters of "village" tearooms and studios. A friend of mine was asked by an acquaintance to accompany him to the studio of a well-known "villager" to Sunday afternoon tea. There was a large group there. The men were smoking and talking in one end of the room, the women in the other. There was a good deal of taking one another's arms, sitting on the arms of one another's chairs, and of throwing an arm about one another's shoulders. But he thought it was merely that the group were old friends. He was asked to tea again a few weeks later. This time he remained in the evening. Soon the men were fondling one another, as were the women. A man he had met that afternoon threw an arm about him. He got up, went over to the acquaintance who had brought him, and said, "I'm leaving." When they got out on the street he asked, "What sort of a place was that, anyhow?" "Why, I thought you knew," his companion replied, "the best-known fairies and lesbians in Chicago were there."

The intimate and artistic life of the "village" is passed unnoticed by the rest of the city, to which Towertown stands only for these bizarre garret and stable studios, long hair, eccentric dress, and free love. This is due largely to the fact that certain shrewd individuals were not slow to see possibilities in the commercialization of bohemia. Some of these individuals were of bohemia themselves. A group of young women writers in Towertown organized "Seeing Bohemia" trips, at seventy-five cents a head, and conducted curious persons from the outside world through tearooms and studios bizarrely decorated for the occasion.

125

Chicago Through the Eyes of Business

CHICAGO BETTER BUSINESS BUREAU INC.

Published in 1930 by the Chicago Better Business Bureau, this is very much part of a public relations exercise to "boost" the image of the city as a vibrant commercial centre. Its approach is to engender as positive a view as possible. In this "great city" even its slums "are but a dull streak across its face".

It is high time the business man talked about Chicago and told the truth about the city for Chicago is suffering from the sins of exaggeration. Regardless of who is to blame, Chicago has acquired a bad reputation. The members of the Better Business Bureau realize that the time has come to care about what the world thinks of the city for the city's bad name has ceased to be a joke. It is a detriment to community welfare. Not only does it injure the city's good name; it affects property and business.

The business men who are members of the Better Business Bureau in cooperation with other civic bodies, have determined to rescue the city's good name—not to gloss over crimes and deny facts, but to produce facts and tell the truth. The truth is that Chicago is a prosperous and industrious city where life and property are as safe as anywhere else, where rewards for hard work and decent living are as great as in any other community.

Chicago! Growing, glowing, noisy, wind swept Chicago, with her towers and her parks, her squalor and her dust! A prodigy among cities, so acclaimed by friends and foes—a city that so grips the imagination and the curiosity that all who know her talk about her. Everyone who knows anything at all about Chicago has presented his impression to the world. Everyone has talked about the city except the business man. He has been too busy making the city worth talking about, and yet he alone knows and understands the city for what it really is.

No community has more to offer the average man. In no large city are general conditions more pleasant than in Chicago. It is a city of homes above the

Source: Chicago Better Business Bureau Inc., "Chicago Through the Eyes of Business", 1930, pp. 2–3, 13–15, 25–9.

the regular habitues of the establishment. Many of them were poor and most were people, young and old, who were misfits in American life, who were maladjusted but turned their maladjustments into virtues. In her own mind, Bridget knew that she was play-acting. Whatever she did at the Sour Apple and in the circles of the near-North Side Bohemia did not count, just as years ago, when she had been a little girl on the West Side of Chicago, the games she had played with herself and had acted out had never really counted. She had, in those far-off days, pretended all kinds of things, and she had loved these games of hers. Sometimes she had played that she was her own mother. She used to imagine herself, even before she knew what it meant, going to sleep with her father, just as her mother did every night. And she played at having babies, taking care of them, and at everything else that her mother and other grown-ups did. All during her life, it had been like this. What she played at would for a time seem very real to her, more real than anything else in the world. She believed in her pretending and, at the same time, she knew that they weren't real. She had never attempted to explain this to anyone, but she resented everyone who did not understand her and would not participate in her games. Play-acting like this was one of her secrets. She even play-acted with her two lovers and when she would be in their arms, she would often imagine that they were men whom she did not even know. Bridget had done this with boys and men ever since she had lost her virginity to a first cousin at the age of sixteen, and in her imagination she had had hundreds and hundreds of lovers.

She knew that she did this kind of play-acting. It was fun for her, but it wasn't real. What was real was her character underneath everything she pretended. And this, she believed, was the character of a good honest, respectable, conventional woman. And seeing her real self in these terms, she had contempt for her Bohemian friends and acquaintances. If they were play-acting as she was, then they were bad actors, just as her husband, Pete, had been, while she was a good actress, and it was a pity that she had never gone on the stage. And if they were not play-acting then they were shiftless, no-good and not respectable. Not one of them was, she also believed, worthy of her, just as Pete had been unworthy of her. Most of them, too, were poor. She wasn't. She owned her home, and she had over seven thousand dollars in the bank, although no one, not even her children, knew about this. She was a woman of standing, not a shiftless Bohemian. This, also, was part of her secret.

Her secrets and her play-acting made life exciting. No one, she was convinced, lived a more exciting life than she did.

III

Frank O'Dair, Bridget's younger son, and his wife, Teresa, lived in Martha Swanson's rooming house on the two top floors of an old building on North Michigan Avenue near Ohio Street. Bridget decided to move in with them. She easily convinced Martha to give her a room at five dollars a week instead of the seven which Martha had asked. She didn't know that Martha was planning to move to New York and didn't care.

The top floors were rambling and the plumbing was old. Many of the rooms were dirty and there was an air of disorderliness about the place. Bridget liked this because it permitted her to believe and to tell her children and others that this was what she had been reduced to in life, and she also used this as the reason for making still more accusations against her husband as the man who had ruined her life and had reduced her to misery.

After moving into her room, a square medium-sized one with a bed, an old dresser, a rickety table and several chairs, Bridget sat and waited for Frank and Teresa to come home. They were out somewhere. It was a dull and cold March day. She tried to look as gloomy and as unhappy as she could. She lit a cigarette and, puffing on it, imagined how she would tell Frank and Teresa that she was reduced to living in this room, a poor and homeless woman. But what did Frank see in Teresa? A common girl, the daughter of people who were no good and a girl with no ambition. It was Pete's influence that had led her baby, Frank, to take up with this slut.

She heard footsteps outside her door and waited. The footsteps died away. it wasn't anyone coming to see her. She was dispirited. There were many things she could do, and she didn't have to sit alone like this in her miserable five-dollar-a-week room. It wasn't worth five dollars, and to think that Martha had wanted to charge her seven for it. She would have to watch Martha. That girl would scheme and over-charge. But she wouldn't get away with over-charging Bridget O'Dair.

She would sit here alone until her son came back. This would emphasize her plight and her loneliness and it would make him understand and love his mother more. None of her three children really loved her. They thought more of Pete than of her. She knew this. But one day, they would feel sorry for this .One day they would understand.

She squashed out her cigarette.

Bridget became nervous. Allie was at work. She would see him tonight and make him pay her rent. Why didn't Bill come to see her? He lived here now. Frank had convinced Martha to take him in because he didn't have a penny. He was a worn-out bum. What did she see in him? A man over sixty trying to make love to her. Allie, at least, was young and vigorous.

And so was she. Physically she was years younger than her age, and that was why she had. ... What should she call it? Capacity?

Bridget smiled and glowed within herself, remembering that conversation she had had with her daughter, Geraldine, about a month or two ago. She didn't have a good memory for time, and she wouldn't know if something happened one month or six months ago. She had gone to see Dr. Adam Bergman, whose name she had heard mentioned at the Sour Apple. There had been nothing really wrong with her. Her health was remarkable, a phenomenon. But she had been nervous and hadn't been able to sleep, and even when Allie would stay with her, and he would be sleeping and snoring at her side, tired out, she'd lay there unsatisfied. Dr. Bergman had asked her questions about her sex life and she had told him. He was a doctor, wasn't he? She'd told him about Bill and Allie, and after listening to her, he'd told her to get a third lover or to masturbate. She'd told all this to Geraldine. That was the kind of woman she was. Why even now when she was a grandmother, she was as good as three women.

Bridget suddenly left her room in a nervous state.

128

Humboldt's Gift

SAUL BELLOW

Saul Bellow (1915–), one of the greatest of twentieth-century American novelists, was born in Quebec, Canada. His family moved to Chicago in 1924, and Bellow went on to attend Northwestern and Chicago (as well as Wisconsin) Universities. His writing has always been informed by Chicago as both a dense and immediate daily experience as well as a symbol of the pattern of twentieth-century life. His Jewish background has been equally as influential, and Bellow's significance as a novelist forms part of the post-Second World War rise of such Jewish writers as Malamud, [Philip] Roth, and Ginsberg.

Bellow however tests his inheritance in terms of a subtle and complex philosophical context where the moral perspectives of modern culture are judged accordingly. The novels, in that sense, form an extended dramatic investigation of the terms of twentieth-century urban life. This is the basis of his first novel, *Dangling Man* (1944), an existentialist story reflecting the pervasive uncertainties of the decade. He developed such preoccupations in later novels, notably, *The Adventures of Augie March* (1953), *Seize the Day* (1956), and *Henderson The Rain King* (1959).

Herzog makes the urban seeing central, although it is *Mr. Sammler's Planet* (1970) which most vehemently reflects Bellow's increasing *angst* against what he regards as a crass, materialistic society. Set in New York City, it reflects an urban atmosphere of incipient breakdown and violence. Its anti-hero, Mr. Sammler, a survivor of Auschwitz Concentration Camp, observes a post-modern condition from the double perspective of the hell of Auschwitz and the civilized atmosphere of Bloomsbury in pre-war London. In *Humboldt's Gift* (1975), the setting is once again Chicago.

A brilliant observer of the age, Bellow extends American realism into a web of the psychological and moral within the specific context of particular environments. See Tony Tanner, *Saul Bellow* (1965) and Maxwell Geismar, *American Moderns* (1958).

Source: Saul Bellow, *Humboldt's Gift*, New York, 1975.
Page references are to the 1976 Penguin edition, pp. 72–106.

At the Mercedes shop the distinguished official and technician in the white smock was naturally curious but I refused to answer questions. "I don't know how this happened, Fritz. I found it this way. Fix it. I don't want to see the bill, either. Just send it to the Continental Illinois. They'll pay it." Fritz charged like a brain surgeon.

I flagged a taxi in the street. The driver was wild-looking with an immense Afro like a shrub from the gardens at Versailles. The back of his cab was dusty with cigarette ashes and had a tavern odour. There was a bullet-proof screen between us. He made a fast turn and charged due west on Division Street. I could see little, because of the blurred Plexiglas and the Afro, but I didn't really need to look, I knew it all by heart. Large parts of Chicago decay and fall down. Some are rebuilt, others just lie there. It's like a film montage of rise fall and rise. Division Street where the old Bath stands used to be Polish and now is almost entirely Puerto Rican. In the Polish days, the small brick bungalows were painted fresh red, maroon, and candy green. The grass plots were fenced with iron pipe. I always thought that there must be Baltic towns that looked like this, Gdynia for instance, the difference being that the Illinois prairie erupted in vacant lots and tumbleweed rolled down the streets. Tumbleweed is so melancholy.

In the old days of ice wagons and coal wagons householders used to cut busted boilers in half, set them out on the grass plots, and fill them with flowers. Big Polish women in ribboned caps went out in the spring with cans of Sapolio and painted these boiler-planters so that they shone silver against the blaring red of the brick. The double rows of rivets stood out like the raised-skin patterns of African tribes. Here the women grew geraniums, sweet William, and other low-grade dusty flowers. I showed all of this to Humboldt Fleisher years ago. He came to Chicago to give a reading for *Poetry* magazine and asked me for a tour of the city. We were dear friends then. I had come back to see my father and to put the last touches on my book, New Deal Personalities, at the Newberry Library. I took Humboldt on the El to the stockyards. He saw the Loop. We went to the lakeshore and listened to the foghorns. They bawled melancholy over the limp silk fresh lilac drowning water. But Humboldt responded mostly to the old neighbourhood. The silvered boiler rivets and the blazing Polish geraniums got him. He listened pale and moved to the buzzing of roller-skate wheels on the brittle cement. I too am sentimental about urban ugliness. In the modern spirit of ransoming the commonplace, all this junk and wretchedness, through art and poetry, by the superior power of the soul.

Mary, my eight-year-old daughter, has discovered this about me. She knows my weakness for ontogeny and phylogeny. She always asks to hear what life was like way-back-when.

"We had coal stoves," I tell her. "The kitchen range was black, with a nickel trim—huge. The parlour stove had a dome like a little church, and you could watch the fire through the isinglass. I had to carry up the scuttle and take down the ashes."

"What did you wear?"

"A leatherette war-ace cap with rabbit-fur flaps, high-top boots with a sheath for a rusty jack-knife, long black stockings, and plus fours. Underneath, woolly combinations which left lint in my navel and elsewhere."

"What else was it like?" my younger daughter wanted to know. Lish, who is ten years old, is her mother's child and such information would not interest her. But Mary is less pretty, though to my mind she is more attractive (more like her father). She is secretive and greedy. She lies and steals more than most small girls, and this is also endearing. She hides chewing gum and chocolates with stirring ingenuity. I find her candy buried under the upholstery or in my filing cabinet. She has learned that I don't often look at my research materials. She flatters and squeezes me precociously. And she wants to hear about old times. She has her own purposes in evoking and manipulating my emotions. But Papa is quite willing to manifest the old-time feelings. In fact I must transmit these feelings. For I have plans for Mary. Oh, nothing so definite as plans, perhaps. I have an idea that I may be able to pervade the child's mind with my spirit so that she will later take up the work I am getting too old or too weak or too silly to continue. She alone, or perhaps she and her husband. With any luck. I worry about the girl. In a locked drawer of my desk I keep notes and memos for her, many of them written under the influence of liquor. I promise myself to censor these one day, before death catches me off base on the racquet-ball court or on the Posturepedic mattress of some Renata or other. Mary is sure to be an intelligent woman. She interprets "Für Elise" much better than Lish. She feels the music. My heart is often troubled for Mary, however. She will be a straight-nosed thin broad who feels the music. And personally I prefer plump women with fine breasts. So I felt sorry for her already. As for the project or purpose I want her to carry on, it is a very personal overview of the Intellectual Comedy of the modern mind. No one person could do this comprehensively. By the end of the nineteenth century what had been the ample novels of Balzac's Comedy had already been reduced to stories by Chekhov in his Russian *Comédie Humaine.* Now it's even less possible to be comprehensive. I never had a work of fiction in mind but a different kind of imaginative projection. Different also from Whitehead's *Adventures of Ideas* ... This is not the moment to explain it. Whatever it was, I conceived of it while still a youngish man. It was actually Humboldt who lent me the book of Valéry that suggested it. Valéry wrote of Leonardo, "*Cet Apollon me ravissait au plus haut degré de moi-même.*" I too was ravished with permanent effect–perhaps carried beyond my mental means. But Valéry had added a note in the margin: "*Trouve avant de chercher.*" This finding before seeking was my special gift. If I had any gift.

However, my small daughter would say to me with deadly accuracy of instinct. "Tell me what your mother used to do. Was she pretty?"

"I think she was very pretty. I don't look like her. And she did cooking, baking, laundry and ironing, canning and pickling. She could tell fortunes with cards and sing trembly Russian songs. She and my father took turns visiting me at the sanatorium, every other week. In February the vanilla ice cream they brought was so hard you couldn't cut it with a knife. And what else—ah yes, at home when I lost a tooth she would throw it behind the stove and ask the little mouse to bring a better one. You see what kind of teeth those bloody mice palmed off on me."

"You loved your mother?"

Eager swelling feeling suddenly swept in. I forgot that I was talking to a child and I said, "Oh, I loved them all terribly, abnormally. I was all torn up with love. Deep in the heart. I used to cry in the sanatorium because I might never make it home and see them. I'm sure they never knew how I loved them, Mary. I had a TB fever and also a love fever. A passionate morbid little boy. At school I was always in love. At home if I was first to get up in the morning I suffered because they were still asleep. I wanted them to wake up so that the whole marvellous thing could continue. I also loved Menasha the boarder and Julius, my brother, your Uncle Julias."

I shall have to lay aside these emotional data.

At the moment money, cheques, hoodlums, automobiles pre-occupied me.

Another cheque was on my mind. It had been sent by my friend Thaxter, the one whom Huggins accused of being a CIA agent. You see Thaxter and I were preparing to bring out a journal, *The Ark*. We were all ready. Wonderful things were to be printed in it—pages from my imaginative reflections on a world transformed by Mind, for example. But meantime Thaxter had defaulted on a certain loan.

It's a long story and one that I'd rather not go into at this point. For two reasons. One is that I love Thaxter, whatever he does. The other is that I actually do think too much about money. It's no good trying to conceal it. It's there and it's base. Earlier when I described how George saved Sharon's life when her throat was cut, I spoke of blood as a vital substance. Well, money is a vital substance, too. Thaxter was supposed to repay part of the defaulted loan. Broke but grandoise he had ordered a cheque from his Italian bank for me, the Banco Ambrosiano of Milan. Why the Banco? Why Milan? But all of Thaxter's arrangements were out of the ordinary. He had had a transatlantic upbringing and was equally at home in France and in California. You couldn't mention a region so remote that Thaxter didn't have an uncle there, or an interest in a mine, or an old château or villa. Thaxter with his exotic ways was another of my headaches. But I couldn't resist him. However, that too must wait. Only one last word: Thaxter wanted people to believe that he was once a CIA agent. It was a wonderful rumour and he did everything to encourage it. It greatly added to his mysteriousness, and mystery was one of his little rackets. This was harmless and in fact endearing. It was even philanthropic, as charm always is—up to a point. Charm always is a bit of a racket.

The cab pulled up at the Bath twenty minutes early and I wasn't going to loiter there so I said through the perforations of the bulletproof screen, "Go on, drive west. Take it easy. I just want to look around." The cabbie heard me and nodded his Afro. It was like an enormous black dandelion in seed, blown, all its soft spindles standing out.

In the last six months more old neighbourhood landmarks had been torn down. This shouldn't have mattered much. I can't say why it made such a difference. But I was in a state. It almost seemed to me that I could hear myself rustling and fluttering in the back seat like a bird touring the mangroves of its youth, now car dumps. I stared with pulsatory agitation through the soiled windows. A whole block had gone down. Lovi's Hungarian Restaurant had been swept away, plus Ben's Pool Hall and the old brick carbarn and Gratch's Funeral Parlour, out of which both my parents had been buried. Eternity got no picturesque interval here. The ruins of time had been bulldozed, scraped, loaded in trucks, and dumped as fill. New steel beams were going up. Polish kielbasa no longer hung in butchers' windows. The sausages in the *carniceria* were Caribbean, purple and wrinkled. The old shop signs were gone. The new ones said HOY. MUDANZAS. IGLESIA.

"Keep going west," I said to the driver. "Past the park. Turn right on Kedzie."

The old boulevard now was a sagging ruin, waiting for the wreckers. Through great holes I could look into apartments where I had slept, eaten, done my lessons, kissed girls. You'd have to loathe yourself vividly to be indifferent to such destruction or, worse, rejoice at the crushing of the locus of these middle-class sentiments, glad that history had made rubble of them. In fact I know such tough guys. This very neighbourhood produced them. Informers to the metaphysical-historical police against fellows like me whose hearts ache at the destruction of the past. But I had come here to be melancholy, to be sad about the wrecked walls and windows, the missing doors, the fixtures torn out, and the telephone cables ripped away and sold as junk. More particularly, I had come to see whether the house in which Naomi Lutz had lived was still standing. It was not. That made me feel very low.

In my highly emotional adolescence I had loved Naomi Lutz. I believe she was the most beautiful and perfect young girl I have ever seen, I adored her, and love brought out my deepest peculiarities. Her father was a respectable chiropodist. He gave himself high medical airs, every inch the Doctor. Her mother was a dear woman, slipshod, harum-scarum, rather chinless, but with large glowing romantic eyes. Night after night I had to play rummy with Dr Lutz, and on Sundays I helped him to wash and simonize his Auburn. But that was all right. When I loved Naomi Lutz I was safely *within life*. Its phenomena added up, they made sense. Death was an after all acceptable part of the proposition. I had my own little Lake Country, the park, where I wandered with my Modern Library Plato, Wordsworth, Swinburne, and *Un Cœur Simple*. Even in winter Naomi petted behind the rose garden with me. Among the frozen twigs I made myself warm inside her raccoon coat. There was a delicious mixture of coon skin and maiden fragrance. We breathed frost and kissed. Until I met Demmie Vonghel many years later, I loved no one so much as Naomi Lutz. But Naomi, while I was away in Madison, Wisconsin, reading poetry and studying rotation pool at the

Rathskeller, married a pawnbroker. He dealt also in rebuilt office machinery and had plenty of money. I was too young to give her the charge accounts she had to have at Field's and Saks, and I believe the mental burdens and responsibilities of an intellectual's wife had frightened her besides. I had talked all the time about my Modern Library books, of poetry and history, and she was afraid that she would disappoint me. She told me so. I said to her, if a tear was an intellectual thing how much more intellectual pure love was. It needed no cognitive additives. But she only looked puzzled. It was this sort of talk by which I had lost her. She did not look me up even when her husband lost all his money and deserted her. He was a sporting man, a gambler. He had to go into hiding at last, because the juice men were after him. I believe they had even broken his ankles. Anyway, he changed his name and went or limped to the Southwest. Naomi sold her classy Winnetka house and moved to Marquette Park, where the family owned a bungalow. She took a job in the linen department at Field's.

As the cab went back to Division Street I was making a wry parallel between Naomi's husband's Mafia troubles and my own. He had muffed it, too. I couldn't help thinking what blessed life I might have led with Naomi Lutz. Fifteen thousand nights embracing Naomi and I would have smiled at the solitude and boredom of the grave. I would have needed no bibliography, no stock portfolios, no medal from the Legion of Honour.

So we drove again through what had become a tropical West Indies slum, resembling the parts of San Juan that stand beside lagoons which bubble and smell like stewing tripe. There was the same crushed plaster, smashed glass, garbage in the streets, the same rude amateur blue chalk lettering on the shops.

But the Russian Bath where I was supposed to meet Rinaldo Cantabile stood more or less unchanged. It was also a proletarian hotel or lodging house. On the second floor there had always lived aged workingstiffs, lone Ukrainian grandfathers, retired car-line employees, a pastry cook famous for his icings who had to quit because his hands became arthritic. I knew the place from boyhood. My father, like old Mr Swiebel, had believed it was healthful, good for the blood to be scrubbed with oak leaves lathered in old pickle buckets. Such retrograde people still exist, resisting modernity, dragging their feet. As Menasha the boarder, an amateur physicist (but mostly he wanted to be a dramatic tenor and took voice lessons: he had worked at Brunswick Phonograph Co. as a punch-press operator), once explained to me, human beings could affect the rotation of the earth. How? Well, if the whole race at an agreed moment were to scuff it s feet the revolution of the planet would actually slow down. This might also have an effect on the moon and on the tides. Of course Menasha's real topic was not physics but concord, or unity. I think that some through stupidity and others through perversity would scuff the wrong way. However, the old guys at the Bath do seem to be unconsciously engaged in a collective attempt to buck history.

These Division Street steam-bathers don't look like the trim proud people downtown. Even old Feldstein pumping his Exercycle in the Downtown Club at the age of eighty would be out of place on Division Street. Forty years ago Feldstein was a swinger, a high roller, a good-time Charlie on Rush Street. In spite of his age he is a man of today, whereas the patrons of the Russian Bath are cast in an antique form. They have swelling buttocks and fatty breasts as yellow as buttermilk. They stand on thick pillar legs affected with a sort of creeping verdigris or blue-cheese mottling of the ankles. After steaming, these old fellows eat enormous snacks of bread and salt herring or large ovals of salami and dripping skirt-steak and they drink schnapps. They could knock down walls with their hard stout old-fashioned bellies. Things are very elementary here. You feel that these people are almost conscious of obsolescence, of a line of evolution abandoned by nature and culture. So down in the super-heated subcellars all these Slavonic cavemen and wood demons with hanging laps of fat and legs of stone and lichen boil themselves and splash ice water on their heads by the bucket. Upstairs, on the television screen in the locker-room, little dudes and grinning broads make smart talk or leap up and down. They are unheeded. Mickey who keeps the food concession fries slabs of meat and potato pancakes, and, with enormous knives, he hacks up cabbages for coleslaw and he quarters grapefruits (to be eaten by hand). The stout old men mounting in their bed sheets from the blasting heat have a strong appetite. Below, Franush the attendant makes steam by sloshing water on the white-hot boulders. These lie in a pile like Roman ballistic ammunition. To keep his brains from baking Franush wears a wet felt hat with the brim torn off. Otherwise he is naked. He crawls up like a red salamander with a stick to tip the latch of the furnace, which is too hot to touch, and then on all fours, with testicles swinging on a long sinew and the clean anus staring out, he backs away groping for the bucket. He pitches in the water and the boulders flash and sizzle. There may be no village in the Carpathians where such practices still prevail.

Loyal to this place, Father Myron Swiebel came every day of his life. He brought his own herring, buttered pumpernickel, raw onions, and bourbon whiskey. He drove a Plymouth, though he had no driver's licence. He could see well enough straight ahead, but because there were cataracts on both eyes he sideswiped many cars and did great damage in the parking lot.

I went in to reconnoitre. I was quite anxious about George. His advice had put me in this fix. But then I knew that it was bad advice. Why did I take it? Because he had raised his voice with such authority? Because he had cast himself as an expert on the underworld and I had let him do his stuff? Well, I hadn't used my best mind. But my best mind was now alert and I believed I could handle Cantabile. I reckoned that Cantabile had already worked off his rage against the car and I thought the debt was largely paid.

I asked the concessionaire, Mickey, who stood in the smoke behind the counter searing fatty steaks and frying onions, "Has George come in? Does his old man expect him?"

I thought that if George were here it was not likely that Cantabile would rush fully dressed into the steam to punch or beat or kick him. Of course Cantabile was an unknown quantity. You couldn't guess what Cantabile might do. Either in rage or from calculation.

"George isn't here. The old man is steaming."

"Good. Is he expecting his son?"

"No. George was here Sunday, so he won't come again. He's only once a week with his father."

"Good. Excellent!"

Built like a bouncer with huge bar arms and an apron tied very high under his oxters, Mickey has a twisted lip. During the Depression he had to sleep in the parks and the cold ground gave him a partial paralysis of the cheek. This makes him seem to scoff or jeer. A misleading impression. He is a gentle earnest and peaceful person. A music-lover, he takes a season ticket at the Lyric Opera.

"I haven't seen you in a long time, Charlie. Go steam with the old man, he'll be glad for the company."

But I hurried out again past the cashier's cage with its little steel boxes where patrons left their valuables. I passed the squirming barber pole, and when I got to the sidewalk, which was as dense as the galaxy with stars of broken glass, a white Thunderbird pulled up in front of the Puerto Rican sausage shop across the street and Ronald Cantabile got out. He sprang out, I should say. I saw that he was in a terrific state. Dressed in a brown raglan coat with a matching hat and wearing tan kid boots, he was tall and good-looking. I had noted his dark dense moustache at the poker game. It resembled fine fur. But through the crackling elegance of dress there was a current, a desperate sweep, so that the man came out, so to speak, raging from the neck up. Though he was on the other side of the street I could see how furiously pale he was. He had worked himself up to intimidate me, I thought. But also he was making unusual steps. His feet behaved strangely. Cars and trucks came between us just then so that he could not cross over. Beneath the cars I could see him trying to dodge through. The boots were exquisite. At the first short break in the traffic Cantabile held open his raglan to me. He was wearing a magnificent broad belt. But surely it wasn't a belt that he wanted to display. Just beside the buckle something was sticking out. He clapped his hand to it. He wanted me to know that he was carrying a gun. More traffic came, and Cantabile was jumping up and down, glaring at me over the tops of automobiles. Under the utmost strain he called out to me when the last truck had passed, "You alone?"

"Alone. I'm alone."

He drew himself up towards the shoulders with peculiar twisting intensity. "You got anybody hiding?"

"No. Just me. Nobody."

He threw open the door and brought up two baseball bats from the floor of the Thunderbird. A bat in each hand, he started towards me. A van came between us. Now I could see nothing but his feet moving rapidly in the fancy boots. I thought, He sees I've come to pay. Why should he clobber me? He's got to know I wouldn't pull anything. He's proved his point on the car. And I've seen the gun. Should I run? Since I had discovered on Thanksgiving Day how fast I could still run, I seemed oddly eager to use this ability. Speed was one of my resources. Some people are too fast for their own good, like Asahel in the Book of Samuel. Still it occurred to me that I might dash up the stairs of the Bath and take shelter in the cashier's office where the little steel boxes were. I could crouch on the floor and ask the cashier to pass the four hundred and fifty dollars through the grille to Cantabile. I knew the cashier quite well. But he'd never let me in. He couldn't. I wasn't bonded. He had once referred to this special circumstance when we were having a chat. But I couldn't believe that Cantabile would batter me down. Not in the street. Not as I waited and bowed my head. And just at that moment I remembered Konrad Lorenz's discussion of wolves. The defeated wolf offered his throat, and the victor snapped but wouldn't bite. So I was bowing my head. Yes, but damn my memory! What did Lorenz say next? Humankind was different, but in what respect? How! I couldn't remember. My brain was disintegrating. The day before, in the bathroom, I hadn't been able to find the word for the isolation of the contagious, and I was in agony. I thought, whom should I telephone about this? My mind is going! And then I stood and clutched the sink until the word "quarantine" mercifully came back to me. Yes, quarantine, but I was losing my grip. I take such things hard. In old age my father's memory also failed. So I was shaken. The difference between man and other species such as the wolves never did come back to me. Perhaps the lapse was excusable at a time like this. But it served to show how carelessly I was treading, these days. This inattentiveness and memory-failure boded no good.

As the last of a string of cars passed, Cantabile took a long stride with both bats as if to rush upon me without a pause. But I yelled, "For Christ's sake, Cantabile!"

He paused. I held up open hands. Then he flung one of the bats into the Thunderbird and started for me with the other.

I called out to him, "I brought the money. You don't have to beat my brains out."

"You got a gun?"

"I've got nothing."

"You come over here," he said.

I started willingly to cross the street. He made me stop in the middle.

"Stay right there," he said. I was in the centre of heavy traffic, cars honking and the provoked drivers rolling down their windows, already fighting mad. He tossed the second bat back into the T-bird. Then he strode up and took hold of me roughly. He treated me as if I deserved the extreme penalty. I held out the money, I offered it to him on the spot. But he refused to look at it. Furious he pushed me on to the sidewalk and towards the stairs of the Bath and past the squirming barbershop cylinders of red, white and blue. We hurried in, past the cashier's cage and along the dirty corridor.

"Go on, go on," said Cantabile.

"Where do you want to go?"

"To the can. Where is it?"

"Don't you want the dough?"

"I said the can! The can!"

I then understood, his bowels were acting up, he had been caught short, he had to go to the toilet, and I was to go with him. He wouldn't allow me to wait in the street. "Okay," I said, "just take it easy and I'll lead you." He followed me through the locker room. The john entrance was doorless. Only the individuals stalls have doors. I motioned him forward and was about to sit down on one of the locker-room benches nearby but he gave me a hard push on the shoulder and drove me forward. These toilets are the Bath at its worst. The radiators put up a stunning dry heat. The tiles are never washed, never disinfected. A hot dry urine smell rushes to your eyes like onion fumes. "Jesus!" said Cantabile. He kicked open a stall, still keeping me in front of him. He said, "You go in first."

"The both of us?" I said.

"Hurry up."

"There's space only for one."

He tugged out his gun and shook the butt at me. "You want this in your teeth?" The black fur of his moustache spread as the lip of his distorted face stretched. His brows were joined above the nose like the hilt of a large dagger. "In the corner, you!" He slammed the door and panting, took of his things. He thrust the raglan and the matching hat into my arms, although there was a hook. There was even a piece of hardware I had never before noticed. Attached to the door was a brass fitting, a groove labelled *Cigar*, a touch of class from the old days. He was seated now with the gun held in both palms, his hands between his knees, his eyes first closing then dilating greatly.

In a situation like this I can always switch out and think about the human condition over-all. Of course he wanted to humiliate me. Because I was a *chevalier* of the *Légion d'honneur*? Not that he actually knew of this. But he was aware that I was as they would say in Chicago a *Brain*, a man of culture or intellectual attainments. Was this why I had to listen to him rumbling and slopping and smell his stink? Perhaps fantasies of savagery and monstrosity, of beating my brains out, had loosened his bowels. Humankind is full of nervous invention of this type, and I started to think (to distract myself) of all the volumes of ape behaviour I had read in my time, of Kohler and Yerkes and Zuckerman, of Marais on baboons and Schaller on gorillas, and of the rich repertory of visceral-emotional sensitivities in the anthropoid branch. It was even possible that I was a more limited person than a fellow like Cantabile in spite of my concentration on intellectual achievement. For it would never have occurred to me to inflict anger on anyone by such means. This might have been a sign that his vital endowment or natural imagination was more prodigal and fertile than mine. In this way, thinking improving thoughts, I waited with good poise while he crouched there with his hardened dagger brows. He was a handsome slender man whose hair had a natural curl. It was cropped so close that you cold see the roots of his curls and I observed the strong contraction of his scalp in this moment of stress. He wanted to inflict a punishment on me but the result was only to make us more intimate.

As he stood and then wiped, and then pulled his shirt-tails straight, belting his pants with the large oval buckle and sticking back the gun (I hoped the safety catch was on), as I say, when he pulled his shirt-tails straight and buckled his stylish belt on the hip-huggers, thrusting the gun in, flushing the toilet with his pointed soft boot, to fastidious to touch the lever with his hand—he said, "Christ, if I catch the crabs here ... !" As if that would be my fault. He was evidently a violent reckless blamer. He said, "You don't know how I hated to sit here. These old guys must piss on the seats." This too he entered on the debit side against me. Then he said, "Who owns this joint?"

Now this was a fascinating question. It had never occurred to me, you know. The Bath was so ancient, it was like the Pyramids of Egypt, the Gardens of Ashurbanipal. It was like water seeking its level, or like gravitational force. But who in fact was its proprietor? "I've never heard of an owner," I said. "For all I know it's some old party out in British Columbia."

"Don't get smart. You're too fucking smart. I only asked for information. I'll find out."

To turn the faucet he used a piece of toilet paper. He washed his hands without soap, none was provided by the management. At this moment I offered him the nine fifty-dollar bills again. He refused to look at them. He said, "My hands are wet." He wouldn't use the roller towel. It was, I must admit, repulsively caked, filthy, with a certain originality in the way of filth. I held out my pocket handkerchief, but he ignored it. He didn't want his anger to diminish. Spreading his fingers wide he shook them dry. Full of the nastiness of the place he said, "the bathing is all downstairs."

They had two long rows of showers, below, which led to the heavy wooden doors of the steam room. There also was a small cistern, the cold plunge. The water was unchanged from year to year, and it was a crocodile's habitat if I ever saw one.

Cantabile now hurried out to the lunch counter, and I followed him. There he dried his hands with paper napkins which he pulled from the metal dispenser angrily. He crumpled these embossed flimsy papers and threw them on the floor. He said to Mickey, "Why don't you have soap and towels in the can? Why don't you wash the goddamn place out? There's no disinfectant in there."

Mickey was very mild, and he said, "No? Joe is supposed to take care of it. I buy him Top Job, Lysol." He spoke to Joe. "Don't you put in mothballs any more?" Joe was black and old, and he answered nothing. He was leaning on the shoe-shine chair with its brass pedestals, the upside-down legs and rigid feet (reminiscent of my own feet and legs during the Yoga headstand). He was there to remind us all of some remote, grand considerations and he would not answer any temporal questions.

"You guys are gonna buy supplies from me," said Cantabile. "Disinfectant, liquid soap, paper towels, everything. The name is Cantabile. I've got a supply business on Clybourne Avenue." He took out a long pitted ostrich-skin wallet and threw several business cards on the counter.

"I'm not the boss," said Mickey. "All I have is the restaurant concession." But he picked up a card with deference. His big fingers were covered with black knife-marks.

"I better hear from you."

"I'll pass it along to the Management. They're downtown."

"Mickey, who owns the Bath?" I said.

"All I know is the Management, downtown."

It would be curious, I thought, if the Bath should turn out to belong to the Syndicate.

"Is George Swiebel here?" said Cantabile.

"No."

"Well, I want to leave him a message."

"I'll give you something to write on," said Mickey.

"There's nothing to write. Tell him he's a dumb shit. Tell him I said so."

Mickey had put on his specs to look for a piece of paper, and now he turned his spectacled face towards us as if to say that his only business was the coleslaw and skirt-steaks and whitefish. Cantabile did not ask for old Father Myron, who was steaming himself below.

We went out into the street. The weather had suddenly cleared. I couldn't decide whether gloomy weather suited the environment better than bright. The air was cold, the light was neat, and the shadows thrown by blackened buildings divided the sidewalks.

I said, "Well, now let me give you this money. I brought new bills. This ought to wrap the whole thing up, Mr Cantabile."

"What—just like that? You think it's so easy?" said Rinaldo.

"Well, I'm sorry. It shouldn't have happened. I really regret it."

"You regret it! You regret your hacked-up car. You stopped a cheque on me, Citrine. Everybody blabbed. Everybody knows. You think I can allow it?"

"Mr Cantabile, who knows—who is everybody? Was it really so serious? I was wrong—"

"Wrong, you fucking ape ...!"

"Okay, I was stupid."

"Your pal George tells you to stop a cheque, so you stop it. Do you take that asshole's word for everything? Why didn't he catch Emil and me in the act? He has you pull this sneaky stunt and then you and he and the undertaker and the tuxedo guy and the other dummies spread around the gossip that Ronald Cantabile is a punk. Man! You could never get away with that. Don't you realize!"

"Yes, now I realize."

"No, I don't know what you realize. I was watching at the game, and I don't dig you. When are you going to do something *and know what you're doing?*" Those last words he spaced, he accented vehemently and uttered into my face.

Then he snatched away his coat, which I was still holding for him, the rich brown raglan with its large buttons. Circe might have had buttons like those in her sewing box. They were very beautiful, really, rather Oriental-treasure buttons.

The last garment I had seen resembling this one was worn by the late Colonel McCormick. I was then about twelve years old. His limousine had stopped in front of the Tribune Tower, and two short men came out. Each man held two pistols, and they circled on the pavement, crouching low. then, in this four-gun setting, the Colonel stepped out from his car in just such a tobacco-coloured coat as Cantabile's and a pinch hat with gleaming harsh fuzz. The wind was stiff, the air pellucid, the hat glistened like a bed of nettles.

"You don't think I know what I'm doing, Mr Cantabile?"

"No you don't. You couldn't find your ass with both hands."

Well, he may have been right. But at least I wasn't crucifying anyone. Apparently life had not happened to me as it had happened to other people. For some indiscernible reason it happened differently to them, and so I was not a fit judge of their concerns and desires. Aware of this I acceded to more of these desires than was practical. I gave in to George's low-life expertise. Now I bent before Cantabile. My only resource was to try to remember useful things from my ethological reading about rats, geese, sticklebacks, and dancing flies. What good is all this reading if you can't use it in the crunch? All I asked was a small mental profit.

"Anyway, what about these fifty-dollar bills?" I said.

"I'll let you know when I'm ready to take them," he said. "You didn't like what happened to your car, did you?"

I said, "It's a beautiful machine. It was really heartless to do that."

Apparently the bats he had threatened me with were what he had used on the Mercedes and there were probably more assault weapons in the back seat of the Thunderbird. He made me get into this showy auto. It had leather bucket seats red as spilt blood and an immense instrument panel. He took off at top speed from a standstill, like an adolescent drag-racer, the tyres wildly squealing.

In the car I got a slightly different impression of him. Seen in profile, his nose ended in a sort of white bulb. It was intensely, abnormally white. It reminded me of gypsum and it was darkly lined. His eyes were bigger than they ought to have been, artificially dilated perhaps. His mouth was wide, with an emotional underlip in which there was the hint of an early struggle to be thought full grown. His large feet and dark eyes also hinted that he aspired to some ideal, and that his partial attainment or non-attainment of the ideal was a violent grief to him. I suspected that the ideal itself might be fitful.

"Was it you or your cousin Emil that fought in Vietnam?"

We were speeding eastward on Division Street. He held the wheel in both hands as though it were a pneumatic drill to chop up the macadam. "What! Emil in the Army? Not that kid. He was 4-F, practically psycho. No, the most action Emil ever saw was during the 1968 riots in front of the Hilton. He was twigged out and didn't even know which side he was on. No, I was in Vietnam.

The folks sent me to that smelly Catholic college near St Louis that I mentioned at the game, but I dropped out and enlisted. That was some time back."

"Did you fight?"

"I'll tell you what you want to hear. I stole a tank of gasoline—the truck, trailer, and all. I sold it to some blackmarket guys. I got caught but my folks made a deal. Senator Dirksen helped. I was only eight months in jail."

He had a record of his own. He wished me to know that he was a true Cantabile, a throwback to the twenties and no mere Uncle Moochy. A military prison—he had a criminal pedigree and he could produce fear on his own credentials. Also the Cantabiles were evidently in small rackets of the lesser hoodlum sort, as witness the toilet-disenfectant business on Clybourne Avenue. Perhaps also a currency exchange or two—currency exchanges were often owned by former small-time racketeers. Or in the extermination business, another common favourite. But he was obviously in the minor leagues. Perhaps he was in no league at all. As a Chicagoan I had some sense of this. A real big shot used hired muscle. No Vito Langobardi would carry baseball bats in the back seat of his car. A Langobardi went to Switzerland for winter sports. Even his dog travelled in class. Not in decades had a Langobardi personally taken part in violence. No, this restless striving smoky-souled Cantabile was on the outside trying to get in. He was the sort of unacceptable entrepreneur that the sanitation department still fished out of the sewers after three months of decomposition. Certain persons of this type were occasionally found in the trunks of automobiles parked at O'Hare. The weight of the corpse at the back was balanced by a cinderblock laid on the motor.

Deliberately, at the next corner, Rinaldo ran a red light. He rode the bumper of the car ahead and he made other motorists chicken out. He was elegant, flashy. The seats of the T-bird were specially upholstered in soft leather—so soft, so crimson! He wore the sort of gloves sold to horsemen at Abercrombie & Fitch. At the expressway he swept right and gunned up the slope, running into merging traffic. Cars braked behind us. His radio played rock music. And I recognized Cantabile's scent. It was Canoe. I had once gotten a bottle of it for Christmas from a blind woman named Muriel.

In the squalid closet at the Bath when his pants were down and I was thinking about Zuckerman's apes at the London Zoo it had been clear that what was involved here were the plastic and histrionic talents of the human creature. In other words I was involved in a dramatization. It wouldn't have done much for the image of the Cantabiles, however, if he had actually shot off the gun that he held between his knees. It would make him too much like the crazy uncle who disgraced the family. That, I thought, was the whole point.

Was I afraid of Cantabile? Not really. I don't know what he thought, but what I thought was perfectly clear to me. Absorbed in determining what a human being is, I went along with him. Cantabile may have believed that he was abusing a passive man. Not at all. I was a man active elsewhere. At the poker game, I received a visionary glimpse of this Cantabile. Of course, I was very high that night, if not downright drunk, but I saw the edge of his spirit rising from him, behind him. So when Cantabile yelled and threatened I didn't make a stand on grounds of proper pride—"Nobody treats Charlie Citrine like this, I'm going to the pole," and so forth. No, the police had no such things to show me. Cantabile had made a very peculiar and strong impression on me.

What a human being is—I always had my own odd sense of this. For I did not have to live in the land of the horses, like Dr Gulliver, my sense of mankind was strange enough without travel. In fact I travelled not to seek foreign oddities but to get away from them. I was drawn also to philosophical idealists because I was perfectly sure that *this* could not be *it*. Plato in the Myth of Er confirmed my sense that this was not my first time around. We had all been here before and would presently be here again. There was another place. Maybe a man like me was imperfectly reborn. The soul is supposed to be sealed by oblivion before its return to earthly life. Was it possible that my oblivion might be slightly defective? I never was a thorough Platonist. I never could believe that you could be reincarnated a bird or a fish. No soul once human was locked into a spider. In my case (which I suspect is not so rare as all that) there may have been an incomplete forgetting of the pure soul-life, so that the mineral condition of re-embodiment seemed abnormal, so that from an early age I was taken aback to see eyes move in faces, noses breathe, skins sweat, hairs grow, and the like, finding it comical. This was sometimes offensive to people born with full oblivion of their immortality.

This leads me to recall and reveal a day of marvellous spring and a noontime full of the most heavy silent white clouds, clouds like bulls, behemoths, and dragons. The place is Appleton, Wisconsin, and I am a grown man standing on a crate trying to see into the bedroom where I was born in the year 1918. I was probably conceived there, too, and directed by divine wisdom to appear in life as so-and-so, such-and-such (C. Citrine, Pulitzer Prize, Legion of Honour, father of Lish and Mary, husband of A, lover of B, a serious person, and a card). And why should this person be perched on a box, partly hidden by the straight twigs and glossy leaves of a flowering lilac? And without asking permission of the lady of the house? I had knocked and rung but she did not answer. And now her husband was standing at my back. He owned a gas station. I told him who I was. At first he was very hard-nosed. But I explained that this was my birthplace and I asked for old neighbours by name. Did he remember the Saunderses? Well, they were his cousins. This saved me a punch in the nose as a Peeping Tom. I could not say, "I am standing on this crate among these lilacs trying to solve the riddle of man, and not to see your stout wife in her panties." Which was indeed what I saw. Birth is sorrow (a sorrow that may be cancelled by intercession) but in the room where my birth took place I beheld with sorrow of my own a fat old woman in underpants. With great presence of mind she pretended not to see my face at the screen but slowly left the room and phoned her husband. He ran from the gas pumps and nabbed me, laying oily hands on my exquisite grey suit—I was at the peak of my elegant period.Bbut I was able to explain that I was in Appleton to prepare that article on Harry Houdini, also a native—as I have obsessively mentioned—and I experienced a sudden desire to look into the room where I was born.

"So what you got was an eyeful of my Missus."

He didn't take this hard. I think he understood. These matters of the spirit are widely and instantly grasped. Except of course by people who are in heavily fortified positions, mental opponents trained to resist what everyone is born knowing.

As soon as I saw Rinaldo Cantabile at George Swiebel's kitchen table I was aware that a natural connection existed between us.

I was now taken to the Playboy Club. Rinaldo was a member. He walked away from his supercar, the Bechstein of automobiles, leaving it to the car jockey. The checkroom Bunny knew him. From his behaviour here I began to understand that my task was to make amends publicly. The Cantabiles had been defied. Maybe Rinaldo had been ordered at a family council to go out and repair the damage to their good bad name. And this matter of his reputation would consume a day—an entire day. And there were so many pressing needs, I had so many headaches already that I might justifiably have begged fate to give me a pass. I had a pretty good case.

"Are the people here?"

He threw over his coat. I also dropped mine. We stepped into the opulence, the semi-darkness, the thick carpets of the bar where bottles shone, and sensual female forms went back and forth in an amber light. He took me by the arm into an elevator and we rose immediately to the top. Cantabile said, "We're going to see some people. When I give you the high sign, then you pay me the money and apologize."

We were standing before a table.

"Bill, I'd like to introduce Charlie Citrine," said Ronald to Bill.

"Hey, Mike, this is Ronald Cantabile," Bill said, on cue.

The rest was, Hey how are you, sit down, what'll you drink.

Bill was unknown to me, but Mike was Mike Schneiderman the gossip columnist. He was large heavy strong tanned sullen fatigued, his hair was razor styled, his cufflinks were as big as his eyes, his necktie was a clumsy flap of silk brocade. He looked haughty, creased and sleepy, like certain oil-rich American Indians from Oklahoma. He drank an old-fashioned and held a cigar. His business was to sit with people in bars and restaurants. I was much too volatile for sedentary work like this, and I couldn't understand how it was done. But then I couldn't understand office jobs, either, or clerking or any of the confining occupations or routines. Many Americans described themselves as artists or intellectuals who should only have said that they were incapable of doing such work. I had many times discussed this with Von Humboldt Fleisher, and now and then with Gumbein the art critic. The work of sitting with people to discover what was interesting didn't seem to agree with Schneiderman either. At certain moments he looked blank and almost ill. He knew me, of course, I had once appeared on his television programme, and he said, "Hello, Charlie." Then he said to Bill, "Don't you know Charlie? He's a famous person who lives in Chicago incognito."

I began to appreciate what Rinaldo had done. He had gone to great trouble to set up this encounter, pulling many strings. This Bill, a connection of his, perhaps owed the Cantabiles a favour and had agreed to produce Mike Schneiderman the columnist. Obligations were being called in all over the place. The accountancy must be very intricate, and I could see that Bill was not pleased. Bill had a Cosa Nostra look. There was something corrupt about his nose. Curving deeply at the nostrils it was powerful yet vulnerable. He had a foul nose. In a different context I would have guessed him to be a violinist who had become disgusted with music and gone into the liquor business. He had just returned from Acapulco and his skin was dark, but he was not exactly shining with health and well-being. He didn't care for Rinaldo; he appeared contemptuous of him. My sympathy at this moment was with Cantabile. He had attempted to organize what should have been a beautiful spirited encounter, worthy of the Renaissance, and only I appreciated it. Cantabile was trying to crash Mike's column. Mike of course was used to this. The would-be happy few were always after him and I suspected that there was a good deal of trading behind the scenes, quid pro quo. You gave Mike an item of gossip and he printed your name in bold type. The Bunny took our drink order. Up to the chin she was ravishing. Above, all was commercial anxiety. My attention was divided between the soft crease of her breasts and the look of business difficulty on her face.

We were on one of the most glamorous corners of Chicago. I dwelt on the setting. The lakeshore view was stupendous. I couldn't see it but I knew it well and felt its effect–the shining road beside the shining gold vacancy of Lake Michigan. Man had overcome the emptiness of his land. But the emptiness had given him a few good licks in return. And here we sat amid the flatteries of wealth and power with pretty maidens and booze and tailored suits, and the men wearing jewels and using scent. Schneiderman was waiting, most sceptically, for an item he could use in his column. In the right context, I was good copy. People in Chicago are impressed with the fact that I am taken seriously elsewhere. I have now and then been asked to cocktail parties by culturally ambitious climbing people and have experienced the fate of a symbol. Certain women have said to me, "You *can't* be Charles Citrine!" Many hosts are pleased by the contrast I offer. Why, I look like a man intensely but incompletely thinking. My face is no match for their shrewd urban faces. And it's especially the ladies who can't mask their disappointment when they see what the well-known Mr Citrine actually looks like.

Whisky was set before us. I drank down my double Scotch eagerly and, being a quick expander, started to laugh. No one joined me. Ugly Bill said, "What's funny?"

upholstery with my scotch on the rocks, his hat coat suit boots (the boots may have been unborn calf) his equestrian gloves, and I made an effort to imagine how he had obtained these articles through criminal channels, from Field's, from Saks Fifth Avenue, from Abercrombie & Fitch. He was not, so far as I could judge, taken absolutely seriously by the old fence.

Rinaldo was intrigued with one of the watches and slipped it on. His old watch he tossed to the Japanese who caught it. I thought the moment had come to recite my piece and I said, "Oh, by the way, Ronald, I owe you some dough from the other night."

"Where from?" said Cantabile.

"From the poker game at George Swiebel's. I guess it slipped your mind."

"Oh I know that guy Swiebel with all the muscles," said the old gentleman. "He's terrific company. And you know he cooks a great bouillabaisse, I'll give him that."

"I inveigled Ronald and his cousin Emil into this game," I said. "It really was my fault. Anyhow, Ronald cleaned up on us. Ronald is one of the poker greats. I ended up about six hundred dollars in the hole and he had to take my IOU—I've got the dough on me, Ronald, and I better give it to you while we both remember."

"Okay." Again Cantabile, without looking, crumpled the notes into his jacket pocket. His performance was better than mine, though I was doing my very best. But then he had the honour side of the deal, the affront. To be angry was his right and that was no small advantage.

When we were out of the building again I said, "Wasn't that okay?"

"Okay—yes! Okay!" he said loud and bitter. Clearly he wasn't ready to let me off. Not yet.

"I figure that old pelican will pass the word around that I paid you. Wasn't that the object?"

I added, almost to myself, "I wonder who makes pants like the pants the old boy was wearing. The fly alone must have been three feet long."

But Cantabile was still stoking his anger. "Christ!" he said. I didn't like the way he was staring at me under those straight bodkin brows.

"Well, then, that does it," I said. "I can get a cab."

Cantabile caught me by the sleeve. "You wait," he said. I didn't really know what to do. After all, he carried a gun. I had for a long time thought about having a gun too, Chicago being what it is. But they'd never give me a licence. Cantabile, without a licence, packed a pistol. There was one index of the difference between us. Only God knew what consequences such differences might bring. "Aren't you enjoying our afternoon?" said Cantabile, and grinned.

Attempting to laugh this off I failed. The globus hystericus interfered. My throat felt sticky.

"Get in, Charlie."

Again I sat in the crimson bucket seat (the supple fragrant leather kept reminding me of blood, pulmonary blood) and fumbled for the seat belt—you never can find those cursed buckles.

"Don't fuck with the belt, we're not going that far."

Out of this information I drew what relief I could. We were on Michigan Boulevard, heading south. We drew up beside a skyscraper under construction, a headless trunk swooping up, swarming with lights. Below the early darkness now closing with December speed over the listening west, the sun like a bristling fox jumped beneath the horizon. Nothing but a scarlet afterglow remained. I saw it between the El pillars. As the tremendous trusses of the unfinished skyscraper turned black, the hollow interior filled with thousands of electric points resembling champagne bubbles. The completed building would never be so beautiful as this. We got out, slamming the car doors, and I followed Cantabile over some plank-bedding laid down for the trucks. He seemed to know his way around. Maybe he had clients among the hard-hats. If he was in the juice racket. Then again if he was a usurer he wouldn't come here after dark and risk getting pushed from a beam by one of these tough guys. They must be reckless. They drink and spend recklessly enough. I like the way these steeplejacks paint the names of their girlfriends on inaccessible girders. From below you often see DONNA or SUE. I suppose they bring the ladies on Sunday to point to their love-offerings eight hundred feet up. They fall to death now and then. Anyway Cantabile had brought his own hard hats. We put them on. Everything was prearranged. He said he was related by blood to some of the supervisory personnel. He also mentioned that he did lots of business hereabouts. He said he had connections with the contractor and the architect. He told me things much faster than I could discount them. However, we rose in one of the big open elevators, up, up.

How should I describe my feelings? Fear, thrill, appreciation, glee—yes I appreciated his ingenuity. It seemed to me, however, that we were rising too high, too far. Where were we? Which button had he pressed? By daylight I had often admired the mantis-like groups of cranes, tipped with orange paint. The tiny bulbs, which seemed so dense from below, were sparsely strung through. I don't know how far we actually went, but it was far enough. We had as much light about us as the time of day had left to give, steely and freezing, keen, with the wind ringing in the empty squares of wound-coloured rust and beating against the hanging canvases. On the east, violently rigid was the water, icy, scratched, like a plateau of solid stone, and the other way was a tremendous effusion of low-lying colour, the last glow, the contribution of industrial poisons to the beauty of the Chicago evening. We got out. About ten hard-hats who had been waiting pushed into the elevator at once. I wanted to call to them "Wait!" They went down in a group, leaving us nowhere. Cantabile seemed to know where he was going, but I had no faith in him. He was capable of faking anything. "Come on," he said. I followed, but I was going slowly. He waited for me. There were a few windbreaks up here on the fiftieth or sixtieth floor, and those, the wind was storming. My eyes ran. I held on to a pillar and he said, "Come on Granny, come on cheque-stopper."

I said, "I have leather heels. They skid."

"You better not chicken out."

"No, this is it," I said. I put my arms around the pillar. I wouldn't move.

Actually we had come far enough to suit him. "Now," he said, "I want to show you just how much your dough means to me. You see this?" He held up a fifty-dollar bill. He rested his back on a steel upright and stripping off his fancy equestrian gloves began to fold the money. It was incomprehensible at first. Then I understood. He was making a child's paper glider of it. Hitching back his raglan sleeve, he sent the glider off with two fingers. I watched it speeding through the strung lights with the wind behind it out into the steely atmosphere, darker and darker below. On Michigan Boulevard they had already put up the Christmas ornaments, winding tiny bubbles of glass from tree to tree. They streamed down there like cells under a microscope.

My chief worry now was how to get down. Though the papers underplay it people are always falling off. But however scared and harassed, my sensation-loving soul also was gratified. I knew that it took too much to gratify me. The gratification-threshold of my soul had risen too high. I must bring it down again. It was excessive. I must, I knew, change everything.

He sailed off more of the fifties. Tiny paper planes. Origami (my knowledgeable mind, keeping up its indefatigable pedantry—my lexical busybody mind!), the Japanese paper-folder's art. An international congress of paper-aircraft freaks had been held, I think, last year. It seemed last year. The hobbyists were mathematicians and engineers.

Cantabile's green bills went off like finches, like swallows and butterflies, all bearing the image of Ulysses S. Grant. They brought crepuscular fortune to people down in the streets.

"The last two I'm going to keep," said Cantabile. "To blow them on drinks and dinner for us."

"If I ever get down alive."

"You did fine. Go on, lead the way, start back."

"These leather heels are awfully tricky. I hit an ordinary piece of wax paper in the street the other day and went down. Maybe I should take my shoes off."

"Don't be crazy. Go on your toes."

If you didn't think of falling, the walkways were more than adequate. I crept along, fighting paralysis of the calves and the thighs. My face was sweating faster than the wind could dry it as I took hold of the final pillar. I thought that Cantabile had been much too close behind. More hard-hats waiting for the elevator probably took us for union guys or architect's men. It was night now and the hemisphere was frozen all the way to the Gulf. Gladly I fell into the seat of the Thunderbird when we got down. He removed his hard hat and mine. He cocked the wheel and started the motor. He should really let me go now. I had given him enough satisfaction.

But he was off again, driving fast. He sped away towards the next light. My head hung back over the top of the seat in the position you take to stop a nosebleed. I didn't know exactly where we were. "Look, Rinaldo," I said. "You've made your point. You bashed my car, you've run me all day long, and you've just given me the scare of my life. Okay, I see it wasn't the money that upset you. Let's stuff the rest of it down a sewer so I can go home."

"You've had it with me?"

"It's been a whole day of atonement."

"You've seen enough of the whatchamacallems?—I learned some new words at the poker game from you."

"Which words?"

"Proles," he said, "*Lumps. Lumpenproletariat.* You gave us a little talk about Karl Marx."

"My lord, I did carry on, didn't I. Completely unbuttoned. What got into me!"

"You wanted to mix with riffraff and the criminal element. You went slumming, Charlie, and you had a great time playing cards with us dumbheads and social rejects."

"I see. I was insulting."

"Kind of. But you were interesting, here and there, about the social order and how obsessed the middle class was with the *Lumpenproletariat.* The other fellows didn't know what in hell you were talking about." For the first time, Cantabile spoke more mildly to me. I sat up and saw the river flashing night-lights on the right, and the Merchandise Mart decorated for Christmas. We were going to Gene and Georgetti's old steak house, just off the spur of the Elevated train. Parking among other sinister luxury cars we went into the drab old building where—hurrah for opulent intimacy!—a crash of jukebox music fell on us like Pacific surf. The high-executive bar was crowded with executive drinkers and lovely companions. The gorgeous mirror was peopled with bottles and resembled a group photograph of celestial graduates.

"Giulio," Rinaldo told the waiter. "A quiet table, and we don't want to sit by the rest rooms."

"Upstairs, Mr Cantabile?"

"Why not?" I said. I was shaky and didn't want to wait at the bar for seating. It would lengthen the evening, besides.

Cantabile stared as if to say, Who asked you! But he then consented. "Okay, upstairs. And two bottles of Piper Heidsieck."

"Right away, Mr Cantabile."

In the Capone days hoodlums fought mock battles with champagne at banquets. They jigged the bottles up and down and shot each other with corks and foaming wine, all in black tie, and like a fun-massacre.

"Now I want to tell you something," said Rinaldo Cantabile, "and it's a different subject altogether. I'm married, you know."

"Yes, I remember."

"To a marvellous beautiful intelligent woman."

"You mentioned your wife in South Chicago. That night ... Do you have children? What does she do?"

Indeed this *visual* quality is made more obvious by the city's pop architecture. If for Saul Steinberg Los Angeles was the first American "highway city", it was also "the avant-garde city of parody in architecture and even in nature (canyons and palm-trees)".[24] Once again the visual mix speaks to an especial sense of the surreal and bizarre: a city which advertises and inculcates "desire" into its very texture. I do not mean, here, the extravagances of Beverly Hills or the strange mixture of domestic architecture we find in Raymond Chandler and Fitzgerald: the Californian bungalow and Spanish vernacular; nor even Simon Rodia's extraordinary Watts Towers. Rather I have in mind the commercial buildings, shops and restaurants built as absurd objects which take their place within this larger roadside environment of billboards, letters and neon constructions. A mixture of the real and surreal: of a fantastic cityscape reminiscent of the disorientated images of Los Angeles caught by the photographs of Hideko Kembe.[25] Once again these suggest how much of the art of the city is related to seeing it from the road. The extraordinary hand-painted billboards, for example, or the unique range of buildings from the 1930s and 1940s: a "pop architecture" of the West Coast that we have come to associate more with the franchise restaurants of a newer (and more uniform) corporate America. One thinks of the "Big Red Piano" in Venice (1930), of the Brown Derby Restaurant, Wilshire Boulevard (1936), Pinnochio's Hot Dog Stand, in Venice (1946) and, of course, Grauman's Chinese Theater (1926) on Hollywood Boulevard. Such buildings reveal an extravagance and frivolity which takes a product to its ultimate statement as an advertised image but, equally, relate it to a larger symbolism of fantasy and dream; for the enormous mouths, massive hamburgers, and outsize Coke bottles which form these buildings are part of a larger myth: the culmination, at road level, of that language of desire grounded in Hollywood and Disneyland.

3

If Wolfe celebrates this sense of the city's visual presence, other writers have seen it as evidence of an urban chaos symptomatic of a wider cultural disarray. In *After Many a Summer* (1942), for example, Aldous Huxley's Los Angeles novel, his *English* hero (Jeremy Pordage) arrives in the city for an initiation drive from the airport:

> ... suddenly the car plunged into a tunnel and emerged into another world, a vast, untidy suburban world of filling-stations and billboards, of low houses in gardens, of vacant lots and waste-paper, of occasional shops and office buildings and churches—Primitive Methodist churches built, surprisingly enough, in the style of the Cartuja at Granada, Catholic churches like Canterbury Cathedral, synagogues disguised as Hagia Sophia, Christian Science churches with pillars and pediments, like banks. It was a winter day and early in the morning: but the sun shone brilliantly, the sky was without a cloud. The car was travelling westwards, and the sunshine, slanting from behind them as they advanced, lit up each building, each sky-sign and billboard, as though with a spot-light, as though on purpose to show the new arrival all the sights,
>
> EATS. COCKTAILS. OPEN NITES.

> DO THINGS, GO PLACES WITH CONSOL SUPER GAS!
> JUMBO MALTS.
> AT BEVERLY PANTHEON FINE FUNERALS ARE *NOT* EXPENSIVE.
> The car sped onwards, and here in the middle of a vacant lot was a restaurant in the form of a seated bulldog, the entrance between the front paws, the eyes illuminated.[26]

And so they continue, "mile after mile" in which shops, gas-stations, "vacant lots" and houses "went along with them, interminably". This is, of course, partly an English eye responding to the difference Los Angeles offers—thus the almost incongruous points of comparison. But it is also a passage which suggests an appropriate sense of the kind of urban sprawl indicative of so much of Los Angeles. In part it recalls the mix of styles we have in the studio lots of Hollywood—as if the city itself is a single, extensive film set. In turn, it suggests a surreal dimension to the most mundane of urban sights—the mix of buildings themselves a juxtaposition of the endlessly unexpected. But the passage equally responds to a more distinctive aspect of the city. Not only *is* there no perspective—visual, cultural, historical—there is no organizing principle at work. The cityscape is both random and profuse—speaking (advertising) endlessly a process which will not be made still. The effect, in the end, is for the eye to be worn down as the *mass* of images impinges upon the participant. Everything, as it were, has equal significance—everything has become, once again, a sign.

Huxley's novel stresses the way the city spreads out as a chaotic text always on the edge of the surreal. In contrast, although William Faulkner responded to Los Angeles in a similar form, his sense of the city (as we might expect) is very much bound to his Southern background. In "Golden Land" (1934) for example, a short story related to his period in Hollywood as a script-writer, the city, as ever, is experienced from inside a car:

> ... the car ran powerful, smooth, and fast beneath him, performing its afternoon's jaunt over the incredible distances of which the city was composed; from time to time, had he looked, he could have seen the city in the bright soft vague hazy sunlight, random, scattered about the arid earth like so many gay scraps of paper, without order, with its curious air of being rootless—of houses bright, beautiful and gay, without basements or foundations, lightly attached to a few inches of light penetrable earth, lighter even than dust and laid lightly in turn upon the profound and primeval lava, which one good hard rain would wash forever from the sight and memory of a man as a firehose flushes down a gutter. ...[27]

Once again the city here is casual and chaotic: a limitless sprawl. Faulkner's interest, however, lies elsewhere, for his concern in with depth rather than breadth. Los Angeles is, thus, rootless: it actively denies the past to the extent that it has no foundations, no memory. One could not be further from Faulkner's south: a country of sediment and osmotic acretion where meaning, and the past, saturates the present and shapes an identity hidden as it is ambiguous. In contrast Los Angeles is viewed as a spectacle lacking solidity and substance. And yet, in part, Faulkner's response misses the point, for in this environment the houses require no basements or cellars. The underside of the family house—so prevalent in Faulkner and Poe—has literally been brought to the surface. Architecturally, and in the environment created, Los Angeles exists as the antipathy of the South. It deposits, as it were, its language of desire and the unconscious on *to* its streets: it does not hide them in cellars. its rootlessness is not so much a divorce from the past as a structuring *of* that past into the fetish and fantasy of the city's visual iconography. The restrictive mental space of Poe's Southern Gothic has been freed into the endless imaginative space of the Los Angeles cityscape—the hidden is given specific and enlarged visual form.

This has, of course, underpinned the sense of Los Angeles as both apogee of commercialism and of a popular culture lacking in significance. Indeed, Faulkner's sense of "roots" is precisely the imagery Mailer uses in his view of the city in *The Presidential Papers* (1964):

> Not all the roots of American life are uprooted, but almost all, and the spirit of the supermarket, that homogenous extension of stainless surfaces and psychoanalyzed people, packaged commodities and ranch homes, interchangeable, geographically unrecognizable, that essence of the new postwar super America is found nowhere so perfectly as in Los Angeles' ubiquitous acres. One gets the impression that people come to Los Angeles in order to divorce themselves from the past, here to live or try to live in the rootless pleasure world of an adult child.[28]

Mailer here speaks to an Easterner's eye view similar to that found in *The Nowhere City*. He looks for a cityscape, a weight almost, redolent of an older heartland and industrial America. but what Mailer sees is, for him, the ultimate image of the commercial spirit: a blandness which borders on vacuum. Mailer views it as an anaesthetized city: a de-historicized and continuous present; a pleasure world constructed through the auspices of the mass-media. Although Los Angeles is "a city to drive in", all that Mailer notes are "the endless repetitions" of "milky pinks", "washed-out oranges" and "lime-yellows of pastel". Once again, a blandness devoid of substance: an unreal atmosphere constantly at a distance. Indeed, Mailer's response is similar to Raymond Chandler's sense of California as a "department-store state", for he views the city as an image of consumerism sustained by a manufactured desire and fantasy. Thus the city is seen as if it were a film: an endless series of images which advertises possibility. It is, for example, the Los Angeles Hugo Williams saw in *No Particular Place to Go* (1981):

> Bank, temple, gas station, motel, bank, temple, gas station, the endless forecourts of Wilshire Boulevard seemed to be on a loop, like some half-hearted attempt at back projection. Everything was slightly out of focus, like early colour film.[29]

4

Thus the difference between San Francisco and Los Angeles as West Coast cities: a difference made clear by Herbert Gold when he sees California as a "a country of the mind" with San Francisco "its ego" and Los Angeles "its id".[30] Or again by Edmund Wilson, suggesting that

> the real cultural center, San Francisco, with its cosmopolitanism and its Bohemian clubs ... was arrested in its natural development by the earthquake of 1906 ... and thereafter the great anti-cultural amusement-producing center, Los Angeles, grew-up, gigantic and vulgar. ...[31]

In part, of course, Wilson's distinction points to a literary tradition one associates with San Francisco in a way one could not with Los Angeles. A tradition which includes Mark Twain, Bret Harte, Ambrose Bierce, Jack London, Frank Norris, Robinson Jeffers and, more latterly, Richard Brautigan, and the Beats.[32] Indeed the Beat writers underscore the extent to which San Francisco has housed "unofficial" groups as part of its cultural heritage, for one adds to the "Beat" presence the Hippies in the '60s (in Haight-Ashbury) and, more recently, the "Gay" community in the Castro area.[33] Thus, although San Francisco, in Dashiell Hammett's fiction, becomes very much a city akin to Chandler with its "blurred" streets and "night-fog, thin, clamming, and penetrant",[34] a city of Alcatraz and a dangerous Chinatown, the Beats as characteristic outsiders signify an urban ambience quite distinct from Los Angeles.

San Francisco, for example, has a more distinct working relationship with the ocean, whereas that of Los Angeles appears to be primarily based on pleasure. It also underlines the extent to which San Francisco is a city in which to walk rather than drive: a city in which areas retain a recognizable local sense of scale. In brief, a city at once oriental and European: a mix of atmospheres and scales; as much figured in the range of the city's indigenous (rather than imagined) architecture as in the steep incline of the streets as they run down to the Bay. It is a difference underlined by Kenneth Rexroth when he speaks of San Francisco as an "international city" having "a living contact with the Orient".[35] A claim which emphasizes its image as a base for alternative cultures: ecological, spiritual and sexual. Thus for Jack Kerouac San Francisco

> was the end of the land, and for many reasons it was different. ... The beauty of the setting and the Mediterranean *dolce far niente*. ... Perhaps the atmosphere dated all the way back to the 1840s, when the city was settled ... not by protestant farmers and merchants ... but by lunatic miners, whores, pirates, latinos, and Asians. ... It was freer.[36]

It is, thus, appropriate that the Beats belonged, as it were, *to* San Francisco and that, as writers, they were essentially poetic in their concerns: Allen Ginsberg, Kenneth Rexroth, Laurence Ferlinghetti, Michael McClure, Gary Snyder, Lew Welch and Jack Kerouac (and, in some ways, Ken Kesey) all form part of what Donald M. Allen understood as the "San Francisco Renaissance".[37] Such "West Coast" and "Berkeley" poets look to San Francisco rather than to Los Angeles as the point at which America finds its "holy" destiny. Los Angeles remains its material other. Indeed Los Angeles, despite its name, becomes the image of a frenzied psyche: a neurotic and nightmarish *alter* cityscape. Not, as it were, Whitman's imagined West Coast ideal but rather Ginsberg's image of a prophetic American in *Howl* (1956): a daunting "Supermarket in California".

own meaninglessness. In Pynchon the city remains an enigma: a sign. How appropriate, then, that a city the size of Los Angeles has become known as L.A. What other city could reduce itself to an abbreviation of two single letters? What other metropolitan area of some 4,000 square miles could be so hard to *find*:

> And I saw some lights and I thought, that must be [Los Angeles]. I walked two miles, and when I got there all it was was a big gas station, so brightly lit I'd thought it was the city.[58]

Notes

1. Horace McCoy, *I Should Have Stayed Home* (London, 1938), pp. 5, 6.

2. Robert Frank, *The Americans* (New York, 1978).

3. Jane Jacobs, *The Death and Life of Great American Cities* (1961; Harmondsworth, 1965), p. 368.

4. Herbert Gold, *A Walk on the West Side, California on the Brink*, (New York, 1981), p. 25. The whole volume is of significance for those interested in San Francisco and Los Angeles.

5. Kevin Lynch, *The Image of the City* (Cambridge, Mass., 1960), p. 43.

6. J. T. Farrell, "The Language of Hollywood" in *The League of Frightened Philistines* (New York, 1944), p. 148.

7. Edmund Wilson, "The Boys in the Back Room" in *Classics and Commercials: A Literary Chronicle of the Forties* (London, 1951), p. 46.

8. Robert Lowell, *Notebook* (London, 1970), p. 53.

9. Alison Lurie, *The Nowhere City* (London, 1986: Abacus paperback edition), p. 39.

10. In many ways the same is true of Las Vegas, or at least the central area of "the strip". See, for example, Robert Venturi's *Learning from Las Vegas* (M.I.T. Press, 1972). In *The Kandy-Kolored Tangerine-Flake Streamline Baby* (1965), Tom Wolfe says that "Las Vegas is the only town in the world whose skyline is made up ... of signs" (Mayflower, 1968 edition), p. 18.

11. *The Nowhere City*, p. 279.

12. Ibid., p. 232.

13. Joan Didion, *Play it as it Lays* (London, 1971), pp. 15, 16.

14. Rayner Banham, *Los Angeles: The Architecture of Four Ecologies* (Harmondsworth, Penguin edition, 1971), p. 35. Banham's study remains a central assessment of the city.

15. Ibid., p. 23.

16. All published by Heavy Industry Publications, Hollywood. See also David Bourdan's essay on Ruscha, "A Heap of Words About Ed Ruscha" in *Art International*, vol. 15, no. 9, November 1971, 25–8, 38.

17. Created in the 1920s.

18. Evelyn Waugh, *The Loved One* (Harmondsworth, Penguin edition, 1951), p. 35.

19. Quoted by Bourdan in "A Heap of Words About Ed Ruscha".

20. *Los Angeles: The Architecture of Four Ecologies*, p. 75.

21. Ibid., p. 139.

22. Tom Wolfe, "Electrographic Architecture" in *Architectural Design*, July 1969, 380.

23. Tom Wolfe, "Chester Gould Versus Roy Lichtenstein" in *California: 5 Footnotes to Modern Art History*, ed. Stephanie Barron (Los Angeles, 1977), p. 98.

24. Quoted in Harold Rosenberg, *Saul Steinberg* (New York and London, 1979), p. 238.

25. See *California: 5 Footnotes to Modern Art History*. D. Gebhard and R. Winter note in the *Guide to Architecture in Southern California*: "How suggestive that Los Angeles' great contribution to fantastic architecture", the Watts Towers, "should be made out of junk."

26. Aldous Huxley, *After Many a Summer* (London, 1942), p. 5.

27. William Faulkner, *Collected Stories* (New York, 1941), p. 719.

28. Norman Mailer, *The Presidential Papers* (London, Panther, 1976), p. 45. The whole section, "The Existential Hero" is appropriate.

29. Hugo Williams, *No Particular Place to Go* (London, 1981), p. 120.

30. *A Walk on the West Side*, p. 31.

31. *Classics and Commercials*, p. 47.

32. I can do no more than allude to the names here. See, for example, Stoddard Martin, *California*

Writers (London, 1983).

33. For a critical consideration of the Hippie phenomenon in San Francisco see Joan Didion, *Slouching Towards Bethlehem* (New York, 1968; Penguin edition, 1974). The Castro area is analysed in Francis Fitzgerald's *Cities on a Hill* (New York, 1986), a study which first appeared in *The New Yorker*, 1986.

34. Dashiell Hammett, *The Maltese Falcon*, (1929). See Ch. 2.

35. Kenneth Rexroth in *The San Francisco Poets*, ed. David Meltzer (New York, 1971), p. 30.

36. Quoted in *Californian Writers*, p. 190.

37. See Donald M. Allen, *The New American Poetry* (New York, 1960).

38. See, for example, Jonas Spatz, *Hollywood in Fiction* (The Hague and Paris, 1969).

39. Nathanael West, *Miss Lonelyhearts and the Day of the Locust* (New Directions, 1962). See Ch. 18.

40. Ibid., p. 184.

41. *Slouching Towards Bethlehem* (Harmondsworth, Penguin edition), p. 179.

42. See Ed Sanders, *The Family* (New York, 1971).

43. Henry Miller, *The Air-Conditioned Nightmare* (1947; 1965 Panther edition), p. 169.

44. The phrase, of course, is W. H. Auden's from "The Guilty Vicarage" in *The Dyer's Hand and Other Essays* (London, 1963).

45. *I Should Have Stayed Home*, p. 1.

46. John Rechy, *City of Night* (London, 1965 Panther edition), p. 175.

47. Raymond Chandler, *The Little Sister* (1949). See Ch. 13. Vol. 1, *The Chandler Collection* (London, 1983), especially pp. 441-521.

48. *The Big Sleep* (Harmondsworth, Penguin edition, 1978), p. 44.

49. *The High Window* (London, Pan edition, 1979), pp. 142, 12, 54.

50. *Farewell my Lovely* (Harmondsworth, Penguin edition, 1975), p. 51.

51. *Trouble is my Business and Other Stories* (Harmondsworth, Penguin edition, 1976), p. 160 and 130.

52. Ibid., pp. 124, 102.

53. Alain Silver and Elizabeth Ward (eds.), *Film Noir* (Woodstock, New York, 1979), p. 1. See also Raymond Durgnat, "Paint it Black: The Family Tree of Film Noir", in *Cinema* (U.K.) 617 (1970), 49-56.

54. *Film Noir*, p. 204.

55. *City of Night*, p. 94.

56. See the discussion of Hockney's Californian paintings in Marco Livingstone, *David Hockney* (London, Thames and Hudson, 1981), pp. 63-76.

57. Thomas Pynchon, *The Crying of Lot 49* (Bantam, 1966 edition), p. 12. See Tony Tanner's discussion of Pynchon in *City of Words: American Fiction 1950-1970* (London, 1971), pp. 141-80.

58. David Hockney in *Pictures*, ed. Nikos Stangos (London, 1976), p. 36.

131
Golden Land

WILLIAM FAULKNER

William Faulkner (1897–1962) is perhaps *the* central southern writer in the American tradition. Born in Albany, Mississippi, he lived for much of his life in Oxford, Mississippi, which formed the basis of his mythic fictional area, the Yoknapatawpha County which is the setting of his novels. Based on life in the South, they follow the fortunes (and misfortunes) of a series of families which reflect the larger cultural and historical changes of the region from the Civil War into the twentieth century. Densely plotted, they are saturated with an underlying sense of violence, loneliness, and the tragic. Both individually and collectively they offer an intense psychological drama of contemporary culture, and move beyond their local concerns to fundamental aspects of human existence.

The Sound and the Fury (1929), one of his most experimental novels, shows the influence of European modernism, particularly that of James Joyce. *As I Lay Dying* (1930), *Sanctuary* (1931), *Light in August* (1932), and *Absalom, Absalom!* (1936) extend and develop the cycle of family and cultural decline. Although fiercely associated with the South, Faulkner spent time working in Hollywood, and "Golden Land" (1934) is a significant story in the way it views Western Californian urban life-styles from its deeply embedded Mississippi perspectives. See Michael Millgate, *The Achievement of William Faulkner* (1967), and Richard Gray, *William Faulkner and the Literature of the South* (1992).

If he had been thirty, he would not have needed the two aspirin tablets and the half glass of raw gin before he could bear the shower's needling on his body and steady his hands to shave. But then when he had been thirty neither could he have afforded to drink as much each evening as he now drank; certainly he would not have done it in the company of the men and the women in which, at forty-eight, he did each evening, even though knowing during the very final hours filled with the breaking of glass and the shrill cries of drunken women above the drums and saxophones—the hours during which he carried a little better than his weight both in the amount of

Source: William Faulkner, "Golden Land", *Collected Stories*, New York, 1934, pp. 701–26.

liquor consumed and in the number and sum of checks paid—that six or eight hours later he would rouse from what had not been sleep at all but instead that dreamless stupefaction of alcohol out of which last night's turgid and licensed uproar would die, as though without any interval for rest or recuperation, into the familiar shape of his bedroom—the bed's foot silhouetted by the morning light which entered the bougainvillaea-bound windows beyond which his painful and almost unbearable eyes could see the view which might be called the monument to almost twenty-five years of industry and desire, of shrewdness and luck and even fortitude—the opposite canyonflank dotted with the white villas halfhidden in imported olive groves or friezed by the sombre spaced columns of cypress like the façades of eastern temples, whose owners' names and faces and even voices were glib and familiar in back corners of the United States and of America and of the world where those of Einstein and Rousseau and Esculapius had never sounded.

He didn't waken sick. He never wakened ill nor became ill from drinking, not only because he had drunk too long and too steadily for that, but because he was too tough even after the thirty soft years ago when at fourteen he had fled, on the brakebeam of a westbound freight, the little lost Nebraska town named for, permeated with, his father's history and existence—a town to be sure, but only in the sense that any shadow is larger than the object which casts it. It was still frontier even as he remembered it at five and six—the projected and increased shadow of a small outpost of sodroofed dugouts on the immense desolation of the plains where his father, Ira Ewing too, had been first to essay to wring wheat during the six days between those when, outdoors in spring and summer and in the fetid halfdark of a snowbound dugout in the winter and fall, he preached. The second Ira Ewing had come a long way since then, from that barren and treeless village which he had fled by a night freight to where he now lay in a hundred-thousand-dollar house, waiting until he knew that he could rise and go to the bath and put the two aspirin tablets into his mouth. They—his mother and father—had tried to explain it to him—something about fortitude, the will to endure. At fourteen he could neither answer them with logic and reason nor explain what he wanted: he could only flee. Nor was he fleeing his father's harshness and wrath. He was fleeing the scene itself—the treeless immensity in the lost center of which he seemed to see the sum of his father's and mother's dead youth and bartered lives as a tiny forlorn spot which nature permitted to green into brief and niggard wheat for a season's moment before blotting it all with the primal and invincible snow as though (not even promise, not even threat) in grim and almost playful augury of the final doom of all life. And it was not even this that he was fleeing because he was not fleeing: it was only that absence, removal, was the only argument which fourteen knew how to employ against adults with any hope of success. He spent the next ten years half tramp half casual laborer as he drifted down the Pacific Coast to Los Angeles; at thirty he was married, to a Los Angeles girl, daughter of a carpenter, and father of a son and a daughter and with a foothold in real estate; at forty-eight he spent fifty thousand dollars a year, owning a business which he had built up unaided and preserved intact through nineteen-twenty-nine; he had given to his children luxuries and advantages which his own father not only could not have conceived in fact but would have condemned completely in theory—as it proved, as the paper which the Filipino chauffeur, who each morning carried him into the house and undressed him and put him to bed, had removed from the pocket of his topcoat and laid on the reading table proved, with reason. On the death of his father twenty years ago he had returned to Nebraska, for the first time, and fetched his mother back with him, and she was now established in a home of her own only the less sumptuous because she refused (with a kind of abashed and thoughtful unshakability which he did not remark) anything finer or more elaborate. It was the house in which they had all lived at first, though he and his wife and children had moved within the year. Three years ago they had moved again, into the house where he now waked in a select residential section of Beverley Hills, but not once in the nineteen years had he failed to stop (not even during the last five, when to move at all in the mornings required a terrific drain on that character or strength which the elder Ira had bequeathed him, which had enabled the other Ira to pause on the Nebraska plain and dig a hole for his wife to bear children in while he planted wheat) on his way to the office (twenty miles out of his way to the office) and spend ten minutes with her. She lived in as complete physical ease and peace as he could devise. He had arranged her affairs so that she did not even need to bother with money, cash, in order to live; he had arranged credit for her with a neighboring market and butcher so that the Japanese gardener who came each day to water and tend the flowers could do her shopping for her; she never even saw the bills. And the only reason she had no servant was that even at seventy she apparently clung stubbornly to the old habit of doing her own cooking and housework. So it would seem that he had been right. Perhaps there were times when, lying in bed like this and waiting for the will to rise and take the aspirin and the gin (mornings perhaps following evenings when he had drunk more than ordinarily and when even the six or seven hours of oblivion had not been sufficient to enable him to distinguish between reality and illusion) something of the old strong harsh Campbellite blood which the elder Ira must have bequeathed him might have caused him to see of feel or imagine his father looking down from somewhere upon him, the prodigal, and what he had accomplished. If this were so, then surely the elder Ira, looking down for the last two mornings upon the two tabloid papers which the Filipino removed from his master's topcoat and laid on the reading table, might have taken advantage of that old blood and taken his revenge, not just for that afternoon thirty-four years ago but for the entire thirty-four years.

When he gathered himself, his will, his body, at last and rose from the bed he struck the paper so that it fell to the floor and lay open at his feet, but he did not look at it. He just stood so, tall, in silk pyjamas, thin where his father had been gaunt with the years of hard work and unceasing struggle with the unpredictable and implacable earth (even now, despite the life which he had led, he had very little paunch) looking at nothing while at his feet the black headline flared above the row of five or six tabloid photographs from which his daughter alternately stared back of flaunted long pale shins: APRIL LALEAR BARES ORGY SECRETS. When he moved at last he stepped on the paper, walking on his bare feet into the bath; now it was his trembling and jerking hands that he watched as he shook the two tablets onto the glass shelf and set the tumbler into the rack and unstoppered the gin bottle and braced his knuckles against the wall in order to pour into the tumbler. But he did not look at the paper, not even when, shaved, he re-entered the bedroom and went to the bed beside which his slippers sat and shoved the paper aside with his foot in order to step into them. Perhaps, doubtless, he did not need to. The trial was but entering its third tabloidal day now, and so for two days his daughter's face had sprung out at him, hard, blonde and inscrutable, from every paper he opened; doubtless he had never forgot her while he slept even, that he had waked into thinking about remembering her as he had waked into the dying drunken uproar of the evening eight hours behind him without any interval between for rest or forgetting.

Nevertheless as, dressed, in a burnt orange turtleneck sweater beneath his gray flannels, he descended the Spanish staircase, he was outwardly calm and possessed. The delicate iron balustrade and the marble steps coiled down to the tile-floored and barnlike living room beyond which he could hear his wife and son talking on the breakfast terrace. The son's name was Voyd. He and his wife had named the two children by what might have been called mutual contemptuous armistice—his wife called the boy Voyd, for what reason he never knew; he in his turn named the girl (the child whose woman's face had met him from every paper he touched for two days now beneath or above the name, April Lalear) Samantha, after his own mother. He could hear them talking—the wife between whom and himself there had been nothing save civility, and not always a great deal of that, for ten years now; and the son who one afternoon two years ago had been delivered at the door drunk and insensible by a car whose occupants he did not see and, it devolving upon him to undress the son and put him to bed, whom he discovered to be wearing, in place of underclothes, a woman's brassière and step-ins. A few minutes later, hearing the blows perhaps, Voyd's mother ran in and found her husband beating the still unconscious son with a series of towels which a servant was steeping in rotation in a basin of ice-water. He was beating the son hard, with grim and deliberate fury. Whether he was trying to sober the son up or was merely beating him, possibly he himself did not know. His wife though jumped to the latter conclusion. In his raging disillusionment he tried to tell her about the woman's garments but she refused to listen; she assailed him in turn with virago fury. Since that day the son had contrived to see his father only in his mother's presence (which neither the son nor the mother found very difficult, by the way) and at which times the son treated his father with a blend of cringing spite and vindictive insolence half a cat's and half a woman's.

He emerged onto the terrace; the voices ceased. The sun, strained by the vague high soft almost nebulous California haze, fell upon the terrace with a kind of treacherous unbrightness. The terrace, the sundrenched terra cotta tiles, butted into a rough and savage shear of canyonwall bare yet without dust, on or against which a solid mat of flowers bloomed in fierce lush myriad-colored paradox as though in place of being rooted into and drawing from the soil they lived upon air alone and had been merely leaned intact against the sustenanceless lavawall by someone who would later return and take them away. The son, Voyd, apparently naked save for a pair of straw-colored shorts, his body brown with sun and scented faintly by the depilatory which he used on arms, chest and legs, lay in a wicker chair, his feet in straw beach shoes, an open newspaper across his brown legs. The paper was the highest class one of the city, yet there was a black headline across half of it too, and even without pausing, without even being aware that he had looked, Ira saw there too the name which he recognized. He went on to his place; the Filipino who put him to bed each night, in a white service jacket now, drew his chair. Beside the glass of orange juice and the waiting cup lay a neat pile of mail topped by a telegram. He sat down and took up the telegram; he had not glanced at his wife until she spoke:

"Mrs. Ewing telephoned. She says for you to stop in there on your way to town."

He stopped; his hands opening the telegram stopped. Still blinking a little against the sun he looked at the face opposite him across the table—the smooth dead makeup, the thin lips and the thin nostrils and the pale blue unforgiving eyes, the meticulous platinum hair which looked as though it had been transferred to her skull with a brush from a book of silver leaf such as window painters use. "What?" he said. "Telephoned? Here?"

"Why not? Have I ever objected to any of your women telephoning you here?"

The unopened telegram crumpled suddenly in his hand. "You know what I mean," he said harshly. "She never telephoned me in her life. She don't have to. Not that message. When have I ever failed to go by there on my way to town?"

"How do I know?" she said. "Or are you the same model son you have been a husband and seem to be a father?" Her voice was not shrill yet, nor even very loud, and none could have told how fast her breathing was because she sat so still, rigid beneath the impeccable and unbelievable hair, looking at him with that pale and outraged unforgiveness. They both looked at each other across the luxurious table—the two people who at one time twenty years ago would have turned as immediately and naturally and unthinkingly to one another in trouble, who even ten years ago might have done so.

"You know what I mean," he said, harshly again, holding himself too against the trembling which he doubtless believed was from last night's drinking, from the spent alcohol. "She don't read papers. She never even sees one. Did you send it to her?"

"I?" she said. "Send what?"

"Damnation!" he cried. "A paper! Did you send it to her? Don't lie to me."

"What if I did?" she cried. "Who is she, that she must not know about it? Who is she, that you should shield her from knowing it? Did you make any effort to keep it from happening? Why didn't you think about that all those years while you were too drunk, too besotted with drink, to know or notice or care what Samantha was—"

"Miss April Lalear of the cinema, if you please," Voyd said. They paid no attention to him; they glared at one another across the table.

"Ah," he said, quiet and rigid, his lips scarcely moving. "So I am to blame for this too, am I? I made my daughter a bitch, did I? Maybe you will tell me next that I made my son a f—"

"Stop!" she cried. She was panting now; they glared at one another across the suave table, across the five feet of irrevocable division.

"Now, now," Voyd said. "Don't interfere with the girl's career. After all these years, when at last she seems to have found a part that she can—" He ceased; his father had turned and was looking at him. Voyd lay in his chair, looking at his father with that veiled insolence that was almost feminine. Suddenly it became completely feminine; with a muffled halfscream he swung his legs out to spring up and flee but it was too late; Ira stood above him, gripping him not by the throat but by the face with one hand, so that Voyd's mouth puckered and slobbered in his father's hard, shaking hand. Then the mother sprang forward and tried to break Ira's grip but he flung her away and then caught and held her, struggling too, with the other hand when she sprang in again.

"Go on," he said. "Say it." But Voyd could say nothing because of his father's gripping his jaws open, or more than likely because of terror. His body was free of the chair now, writhing and thrashing while he made his slobbering, moaning sound of terror while his father held him with one hand and held his screaming mother with the other one. Then Ira flung Voyd free, onto the terrace; Voyd rolled once and came onto his feet, crouching, retreating toward the French windows with one arm flung up before his face while he cursed his father. Then he was gone. Ira faced his wife, holding her quiet too at last, panting too, the skilful map of makeup standing into relief now like a paper mask trimmed smoothly and pasted onto her skull. He released her.

"You sot," she said. "You drunken sot. And yet you wonder why your children—"

"Yes," he said quietly. "All right. That's not the question. That's all done. The question is, what to do about it. My father would have known. He did it once." He spoke in a dry light pleasant voice: so much so that she stood, panting still but quiet, watching him. "I remember. I was about ten. We had rats in the barn. We tried everything. Terriers. Poison. Then one day father said, "Come." We went to the barn and stopped all the cracks, the holes. Then we set fire to it. What do you think of that?" Then she was gone too. He stood for a moment, blinking a little, his eyeballs beating faintly and steadily in his skull with the impact of the soft unchanging sunlight, the fierce innocent mass of the flowers. "Philip!" he called. The Filipino appeared, brownfaced, impassive, with a pot of hot coffee, and set it beside the empty cup and the icebedded glass of orange juice. "Get me a drink," Ira said. The Filipino glanced at him, then he became busy at the table, shifting the cup and setting the pot down and shifting the cup again while Ira watched him. "Did you hear me?" Ira said. The Filipino stood erect and looked at him.

"You told me not to give it to you until you had your orange juice and coffee."

"Will you or won't you get me a drink?" Ira shouted.

"Very good, sir," Filipino said. He went out. Ira looked after him; this had happened before: he knew well that the brandy would not appear until he had finished the orange juice and the coffee, though just where the Filipino lurked to watch him he never knew. He sat again and opened the crumpled telegram and read it, the glass of orange juice in the other hand. It was from his secretary: MADE SETUP BEFORE I BROKE STORY LAST NIGHT STOP THIRTY PERCENT FRONT PAGE STOP MADE APPOINTMENT FOR YOU COURTHOUSE THIS P.M. STOP WILL YOU COME TO OFFICE OR CALL ME. He read the telegram again, the glass of orange juice still poised. Then he put both down and rose and went and lifted the paper from the terrace where Voyd had flung it, and read the half headline: LALEAR WOMAN DAUGHTER OF PROMINENT LOCAL FAMILY. Admits Real Name Is Samantha Ewing, Daughter of Ira Ewing, Local Realtor. He read it quietly; he said quietly, aloud:

"It was that Jap that showed her the paper. It was that damned gardener." He returned to the table. After a while the Filipino came, with the brandy-and-soda, and wearing now a jacket of bright imitation tweed, telling him that the car was ready.

II

His mother lived in Glendale; it was the house which he had taken when he married and later bought, in which his son and daughter had been born—a bungalow in a cul-de-sac of pepper trees and flowering shrubs and vines which the Japanese tended, backed into a barren foothill combed and curried into a cypress-and-marble cemetery dramatic as a stage set and topped by an electric sign in red bulbs which, in the San Fernando valley fog, flared in broad sourceless ruby as though just beyond the crest lay not heaven but hell. The length of his sports model car in which the Filipino sat reading a paper dwarfed it. But she would have no other, just as she would have neither servant, car, nor telephone—a gaunt spare slightly stooped woman upon whom even California and ease had put no flesh, sitting in one of the chairs which she had insisted on bringing all the way from Nebraska. At first she had been content to allow the Nebraska furniture to remain in storage, since it had not been needed (when Ira moved his wife and family out of the house and into the second one, the intermediate one, they had bought new furniture too, leaving the first house furnished complete for his mother) but one day, he could not recall just when, he discovered that she had taken the one chair out of storage and was using it in the house. Later, after he began to sense that quality of unrest in her, he had suggested that she let him clear the house of its present furniture and take all of hers out of storage but she declined, apparently preferring or desiring to leave the Nebraska furniture where it was. Sitting so, a knitted shawl about her shoulders, she looked less like she lived in or belonged to the house, the room, than the son with his beach burn and his faint theatrical gray temples and his bright expensive suavely antiphonal garments did. She had changed hardly at all in the thirty-four years; she and the older Ira Ewing too, as the son remembered him, who, dead, had suffered as little of alteration as while he had been alive. As the sod Nebraska outpost had grown into a village and then into a town, his father's aura alone had increased, growing into the proportions of a giant who at some irrevocable yet recent time had engaged barehanded in some titanic struggle with the pitiless earth and endured and in a sense conquered—it too, like the town, a shadow out of all proportion to the gaunt gnarled figure of the actual man. And the actual woman too as the son remembered them back in that time. Two people who drank air and who required to eat and sleep as he did and who had brought him into the world, yet were strangers as though of another race, who stood side by side in an irrevocable loneliness as though strayed from another planet, not as husband and wife but as blood brother and sister, even twins, of the same travail because they had gained a strange peace through fortitude and the will and strength to endure.

"Tell me again what it is," she said. "I'll try to understand."

"So it was Kazimura that showed you the damned paper," he said. She didn't answer this; she was not looking at him.

"You tell me she has been in the pictures before, for two years. That that was why she had to change her name, that they all have to change their names."

"Yes. They call them extra parts. For about two years, God knows why."

"And then you tell me that this—that all this was so she could get into the pictures—"

He started to speak, then he caught himself back out of some quick impatience, some impatience perhaps of grief or despair or at least rage, holding his voice his tone, quiet: "I said that was one possible reason. All I know is that the man has something to do with pictures, giving out the parts. And that the police caught him and Samantha and the other girl in an apartment with the doors all locked and that Samantha and the other woman were naked. They say that he was naked too and he says he was not. He says in the trial that he was framed—tricked; that they were trying to blackmail him into coming there and arranged for the police to break in just after they had taken off their clothes; that one of them made a signal from the window. Maybe so. Or maybe they were all just having a good time and were innocently caught." Unmoving, rigid, his face broke, wrung with faint bitter smiling as though with indomitable and impassive suffering, or maybe just smiling, just rage. Still his mother did not look at him.

"But you told me she was already in the pictures. That that was why she had to change her—"

"I said, extra parts," he said. He had to catch himself again, out of his jangled and outraged nerves, back from the fierce fury of the impatience. "Can't you understand that you don't get into the pictures just by changing your name? and that you don't even stay there when you get in? that you can't even stay there by being female? that they come here in droves on every train—girls younger and prettier than Samantha and who will do anything to get into the pictures? So will she, apparently; but who know or are willing to learn to do more things than even she seems to have thought of? But let's don't talk about it. She has made her bed; all I can do is to help her up: I can't wash the sheets. Nobody can. I must go, anyway; I'm late." He rose, looking down at her. "They said you telephoned me this morning. Is this what it was?"

"No," she said. Now she looked up at him; now her gnarled hands began to pick faintly at one another. "You offered me a servant once."

"Yes. I thought fifteen years ago that you ought to have one. Have you changed your mind? Do you want me to—"

Now she stopped looking at him again, though her hands did not cease. "That was fifteen years ago. It would have cost at least five hundred dollars a year. That would be—"

He laughed, short and harsh. "I'd like to see the Los Angeles servant you could get for five hundred dollars a year. But what—" He stopped laughing, looking down at her.

"That would be at least five thousand dollars," she said.

He looked down at her. After a while he said, "Are you asking me again for money?" She didn't answer nor move, her hands picking slowly and quietly at one another. "Ah," he said. "You want to go away. You want to run from it. So do I!" he cried, before he could catch himself this time; "so do I! But you did not choose me when you elected a child; neither did I choose my two. But I shall have to bear them and you will have to bear all of us. There is no help for it." He caught himself now, panting, quieting himself by will as when he would rise from bed, though his voice was still harsh: "Where would you go? Where would you hide from it?"

"Home," she said.

"Home?" he repeated; he repeated in a kind of amazement: "home?" before he understood. "You would go back there? with those winters, that snow and all? Why, you wouldn't live to see the first Christmas: don't you know that?" She didn't move nor look up at him. "Nonsense," he said. "This will blow over. In a month there will be two others and nobody except us will even remember it. And you don't need money. You have been asking me for money for years, but you don't need it. I had to worry about money so much at one time myself that I swore that the least I could do was to arrange your affairs so you would never even have to look at the stuff. I must go; there is something at the office today. I'll see you tomorrow."

It was already one o'clock. "Courthouse," he told the Filipino, settling back into the car. "My God, I want a drink." He rode with his eyes closed against the sun; the secretary had already sprung onto the runningboard before he realized that they had reached the courthouse. The secretary, bareheaded too, wore a jacket of authentic tweed; his turtleneck sweater was dead black, his hair was black too, varnished smooth to his skull; he spread before Ira a dummy newspaper page laid out to embrace the blank space for the photograph beneath the caption: APRIL LALEAR'S FATHER. Beneath the space was the legend: IRA EWING, PRESIDENT OF THE EWING REALTY CO.,—WILSHIRE BOULEVARD, BEVERLY HILLS.

"Is thirty percent all you could get?" Ira said. The secretary was young; he glared at Ira for an instant in vague impatient fury.

"Jesus, thirty percent is thirty percent. They are going to print a thousand extra copies and use our mailing list. It will be spread all up and down the Coast and as far East as Reno. What do you want? We can't expect them to put under your picture, 'Turn to page fourteen for halfpage ad,' can we?" Ira sat again with his eyes closed, waiting for his head to stop.

"All right," he said. "Are they ready now?"

"All set. You will have to go inside. They insisted it be inside, so everybody that sees it will know it is the court-house."

"All right," Ira said. He got out; with his eyes half closed and the secretary at his elbow he mounted the steps and entered the courthouse. The reporter and the photographer were waiting but he did not see them yet; he was aware only of being enclosed in a gaping crowd which he knew would be mostly women, hearing the secretary and a policeman clearing the way in the corridor outside the courtroom door.

"This is O.K.," the secretary said. Ira stopped; the darkness was easier on his eyes though he did not open them yet; he just stood, hearing the secretary and the policeman herding the women, the faces, back; someone took him by the arm and turned him; he stood obediently; the magnesium flashed and glared, striking against his painful eyeballs like blows; he had a vision of wan faces craned to look at him from either side of a narrow human lane; with his eyes shut tight now he turned, blundering until the reporter in charge spoke to him:

"Just a minute, chief. We better get another one just in case." This time his eyes were tightly closed; the magnesium flashed, washed over them; in the thin acrid smell of it he turned and with the secretary again at his elbow he moved blindly back and into the sunlight and into his car. He gave no order this time, he just said, "Get me a drink." He rode with his eyes closed again while the car cleared the downtown traffic and then began to move quiet, powerful and fast under him; he rode so for a long while before he felt the car swing into the palmbordered drive, slowing. It stopped; the doorman opened the door for him, speaking to him by name. The elevator boy called him by name too, stopping at the right floor without direction; he followed the corridor and knocked at a door and was fumbling for the key when the door opened upon a woman in a bathing suit beneath a loose beach cloak—a woman with treated hair also and brown eyes, who swung the door back for him to enter and then to behind him, looking at him with the quick bright faint serene smiling which only a woman nearing forty can give to a man to whom she is not married and from whom she has had no secrets physical and few mental over a long time of pleasant and absolute intimacy. She had been married though and divorced; she had a child, a daughter of fourteen, whom he was now keeping in boarding school. He looked at her, blinking, as she closed the door.

"You saw the papers," he said. She kissed him, not suddenly, without heat, in a continuation of the movement which closed the door, with a sort of warm envelopment; suddenly he cried, "I can't understand it! After all the advantages that ... after all I tried to do for them—"

"Hush," she said. "Hush, now. Get into your trunks; I'll have a drink ready for you when you have changed. Will you eat some lunch if I have it sent up?"

"No. I don't want any lunch.—after all I have tried to give—"

"Hush, now. Get into your trunks while I fix you a drink. It's going to be swell at the beach." In the bedroom his bathing trunks and robe were laid out on the bed. He changed, hanging his suit in the closet where her clothes hung, where there hung already another suit of his and clothes for the evening. When he returned to the sitting room she had fixed the drink for him; she held the match to his cigarette and watched him sit down and take up the glass, watching him still with that serene impersonal smiling. Now he watched her slip off the cape and kneel at the cellarette, filing a silver flask, in the bathing costume of the moment, such as ten thousand wax female dummies wore in ten thousand shop windows that summer, such as a hundred thousand young girls wore on California beaches; he looked at her, kneeling—back, buttocks and flanks trim enough, even firm enough (so firm in fact as to be a little on the muscular side, what with unremitting and perhaps even rigorous care) but still those of forty. But I don't want a young girl, he thought. Would to God that all young girls, all young female flesh, were removed, blasted even, from the earth. He finished the drink before she had filled the flask.

"I want another one," he said.

"All right," she said. "As soon as we get to the beach."

"No. Now."

"Let's go on to the beach first. It's almost three o'clock. Won't that be better?"

"Just so you are not trying to tell me I can't have another drink now."

"Of course not," she said, slipping the flask into the cape's pocket and looking at him again with that warm, faint, inscrutable smiling. "I just want to have a dip before the water gets too cold." They went down to the car; the Filipino knew this too: he held the door for her to slip under the wheel, then he got himself into the back. The car moved on; she drove well. "Why not lean back and shut your eyes," she told Ira, "and rest until we get to the beach? Then we will have a dip and a drink."

"I don't want to rest," he said. "I'm all right." But he did close his eyes again and again the car ran powerful, smooth, and fast beneath him, performing its afternoon's jaunt over the incredible distances of which the city was composed; from time to time, had he looked, he could have seen the city in the bright soft vague hazy sunlight, random, scattered about the arid earth like so many gay scraps of paper blown without order, with its curious air of being rootless—of houses bright beautiful and gay, without basements or foundations, lightly attached to a few inches of light penetrable earth, lighter even than dust and laid lightly in turn upon the profound and primeval lava, which one good hard rain would wash forever from the sight and memory of man as a firehose flushes down a gutter—that city of almost incalculable wealth whose queerly appropriate fate it is to be erected upon a few spools of a substance whose value is computed in billions and which may be completely destroyed in that second's instant of a careless match between the moment of striking and the moment when the striker might have sprung and stamped it out.

"You saw your mother today," she said. "Has she—"

"Yes." He didn't open his eyes. "That damned Jap gave it to her. She asked me for money again. I found out what she wants with it. She wants to run, to go back to Nebraska. I told her, so did I. ... If she went back there, she would not live until Christmas. The first month of winter would kill her. Maybe it wouldn't even take winter to do it."

She still drove, she still watched the road, yet somehow she had contrived to become completely immobile. "So that's what it is," she said.

He did not open his eyes. "What what is?"

"The reason she has been after you all this time to give her money, cash. Why, even when you won't do it, every now and then she asks you again."

"What what ..." He opened his eyes, looking at her profile; he sat up suddenly. "You mean, she's been wanting to go back there all that time: That all these years she has been asking me for money, that that was what she wanted with it?"

She glanced at him swiftly, then back to the road. "What else can it be? What else could she use money for?"

"Back there?" he said. "To those winters, that town, that way of living, where she's bound to know that the first winter would ... You'd almost think she wanted to die, wouldn't you?"

"Hush," she said quickly. "Shhhhh. Don't say that. Don't say that about anybody." Already they could smell the sea; now they swung down toward it; the bright salt wind blew upon them, with the long-spaced sound of the rollers; now they could see it—the dark blue of water creaming into the blanched curve of beach dotted with bathers. "We won't go through the club," she said. "I'll park in here and we can go straight to the water." They left the Filipino in the car and descended to the beach. It was already crowded, bright and gay with movement. She chose a vacant space and spread her cape.

"Now that drink," he said.

"Have your dip first," she said. He looked at her. Then he slipped his robe off slowly; she took it and spread it beside her own; he looked down at her.

"Which is it? Will you always be too clever for me, or is it that every time I will always believe you again?"

She looked at him, bright, warm, fond and inscrutable. "Maybe both. Maybe neither. Have your dip; I will have the flask and a cigarette ready when you come out." When he came back from the water, wet, panting, his heart a little too hard and fast, she had the towel ready, and she lit the cigarette and uncapped the flask as he lay on the spread robes. She lay too, lifted to one elbow, smiling down at him, smoothing the water from his hair with the towel while he panted, waiting for his heart to slow and quiet. Steadily between them and the water, and as far up and down the beach as they could see, the bathers passed—young people, young men in trunks, and young girls in little more, with bronzed, unselfconscious bodies. Lying so, they seemed to him to walk along the rim of the world as though they and their kind alone inhabited it, and he with his forty-eight years were the forgotten last survivor of another race and kind, and they in turn precursors of a new race not yet seen on the earth: of men and women without age, beautiful as gods and goddesses, and with the minds of infants. He turned quickly and looked at the woman beside him—at the quiet face, the wise, smiling eyes, and grained skin and temples, the hairroots showing where the dye had grown out, the legs veined faint and blue and myriad beneath the skin. "You look better than any of them!" he cried. "You look better to me than any of them!"

III

The Japanese gardener, with his hat on, stood tapping on the glass and beckoning and grimacing until old Mrs. Ewing went out to him. He had the afternoon's paper with its black headline: LALEAR WOMAN CREATES SCENE IN COURTROOM. "You take," the Japanese said. "Read while I catch water." But she declined; she just stood in the soft halcyon sunlight, surrounded by the myriad and almost fierce blooming of flowers, and looked quietly at the headline without even taking the paper, and that was all.

"I guess I won't look at the paper today," she said. "Thank you just the same." She returned to the living room. Save for the chair, it was exactly as it had been when she first saw it that day when her son brought her into it and told her that it was now her home and that her daughter-in-law and her grandchildren were now her family. It had changed very little, and that which had altered was the part which her son knew nothing about, and that too had changed not at all in so long that she could not even remember now when she had added the last coin to the hoard. This was in a china vase on the mantel. She knew what was in it to the penny; nevertheless, she took it down and sat in the chair which she had brought all the way from Nebraska and emptied the coins and the worn timetable into her lap. The timetable was folded back at the page on which she had folded it the day she walked downtown to the ticket office and got it fifteen years ago, though that was so long ago now that the pencil circle about the name of the nearest junction point to Ewing, Nebraska, had faded away. But she did not need that either; she knew the distance to the exact halfmile, just as she knew the fare to the penny, and back in the early twenties when the railroads began to become worried and passenger fares began to drop, no broker ever watched the grain and utilities market any closer than she watched the railroad advertisements and quotations. Then at last the fares became stabilized with the fare back to Ewing thirteen dollars more than she had been able to save, and at a time when her source of income had ceased. This was the two grandchildren. When she entered the house that day twenty years ago and looked at the two babies for the first time, it was with diffidence and eagerness both. She would be dependent for the rest of her life, but she would give something in return for it. It was not that she would attempt to make another Ira and Samantha Ewing of them; she had made that mistake with her own son and had driven him from home. She was wiser now; she saw now that it was not the repetition of hardship: she would merely take what had been of value in hers and her husband's hard lives—that which they had learned through hardship and endurance of honor and courage and pride—and transmit it to the children without their having to suffer the hardship at all, the travail and the despairs. She had expected that there would be some friction between her and the young daughter-in-law, but she had believed that her son, the actual Ewing, would be her ally; she had even reconciled herself after a year to waiting, since the children were still but babies; she was not alarmed, since they were Ewings too: after she had looked that first searching time at the two puttysoft little faces feature by feature, she had said it was because they were babies yet and so looked like no one. So she was content to bide and wait; she did not even know that her son was planning to move until he told her that the other house was bought and that the present one was to be hers until she died. She watched them go; she said nothing; it was not to begin then.

It did not begin for five years, during which she watched her son making money faster and faster and easier and easier, gaining with apparent contemptible and contemptuous ease that substance for which in niggard amounts her husband had striven while still clinging with undeviating incorruptibility to honor and dignity and pride, and spending it, squandering it, in the same way. By that time she had given up the son and she had long since learned that she and her daughter-in-law were irrevocable and implacable moral enemies. It was in the fifth year. One day in her son's home she saw the two children take money from their mother's purse lying on a table. The mother did not even know how much she had in the purse; when the grandmother told her about it she became angry and dared the older woman to put it to the test. The grandmother accused the children, who denied the whole affair with perfectly straight faces. That was the actual break between herself and her son's family; after that she saw the two children only when the son would bring them with him occasionally on his unfailing daily visits. She had a few broken dollars which she had brought from Nebraska and had kept intact for five years, since she had no need for money here; one day she planted one of the coins while the children were there, and when she went back to look, it was gone too. The next morning she tried to talk to her son about the children, remembering her experience with the daughter-in-law and approaching the matter indirectly, speaking generally of money. "Yes," the son said. "I'm making money. I'm making it fast while I can. I'm going to make a lot of it. I'm going to give my children luxuries and advantages that my father never dreamed a child might have."

"That's it," she said. "You make money too easy. This whole country is too easy for us Ewings. It may be all right for them that have been born here for generations; I don't know about that. But not for us."

"But these children were born here."

"Just one generation. The generation before that they were born in a sodroofed dugout on the Nebraska wheat frontier. And the one before that in a log house in Missouri. And the one before that in a Kentucky blockhouse with Indians around it. This world has never been easy for Ewings. Maybe the Lord never intended it to be."

"But it is from now on," he said; he spoke with a kind of triumph. "For you and me too. But mostly for them."

And that was all. When he was gone she sat quietly in the single Nebraska chair which she had taken out of storage—the first chair which the older Ira Ewing had bought for her after he built a house and in which she had rocked the younger Ira to sleep before he could walk, while the older Ira himself sat in the chair which he had made out of a flour barrel, grim, quiet and incorruptible, taking his earned twilight ease between a day and a day—telling herself quietly that that was all. Her next move was curiously direct; there was something in it of the actual pioneer's opportunism, of taking immediate and cold advantage of Spartan circumstance; it was as though for the first time in her life she was able to use something, anything, which she had gained by bartering her youth and strong maturity against the Nebraska immensity, and this not in order to live further but in order to die; apparently she saw neither paradox in it nor dishonesty. She began to make candy and cake of the materials which her son bought for her on credit, and to sell them to the two grandchildren for the coins which their father gave them or which they perhaps purloined also from their mother's purse, hiding the coins in the vase with the timetable, watching the niggard hoard grow. But after a few years the children outgrew candy and cake, and then she had watched railroad fares go down and down and then stop thirteen dollars away. But she did not give up, even then. Her son had tried to give her a servant years ago and she had refused; she believed that when the time came, the right moment, he would not refuse to give her at least thirteen dollars of the money which she had saved him. Then this had failed. "Maybe it wasn't the right time," she thought. "Maybe I tried too quick. I was surprised into it," she told herself, looking down at the heap of small coins in her lap. "Or maybe he was surprised into saying No. Maybe when he has had time ..." She roused; she put the coins back into the vase and set it on the mantel again, looking at the clock as she did so. It was just four, two hours yet until time to start supper. The sun was high; she could see the water from the sprinkler flashing and glinting in it as she went to the window. It was still high, still afternoon; the mountains stood serene and drab against it; the city, the land, lay sprawled and myriad beneath it—the land, the earth which spawned a thousand new faiths, nostrums and cures each year but no disease to even disprove them on—beneath the golden days unmarred by rain or weather, the changeless monotonous beautiful days without end countless out of the halcyon past and endless into the halcyon future.

"I will stay here and live forever," she said to herself.

132
The Day of the Locust

NATHANAEL WEST

Nathanael West (Nathan Wallenstein Weinstein) (1904–40) was born in New York City, but spent the most significant period of his life as a writer in Hollywood (1935–40). He was killed in a car crash in California. West's output as a writer was relatively small, although his influence and significance is great. Four brief novels, *The Dream Life of Balso Snell* (1931), *Miss Lonelyhearts* (1933), *A Cool Million* (1934), and *The Day of the Locust* (1939) form his *oeuvre*. Limited as it is, the four novels constitute a sustained and highly individual view of American culture, the very opposite of the Hollywood "dream-machine" for which he worked.

The Day of the Locust is a trenchant, almost surreal satire on the significance of Hollywood (and Los Angeles) within the American psyche and, as it develops, shows the influence of psychological theory which places it ahead of its time. See Randall Reid, *The Fiction of Nathanael West* (1968), and Victor Comerchero, *Nathanael West: The Ironic Prophet* (1964).

1

Around quitting time, Tod Hackett heard a great din on the road outside his office. The groan of leather mingled with the jangle of iron and over all beat the tattoo of a thousand hooves. He hurried to the window.

An army of cavalry and foot was passing. it moved like a mob; its lines broken, as though fleeing from some terrible defeat. The dolmans of the hussars, the heavy shakos of the guards, Hanoverian light horse, with their flat leather caps and flowing red plumes, were all jumbled together in bobbing disorder. Behind the cavalry came the infantry, a wild sea of waving sabretaches, sloped muskets, crossed shoulder belts, and swinging cartridge boxes. Tod recognized the scarlet infantry of England with their white shoulder pads, the black infantry of the Duke of Brunswick, the French grenadiers with their enormous white gaiters, the Scotch with bare knees under plaid skirts.

Source: Nathanael West, *The Day of the Locust*, 1939, Chs. 1, 18, 27.

While he watched, a little fat man, wearing a cork sun-helmet, polo shirt, and knickers, darted around the corner of the building in pursuit of the army.

"Stage Nine—you bastards—Stage Nine!" he screamed through a small megaphone.

The cavalry put spur to their horses and the infantry broke into a dogtrot. The little man in the cork hat ran after them, shaking his fist and cursing.

Tod watched until they had disappeared behind half a Mississippi steamboat, then put away his pencils and drawingboard, and left the office. On the sidewalk outside the studio he stood for a moment trying to decide whether to walk home or take a streetcar. He had been in Hollywood less than three months and still found it a very exciting place, but he was lazy and didn't like to walk. He decided to take the streetcar as far as Vine Street and walk the rest of the way.

A talent scout for National Films had brought Tod to the Coast after seeing some of his drawings in an exhibit of undergraduate work at the Yale School of Fine Arts. He had been hired by telegram. If the scout had met Tod, he probably wouldn't have sent him to Hollywood to learn set and costume designing. His large, sprawling body, his slow blue eyes and sloppy grin made him seem completely without talent, almost doltish in fact.

Yet, despite his appearance, he was really a very complicated young man with a whole set of personalities, one inside the other like a nest of Chinese boxes. And, *The Burning of Los Angeles*, a picture he was soon to paint, definitely proved he had talent.

He left the car at Vine Street. As he walked along, he examined the evening crowd. A great many of the people wore sports clothes which were not really sports clothes. Their sweaters, knickers, slacks, blue-flannel jackets with brass buttons were fancy dress. The fat lady in the yachting cap was going shopping, not boating; the man in the Norfolk jacket and Tyrolean hat was returning, not from a mountain, but an insurance office; and the girl in slacks and sneaks with a bandanna around her head had just left a switchboard, not a tennis court.

Scattered among these masquerades were people of a different type. Their clothing was sombre and badly cut, bought from mail-order houses. While the others moved rapidly, darting into stores and cocktail bars, they loitered on the corners or stood with their backs to the shop windows and stared at everyone who passed. When their stare was returned, their eyes filled with hatred. At this time Tod knew very little about them except that they had come to California to die.

He was determined to learn much more. They were the people he felt he must paint. He would never again do a fat red barn, old stone wall, or sturdy Nantucket fisherman. From the moment he had seen them, he had known that, despite his race, training, and heritage, neither Winslow Homer nor Thomas Ryder could be his masters and he turned to Goya and Daumier.

He had learned this just in time. During his last year in art school, he had begun to think that he might give up painting completely. The pleasures he received from the problems of composition and colour had decreased as his facility had increased and he had realized that he was going the way of all his classmates, towards illustration or mere handsomeness. When the Hollywood job had come along, he had grabbed it despite the arguments of his friends who were certain that he was selling out and would never paint again.

He reached the end of Vine Street and began the climb into Pinyon Canyon. Night had started to fall.

The edges of the trees burned with a pale violet light and their centres gradually turned from deep purple to black. The same violet piping, like a Neon tube, outlined the tops of the ugly, humpbacked hills and they were almost beautiful.

But not even the soft wash of dusk could help the houses. Only dynamite would be of any use against the Mexican ranch houses, Samoan huts, Mediterranean villas, Egyptian and Japanese temples, Swiss chalets, Tudor cottages, and every possible combination of these styles that lined the slopes of the canyon.

When he noticed that they were all of plaster, lath, and paper, he was charitable and blamed their shape on the materials used. Steel, stone, and brick curb a builder's fancy a little, forcing him to distribute his stresses and weights and to keep his corners plumb, but plaster and paper know no law, not even that of gravity.

On the corner of La Huerta Road was a miniature Rhine castle with tarpaper turrets pierced for archers. Next to it was a little highly coloured shack with domes and minarets out of the *Arabian Nights*. Again he was charitable. Both houses were comic, but he didn't laugh. Their desire to startle was so eager and guileless.

It is hard to laugh at the need for beauty and romance, no matter how tasteless, even horrible, the results of that need are. But it is easy to sigh. Few things are sadder than the truly monstrous.

18

Faye moved out of the San Berdoo the day after the funeral. Tod didn't know where she had gone and was getting up the courage to call Mrs. Jenning when he saw her from the window of his office. She was dressed in the costume of a Napoleonic vivandière. By the time he got the window open, she had almost turned the corner of the building. He shouted for her to wait. She waved, but when he got downstairs she was gone.

From her dress, he was sure that she was working in the picture called Waterloo. He asked a studio policeman where the company was shooting and was told on the back lot. He started towards it at once. A platoon of cuirassiers, big men mounted on gigantic horses, went by. He knew that they must be headed for the same set and followed them. They broke into a gallop and he was soon outdistanced.

The sun was very hot. His eyes and throat were choked with the dust thrown up by the horses' hooves and his head throbbed. The only bit of shade he could find was under an ocean liner made of painted canvas with real lifeboats hanging from its davits. He stood in its narrow shadow for a while, then went on towards a great forty-foot papiermâché sphinx that loomed up in the distance. He had to cross a desert to reach it, a desert that was continually being made larger by a fleet of trucks dumping white sand. He had gone only a few feet when a man with a megaphone ordered him off.

He skirted the desert, making a wide turn to the right, and came to a Western street with a plank sidewalk. On the porch of the Last Chance Saloon was a rocking-chair. He sat down on it and lit a cigarette.

From there he could see a jungle compound with a water buffalo tethered to the side of a conical grass hut. Every few seconds the animal groaned musically. Suddenly an Arab charged by on a white stallion. He shouted at the man, but got no answer. A little while later he saw a truck with a load of snow and several malamute dogs. He shouted again. The driver shouted something back, but didn't stop.

Throwing away his cigarette, he went through the swinging doors of the saloon. There was no back to the building and he found himself in a Paris street. He followed it to its end, coming out in a Romanesque courtyard. He heard voices a short distance away and went towards them. On a lawn of fibre, a group of men and women in riding costume were picnicking. They were eating cardboard food in front of a cellophane waterfall. He started towards them to ask his way, but was stopped by a man who scowled and held up a sign—"Quiet, Please, We're Shooting". When Tod took another step forward, the man shook his fist threateningly.

Next he came to a small pond with large celluloid swans floating on it. Across one end was a bridge with a sign that read, "To Kamp Komfit". He crossed the bridge and followed a little path that ended at a Greek temple dedicated to Eros. The god himself lay face downward in a pile of old newspapers and bottles.

From the steps of the temple, he could see in the distance a road lined with Lombardy poplars. It was the one on which he had lost the cuirassiers. He pushed his way through a tangle of briars, old flats, and iron junk, skirting the skeleton of a Zeppelin, a bamboo stockade, an adobe fort, the wooden horse of Troy, a flight of baroque palace stairs that started in a bed of weeds and ended against the branches of an oak, part of the Fourteenth Street elevated station, a Dutch windmill, the bones of a dinosaur, the upper half of the Merrimac, a corner of a Mayan temple, until he finally reached the road.

He was out of breath. He sat down under one of the poplars on a rock made of brown plaster and took off his jacket. There was a cool breeze blowing and he soon felt more comfortable.

He had lately begun to think not only of Goya and Daumier but also of certain Italian artists of the seventeenth and eighteenth centuries, of Salvator Rosa, Francesco Guardi, and Monsu Desiderio, the painters of Decay and Mystery. Looking downhill now, he could see compositions that might have actually been arranged from the Calabrian work of Rosa. There were partially demolished buildings and broken monuments, half-hidden by great, tortured trees, whose exposed roots writhed dramatically in the arid ground, and by shrubs that carried, not flowers or berries, but armouries of spikes, hooks, and swords.

For Guardi and Desiderio there were bridges which bridged nothing, sculpture in trees, palaces that seemed of marble until a whole stone portico began to flap in the light breeze. And there were figures as well. A hundred yards from where Tod was sitting a man in a derby hat leaned drowsily against the gilded poop of a Venetian barque and peeled an apple. Still farther on, a charwoman on a stepladder was scrubbing with soap and water the face of a Buddha thirty feet high.

He left the road and climbed across the spine of the hill to look down on the other side. From there he could see a ten-acre field of cockleburs spotted with clumps of sunflowers and wild gum. In the centre of the field was a gigantic pile of sets, flats, and props. While he watched, a ten-ton truck added another load to it. This was the final dumping ground. He thought of Janvier's *Sargasso Sea.* Just as that imaginary body of water was a history of civilization in the form of a marine junkyard, the studio lot was one in the form of a dream dump. A Sargasso of the imagination! And the dump grew continually, for there wasn't a dream afloat somewhere which wouldn't sooner or later turn up on it, having first been made photographic by plaster, canvas, lath, and paint. Many boats sink and never reach the Sargasso, but no dream ever entirely disappears. Somewhere it troubles some unfortunate person and some day, when that person has been sufficiently troubled, it will be reproduced on the lot.

When he saw a red glare in the sky and heard the rumble of cannon, he knew it must be Waterloo. From around a bend in the road trotted several cavalry regiments. They wore casques and chest armour of black cardboard and carried long horse pistols in their saddle holsters. They were Victor Hugo's soldiers. He had worked on some of the drawings for their uniforms himself, following carefully the descriptions in *Les Misérables.*

He went in the direction they took. Before long he was passed by the men of Lefebvre-Desnouttes, followed by a regiment of *gendarmes d'élite,* several companies of chasseurs of the guard, and a flying detachment of Rimbaud's lancers.

They must be moving up for the disastrous attack on La Haite Santée. He hadn't read the scenario and wondered if it had rained yesterday. Would Grouchy or Bulcher arrive? Grotenstein, the producer, might have changed it.

The sound of cannon was becoming louder all the time and the red fan in the sky more intense. He could smell the sweet, pungent odour of blank powder. It might be over before he could get there. He started to run. When he topped a rise after a sharp bend in the road, he found a great plain below him covered with early nineteenth-century troops, wearing all the gay and elaborate uniforms that used to please him so much when he was a child and spent long hours looking at the soldiers in an old dictionary. At the far end of the field, he could see an enormous hump around which the English and their allies were gathered. It was Mont St Jean and they were getting ready to defend it gallantly. It wasn't quite finished, however, and swarmed with grips, property men, set dressers, carpenters, and painters.

Tod stood near a eucalyptus tree to watch, concealing himself behind a sign that read, "*Waterloo*–A Charles H. Grotenstein Production". Near by a youth in a carefully torn horse guard's uniform was being rehearsed in his lines by one of the assistant directors.

"*Vive l'Empereur!*" the young man shouted, then clutched his breast and fell forward dead. The assistant director was a hard man to please and made him do it over and over again.

In the centre of the plain, the battle was going ahead briskly. Things looked tough for the British and their allies. The Prince of Orange commanding the centre, Hill the right and Picton the left wing, were being pressed hard by the veteran French. The desperate and intrepid Prince was in an especially bad spot. Tod heard him cry hoarsely above the din of battle, shouting to the Hollande-Belgians, "Nassau! Brunswick! Never retreat!" Nevertheless, the retreat began. Hill, too, fell back. The French killed General Picton with a ball through the head and he returned to his dressing-room. Alten was put to the sword and also retired. The colours of the Lunenberg battalion, borne by a prince of the family of Deux-Ponts, were captured by a famous child star in the uniform of a Parisian drummer boy. The Scots Greys were destroyed and went to change into another uniform. Ponsonby's heavy dragoons were also cut to ribbons. Mr. Grotenstein would have a large bill to pay at the Western Costume Company.

Neither Napoleon nor Wellington was to be seen. In Wellington's absence, one of the assistant directors, a Mr. Crane, was in command of the allies. He reinforced his centre with one of Chasse's brigades and one of Wincke's. He supported these with infantry from Brunswick, Welsh foot, Devon yeomanry, and Hanoverian light horse with oblong leather caps and flowing plumes of horsehair.

For the French, a man in a checked cap ordered Milhaud's cuirassiers to carry Mont St Jean. With their sabres in their teeth and their pistols in their hands, they charged. It was a fearful sight.

The man in the checked cap was making a fatal error. Mont St Jean was unfinished. The paint was not yet dry and all the struts were not in place. Because of the thickness of the cannon smoke, he had failed to see that the hill was still being worked on by property men, grips, and carpenters.

It was the classic mistake, Tod realized, the same one Napoleon had made. Then it had been wrong for a different reason. The Emperor had ordered the cuirassiers to charge Mont St Jean not knowing that a deep ditch was hidden at its foot to trap his heavy cavalry. The result had been disaster for the French; the beginning of the end.

This time the same mistake had a different outcome. Waterloo, instead of being the end of the Grand Army, resulted in a draw. Neither side won, and it would have to be fought over again the next day. Big losses, however, were sustained by the insurance company in workmen's compensation. The man in the checked cap was sent to the dog house by Mr. Grotenstein just as Napoleon was sent to St Helena.

When the front rank of Milhaud's heavy division started up the slope of Mont St Jean, the hill collapsed. The noise was terrific. Nails screamed with agony as they pulled out of joists. The sound of ripping canvas was like that of little children whimpering. Lath and scantling snapped as though they were brittle bones. The whole hill folded like an enormous umbrella and covered Napoleon's army with painted cloth.

It turned into a rout. The victors of Bersina, Leipsic, Austerlitz, fled like schoolboys who had broken a pane of glass, "*Sauve qui peut!*" they cried, or, rather, "Scram!"

The armies of England and her allies were too deep in scenery to flee. They had to wait for the carpenters and ambulances to come up. The men of the gallant Seventy-fifth Highlanders were lifted out of the wreck with block and tackle. They were carted off by the stretcher-bearers, still clinging bravely to their claymores.

27

When Tod reached the street, he saw a dozen great violet shafts of light moving across the evening sky in wide crazy sweeps. Whenever one of the fiery columns reached the lowest point of its arc, it lit for a moment the rose-coloured domes and delicate minarets of Kahn's Persian Palace Theatre. The purpose of this display was to signal the world première of a new picture.

Turning his back on the searchlights, he started in the opposite direction, towards Homer's place. Before he had gone very far, he saw a clock that read a quarter past six and changed his mind about going back just yet. He might as well let the poor fellow sleep for another hour and kill some time by looking at the crowds.

When still a block from the theatre, he saw an enormous electric sign that hung over the middle of the street. In letters ten feet high he read that—

MR. KAHN A PLEASURE DOME DECREED

Although it was still several hours before the celebrities would arrive, thousands of people had already gathered. They stood facing the theatre with their backs towards the gutter in a thick line hundreds of feet long. A big squad of policemen was trying to keep a lane open between the front rank of the crowd and the façade of the theatre.

Tod entered the lane while the policeman guarding it was busy with a woman whose parcel had torn open, dropping oranges all over the place. Another policeman shouted for him to get the hell across the street, but he took a chance and kept going. They had enough to do without chasing him. He noticed how worried they looked and how careful they tried to be. If they had to arrest someone, they joked good-naturedly with the culprit, making light of it until they got him around the corner, then they whaled him with their clubs. Only so long as the man was actually part of the crowd did they have to be gentle.

Tod had walked only a short distance along the narrow lane when he began to get frightened. People shouted, commenting on his hat, his carriage, and his clothing. There was continuous roar of catcalls, laughter, and yells, pierced occasionally by a scream. The scream was usually followed by a sudden movement in the dense mass and part of it would surge forward wherever the police line was weakest. As soon as that part was rammed back, the bulge would pop out somewhere else.

The police force would have to be doubled when the stars started to arrive. At the sight of their heroes and heroines, the crowd, would turn demoniac. Some little gesture, either too pleasing or too offensive, would start it moving and then nothing but machine-guns would stop it. Individually the purpose of its members might simply be to get a souvenir, but collectively it would grab and rend.

A young man with a portable microphone was describing the scene. His rapid, hysterical voice was like that of a revivalist preacher whipping his congregation towards the ecstasy of fits.

"What a crowd, folks! What a crowd! There must be ten thousand excited, screaming fans outside Kahn's Persian tonight. The police can't hold them. Here, listen to them roar."

He held the microphone out and those near it obligingly roared for him.

"Did you hear it? It's a bedlam, folks. A veritable bedlam! What excitement! Of all the premières I've attended, this is the most ... the most ... stupendous, folks. Can the police hold them? Can they? It doesn't look so, folks. ..."

Another squad of police came charging up. The sergeant pleaded with the announcer to stand farther back so the people couldn't hear him. His men threw themselves at the crowd. It allowed itself to be hustled and shoved out of habit and because it lacked an objective. It tolerated the police, just as a bull elephant does when he allows a small boy to drive him with a light stick.

Tod could see very few people who looked tough, nor could he see any working men. The crowd was made up of the lower middle classes, every other person one of his torch-bearers.

Just as he came near the end of the lane, it closed in front of him with a heave, and he had to fight his way through. Someone knocked his hat off and when he stooped to pick it up, someone kicked him. He whirled around angrily and found himself surrounded by people who were laughing at him. He knew enough to laugh with them. The crowd became sympathetic. A stout woman slapped him on the back, while a man handed him his hat, first brushing it carefully with his sleeve. Still another man shouted for a way to be cleared.

By a great deal of pushing and squirming, always trying to look as though he were enjoying himself, Tod finally managed to break into the open. After rearranging his clothes, he went over to a parking lot and sat down on the low retaining wall that ran along the front of it.

New groups, whole families, kept arriving. He could see a change come over them as soon as they had become part of the crowd. Until they reached the line, they looked difficult, almost furtive, but the moment they had become part of it, they turned arrogant and pugnacious. It was a mistake to think them harmless curiosity seekers. They were savage and bitter, especially the middle-aged and the old, and had been made so by boredom and disappointment.

All their lives they had slaved at some kind of dull, heavy labour, behind desks and counters, in the fields and at tedious machines of all sorts, saving their pennies and dreaming of the leisure that would be theirs when they had enough. Finally that day came. They could draw a weekly income of ten or fifteen dollars. Where else should they go but California, the land of sunshine and oranges?

Once there, they discover that sunshine isn't enough. They get tired of oranges, even of avocado pears and passion fruit. Nothing happens. They don't know what to do with their time. They haven't the mental equipment for leisure, the money nor the physical equipment for pleasure. Did they slave so long just to go to an occasional Iowa picnic? What else is there? They watch the waves come in at Venice. There wasn't any ocean where most of them came from, but after you've seen one wave, you've seen them all. The same is true of the aeroplanes at Glendale. If only a plane would crash once in a while so that they could watch the passengers being consumed in a "holocaust of flame", as the newspapers put it. But the planes never crash.

Their boredom becomes more and more terrible. They realize that they've been tricked and burn with resentment. Every day of their lives they read the newspapers and went to the movies. Both fed them on lynchings, murder, sex crimes, explosions, wrecks, love-nests, fires, miracles, revolutions, war. This daily diet made sophisticates of them. The sun is a joke. Oranges can't titillate their jaded palates. Nothing can ever be violent enough to make taut their slack minds and bodies. They have been cheated and betrayed. They have slaved and saved for nothing.

Tod stood up. During the ten minutes he had been sitting on the wall, the crowd had grown thirty feet and he was afraid that his escape might be cut off if he loitered much longer. He crossed to the other side of the street and started back.

He was trying to figure what to do if he were unable to wake Homer when, suddenly, he saw his head bobbing above the crowd. He hurried towards him. From his appearance, it was evident that there was something definitely wrong.

Homer walked more than ever like a badly made automaton and his features were set in a rigid, mechanical grin. He had his trousers on over his nightgown and part of it hung out of his open fly. In both of his hands were suitcases. With each step, he lurched to one side then the other, using the suitcases for balance weights.

Tod stopped directly in front of him, blocking his way.

"Where're you going?"

"Wayneville," he replied, using an extraordinary amount of jaw movement to get out this single word.

"That's fine. But you can't walk to the station from here. It's in Los Angeles."

Homer tried to get around him, but he caught his arm.

"We'll get a taxi. I'll go with you."

The cabs were all being routed around the block because of the preview. He explained this to Homer and tried to get him to walk to the corner.

"Come on, we're sure to get one on the next street."

Once Tod got him into a cab, he intended to tell the driver to go to the nearest hospital. But Homer wouldn't budge, no matter how hard he yanked and pleaded. People stopped to watch them, others turned their heads curiously. He decided to leave him and get a cab.

"I'll come right back," he said.

He couldn't tell from either Homer's eyes or expression whether he heard, for they both were empty of everything, even annoyance. At the corner he looked around and saw that Homer had started to cross the street, moving blindly. Brakes screeched and twice he was almost run over, but he didn't swerve or hurry. He moved in a straight diagonal. When he reached the other curb, he tried to get on the sidewalk at a point where the crowd was very thick and was shoved violently back. He made another attempt and this time a policeman grabbed him by the back of the neck and hustled him to the end of the line. When the policeman let go of him, he kept on walking as though nothing had happened.

Tod tried to get over to him, but was unable to cross until the traffic lights changed. When he reached the other side, he found Homer sitting on a bench, fifty or sixty feet from the outskirts of the crowd.

He put his arm around Homer's shoulder and suggested that they walk a few blocks farther. When Homer didn't answer, he reached over to pick up one of the valises. Homer held on to it.

"I'll carry it for you," he said, tugging gently.

"Thief!"

Before Homer could repeat the shout, he jumped away. It would be extremely embarrassing if Homer shouted thief in front of a cop. He thought of phoning for an ambulance. But then, after all, how could he be sure that Homer was crazy? He was sitting quietly on the bench, minding his own business.

Tod decided to wait, then try again to get him into a cab. The crowd was growing in size all the time, but it would be at least half an hour before it overran the bench. Before that happened, he would think of some plan. He moved a short distance away and stood with his back to a store window so that he could watch Homer without attracting attention.

About ten feet from where Homer was sitting grew a large eucalyptus tree and behind the trunk of the tree was a little boy. Tod saw him peer around it with great caution, then suddenly jerk his head back. A minute later he repeated the manoeuvre. At first Tod thought he was playing hide-and-seek, then noticed that he had a string in his hand which was attached to an old purse that lay in front of Homer's bench. Every once in a while the child would jerk the string, making the purse hop like a sluggish toad. Its torn lining hung from its iron mouth like a furry tongue and a few uncertain flies hovered over it.

Tod knew the game the child was playing. He used to play it himself when he was small. If Homer reached to pick up the purse, thinking there was money in it, he would yank it away and scream with laughter.

When Tod went over to the tree, he was surprised to discover that it was Adore Loomis, the kid who lived across the street from Homer. Tod tried to chase him, but he dodged around the tree, thumbing his nose. He gave up and went back to his original position. The moment he left, Adore got busy with his purse again. Homer wasn't paying any attention to the child, so Tod decided to let him alone.

Mrs. Loomis must be somewhere in the crowd, he thought. Tonight when she found Adore, she would give him a hiding. He had torn the pocket of his jacket and his Buster Brown collar was smeared with grease.

Adore had a nasty temper. The completeness with which Homer ignored both him and his pocket-book made him frantic. He gave up dancing it at the end of the string and approached the bench on tiptoes, making ferocious faces, yet ready to run at Homer's first move. He stopped when about four feet away and stuck his tongue out. Homer ignored him. He took another step forward and ran through a series of insulting gestures.

If Tod had known that the boy held a stone in his hand, he would have interfered. But he felt sure that Homer wouldn't hurt the child and was waiting to see if he wouldn't move because of his pestering. When Adore raised his arm, it was too late. The stone hit Homer in the face. The boy turned to flee, but tripped and fell. Before he could scramble away, Homer landed on his back with both feet, then jumped again.

Tod yelled for him to stop and tried to yank him away. He shoved Tod and went on using his heels. Tod hit him as hard as he could, first in the belly, then in the face. He ignored the blows and continued to stamp on the boy. Tod hit him again and again, then threw both arms around him and tried to pull him off. He couldn't budge him. He was like a stone column.

The next thing Tod knew, he was torn loose from Homer and sent to his knees by a blow in the back of the head that spun him sideways. The crowd in front of the theatre had charged. He was surrounded by churning legs and feet. He pulled himself erect by grabbing a man's coat, then let himself be carried along backwards in a long, curving swoop. He saw Homer rise above the mass for a moment, shoved against the sky, his jaw hanging as though he wanted to scream but couldn't. A hand reached up and caught him by his open mouth and pulled him forward and down.

There was another dizzy rush. Tod closed his eyes and fought to keep upright. He was jostled about in a hacking cross-surf of shoulders and backs, carried rapidly in one direction and then in the opposite. He kept pushing and hitting out at the people around him, trying to face in the direction he was going. Being carried backwards terrified him.

Using the eucalyptus tree as a landmark, he tried to work towards it by slipping sideways against the tide, pushing hard when carried away from it and riding the current when it moved towards his objective. He was within only a few feet of the tree when a sudden, driving rush carried him far past it. He struggled desperately for a moment, then gave up and let himself be swept along. He was the spearhead of a flying wedge when it collided with a mass going in the opposite direction. The impact turned him around. As the two forces ground against each other, he was turned again and again, like a grain between millstones. This didn't stop until he became part of the opposing force. The pressure continued to increase until he thought he must collapse. He was slowly being pushed into the air. Although relief for his cracking ribs could be got by continuing to rise, he fought to keep his feet on the ground. Not being able to touch was an even more dreadful sensation than being carried backwards.

There was another rush, shorter this time, and he found himself in a dead spot where the pressure was less and equal. He became conscious of a terrible pain in his left leg, just above the ankle, and tried to work it into a more comfortable position. He couldn't turn his body, but managed to get his head around. A very skinny boy, wearing a Western Union cap, had his back wedged against his shoulder. The pain continued to grow and his whole leg as high as the groin throbbed. He finally got his left arm free and took the back of the boy's neck in his fingers. he twisted as hard as he could. The boy began to jump up and down in his clothes. He managed to straighten his elbow, by pushing at the back of the boy's head, and so turn half-way around and free his leg. The pain didn't grow less.

There was another wild surge forward that ended in another dead spot. He now faced a young girl who was sobbing steadily. Her silk print dress had been torn down the front and her tiny brassière hung from one strap. He tried by pressing back to give her room, but she moved with him every time he moved. Now and then, she would jerk violently and he wondered if she was going to have a fit. One of her thighs was between his legs. He struggled to get free of her, but she clung to him, moving with him and pressing against him.

She turned her head and said, "Stop, stop," to someone behind her.

He saw what the trouble was. An old man, wearing a Panama hat and horn-rimmed glasses, was hugging her. He had one of his hands inside her dress and was biting her neck.

Tod freed his right arm with a heave, reached over the girl, and brought his fist down on the man's head. He couldn't hit very hard but managed to knock the man's hat off, also his glasses. The man tried to bury his face in the girl's shoulder, but Tod grabbed one of his ears and yanked. They started to move again. Tod held on to the ear as long as he could hoping that it would come away in his hand. The girl managed to twist under his arm. A piece of her dress tore, but she was free of her attacker.

Another spasm passed through the mob and he was carried towards the curb. He fought towards a lamp-post, but he was swept by before he could grasp it. He saw another man catch the girl with the torn dress. She screamed for help. He tried to get to her, but was carried in the opposite direction. This rush also ended in a dead spot. Here his neighbours were all shorter than he was. He turned his head upward towards the sky and tried to pull some fresh air into his aching lungs, but it was all heavily tainted with sweat.

In this part of the mob no one was hysterical. In fact, most of the people seemed to be enjoying themselves. Near him was a stout woman with a man pressing hard against her from in front. His chin was on her shoulder, and his arms were around her. She paid no attention to him and went on talking to the woman at her side.

"The first thing I knew," Tod heard her say, "there was a rush and I was in the middle."

"Yeah. Somebody hollered, 'Here comes Gary Cooper,' and then wham!"

"That ain't it," said a little man wearing a cloth cap and pullover sweater. "This is a riot you're in."

"Yeah," said a third woman, whose snaky grey hair was hanging over her face and shoulders. "A pervert attacked a child."

"He ought to be lynched."

Everybody agreed vehemently.

"I come from St Louis," announced the stout woman, "and we had one of them pervert fellers in our neighbourhood once. He ripped up a girl with a pair of scissors."

"He must have been crazy," said the man in the cap. "What kind of fun is that?"

Everybody laughed. The stout woman spoke to the man who was hugging her.

"Hey, you," she said. "I ain't no pillow."

The man smiled beatifically but didn't move. She laughed, making no effort to get out of his embrace.

"A fresh guy," she said.

The other woman laughed.

"Yeah," she said, "this is a regular free-for-all."

The man in the cap and sweater thought there was another laugh in his comment about the pervert.

"Ripping up a girl with scissors. That's the wrong tool."

He was right. They laughed even louder than the first time.

"You'd a done it different, eh, kid?" said a young man with a kidney-shaped head and waxed moustaches.

The two women laughed. This encouraged the man in the cap and he reached over and pinched the stout woman's friend. She squealed.

"Lay off that," she said good-naturedly.

"I was shoved," he said.

An ambulance siren screamed in the street. Its wailing moan started the crowd moving again and Tod was carried along in a slow, steady push. He closed his eyes and tried to protect his throbbing leg. This time, when the movement ended, he found himself with his back to the theatre wall. He kept his eyes closed and stood on his good leg. After what seemed like hours, the pack began to loosen and move again with a churning motion. It gathered momentum and rushed. He rode it until he was slammed against the base of an iron rail which fenced the driveway of the theatre from the street. He had the wind knocked out of him by the impact, but managed to cling to the rail. He held on desperately, fighting to keep from being sucked back. A woman caught him around the waist and tried to hang on. She was sobbing rhythmically. Tod felt his fingers slipping from the rail and kicked backwards as hard as he could. The woman let go.

Despite the agony in his leg, he was able to think clearly about his picture, *The Burning of Los Angeles*. After his quarrel with Faye, he had worked on it continually to escape tormenting himself, and the way to it in his mind had become almost automatic.

As he stood on his good leg, clinging desperately to the iron rail, he could see all the rough charcoal strokes with which he had blocked it out on the big canvas. Across the top, parallel with the frame, he had drawn the burning city, a great bonfire of architectural styles, ranging from Egyptian to Cape Cod colonial. Through the centre, winding from left to right, was a long hill street and down it, spilling into the middle foreground, came the mob carrying baseball bats and torches. For the faces of its members, he was using the innumerable sketches he had made of the people who come to California to die; the cultists of all sorts, economic as well as religious, the wave, aeroplane, funeral, and preview watchers—all those poor devils who can only be stirred by the promise of miracles and then only to violence. A super "Dr Know-All Pierce-All" had made the necessary promise and they were marching behind his banner in a great united front of screwballs and screwboxes to purify the land. No longer bored, they sang and danced joyously in the red light of the flames.

In the lower foreground, men and women fled wildly before the vanguard of the crusading mob. Among them were Faye, Harry, Homer, Claude, and himself. Faye ran proudly, throwing her knees high. Harry stumbled along behind her, holding on to his beloved derby hat with both hands. Homer seemed to be falling out of the canvas, his face half-asleep, his big hands clawing the air in anguished pantomime. Claude turned his head as he ran to thumb his nose at his pursuers. Tod himself picked up a small stone to throw before continuing his flight.

He had almost forgotten both his leg and his predicament, and to make his escape still more complete he stood on a chair and worked at the flames in an upper corner of the canvas, modelling the tongues of fire so that they licked even more avidly at a Corinthian column that held up the palm-leaf roof of a nutburger stand.

He had finished one flame and was starting on another when he was brought back by someone shouting in his ear. He opened his eyes and saw a policeman trying to reach him from behind the rail to which he was clinging. He let go with his left hand and raised his arm. The policeman caught him by the wrist, but couldn't lift him. Tod was afraid to let go until another man came to aid the policeman and caught him by the back of his jacket. He let go of the rail and they hauled him up and over it.

When they saw that he couldn't stand, they let him down easily to the ground. He was in the theatre driveway. On the curb next to him sat a woman crying into her skirt. Along the wall were groups of other dishevelled people. At the end of the driveway was an ambulance. A policeman asked him if he wanted to go to the hospital. He shook his head no. He then offered him a lift home. Tod had the presence of mind to give Claude's address.

He was carried through the exit to the back street and lifted into a police car. The siren began to scream and at first he thought he was making the noise himself. He felt his lips with his hands. They were clamped tight. He knew then it was the siren. For some reason this made him laugh and he began to imitate the siren as loud as he could.

133

The Homes of the Stars

F. SCOTT FITZGERALD

For an introductory note to F. Scott Fitzgerald, see Chapter 103.

Beneath a great striped umbrella at the side of a boulevard in a Hollywood heat wave, sat a man. His name was Gus Venske (no relation to the runner) and he wore magenta pants, cerise shoes and a sport article from Vine Street which resembled nothing so much as a cerulean blue pajama top.

Gus Venske was not a freak nor were his clothes at all extraordinary for his time and place. He had a profession—on a pole beside the umbrella was a placard:

VISIT THE HOMES OF THE STARS

Business was bad or Gus would not have hailed the unprosperous man who stood in the street beside a panting, steaming car, anxiously watching its efforts to cool.

"Hey fella," said Gus, without much hope. "Wanna visit the homes of the stars?"

The red-rimmed eyes of the watcher turned from the automobile and looked superciliously upon Gus.

"I'm *in* pictures," said the man, "I'm in 'em myself."

"Actor?"

"No. Writer."

Pat Hobby turned back to his car, which was whistling like a peanut wagon. He had told the truth—or what was once the truth. Often in the old days his name had flashed on the screen for the few seconds allotted to authorship, but for the past five years his services had been less and less in demand.

Presently Gus Venske shut up shop for lunch by putting his folders and maps into a briefcase and walking off with it under his arm. As the sun grew hotter moment by moment, Pat Hobby took refuge under the faint protection of

Source: F. Scott Fitzgerald, "The Homes of the Stars", *The Pat Hobby Stories*, New York, 1962,

the umbrella and inspected a soiled folder which had been dropped by Mr. Venske. If Pat had not been down to his last fourteen cents he would have telephoned a garage for aid—as it was, he could only wait.

After a while a limousine with a Missouri license drew to rest beside him. Behind the chauffeur sat a little white moustached man and a large woman with a small dog. They conversed for a moment—then, in a rather shamefaced way, the woman leaned out and addressed Pat.

"What stars' homes can you visit?" she asked.

It took a moment for this to sink in.

"I mean can we go to Robert Taylor's home and Clark Gable's and Shirley Temple's—"

"I guess you can if you can get in," said Pat.

"Because—" continued the woman, "—if we could go to the very best homes, the most exclusive—we would be prepared to pay more than your regular price."

Light dawned upon Pat. Here together were suckers and smackers. Here was that dearest of Hollywood dreams—the angle. If one got the right angle it meant meals at the Brown Derby, long nights with bottles and girls, a new tire for his old car. And here was an angle fairly thrusting itself at him.

He rose and went to the side of the limousine.

"Sure. Maybe I could fix it." As he spoke he felt a pang of doubt. "Would you be able to pay in advance?"

The couple exchanged a look.

"Suppose we gave you five dollars now," the woman said, "and five dollars if we can visit Clark Gable's home or somebody like that."

Once upon a time such a thing would have been so easy. In his salad days when Pat had twelve or fifteen writing credits a year, he could have called up many people who would have said, "Sure, Pat, if it means anything to you." But now he could only think of a handful who really recognized him and spoke to him around the lots—Melvyn Douglas and Robert Young and Ronald Colman and Young Doug. Those he had known best had retired or passed away.

And he did not know except vaguely where the new stars lived, but he had noticed that on the folder were type-written several dozen names and addresses with penciled checks after each.

"Of course you can't be sure anybody's at home," he said, "they might be working in the studios."

"We understand that." The lady glanced at Pat's car, glanced away. "We'd better go in our motor."

"Sure."

Pat got up in front with the chauffeur—trying to think fast. The actor who spoke to him most pleasantly was Ronald Colman—they had never exchanged more than conventional salutations but he might pretend that he was calling to interest Colman in a story.

Better still, Colman was probably not at home and Pat might wangle his clients an inside glimpse of the house. Then the process might be repeated at

Robert Young's house and Young Doug's and Melvyn Douglas's. By that time the lady would have forgotten Gable and the afternoon would be over.

He looked at Ronald Colman's address on the folder and gave the direction to the chauffeur.

"We know a woman who had her picture taken with George Brent," said the lady as they started off, "Mrs. Horace J. Ives, Jr."

"She's our neighbor," said her husband. "She lives at 372 Rose Drive in Kansas City. And we live at 327."

"She had her picture taken with George Brent. We always wondered if she had to pay for it. Of course I don't know that I'd want to go so far as that. I don't know what they'd say back home."

"I don't think we want to go as far as all that," agreed her husband.

"Where are we going first?" asked the lady, cosily.

"Well, I had a couple calls to pay anyhow," said Pat. "I got to see Ronald Coleman about something."

"Oh, he's one of my favorites. Do you know him well?"

"Oh yes," said Pat, "I'm not in this business regularly. I'm just doing it today for a friend. I'm a writer."

Sure in the knowledge that not so much as a trio of picture writers were known to the public he named himself as the author of several recent successes.

"That's very interesting," said the man, "I knew a writer once–this Upton Sinclair or Sinclair Lewis. Not a bad fellow even if he was a socialist."

"Why aren't you writing a picture now?" asked the lady.

"Well, you see we're on strike," Pat invented. "We got a thing called the Screen Playwriters' Guild and we're on strike."

"Oh." His clients stared with suspicion at this emissary of Stalin in the front seat of their car.

"What are you striking for?" asked the man uneasily.

Pat's political development was rudimentary. He hesitated.

"Oh, better living conditions," he said finally, "free pencils and paper. I don't know–it's all in the Wagner Act." After a moment he added vaguely, "Recognize Finland."

"I didn't know writers had unions," said the man. "Well, if you're on strike who writes the movies?"

"The producers," said Pat bitterly. "That's why they're so lousy."

"Well, that's what I would call an odd state of things."

They came in sight of Ronald Coleman's house and Pat swallowed uneasily. A shining new roadster sat out in front.

"I better go in first," he said. "I mean we wouldn't want to come in on any–on any family scene or anything."

"Does he have family scenes?" asked the lady eagerly.

"Oh, well, you know how people are," said Pat with charity. "I think I ought to see how things are first."

The car stopped. Drawing a long breath Pat got out. At the same moment the door of the house opened and Ronald Colman hurried down the walk. Pat's heart missed a beat as the actor glanced in his direction.

"Hello Pat," he said. Evidently he had no notion that Pat was a caller for he jumped into his car and the sound of his motor drowned out Pat's responses as he drove away.

"Well, he called you "Pat", said the woman impressed.

"I guess he was in a hurry," said Pat. "But maybe we could see his house."

He rehearsed a speech going up the walk. He had just spoken to his friend Mr. Colman, and received permission to look around.

But the house was shut and locked and there was no answer to the bell. He would have to try Melvyn Douglas whose salutations, on second thought, were a little warmer than Ronald Colman's. At any rate his clients' faith in him was now firmly founded. The "Hello, Pat," rang confidently in their ears; by proxy they were already inside the charmed circle.

"Now let's try Clark Gable's," said the lady. "I'd like to tell Carole Lombard about her hair."

The lese majesty made Pat's stomach wince. Once in a crowd he had met Clark Gable but he had no reason to believe that Mr. Gable remembered.

"Well, we could try Melvyn Douglas' first and then Bob Young or else Young Doug. They're all on the way. You see Gable and Lombard live away out in the St Joaquin valley."

"Oh," said the lady disappointed, "I did want to run up and see their bedroom. Well then, our next choice would be Shirley Temple." She looked at her little dog. "I know that would be Boojie's choice too."

"They're kind of afraid of kidnappers," said Pat.

Ruffled, the man produced his business card and handed it to Pat.

DEERING R. ROBINSON
Vice President and Chairman
of the Board
Robdeer Food Products

"Does *that* sound as if I want to kidnap Shirley Temple?"

"They just have to be sure," said Pat apologetically. "After we go to Melvyn—"

"No—let's see Shirley Temple's *now*," insisted the woman. "Really! I told you in the first place what I wanted."

Pat hesitated.

"First I'll have to stop in some drugstore and phone about it."

In a drugstore he exchanged some of the five dollars for a half pint of gin and took two long swallows behind a high counter, after which he considered the situation. He could, of course, duck Mr. and Mrs. Robinson immediately—after all he had produced Ronald Colman, with sound, for their five smackers. On the other hand they just might catch Miss Temple on her way in or out—and for a pleasant day at Santa Anita tomorrow Pat needed five smackers more. In the glow of the gin his courage mounted, and returning to the limousine he gave the chauffeur the address.

But approaching the Temple house his spirit quailed as he saw that there was a tall iron fence and an electric gate. And didn't guides have to have a license?

"Not here," he said quickly to the chauffeur. "I made a mistake. I think it's the next one, or two or three doors further on."

He decided on a large mansion set in an open lawn and stopping the chauffeur got out and walked up to the door. He was temporarily licked but at least he might bring back some story to soften them—say, that Miss Temple had mumps. He could point out her sick-room from the walk.

There was no answer to his ring but he saw that the door was partly ajar. Cautiously he pushed it open. He was staring into a deserted living room on the baronial scale. He listened. There was no one about, no footsteps on the upper floor, no murmur from the kitchen. Pat took another pull at the gin. Then swiftly he hurried back to the limousine.

"She's at the studio," he said quickly. "But if we're quiet we can look at their living-room."

Eagerly the Robinsons and Boojie disembarked and followed him. The living-room might have been Shirley Temple's, might have been one of many in Hollywood. Pat saw a doll in a corner and pointed at it, whereupon Mrs. Robinson picked it up, looked at it reverently and showed it to Boojie who sniffed indifferently.

"Could I meet Mrs. Temple?" she asked.

"Oh, she's out—nobody's home," Pat said—unwisely.

"Nobody. Oh—then Boojie would so like a wee little peep at her bedroom."

Before he could answer she had run up the stairs. Mr. Robinson followed and Pat waited uneasily in the hall, ready to depart at the sound either of an arrival outside or a commotion above.

He finished the bottle, disposed of it politely under a sofa cushion and then deciding that the visit upstairs was tempting fate too far, he went after his clients. On the stairs he heard Mrs. Robinson.

"But there's only *one* child's bedroom. I thought Shirley had brothers."

A window on the winding staircase looked upon the street, and glancing out Pat saw a large car drive up to the curb. From it stepped a Hollywood celebrity who, though not one of those pursued by Mrs. Robinson was second to none in prestige and power. It was old Mr. Marcus, the producer, for whom Pat Hobby had been press agent twenty years ago.

At this point Pat lost his head. In a flash he pictured an elaborate explanation as to what he was doing here. He would not be forgiven. His occasional weeks in the studio at two-fifty would now disappear altogether and another finis would be written to his almost entirely finished career. He left, impetuously and swiftly—down the stairs, through the kitchen and out the back gate, leaving the Robinsons to their destiny.

Vaguely he was sorry for them as he walked quickly along the next boulevard. He could see Mr. Robinson producing his card as the head of Robdeer Food Products. He could see Mr. Marcus' skepticism, the arrival of the police, the frisking of Mr. and Mrs. Robinson.

Probably it would stop there—except that the Robinsons would be furious at him for his imposition. They would tell the police where they had picked him up.

Suddenly he went ricketing down the street, beads of gin breaking out profusely on his forehead. He had left his car beside Gus Venske's umbrella. And now he remembered another recognizing clue and hoped that Ronald Colman didn't know his last name.

134

After Many a Summer

ALDOUS HUXLEY

Aldous Huxley (1894–1964), the English novelist and essayist, is best known for his "scientific" novels, *Chrome Yellow* (1921), *Point Counter Point* (1928), and *Brave New World* (1932). The grandson of Thomas Huxley, he established himself as one of the leading intellectuals of the period. *After Many a Summer* (1942), like Evelyn Waugh's *The Loved Ones*, is a wry satire on Californian life-styles and values, seen from a caustic English perspective. Chapter One, however is also notable for the way it presents an urban imagery almost archetypal of the special "language" of Lost Angeles as a city.

It had all been arranged by telegram; Jeremy Pordage was to look out for a coloured chauffeur in a grey uniform with a carnation in his button-hole; and the coloured chauffeur was to look out for a middle-aged Englishman carrying the Poetical Works of Wordsworth. In spite of the crowds at the station, they found one another without difficulty.

"Mr. Stoyte's chauffeur?"

"Mr. Pordage, sah?"

Jeremy nodded and, his Wordsworth in one hand, his umbrella in the other, half extended his arms in the gesture of a self-deprecatory mannequin exhibiting, with a full and humorous consciousness of their defects, a deplorable figure accentuated by the most ridiculous clothes. "A poor thing," he seemed to be implying, "but myself." A defensive and, so to say, prophylactic disparagement had become a habit with him. He resorted to it on every sort of occasion. Suddenly a new idea came into his head. Anxiously he began to wonder whether, in this democratic Far West of theirs, one shook hands with the chauffeur—particularly if he happened to be a blackamoor, just to demonstrate that one wasn't a pukka sahib even if one's country did happen to be bearing the White Man's burden. In the end he decided to do nothing. Or, to be more accurate, the decision was forced upon him—as usual, he said to himself, deriving a curious wry pleasure from the recognition of his own shortcomings. While he was

Source: Aldous Huxley, *After Many a Summer*, Random House Inc., London, 1942, Ch. 1.

hesitating what to do, the chauffeur took off his cap and, slightly over-acting the part of an old-world negro retainer, bowed, smiled toothily and said, "Welcome to Los Angeles, Mr. Pordage, sah!" Then, changing the tone of his chanting drawl from the dramatic to the confidential, "I should have knowed you by your voice, Mr. Pordage," he went on, "even without the book."

Jeremy laughed a little uncomfortably. A week in America had made him self-conscious about that voice of his. A product of Trinity College, Cambridge, ten years before the War, it was a small, fluty voice, suggestive of evensong in an English cathedral. At home, when he used it, nobody paid any particular attention. He had never had to make jokes about it, as he had done, in self-protection, about his appearance for example, or his age. Here, in America, things were different. He had only to order a cup of coffee or ask the way to the lavatory (which anyhow wasn't called the lavatory in this disconcerting country) for people to stare at him with an amused and attentive curiosity, as though he were a freak on show in an amusement park. It had not been at all agreeable.

"Where's my porter?" he said fussily in order to change the subject.

A few minutes later they were on their way. Cradled in the back seat of the car, out of range, he hoped, of the chauffeur's conversation, Jeremy Pordage abandoned himself to the pleasure of merely looking. Southern California rolled past the windows; all he had to do was to keep his eyes open.

The first thing to present itself was a slum of Africans and Filipinos, Japanese and Mexicans. And what permutations and combinations of black, yellow and brown! What complex bastardies! And the girls—how beautiful in their artificial silk! "And negro ladies in white muslin gowns." His favourite line in *The Prelude*. He smiled to himself. And meanwhile the slum had given place to the tall buildings of a business district.

The population took on a more Caucasian tinge. At every corner there was a drug-store. The newspaper boys were selling headlines about Franco's drive on Barcelona. Most of the girls, as they walked along, seemed to be absorbed in silent prayer; but he supposed, on second thoughts, it was only gum that they were thus incessantly ruminating. Gum, not God. Then suddenly the car plunged into a tunnel and emerged into another world, a vast, untidy, suburban world of filling-stations and billboards, of low houses in gardens, of vacant lots and waste-paper, of occasional shops and office buildings and churches—Primitive Methodist churches built, surprisingly enough, in the style of the Cartuja at Granada, Catholic churches like Canterbury Cathedral, synagogues disguised as Hagia Sophia, Christian Science churches with pillars and pediments, like banks. It was a winter day and early in the morning; but the sun shone brilliantly, the sky was without a cloud. The car was travelling westwards, and the sunshine, slanting from behind them as they advanced, lit up each building, each sky-sign and billboard, as though with a spot-light, as though on purpose to show the new arrival all the sights.

EATS. COCKTAILS. OPEN NITES.

JUMBO MALTS.

Do Things, Go Places With Consol Super Gas!

At Beverly Pantheon Fine Funerals Are *Not* Expensive.

The car sped onwards, and here in the middle of a vacant lot was a restaurant in the form of a seated bulldog, the entrance between the front paws, the eyes illuminated.

"Zoomorph," Jeremy Pordage murmured to himself, and again, "zoomorph." He had the scholar's taste for words. The bulldog shot back into the past.

Astrology, Numerology, Psychic Readings.

Drive In For Nutbergers—whatever they were. He resolved at the earliest opportunity to have one. A nutberger and a jumbo malt.

Stop Here For Consol Super Gas.

Surprisingly, the chauffeur stopped. "Ten gallons of Super-Super," he ordered; then, turning back to Jeremy, "This is our company," he added. Mr. Stoyte, he's the president." He pointed to a billboard across the street. Cash Loans In Fifteen Minutes, Jeremy read; Consult Community Service Finance Corporation. "That's another of ours," said the chauffeur proudly.

They drove on. The face of a beautiful young woman, distorted, like a Magdalene's, with grief, stared out of a giant billboard. Broken Romance, proclaimed the caption. Science Proves That 73 Per Cent. Of All Adults Have Halitosis.

In Time Of Sorrow Let Beverly Pantheon Be Your Friend.

Facials, Permanents, Manicures.

Betty's Beauty Shoppe.

Next door to the beauty shoppe was a Western Union office. That cable to his mother ... Heavens, he had almost forgotten! Jeremy leaned forward and, in the apologetic tone he always used when speaking to servants, asked the chauffeur to stop for a moment. The car came to a halt. With a preoccupied expression on his mild, rabbit-like face, Jeremy got out and hurried across the pavement, into the office.

"Mrs. Pordage, The Araucarias, Woking, England," he wrote, smiling a little as he did so. The exquisite absurdity of that address was a standing source of amusement. "The Araucarias, Woking." His mother, when she bought the house, had wanted to change the name, as being too ingenuously middle-class, too much like a joke by Hilaire Belloc. "But that's the beauty of it," he had protested. "That's the charm." And he had tried to make her see how utterly right it would be for them to live at such an address. The deliciously comic incongruity between the name of the house and the nature of its occupants! And what a beautiful, topsy-turvy appositeness in the fact that Oscar Wilde's old friend, the witty and cultured Mrs. Pordage, would write her sparkling letters from The Araucarias, and that from these same Araucarias, these Araucarias, mark you, at *Woking*, should come the works of mingled scholarship and curiously rarefied wit for which her son had gained his reputation. Mrs. Pordage had almost instantly seen what he was driving at. No need, think goodness, to labour your points where she was concerned. You could talk entirely in hints and anacoluthons; she could be relied on to understand. The Araucarias had remained The Araucarias.

Having written the address, Jeremy paused, pensively frowned and initiated the familiar gesture of biting his pencil—only to find, disconcertingly, that this particular pencil was tipped with brass and fastened to a chain. "Mrs. Pordage, The Araucarias, Woking, England," he read out aloud, in the hope that the worlds would inspire him to compose the right, the perfect message—the message his mother expected of him, at once tender and witty, charged with a genuine devotion ironically worded, acknowledging her maternal domination, but at the same time making fun of it, so that the old lady could salve her conscience by pretending that her son was entirely free, and herself the least tyrannical of mothers. It wasn't easy—particularly with this pencil on a chain. After several abortive essays he decided, though it was definitely unsatisfactory, on: "Climate being subtropical shall break vow re underclothes stop Wish you were here my sake not yours as you would scarcely appreciate this unfinished Bournemouth indefinitely magnified stop."

"Unfinished what?" questioned the young woman on the further side of the counter.

"B-o-u-r-n-e-m-o-u-t-h," Jeremy spelled out. He smiled; behind the bi-focal lenses of his spectacles his blue eyes twinkled, and, with a gesture of which he was quite unconscious, but which he always, automatically, made when he was about to utter one of his little jokes, he stroked the smooth bald spot on the top of his head. "*You* know," he said, in a particularly fluty tone, "the bourne to which no traveller goes, if he can possibly help it."

The girl looked at him blankly; then, inferring from his expression that something funny had been said, and remembering that courteous Service was Western Union's slogan, gave the bright smile for which the poor old chump was evidently asking, and went on reading: "Hope you have fun at Grasse stop Tendresses Jeremy."

It was an expensive message; but luckily, he reflected, as he took out his pocket-book, luckily Mr. Stoyte was grossly overpaying him. Three months' work, six thousand dollars. So damn the expense.

He returned to the car and they drove on. Mile after mile they went, and the suburban houses, the gas-stations, the vacant lots, the churches, the shops went along with them, interminably. To right and left, between palms, or pepper trees, or acacias, the streets of the enormous residential quarter receded to the vanishing point.

CLASSY EAST. MILE HIGH CONES.

JESUS SAVES.

HAMBURGERS.

Yet once more the traffic lights turned red. A paper-boy came to the window. "Franco claims gains in Catalonia." Jeremy read, and turned away. The frightfulness of the world had reached a point at which it had become for him merely boring. From the halted car in front of them, two elderly ladies, both with permanently waved white hair and both wearing crimson trousers, descended, each carrying a Yorkshire terrier. The dogs were set down at the foot of the traffic signal. Before the animals could make up their minds to use the convenience, the lights had changed. The negro shifted into first, and the car swerved forward, into the future. Jeremy was thinking of his mother. Disquietingly enough, she too had a Yorkshire terrier.

FINE LIQUORS.

TURKEY SANDWICHES.

GO TO CHURCH AND FEEL BETTER ALL THE WEEK.

WHAT IS GOOD FOR BUSINESS IS GOOD FOR YOU.

Another zoomorph presented itself, this time a real estate agent's office in the form of an Egyptian sphinx.

JESUS IS COMING SOON.

YOU TOO CAN HAVE ABIDING YOUTH WITH THRILL-PHORM BRASSIERES.

BEVERLY PANTHEON, THE CEMETERY THAT IS *DIFFERENT*.

With the triumphant expression of Puss-in-Boots enumerating the possessions of the Marquis of Carabas, the negro shot a glance over his shoulder at Jeremy, waved his hand towards the billboard and said, "That's ours too."

"You mean, the Beverly Pantheon?"

The man nodded. "Finest cemetery in the world, I guess," he said: and added, after a moment's pause, "Maybe you's like to see it. It wouldn't hardly be out of our way."

"That would be very nice," said Jeremy with upper-class English graciousness. Then, feeling that he ought to express his acceptance rather more warmly and democratically, he cleared his throat and, with a conscious effort to reproduce the local vernacular, added that it would be swell. Pronouced in his Trinity-College-Cambridge voice, the word sounded so unnatural that he began to blush with embarrassment. Fortunately, the chauffeur was to busy with the traffic to notice.

They turned to the right, sped past a Rosicrucian Temple, past two cat-and-dog hospitals, past a School for Drum-Majorettes and two more advertisements of the Beverly Pantheon. As they turned to the left on Sunset Boulevard, Jeremy had a glimpse of a young woman who was doing her shopping in a hydrangea-blue strapless bathing-suit, platinum curls and a black fur jacket. Then she too was whirled back into the past.

The present was a road at the foot of a line of steep hills, a road flanked by small, expensive-looking shops, by restaurants, by night-clubs shuttered against the sunlight, by offices and apartment houses. Then they too had taken their places in the irrevocable. A sign proclaimed that they were crossing the city limits of Beverly Hills. The surroundings changed. The road was flanked by the gardens of a rich residential quarter. Through trees, Jeremy saw the façades of houses, all new, almost all in good taste—elegant and witty pastiches of Lutyens manor houses, of Little Trianons, of Monticellos; light-hearted parodies of Le Corbusier's solemn machines-for-living-in; fantastic Mexican adaptations of

Mexican haciendas and New England farms.

They turned to the right. Enormous palm trees lined the road. In the sunlight, masses of mesembryanthemums blazed with an intense magenta glare. The houses succeeded one another, like the pavilions at some endless international exhibition. Gloucestershire followed Andalusia and gave place in turn to Touraine and Oaxaca, Düsseldorf and Massachusetts.

"That's Harold Lloyd's place," said the chauffeur, indicating a kind of Boboli. "And that's Charlie Chaplin's. And that's Pickfair."

The road began to mount, vertiginously. The chauffeur pointed a cross an intervening gulf of shadow at what seemed a Tibetan lamasery on the opposite hill, "That's where Ginger Rogers lives. Yes, *sir*," he nodded triumphantly, as he twirled the steering-wheel.

Five or six more turns brought the car to the top of the hill. Below and behind lay the plain, with the city like a map extending indefinitely into a pink haze.

Before and to either hand were mountains—ridge after ridge as far as the eye could reach, a desiccated Scotland, empty under the blue desert sky.

The car turned a shoulder of orange rock, and there all at once, on a summit hitherto concealed from view, was a huge sky sign, with the words, BEVERLY PANTHEON, THE PERSONALITY CEMETERY, in six-foot neon tubes and, above it, on the very crest, a full-scale reproduction of the Leaning Tower of Pisa—only this one didn't lean.

"See that?" said the negro impressively. "That's the Tower of Resurrection. Two hundred thousand dollars, that's what it cost. Yes, *sir*." He spoke with an emphatic solemnity. One was made to feel that the money had all come out of his own pocket.

great career of love and crime. And yet "it was like all I had done in California was just a dream. And at first it felt good, and then it felt worse, because Sheila was only a dream with everything else. And that was bad. I could remember everything about California, but I couldn't feel it. I tried to get my mind to remember something that it could feel, too, but it was no use. It was all gone. All of it. The pink stucco houses and the palm trees and the stores built like cats and dogs and frogs and ice-cream freezers and the neon lights round everything."

This is partly no doubt a matter of climate: the empty sun and the incessant rains; and of landscape: the dry mountains and the void of the vast Pacific; of the hypnotic rhythms of day and night that revolve with unblurred uniformity, and of the surf that rolls up the beach with a beat that seems expressionless and purposeless after the moody assaults of the Atlantic. Add to this the remoteness from the East and the farther remoteness from Europe, New York has its own insubstantiality that is due to the impermanence of its people, of its buildings, of its business, of its thoughts; but all the wires of our western civilization are buzzing and crossing here. California looks away from Europe, and out upon a wider ocean toward an Orient with which as yet any cultural communication is difficult.

This problem of the native Californian to find a language for the reality of his experience is touched upon in Hans Otto Storm's *Count Ten*. "If things now and then did not look real to you; if you were bothered by that particular question, Eric thought, then you ought certainly to keep off the Gulf of California. It hadn't looked real the time they did or did not bathe their feet in it and eat the clams, and it certainly did not look real now, this deadish place where no ships ever came and where the waves move with such an unutterable weariness." The hero is puzzled but his interest is pricked by an Easterner he meets at Berkeley, who misses the New England seasons and tries to explain to him the dramatic character which they impart to the cycle of the year; and when, gazing over San Francisco bay, he quotes Heine to one of his girls, she objects: "'That isn't Heine any more. It's a hakku. It makes me think of tea-cakes without salt.' She shivered a little. 'It's getting cold. No, that doesn't click in California. In California you can't sit and meditate on through the sunset.'" The young man applies himself to learning Chinese.

Add to this that the real cultural center, San Francisco, with its cosmopolitanism and its Bohemian clubs, the city of Bret Harte and Ambrose Bierce, was arrested in its natural development by the earthquake of 1906, and that thereafter the great anti-cultural amusement-producing center, Los Angeles, grew up, gigantic and vulgar, like one of those synthetic California flowers, and tended to drain the soil of the imaginative life of the State. (It is a question how much the movies themselves have been affected by the California atmosphere: might they not have been a little more interesting under the stress of affairs in the East?) In this city that swarms with writers, none yet has really mustered the gumption to lay bare the heart and bowels of the moving-picture business. The novels I have mentioned above only trifle with the fringes of Hollywood, as the stage comedies like *Boy Meets Girl* only kid it in a superficial way. A novel on a higher level of writing than any of those I have mentioned—*The Day of the Locust* by Nathanael West—is also mostly occupied with extras and gives mere glimpses into the upper reaches. Aldous Huxley's California novel, *After Many a Summer dies the Swan*, does not get even so far into the subject as his compatriot Mr. Eric Knight, the author, under a pseudonym, of *You Play the Black etc.* Mr. Huxley here seems well on his way to becoming a second-rate American novelist. Satirizing in more or less conventional fashion the Hearstian millionaire, the vapid Hollywood beauty and the burlesque pomps of a Los Angeles cemetery, he has succumbed to one of the impostures with which the Golden State deludes her victims: the Burbankized West Coast religion; and Mr. Huxley and his ally, Mr. Gerald Heard, will be lucky if they do not wake up some morning to find themselves transformed into Yogis and installed in one of those Wizard-of-Oz temples that puff out their bubble-like domes among the snack bars and the lion ranches.

The novel about Hollywood with most teeth in it is still that intrepid satire by Miss Anita Loos called *The Better Things of Life*, which came out serially in the *Cosmopolitan* and was repeatedly announced by her publishers, but which never appeared between covers. It seems to be true, in general, of Hollywood as a subject for fiction that those who write about it are not authentic insiders and that those who know about it don't write.[1]

But, as I say, it is not merely in Los Angeles that the purposes and passions of humanity have the appearance of playing their roles in a great open-air amphitheater which lacks not only acoustics to heighten and clarify the speeches but even an attentive audience at whom they may be directed. The paisanos of *Tortilla Flat* also eat, love and die in a golden and boundless sunlight that never becomes charged with their energies; and the rhapsodies of William Saroyan, diffused in this non-vibrant air, pass without repercussions. Even the monstrous, the would-be elemental, the would-be barbaric tragedies which Robinson Jeffers heaps up are a little like amorphous cloud-dramas that eventually fade out to sea, leaving only on our faces a slight moisture and in our ears an echo of hissing. It is probably a good deal too easy to be a nihilist on the coast at Carmel: your very negation is a negation of nothing.

One theme does, however, it must be said, remain serious for the California novelists: the theme of the class war. The men and women of the Cain-O'Hara novels are doomed: they are undone by their own characters or by circumstances. But in time—as in Cain's *Serenade* and O'Hara's *Hope of Heaven*[2]—the socialist diagnosis and the socialist hope begin to appear in the picture. This had been true, of course, during the thirties, of our American fiction in general; but the labor cause has been dramatized with more impact by these writers of the Western coast than it has been, on the whole, in the East, where the formulas of Marxist theory have been likely to take the place of experience. I do not mean the Hollywood Stalinism which is satirized by Mr. McCoy in the swimming-pool scene of *I Should Have Stayed Home*: I mean the tradition of radical writing which Californians like Storm and Steinbeck are carrying on from Frank Norris,[3] Jack London and Upton Sinclair.

This tradition dates from Henry George, who witnessed, in the sixties and seventies, the swallowing-up of the State—in what must have been record time—by capital; and California has since been the scene of some of the most naked and savage of American labor wars. The McNamaras, Mooney and Billings, the Wobblies and Vigilantes, the battles of the longshoremen and the fruit-pickers, the San Francisco general strike—these are names and events that have wrung blood and tears in the easy California climate; and it is this conflict that has kept Mr. Storm afloat in the Pacific vacuum, fixed securely in his orientation toward the east of the social world, and that has communicated to Mr. Steinbeck the impetus that has carried the Joad jalopy into the general consciousness of the nation.

Here the novelists of California know what they are talking about, and they have something arresting to say. In describing their special mentality, I do not, of course, in the least, mean to belittle their interest or value. The writing of the Coast, as I say, may seem difficult to bring into focus with the writing that we know in the East. But California, since we took it from the Mexicans, has always presented itself to Americans as one of the strangest and most exotic of their exploits; and it is the function of the literary artist to struggle with new phases of experience, and to try to give them beauty and sense.

Postscript

These notes were first written during the autumn and early winter of 1940. Since then, several events have occurred which require a few words of postscript.

On December 21, 1940, F. Scott Fitzgerald suddenly died in Hollywood; and, the day after, Nathanael West was killed in a motor accident on the Ventura boulevard. Both men had been living on the West Coast; both had spent several years in the studios; both, at the time of their deaths, had been occupied with novels about Hollywood.

The work of Nathanael West derived from a different tradition than that of these other writers. He had been influenced by those post-war Frenchmen who had specialized, with a certain preciosity, in the delirious and diabolic fantasy that descended from Rimbaud and Lautréamont. Beginning with *The Dream Life of Balso Snell*, a not very successful exercise in this vein of phantasmagoria, he published, after many revisions, a remarkable short novel called *Miss Lonelyhearts*. This story of a newspaper hack who conducts an "advice to the lovelorn" department and eventually destroys himself by allowing himself to take too seriously the sorrows and misfortunes of his clients, had a poetic-philosophical point of view and a sense of phrase as well as of chapter that made it seem rather European than American. It was followed by *A Cool Million*, a less ambitious book, which both parodied Horatio Alger and more or less reproduced *Candide* by reversing the American success story. In his fourth book, *The Day of the Locust*, he applied his fantasy and irony to the embarrassment of rich materials offered by the movie community. I wrote a review of this novel in 1939, and I shall venture to append it here—with apologies for some repetition of ideas expressed above—to make the California story complete:

Nathanael West, the author of *Miss Lonelyhearts*, went to Hollywood a few years ago, and his silence had been causing his readers alarm lest he might have faded out on the Coast as so many of his fellows have done. But Mr. West, as this new book happily proves, is still alive beyond the mountains, and quite able to set down what he feels and sees—has still, in short, remained an artist. His new novel, *The Day of the Locust*, deals with the nondescript characters on the edges of the Hollywood studios: an old comic who sells shoe polish and his filmstruck daughter; a quarrelsome dwarf; a cock-fighting Mexican; a Hollywood cowboy and a Hollywood Indian; and an undeveloped hotel clerk from Iowa, who has come to the Coast to enjoy his savings—together with a sophisticated screen-writer, who lives in a big house that is "an exact reproduction of the old Dupuy mansion near Biloxi, Mississippi." And these people have been painted as distinctly and polished up as brightly as the figures in Persian miniatures. Their speech has been distilled with a sense of the flavorsome and the characteristic which makes John O'Hara seem pedestrian. Mr. West has footed a precarious way and has not slipped at any point into relying on the Hollywood values in describing the Hollywood people. The landscapes, the architecture and the interior decoration of Beverly Hills and vicinity have been handled with equal distinction. Everyone who has ever been in Los Angeles knows how the mere aspect of things is likely to paralyze the aesthetic faculty by providing no *point d'appui* from which to exercise its discrimination, if it does not actually stun the sensory apparatus itself, so that accurate reporting becomes impossible. But Nathanael West has stalked and caught some fine specimens of these Hollywood lepidoptera and impaled them on fastidious pins. Here are Hollywood restaurants, apartment houses, funeral churches, brothels, evangelical temples and movie sets—in this latter connection, an extremely amusing episode of a man getting nightmarishly lost in the Battle of Waterloo. Mr. West's surrealist beginnings have stood him in good stead on the Coast.

The doings of these people are bizarre, but they are also sordid and senseless. Mr. West has caught the emptiness of Hollywood; and he is, as far as I know, the first writer to make this emptiness horrible. The most impressive thing in the book is his picture of the people from the Middle West who, retiring to sunlit leisure, are trying to leave behind them the meagerness of their working lives; who desire something different from what they have had but do not know what they desire, and have no other resources for amusement than gaping at movie stars and listening to Aimee McPherson's sermons. In the last episode, a crowd of these people, who have come out to see the celebrities at an opening, is set off by an insane act of violence on the part of the cretinous hotel clerk, and gives way to an outburst of mob mania. The America of the murders and rapes which fill the Los Angeles papers is only the obverse side of the America of the inanities of the movies. Such people—Mr. West seems to say—dissatisfied, yet with no ideas, no objectives and no interest in anything vital, may in the mass be capable of anything. The day-dreams purveyed by Hollywood, the romances that in movie stories can be counted on to have whisked around all obstacles and adroitly knocked out all "menaces" by the time they have run off their reels, romances which their fascinated audiences have never been able to live themselves—only cheat them and embitter their frustration. Of such mobs are the followers of fascism made.

I think that the book itself suffers a little from the lack of a center in the community with which it deals. It has less concentration than *Miss Lonelyhearts*. Mr. West has introduced a young Yale man who, as an educated and healthy human being, is supposed to provide a normal point of view from which the deformities of Hollywood may be criticized; but it is also essential to the story that this young man should find himself swirling around in the same aimless eddies as the others. I am not sure that it is really possible to do anything substantial with Hollywood except by making it, as John Dos Passos did in *The Big Money*, a part of a larger picture which has its center in a larger world. But in the meantime Nathanael West has survived to write another distinguished book—in its peculiar combination of amenity of surface and felicity of form and style with ugly subject matter and somber feeling, quite unlike—as *Miss Lonelyhearts* was—the books of anyone else.

Scott Fitzgerald, who at the time of his death had published only short stories about the movies, had been working for some time on a novel[4] in which he had tackled the key figure of the industry: the successful Hollywood producer. This subject has also been attempted, with sharp observation and much humor, by Mr. Budd Schulberg, Jr.; whose novel *What Makes Sammy Run* has been published since my articles were written. But Mr. Schulberg is still a beginner, and his work in *What Makes Sammy Run* does not rise above the level of a more sincere and sensitive George Kaufman; whereas Scott Fitzgerald, an accomplished artist, had written a considerable part of what promised to be by all odds the best novel ever devoted to Hollywood. Here you are shown the society and the business of the movies, no longer through the eyes of the visitor to whom everything is glamorous or ridiculous, but from the point of view of people who have grown up or lived with the industry and to whom its values and laws are their natural habit of life. These are criticized by higher standards and in the knowledge of wider horizons, but the criticism is implicit in the story; and in the meantime, Scott Fitzgerald, by putting us inside their group and making us take things for granted, is able to excite an interest in the mixed destiny of his Jewish producer of a kind that lifts the novel quite out of the class of this specialized Hollywood fiction and relates it to the story of man in all times and all places.

Both West and Fitzgerald were writers of a conscience and with natural gifts rare enough in America or anywhere; and their failure to get the best out of their best years may certainly be laid partly to Hollywood, with its already appalling record of talent depraved and wasted.

Notes

1. The relation between the movies and prose fiction works in two ways. There are the actual writers for the pictures like Mr. West and Mr. Cain who produce sour novels about Hollywood. And there are the serious novelists who do not write for the films but are influenced by them in their novels. Since the people who control the movies will not go a step of the way to give the script-writer a chance to do a serious script, the novelist seems, consciously or unconsciously, to be going part of the way to meet the producers. John Steinbeck, in *The Grapes of Wrath*, has certainly learned from the films—and not only from such documentary pictures as those of Pare Lorentz, but from the sentimental symbolism of Hollywood. The result is that the *Grapes of Wrath* has poured itself on to the screen as easily as if it had been written in the studios, and that it is probably the sole serious story on record that seems almost equally effective as a book and as a film. Ernest Hemingway's *For Whom the Bell Tolls*, which also has elements of movie romance, was instantly snapped up by Hollywood.

2. O'Hara is not yet a Californian either by birth or by adoption. Except in *Hope of Heaven*, he had always had the Eastern edge and tension.

3. Steinbeck's close relationship with Norris is indicated by what is evidently a borrowing from *McTeague* in *Of Mice and Men*. The conversation that is so often repeated between Norris's Polish junk dealer and the cracked Spanish-American girl, in which he is always begging her to describe for him the gold table service she remembers from her childhood, must have suggested the similar dialogue that recurs between Lennie and George, in which the former is always begging the latter to tell him more about the rabbit farm they are going to have together. Steinbeck's attitude toward his rudimentary characters may, also, owe something to Norris—who, like him, alloys his seriousness with trashiness.

4. Later published as *The Last Tycoon*.

137

The Presidential Papers

NORMAN MAILER

Norman Mailer (1923–), a major novelist, essayist and critic of the post-war era, was born in New jersey, spent his childhood in Brooklyn and graduated from Harvard in 1943. He spent the remaining period of the war in the Pacific. His military experiences went into his major first novel *The Naked and the Dead* (1948). War is a central metaphor in his work and, with Hemingway, reflects a pervasive condition of life as the individual struggles against anonymous powers–especially in the context of modern urban life. Routine and bureaucracy have become two of the major enemies. Amongst his early work is *Advertisements for Myself* (1959), a series of essays and prose pieces including "The White Negro", an overtly radical (and romantic) essay of "hip" existence in a violent urban context. It attracted much criticism. Other major writing in a prolific career includes *An American Dream* (1965), *Why are we in Vietnam?* (1967), *The Presidential Papers* (1963), and *The Executioner's Song* (1989).

Although uneven in its effect, Mailer's vision is fired by a philosophy of radical individualism. His work views an increasingly corporate and technological America in a negative light, part of the standardisation of thought and feeling. Architecture is a crucial symbol of such a process-the outward manifestation of inner cultural values and needs. The anonymity and blandness of much American building is, for Mailer, a dangerous and pessimistic development. See B. H. Leeds, *The Unstructured Vision of Norman Mailer* (1969) and Richard Poirier, *Norman Mailer*, (1972).

Seeing Los Angels after ten years away, one realizes all over again that America is an unhappy contract between the East (that Faustian thrust of a most determined human will which reaches up and out above the eye into the skyscrapers of New York) and those flat lands of compromise and mediocre self-

Source: Norman Mailer, *The Presidential Papers*, from "The Third Presidential Paper–The Existential Hero" and "The Ninth Presidential Paper–Totalitarianism", London, 1964, pp. 44–6 & 194–5.

expression, those endless half-pretty repetitive small towns of the Middle and the West, whose spirit is forever horizontal and whose marrow comes to rendezvous in the pastel monotonies of Los Angeles architecture.

So far as America has a history, one can see it in the severe heights of New York City, in the glare from the Pittsburgh mills, by the color in the brick of Louisburg Square, along the knotted greedy façades of the small mansions on Chicago's North Side, in Natchez' antebellum homes, the wrought-iron balconies off Bourbon Street, a captain's house in Nantucket, by the curve of Commercial Street in Provincetown. One can make a list; it is probably finite. What culture we have made and what history has collected to it can be found in those few hard examples of an architecture which came to its artistic term, was born, lived and so collected some history about it. Not all the roots of American life are uprooted, but almost all, and the spirit of the supermarket, that homogenous extension of stainless surfaces and psychoanalyzed people, packaged commodities and ranch homes, interchangeable, geographically unrecognizable, that essence of the new postwar SuperAmerica is found nowhere so perfect as in Los Angeles' ubiquitous acres. One gets the impression that people come to Los Angeles in order to divorce themselves from the past, here to live or try to live in the rootless pleasure world of an adult child. One knows that if the cities of the world were destroyed by a new war, the architecture of the rebuilding would create a landscape which looked, subject to specifications of climate, exactly and entirely like the San Fernando Valley.

It is not that Los Angeles is altogether hideous, it is even by degrees pleasant, but for an Easterner there is never any salt in the wind; it is like Mexican cooking without chilli, or Chinese egg rolls missing their mustard; as one travels through the endless repetitions of that city which is the capital of suburbia with its milky pinks, its washed-our oranges, its tainted lime-yellows of pastel on one pretty little architectural monstrosity after another, the colors not intense enough, the styles never pure, and never sufficiently impure to collide on the eye, one conceives the people who live here—they have come out to express themselves, Los Angeles is the home of self-expression, but the artists are middle-class and middling-minded; no passions will calcify here for years in the gloom to be revealed a decade later as the tessellations of a hard and fertile work, no, it is all open, promiscuous, borrowed, half bought, a city without iron, eschewing wood, a kingdom of stucco, the playground for mass men—one has the feeling it was built by television sets giving orders to men. And in this land of the pretty-pretty, the virility is in the barbarisms, the vulgarities, it is in the huge billboards, the screamers of the neon lighting, the shouting farm-utensil colors of the gas stations and the monster drugstores, it is in the swing of the sports cars, hot rods, convertibles, Los Angeles is a city to drive in, the boulevards are wide, the traffic is nervous and fast, the radio stations play bouncing , blooping, rippling tunes, one digs the pop in a pop tune, no one of character would make love by it but the sound is good for swinging a car, electronic guitars and Hawaiian harps.

So this is the town the Democrats came to, and with their unerring instinct (after being with them a week, one thinks of this party as a crazy, half-rich family, loaded with poor cousins, traveling always in caravans with Cadillacs and Okie Fords, Lincolns and quarter-horse mules, putting up every night in tents to hear the chamber quartet of Great Cousin Eleanor invaded by the Texas-twanging steel-stringing geetarists of Bubber Lyndon, carrying it own mean high-school principal, Doc Symington, chided for its manners by good Uncle Adlai, told the route of march by Navigator Jack, cut off every six months from the rich will of Uncle Jim Farley, never listening to the mechanic of the caravan, Bald Sam Rayburn, who assures them they'll all break down unless Cousin Bubber gets the concession on the garage; it's the Snopes family married to Henry James, with the labor unions thrown in like a Yankee dollar, and yet it's true, in tranquility one recollects them with affection, their instinct is good, crazy family good) and this instinct now led the caravan to pick the Biltmore Hotel in downtown Los Angeles for their family get-together and reunion.

The Biltmore is one of the ugliest hotels in the world. Patterned after the flat roofs of an Italian Renaissance palace, it is eighty-eight times as large, and one-millionth as valuable to the continuation of man, and it would be intolerable if it were not for the presence of Pershing Square, that square block of park with cactus and palm trees, the three-hundred-and-sixty-five-day-a-year convention of every junkie, pot-head, pusher, queen (but you have read that good writing already). For years Pershing Square has been one of the three or four places in America famous to homosexuals, famous not for its posh, the chic is round-heeled here, but because it is one of the avatars of the good old masturbatory sex, dirty with the crusted sugars of smut, dirty rooming houses around the corner where the score is made, dirty book and photograph stores down the street, old-fashioned out-of-the-Thirties burlesque house, cruising bars, jukeboxes, movie houses; Pershing Square is the town plaza for all those lonely, respectable, small-town homosexuals who lead a family life, make children, and have the Philbrick psychology (How I Joined the Communist Party and Led Three Lives). Yes, it is the open-air convention hall for the small-town inverts who live like spies, and it sits in the center of Los Angeles, facing the Biltmore, that hotel which is a mausoleum, that Pentagon of traveling salesmen the Party chose to house the headquarters of the Convention.

For most of us death may not be peace but an expedition into all the high terror and deep melancholy we sought to avoid in our lives. So the act of travel is a grave hour to some part of the unconscious, for it may be on a trip that we prepare a buried corner of ourselves to be ready for what happens once we are dead.

By this logic, the end of a trip is a critical moment of transition. Railroad stations in large cities should properly be monumental, heavy with dignity, reminiscent of the past. We learn little from travel, not nearly so much as we need to learn, if everywhere we are assaulted by the faceless plastic surfaces of everything which has been built in America since the war, that new architecture of giant weeds and giant boxes, of children's colors on billboards and jagged electric signs. Like the metastases of cancer cells, the plastic shacks, the motels, the drive-in theatres, the highway restaurants and the gas stations proliferate year by year until they are close to covering the highways of America with a new country which is laid over the old one the way a transparent sheet with new drawings is set upon the original plan. It is an architecture with no root to the past and no suggestion of the future, for one cannot conceive of a modern building growing old (does it turn dingy or will the colors stain?); there is no way to age, it can only cease to function. No doubt these buildings will live for twenty years and then crack in two. They will live like robots, or television sets which go out of order with one whistle of the wind.

In the suburbs it is worse. To live in leisure in a house much like other houses, to live in a landscape where it is meaningless to walk because each corner which is turned produces the same view, to live in comfort and be bored is a preparation for one condition: limbo.

The architectural face of the enemy has shifted. Twenty years ago Pennsylvania Station in New York City seemed a monstrosity, forbidding, old, dingy, unfunctional, wasteful of space, depressing in its passages and waiting rooms. The gloomy exploitative echoes of the industrial revolution sounded in its grey stone. And yet today the plan to demolish it is a small disaster.

Soon the planners will move in to tear down the majestic vaults of the old building in order to rear up in its place a new sports arena, a twenty-, thirty-, forty-story building. One can predict what the new building will look like. It will be made of steel, concrete and glass, it will have the appearance of a cardboard box which contains a tube of toothpaste, except that it will be literally one hundred million times larger in volume. In turn, the sports arena will have plastic seats painted in pastel colors, sky-blue, orange-pink, dead yellow. There will be a great deal of fluorescent lighting, an electronically operated scoreboard (which will break down frequently) and the acoustics will be particularly poor, as they invariably are in new auditoriums which have been designed to have good acoustics.

The new terminal will be underground. It will waste no space for high vaulted ceilings and monumental columns, it will look doubtless like the inside of a large airport. And one will feel the same subtle nausea coming into the city or waiting to depart from it that one feels now in such plastic catacombs as O'Hare's reception center in Chicago, at United or American Airlines in Idlewild, in the tunnels and ramps and blank gleaming corridors of Dallas' airport, which is probably one of the ten ugliest buildings in the world.

Now in the cities, an architectural plague is near upon us. For we have tried to settle the problem of slums by housing, and the void in education by new schools. So we have housing projects which look like prisons and prisons which look like hospitals which in turn look like schools, schools which look like luxury hotels, luxury hotels which seem to confuse themselves with airline terminals, and airline terminals which cannot be told apart from civic centers, and the civic centers look like factories. Even the new churches look like recreation centers at large ski resorts. One can no longer tell the purpose of a building by looking at its face. Modern buildings tend to look like call girls who came out of it intact except that their faces are a touch blank and the expression in their eyes is as lively as the tip on a filter cigarette.

Our modern architecture reminds me a little of cancer cells. Because the healthy cells of the lung have one appearance and those in the liver another. But if both are cancerous they tend to look a little more alike, they tend to look a little less like anything very definite.

138

Los Angeles Notebook

JOAN DIDION

Joan Didion (1934–) was born in Sacramento, California and attended the University of California at Berkeley. Her writing includes the novels *Run River* (1963), *Play It as It Lays* (1970), and *A Book of Common Prayer* (1977). She has published two significant collections of essays on America, especially West Coast life and urban mores: *Slouching Towards Bethlehem* (1968) and *The White Album* (1979). She is an acute observer of urban life and achieves a vibrant yet philosophical sense of contemporary American culture. She is one of the most important of current writers on the urban and social "scene".

There is something uneasy in the Los Angeles air this afternoon, some unnatural stillness, some tension. What it means is that tonight a Santa Ana will begin to blow, a hot wind from the northeast whining down through the Cajon and San Gorgonio Passes, blowing up sandstorms out along Route 66, drying the hills and the nerves to the flash point. For a few days now we will see smoke back in the canyons, and hear sirens in the night. I have neither heard nor read that a Santa Ana is due, but I know it, and almost everyone I have seen today knows it too. We know it because we feel it. The baby frets. The maid sulks. I rekindle a waning argument with the telephone company, then cut my losses and lie down, given over to whatever it is in the air. To live with the Santa Ana is to accept, consciously or unconsciously, a deeply mechanistic view of human behaviour.

I recall being told, when I first moved to Los Angeles and was living on an isolated beach, that the Indians would throw themselves into the sea when the bad wind blew. I could see why. The Pacific turned ominously glossy during a Santa Ana period, and one woke in the night troubled not only by the peacocks screaming in the olive trees but by the eerie absence of surf. The heat was

Source: Joan Didion, "Los Angeles Notebook", *Slouching Towards Bethlehem*, New York, 1968, pp. 177–82.

surreal. The sky had a yellow cast, the kind of light sometimes called "earthquake weather". My only neighbour would not come out of her house for days, and there were no lights at night, and her husband roamed the place with a machete. One day he would tell me that he had heard a trespasser, the next a rattlesnake.

"On nights like that," Raymond Chandler once wrote about the Santa Ana, "every booze party ends in a fight. Meek little wives feel the edge of the carving knife and study their husbands' necks. Anything can happen." That was the kind of wind it was. I did not know then that there was any basis for the effect it had on all of us, but it turns out to be another of those cases in which science bears out folk wisdom. The Santa Ana, which is named for one of the canyons it rushes through, is a *foehn* wind, like the *foehn* of Austria and Switzerland and the *hamsin* of Israel. There are a number of persistent malevolent winds, perhaps the best known of which are the *mistral* of France and the Mediterranean *sirocco*, but a *foehn* wind has distinct characteristics: it occurs on the leeward slope of a mountain range and, although the air begins as a cold mass, it is warmed as it comes down the mountain and appears finally as a hot dry wind. Whenever and wherever a *foehn* blows, doctors hear about headaches and nausea and allergies, about "nervousness", about "depression". In Los Angeles some teachers do not attempt to conduct formal classes during a Santa Ana, because the children become unmanageable. In Switzerland the suicide rate goes up during the *foehn*, and in the courts of some Swiss cantons the wind is considered a mitigating circumstance for crime. Surgeons are said to watch the wind, because blood does not clot normally during a *foehn*. A few years ago an Israeli physicist discovered that not only during such winds, but for the ten or twelve hours which precede them, the air carries an unusually high ratio of positive to negative ions. No one seems to know exactly why that should be; some talk about friction and others suggest solar disturbances. In any case the positive ions are there, and what an excess of positive ions does, in the simplest terms, is make people unhappy. One cannot get much more mechanistic than that.

Easterners commonly complain that there is no "weather" at all in Southern California, that the days and the seasons slip by relentlessly, numbingly bland. That is quite misleading. In fact the climate is characterized by infrequent but violent extremes: two periods of torrential subtropical rains which continue for weeks and wash out the hills and send subdivisions sliding towards the sea; about twenty scattered days a year of the Santa Ana, which, with its incendiary dryness, invariably means fire. At the first prediction of a Santa Ana, the Forest Service flies men and equipment from northern California into the southern forests, and the Los Angeles Fire Department cancels its ordinary non-firefighting routines. The Santa Ana caused Malibu to burn the way it did in 1956, and Bel Air in 1961, and Santa Barbara in 1964. In the winter of 1966–7 eleven men were killed fighting a Santa Ana fire that spread through the San Gabriel Mountains.

Just to watch the front-page news out of Los Angeles during a Santa Ana is to get very close to what it is about the place. The longest single Santa Ana period in recent years was in 1957, and it lasted not the usual three or four days but fourteen days, from 21 November until 4 December. On the first day 25,000 acres of the San Gabriel Mountains were burning, with gusts reaching 100 miles an hour. In town, the wind reached Force 12, or hurricane force, on the Beaufort Scale; oil derricks were toppled and people ordered off the downtown streets to avoid injury from flying objects. On 22 November the fire in the San Gabriels was out of control. On 24 November six people were killed in automobile accidents, and by the end of the week the Los Angeles *Times* was keeping a box score of traffic deaths. On 26 November a prominent Pasadena attorney, depressed about money, shot and killed his wife, their two sons, and himself. On 27 November a South Gate divorcée, twenty-two, was murdered and thrown from a moving car. On 30 November the San Gabriel fire was still out of control, and the wind in town was blowing eighty miles an hour. On the first day of December four people died violently, and on the third the wind began to break.

It is hard for people who have not lived in Los Angeles to realize how radically the Santa Ana figures in the local imagination. The city burning is Los Angeles's deepest image of itself: Nathanael West perceived that, in *The Day of the Locust*; and at the time of the 1965 Watts riots what struck the imagination most indelibly were the fires. For days one could drive the Harbour Freeway and see the city on fire, just as we had always known it would be in the end. Los Angeles weather is the weather of catastrophe, of apocalypse, and, just as the reliably long and bitter winters of New England determine the way life is lived there, so the violence and the unpredictability of the Santa Ana affect the entire quality of life in Los Angeles, accentuate its impermanence, its unreliability. The wind shows us how close to the edge we are.

2

"Here's why I'm on the beeper, Ron," said the telephone voice on the all-night radio show. "I just want to say that this *Sex for the Secretary* creature—whatever her name is—certainly isn't contributing anything to the morals in this country. It's pathetic. Statistics *show*."

"It's *Sex and the Office*, honey," the disc jockey said. "That's the title. By Helen Gurley Brown. Statistics show what?"

"I haven't got them right here at my fingertips, naturally. But they *show*."

"I'd be interested in hearing them. Be constructive, you Night Owls."

"All right, let's take *one* statistic," the voice said, truculent now. "Maybe I haven't read the book, but what's this business she recommends about *going out with married men for lunch?*"

So it went, from midnight until 5 a.m., interrupted by records and by occasional calls debating whether or not a rattlesnake can swim. Misinformation about rattlesnakes is a leitmotiv of the insomniac imagination in Los Angeles. Towards 2 a.m. a man from "out Tarzana way" called to protest. "The Night

Owls who called earlier must have been thinking about, uh, *The Man in the Grey Flannel Suit* or some other book," he said, "because Helen's one of the few authors trying to tell us what's really going *on*. Hefner's another, and he's also controversial, working in, uh, another area."

An old man, after testifying that he "personally" had seen a swimming rattlesnake, in the Delta-Mendota Canal, urged "moderation" on the Helen Gurley Brown question. "We shouldn't get on the beeper to call things pornographic before we've read them," he complained, pronouncing it porn-ee-oh-graphic. "I say, get the book. Give it a chance." The original *provocateur* called back to agree that she would get the book. "And then I'll burn it," she added.

"Book burner, eh?" laughed the disc jockey good-naturedly.

"I wish they still burned witches," she hissed.

3

It is three o'clock on a Sunday afternoon and 105° and the air so thick with smog that the dusty palm trees loom up with a sudden and rather attractive mystery. I have been playing in the sprinklers with the baby and I get in the car and go to Ralph's Market on the corner of Sunset and Fuller wearing an old bikini bathing suit. This is not a very good thing to wear to the market but neither is it, at Ralph's on the corner of Sunset and Fuller, an unusual costume. Nonetheless a large woman in a cotton muumuu jams her cart into mine at the butcher counter. "*What a thing to wear to the market*," she says in a loud but strangled voice. Everyone looks the other way and I study a plastic package of rib lamb chops and she repeats it. She follows me all over the store, to the Junior Foods, to the Dairy Products, to the Mexican Delicacies, jamming my cart whenever she can. Her husband plucks at her sleeve. As I leave the check-out counter she raises her voice one last time: "*What a thing to wear to Ralph's*," she says.

4

A party at someone's house in Beverly Hills: a pink tent, two orchestras, a couple of French Communist directors in Cardin evening jackets, chili and hamburgers from Chasen's. The wife of an English actor sits at a table alone; she visits California rarely although her husband works here a good deal. An American who knows her slightly comes over to the table.

"Marvellous to see you here," he says.

"Is it," she says.

"How long have you been here?"

"Too long."

She takes a fresh drink from a passing waiter and smiles at her husband, who is dancing.

The American tries again. He mentions her husband.

"I hear he's marvellous in this picture."

She looks at the American for the first time. When she finally speaks she enunciates every word very clearly. "He ... is ... also ... a ... fag," she says pleasantly.

5

The oral history of Los Angeles is written in piano bars. "Moon River", the piano player always plays, and "Mountain Greenery". "There's a Small Hotel" and "This Is Not the First Time". People talk to each other, tell each other about their first wives and last husbands. "Stay funny," they tell each other, and "This is to die over." A construction man talks to an unemployed screenwriter who is celebrating, alone, his tenth wedding anniversary. The construction man is on a job in Montecito: "Up in Montecito," he says, "they got one square mile with 135 millionaires."

"Putrescence," the writer says.

"That's all you got to say about it?"

"Don't read me wrong, I think Santa Barbara's one of the most—Christ, *the* most—beautiful places in the world, but it's a beautiful place that contains a ... *putrescence.* They just live on their putrescent millions."

"So give me putrescent."

"No, no," the writer says. "I just happen to think millionaires have some sort of lacking in their ... in their elasticity."

A drunk requests "The Sweetheart of Sigma Chi". The piano player says he doesn't know it. "Where'd you learn to play the piano?" the drunk asks. "I got two degrees," the piano player says. "One in musical education." I go to a coin telephone and call a friend in New York. "Where are you?" he says. "In a piano bar in Encino," I say. "Why?" he says. "Why not," I say.

1965–7

139
Electrographic Architecture

TOM WOLFE

Tom Wolfe (1931–), not be confused with Thomas Wolfe (1900–38) was born in Virginia, but undertook his graduate degree at Yale University. Essentially a cultural critic, especially of the quiddities of the "chic" scene, he came to prominence as a reporter in the 1960s with collections such as *The Kandy-Kolored Tangerine—Flake Streamline Baby (1965)* and *The Electric Kool-Aid Acid Test* (1968). His viewpoint is underpinned by a pervasive sense of irony and humour, a critical perspective which is reflected in his two studies of modern art and architecture (especially in the American context), *The Painted Word* (1975) and *From Bauhaus to Our House* (1981). His most sustained rendition of contemporary fads and mores is *Bonfire of the Vanities* (1989), a novel based on the yuppie culture of Manhattan and its Wall Street executives. Wolfe remains one of the most acute critics of urban life.

This is a show, this set of pictures ... of electro-graphic architecture from around Los Angeles and San Diego. Electro-graphic ... I coined the term myself ... why be bashful! The existing vocabulary of art history is helpless before what commercial artists are now doing in the western USA. Commercial artists in America are now at least 10 years ahead of serious artists in almost every field, including architecture. ... It's a revelation, you might say ... which first came to me one evening on Park Avenue, in New York. I stopped by the lobby of the Pepsi-Cola building to see a show of neon sculpture by Billy Apple. Apple is a serious artist. *Avant-Garde* is the word. He "combines art and technology" ... "He is a lyrical user of neon with a very personal sense of colour," in the words of Jack Burnham ... The praise is running deep ... I walk in and here is neon tubing hung from wires and bent into simple geometric shapes ... The colours are curiously pallid, for neon ... Everything is a sick apricot in here ... They're limp ... They splutter ... They're like the neon outlines you can still see sometimes in the windows of the old bars with glass brick facing

Source: Tom Wolfe, "Electrographic Architecture", *Architectural Design*, Vol. XXXIX, July, 1969, No. 7. pp. 379–84. © Tom Wolfe

and other remains of 1930's ... Glamour ... Frankly, I'm embarrassed for the guy! ... All I can think of is that I could walk over a few blocks to almost any inter-section along the avenues on the West Side or drive out Route 22 in New Jersey and see some common commercial electric signs that do it better ... There's not a drive-in or all-night cafeteria or bar & grill in the lot that doesn't give the glories of electric tubing a better ride.

... A lyrical user of neon with a ...

All of this came back to me last week as I drove around Los Angeles and San Diego. Here is an electric sign *Buick* I saw on El Cajon Boulevard in San Diego, near the Route 395 freeway ... By Melvin Zeitvogel of the California Neon Co.—why be bashful! ... I wish I could show it in action, or at least in colour ... Each letter of *Buick* is on a baroque rocket ... The lights work in a series ... In phase 2 the rockets light up orange and yellow ... They shoot off red jet flames ... They take off to the left ... A terrific rush of light shoots up the main stem there, the big parabola ... It explodes in the crazed atomic nucleus at the top ... The sign is 105 feet high, 11 stories up in the air, in other words ... It's insane! ... It's marvellous!

Melvin Zeitvogel did this sign 10 years ago. Serious artists and architects are only just now approaching the ideas commercial artists like him have been working with for years ... I notice in the October 1968 issue of *Progressive Architecture* that Kenneth Carbajal is saying: "What is happening in architecture today is a revolution. It is a complete readjustment of aesthetics that puts it more in step with the Space Age and its materials and forms." ... More statements about the revolution ... They love this word revolution ... They set about illustrating it. They present a special section on electric light experiments ... The Pulsa group at Yale, in Project Angus ... A California group designs "neon banners" for Charles Moore's Faculty Club building at the University of California's Santa Barbara campus ... Here are designers working with Super-graphics, as they call it, for interiors ... Everybody comes skipping and screaming into the million-volt future, of course ... Another magazine, *Domus* ... they're excited about some simple rectangles of light used on the exterior and interior of a club in Rimini, Italy, called L'Altro Mondo, and about some light show effects in the Piper-Pluriclub ... I pick up a new book entitled *Beyond Modern Sculpture.* It calls light sculpture the new wave in this age of new technologies ... They're all in there, serious artists like Apple, Dan Flavin, Martial Raysse, Robert Rauschenberg, Robert Whitman ... They have terrific theories, especially Rauschenberg and Whitman, about cybernetic art, computer art, holographic art, laser art. But I look at what they have actually done and then at Melvin Zeitvogel's *Buick*—it's crazy! the art world is upside down. All of a sudden the *avant-garde*, the serious artists, are the primitives, the Grandma Moseses ... The commercial artists, the Melvin Zeitvogels, are the classicists[1] ...

Melvin Zeitvogel! I have to call the guy up ... He's 54, it turns out. He tells me he started out as a glass blower. He was hired by California Neon 25 years ago, when he was 29, because he could work with the glass that goes into neon and fluorescent tubing. He gradually moved into designing ... He was 44 when he did Buick ... I asked him if most electric sign designers get into it indirectly like he did ... No, he says, quite a few today have some art training ... "You kind of need a fellow who has–you know ... kind of an arty side to him"–

Kind of an arty side to him! Perfect. The notion that he himself *is* an artist– none of the great sign artists seem to lose any sleep over that ... Which is their secret, of course. They're free souls! The hell with art history! and the New York art status sphere! The hell with *Art Forum* and the new academy! The hell with the Bauhaus, Mies, Corbu, and Billy Apple! and all lyrical users of neon with a very personal sense of colour!–

Yahhhh!–if anybody ever heard of them. Practically all the men in the new electro-graphic architecture have been engaged first of all in a highly competitive business ... They have been building not to catch the eye of the art world but of people driving by in cars ... It's as simple as that ... A very liberating thing, the car ... Millions of Americans roaring down the boulevards and strips and freeways in 327-horsepower family car dreamboat fantasy creations ...

... Daddy Dreamboat Family Car ...

Designing for the eyes of people moving–it shook California's commercial artist and engineers free of the whole historic baggage of serious architects ... who still think chiefly in terms of static solids ... Zeitvogel's Buick is 1960-style Las Vegas electro-graphic architecture ... He added an 11-story electric sign to a conventional one-storey commercial building, the Dick Grihalva Buick agency ... Since then Los Angeles commercial artists have unified the concept. They don't just add the lighting. they combine lighting, graphics and building structure in a single architectural form *Mobil station in the Crenshaw shopping centre* ... They convert the building itself into one vast electrical advertisement ... The structure itself takes on the hyperbole of advertising ...

Here is a Union 76 station 4 in Beverly Hills, at Santa Monica Boulevard and Crescent Drive, built in 1964. Jim Wong of Pereira Associates designed it. He actually designed it in 1960, for the Los Angeles airport. He told me he wanted to express the sense of motion around the airport ... the flow of cars as well as planes ... It looks like a pagoda style from most angles, but it is really a huge spherical triangle resting on three piers with curving soffits ... Standard Oil bid lower for the airport station and got the site. As a matter of fact, they put up a remarkable piece of electro-graphic architecture of their own ... Anyway, Union 76 eventually decided to build Wong's fantasy in Beverly Hills ... If any building ever proved that electro-graphic architecture works commercially, it was this one. ... There was a Union 76 station on the site already. It was pumping 100,000 gallons of petrol a month, which was high, even by Los Angeles standards ... A month after Wong's building went up, business increased 50 per cent, to 150,000 gallons a month ...

Here is one of the first large buildings in Los Angeles that was designed to express not a structural form but a graphic form ... the Crenshaw Ford agency on Crenshaw Boulevard at 52nd Street in Los Angeles ... The whole building is designed around the big curved corner façade. The corner was designed solely to accommodate the shape of the F in *Ford* ... Since then the graphics in electrographic architecture have moved from mere lettering to whole structures designed primarily as pictures or representational sculpture, everything from drive-in theatres 5 to a restaurant in Long Beach (no longer standing) in which the walls were huge and very sharply defined colour photographs of steaks, chops, salads, sundaes, drinks ... Entire walls were backlit, like the huge photo-mural in Grand Central Station advertising Kodak ... A whole building expressing a gigantic sirloin, medium-rare, with french fries ... and why not! ... That 's what we have here, motoring friends ...

I talked to Sal Merendino, a Los Angeles industrial designer and teacher. He told me he sees this kind of super-electro-graphics as a great new wave of urban design: "I can see these sort of panels being done by really first-rate graphic designers, like Saul Bass or George Kepes. Why should buildings always express merely their own structure? Why shouldn't they express what's inside? I think panels like this could be used with great warmth, joy and good taste. A city ought to be joyous. There's enough severity in a city anyway, without striving for it in architecture. In one sense we ought to forget the idea of Architecture in cities. I think if you call it Architecture, you get screwed up. You end up setting these old standards for yourself. Architects want something that makes them look good when it's photographed and printed on coated stock in some grand book on the history of architecture. It's time we started thinking about what people who live in cities really want and need. All my beliefs end up with that. I think people want warmth and love and joy and good taste in their environment, and I think really good graphic panels would be a big step in that direction."

The whole idea is so far away from the conventional Bauhaus notion of what a structure ought to express that it's—exhilarating. It's beyond baroque! beyond mannerist! ... In fact, it is really hard to figure out how the old Bauhaus ideals of "structural honesty" and "a pure art of use of usefulness" ... of functionalism, in short ...have hung on so long. After all, the whole idea came out of the political atmosphere of post-World War I Europe. A desperate time, brothers ... "Brothers of the world bend your knees ... The proletarian armies of the world have grasped at the stars, destroying and building at the same time in a heavenly craving for justice and love ... brothers, lift up your hearts and eyes high to the firmament, and the ridiculous national boundary stone will be no obstacle to a single fatherland for us all—the World—the Earth!" This was a manifesto of the November Group in 1919, a group of radical German artists concerned chiefly with architecture ... Out of the November Group grew the Workers Circle, including Walter Gropius, guru of the Bauhaus ... which, in turn, was the mother of it all, the rectangular straight-line functional serious "modern" architecture of Europe and America ... Serious architects became obsessed with the idea that structure should be "expressed honestly" ... Honesty usually meant straight lines and right angles! Serious architects were very slow to shape newer materials like reinforced concrete into the sort of fantastic curved shells and soffits that Saarinen became famous for in the early 1960s[2] ... Serious architects still tend to regard exterior decoration as dishonest. Electric tubing is still *gauche* ... or, at best, camp[3] ... Back-lit plastic facings and acrylic paints—I doubt if many serious architects have ever thought about them in terms of architecture. Underneath it all, they have a terrific *nostalgie du chateau*. They can't get it out of their systems ...

It was left to commercial artists in towns like Los Angeles, Las Vegas, and San Diego to create something wild enough and baroque enough to express the new age of motion and mass wealth. There is a terrific Eastern intellectual snobbery about Los Angeles as a city of sprawl, chaos, madness, strangled by the automobile.

... *Nostalgie du chateau!* ... I still hear people in New York say that the trouble with Los Angeles is that it has no landmarks, you can never orient yourself. I doubt that anybody who lives in Los Angeles feels that way. In fact, Los Angeles has the most monumental landmarks ever built, namely, the freeways. Periodically, the upper social orders of Los Angeles try to bring the city's architecture in line with the dictates of the New York art status sphere and its ancient ideas of monumentality—*nostalgie du Lincoln Center!*—by sponsoring museums, culture centres, grand plazas ... Invariably they end up as great ... *lumps*, compared to the curvilinear forms of the freeways (6, *an unfinished ramp to the San Diego Freeway at Jefferson Boulevard*) and all the forms of car fantasy architecture that go with them ...

And so much goes with them; yes. The freeways are elevated at many points, and for many miles, in the form of what in New York would be called skyways. They are anywhere from 20 to 100 feet above the ground in curving shapes, with these great heron-neck light stanchions curving over them like some endless Yves Tanguy decoration ... The great spaces between the skyways are unified by a constellation of other objects of light and colour thrust high up into the air: signs, electric displays, banners, bunting 8, towers, spires ... like the scores of lit-up orange globes of the Union 76 stations (7 *designed by Raymond Loewy*) ... full-fledged electro-graphic architecture, like the McDonald's Hamburger golden arches ... and, everywhere you go, clusters of light stanchions over car lots with flat wing-shaped banks of electric tubing at the top 8 ... these light displays in themselves are more interesting than most of what serious light sculptors have accomplished, for my money ...

Many of the spires and luminous objects, shooting up or floating in the atmosphere, have no function whatsoever other than display ... They are there for visual excitement. Functionalism—the hell with it!—The Los Angeles car washes especially ... They violate all the canons of 50-year-old Modernism with a verve that would drive Mies off the platter ... The car washes are very simple structures, basically, just open sheds, but they send their supporting columns

10, 20, 30 feet up into the air with a kind of pure Low-Rent LA exuberance (9 *Cinema city car wash*) ... Other shed structures, like the roofs of drive-ins, are given a massive and often whimsical treatment ...

Other structures of the most massive or towering sort will have little ornaments stuck on top after a kind of Christmas Tree Star principle, like Zeitvogel's *Buick* ... I noticed the same thing throughout Las Vegas. At first it just seemed like Googie decoration. But gradually I saw that it has an important psychological function in the modern city ... It *tames* the impersonal massiveness and severity ... Hey! it says, This is a laugh and a half! ... It's like the old Low-Rent car jockeys with a pair of Styrofoam dice hanging from the rear-view mirror of their Cadillac and a da-da-da-da-dum-dum-dum musical horn under the hood ... Domesticate the beast ...

Frankly, it is very ironic that the national Beautification programme is now beginning to catch on around Los Angeles in the form of local zoning ordinances requiring that commercial buildings and displays conform to conventional local building designs ... in other words, to the traditional static forms, the bungalows, the two-storey stores, that have been there longer ... The new genre of petrol stations has pitched roofs and rubble facing—*nostalgie du Quaint & Rural* ... The truth is ... how drab Los Angeles, San Diego and hundreds of other American cities and towns and crossroads would be without the electro-graphic car fantasy mobile architecture that America's *avant-garde* commercial artists have given them ... Someone must write the new book, now, fast, on the most lavish coated stock $18.50 a copy, called *Beyond Modern Architecture*, featuring ... well, for a start—Melvin Zeitvogel ...

Notes

1. Serious light sculptors have a strangely old-fashioned, rear-view taste in technology. They have a nostalgia for neon. Neon was introduced into the electric sign business in the late 1920s and enjoyed quite a vogue. But it was a fragile material and unsuited for large-scale or really spectacular work. In the 1930s glass signs were developed, using interior incandescent lighting and ceramic-fired colours for the lettering and art. In the late 1940s back-lit plastic signs were developed. The trouble with plastic had been that there was no way to apply colour to it for the art work. Acrylic colours solved that. Signs today use all devices, from the oldest to the newest. The most spectacular effects, as in the new 188-feet-high *Stardust* (hotel and casino) sign in Las Vegas, still use fields of light bulbs for the most brilliant effects, plus plastic facings, acrylic colours, and neon for outlining letters and other highlight effects. The *Stardust* sign, by Ad Art Co. of Stockton, California, has 25,000 bulbs, 611,000 watts of power, and a solid-state programming with 27 lighting sequences.

2. Other architects had dreamed up fantastic dome and shell designs, of course, notably, Gunter Günschel, Enrico Castiglioni, Eduardo Catalano, Luciano Baldessari; but few had been built.

3. Robert Venturi is one of the few serious American architects to comprehend the possibilities of electric sign technology and to conceive of full-scale electro-graphic architecture. In fact, this month (October) he has taken his third-year studio class at Yale to Nevada to study the electro-graphic landscape of Las Vegas with the same objective and scholarly thoroughness that might be applied to Athens or Pompeii. A few architects in Germany and Tokyo have used electric sign technology as an integral part of design, sometimes in the form of fluorescent tubing outlining the entire face of a building, something I have never seen done in the USA; also in the form of electric designs covering a main façade, as in the case of the ascending burst of stars on the face of the Stern (Star) magazine building in Frankfurt.

140

In the Rear-view Mirror

RAYNER BANHAM

Rayner Banham (1922–) was born in Norwich, England. After teaching at University College, London, he taught at the University of Southern California and Buffalo, New York State. His publications include *Theory and Design in the First Machine Age* and *The New Brutalism*. His *Rayner Banham Loves Los Angeles* was shown on BBC television in 1972. *Los Angeles The Architecture of Four Ecologies* has become a classic study of Los Angeles and it remains essential reading for any understanding of the special image of the city both as an environment and as a visual spectacle.

A city seventy miles square but rarely seventy years deep apart from a small downtown not yet two centuries old and a few other pockets of ancientry, Los Angeles is instant architecture in an instant townscape. Most of its buildings are the first and only structures on their particular parcels of land; they are couched in a dozen different styles, most of them imported, exploited, and ruined within living memory. Yet the city has a comprehensible, even consistent, quality to its built form, unified enough to rank as a fit subject for an historical monograph.

Historical monograph? Can such an old-world, academic, and precedent-laden concept claim to embrace so unprecedented a human phenomenon as this city of Our Lady Queen of the Angels of Porciuncula?—otherwise known as Internal Combustion City, Surfurbia, Smogville, Aerospace City, Systems Land, the Dream-factory of the Western world. It's a poor historian who finds a human artefact alien to his professional capacities, a poorer one who cannot find new bottles for new wine. In any case, the new wine of Angeleno architecture has already been decanted into one of the older types of historical bottle with a success that I will not even try to emulate.

Architecture in Southern California by David Gebhard and Robert Winter is a

Source: Rayner Banham, "In the Rear-view Mirror", *Los Angeles: The Architecture of Four Ecologies*, Harmondsworth, 1971, pp. 21–36, © Rayner Banham.

model version of the classical type of architectural gazetteer—erudite, accurate, clear, well-mapped, pocket-sized. No student of the architecture of Los Angeles can afford to stir out of doors without it. But there is no need to try and write it again; all I wish to do here is to record my profound and fundamental debt to the authors, and echo their admission of even more fundamental indebtedness—to Esther McCoy and her "one-woman crusade" to get Southern California's modern architectural history recorded and its monuments appreciated.

Yet even the professed intention of Gebhard and Winter to cover "a broad cross-section of the varieties of Angeleno architecture", is inhibited by the relatively conventional implicit definition of "architecture" accepted by these open-minded observers; their spectrum includes neither hamburger bars and other Pop ephemeridae at one extreme, nor freeway structures and other civil engineering at the other. However, both are as crucial to the human ecologies and built environments of Los Angeles as are dated works in classified styles by named architects.

In order to accommodate such extremes, the chapters that follow will have to deviate from accepted norms for architectural histories of cities. What I have aimed to do is to present the architecture (in a fairly conventional sense of the word) within the topographical and historical context of the total artefact that constitutes Greater Los Angeles, because it is this double context that binds the polymorphous architectures into a comprehensible unity that cannot often be discerned by comparing monument with monument out of context.

So when most observers report monotony, not unity, and within that monotony, confusion rather than variety, this is usually because the context has escaped them; and it has escaped them because it is unique (like all the best unities) and without any handy terms of comparison. It is difficult to register the total artefact as a distinctive human construct because there is nothing else with which to compare it, and thus no class into which it many be pigeonholed. And we historians are too prone to behave like Socrates in Paul Valéry's *Eupalinos*, to reject the inscrutable, to hurl the unknown in the ocean.

How then to bridge this gap of comparability. One can most properly begin by learning the local language; and the language of design, architecture, and urbanism in Los Angeles is the language of movement. Mobility outweighs monumentality there to a unique degree, as Richard Austin Smith pointed out in a justly famous article in 1965, and the city will never be fully understood by those who cannot move fluently through its diffuse urban texture, cannot go with the flow of its unprecedented life. So, like earlier generations of English intellectuals who taught themselves Italian in order to read Dante in the original, I learned to drive in order to read Los Angeles in the original.

But whereas knowledge of Dante's tongue could serve in reading other Italian texts, full command of Angeleno dynamics qualifies one only to read Los Angeles, the uniquely mobile metropolis. Again that word "uniquely" ... I make no apology for it. The splendours and miseries of Los Angeles, the graces and grotesqueries, appear to me as unrepeatable as they are unprecedented. I share neither the optimism of those who see Los Angeles as the prototype of all future cities, nor the gloom of those who see it as the harbinger of universal urban doom. Once the history of the city is brought under review, it is immediately apparent that no city has ever been produced by such an extraordinary mixture of geography, climate, economics, demography, mechanics and culture; nor is it likely that an even remotely similar mixture will ever occur again. The interaction of these factors needs to be kept in constant historical view—and since it is manifestly dangerous to face backwards while at the steering wheel, the common metaphor of history as the rear-view mirror civilization seems necessary, as well as apt, in any study of Los Angeles.

First, observe an oddity in the "Yellow Pages" of the local phone books; many firms list, in the same size type and without comment, branches in Hawaii, New Zealand, and Australia. This is neither a picturesque curiosity nor commercial bragging—it is simply the next natural place to have branches, a continuation of the great westward groundswell of population that brought the Angelenos to the Pacific shore in the first place, a groundswell that can still be felt throughout the life of the city.

Los Angeles looks naturally to the Sunset, which can be stunningly handsome, and named one of its great boulevards after that favourite evening view. But if the eye follows the sun, westward migration cannot. The Pacific beaches are where young men stop going West, where the great waves of agrarian migration from Europe and the Middle West broke in a surf of fulfilled and frustrated hopes. The strength and nature of this westward flow need to be understood; it underlies the differences of mind between Los Angeles and its sister-metropolis to the north.

San Francisco was plugged into California from the sea; the Gold Rush brought its first population and their culture round Cape Horn; their prefabricated Yankee houses and prefabricated New England (or European) attitudes were dumped unmodified on the Coast. Viewed from Southern California it looks like a foreign enclave, like the Protestant Pale in Ireland, because the Southern Californians came, predominantly, overland to Los Angeles, slowly traversing the whole North American land-mass and its evolving history.

They brought with them—and still being—the prejudices, motivations, and ambitions of the central heartland of the USA. The first major wave of immigration came from Kansas City on excursion tickets after 1885; later they came in second-hand cars out of the dust-bowl—not for nothing is Mayor Yorty known (behind his back) as the Last of the Okies, and Long Beach as the Main Seaport of Iowa! In one unnervingly true sense, Los Angeles is the Middle West raised to flash-point, the authoritarian dogmas of the Bible Belt and the perennial revolt against them colliding at critical mass under the palm trees. Out of it comes a cultural situation where only the extreme is normal, and the Middle Way is just the unused reservation down the centre of the Freeway.

Yet these extremes contrive to co-exist with only sporadic flares of violence—on Venice Beach, in Watts, or whatever is the fashionable venue for confrontations. Miraculously the city's extremes include an excessive tolerance. Partly this is that indifference which is Los Angeles's most publicized vice, but it is also a heritage from the extraordinary cultural mixture with which the city began. If Los Angeles is not a monolithic Protestant moral tyranny—and it notoriously is not!—it is because the Mid-western agrarian culture underwent a profound transformation as it hit the coast, a sun-change that pervades moral postures, political attitudes, ethnic groupings, and individual psychologies. This change has often been observed, and usually with bafflement, yet one observer has bypassed the bafflement and gone straight to an allegory of Californiation that seems to hold good from generation to generation—Ray Bradbury in the most fundamental of his Martian stories, *Dark they were and Golden Eyed*, where the earth-family are subtly transformed, even against their wills, into tall, bronzed, gold-eyed Martians who abandon their neat Terran cities and the earthly cares and duty they symbolize, and run free in the mountains.

In one sense, this Martian transformation was forced upon the arriving agriculturalists by their daily occupations. Whereas a wheat-farming family relocating itself in the Central Valley, around Stockton in mid California, might expect to continue wheat-farming, those who went to Southern California could hardly hope even to try. Where water was available, Mediterranean crops made better sense and profit, olives, vines and—above all—citrus fruits, the first great source of wealth in Southern California after land itself. Horny-handed followers of the plough and reaper became gentlemen horticulturalists among their "groves and fountains".

The basic plant and crops for this transformed rural culture were already established on the land before the Mid-westerners and North Europeans arrived, for the great wave of westward migration broke across the backwash of a receding wave from the south—the collapsing Mexican regime that was in itself the successor to the original Spanish colonization of California. The two currents swirled together around some very substantial Hispanic relics: the Missions, where the fathers had introduced the grape, olive, and orange as well as Christianity, the military communication line of the Camino Real and the Presidio forts, the very Pueblo de Nuestra Señora Reina de Los Angeles de Porciuncula.

And, above all, a system of ranching whose large scale, open-handedness and al fresco style were infectious, and whose pattern of land-holding still gives the ultimate title to practically every piece of land in Greater Los Angeles. Most of the original titles granted by the kings of Spain and by the Mexican governors were confirmed by patents granted by the US after 1848 (often a long while after; land-grant litigation became almost a national sport in California) and thus bequeathed to the area a pattern of property lines, administrative boundaries, and place-names that guarantee a kind of cultural immortality to the Hispanic tradition.

So the predominantly Anglo-Saxon culture of Los Angeles ("Built by the British, financed by the Canadians") is deeply entangled with remnants of

Spain, and has been so ever since an early-arriving *Yanqui* like Benjamin Wilson could translate himself into a "Don Benito" by marrying into the Yorba clan, and thus into a ranching empire that spread over vast acreages of the east of the Pueblo. This ancient entanglement is still deeply felt, even if it is not officially institutionalized (as in the Spanish *Fiesta* in Santa Barbara, up the coast). It still provides psychological support for the periodical outbursts of pantiled roofs, adobe construction, arcaded courtyards, that constitute the elusive but ever-present Spanish Colonial Revival style, in all its variants from the simplest stuccoed shed to fantasies of fully-fledged Neo-Churrigueresque. Such architecture should never be brushed off as mere fancy-dress; in Los Angeles it makes both ancestral and environmental sense, and much of the best modern architecture there owes much to its example.

As this architecture shows, the mixture of Hispanic and Anglo-Saxon traditions could have provided the basis for an interesting culture, even if its economic basis had remained agrarian. But the Yankees were coming because they knew a better trick with land than just ranching it; they stormed in on the crest of a wave of technological self-confidence and entrepreneurial abandon that left simple ranching little hope of survival. Land was acquired from the grant holders by every means in the rule book and some outside it, was subdivided, watered, put down to intensive cropping, and ultimately offered as residential plots in a landscape that must have appeared to anyone from east of the Rockies like an earthly Paradise.

Whatever man has done subsequently to the climate and environment of Southern California, it remains one of the ecological wonders of the habitable world. Given water to pour on its light and otherwise almost desert soil, it can be made to produce a reasonable fascimile of Eden. Some of the world's most spectacular gardens are in Los Angeles, where the southern palm will literally grow next to northern conifers, and it was this promise of an ecological miracle that was the area's first really saleable product—the "land of perpetual spring".

But to produce instant Paradise you have to add water—and keep on adding it. Once the scant local sources had been tapped, wasted, and spoiled, the politics of hydrology became a pressing concern, even a deciding factor in fixing the political boundaries of Los Angeles. The City annexed the San Fernando Valley, murdered the Owens Valley in its first great raid on hinterland waters under William Mulholland, and its hydrological frontier is now on the Colorado River. Yet fertile watered soil is no use if it is inaccessible; transportation was to be the next great shaper of Los Angeles after land and water. From the laying of the first railway down to the port at Wilmington just over a century ago, transport has been an obsession that grew into a way of life.

Lines were hardly laid before commuting began along them; scattered communities were joined in a diffuse and unprecedented super-community, whose empty interstices filled up with further townships, vineyards, orchards, health resorts, and the fine tracery of the second generation of railroads—the inter-urbans. By 1910 when amalgamations and rationalizations had unified these inter-urban commuter lines into the Pacific Electric Railway, the map of its network was a detailed sketch for the whole Los Angeles that exists today. In part this must have been due to the way in which any major investment in transport tends to stabilize a new pattern more permanent than the old one which was disrupted by the investment, but it must have been at least equally due to the coincidence in time of the construction of the PE and a new phase of economic and industrial development.

In the decades on either side of 1900 the economic basis of Angeleno life was transformed. While land and field-produce remained the established basis of wealth, an important new primary industry was added—oil. Its existence had been long known from the natural seepages at the La Brea tar-pits in what is now Hancock Park, but commercial working did not begin until the mid-nineties and large-scale exploitation grew throughout the first quarter of the present century as new fields were discovered. Nowadays drilling rigs or nodding pumps are liable to be found almost anywhere on the plains or along the coast, and the olfactory evidence of the existence of the oil industry is as ubiquitous as the visual.

In those same years of the full florescence of the Pacific Electric, Los Angeles also acquired a major secondary industry and a most remarkable tertiary. The secondary was its port. There had always been harbour facilities on its coast, but the building of the Point Fermin breakwater to enclose the harbour at Wilmington/San Pedro from 1899 onwards was in good time to catch the greatly expanded trade promoted by the opening of the short sea-route from coast to coast through the Panama Canal after 1914. Within the breakwater now are a spreading complex of artificial islands and basins that constitute the largest man-made harbour in the world, clearing three billion dollars worth of goods a year.

And in 1910, the tertiary industry that sets Los Angeles apart even from other cities that now possess the same tertiary, was founded, when the first Hollywood movie was made in a barn at the corner of Sunset and Gower. The movies seem to have been the great imponderable in the history of the area; their economic consequences were undoubtedly great, but it was mad money that the film industry brought in, and in any case it is the cultural consequences that now seem most important. Hollywood brought to Los Angeles an unprecedented and unrepeatable population of genius, neurosis, skill, charlatanry, beauty, vice, talent, and plain old eccentricity, and it brought that population in little over two decades, not the long centuries that most metropolitan cities have required to accumulate a cultured and leisured class. So Hollywood was also the end of innocence and provincialism—the movies found Los Angeles a diffuse fruit-growing super-village of some eight hundred thousand souls, and handed it over to the infant television industry in 1950 a world metropolis of over four million.

Now all these economic and cultural developments tended to go with the flow of urbanization that the Pacific Electric both served and stimulated. Oil was

extended families of those faithful to UFOs and Scientology, and you can listen to soft Scientological rock on an L. Ron Hubbard radio station. There are those who converse in tongues and those awaiting a call from mail-order prophets who bless cripples and change the tires on their wheelchairs. The Mexicans live uneasily beside the blacks and the transplanted southerners and dustbowl refugees who have, in general and relatively, prospered. East Los Angeles College, where I once lectured, has a mainly black and brown student body. A professor of English, who had spent a previous career as an Army officer stationed in Germany, informed me: "This is not one of those fancy classic educations we give here. We teach them to fill out forms and put the commas inside the quotation marks and how to write the possessives. I want my students to make good cops, soldiers, and clerks. I want them to know how to use credit cards. They're good kids, and if I kick ass a little, they learn."

No, East Los Angeles College is not Harvard or Stanford, but when I spoke to these students about American literature, they wanted to know: Who are the great black writers and why? Who are the great brown writers and why? Where is the epic novel about how the Chinese worked the railroads that made this town prosper? Sir, have you read *Longtime Californ*, that anthology of Asian writing about California?

In the census of 1970, Los Angeles and New York showed great similarities as the commanding metropolises of the Pacific and Atlantic coasts. As ports and commercial centers they were comparable, and they came out about the same for population stability, educational levels, crime levels, numbers of doctors and dentists (more faith healers in L.A., more voodoo doctors in N.Y.), average family income (about $11,000 per year in 1970, before the recent inflation). The great difference was population growth and exchange. New Yorkers move to California, rarely the reverse. And nearly forty-five thousand people from New York City had moved to Los Angeles during the previous decade.

They were not going for the clean air or the tacos. They were not going for money, since Los Angeles is not richer than New York. They were going because it is still El Dorado, the golden promised land, to which Americans pay soul service. And the blue VW vans of the kids, and the piled-high Avis rent-a-trucks of the young families, still continued the trek westward during the slowed-down, less-prosperous, less-mobile seventies.

Near the campus of Short Hills Community College a middle-aged man in the uniform of a professor of the fifties, tweed jacket, pipe, neatly trimmed pepper-and-salt mustache (regimental in England, professorial here), was walking along the street at dusk with a toddler. He was smiling. The child could have been his grandson or his son by a second or third marriage. He was puffing his pipe and smiling and sharply cracking the child on the rear and legs while the child screamed and begged him to stop and alternately ran away (man caught up with him and gave him a harder swat) or clung to his legs, crying, "Please don't don't don't I promise," and there was a clawing jerk out of this embrace from below which seemed to enrage the smiling man and another hard crack. Before my eyes—cling and beg? run away?—I could see the child receiving an adult lesson in hopelessness. He had no chance.

I crossed the street and ran toward the two. I was a stranger in town. They belonged. The man looked up at me quizzically, took the pipe out of his mouth, and said in soft easy tones, "He has to learn not to run into the street. He crosses the curb before I tell him to."

The boy was hiccuping and sobbing at this respite, and staring at me. The only thing I could think to do was to stand there and watch. Still sobbing, the child toddled along beside his guardian. The man puffed his pipe and did not hit him. They turned the corner, and as they disappeared from sight, I heard a piercing shriek.

On that quiet suburban street there was chaos. There had always been chaos on that street, but now the man and his child made it visible. They had together even brought a bit of excitement into this clean, calm world—the child's hysteria, the man's sadism and pleasure made sweeter by his sense that it was a necessary discipline, the communication of energy which flooded me like sexual bliss. And since none of this could have a happy outcome, it was chaos.

In Westwood, near the University of California campus, even the beggars are stylish. A bum looked at my beard and jeans and said, "Are you one of them or one of us?" And another asked me not for whiskey or coffee, but: "Hey, Mister, gimme a quarter for a frozen yogurt."

Angelenos often have a large provincial sophistication about the rest of the world. They think big and they think possessively. In a real estate office in Westwood, the boom in property values makes the air vibrate with bizarre prosperity. Inner cities die, the barrio explodes with music from radios on windowsills, ghettoes burn, but Malibu, Westwood, Marina del Mar, Santa Monica inflate. A salesman who has earned "too much" this year—taxes—told me, "I gotta go to Europe in October. I've never seen that part of the country."

If you slide onto a Los Angeles freeway and drive and drive and drive, and then pull off the freeway, you might find something different from what you left. Or you might find another stretch of neighborhood, many canyons and hills and plains away, which is just like the one you left—palm trees, palmy breezes, swimming pools, gray photosynthetic air. It is written in a holy text: "Paradise is only for those who have already been there." To escape L.A., you may have to go there.

I remember when the dust bowl farmers of the thirties fled to California, their belongings heaped on their Fords, their faces drawn and embittered. Many of them grew rich on ranches which later became urban L.A. The grapes of wrath were stamped into wine.

I remember when the aging of Cleveland and Detroit and Chicago and New York decided, after the war, to strike out anew for the all-year garden cuddliness of Los Angeles. It was before the word smog had come into the vocabulary. Some of them died of emphysema; now, if they made their fortunes and have grown old, they have fled to Palm Springs, where little tendrils of smog follow them.

The air. How can we talk about Los Angeles, that basin of thermal anarchy, without the Smog? It provides a moral haze while it breaks down the lung tissue. The rich try to escape it by moving to Malibu or Santa Monica, or by climbing the hills; but smears and wisps follow silently after them, like werewolves, like Dracula, like the sins of Man, sucking at their lives. Shoeleather erodes. Eyes smart. School children are told on certain days not to play. The freeways snake throughout this world larger than many nations and the motors emit, emit, emit. Photosynthesis. Ozone. Inversion. The radio weather helicopters hover over the stalled rush-hour traffic and, between Scientology rock music and sweet whispers of laid-back true love, tell the world: "Air quality today not so good ... turn off your engines if you can ..." And the commuters are late because of an accident, jamming the freeway. Francis Gary Powers, once the U-2 pilot shot down over the USSR, the one who didn't use his CIA cyanide needle, who caused Ike to squirm and Khrushchev to bellow, died in the crash of a weather helicopter. Someone had forgotten to fill the gas tanks.

Sing a Song of L.A. air, that product which sometimes makes one want to be a minnow or a shark, living in a friendlier salt element. No wonder people smoke, drink, brag, and switch wives. And yet there are gardens growing, space in the alleys for flowers, poolside loungers—pools everywhere—old people, on Social Security, and young folks, starting out in life as post office clerks, who live in apartment complexes constructed around the pool.

When San Francisco was in a water panic due to drought, and angry with L.A. for the canals which divert its water southwards, and rationing water, friends from the Southland were telephoning long distance and playing the sounds of flushing toilets and giggling madly.

Society West, an attempt to authenticate for Los Angeles and its satellites the idea of an aristocracy, is a magazine filled with horse shows, news of formal dances for children, and flashes like: "Mort Ballagh sold his house in Trousdale and has taken an apartment in one of those high rises on the beach. It's a lot chummier ... Speaking of moving, I understand that Jack Hupp, realtor, has just sold a house in Trousdale to a Saudi Arabian for $800,000." The 10th Diamond Horseshoe Tie Ball was held in the Grand Trianon Ballroom of the Beverly Wilshire Hotel. The Ambassador of "Free China" was honored by the Americanism Educational League at the same time as the police chief of L.A., Ed Davis, was given the "Outstanding American of the Year Award" by the L.A. Philanthropic Foundation, also at a hotel meal. Carroll Righter, astrologer to the stars, was giving crisp advice to the readers of *Society West*: "Geminis, public charities are good outlets to bring you prestige. Moonchild, enjoy some very happy romantic moments. Be Happy. Scorpio, charm everyone by that special warmth that you so easily can turn on. Sagittarius, some very happy romantic moments." (Moonchild and Sagitarius might collaborate, it seems.) And Pisces? "Society interests are now excellent for you. Meet the finest possible persons."

In the same issue, Doug Gross and Stanley Garner are thanked for hosting "a Saturday night luau that was more Hawaiian than Hawaii itself. Some stayed at the party until dawn threw a pink frown across the forehead of the night." Rachel Anderson's poodle, Agnes Anderson, also gave a party. "Beware of Rachel, she can lick you to death, and almost did when her hostess gifts of pure red beef arrived." A Ms. Wonderful Award was given to Rita Hayworth. An artist is described with the words, "In the very near future his price will at least double or triple." Malibu Navy officers dressed in female Hawaiian garb for another party, "each a sight to behold." And Ruth Carter Stapleton, the President's sister, discussed her need for "Unconditional Love for All Humanity" at a conference sponsored by the Association for Holistic Health.

And that's just for November. But somebody seems to know what all this pure red poodle beef means, for buried in the newspaper is one more item, entitled, "Nostalgic Night in Old California"—"An Evening in Old California dinner dance, dancing, Mexican food, in an early California hacienda like Daddy's ... *All proceeds are directed to the Emphysema Foundation.*"

> Joke from Cyrano's on the Sunset Strip: "My wife ran away with my best friend, and I really miss him."
>
> Headline: MISS UNIVERSE ARREST
>
> Los Angeles (AP) November 9
>
> Miss Universe of 1961 was being held for $50,000 bail yesterday following her second arrest on a drug-related charge in a week.
>
> Police said Constance Meyer, 36, was arrested and booked for investigation of possessing cocaine Wednesday by Hollywood police she summoned to her apartment, saying she was being harassed by a former boyfriend.

Years ago, my favorite literary item from L.A. was the news in a Hollywood gossip column that "Natalie Wood will be playing the title role in the film to be made from the book 'Arma Gedden.'" There are real people playing the Apocalypse out there (starring Pock Alypse?).

"Are you a Pisces?" asked the woman gas station attendant. "Because I can't hack it with Pisceans."

"Could you check my oil?"

"You're really into checking your oil, aren't you? I'm a Capricorn. Only certain men please me. You're half a quart low."

"What do I need?"

She stared. "Like most men around here, you need to get your act together."

A sincere-type actress and model said to me at the Troubador, where she was looking for ... looking for ... looking for what might happen in a discotheque, but she had heard of this ancient, ten-year-old rock showplace: "I believe in karma, that's my religion, whatever you do comes back to you double or triple. If you rip people off, you get ripped off. but if you're just nice to people, they'll be wonderful to you. And you won't necessarily have to fuck them, but you'll want to."

The nearsighted bandit demands, "Stick 'em up! ... Are they up?" In the same way, the proud Angeleno announces, "You love it here, it's wonderful whole place! ... *Don't you?*"

Sometimes, driving in the rain down one of the older streets, the toy houses and decor make it look, through the working wipers, like the pages of a children's book, tattered and abandoned in a summer house. It could be real for the people who live there, but something nostalgic, sad, and colorful is emerging through the aging of Los Angeles. History finally begins to exist; or at least a wistful child's history.

The hood of my car flew up on the freeway. I pulled blindly off the road. I tied it with rope. I searched in low gear for someone to repair it. WELDING SHOP. I headed in. A bull-necked crewcut old man with huge mandible gloves said, "Naw, I don't do car work."

"What am I going to do?"

I started for my car. I was lost in a part of the Valley which was as far from home as any place I could imagine.

"Okay, let me get at that job," he said.

He welded a new catch onto the hood. He charged me a couple of dollars. I thanked him. After his griping and complaining that it was not his work, he said: "If you can't do a favor for someone, you might as well not do it."

"The favor?"

"You might as well," he said.

I understood the generous thought if not the language. The welder was a human being in his gloves and mask and asbestos armor; he was the knight guardian of my safety; I was a voyager in need.

Los Angeles pioneered Los Angeles-style architecture. The tautology conceals some moderate wisdom. This country is fantasy and need. So there are skyscrapers of glass and aluminum lining Wilshire Boulevard, the children of Bauhaus, and there also are drive-ins built like hamburgers, sundaes, ships, Japanese temples, and seraglios. People live in grand pianos, giant Hansel-and-Gretel huts, petit Trianons and Bavarian castles. What seems more authentic and sweet, the redwood spidery constructions sometimes found clinging to steep canyon walls, is really borrowed from that other state which we can call Northern California. The true architecture is horizontal, the freeway system. Pasadena has millionaire tracts, like Shaker Heights, Ohio. The Valley has Levittowns. Malibu has modified fishing huts for movie stars and electronic millionaires along the ocean. Bob Dylan built a two-million-dollar hideaway on the beach, with instructions that he wanted a living room large enough for a horse to canter through, but then had to debate proprietorship with his wife. Divorce ends most living arrangements down here, not death or horses. There is a tract, Brentwood, Truesdale Heights, some such names, where the houses are mostly Greek temples. I visited one where a sentimental New York producer of soft porn kept a floodlight between the Doric columns, shining on a Central Park bench kept in a cage, his pet memory.

An actor friend of mine puts his income into his house. Here a tennis court (spaghetti western), there a hot tub and Jacuzzi added to the swimming pool (taco commercial). Mud slides wear into his miniature eucalyptus grove. The native redwoods are disappearing. The eucalyptus, a handsome and useless tree, smelling strong and cool, was brought from the East with the thought it might be useful as wood. It is useful for pleasure; that's enough.

The widow of a famous actor rents out their house, and lives off the income in a palatial camper in which she cruises from estate to estate, until her dead husband's friends ask her to please park elsewhere awhile. She keeps hair drier, electric coffee maker, stereo console, a whole discount shop of appliances in her camper, and hooks up to the electric security gates. She has not yet decided what to do with her life. So far, she might write. She has written the first chapter of her autobiography, describing her sexual experiences before and after the funeral. One week makes an interesting story; I tell her, reading the manuscript, I'm not sure it's a full-length book. "What do you know about commerce?" she asks me.

The architectural spaghetti of Los Angeles—all right, call it bouillabaisse in elegant Westwood and Beverly Hills and Malibu—makes living there a form of desolate theater if you too are not a star. If all the world's a stage, and all of us merely players, what profiteth a man to be merely an extra? To drive a clunker, to live in a tract or decaying section of Hollywood if you're older than twenty-eight, does not feel marvelous. You are supposed to feel marvelous among the bougainvillea, the palms, the Mercedes-Benz, the expense account dining. (Sign on a Mexican restaurant: WE SERVE LUNCHO.) The sense of theater here is traditional. Nathanael West wrote that paper has been made to look like wood, wood like rubber, rubber like steel, steel like cheese. That was a generation ago. Alive now, he might report that hairdressers look like movie producers and, amazingly, it has become chic for movie producers to look like hairdressers, psychiatrists like surfers.

To avoid Forest Lawn, Nathanael West's ashes were scattered over the coastline. This great chronicler of the Los Angeles bizarre seems to have sprouted lots of little Westlings. Every Hollywood writer, during his period of unemployment, writes a Hollywood novel. During one of the writers' strikes, an ardent proletarian leader in cashmere sweater and tailored Dacs pounded his desk at a meeting and cried out the agony of the Workers: "My fellow craftsmen! I happen to know there are still writers in this town earning less than a thousand dollars a week!"

So if you are feeling marvelous and up for all this play, the Theater of Hallucinatory Reality makes every day a fantasy feast carried into reality, like a dream remembered, or more precisely, like a movie. Lives unreel on endless tape loops. A flat of a Paris café is knocked down, and Nevada appears behind it—fine! A man in a three-piece suit drives home in his native-born compact car from his law office, puts on his leathers and jumps on his BMW cycle and roars down the Sunset Strip—he has any life he chooses! Occasionally a volcano explodes, as one did at Pompeii; the depression in aerospace at Lockheed, or a no-hit year in the stock market, when the bankers rip out the rugs, tends to slow things down for a moment or two. A few private clubs or discotheques close. Others always open.

Los Angeles is in some ways the mobile version of Manhattan. There is a desire for richness, variety, pleasure, the invention of self in an image which will surely come clear some day. It is the place where the automobile is treated like the cow in India. It is also a holy place of the human spirit, as India is holy—holy for suffering, holy as devils are holy, damned by passionately stubborn and slippery will. Angelenos may not have read Goethe's *Faust*, but they are looking to make a deal with the devil. Every night can be *Walpurgisnacht*. Every man can dance with a witch, every woman find a sorcerer someplace (maybe only a tennis pro or a hairdresser).

"One always begins to forgive a place as soon as it's left behind," someone says in one of Dickens's novels. But I haven't left Los Angeles behind; I still go there; I don't have to forgive it. I have gone through my horror to find some love for this place which will never be a city. I found a welder who fixed the hood of my car although this was not his job.

Desert and mountain, sea and plain, splendor of landscape are preserved beneath the tar of industry and population. The portmanteau word "slurb" describes the post-urban ooze which flows over what used to be a tiny Spanish settlement. And yet, like the gypsy girl in Tennessee Williams's play *Camino Real*, Los Angeles seems to regain its virginity with each full moon. When the smog clears, and the mountains shine in the reflection of the Pacific, and hope springs eternal in the breasts of the orphan sons and daughters who came to California, choosing new names and identities and roles and futures—not so much making a new past for themselves, as liars might do, but simply wiping out the past—we are all virgins filled with expectation once more. We are a city of Angels, holding the demons at bay. And if any devils find their way through our protective network of highways, we can always solve the problem by naming them angels, too.

L.A. MINI SUPERETTE
Gas, Food, Tums
OPEN 24 HOURS A DAY!
(Closed Midnight to 7 A.M.)

143

San Francisco: The City That Asks If You Came

HERBERT GOLD

For an introductory note to Herbert Gold, see the previous Chapter 142.

The story is told that a Mill Valley video freak commune decided to make the bread for some new equipment with a little advanced, underground, commercial, sell-out short subject. Participatory democracy means you never have to say, "I'm sorry, I'd rather deal dope than rip off Allen Funt." So they dressed a woman in the compleat nun's habit and installed her at the San Francisco International Airport, where she was greeted at the gate for the hip, cheap midnight PSA flight from L.A. by a rabbi who began by chastely kissing her. The video crew filmed audience response as the rabbi embraced her sweetly. He put his hand under her habit. They began to struggle. She was gasping. Her cowl was knocked awry. Also his tie. They were both panting and biting, and his tongue was in her mouth, darting in and out, as she bent backward and eventually tumbled to the vinyl-marble floor, and they rolled around in an ecstasy of Welcome to San Francisco while the hidden cameras rolled. Allen Funt time in the counterculture. Tongues, zippers, cowls, pink folds and crevices undulating.

Well, the people streamed by without noticing.

Finally, one very straight citizen, maybe an insurance executive just in from a bit of desert sun, bent over the ecumenical thumping forms where they lay, tapped the pseudo-nun on the shoulder, and asked, "*Did you come?*"

Despite encroachments of smog from Oakland and high rises from Manhattan, San Francisco remains a name and place apart from other American places and names. Narcissistic, yes; but sexually narcissistic. Another American metropolis,

Source: Herbert Gold, "San Francisco: The City That Asks If You Came", *A Walk on the West Side: California on the Brink*, New York, 1981, pp. 48–67.

drilling subways, crowding highways, yes; but with a certain juice and languor to its making out and making do. The time of the flower children is over—partly because everyone believes in being turned-on now. The police joke with the whores as of old, they tease the transvestites, they laugh along with the tourists at the parade of post-Cockettes near the Castro Theater at midnight on weekends, they don't beat them up as much as they do in my ancestral Cleveland. There is a Polk Street bar called the White Swallow, located near Hard On Leathers and other shoppes and oases whose signals remain to be decoded. The jeans in the windows of the men's shops face the front with their backs. Perhaps the structure of that sentence is inverted, too. A friend, a proctologist, is writing a book about anal intercourse which should be entitled, *Above and Behind the Call of Duty*. (He sees lots of problems, and is thinking of changing his practice to dermatology or psychiatry—something more comfortable for his riper years.) Hip Sheriff Hongisto introduced a gay minister to serve the gay community in the county jail.

Police, real estate promoters, and big-city thugs are never quite Gilbert & Sullivan characters, or even lovable rogues from *Guys and Dolls*, but Veblenian marginal differentiation shows its power in San Francisco. So it's a big American city, true—but not just another big American city. Many visitors and transplants grind their teeth and hate it. It doesn't solve a fellow's problems. It can be a zap of mother's milk straight into the eyes, blindingly sweet. The Chamber of Commerce Tourist Bureau's gulls, cable cars, Golden Gate Bridge, and romantic fog tend to zap hometown kids straight in the liver, providing instant hepatitis, or at least a jaundiced gaze. The town is being stripmined for movie-of-the-week atmosphere. Disney discovers crookedest-street-in-the-world. The Ford Times borrows Picturesque Telegraph Hill. The Gray Line ships in busloads of chiropractors with aching backs for a dose of female impersonation (Finocchio's) or here's-where-the-stars-got-their-start (Purple Onion).

San Francisco is not Positano or Acapulco. They are tired, too. But despite media overload, despite its being fed into the great international media meat-grinder, and coming out Hilton Hamburger and Fisherman's Wharf link sausage, San Francisco remains something of what people have always thought about it. While New York and Paris seem to be yearning to become larger versions of Cleveland, and Cleveland is becoming Detroit, San Francisco remains mysteriously itself. This may last for our lifetime.

One day an old friend came to visit for the first time. It happened to be the season of the Chinese New Year, and the streets were filled with costumes, dragons, papier-mâché, firecrackers, and clanking bands dancing like segmented metal caterpillars. The day had been sunny and dry, with the parks occupied by easy strollers. I said this was a city for strolling, and we strolled. The Mime Troupe performed its guerilla theater, with a medieval pope portrayed by a beautiful male actress. A clone of Bobby Shields, the genial white-face, did his fantastic energy-raising acrobatics in Union Square. A time-lag rock band set up in the Panhandle for an audience of speed freaks who thought it was 1967 again.

It happened that night that my friend had a meal in one of the Italian family-style restaurants on upper Grant, along with a Japanese opera troupe, which rose after the spumoni to sing "Oh! Susanna" in Japanese, in order to show their appreciation. Then my friend fell into conversation with a pretty woman, who described herself as an actor and sex researcher. They discussed the theater. They discussed science. She said good-bye to the group she had come with and they went for a cappuccino at La Tosca, continuing their getting-to-know-you joint arias. Two cappuccinos on the leather banks of La Tosca. Little flutterings in the heart and elsewhere. She took him home with her that night.

The next day my friend asked me with a certain incredulity, "Is it always like this here?"

"Not every day," I was forced to admit. "On Sunday, for example, I drive my daughter to Sunday school. And Chinese New Year is over soon. Next month, I think."

But for some who come to San Francisco, Chinese New Year never ends, despite the alcoholism and breakdown rates, the busing and ghetto issues, the complacent hustle of city politics. It's possible to treat San Francisco as a continuous costume party, Halloween-by-the-bay, and amazingly enough—the flower-child spasm was partly about this—some manage to make of Halloween a way of life. It's not real, but it really happens. San Francisco is not authentic, but it would be genocide to say it isn't as it is. The market for antique funny clothes, outer-space brooms, and witches' brew, seems nearly inexhaustible.

Here is a birthday party at Sally Stanford's humorously posh New Orleans-brothel glass-and-crossword-Tiffany restaurant on the bay in Sausalito. The fest cost thousands. Young Lenny Norton, twenty-one, ex-car parker, was honoring his lawyer, Neil Murphy, dope lawyer, just turning thirty. Oysters flown west, steaks, girls in various stages of stoned and groovy silence, pink and chartreuse sweet liquids; and pilots, lawyers, groupies, coaches, rugby buddies, and even a few proud parents of the businessmen. Lenny's mom and dad, glad that their son the dealer could afford to spend a couple-three thousand on a little birthday party, walked about in their Macy's groove-clothes and said, "Yes, Lenny has a good head for business. Yes, Lenny bought us a little house in El Cerrito, plus some income property in Oakland. Yes, we're Lenny's mom and pop, man. Right on."

Lenny was wearing hotpants, full pancake makeup, dark red Cockette lipstick, and, resting on his skinny arms, the two girls he was planning to ball later. Sally Stanford herself, the ancient madam now playing at crone's career, beamed over the money she was making and poured champagne. A satisfying fiscal popping filled the air under the chandeliers.

I don't want you to think this chic orgy, with all the good food and drink and beautiful girls and men grown rich and dramatic in the dope trade was actually very rowdy and joyous. Everybody was too stoned to do much in the social line. But I enjoyed the fish and meat proteins and a cholesterol dessert. In the john two chauffeurs were discussing the virtues of Cessnas and Beechcrafts of various models in making the run up the coast from Baja. The Staff Headquarters of the Dope Air Force, a combination mercy and Mafia and general teenage rip-off operation, are in Sausalito. More planes than most nations with seats at the U.N.; the largest private air force on a war footing since Mike Nichols gathered his fleet for Catch-22. The unzipped pilots, relieving themselves of early champagne ballast, didn't stop their professional murmuring just because I happened to be standing there alongside. "What if I were a narc?" I asked the crew-cut one.

He looked at me and said to the other, "I think the radar screen just made it easier. They're overconfident." And he shook himself dry and free, twenty-eight, a veteran of Viet Nam, cool as Kool-Aid.

On the way out, a desperate group of tourists from a nearby table clutched my arm. They were ready to weep with frustration and desire. They watched a hundred freaks gobbling up caviar, French wines, steaks, oysters, cool, so cool, and these Latter-Day-Saint tourists from Salt Lake City felt that I, perhaps the eldest member of that crowd, was their last hope for salvation short of the return of bearded Joseph Smith. "*Who are those people?*" one hissed, his fundamentalist talons scrabbling against my corduroy jacket.

"The strike committee from Pacific Telephone," I said, and they nodded. They too always knew San Francisco would be like this.

No picturesque weirdness means that San Francisco escapes being an American city, with all the problems of an American city, while it also has some of the provincial, exempted charm of other hilly and provincial port cities, such as Leningrad, Marseilles, Naples, and Haifa, which live freed from the responsibilities of capitals—Moscow, Paris, Rome, Jerusalem—and therefore preserve something traditional, both highly colored by the sea and less hectic in the culture. Once, thanks to the gold rush, San Francisco had an intense hour in the sun. Mainland China Trade Stores have opened with soft commercial smiles in the wake of the various presidential China spectaculars, and perhaps San Francisco could have another gold rush if shipping and trade really begins to shuttle between the old opium states and the West Coast. Whether or not the town becomes Venice again, a window to elsewhere, it shares certain household frets in common with all other American centers—race, poverty, welfare, slums, freeways, school systems, smog, the resentments of Middle America, the rage of deprived America, the flight of money from the central city. It is not exempt from the times. Despite all the money, power, shipping, unions, major corporations, it's still consumer's easy garden city, a terrarium in America.

But gardens, as everyone knows, are filled with worms and other beasties. The green hides violence, red in tooth and claw. They fire at the President here. And Dan White, a disgruntled nice boy, ex-fireman, ex-policeman, ex-supervisor, crawled through a window of City Hall to murder Mayor Moscone and Harvey Milk, the homosexual supervisor. And was given a wristslap sentence by a San Francisco jury which found he was just a nice boy led astray by concern for his city, an I.Q. not equal to his aspirations, and overindulgence in Twinkies, causing sugar panic and psychiatric testimony.

The barker at The Condor in North Beach looks like the star of a teevee series pilot called "The Young Dentist," but on speed. He is skinny, sharp-featured, very fast, and suggests slurping eroticism while doing busy work with his teeth. His hair is as short as an Orange County football coach's, yet you don't see the scalp through it. He paces back and forth with methamphetamine rancor, chanting, "Come on in, organic sex! Sex is the best aphrodisiac! Come on in, all topless and bottomless college coeds!" He doesn't specify the school.

The Jesus people on the sidewalk outside The Condor are no longer shooting, sniffing, or smoking; they have found Jesus, or at least Pat Boone. They have long hair. Their complexions look up at their scalps reproachfully, if complexions could look, saying, *Shampoo a little.* Keep clean, a little shampoo isn't dirty. One is selling Jesus Now, with a headline: MOSHE FINDS CHRIST, LEARNS LOVE. "It's free, it's true," whispers a girl in a granny dress. She is thrusting the paper into hands which promptly litter. A long-haired young man, square wire glasses, like a lobotomized Harvard kid, is crying out with fixed Teutonic smile: "Abstain from filth!"

Meanwhile, he too is handing out leaflets which fall to the street from the nerveless fingers of tourists.

"Aw, knock it off," says the pacing Young Dentist. "I'm working this doorway, not you, kinds."

"Knock off this abomination!" cries the ambassador from Jesus-in-San Rafael. "Here, read the Truth as we learned it!"

The battle between the drag-em-off-the-street barker at the topless bar and the Jesus freaks. "Be saved by Jee-zuz!"

"Get some sex! It's organic!"

"Christ will save you!"

"For Christ's sake, get the fuck out of here!"

"Tell you what you can do for me, go across the street and let Jesus love the Garden of Allah."

It was a countdown between the short-haired businessmen selling sex and the long-haired freaky Christians selling salvation. Some leather-jacketed allies of The Condor gathered about the barker to consider extreme unction; that is, kicks in rear, shoves over curb. But in the typical distortion brought about by the media, the fact of my standing there, gaping like a journalist, changed history. They said, "Aw, fuck," and went inside to drink and enjoy bottomless dancing, not living up to their promise. The Jesus freaks eventually climbed into a blue VW bus and drove back to their commune in the Haight, where they get high on Christ and brown rice. They mix the traditions.

A few weeks later they were busted for housing runaways.

Heroin is still sold in adjacent doorways.

When I packed my wagon and hit the trail from New York in 1960, I had plans to spend a year in Friscoville, where there had been happy times on a visit in 1957—Alan Ginsberg, the Co-Existence Bagel Bar, Mad Alex the Talker, Bob Kaufman the poet ("Notes Found at the Tomb of the Unknown Draft Dodger"), my brother beatniks getting beaten around the head by Officer Bigarani on upper Grant. By the time I came to stay, the beat movement was frazzled away by a combination of media overload, changing times, and natural wear. Guitars were being traded in for washer-dryers, wine for grass, and the long somnolence which would suddenly erupt in 1966–67 (flower children, Haight-Ashbury, "we are the children of the beats") needed a certain incubation period. Still, doorways and chess bars were filled with patient dissemblers, awaiting the next call. San Francisco was a town in which no one had to decide whether or not to open the windows. good working. A host of lawyers, doctors, architects, post-analysands were deciding not to get rich but to get happy on the Bay. A nice place to idle away the rest of the century.

Then, around 1965–66 ... No, let's name the night. On the night when I heard the Jefferson Airplane in the Matrix on Fillmore—amplified? what's this? Speak a little louder, I can't hear you—it was clear that a new implosion had occurred, and explosion would follow. The cybernetic revolution had hit the beat guitar. It was as if every washer-dryer in the universe was churning out its Bendix slurp-and-roll. I was, I'll admit it—*charmed.*

The rest is the history of the micro-moment. The primal horde discovered Levi's. Old Kronos was dealing at the corner of Haight and Ashbury. Poster art became visual rock and roll; the youthquake become a market. Both Bechtel Corporation and the Greening of America industry had their headquarters here. Into the great media machine was fed the hope and dream of a time. "I'm not putting down the Viet Nam War," declared a retired activist from Berkeley, no longer interested in politics, tuned in, turned on, dropped out, and cured like beef jerky. "After all, Viet Nam brought us all together, so it was a real good thing."

And in the flash of a season, it was Mafia-hip, MGM groovy, a style for every college and big city in the country. A revolution, a fashion, and an industry all in one. The bands were no longer playing for free in the park, they were playing for fortunes for Bill Graham Presents. The Diggers stopped serving their buffalo stew in the Panhandle. Emmett Grogan wrote his memoirs for Little, Brown. Post-hip in San Francisco is like post-beat: there are still people in doorways, hiding out, waiting for the next movement. The town staggers along, looking for its next movement. There are those who swear that when it happens they won't tell anyone. But if they don't, will it be a Movement? Guru poets on the Great Highway, beating old coffee cans till their heads spin, expanding their consciousness and destroying their eardrums, are they really a Movement? One says, "I'm a Countercultural Biggie," and maybe he is, but the traffic whooshes by and not many stop to receive the message. The Jews for Jesus Country Western band chants its latest hit:

I knew Jesus
Before he was a Gentile

On Haight Street a strung-out speed-freak in dirty denims stopped a passer-by and invited him to her pad. "I may not be a flower child anymore," she said enticingly, "but come with me anyway. Have you ever had a real pig?"

No, she was not really a flower child anymore. Haight Street for awhile was a teenage slum; then a speed-and-heroin-real-estate hell, dropped all the way out. Now it is being revived as a Madison Avenue or Union street for unisex speculators, middle-class blacks, and a few fix-it young couples with adventure in their hearts.

The special story about San Francisco may be that it is a place to drop out while not absolutely dropping out. A former graduate student and mad bomber, fled to Canada after trying to end the war in Viet Nam by ending the Bank of America, now dwells at relative peace with himself in Bernal Heights. He confessed, regretted, returned, did a bit of prison, had his skull fractured in the showers by a patriotic felon, recovered, wears a steel plate in his head, and now works for Sparkies, delivering packages. He has a pretty wife. "That's not the way," he says about bombing. The urban-rural slum, an interracial community on the hilly slope of Bernal, now gives him a home. There are even unpaved streets, and chickens, and backyard gardens, plus coffee houses and theater groups and action art galleries. Despite his periodic headaches and dizzy spells, life isn't too bad. The doctor says he won't necessarily develop epilepsy.

A former hotshot editor, once quick and randy, now reformed, ecstatic, transformed, says calmly about his projects for the future: "I'll neither make plans for the future nor not make plans. I'll neither do things nor not do things. I'm learning about my body and soul these days, but I don't care if I'm really learning, either." His smile is beatific. His walk is smooth. His heart is pure.

A former Manhattan women's liberation activist has come to San Francisco and is losing the struggle against her sexist hang-ups. She still raises her consciousness at consciousness-raising meetings, and exchanges clitoral know-how with her sisters, but more and more she tends to regard her husband as a human being. She can't fight the town.

The habits of transferees from major corporations—insurance, banking, real estate, conglomerates left over from the great mergers of the sixties, advertising agency managers and media organizers—are known for a certain inevitable life direction. The pattern can be predicted. They arrive in their eastern J. Press or Brooks Brothers neatness, look around with hauteur at the gray-haired, long-haired groovers, and they swear on their honor: "Well, I won't wear the vest. I'll wear the three-piece suit without the vest. But that's as far as I'll go."

"Don't swear," I tell them, "it's impious."

Pretty soon some little State University of New York at Buffalo dropout, now waitressing at the Trident or MacArthur Park while she "gets her shit together," begins to recount her life story: "Neil broke my heart three weeks ago. Maybe, I'm not a woman, just a little girl, but my heart breaks, too. So three weeks ago, when Neil broke my heart, I decided—"

And Mr. Media Transferee is nodding, nodding, nodding. tell me more.

A few weeks later, as he sits there still nodding, he is telling Neil's ex-old lady "I chose a lower-paying job to live out here, because six months ago, when my wife broke my heart, I knew I couldn't stand that uptight scene anymore—"

It's the Sports Car Menopause all the way. What looked like the Groovy Horde, maddened flower ghouls and pagan flits, is now, in the flash of a season, just Standard American to Mr. Media Transferee. He may not have qualified as a card-carrying teenager in twenty years. That's no reason for not changing his life.

I speak with due diffidence as one of his spiritual cousins. I have lived in Cleveland, New York, Paris, Port-au-Prince, Detroit, and New York—a tipsy itinerary, I'll admit—with way stations in Havana, Key West, and Fort Bragg—and until I came to San Francisco, I always dreamed of eventually settling in Paris, the City of Light, where I had spent idle student and dreamy bohemian years. I would be a stroller on two sides of the river. In the capital of misery and the paradise of hope would I dwell forever, just like Villon, Carco, and Jean-Paul Sartre.

So when I arrived to pass a season in San Francisco, having sublet my flat in Greenwich Village, it was just to do a job. I was having a play produced at the old Actors' Workshop. Hmm, so this is Frisco, I thought.

Two weeks later I phoned back to New York and told my tenants to keep the place. I was staying. I left my clothes there so long they came back into style. My blue suit, fit only to wear at Stalin's funeral, is now just right for the midnight show, Reefer Madness, and the Cockettes' Sylvester's newest comeback stage presentation. I still have things in storage with various friends around Manhattan, though I now recognize the law which states that a loan for more than a year is a gift. Never mind those lampshades, Japanese prints, and wide pants, Marcus: they're yours.

Why? Why have I sold out Paris, abandoned Manhattan?

I'm trying to say it's fun here. The town has really succeeded in limiting high-rise development. The morning and evening tides really wash the pollution out of the bay, so that we dolphins can scream and swim in the chill waters. The TransAmerica Pyramid wasn't so ugly as I thought it would be when I harangued the Board of Supervisors about destroying North Beach. A few years earlier, in another great battle, I was co-chairman of the Anti-Digit-Dialing League, along with S.I. Hayakawa. Well, we've got nothing but digits now. You can't win them all. We voted a city-wide initiative against the Viet Nam War. We cleaned up the oil slick on the beaches. We are not a sweet garden separated from the real world, like Italy. It feels here as if we are living real life, only in a more advanced stage. Italy may feel the same way about itself and the habit of political kneecapping and murder.

For example, take Project Artaud and Project One, warehouses to the people. They were defunct real estate disaster areas, gloomy brick and space in perishing parts of the town. "What is valuable?" asked a few revolutionary innovators. Well, for one thing, bricks, space, windows, doors, rooms, roofs—these things we love. The gloom we can do away with. Artists need space, and so do galleries, filmmakers, literary magazines, free schools, consciousness-raising women's groups, revolutionary action societies, Zen meditators, musicians (especially rock musicians, who tend to shiver foundations and send neighbors to the emergency telephone); gropers and rappers need space, embryo feeling orgs need space—people need space. Dollars per square foot are real issues. Project Artaud formed a cooperative, including even automobile repair gurus in the courtyard, to take over the moribund buildings and give them to the people, spelled The People, at minimum rents plus occasional basic metaphysic sessions. This is countercultural real estate ferment, and it works. Project One followed Project Artaud, just as a few years ago, the *Free Press* followed the *Berkeley Barb*. Home organic food bakeries, yogurteries, leather connivers, all the enterprises of the countercultural ferment found an amiable environment south of Market in an old blue-collar, light-industry, heavy-trucking part of town. One winter they even had a reading by Yevtushenko, with mobs waiting to support a new concept in square footage.

When Project One became valuable, the owners decided to put out the artists and put in real people. It's a familiar story.

Countercultural San Franciscans sometimes think they are all of San Francisco, somewhat in the state of mind of the Dupont executive of the thirties, who refused to sponsor a Sunday afternoon radio program on the grounds that: "On Sunday afternoon everyone is playing polo." In fact, San Francisco is middle-class strivers, union people, dockmen, straight insurance clerks, Chinese and Japanese immigrants looking to make out okay, a large black and Chicano population—the usual mix of a great American city. All the minority of the turned-on do is what is most important: give the city its tone and reputation, its style in the breeze of the mind. The flower children, the traditional bohemians, and the polo players are merely the minority which sets the tone. Out in Daly City and South San Francisco, in the Sunset and the Richmond, there are the standard-sized okay Americans who attend services at the First Church of Christ Discounter (All Prayers Guaranteed) and think Ché Guevara was somebody's girlfriend. They are decent people who lead decent lives and read the *San Francisco Examiner*, flagship of the Hearst empire.

But a stroller, looking for other news of the city, might have found, say, the Physicians Exchange Pharmaceutical Service (PEPS) storefront office on Powell along the cable car tracks. Inside, instead of doctors or clerks, there were cots with freaks sleeping, a few drug house magazines, and nothing much happening. Every once in a while I'd hang around. They'd give me coffee and I'd feel so good. "Say," I might ask, "what are you chaps *really*—"

The shrugs were beginning.

"—really, really doing?"

The shrugs were continuing.

"Don't tell me, I don't want to know," I added.

"Okay, you're a friend mumble-mumble," they'd say. They were all lank, cadaverous young men with beards, like young Howard Hugheses fresh out of San Jose State. There were bunches of pencils in their pockets. They would write little things down, sleep a while, then write some more. They didn't speak much to each other, in the fashion of family, as if they communicated by smell and felt no need of conversation. They had the electronic genius look, and old laundry smell. They read *Mad Magazine* and the underground press, and only occasionally I noticed a ravishing pink blonde girl waking up on the cot in the back room.

"I didn't hear a word," I said in response to an explanation I couldn't make out.

Somehow it was nice to laze and gefuffle in that room, until one day it was closed and sealed BY ORDER OF U.S. MARSHAL and the beards and cots were gone. And now it's rented to a gift shop.

Who, what, where, why, how? Weathermen, underground press service, dope exchange, con rip-off freaks, kids playing send-away-for-samples? A pure exercise of style?

Really don't know.

Frisco days and nights. Paris used to be like this. I remember the pretenders to the throne of Holy Russia, printing posters, plotting their White revolution; probably they still have an office in Montmartre, three-generation refugees from Lenin.

Once I thought I saw the pink blonde girl on a cable car, but I couldn't catch her to ask what happened, where our friends were meeting now. She was rubbing her chin in the collar of her suede coat. Perhaps that was a signal to me. I rubbed my own chin in response, but she just rode the cable car up Hyde Street to the summit. Maybe I chose the wrong signal.

Who are those other ghostly figures walking down Russian, Nob, and Telegraph hills at dawn? Those samurai knights shrouded in mist are the stockbrokers, who must be at work by 7.00 A.M. to keep up with Wall Street. Due to the time change, when it's three o'clock in the morning in the dark night of the soul of Manhattan, it's only midnight in San Francisco. Bill Graham, now fifty, is an ancient San Francisco rock millionaire. Soon he'll be starting a new career, a new marriage, new family; watch and see. It's only midnight in the dark night of the soul. The girl from PEPS may be haunting someplace, too, waiting for the next federal padlock. (Or maybe she's hijacking a plane someplace, holding it for ransom, getting bills in small denominations and trying to decide whether to ask for the halibut or the roast beef dinner.) It does sometimes seem as if the heist artists have more style in San Francisco: the check-writer who keeps buying Bentleys (his psychiatrist says he has a Bentley fixation), the would-be rapist who rejected his victim at the last minute, morosely describing her as a ball-breaker. A woman named Gloria Something sued the transit authority, charging that a cable car accident transformed her into a nymphomaniac, and a San Francisco jury awarded her a judgment of $50,000 for her psychic wounds. Suggested headline: GLORIA SICS TRANSIT. Later a local porn producer made a film inspired by this tragic episode in the history of transportation.

The city is not immune to all the American troubles of violence, spite, and anomie. A young actress, raped at knifepoint in the hall of her apartment house, proceeded afterward to trudge upstairs to her flat, telephone her boyfriend, and say, "A funny thing just happened to me. We could use it in an improvisation ..."

Another well-known social lady had the following conversation with a rapist who invaded her house and forced herself and her children to parade nude in front of him:

RAPIST: (as she reported the conversation to the police) Gosh, you're beautiful.

LADY: Well, I'm a little overweight these days.

The rapist thought about it, then raped the maid while his accomplices held the family at bay. The rapist returned to the lady.

RAPIST: Would you like me to rape you, too?

LADY: No, thanks.

The rape team then gathered up a few baubles and left. The lady reported to her friends that the leader stopped raping the maid when his accomplices approached. "And I think that shows a glimmer of sensitivity in the man, don't you?"

I don't mean to imply that random violence, drug fiends, the assassination of political leaders, and sexual tensions are just cute in San Francisco. But they sometimes seem to be different. When I was slugged on the neck by a disappointed stock market investor, and knocked sprawling into Montgomery Street, his first question as I came up was why Fannie Mae, Federal National Mortgage, hadn't lived up to its early promise. It had gone up, then it went down, then up again, and now back down. How can you count on a stockbroker who recommends a stock like that? I wasn't a stockbroker, but I deserved to be hit because I couldn't explain it to him, either. I think it showed a glimmer of sensitivity in the man that he didn't stab me, too.

I didn't mind getting married, because my wife told me to go on walking in North Beach. It's good for the legs, wind, and cardio-vascular system, and therefore the heart; my soul is aired in fogs salted by the sea, peppered by human spices; and although not the same—I wasn't what you'd call *prowling* anymore—I took a new perspective on the tiny implosions of animus and entertainment in the Barbary Coast, the International Settlement, on Broadway, up and down Columbus and Grant where ghosts, shades, artists, tourists, pimps and would-be-pimps, dealers and dealees, marks and targets wandered the time-lag evening.

For example, Ken Rand, proprietor of the Minimum Daily Requirement café, had a little problem with the speed freaks, junkies, whores, two-baggie businessmen, runaways, and pouting poets who hang out without buying more than coffee. One evening he just got fed up with this near-albino lady, very ugly, about twenty-two; huge doughnut buttocks, whitish hair a little darker at the roots, complexion of blah and bump, about forty pounds overweight, poorly distributed. She looked like a girlfriend of Papa Boy Duvalier, I thought (I had just come home from a stroll in Port-au-Prince). She was talking too much, and she wasn't talking to anyone visible. Ken approached her with his neat, mustachioed suave (he attended various eastern schools and enjoys his scene with a certain Charles River hauteur). "All right, Marlene, you should go someplace else now."

She said, "Unh."

"Come on, Marlene, give us a rest. Let's move, Marlene. I'll walk you to the door."

"Unh." This was half of unh-unh.

He took her by the elbow, firmly, between several fingers, and urged her forward. She flounced. Shielding half the squeezed, puddled doughnuts, she was wearing some kind of semi-Bermuda shorts and bare feet. His pressure around elbow got through to her, because she was angry, but he walked, still gracious and smiling, as far as the door with her. Whereupon she turned, stared balefully out of eyes that could oink if eyes made oinks, and raised her sweater. Underneath there was nothing. That is, there was plenty, but nothing else. She took a breast and, still fixing Ken with that silent oink, lifted it between suddenly skillful fingers. And shot him a jet of milk straight between the eyes.

Ken closed the MDR and opened the Sand Dollar, a relaxed and elegant seaside restaurant in Stinson Beach, down the coast of Route 1 a few miles from North Beach.

I get up in the morning and now it's time once more to go where the city leads me. Now that I'm divorced, I can both stroll and prowl. A piece of strange is San Francisco.

Richard Brautigan is writing a poem about a girl with hair down to her ass, and everybody wants her, and there is Richard Brautigan, lonely with his brandy on the terrace at Enrico's, looking to find the girl he has just written about. The parade of girls with hair down to their asses passes.

I am an anti-guru. I too am sitting there alone, inspired by the sight of Richard Brautigan, but determined not to write a poem about girls with hair down to their asses.

SAN FRANCISCO ANTI-GURU POEM

The anti-guru
Stood on the mountain
Extended his arms to the masses below
    below
        below
            below
and cried
            cried
        cried
    cried
"Do not follow me!"

Washington D. C.

144
The Truths of Washington D.C.

JULIAN G. HURSTFIELD

Washington was always amusing ...
The Education of Henry Adams

The arts, you know,—they're Jews, they're left-wing—in other words, stay away.
Richard Nixon, the White House, 23 June 1972

Last night I watched the news from Washington, the capital ...
Jackson Browne, *Lawyers in Love* (1983)

1

Washington, District, Columbia: the words do not even sound like the name of a city, only an incongruous blending of monument, municipal subdivision, and a seemingly classical allusion (a reminder of Columbus, obviously, but also, perhaps, an intended comparison with Britannia).

The city's distinctiveness extends far beyond its name. Washington also defies customary notions of what an American city should be like. It lacks, for example, what that exacting student of American cities, Jane Jacobs, has recently termed their defining characteristic: it is not an "import-replacing" region.[1] It did not grow upon an economic base, and remains neither a commercial artery nor an industrial centre. Second, this is a city planned from its inception, unlike the haphazard sprawl of most other American cities. Planning may have been a commonplace of colonial and Enlightenment thought, but there is a geometrical exactness, a ruthless, rectilinear precision about Washington's streets, named with alphabetical and numerical correctness, the syllables increasing towards the north, as there is about its avenues, one named for every state, crossing, with crazy-quilt logic, the letters and digits of the grid. These constitute the "Lines or Avenues of direct communication" which the city's first architect, Pierre Charles L'Enfant, devised, "in order to connect the separate and most distant objects with the principal, and to preserve through the whole a reciprocity of sight at the same time".[2]

Source: Julian G. Hurstfield, "The Truths of Washington D.C.", *The American City: Literary and Cultural Perspectives*, ed. Graham Clarke, London and New York, 1988, Ch. 5. pp. 105–23,

Third, the city departs from the pattern of American urban politics. It lacked, until recently, home rule; its residents are unrepresented in Congress. It was not therefore worthy of Lincoln Steffens' investigations into *The Shame of the Cities* (1904). The only boss it ever had, Alexander Robey Shepherd, the friend and protégé of President Grant, was a boss in nickname only. An exception to the rule of Gilded Age politics, he was a resourceful, energetic, and honest civic administrator. He was a precursor of a more modern type of urban renewal expert, sending out one night a force of 200 men to tear up the entire line of the Alexandria and Washington railroad along Maryland avenue.[3] Since his time railroads have tended to observe city codes.

Fourth, this city—with the Mall, Cleveland Park, Rock Creek Park, Constitution Gardens, its small town atmosphere—seems like an accidental constellation of old villages, Georgetown, Capitol Hill, Foggy Bottom, whose pre-urban names suggest that this may be the most rural of American cities. Finally, and to the visitor, rather than the student, most important of all, Washington lacks one essential constituent element of all other American cities, what makes them individual, recognizable, unique. It has, by government edict, no skyline: the nineteenth-century city fathers prescribed exact, and still enforced, limits to the height of any building. The 555-foot Washington Memorial (1884) remains the city's tallest construction.

These are all different ways of expressing one central feature of the city: its rootlessness, literal and figurative. The concrete poured over a stretch of Virginia swampland, a populace whose most prominent members flit in and out at electoral fancy, the marked ambassadorial and journalistic presence: these all suggest the difficulty of locating a specific urban identity. And since it lacks the usual economic, political and topographical requisites, we may begin to ask what entitles Washington to be numbered among America's more revealing cities? It may be the nation's capital, but that sets it alongside Albany, Springfield and Sacramento rather than New York, Chicago and Los Angeles. And even as a political capital it is unusual. European capitals grew around a market, the head of a river, or a religious centre. But Washington, while it contains a National cathedral, and lies at the head of the Potomac River, is a relentlessly and exclusively political capital. Its English counterpart is not London, nor even the City of London, but rather the City of Westminster, with its attendant apparatus of Whitehall, Fleet Street and the Inns of Court.

Washington's business is the transaction of political affairs; and a part of its interest is that this is one of the very few American cities (New Orleans being perhaps another) where Americans themselves may share the foreign tourist's sense of being an outsider, a stranger. This is true today, but it was also true at the very outset, the foundation of the city, when office-seekers, influence peddlars and lobbyists flocked to the new city looking for jobs. And this in turn suggests a further interest in the city: that it is, palpably, the chief arena in which the American past and the American present intersect. Present-day politicians are measured against ancient standards; the monuments and memorials stand guard on the old virtues; and the homeless and the strays who today throng the capital, in unprecedented numbers, are but the descendants of those "straggling vagabond beggars, which the seat of government draws together", who had journeyed there from the start, making of it "the nation's poorhouse".[4]

2

Washington, we have been suggesting, deserves attention not because of its resemblance to other American cities, but its representative quality about American life. Before America even industrialized, this was America's first post-industrial city, whose chief activities were bureaucratic, administrative, financial, political. Thus one step towards understanding the city is the recognition that it was founded as the centre of power within a political culture profoundly hostile to the exercise of power, and of centralized power especially. Unlike the poor and the destitute, its permanent denizens, the actual office-holders went there reluctantly and stayed only briefly, to conduct necessary, often distasteful business.

It is amusing, in this regard, to find a series of recent authors, writing independently, announcing, as fresh insights, some of the oldest commonplaces of Washington life: to learn, from Alfred Kazin, that the city contains a "governmental medium that excludes lies, propaganda, misinformation, plain ignorance"[5]; to discern, with James Fallows, an increasing weight given to mere opinion-mongering[6]; and to locate, with Fred Barnes, a "new parasite culture in Washington"[7], feeding off not graft, the conventional form of political corruption, but expense accounts, book contracts, cable television performances, and, among government officials, the peddling of influence, or what has come to be known as "access", the contraband of a post-industrial world.

Techniques (and technology) may evolve. But we are hardly confronted by a revolutionary alteration in the city's life. Such writers are offering only a reminder of an older, familiar tradition of viewing the city. It was Mark Twain who, over a century ago, co-authored the novel which fixed upon this city, and that epoch, its lasting metaphor, *The Gilded Age* (1872): an era when high ideals and noble professions only masked (like the fashionably worn beards or, on the opposite sex, the costume jewellery) base, ugly, selfish and materialistic purposes. The novel's plot requires the pretended construction of a railroad for no other purpose than to float investments rather than accommodate passengers or freight. A generation later Henry Adams would astonish himself "by remarking what a purified charm was lent to the Capitol by the greatest possible distance, as one caught glimpses of the dome over miles of forest foliage."[8]

Henry James likewise saw in Washington a city whose sole activity was talk; and it was talk of a rather specialized nature, not the "direct communication" which L'Enfant had hoped would ease the nation's progress, but a rather more informal, less productive exchange, the conversation which easily becomes gossip:

> One had put one's finger on it when one had seen disengage itself from many anomalies, from not a few drolleries, the superior, the quite majestic fact of the City of Conversation pure and simple, and positively of the only specimen, of any such intensity, in the world.

It was, moreover, to James a city whose conversation was remorselessly self-obsessed: "It is about herself *as* the City of Conversation precisely that she incessantly converses; adorning the topic, moreover, with endless ingenuity and humour."[9] A generation later, H. L. Mencken would capture, in sonorous prose, the rhythms of a city which had long attracted a parasitic class:

> The secretary to the secretary to the Secretary of Labor ... the former wife of the former secretary to the former member of the Interstate Commerce Commission ... the press agent to the chaplain of the House ... the brother to the wife of the brother-in-law of the Vice President.[10]

And, for a contemporary view, Joseph Heller has exposed, in *Good as Gold* (1979) a Washington whose contradictions and absurdities update those he previously recounted in *Catch-22*: a speechwriter who cannot write (or know) the truth; a White House post of undiscoverable responsibility ("This Administration", the appointee is told, "will back you all the way until it has to") and a serious speculation that Dr. Kissinger may not be Jewish.[11]

3

Alongside its officeholders and placemen, the world of public relations and official spokesmen, Washington also offers, most famously, its monuments. These lend permanence to a city whose most public inhabitants have only a shifting, transient, temporary presence. And it is to these monuments that American poets and artists return when they wish to recall America's past, or Washington's present. Robert Lowell understood the promise that the capital, untarnished, once offered the world: "On the circles, green statues ride like South American liberators above the breeding vegetation—/ prongs and spearheads of some equatorial backland that will inherit the globe."[12] Allen Tate likewise sensed the descent the city had fallen from classical grace:

> *I stood in the rain, far from home at nightfall*
> *By the Potomac, the great Dome lit the water*
> *The city my blood had built I knew no more*
> *... I thought of Troy, what we had built her for.*[13]

The city of monuments, and the city of politics—with its associated journalistic, public relations retinue—have recently met. Washington's earliest memorials—the Washington Monument (1884), the Lincoln Memorial (1922), the Jefferson Memorial (1938)—were all completed at some distance from their subjects' lifetimes. Briefer interludes now elapse, and a more faithful contemporary verdict may be recorded. The city now contains the John F. Kennedy Center for the Performing Arts (1971) which all too accurately reveals the overarching ambitions (and, a critic might add, the slim performance) of its namesake. But the city also holds the Martin Luther King Memorial Library (1972) whose site, in a low-income shopping district, and whose simple, unadorned design no less accurately reflect its namesake's democratic hopes and educational faith. But above all, or rather beneath all—as it is carved into the very soil of the city—lies the Vietnam Veterans War Memorial (1983).

Of all Washington's monuments and memorials, this may be the most democratic. A historian has to reach back to the turn of the century, and the cult which then arose around General Grant, to find a comparable burst of popular activity. Purchased through public subscription, designed by the youthful winner of a competition open to all architectural students, this memorial evades the establishment aura of all the others we have considered. Yet, as Charles Griswold has shown, it also supplements and completes them; and it does so with a formality and a seriousness which forbid the kind of easygoing, touristic festiveness which the others, for all their grandeur, invite.[14]

It consists of two walls of shiny, black granite, set at an angle which points the rims towards the Washington and Lincoln monuments. Carved into the marble are the names of the 58,132 Americans killed in Vietnam: not alphabetically, but chronologically, beginning and ending in the same place. It is a capsule history of the most telling American aspect of the war: its human cost. But also it acts as a reminder of a frequently neglected feature of war. As we look at the names we also see, gazing back at us, reflected in the polished marble, ourselves. We witness ourselves in the act of witnessing, and are prompted to consider the democratic seed of governmental policy, the final, and in the United States also the earliest, responsibility for governmental actions. Two decades before the memorial was completed, Robert Lowell had warned us, in a different Washington context: "We cannot name their names or number their duties."[15]

Washington's monuments have this habit of recalling to their observers ancient and often neglected truths. It is for that reason that Henry Adams, in *Democracy* (1880), has his party of visitors make an excursion to Mount Vernon, moving his idealistic heroine, Mrs. Lightfoot Lee, to remark:

> Why was it ... that everything Washington touched, he purified, even down to the associations of his house? and why is it that everything that we touch seemed soiled. Why do I feel unclean when I look at Mount Vernon?[16]

American filmmakers might have been expected to exploit the artistic opportunities afforded by such a landscape. Yet, for all the political melodramas and espionage tales set in the capital, only one film by a director of the first rank has successfully employed this setting as something more than background scenery. In *Mr. Smith Goes to Washington* (1939), Frank Capra incorporated the sights of Washington within a consistent and serious vision of the capital's life. The past is ever present: in the character's names, Jefferson Smith and Joseph Paine; in a backdrop which continuously issues judgement on the action of the plot (a two-day tour of the capital, which occupies three minutes of the film, amazes its innocent hero with the extent of American history); and above all within the narrative itself: of a narrowly won victory of moral integrity over political corruption, secured only with the inspiration of the city's icons, and the (hastily crammed) precedents of the Senate.

Again and again Capra, and his screenwriter Sidney Buchman, emphasize Mr. Smith's understanding of the spiritual authority of the city's landmarks. On his first visit to the Lincoln Memorial, Smith notes Lincoln looking down at him, "just waiting for someone to come along". He will return there to summon up the courage to conduct a Senate filibuster on behalf of an honest cause, as well as to rescue his own integrity. Mr. Smith, the fire-fighter, the Boys Club hero, is alone among the characters in the film in possessing an intuitive belief in the inspirational worth of his country's history, a populist faith in its perceived traditions.

Yet while it may once have been fashionable to disparage Capra as a sentimentalist, we should note that this is not an optimistic film. It does not end on a happy note. A small, personal victory has been won. But there is no suggestion that the political system has been purged of corruption, or that the Montana bosses (who murdered, twenty years earlier, Senator Paine's father) have been dislodged from power. On the contrary, the view has been returned, at the film's end, to a darker and more familiar understanding of Washington.

For the Senate, not for the first time, is in turmoil; but its proceedings, though shaken, show no signs of reform. And the viewer's mind may go back to the closing pages of *The Gilded Age*, where a similarly convulsed Senate soon resumes its proper business:

> ... the President's salary was proposed to be doubled and every Congressman paid several thousand dollars extra for work previously done, under an accepted contract, and already paid for once and receipted for.

Similarly at the start of the film, when Mr. Smith vows "never to do anything to disgrace the name of the Senate", there is a distant echo of Mark Twain's ironic comment, from the lips of an earlier fictional Senator, that a disgraced and corrupt Senator's continued presence would not "contaminate the Senate to a dreadful degree".[17] And finally, if we have understood the film correctly, its unsettled and unhappy conclusion will only bring to mind the sad, disillusioned departure from the city of Henry Adams' heroine in *Democracy*: "The idea of my purifying politics is absurd."[18]

4

Henry Adams has a distinct place within Washington's history, owing to his residence there during the last four decades of his life: a living, rather than monumental reminder of the Founding Fathers, a breathing reproach to the current generation of politicians. As he remarks in his *Education*, "The progress of evolution from President Washington to President Grant, was alone enough to upset Darwin."[19]

It was in Washington that he wrote his account, based on personal observation, of the capital's life during the Secession winter of 1860–61; his journalistic investigations into Gilded Age corruption[20]; his historical researches into the more distant epoch of the presidencies of his grandfather's and great-grandfather's rivals[21]; and his fictional account, in *Democracy*, of Gilden Age morality, in which the reader may learn, from Baron Jacobi, the Bulgarian minister, an unnerving prediction of the climate which would overwhelm the city in a century's time, that is, during its recent past:

> I do much regret that I have not yet one hundred years to live. If I could then come back to this city, I should find myself very content—much more than now. I am always content where there is much corruption, and ... the United States will then be more corrupt than Rome under Caligula; more corrupt than the Church under Leo X; more corrupt than France under the Republic![22]

Here too, Adams maintained, across from the White House, on Lafayette Square, an intellectual and social salon to rival and rebuke that of successive presidents. His *Education* discloses little of this life, the alternative culture, as it might seem, which shadowed official Washington. But we do possess, in Henry James's short story "Pandora" (1884), a portrait of a Washington aristocrat who tells his wife, as they draw up their guest list, "Hang it ... let us have some fun—let us invite the President."[23]

Adams, one of the last direct descendants of the Founding Fathers, left no heirs. But he has had successors, or claimants to his lingering eminence: Robert Lowell, for example, last of a very different Massachusetts dynasty and no less burdened by his distinguished ancestors, was awed, during 1967's protest march on the Pentagon, by "... the too white marmoreal Lincoln Memorial, the too tall marmoreal Washington obelisk ... the too long reflecting pool"[24]; or Lowell's companion on the march, Norman Mailer, whose resemblance to Adams, in his awareness of historical forces as well as in his occasional use of the third-person narrator, inside and outside the events he describes, seems clear, though never directly acknowledged by Mailer. On the eve of that same march, Mailer stayed at the Hay-Adams hotel, the two conjoined red-brick houses H. H. Richardson had built for Adams and John Hay; and he pondered, for only half a sentence, "if the name of his hotel bore any relation to Henry".[25]

But Adams has acquired a more consistent, and more self-conscious, contemporary heir. "I cannot remember", Gore Vidal has written, "when I was not fascinated by Henry Adams."[26] Like Adams, Vidal has written history, fiction, essays. Like Adams, he has written pseudonymously about Washington life: a detective mystery, *Death before Bedtime,* which obeys the conventions to the extent that its solution depends not on the public, political activities of its characters, but the exposure of their domestic intrigues.[27] Like Adams, Vidal maintains an aloof distance from the sources of power, and a disdain for its wielders.

Vidal has referred to Washington as his "native city"[28]; and an early short story, "A Moment of Green Laurel" (1956) does convey the atmosphere of Rock

Creek Park (where, earlier, Adams had been enraptured by "the brooding heat of the profligate vegetation, the cool charm of the running water"[29]). This story also demonstrates, as a middle-aged man confronts an incarnation of his younger self, the familiar Washington interaction of present and past.[30] Above all, Vidal resembles Adams in his uneasy relationship with history, especially the history Washington embodies.

Vidal has called himself America's "current biographer".[31] He has referred to the "national amnesia", which dissolves the distinction between history and fiction: the politician "can reinvent himself every morning".[32] And against this he has attempted, through a sequence of historical novels, all set in or around Washington, to propose an alternative reading of official American history. Together they suggest a direct, if illicit line of succession from the disgraced Aaron Burr, Washington's protégé, Jefferson's rival, Hamilton's foe, down to the Kennedys: a descent followed through a series of deceits, each generation unravelling the secrets of its predecessor. These secrets range from eighteenth-century cabinet intrigue through Victorian hypocrisy to modern corruption. They encompass illegitimacy, adultery, bribery, fraud, insanity, a rumour of incest, a suggestion of murder. Vidal, the stepson of Hugh D. Auchincloss, whose mother was a descendant of the Burrs, himself belongs to this cadet line as surely as Henry Adams was the last member of the senior line.

Vidal's *1876* (1976), a Gilded Age novel to place beside *The Gilded Age* itself as well as *Democracy*, captures, like its models, the mingling of private and public corruptions, as the heroine's murder of her friend mirrors the Republican Party's crushing of reform. This is also the novel in which Vidal first resurrects Adams' Baron Jacobi. Before that, in his play *An Evening with Richard Nixon* (1972) he used the president's own words, from the public record of a lifetime in politics, to condemn him, not with ridicule but with verifiable facts. One scene records Nixon's studiedly informal meeting with war protestors one night in 1970 (after the Cambodian invasion) at the Lincoln Memorial—that same memorial which had once inspired Mr. Smith: "Have a good time in Washington," the President told them, "and don't go away bitter."[34] Vidal was thus a happy choice to examine the literary merits (which were slight) and the political significance (which was great) of the pseudonymous espionage novels of the convicted Watergate burglar, and Washington habitué, E. Howard Hunt: and an appropriate literary figure to enquire, as a result of his examination, whether "during the dark night of our empire's defeat in Cuba and Asia the American story shifted from cheerful familiar farce to Jacobean tragedy—to murder, chaos?"[35]

5

Jacobean tragedies, composed at the very moment of America's first colonization, hinged on conspiracies. These were often obscurely motivated and incompetently conducted; they tended also to have unfortunate consequences for their members. This is not the occasion to explore in detail the nature of the Watergate affair, an event of national (and international) rather than merely civic importance. But we may parenthetically note that the series of events which followed the burglary attempt, on 17 June 1972, at the Democratic Party's headquarters in the Watergate apartment complex—named for another monument, the nearby ceremonial steps, completed in 1932, which lead to the bank of the Potomac—has not ended. Speculation and rumour were not stilled, they may even have been quickened, by President Nixon's resignation in August 1974, and his speedy pardon, for offences as yet undisclosed, by his successor. A steady, though unbalanced diet of interpretation has ever since been fed to the curious.

As late as 1976 the journalist Renata Adler, a member of the House Judiciary Committee's impeachment inquiry staff, could avow that the undisclosed secret of Watergate was a consistent pattern of South Vietnamese bribery of the American president.[36] As late as 1984 an investigative journalist, Jim Hougan would publish a book, *Secret Agenda*, which documented the intuitive suspicions of earlier observers, that the C.I.A. had played an active not an accidental rôle in the affair, concealing domestic activities prohibited by law.[37] And as recently as May 1986, a Washington journalist, Christopher Hitchens, could propose that the real purpose of the break-in was to discover what damaging material the Democrats might possess on corrupt links between the Nixon administration and the Greek junta.[38]

The mysteries and secrets endure. But for our purposes it is the overall atmosphere, thick with Washington culture, which impresses. When honour and integrity were banished from the White House, they slipped into other, unlikely quarters: a specially convened Senate committee, or the House Judiciary Committee. Walt Whitman had seen how this could come about, in the bleakest days of the American Civil War, in a besieged capital:

> One is not without impression ... amid these members of Congress, of both the Houses, that if the flat routine of their duties should ever be broken in upon by some great emergency involving real danger, and calling for first-class personal qualities, those qualities would be found generally forthcoming, and from men not now credited with them.[39]

More than a generation later, Henry Adams who had already, in *Democracy*, glimpsed a future which might include Watergate, also foresaw the growing popular revulsion at the mounting evidence of Nixon's guilt. Adams had had, he recalled in the *Education*, a similar experience while scrutinizing British duplicity during the Civil War: "...there could be no sense in history unless a constant course of faults implied a constant motive."[40] And Henry James, recalling Washington as the "City of Conversation", might not have been surprised to learn that it was precisely through the recording, and publication, of certain conversations, public and private, that a President had been brought down. He might, however, have been startled at some of the language.

But Watergate has other dimensions, which bear more directly upon the city's life. Consider the following sequence of events. Two journalists, working for the metropolitan pages of the *Washington Post*, win a Pulitzer prize for exposing the activities of a corrupt president. A book recounting their early successes, is later made into a film. One of them marries a journalist, and they raise two sons. But the father has embarked on an affair with (and here the Jamesian echoes pound the ear) the wife of the British ambassador. The marriage collapses, and the wife writes a novel whose protagonists are barely disguised. The novel is about to be made into a film, when the father's lawyers intervene. On 26 June 1985 the author of the novel, and the screenplay, files "Attachment A to the Marital Separation Agreement between Nora Ephron and Carl Bernstein" in the Superior Court of Washington D.C. It announces that "The Book and the script ... are fiction." A pseudonymous columnist for *Vanity Fair* meanwhile compares that author's artistic treatment of her children's lives to "child abuse".[41]

That is one trail out of Watergate, into a polite, genteel, elegant society, whose secrets and intrigues would not surprise any of the nineteenth-century authors we have been considering, any more than the teasing mixture of fact and invention, the multi-media quality of the affair, would puzzle a contemporary structuralist critic. It is of course precisely at this world that another pseudonymous correspondent for the *Washington Post*, "Miss Manners", addresses her regular homilies on polite behaviour, stressing, to an apprentice aristocracy, the traditional bourgeois virtues of correct form, decorum and civility.[42] Cities are, after all, where one is "civil". But Watergate also opened another path, an indirect one, into a very different quarter.

On 28 September 1980 readers of the *Washington Post* were informed that living in the nation's capital was an 8-year-old heroin addict, "Jimmy", fired up, each morning, by his mother, or her lover, or some friend, "sending the 4th grader into a hypnotic nod". The sensational nature of this story, published under the title "Jimmy's World", and the care which had gone into reporting it, won for the newspaper a second Pulitzer prize. But the story was, like so much in and out of Washington, a fiction. The journalist had not only invented "Jimmy", she had also, with the sure instinct of a modernist writer, invented herself. She had faked her own resumé in order to obtain her job at the *Post*. She now had to return the Pulitzer prize in disgrace.

"Jimmy" never existed. But his world may. When the accuracy of the story was initially questioned by one member of the Pulitzer Board, he was told, by the associate editor of the *Washington Star*, that this was a familiar tale: a "Jimmy" could be found within ten blocks of where the Board was meeting. The damage the journalist inflicted was by rendering as fact what was fiction: an old Washington custom. She would later claim that "Jimmy" was a composite of several drug users.[43]

So perhaps these two strands, reaching into two distinct regions, apparently two worlds, are not so far apart after all. As Sissela Bok has reminded us, in her study of *Lying*, the Watergate journalists themselves engaged in their own species of deception: people being questioned were told, falsely, that others had already revealed certain information which now only needed to be confirmed; one reporter impersonated a campaign official on the telephone; the other lied to his secret informant, known as "Deep Throat", in order to corroborate a fact which was dangerous to reveal; and the *Washington Post* repeatedly ran stories on inadequate evidence.[44]

6

In all this the actuality of the lives of the black residents of Washington—who have constituted its majority since at least 1959, longer than in any other city[45]—risks being lost. We cannot, at the close of a brief essay, even attempt to do justice to residential Washington in the same detail as monumental or political Washington. We can, however, note how faithfully it echoes the hidden, secretive quality of Washington as a whole. There are entire tracts of the city which will remain forbidding to the tourist or the mere observer—places with names like Kalorama (Greek for "beautiful view"), or Anacostia, on the old Indian settlement of Anaquashatanick.

The residential history of Washington defies condescension, though it suffers, outside the city, from a lack of interest. It possesses many honourable moments, from the time of its site as a centre of abolitionist activity within a slave South, a haven for free blacks, to the symbolic power of Martin Luther King's address on the Mall in August 1963. Its citizens have offered hospitality to Coxey's Army (1894), to the Bonus Marchers (1931), and to countless Vietnam veterans on their pilgrimage to their own memorial.

Yet the residents themselves remain elusive, sometimes forgotten, often excluded. When the Federal Writers' Project produced its guide to Washington in 1937, it included several references to discrimination against blacks, and to their current reduced state. Such references had been evicted when the second edition appeared in 1942, in the thick of an anti-Nazi crusade.[46] Honourably reversing this process the city's leading historian, Constance McLaughlin Green, supplemented her great history of the city with a third volume, entirely devoted to its black population. This she entitled *The Secret City*.[47]

This term, the secret city, was first employed to describe black life within the capital by an anonymous writer in *Crisis* in 1932 and, as Professor Green remarks, it never entered popular use.[48] Yet it serves admirably to portray that hidden, unapproachable quality which has long characterized not the black community alone, but the pattern of white behaviour towards it, through all the years of indifference and neglect, the imposition of segregation and the construction of ghettoes.

But the idea of secrecy has an even larger use. Outside the black community it also seems an appropriate civic theme. Secrets are, almost by definition, what are important, to individuals as to cultures; and any serious exploration of Washington must in time turn away from those deceptively open spaces and tangible memorials, however inspiring, and search out hidden, obscure, and sometimes deliberately concealed meanings. Mr. Smith is, in this sense, Everyman. But these secrets may often be very carefully guarded, as one final illustration, drawn from the modern period, will suggest.

St. Elizabeth's Hospital, on Nichols Avenue, was established in 1855 as the Government Hospital for the Insane. During the Civil War it became a Union Army Hospital, whose commanding officer was for a while General Joseph Hooker. Here he rescued a most undistinguished military career (the defeat at Chancellorsville) and earned immortality, or at least a place in the American language, by developing previously unsuspected talents at procuring. Among its many other distinctions, Washington had the first prostitutes to be known as "hookers", the comforters of stricken soldiers. These wounded men also had, we may suppose, a rather different visitor, Walt Whitman, whose war years were passed mainly tending the sick in Washington's freshly converted hospitals ("I am in the habit of going to all"[44]), Patent Office, Finley, Campbell, Carver, Emory, Harewood, Mount Pleasant, Armory Square, Judiciary. The entire wartime capital must have seemed as much a sanitorium as a command post.

Eighty years later, St. Elizabeth's would house another distinguished American poet, this time as an inmate. In 1946 Ezra Pound was judged insane, and thus incapable of standing trial for the treason charges which the government had brought against him for his wartime broadcasts from Fascist Italy. These broadcasts offered, incidentally, an eerie mirror-image of President Nixon's later, private reflections. While the President counselled his chief of staff against "the arts", which were "Jews ... left-wing", the artist, thirty years earlier, had warned his countrymen against "the sub-jew in the White House".[50] So Pound spent the following twelve years in the hospital, safe from prosecution, the host and correspondent of writers and scholars, but otherwise uninterrupted in his literary work. It was, nonetheless, regarded in some quarters as an affront and an injustice thus to incarcerate a man whom many considered America's leading poet. A campaign was opened to secure his release. Through the petitions and the publicity secured by such as T. S. Eliot, Ernest Hemingway, Robert Frost, and above all Archibald MacLeish, the government dropped its charges, and Pound was released, free to return to Italy. A major psychiatric injustice had been undone.

Or had it? That was undoubtedly what was believed at the time, and for many years since. Then in the early 1980s two researchers, working independently on separate projects,[51] discovered from government records and medical files what might have been suspected all along. Pound had never been insane. His confinement had only ever been a ruse to escape prosecution. He was protected by Dr. Winifred Overholser, Superintendent of St. Elizabeth's, against the weight of medical opinion that Pound was competent to stand trial. And, in time, his release was championed by Archibald MacLeish, a former Librarian of Congress and devout anti-fascist crusader. Washington saved Pound.

His was only a temporary residence in Washington. But Pound does resemble its more established inhabitants, as they in turn resemble the other, even more shadowy, transient figures we have considered, invented and historical, pseudonymous and anonymous–the lobbyists on Capitol Hill, the miscreants of Watergate, the perpetrators, real, fictional, and metaphorical, of "child abuse", the plumbers, moles, investigators, adulterers, and informers, "Deep Throat" and "Jimmy", the prisoner of the White House and the prisoner of St. Elizabeth's–but also those rows of named, but still barely known, war dead at the Vietnam Memorial. They are all alike in one regard. They have retained their secrets. It is a Washington tradition.

Notes

1. Jane Jacobs, *Cities and the Wealth of Nations* (New York, 1984).
2. "Inscriptions on the Plan of the City" (1791), transcribed by Elizabeth A. Kite, editor of *L'Enfant and Washington, 1791–1792* (Baltimore, 1929), and reproduced in David T. Weimer (ed.), *City and Country in America* (New York, 1962), p. 22.
3. Frederick Gutheim, *The Potomac* (New York, 1949, repr. Baltimore, 1986), p. 342.
4. James Sterling Young, *The Washington Community, 1800–1828* (New York, 1966), pp. 25–6.
5. Alfred Kazin, "In Washington", *New York Review*, 29 May 1986.
6. James Fallows, "The New Celebrities of Washington", *ibid.*, 12 June 1986.
7. Fred Barnes, "The New Parasite Culture of Washington", *New Republic*, 28 July 1986.
8. *The Education of Henry Adams*, ed. Ernest Samuels (Boston: Houghton Mifflin, 1973), p. 282.
9. Henry James, *The American Scene*, ed. Leon Edel (Midland Books, Indiana University Press, 1968), pp. 341, 343.
10. H. L. Mencken, "People and Things: 1. The Capital of a Great Republic", *Prejudices, Fourth Series* (New York, 1924), pp. 294–95.
11. Joseph Heller, *Good as Gold* (London, 1979); the quotation is on p. 201.
12. Robert Lowell, "July in Washington" in *For the Union Dead* (New York, 1964), p. 58.
13. Allen Tate, "Aeneas at Washington" (1933) in *Collected Poems 1919–1976* (New York, 1977), p. 68.
14. Charles I. Griswold, "The Vietnam Veterans Memorial and the Washington Mall: Philosophical Thoughts on Political Iconography", *Critical Inquiry* 12 (Summer 1986), 688–719.
15. See above, note 12. See also, for comparable responses to this particular memorial, William Hubbard, "A meaning for monuments", *Public Interest* 74 (winter, 1984), and *New Yorker*, 14 July 1986, pp. 19–20.
16. Henry Adams, *Democracy* (Signet, New American Library, 1961), p. 82.
17. Mark Twain and Charles Dudley Warner, *The Gilded Age* (Meridian Classic, New American Library, 1969), pp. 414, 413.
18. Adams, *Democracy*, p. 185.
19. *Education of Henry Adams*, p. 266.
20. These have been collected as Henry Adams, *The Great Secession Winter of 1860–61, and Other Essays*, ed. George E. Hochfield (New York: A. S. Barnes, 1958).
21. Henry Adams, *The History of the United States during the Administration of Jefferson and Madison* (1889–91), now available in the Library of America series (1986).
22. Adams, *Democracy*, p. 48.
23. Leon Edel (ed.), *The Complete Tales of Henry James*, vol. 5, 1883–84 (London, 1963), pp. 357–412; the quotation is on p. 383.
24. Robert Lowell. "The March", *Notebook 1967–68* (New York, 1969), p. 27.
25. Norman Mailer, *The Armies of the Night* (New American Library, 1968), p. 54; on Mailer's resemblance to Adams, see Gordon O. Taylor, "Of Adams and Aquarius: Henry Adams and Norman Mailer", *Studies in Modern American Autobiography* (London, 1983), pp. 1–15.
26. Gore Vidal, "The Four Generations of the Adams Family", *Matters of Fact and of Fiction* (London, 1977), p. 205.
27. [Edgar Box], *Death Before Bedtime* (New York, 1953).
28. Gore Vidal, "The Art and Arts of E. Howard Hunt", *Matters of Fact*, p. 256.
29. *Education of Henry Adams*, p. 268.

30. In Gore Vidal, A *Thirsty Evil: Seven Short Stories* (New York, 1956), pp. 31–42.
31. *The Nation*, 22 March 1986.
32. Gore Vidal, *An Evening with Richard Nixon* (New York, 1972), pp. ix, x.
33. Gore Vidal, *Washington D.C., Burr, 1876* (new York, 1967, 1973, 1984).
34. Vidal, *Evening with Richard Nixon*, p. 118.
35. Above, note 28, p. 277.
36. Renata Adler, "Searching for the real Nixon scandal; a last inference", *Atlantic Monthly*, August 1976.
37. Jim Hougan, *Secret Agenda* (New York, 1984).
38. Christopher Hitchens, "Watergate—The Greek Connection", *The Nation*, 31 May 1986.
39. Walt Whitman, *Specimen Days* (*The Portable Walt Whitman*, rev. ed., 1974), p. 465.
40. *Education of Henry Adams*, p. 151.
41. The published works referred to are: Bob Woodward and Carl Bernstein, *All the President's Men* (New York, 1974); Nora Ephron, *Heartburn* (N.Y., 1983); "Tristan Vox", "Carl and Nora and Jack and Meryl", *Vanity Fair*, October, 1985; the Ephron-Bernstein marital separation agreement was published, in part, in *Harper's* September 1985.
42. These have been collected in Judith Martin, *Miss Manners' Guide to Excruciatingly Correct Behaviour* (London, 1983).
43. Helpful accounts of these events may be found in, David Shaw, "Due Process for the Pulitzer Prizes", *Washington Journalism Review*, June 1981, 16–19; Ben Bagdikian, "Are Pulitzers still the greatest?" *Journalism Studies Review*, July 1982, pp. 13-15; and Douglas A. Anderson, "How Newspaper Editors Reacted to *Post's* Pulitzer Prize Hoax", *Journalism Quarterly*, Autumn 1982, pp. 363-66.
44. Sissela Bok, *Lying: Moral Choice in Public and Private Life* (London, 1978), pp. 120–21.
45. Constance McLaughlin Green, *The Secret City, a History of Race Relations in the Nation's Capital* (Princeton, New Jersey, 1967), pp. 236, 316.
46. *The W.P.A. Guide to Washington, D.C.* (new York: Random House, 1983).
47. See above, note 45. Professor Green's previous volumes were, *Washington, Village and Capital, 1800–1878* and *Washington, Capital City, 1879–1950* (Princeton, New Jersey, 1962, 1963).
48. Green, *Secret City*, vii.
49. Whitman, *Speciman Days*, p. 438.
50. The text of Nixon's conversation may be most easily consulted in the *Washington Post's* staff's compilation, *The Fall of a President* (New York, 1974), p. 222; Pound's utterance is cited in Stanley I. Kutler, *The American Inquisition: Justice and Injustice in the Cold War* (New York, 1982), p. 62.
51. Kutler, op. cit., and E. Fuller Torrey, *The Roots of Treason: Ezra Pound and the Secret of St. Elizabeth's* (New York, 1984), pp. 177–260.

145
Washington

JAMES FENIMORE COOPER

For an introductory note to James Fenimore Cooper, see Chapter 94. It is useful to compare and contrast Cooper's response to the "new" capital with that of his response to new York in the same period. (See Chapter 94, *Notions of the Americans.*)

To the Count Jules De Bethizy,
Colonel en Retraite of the Imperial Guard.

Washington, —

I write you from the little capital of this great republic. After lingering at Baltimore until reasons for all further delay were exhausted, we reluctantly turned our faces westward. Cadwallader had pointed out to me sundry busy-looking travellers, who were strolling through the streets of the town, with more gravity of mien (assumed or natural) than is common to meet in a city, and whispered in my ears that they were members of Congress, on their way to the seat of government. This was a hint not to be disregarded. Tearing ourselves from the attraction of bright eyes and soft voices, we gallantly entered a coach, and broke the chain of attraction which, like the fabled magnet of Mahomet's coffin, had so long kept me suspended between heaven and earth. Heigho! dear Jules, I confess to twenty-four hours, when a treacherous intention of resigning, to some less inexorable successor, the stall which I so unworthily fill in our self-denying chapter, was insidiously floating before my imagination. But a resolution which has borne me through so many similar dangers in triumph, (aided by the members of Congress), was victorious. By-the-bye, I am grieved to the heart to hear of the sad accident that has befallen the professor, and most sincerely do I pray that the time may be long averted when it shall become necessary to supply a vacancy in our numbers, from a cause so fatal as a marriage. The grave might be wept over, and time would soften grief for the death of even a bosom friend,

James Fenimore Cooper, 'Washington', *Notions of the Americans*, London, 1828.

but what could time do towards mitigating a penance performed at the *confessional* of Hymen? The more sincere, and the more frequent the acknowledgments, the more keen and helpless would the bitterness of a spirit so thoroughly bruised become. If you pass through the queen of cities this winter, order a new cushion to my chair; I intend that the sittings of 1827 shall wear well into the mornings!

The road between Baltimore and Washington is neither particularly bad nor particularly good. It passes through a comparatively barren, and a little inhabited country. It was here that I first observed the great difference between the aspect of the slave-holding and the non-slave-holding States. In Pennsylvania, at the distance of sixty miles north of our present route, we should have seen a landscape, over which farm-houses, barns, and all the ordinary objects of a prosperous husbandry, were profusely sprinkled, while here the houses began to be distant from each other, or were grouped in little clusters apart from the highways. This portion of America bears a greater resemblance to continental Europe, than the States we have quitted. The dwelling of the planter is the château; and the huts of the slaves form the contiguous village. A difference in the moral condition of the ages in which the two have been constructed, has induced some very sensible alterations in the plans of the buildings; but, still the outline is the same.

I was surprised at the sterility and nakedness of the country through which we journeyed, though I was given to understand that a great deal of the State of Maryland is land of the richest quality. There were one or two small villages on the route, but which, after those we had seen further north, wore a miserable air. I am not certain, however, that they are not quite as good in every particular as the ordinary villages of Europe. Here I first saw fields for the tobacco plant. It grows in hills, not unlike the maize, and is rarely, or never, fenced, no animal but man having a relish for the unsavoury weed.

At the distance of six or seven miles from Washington, we stopped at the village of Bladensburgh, a place notorious for two circumstances. It lies just without the territory of the district of Columbia, and is the spot usually chosen for the decision of private combats; and it is the place where the affair between the English and the Americans was fought a few hours before the former entered the city.

I confess I had thought it surprising that so small a force (about 5000 men) could have taken possession of the capital of so powerful a nation; but a nearer view has entirely dissipated the wonder. It was a point where the Americans, having nothing of military importance to defend, had assembled no force, and there is not probably on the whole line of their coast, a more deserted and tenantless region than the country traversed by the invaders. The troops rallied to resist the English, as their intention became known, were merely the citizens of the adjoining country, who assembled in a very imperfect state of preparation, and who were very little, if at all, superior in numbers to their antagonists. They had not even the ordinary inducements to risk their lives against those of hireling troops; for, even to this hour, it is difficult to find what object General Ross could have had in hazarding his army in an expedition that might have been attended with destruction. A man like Jackson to oppose him would have insured it.

I alighted at Bladensburgh, and, accompanied by my friend, walked in advance of the carriage over the ground, attended by a sufficiently intelligent man who had witnessed the whole affair. As it is a little in your way, the details I gleaned shall be rendered as an offering to your military *goût*. Should they fail of the interest which has so often been thrown over the entrances of Moscow and Paris, you know how to make allowances for an inferiority in dramatic effect, which is not more than a natural consequence of the difference between the conquest of a city of half a million of inhabitants, and of a town of eight or nine thousand.

The country around Bladensburgh is gently undulating and moderately wooded. A small stream lies near the village, and between it and the capital. It is crossed by a wooden bridge. So much hurry and indecision appear to have existed among the defenders, that even this bridge was not destroyed, though it might have been rendered impassable in ten minutes. It would seem, however, that many of their troops, such as they were, only reached the ground at the critical moment when they were wanted in the combat. The dispositions for resistance were made along the crest of a gentle acclivity, at the distance of rather more than a mile from this bridge. The centre of their position was on the highway, and its defence was intrusted to a few seamen and two or three hundred marines, the only disciplined forces on the ground. A few light troops (all militia) were pushed in front to the banks of the stream, and two pieces of artillery were placed at a point to command the passage of the bridge. There was a little skirmishing here; and it seems, by the English accounts, that they suffered severely from the artillery in crossing the bridge. The ground in front of the seamen and marines was a gentle acclivity, and perfectly open. Here there was some sharp fighting. The British columns were obliged to open, and General Ross began to manœuvre. But the militia did not wait to be turned, for they retired to a man (the skirmishers excepted), without firing a gun. The seamen and marines stood well, and were necessarily brought off to prevent capture. The artillery was all, or nearly all, taken. This is, in substance, what is called the Battle of Bladensburgh. The American loss was trifling, less than two hundred, and that of the English perhaps three or four hundred.

It is easy to criticise the disposition of the American commander. This gentleman was an able lawyer of the adjoining State of Maryland, who had listened to the whisperings of that uneasy ambition which sometimes makes men heroes. He had quitted the gown for the sword a short time before, and probably knew as little about his new profession as you know of the one he had deserted. Lawyer or not, had this gentleman placed his fellow-citizens (for soldiers they cannot be called) in and about the Capitol, and had they only fought as well as they did, he taking care not to give them any particularly favourable opportunity of dispersing, I think General Ross would have been spared the very equivocal glory of burning all that then existed of that edifice; viz. the two wings. He listened to other counsels.

As we approached the capital, we saw before us an extent of open country that did not appear to be used for any agricultural purposes. It lay, without fences, neglected, and waste. This appearance is common just here, and is owing to the circumstance that tobacco exhausts the soil so much, that, in a country where land and its products are still so cheap, it is not worth the cost of restoring it. We soon got a view of the dome of the Capitol, and the whole of the facade of that noble edifice came into view, as we mounted a slight eminence which had partly concealed it. As my eye first wandered eagerly around, at this point, to gather together the scattered particles of the city, I will take the present occasion to convey a general impression of its appearance.

The seat of government was removed from Philadelphia to this place, in order that it might be more central. So far as a line drawn north and south is in question, this object is sufficiently answered. But Washington stands so very far east of a central meridian as to render it probable that other considerations influenced the change. I have never heard it so said, but nothing is more probable than that the slave-holding States required some such concession to their physical inferiority. At all events, everybody appears perfectly satisfied with the present position of the capital. Perhaps, notwithstanding the difference on the map, the place is practically nearer the centre than if it stood farther west. The member from Alabama, or Louisiana, or Missouri, arrives by sea, or by means of the great rivers of the west, with about the same expense of money and of labour as the member from Vermont, Maine, or New Hampshire. Some one must always have the benefit of being nearest the political centre, and it is of no great moment whether he be a Virginian or an Ohiese. As the capital is now placed, it is more convenient for quick communication with Europe that if farther inland, and it is certainly nearer the centre of interests where it stands, than it would be in almost any other spot in the confederation.

Had the plan of the city been as well conceived as its locality, there would be less ground of complaint. The perspective of American character was certainly exhibited to great advantage in the conceptions of the individual who laid out the site of this town. It is scarcely possible to imagine a more unfortunate theory than the one he assumed for the occasion. He appears to have egregiously mistaken the relative connexion between streets and houses, since it is fair to infer he would not have been so lavish of the one without the aid of the other, did he not believe the latter to be made use of as accessories to the former, instead of the reverse, as is everywhere else found to be the case. And, yet I think, both nature and art had united to point out the true plan for this city, as I shall endeavour to convince you without delay.

The ground occupied by the city of Washington, may be described as forming a tolerably regular triangle. Two of its sides are washed by the two branches of the Potomac, which diverge towards the north-east and north-west, while on its third, there are no limits to its extent, the land being a somewhat gentle acclivity, gradual on the whole, though undulating, and often broken in its minute parts. The river below the point is a noble stream, stretching for many miles to the southward, in full view of the town. Both of its branches are navigable for near a league. At the distance of about two miles from the point, the main river (west branch), which had hitherto washed a champaign country, enters a range of low mountains, and makes a still more decided inclination to the west. Here is the head of tide and of navigation. The latter circumstance had early pointed out the place for the site of a town, and accordingly a little city grew on the spot, whence tobacco and lumber were shipped for other ports, long before the neighbourhood was thought of, as the capital of a great nation. This place is called Georgetown. It is rather well built than otherwise, and the heights, in the rear, for it lies against an acclivity, are not only beautiful in themselves, but they are occupied by many pretty villas. It contains in itself, perhaps 9000 inhabitants. It has a college and five churches, two of which are Episcopal.

Georgetown is divided, from what is termed Washington City, by a rapid little stream called Rock Creek. The land, for a considerable distance after the creek is crossed, is well adapted for a town. It is sufficiently unequal to carry off the water, and yet sufficiently level for convenient streets. Here is the spot, I think, where the buildings should have been collected for the new city. But at the distance of about a mile and a quarter from the bridge, a vast square is laid out. On one of its sides is the President's House, flanked by the public offices. A few houses and a church are on two more of its sides, though the one opposite to the "White House" is as yet entirely naked. From this square, sundry great avenues diverge, as do others from another centre, distant a mile and half still further east. The latter square is adorned by the Capitol. Across all these avenues, which are parallel to nothing, there is a sort of net-work of streets, running at right angles with each other. Such is Washington on the map.

In point of fact, but few of the avenues or streets are opened, and fewer still are built on. There is one of the former running from the bridge at Georgetown to the first square, and another leads from the President's House to the capitol. There are two or three more which connect important points, though only the two named are sufficiently built on to have the least of the character of a town. There are rather more streets open, though not one of them all is absolutely built up from one end to the other.

In consequence of the gigantic scale on which Washington is planned, and the different interests which influence the population, its inhabitants (including Georgetown) are separated into four distinct little towns, distant from each other about a mile. Thus we have Georgetown in the west, containing 9000 souls; the town immediately around the President's House, (extending towards the Capitol), with perhaps 10,000; that around the Capitol, of some two or three thousand souls; and the buildings at the Navy-Yard, which lies on the east branch, still a mile further. The whole *city*, including its three divisions, with here and there a few scattered buildings, may now contain about 16,000 souls.

When the people of the United States determined to have a more central capital, it was thought best to give the general government absolute jurisdiction over it. In order to effect this object, it was necessary to extinguish the State rights. This was done by Virginia and Maryland ceding sufficient territory to make a district of ten miles square at the point I have described. In this little territory the President exercises the authority which a governor commonly exercises in a State, or rather, there is no intermediate or concurrrent executive authority between him and the people, as in the several States; and Congress, though in fact elected by the citizens of the States, does all the legislation. Thus the inhabitants of this territory have no representation whatever; neither voting for members of Congress, nor for members of any State legislation. But their voices are often heard in the way of petitions and demands. It is probable that when they shall become as numerous as the smallest State, they will receive the right of electing representatives.[1]

I think you must be enabled to understand the anomaly of the district of Columbia. It has been necessarily fostered by the nation, for as it has been entirely called into existence, as a separate community, for their use, it owes most of all it possesses to the public grants and to the presence of the ministers of the government. With a view to *force a town*, establishments have been formed which will probably linger in a doubtful state of existence for a long time to come, if, indeed, they ever prosper. Among others is that of the Navy-Yard.

The village around the Navy-Yard is the least important of the three which properly constitute the community assembled at Washington Proper. You will remember that I now exclude Georgetown from this enumeration. It possesses a different city government, though it is, in fact, quite as near the centre, or the President's House, as the Capitol. Alexandria, a little city, also, of about 9000 inhabitants, is equally within the limits of the District, but it lies on the opposite side of the Potomac, and at a distance of six miles. There are not many good houses in the quarter of the Navy-Yard, and I should think that a great portion of its inhabitants are people dependent on the establishment for support. Notwithstanding there is a long river to navigate before a ship can get into the bays below, a very considerable number of the public vessels are built and repaired at this spot. Seamen, there are none at Washington, for the simple reason that there is no commerce. A few ships are, indeed, seen at the wharfs of Georgetown and Alexandria, but the navigation of the two places united is far less than that of most of the fourth-rate commercial towns of the Union.

As the department of the navy, and the board of naval commissioners, are both established at Washington, this yard may be of some service in the way of modelling, and for the superintendence of inventions. A shop built here is said to cost more than one built in any of the more northern ports, and it is therefore plain, that when the size of their marine shall compel the Americans to observe a rigid economy in its construction, the relative importance of this yard must cease. It may long continue a school for experiments, but it can never become what was once anticipated for it, a large and flourishing building establishment.

I saw, in the Navy-Yard at Washington, the only public monument in commemoration of the dead that I could find in the city, unless a few simple stones, erected around the graves of members of Congress, who have died while here in the discharge of their official duties, can be so termed. This little monument was erected to commemorate the deaths of the officers who fell in the war with Tripoli; a war to which the United States' marine owes its present high and merited character. It is a simple column, wrought in Italy at the expense of the survivors, and erected on this spot under the impulse of that stubborn feeling of independence which distinguishes this people. The high-spirited contributors of the little work, thought the congress did not pay a suitable respect to their petition for a site in a more public situation. They were masters of the Navy-Yard, and in disgust they caused their modest memorial to be put up in the centre of its area. It may be doubted, after all, if any other situation so appropriate, or so touching, could have been found. This monument has received some injury, by having one or two of its ornamental figures broken. On one of its sides I read the following inscription: "Mutilated by Britons, August, 1814." This was the date of the inroad of the English.

Now it struck me that this inscription was in singularly bad taste. The incursion of General Ross was not an affair in which either party should exult. It was no extraordinary military achievement for four or five thousand highly disciplined troops, to land under the protection of an overwhelming naval force, and to make a forced march, for a few days, through a perfectly defenceless, and nearly uninhabited country; to attack and disperse a hastily assembled body of armed citizens, who were but little, if any, superior to them in numbers; to enter a line of straggling villages; to remain one night, and then to retreat at a rate that was quite as precipitate as their advance. Perhaps it was not bad policy, in the abstract, for a people who possessed the advantages of the British, to take this means of harassing their enemy. But I doubt the policy, in a nation situated precisely as England was and is, of proving so practically to a nation with the spirit, the resources, maritime character, and prospects of this, that a powerful navy is so absolutely necessary to defend their coast. The use that was made of the success, too, might admit of some cavilling. But, on the other hand, the Americans fell so far short in their defence of what even the case admitted, and so very far short of what, even under less propitious circumstances, they themselves effected at New-Orleans, that wisdom would prescribe silence as the better course. It is permitted for the defenders of Bunker's hill to allude to their defeat, but the chisel of the Americans should have been industriously employed to erase every vestige of, and not to commemorate, even thus indirectly, the occupation of their capital by an enemy. But, even admitting that the defence of the town had been quite equal to the means at hand, what was the immediate offence, that called for this particular punishment? The English occupied the Navy-Yard, and, although a little hurried, they certainly had time to have *destroyed* this small monument, instead of *mutilating* it, by knocking the heads off one or two small marble angels. The very nature of the injury proves it was the act of an individual, and not of the authority, which alone should be considered responsible for any grave national accusation. Cadwallader is of my opinion, as, indeed, were half-a-dozen naval officers who showed us through the yard. The latter said that the inscription was by order of an officer of rank, who had reasons for a special degree of antipathy against their late enemy. No man, especially in a country like this, should be permitted, however, thus to interpose his personal resentments between a nation and its dignity.

It is more than a mile from the quarter of the Navy-Yard to that of the Capitol. I have read accounts of this place, which convey an idea that it was lately a forest, and that the wood had been felled in order to make a space to receive the town. There is some error in this impression. Most of the country, for miles around Washington, was early devoted to the growth of tobacco. It is a baneful consequence of the cultivation of this weed, that, for a long time, it destroys the fertility of the soil. Thus, one sees vast fields here, which wear the appearance of neglected heaths. A growth of low, stunted, dwarfish trees succeeds in time, and bushes must, of course, first make their appearance. I could see no traces of wood in any part of this city, nor for some distance around it, though it is not improbable that some copses of a second growth did exist at the time the plan was formed. All I mean to say is, that the vicinity of the Capitol has rather the appearance of an old and an exhausted, than of what is here called a new country. A great deal of the land in and about the town is not fenced, and the whole appearance of the place is that produced by the separate villages I have described, lying on a great heath, which is beginning to be cultivated, and whose surface is irregularly waving. The avenues in those parts which are not built, consequently, cross these open fields, and the view is perfectly unobstructed on every side.

The quarter of the Capitol stands on elevated ground, and is certainly the most picturesque portion of the city proper. The Capitol itself is placed on the brow of a considerable declivity, and commands a noble view. There is something exceedingly imposing in the aspect of this building, with its powerful accessories of scenery and of moral association. I shall beg your patience while I attempt an imperfect description.

The edifice is of a light greyish freestone. It has been found necessary to paint it white, in order to conceal the marks of the smoke left by the conflagration of 1814. This is in better taste than the inscription on the monument. The effect of a clear, brilliant white, under so fine a sun, is in itself exceedingly striking. The antiquarian may riot in the rust, but every plain-viewing man sees that the coin is never so beautiful as when it is new from the mint. This freshness of air is rather a peculiarity throughout most of the United States, and it is exactly the appearance the country should wear in order to be in keeping with its recollections.

The Capitol is composed of a centre and two wings. The former is something more than 150 feet square, or nearly square, and the latter are each just 100. The several parts are in a line on the eastern front, and consequently the wings are thrown back on the western. This irregularity of the western facade is a

we have no small advantage over all the rest of the world. If you doubt the fact, compare our actual situation, the past, and what we have done and are doing, with what other governments have done and are about, and let the result speak for itself.

"You will see on the floors of Congress men belonging to every condition of society known to our community, with the exception of that which necessarily infers great ignorance and vulgarity. All the members are respectable, and very many of them are gentlemen. There are some who are scholars, and not a few have been improved by travel and by observation of other countries. A remote frontier district, however, must send such men as it possesses, or trust its peculiar interests to those who have but little concern in its welfare. The Senate is, in some respects, rather more select than the lower house, because their constituents have a State instead of a district to choose from, and because that body is expected to temper the proceedings of legislation with a peculiar degree of moderation and dignity.

"In the British Parliament there is some show of this universality of representation. Certain corporations send men of their own stamp; but in England every thing has a tendency to aristocracy, while, in this country, every thing which pertains to the government must seek its support in the democracy. The "worthy alderman," who may have commenced life behind a counter, endeavours to forget his apron when he takes his seat on the opposition benches. Instead of returning to his shop when the session is ended, he becomes a deserter to aristocracy, the moment he has received the seal of office from the people. How far he may contribute to the boasted refinement of the higher classes, I cannot pretend to say; but it is certain that he does not, like his American prototype, assist to give respectability and elevation to that of which he was originally a member. It is this elevation of character among the middling, and even among the more inferior classes of our community, which chiefly distinguishes us from all other nations. Europe must show a population as much accustomed to political power, as moderate in its exercise, as practised in all that controls the general interest of life, and as shrewd in their estimate of character, as this of ours, before she should pretend to infer the results of democratic institutions by any facts drawn from her own experience. We do not deny the universality of human impulses, we only insist that governments have not the habit of giving them fair play. The two houses of Congress are, and ever have been, living proofs that the majority of men are not disposed to abuse power when it is once fairly intrusted to them. There is not a doubt that the comparatively poor and ignorant might fill all our legislative chairs with men of their own class, and yet they rather take pride in seeing the representation respectable for information. Some part of this seeming generosity is, no doubt, owing to the superior influence of intelligence; but you must allow there is a prospect of quiet and durability under a system in which the majority find no reason to complain, and in which the minority must see the folly of usurpation. But as the two houses are by this time organized, we will go to the Capitol, and hear the message. When on the spot, I will endeavour to direct your attention to such individuals as may serve to elucidate what you have just heard."

We proceeded to the Capitol in a coach. Alighting at the foot of the hill, we mounted it to a door on the western façade, and entered the edifice through its *substratum*. Passing among a multitude of eating rooms, &c. &c., we ascended, by a noble flight of massive steps, to the true basement, or to that story which runs through the whole building. Directly under the dome is a gloomy vaulted hall, that I have heard called the "caucus;" more, I believe, from its fancied fitness for the political meetings that are thus termed, than from the fact that it has ever actually been appropriated to such an use. It has the air, however, of being admirably adapted to the purposes of a secret conclave, though, in truth, it is a common thoroughfare of the building. Immediately above the "caucus" is the principal hall. It is circular, large, high, and covered with a fine dome. There is not much richness in the ornaments of this hall, though it is sufficiently wrought to prevent the appearance of nakedness. It contains, among other things, four bas-reliefs in stone, which are intended to illustrate as many of the most striking incidents in the original settlement of the country. I have no disposition to criticise their execution. Historical pictures are to be placed in the panels beneath.

From the great hall we passed into that of the House of Representatives. My friend was formerly a member, and by an usage he is permitted to enter the body of the chamber, or rather to occupy a seat that is only separated from those of the actual members by a slight division. Under his auspices, and by the aid of a little interest, I was permitted to be his companion.

The hall of the House of Representatives, without being particularly rich, or highly wrought, is one of the most beautiful apartments I have ever entered. The form is semicircular. It is lighted from above, and from windows on its straight side. Between these windows and the body of the hall, is a sort of lobby or gallery, which is separated from the other parts by a colonnade. Here the members and privileged persons promenade, converse, stand, listen, or repose, without, in fact, quitting the room. It is sufficiently withdrawn to prevent the appearance of disorder, and yet near enough to render the debates audible.

In the centre of the diameter which cuts the circle is the Speaker's chair. It is, in fact, a little sofa, sufficiently large to hold, on occasion, the President of the United States, the President of the Senate, and the Speaker. Immediately in front, and four or five feet lower, is a chair for the presiding member, when the house acts as a committee. On a line with the Speaker the clerks have their places. In front of the chair there is a vacant semicircular space of perhaps five-and-twenty feet in diameter. Then the seats of the members commence. They are arranged in semi-circular rows, preserving the form of the exterior walls, and are separated by a great number of little openings, to admit of a passage between them. Each member has an arm-chair and a low desk, in mahogany. In the first row, they sit in pairs, or there is a vacant space between every two, and each successive row increases its number by one member. Thus, in the last row, some six or seven are placed side by side, as on a bench (though actually on chairs), while those in front are in pairs. The practice is for those who arrive first to choose their seats, and the choice is invariably respected.

There is no such thing known as a political division of seats. Members of the same politics certainly often choose to be placed near to each other, and sometimes the entire representation of a particular State is to be seen as near together as possible. But there is no rule in the matter.

The seats of the members are separated from the semicircular passage in which Cadwallader and myself were placed, by no other division than a low railing. Sofas lined the whole of the exterior wall: and as the floor rises a little from the centre, or the area in front of the Speaker, we had the best possible opportunity for seeing and hearing. A spacious and commodious gallery, of the same form as the hall, completed the outline of the apartment. It was raised several feet above the level of the chamber, and is intended for the use of spectators.

The house was organized when we entered, and was engaged in some business of form. Nearly all the seats were occupied; and, as the message was expected, the gallery was crowded with ladies and well-dressed men. The privileged places around the floor of the hall were nearly all filled. The Speaker was uncovered, but most of the members wore their hats. No one appeared in costume, nor is there any official dress prescribed to the members of Congress for any ceremony whatever.

After what Cadwallader had told me of the true character of the representation of his country, I confess I was rather surprised with the appearance of the individuals who composed this assembly. It was to be expected that they should all be well attired, but, on the whole, with some very few exceptions, they had quite as much the air of the world about them as those who compose the chambers of the two first nations of Europe. No one is allowed to sit in the lower house who has not attained the age of five-and-twenty; but, in point of act, there is not, probably, a single member of Congress who has seen less than thirty years. The greater number seemed to be men between the ages of thirty-five and fifty-five. There were but very few who could be termed old. All, or very nearly all, were natives of the country.

I was struck with the simple but imposing aspect of this assembly. Though so totally destitute of any personal decorations, the beauty of the hall, with its magnificent row of massive columns,[2] the great neatness of the fautëuil and desks, the beautifully carpeted floors, and the long range of sofas, serve to relieve a scene that might otherwise have been too naked. It appeared as if the members had said, thus much may you do for the benefit of comfort, for the encouragement of the arts, and, perhaps, as a testimonial of the respect due to the sacred uses of the place, but man must be left in the fullest force of his simplicity. None of the attendants even wore any badges of their offices. There were neither swords, chains, collars, stars, bayonets, nor maces, seen about the place, though a quiet, and order, and decency, reigned in the hall that bespoke the despotic dominion of that mighty, though invisible, monarch—the Law.

A discussion on some question of order was getting to be a little general, and one member was addressing the chair [they speak from their places, as in the British Parliament] with some earnestness, when the principal door was thrown open, and an officer proclaimed aloud, "A message from the President." The members all rose in their places, the Speaker included, when a young gentleman entered, and passed through the body of the house to the chair. He was attired in a neat morning-dress, and having placed his document in the hand of the Speaker, he bowed and withdrew. It was then decided that the communication should be read. There was much interest to hear this document, which always contains a great outline of the state of the republic. It was a clear, succinct narrative of what had been done in the course of the past year, of the condition of the finances, of the several negotiations, and concluded with a statement of what the people had a right to anticipate for the future.

When the message was ended, Cadwallader introduced me to several of the members to whom he was personally known. Most of them were men of good manners, and of education, though one or two were certainly individuals who had paid far more attention to the substance of things than to forms. The former were of course of that class of society which, in Europe, would be termed the gentry, and the others were probably farmers, if not mechanics. There was an air of great self-possession and decorum in the latter; nor could the slightest visible difference be traced between the respect which they received, and that which their more polished confederates bestowed on each other. A simple, quiet courtesy is certainly the tone of manners in Congress. While we stood together in the lobby, a grave-looking, middle-aged man, of a slightly rustic air, approached, and addressed my companion. His manner was manly and independent, but at the same time decent, and I think it was to be distinguished by a shade of respect. They shook hands, and conversed a little concerning some questions of local politics. Promises were made of exchanging visits. "This is my friend, the ——," said Cadwallader; "a gentleman who is travelling in our country." The stranger saluted me, offering his hand with the utmost simplicity. "If this gentleman comes into our part of the country, I hope to see him," he said, and soon after took his leave. When he was gone, I learned that this individual was a member of Congress from the county in which the paternal estates of my friend lie; that he was a farmer of moderate means and good character, whom his fellow-citizens had sent to represent them. His constituents might very possibly have made a better choice, and yet this man was not useless, since he served as a check on the schemes of those who would be legislating for effect. A gentleman-like man of sixty came next, and he and my friend met as equals in all respects, except that the latter paid a slight deference to the years of his acquaintance. I was introduced. We touched our hats, and exchanged a few words. The next day, I received his gentleman's card, and as soon as his visit was returned, an invitation to dine in his private lodgings followed. This was Mr. ——, a man of immense hereditary landed estate. His alliances, fortune, and habits, (though tempered by the institutions of his country), are, to all

used as freely as if they were common blue flags—with rich door-frames and window-casings of bronze and gold—heavy chandeliers and mantels, and clocks in every room—and indeed by far the richest and gayest, and most unAmerican and inappropriate ornamenting and finest interior workmanship I ever conceived possible, spread in profusion through scores, hundreds, (and almost thousands) or rooms—such are what I find, or rather would find to interest me, if I devoted time to it—But a few of the rooms are enough for me—the style is without grandeur, and without simplicity—These days, the state our country is in, and especially filled as I am from top to toe, of late with scenes and thoughts of *the hospitals*, (America seems to me now, though only in her youth, but brought *already here* feeble, bandaged and bloody *in hospital)—these* days I say, Jeff, all the poppy-show goddesses and all the pretty blue & gold in which the interior Capitol is got up, seem to me out of place beyond any thing I could tell—and I get away from it as quick as I can when that kind of thought comes over me. I suppose it is to be described throughout—those interiors—as all of them got up in the French style—well enough for a New York [*incomplete*]

From a Letter To Nathaniel Bloom and John F. S. Gray

Washington, March 19, 1863

Washington and its points I find bear a second and a third perusal, and doubtless indeed many. My first impressions, architectural, &c. were not favorable; but upon the whole, the city, the spades, buildings, &c make no unfit emblem of our country, so far, so broadly planned, every thing in plenty, money & materials staggering with plenty, but the fruit of the plans, the knit, the combination yet wanting—Determined to express ourselves greatly in a capital but no fit capital yet here—(time, associations, wanting, I suppose)—many a hiatus yet—many a thing to be taken down and done over again yet—perhaps an entire change of base—may-be a succession of changes. Congress does not seize very hard upon me—I studied it and its members with curiosity, and long—much gab, great fear of public opinion, plenty of low business talent, but no masterful man in Congress, (probably best so.) I think well of the President. He has a face like a hoosier Michael Angelo, so awful ugly it becomes beautiful, with its strange mouth, its deep cut, criss-cross lines, and its doughnut complexion. My notion is, too, that underneath his outside smutched mannerism, and stories from third-class county bar-rooms, (it is his humor,) Mr. Lincoln keeps a fountain of first-class practical telling wisdom. I do not dwell on the supposed failures of his government, he has shown, I sometimes think, an almost supernatural tact in keeping the ship afloat at all, with head steady, not only going down, and now certain not to, but with proud and resolute spirit, and flag flying in sight of the world, menacing and high as ever. I say never yet captain, never ruler, had such a perplexing, dangerous task as his, the past two years. I more and more rely upon his idiomatic western genius, careless of court dress or court decorums.

147

Patent-Office Hospital *and* The White House by Moonlight

WALT WHITMAN

For an introductory note, see Chapters 95 and 146.

Patent-Office Hospital

February 23. [*1863*]—I must not let the great hospital at the Patent-office pass away without some mention. A few weeks ago the vast area of the second story of that noblest of Washington buildings was crowded close with rows of sick, badly wounded and dying soldiers. They were placed in three very large apartments. I went there many times. It was a strange, solemn, and, with all its features of suffering and death, a sort of fascinating sight. I go sometimes at night to soothe and relieve particular cases. Two of the immense apartments are fill'd with high and ponderous glass cases, crowded with models in miniature of every kind of utensil, machine or invention, it ever enter'd into the mind of man to conceive; and with curiosities and foreign presents. Between these cases are lateral openings, perhaps eight feet wide and quite deep, and in these were placed the sick, besides a great long double row of them up and down through the middle of the hall. Many of them were very bad cases, wounds and amputations. Then there was a gallery running above the hall in which there were beds also. It was, indeed, a curious scene, especially at night when lit up. The glass cases, the beds, the forms lying there, the gallery above, and the marble pavement under foot—the suffering, and the fortitude to bear it in various degrees—occasionally, from some, the groan that could not be repress'd—sometimes a poor fellow dying, with emaciated face and glassy eye, the nurse by his side, the doctor also there, but no friend, no relative—such were the sights but lately in the Patent-office. (The wounded have since been removed from there, and it is now vacant again.)

Source: Walt Whitman, "Patent-Office Hospital", "The White House by Moonlight", *Specimen Days*, 1882.

The White House by Moonlight

February 24th. [*1863*]—A spell of fine soft weather. I wander about a good deal, sometimes at night under the moon. To-night took a long look at the President's house. The white portico—the palace-like, tall, round columns, spotless as snow—the walls also—the tender and soft moonlight, flooding the pale marble, and making peculiar faint languishing shades, not shadows—everywhere a soft transparent hazy, thin, blue moon-lace, hanging in the air—the brilliant and extra-plentiful clusters of gas, on and around the façade, columns, portico, &c.—everything so white, so marbly pure and dazzling, yet soft—the White House of future poems, and of dreams and dramas, there in the soft and copious moon—the gorgeous front, in the trees, under the lustrous flooding moon, full of reality, full of illusion—the forms of the trees, leafless, silent, in trunk and myriad-angles of branches, under the stars and sky—the White House of the land, and of beauty and night—sentries at the gates, and by the portico, silent, pacing there in blue overcoats—stopping you not at all, but eyeing you with sharp eyes, whichever way you move.

148

Washington's Monument

WALT WHITMAN

For an introductory note, see Chapters 95 and 146.

Washington's Monument, February, 1885.

Ah, not this marble, dead and cold:
Far from its base and shaft expanding—the round zones circling, comprehending,
Thou, Washington, art all the world's, the continents' entire—not yours alone, America,
Europe's as well, in every part, castle of lord or laborer's cot,
Or frozen North, or sultry South—the African's—the Arab's in his tent,
Old Asia's there with venerable smile, seated amid her ruins;
(Greets the antique the hero new? 'tis but the same—the heir legitimate, continued ever,
The indomitable heart and arm—proofs of the never-broken line,
Courage, alertness, patience, faith, the same—e'en in defeat defeated not, the same:)
Wherever sails a ship, or house is built on land, or day or night,
Through teeming cities' streets, indoors or out, factories or farms,
Now, or to come, or past—where patriot wills existed or exist,
Wherever Freedom, pois'd by Toleration, sway'd by Law,
Stands or is rising thy true monument.

Source: Walt Whitman, "Washington's Monument, February, 1885"

149
Washington

HENRY JAMES

For the context of this extract from *The American Scene*, see the introductory note to Chapter 96.

Washington

I was twice in Washington, the first time for a winter visit, the second to meet the wonderful advance of summer, to which, in that climate of many charms, the first days of May open wide the gates. This latter impression was perforce much the more briefly taken; yet, though I had gathered also from other past occasions, far-away years now, something of the sense of the place at the earlier season, I find everything washed over, at the mention of the name, by the rare light, half green, half golden, of the lovely leafy moment. I see all the rest, till I make the effort to break the spell, through that voluminous veil; which operates, for memory, quite as the explosion of spring works, even to the near vision, in respect to the American scene at large—dressing it up as if for company, preparing it for social, for human intercourse, making it in fine publicly presentable, with an energy of renewal and an effect of redemption not often to be noted, I imagine, on other continents. Nowhere, truly, can summer have such work cut out for it as here—nowhere has it to take upon itself to repaint the picture so completely. In the "European" landscape, in general, some, at least, of the elements and objects remain upon the canvas; here, on the other hand, one seems to see intending Nature, the great artist of the season, decline to touch that surface unless it be first swept clean—decline, at any rate, to deal with it save by ignoring all its perceived pretensions. Vernal Nature, in England, in France, in Italy, has still a use, often a charmed or amused indulgence, for the material in hand, the furniture of the foreground, the near and middle distances, the heterogeneous human features of the face of the land. She looks at her subject much as the portrait-painter looks at the personal properties, this or that household object, the official uniform, the badges and ornaments, the favourite dress, of his sitter—

Source: Henry James, "Washington", *The American Scene*, 1907, Ch XI.

with an "Oh, yes, I can bring them in; they're just what I want, and I see how they will help me out." But I try in vain to recall a case in which, either during the New England May and June, or during those of the Middle States (since these groups of weeks have in the two regions a differing identity and value), the genius in question struck me as adopting with any frankness, as doing more than passively, helplessly accept, the supplied paraphernalia, the signs of existing life. The business is clearly to get rid of them as far as may be, to cover and smother them; dissimulating with the biggest, freest brush their impertinence and their ugliness.

I must ask myself, I meanwhile recognize, none the less, why I should have found Mount Vernon exquisite, the first of May, if the interest had all to be accounted for in the light of nature. The light of nature was there, splendid and serene; the Potomac opened out in its grandest manner; the bluff above the river, before the sweep of its horizon, raised its head for the historic crown. But it was not for a moment to be said that this was the whole story; the human interest and the human charm lay in wait and held one fast—so that, if one had been making light, elsewhere, of their suggestion and office, one had at least this case seriously to reckon with. I speak straightway, thus, of Mount Vernon, though it be but an outlying feature of Washington, and at the best a minor impression; the image of the particular occasion is seated so softly in my path. There was a glamour, in fine, for the excursion—that of an extraordinary gracious hospitality; and the glamour would still have been great even if I had not, on my return to the shadow of the Capitol, found the whole place transfigured. The season was over, the President away, the two Houses up, the shutters closed, the visitor rare; and one lost one's way in the great green vistas of the avenues quite as one might have lost it in a "sylvan solitude"—that is in the empty alleys of a park. The emptiness was qualified at the most, here and there, by some encounter with a stray diplomatic agent, wreathed for the most part in sincerer smiles than we are wont to attribute to his class. "This"—it was the meaning of these inflections—"was the *real* Washington, a place of enchantment; so that if the enchantment were never less who could ever bring himself to go away?" The enchantment had been so much less in January—one could easily understand; yet the recognition seemed truly the voice of the hour, and one picked it up with a patriotic flutter not diminished by the fact that the speaker would probably be going away, and with delight, on the morrow.

The memory of some of the smiles and inflections comes back in that light; Washington being the one place in America, I think, where those qualities are the values and vehicles, the medium of exchange. No small part of the interest of the social scene there consists, inevitably, for any restless analyst, in wonder about the "real" sentiments of appointed foreign participants, the delegates of Powers and pledged alike to penetration and to discretion, before phenomena which, whatever they may be, differ more from the phenomena of other capitals and other societies than they resemble them. This interest is susceptible, on occasion, of becoming intense; all the more that curiosity must, for the most part, pursue its object (that of truly looking over the alien shoulder and of seeing, judging, building, fearing, reporting with the alien sense) by subtle and tortuous ways. This represents, first and last, even for a watcher abjectly irresponsible, a good deal of speculative tension; so that one's case is refreshing in presence of the clear candour of such a proposition as that the national capital *is* charming in proportion as you don't see it. For that is what it came to, in the bowery condition; the as yet unsurmounted bourgeois character of the whole was screened and disguised; the dressing-up in other words, was complete, and the great park-aspect gained, and became nobly artificial, by the very complexity of the plan of the place—the perpetual perspectives, the converging, radiating avenues, the frequent circles and crossways, where all that was wanted for full illusion was that the bronze generals and admirals, on their named pedestals, should have been great garden-gods, mossy mythological marble. This would have been the perfect note; the long vistas yearned for it, and the golden chequers scattered through the gaps of the high arches waited for some bending nymph or some armless Hermes to pick them up. The power of the scene to evoke such visions sufficiently shows, I think, what had become, under the mercy of nature, of the hard facts, as one must everywhere call them; and yet though I could diplomatically, patriotically pretend, at the right moment, that such a Washington *was* the "real" one, my assent had all the while as still finer meaning for myself.

I am hanging back, however, as with sacred terror, from Mount Vernon, where indeed I may not much linger, or only enough to appear not to have shirked the responsibility incurred at the opening of these remarks. There, in ample possession, was masking, dissimulating summer, the envelope and disguise to which I have hinted that the American picture owes, on its human side, *all* its best presentability; and at the same time, unmistakably, there was the spell, as quite a distinct matter, of the hard little facts in themselves. How came it that if they had no intrinsic sweetness, no visible dignity, they could yet play their part in so unforgettable an impression? The answer to this can only be, I think, that we happen here to "strike," as they say, one of the rarest of cases, a spot on which all sorts of sensibilities are touched and on which a lively emotion, and one yet other than the æsthetic, makes us its prey. The old high-placed house, unquestionably, is charming, and the felicity of the whole scene, on such a day as that of my impression, scarce to be uttered. The little hard facts of form, of substance, of scale, facts of essential humility and exiguity, none the less, look us straight in the face, present themselves literally to be counted over—and reduce us thereby to the recognition of our supreme example of the rich interference of association. Association does, at Mount Vernon, simply what it likes with us—it is of so beautiful and noble a sort; and to this end it begins by making us unfit to say whether or no we would in its absence have noticed the house for any material grace at all. We scarce care more for its being proved picturesque, the house, than for its being proved plain; its architectural interest and architectural nullity becomes one and the same thing for us. If asked what we should think of it if it hadn't been, or if we hadn't known it for, Washington's, we retort that the inquiry is inane, since it is not the possessive case, but the straight, serene nominative, that we are dealing with. The whole thing *is* Washington—not his invention and his property, but his presence and his person; with discriminations (as distinguished from enthusiasms) as invidious and unthinkable as if they were addressed to his very ears.

The great soft fact, as opposed to the little hard ones, is the beauty of the site itself; that is definitely, if ever so delicately, sublime, but it fails to rank among the artificial items that I began by speaking of, those of so generally compromising an effect in the American picture. Everything else is *communicated* importance, and the magic so wrought for the American sensibility—by which I mean the degree of the importance and the sustained high pitch of the charm—place it, doubtless, the world over, among the few supreme triumphs of such communication. The beauty of the site, meanwhile, as we stand there becomes but the final aspect of the man; under which everything conduces to a single great representative image, under which every feature of the scene, every object in the house, however trivial, borrows from it and profits by it. The image is the largest, clearest possible of the resting, as distinguished from the restless, consciousness of public service consummately rendered. The terms we commonly use for that condition—peace with honour, well-earned repose, enjoyment of homage, recognition of facts—render but dimly the luminous stillness in which, on its commanding eminence, we see our image bathed. It hangs together with the whole bright immensity of air and view. It becomes truly the great white, decent page on which the whole sense of the place is written. It does more things even besides; attends us while we move about and goes with us from room to room; mounts with us the narrow stairs, to stand with us in these small chambers and look out of the low windows; takes up for us, to turn them over with spiritual hands, the objects from which we respectfully forbear, and places an accent in short, through the rambling old phrase, wherever an accent is required. Thus we arrive at the full meaning, as it were—thus we know, at least, why we are so moved.

It is for the same reason for which we are always inordinately moved, on American ground, I think, when the unconscious minor scale of the little old demonstrations to which we owe everything is made visible to us, when their disproportionate modesty is proved upon them. The reason worked at Mount Vernon, for the restless analyst, quite as it had worked a few months before, on the small and simple scene of Concord Fight: the slight, pale, bleeding Past, in a patched homespun suit, stands there taking the thanks of the bloated Present—having woundedly rescued from thieves and brought to his door the fat, locked pocket-book of which that personage appears the owner. The pocket-book contains, "unbeknown" to the honest youth, bank-notes of incredible figure, and what breaks our heart, if we be cursed with the historic imagination, is the grateful, wan smile with which the great guerdon of sixpence is received. I risk, floridly, the assertion that half the intensity of the impression of Mount Vernon, for many a visitor, will ever be in this vision there of Washington only (so far as consciously) so rewarded. Such fantastications, I indeed admit, are refinements of response to any impression, but the ground had been cleared for them, and it ministered to luxury of thought, for instance, that we were a small party at our ease there, with no other circulation—with the prowling ghosts of fellow-pilgrims, too harshly present on my previous occasion, all conveniently laid. This alone represented privilege and power, and they in turn, with their pomp and circumstance of a charming Government launch, under official attendance, at the Navy-Yard steps, amid those large, clean, protecting and protected properties of the State which always make one think much of the State, whatever its actual infirmities—these things, to say nothing of other rich enhancements, above all those that I may least specify, flung over the day I scarce know what iridescent reflection of the star-spangled banner itself, in the folds of which I had never come so near the sense of being positively wrapped. That consciousness, so unfamiliar, was, under the test, irresistible; it pressed the spring, absolutely, of intellectual exaltation—with the consequent loud resonance that my account of my impressions doubtless sufficiently translates.

II

Washington itself meanwhile—the Washington always, I premise, of the rank outsider—had struck me from the first as presenting two distinct faces; the more obvious of which was the public and official, the monumental, with features all more or less majestically playing the great administrative, or, as we nowadays put it, Imperial part. This clustered, yet at the same time oddly scattered, city, a general impression of high granite steps, of light grey corniced colonnades, rather harmoniously low, contending for effect with slaty mansard roofs and masses of iron excrescence, a general impression of somewhat vague, empty, sketchy, fundamentals, however expectant, however spacious, overweighted by a single Dome and overaccented by a single Shaft—this loose congregation of values seemed, strangely, a matter disconnected and remote, though remaining in its way portentous and bristling all incoherently at the back of the scene. The back of the scene, indeed, to one's quite primary sense, might have been but an immense painted, yet unfinished cloth, hung there to a confessedly provisional end and marked with the queerness, among many queernesses, of looking always the same; painted once for all in clear, bright, fresh tones, but never emerging from its flatness, after the fashion of other capitals, into the truly, the variously, modelled and rounded state. (It appeared provisional therefore because looking as if it might have been unhooked and removed as a whole; because any one object in it so treated would have made the rest also come off.) The foreground was a different thing, a thing that, ever so quaintly, seemed to represent the force really in possession; though consisting but of a small company of people engaged perpetually in conversation and (always, I repeat, for the rank outsider) singularly destitute of conspicuous marks or badges. This little society easily became for the detached visitor, the city itself, *the* national capital and the greater part of the story; and that, ever, in spite of the comparatively scant intensity of its political permeation. The political echo was of course to be heard in it, and the public character, in his higher forms, to be encountered—though only in "single spies," not in battalions; but there was something that made it much more individual than any mere predominance of political or administrative colour would have made it; leaving it in that case to do no more than resemble the best society in London, or that in best possession of the field in Paris.

Two sharp signs my remoter remembrance had shown me the then Washington world, and the first met, as putting forth; one of these the fact of its being extraordinary easy and pleasant, and the other that of one's appearing to make out in it not more than half-a-dozen members of the Lower House and not more than a dozen of the Upper. This kept down the political permeation, and was bewildering, if one was able to compare, in the light of the different London condition, the fact of the social ubiquity there of the acceptable M.P. and that of the social frequency even of his more equivocal hereditary colleague. A London nestling under the towers of Westminster, yet practically void of members of the House of Commons, and with the note of official life far from exclusively sounding, that might have been in those days the odd image of Washington, had not the picture been stamped with other variations still. These were a whole cluster, not instantly to be made out, but constituting the unity of the place as soon as perceived; representing that finer extract or essence which the self-respecting observer is never easy till he be able to shake up and down in bottled form. The charming company of the foreground then, which referred itself so little to the sketchy back-scene, the monstrous Dome and Shaft, figments of the upper air, the pale colonnades and mere myriad-windowed Buildings, was the second of the two faces, and the more one lived with it the more, up to a certain point, one lived away from the first. In time, and after perceiving *how* it was what it so agreeably was, came the recognition of common ground; the recognition that, in spite of strange passages of the national life, liable possibly to recur, during which the President himself was scarce thought to be in society, the particular precious character that one had apprehended could never have ripened without a general consensus. One had put one's finger on it when one had seen disengaged itself from many anomalies, from not a few drolleries, the superior, the quite majestic fact of the City of Conversation pure and simple, and positively by the only specimen, of any such intensity, in the world.

That had remained for me, from the other time, the properest name of Washington, and nothing could so interest me, on a renewal of acquaintance, too long postponed and then too woefully brief, as to find my description wholly justified. If the emphasis added by "pure and simple" be invariably retained, the description will continue, I think, to embrace and exhaust the spectacle, while yet leaving it every inch of its value. Clearly quite immeasurable on American ground, the value of such an assertion of a town-type directly opposed to the unvarying American, and quite unique, on any ground, so organized a social indifference to the vulgar vociferous Market. Washington may of course *know* more than she confesses—no community could perhaps really be as ignorant as Washington used at any rate to look, and to like to look, of this particular thing, of "goods" and shares and rises and falls and all such sordidities; but she knows assuredly still the very least she can get off with, and nothing even yet pleases her more than to forget what she does know. She unlearns, she turns her back, while London, Paris, Berlin, Rome, in their character of political centres, strike us as, on the contrary, feverishly learning, trying more and more to do the exact opposite. (I speak, naturally, as to Washington, of knowing actively and interestedly, in the spirit of gain—not merely of the enjoyed lights of political and administrative science, doubtless as abundant there as anywhere else.) It might fairly have been, I used to think, that the charming place—charming in the particular connection I speak of—had on its conscience to make one forget for an hour the colossal greed of New York. Nothing, in fact, added more to its charm than its appearing virtually to invite one to impute to it some such vicarious compunction.

If I be reminded, indeed, that the distinction I here glance at is negative, and be asked what then (if she knew nothing of the great American interest) Washington did socially know, my answer, I recognize, has at once to narrow itself, and become perhaps truly the least bit difficult to utter. It none the less remains distinct enough that, the City of Conversation being only in question, and a general subject of all the conversation having thereby to be predicated, our responsibility is met as soon as we are able to say what Washington mainly talks, and appears always to go mainly talking, about. Washington talks about herself, and about almost nothing else; falling superficially indeed, on that ground, but into line with the other capitals. London, Paris, Berlin, Rome, goodness knows, talk about themselves: that is each member of this sisterhood talks, sufficiently or inordinately, of the great number of divided and differing selves that form together her controlling identity. London, for instance, talks of everything in the world without thereby for a moment, as it were, ceasing to be egotistical. It has taken everything in the world to make London up, so that she is in consequence simply doomed never to get away from herself. Her conversation is largely, I think, the very effort to do that; but she inevitably figures in it but as some big buzzing insect which keeps bumping against a treacherous mirror. It is in positive quest of an identity of some sort, much rather—an identity other than merely functional and technical—that Washington goes forth, encumbered with no ideal of avoidance or escape: it is about herself *as* the City of Conversation precisely that she incessantly converses; adorning the topic, moreover, with endless ingenuity and humour. But that, absolutely, remains the case; which thus becomes one of the most thorough, even if probably one of the most natural and of the happiest, cases of collective self-consciousness that one knows. The spectacle, as it at first met my senses, was that of a numerous community in ardent pursuit of some workable conception of its social self, and trying meanwhile intelligently to talk itself, and even this very embarrassment, into a *subject* for conversation. Such a picture might not seem purely pleasing, on the side of variety of appeal, and I admit one may have had one's reserves about it; reserves sometimes reflected, for example, in dim inward speculation—one of the effects of the Washington air I have already glanced at—as to the amount of response it might evoke in the diplomatic body was liable to strike one there as more characteristically "abysmal" than elsewhere, more impenetrably bland and inscrutable blank; and it was obvious, certainly, that their concern to help the place intellectually to find itself was not to be expected to approach in intensity the concern even of a repatriated absentee. You were concerned only if you had, by your sensibility, a stake in the game; which was the last thing a foreign representative would wish to confess to, this being directly opposed to all his enjoined duties. It is no part of the office of such personages to assist the societies to which they are accredited to find themselves—it is much more their mission to leave all such vaguely and, so far as may be, grotesquely groping: so apt are societies, in finding themselves, to find other things too. This detachment from the whole mild convulsion of effort, the considerate pretence of not being too aware of it, combined with latent probabilities of alarm about it no less than of amusement, represented, to the unquiet fancy, much more the spirit of the old-time Legations.

What *was*, at all events, better fun, of the finer sort, than having one's self a stake in the outcome?—what helped the time (so much of it as there was!) more to pass than just to join in the so fresh experiment of constitutive, creative talk? The boon, it should always be mentioned, meanwhile went on not in the least in the tone of solemnity. That would have been fatal, because probably irritating, and it was where the good star of Washington intervened. The tone was, so to speak, of *conscious* self-consciousness, and the highest genius for conversation doubtless dwelt in the fact that the ironic spirit was ready always to give its very self away, fifty times over, for the love, or for any quickening, of the theme. The foundation for the whole happy predicament remained, moreover, of the firmest, and the essence of the case was to be as easily stated as the great social fact is, in America, whether through exceptions or aggravations, everywhere to be stated. Nobody was in "business"—that was the sum and substance of it; and for the one large human assemblage on the continent of which this was true the difference made was huge. Nothing could strike one more than that it was the only way in which, over the land, a difference *could* be made, and than how, in our vast commercial democracy, almost any difference—by which I mean almost any exception—promptly acquires prodigious relief. The value here was at once that the place could offer to view a society, the only one in the country, in which Men existed, and that that rich little fact became the key to everything. Superficially taken, I recognize, the circumstance fails to look portentous; but it looms large immediately, gains the widest bearing, in the light of any direct or extended acquaintance with American conditions. From the moment it is adequately borne in mind that the business-man, in the United States, may, with no matter what dim struggles, gropings, yearnings, never hope to be anything *but* a business-man, the size of the field he so abdicates is measured, as well as the fact of the other care to which his abdication hands it over. It lies there waiting, pleading from all its pores, to be occupied—the lonely waste, the boundless gaping void of "society"; which is but a rough name for all the other so numerous relations with the world he lives in that are imputable to the civilized being. Here it is then that the world he lives in accepts its doom and becomes, by his default, subject and plastic to his mate; his default having made, all around him, the unexampled opportunity of the woman—which she would have been an incredible fool not to pounce upon. It needs little contact with American life to perceive how she has pounced, and how, outside business, she has made it over in her image. She has been, up to now, on the vast residual tract, in peerless possession, and is occupied in developing and extending her wonderful conquest, which she appreciates to the last inch of its extent.

III

She has meanwhile probably her hours of amazement at the size of her windfall; she cannot quite live without wonder at the oddity of her so "sleeping" partner, the strange creature, by her side, with his values and his voids, but who is best known to her as having yielded what she would have clutched to the death. Yet these are mere mystic, inscrutable possibilities—dreams, for us, of her hushed, shrouded hours: the face she shows, on all the facts, is that of mere unwinking tribute to the matter of course. The effect of these high signs of assurance in her has been—and it is really her master-stroke—to represent the situation as perfectly normal. Her companion's attitude, totally destitute of high signs, does everything it can to further this feat; so that, as disposed together in the American picture, they testify, extraordinarily, to the *successful* rupture of a universal law, the sight is at first, for observation, most mystifying. Then the impunity of the whole thing gains upon us; the equilibrium strikes us, however strangely, as at least provisionally stable; we see that a society in many respects workable would seem to have been arrived at, and that we shall in any case have time to study it. The phenomenon may easily become, for a spectator, the sentence written largest in the American sky: when he is in search of the characteristic, what else so plays the part? The woman is two-thirds of the apparent life—which means that she is absolutely all of the social; and, as this is nowhere else the case, the occasion is unique for seeing what such a situation may make of her. The result elsewhere, in Europe generally, of conditions in which men have actively participated and to which, throughout, they personally contribute, she has only the old story to tell, and keeps telling it after her fashion. The woman produced by a women-made society alone has obviously quite a new story—to which it is not for a moment to be gainsaid that the world at large has, for the last thirty years in particular, found itself lending an attentive, at times even a charmed, ear. The extent and variety of this attention have been the specious measure of the personal success of the type in question, and are always referred to when its value happens to be challenged. "The American woman?—why, she has beguiled, she has conquered, the globe: look at her fortune everywhere and fail to accept her if you can."

She has been, accordingly, about the globe, beyond all doubt, a huge success of curiosity; she has at her best—and far beyond any consciousness and intention of her own, lively as these for the most part usually are—infinitely amused the nations. It has been found among them that, for more reasons that we can now go into, her manner of embodying and representing her sex has fairly made of her a new human convenience, not unlike fifty of the others, of a slightly different order, the ingenious mechanical appliances, stoves, refrigerators, sewing-machine, type-writers, cash-registers, that have done so much, in the household and the place of business, for the American name. By which I am of course far from meaning that the revelation has been of her utility as a domestic drudge; it has been much rather in the fact that the advantages attached to her being a woman at all have been so happily combined with the absence of the drawbacks, for persons intimately dealing with her, traditionally suggested by that condition. The corresponding advantages, in the light of almost any old order, have always seemed inevitably paid for by the drawbacks; but here, unmistakably, was a case in which—as at first appeared, certainly—they were to be enjoyed very nearly for nothing. What it came to, evidently, was that she had been grown in an air in which a hundred of the "European" complications and dangers didn't exist, and in which also she had had to take upon herself a certain training for freedom. It was not that she had had, in the vulgar sense, to "look out" for herself, inasmuch as it was of the very essence of her position not to be threatened or waylaid; but that she could develop her audacity on the basis of her security, just as she could develop her "powers" in a medium from which criticism was consistently absent. Thus she arrived, full-blown, on the general scene, the least criticized object, in proportion to her importance, that had ever adorned it. It would take long to say why her situation, under this retrospect, may affect the inner fibre of the critic himself as one of the most touching on record; he may merely note his perception that she was to have been after all but the sport of fate. For why need she originally, he wonders, have embraced so confidently, so gleefully, yet so unguardedly, the terms offered her to an end practically so perfidious? Why need she, unless in the interest of her eventual discipline, have turned away with so light a heart after watching the Man, the deep American man, retire into his tent and let down the flap? She had her "paper" from him, their agreement signed and sealed; but would she not, in some other air and under some other sky, have been visited by a saving instinct? Would she not have said "No, this is too unnatural; there must be a trap in it somewhere—it's addressed really, in the long run, to making a fool of me?" It is impossible, of course, to tell; and her case, as it stands for us, at any rate, is that she showed no doubts. It is not on the American scene and in the presence of mere American phenomena that she is even yet to be observed as showing them; but does not my digression find itself meanwhile justified by the almost clear certainty that the first symptoms of the revulsion—of the *convulsion*, I am tempted to say—must break out in Washington?

For here—and it is what I have been so long in coming to—here alone in the American world, do we catch the other sex not observing the agreement. I have described this anomaly, at Washington, as that of Man's socially "existing"; since we have seen that his fidelity to his compact throughout the country in general has involved his not doing so. What has happened, obviously, has been that his reasons, at a stroke, have dropped, and that he finds himself, without them, a different creature. He has discovered that he *can* exist in other connections than that of the Market, and that all he has therefore to settle is the question of whether he may. The most delicate interest of Washington is the fact that it is quite practically *being* settled there—in the practical way which is yet also the dramatic. *Solvitur ambulando*; it is being settled—that is the charm—as it goes, settled without discussion. It would be awkward and gross to say that Man has dealt any conscious blow at the monopoly of his companion, or that her prestige, as mistress of the situation, has suffered in any manner a noted abatement. Yet none the less, as he has there, in a degree, socially found himself and, allured by the new sense, is evidently destined to seek much further still, the sensible effect, the change of impression on one's coming from other places, is of the most marked. Man is solidly, vividly present, and the presence of Woman has consequently, for the proposed intensity, to reckon with it. The omens on behalf of the former appearance are just now strikingly enhanced, as happens, by the accident of the rare quality, as it were, of the particular male presence supremely presiding there; and it would certainly be strange that this idea of the re-committal to masculine hands of some share at least in the interest of civilisation, some part of the social property and social office, should not, from so high an example, have received a new impulse and a new consecration. Easily enough, if we had space here to consider it, might come up the whole picture of the new indications thus afforded, the question of the degree in which a sex capable, in the American air, of having so despoiled itself may really be capable of retracing its steps and repairing its mistake. It would appear inevitable to ask whether such a mistake on such a scale *can* prove effectively reparable—whether ground so lost can be effectively recovered. Has not the American woman, with such a start, gained such an irreducible advance, on the whole high plane of the amenities, that her companion will never catch up with her? This last is an inquiry that I must, alas, brush aside, though feeling it, as I have already noted, *the* most oddly interesting that the American spectacle proposes to us; only saying, provisionally, that the aspect of manners through the nation at large offers no warrant whatever for any prompt "No" to it.

It is not, however, of the nation at large I here speak; the case is of the extremely small, though important and significant, fraction of the whole represented by the Washington group—which thus shows us the Expropriated Half in the very act of itself pondering that issue. Is the man "up to it," up to the major heritage, the man who *could*, originally, so inconceivably, and for a mere mess of pottage if there ever was one, let it go? "Are we up to it, really, at this time of day, and what on earth will awfully become of us if the question, once put to the test, shall have to be decided against us?" I think it not merely fanciful to say that some dim, distressful interrogative sound of that sort frequently reached, in the Washington air, the restless analyst—though not to any quickening of his own fear. With a perfect consciousness that it was still early to say, that the data are as yet insufficient and that the missing quantity must absolutely be found before it can be weighted and valued, he was none the less struck with the felicity of many symptoms and would fairly have been able to believe at moments that the character hitherto so effaced has but to show the confidence of taking itself for granted. That act of itself reveals, restores, reinstates and completes this character. Is it not, for that matter, essentially implied in our recognition of the place as the City of Conversation? The victim of effacement, the outcast at the door, has, all the while we have been taking of him, *talked himself* back; and if anything could add to this happy portent it would be another that had scarcely less bearing. Nowhere more than in Washington, positively, were the women to have struck me as naturally and harmoniously in the social picture—as happily, soothingly, proportionately, and no more than proportionately, participant and ministrant. Hence the irresistible conclusion that with the way really shown them they would only ask to take it; the way being their assent to the truth that the abdication of the Man proves even (after the first flush of their triumph) as bad really for their function as for his. Hence, in fine, the appearance that, with the proportions re-established, they will come to recognize their past world as a fool's paradise, and their present, and still more their future, as much more made to endure. They could not, one reasoned, have been in general, so perfectly agreeable unless they had been pleased, and they could not have been pleased without the prospect of gaining, by the readjusted relation, more, on the whole, than they were to lose; without the prospect even again perhaps of truly and insidiously gaining more than the other beneficiary. That *would* be, I think, the feminine conception of a readministered justice. Washington, at such a rate, in any case, might become to them as good as "Europe," and a Europe of their own would obviously be better than a Europe of other people's. There are, after all, other women on the other continents.

IV

One might have been sure in advance that the character of a democracy would nowhere more sharply mark itself than in the democratic substitute for a court city, and Washington is cast in the mould that expresses most the absence of salient social landmarks and constituted features. Here it is that conversation, as the only invoked presence, betrays a little in its adequacy to the furnishing forth, all by itself, of an outward view. It tells us it must be there, since in all the wide empty vistas nothing else is, and the general elimination can but have left it. A pleading, touching effect, indeed, lurks in this sense of it as seated, at receipt of custom, by any decent door of any decent domicile and watching the vacancy for reminder and appeal. It is left to conversation alone to people the scene with accents; putting aside two or three objects to be specified, there is *never* an accent in it, up and down, far and wide, save such as fall rather on the ear of the mind: those projected by the social spirit starved for the sense of an occasional emphasis. The White House is an accent—one of the lightest, sharpest possible; and the Capitol, of course, immensely another; though the latter falls on the exclusively political page, as to which I have been waiting to say a word. It should meanwhile be mentioned that we are promised these enhancements, these illustrations, of the great general text, on the most magnificent scale; a splendid projected and announced Washington of the future, with approaches even now grandly outlined and massively marked; in face of which one should perhaps confess to the futility of any current estimate. If I speak thus of the Capitol, however, let me not merely brush past the White House to get to it—any more than feel free to pass into it without some preliminary stare at the wondrous Library of Congress which glitters in fresh and almost unmannerly emulation, almost frivolous irrelevance of form, in the neighbourhood of the greater building. About the ingenuities and splendours of this last costly structure, a riot of rare material and rich ornament, there would doubtless be much to say—did not one everywhere, on all such ground, meet the open eye of criticism simply to establish with it a private intelligence, simply to respond to it by a deprecating wink. The guardian of that altar, I think, is but too willing, on such a hint, to let one pass without the sacrifice.

It is a case again here, as on fifty other occasions, of the tribute instantly paid by the revisiting spirit; but paid, all without question, to the general kind of presence for which the noisy air, over the land, feels so sensibly an inward ache—the presence that corresponds there, no matter how loosely, to that of the housing and harbouring European Church in the ages of great disorder. The Universities and the greater Libraries (the smaller, for a hundred good democratic reasons, are another question), repeat, in their manner, to the imagination, East and West, the note of the old thick-walled convents and quiet cloisters: they are large and charitable, they are sturdy, often proud and often rich, and they have their incalculable value that they represent the only intermission to inordinate rapacious traffic that the scene offers to view. With this suggestion of sacred ground they play even upon the most restless of analysts as they will, making him face about, with ecstasy, any way they seem to point; so that he feels it his business much less to count over their shortcomings than to proclaim them places of enchantment. They are better at their worst than anything else at its best, and the comparatively sweet sounds that stir their theoretic stillness are for him as echoes of the lyre of Apollo. The Congressional Library is magnificent, and would become thus a supreme sanctuary even were it ten times more so: there would seem to be nothing then but to pronounce it a delight and have done with it—or let the appalled imagination, in other words, slink into it and stay there. But here is pressed precisely, with particular force, the spring of the question that takes but a touch to sound: is the case of this remarkable creation, by exception, a case in which the violent waving of the pecuniary wand *has* incontinently produced interest? The answer can only be, I feel, a shy assent—though shy indeed only till the logic of the matter is apparent. This logic is that, though money alone can gather in on such a scale the treasures of knowledge, these treasures, in the form of books and documents, themselves organize and furnish their world. They appoint and settle the proportions, they thicken the air, they people the space, they create and consecrate all their relations, and no one shall say that, where they scatter life, which they themselves in fact *are*, history does not promptly attend. Emphatically yes, therefore, the great domed and tiered, galleried and statued central hall of the Congressional, the last word of current constructional science and artistic resource, already crowns itself with that grace.

The graceful thing in Washington beyond any other, none the less, is the so happily placed and featured White House, the late excellent extensions and embellishments of which have of course represented expenditure—but only of the refined sort imposed by some mature portionless gentlewoman on relatives who have accepted the principle of making her, at a time of life, more honourably comfortable. The whole ample precinct and margin formed by the virtual continuity of its grounds with those expanses in which the effect of the fine Washington Obelisk rather spends or wastes itself (not a little as if some loud monosyllable had been uttered, in a preoccupied company, with a due production of sympathy or sense)—the fortunate isolation of the White House, I say, intensifies its power to appeal to that musing and mooning visitor whose perceptions alone, in all the conditions, I hold worthy of account. Hereabouts, beyond doubt, history had from of old seemed to me insistently seated, and I remember a short spring-time of years ago when Lafayette Square itself, contiguous to the Executive Mansion, could create a rich sense of the past by the use of scarce other witchcraft than its command of that pleasant perspective and its possession of the most prodigious of all Presidential effigies, Andrew Jackson, as archaic as a Ninevite king, prancing and rocking through the ages. If that atmosphere, moreover, in the fragrance of the Washington April, was even a quarter of a century since as a liquor of bitter-sweet taste, overflowing its cup, what was the ineffable mixture, now, with all the elements further distilled, all the life further sacrificed, to make it potent? One circled about the place as for meeting the ghosts, and one paused, under the same impulse, before the high palings of the White House drive, as if wondering at haunted ground. There the ghosts stood in their public array, spectral enough and clarified; yet scarce making it easier to "place" the strange, incongruous blood-drops, as one looked through the rails, on that revised and freshened page. But one fortunately has one's choice, in all these connections, as one turns away; the mixture, as I have called it, is really here so fine. General Jackson, in the centre of the Square, still rocks his hobby and the earth; but the fruit of the interval, to my actual eyes, hangs nowhere brighter than in the brilliant memorials lately erected to

Lafayette and to Rochambeau. Artful, genial, expressive, the tribute of French talent, these happy images supply, on the spot, the note without which even the most fantasticating sense of our national past would feel itself rub forever against mere brown homespun. Everything else gives way, for me, I confess, as I again stand before them; everything, whether as historic fact, or present *agrément*, or future possibility, yields to this one high luxury of our old friendship with France.

The "artistic" Federal city already announced spreads itself then before us, in plans elaborated even to the finer details, a city of palaces and monuments and gardens, symmetries and circles and far radiations, with the big Potomac for water-power and water-effect and the recurrent Maryland spring, so prompt and so full-handed, for a perpetual benediction. This imagery has, above all, the value, for the considering mind, that it presents itself as under the wide-spread wings of the general Government, which fairly make it figure to the rapt vision as the object caught up in eagle claws and lifted into fields of air that even the high brows of the municipal boss fail to sweep. The wide-spread wings affect us, in the prospect, as great fans that, by their mere tremor, will blow the work, at all steps and stages, clean and clear, disinfect it quite ideally of any germ of the job, and prepare thereby for the American voter, on the spot and in the pride of possession, quite a new kind of civic consciousness. The scheme looms largest, surely, as a demonstration of the possibilities of that service to him, and nothing about it will be more interesting than to measure—though this may take time—the nature and degree of his alleviation. Will the new pride I speak of sufficiently inflame him? Will the taste of the new consciousness, finding him so fresh to it, prove the right medicine? One can only regret that we must still rather indefinitely wait to see—and regret it all the more that there is always, in America, yet another lively source of interest involved in the execution of such designs, and closely involved just in proportion as the high intention, the formal majesty, of the thing seems assured. It comes back to what we constantly feel, throughout the country, to what the American scene everywhere depends on for half its appeal or its effect; to the fact that the social conditions, the material, pressing and pervasive, make the particular experiment or demonstration, whatever it may pretend to, practically a new and incalculable thing. This general Americanism is often the one tag of character attaching to the case after every other appears to have abandoned it. The thing is happening, or will have to happen, in the American way—that American way which is more different from all other native ways, taking country with country, than any of these latter are different from each other; and the question is of how, each time, the American way will see it through.

The element of suspense—beguilement, ever, of the sincere observer—is provided for by the fact that, though this American way never fails to come up, he has to recognize as by no means equally true that it never fails succeed. It is inveterately applied, but with consequences bewilderingly various; which means, however, for our present moral, but that the certainty of the *determined* American effect is an element to attend quite especially such a case as the employment of the arts of design, on an unprecedented scale, for public uses, the adoption on this scale of the whole æsthetic law. Encountered in America, phenomena of this order strike us mostly as occurring in the historic void, as having to present themselves in the hard light of that desert, and as needing to extort from it, so far as they can, something of the shading of their interest. Encountered in older countries, they show, on the contrary, as taking up the references, as consenting perforce to the relations, of which the air is already full, and as having thereby much rather to get themselves expressive by charm than to get themselves expressive by weight. The danger "in Europe" is of their having too many things to say, and too many others to distinguish these from; the danger in the States is of their not having things enough—with enough tone and resonance furthermore to give them. What therefore will the multitudinous and elaborate forms of the Washington to come have to "say," and what, above all, besides gold and silver, stone and marble and trees and flowers, will they be able to say it *with*? That is one of the questions in the mere phrasing of which the restless analyst finds a thrill. There is a thing called interest that has to be produced for him—positively as if he were a rabid usurer with a clutch of his imperilled bond. He has seen again and again how the most expensive effort often fails to lead up to interest, and he has seen how it may bloom in soil of no more worth than so many layers of dust and ashes. He has learnt in fact—he learns greatly in America—to mistrust any plea for it *directly* made by money, which operates too often as the great puffing motor-car framed for whirling him, in his dismay, quite away from it. And he has inevitably noted, at the same time, from how comparatively few other sources this rewarding dividend on his invested attention may be drawn. He thinks of these sources as few, that is, because he sees the same ones, which are the references by which interest is fed, used again and again, with a desperate economy; sees the same ones, even as the human heroes, celebrities, extemporized lions or scapegoats, required social and educational figure-heads and "values," having to serve in *all* the connections and adorn all the tales. That is one of the liveliest of his American impressions. He has at moments his sense that, in presence of such vast populations, and instilled, emulous demands, there is not, outside the mere economic, enough native history, recorded or current, to go round.

V

It seemed to me on the spot, moreover, that such reflections were rather more than less pertinent in face of the fact that I was again to find the Capitol, whenever I approached, and above all whenever I entered it, a vast and many-voiced creation. The thing depends of course somewhat on the visitor, who will be the more responsive, I think, the further back into the "origins" of the whole American spectacle his personal vision shall carry him; but this hugest, as I suppose it, of all the homes of debate only asks to put forth, on opportunity, an

of President, Vice-President and representatives in Congress. ... The acting assistant doorkeeper of the House visitors' gallery. ... The junior Senator from Delaware. ... The assistant to the secretary to the chief clerk of the Division of Audits and Disbursements, Bureau of Stationary and Supplies, Postoffice Department. ... The press-agent to the chaplain of the House. ... The commercial attaché to the American legation at Quito. ... The chauffeur to the fourth assistant Post-master General. ... The acting substitute elevator-man in the Washington monument. ... The brother to the wife of the brother-in-law of the Vice-President. ... The aunt to the sister of the wife of the officer in charge of ceremonials, State Department. ... The neighbor of the cousin of the step-father of the sister-in-law of the President's pastor. ... The superintendent of charwomen in Temporary Storehouse B7, Bureau of Navy Yards and Docks. ... The assistant confidential clerk to the acting chief examiner of the Patent Office. ... The valet to the Chief Justice.

151
Architecture

ELBERT PEETS

This article on Washington's architecture is part of a larger undertaking, the *WPA Guides* (Works Progress Administration) which were very much a product of 1930s America, and were produced for a number of cities (most obviously New York and Los Angeles). As such they are virtually cultural documents in their own right, especially in the way they "construct" an image of the city. Peets's essay is both historical and touristic. Its interest lies in the way it maps a significant geography as symptomatic of what constitutes the meaningful architecture (and habitats) of Washington D.C. in the 1930s.

This chapter has to do with the buildings of the city, primarily as visible things—their appearance and how they came to be given the external form they have. This chapter is written to help you enjoy Washington, to guide you toward high adventure of the spirit as you ride and walk through the Capital City of these States. Or, if at such times your spirit be not set a-singing, this chapter wants you at least to have the experience of viewing curious things, of accounting for them in some degree, and of comprehending their place in the flow of architectural form.

To keep the buildings of Washington from impinging upon the mind as a chaos of unrelated phenomena is not easy. Because, although Washington has a certain totality of expression, very few buildings contribute much to the peculiar feel of the city. The soul of Washington is in its plan, its streets and squares and radiating avenues. Without this mastering plan the buildings, in the first view, would be a bedlam. But beyond the conspicuous variety of the first impression lies a mass of substantial uniformity—the red-brick row houses that form the city's great pool of human habitation. This is not true of the shopping-and-theater blocks along F Street nor of lower Connecticut Avenue—in smart streets such as these everything is yellow brick, stucco, enamel, glass,

Source: Elbert Peets, "Architecture", *The WPA Guide to Washington D.C.* (published in 1937 as *Washington: City and Capital*), Washington D.C. pp. 68–79.

and gray stone. And everywhere through the city there are a few houses of stone and many brick houses painted buff, white or gray. Whole suburbs are built of single houses. But a sampling of the city, at random, including all its four sections, will prove that it is a city of row houses, and that a warm dark red is its basic color.

There is good clay in the region, rich in the iron that makes bricks red. And the row house is the ancient English folkway of urban residence. To a visitor from Detroit or Los Angeles, talk of brick houses will arouse expectations of quaintness and Colonial charm. As a general picture, these hopes will be disappointed. Washington was born in the fine afternoon of the Georgian style, but it was born poor; most of the lovely houses of "circa 1800" were built in such truly Colonial towns as Charleston, Philadelphia, and Salem. Yet here and there, throughout the older regions of the city, there are veterans that have the unmistakable distinction of Georgian building. Many are fat bourgeois houses with big chimneys, honest pitched roofs, and well-proportioned windows of small panes. A few are really distinguished town houses, worthy of Savannah or New Castle. The yellow-and-white Blair House near Lafayette Square is one of the best. Another, on Eye Street near 20th, is now the home of the Arts Club. This [view] about the paucity of Colonial architecture in Washington obviously does not apply to Georgetown, where one can stroll for an hour without leaving the eighteenth century. The feel of the Georgetown streets is quite unlike Washington. The Post Office Department draws no line between the two communities, but to the town planner they are wholly apart. Poetically speaking, Washington is like an oak in its prime that stands beside a beautiful old dogwood, always in flower.

In the Capital's third or fourth decade new forms crept in. The swing from Georgian began with taller windows, jamb mouldings carried around arched openings without a break at the impost, ornamentations suggesting foliage forms—all details shifting slightly toward medieval motifs, perhaps a good deal affected by baroque. In much the same way the latest Gothic buildings shifted toward grotesque classic details. Cornices increased in projection, modillions developing into brackets enriched with details that exhibited the powers of the new woodworking machinery. Some of these first frontier fruits of styles already sophisticated in London and New York have much charm of pattern, like a perfectly designed sampler or title page.

Contemporary with this softening of the Georgian was another movement, almost contrary in spirit. This was the Greek Revival, of which not many strongly marked creations survive in the residential architecture of Washington. The first considerable growth of the city was at the time of the Civil War and it fell within an architectural era more influenced by pressed brick than by any of the historical styles. The invention of pressed brick (always deplored by persons of a nostalgic cast) changed quite radically the face of Washington's houses. It came at a moment when, simultaneously, the nineteenth century group-soul yearned for good mechanical finish, for fancy workmanship, and for a flavor of medieval picturesqueness. Pressed brick made all of these things possible. They could be laid with narrow joints, forming a neat smooth wall; their uniform size and sharp edges made possible all sorts of picturesque patterns—picturesqueness was thought to be essence of medieval art—that would have been lost in the crude approximations of the old handmade bricks. The skilled bricklayers of Washington took full advantage of the qualities of the new material. They built a prodigious quantity and variety of bay windows, corner towers, dormers, parapets, corbelled cornices, porches, entrance arches, window enframements, string courses, mouldings, ornamental panels, and many things for which orderly architecture has no recognized designation.

Externally, the conspicuous thing about these nineteenth-century row houses is their bay windows. For this, there is a particular reason. Washington streets are wide and the city-owned right of way goes right up to the front wall of the buildings. The sidewalk is from 5 to 30 feet away from the house. The front yard, therefore, although normally used as if it were private property, is part of the street. The city permits lot owners to erect porches projecting 5 feet and bay windows projecting 4 feet beyond the property line. A great majority of the older houses accordingly have projecting bays extending from the ground to the roof, or beyond it. A few of these are half-round, like the Bullfinch bow windows of Boston; most are square or half-octagonal. They catch sunlight and afford long views along the street, but they rob Washington of the reposeful street-walls that are so pleasant in many row-house towns.

During the 1870's and 1880's, square miles of these brick row houses were put up by speculative builders. Most of them are three stories, plus a high basement. Very often there is a service entrance under the porch or iron steps. The kitchen is often in the basement with dumb-waiter service to a butler's pantry. Or the kitchen is on the main floor, in an ell. The stairs are against a side wall. There is often an alcove (above the entrance hall) in connection with the front bedroom. The bathroom is often attenuated in plan. There is rarely need for a second stairway because Washington maids usually go home in the evening.

These streets of quaint-to-ugly—but fairly comfortable—row houses form the bulk of the city's shelter. They should not be high-hatted by wandering citizens of western towns in which everyone lives in a white-painted vine-covered cottage. No wood houses and landscaped lawns could give 60 years of use at moderate rentals and come through looking as neat and decent as most of the Washington row houses do.

The expression "row house" does not necessarily imply identity in the row. It is applied also to contiguous houses built separately, as the finest row houses in Washington were built. Until about 1920 quite expensive residences of the row-house type were still being erected, such as the house Secretary McAdoo built on 16th Street just above Scott Circle. On Massachusetts and New Hampshire Avenues and on all the streets around Dupont Circle are other specimens of the genre worth coming upon. The best of these houses are not invariably the latest to be built nor the most expensive. Scattered through the city there are row houses of all periods—most often dating from the eighties and nineties—that are sincere and sympathetic architecture. Perhaps some of them were influenced by the houses Richardson built for Hay and Adams on Lafayette Square and by LaFarge's scholarly brickwork in St. Matthew's Church and its parish house. Some of them embody delightfully both the dignity and the geniality of comfortable living. Many are by unknown masters, in styles long left behind. But these houses, along with the happy blunders and strange antics of less thoughtful designers, give to the old and middle-aged streets of Washington a fascination that few cities can equal.

It is fortunate for Washington that the mass of its residential construction has been done in permanent materials and that most of its workers are of the white-collar class—and, further, that so many of them are single and that so many want to live within walking distance of their work. These circumstances, shielded by an intelligently enforced zoning law, have preserved the prosperity of large sections which, in Cleveland or Chicago, would have degenerated into slums or blighted areas. It is quite possible, in Washington, for a street to change in type of occupancy without conspicuous evidence of physical and aesthetic decay. In most cities the aesthetic decay of a street begins with an invasion of boarding houses. In Washington the boarding houses do not necessarily have that result. Government clerks must live economically but are used to living moderately well. The big but-homelike boarding house is for such as these a happy compromise. They listen to the radio in the senator's parlor and dine comfortably in his basement billiard-room. By cutting a few doors through party walls, this profitable co-operation can spread into two or three adjacent houses. And the only outward sign of the changed occupancy is a brass plate letting you know that this is the Wyoming Club.

In recent years the new residences in what might be called the upper brackets have been built as free-standing houses, though rather closely grouped. In the Kalorama district, for example, and in other neighborhoods lying northerly and westerly of the city, there are hundreds of sumptuous homes. And in other suburbs, as in Chevy Chase and Takoma Park, there are even larger areas of free-standing houses occupied by people of moderate means. Around the outer fringe there are now the usual clusters of ducky little FHA love-nests with red or blue shutters tacked up beside the windows. Yet the brick row house has not been abandoned. There are broad areas of new brick rows near the city—notably around the outlying section of New Hampshire Avenue. Most of them have become "group houses"—each unit in the row is tricked out with a half-timber gable end or a patch of stone to give it "individuality."

Then there are the apartments. Relatively few in number until the "other war," they began to grow like popcorn when the New Deal came to town. Some of them are of a magnitude and completeness that make them impressive machines for that way of living. Take Westchester Apartments, for example. And more recently the outlying apartment groups—as Falkland, at the end of the 16th Street, Colonial Village and Buckingham across the Potomac in Arlington—have developed a new manner of suburban living in which the amenities of space and pleasant environment compensate for relative remoteness from urban bright lights. The formula, one sees, is based on car ownership and cheap land.

In these apartment groups a sophisticated Rip van Winkle, just awakening, would note something passing strange. The side and rear walls of these buildings are made of the same brick as the front! Since the Civil War it has been the American custom to build apartments on the Queen-Anne-Mary Ann principle—yellow-brick front and red-brick for the rest, or vice versa in towns where red brick costs more than yellow. The decay of that custom is a major architectural phenomenon. To explain this change some observers say it was pioneered by Government housing projects. These, since they must be built of the cheapest permanent material, are built, all four sides, of one thing, usually a hard common brick. Perhaps the current fashion in windows also has some bearing on the phenomenon; you really have to design in three dimensions if you use corner windows. Which reminds one that the city has lately been peppered with smart and likable apartment house creations in yellow brick with corner windows and glass doors. This is the chic of 1942. Which is true, doubtless, of every other city in the country.

Washington is not like other cities, however, in respect to two sorts of buildings, the headquarters of national organizations and the embassies of foreign countries. In each of these classifications a numerical majority occupy quarters built originally as sumptuous private residences. In recent decades, however, many countries have erected embassy buildings—those of Great Britain and Japan are pointed out to every tourist. In material and style the proud-yet-gracious British group is perhaps a reminder that the word "ours" at one time did not dissociate English ways from American. The fascinating little home of the Venezuelan delegation is a tactful reminder that our South American neighbors know as much as we do about what goes on in the world of shelter-construction.

The commercial buildings of a city traverse in their evolution the same cultural valleys that the road of residential construction passes through. But the ways in which they are alike are often hard to see. And, as time passes, the bifurcation widens. The early shops and offices of Washington have not survived well—nothing like as well as they have in Frederick and Annapolis. There have been such constant remodelling and rebuildings here, and whole regions of old commercial buildings—such as the site of the Triangle—have been razed. There is no building in Washington to match the old Iron Block in Milwaukee. Indeed there is probably not in the city a good specimen of the castiron store fronts that Bogardus of New York sold by the yard in the 1870's. Of the beetling rococo pediments that flourished in those days only a few gallant examples still exist.

The passing of these old store fronts is a loss to American street architecture. The modern stores, all trying to be unlike their neighbors, each purposely singing in a different key, are inimical to all civility and community expression. At least so it seems when the transvaluation begins. A fashionable retail street, after the stores have built up their own smart society, has its fetching qualities. As examples: three or four blocks in the vicinity of F Street and 14th, various uptown shopping centers, and scattered gatherings of chic modern shops.

Washington's office buildings are not high; none of them would rate as skyscrapers in New York or Chicago. They tend, rather, to have great bulk. That is conspicuously true of the Federal Loan Building (1940), one in which simple bulk is given dramatic value. It is utterly plain, the surest way to attain distinction in an environment somewhat overrich in architectural insistency. There is a fine view down 15th Street (from the east sidewalk, well up toward Massachusetts Avenue) in which this geometric mass composes with the Washington Monument. The building seems, in this view, quite contemporary in form-feeling with the Monument.

The Longfellow Building (1914), Connecticut and Rhode Island Avenues, is so modern that it has a horizontal flagpole. It is also noteworthy as the first radically modern office of a Government agency. Its design is clearly iconoclastic; the building might be thought of as a favorable portent if the location were favorable from any point of view but its advertising value. It is at a busy and noisy corner; land in the vicinity is too expensive to clear for car parking. Incidentally, the concentrated bulk of the building makes it what should be technically known as a bomber's delight.

Half this chapter has been written and hardly a word has been said about marble and granite and limestone, about domes and columns and porticos. Surely it is time, in Shakespeare's Shakespearean phrase, for us to feed our eyes upon the monuments and things of fame that do renown this city! It seems to be a tenet of American opinion—at least of Washington official opinion—that all governmental buildings should be monumental and, further, that monumental means built of stone. That is not at all logical but it does give a shade of sense to the statement that in Washington brick is the building material of the people and stone the building material of the Government. In any case, the history of Government building in Washington has paralleled pretty closely the evolution of stone architecture through the same years.

Architecture is as international as music. The story of Government building through the century and a half from Dr. Thornton's Capitol to the latest defense office building, has continuity and reason only when it is correlated with the flow of architecture in the world outside Washington. Buildings are preceded (and followed!) by thinking. Colonial thinking about architecture was based on European ideas—with a certain lag in time. Palladio and Vignola, in 1791, were a little old-fashioned in several European capitals, but they still ruled architectural thought in the young United States. In detailing the general style of the Capitol, Thornton and the rest had the good sense to play safe. What is astounding about it, even as it was first built, is the Capitol's great size. That was not merely a good guess that the country would grow in population. It was part of the architectural thought of such men as Jefferson to do things on a large open, and dignified scale. They lived in the Renaissance tradition.

While the Capitol was being completed, new ferments were at work in the architectural world. The Greek Revival came; to it the new States of the west owe many buildings—among them the beautiful State Capitol of Ohio. In Washington, Elliott made the south portico of the old Patent Office a copy of the Parthenon front. In 1836 Robert Mills did the first section of the Treasury—the east side, with its 30 lovely Ionic columns. The next great work was the construction of the wings of the Capitol, carried through by Thomas Walter. Quite consciously he respected and followed the style of the old building, just as he respected Mills' work in his completion of the Treasury. Walter was quite aware of the new ways that were coming in. He saw the growing vogue of the Gothic Revival—in some of its forms an unquitting revival of baroque—of which the first non ecclesiastical work in this country, the old Smithsonian, was completed in 1856.

Thomas Walte saw also the development of a technical means of producing cheaply the foliage forms and medieval motifs for which people were asking. This was cast iron. It was also used in the manufacture of beams, columns, and plates for building construction. Cast iron made it possible to build a high dome over the Capitol. In designing it, Walter was not controlled by any existing work, as he had been in designing the wings, and he used, on the dome, a good deal of tactful ornamentation of the wreath and garland type. Walter knew how to weave in the new forms without offense to his Renaissance dome.

But our luck could not continue. By the 1870's the universal romantic taste had taken possession of the new building materials and the new machines for cutting wood and stone. In the buildings that resulted there was often confusion between purpose and means, but there was at least restless experimentation—the dead hand of the past lay more lightly on the period than is supposed. The old national Museum, built in 1879, was presumed to be Byzantine, but essentially it was a fairly efficient enclosure of space for the exhibition of a lot of things to a lot of people.

Thus always the stream of thought swirled around the beloved past and the exciting present. A vigorous eddy was caused by the physical as well as creative bulk of H. H. Richardson. His cousins of the spirit turned granite quarries into post offices—one of them stands alongside Pennsylvania Avenue. The planners of the Triangle hatched a clever scheme to get this building torn down. They laid out a circular plaza which cannot be completed while the Old Post Office stands. But the plaza forms a rather pleasant setting for the huge old veteran, whose demolition does not seem imminent.

Another architectural current that caused important erosions along these shores was the French École des Beaux Arts. It brought Washington the Library of Congress, begun in 1886. Before it was completed, came the Chicago Fair. The World's Fair of 1893 was Beaux-Arts too, but it had the advantage of being done by such men as Charles Follen McKim and the further advantage of being executed in plaster of Paris, a beautiful material. Louis Sullivan said, "The damage wrought by the World's Fair will last for half a century from its date." Adding 50 to 1893 gives 1943. We are at the end of the prophesied period. In Washington, at least, Sullivan has proved to be right. With but few exceptions, every piece of official architecture built in this city during that period has had some of the Chicago plaster of Paris at its core, though over each has been laid a pretty veneer in some acceptable style.

The Commission of 1901, which laid down the lines on which modern Washington has developed, included in its membership the principal designers of the Chicago Fair. Their tenets were these: (1) "Classical" style; (2) uniform cornice height; (3) concentration of buildings in the Triangle, along the Mall, and around the Capitol and White House.

The Senate and House Office buildings were the first result of the program. They were handsome adaptations of Gabriel's Garde-Meuble on the Place de la Concorde. The Lincoln Memorial and Cass Gilbert's Treasury Annex, first section of the intended frame around Lafayette Square, were started during the World War. Then there was a pause; the Triangle plans were initiated about 1925. By that time architects had learned and unlearned. The San Francisco Fair had taught the beauty of enclosed courts. More was known about the French plaza designs of the eighteenth century. Charles Platt had designed skyscrapers that were Florentine palaces. The Federal Reserve Banks had explored new ways to give office buildings the appearance of being stone and not steel. And the Beaux-Arts clichés, as painfully illustrated by the now-disdained District Building, had definitely shifted to the shady side of the ledger. So, when the Triangle plans appeared, they were very different from the plans that would have been made two decades before. Of course there was no disloyalty to the three basic rules of 1901. No one questioned the importance of making the Triangle symbolize America by building beautiful Italian palaces for our file clerks. None of the first-flight architects questioned the architectural taste of the Secretary of the Treasury, nor did he question theirs. So the Triangle was built. It contains a pair of plazas in the French mode of 1760 (Contant d'Ivry made a somewhat similar plan for a proposed town hall in Paris) and the buildings are done in delicately modulated French and Italian palatial styles, the precise identification of each being a matter that could interest only a professor of architecture. One of them, to be sure, the Justice Building, is modern—in the sense of using a Greek style more primitive than the standard.

Though still pointed to with official pride, the Triangle has had in recent years a very poor press. The location is usually described as atrocious city planning and the common attitude toward the monumental office buildings is simply satirical. The cost, also monumental, is mentioned with chiding.

Perhaps the Triangle ought never to have been built, but there it is, and any pile of stones has within it certain fundamental verities which no stupidity of client or architect can quite take away. That melodramatic group of porticos on Constitution Avenue—how easily, on a foggy evening, can be imagined the incredulous joy of some long-future Hugo Robert, searching the ruined city for scenes to paint, when he should first come upon those ingratiating, vainglorious columns and cornices. ... While its red-tile roofs were still being laid, the Triangle became a landmark, a thing of the past. Waddy Wood's South Interior Building was designed in an avowed mood of "No more Seicento, no more Louis Seize, no more enclosed light courts." So the style of the building is a stripped-down Patent Office or Treasury; the few columns are purified by being square and lacking entasis.

The new burst of office construction has still further high-lighted the Triangle as the-thing-to-do-it-different-from. The new buildings south of the Mall, around 4th Street SW., are about as modern as they could be without being Modern. Since the Renaissance tradition of wall-membering is easily adapted to long vertical openings but not to horizontal ones, simplicity in the glass area has been attained by carrying vertical windows through three or four stories. A large simplicity of scale results; whether that is a good thing is less a matter of architecture than of town planning.

The War Department Building (1941) is still a little farther post-Triangle. It disclaims any controlling cornice-height. It is not a composition carried out upon flat facades but a masculine composition of great masses mortised together. This building truly looks like a war department; if its functions were something like the Battle Abbey in Richmond—if it contained the sacred things of the Department, the maps, rosters, and records of wars, old weapons, stands of frayed battle flags; if it had a distinguished place in the street plan of the city; if, further, the clerks and typewriters and desks and ash trays were housed somewhere else in well-oriented offices—this would be a first-rate building.

As every new building has been planned and built it has become more and more clear that the town planning factors are becoming absolutely crucial to the success of new buildings in Washington. There are already so many huge buildings around the Mall, with many more sites not yet filled, that each new construction finds itself with numerous inevitable relationships—and if these relationships are not well managed, the whole group suffers. Then too, the law of diminishing returns operates to destroy the value of purely individual architectural effects. From now on, in Washington, the effort to give strong and independent character to a building will be useless. The only large satisfactions must come from position, logical environment, relationships, and the embracing totalities of town planning. Architects who disregard this condition will go down in defeat and will carry their friends with them

The Mellon Gallery—as people persist in calling the National Gallery of Art—can be used to illustrate some of these relationships. The Gallery has as its central element a large saucer dome. Considered in detachment from the function of the building and from the social responsibilities of art, it is a very lovely dome. If the plan of a large garden and a little town were organized under the control of that dome, the whole composition might be magnificent. But here it is a secondary mass and stands near another dome, that of the National Museum (now called the Natural History Building), which is somewhat suppressed in character (though vigorously detailed), with the evident purpose of deferring to the Capitol. Approaching the Capitol now, along the Mall, one is extremely conscious of the domes of the Museum and the Gallery, so different in color and in feel of contour. They are obviously unfriendly, and the Capitol suffers from this feud within its guard of honor. If other buildings set down along the Mall continue to be of the egocentric sort, each piping its own tune, the result will be pandemonium. The first law of aesthetic town planning is that the many must efface themselves so that the few may stand forth in dignity and dominance.

By way of technical comment on the Mellon Gallery, something should be said as warning against calling it "pure Greek." The building is more Roman than Greek, but more Renaissance than either. The use of shallow rectangular niches at a corner of various wall-surfaces—the purpose being to destroy secondary symmetries in order to strengthen the dominant axis—is a baroque conception. If the building must be ticketed with a style, it might be called Beaux-Arts in the purity of death.

Mr. Pope's other Pantheon, the Jefferson Memorial, has one great advantage over its sister on the Mall—it will have a fine garden of its own to stand in. It will in fact be a jewel of garden art, a very gracious thing as you see the dome, in the afternoon, from across the Potomac—likable, yet a little soft. Perhaps we have here a materialization of the cherry-blossom sentiment which hangs heavily upon the site. But inevitably, in this garden Pantheon, one questions the use of a portico with a circular colonnade. It is normally, as in the Pantheon itself, the contrast of the columns of the portico against the solid wall of the rotunda that gives the portico its contrast, its "value." That Mr. Jefferson, standing within, will be comfortably illuminated, is the anxious prayer of the Society for the Prevention of Cruelty to Statuary.

Since all these capitoline structures were the fruits of ideas, things that were first built in the ever-wandering faith of men, it may be well to mention two buildings that are as yet (1942) only images. One is Frank Lloyd Wright's fairyland design for a "crystal city" on a fine site near the intersection of Connecticut and Florida Avenues. There would be a hotel, shops, recreation. The land cost compels high buildings—which the District authorities refuse to authorize.

The other is the Saarinens' plan for the proposed new Smithsonian. At the instigation of Edward Bruce, Congress in 1938 authorized a competition for the design of the building. To no sophisticated surprise, the award went to a "modernistic" design. No money has been appropriated for the building, but the plan hovers over the Mall, an angel of hope to some, an evil ghost to others.

These words were caught together as Washington seethed with defense work and workers. A chapter about buildings in Washington is being assembled in more lasting stuff than words. Every day there are rumors of new buildings, temporary and permanent, to be located downtown, uptown, or across the Anacostia River. Persons of optimistic temperament are saying that the incubus of monumentality will be thrown off and that no more office buildings will be designed and located to ornament the Mall. Persons of more realistic temperament base similar hopes upon the purifying effect of budgetary limitations. Well, the pendulum was swinging back, long before defense crept upon us. The flight from plaster of Paris has now become a race. We shall see....

Washington, however, is not, even in defense time, a place exclusively of work and conferences and air-conditioning. It is a place of recreation also, where people walk or drive on a summer evening, and a place of pilgrimage, where hundreds of people go late at night to the Lincoln Memorial. It is a beautiful place, as American cities go, made beautiful by its trees, skies, fogs, rivers, and low green hills, even by the rich chaos of its buildings, a chaos subdued by the city's magnificently ordered plan. To gain these values of the spirit and the eye, the visitor to Washington should explore persistently, should go into all parts of the city, wander through unknown streets and famous ones, go to the terrace of the Capitol before sunset until the lights are on, walk up Meridian Hill during a snowstorm. Upon all this material the lights and shadows play, giving golden moments of beauty equally to true and false, old and new. Washington has inexhaustible resources for those who have the gift of fashioning dramatic experiences out of architecture.

152

Aeneas at Washington

ALLEN TATE

For an introductory note to Tate, see Chapter 99. Tate's response to the symbolic grandeur of Washington is matched by the ambiguous meaning he gives to its icons. However, it is obviously contrasted with his experience in the New York subway (see Chapter 99). The classical allusions in the poem to Washington are both characteristic and central. Aeneas was, of course, the hero of Virgil's *Aeneid.*

I myself saw furious with blood
Neoptolemus, at his side the black Atridae,
Hecuba and the hundred daughters, Priam
Cut down, his filth drenching the holy fires.
In that extremity I bore me well,
A true gentleman, valorous in arms,
Disinterested and honourable. Then fled:
That was a time when civilization
Run by the few fell to the many, and
Crashed to the shout of men, the clang of arms:
Cold victualing I seized, I hoisted up
The old man my father upon by back,
In the smoke made by sea for a new world
Saving little—a mind imperishable
If time is, a love of past things tenuous
As the hesitation of receding love.

(To the reduction of uncitied littorals
We brought chiefly the vigor of prophecy,
Our hunger breeding calculation
And fixed triumphs.)

Source: Allen Tate, "Aeneas at Washington", *Collected Poems*, New York, 1977, pp. 68–69.

I saw the thirsty dove
In the glowing fields of Troy, hemp ripening
And tawny corn, the thickening Blue Grass
All lying rich forever in the green sun.
I see all things apart, the towers that men
Contrive I too contrived long, long ago.
Now I demand little. The singular passion
Abides its object and consumes desire
In the circling shadow of its appetite.
There was a time when the young eyes were slow,
Their flame steady beyond the firstling fire,
I stood in the rain, far from home at nightfall
By the Potomac, the great Dome lit the water,
The city my blood had built I knew no more
While the screech-owl whistled his new delight
Consecutively dark.

Struck in the wet mire
Four thousand leagues from the ninth buried city
I thought of Troy, what we had built her for.

1933

153

July in Washington

ROBERT LOWELL

Robert Lowell (1911–77) was born in Boston, Massachusetts into a New England family, whose "famous" forebears included Amy Lowell. Lowell attended Harvard University but came under the influence of the Southern writer, Allen Tate, and spent time at Kenyon College–very much against the grain of his family's traditions. Lowell's Protestant family could trace its roots back to *The Mayflower*. His subsequent life was as complex as his poetry. He became a Catholic, was imprisoned as a conscientious objector, suffered from periods of extreme depression, and lived through a series of unhappy personal circumstances.

Lord Weary's Castle (1946) established his reputation, although it was the intensely personal writing of *Life Studies* (1959) which gave him the status of "confessional" poet of the age. *For the Union Dead*, (1964) seeks to render private perspectives in the context of public life and history, while *Notebook* (1970) virtually reduces the poetic enterprise to sonnet-like snatches of clarity in a swirling world of incipient chaos. Very much a poet of the age, his form uses both the traditional and the modern, and is characterised by a dense moral tension cast against the certainties of the past against the anxieties of the present.

See Ian Hamilton, *Robert Lowell—A Biography* (1983) and Marjorie Perloff, *The Poetic Themes of Robert Lowell* (1973). See also Chapter 159.

July in Washington

The stiff spokes of this wheel
touch the sore spots of the earth.

On the Potomac, swan-white
power launches keep breasting the sulphurous wave.

Source: Robert Lowell, "July in Washington", *For the Union Dead*, New York, 1964, p. 58,

Otters slide and dive and slick back their hair,
raccoons clean their meat in the creek.

On the circles, green statues ride like South American
liberators above the breeding vegetation—

prongs and spearheads of some equatorial
backland that will inherit the globe.

The elect, the elected ... they come here bright as dimes,
and die dishevelled and soft.

We cannot name their names, or number their dates—
circle on circle, like rings on a tree—

but we wish the river had another shore,
some further range of delectable mountains,

distant hills powdered blue as a girl's eyelid.
It seems the least little shove would land us there,

that only the slightest repugnance of our bodies
we no longer control could drag us back.

Boston

154

A Week's Visit to Boston *and* The Boston of Today

WALT WHITMAN

See Chapter 95 for an introductory note to Walt Whitman and see also Chapters 146, 147 and 148 in order to "place" Whitman's response to Boston against that of New York and Washington.

A Week's Visit to Boston

May 1, '81—Seems as if all the ways and means of American travel today had been settled, not only with reference to speed and directness, but for the comfort of women, children, invalids, and old fellows like me. I went on by a through train that runs daily from Washington to the Yankee metropolis without change. You get in a sleeping car soon after dark in Philadelphia, and after ruminating an hour or two, have your bed made up if you like, draw the curtains, and go to sleep in it—fly on through Jersey to New York—hear in your half-slumbers a dull jolting and bumping sound or two—are unconsciously toted from Jersey City by a midnight steamer around the Battery and under the big bridge to the track of the New Haven road—resume your flight eastward, and early the next morning you wake up in Boston. All of which was my experience. I wanted to go to the Revere House. a tall unknown gentleman (a fellow passenger on his way to Newport, he told me; I had just chatted a few moments before with him) assisted me out through the depot crowd, procured a hack, put me in it with my traveling bag, saying smilingly and quietly, "Now I want you to let this be *my* ride," paid the driver, and before I could remonstrate, bowed himself off.

The occasion of my jaunt, I suppose I had better say here, was for a public reading of "The death of Abraham Lincoln" essay, on the sixteenth anniversary of that tragedy, which reading duly came off, night of April 15. Then I lingered a week in Boston—felt pretty well (the mood propitious, my paralysis lulled)—

Source: Walt Whitman, "A Week's Visit to Boston" and "The Boston of Today", *Specimen Days*, 1882.

went around everywhere, and saw all that was to be seen, especially human beings. Boston's immense material growth—commerce, finance, commission stores, the plethora of goods, the crowded streets, and sidewalks—made of course the first surprising show. In my trip out West, last year, I thought the wand of future prosperity, future empire, must soon surely be wielded by St. Louis, Chicago, beautiful Denver, perhaps San Francisco; but I see the said wand stretched out just as decidedly in Boston, with just as much certainty of staying; evidences of copious capital—indeed no center of the New World ahead of it (half the big railroads in the West are built with Yankees' money, and they take the dividends). Old Boston with its zigzag streets and multitudinous angles (crush up a sheet of letter paper in your hand, throw it down, stamp it flat, and that is a map of old Boston)—new Boston with its miles upon miles of large and costly houses—Beacon Street, Commonwealth Avenue, and a hundred others. But the best new departures and expansions of Boston, and of all the cities of New England, are in another direction.

The Boston of Today

In the letters we get from Dr. Schliemann (interesting but fishy) about his excavations there in the far-off Homeric area, I notice cities, ruins, etc., as he digs them out of their graves, are certain to be in layers—that is to say, upon the foundation of an old concern, very far down indeed, is always another city or set of ruins, and upon that another superadded—and sometimes upon that still another—each representing either a long or rapid stage of growth and development, different from its predecessor, but unerringly growing out of and resting on it. In the moral, emotional, heroic, and human growths (the main of a race in my opinion), something of this kind has certainly taken place in Boston. The New England metropolis of today may be described as sunny (there is something else that makes warmth, mastering even winds and meteorologies, though those are not to be sneezed at), joyous, receptive, full of ardor, sparkle, a certain element of yearning, magnificently tolerant, yet not to be fooled; fond of good eating and drinking—costly in costume as its purse can buy; and all through its best average of houses, streets, people, that subtle something (generally thought to be climate, but it is not—it is something indefinable in *the race*, the turn of its development) which effuses behind the whirl of animation, study, business, a happy and joyous public spirit, as distinguished from a sluggish and saturnine one. Makes me think of the glints we get (as in Symonds's books) of the jolly old Greek cities. Indeed there is a good deal of the Hellenic in B., and the people are getting handsomer too—padded out, with freer motions, and with color in their faces. I never saw (although this is not Greek) so many fine-looking gray-haired women. At my lecture I caught myself pausing more than once to look at them, plentiful everywhere through the audience—healthy and wifely and motherly, and wonderfully charming and beautiful—I think such as no time or land but ours could show.

155

Looking Backward: 2000–1887

EDWARD BELLAMY

Edward Bellamy (1850–98) was born in Massachusetts, where he lived for most of his life. He is best known for *Looking Backward: 2000–1887*, published in 1888. *Looking Backward* is a Utopian novel in which the main character, Julian West, is "transported" from the Boston of 1887 to the Boston of 2000. He views a city based on the principles of collective equality. Socialist in its outlook, it gained immense popularity in the period and led to the formation of a "Nationalist" party based on its values. Bellamy developed his socialist outlook in his journal *New Nation* (1891–94). Inevitably, *Looking Backward* contrasts the future and the present very much to the detriment of Bellamy's contemporary Boston. See A. E. Morgson, *Edward Bellamy*, 1944.

... "You are probably surprised," said my companion, "to see that, although you are a century older than when you lay down to sleep in that underground chamber, your appearance is unchanged. That should not amaze you. It is by virtue of the total arrest of the vital functions that you have survived this great period of time. If your body could have undergone any change during your trance, it would long ago have suffered dissolution."

"Sir," I replied, turning to him, "what your motive can be in reciting to me with a serious face this remarkable farrago, I am utterly unable to guess, but you are surely yourself too intelligent to suppose that anybody but an imbecile could be deceived by it. Spare me any more of this elaborate nonsense and once and for all tell me whether you refuse to give me an intelligible account of where I am and how I came here. If so, I shall proceed to ascertain my whereabouts for myself, whoever may hinder."

"You do not, then, believe that this is the year 2000?"

"Do you really thing it necessary to ask me that?" I returned.

"Very well," replied my extraordinary host. "Since I cannot convince you, you shall convince yourself. Are you strong enough to follow me upstairs?"

Source: Edward Bellamy, *Looking Backward: 2000–1887*, 1888, from Chs. III, IV, X, XXVIII.

"I am as strong as I ever was," I replied angrily, "as I may have to prove if this jest is carried much further."

"I beg, sir," was my companion's response, "that you will not allow yourself to be too fully persuaded that you are the victim of a trick, lest the reaction, when you are convinced of the truth of my statements, should be too great."

The tone of concern, mingled with commiseration, with which he said this, and the entire absence of any sign of resentment at my hot words, strangely daunted me, and I followed him from the room with an extraordinary mixture of emotions. He led the way up two flights of stairs and then up a shorter one, which landed us upon a belvedere on the housetop. "Be pleased to look around you," he said, as we reached the platform, "and tell me if this is the Boston of the nineteenth century."

At my feet lay a great city. Miles of broad streets, shaded by trees and lined with fine buildings, for the most part not in continuous blocks but set in larger or smaller enclosures, stretched in every direction. Every quarter contained large open squares filled with trees, along which statues glistened and fountains flashed in the late-afternoon sun. Public buildings of a colossal size and architectural grandeur unparalleled in my day raised their stately piles on every side. Surely I had never seen this city nor one comparable to it before. Raising my eyes at last toward the horizon, I looked westward. That blue ribbon winding away to the sunset—was it not the sinuous Charles? I looked east—Boston harbor stretched before me within its headlands, not one of its green islets missing.

I knew then that I had been told the truth concerning the prodigious thing which had befallen me.

IV

I did not faint, but the effort to realize my position made me very giddy, and I remember that my companion had to give me a strong arm as he conducted me from the roof to a roomy apartment on the upper floor of the house, where he insisted on my drinking a glass or two of good wine and partaking of a light repast.

"I think you are going to be all right now," he said cheerily. "I should not have taken so abrupt a means to convince you of your position if your course, while perfectly excusable under the circumstances, had not rather obliged me to do so. I confess," he added, laughing, "I was a little apprehensive at one time that I should undergo what I believe you used to call a knockdown in the nineteenth century, if I did not act rather promptly. I remember that the Bostonians of your day were famous pugilists, and thought best to lose no time. I take it you are now ready to acquit me of the charge of hoaxing you."

"If you had told me," I replied profoundly awed, "that a thousand years instead of a hundred had elapsed since I last looked on this city, I should now believe you."

"Only a century has passed," he answered, "but many a millennium in the world's history has seen changes less extraordinary.

"And now," he added, extending his hand with an air of irresistible cordiality, "let me give you a hearty welcome to the Boston of the twentieth century and to this house. My name is Leete, Doctor Leete they call me."

"My name," I said as I shook his hand, "is Julian West."

"I am most happy in making your acquaintance, Mr. West," he responded. "Seeing that this house is built on the site of your own, I hope you will find it easy to make yourself at home in it."

After my refreshment Doctor Leete offered me a bath and a change of clothing, of which I gladly availed myself.

It did not appear that any very startling revolution in men's attire had been among the great changes my host had spoken of, for, barring a few details, my new habiliments did not puzzle me at all.

Physically, I was now myself again. But mentally, how it was with me, the reader will doubtless wonder. What were my intellectual sensations, he may wish to know, on finding myself so suddenly dropped as it were into a new world. In reply let me ask him to suppose himself suddenly, in the twinkling of an eye, transported from earth, say, to Paradise or Hades. What does he fancy would be his own experience? Would his thoughts return at once to the earth he had just left, or would he, after the first shock, well-nigh forget his former life for a while, albeit to be remembered later, in the interest excited by his new surroundings? All I can say is, that if his experience were at all like mine in the transition I am describing, the latter hypothesis would prove the correct one. The impression of amazement and curiosity which my new surroundings produced occupied my mind, after the first shock, to the exclusion of all other thoughts. For the time the memory of my former life was, as it were, in abeyance.

No sooner did I find myself physically rehabilitated through the kind offices of my host, than I became eager to return to the housetop; and presently we were comfortably established there in easy chairs, with the city beneath and around us. After Doctor Leete had responded to numerous questions on my part, as to the ancient landmarks I missed and the new ones which had replaced them, he asked me what point of the contrast between the new and the old city struck me most forcibly.

"To speak of small things before great," I responded, "I really think that the complete absence of chimneys and their smoke is the detail that first impressed me."

"Ah!" ejaculate my companion with an air of much interest. "I had forgotten the chimneys, it is so long since they went out of use. It is nearly a century since the crude method of combustion on which you depended for heat became obsolete."

"In general," I said, "what impresses me most about the city is the material prosperity on the part of the people which its magnificence implies."

"I would give a great deal for just one glimpse of the Boston of your day," replied Doctor Leete. "No doubt, as you imply, the cities of that period were rather shabby affairs. If you had the taste to make them splendid, which I would not be so rude as to question, the general poverty resulting from your extraordinary industrial system would not have given you the means. Moreover, the excessive individualism which then prevailed was inconsistent with much public spirit. What little wealth you had seems almost wholly to have been lavished in private luxury. Nowadays, on the contrary, there is no destination of the surplus wealth so popular as the adornment of the city, which all enjoy in equal degree."

The sun had been setting as we returned to the housetop, and as we talked night descended upon the city.

"It is growing dark," said Doctor Leete. "Let us descend into the house. I want to introduce my wife and daughter to you."

His words recalled to me the feminine voices which I had heard whispering about me as I was coming back to conscious life; and, most curious to learn what the ladies of the year 2000 were like, I assented with alacrity to the proposition. The apartment in which we found the wife and daughter of my host, as well as the entire interior of the house, was filled with a mellow light, which I knew must be artificial, although I could not discover the source from which it was diffused. Mrs. Leete was an exceptionally fine-looking and well-preserved woman of about her husband's age, while the daughter, who was in the first blush of womanhood, was the most beautiful girl I had ever seen. Her face was as bewitching as deep-blue eyes, delicately tinted complexion, and perfect features could make it, but even had her countenance lacked special charms, the faultless luxuriance of her figure would have given her place as a beauty among the women of the nineteenth century. Feminine softness and delicacy were in this lovely creature deliciously combined with an appearance of health and abounding physical vitality too often lacking in a maidens with whom alone I could compare her. It was a coincidence trifling in comparison with the general strangeness of the situation, but still striking, that her name should be Edith.

The evening that followed was certainly unique in the history of social intercourse, but to suppose that our conversation was peculiarly strained or difficult would be a great mistake. I believe indeed that it is under what may be called unnatural, in the sense of extraordinary, circumstances that people behave most naturally, for the reason, no doubt, that such circumstances banish artificiality. I know at any rate that my intercourse that evening with these representatives of another age and world was marked by an ingenuous sincerity and frankness such as but rarely crown long acquaintance. No doubt the exquisite tact of my entertainers had much to do with this. Of course there was nothing we could talk of but the strange experience by virtue of which I was there, but they talked of it with an interest so naive and direct in its expression as to relieve the subject to a great degree of the element of the weird and the uncanny which might so easily have been overpowering. One would have supposed that they were quite in the habit of entertaining waifs from another century, so perfect was their tact.

For my own part, never do I remember the operations of my mind to have been more alert and acute than that evening, or my intellectual sensibilities more keen. Of course I do not mean that the consciousness of my amazing situation was for a moment out of mind, but its chief effect thus far was to produce a feverish elation, a sort of mental intoxication.[1]

Edith Leete took little part in the conversation, but when several times the magnetism of her beauty drew my glance to her face, I found her eyes fixed on me with an absorbed intensity, almost like fascination. It was evident that I had excited her interest to an extraordinary degree, as was not astonishing, supposing her to be a girl of imagination. Though I supposed curiosity was the chief motive of her interest, it could but affect me as it would not have done had she been less beautiful.

Doctor Leete, as well as the ladies, seemed greatly interested in my account of the circumstances under which I had gone to sleep in the underground chamber. All had suggestions to offer to account for my having been forgotten there, and the theory which we finally agreed on offers at least a plausible explanation, although whether it be in its details the true one, nobody, of course, will ever know. The layer of ashes found above the chamber indicated that the house had been burned down. Let it be supposed that the conflagration had taken place the night I fell asleep. It only remains to assume that Sawyer lost his life in the fire or by some accident connected with it, and the rest follows naturally enough. No one but he and Doctor Pillsbury either knew of the existence of the chamber or that I was in it, and Doctor Pillsbury, who had gone that night to New Orleans, had probably never heard of the fire at all. The conclusion of my friends, and of the public, must have been that I had perished in the flames. An excavation of the ruins, unless thorough, would not have disclosed the recess in the foundation walls connecting with my chamber. To be sure, if the site had been again built upon, at least immediately, such an excavation would have been necessary, but the troublous times and the undesirable character of the locality might well have prevented rebuilding. The size of the trees in the garden now occupying the site indicated, Doctor Leete said, that for more than half a century, at least, it had been open ground.

X

"If I am going to explain our way of shopping to you," said my companion, as we walked along the street, "you must explain your way to me. I have never been able to understand it from all I have read on the subject. For example, when you had such a vast number of shops, each with its different assortment, how could a lady ever settle upon any purchase till she had visited all the shops, for, until she had, she could not know what there was to choose from."

"It was as you suppose. That was the only way she could know," I replied.

"Father calls me an indefatigable shopper, but I should soon be a very fatigued one if I had to do as they did," was Edith's laughing comment.

"The loss of time in going from shop to shop was indeed a waste which the busy bitterly complained of," I said. "But as for the ladies of the idle class, though they complained also, I think the system was really a godsend by furnishing a device to kill time."

"But say there were a thousand shops in a city, hundreds, perhaps, of the same sort, how could even the idlest find time to make their rounds?"

"They really could not visit all, of course," I replied. "Those who did a great deal of buying, learned in time where they might expect to find what they wanted. This class had made a science of the specialities of the shops, and bought at advantage, always getting the most and best for the least money. It required, however, long experience to acquire this knowledge. Those who were too busy, or bought too little to gain it, took their chances and were generally unfortunate, getting the least and worst for the most money. it was the merest chance if persons not experienced in shopping received the value of their money."

"But why did you put up with such a shockingly inconvenient arrangement when you saw its faults so plainly?" Edith asked me.

"It was like all our social arrangements," I replied. "You can see their faults scarcely more plainly than we did, but we saw no remedy for them."

"Here we are at the store of our ward," said Edith, as we turned in at the great portal of one of the magnificent public buildings I had observed in my morning walk. There was nothing in the exterior aspect of the edifice to suggest a store to a representative of the nineteenth century. There was no display of goods in the great windows, or any device to advertise wares, or attract custom. Nor was there any sort of sign or legend on the front of the building, a majestic life-size group of statuary, the central figure of which was a female ideal of Plenty, with her cornucopia. Judging from the composition of the throng passing in and out, about the same proportion of the sexes among shoppers obtained as in the nineteenth century. As we entered, Edith said that there was one of these great distributing establishments in each ward of the city, so that no residence was more than five or ten minutes' walk from one of them. It was the first interior of a twentieth-century public building that I had ever beheld, and the spectacle naturally impressed me deeply. I was in a vast hall full of light, received not alone from the windows on all sides, but from the dome, the point of which was a hundred feet above. Beneath it, in the center of the hall, a magnificent fountain played, cooling the atmosphere to a delicious freshness with its spray. The walls and ceiling were frescoed in mellow tints, calculated to soften without absorbing the light which flooded the interior. Around the fountain was a space occupied with chairs and sofas, on which many persons were seated conversing. Legends on the walls all about the hall indicated to what classes of commodities the counters below were devoted. Edith directed her steps toward one of these, where samples of muslin of a bewildering variety were displayed, and proceeded to inspect them.

"Where is the clerk?" I asked, for there was no one behind the counter, and no one seemed coming to attend to the customer.

"I have no need of the clerk yet," said Edith. "I have not made my selection."

"It was the principal business of clerks to help people to make their selections in my day," I replied.

"What! To tell people what they wanted?"

"Yes. And oftener to induce them to buy what they didn't want."

"But did not ladies find that very impertinent?" Edith asked, wonderingly. "What concern could it possibly be to the clerks whether people bought or not?"

"It was their sole concern," I answered. "They were hired for the purpose of getting rid of the goods, and were expected to do their utmost, short of the use of force, to compass that end."

"Ah, yes! How stupid I am to forget!" said Edith. "The storekeeper and his clerks depended for their livelihood on selling the goods in your day. Of course that is all different now. The goods are the nation's They are here for those who want them, and it is the business of the clerks to wait on people and take their order; but it is not the interest of the clerk or the nation to dispose of a yard or a pound of anything to anybody who does not want it." She smiled as she added, "How exceedingly odd it must have seemed to have clerks trying to induce one to take what one did not want, or was doubtful about!"

"But even a twentieth-century clerk might make himself useful in giving you information about the goods, though he did not tease you to buy them," I suggested.

"No," said Edith, "that is not the business of the clerk. These printed cards, for which the government authorities are responsible, give us all the information we can possibly need."

I saw then that there was fastened to each sample a card containing in succinct form a complete statement of the make and materials of the goods and all its qualities, as well as price, leaving absolutely no point to hang a question on.

"The clerk has, then, nothing to say about the goods he sells?" I said.

"Nothing at all. It is not necessary that he should know or profess to know anything about the. Courtesy and accuracy in taking orders are all that are required of him."

"What a prodigious amount of lying that simple arrangement saves!" I ejaculated.

"Do you mean that all the clerks misrepresented their goods in your day?" Edith asked.

"God forbid that I should say so!" I replied. "For there were many who did not, and they were entitled to especial credit, for when one's livelihood and that of his wife and babies depended on the amount of goods he could dispose of, the temptation to deceive the customer—or let him deceive himself—was well-nigh overwhelming. But, Miss Leete, I am distracting you from your task with my talk."

"Not at all. I have made my selections." With that she touched a button, and in a moment a clerk appeared. He took down her order on a table with a pencil which made two copies, of which he gave one to her, and enclosing the counterpart in a small receptacle, dropped it into a transmitting tube.

"The duplicate of the order," said Edith as she turned away from the counter, after the clerk had punched the value of her purchase out of the credit card she gave him, "is given to the purchaser, so that any mistakes in filling it can be easily traced and rectified."

"You were very quick about your selections," I said. "May I ask how you knew that you might not have found something to suit you better in some of the other stores? But probably you are required to buy in your own district."

"Oh, no," she replied. "We buy where we please, though naturally most often near home. But I should have gained nothing by visiting other stores. The assortment in all is exactly the same, representing as it does in each case samples of all the varieties produced or imported by the United States. That is why one can decide quickly, and never need visit two stores."

"And is this merely a sample store? I see no clerks cutting off goods or marking bundles."

"All our stores are sample stores, except as to a few classes of articles. The goods, with these exceptions, are all at the great central warehouse of the city, to which they are shipped directly from the producers. We order from the sample and the printed statement of texture, make, and qualities. The orders are sent to the warehouse, and the goods distributed from there."

"That must be a tremendous saving of handling," I said. "By our system, the manufacturer sold to the wholesaler, the wholesaler to the retailer, and the retailer to the consumer, and the goods had to be handled each time. You avoid one handling of the goods, and eliminate the retailer altogether, with his big profit and the army of clerks it goes to support. Why, Miss Leete, this store is merely the order department of a wholesale house, with no more than a wholesaler's complement of clerks. Under our system of handling the goods, persuading the customer to buy them, cutting them off, and packing them, ten clerks would not do what one does here. The saving must be enormous."

"I suppose so," said Edith, "but of course we have never known any other way. But, Mr. West, you must not fail to ask Father to take you to the central warehouse some day, where they receive the orders from the different sample houses all over the city and parcel out and send the goods to their destinations. He took me there not long ago, and it was a wonderful sight. The system is certainly perfect; for example, over yonder in that sort of cage is the dispatching clerk. The order, as they are taken by the different departments in the store, are sent by transmitters to him. His assistants sort them and enclose each class in a carrier-box by itself. The dispatching clerk has a dozen pneumatic transmitters before him answering to the general classes of goods, each communicating with the corresponding department at the warehouse. He drops the box of orders into the tube it calls for, and a few moments later it drops on the proper desk in the warehouse, together with all the orders of the same sort from the other sample stores. The orders are read off, recorded, and sent to be filled, like lightening. The filing I thought the most interesting part. Bales of cloth are placed on spindles and turned by machinery, and the cutter, who also has a machine, works right through one bale after another till exhausted, when another man takes his place; and it is the same with those who fill the orders in any other staple. The packages are then delivered by larger tubes to the city districts, and thence distributed to the houses. You may understand how quickly it is all done when I tell you that my order will probably be at home sooner than I could have carried it from here."

"How do you manage in the thinly settled rural districts?" I asked.

"The system is the same," Edith explained, "the village sample shops are connected by transmitters with the central county warehouse, which may be twenty miles away. The transmission is so swift, though, that the time lost on the way is trifling. But, to save expense, in many counties one set of tubes connect several villages with the warehouse, and then there is time lost waiting for one another. Sometimes it is two or three hours before goods ordered are received. It was so where I was staying last summer, and I found it quite inconvenient."[2]

"There must be many other respects also, no doubt, in which the country stores are inferior to the city stores," I suggested.

"No," Edith answered, "they are otherwise precisely as good. The sample shop of the smallest village, just like this one, gives you your choice of all the varieties of goods the nation has, for the county warehouse draws on the same source as the city warehouse."

As we walked home I commented on the great variety in the size and cost of the houses. "How is it," I asked, "that this difference is consistent with the fact that all citizens have the same income?"

"Because," Edith explained, "although the income is the same, personal taste determines how the individual shall spend it. Some like fine houses; others, like myself, prefer pretty clothes; and still others want an elaborate table. The rents which the nation receives for these houses vary, according to size, elegance, and location, so that everybody can find something to suit. The larger houses are usually occupied by large families, in which there are several to contribute to the rent; while small families, like ours, find smaller houses more convenient and economical. It is a matter of taste and convenience wholly. I have read that in old times people often kept up establishments and did other things which they could not afford for ostentation, to make people think them richer than they were. Was it really so, Mr. West?"

"I shall have to admit that it was," I replied.

"Well, you see, it could not be so nowadays; for everybody's income is known, and it is known that what is spent one way must be saved another."

XXVIII

"It's a little after the time you told me to wake you, sir. You did not come out of it as quick as common, sir." The voice was the voice of my man Sawyer. I sat bolt upright in bed and stared around. I was in my underground chamber. The mellow light of the lamp which always burned in the room when I occupied it illuminated the familiar walls and furnishings. By my bedside, with the glass of sherry in his hand which Doctor Pillsbury prescribed on first rousing from a mesmeric sleep, by way of awakening the torpid physical functions, stood Sawyer.

"Better take this right off, sir," he said, as I stared blankly at him. "You look kind of flushed like, sir, and you need it."

I tossed off the liquor and began to realize what had happened to me. It was, of course, very plain. All that about the twentieth century had been a dream. I had but dreamed of that enlightened and carefree race of men and their ingeniously simple institutions, of the glorious new Boston with its domes and pinnacles, its gardens and fountains, and its universal reign of comfort. The amiable family which I had learned to know so well, my genial host and mentor, Doctor Leete, his wife, and their daughter, the second and more beauteous Edith, my betrothed—these, too, had been but figments of a vision.

For a considerable time I remained in the attitude in which this conviction had come over me, sitting up in bed gazing at vacancy, absorbed in recalling the scenes and incidents of my fantastic experience. Sawyer, alarmed at my looks, was meanwhile anxiously inquiring what was the matter with me. Roused at length by his importunities to a recognition of my surroundings, I pulled myself together with an effort and assured the faithful fellow that I was all right. "I have had an extraordinary dream, that's all, Sawyer," I said, "a most-ex-traor-dinary-dream."

I dressed in a mechanical way, feeling lightheaded and oddly uncertain of myself, and sat down to the coffee and rolls which Sawyer was in the habit of providing for my refreshment before I left the house. The morning newspaper lay by the plate. I took it up, and my eye fell on the date, May 31, 1887. I had known, of course, from the moment I opened my eyes that my long and detailed experience in another century had been a dream, and yet it was startling to have it so conclusively demonstrated that the world was but a few hours older than when I had lain down to sleep.

Glancing at the table of contents at the head of the paper, which reviewed the news of the morning, I read the following summary:

> FOREIGN AFFAIRS. The impending war between France and Germany. The French Chambers asked for new military credits to meet Germany's increase of her army. Probability that all Europe will be involved in case of war.—Great suffering among the unemployed in London. They demand work. Monster demonstration to be made. The authorities uneasy.—Great strikes in Belgium. The government preparing to repress outbreaks. Shocking facts in regard to the employment of girls in Belgium coal mines.—Wholesale evictions in Ireland.
>
> HOME AFFAIRS. The epidemic of fraud unchecked. Embezzlement of half a million in New York.—Misappropriation of a trust fund by executors. Orphans left penniless.—Clever system of thefts by a bank teller; $50,000 gone.—The coal barons decide to advance the price of coal and reduce production.—Speculators engineering a great wheat corner at Chicago.—A clique forcing up the price of coffee.—Enormous

land-grabs of Western syndicates.—Revelations of shocking corruption among Chicago officials. Systematic bribery.—The trials of the Boodle alderman to go on at New York.—Large failures of business houses. Fears of a business crisis.—A large grist of burglaries and larcenies.—A woman murdered in cold blood for her money at New Haven.—A householder shot by a burglar in this city last night.—A man shoots himself in Worcester because he could not get work. A large family left destitute.—An aged couple in New Jersey commit suicide rather than go to the poorhouse.—Pitiable destitution among the women wage workers in the great cities.—Startling growth of illiteracy in Massachusetts.—More insane asylums wanted.—Decoration Day addresses. Professor Brown's oration on the moral grandeur of nineteenth-century civilization.

It was indeed the nineteenth century to which I had awaked; there could be no kind of doubt about that. Its complete microcosm this summary of the day's news had presented, even to that last unmistakable touch of fatuous self-complacency. Coming after such a damning indictment of the age as that one day's chronicle of worldwide bloodshed, greed, and tyranny, was a bit of cynicism worthy of Mephistopheles, and yet of all whose eyes it had met this morning I was, perhaps, the only one who perceived the cynicism and but yesterday I should have perceived it no more than the others. That strange dream it was which had made all the difference. For I know not how long, I forgot my surroundings after this, and was again in fancy moving in that vivid dream world, in that glorious city, with its homes of simple comfort and its gorgeous public places. Around me were again faces unmarred by arrogance or servility, by envy or greed, by anxious care or feverish ambition, and stately forms of men and women who had never known fear of a fellow man or depended on his favor, but always, in the words of that sermon which still rang in my ear, had "stood up straight before God."

With a profound sigh and sense of irreparable loss, not the less poignant that it was a loss of what had never really been, I roused at last from my reverie, and soon after left the house.

A dozen times between my door and Washington Street I had to stop and pull myself together, such power had been in that vision of the Boston of the future to make the real Boston strange. The squalor and malodorousness of the town struck me, from the moment I stood upon the street, as facts I had never before observed. But yesterday, moreover, it had seemed quite a matter of course that some of my fellow-citizens should wear silks, and others rags, that some should look well-fed, and others hungry. Now on the contrary the glaring disparities in the dress and condition of the men and women who brushed each other on the sidewalks shocked me at every step, and yet more the entire indifference which the prosperous showed to the plight of the unfortunate. Were these human beings, who could behold the wretchedness of their fellows without so much as a change of countenance? And yet, all the while, I knew well that it was I who had changed, and not my contemporaries. I had dreamed of a city whose people fared all alike as children of one family and were one another's keepers in all things.

Another feature of the real Boston, which assumed the extraordinary effect of strangeness that marks familiar things seen in a new light, was the prevalence of advertising. There had been no personal advertising in the Boston of the twentieth century, because there was no need of any, but here the walls of the buildings, the windows, the broadsides of the newspapers in every hand, the very pavements, everything in fact, save the sky, were covered with the appeals of individuals who sought, under innumerable pretexts, to attract the contributions of others to their support. However the wording might vary, the tenor of all these appeals was the same:

"Help John Jones. Never mind the rest. They are frauds. I, John Jones, am the right one. Buy of me. Employ me. Visit me. Hear me, John Jones. Look at me. Make no mistake. John Jones is the man and nobody else. Let the rest starve, but for God's sake remember John Jones!"

Whether the pathos or the moral repulsiveness of the spectacle most impressed me, so suddenly become a stranger in my own city, I know not. Wretched men, I was moved to cry, who, because they will not learn to be helpers of one another, are doomed to be beggers of one another from the least to the greatest! This horrible babel of shameless self-assertion and mutual depreciation, this stunning clamor of conflicting boasts, appeals, and adjurations, this stupendous system of brazen beggary, what was it all but the necessity of a society in which the opportunity to serve the world according to his gifts, instead of being secured to every man as the first object of social organization, had to be fought for!

I reached Washington Street at the busiest point, and there I stood and laughed aloud, to the scandal of the passer-by. For my life I could not have helped it, with such a mad humour was I moved at sight of the interminable rows of stores on either side, up and down the street so far as I could see—scores of them, to make the spectacle more utterly preposterous, within a stone's throw devoted to selling the same sort of goods. Stores! stores! stores! miles of stores! ten thousand stores to distribute the goods needed by this one city, which in my dream had been supplied with all things from a single warehouse, as they were ordered through one great store in every quarter, where the buyer, without waste of time or labor, found under one roof the world's assortment in whatever line he desired. There the labor of distribution had been so slight as to add but a scarcely perceptible fraction to the cost of commodities to the user. The cost of production was virtually all he paid. But here the mere distribution of goods, their handling alone, added a fourth, a third, a half and more, to the cost. All these ten thousand plants must be paid for, their rent, their staffs of superintendence, their platoons of salesmen, their ten thousand sets of accountants, jobbers, and business dependents, with all they spent in advertising themselves and fighting one another, and the consumers must do the paying. What a famous process for beggaring a nation!

Were these serious men I saw about me, or children, who did their business on such a plan? Could they be reasoning beings, who did not see the folly which, when the product is made and ready for use, wastes so much of it in getting it to the user? If people eat with a spoon that leaks half its contents between bowl and lip, are they not likely to go hungry?

I had passed through Washington Street thousands of times before and viewed the ways of those who sold merchandise, but my curiosity concerning them was as if I had never gone by their way before. I took wondering note of the show windows of the stores, filled with goods arranged with a wealth of pains and artistic device to attract the eye. I saw the throngs of ladies looking in, and the proprietors eagerly watching the effect of the bait. I went within and noted the hawk-eyed floor-walker watching for business, overlooking the clerks, keeping them up to their task of inducing the customers to buy, buy, buy, for money if they had it, for credit if they had it not, to buy what they wanted not, more than they wanted, what they could not afford. At times I momentarily lost the clue and was confused by the sight. Why this effort to induce people to buy? Surely that had nothing to do with the legitimate business of distributing products to those who needed them. Surely it was the sheerest waste to force upon people what they did not want, but what might be useful to another. The nation was so much the poorer for every such achievement. What were those clerks thinking of? Then I would remember that they were not acting as distributors like those in the store I had visited in the dream Boston. They were not serving the public interest, but their immediate personal interest, and it was nothing to them what the ultimate effect of their course on the general prosperity might be, if but they increased their own hoard, for these goods were their own, and the more they sold and the more they got for them, the greater their gain. The more wasteful the people were, the more articles they did not want which they could be induced to buy, the better for these sellers. To encourage prodigality was the express aim of the ten thousand stores of Boston.

Nor were these storekeepers and clerks a whit worse men than any others in Boston. They must earn a living and support their families, and how were they to find a trade to do it by which did not necessitate placing their individual interests before those of others and that of all? They could not be asked to starve while they waited for an order of things such as I had seen in my dream, in which the interests of each and that of all were identical. But, God in heaven! what wonder, under such a system as this about me—what wonder that the city was so shabby, and the people so meanly dressed, an so many of them ragged and hungry!

Some time after this it was that I drifted over into South Boston and found myself among the manufacturing establishments. I had been in this quarter of the city a hundred times before, just as I had been on Washington Street, but here, as well as there, I now first perceived the true significance of what I witnessed. Formerly I had taken pride in the fact that, by actual count, Boston had some four thousand independent manufacturing establishments; but in this very multiplicity and independence I recognized now the secret of the insignificant total product of their industry.

If Washington Street had been like a lane in Bedlam, this was a spectacle as much more melancholy as production is a more vital function than distribution. For not only were these four thousand establishments not working in concert, and for that reason alone operating at prodigious disadvantage, but, as if this did not involve a sufficiently disastrous loss of power, they were using their utmost skill to frustrate one another's effort, praying by night and working by day for the destruction of one another's enterprises.

The roar and rattle of wheels and hammers resounding from every side was not the hum of a peaceful industry, but the clangor of swords wielded for foemen. These mills and shops were so many forts, each under its own flag, its guns trained on the mills and shops about it, and its sappers busy below, undermining them.

Within each one of these forts the strictest organization of industry was insisted on; the separate gangs worked under a single central authority. No interference and no duplicating of work were permitted. Each had his allotted task, and none were idle. By what hiatus in the logical faculty, by what lost link of reasoning, account, then, for the failure to recognize the necessity of applying the same principle to the organization of the national industries as a whole, to see that if lack of organization could impair the efficiency of a shop, it must have effects as much more disastrous in disabling the industries of the nation at large as the latter are vaster in volume and more complex in the relationship of their parts.

People would be prompt enough to ridicule an army in which there were neither companies, battalions, regiments, brigades, divisions, nor army corps—no unit of organization, in fact, larger than the corporal's equal in authority. And yet just such an army were the manufacturing industries of nineteenth-century Boston, an army of four thousand independent squads led by four thousand independent corporals, each with a separate plan of campaign.

Knots of idle men were to be seen here and there on every side, some idle because they could find no work at any price, others because they could not get what they thought a fair price.

I accosted some of the latter, and they told me their grievances. It was very little comfort I could give them. "I am sorry for you," I said. "You get little enough, certainly, and yet the wonder to me is, not that industries conducted as these are do not pay you living wages, but that they are able to pay you any wages at all."

Making my way back again after this to the peninsular city, toward three o'clock I stood on State Street, staring, as if I had never seen them before, at the banks and brokers' offices, and other financial institutions, of which there had been in the State Street of my vision no vestige. Businessmen, confidential clerks, and errand boys were thronging in and out of the banks, for it wanted but a few minutes of the closing hour. Opposite me was the bank where I did business, and presently I crossed the street, and, going in with the crowd, stood in a recess of the wall looking on at the army of clerks handling money, and the cues of depositors at the tellers' windows. An old gentleman whom I knew, a director of the bank, passing me and observing my contemplative attitude, stopped a moment.

"Interesting sight, isn't it, Mr. West," he said. "Wonderful piece of mechanism; I find it so myself. I like sometimes to stand and look on at it just as you are doing. It's a poem, sir, a poem, that's what I call it. Did you ever think, Mr. West, that the bank is the heart of the business system? From it and to it, in endless flux and reflux, the life blood goes. It is flowing in now. It will flow out again in the morning." And pleased with his little conceit, the old man passed on smiling.

Yesterday I should have considered the simile apt enough, but since then I had visited a world incomparably more affluent than this, in which money was unknown and without conceivable use. I had learned that it had a use in the world around me only because the work of producing the nation's livelihood, instead of being regarded as the most strictly public and common of all concerns, and as such conducted by the nation, was abandoned to the haphazard efforts of individuals. This original mistake necessitated endless exchanges to bring about any sort of general distribution of products. These exchanges money effected—how equitably, might be seen in a walk from the tenement-house districts to the Back Bay—at the cost of an army of men taken from productive labor to manage it, with constant ruinous breakdowns of its machinery, and a generally debauching influence on mankind which had justified its description, from ancient time, as the "root of all evil."

Alas for the poor old bank director with his poem! He had mistaken the throbbing of an abscess for the beating of the heart. What he called "a wonderful piece of mechanism" was an imperfect device to remedy an unnecessary defect, the clumsy crutch of a self-made cripple.

After the banks had closed I wandered aimlessly about the business quarter for an hour or two, and later sat awhile on one of the benches of the Common, finding an interest merely in watching the throngs that passed, such as one has in studying the populace of a foreign city, so strange since yesterday had my fellow citizens and their ways become to me. For thirty years I had lived among them, and yet I seemed to have never noted before how drawn and anxious were their faces, of the rich as of the poor, the refined, acute faces of the educated as well as the dull masks of the ignorant. And well it might be so, for I saw now, as never before I had seen so plainly, that each as he walked constantly turned to catch the whispers of a specter at his ear, the specter of Uncertainty. "Do your work never so well," the specter was whispering—"rise early and toil till late, rob cunningly or serve faithfully, you shall never know security. Rich you may be now and still come to poverty at last. Leave never so much wealth to your children, you cannot buy the assurance that your son may not be the servant of your servant, or that your daughter will not have to sell herself for bread."

A man passing by thrust an advertising card in my hand, which set forth the merits of some new scheme of life insurance. The incident reminded me of the only device, pathetic in its admission of the universal need it so poorly supplied, which offered these tired and hunted men and women even a partial protection from uncertainty. By this means, those already well-to-do, I remembered, might purchase a precarious confidence that after their death their loved ones would not, for a while at least, be trampled under the feet of men. But this was all, and this was only for those who could pay well for it. What idea was possible to these wretched dwellers in the land of Ishmael, where every man's hand was against each and the hand of each against every other, of true life insurance as I had seen it among the people of that dreamland, each of whom, by virtue merely of his membership in the national family, was guaranteed against need of any sort, by a policy underwritten by one hundred million fellow countrymen.

Some time after this it was that I recall a glimpse of myself standing on the steps of a building on Tremont Street, looking at a military parade. A regiment was passing. It was the first sight on that dreary day which had inspired me with any other emotions that wondering pity and amazement. Here at last were order and reason, an exhibition of what intelligent co-operation can accomplish. The people who stood looking on with kindling faces—could it be that the sight had for them no more than but a spectacular interest? Could they fail to see that it was their perfect concert of action, their organization under one control, which made these men the tremendous engine they were, able to vanquish a mob ten times as numerous? Seeing this so plainly, could they fail to compare the scientific manner in which the nation went to war with the unscientific manner in which it went to work? Would they not query since what time the killing of men had been a task so much more important than feeding and clothing them, that a trained army should be deemed alone adequate to the former, while the latter was left to a mob?

It was now toward nightfall, and the streets were thronged with the workers from the stores, the shops, and mills. Carried along with the stronger part of the current, I found myself, as it began to grow dark, in the midst of a scene of squalor and human degradation such as only the South Cove tenement district could present. I had seen the mad wasting of human labor; here I saw in direct shape the want that waste had bred.

From the black doorways and windows of the rookeries on every side came gusts of fetid air. The streets and alleys reeked with the effluvia of a slave ship's between-decks. As I passed I had glimpses within of pale babies gasping out their lives amid sultry stenches, of hopeless-faced women deformed by hardship, retaining of womanhood no trait save weakness, while from the windows leered girls with brows of brass. Like the starving bands of mongrel curs that infest the streets of Moslem towns, swarms of half-clad brutalized children filled the air with shrieks and curses as they fought and tumbled among the garbage that littered the courtyards.

There was nothing in all this that was new to me. Often had I passed through this part of the city and witnessed its sights with feelings of disgust mingled with a certain philosophical wonder at the extremities mortals will endure and still cling to life. But not alone as regarded the economical follies of this age, but equally as touched its moral abominations, scales had fallen from my eyes since that vision of another century. No more did I look upon the woeful dwellers in this Inferno with a callous curiosity as creatures scarcely human. I saw in them my brothers and sisters, my parents, my children, flesh of my flesh, blood of my blood. The festering mass of human wretchedness about me offended not now my senses merely, but pierced my heart like a knife, so that I could not repress my sighs and groans. I not only saw but felt in my body all that I saw.

Presently, too, as I observed the wretched beings about me more closely, I perceived that they were all quite dead. Their bodies were so many living sepulchers. On each brutal brow was plainly written the *hic jacet* of a soul dead within.

As I looked, horrorstruck, from one death's head to another, I was affected by a singular hallucination. Like a wavering translucent spirit face superimposed upon each of these brutish masks I saw the ideal, the possible face that would have been the actual if mind and soul had lived. It was not till I was aware of these ghostly faces, and of the reproach that could not be gainsaid which was in their eyes, that the full piteousness of the ruin that had been wrought was revealed to me. I was moved with contrition as with a strong agony, for I had been one of those who had endured that these things should be. I had been one of those who, well knowing that they were, had not desired to hear or be compelled to think mush of them, but had gone on as if they were not, seeking my own pleasure and profit. Therefore now I found upon my garments the blood of this great multitude of strangled souls of my brothers. The voice of their blood cried out against me from the ground. Every stone of the reeking pavements, every brick of the pestilential rookeries, found a tongue and called after me as I fled: "What hast thou done with thy brother Abel?"

I have no clear recollection of anything after this till I found myself standing on the carved stone steps of the magnificent home of my betrothed in Commonwealth Avenue. Amid the tumult of my thoughts that day, I had scarcely once thought of her, but now obeying some unconscious impulse my feet had found the familiar way to her door. I was told that the family were at dinner, but word was sent out that I should join them at table. Besides the family, I found several guests present, all known to me. The table glittered with plate and costly china. The ladies were sumptuously dressed and wore the jewels of queens. The scene was one of costly elegance and lavish luxury. The company was in excellent spirits, and there was plentiful laughter and a running fire of jests.

To me it was as if, in wandering through the place of doom, my blood turned to tears by its sights, and my spirit attuned to sorrow, pity, and despair, I had happened in some glade upon a merry party of roisterers. I sat in silence until Edith began to rally me upon my somber looks. What ailed me? The others presently joined in the playful assault, and I became a target for quips and jests. Where had I been, and what had I seen to make such a dull fellow of me?

"I have been in Golgotha," at last I answered. "I have seen Humanity hanging on a cross! Do none of you know what sights the sun and stars look down on in this city, that you can think and talk of anything else? Do you not know that close to your doors a great multitude of men and women, flesh of your flesh, live lives that are one agony from birth to death? Listen! Their dwellings are so near that if you hush your laughter you will hear their grievous voices, the piteous crying of the little ones that suckle poverty, the hoarse curses of men sodden in misery, turned halfway back to brutes, the chaffering of an army of women selling themselves for bread. With what have you stopped your ears that you do not hear these doleful sounds? For me, I can hear nothing else."

Silence followed my words. A passion of pity had shaken me as I spoke, but when I looked around upon the company, I saw that, far from being stirred as I was, their faces expressed a cold and hard astonishment, mingled in Edith's with extreme mortification, in her father's with anger. The ladies were exchanging scandalized looks, while one of the gentlemen had put up his eyeglass and was studying me with an air of scientific curiosity. When I saw that things which were to me so intolerable moved them not at all, that words that melted my heart to speak had only offended them with the speaker, I was at first stunned and then overcome with a desperate sickness and faintness at the heart. What hope was there for the wretched, for the world, if thoughtful men and tender women were not moved by things like these! Then I bethought myself that it must be because I had not spoken aright. No doubt I had put the case badly. They were angry because they thought I was berating them, when God knew I was merely thinking of the horror of the fact without any attempt to assign the responsibility for it.

I restrained my passion, and tried to speak calmly and logically that I might correct this impression. I told them that I had not meant to accuse them, as if they, or the rich in general, were responsible for the misery of the world. True indeed it was that the superfluity which they wasted would, otherwise bestowed, relive much bitter suffering. These costly viands, these rich wines, these gorgeous fabrics and glistening jewels represented the ransom of many lives. They were verily not without he guiltiness of those who waste in a land stricken with famine. Nevertheless, all the waste of all the rich, were it saved, would go but a little way to cure the poverty of the world. There was so little to divide that even if the rich went share-and-share with the poor, there would be but a common fare of crusts, albeit made very sweet then by brotherly love.

The folly of men, not their hard-heartedness, was the great cause of the world's poverty. It was not the crime of man, nor of any class of men, that made the race so miserable, but a hideous, ghastly mistake, a colossal world-darkening blunder. And then I showed them how four-fifths of the labor of men was utterly wasted by the mutual warfare, the lack of organization and concert among the workers. Seeking to make the matter very plain, I instanced the case of arid lands where the soil yielded the means of life only by careful use of the watercourses for irrigation. I showed how in such countries it was counted the most important function of the government to see that the water was not wasted by the selfishness or ignorance of individuals, since otherwise there would be famine. To this end its use was strictly regulated and systematized, and individuals of their mere caprice were not permitted to dam it or divert it, or in any way to tamper with it.

The labor of men, I explained, was the fertilizing stream which alone rendered earth habitable. It was but a scanty stream at best, and its use required to be regulated by a system which expended every drop to the best advantage, if the world were to be supported in abundance. But how far from any system was the actual practice! Every man wasted the precious fluid as he wished, animated only by the equal motives of saving his own crop and spoiling his neighbor's, that his might sell the better. What with greed and what with spite some fields were flooded while others were parched, and half the water ran wholly to waste. In such a land, though a few by strength or cunning might win the means of luxury, the lot of the great mass must be poverty, and of the weak and ignorant bitter want and perennial famine.

Let but the famine-stricken nation assume the function it had neglected, and regulate for the common good the course of the life-giving stream, and the earth would bloom like on garden, and one of its children lack any good thing. I described the physical felicity, mental enlightenment, and moral elevation which would then attend the lives of all men. With fervency I spoke of that new world, blessed with plenty, purified by justice and sweetened by brotherly kindness, the world of which I had indeed but dreamed, but which might so easily be made real. But when I had expected now surely the faces around me to light up with emotions akin to mine, they grew even more dark, angry, and scornful. Instead of enthusiasm, the ladies showed only aversion and dread, while the men interrupted me with shouts of reprobation and contempt. "Madman!" "Pestilent fellow!" "Fanatic!" "Enemy of society!" were some of their cries, and the one who had before taken his eyeglass to me exclaimed, "He says we are to have no more poor. Ha! ha!"

"Put the fellow out!" exclaimed the father of my betrothed, and at the signal the men sprang from their chairs and advanced upon me.

It seemed to me that my heart would burst with the anguish of finding that what was to me so plain and so all-important was to them meaningless, and that I was powerless to make it other. So hot had been my heart that I had thought to melt an iceberg with its glow, only to find at last the overmastering chill seizing my own vitals. It was not enmity that I felt toward them as they thronged me, but pity only, for them and for the world.

Although despairing, I could not give over. Still I strove with them. Tears poured from my eyes. In my vehemence I became inarticulate. I panted, I sobbed, I groaned, and immediately afterwards found myself sitting upright in bed in my room in Doctor Leete's house, and the morning sun shining through the open window into my eyes. I was gasping. The tears were streaming down my face, and I quivered in every nerve.

As with an escaped convict who dreams that he has been recaptured and brought back to his dark and reeking dungeon, and opens his eyes to see the heaven's vault spread above him, so it was with me, as I realized that my return to the nineteenth century had been the dream, and my presence in the twentieth was the reality.

The cruel sights which I had witnessed in my vision, and could so well confirm from the experience of my former life, though they had, alas! once been, and most in the retrospect to the end of time move the compassionate to tears, were, God be thanked, forever gone by. Long ago oppressor and oppressed, prophet and scorner, had been dust. For generations, rich and poor had been forgotten words.

But in that moment, while yet I mused with unspeakable thankfulness upon the greatness of the world's salvation and my privilege in beholding it, there suddenly pierced me like a knife a pang of shame, remorse, and wondering self-reproach, that bowed my head upon my breast and made me wish the grave had hid me with my fellows from the sun. For I had been a man of that former time. What had I done to help on the deliverance whereat I now presumed to rejoice? I who had lived in those cruel, insensate days, what had I done to bring them to an end? I had been every whit as indifferent to the wretchedness of my brothers, as cynically incredulous of better things, as besotted a worshipper of Chaos and Old Night, as any of my fellows. So far as my personal influence went, it had been exerted rather to hinder than to help forward the enfranchisement of the race which was even then preparing. What right had I to hail a salvation which reproached me, to rejoice in a day whose dawning I had mocked?

"Better for you, better for you," a voice within me rang, "had this evil dream been the reality, and this fair reality the dream; better your part pleading for crucified humanity with a scoffing generation, than here, drinking of wells you digged not, and eating of trees whose husbandmen you stoned." And my spirit answered, "Better, truly."

When at length I raised my bowed head and looked forth from the window, Edith, fresh as the morning, had come into the garden and was gathering flowers. I hastened to descend to her. Kneeling before her, with my face in the dust, I confessed with tears how little was my worth to breathe the air of this golden century, and how infinitely less to wear upon my breast its consummate flower. Fortunate is he who, with a case so desperate as mine, finds a judge so merciful.

Notes

1. In accounting for this state of mind it must be remembered that, except for the topic of our conversations, there was in my surroundings next to nothing to suggest what had befallen me. Within a block of my home in the old Boston I could have found social circles vastly more foreign to me. The speech of the Bostonians of the twentieth century differs even less from that of their cultured ancestors of the nineteenth than did that of the latter from the language of Washington and Franklin, while the differences between the style of dress and furniture of the two epochs are not more marked than I have known fashion to make in the time of one generation.

2. I am informed since the above is in type that this lack of perfection in the distributing service of some of the country districts is to be remedied, and that soon every village will have its own set of tubes.

156

Quincy 1838–1848

HENRY ADAMS

Henry Brooks Adams (1838–1918) was born in Boston, Massachusetts, into one of New England's leading families (members of which included two former Presidents of the United States). Adams established himself as one of the leading American historians of his time. Educated at Harvard, he also spent time in Europe, most notably in France, which was to have an important influence on his ideas and historical theories.

The Education of Henry Adams (1918, but published privately in 1906), is a "third" person autobiographical account of Adams's life and ideas. It reflects a general sense of loss and confusion–indeed, the "education" he received is rejected as not offering anything like the education he required in order to understand the modern world. Adams confronted an increasingly urban, technological, and industrial America–the very opposite to the "gentler" and urbane rhythm of the Boston into which he was born.

He increasingly viewed the modern period in terms of chaos and breakdown, appropriating the Second Law of Thermodynamics as an historical theory based on entropy. Against this he placed the supposed unity of the Middle Ages and its Catholic faith symbolised in the holistic image of cathedrals. This is the basis of *Mont Saint-Michel and Chartres.*

Adams's ideas, while complex, have had a significant influence on contemporary American writers, most obviously Thomas Pynchon. See J. C. Levenson, *The Mind and Art of Henry Adams* (1957), and Tony Tanner *City of Words* (1971). See also Adams's two novels, *Democracy* (1880) and *Esther* (1884).

Under the shadow of Boston State House, turning its back on the house of John Hancock the little passage called Hancock Avenue runs, or ran, from Beacon Street, skirting the State House grounds, to Mount Vernon Street, on the summit of Beacon Hill; and there, in the third house below Mount Vernon

Source: Henry Adams, "Quincy–1838–1848", *The Education of Henry Adams*, privately printed, 1907, Ch. 1.

Place, February 16, 1838, a child was born, and christened later by his uncle, the minister of the First Church after the tenets of Boston Unitarianism, as Henry Brooks Adams.

Had he been born in Jerusalem under the shadow of the Temple and circumcised in the Synagogue by his uncle the high priest, under the name of Israel Cohen, he would scarcely have been more distinctly branded, and not much more heavily handicapped in the races of the coming century, in running for such stakes as the century was to offer; but, on the other hand, the ordinary traveller, who does not enter the field of racing, finds advantage in being, so to speak, ticketed through life, with the safeguards of an old, established traffic. Safeguards are often irksome, but sometimes convenient, and if one needs them at all, one is apt to need them badly. A hundred years earlier, such safeguards as his would have secured any young man's success; and although in 1838 their value was not very great compared with what they would have had in 1738, yet the mere accident of starting a twentieth-century career from a nest of associations so colonial—so troglodytic—as the First Church, the Boston State House, Beacon Hill, John Hancock and John Adams, Mount Vernon Street and Quincy, all crowding on ten pounds of unconscious babyhood, was so queer as to offer a subject of curious speculation to the baby long after he had witnessed the solution. What could become of such a child of the seventeenth and eighteenth centuries, when he should wake up to find himself required to play the game of the twentieth? Had he been consulted, would he have cared to play the game at all, holding such cards as he held, and suspecting that the game was to be one of which neither he nor anyone else back to the beginning of time knew the rules or the risks or the stakes? He was not consulted and was not responsible, but had he been taken into the confidence of his parents, he would certainly have told them to change nothing as far as concerned him. He would have been astounded by his own luck. Probably no child, born in the year, held better cards than he. Whether life was an honest game of chance, or whether the cards were marked and forced, he could not refuse to play his excellent hand. He could never make the usual plea of irresponsibility. He accepted the situation as though he had been a party to it, and under the same circumstances would do it again, the more readily for knowing the exact values. To his life as a whole he was a consenting, contracting party and partner from the moment he was born to the moment he died. Only with that understanding—as a consciously assenting member in full partnership with the society of his age—had his education an interest to himself or to others.

As it happened, he never got to the point of playing the game at all; he lost himself in the study of it, watching the errors of the players; but this is the only interest in the story, which otherwise has no moral and little incident. A story of education—seventy years of it—the practical value remains to the end in doubt, like other values about which men have disputed since the birth of Cain and Abel; but the practical value of the universe has never been stated in dollars. Although everyone cannot be a Gargantua-Napoleon-Bismarck and walk off with the great bells of Notre Dame, everyone must bear his own universe, and most persons are moderately interested in learning how their neighbors have managed to carry theirs.

This problem of education, started in 1838, went on for three years, while the baby grew, like other babies, unconsciously, as a vegetable, the outside world working as it never had worked before, to get his new universe ready for him. Often in old age he puzzled over the question whether, on the doctrine of chances, he was at liberty to accept himself or his world as an accident. No such accident had ever happened before in human experience. For him, alone, the old universe was thrown into the ash-heap and a new one created. He and his eighteenth-century, troglodytic Boston were suddenly cut apart—separated forever—in act if not in sentiment, by the opening of the Boston and Albany Railroad; the appearance of the first Cunard steamers in the bay; and the telegraphic messages which carried from Baltimore to Washington the news that Henry Clay and James K. Polk were nominated for the Presidency. This was in May, 1844; he was six years old; his new world was ready for use, and only fragments of the old met his eyes.

Of all this that was being done to complicate his education, he knew only the color of yellow. He first found himself sitting on a yellow kitchen floor in strong sunlight. He was three years old when he took this earliest step in education; a lesson of color. The second followed soon; a lesson of taste. On December 3, 1841, he developed scarlet fever. For several days he was as good as dead, reviving only under the careful nursing of his family. When he began to recover strength, about January 1, 1842, his hunger must have been stronger than any other pleasure or pain, for while in after life he retained not the faintest recollection of his illness, he remembered quite clearly his aunt entering the sickroom bearing in her hand a saucer with a baked apple.

The order of impressions retained by memory might naturally be that of color and taste, although one would rather suppose that the sense of pain would be first to educate. In fact, the third recollection of the child was that of discomfort. The moment he could be removed, he was bundled up in blankets and carried from the little house in Hancock Avenue to a larger one which his parents were to occupy for the rest of their lives in the neighboring Mount Vernon Street. The season was midwinter, January 10, 1842, and he never forgot his acute distress for want of air under his blankets, or the noises of moving furniture.

As a means of variation from a normal type, sickness in childhood ought to have a certain value not to be classed under any fitness or unfitness of natural selection; and especially scarlet fever affected boys seriously, both physically and in character, though they might through life puzzle themselves to decide whether it had fitted or unfitted them for success; but this fever of Henry Adams took greater and greater importance in his eyes, from the point of view of education, the longer he lived. At first, the effect was physical. He fell behind his brothers two or three inches in height, and proportionally in bone and weight. His character and processes of mind seemed to share in this fining-down process of scale. He was not good in a fight, and his nerves were more delicate than boys' nerves ought to be. He exaggerated these weaknesses as he grew older. The habit of doubt; of distrusting his own judgment and of totally rejecting the judgment of the world; the tendency to regard every question as open; the hesitation to act except as a choice of evils; the shirking of reponsibility; the love of line, form, quality; the horror of ennui; the passion for companionship and the antipathy to society—all these are well-known qualities of New England character in no way peculiar to individuals but in this instance they seemed to be stimulated by the fever, and Henry Adams could never make up his mind whether, on the whole, the change of character was morbid or healthy, good or bad for his purpose. His brothers were the type; he was the variation.

As far as the boy knew, the sickness did not affect him at all, and he grew up in excellent health, bodily and mental, taking life as it was given; accepting its local standards without a difficulty, and enjoying much of it as keenly as any other boy of his age. He seemed to himself quite normal, and his companions seemed always to think him so. Whatever was peculiar about him was education, not character, and came to him, directly and indirectly, as the result of that eighteenth-century inheritance which he took with his name.

The atmosphere of education in which he lived was colonial, revolutionary, almost Cromwellian, as though he were steeped, from his greatest grandmother's birth, in the odor of political crime. Resistance to something was the law of New England nature; the boy looked out on the world with the instinct of resistance; for numberless generations his predecessors had viewed the world chiefly as a thing to be reformed, filled with evil forces to be abolished, and they saw no reason to suppose that they had wholly succeeded in the abolition; the duty was unchanged. That duty implied not only resistance to evil, but hatred of it. Boys naturally look on all force as an enemy, and generally find it so, but the New Englander, whether boy or man, in his long struggle with a stingy or hostile universe, had learned also to love the pleasure of hating; his joys were few.

Politics, as a practice, whatever its professions, had always been the systematic organization of hatreds, and Massachusetts politics had been as harsh as the climate. The chief charm of New England was harshness of contrasts and extremes of sensibility—a cold that froze the blood, and a heat that boiled it—so that the pleasure of hating—oneself if no better victim offered—was not its rarest amusement; but the charm was a true and natural child of the soil, not a cultivated weed of the ancients. The violence of the contrast was real and made the strongest motive of education. The double exterior nature gave life its relative values. Winter and summer, cold and heat, town and country, force and freedom, marked two modes of life and thought, balanced like lobes of the brain. Town was winter confinement, school, rule, discipline; straight, gloomy streets, piled with six feet of snow in the middle; frosts that made the snow sing under wheels or runners; thaws when the streets became dangerous to cross; society of uncles, aunts, and cousins who expected children to behave themselves, and who were not always gratified; above all else, winter represented the desire to escape and go free. Town was restraint, law, unity. Country, only seven miles away, was liberty, diversity, outlawry, the endless delight of mere sense impressions given by nature for nothing, and breathed by boys without knowing it.

Boys are wild animals, rich in the treasures of sense, but the New England boy had a wider range of emotions than boys of more equable climates. He felt his nature crudely, as it was meant. To the boy Henry Adams, summer was drunken. Among senses, smell was the strongest—smell of hot pine-woods and sweet-fern in the scorching summer noon; of new-mown hay; of ploughed earth; of box hedges; of peaches, lilacs, syringas; of stables, barns, cow-yards; of salt water and low tide on the marshes; nothing came amiss. Next to smell came taste, and the children knew the taste of everything they saw or touched, from pennyroyal and flagroot to the shell of a pignut and the letters of a spelling-book—the taste of A-B, AB, suddenly revived on the boy's tongue sixty years afterwards. Light, line, and color as sensual pleasures, came later and were as crude as the rest. The New England light is glare, and the atmosphere harshens color. The boy was a full man before he ever knew what was meant by atmosphere; his idea of pleasure in light was the blaze of a New England sun. His idea of color was a peony, with the dew of early morning on its petals. The intense blue of the sea, as he saw it a mile or two away, from the Quincy hills; the cumuli in a June afternoon sky; the strong reds and greens and purples of colored prints and children's picture-books, as the American colors then ran; these were ideals. The opposites or antipathies, were the cold grays of November evenings, and the thick, muddy thaws of Boston winter. With such standards, the Bostonian could not but develop a double nature. Life was a double thing. After a January blizzard, the boy who could look with pleasure into the violent snow-glare of the cold white sunlight, with its intense light and shade, scarcely knew what was meant by tone. He could reach it only by education.

Winter and summer, then, were two hostile lives, and bred two separate natures. Winter was always the effort to life; summer was tropical license. Whether the children rolled in the grass, or waded in the brook, or swam in the salt ocean, or sailed in the bay, or fished for smelts in the creeks, or netted minnows in the salt-marshes, or took to the pine-woods and the granite quarries, or chased muskrats and hunted snapping-turtles in the swamps, or mushrooms or nuts on the autumn hills, summer and country were always sensual living, while winter was always compulsory learning. Summer was the multiplicity of nature; winter was school.

The bearing of the two seasons on the education of Henry Adams was not fancy; it was the most decisive force he ever knew; it ran through life, and made the division between its perplexing, warring, irreconcilable problems, irreducible opposites, with growing emphasis to the last year of study. From earliest childhood the boy was accustomed to feel that, for him, life was double. Winter and summer, town and country, law and liberty, were hostile, and man who pretended they were not, was in his eyes a schoolmaster—that is, a man employed to tell lies to little boys. Though Quincy was but two hours' walk from Beacon

Hill, it belonged in a different world. For two hundred years, every Adams, from father to son, had lived within sight of State Street, and sometimes had lived in it, yet none had ever taken kindly to the town, or been taken kindly by it. The boy inherited his double nature. He knew as yet nothing about his great-grandfather, who had died a dozen years before his own birth: he took for granted that any great-grandfather, of his must have always been good, and his enemies wicked; but he divined his great-grandfather's character from his own. Never for a moment did he connect the two ideas of Boston and John Adams; they were separate and antagonistic; the idea of John Adams went with Quincy. He knew his grandfather John Quincy Adams only as an old man of seventy-five or eighty who was friendly and gentle with him, but except that he heard his grandfather always called "the President," and his grandmother "the Madam," he had no reason to suppose that his Adams grandfather differed in character from his Brooks grandfather who was equally kind and benevolent. He liked the Adams side best, but for no other reason than that it reminded him of the country, the summer, and the absence of restraint. Yet he felt also that Quincy was in a way inferior to Boston, and that socially Boston looked down on Quincy. The reason was clear enough even to a five-year-old child. Quincy had no Boston style. Little enough style had either; a simpler manner of life and thought could hardly exist, short of cave-dwelling. The flint-and-steel with which his grandfather Adams used to light his own fires in the early morning was still on the mantelpiece of his study. The idea of a livery or even a dress for servants, or of an evening toilette, was next to blasphemy. Bathrooms, water-supplies, lighting, heating, and the whole array of domestic comforts, were unknown at Quincy. Boston had already a bathroom, a water supply, a furnace, and gas. The superiority of Boston was evident, but a child liked it no better for that.

The magnificence of his grandfather Brooks's house in Pearl Street or South Street has long ago disappeared, but perhaps his country house at Medford may still remain to show what impressed the mind of a boy in 1845 with the idea of city splendor. The President's place at Quincy was the larger and older and far the more interesting of the two; but a boy felt at once its inferiority in fashion. It showed plainly enough its want of wealth. It smacked of colonial age, but not of Boston style or plush curtains. To the end of his life he never quite overcame the prejudice thus drawn in with his childish breath. He never could compel himself to care for nineteenth-century style. He was never able to adopt it, any more than his father or grandfather or great-grandfather had done. Not that he felt it as particularly hostile, for he reconciled himself to much that was worse; but because, for some remote reason, he was born an eighteenth-century child. The old house at Quincy was eighteenth century. What style it had was in its Queen Anne mahogany panels and its Louis Seize chairs and sofas. The panels belonged to an old colonial Vassall who built the house; the furniture had been brought back from Paris in 1789 or 1801 or 1817, along with porcelain and books and much else of old diplomatic remnants; and neither of the two eighteenth-century styles—neither English Queen Anne nor French Louis Seize—

was comfortable for a boy, or for anyone else. The dark mahogany had been painted white to suit daily life in winter gloom. Nothing seemed to favor, for a child's objects, the older forms. On the contrary, most boys, as well as grown-up people, preferred the new, with good reason, and the child felt himself distinctly at a disadvantage for the taste.

Nor had personal preference any share in his bias. The Brooks grandfather was as amiable and as sympathetic as the Adams grandfather. Both were born in 1767, and both died in 1848. Both were kind to children, and both belonged rather to the eighteenth than to the nineteenth centuries. The child knew no difference between them except that one was associated with winter and the other with summer; one with Boston, the other with Quincy. Even with Medford, the association was hardly easier. Once as a very young boy he was taken to pass a few days with his grandfather Brooks under charge of his aunt, but became so violently homesick that within twenty-four hours he was brought back in disgrace. Yet he could not remember ever being seriously homesick again.

The attachment to Quincy was not altogether sentimental or wholly sympathetic. Quincy was not a bed of thornless roses. Even there the curse of Cain set its mark. There as elsewhere a cruel universe combined to crush a child. As though three or four vigorous brothers and sisters, with the best will, were not enough to crush any child, every one else conspired towards an education which he hated. From cradle to grave his problem of running order through chaos, direction through space, discipline through freedom, unity through multiplicity, has always been, and must always be the task of education as it is the moral of religion , philosophy, science, art, politics, and economy; but a boy's will is his life, and he dies when it is broken, as the colt dies in harness,, taking a new nature in becoming tame. Rarely has the boy felt kindly towards his tamers. Between him and his master has always been war. Henry Adams never knew a boy of his generation to like a master, and the task of remaining on friendly terms with one's own family, in such a relation, was never easy.

All the more singular it seemed afterwards to him that his first serious contact with the President should have been a struggle of will, in which the old man almost necessarily defeated the boy, but instead of leaving, as usual in such defeats, a lifelong sting, left rather an impression of as fair treatment as could be expected from a natural enemy. The boy met seldom with such restraint. He could not have been much more than six years old at the time—seven at the utmost—and his mother had taken him to Quincy for a long stay with the President during the summer. What became of the rest of the family he quite forgot; but he distinctly remembered standing at the house door one summer morning in a passionate outburst of rebellion against going to school. Naturally his mother was the immediate victim of his rage; that is what mothers are for, and boys also; but in this case the boy had his mother at unfair disadvantage, for she was a guest, and had no means of enforcing obedience. Henry showed a certain tactical ability by refusing to start, and he met all efforts at compulsion by successful, though too vehement protest. He was in fair way to win, and was holding his own, with sufficient energy, at the bottom of the long staircase which led up to the door of the President's library, when the door opened, and the old man slowly came down. Putting on his hat, he took the boy's hand without a word, and walked with him, paralyzed by awe, up the road to the town. After the first moments of consternation at this interference in a domestic dispute, the boy reflected that an old gentleman close on eighty would never trouble himself to walk near a mile on a hot summer morning over a shadeless road to take a boy to school, and that it would be strange if a lad imbued with the passion of freedom could not find a corner to dodge around, somewhere before reaching the school door. Then and always, the boy insisted that this reasoning justified his apparent submission; but the old man did not stop, and the boy saw all his strategical points turned, one after another, until he found himself seated inside the school, and obviously the centre of curious if not malevolent criticism. Not till then did the President release his hand and depart.

The point was that this act, contrary to the inalienable rights of boys, and nullifying the social compact, ought to have made him dislike his grandfather for life. He could not recall that it had this effect even for a moment. With a certain maturity of mind, the child must have recognized that the President, though a tool of tyranny, had done his disreputable work with a certain intelligence. He had shown no temper, no irritation, no personal feeling, and had made no display of force. Above all, he had held his tongue. During their long walk he had said nothing; he had uttered no syllable of revolting cant about the duty of obedience and the wickedness of resistance to law; he had shown no concern in the matter; hardly even a consciousness of the boy's existence, probably his mind at that moment was actually troubling itself little about his grandson's iniquities, and much about the iniquities of President Polk but the boy could scarcely at that age feel the whole satisfaction of thinking that President Polk was to be the vicarious victim of his own sins, and he gave his grandfather credit for intelligent silence. For this forbearance he felt instinctive respect. He admitted force as a form of right; he admitted even temper, under protest; but the seeds of a moral education would at that moment have fallen on the stoniest soil in Quincy, which is, as everyone knows, the stoniest glacial and tidal drift known in any Puritan land.

Neither party to this momentary disagreement can have felt rancor, for during these three or four summers the old President's relations with the boy were friendly and almost intimate. Whether his older brothers and sisters were still more favored he failed to remember, but he was himself admitted to a sort of familiarity which, when in his turn he had reached old age, rather shocked him, for it must have sometimes tried the President's patience. He hung about the library; handled the books; deranged the papers; ransacked the drawers; searched the old purses and pocket-books for foreign coins; drew the sword-cane, snapped the travelling-pistols; upset everything in the corners, and penetrated the President's dressing-closet where a row of tumblers, inverted on the shelf, covered caterpillars which were supposed to become moths or butterflies, but never did. The Madam bore with fortitude the loss of the tumblers which her husband purloined for these hatcheries; but she made protest when he carried off her best cut-glass bowls to plant with acorns or peachstones that he might see the roots grow, but which, she said, he commonly forgot like the caterpillars.

At that time the President rode the hobby of tree-culture, and some fine old trees should still remain to witness it, unless they have been improved off the ground; but his was a restless mind, and although he took his hobbies seriously and would have been annoyed had his grandchild asked whether he was bored like an English duke, he probably cared more for the processes than for the results, so that his grandson was saddened by the sight and smell of peaches and pears, the best of their kind, which he brought up from the garden to rot on his shelves for seed. With the inherited virtues of his Puritan ancestors, the little boy Henry conscientiously brought up to him in his study the finest peaches he found in the garden, and ate only the less perfect. Naturally he ate more by way of compensation, but the act showed that he bore no grudge. As for his grandfather, it is even possible that he may have felt a certain self-reproach for his temporary rôle of schoolmaster—seeing that his own career did not offer proof of the worldly advantages of docile obedience—for there still exists somewhere a little volume of critically edited Nursery Rhymes with the boy's name in full written in the President's hand on the fly-leaf; while their grandfather Brooks supplied the silver mugs.

So many Bibles and silver mugs had to be supplied, that a new house, or cottage, was built to hold them. It was "on the hill," five minutes' walk above "the old house," with a far view eastward over Quincy Bay, and northward over Boston. Till his twelfth year, the child passed his summers there, and his pleasures of childhood mostly centred in it. Of education he had as yet little to complain. Country schools were not very serious. Nothing stuck to the mind except home impressions, and the sharpest were those of kindred children; but as influences that warped a mind, none compared with the mere effect of the back of the President's bald head, as he sat in his pew on Sundays, in line with that of President Quincy, who, though some ten years younger, seemed to children about the same age. Before railways tendered the New England town, every parish church showed half-a-dozen of these leading citizens, with gray hair, who sat on the main aisle in the best pews, and had sat there, or in some equivalent dignity, since the time of St. Augustine, if not since the glacial epoch. It was unusual for boys to sit behind a President grandfather, and to read over his head the tablet in memory of a President great-grandfather, who had "pledged his life, his fortune, and his sacred honor" to secure the independence of his country and so forth; but boys naturally supposed, without much reasoning, that other boys had the equivalent of President grandfathers, and that churches would always go on, with the bald-headed leading citizens on the main aisle, the Presidents or their equivalents on the walls. The Irish gardener once said to the child: "You'll be thinkin' you'll be President too!" The casuality of the remark made so strong an impression on his mind that he never forgot it. He could not remember ever to have thought on the subject; to him, that there should be a doubt of his being President was a new idea. What had been would continue to be. He doubted neither about President nor about Churches, and no one suggested at that time a doubt whether a system of society which had lasted since Adam would outlast one Adams more.

The Madam was a little more remote than the President, but more decorative. She stayed much in her own room with the Dutch tiles, looking out on her garden with the box walks, and seemed a fragile creature to a boy who sometimes brought her a note or a message, and took distinct pleasure in looking at her delicate face under what seemed to him very becoming caps. He liked her refined figure; her gentle voice and manner; her vague effect of not belonging there, but to Washington or to Europe, like her furniture, and writing-desk with little glass doors above and little eighteenth-century volumes in old binding, labelled "Peregrine Pickle" or "Tom Jones" or "Hannah More." Try as she might, the Madam could never be Bostonian, and it was her cross in life, but to the boy it was her charm. Even at that age, he felt drawn to it. The Madam's life had been in truth far from Boston. She was born in London in 1775, daughter of Joshua Johnson, an American merchant, brother of Governor Thomas Johnson of Maryland; and Catherine Nuth, of an English family in London. Driven from England by the Revolutionary War, Joshua Johnson took his family to Nantes, where they remained till the peace. The girl Louisa Catherine was nearly ten years old when brought back to London, and her sense of nationality must have been confused; but the influence of the Johnsons and the services of Joshua obtained for him from President Washington the appointment of Consul in London on the organization of the Government in 1790. In 1794 President Washington appointed John Quincy Adams Minister to The Hague. He was twenty-seven years old when he returned to London, and found the Consul's house a very agreeable haunt. Louisa was then twenty.

At that time, and long afterwards, the Consul's house, far more than the Minister's, was the centre of contact for travelling Americans, either official or other. The Legation was a shifting point, between 1785 and 1815; but the Consulate, far down in the City, near the Tower, was convenient and inviting; so inviting that it proved fatal to young Adams. Louisa was charming, like a Romney portrait, but among her many charms that of being a New England woman was not one. The defect was serious. Her future mother-in-law, Abigail, a famous New England woman whose authority over her turbulent husband, the second President, was hardly so great as that which she exercised over her son, the sixth to be, was troubled by the fear that Louisa might not be made of stuff stern enough, or brought up in conditions severe enough, to suit a New England climate, or to make an efficient wife for her paragon son, and Abigail was right on that point, as on most others where sound judgment was involved; but sound judgment is sometimes a source of weakness rather than of force,, and John Quincy already had reason to think that his mother held sound judgments on the subject of daughters-in-law which human nature, since the fall of Eve, made Adams helpless to realize. Being three thousand miles away from his mother, and equally far in love, he married Louisa in London, July 26, 1797, and took her to Berlin to be the head of the United States Legation. During three or four exciting years, the young bride lived in Berlin; whether she was happy or not, whether she was content or not, whether she was socially successful or not, her descendants did not surely know; but in any case she could by no chance have become educated there for a life in Quincy or Boston. In 1801 the overthrow of the Federalist Party drove her and her husband to America, and she became at last a member of the Quincy household, but by that time her children needed all her attention, and she remained there with occasional winters in Boston and Washington, till 1809. Her husband was made Senator in 1803, and in 1809 was appointed Minister to Russia. She went with him to St. Petersburg, taking her baby, Charles Francis, born in 1807; but broken-hearted at having to leave her two older boys behind. The life at St. Petersburg was hardly gay for her; they were far too poor to shine in that extravagant society; but she survived it, though her little baby girl did not, and in the winter of 1814–15, alone with the boy of seven years old, crossed Europe from St. Petersburg to Paris, in her travelling-carriage, passing through the armies, and reaching Paris in the *Cent Jours* after Napoleon's return from Elba. Her husband next went to England as Minister, and she was for two years at the Court of the Regent. In 1817 her husband came home to be Secretary of State, and she lived for eight years in F Street, doing her work of entertainer for President Monroe's administration. Next she lived four miserable years in the White House. When that chapter was closed in 1829, she had earned the right to be tired and delicate, but she still had fifteen years to serve as wife of a Member of the House, after her husband went back to Congress in 1833. Then it was that the little Henry, her grandson, first remembered her, from 1843 to 1848, sitting in her panelled room, at breakfast, with her heavy silver teapot and sugar-bowl and cream-jug, which still exist somewhere as an heirloom of the modern safety-vault. By that time she was seventy years old or more, and thoroughly weary of being beaten about a stormy world. To the boy she seemed singularly peaceful, a vision of silver gray, presiding over her old President and her Queen Anne mahogany; an exotic, like her Sèvres china; an object of deference to everyone, and a great affection to her son Charles; but hardly more Bostonian than she had been fifty years before, on her wedding-day, in the shadow of the Tower of London.

Such a figure was even less fitted than that of her old husband, the President, to impress on a boy's mind the standards of the coming century. She was Louis Seize, like the furniture. The boy knew nothing of her interior life, which had been, as the venerable Abigail, long since at peace, foresaw, one of severe stress and little pure satisfaction. He never dreamed that from her might come some of those doubts and self-questionings, those hesitations, those rebellions against law and discipline, which marked more than one of her descendants; but he might even then have felt some vague instinctive suspicion that he was to inherit from her the seeds of the primal sin, and fall from grace, the curse of Abel, that he was not of pure New England stock, but half exotic. As a child of Quincy he was not a true Bostonian, but even as a child of Quincy he inherited a quarter taint of Maryland blood. Charles Francis, half Marylander by birth, had hardly seen Boston till he was ten years old, when his parents left him there at school in 1817, and he never forgot the experience. He was to be nearly as old as his mother had been in 1845, before he quite accepted Boston, or Boston quite accepted him.

A boy who began his education in these surroundings, with physical strength inferior to that of his brothers, and with a certain delicacy of mind and bone, ought rightly to have felt at home in the eighteenth century and should, in proper self-respect, have rebelled against the standards of the nineteenth. The atmosphere of his first ten years must have been very like that of his grandfather at the same age, from 1767 till 1776, barring the battle of Bunker Hill, and even as late as 1846, the battle of Bunker Hill remained actual. The tone of Boston society was colonial. The true Bostonian always knelt in self-abasement before the majesty of English standards; far from concealing it as a weakness, he was proud of it as his strength. The eighteenth century ruled society long after 1850. Perhaps the boy began to shake it off rather earlier than most of his mates.

Indeed this prehistoric stage of education ended rather abruptly with his tenth year. One winter morning he was conscious of a certain confusion in the house in Mount Vernon Street, and gathered, from such words as he could catch, that the President, who happened to be then staying there, on his way to Washington, had fallen and hurt himself. Then he heard the word paralysis. After that day he came to associate the word with the figure of his grandfather, in a tall-backed, invalid armchair, on one side of the spare bedroom fireplace, and one of his old friends, Dr. Parkman or P. P. F. Degrand, on the other side, both dozing.

The end of this first, or ancestral and Revolutionary, chapter came on February 21, 1848—and the month of February brought life and death as a family habit—when the eighteenth century, as an actual and living companion, vanished. If the scene on the floor of the House, when the old President fell, struck the still simple-minded American pubic with a sensation unusually dramatic, its effect on a ten-year-old boy, whose boy-life was fading away with the life of his grandfather, could not be slight. One had to pay for Revolutionary patriots; grandfathers, and grandmothers; Presidents; diplomats; Queen Anne mahogany and Louis Seize chairs, as well as for Stuart portraits. Such things warp young life. Americans commonly believed that they ruined it, and perhaps the practical common-sense of the American mind judged right. Many a boy might be ruined by much less than the emotions of the funeral service in the Quincy church, with its surroundings of national respect and family pride. By another dramatic chance it happened that the clergyman of the parish, Dr. Lunt, was an unusual pulpit orator, the ideal of a somewhat austere intellectual type, such as the school of Buckminister and Channing inherited from the old Congregational clergy. His extraordinarily refined appearance, his dignity of manner, his deeply cadenced voice, his remarkable English and his fine appreciation, gave the funeral service a character that left an overwhelming impression on the boy's mind. He was to see many great functions—funerals and festivals—in after-life, till his only thought was to see no more, but he never again witnessed anything nearly so impressive to him as the last services at Quincy over the body of one President and the ashes of another.

The effect of the Quincy service was deepened by the official ceremony which afterwards took place in Faneuil Hall, when the boy was taken to hear his uncle, Edward Everett, deliver a Eulogy. Like all Mr. Everett's orations, it was an admirable piece of oratory, such as only an admirable orator and scholar could create; too good for a ten-year-old boy to appreciate at its value; but already the boy knew that the dead President could not be in it, and had even learned why he would have been out of place there; for knowledge was beginning to come fast. The shadow of the War of 1812 still hung over State Street; the shadow of the Civil War to come had already begun to darken Faneuil Hall. No rhetoric could have reconciled Mr. Everett's audience to his subject. How could he say there, to an assemblage of Bostonians in the heart of mercantile Boston, that the only distinctive mark of all the Adamses, since old Sam Adams's father a hundred and fifty years before, had been their inherited quarrel with State Street, which had again and again broken out into riot, bloodshed, personal feuds, foreign and civil war, wholesale banishments and confiscations, until the history of Florence was hardly more turbulent than that of Boston? How could he whisper the word Hartford Convention before the men who had made it? What would have been said had he suggested the chance of Secession and Civil War?

Thus already, at ten years old, the boy found himself standing face to face with a dilemma that might have puzzled an early Christian. What was he?—where was he going? Even then he felt that something was wrong, but he concluded that it must be Boston. Quincy had always been right, for Quincy represented a moral principle—the principle of resistance to Boston. His Adams ancestors must have been right, since they were always hostile to State Street. If State Street was wrong, Quincy must be right! Turn the dilemma as he pleased, he still came back on the eighteenth century and the law of Resistance; of Truth; of Duty, and of Freedom. He was a ten-year-old priest and politician. He could under no circumstances have guessed what the next fifty years had in store, and no one could teach him; but sometimes, in his old age, he wondered—and could never decide—whether the most clear and certain knowledge would have helped him. Supposing he had seen a New York stocklist of 1900, and had studied the statistics of railways, telegraphs, coal, and steel—would he have quitted his eighteenth-century, his ancestral prejudices, his abstract ideals, his semi-clerical training, and the rest, in order to perform an expiatory pilgrimage to State Street, and ask for the fatted calf of his grandfather Brooks and a clerkship in the Suffolk Bank?

Sixty years afterwards he was still unable to make up his mind. Each course had its advantages, but the material advantages, looking back, seemed to lie wholly in State Street.

157

Boston

HENRY JAMES

See the introductory note to Chapter 86 for a note on Henry James. The Boston section of *The American Scene* is, of course, to be compared to his depiction of Boston in *The Bostonians* (1886). Although primarily concerned with nineteenth-century feminist principles and experiences, its view of Boston placed the transcendentalism of Emerson into the context of late nineteenth-century realism. It is a central text, although it has been criticised on several fronts.

It sometimes uncomfortably happens for a writer, consulting his remembrance, that he remembers too much and finds himself knowing his subject too well; which is but the case of the bottle too full for the wine to start. There has to be room for the air to circulate between one's impressions, between the parts of one's knowledge, since it is the air, or call it the intervals on the sea of one's ignorance, of one's indifference, that sets these floating fragments into motion. This is more or less what I feel in presence of the invitation—even the invitation written on the very face of the place itself, of its actual aspects and appearances—to register my "impression" of Boston. Can one *have*, in the conditions, an impression of Boston, any that has not been for long years as inappreciable as a "sunk" picture?—that dead state of surface which requires a fresh application of varnish. The situation I speak of is the consciousness of "old" knowledge, knowledge so compacted by the years as to be unable, like the bottled wine, to flow. The answer to such questions as these, no doubt, however, is the practical one of trying a shake of the bottle or a brushful of the varnish. My "sunk" sense of Boston found itself vigorously varnished by mere renewal of vision at the end of long years; though I confess that under this favouring influence I ask myself why I should have had, after all, the notion of overlaid deposits of experience. The experience had anciently been small—so far as smallness may be imputed to any of our prime initiations; yet it had left consequences out of proportion to its limited seeming self. Early contacts had been brief and few,

Source: Henry James, "Boston", *The American Scene*, 1907, Ch.VII.

and the slight bridge had long ago collapsed; wherefore the impressed condition that acquired again, on the spot, an intensity, struck me as but half explained by the inordinate power of assimilation of the imaginative young. I should have had none the less to content myself with this evidence of the magic of past sensibilities had not the question suddenly been lighted for me as by a sudden flicker of the torch—and for my special benefit—carried in the hand of history. This light, waving for an instant over the scene, gave me the measure of my relation to it, both as to immense little extent and to quite subjective character.

II

It was in strictness only a matter of noting the harshness of change—since I scarce know what else to call it—on the part of the approaches to a particular spot I had wished to revisit. I made out, after a little, the entrance to Ashburton Place; but I missed on that spacious summit of Beacon Hill more than I can say the pleasant little complexity of the other time, marked with its share of the famous old-world "crookedness" of Boston, that element of the mildly tortuous which did duty, for the story-seeker, as an ancient and romantic note, and was half envied, half derided by the merely rectangular criticism. Didn't one remember the day when New Yorkers, when Philadelphians, when pilgrims from the West, sated with their eternal equidistances, with the quadrilateral scheme of life, "raved" about Cornhill and appeared to find in the rear of the State House a recall of one of the topographical, the architectural jumbles of Europe or Asia? And did not indeed the small happy accidents of the disappearing Boston exhale in a comparatively sensible manner the warm breath of history, the history of something as against the history of nothing?—so that, being gone, or generally going, they enabled one at last to feel and almost to talk about them as one had found one's self feeling and talking about the sacrificed relics of old Paris and old London. In this immediate neighbourhood of the enlarged State House, where a great raw clearance has been made, memory met that pang of loss, knew itself sufficiently bereft to see the vanished objects, a scant but adequate cluster of "nooks," of such odds and ends as parochial schemes of improvement sweep away, positively overgrown, within one's own spirit, by a wealth of legend. There was at least the gain, at any rate, that one was now going to be free to picture them, to embroider them, at one's ease—to tangle them up in retrospect and make the real romantic claim for them. This accordingly is what I am doing, but I am doing it in particular for the sacrificed end of Ashburton Place, the Ashburton Place that I anciently knew. This eminently respectable by-way, on my return to question it, opened its short vista for me honestly enough, though looking rather exposed and undermined, since the mouth of the passage to the west, formerly measured and narrow, had begun to yawn into space, a space peopled in fact, for the eye of appreciation, with the horrific glazed perpendiculars of the future. But the pair of ancient houses I was in quest of kept their tryst; a pleasant individual pair, mated with nothing else in the street, yet looking at that hour as if their old still faces had lengthened, their shuttered, lidded eyes had closed, their brick complexions had paled, above the good granite basements, to a fainter red—all as with the cold consciousness of a possible doom.

That possibility, on the spot, was not present to me, occupied as I was with reading into one of them a short page of history of two years of far-away youth spent there at a period—the closing-time of the War—full both of public and of intimate vibrations. The two years had been those of a young man's, a very young man's, earliest fond confidence in a "literary-career," and the effort of actual attention was to recover on the spot some echo of ghostly footsteps—the sound as of taps on the window-pane heard in the dim dawn. The place itself was meanwhile, at all events, a conscious memento, with old secrets to keep and old stories to witness for, a saturation of life as closed together and preserved in it as the scent lingering in a folded pocket-handkerchief. But when, a month later, I returned again (a justly-rebuked mistake) to see if another whiff of the fragrance were not to be caught, I found but a gaping void, the brutal effacement, at a stroke, of every related object, of the whole precious past. Both the houses had been levelled and the space to the corner cleared; hammer and pickaxe had evidently begun to swing on the very morrow of my previous visit—which had moreover been precisely the imminent doom announced, without my understanding it, in the poor scared faces. I had been present, by the oddest hazard, at the very last moments of the victim in whom I was most interested; the act of obliteration had been breathlessly swift, and if I had often seen how fast history could be made I had doubtless never so felt that it could be unmade still faster. It was as if the bottom had fallen out of one's own biography, and one plunged backward into space without meeting anything. That, however, seemed just to give me, as I have hinted, the whole figure of my connection with everything about, a connection that had been sharp, in spite of brevity, and then had broken short off. Thus it was the sense of the rupture, more than of anything else, that I was, and for a still much briefer time, to carry with me. It seemed to leave me with my early impression of the place on my hands, inapt, as might be, for use; so that I could only try, rather vainly, to fit it to present conditions, among which it tended to shrink and stray.

It was on two or three such loitering occasions, wondering and invoking pauses that had, a little vaguely and helplessly perhaps, the changed crest of Beacon Hill for their field—it was at certain of these moments of charged, yet rather chilled, contemplation that I felt my small cluster of early associations shrivel to a scarce discernible point. I recall a Sunday afternoon in particular when I hung about on the now vaster platform of the State House for a near view of the military monuments erected there, the statues of Generals Hooker and Devens, and for the charm at once and the pang of feeling the whole backward vista, with all its features, fall from that eminence into grey perspective. The top of Beacon Hill quite rakes, with a but slightly shifting range, the old more definite Boston; for there seemed no item, nor any number, of that remarkable sum that it would not anciently have helped one to distinguish or divine. There all these things essentially were at the moment I speak of, but only again as something ghostly and dim, something overlaid and smothered by the mere modern thickness. I lingered half-an-hour, much of the new disposition of the elements here involved being duly impressive, and the old uplifted front of the State House, surely, in its spare and austere, its ruled and pencilled kind, a thing of beauty, more delightful and harmonious even than I had remembered it; one of the inestimable values again, in the eye of the town, for taste and temperance, as the perfectly felicitous "Park Street" Church hard by, was another. The irresistible spell, however, I think, was something sharper yet—the coercion, positively, of feeling one's case, the case of one's deeper discomfiture, completely made out. The day itself, toward the winter's end, was all benignant, like the immense majority of the days of the American year, and there went forward across the top of the hill a continuous passage of men and women, in couples and talkative companies, who struck me as labouring wage-earners, of the simpler sort, arrayed, very comfortable, in their Sunday best and recently enjoying their leisure. They came up as from over the Common, they passed or they paused, exchanging remarks on the beauty of the scene, but rapidly presenting themselves to me as of more interest, for the moment, than anything it contained.

For no sound of English, in a single instance, escaped their lips; the greater number spoke a rude form of Italian, the others some outland dialect unknown to me—though I waited and waited to catch an echo of antique refrains. No one of any shade of American speech struck my ear, save in so far as the sounds in question represent today so much of the substance of that idiom. The types and faces bore them out; the people before me were gross aliens to a man, and they were in serene and triumphant possession. Nothing, as I say, could have been more effective for figuring the hitherward bars of a grating through which I might make out, far-off in space, "my" small homogeneous Boston of the more interesting time. It was not of course that our gross little aliens were immediate "social" figures in the narrower sense of the term, or that any personal commerce of which there might be question could colour itself, to its detriment, from their presence; but simply that they expressed, as everywhere and always, the great cost at which every place on my list had become braver and louder, and that they gave the measure of the distance by which the general movement was *away*—away, always and everywhere, from the old presumptions and conceivabilities. Boston, the bigger, braver, louder Boston, was "away," and it was quite, at that hour, as if each figure in my procession were there on purpose to leave me no doubt of it. Therefore had I the vision, as filling the sky, no longer of the great Puritan "whip," the whip for the conscience and the nerves, of the local legend, but that of a huge applied sponge, a sponge saturated with the foreign mixture and passed over almost everything I remembered and might still have recovered. The detail of this obliteration would take me too far, but I had even then (on a previous day as well as only half-an-hour before) caught at something that might stand for a vivid symbol of the general effect of it. To come up from School Street into Beacon was to approach the Athenæum—exquisite institution, to fond memory, joy of the aspiring prime; yet to approach the Athenæum only to find all disposition to enter it drop as dead as if from quick poison, what did *that* denote but the dreadful chill of change, and of the change in especial that was most completely dreadful? For had not this honoured haunt of all the most civilized—library, gallery, temple of culture, the place that was to Boston at large as Boston at large was to the rest of New England—had it not with peculiar intensity had a "value," the most charming of its kind, no doubt, in all the huge country, and had not this value now, evidently, been brought so low that one shrank, in delicacy, from putting it to the test?

It was a case of the detestable "tall building" again, and of its instant destruction of quality in everything it overtowers. Put completely out of countenance by the mere masses of brute ugliness beside it, the temple of culture looked only rueful and snubbed, hopelessly down in the world; so that, far from being moved to hover or to penetrate, one's instinct was to pass by on the other side, averting one's head from an humiliation one could do nothing to make less. And this indeed though one would have liked to do something; the brute masses, above the comparatively small refined façade (one saw how happy one had always thought it) having for the inner ear the voice of a pair of school-bullies who hustle and pummel some studious little boy. "'Exquisite' was what they called you, eh? We'll teach you, then, little sneak, to be exquisite! We allow none of that rot round here." It was heart-breaking, this presentation of a Boston practically void of an Athenæum; though perhaps not without interest as showing how much one's own sense of the small city of the earlier time had been dependent on that institution. I found it of no use, at any rate, to think, for a compensatory sign of the new order, of the present Public Library; the present Public Library, however remarkable in its pomp and circumstance, and of which I had at that hour received my severe impression, being neither exquisite nor on the way to become so—a difficult, an impassable way, no doubt, for Public Libraries. Nor did I cast about, in fact, very earnestly, for consolation—so much more was I held by the vision of the closed order which shaped itself, continually, in the light of the differing present; an order gaining an interest for this backward view precisely as one felt that all the parts and tokens of it, while it lasted, had hung intimately together. Missing those parts and tokens, or as many of them as one could, became thus a constant slightly painful joy: it made them fall so into their place as items of the old character, or proofs, positively, as one might say, of the old distinction. It was impossible not to see Park Street itself, for instance—while I kept looking at the matter from my more "swagger" hilltop as violently vulgarized; and it was incontestable that, whatever might be said, there had anciently not been, on the whole continent, taking everything together, an equal animated space more exempt from vulgarity. There had probably been comparable spaces—impressions, in New York, in Philadelphia, in Baltimore, almost as good; but only almost, by reason of their lacking (which was just the point) the indefinable perfection of Park Street.

It seems odd to have to borrow from the French the right word in this association—or would seem so, rather, had it been less often indicated that that people have better names than ours even for the qualities we are apt to suppose ourselves more in possession of than they. Park Street in any case, had been magnificently *honnête*—the very type and model, for a pleasant street-view, of the character. The aspects that might elsewhere have competed were *honnêtes* and weak, whereas Park Street was *honnête* and strong—strong as founded on *all* the moral, material, social solidities, instead of on some of them only; which made again all the difference. Personal names, as notes of that large emanation, need scarcely be invoked—they might even have a weakening effect; the force of the statement was in its collective, cumulative look, as if each member of the row, from the church at the Tremont Street angle to the amplest, squarest, most purple presence at the Beacon Street corner (where it always had a little the air of a sturdy proprietor with back to the fire, legs apart and thumbs in the armholes of an expanse of high-coloured plush waistcoat), was but a syllable in the world Respectable several times repeated. One had somehow never heard it uttered with so convincing an emphasis. But the shops, up and down, are making all this as if it had never been, pleasant "premises" as they have themselves acquired; and it was to strike me from city to city, I fear, that the American shop in general pleads but meagrely—for indulgence to its tendency to swarm, to bristle, to vociferate. The shop-front, observed at random, produced on me from the first, and almost everywhere alike, a singular, a sinister impression, which left me uneasy till I had found a name for it: a sense of an economic law of which one had not for years known the unholy rigour, the vision of "protected" production and of commodities requiring certainly, in many cases, every advantage Protection could give them. They looked to me always, these exhibitions, consciously and defiantly protected—insolently safe, able to be with impunity anything they would; and when once that lurid light had settled on them I could see them, I confess, in none other; so that the objects composing them fell, throughout, into a vicious and villainous category—quite as if audibly saying: "Oh come; don't look among us for what you won't, for what you shan't find, the best quality attainable; but only for that quite other matter, the best value we allow you. You must take us or go without, and if you feel your nose thus held to the grindstone by the hard fiscal hand, it's no more than you deserve for harbouring treasonable thoughts."

So it was, therefore, that while the imagination and the memory strayed—strayed away to other fiscal climates, where the fruits of competition so engagingly ripen and flush—the streets affected one at moments as a prolonged show-case for every arrayed vessel of humiliation. The fact that several classes of the protected products appeared to consist of articles that one might really anywhere have preferred did little, oddly enough, to diminish the sense of severe disciple awaiting the restored absentee on contact with these occasions of traffic. The discipline indeed is general, proceeding as it does from so many sources, but it earns its name, in particular, from the predicament of the ingenuous inquirer who asks himself if he can "really bear" the combination of such general manners and such general prices, of such general prices and such general manners. He has a helpless bewildered moment during which he wonders if he mightn't bear the prices a little better if he were a little better addressed, or bear the usual form of address a little better if the prices were in themselves, given the commodity offered, a little less humiliating to the purchaser. Neither of these elements of his dilemma strikes him as likely to abate—the general cost of the things to drop, or the general grimness of the person he deals with over the counter to soften; so that he reaches out again for balm to where he has had to seek it under other wounds, falls back on the cultivation of patience and regret, on large international comparison. He is confronted too often, to his sense, with the question of what may be "borne"; but what does he see about him if no a vast social order in which the parties to certain relations are all the while marvellously, inscrutably, desperately "bearing" each other? He may wonder, at his hours, how, under the strain, social cohesion does not altogether give way; but that is another question, which belongs to a different plane of speculation. For he asks himself quite as much as anything else how the shopman or the shoplady can bear to be barked at in the manner he constantly hears used to them by customers—he recognizes that no agreeable form of intercourse *could* survive a day in such air: so that what is the only relation finding ground there but a necessary vicious circle of gross mutual endurance?

These reflections connect themselves moreover with that most general of his restless hauntings in the United States—not only with the lapse of all wonderment at the immense number of absentees unrestored and making their lives as they may in other countries, but with the preliminary American postulate or basis for any successful accommodation of life. This basis is that of active pecuniary gain and of active pecuniary gain only—that of one's making the conditions so triumphantly pay that the prices, the manners, the other inconveniences, take their place as a friction it is comparatively easy to salve, wounds directly treatable with the wash of gold. What prevails, what sets the tune, is the American scale of gain, more magnificent than any other, and the fact that the whole assumption, the whole theory of life, is that of the individual's participation in it, that of his being more or less punctually and more or less effectually "squared." To make so much money that you won't, that you don't "mind," don't mind anything—that is absolutely, I think, the main American formula. Thus your making no money—or so little that it passes there for none—and being thereby distinctly reduced to minding, amounts to your being reduced to the knowledge that America is no place for you. To mind as one minds, for instance, in Europe, under provocation or occasion offered, and yet to have to live under the effect of American pressure, is speedily to perceive that the knot can be untied but by a definite pull of one or the other string. The immense majority of people pull, luckily for the existing order, the string that consecrates their connection with it; the minority (small, however, only in comparison) pull the string that loosens that connection. The existing order is meanwhile safe, inasmuch as the faculty of making money is in America the commonest of all and fairly runs the streets: so simple a matter does it appear there, among vast populations, to make betimes enough *not* to mind. Yet the withdrawal of the considerable group of the pecuniary disqualified seems no less, of the present, an assured movement; there will always be scattered individuals condemned to mind on a scale beyond any scale of making. The relation of this modest body to the country of their birth, which asks so much, on the whole—so many surrenders and compromises, and the possession above all of such a prodigious head for figures—before it begins, in its wonderful way, to give or to "pay," would appear to us supremely touching, I think, as a case of communion baffled and blighted, if we had time to work it out. It would bathe in something of a tragic light the vivid truth that the "great countries" are all, more and more, happy lands (so far as any can be called such) for any, for every sort of person rather than the middle sort. The upper sort—in the scale of wealth, the only scale now—can to their hearts' content build their own castles and move by their own motors; the lower sort, masters of gain in *their* degree, can profit, also to their heart's content, by the enormous extension of those material facilities which may be gregariously enjoyed; they are able to rush about, as never under the sun before, in promiscuous packs and hustled herds, while to the act of so rushing about all felicity and prosperity appear for them to have been comfortably reduced. The frustrated American, as I have hinted at him, scraping for *his* poor practical solution in the depleted silver-mine of history, is the American who "makes" too little for the castle and yet "minds" too much for the hustled herd, who can neither achieve such detachment nor surrender to such society, and who most of all accordingly, in the native order, fails of a working basis. The salve, the pecuniary salve, in Europe, is sensibly less, but less on the other hand also the excoriation that makes it necessary, whether from above or below.

III

Let me at all events say for the Park Street Church, while I may still, on my hilltop, keep more or less in line with it, that this edifice persistently "holds the note," as yet, the note of the old felicity, and remains by so doing a precious public servant. Strange enough, doubtless, to find one's self pleading sanctity for a theological structure sanctified only by such a name—as who should say the Park Street Hotel or the Park Street Post-office; so much clearer would the claim seem to come were it the case of another St. Clement Danes or of another St. Mary-le-Strand. But in America we get our sanctity as we can, and we plead it, if we are wise, wherever the conditions suffer the faintest show of colour for it to flush through. Again and again it is a question, on behalf of the memorial object (and especially when preservation is at stake), of an interest and an appeal proceeding exactly *from* the conditions, and thereby not of an absolute, but of a relative force and weight; which is exactly the state of the matter with the Park Street Church. This happy landmark is, in strictness, with its mild recall, by its spire, of Wren's bold London examples, the comparatively thin echo of a far-away song—playing its part, however, for harmonious effect, as perfectly as possible. It is admirably placed quite peculiarly *present,* on the Boston scene, and thus, for one reason and another, points its moral as not even the State House does. So we see afresh, under its admonition, that charm is a flower of wild and windblown seed—often not to be counted on when most anxiously planted, but taking its own time and its own place both for enriching and for mocking us. It mocks assuredly, above all, our money and our impatience, elements addressed to buying or "ordering" it, and only asks that when it does come we shall know it and love it. When we fail of this intelligence it simply, for its vengeance, boycotts us—makes us vulgar folk who have no concern with it. Then if we ever miss it we can never get it back—though our deepest depth of punishment of course is to go on fatuously not missing it, the joy of ourselves and of each other and the derision of those who know. These reflections were virtually suggested to me, on the eve of my leaving Boston, by ten words addressed to my dismay; the effect of which was to make Part Street Church, for the hour, the most interesting mass of brick and mortar and (if I may risk the supposition) timber in America.

The words had been spoken, in the bright July air, by a friend encountered in the very presence of the mild monument, on the freshly-perceived value of which, for its position, for its civil function, I had happened irrepressibly to exclaim. Thus I learned that its existence might be spoken of as gravely menaced—menaced by a scheme for the erection of a "business block," a huge square of innumerable tiers and floors, thousands of places of trade, the trade that in such a position couldn't fail to be roaring. In the eye of financial envy the church was but a cumberer of the ground, and where, about us, had we seen financial envy fail when it had once really applied the push of its fat shoulders? Drunk as it was with power, what was to be thought of as resisting it? This was a question, truly, to frighten answers away—until I presently felt the most pertinent of all return as if on tiptoe. The perfect force of the case *as* a case, as an example, that was the answer of answers; the quite ideal pitch of the opportunity for virtue. Ideal opportunities are rare, and this occasion for not sacrificing the high ornament and cynosure of the town to the impudence of private greed just happens to be one, and to have the finest marks of the character. One had but to imagine a civilized community reading these marks, feeling that character, and then consciously and cynically falling below its admirable chance, to take in the impossibility of any such blot on the page of honour, any such keen appetite for the base alternative. It would be verily the end—the end of the old distinguished life, of the common intelligence that had flowered formerly, for attesting fame, from so strong a sap and into so thick and rich a cluster. One had thought of these things as one came and went—so interesting today in Boston are such informal consultations of the oracle (that of the very air and "tone"), such puttings to it of the question of what the old New England spirit may have still, intellectually, æsthetically, or for that matter even morally, to give; of what may yet remain, for productive scraping, of the formula of the native Puritanism educated, the formula once capacious enough for the "literary constellation" of the Age of Emerson. Is that cornucopia empty, or does some handful of strong or at least sound fruit lurk to this day, a trifle congested by keeping, up in the point of the horn? What, if so, are, in the ambient air, the symptoms of this possibility? what are the signs of intellectual promise, poetic, prosaic, philosophic, in the current generations, those actually learning their principal lesson, as one assumes, from the great University hard by? The old formula, that of Puritanism educated, has it, in fine, except for "business," anything more to communicate?—or do we perhaps mistake the case in still speaking, by reason of the projected shadow of Harvard, of "education" as at all involved?

Oh, for business, for a commercial, an organizing energy of the first order, the indications would seem to abound; the air being full of them as one loud voice, and nowhere so full perhaps as at that Park Street corner, precisely, where it was to be suggested to me that their meaning was capable on occasion of turning to the sinister. The commercial energy at least was educated, up to the eyes—Harvard was still caring for that more than for anything else—but the wonderments, or perhaps rather the positive impressions I have glanced at, bore me constant company, keeping the last word, all emphasis of answer, back as if for the creation of a dramatic suspense. I liked the suspense, none the less, for what it had in common with "intellectual curiosity," and it gave me a light, moreover, which was highly convenient, helping me to look at everything in some related state to this proposition of the value of the Puritan residuum—the question of whether value *is* expressed, for instance, by the little tales, mostly by ladies, and about and for children romping through the ruins of the Language, in the monthly magazines. Some of my perceptions of relation might seem forced, for other minds, but it sufficed me that they were straight and clear for myself—straight and clear again, for example, when (always on my hilltop and raking the prospect over for memories) I quite assented to the tacit intimation that a long æsthetic period had closed with the disappearance of the old Museum Theatre. This had been the theatre of the "great" period—so far as such a description may fit an establishment that never produced during that term a play either by a Bostonian or by any other American; or it had at least, with however unequal steps, kept the great period company, made the Boston of those years quite complacently participate in its genial continuity. This character of its *being* an institution, its really being a theatre, with a repertory and a family of congruous players, not one of them the baleful actor-manager, head and front of all the so rank and so acclaimed vulgarities of our own day—this nature in it of not being the mere empty shell, the indifferent cave of the winds, that yields a few nights' lodging, under stress, to the passing caravan, gave it a dignity of which I seemed to see the ancient city gratefully conscious, fond and jealous, and the thought of which invites me to fling over it now perhaps to free a fold of the mantle of romance. And yet why too free? is what I ask myself as I remember that the Museum had for long years a repertory—the repertory of its age—a company and a cohesion, theatrical trifles of the cultivation of which no present temple of the drama from end to end of the country appears to show a symptom. Therefore I spare a sigh to its memory, and, though I doubtless scarce think of it as the haunt of Emerson, of Hawthorne or of Mr. Ticknor, the common conscience of the mid-century in the New England capital insists on showing, at this distance of time, as the richer for it.

That then was one of the missed elements, but the consequent melancholy, I ought promptly to add, formed the most appropriate soil for stray sprouts of tenderness in respect to the few aspects that had not suffered. The old charm of Mount Vernon Street, for instance, wandering up the hill, almost from the waterside, to the rear of the State House, and fairly hanging about there to rest like some good flushed lady, of more than middle age, a little spent and "blown"—this ancient grace was not only still to be felt, but was charged, for depth of interest, with intenser ghostly presences, the rich growth of time, which might have made the ample slope, as one mounted, appear as beautifully peopled as Jacob's Ladder. That was exactly the kind of impression to be desired and welcomed; since ghosts belong only to places and suffer and perish with them. It was as if they themselves moreover were taking pleasure in this place, fairly indeed commending to me the fine old style of the picture. Nothing less appeared to account for my not having, in the other age, done it, as the phrase is, full justice, recognized in it so excellent a peace, such a clear Boston bravery—all to the end that it should quite strike me, on the whole, as not only, for the minor stretch and the domestic note, the happiest street-scene the country could show, but as pleasant, on those respectable lines, in a degree not surpassed even among outland pomps. Oh, the wide benignity of brick, the goodly, friendly, ruddy fronts, the felicity of scale, the solid *seat* of everything, even to the handful of happy deviations from the regular produced, we may fancy, by one of those "historic" causes which so rarely complicate, for humanization, the blankness of the American street-page, and the occasional occurrence of which, in general, as I am perhaps too repeatedly noting, excites on the part of the starved story-seeker a fantastic insistence. I find myself willing, after all, to let my whole estimate of these mere mild monuments of private worth pass for extravagant if it but leave me a perch for musing on the oddity of our nature which makes us still like the places we have known or loved to grow old, when we can scarcely bear it in the people. To walk down Mount Vernon Street to Charles was to have a brush with that truth, to recognize at least that we like the sense of age to come, locally, when it comes with the right accompaniments, with the preservation of character and the continuity of tradition, merits I had been admiring on the brow of the eminence. From the other vision, the sight of the "decline in the social scale," the lapse into shabbiness and into bad company, we only suffer, for the ghosts in that case either refuse to linger, or linger at the most with faces ashamed and as if appealing against their association.

Such was the condition of the Charles Street ghosts, it seemed to me—shades of a past that had once been so thick and warm and happy; they moved, dimly, through a turbid medium in which the signs of their old life looked soiled and sordid. Each of them was there indeed, from far, far back; they met me on the pavement, yet it was if we could pass but in conscious silence, and nothing could have helped us, for any courage of communion, if we had not enjoyed the one merciful refuge that remained, where indeed we could breathe again, and with intensity, our own liberal air. Here, behind the effaced anonymous door, was the little ark of the modern deluge, here still the long drawing-room that looks over the water and toward the sunset, with a seat for every visiting shade, from far-away Thackeray down, and relics and tokens so thick on its walls as to make it positively, in all the town, the votive temple to memory. Ah, if it hadn't been for that small patch of common ground, with its kept echo of the very accent of the past, the revisiting spirit, at the bottom of the hill, could but have muffled his head, or but have stifled his heart, and turned away for ever. Let me even say that—always now at the bottom of the hill—it was in this practical guise he afterwards, at the best, found himself roaming. It is from about that point southward that the new splendours of Boston spread, and will clearly continue to spread, but it opened out to me as a tract pompous and prosaic, with which the little interesting city, the city of character and genius, exempt as yet from the Irish yoke, had had absolutely nothing to do. This disconnection was complete, and the southward, the westward territory made up, at the most, a platform or stage from which the other, the concentrated Boston of history, the Boston of Emerson, Thoreau, Hawthorne, Longfellow, Lowell, Holmes, Ticknor, Motley, Prescott, Parkman and the rest (in the sense either of birthplace or of central or sacred city) could be seen in as definite, and indeed now in almost as picturesquely mediæval, a concretion, appear to make as black and minute and "composed" a little pyramidal image, as the finished background of a Dürer print. It seemed to place itself there, in the middle distance, on the sharp salience of its commingled Reforms and Reserves—reformers and reservists, rubbing shoulders in the common distinctness of their detachment from an inexpressive generation, and the composition rounding itself about as with the very last of its loose-ends snipped off or tucked in.

IV

There are neither loose ends nor stray flutters, whether of the old prose or the old poetry, to be encountered on the large lower level, though there are performances of a different order, in the shadow of which such matters tend to look merely, and perhaps rather meagrely, subjective. It is all very rich and prosperous and monotonous, the large lower level, but oh, so inexpressibly vacant! Where the "new land" corresponds most to its name, rejoices most visibly and complacently in its newness, its dumped and shovelled foundations, the home till recently of a mere vague marine backwater, there the long, straight residential avenues, vistas quite documentary, as one finds one's self pronouncing them, testify with a perfection all their own to a whole vast side of American life. The winter winds and snows, and the eternal dust, run races in them over the clearest course anywhere provided for that grim competition; the league-long brick pavements mirror the expansive void, for many months of the year, in their smooth, tight ice-coats (and ice over brick can only be described as heels over head), and the innumerable windows, up and down, watch each other, all hopelessly, as for revelations, indiscretions, audible, resonant, rebellious or explosive breakages of the pane from within, that never disturb the peace. (No one will begin, and the buried hatchet, in spite of whatever wistful looks to where it lies, is never dug up.) So it is that these sustained affirmations of one of the smoothest and the most settled social states "going" excite perversely, on the part of the restless analyst, questions that would seem logically the very last involved. We call such aspects "documentary" because they strike us, more than any others, as speaking volumes for the possible *serenity*, the common decency, the quiet cohesion, of a vast commercial and professional bourgeoisie left to itself. Here was such an order caught in the very fact, the fact of its living maximum. A bourgeoisie without an aristocracy to worry it is of course a very different thing from a bourgeoisie struggling in that shade, and nothing could express more than these interminable perspectives of security the condition of a community leading its life in the social sun.

Why, accordingly, of December afternoons, did the restless analyst, pausing at eastward-looking corners, find on his lips the vague refrain of Tennyson's "long, unlovely street"? Why, if Harley Street, if Wimpole, is unlovely, should Marlborough Street, Boston, be so—beyond the mere platitude of its motiveless name? Here is no monotony of black leasehold brick, no patent disavowal, in the interest of stale and strictly subordinate gentilities, of expression, animation, variety, curiosity; here, on the contrary, is often the individual house-front in all its independence and sometimes in all its felicity: this whole region being, like so many such regions in the United States today, the home of the free hand, a field for the liveliest architectural experiment. There are interesting, admirable houses—though always too much of the detestable vitreous "bow"—and there is above all what there is everywhere in America for saving, or at least for propping up, the situation, that particular look of the clear course and large opportunity ahead, which, when taken in conjunction with all the will to live, all the money to spend, all the knowledge to acquire and apply, seems to marshal the material possibilities in glittering illimitable ranks. Beacon Street, moreover, used to stretch back like a workable telescope for the focussing, at its higher extremity, in an air of which the positive defect is to be too seldom prejudicial, of the gilded dome of the State House—fresh as a Christmas toy seen across the floor of a large salubrious nursery. This made a civic vignette that furnished a little the desert of cheerful family life. But Marlborough Street, for imperturbable reasons of it own, used periodically to break my heart. It was of no use to make a vow of hanging about till I should have sounded my mystery—learned to say *why* black, stale Harley Street, for instance, in featureless row after row, had character and depth, while what was before me fell upon my sense with the thinness of tone of a precocious child—and still more why this latter effect should have been, as it were, so insistently irritating. If there be strange ways of producing an interest, to the critical mind, there are doubtless still stranger ways of not producing one, and it was important to me, no doubt, to make "my" defunct and compact and expressive little Boston appear to don all the signs of that character that the New Land, and what is built thereon, miss. How could one consider the place at all unless in a light?—so that one had to decide definitely on one's light.

This it was after all easy to do from the moment one had determined to concede to the New Land the fact of possession of everything convenient and handsome under heaven. Peace could always come with this recognition of all the accessories and equipments, a hundred costly things, parks and palaces and institutions, that the earlier community had lacked; and there was an individual connection—only one, presently to be noted—in which the actual city might seem for an hour to have no capacity for the uplifting idea, no aptitude for the finer curiosity, to envy the past. But meanwhile it was strange that even so fine a conception, finely embodied, as the new Public Library, magnificently superseding all others, was committed to speak to one's inner perception still more of the power of the purse and of the higher turn for business than of the old intellectual, or even of the old moral, sensibility. Why else then should one have thought of some single, some admirable hour of Emerson, in one of the dusky, primitive lecture-halls that have ceased to be, or of some large insuperable anti-slavery eloquence of Wendell Phillip's, during the same term and especially during the War, as breathing more of the consciousness of literature and of history than all the promiscuous bustle of the Florentine palace by Copley Square? Not that this latter edifice, the fruit of immense considerations, has not its honourable interest too; which it would have if only in the light of the constant truth that almost any American application or practice of a general thought puts on a new and original aspect. Public libraries are a thoroughly general thought, and one has seen plenty of them, one is seeing dreadfully many, in these very days, the world over; yet to be confronted with an American example is to have sight straightway of more difference than community, and to glean on the spot fresh evidence of that democratic way of dealing which it has been the American office to translate from an academic phrase into a bristling fact. The notes of difference of the Florentine palace by Copley Square—more delicately elegant, in truth, if less sublimely rugged, than most Florentine palaces—resolve themselves, like so many such notes everywhere, into our impression here, once more, that every one is "in" everything, whereas in Europe so comparatively few persons are in anything (even as yet in "society," more and more the common refuge or retreat of the masses).

The Boston institution then is a great and complete institution, with this reserve of its striking the restored absentee as practically without *penetralia*. A library without *penetralia* may affect him but as a temple without altars; it will at any rate exemplify the distinction between a benefit given and a benefit taken, a borrowed, a lent, and an owned, an appropriated convenience. The British Museum, the Louvre, the Bibliothèque Nationale, the treasures of South Kensington, are assuredly, under forms, at the disposal of the people; but it is to be observed, I think, that the people walk there more or less under the shadow of the right waited for and conceded. It remains as difficult as it is always interesting, however, to trace the detail (much of it obvious enough, but much more indefinable) of the personal port of a democracy that, unlike the English, is social as well as political. One of these denotements is that social democracies are unfriendly to the preservation of *penetralia*; so that when *penetralia* are of the essence, as in a place of study and meditation, they inevitably go to the wall. The main staircase, in Boston, has, with its amplitude of wing and its splendour of tawny marble, a high and luxurious beauty—bribing the restored absentee to emotion, moreover, by expanding, monumentally, at one of its rests, into admirable commemoration of the Civil War service of the two great Massachusetts Volunteer regiments of *élite*. Such visions, such felicities, such couchant lions and recorded names and stirred memories as these, encountered in the early autumn twilight, *colour* an impression—even though to say so be the limit of breach of the silence in which, for persons of the generation of the author of these pages, appreciation of them can best take refuge: the refuge to which I felt myself anon reduced, for instance, opposite the State House, in presence of Saint-Gaudens's noble and exquisite monument to Robert Gould Shaw and the Fifty-fourth Massachusetts. There are works of memorial art that may suddenly place themselves, by their operation in a given case, outside articulate criticism—which was what happened, I found, in respect to the main feature, the rich staircase of the Library. Another way in which the bribe, as I have called it, of that masterpiece worked on the spot was by prompting one to immediate charmed perception of the character of the deep court and inner arcade of the place, where a wealth of science and taste has gone to producing a sense, when the afternoon light sadly slants, of one of the myriad gold-coloured courts of the Vatican.

These are the refinements of the present Boston—keeping company as they can with the healthy animation, as it struck me, of the rest of the building, the multitudinous bustle, the coming and going, as in a railway-station, of persons, with carpet-bags and other luggage, the simplicity of plan, the open doors and immediate accesses, admirable *for* a railway-station, the ubiquitous children, *most* irrepressible little democrats of the democracy, the vain quest, above all, of the deeper depths aforesaid, some part that should be sufficiently *within* some other part, sufficiently withdrawn and consecrated, not to constitute a thoroughfare. Perhaps I didn't adequately explore; but there was always the visible scale and scheme of the building. It was a shock to find the so brave decorative designs of Puvis de Chavannes, of Sargent and Abbey and John Elliott, hanging over mere chambers of familiarity and resonance; and then, I must quickly add, it was a shock still greater perhaps to find one had no good reason for defending them against such freedoms. What was sauce for the goose was sauce for the gander: had one not in other words, in the public places and under the great loggias of Italy, acclaimed it as just the charm and dignity of these resorts that, in their pictured and embroidered state, they still serve for the graceful common life? It was true that one had not been imprisoned in that consistency in the Laurentian, in the Ambrosian Library—and at any rate one was here on the edge of abysses. Was it not splendid, for example, to see, in Boston, such large provision made for the amusement of children on rainy afternoons?—so many little heads bent over their story-books that the edifice took on at moments the appearance worn, one was to observe later on, by most other American edifices of the same character, that of a lively distributing-house of the new fiction for the young. The note was bewildering—yet would one, snatching the bread-and-molasses from their lips, cruelly deprive the young of rights in which they have been installed with a majesty nowhere else approaching that of their American installation? I am not wrong, probably, at all events, in qualifying such a question as that as abysmal, and I remember how, more than once, I took refuge from it in craven flight, straight across the Square, to the already so interesting, the so rapidly-expanding Art Museum.

There, for some reason, questions exquisitely dropped; perhaps only for the reason that things sifted and selected have, very visibly, the effect of challenging the confidence even of the rash. It is of the nature of objects doomed to show distinction that they virtually make a desert round them, and peace reigned unbroken, I usually noted, in the two or three Museum rooms that harbour a small but deeply-interesting and steadily-growing collection of fragments of the antique. Here the restless analyst found work to his hand—only too much; and indeed in presence of the gem of the series, of the perhaps just too conscious grace of a certain little wasted and dim-eyed head of Aphrodite, he felt that his function should simply give way, in common decency, to that of the sonneteer. For it is an impression by itself, and I think quite worth the Atlantic voyage, to catch in the American light the very fact of the genius of Greece. There are things we don't know, feelings not to be foretold, till we have had that experience—which I commend to the *raffiné* of almost any other clime. I should say to him that he has not *seen* a fine Greek thing till he has seen it in America. It is of course on the face of it the most merciless case of transplanting—the mere moral of which, none the less, for application, becomes by no means flagrant. The little Aphrodite, with her connections, her antecedents and references exhibiting the maximum of breakage, is no doubt as *lonely* a jewel as ever strayed out of its setting; yet what does one quickly recognize but that the intrinsic lustre will have, so far as that may be possible, doubled? She has lost her background, the divine creature—has lost her company, and is keeping, in a manner, the strangest; but so far from having lost an iota of her power, she has gained unspeakably more, since what she essentially stands for she here stands for alone, rising ineffably to the occasion. She has in short, by her single presence, as yet, annexed an empire, and there are strange glimmers of moments when, as I have spoken of her consciousness, the very knowledge of this seems to lurk in the depth of her beauty. Where was she ever more, where was she ever so much, a goddess—and who knows but that, being thus divine, she foresees the time when, as she has "moved over," the place of her actual whereabouts will have become one of her shrines? Objects doomed to distinction make round them a desert, I have said; but that is only for any gross confidence in other matters. For confidence in *them* they make a garden, and that is why I felt this quarter of the Boston Art Museum bloom, under the indescribable dim eyes, with delicate flowers. The impression swallowed up every other; the place, whatever it was, was supremely justified, and I was left cold by learning that a much bigger and grander and richer place is presently to overtop it.

The present establishment "dates back," back almost to the good Boston of the middle years, and is full of all sorts of accumulated and concentrated pleasantness; which fact precisely gives the signal, by the terrible American law, for its coming to an end and giving a chance to the untried. It is a consistent application of the rotary system—the untried always awaiting its turn, and quite perceptibly stamping and snorting while it waits; all heedless as it is, poor innocent untried, of the certain hour of the impatiences before which it too will have to retreat. It is not indeed that the American laws, so operating, have not almost always their own queer interest; founded as they are, all together, on one of the strongest of the native impulses. We see this characteristic again and again at play, see it in especial wherever we see (which is more than frequently enough) a university or a college "started" or amplified. This process almost always takes the form, primarily, of more lands and houses and halls and rooms, more swimming-baths and football-fields and gymnasia, a greater luxury of brick and mortar, a greater ingenuity, the most artful conceivable, of accommodation and installation. Such is the magic, such the presences, that tend, more than any other, to figure *as* the Institution, thereby perverting not a little, as need scarce be remarked, the finer collegiate idea: the theory being, doubtless, and again most characteristically, that with all the wrought stone and oak and painted glass, the immense provision, the multiplied marbles and tiles and cloisters and acres, "people will come," that is, individuals of value will, and in some manner work some miracle. In the early American time, doubtless, individuals of value had to wait too much for things; but that is now made up by the way things are waiting for individuals of value. To which I must immediately add, however—and it is the ground of my allusion of a moment ago—that no impression of the "new" Boston can feel itself hang together without remembrance of what it owes to that rare exhibition of the living spirit lately achieved, in the interest of the fine arts, and of all that is noblest in them, by the unaided and quite heroic genius of a private citizen. To attempt to tell the story of the wonderfully-gathered and splendidly-lodged Gardner Collection would be to displace a little the line that separates private from public property; and yet to find no discreet word for it is to appear to fail of feeling for the complexity of conditions amid which so undaunted a devotion to a great idea (undaunted by the battle to fight, losing, alas, with State Protection of native art, and with other scarce less uncanny things) has been able consummately to flower. It is in presence of the results magnificently attained, the energy triumphant over everything, that one feels the fine old disinterested tradition of Boston least broken.

158

Two Boston Poems

T. S. ELIOT

Thomas Stearns Eliot (1888–1965) is one of the outstanding poets of the twentieth century, whose influence on writers and intellectuals seems pervasive. Born in St. Louis, Missouri, Eliot came from a Unitarian family of New England descent—an aspect of his personal history which has an important influence on the rest of his life and attitudes. He attended Harvard University where he met such luminaries as Santayana and Irving Babbit. His Boston years involved the "discovery" of the French symbolist poets, most notably Laforgue and Baudelaire. Their work suggested a new kind of aesthetic for dealing with the moods and nuances of modern city life. Eliot moved to London in 1915 and effectively ended his connections with the United States. Indeed, he became a British citizen in 1927.

His major poem remains *The Waste Land* (1922), a dense and often obscure poem, which, through a cubist-like series of multiple perspectives, develops a dramatic rendition of a modern urban consciousness on the point of breakdown. The London of its setting is placed against the larger symbolic landscape of myth and religion which offer hope and fecundity rather than the sterility and emptiness of modern life. "Ash-Wednesday" (1930) confirms his Christian perspectives which are placed to the fore in the major poem of his mature period, *Four Quartets* (1943). Eliot was often negative towards the modern period but remains a central modern poet. Such a paradox is evident in *Selected Prose* (1975). Eliot was also a major dramatist of which, perhaps, *Murder in the Cathedral* (1935) is his most famous work. See Bernard Bergonzi, *T. S. Eliot* (1972), Peter Ackroyd, *T. S. Eliot* (1984) and Graham Clarke (ed), *T. S. Eliot: Critical Assessments* (4 vols, 1988).

Source: T. S. Eliot, "The 'Boston Evening Transcript'" and "Morning at the Window", 1917,

The "Boston Evening Transcript"

The readers of the Boston Evening Transcript
Sway in the wind like a field of ripe corn.

When evening quickens faintly in the street,
Wakening the appetites of life in some
And to others bringing the Boston Evening Transcript,
I mount the steps and ring the bell, turning
Wearily, as one would turn to nod good-bye to La Rochefoucauld,
If the street were time and he at the end of the street,
And I say, "Cousin Harriet, here is the Boston Evening Transcript."

Morning at the Window

They are rattling breakfast plates in basement kitchens,
And along the trampled edges of the street
I am aware of the damp souls of housemaids
Sprouting despondently at area gates.

The brown waves of fog toss up to me
Twisted faces from the bottom of the street,
And tear from a passer-by with muddy skirts
An aimless smile that hovers in the air
And vanishes along the level of the roofs.

159

For the Union Dead

ROBERT LOWELL

For an introductory note to Robert Lowell, see Chapter 153.

For the Union Dead
"Relinquunt Omnia Servare Rem Publicam."

The old South Boston Aquarium stands
in a Sahara of snow now. Its broken windows are boarded.
The bronze weathervane cod has lost half its scales.
The airy tanks are dry.

Once my nose crawled like a snail on the glass;
my hand tingled
to burst the bubbles
drifting from the noses of the cowed, compliant fish.

My hand draws back. I often sigh still
for the dark downward and vegetating kingdom
of the fish and reptile. One morning last March,
I pressed against the new barbed and galvanized

fence on the Boston Common. Behind their cage,
yellow dinosaur steamshovels were grunting
as they cropped up tons of mush and grass
to gouge their underworld garage.

Parking spaces luxuriate like civic
sandpiles in the heart of Boston.
A girdle of orange, Puritan-pumpkin colored girders
braces the tingling Statehouse,

Source: Robert Lowell, "For the Union Dead", *For the Union Dead*, London, 1964.

shaking over the excavations, as it faces Colonel Shaw
and his bell-cheeked Negro infantry
on St. Gaudens' shaking Civil War relief,
propped by a plank splint against the garage's earthquake.

Two months after marching through Boston,
half the regiment was dead;
at the dedication,
William James could almost here the bronze Negroes breathe.

Their monument sticks like a fishbone
in the city's throat.
Its Colonel is as lean
as a compass-needle.

He has an angry wrenlike vigilance,
a greyhound's gentle tautness;
he seems to wince at pleasure,
and suffocate for privacy.

He is out of bounds now. He rejoices in man's lovely,
peculiar power to choose life and die—
when he leads his black soldiers to death,
he cannot bend his back.

On a thousand small town New England greens,
the old white churches hold their air
of sparse, sincere rebellion: frayed flags
quilt the graveyards of the Grand Army of the Republic.

The stone statues of the abstract Union Soldier
grow slimmer and younger each year—
wasp-wasted, they doze over muskets
and muse through their sideburns ...

Shaw's father wanted no monument
except the ditch,
where his son's body was thrown
and lost with his "niggers."

The ditch is nearer.
There are no statues for the last war here;
on Boylston Street, a commercial photograph
shows Hiroshima boiling

over a Mosler Safe, the "Rock of Ages"
that survived the blast. Space is nearer.

When I crouch to my television set,
the drained faces of Negro school-children rise like balloons.

Colonel Shaw
is riding on his bubble,
he waits
for the blessèd break.

The Aquarium is gone. Everywhere,
giant finned cars nose forward like fish;
a savage servility
slides by on grease.

❧160❧

One American City

JONATHAN RABAN

Jonathan Raban (1942–) was born in Norfolk, England, and was a university lecturer until 1969 when he became a full-time writer. His publications include the novel *Foreign Land* (1985), and travel writing such as *Old Glory* (1982) and *Coasting* (1986). *Soft City* (1974) is a critical but personal deliberation on the nature of the modern city. Raban is a significant travel writer and critic and, since his settling in Seattle, Washington State, he has continued to offer distinctive observations on urban life in the United States of the 1980s and 1990s.

At ten o'clock on Saturday night, the old black man and his wife set up their piles of *Boston Sunday Herald-Americans* at the corner of Inman Square. But this is not a square; it's a deserted intersection, eerily darkened because of the Energy Crisis. The blacks, wrapped up like parcels against the December weather, have no customers. They flap their arms forlornly to keep warm, mooch five steps up the street, and five steps back. A big yellow car with a jagged fender skips the red light and heads towards whatever action there may be in downtown Boston. Crossing the road to get to the Gaslight Pub I notice a laundry-bundle in a doorway which, seeing me, gets up and turns into the remains of a woman; a stunted thing with a big head and a frizzy mop of ochre-coloured hair. She starts singing gibberish first at me, then at her reflection in the glass of a shop door. Only the word "babylove" is distinguishable.

"Babyloveshamingamingaliveaplingalove." And cackles at me, her face as creased as Auden's. But something about the mouth is still only in its late teens or very early twenties; it has the raw-meat floppiness of adolescence.

"Is-scher-schplitzer-mishder-kwicks-a-schpearer-quarter."

I hurry past.

"Fuck you!"

In the pub that is not a pub in the square that is not a square, there is an

Source: Jonathan Raban, "One American City", *Soft City*, Jonathan Raban. London, 1974, Ch. 9, pp. 209–22, (1988 edition), © Jonathan Raban, 1974.

amiable seedy huddle around the bar. Plaid donkey jackets, a couple of tarts who look as though they've strayed in from the 1950s, one or two crimped underfed faces from the Great Depression, and a man with a watch chain and hat from another era altogether. The rest of the place is laid out like a workman's café, in barren lines of tables and chairs. There's an unplayed-at club pool table with bald baize, a glass phone kiosk that looks as if it had been smuggled in off the street, and an electric tennis machine that has a cardiogram for a face and is hungry for quarters. Everything is out of kilter. Nothing in the room, except for the plaid jackets, comes together.

It takes a few minutes to notice the three men at separate tables, they are so still, so much a part of the bar furniture. Each one has his head sunk into his chest, an empty bottle of Schlitz on the table in front of him. Their coats trail in straight lines from shoulders to floor. Their eyes are closed tight as zip-fasteners. The man nearest to me seems to have forgotten his lips; they twitch and blink as if he were speaking in tongues. His thumb mashes what's left of a stale bagel to dust on the tabletop.

Outside on the street, the black couple are doing a joyless shuffle-dance on the sidewalk, like a lumpish parody of Fred Astaire and Ginger Rogers. Business is bad. They blow on their hands and gaze uptown for car lights. Nothing doing.

The Gaslight Pub, with its browbeaten collection of people and things in the wrong time and the wrong place, is true to the spirit of Boston as a city—a raw, dislocated place that never seems to quite come right. It is not even a city, exactly; rather, it is a shabby galaxy of more or less independent townships. Boston proper has less than three-quarters of a million inhabitants, but "metropolitan Boston" is as big as Birmingham, swollen by more than a dozen separate "communities" which have kept their autonomy ever since the Puritans settled in the area in the seventeenth century. They have their own town meetings, their own police forces, schools, courts, newspapers. Boston has a metropolitan economy and metropolitan-scale commuter routes—a gigantic tangle of expressways, subways and streetcar lines. But it has never coalesced into a metropolitan city. Its style is resolutely small-town—small-town emptiness, small-town sprawl, small-town isolation; it exudes the wet Sunday afternoon atmosphere of the dull province where there's no place to go, no big-city freedom, no glamour. Everything about Boston—its architecture and size, its strange concentration of eccentric talents—should have made it an exciting city. But no. That is not what Boston wanted. It craved discreet uneventfulness, the calm of a vast, woody suburb. Like so many American cities, it has succeeded in landing itself up in a terrible, anomalous mess.

When I first arrived here for a three-month stay, I was lost in a labyrinth of names and boundaries that were quite incomprehensible to an outsider. There was a fifteen-minute taxi ride from the airport on a looping expressway, through tunnels, on flyovers, past an architecture of ruddy brick, white-painted wood, sharp angles, bowfronts, balconies, pretty spires and small cluster of skyscrapers that looked as if they had been hired from New York for the day. There were changes of colour and texture in the journey but were these the outskirts or the city centre? I couldn't tell. We crossed a river, and on all sides I saw the same jerky, up-and-down look. *There* must be the centre ... no *there*; but there was no area of sufficient intensity on the skyline to be sure. We stopped at the great redbrick shoebox of an apartment house where I was to be living. This was ... Boston? No, Cambridge. But isn't Cambridge part of Boston? No, Cambridge is Cambridge. A few days before, I'd read in the English papers of the murder of a woman by immolation on a vacant lot in Boston. Was that near here? No, that was in Roxbury. Is Roxbury part of Boston? Well, sort of ... yes, you could say Roxbury is a part of Boston. How far from here? About, oh, three miles. My second night, still giddy with these names, there was a huge fire in Chelsea; we could see the flames from the top of our block. But Chelsea, of course, is not in Boston, and it's not even next door to Cambridge, so the fire was none of our business: it was an interesting blaze in another country, to hear about on the radio.

Never have I been so confined to quarters. It was like being back at boarding school, for nearly everywhere turned out to be out of bounds. The newcomer to the American city finds himself being constantly buttonholed by his acquaintances. "How well do you actually *know* Boston?" they inquire, as if you were not to be trusted with your frivolous European idea of the freedom of the city. Then come the warnings. "You mustn't think it's like London, you know." By the end of the first day, I had learned that I was not to cross the river, go on to or beyond the Cambridge Common; that I could go to Harvard Square, but not as far as Central Square, a mile further down. Somerville, the neighbouring "community" was unsafe. I must not take taxis, they were much too expensive, and I mustn't ride on the subway because a lot of people were getting mugged there. I found that I was stuck, and that during daylight hours only, with an area of about a square mile; a small, frustrating cell of city space, beset by phantoms on every side.

Within a few days, these boundaries had become as real and oppressive as the walls of ghetto. They enclosed Harvard University and a few leafy suburban streets of wooden mansions, their fronts as full of rigging, balconies and quarter-decks as Mississippi steamboats. There were lots of nice old ladies who got blown along the sidewalks with the fall leaves, their voices dry and querulous—the characteristic note of the old Boston accent, genteel as an embroidery needle stitching a sampler. There were rangy students, and triumphantly androgynous young women, and squat European sages in berets and mufflers, but there was no sense at all of a city. Here was "The Square", "The Yard"; one department store, two cinemas, a clutch of second-rate restaurants ... enough, perhaps, to make a life, but the life would have the small, defensive certitude of a scholarly village parson's. You could enclose it in a little glass dome, adding water and a snowstorm of plastic chips, then sell it in the gift shop on Brattle Street: "A Souvenir from Harvard College."

It is a pretty toy ghetto. Like a nanny's frightening stories of the outside world, designed to keep the children safe inside the nursery, there are scary rumours about the rest of the city. Everywhere else in Greater Boston, so it would seem, is the exclusive territory of some group, patrolled by vigilantes on the look out for strangers like you. Never go to Roxbury or Dorchester, or you will be murdered by "the blacks" ... in the North End, the Italians will get you ... in Somerville, the poor whites ... in Chelsea, the poor Jews ... in Brookline, the rich Jews ... on the back of Beacon Hill, the junkies ... on the front of Beacon Hill, the Brahmins ... and if you go near water, you will be bitten by the snapping turtles. A graduate student, who had displayed no other signs of insane paranoia, solemnly asserted that the Back Bay "had been taken over by the Jews". From the perspective of Cambridge, Boston is a chequerboard of enemy camps, and anyone who moves from his square is taking his life in his hands.

Yet, looking over the city from the safe vantage point of the restaurant on the fifty-second floor of the Prudential Center, all I could see was miles and miles of the same, infinitely extended small town—low, bricky, sprouting elms and maples in every available gap between the buildings. The two tallest blocks in Boston are owned by rival insurance companies—the stockily provincial Prudential building and the rakish, slender, very New York, John Hancock Tower—and that seems appropriate for the city, with its detached suburban spaciousness, its deceptive owner-occupier air. Dogs ... year-old cars ... the funny-sections of the Sunday *Globe* .. a night out at a family movie, followed by the weary exotica of sweet-and-sour pork and chicken chop suey. I went underground, to Filene's basement, where women squabble over cut-price frocks, upending themselves in floral heaps of mark downs. It all seemed a long way from the nightmare city I had been warned of by experienced Bostonians; a place where, I would have thought, one was more likely to die from dullness than from gunshot wounds.

Crime figures, of all statistics, are the most misusable; but Boston's do raise an ugly question mark over my innocent perception of the city's tedious homeliness. There were 136 murders here in 1973, a number that climbs appallingly close to the annual death toll in the Ulster war (something over 200). Even inside Cambridge's glass globe, with the snow settling prettily over the Colonial churches, the nightmare was coming real. Across the street from Longfellow's house with its elegant pilasters, Harvard professor's wife was dragged screaming into a park and shot. Another woman was blinded when a man rammed a broken brick into her face. On Thanksgiving Day, a robber with a gun was threatening people in the apartment house where I was staying; he rode away with his loot on a yellow ten-speed bicycle, a travelling man, from another part of town. In November, the fire-raisers were on our avenue, setting light to heaps of gasoline-soaked newspapers in garages.

As the catalogue of these events, some tragic, others merely ominous and dispiriting, grew longer, so they seemed to thicken the brickwork of the walls of our ghetto. Illogically, they made the boundaries even tighter. They did not so much make Cambridge a bad place, as strengthen our terrors of Roxbury and

Dorchester and Somerville. Evil deeds were attributed to outsiders; they were taken as signs of what happens when the rottenness of the city beyond the walls reaches into the protected Eden of "our neighbourhood". They just went to show that Nanny was right. As the fall wore on, we huddled closer to each other, telling blood-curdling stories at dinner parties, praying that the phantoms of the city at large would withdraw to their proper quarters and leave us safe inside our globe.

With a borrowed car, all windows up and doors securely locked from the inside, I did some timid trespassing. I crossed the river into a scrawny landscape of marsh, abandoned gas stations, and craven redbrick public housing projects that looked like vandalised urinals. Wire-mesh fencing bulged and tottered; the sidewalks were cracked and broken, and the roads seemed subject to a continuous, mild volcanic action—a subterranean bubbling of earth and water which might at any moment simply swallow what little human life was left. The people I saw looked too vanquished for violence. A great deal of English poverty is borne amiably, with the air of long, tolerant habituation. No London slum has the raw, exposed, beaten appearance of these sinks of American urban poverty. Nobody was making an attempt to keep up, to put on their best face; there were no lone geraniums, no flowers of any kind. Broken glass lay where it had fallen out of windows, half-covered with straggling tendrils of tangleweed. Black women were leading their children to an evangelist's shack (it was a Sunday afternoon); their faces had gone to the livid purple of a bruise in the cold.

But this was not a place in Boston's mythology; it was a nowhere, a bit of seedy emptiness in the shadow of an expressway, too dead and desolate to warrant a name. An American woman was scornful of my shock. "It's just a public housing project; you've seen nothing. They're all like that. That's not *Roxbury*." I had thought it was—at least, I wanted to go nowhere that was worse. I like cities on principle; but in America, my liking was rapidly turning sour, my enthusiasm was beginning to seem to me glib and blinkered.

Roxbury—real Roxbury—shocks in the most unexpected way of all. I knew exactly what a "black ghetto" was. It was the steep scabrous tenements of Harlem, the intense, murky street-life, as thick with infection and activity as a slide of pond mud under a microscope. It was close clumps of grey concrete high rises, built on the ash-and-brick ruins of older slums. I was not prepared for a ghetto that was a precise mirror image of the ghetto from which I had come—another dainty suburb fresh from the gift shop in the December sun.

Roxbury was the first and the sweetest of the nineteenth-century "streetcar suburbs" of Boston. Every wooden cottage had a baby country estate for its backyard; its whiteness shone through a tangle of greenery, and, rocking on the balconied porch with the *Evening Transcript*, one would have looked out over a dreamland where all the nicest people lived in the nicest possible American way. This was the garden where Adam could buy a tidy lot with a gabled doll's house set square in its centre. He could fall asleep with green shutters murmuring in a country breeze and, in the morning, ride the car into town. To his ear,

"Roxbury" and "rus in urbe" ran tranquilly into a single word. The commanding spires of the Unitarian churches, with their genial ethical theology of God, Man and Nature all in harmony, were fitting landmarks in this innocently prelapsarian quarter of the city.

The churches, the houses, the tall trees on the streets, are there still. The paint is pocky, much of the wood is rotten, and slats of shingling have fallen away exposing the skeletal frames, but the basic lineaments of the old dream are clear enough even now. It takes a few minutes before you notice that the windows are mostly gone and only a few shutters are left. Each house stares blindly through eyes of cardboard and torn newspaper. Burn marks run in tongues up their sides, and on most blocks there is a gutted shell, sinking onto its knees in a flapping ruin of blackened lath and tarpaper. Our own century has added rows of single-storey brick shacks, where bail-bondsmen and pawnbrokers do their business. What were once front lawns are now oil patches of bare earth. The carcasses of wrecked Buicks, Chevrolets and Fords are jacked up on bricks, their hoods open like mouths, their guts looted. No-one is white. Stopped at the lights, I am inspected blankly by the drivers alongside me. A kid on the sidewalk yells "Honky! ... Hey, Honky!"

It is hard not to feel both scared and guilty. One should not trespass, and this is no place for tourists. This is not my country, my city, or my quarter; probably the most one can learn from a voyeuristic trip like this is that there are parts of other people's cities that are as inhospitable and remote as moon-craters. If I had believed before in a city-freedom that permits everyone to roam into other social worlds, here was proof of the reality of those boundaries about which I'd been so sceptical. I was in the wrong place and anxious to get out.

Yet Roxbury was like an optical maladjustment, a troubling double image; each time one looked at it one saw a pretty tranquil suburb and an angry wound—each image stubbornly refused to take precedence. Its prettiness turned into an insult, its anger into an irony. Much of its incongruity seemed perversely deliberate. The word *KILL* spray-gunned on a wall had been executed with a sign-painter's shapely precision. A family on the sidewalk arranged itself as formally as a portrait-group in an early American painting. The speed of the traffic was slow and stately in comparison to the precipitate, shoving style of most Boston driving. A very slight blurring of vision, and one might be in that ideal pastoral place which Cambridge has tried so hard to be and failed.

I got back to our apartment block. The air in the corridors is thick, burnt and biscuity; the walls are thin, the lifts shudder and creak. With the mythological arbitrariness that is Boston's special gift, it has been consecrated as a respectable middle-class place in a "good area". But were a blindfolded man to be driven to it, and allowed to look only when he was inside the hall, he would say with some certainty that he was in a ruinous tenement. It might just as well be a den of thieves living off welfare and plunder as a den of teachers, psychoanalysts, secretaries and small-businessmen. What counts here, though, is the mythology. There is a logic that dictates why rich Bostonians should cluster in the splendid Georgian houses round Louisberg Square on Beacon Hill. But why should the Italians all cram themselves behind the expressway in the North End? Why should Negroes live in Roxbury, and Jews in Chelsea? By what law do Boston suburbs turn into rigidly circumscribed ghettoes, when they look so much alike, so quaintly attractive, so prim, so dull? For it is as if someone had taken a map of the city and, resolutely blind to its topography, had coloured in irregularly shaped lumps labelled "Black", "Jews", "Irish", "Academics", "Gentry", "Italians", "Chinese", "Assorted Others".

Clearly the civic authorities are very keen on ghettoes. On the Fitzgerald Expressway, there is an exit sign marked "To Chinatown". One then has to weave through a signposted maze, one's expectations rising as the trip to this obviously important place lengthens. Just off Washington Street, there are a few Chinese restaurants, oriental groceries and Hong Kong kitsch shops. They are dwarfed by looming warehouses, and one would barely notice them if one had not been alerted by the string of signs. The Bell Telephone Company has chipped in with phone boxes rigged out as pagodas, and the National Shawmut Bank advertises itself with illuminated Mandarin characters. "Chinatown" is a fake ghetto, an exercise in official image-projection. But in a city that has so many real ghettoes, why should it have seemed desirable to fabricate one?

There are some answers to these questions to be sniffed out in the ghetto in which I was staying. All Cambridge academic life bears down on Harvard Square, a queer grey tangle of spotlights, kiosks, pretentious neo-Georgian architecture and telegraph wires. Winds collect here, laden with garbage; so do automobiles, hippie-entrepreneurs selling political stick-ons, candles, pottery and fortunes, Salvation Army bands, boys waiting for their girls, and sandwich-board men grim with cold, deep in conversation with topknotted religious fanatics. Here all routes collide, and one might on first glance mistake the square for the local version of Piccadilly Circus. But it is not. Rather it is Cambridge's village green. Here one bumps into the people one was having dinner with last night; the phrase "Oh, *hi*" whines and tinkles all round. In the tobacconist's, a drink is fixed, at the subway entrance, a supper-date for next week.

For the first few days, this smallness seems delightful, then it starts to suffocate. For Cambridge, with its intense, pressured containedness, repeats itself like a mouse's wheel. At dinner after dinner, the same knot of intelligent, ironic faces; the same topics of conversation; the same wry jokes. There are half a dozen celebrities held in common by the village, and in gossip they loom infinitely larger than life; practice and study have made their every twitch and gesture famous, so that stories about them hinge on the teller's discovery of a new tiny detail that will become public and accrete to the myth. On those rare occasions when the celebrities are actually present (they are heavily in demand, greedily hoarded, and unwillingly shared around among the villagers), there is a breathless unease: with X leaning heavily over the claret at the far end of the table, Jack has to be kicked by his wife before he stops telling his great story about X which went down so well at the Herzbergers last week. The famous village dead still live on in gossip, like the ancestors who brood over conversations in the bars of Irish hamlets. Professor Perry Miller stalks by candlelight nightly, at a score of Harvard parties. Every inflection of his has been perfected and preserved in mimicry; and the manner of his dying is told, again and again, with a reverent Shakespearian regard for irony, narrative and pathos. As Longfellow knew, there are great consolations for the man who dies popular at Harvard; one kind of immortality, at least, is guaranteed for him.

The tightly circumscribed limits of conversation correspond exactly to those limits which forbade me to travel to Somerville and Roxbury. They stake out Cambridge and its confines against the rest of Boston. But I was not at Harvard, I was a visitor on its fringes and lacked the anchor of a position to keep me safe inside the walls. I made a point of breaking bounds, lunching several days a week in Boston proper. "You go to lunch in *Boston*?" I might as well have said that I was going to a favourite Howard Johnson's in Woonsocket. The journey takes twelve minutes, and costs a dime, on the subway—about half the cost and half the time of a trip from where I live in England to a lunch-date in London.

But there is a deep suspicion in Cambridge that the name of Perry Miller might lose some of its shine at the wrong end of the subway—that in Boston certain persons might not even have *heard* of Professor Miller.

Indeed, in Boston, Cambridge does seem to recede into a far, upriver distance. Sometimes I lunched at the Tavern Club, a generous, genial, timbered place in a secret alley off Boston Common. Its members are lawyers, painters, publishers, newspapermen; its tone is worldly and jovial. Under a chandelier at a huge round table, it is easy to slide crabwise back into the old, compact, genteel city of the nineteenth century. Talk here is much more rangy and unbuttoned than in Cambridge; appetites, of every kind, are more expansive. Yet there is still a curious sense that one is somehow living in miniature. Across the Common, with its frozen, greying turf and modest statuary, lie the State House, law courts, and Athenaeum Library. The office of the two major Boston publishers, Little, Brown and Houghton Mifflin, are close by; so are the headquarters of the *Boston Globe* and *Christian Science Monitor*. For most of the men at lunch, work is only a digestive stroll away. Many of them now live in the country or the outer suburbs, but a good number still have houses on Beacon Hill, or, another short step across the public Gardens, in Back Bay. "Oh, you've come in from *Cambridge?*" The candles flicker on the chandelier; the wine passes round the table. I feel like a traveller, short of suitable tales about the land from which I've come; perhaps a remark or two about how the weather was when I left Cambridge would be in order.

In London, villaging is an expensive game, played self-consciously, with a constant sense that it is an enjoyable indulgence, that it goes against the grain of the city. In Canonbury and Camden Town, it's largely an evening hobby valued precisely because most people spend most of the day trekking through areas of the city far from their own quarter. But the Boston "village" is stiflingly real—and the word *village*, fitting enough, perhaps, for privileged places like Harvard and the Tavern Club, turns into a bleak irony when tagged to Roxbury, Dorchester or Somerville. One man's village is another's ghetto, and both proceed from a single vision of what the city ought to be.

During the 1860s and 1870s there was real local pride in Boston's success as a metropolis. The suburbs of Roxbury and Dorchester voted to annex themselves to the central city, to share its bigness and bustle, to help pay for the new civic amenities—the concert halls, monuments, transit systems. But the "annexation movement" soon wore through. Brookline voted to stay separate, so did Cambridge, Somerville and the others. Enthusiasm for the city is not an American weakness. The independent township, "the small, self-contained center of life" (in the words of the southern agrarian manifesto *I'll Take My Stand*) is where most Americans would prefer to stake out the perimeters of their backyards. They may need the enlarged economy and technology of the big city to earn their living, but, by hook or crook, they'll sleep where the grass and the trees are. The *neighbourhood* is all-important; the city is a mere abstraction—vague, threatening, impersonal. The crazy-quilt of town-lines that enmeshes Greater Boston flies in the face of visible fact. But the further the city spreads and congeals, the more passionately do people cling to "communities" which are really only nostalgic dreams and historical relics.

By sheer force of will, Bostonians have made these ancient cartographers' divisions real, mythologising them into actuality by a massive conspiracy of Cartesian concentration. They have had local taxes to help them, so that Brookline, for instance, was able to spend $1,470 per pupil in its schools in 1970–71, while Somerville only managed $756. There were comparable inequalities of expenditure on policing, streetlighting, garbage disposal and fire services. Taxes diverted in the interests of an ideology are powerful weapons. As one stands on Beacon Street, midway between Cambridge and Somerville, one is suspended between two quite different worlds. Behind one, there are shady avenues and handsome houses; new cars, faces bathed in all the creams that keep skin soft and youthful, an air of proper and discreet prosperity. In front, the streets narrow to alleys, the temperature is colder, rubbish skids across soiled sidewalks, and people have the bent, furtive look of habitual scurriers, always on the lookout for trouble. To a European, these sudden abrupt transitions within the city are amazing; he can measure to the inch where poverty stops and starts, and soon learns to translate these maplike lines into other, more subtle divisions of race and nationality. It takes much longer to realise that these boundaries are simply and effectively enforced by a mad system of tax differentials.

Yet behind the madness lies a dream of an independent life away from the destructive abstraction of the city. The ghettoes—or villages—are real because Boston, in common with the majority of American cities, feared the unmanageable bigness of New York or London. It has tried to remain a little city on a hill, surrounded by a pretty cluster of small towns and villages. To do so, it has had, like the city-elders in Plato's Republic, to conscientiously fake its history, its geography, its economy, even the individual memories of its citizens. A painter in Cambridge, whom I spoke to because he was mounting a campaign to shift the Kennedy Memorial Library to the far side of the river Charles (where it would turn into Boston's problem), said sadly: "Ten years ago, Cambridge was a village. Everybody knew each other. Now look at it." *Ten years?* That was not true fifty years ago, or even a hundred years ago, when W. D. Howells used the place as a setting for his *Suburban Sketches*. Mythological taboos and hectic rounds of dinner parties make ghettoes, not villages.

Nor am I using "ghetto" lightly. The preserved, exemplary lives of Cambridge and Beacon Hill have been instrumental in making Roxbury what it is. And Roxbury is a real ghetto. Brookline, Cambridge, and the rich end of Boston have dug a deep moat around it, isolating it with fear and rumour. The constituent parts of Boston are now so separated, and so inequitably served, that it is almost impossible to imagine the place ever coming together again as a city. Expressways and rapid transit systems will not connect it up when the Bostonian's whole habit of mind is superstitiously bent on staying out, on sticking to his village, on loathing what "the city" stands for in America at present. Ironically, Boston has succeeded in attracting big-city virtues. There is no freedom of movement in it; socially, it is as tight as three separate drawing-rooms with a warren of unspeakable quarters below stairs. It has no flair, and its surprises are nearly always unpleasant ones. In Harvard and MIT it has two of the best universities in the country, it has a superb symphony orchestra, some of the finest libraries, a marvellously varied architectural texture in its individual buildings (though they, too, never cohere into a recognisable city). Yet it stays stubbornly beset by the conviction that it is better not to be a city; it is a great, sluggardly, anomalous Peter Pan of a place, which has preferred never to grow up.

If one belongs somewhere in it, one is very lucky. The people in the Gaslight Pub had the weary, peculiarly Boston look of those who fit nowhere. They too were on the boundary line between Cambridge and Somerville, but they had fallen through. Without a village, without even a ghetto, they were people of the gaps between, with little more than their dislocation in common. That may be the hardest of all Boston fates, even, perhaps the most frequent, certainly the strongest charge with which the place might be indicted—to be a citizen without a city.

New Orleans

161

Life and Death in New Orleans

ARNOLD GOLDMAN

In 1883, the title of the first of the New Orleans chapters in Mark Twain's *Life on the Mississippi*, "The Metropolis of the South", invited the response "a paradox, even a contradiction in terms". The implied prior question of the book's title, "*Is* there life on the Mississippi?"–life now, after the Civil War and a hated "reconstruction"–is also tackled in Twain's consideration of the South's putative metropolis.[1]

Twain measures contemporary New Orleans by his long-past visits. Much appears unchanged, but there lie beneath superficial similarities some hidden or incipient transformations: "The old brick salt-warehouses clustered at the upper end of the city looked as they had always looked" (473), but they "had had a kind of Aladdin's lamp experience ... since I had [last] seen them". There are "deep trough-like gutters alongside the curbstones ... still half full of reposeful water with a dusty surface", but "the gutters are flushed now, two or three times a day, by powerful machinery; in many of the gutters the water never stands still, but has a steady current" (474). That which is as it was is static ("still", "reposeful"); that which is changed, is dynamic ("flushed", "powerful", "current").

"The spirit of the city" is reflected in the "progressive men" with whom New Orleans is "well outfitted"–"thinking, sagacious, long-headed". "It is a driving place commercially" (475), he notes, and his praise mingles the language of business ("powerful machinery", "ice manufactured in the town", "the best-lighted city in the Union, electrically-speaking") and of culture:

> There are good clubs in the city now—several of them but recently organised—and inviting modern-style pleasure resorts at West End and Spanish Fort. The telephone is everywhere. One of the most notable advances is in journalism. ... The editorial work is not hack-grinding, but literature. As an example of New Orleans journalistic achievement, it may be mentioned that the "Times-Democrat" of August 26, 1882, ... consisted of *forty* pages. ... [N]ot much short of three times as many words as are in this book. One may with sorrow contrast this with the architecture of New Orleans.

Source: Arnold Goldman, "Life and Death in New Orleans", *The American City: Literary and Cultural Perspectives*, ed. Graham Clarke, London and New York, 1988, Ch. 7 pp. 146–78,

The human spirit "is like the contrast between waking and sleep" (474), "public architecture" a troubling reminder of the latter state, a visible sign of civic stasis: "there is no architecture in New Orleans, except in the cemeteries", a "'city of the dead" (477), a parody of what a "Crescent City" should have. Since New Orleans, being below the level of the Mississippi, cannot have graves, "They bury their dead in vaults, above the ground. These vaults have a resemblance to houses–sometimes to temples", with "white roofs and gables stretching into the distance on every hand". Though he notes these are "architecturally graceful and shapely", paragraph by paragraph Twain's appreciation wanes. The ubiquity of "the coarse and ugly but indestructible" grave decoration, the "immortelle", provokes a sudden vernacular shaft:

> you just hang it up, and there you are; just leave it alone, it will take care of your grief for you, and keep it in mind better than you can; stands weather first-rate, and lasts like boiler-iron.

He cannot abandon the cemeteries: "It is all grotesque, ghastly, horrible" (478).[2] Having postulated two cities, Twain has been more drawn to the city of death, against his wishes. Necropolis is the city which he has been trying to repress, and it has returned to haunt the living one, which it mimics.

Twain's underlying metaphor is now clear. To the extent that "the metropolis" is "still" as it was (when Twain was a "cub" and a pilot), it is asleep, entranced or worse. If it is changed (for the better), it has awakened–or is at least awakening. Waking is waking to life, but continued torpor is the sleep of death. Having acknowledged this, and after taking a whole burlesque chapter ("The Art of Inhumation") to laugh death off, Twain can return for the time being to the metropolis. He sets out with George Washington Cable to view private architecture, "the deep, warm, varicolored [plaster] stain" of the houses in the "ancient quarter of New Orleans" and their iron railings with "light and dainty, and airy and graceful" patterns (485). Cable is "the South's finest literary genius, the author of 'the Grandissimes'", through whose books Twain has come closer to the "interior life and ... history" of the South "than by personal contact". With the genius of the place himself as your guide, you may begin to approach that inner life, for in his presence "you have a vivid *sense* as of unseen or dimly seen things–vivid, and yet fitful and darkling; you glimpse salient features"; though you may "lose the fine shades". you may "catch them imperfectly through the vision of the imagination".

Twain's report on the old St. Louis Hotel and on the cathedral is, however, perfunctory, and his visits to Lake Pontchartrain and "an editorial dinner at one of the clubs in the city" (487) are remembered mainly for "the chief dish the renowned fish called pompano". It is all anecdotes, like "the Broom Brigade"–young ladies who "do everything which a human being can possibly do with a broom, except sweep". Twain reflects on Southern pronunciation, grammar and vocabulary. After the passionate outburst about cemeteries, he is slowly warming to the life of his subject, and indeed the prose rekindles to a "*sense* as of unseen or dimly seen things" only when he enters upon the subject of the late war.

"The war is the great chief topic of conversation ... what A.D. is elsewhere: they date from it" (491). Time is measured by "since the waw; or du'in' the waw; or befo' the waw; or right aftah the war [etc.]". "At a club one evening, a gentleman" bets Twain that any topic of conversation broached will revert to the war before long. A poet "began to speak—about the moon" (492). He is interrupted:

> "Reminds me of an anecdote. Everything is changed since the war, for better or for worse; but you'll find people down here born grumblers, who see no change except the change for the worse. There was an old negro woman of this sort. A young New-Yorker said in her presence, 'What a wonderful moon you have down here!' She sighed and said, 'Ah, bless yo' heart, honey, you ought to seen dat moon befo' de waw!'"
>
> The new topic was dead already. But the poet resurrected it, and gave it a new start.

Death, resurrection and a "new start": the progress of the conversation mirrors a wider history. The "new start" too soon becomes "war talk"—how Farragut advancing on Port Hudson painted his decks white to enable his men to see their way without alerting the Confederate gunners to the presence of his ships.[3] The progressive post-bellum Southerner does not repine; he admires the know-how of the Yankee though it led to his own defeat. Twain is "not sorry" (493) at the turn of conversation; among the cosmopolitan gentlemen of a Southern metropolis, that talk is practical, "war talk by men who have been in a war", better than "moon talk by a poet who has not been in the moon".

By "the vision of the imagination", we begin to discern that change is not wholly dependent on outward signs even such as public architecture. Even where the moon shines still, Southern recognition that the "vast and comprehensive calamity" of the invasion (491) did not change everything for the worse is the beginning of Southern wisdom. So is the ability dispassionately to remember, articulate and evaluate what actually happened. But the sudden possibility that this new wisdom and articulation may not be fully attained or may be thrown away rekindles Twain's fears that the "metropolis of the South", as the expression of the potential development of the South, may yet become Necropolis, the "city of the dead".

Twain's apprehensions are raised by the pseudo-poetic language Southerners also use to describe their society. He is at a mule-race:

> The grand stand was well filled with the beauty and the chivalry of New Orleans. That phrase is not original with me. It is the Southern reporter's. He has used it for two generations. He uses it twenty times a day, or twenty thousand times a day; or a million times a day—according to the exigencies. ... He never tires of it; it always has a fine sound to him. There is a kind of swell, mediæval bulliness and tinsel about it that pleases his gaudy, barbaric soul. (494)

Compared to the workmanlike prose of the New Orleans editor, who has "a strong, compact, direct, unflowery style; wastes no words, and does not gush", the "tinsel" language of Southern reportage is offensive. (In an Appendix, Twain provides "a good letter, penned by a trained hand".) Twain exemplifies—"'On Saturday, early in the morning, the beauty of the place graced our cabin, and proud of her fair freight the gallant little boat glided up the bayou'" (495)—and provides his vernacular and mostly monosyllabic alternative:

> Twenty-two words to say the ladies came aboard and the boat shoved out up the creek, is a clean waste of ten good words. ...
>
> The trouble with the Southern reporter is—Women. They unsettle him; they throw him off his balance. He is plain, and sensible, and satisfactory, until a woman heaves in sight. Then he goes all to pieces; his mind totters, becomes flowery and idiotic. ... [T]his student of Sir Walter Scott ... knows well enough how to handle it when the women are not around to give him the artificial-flower complaint.

Thus, in "Enchantments and Enchanters" (Ch. XLVI), Twain symbolizes his fears of potential social stagnation and regression in the notorious attack on the presumptive influence of Sir Walter Scott on the South ("in great measure responsible for the war" (501)). This comes in a description of the Mardi Gras (actually the Carnival before it), no mere mule-race but the renowned apex of New Orleans social calendar. Since the war: "I judge that the religious feature has been pretty well knocked out. ... Sir Walter has got the advantage of the gentlemen of the cowl and rosary, and he will stay." The "crimes of the French Revolution and of Bonaparte" had "compensating benefactions", freedom and careers opened to men of talent, "great and permanent services to liberty, humanity, and progress" (500); not so the romanticism of Scott and, worse, its imitation:

> by his single might [he] checks this wave of progress, and even turns it back; sets the world in love with dreams and phantoms; with decayed and swinish forms of religion; with decayed and degraded systems of government; with the sillinesses and emptinesses, sham grandeurs, sham gauds, and sham chivalries of a brainless and worthless long-vanished society.

For Twain, the Carnival procession, complete with its "Mystic Crew of Comus" (499), suggests social paralysis in the guise of licensed misrule: "with knights and nobles and so on ... and in their train all manner of giants, dwarfs, monstrosities, and other diverting grotesquerie". Then he generalizes:

> Most of the world has now outlived a good part of these harms, though by no means all of them; ... [but] in our South they flourish pretty forcefully still. ... There, the genuine and wholesome civilization of the nineteenth century is curiously confused and commingled with the Walter Scott Middle-Age sham civilization, and so you have practical, common-sense, progressive ideas, and progressive works, mixed up with the duel, the inflated speech, and the jejune romanticism of an absurd past that is *dead, and out of charity ought to be buried.* But for the Sir Walter disease, the character of the Southerner ... would be wholly modern, in place of modern and mediæval mixed, and the South would be fully a generation further advanced than it is. (500–1; my emphasis)

While "the North has thrown out that old inflated style, ... the Southern writer still clings to it—clings to it and has a restricted market for his wares, as a consequence" (501). With unabashed use of commercial language for literary "wares", Twain notes that Southern literary work "can gain but slight currency ... the authors write for the past, not the present" (502). However, all is not lost—though it yet might be—and

> when a Southerner of genius writes modern English, his book goes ... upon wings; and they carry it swiftly all about America and England, and ... Germany—as witness the experience of Mr. Cable and Uncle Remus, two of the very few Southern authors who do not write in the southern style.

Twain gives little example of Cable's "interior life and history" of the South, noting more his prowess as a public performer: it is "a great treat to hear him read about Jean-ah Poquelin, and about Innerarity and his famous 'pigshoo' representing 'Louisihanna *Rif*-fusing to Hanter the Union'" (504). The few remarks on Cable bear, however, on the contrast between the progressive, practical and energetic potential of the city—"life on the Mississippi"—and the sham, stasis and death which can also characterize even "the metropolis of the South". Twain's allusions place a great responsibility on the Southern writer, who must labour to dispel the baleful effects of "dreams and phantoms", "enchantments and enchanters", which threaten metropolis with the city of death.

In the story which Twain so admired, "Jean-ah Poquelin" (in *Old Creole Days*, 1879),[4] Cable also confronts the expanding city with a dark antithesis, the "*Terre aux Lépreux*", land of the living dead, at "the rear of the ancient city" (123), but the comparison is not to the advantage of the modern. A true historical novelist, Cable consistently treats moments of potential historical shift.[5] "Jean-ah Poquelin" is set in the fluid aftermath of the Louisiana Purchase, "when the newly established American Government was the most hateful thing in Louisiana—when the Creoles were still kicking" at the new regularizing laws (102). In "an old colonial plantation house half in ruin ... aloof from [the new] civilization ... its massive build a strong reminder of days still earlier, when every man had been his own peace officer" (102–3), lives Jean Marie Poquelin, "once an opulent indigo planter", who had turned to "smuggling, and later ... the African slave trade" (104). Seven years earlier, his beloved younger brother had accompanied him on a slaving voyage to the Guinea coast and apparently had not returned. Thereafter Poquelin became a hermit and "'The last of his line', say the gossips" (103). "A dark suspicion fell upon the old slave trader", and in the passage of time, "the house ... [became] an object of a thousand superstitions" and "the name of Jean Marie Poquelin became a symbol of witchery, devilish crime, and hideous nursery fictions" (105). Children carry after him, "O Jean-ah Poquelin! O Jean-ah! Jean-ah Poquelin!": Cable's title is thus "the name and tone of mockery".

The new "*Américains*", the "alien races pouring into New Orleans[,] began to find the few streets named for the Bourbon princes too strait for them" (106). "Civilization and even trade" propel them "beyond the ancient corporation", with "leveler ... peering through his glass and rodsmen ... whacking" until they come to the boundary of the Poquelin land, symbol of the unsubdued and unredeemed past: "a *line* of tiny rods, with bits of white paper in their split tops, gradually extended its way *straight* through the haunted ground, and across the canal *diagonally*" (my emphases). Cable stresses throughout the equivocal attitude of the "the many", "the Jean-Baptistes", at the hands of "an enterprise that asked neither co-operation nor advice of them"; they are like the taunting children, and they are finally the villains of the piece, neither truly for "enterprise" and American progress, nor for the dark mysteries of an earlier day, neither for the surveyor's plumb line nor for the marsh and "the jungle" (123). For them it is all one "whether the streetmakers mired in the marsh, or contrived to cut through old 'Jean-ah's property'" (106).

Applying to the Governor of the Territory of Orleans to prevent the imminent incursion, Poquelin is disgusted to hear merely that "the city will indemnify you for any loss you may suffer" (107). "[T]he canal is a private", says Poquelin,[6] at which the projectors mutter, "*that* old ditch; that's to be filled up. Tell the old man we're going to fix him up nicely" (109). "The street, or rather a sunny road" (110) is built along the edge of the Poquelin land. Others build "bright new houses" (111) along it, "prying in upon the old man's privacy": "Ah! then the common people began to hate him. ... [W]hy don't he build when the public need demands it?" Poquelin, who never had a neighbour, is now "unneighborly".

The new bourgeoisie determines to "employ all possible means to oust this old nuisance from among us" (113). The missing brother is remembered; perhaps Poquelin has him "locked up in that old house", or worse: "Now, if this is to, and we can fix it on him, ... we can make the matter highly useful. ... [I]t is an action we owe to the community ...". When the secretary of the "Building and Improvement Company" penetrates the grounds, however, what he sees—and smells, "a strange, sickening odor ... loathsome and horrid" (114)—makes him a changed man:

> The figure of a man, a presence if not a body—but whether clad in some white stuff or naked, the darkness would not allow him to determine—had turned, and now, with a seeming painful gait, moved slowly from him. "Great Heaven! can it be that the dead do walk?" ... Then all was still except the measured tread of Jean Poquelin walking on the veranda. ...
>
> [Poquelin] spoke in a low, tender tone in the French tongue, making some inquiry. An answer came from within. Was it the voice of a human? So unnatural was it—so hollow, so discordant, so unearthly. ... [T]he little secretary actually turned and fled. As he left the enclosure ... now and then he spoke aloud: "Oh, oh! I see, I understand!" (115–16).[7]

The secretary's subsequent defence of Poquelin only angers the "rollicking Creoles" (118), who, if they cannot tar and feather him and "ride him on a rail" (117), have a New Orleans custom ready to hand, the "shivaree" (charivari). The "mob"—Cable elaborately justifies his term—goes for Poquelin: "Swiftly they

... enter the willowy jungles of the haunted ground ... tearing the air with their clamor" (121).[8] Death has preceded them: they encounter the coffin of Jean Marie, tended by the old African mute who was Poquelin's faithful slave and with him the ghostly white figure the secretary earlier saw. They recoil, but the secretary bids them attend "the funeral" (122), where they too see

> behind the bier, with eyes cast down and labored step, ... the living remains—all that was left—of little Jacques Poquelin, the long-hidden brother—a leper, as white as snow.
>
> Dumb with horror, the cringing crowd gazed upon the walking death. They watched, in silent awe, the slow *cortège* creep down the long, straight road and lessen on the view, until by and by it stopped where a wild, unfrequented path branched off into the undergrowth toward the rear of the ancient city.
>
> "They are going to the *Terre aux Lépreux*," said one in the crowd. The rest watched them in silence.
>
> ... For a moment more the mute and the leper stood in sight ...; then without one backward glance upon the unkind human world, turning their faces toward the ridge in the depths of the swamp known as the Leper's Land, they stepped into the jungle, disappeared, and were never seen again. (123)

Américains, officials, men of business, "mob"—all are all modern New Orleans, and if they are finally not to be resisted, they are not to be admired: something hard and mechanical has defeated that whose time was up, and which has returned to the dark "jungle". Does the revelation that the slaver Poquelin lived a fraternity beyond their conception affect them? There is a thin thread of hope in "Little White", the secretary. It is only he who could transmit the "inner history" of Jean Poquelin. Are there other secretaries of society, and what histories do they preserve?

Cable set The Grandissimes (1880) at the same historical moment as "Jean-ah Poquelin". An outsider, the apothecary Joseph Frowenfeld, is welcomed to New Orleans by the senior member of the Creole Grandissime clan, the martinet Agricola Fusilier:

> I might have hoped, had not Louisiana just passed into the hands of the most claptrap government in the universe, ... that you had come among us to fasten the lie direct upon a late author, who writes of us that "the air of this region is deadly to the Muses". (50)[9]

Having seen events of "the first week of American jurisdiction" (48), having heard something of the story of the "wonderful family" of the Grandissimes (109), and having had "the circumference of his perceptions consciously enlarged" (110), Joseph resolves

> to begin at once this perusal of this newly-found book, the community of New Orleans. ... [I]t was a volume whose displaced leaves would have to be lifted tenderly, blown free of much dust, re-arranged, some torn fragments laid together again with much painstaking, and even the purport of some pages guessed out. (111)

Thus he looks at New Orleans and sees that

> The human life which dotted the view displayed a variety of tints and costumes such as a painter would be glad to take just as he found them: the gaily-feathered

> Indian, the slashed and tinselled Mexican, the leather-breeched raftsmen, the blue or yellow-turbaned *négresse*, the sugar-planter in white flannel and moccasins, the average townsman in the last suit of clothes of the lately deceased century, and now and then a fashionable man in that costume whose union of tight-buttoned martial severity, swathed throat, and effeminate superabundance of fine linen seemed to offer a sort of state's evidence against the pompous tyrannies and frivolities of the times. (111–12)

How to assimilate this? The Grandissime network is vast: in his need there appears at his door the "cousin" Raoul Innerarity, requesting that his "pigshoe" of "Louisiana rif-using to hanter de h-Union" be placed in the Frowenfeld shop-window alongside other bric-à-brac (124), and willing to be employed as a shop assistant:

> To a student of the community [Raoul] was a key, a lamp, a lexicon, a microscope, a tabulated statement, a book of heraldry, a city directory, a glass of wine, a Book of Days, a pair of wings, a comic almanac, a diving bell, a Creole *veritas*. Before the day had had time to cool, his continual stream of words had done more to elucidate the mysteries in which his employer had begun to be befogged than half a year of the apothecary's scrupulous guessing. (128)

Joseph, however, holds strong (and rather precocious) views about such efforts as "Louisiana": "A passably good example of Creole art" (125), but demonstrating that "The bane of all Creole art-effort ... [is] amateurism ... a kind of ambitious indolence ..." (153). His broader criticism angles towards Twain's:

> Nothing on earth can take the place of hard and patient labour. But that, in this community, is not esteemed; most sorts of it are condemned; the humbler sorts are despised, and the higher are regarded with mingled patronage and commiseration. ... Industry is not only despised, but has been degraded and disgraced, handed over into the hands of African savages.

To Joseph, the South is falling behind in the world's social development:

> Human rights is, of all subjects, the one upon which this community is most violently determined to hear no discussion. It has pronounced that slavery and caste are right, and sealed up the whole subject. What, then, will they do with the world's literature? ...
>
> ... what a bondage it is which compels a community, in order to preserve its established tyrannies, to walk behind the rest of the intelligent world! (155)

Once the burden of social criticism is established through the outsider Joseph, we are told of Bras-Coupé, the African prince who had insisted on being a prisoner of war not a slave: for striking his Grandissime "master" (*sc.* captor) his sentence of death was commuted, but his ears were docked and he hamstrung. This episode, the origin of Cable's novel, casts "the shadow of the Ethiopian" over it. The twin evils of slavery and familial pride—Cable regarded caste as the underlying factor comprehending both—threaten the fluid present with stagnation. As the Grandissimes, so the South: hence the heroism and the "historical" significance of the attempt by the scion of the Grandissimes, Honoré, to square family (the Creole and Southern "way") and human progress.

Honoré is the Grandissime Waverley,[10] the representative protagonist through whom the old ways might be mediated into the new era, through whom Louisiana may enter the Union without defeat and humiliation. Honoré tells the new American governor-general, Claiborne, that his "principal danger—at least, I mean difficulty" (101) is that not only will no native participate in the new government but that "all sympathy with it, all advocacy of its principles, and especially all office-holding under it" will be rendered "odious—disreputable—infamous". He then solves Claiborne's problem, by inventing a formula which makes Creole "riff-using" public service practically impossible—it would compromise their pride. Thus in the first phase of the novel, he proposes what is simultaneously progressive and holds his clan together. "Slavery ... or rather caste" (167), the "main defect" (166), is so stressful for Honoré that his usually impeccable English pronunciation lapses: "I am *ama-aze* at the length, the blackness of that shadow. ... It is the *Némésis* ...! It blanches, my-de'seh, ow whole civilization! it drhags us a centurhy behind the rhes' of the world! It rhetahds and poisons everhy industrhy we got!" (169). He considers "reparations", first to the de Grapions who are the Grandissimes' Creole antagonists, but more challengingly to "the caste" itself, symbolically in the person of his "free-mulatto" namesake and half-brother. Though he anticipates difficulties over the former, he can contain them; his attempt at the latter founders, and with it the city's and the South's broader social progress.

That the scion of the Grandissimes has gone into commerce is bearable; that he should make the "other" Honoré Grandissime his partner, even renaming the family from Grandissime Frères, strains the credulity not only of New Orleans but of the reader. The result is a fatal replay of the story of Bras-Coupé: when the senior Grandissime, Agricola Fusilier, attacks the free-mulatto, the dark Honoré stabs him to death. The "Black code" condemned Bras-Coupé; now the populace sets out to lynch the offender, who is, however, inexplicably hidden from it, apparently by the very whites whose kinsman he has slain, and spirited off to Paris where he commits suicide over unrequited love for Bras-Coupé's woman. Though the white Honoré needed his half-brother's financial assistance to survive the American refusal to honour Spanish and French titles to land ownership, we never learn what preserves the family business after the suicide, even if the white Honoré, having consigned $100,000 to the widow de Grapion as reparation for past family close dealing, later marries her.

Similarly the progress of the outsider Frowenfeld is towards apparent disaster. The Creoles (barring the cynosure Honoré) constitute "a hive of patriots who don't know where to swarm" (49). They pose, strut and sham at the edge of violence. Of Frowenfeld they think, "We ought to hang that fellow. ... It is no more than we owe to the community to go and smash his shop-window ..." (95). Later, as "He has given us good reason half a dozen times, with his too free speech and his high moral whine, to hang him with the lamp-post rope" (269), his shop is destroyed, and his safety menaced. His troth pledged to the de Grapion ingenue, daughter of Honoré's beloved, apparently alters everything.

The trajectory of social movement in the novel is towards arrest or even catastrophe, and catastrophe is averted at a price: the terms of social progress which were established by Frowenfeld and by Honoré are tacitly abandoned. Frowenfeld's book of the city becomes an "unwriteable volume" (148). Cable ignores the fact that the novel's ending abandons the pursuit of progressive social movement and settles for romance and domestic felicity. He diverts our attention to the resolution of the Creole clan division (though not the caste division) and to the acceptance of the outsider through marriage. It is not just that society makes a grand refusal; one's disappointment is that the author's language does not acknowledge the meaning of his action. Louisiana enters the Union, but Cable cannot bring himself to name the purchase price. The New Orleans of *The Grandissimes* starts as a proxy measure of Southern society, of *l'état*—and symbolically of events after the recent war. It ends as a protected enclave, on the one hand a romantic haven and on the other a commercial locus. That which might mediate them has foundered: no doubt it did.

The split and diminished rôle of New Orleans into a city of commerce (masculine) and a city of feeling (feminine), presides in the fiction of Kate Chopin. In *The Awakening* (1899), we see the gravity and entrenchment of it. There is a paralysis about society in the novel. Chopin exposes as shabby and life-sapping the compromises which give the two worlds an appearance of co-existence. Edna Pontellier, trapped and thwarted, attempts to break out: if the city functions by an unholy arrangement, what can it offer her?

The first appearance of New Orleans in the novel is telling and characteristic:

> A few days later a box arrived for Mrs. Pontellier from New Orleans. It was from her husband. It was filled with *friandises*, with luscious and toothsome bits—the finest of fruits, *patés*, a rare bottle or two, delicious syrups, and bonbons in abundance.[11]

New Orleans is the source of physical satisfaction refined to the point of a pretension of taste and even culture. Why this gift? Léonce Pontellier, a successful New Orleans broker, with his wife and children for the weekend at their summer cottage on nearby Grand Isle, had been restless and "unable to read his newspaper with any degree of comfort" (881):

> He was already acquainted with the market reports, and he glanced restlessly over the editorials and bits of news which he had not had time to read before quitting New Orleans the day before.

He looks at his wife Edna "as one looks at a valuable price of personal property" (882), and regrets that she

> evinced so little interest in things which concerned him, and valued so little his conversation.
>
> Mr. Pontellier had forgotten the bonbons and peanuts for the boys. Notwithstanding he loved them very much, and went into the adjoining room where they slept to take a look at them. ...
>
> Mr. Pontellier returned to his wife with the information that Raoul had a high fever and needed looking after. Then he lit a cigar and went and sat near the open

door to smoke it. ...

He reproached his wife with her inattention, her habitual neglect of the children. If it was not a mother's place to look after children, whose on earth was it? He himself had his hands full with his brokerage business. He could not be in two places at once; making a living for his family on the street, and staying at home to see that no harm befell them. (885)

The next morning, Pontellier "had regained his composure, which seemed to have been somewhat impaired the night before. He was eager to be gone, as he looked forward to a lively week in Carondelet Street" (886). The box filled with *friandises* is simultaneously a peace offering which he expects to find acceptable and a statement and reinforcement of his rôle and its essential rightness.

A form of "chivalry", much as described by Twain,[12] plays an important and accepted rôle in this Creole society. Married women have young admirers. The husband feels no jealousy. Flirtation has strict limits, and Creole wives do not engage their affections. The young man provides what the husband no longer wishes to offer, and his attentions are understood to be useful to ease the transition from maidenhood to matronhood.

Pontellier refuses to accept that Edna, an outsider (an American, a Kentucky Presbyterian), finds her duties less than satisfying, and he cannot see that she is beginning to take her "devoted attendant" (890), Robert Lebrun, too seriously. Thus he is solicitous when Robert absents himself from Grand Isle:

"How do you get on without him, Edna?" he asked.

"It's very dull without him," she admitted. Mr. Pontellier had seen Robert in the city, and Edna asked him a dozen questions or more. Where had they met? On Carondelet Street, in the morning. They had gone "in" and had a drink and a cigar together. What had they talked about? Chiefly about [Robert's] prospects in Mexico, which Mr. Pontellier thought were promising. How did he look? How did he seem—grave, or gay, or how? Quite cheerful, and wholly taken up with the idea of his trip, which Mr. Pontellier found altogether natural in a young fellow. ... (928)

Pontellier means that Robert is a man among men, no different to himself. Robert knows how to relax like a man in the city, with a drink and a cigar. In New Orleans, at least on Carondelet Street (where Pontellier's office is), commerce is in its place and eros is relegated.

At home, on Esplanade Street, similar conventions are to be followed. Pontellier looks at the house's "various appointments and details" (931) much as he looked at his wife on Grand Isle:

He greatly valued his possession, chiefly because they were his, and derived genuine pleasure from contemplating a painting, a statuette, a rare lace curtain—no matter what—after he had bought it and placed it among his household gods.

The Pontelliers' routine includes Edna's Tuesday callers,

who came in carriages or in the streetcars, or walked when the air was soft and distance permitted. ... A maid, in white fluted cap, offered the callers liqueur,

> coffee, or chocolate, as they might desire. Mrs. Pontellier, attired in a handsome reception gown, remained in the drawing room the entire afternoon receiving her visitors. (931–32)

Chopin's prose sets out the constrained variety of permitted options. It is thus the more shocking when Pontellier realizes that Edna has stopped playing the game: "Many callers?" ... "There were a good many. ... I found their cards when I got home ..." Pontellier knows that "people don't do such things; we've got to observe *les convenances* if we ever expect to get on and keep up with the procession". Edna's action will have consequences:

> Mr. Pontellier scanned the names of his wife's callers [on their visiting cards], reading some of them aloud, with comments as he read.
>
> "'The Misses Delasidas.' I worked a big deal in futures for their father this morning; nice girls; it's time they were getting married. 'Mrs. Belthrop.' I tell you what it is, Edna; you can't afford to snub Mrs. Belthrop. Why, Belthrop could buy and sell us ten times over. His business is worth a good, round sum to me. You better write her a note." (933)

"Buy and sell us" could just mean "ruin" to a broker, but Edna persists, doing "as she liked" (938), and abandons her Tuesdays at home altogether. When Pontellier goes to the office, she retreats to her "atelier—a bright room in the top of the house" (939) where she paints and feeds her "infatuation" and "obsession" with Robert (936). The pursuit of art and an artistic life are summoned as an alternative to the commercial-domestic complex. Here, surely, the passional life may be satisfied. Edna takes up painting to the exclusion of her duties, and enrols "the whole household ... in the service of art" (1939), posing the children and servants, humming a tune of Robert's the while. It is, alas, "amateurism".

The house on Esplanade Street is too restrictive even when Edna stops conducting its affairs, and she uses the absences of Pontellier in New York and her children at their grandparents to move to "a little four-room house around the corner ... so cozy, so inviting and restful" (962). She will no longer live on Pontellier's money; money from her mother's estate will buy her own house,

> and I am beginning to sell my sketches. Laidpore is more and more pleased with my work. ... I have sold a good many through Laidpore. ... I know I shall like it, like the feeling of freedom and independence. (963)

Before she leaves Esplanade Street, Edna gives a dinner which Alcée Arobin, the dangerous roué who has insinuated himself into her favour, calls a "coup d'état" (969). The dinner is a grim parody of the orderly and socially approved dinners the Pontelliers gave in the six years of their conventional marriage. This one intends the gaiety of free spirits; it is in fact stilted and forced. The diminished social city is momentarily overthrown, but the very meaning of its opposition lies in its dependence. Pontellier, hearing of Edna's move, "saved appearances" (977) by having it announced that he has closed his house for major renovation. But Pontellier does not return, and Edna, in her "pigeon house" (968), finds that playing the free artist is not enough. Between distraction and distraction, while dreaming of Robert, she gives herself to Arobin.

An alternative life is presented: what Edna might have been if she had been able to accept what she cannot. In New Orleans, the Ratignolles embody domestic felicity, but Edna's visits to them "depressed rather than soothed" her (936): "It was not a condition of life which fitted her, and she could see in it but an appalling and hopeless ennui."

Events gather momentum. Alone of the company of Grand Isle Edna has appreciated the artistry and commitment of the unpleasant "little musician" Mademoiselle Reisz, and she seeks her out. Robert, Mlle. Reisz had said, "comes to see me often in the city. I like to play to him" (930). It transpires that the absent Lebrun corresponds with "the little musician" and Edna is permitted to read his letters from Mexico. At Mlle. Reisz's, Edna meets the returned Robert. He has discovered that "After all there is as much chance for me here as there was there—that is, I might find it profitable some day" (981). So he has "started in at once ... with the old firm". While Edna regains the hope of happiness, we note Robert's acceptance of the economic nexus. When, under pressure of Edna's insistence, Robert indicates that he had left New Orleans because he had become attracted to her Edna declares her love. Why had he "been fighting against" it (991)? "Why? because you were not free; you were Léonce Pontellier's wife", but "There in Mexico ... I forgot everything but a wild dream of your some way becoming my wife" (992). Her exclamation, "Your wife!" shows Edna stunned by Robert's conventionality. His intentions are precisely fantasy: "I was demented, dreaming of wild, impossible things, recalling men who had set their wives free". Free to become other men's wives:

> "I am no longer one of Mr. Pontellier's possessions to dispose of or not. I give myself where I choose. If he were to say, 'Here, Robert, take her and be happy, she is yours,' I should laugh at you both."
>
> His face grew a little white. "What do you mean?" he asked.

Madame Ratignolle summons Edna to her annual accounchment: "Think of the children" is her exhausted and knowing whisper (995). Edna returns to the "pigeon house" expecting Robert, but finds only his note: "I love you. Good-by—because I love you" (997). This is the "honourable" alternative to Arobin, who will be only too happy to have her as another man's wife. Pontellier's return from New York is imminent.

Prepared as the home for one scene, the "pigeon house" offers only to become another. Indeed there is no real difference between returning to Esplanade Street as *chatelaine* and remaining "around the corner", wife or kept woman. In each, Alcée Arobin looms, assuring her of "his devotion" (988). There is no New Orleans left for her. Edna returns to Grand Isle, and to the sea where she learned to swim, and gives it the gift of her baffled self.

The domestic solution of *The Grandissimes* breaks down in *The Awakening*. Edna Pontellier's thought of being an artist in the Quarter temporarily gives her dream a local habitation, though she may mis- or re-interpret Mademoiselle Reisz's stern warning: "'To succeed, the artist must possess the courageous soul. ... The brave soul. The soul that dares and defies'" (946). William Faulkner's *Mosquitoes* (1927) is a thorough examination of the city as a home for the spirit through art. It builds with literary references:

> Outside the window, New Orleans, the vieux carré, brooded in a faintly tarnished languor like an ageing yet still beautiful courtesan in a smoke-filled room, avid yet weary too of ardent ways. ... Spring and the cruellest months were gone. ... (14)[13]

As Joyce and Eliot buttress it, the narrative is at first enlisted on the side of art:

> across an undimensional feathered square, across stencilled palms ... [was the statue of] Andrew Jackson in childish effigy bestriding the terrific arrested plunge of his curly balanced horse, ... [and] the long unemphasis of the Pontalba building and three spires of the cathedral *graduated by perspective*. ...
>
> ... Jackson Square was now a green and quiet lake in which abode lights round as jellyfish. ... Pontalba and cathedral were *cut from black paper and pasted flat* on a green sky. ... (17–18; my emphases)

Inside the sculptor's studio is quite specifically New Orleans in its "uneasily boarded floor" and "rough stained walls ... which had housed slaves long ago" (14), and the attractions of the city (as in Joyce's Dublin Nighttown) also contain a darker, seductive call:

> In a doorway slightly ajar were women, their faces in the starlight flat and pallid and rife, odorous and exciting and unchaste. ... A woman laughed, rife and hushed and rich in the ordorous dark come in boys lots of girls cool you off come in boys. (277)

New Orleans's artistic life ranges from the stern, ascetic dedication of the sculptor Gordon to the surrogate "creativity" of the society hostess and would-be art patron Mrs. Maurier. Though in her own estimation "sensitive to the beautiful in Art" (25), Mrs. Maurier's taste is execrable: the "most wonderful thing" which she has found is only "a dull lead plaque from which in dim bas-relief of faded red and white simpered a Madonna with an expression of infantile astonishment identical" to hers (20). That's what pays the rent.

Gordon turns down flat Mrs. Maurier's invitation to "a yachting party, a few days on the lake" (27). Then he meets her niece, Patricia Robyn, "named for me" (19), and is brought up sharp. The younger "Pat" looks uncannily like his chef d'oeuvre, the "virginal breastless torso of a girl, headless, armless, legless, in marble temporarily caught and hushed yet passionate still for escape" (15).[14] "It's like me", Patricia says (25), and Gordon

> examined with growing interest her flat breast and belly, her boy's body which the poise of it and the thinness of her arms belied. Sexless, yet somehow vaguely troubling. Perhaps just young, like calf or a colt. (26)

The two Patricias, old and young, are doubles, both possible needs, both temptations.[15] For the moment Gordon fears Mrs. Maurier less than he fears Patricia:

> fool fool you have work to do o cursed of god cursed and forgotten form shapes cunningly sweated cunning to simplicity shapes out of chaos more satisfactory than bread to the belly form by a madmans dream gat on the body of chaos le garçon vierge of the soul horned by utility o cuckold of derision. (44)

"Form and utility", he calls the problem, artistic form or animal attraction. The narrative unhelpfully notes that the Crescent City's "shore and the river curved away like the bodies of two dark sleepers embracing, curved one to another in slumber"; New Orleans can align itself on the side of utility, too. "What would I say to her", he thinks,

> fool fool you have work to do you have nothing accursed intolerant and unclean too warm you damn bones then whisky will do as well or a chisel and maul any damn squirrel keeps warm in a cage go on go on then. ...

Can any valid artistic life in New Orleans traffic with Mrs. Maurier? Her go-between Talliaferro (né Tarver) appeals to the (Sherwood Anderson-like) novelist Dawson Fairchild. Fairchild is at lunch, stringing along a Yankee evangelist who has been selling the New Orleans Rotary Club on his brand of religion:

> You have a splendid organisation here ... and a city that is worthy of it. Except for this southern laziness of yours. You folks need more northern blood, to bring out all your possibilities. (34)

The Rotary "get-together" provokes discussion between Fairchild and "the Semitic man", Julius Wiseman, on the desire, need and danger (especially for the artist) of "joining things" (37). Fairchild concludes that contact with the America of "joiners" is necessary, survivable and turnable to account. ("I have a kind of firm belief that life is alright" (192), he later affirms.)

Talliaferro notes that Gordon has refused Mrs. Maurier's invitation to one get-together:

> "Oh, he'll come, I guess", Fairchild said. "He'd be a fool not to let her feed him for a few days." "He'd pay a fairly high price for his food," the Semitic man remarked drily. Fairchild looked at him and he added: "Gordon hasn't served his apprenticeship yet, you know. You've got through yours". (40)

When Fairchild and Wiseman meet him, Gordon surprisingly tells them, "I'm coming". We guess that it is the thought of the niece which has caused his change of mind, but Fairchild, believing that Gordon is willing to accept patronage, approves: "You'll be wise to go on and get it over with, then she'll let you alone. After all, you can't afford to ignore people that own food and automobiles, you know." In Fairchild's eyes, Gordon can survive the contact: "He ought to get out of himself more. ... You can't be an artist all the time. You'll go crazy" (47). Wiseman has his doubts:

> You couldn't. ... But then, you are not an artist. There is somewhere within you a bewildered stenographer with a gift for people, but outwardly you might be anything. You are an artist only when you are telling about people, while Gordon is not an artist only when he is cutting at a piece of wood or stone. And it's very difficult for a man like that to establish workable relations with people. ... [His]

> alternatives are misanthropy or an endless gabbling of aesthetic foster sisters of both sexes. Particularly if his lot is cast outside of New York city.

They argue for and against "our Latin Quarter" (48). The feebleness of Fairchild's defence—"lay off New Orleans bohemian life; stay away from us if you don't like it. I like it, myself; there is a kind of charming futility about it ..."—leaves his seriousness in doubt.

On Mrs. Maurier's ominously named yacht *Nausikaa*, the party of artists includes, as well as Gordon and Fairchild, the poets Mark Frost (on his own account "the best poet in New Orleans" (41) and Julius Wiseman's sister Eva, and the painter Dorothy Jameson. Even Patricia Robyn's twin brother is carving, fashioning an intricate cherry wood pipe, in pursuing which he gets the yacht grounded, by removing part of its steering mechanism. But it is on Gordon that the possibility of the life of art in New Orleans hangs. Mrs. Maurier approaches him while he is intent on the sculptural features of his surroundings ("the dimensionless curve of the deck ... the stem of the yacht;: a pure triangle of sheer white with small waves lapping at its horizontal leg"), vainly attempting to write herself into the artistic scene:

> As for we others, the best we can hope for is that sometimes, somewhere, somehow we may be fortunate enough to furnish that inspiration, or the setting for it, at least. But, after all, that would be an end in itself, I think. ... And I do hope that you will find on this voyage something to compensate you for having been taken away from your Work. (129)

His monosyllabic repetition of "Yes" produces an inner "jeering laughter"; his hands "read" her face, causing her "utter fear", and he "commands" her to "Tell me about her ... Why aren't you her mother, so you could tell me how conceiving her must have been. ... There's something in your face, something behind all this silliness ..." (130). Mrs. Maurier is devastated. When Fairchild encourages riotous and drunken behaviour, she draws the line and has their liquor supply jettisoned. Mark Frost later senses that some great change has occurred ("her strange ... not coldness: rather, detachment, aloofness ... callousness. ... Never saw the old girl so bloodless in the presence of genius, he told himself. Didn't seem to give a damn whether I stayed or not" (272–73)). We never find out whether Mrs. Maurier relapses into foolishness or passes beyond her despair to recover from her absurd dream of surrogate artistic fulfilment.

Patricia has fled the grounded yacht with a new admirer, the mooning steward David West. David is what Gordon would be without art. Patricia gone, however, the world goes flat on Gordon, its "Ideas, thoughts, became mere sounds to be bandied about until they were dead" (156). "Form and utility" both fled,

> he seemed to feel about him like an odour that young hard graveness of hers. No wonder she was gone out of it: she who was as a flame among stale ashes, a little tanned flame. ...

Her life— a kind of living sculpture, "graven"; their deathliness—"ashes". Gordon jumps ship, but like Patricia (and David) he cannot get back to New Orleans any other way. They meet again, he "in the hushed happiness of his dram and his arrogant bitter heart" (223). Patricia attempts, as she did earlier, to claim the marble torso, and again he denies her. In frustration at his reiterated "No"—compare the distress he causes by answering Mrs. Maurier only with "yes"—she swears at him, using a word she does not understand. He spanks her, she weeps, and he "moved his hand over her face, slowly and firmly, but lightly" (226), as he had done to Mrs. Maurier. She asks if he can "do a marble of my head" (227) and offers to pose for it: "Learn it good." When, however, she issued "a kind of leering invitation, so palpably theatrical and false that it but served to emphasise the grave, hard sexlessness of hers", he asks "quietly", "What are you trying to do ... vamp me?" (228), and again and later again, he refuses her the torso.

Back in New Orleans, Dawson Fairchild discovers in Gordon's studio a new clay sculpture, a head—surprisingly not of Patricia but of Mrs. Maurier[16].

> It was clay, yet damp, and from out its dull, dead grayness Mrs. Maurier looked at them. Her chins, harshly, and her flaccid jaw muscles with savage verisimilitude. Her eyes were caverns thumbed with two motions into the dead familiar astonishment of her face; and yet, behind them, somewhere within those empty sockets, there was something else—something that exposed her face for the mask it was, and still more, a mask unaware. "Well, I'm damned," Fairchild said slowly, staring at it. "I've known her for a year, and Gordon comes along after four days ... Well, I'll be damned," he said again. (266–67)

Wiseman remarks that Fairchild, "with your faith in your fellow man" (267), should have realized that Mrs. Maurier's "silliness" required "explanation", "You missed it". Fairchild still imagines a stereotype: "But it's the usual thing, ain't it? plantations and things? First family, and all that?" Wiseman then tells the story of Mrs. Maurier's background and marriage, the pathos of which Gordon but not Fairchild had sensed and turned to artistic account. She is a northerner forcibly married to a Reconstruction era *nouveau riche*, formerly an overseer, "during those years immediately following General Butler's assumption of the local purple" (268):

> They never had any children. Maurier may have been too old; she herself may have been barren. Often that type is. But I don't think so. I believe ... But who knows: I don't. Anyway, that explains her, to me. At first you think it's just silliness, lack of occupation—a tub of washing, to be exact. But I see something thwarted back of it all, something stifled, yet which won't quite die. (270)

Gordon has sensed and expressed what Fairchild even now cannot. Gordon has survived his encounter with Mrs. Maurier, and turned it to account, finding life beneath the mask of death.

Fairchild, drunk, Julius and Gordon, walk through the Quarter in the "voluptuous night", solicited by women "odorous and exciting and unchaste" (276). Fairchild, "babbling", reckons that beauty is

> natural and fecund and foul—you don't stop for it; you pass on. ... You want to go into all the streets of all the cities men live in. To look into all the darkened rooms in the world. Not with curiosity, not with dread nor doubt nor disapproval. But humbly, gently ... not to disturb it. (277–78)

Gordon's response is different:

> (They were accosted. Whispers from every doorway, hands unchaste and importunate and rife in the tense wild darkness. ... Gordon stopped again.) "I'm going in here," he said. "Give me money." ... (A door opened in the wall. Gordon entered and before the door closed again they saw him in a narrow passageway lift a woman from the shadow and raise her against the mad stars, smothering her squeal against his tall kiss.) (280)

Michael Millgate considers *Mosquitoes* "in its overall effect a repudiation of New Orleans and of all such literary milieux", noting the "sterility of talk, of the mere proliferation of words" by quoting Gordon's words when abandoned by Patricia Robyn. Faulkner was, he says, "shaking the dust of New Orleans from his shoes".[17] The image of New Orleans in *Mosquitoes* actually sustains to the end a remarkable suspension of elements. If much of its "art" is dubious—Mark Frost's and Eva Wiseman's poetry, Dorothy Jameson's painting, Dawson Fairchild's "Al Jackson" tall tales—Gordon's is not: it continues to come and as a direct result of the action of the novel. It does not of course release him from his frustration and his search. There is no clean bill of health for the air of New Orleans, and pitfalls are real enough, but "the setting" may retain some status as the ground of his art. While Faulkner subsequently found himself more at home in the world of Yoknapatawpha County, the lesson about the complex conditions required and paradoxically survivable for the production of art may have been learned in New Orleans.

Near the end of Walker Percy's *The Moviegoer* (1961), the narrator, Jack ("Binx") Bolling, is dressed down by his aunt Emily Cutrer over "inexcusable" behaviour in permitting her stepdaughter Kate to accompany him from New Orleans to Chicago (155).[18] Binx allows that they have even been intimate, "Though intimate is not quite the word" (162). This euphemism (in Aunt Emily's view) triggers a lengthy statement of her values: persons of their "class", she says, mean "roughly the same thing" by the words they use and they share "a native instinct for behavior, a natural piety or grace". They are "better than other people ... because we do not shirk our obligations either to ourselves or to others":

> I wanted to pass on to you the one heritage of the men of our family, a certain quality of spirit, a gaiety, and sense of duty, a nobility worn lightly, a sweetness, a gentleness with women—the only things the South ever had and the only things that really matter in this life. ... how did it happen that none of this ever meant anything to you?" ...
>
> "That would be difficult for me to say [Binx replies]. You say that none of what you said ever meant anything to me. That is not true. On the contrary. I have never forgotten anything you ever said. In fact I have pondered over it all my life. My objections, though they are not exactly objections, cannot be expressed in the usual way. To tell the truth, I can't express them at all."

Though Aunt Emily's élitist Southern views have been acclaimed as the novel's moral centre, to Binx they disguise unwarranted dramatization:

> All the stray bits and pieces of the past, all that is feckless and gray about people, she pulls together into an unmistakable visage of the heroic or the craven, the noble or the ignoble. So strong is she that sometimes the person and the past are in fact transfigured by her. They become what she sees them to be. Uncle Jules has come to see himself as the Creole member of the gens. ... (41)

This transfigurative impulse is to Binx a deeply misguided mode of perception, expression and living, with manipulative and dire consequences. Aunt Emily expects Binx, named Jack after his father (her late brother), to conform to the pattern of the clan. Hint of this fatalistic imperative in her voice causes in him "a dreadful-but-not-unpleasant eschatological prickling" sensation. The family consider the death of Alex Bolling to the Argonne "fitting since the original Alex Bolling was killed with Roberdaux Wheat in the Hood breakthrough at Gaines Mill in 1862" (23), and Binx sees Kate trapped

> beside the porcelain fireplace with its glassed-in cases of medals ... and the ambrotype of Captain Alex Bolling of the 2nd Louisiana Infantry ... sealed in forever by glass set into the wall. (129)[19]

To Aunt Emily, Kate was—that is, is—"suicidal"; Binx demurs. He sees in Kate not simply a manic-depressive, but a fellow sufferer cursed with the problem of existence. The family but not Binx believe Kate's "nervous" peculiarity stems from the death of her fiancé in a car crash on the eve of their wedding; Binx knows that after the event Kate felt free. Emily believes, and Binx does not, that Kate, on tranquillizers ("taking drugs"), is therefore not morally responsible for herself, and to her Binx's action is moral "default". The interview with his aunt "marks an ending" (165) in their relationship, in that she now sees and acknowledges that Binx is not "uncommon". But what Binx *is*, which he cannot explain to her, and hardly to himself or to the reader, is precisely at question.

As the narrative opens, Binx Bolling has previously

> lived in the Quarter for two years, but in the end I got tired of Birmingham businessmen smirking around Bourbon Street and the homosexuals and patio connoisseurs on Royal Street. My uncle and aunt live in a gracious house in the Garden District and are very kind to me. But whenever I try to live there, I find myself first in a rage ... then in a depression. ... (10–11)

He has preferred the "peaceful" life of the last four years in suburban Gentilly where he "manage[s] a small branch office of my uncle's brokerage firm" (11). He lives in the basement apartment of a raised bungalow on the "undistinguished" thoroughfare Elysian Fields. Here he has consciously avoided confronting what occurred to him in Korea when, in the retreat from the Chongchon River, cut off from the main body of troops, he woke and "knew that something was terribly wrong": "nothing seemed worth doing except something I couldn't even remember" (116, 117).[20] (He shares with Kate the sense that things can suddenly seem "of no account".) When business dictates his having to attend a convention in Chicago, the double blow to his careful post-War life will, Binx fears, put an end to "my life in Gentilly, my Little Way, my secret existence among the happy shades in Elysian Fields" (75).

With the ambiguous reference to "happy shades", a darker meaning to his life in Gentilly and New Orleans opens up: "For some time now the impression has been growing upon me that everyone is dead" (75). He describes how the feeling comes over him in conversation—"yes, beyond a doubt this is death ... At such times it seems that the conversation is spoken by automatons ... and I think to myself: this is death." It is the fate of a "malasian" to see the ordinariness of life as a universe of death: "Everydayness is the enemy" (108). Like Mark Twain, Binx Bolling sees the necropolis of Metaire as an image of that other, lurking New Orleans, the city of death:

> In the gathering dusk the cemeteries look at first like cities, with their rows of white vaults, some two- and three-storied and forming flats and tenements, and the tiny streets and corners and curbs and even plots of lawn, all of such a proportion that ... they set themselves off into the distance like a city seen from far away. (136)

On the other hand, there is a wholly "other" experience of the war, and its recurrence to memory threatens the quiet, evasive pattern of Binx's life from another direction:

> things have suddenly changed. My peaceful existence in Gentilly has been complicated. This morning for the first time in years there occurred to me the possibility of a search. I dreamed of the war, no, not quite dreamed but woke with the taste of it in my mouth ... I remembered the first time the search occurred to me. I came to myself under a chindolea bush. ... As I watched, there awoke in me an immense curiosity. I was onto something. I vowed that if ever I got out of this fix, I would pursue the search. Naturally, as soon as I recovered and got home, I forgot all about it. But this morning ... my belongings ... looked both unfamiliar and at the same time full of clues. ... What was unfamiliar about them was that I could see them. ... the search became possible. (13–14)

"The search" is

> what anyone would undertake if he were not sunk in the everydayness of his own life. ... To become aware of the possibility of the search is to be onto something. Not to be onto something is to be in despair. (15)

The searcher is conscious of the life, unfamiliarity and strangeness of all things (14), and recognizes "the singularities of time and place" (42). In the state of search you cease to be an anyone, anywhere (as are the "research" scientists whom Binx, son of a doctor, is expected to emulate), and you exist "Somewhere" (50), "bewitched by the presence" and the "mystery" of particular things in particular places at particular times (42). When this occurred previously, Binx had

> moved down to the Quarter where I spent the rest of the vacation in quest of the spirit of summer and in the company of an attractive and confused girl from Bennington who fancied herself a poet. (42–3)

So the search first sought the *Mosquitoes*-like conjunction of the Quarter and art, though it soon faded into "everydayness" and worse, just as on the manic edge it can imbue each phenomenon of perception with such intense significance as to transmogrify everything, as it can for Kate, "to horror" (50). So he went to ground in Gentilly.

He also found the movies as a safe reminder: "The movies are onto the search, but they screw it up" (15). They begin by making everything strange and unfamiliar, and it is this which draws him to them again and again; but soon they betray their insight, and their searcher is once again "so sunk in everydayness that he might just as well be dead" (16). In the "anywhere" city of Chicago "the mother and Urwomb of all moviehouses" is "an Aztec mortuary of funeral urns and glyphs" (154). Movies take one through the entire cycle, from the positive "validation" and "certification" of existence to betrayal, "everydayness" and death-in-life, but Binx follows them in hope of new, strange beginnings: "It was here in the Tivoli that I first discovered place and time, tasted it like okra" (58). Moviegoing is a safe version of searching, giving the pleasure but not its fading into the light of day. Can Binx cease to be a Moviegoer without going dead?

Does Binx accept the full burden of searching, ceasing attempts to escape it among the "happy shades" (with moviegoing as a surrogate), and accept that only the search can give an openness to existence, however risky, that will hold at bay the city of death? The events of the New Orleans "Carnival before Mardi Gras" (Binx puts it accurately), already dubious as a measure of social energy to Mark Twain, here stand for the city of death masked as the essence of life. Carnival in New Orleans is the mere pretence of being "somewhere", its reality to Binx (intellectually) and Kate (emotionally) quite different. As the cynosure of civic life it is a powerful coercive symbol, demanding submission. Likewise, Aunt Emily's statement of Southern values, fully rounded and even appealing, threatens to undermine Binx's alternative: "My search has been abandoned: it is no match for my aunt, her rightness and her despair, her despairing of me and her despairing of herself" (166). But at this point, when "I have to find a girl" (any girl)—that is, resume the life of driven, animal ordinariness—Kate seeks him out and he realizes that she continues to credit his all-but-abandoned conception. It affords the only hope of what Joyce's Stephen Dedalus, navigating in *Ulysses* between a comparable Scylla and Charybdis, takes himself to remember: "Hold to the now, the here".[21] Binx holds to the "somewhere" of New Orleans—though Percy is keen to stress that this does not make the author "a Southern writer", that is committed to some essential life-value to be found only in the South.

Binx's references to despair are never casual, like his use of "doubling, or duplication" (173), and his use of "repetition" as a category of experience emanates from the same source, "the great Danish philosopher" Søren Kierkegaard (172). While one is tempted to call the "philosophy" of Aunt Emily a belief in the necessity, rightness and unavailability of repetition, Binx deploys the term with Kierkegaard's distinction:

> What is a repetition? A repetition is the re-enactment of past experience toward the end of isolating the time segment which has lapsed in order that it, the lapsed

> time, can be savored of itself and without the usual adulteration of events that clog time. (61)

Kierkegaard wrote:

> Repetition and recollection are the same movement, only in opposite directions; for what is recollected has been, is repeated backwards, whereas repetition properly so called is recollected forwards. Therefore repetition, if it is possible, makes a man happy, whereas recollection makes him unhappy. ...
>
> In truth, the love of repetition is the only happy love. ... it has the blessed certainty of the instant.[22]

Aunt Emily "recollects", "repeats backwards", expects the present to conform to the past. It is more difficult to conceptualize repetition, the "opposite direction", though Binx tries to illustrate it. Even when lying low in Gentilly, he has tried, characteristically through moviegoing, to lie in wait for his kind of repetition. Though sceptical of his capacity for commitment, Binx not only distrusts grand determining eschatologies, he will take matters one at a time as they come, merely "plant a foot in the right place as the opportunity presents itself" (172).

In an Epilogue, we learn that Binx and Kate married, that they live in New Orleans's Garden District, near Aunt Emily, "who has become fond" of Binx. Their house is "one of the very shotgun cottages done over by my cousin Nell Lovell" (172). (The Lovells always represent automata and death for Binx.) He has enrolled as a medical student, like his father before him. By agreement he doles out little assignments to Kate, still fearful of the great anonymous life around here. He does not know whether in this phase of "acceptance" he has abandoned his search or is waiting for a revelation which will not come or is living, religiously, in a very particularized, wholly revealed existence: "a peculiar word this in the first place, *religion*; it is something to be suspicious of" (172). Thus for him the two metropolises of the South, the cities of life and of death, neither denied, coalesce, and neither he nor the fascinated reader can any longer separate them.

Notes

1. Mark Twain, *Life on the Mississippi*, in *Mississippi Writings* (New York: Library of America, 1982). All references will be to this text, which reprints the first U.S. edition of 1883.

2. Twain expands on the disease-breeding properties of corpse burial, under or especially (as in New Orleans) above ground, providing a scholarly footnote: "During the epidemic in New Orleans in 1853, Dr. E. H. Barton reported that in the Fourth District the mortality was four hundred and fifty-two thousand—more than double that of any other. In this district were three large cemeteries, in which during the previous year more than three thousand bodies had been buried. In other districts the proximity of cemeteries seemed to aggravate the disease. ..."—[Dr. F. Julius Le Moyne,] *North American Review*, No. 3, Vol. 135, 478–79.

3. The particular subject of Twain's interlocutors' "war talk" was crucial to the Civil War history of New Orleans (and the South): the surrender of Vicksburg and of Port Hudson in July 1863 cut the South in two. For a contemporary account of the assault on Port Hudson in May and June of 1863, which resulted in "the opening of the lower Mississippi", see John William De Forest, *A Volunteer's Adventures*, ed. James H. Croushore (New Haven: Yale University Press, 1946), Chapters

VII–VIII, pp. 103–47 (here quoting p. 147). Forest published an earlier draft of these chapter in *Harper's New Monthly Magazine*, August 1867. Admiral David G. Farragut had captured New Orleans in April 1862, so the expressions of admiration for his cleverness which Twain records are particularly dis-interested and urbane, not nostalgic.

4. Stories in *Old Creole Days* will be cited in the text published in *Creoles and Cajuns*, ed. Arlin Turner (Garden City, N.Y.: Doubleday & Co., Inc., Doubleday Anchor Books, 1959).

5. The balance of "human sympathy for, and artistic sensitivity to, the splendid heroic qualities" of "past social formations" and recognition of "the historical necessity of their decline" and supercession by new "social formations" are seen by Georg Lukács, as characteristics of Scott as an historical novelist. (Lukács, "The Classical Form of the Historical Novel", in *The Historical Novel* (1937), trans. Hannah and Stanley Mitchell [Harmondsworth: Penguin Books, 1969], p. 59) Cable and Faulkner constitute a sophisticated variant on Lukács' thesis, describing and analysing (and not as "pseudo-historians of reaction") a society which *itself* resists and refuses the potentiality for historical development. They describe those who credit personal and social stasis; they nonetheless probe for signs of a still-living human and historical potential.

6. See Edmund Wilson, *Patriotic Gore* (New York: Oxford University Press, 1962), p. 599.: "In his handling of the dialogue of his Creole characters, [Cable] seems to be almost bilingual, but the Gallicized English they speak presents some peculiar features. They are made, for example, habitually to talk of 'a difficult,' 'a possible,' 'a necessary,' ... meaning a difficult matter, a beautiful thing, etc. ... Cable is evidently so conscientious in his notation of how people talk that one is bound to assume that he had actually heard the Creoles use it."

7. The ghostly figure is "white"; the secretary's name is White. The secretary becomes a secret sharer of the figure's affliction and Jean Poquelin's only "champion" (116) in New Orleans: his humanity has something common, chivalrous and mysterious about it, like Byron Bunch's in Faulkner's *Light in August*.

8. The mob or "rabble" (121) foreshadows *Light in August*, as do other elements of "Jean-ah Poquelin" (see previous note). Compare the "gossips" and "rumor" of Cable with Faulkner's "they" who speak against Joe Christmas; compare the mobs, intent on "shivaree" (or worse) and lynching, but who may not have been "up" to either; compare the alleged aping of the North. Richard Chase, in *The American Novel and Its Tradition* (Garden City, N.Y.: Doubleday & Co., Inc., 1957), noted, "There is a good deal of highly effective symbolism in ... [*The Grandissimes*], mostly having to do with light and dark and the ambiguity not only of racial strains but of reality itself. This symbolism [is] used with equal effectiveness in American literature perhaps only in *Light in August* and in Melville's *Benito Cereno* ..." (p. 171).

9. George W. Cable, *The Grandissimes A Story of Creole Life*, second edition, (London: Hodder and Stoughton, 1898). All references will be to this text, which reprints Cable's 1883 revised version.

10. Honoré Grandissime has the rôle which Lukács postulates for the "mediocre" protagonists of Scott's novels (Lukács, pp. 32–7). Faulkner gives young Bayard Sartoris this rôle in *The Unvanquished* (1935).

11. Kate Chopin, *The Awakening* (1899), in *The Complete Works of Kate Chopin*, ed. Per Seyersted (Baton Rouge: Louisiana State University Press, 1969), p. 887. All references will be to this text.

12. Chopin lived in New Orleans from October 1870 to late 1879. While there is little to date the events of *The Awakening*, it may be assumed that it is set in the 1870s. Whether, writing in 1899, Kate Chopin regarded the predicament of Edna Pontellier as "historical" (i.e. belonging to an earlier historical phase) is another question.

13. William Faulkner, *Mosquitoes* (London: Chatto & Windus, 1964). First published 1927. All references to the novel will be to the Chatto & Windus text.

14. The torso is an example of "the image of motion in statis which haunted Faulkner throughout his life, especially as embodied in Keats's "Ode to a Grecian Urn" (Michael Millgate, *The Achievement of William Faulkner* (New York: Vintage Books, 1971), p. 96).

15. John T. Irwin, *Doubling and Incest/Repetition and Revenge: A Speculative Reading of Faulkner* (Baltimore and London: Johns Hopkins University Press, 1975), considers that Faulkner sensed "the act of writing as a progressive dismemberment of the self in which parts of the living subject are cut off to become objectified in language ... a kind of doubling in which the author's self is reconstituted" (pp. 158–59). He sees "Faulkner's conscious understanding of this structure as a metaphor for his art ... complete" as early as *Mosquitoes*. Irwin notes certain "doubles" in the novel; this essay suggests other, sometimes contrasting figures who together constitute a complete, ambiguous image: not only the fraternal twins Patricia and Josh, who call each other "Gus" (Irwin,

p. 160), and Gordon and Josh (Irwin, p. 168); but also the two "Pats", Gordon and David West, Gordon and Dawson Fairchild, young Patricia and Jenny Steinbauer, David West and Pete Ginotta. Like Millgate (note 14), Irwin tends to extrapolate from and conflate remarks and thoughts by Fairchild, Julius Wiseman and even Gordon into Faulkner's own view of the relationship between art and life, art and sex; this essay sees those remarks more as dramatized alternatives and oppositions.

16. "Gordon realizes that his love for Patricia is hopeless—that the artist's fated substitute for the real sexual possession of the virgin must be the possession of her in the virgin purity of the work of art" (Irwin, p. 160). Irwin's argument appears to require a head of Patricia Robyn not Mrs. Maurier.

17. Millgate, pp. 68–9.

18. Walker Percy, *The Moviegoer* (London: Granada Publishing, 1985). First published 1961. All references are to the Granada (Panther) edition.

19. Faulkner too saw catastrophic fatalism—expected, demanded and accepted—as characteristic of the stasis of the Southern family or class, as in *Sartoris* (1929): Binx's Aunt Emily is an updated version of young Bayard Sartoris's Aunt Jenny Du Pré. I have treated this preoccupation in "Faulkner's Images of the Past: from *Sartoris* to *The Unvanquished*", in *The Yearbook of English Studies: American Literature Special Number*, eds. G. K. Hunter and C. J. Rawson, Vol. 8 (1978), pp. 108–24; esp. pp. 110–12, 114.

20. In his need for a measured and orderly life, with only severely contained excitements, Binx Bolling, Korean War veteran, can be compared to other (fictional) veterans such as Jake Barnes in Ernest Hemingway's *The Sun Also Rises* (1926).

21. James Joyce, *Ulysses*, ed. Hans Walter Gabler (New York and London: Garland Publishing, Inc., 1984), 9.89.

22. S. Kierkegaard, *Repetition: An Essay in Experimental Psychology*, trans. and ed. Walter Lowrie (London: Oxford University Press, 1941), pp. 33–4. The editor's introduction, pp. xxvii–xxxv, quotes from Kierkegaard's *Journals* and from *The Concept of Dread* in further elucidation of the special meaning Kierkegaard gives to repetition.

162

The Grandissimes: A Story of Creole Life

GEORGE W. CABLE

George Washington Cable (1844–1925), was a novelist, essayist, and short-story writer as well as historian of Creole culture and dialect. He was born in New Orleans, into a slave-owning family. *Old Creole Days* (1879) reflects his deep interest in New Orleans and its Creole past. *The Grandissimes* (1880) is his major account of Louisiana Creole Blacks at the time of the Louisiana Purchase. A complex text, it involves a series of conflicts including those between races. His reforming zeal in relation to race in the American South is evident in *The Silent South* (1885). *The Grandissimes* is as much notable for its attention to dialect, as for its wonderfully evoked atmospheres of a New Orleans very much the reflection of its French and Spanish heritage. See A. Turner, *George W. Cable, A Biography* (1956).

New Light upon Dark Places

As the sun rose and diffused its beams in an atmosphere whose temperature had just been recorded as 50° F., the apothecary stepped half out of his shop-door to face the bracing air that came blowing upon his tired forehead from the north. As he did so, he said to himself:

"How are these two Honoré Grandissimes related to each other, and why should one be thought capable of attempting the life of Agricola?"

The answer was on its way to him.

There is left to our eyes, but a poor vestige of the picturesque view presented to those who looked down the rue Royale before the garish day that changed the rue Enghien into Ingine street, and dropped the "e" from Royale. It was a long, narrowing perspective of arcades, lattices, balconies, *zaguans*, dormer windows, and blue sky—of low, tiled roofs, red and wrinkled, huddled down

Source: George W. Cable, *The Grandissimes: A Story of Creole Life*, 1880. Extracts from Ch. 18, 27, 44, 46.

into their own shadows; of canvas awnings with fluttering borders, and of grimy lamp-posts twenty feet in height, each reaching out a gaunt iron arm over the narrow street and dangling a lamp from its end. The human life which dotted the view displayed a variety of tints and costumes such as a painter would be glad to take just as he found them: the gayly feathered Indian, the slashed and tinselled Mexican, the leather-breeched raftsmen, the blue- or yellow-turbaned *négresse*, the sugar-planter in white flannel and moccasins, the average townsman in the last suit of clothes of the lately deceased century, and now and then a fashionable man in that costume....

The Fête de Grandpère

Sojourners in New Orleans who take their afternoon drive down Esplanade street will notice, across on the right, between it and that sorry streak once fondly known as Champ Elysées, two or three large, old houses, rising above the general surroundings and displaying architectural features which identify them with an irrevocable past—a past when the faithful and true Creole could, without fear of contradiction, express his religious belief that the antipathy he felt for the Américain invader was an inborn horror laid lengthwise in his ante-natal bones by a discriminating and appreciative Providence. There is, for instance, or was until lately, one house which some hundred and fifteen years ago was the suburban residence of the old sea-captain governor, Kerlerec. It stands up among the oranges as silent and gray as a pelican, and, so far as we know, has never had one cypress plank added or subtracted since its master was called to France and thrown into the Bastile. Another has two dormer windows looking out westward, and, when the setting sun strikes the panes, reminds one of a man with spectacles standing up in an audience, searching for a friend who is not there and will never come back. These houses are the last remaining—if, indeed, they were not pulled down yesterday—of a group that once marked from afar the direction of the old highway between the city's walls and the suburb St. Jean. Here clustered the earlier aristocracy of the colony; all that pretty crew of counts, chevaliers, marquises, colonels, dons, etc., who loved their kings, and especially their kings' moneys, with an *abandon* which affected the accuracy of nearly all their accounts.

Among these stood the great mother-mansion of the Grandissimes. Do not look for it now; it is quite gone. The round, white-plastered brick pillars which held the house fifteen feet up from the reeking ground and rose on loftily to sustain the great over-spreading roof, or clustered in the cool, paved basement; the lofty halls, with their multitudinous glitter of gilded brass and twinkle of sweet-smelling wax-candles; the immense encircling veranda, where twenty Creole girls might walk abreast; the great front stairs, descending from the veranda to the garden, with a lofty palm on either side, on whose broad steps forty Grandissimes could gather on a birthday afternoon; and the belvedere, whence you could see the cathedral, the Ursulines', the governor's mansion, and the river, far away, shining between the villas of Tchoupitoulas Coast—all have disappeared as entirely beyond recall as the flowers that bloomed in the gardens on the day of this *fête de grandpère....*

Bad for Charlie Keene

On the same evening of which we have been telling, about the time that Aurora and Clotilde were dropping their last tear of joy over the document of restitution, a noticeable figure stood alone at the corner of the rue du Canal and the rue Chartres. He had reached there and paused, just as the brighter glare of the set sun was growing dim above the tops of the cypresses. After walking with some rapidity of step, he had stopped aimlessly, and laid his hand with an air of weariness upon a rotting China-tree that leaned over the ditch at the edge of the unpaved walk.

"Setting in cypress," he murmured. We need not concern ourselves as to his meaning.

One could think aloud there with impunity. In 1804, Canal street was the upper boundary of New Orleans. Beyond it, to southward, the open plain was dotted with country-houses, brick-kilns, clumps of live-oak and groves of pecan. At the hour mentioned the outlines of these objects were already darkening. At one or two points the sky was reflected from marshy ponds. Out to westward rose conspicuously the old house and willow-copse of Jean-Poquelin. Down the empty street or road, which stretched with arrow-like straightness toward the north-west, the draining-canal that gave it its name tapered away between occasional overhanging willows and beside broken ranks of rotting palisades, its foul, crawling waters blushing and gliding and purpling under the swiftly waning light, and ending suddenly in the black shadow of the swamp. The observer of this dismal prospect leaned heavily on his arm, and cast his glance out along the beautified corruption of the canal. His eye seemed quickened to detect the smallest repellent details of the scene; every cypress stump that stood in or overhung the slimy water; every ruined indigo-vat or blasted tree, every broken thing, every bleached bone of ox or horse—and they were many—for roods around. As his eye passed them slowly over and swept back again around the dreary view, he sighed heavily and said: "Dissolution," and then again— "Dissolution! order of the day—"...

The Pique-en-Terre Loses One of Her Crew

Ask the average resident of New Orleans if his town is on an island, and he will tell you no. He will also wonder how any one could have got that notion,—so completely has Orleans Island, whose name at the beginning of the present century was in everybody's mouth, been forgotten. It was once a question of national policy, a point of difference between Republican and Federalist, whether the United States ought to buy this little strip of semi-submerged land, or whether it would not be more righteous to steal it. The Kentuckians kept the question at a red heat by threatening to become an empire by themselves if one course or the other was not taken; but when the first Consul offered to sell all Louisiana, our commissioners were quite robbed of breath. They had approached to ask a hair from the elephant's tail, and were offered the elephant.

For Orleans Island—island it certainly was until General Jackson closed Bayou Manchac—is a narrow, irregular, flat tract of forest, swamp, city, prairie and sea-marsh lying east and west, with the Mississippi, trending south-eastward, for its southern boundary, and for its northern, a parallel and contiguous chain of alternate lakes and bayous, opening into the river through Bayou Manchac, and into the Gulf through the passes of the Malheureuse Islands. On the narrowest part of it stands New Orleans. Turning and looking back over the rear of the town, one may easily see from her steeples Lake Pontchartrain glistening away to the northern horizon, and in his fancy extend the picture to right and left till Pontchartrain is linked in the west by Pass Manchac to Lake Maurepas, and in the east by the Rigolets and Chef Menteur to Lake Borgne.

An oddity of the Mississippi Delta is the habit the little streams have of running away from the big ones. The river makes its own bed and its own banks, and continuing season after season, through ages of alternate overflow and subsidence, to elevate those banks, creates a ridge which thus becomes a natural elevated aqueduct. Other slightly elevated ridges mark the present or former courses of minor outlets, by which the waters of the Mississippi have found the sea. Between these ridges lie the cypress swamps, through whose profound shades the clear, dark, deep bayous creep noiselessly away into the tall grasses of the shaking prairies. The original New Orleans was built on the Mississippi ridge, with one of these forest-and-water-covered basins stretching back behind her to westward and northward, closed in by Metairie Ridge and Lake Pontchartrain. Local engineers preserve the tradition that the Bayou Sauvage once had its rise, so to speak, in Toulouse street. Though depleted by the city's present drainage system and most likely poisoned by it as well, its waters still move seaward in a course almost due easterly, and empty into Chef Menteur, one of the watery threads of a tangled skein of "passes" between the lakes and the open Gulf, Three-quarters of a century ago this Bayou Sauvage (or Gentilly—corruption of Chantilly) was a navigable stream of wild and sombre beauty.

On a certain morning in August, 1804, and consequently some five months after the events last mentioned, there emerged from the darkness of Bayou Sauvage into the prairie-bordered water of Chef Menteur, while the morning star was still luminous in the sky above and in the water below, and only the practised eye could detect the first glimmer of day, a small, stanch, single-masted, broad and very light-draught boat, whose innocent character, primarily indicated in its coat of many colors,—the hull being yellow below the water line and white above, with tasteful stripings of blue and red,—was further accentuated by the peaceful name of *Pique-en-terre* (the Sandpiper).

She seemed, too, as she entered the Chef Menteur, as if she would have liked to turn southward; but the wind did not permit this, and in a moment more the water was rippling after her swift rudder, as she glided away in the direction of Pointe Aux Herbes. But when she had left behind her the mouth of the passage, she changed her course and, leaving the Pointe on her left, bore down toward Petites Coquilles, obviously bent upon passing through the Rigolets.

We know not how to describe the joyousness of the effect when at length one leaves behind him the shadow and gloom of the swamp, and there bursts upon his sight the widespread, flower-decked, bird-haunted prairies of Lake Catharine. The inside and outside of a prison scarcely furnish a greater contrast; and on this fair August morning the contrast was at its strongest. The day broke across a glad expanse of cool and fragrant green, silver-laced with a net-work of crisp salt pools and passes, lakes, bayous and lagoons, that gave a good smell, the inspiring odor of interclasped sea and shore, and both beautified and perfumed the happy earth, laid bare to the rising sun. Waving marshes of wild oats, drooping like sated youth from too much pleasure; watery acres hid under crisp-growing greenth starred with pond-lilies and rippled by water-fowl; broad stretches of high grass, with thousands of ecstatic wings palpitating above them; hundreds of thousands of white and pink mallows clapping their hands in voiceless rapture, and that amazon queen of the wild flowers, the morning-glory, stretching her myriad lines, lifting up the trumpet and waving her colors, white, azure and pink, with lacings of spider's web, heavy with pearls and diamonds—the gifts of the summer night. The crew of the *Pique-en-terre* saw all these and felt them; for, whatever they may have been or failed to be, they were men whose heart-strings responded to the touches of nature. One alone of their company, and he the one who should have felt them most, showed insensibility, sighed laughingly and then laughed sighingly in the face of his fellows and of all this beauty, and profanely confessed that his heart's desire was to get back to his wife. He had been absent from her now for nine hours!

But the sun is getting high; Petites Coquilles has been passed and left astern, the eastern end of Las Conchas is on the after-larboard-quarter, the briny waters of Lake Borgne flash far and wide their dazzling white and blue, and, as the little boat issues from the deep channel of the Rigolets, the white-armed waves catch her and toss her like a merry babe. A triumph for the helmsman—he it is who sighs, at intervals of tiresome frequency, for his wife. He had, from the very starting-place in the upper waters of Bayou Sauvage, declared in favor of the Rigolets as—wind and tide considered—the most practicable of all the passes. Now that they were out, he forgot for a moment the self-amusing plaint of conjugal separation to flaunt his triumph. Would any one hereafter dispute with him on the subject of Louisiana sea-coast-navigation? He knew every pass and piece of water like A, B, C, and could tell, faster, much faster than he could repeat the multiplication table (upon which he was a little slow and doubtful), the amount of water in each at ebb tide—Pass Jean or Petit Pass, Unknown Pass, Petit Rigolet, Chef Menteur,—

Out on the far southern horizon, in the Gulf—the Gulf of Mexico—there appears a speck of white. It is known to those on board the *Pique-en-terre*, the moment it is descried, as the canvas of a large schooner. The opinion, first expressed by the youthful husband, who still reclines with the tiller held firmly under his arm, and then by another member of the company who sits on the centre-board-well, is unanimously adopted, that she is making for the Rigolets, will pass Petites Coquilles by eleven o'clock, and will tie up at the little port of St. Jean, on the bayou of the same name, before sundown, if the wind holds anywise as it is.....

163

Life on the Mississippi

MARK TWAIN

Mark Twain [Samuel Langhorne Clemens] (1835–1910) remains one of the outstanding prose writers of the nineteenth century and a central figure in the development of a vernacular American literature. When he was four years old his family moved to Hannibal, Missouri, on the banks of the Mississippi. The river (and the area) forms the basis of much of his writing—an ideal *locus* of an earlier pastoral America, the very opposite to the increasingly urban and technological society Twain observed.

In 1857 he trained as a river-boat pilot, a profession that he loved "better than any other I have followed...". In 1867 he settled in Hartford, Connecticut, where he lived until 1890. Despite the vibrant humour which characterises much of his fiction , there is often an underlying pessimism and increasing cynicism which informs his view of America. This is especially so in his later years, after the death of his daughter in 1896.

Twain is perhaps best known for *The Adventures of Huckleberry Finn* (1885), based on the first person narrative of an "uncivilized" orphan, Huck, and his "adventures" as he travels down the Mississippi, deeper and deeper into the slave territory of the Southern States. Accompanied by his friend, Jim, an escaped slave, Huck increasingly questions the society he views, and sees it as both immoral and hypocritical. Huck's questioning is framed in a first person vernacular which brilliantly realises the child's "eye", as it probes an adult world. Huck's voice has a purity about it which is associated with a condition at once ahistorical and pre-social.

Life on the Mississippi (1883) offers an equivalent celebration of the landscape of the river in relation to Twain's own life and his sense of the river's place within the United States as a whole. It is a wonderfully realised celebration of the Mississippi whilst at the same time looking to the inevitable industrial and commercial developments which threaten its "natural" state. See Henry Nash Smith, *Mark Twain: The Development of a Writer* (1962), Tony Tanner, *The Reign of Wonder* (1968) and Leo Marx, *The Machine in the Garden*.

Source: Mark Twain, *Life on the Mississippi*, 1883, Chs. XLI, XLII, XLIII, XLIV.

Chapter XLI: The Metropolis of the South

The approaches to New Orleans were familiar; general aspects were unchanged. When one goes flying through London along a railway propped in the air on tall arches, he may inspect miles of upper bedrooms through the open windows, but the lower half of the houses is under his level and out of sight. Similarly, in high-river stage, in the New Orleans region, the water is up to the top of the enclosing levee rim, the flat country behind it lies low—representing the bottom of a dish—and as the boat swims along, high on the flood, one looks down upon the houses and into the upper windows. There is nothing but that frail breastwork of earth between the people and destruction.

The old brick salt warehouses clustered at the upper end of the city looked as they had always looked; warehouses which had had a kind of Aladdin's lamp experience, however, since I had seen them; for when the war broke out the proprietor went to bed one night leaving them packed with thousands of sacks of vulgar salt, worth a couple of dollars a sack, and got up in the morning and found his mountain of salt turned into a mountain of gold, so to speak, so suddenly and to so dizzy a height had the war news sent up the price of the article.

The vast reach of plank wharves remained unchanged, and there were as many shops as ever: but the long array of steamboats had vanished; not altogether, of course, but not much of it was left.

The city itself had not changed—to the eye. It had greatly increased in spread and population, but the look of the town was not altered. The dust, waste-paper-littered, was still deep in the streets; the deep, troughlike gutters alongside the curbstones were still half full of reposeful water with a dusty surface; the sidewalks were still—in the sugar and bacon region—encumbered by casks and barrels and hogsheads; the great blocks of austerely plain commercial houses were as dusty-looking as ever.

Canal Street was finer, and more attractive and stirring than formerly, with its drifting crowds of people, its several processions of hurrying streetcars, and—toward evening—its broad second-story verandas crowded with gentlemen and ladies clothed according to the latest mode.

Not that there is any "architecture" in Canal Street: to speak in broad, general terms, there is no architecture in New Orleans, except in the cemeteries. It seems a strange thing to say of a wealthy, far-seeing, and energetic city of a quarter of a million inhabitants, but it is true. There is a huge granite U.S. Customhouse—costly enough, genuine enough, but as a decoration it is inferior to a gasometer. It looks like a state prison. but it was built before the war. Architecture in America may be said to have been born since the war. New Orleans, I believe, has had the good luck—and in a sense the bad luck—to have had no great fire in late years. It must be so. If the opposite had been the case, I think one would be able to tell the "burnt district" by the radical improvement in its architecture over the old forms. One can do this in Boston and Chicago.

The "burnt district" of Boston was commonplace before the fire; but now there is no commercial district in any city in the world that can surpass it—or perhaps even rival it—in beauty, elegance, and tastefulness.

However, New Orleans has begun—just this moment, as one may say. When completed, the new Cotton Exchange will be a stately and beautiful building; massive, substantial, full of architectural graces; no shams or false pretences or uglinesses about it anywhere. To the city, it will be worth many times its cost, for it will breed its species. What has been lacking hitherto, was a model to build toward; something to educate eye and taste; a *suggester*, so to speak.

The city is well outfitted with progressive men—thinking, sagacious, long-headed men. The contrast between the spirit of the city and the city's architecture is like the contrast between waking and sleep. Apparently there is a "boom" in everything but that one dead feature. The water in the gutters used to be stagnant and slimy, and a potent disease-breeder; but the gutters are flushed now, two or three times a day, by powerful machinery; in many of the gutters the water never stands still, but has a steady current. Other sanitary improvements have been made; and with such effect that New Orleans claims to be (during the long intervals between the occasional yellow-fever assaults) one of the healthiest cities in the Union. There's plenty of ice now for everybody, manufactured in the town. It is a driving place commercially, and has a great river, ocean, and railway business. At the date of our visit, it was the best lighted city in the Union, electrically speaking. The New Orleans electric lights were more numerous than those of New York, and very much better. One had this modified noonday not only in Canal and some neighboring chief streets, but all along a stretch of five miles of river frontage. There are good clubs in the city now—several of them but recently organized—and inviting modern-style pleasure resorts at West End and Spanish Fort. The telephone is everywhere. One of the most notable advances is in journalism. The newspapers, as I remember then, were not a striking feature. Now they are. Money is spent upon them with a free hand. They get the news, let it cost what it may. The editorial work is not hack grinding, but literature. As an example of New Orleans journalistic achievement, it may be mentioned that the Times-Democrat of August 26, 1882, contained a report of the year's business of the towns of the Mississippi Valley, from New Orleans all the way to St. Paul—two thousand miles. That issue of the paper consisted of forty pages; seven columns to the page; two hundred and eighty columns in all; fifteen hundred words to the column; an aggregate of four hundred and twenty thousand words. That is to say, not much short of three times as many words as there are in this book. One may with sorrow contrast this with the architecture of New Orleans.

I have been speaking of public architecture only. The domestic article in New Orleans is reproachless, notwithstanding it remains as it always was. All the dwellings are of wood—in the American part of the town, I mean—and all have a comfortable look. Those in the wealthy quarter are spacious; painted snow-white usually, and generally have wide verandas, or double-verandas, supported by ornamental columns. These mansions stand in the center of large grounds, and rise, garlanded with roses, out of the midst of swelling masses of shining green foliage and many-colored blossoms. No houses could well be in better harmony with their surroundings, or more pleasing to the eye, or more homelike and comfortable-looking.

One even becomes reconciled to the cistern presently; this is a mighty cask, painted green, and sometimes a couple of stories high, which is propped against the house corner on stilts. There is mansion-and-brewery suggestion about the combination which seems very incongruous at first. But the people cannot have wells, and so they take rain water. Neither can they conveniently have cellars, or graves;[1] the town being built upon "made" ground; so they do without both, and few of the living complain, and none of the others.

Chapter XLII: Hygiene and Sentiment

They bury their dead in vaults, above the ground.

These vaults have a resemblance to houses—sometimes to temples; are built of marble, generally; are architecturally graceful and shapely; they face the walks and driveways of the cemetery; and when one moves through the midst of a thousand or so of them and sees their white roofs and gables stretching into the distance on every hand, the phrase "city of the dead" has all at once a meaning to him. Many of the cemeteries are beautiful and are kept in perfect order. When one goes from the levee or the business streets near it, to a cemetery, he observes to himself that if those people down there would live as neatly while they are alive as they do after they are dead, they would find many advantages in it; and besides, their quarter would be the wonder and admiration of the business world. Fresh flowers, in vases of water, are to be seen at the portals of many of the vaults: placed there by the pious hands of bereaved parents and children, husbands and wives, and renewed daily. A milder form of sorrow finds its inexpensive and lasting remembrancer in the coarse and ugly but indestructible *immortelle*—which is a wreath or cross or some such emblem, made of rosettes of black linen, with sometimes a yellow rosette at the conjunction of the cross's bars—kind of sorrowful breastpin, so to say. The *immortelle* requires no attention: you just hang it up, and there you are; just leave it alone, it will take care of your grief for you, and keep it in mind better than you can; stands weather first rate, and lasts like boiler iron.

On sunny days, pretty little chameleons—gracefullest of legged reptiles—creep along the marble fronts of the vaults, and catch flies. Their changes of color—as to variety—are not up to the creature's reputation. They change color when a person comes along and hangs up an *immortelle*; but that is nothing: any right-feeling reptile would do that.

I will gradually drop this subject of graveyards. I have been trying all I could to get down to the sentimental part of it, but I cannot accomplish it. I think there is no genuinely sentimental part to it. It is all grotesque, ghastly, horrible.

Graveyards may have been justifiable in the bygone ages, when nobody knew that for every dead body put into the ground, to glut the earth and the plant roots and the air with disease germs, five or fifty, or maybe a hundred, persons must die before their proper time; but they are hardly justifiable now, when even the children know that a dead saint enters upon a century-long career of assassination the moment the earth closes over his corpse. It is a grim sort of a thought. The relics of St. Anne, up in Canada, have now, after nineteen hundred years, gone to curing the sick by the dozen. But it is merest matter-of-course that these same relics, within a generation after St. Anne's death and burial, *made* several thousand people sick. Therefore these miracle-performances are simply compensation, nothing more. St. Anne is somewhat slow pay, for a Saint, it is true; but better a debt paid after nineteen hundred years, and outlawed by the statute of limitations, than not paid at all; and most of the knights of the halo do not pay at all. Where you find one that pays—like St. Anne—you find a hundred and fifty that take the benefit of the statute. And none of them pay any more than the principal of what they owe—they pay none of the interest, either simple or compound. A Saint can never *quite* return the principal, however; for his dead body *kills* people, whereas his relics *heal* only—they never restore the dead to life. That part of the account is always left unsettled.

Dr. F. Julius Le Moyne, after fifty years of medical practice, wrote: "The inhumation of human bodies, dead from infectious diseases, results in constantly loading the atmosphere, and polluting the waters, with not only the germs that rise from simply putrefaction, but also with the *specific* germs of the diseases from which death resulted."

The gases (from buried corpses) will rise to the surface through eight or ten feet of gravel, just as coal gas will do, and there is practically no limit to their power of escape.

During the epidemic in New Orleans in 1853, Dr. E. H. Barton reported that in the Fourth District the mortality was four hundred and fifty-two per thousand—more than double that of any other. In this district were three large cemeteries, in which during the previous year more than three thousand bodies had been buried. In other districts the proximity of cemeteries seemed to aggravate the disease.

In 1828 Professor Bianchi demonstrated how the fearful reappearance of the plague at Modena was caused by excavations in ground where, *three hundred years previously* the victims of the pestilence had been buried. Mr. Cooper, in explaining the causes of some epidemics, remarks that the opening of the plague burial-grounds at Eyam resulted in an immediate outbreak of disease.—*North American Review*, No. 3, Vol. 135.

In an address before the Chicago Medical Society, in advocacy of cremation, Dr. Charles W. Purdy made some striking comparisons to show what a burden is laid upon society by the burial of the dead:

"One and one-fourth times more money is expended annually in funerals in the United States than the Government expends for public-school purposes. Funerals cost this country in 1880 enough money to pay the liabilities of all the commercial failures in the United States during the same year, and give each bankrupt a capital of $8,630 with which to resume business. Funerals cost annually more money than the value of the combined gold and silver yield of the United

States in the year 1880! These figures do not include the sums invested in burial grounds and expended in tombs and monuments, nor the loss from depreciation of property in the vicinity of cemeteries.

For the rich, cremation would answer as well as burial; for the ceremonies connected with it could be made as costly and ostentatious as a Hindu *suttee*; while for the poor, cremation would be better than burial, because so cheap[2]—so cheap until the poor got to imitating the rich, which they would do by and by. The adoption of cremation would relieve us of a muck of threadbare burial witticisms; but, on the other hand, it would resurrect a lot of mildewed old cremation jokes that have had a rest for two thousand years.

I have a colored acquaintance who earns his living by odd jobs and heavy manual labor. He never earns above four hundred dollars in a year, and as he has a wife and several young children, the closest scrimping is necessary to get him through to the end of the twelve months debtless. To such a man a funeral is a colossal financial disaster. While I was writing one of the preceding chapters, this man lost a little child. He walked the town over with a friend, trying to find a coffin that was within his means. He bought the very cheapest one he could find, plain wood, stained. It cost him twenty-six dollars. It would have cost less than four, probably, if it had been built to put something useful into. He and his family will feel that outlay a good many months.

Chapter XLIII: The Art of Inhumation

About the same time, I encountered a man in the street, whom I had not seen for six or seven years; and something like this talk followed. I said—

"But you used to look sad and oldish; you don't now. Where did you get all this youth and bubbling cheerfulness? Give me the address."

He chuckled blithely, took off his shining tile, pointed to a notched pink circlet of paper pasted into its crown, with something lettered on it, and went on chuckling while I read, "J. B——, UNDERTAKER." Then he clapped his hat on, gave it an irreverent tilt to leeward, and cried out—

"That's what's the matter! It used to be rough times with me when you knew me—insurance-agency business, you know; mighty irregular. Big fire, all right—brisk trade for ten days while people scared; after that, dull policy business till next fire. Town like this don't have fires often enough—a fellow strikes so many dull weeks in a row that he gets discouraged. But you bet you, *this* is the business! People don't wait for examples to *die*. No, sir, they drop off right along—there ain't any dull spots in the undertaker line. I just started in with two or three little old coffins and a hired hearse, and *now* look at the thing! I've worked up a business here that would satisfy any man, don't care who he is. Five years ago, lodged in an attic; live in a swell house now, with a mansard roof, and all the modern inconveniences."

"Does a coffin pay so well? Is there much profit on a coffin?"

"Go way! How you talk!" Then, with a confidential wink, a dropping of the voice, and an impressive laying of his hand on my arm; "Look here; there's one thing in this world which isn't ever cheap. That's a coffin. There's one thing in this world which a person don't ever try to jew you down on. That's a coffin. There's one thing in this world which a person don't say, "I'll look around a little, and if I find I can't do better I'll come back and take it." That's a coffin. There's one thing in this world which a person won't take in pine if he can go walnut; and won't take in walnut if he can go mahogany; and won't take in mahogany if he can go an iron casket with silver doorplate and bronze handles. That's a coffin. And there's one thing in this world which you don't have to worry around after a person to get him to pay for. And *that's* a coffin. Undertaking?—why it's the dead surest business in Christendom, and the nobbiest.

"Why, just look at it. A rich man won't have anything but your very best; and you can just pile it on, too—pile it on and sock it to him—he won't ever holler. And you take in a poor man, and if you work him right he'll bust himself on a single layout. Or especially a woman. F'r instance: Mrs. O'Flaherty comes in—widow—wiping her eyes and kind of moaning. Unhandkerchiefs one eye, bats it around tearfully over the stock; says—

"And what might ye ask for that wan?"

"Thirty-nine dollars, madam," says I.

"It's a foine big price, sure, but Pat shall be buried like a gintleman, as he was, if I have to work me fingers off for it. I'll have that wan, sor."

"Yes, madam," says I, "and it is a very good one, too; not costly, to be sure, but in this life we must cut our garment to our clothes, as the saying is." And as she starts out, I heave in, kind of casually, "This one with the white satin lining is a beauty, but I am afraid—well, sixty-five dollars *is* a rather—rather—but no matter, I felt obliged to say to Mrs. O'Shaughnessy—"

"D'ye mane to soy that Bridget O'Shaughnessy bought the mate to that joo-ul box to ship that dhrunken divil to Purgatory in?"

"Yes, madam."

"Then Pat shall go to heaven in the twin to it, if it takes the last rap the O'Flaherties can raise; and moind you, stick on some extras, too, and I'll give ye another dollar."

"And as I lay in with the livery stables, of course I don't forget to mention that Mrs. O'Shaughnessy hired fifty-four dollars' worth of hacks and flung as much style into Dennis's funeral as if he had been a duke or an assassin. And of course she sails in and goes the O'Shaughnessy about four hacks and an omnibus better. That *used* to be, but that's all played now; that is, in this particular town. The Irish got to piling up hacks so, on their funerals, that a funeral left them ragged and hungry for two years afterward; so the priest pitched in and broke it all up. He don't allow them to have but two hacks now, and sometimes only one."

"Well," said I, "if you are so lighthearted and jolly in ordinary times, what *must* you be in a epidemic?"

He shook his head.

"No, you're off, there. We don't like to see an epidemic. An epidemic don't pay. Well, of course I don't mean that, exactly; but it don't pay in proportion to the regular thing. Don't it occur to you, why?"

"No."

"Think."

"I can't imagine. What is it?"

"It's just two things."

"Well, what *are* they?"

"One's Embamming."

"And what's the other?"

"Ice."

"How is that?"

"Well, in ordinary times, a person dies, and we lay him up in ice; one day, two days, maybe three, to wait for friends to come. Takes a lot of it—melts fast. We charge jewelry rates for that ice, and war prices for attendance. Well, don't you know, when there's an epidemic, they rush 'em to the cemetery the minute the breath's out. No market for ice in an epidemic. Same with Embamming. You take a family that's able to embam, and you've got a soft thing. You can mention sixteen different ways to do it—though there *ain't* only one or two ways, when you come down to the bottom facts of it—and they'll take the highest-priced way, every time. It's human nature—human nature in grief. It don't reason, you see. 'Time being, it don't care a dam. All it wants is physical immortality for deceased, and they're willing to pay for it. All you've got to do is to just be ca'm and stack it up—they'll stand the racket. Why, man, you can take a defunct that you couldn't *give* away; and get your embamming traps around you and go to work; and in a couple of hours he is worth a cool six hundred—that's what *he's* worth. There ain't anything equal to it but trading rats for di'monds in time of famine. Well, don't you see, when there's an epidemic, people don't wait to embam. No, indeed they don't; and it hurts the business like hellth, as we say—hurts it like hell-th, *health*, see?—our little joke in the trade. Well, I must be going. Give me a call whenever you need any—I mean, when you're going by, sometime."

In his joyful high spirits, he did the exaggerating himself, if any has been done. I have not enlarged on him.

With the above brief references to inhumation, let us leave the subject. As for me, I hope to be cremated. I made that remark to my pastor once, who said, with what he seemed to think was an impressive manner—

"I wouldn't worry about that, if I had your chances."

Much he knew about it—the family all so opposed to it.

Chapter XLIV: City Sights

The old French part of New Orleans—anciently the Spanish part—bears no resemblance to the American end of the city: the American end which lies beyond the intervening brick business center. The houses are massed in blocks; are austerely plain and dignified; uniform of pattern, with here and there a departure from it with pleasant effect; all are plastered on the outside, and nearly all have long, iron-railed verandas running along the several stories. Their chief beauty is the deep, warm, varicolored stain with which time and the weather have enriched the plaster. It harmonizes with all the surroundings, and has as natural a look of belonging there as has the flush upon the sunset clouds. This charming decoration cannot be successfully imitated; neither is it to be found elsewhere in America.

The iron railings are a specialty, also. The pattern is often exceedingly light and dainty, and airy and graceful—with a large cipher or monogram in the center, a delicate cobweb of baffling, intricate forms, wrought in steel. The ancient railings are handmade, and are now comparatively rare and proportionately valuable. They are become bric-a-brac.

The party had the privilege of idling through this ancient quarter of New Orleans with the South's finest literary genius, the author of *The Grandissimes*. In him the South has found a masterly delineator of its interior life and its history. In truth, I find by experience, that the untrained eye and vacant mind can inspect it and learn of it and judge of it more clearly and profitably in his books than by personal contact with it.

With Mr. Cable along to see for you, and describe and explain and illuminate, a jog through that old quarter is a vivid pleasure. And you have a vivid *sense* as of unseen or dimly seen things—vivid, and yet fitful and darkling; you glimpse salient features, but lose the fine shades or catch them imperfectly through the vision of the imagination: a case, as it were, of ignorant nearsighted stranger traversing the rim of wide vague horizons of Alps with an inspired and enlightened longsighted native.

We visited the Old Louis Hotel, now occupied by municipal offices. There is nothing strikingly remarkable about it; but one can say of it as of the Academy of Music in New York, that if a broom or a shovel has ever been used in it there is no circumstantial evidence to back up the fact. It is curious that cabbages and hay and things do not grow in the Academy of Music; but no doubt it is on account of the interruption of the light by the benches, and the impossibility of hoeing the crop except in the aisles. The fact that the ushers grow their buttonhole bouquets on the premises shows what might be done if they had the right kind of an agricultural head to the establishment.

We visited also the venerable cathedral, and the pretty square in front of it; the one dim with religious light, the other brilliant with the worldly sort, and lovely with orange trees and blossomy shrubs; then we drove in the hot sun through the wilderness of houses and out onto the wide dead level beyond, where the villas are, and the water wheels to drain the town, and the commons populous with cows and children; passing by an old cemetery where we were told lie the ashes of an early pirate; but we took him on trust, and did not visit him. He was a pirate with a tremendous and sanguinary history; and as long as he preserved unspotted, in retirement, the dignity of his name and the grandeur of his ancient calling, homage and reverence were his from high and low; but when at last he descended into politics and became a paltry alderman, the public "shook" him, and turned aside and wept. When he died, they set up a monument over him; and little by little he has come into respect again; but it is respect for the pirate, not the alderman. Today the loyal and generous remember only what he was, and charitably forget what he became.

Thence, we drove a few miles across a swamp, along a raised shell road, with a canal on one hand and a dense wood on the other; and here and there, in the distance, a ragged and angular-limbed and moss-bearded cypress, top standing out, clear cut against the sky, and as quaint of form as the apple trees in Japanese pictures—such was our course and the surroundings of it. There was an occasional alligator swimming comfortably along in the canal, and an occasional picturesque colored person on the bank, flinging his statue-rigid reflection upon the still water and watching for a bite.

And by and by we reached the West End, a collection of hotels of the usual light summer-resort pattern, with broad verandas all around, and the waves of the wide and blue Lake Pontchartrain lapping the thresholds. We had dinner on a ground veranda over the water—the chief dish the renowned fish called the pompano, delicious as the less criminal forms of sin.

Thousands of people come by rail and carriage to West End and to Spanish Fort every evening, and dine, listen to the bands, take strolls in the open air under the electric lights, go sailing on the lake, and entertain themselves in various and sundry other ways.

We had opportunities on other days and in other places to test the pompano. Notably, at an editorial dinner at one of the clubs in the city. He was in his last possible perfection there, and justified his fame. In his suite was a tall pyramid of scarlet crayfish—large ones; as large as one's thumb; delicate palatable, appetizing. Also deviled whitebait; also shrimps of choice quality; and a platter of small soft-shell crabs of a most superior breed. The other dishes were what one might get at Delmonico's, or Buckingham Palace; those I have spoken of can be had in similar perfection in New Orleans only, I suppose.

In the West and South they have a new institution—the Broom Brigade. It is composed of young ladies who dress in a uniform costume, and go through the infantry drill, with broom in place of musket. It is a very pretty sight, on private view. When they perform on the stage of a theater, in the blaze of colored fires, it must be a fine and fascinating spectacle. I saw them go through their complex manual with grace, spirit, and admirable precision. I saw them do everything which a human being can possibly do with a broom, except sweep. I did not see them sweep. But I know they could learn. What they have already learned proves that. And if they ever should learn, and should go on the warpath down Tchoupitoulas or some of those other streets around there, those thoroughfares would bear a greatly improved aspect in a very few minutes. But the girls themselves wouldn't; so nothing would be really gained, after all.

The drill was in the Washington Artillery building. In this building we saw many interesting relics of the war. Also a fine oil painting representing Stonewall Jackson's last interview with General Lee. Both men are on horseback. Jackson has just ridden up, and is accosting Lee. The picture is very valuable, on account of the portraits, which are authentic. But, like many another historical picture, it means nothing without its label. And one label will fit it as well as another:

First Interview between Lee and Jackson.
Last Interview between Lee and Jackson.
Jackson Introducing Himself to Lee.
Jackson Accepting Lee's Invitation to Dinner.
Jackson Declining Lee's Invitation to Dinner—with Thanks.
Jackson Apologizing for a Heavy Defeat.
Jackson Reporting a Great Victory.
Jackson Asking Lee for Match.

It tells *one* story, and a sufficient one; for it says quite plainly and satisfactorily, "Here are Lee and Jackson together." The artist would have made it tell that this is Lee and Jackson's last interview if he could have done it. But he couldn't, for there wasn't any way to do it. A good legible label is usually worth, for information, a ton of significant attitude and expression in a historical picture. In Rome, people with fine sympathetic natures stand up and weep in front of the celebrated "Beatrice Cenci the Day Before her Execution." It shows what a label can do. If they did not know the picture, they would inspect it unmoved, and say, "Young Girl with Hay Fever; Young Girl with Her Head in a Bag."

I found the half-forgotten Southern intonations and elisions as pleasing to my ear as they had formerly been. A Southerner talks music. At least it is music to me, but then I was born in the South. The educated Southerner has no use for an *r*, except at the beginning of a word. He says "honah," and "dinnah," and "Gove'nuh," and "befo' the waw," and so on. The words may lack charm to the eye, in print, but they have it to the ear. When did the *r* disappear from Southern speech, and how did it come to disappear? The custom of dropping it was not borrowed from the North, nor inherited from England. Many Southerners—most Southerners—put a *y* into occasional words that begin with the *k* sound. For instance, they say Mr. K'yahtah (Carter) and speak of playing k'yahds or of riding in the k'yahs. And they have the pleasant custom—long ago fallen into decay in the North—of frequently employing the respectful "Sir." Instead of the curt Yes, and the abrupt No, they say "Yes, suh"; "No, suh."

But there are some infelicities. Such as "like" for "as" and the addition of an "at" where it isn't needed. I heard an educated gentleman say, "Like the flag officer did." His cook or his butler would have said, "Like the flag officer done." You hear gentlemen say, "Where have you been at?" And here is the aggravated form—heard a ragged street Arab say it to a comrade: "I was a-ask'n' Tom whah you was a-sett'n' at." The very elect carelessly say "will" when they mean "shall"; and many of them say, "I didn't go to do it," meaning "I didn't mean to do it." The Northern word "guess"—imported from England, where it used to be common, and now regarded by satirical Englishmen as a Yankee original—is but little used among Southerners. They say "reckon." They haven't any "doesn't" in their language; they say "don't" instead. The unpolished often use "went" for "gone." It is nearly as bad as the Northern "hadn't ought." This reminds me that a remark of a very peculiar nature was made here in my neighbourhood (in the North) a few days ago; "He hadn't ought to have went." How is that? Isn't that a good deal of a triumph? One knows the orders combined in this half-breed's architecture without inquiring: one parent Northern, the other Southern. Today I heard a schoolmistress ask, "Where is John gone?" This form is so common—so nearly universal, in fact—that if she had said "whither" instead of "where," I think it would have sounded like an affectation.

We picked up one excellent word—a word traveling to New Orleans to get; a nice limber, expressive, handy word—"lagniappe." They pronounce it lanny-*yap*. It is Spanish—so they said. We discovered it at the head of a column of odds and ends in the Picayune, the first day; heard twenty people use it the second; inquired what it meant the third; adopted it and got facility in swinging it the fourth. It has a restricted meaning, but I think the people spread it out a little when they choose. It is the equivalent of the thirteenth roll in a "baker's dozen." It is something thrown in, gratis, for good measure. The custom originated in the Spanish quarter of the city. When a child or a servant buys something in a shop—or even the mayor or the governor, for aught I know—he finishes the operation by saying—

"Give me something for lagniappe."

The shopman always responds; gives the child a bit of licorice root, gives the servant a cheap cigar or a spool of thread, gives the governor—I don't know what he gives the governor; support, likely.

When you are invited to drink—and this does occur now and then in New Orleans—and you say, "What, again?—no, I've had enough"; the other party says, "But just this one time more—this is for lagniappe." When the beau perceives that he is stacking his compliments a trifle too high, and sees by the young lady's countenance that the edifice would have been better with the top compliment left off, he puts his "I beg pardon—no harm intended," into the briefer form of "Oh, that's for lagniappe." If the waiter in the restaurant stumbles and spills a gill of coffee down the back of your neck, he says. "For lagniappe, sah," and gets you another cup without extra charge.

Notes

1. The Israelites are buried in graves—by permission, I take it, not requirement; but none else, except the destitute, who are buried at public expense. The graves are but three or four feet deep.
2. Four or five dollars is the minimum cost.

164

Willy

LILLIAN HELLMAN

Lillian Hellman (1905–84) was born in New Orleans, although she spent the majority of her life in New York City. Best known as a playwright, especially the contentious *The Children's Hour* (1934), she also wrote important volumes of autobiography, notably *An Unfinished Woman* (1969) and *Pentimento—A Book of Portraits* (1973). *Scoundrel Time* (1976) is a personal account of her conflict in the early 1950s with HUAC (House Un-American Activities Committee) during the McCarthy era.

He was married to my ridiculous great-aunt. But I was sixteen or seventeen by the time I knew she was ridiculous, having before then thought her most elegant. Her jewelry, the dresses from Mr. Worth in Paris, her hand-sewn underwear with the Alençon lace, her Dubonnet with a few drops of spirits of ammonia, were all fine stuff to me. But most of all, I was impressed with her silences and the fineness of her bones.

My first memory of Aunt Lily—I was named for her; born Pansy, she had changed it early because, she told me, "Pansy was a tacky old darky name"—is of watching one of the many fine lavallières swing between the small bumps of her breasts. How, I asked myself in those early years of worship, did my mother's family ever turn out anything so "French," so *raffinée*? It was true that her family were all thin people. and all good-looking, but Lily was a wispy, romantic specimen unlike her brothers and sisters, who were high-spirited and laughed too much over their own vigor and fancy money deals.

That is what I thought about Aunt Lily until I made the turn and the turn was as sharp as only the young can make when they realize their values have been shoddy. It was only then that I understood about the Dubonnet and recognized that the lavallières were too elaborate for the ugly dryness of the breasts, and thought the silences coma-like and stupid. But that, at least, was not the truth.

Source: Lillian Hellman, "Willy" from *Pentimento*, London and New York, 1974.

Lily was so much younger than her brothers and sisters, one of whom was my grandmother, that I don't think she was more than ten years older than my mother. It was whispered that her mother had given birth to her at sixty, and in my bewitched period that made her Biblical and in my turn-against period made her malformed.

I do not know her age or mine when I first met her, because she and her husband, Willy, their son and daughter, had been living in Mobile, and had only then, at the time of my meeting them, moved back to New Orleans. I think I was about nine or ten and I know they lived in a large house on St. Charles Avenue filled with things I thought beautiful and foreign, only to realize, in my turn-against period, that they were ornate copies of French and Italian miseries, cluttering all the tables and running along the staircase walls and newel posts on up to the attic quarters of Caroline Ducky.

Whenever we visited Aunt Lily I was sent off to Caroline Ducky with a gift of chocolate-covered cherries or a jar of pickles, because Caroline Ducky was part of my mother's childhood. Anyway, I liked her. She was an old, very black lady who had been born into slavery in my mother's family and, to my angry eyes, didn't seem to want to leave it. She occupied only part of the large attic and did what was called "the fine sewing," which meant that she embroidered initials on handkerchiefs and towels and Uncle Willy's shirts and was the only servant in the house allowed to put an iron to Aunt Lily's clothes. Caroline Ducky never came downstairs: her meals were brought to her by her daughter, Flo Ducky. Whatever I learned about that house, in the end, came mostly from Caroline Ducky, who trusted me, I think, because my nurse Sophronia was her niece and Sophronia had vouched for me at an early age. But then her own daughter, Flo Ducky, was retarded and was only allowed to deal with the heavy kitchen pans. There were many other servants in that house, ten, perhaps, but I remember only Caroline Ducky and a wheat-colored chauffeur called Peters. Peters was a fine figure in gray uniform, very unlike my grandmother's chauffeur, who was a mean-spirited slob of a German mechanic without any uniform. My grandmother and the other sister, Hattie, would often discuss Peters in a way that was clear to me only many years later, but even my innocent mother would often stop talking when Peters came into the room with Aunt Lily's Dubonnet or to suggest a cooling drive to Lake Pontchartrain.

Aunt Lily's daughter died so early after they returned to New Orleans that I do not even remember what she looked like. It was said officially that she died of consumption, supposedly caused by her insistence on sleeping on the lawn, but when anybody in my mother's family died there was always the rumor of syphilis. In any case, after her daughter's death, Aunt Lily never again appeared in a "color"—all her clothes, for the rest of her life, were white, black, gray and purple and, I believed in the early days, another testament to her world of sensibility and the heart.

The son was called Honey and to this day I do not know any other name for him. (He died about fifteen years ago in a loony bin in Mobile and there's nobody left to ask his real name.) Honey looked like his mother, thin-boned, yellowish, and always sat at dinner between Lily and his father, Uncle Willy, to "interpret" for them.

I suppose I first remember Willy at the dinner table, perhaps a year after they had moved to New Orleans, although because he was a legend I had heard about him all my life. For years I thought he was a legend only to my family, but as I grew up I realized that he was a famous character to the rest of the city, to the state, and in certain foreign parts. Depending, of course, on their own lives and natures, people admired him, envied him, or were frightened of him: in my mother's family his position in a giant corporation, his demotions, his reinstatements, his borrowings, his gamblings, were, as Jake, my grandmother's brother, said, "a sign of a nation more interested in charm than in stability, the road to the end." By which my grandmother's brother meant that Willy had gone beyond their middle-class gains made by cheating Negroes on cotton crops. But, in fairness to her family, I was later to discover that Willy had from time to time borrowed a large part of Lily's fortune, made money with it, lost it, returned it, borrowed it again, paid interest on it, and finally, by the time I met him, been refused it altogether.

I do not think that is the only reason Aunt Lily and her husband no longer spoke to one another, but that's what Honey's "interpretations" seemed to be about. Uncle Willy, his pug, good-looking, jolly face, drawn by nature to contrast with my aunt's sour delicacy, would say to Honey such things as, "Ask your mother if I may borrow the car, deprive her of Peters for a few hours, to go to the station. I will be away for two weeks, at the Boston office." Honey would repeat the message word for word to his mother on the other side of him and, always after a long silence, Aunt Lily would shrug and say, "Tell your father he does not need to ask for his car. *His* money bought it. I would have been happier with something more modest."

There were many "interpretations" about trips or cars, but the day of that particular one, Willy looked down at his plate for a long time and then, looking up, laughed at my mother's face. "Julia, Julia," he said. "You are the charming flower under the feet of the family bulls." Then, puzzling to a child, his laughter changed to anger and he rose, threw his napkin in Honey's face and said, "Tell your mother to buy herself another more modest car. Tell her to buy it with a little piece of the high interest she charged me for the loan she made." We stayed for a longer time than usual that day, although Lily didn't speak again, but on the way home my mother stopped in the nearest church, an old habit when she was disturbed, any church of any belief, and I waited outside, impatient, more than that, the way I always was.

Aunt Jenny, my father's sister, who ran a boarding-house, would take me each Saturday to the French market for the weekly food supplies. It was our custom to have lunch in the Quarter at Tujague's, and my watered wine and her unwatered wine always made for a nice time. And so the next day after Willy had told my mother she was a charming flower, I said to Jenny, "Everybody likes Mama, don't they?"

"Almost," she said, "but not you. You're jealous of your mama and you ought to get over that before it's too late."

"Mama nags," I said. "Papa understands."

"*Ach.* You and your papa. Yes, she does nag. But she doesn't know it and is a nice lady. I said you must know your mother before it is too late."

She was right. By the time I knew how much I loved my mother and understood that her eccentricities were nothing more than that and could no more be controlled than the blinking of an eye in a high wind, it was, indeed, too late. But I didn't like lectures even from Jenny.

"Uncle Willy likes Mama," I said. "I think that's hard for Aunt Lily."

Jenny stared at me. "Hard for *Lily*? Hard for your Aunt Lily?"

"You don't like her because she's thin," I said to Jenny, who was six feet tall, and heavy, and had long been telling me that my rib bones showed. "I think she's the most interesting, the only interesting, part of our family."

"Thank you," said Jenny. "Your *mother's* family. Not mine."

"I didn't mean you or Hannah," I said, "really, I ..."

"Don't worry," Jenny said as she rose, "about me, worry about yourself and why you like very thin people who have money."

I asked her what she meant, and she said that someday she would tell me if I didn't find out for myself. (I did find out, and when I told her she laughed and said I was thirty years old, but better late than never.)

It was that year, the year of my mother being a flower, and now, in my memory, the year before my sharp turn, that I saw most of Aunt Lily. I went to the house two or three times a week and whatever she was doing, and she was never doing much, she would put aside to give me hot chocolate, sending Honey to another room as if she and I were ready to exchange the pains of women. I usually went in the late afternoons, after school, but sometimes I was invited to Saturday lunch. The visits were hung in a limbo of fog over water, but I put that down to the way people who had greater culture and sensibility than the rest of us lived their special lives. I don't know what I meant by culture: in Aunt Lily's house there were not books other than a set of Prescott, and once when Jenny and I went to our second-balcony seats for a concert of Verdi's *Requiem* Aunt Lily sent for us to join her in her box. After a while, Jenny said to me, "Would you ask your Cultivated Majesty Aunt please not to hum the Wedding March? It doesn't go well with the 'Libera me' and there are other reasons she should forget it." But I put that down to Jenny's customary sharpness and went on with my interest in Aunt Lily.

Ever since her daughter's death Aunt Lily made soft sounds from time to time and talked even less than before, although unconnected phrases like "lost life," "the hopes of youth," "inevitable waste," would come at intervals. I was never sure whether she was talking of her daughter or of herself, but I did know that, for a woman who had never before used her hands, she now often touched my hair, patted my arm, or held Honey firmly by the hand.

And I thought it was the need to deny the death of her child that made possible the scene I once saw when I arrived for a visit while Lily was out shopping. The car came into the driveway to the side door and from the window I saw Peters reach in for Lily's hand. As she stepped from the car, she twisted and slipped. Peters caught her and carried her to the door. On the way there, her head moved down to kiss his hair.

I did not know how to cross the room away from the window, how to face what I had seen, so I ran up to the third floor to call upon Caroline Ducky. Past the second landing I heard Honey's voice behind me. He said, "He does it to her."

"Does what?"

"You're older than me," he said, and ran up ahead of me. He was larger, taller than I, and his face was now sweaty and vacant.

I said, "What's the matter?"

"Ssh and I'll show it to you."

I went by him and was caught by the arm. "Want to see it?"

"See what?"

"My thingy."

I hadn't seen a thingy since I was four years old and maybe my no came too slow, because my shoulders were held with his one hand, my dress lifted with the other, and I felt something knocking against my stomach.

"Open up," he shouted into his future. "Open up." I sneezed so hard that he fell back against the staircase wall. I was subject to sneezing fits and now I stood in the full force of one violent rack after another. When the sneezing was over, Honey had disappeared and Caroline Ducky was standing a few steps above me. I don't know how long she had been there but I followed her to the attic, was told to press my upper lip and given a Coca-Cola spiced heavily with spirits of ammonia, an old and perhaps dangerous New Orleans remedy for anything you didn't understand.

Caroline Ducky looked up from her sewing. "You be careful of that Honey." (She was to be right: at twenty he raped a girl at a picnic, at twenty-two or -three he was sued by a Latvian girl for assault, and his later years in the Mobile loony bin were in some way connected with an attack on a woman who was fishing in the Dog River.)

Caroline Ducky said, "I knew what he was going to be the day it took him three days to get himself out."

"Out of what?"

"Out of the stomach of his mother."

"What did you know?"

"I knew what I knew."

I laughed with an old irritation. Such answers were, perhaps still are, a Southern Negro form of put-down to the questions of white people.

"His mama didn't want him, his papa didn't want him, and a child nobody wants got nothing ahead but seeping sand."

"Then what did they have him for? They don't like each other."

"She trapped him," said Caroline Ducky. "Mr. Willy, he was drunk."

"Things can't start from birth, that early," I said from the liberalism I was learning.

"That ain't early, the day you push out, that's late."

"What did you mean Aunt Lily trapped him? How can a man be trapped?"

"You too young for the question, I too old for the answer." She was pleased with herself and laughed.

"Then what did you start it for? You all do that. It's gotten mean."

Grown people were always on the edge of telling you something valuable and then withdrawing it, a form of bully-teasing. (Little of what they withdrew had any value, but the pain of learning that can be unpleasant.) And I was a particular victim of this empty mystery game because, early and late, an attempt was made to hide from me the contempt of my mother's family for my father's lack of success, and thus there was a kind of patronizing pity for me and my future. I think I sensed that mystery when I was very young and to protect what little I had to protect I constructed the damaging combination that was not to leave me until I myself made money: I rebelled against my mother's family, and thus all people who were rich, but I was frightened and impressed by them; and the more frightened and impressed I grew the more aimless became my anger, which sometimes expressed itself in talk about the rights of Negroes and on two Sundays took the form of deliberately breaking plates at my grandmother's table. By fourteen my heart was with the poor except on the days when it was with those who ground them under. I remember that period as a hell of self-dislike, but I do not now mean to make fun of it: not too many years later, although old shriveled leaves remain on the stump to this day, I understood that I lived under an economic system of increasing impurity and injustice for which I, and all those like me, pay with ridiculous wounds to the spirit.

"What's rotten mean," asked Caroline Ducky, "you snip-talking girl?"

"Rotten mean, all of you."

"I like your Uncle Willy," she said, "but he ain't no man of God."

She closed her eyes and crossed herself and that meant my visit was finished. She was the only Baptist I ever knew who crossed herself and I doubt if she knew that she used the Greek cross. I left the house and went far out of my way to back-of-town, the Negro section, to put a dime in the poor box of the Baptist Church. I did this whenever I had an extra dime and years before, when my nurse Sophronia had proudly told my father about it, he said to me, "Why don't you give it to the Synagogue? Maybe we never told you that's where you belong." I said I couldn't do that because there was no synagogue for Negroes and my father said that was perfectly true, he'd never thought about that before.

For years I told myself that it was from that day, the day Caroline Ducky said he was no man of God, that I knew about Uncle Willy, but now I am not sure—diaries carry dates and pieces of conversation, but no record of family gossip—when I knew that he had been a poor boy in Mobile, Alabama, working young on the docks, then as a freight boss for a giant company doing business in Central America, and had married Lily when he was twenty-four and she was thirty. It was said that he had married her for money and respectability, but after six or seven years he couldn't have needed either because by that time he was vice-president of the company, living with the first fast cars, a hundred-foot yacht, the St. Charles Avenue great house, an apartment at the old Waldorf in New York, a hunting place on Jekyll Island, an open and generous hand with everybody, including, I think, my father in his bad years.

Sometimes in those years, years of transition for me, the dinner table of the St. Charles Avenue house included other guests—the "interpretations" of Honey between his mother and father still went on but were circumspect when these people were present—fine-looking, heavy men, with blood in their faces and sound to their voices, and then I heard talk of what they did and how they did it. I don't know when I understood it, or if anybody explained it to me, but there were high tales of adventure, with words like "good natives," "troublemakers," and the National City Bank, ships and shipments that had been sabotaged, teaching lessons to peons, and long, highly relished stories of a man called Christmas, a soldier of fortune who worked for my uncle's company as a mercenary and had a great deal to do with keeping the peons quiet. At one dinner the talk was of "outbreaks," arranged by "native troublemakers"—two men who worked for my uncle's company had been murdered—and the need for firm action, revenge. The firm action was taken by Mr. Christmas, who strung up twenty-two men of a Guatemalan village, cut out their tongues, and burned down the village, driving the others into the jungle. Uncle Willy did not join in the pleasure of that tale, but he said nothing to stop it, nor to interfere with a plan to send a boat-load of guns to Christmas to "insure the future."

The terrors and exploitations of this company were to become a world scandal, the first use of the U.S. Marines as private mercenaries to protect American capital. But even in my uncle's time, the scandal was of such proportions that the guns and the killings tapered off enough to convince me that the company had grown "liberal" as it established schools, decent houses and hospitals for the natives. When, in 1969, I told that to a graduate student from Costa Rica, he laughed and said he thought I should come and see for myself.

In any case, my reaction to those dinner tales at Aunt Lily's was an unpleasant mixture: my distaste for what I heard did not stop my laughter, when they laughed, at the shrewdness and heroics of "our boys" as they triumphed over the natives. I believed in Willy's personal affection and generosity toward the poor people he exploited. But the values of grown people had long pounded at my head, torn me apart with their contradictions.

But I could not now, in truth, get straight the tangled mess of that conflict which went so many years past my childhood: I know only that there were changes and that one day I felt that Aunt Lily was silly and that I had been a fool for ever thinking anything else. But I went on being sympathetic and admiring of Uncle Willy, interested in the day of his youth when he had ridden mules through Central and South American jungles, speaking always with an almost brotherly admiration of the natives from whom he "bought" the land. I am sure that his adventures made him interesting, the money he earned from them was different to me than money earned from a bank or a store, that his fall from high position seemed to me a protest, which it wasn't. And I had other feelings for him, although I didn't know about them for years after the time of which I speak.

But I already thought Aunt Lily foolish stuff the day of the outbreak. We had arrived in New Orleans only a few hours before she telephoned to ask my mother to come immediately. My mother said she was tired from the long journey, but that evidently didn't suit Aunt Lily because my mother told Jenny she guessed she'd have to go immediately, something bad must have happened. Jenny sniffed and said the something bad that had happened was probably the lateness of the Paris mails that failed to bring Aunt Lily's newest necklace. My mother said it was her duty to go and I said I would go along with her. Since I didn't often volunteer to go anywhere with my mother, she was pleased, and we set off at my mother's slow pace. Lily was pacing around her upstairs sitting room, her eyes blank and unfocused, and, annoyed with seeing me, she said immediately that it was too bad my hair was so straight and muddy-blonde, now that I was fourteen. But she sent for my hot chocolate and her watered Dubonnet, and my mother nervously chatted about our New York relatives until I went to a corner with a copy of *Snappy Stories*.

I guess Lily forgot about me because she said to my mother, "You've heard about Willy."

My mother said no, she hadn't heard about Willy, what was the matter, and Aunt Lily said, "I don't believe you. Jenny Hellman must have told you."

I don't think anybody in her life had ever before told my mother they didn't believe her, and I was amazed at the firmness with which she said that Jenny had told her nothing, Jenny didn't move in large circles, worked too hard, and she, my mother, always tried not to lie before God.

"God," said Aunt Lily. "*God*? He hasn't kept everybody else in town from lying at me. Me and Honey and my brothers and sisters who warned me early against Willy. It isn't the first time, but now it's in the open, now that he says he's paid me back when, of course, he still owes me sixty thousand," and she began to cry.

I saw my mother's face, the pity, the getting ready, and knew that she was going to walk into, be a part of, one of those messes the innocent so often walk into, make worse, and are victimized by. I left the room.

I met Peters in the hall. When he spoke to me, I realized he had never spoken to me before. "Miss Lily with your mama? Miss Lily upsetting herself?"

"I guess so," and started up the stairs toward Caroline Ducky.

"Miss Caroline Ducky don't feel good," he said. "I wouldn't bother her today." I went past him.

When Caroline Ducky answered my knock and we had kissed, I said, "Sorry you don't feel good. Your rheumatism?"

"One thing, five things. They mix around when you getting old. Sit you down and tell me what you reading."

This was an old habit between us. She liked stories and I would sum up for her a book I had read, making the plot more simple, cutting down the number of people, and always, as the story went on, she forgot it came from a book, thought it came from life, and would approve or disapprove. But I didn't want to fool around that day.

"What's Aunt Lily so upset about? She made Mama come right away. Something about Uncle Willy and the whole town knowing."

Caroline Ducky said, "The whole town don't know and don't care. Has to do with that Cajun girl, up Bayou Teche."

I was half crazy with pleasure, as I always was with this kind of stuff, but I had ruined it so many times before by going fast with questions that now I shut up. Caroline Ducky, after a while, handed me her embroidery hoop to work on and went to stand by her small window, leaning out to look at the street. In the last few years she had done this a good deal and I figured it had to do with age and never going into the street except for a funeral, and never liking a city where she had been made to live.

She said, over her shoulder, "I'm making a plan to die in high grass. All this Frenchy stuff in this town. Last night, I ask for greens and pot likker. That shit nigger at the stove send me up gumbo, Frenchy stuff. Tell your ma to cook me up some greens and bring 'em here. Your ma used to be a beauty on a wild horse. A wild Alabama horse."

I suppose there was something wrong with my face because she said, "Your ma's changed. City no good for country folk, your ma and me."

"What's that mean?"

"Your ma's a beauty inside out."

I didn't know why she was talking about my mother and I didn't want to talk about her that day, but I think Caroline Ducky meant that my mother was a country girl and the only comfortable period of her life had been with the Alabama Negroes of her childhood. New Orleans and New York, a worldly husband, a difficult child, unloving sisters and a mother of formidable coldness had made deep marks on my mother by the time I was old enough to understand her eccentric nature.

I said, "Uncle Willy going to marry a Cajun girl?"

"What? *What?* There ain't a white child born to woman ain't crazy," said Caroline Ducky. "Niggers sit around wasting time talk about white folk being pig-shit mean. Not me. All I ever say, they crazy. Lock up all white folk, give 'em to eat, but lock 'em up. Than all the trouble be over. What you talking about, *marry* Cajun girl?"

"All I meant was it must be kind of hard for Aunt Lily. Uncle Willy's being in love. I guess nobody wants to share their husband. My father isn't faithful to my mother."

"How you know that?"

"I found out years ago at a circus when ..."

"Shut up," said Caroline Ducky, "this house pushing me to my grave."

There were sudden sounds from downstairs, as if somebody was calling. I opened Caroline Ducky's door but nobody seemed to be calling me, so I closed it again and went back to the embroidery hoop hoping to please Caroline Ducky into more talk, but the sounds downstairs grew louder and Caroline Ducky was too busy listening to pay any attention to anything I might ask.

She laughed. "Well, well. Time now for Miss Lily's morphine shot."

This was the richest hour I had ever spent and I was willing to try anything.

"Look, Caroline Ducky, I'll take you back to Demopolis. I'll get the money from Papa or I can sell my squirrel coat and books. I'll take you back, I swear."

"Shut the shit," said Caroline Ducky, good and mad. "Take me home! What I going to do when I get there? Nobody there for me except the rest of your shit catfish family. Home. What home I got?"

The door opened and Uncle Willy came in. "What's going on?" he said to Caroline Ducky.

"She's calling in the securities," said Caroline Ducky, in a new kind of English, almost without an accent. "Taking 'em from the bank."

"Christ," said Uncle Willy. "When?"

"Today's Sunday, tomorrow's Monday."

"God in Heaven," said Uncle Willy. "What a bastard she is, without telling me. That gives me sixteen hours to borrow three hundred thousand dollars. Maybe Peters just told you that to scare me."

Caroline Ducky smiled. "You too smart for what you're saying."

I had never heard anything so wonderful in my life and, although I didn't know what they were talking about, I knew I would, it was just around the corner. I suppose I was straining with the movements of body and face that have worried so many people in the years after that, because Uncle Willy realized I was in the room.

He smiled at me. "Hello, Lillian. Would you lend me three hundred thousand dollars for a month?"

I said, "You bet. If I had it, I'd ..."

He bowed. "Thank you. Then maybe somebody else will. If they do, I'll take you fishing."

Several years before, Willy had taken my father and me and one of the big-faced men called Hatchey on his large boat and we had had a fine two days fishing in the Gulf. My pleasure in the boat had pleased Willy and there had always been talk of another trip after that. Now he left the room, patting my head as he passed me, and Caroline Ducky fell asleep by the window. I went downstairs. I heard my mother say to somebody that things would be better now that the doctor had arrived.

Walking back to my Aunt Jenny's boarding-house, I said, "So she is having her morphine. Gets it often, I guess."

My mother stared at me. "What makes you think anything like that?"

"Caroline Ducky. Plenty makes me think plenty. Like what about all that money she's making Uncle Willy pay back because of his Cajun girl?"

"My goodness," my mother whispered. "Please don't speak that way. Please."

And I knew I had gold if I could get the coins together. But it was no use because my mother was moving her lips in prayer and that meant she had left the world for a while.

For the next few days I tried games on Jenny, hinting at the morphine, deliberately mispronouncing it, giving her pieces of the conversation between Uncle Willy and Caroline Ducky, saying that I had read in books that men often had outside women like the Cajun girl and what did she think, but I got nowhere. Jenny said we should mind our own business because rich people like my ma's family often got into muddles not meant for the rest of us.

It was a difficult time for me. I wandered about the house at night and Mrs. Caronne, Aunt Jenny's oldest boarder, complained; I wrote two poems about the pleasures of autumn love; I skipped school and spent the days sitting in front of St. Louis Cathedral and one night I wandered back-of-town and got chased home by a cop. I was, of course, at an age of half understanding the people of my world, but I was sure, as are most young people, that there were simple answers and the world, or my own limitations, were depriving me of a mathematical solution. I began, for the first time in my life, to sulk and remain silent, no longer having any faith in what I would say if I did talk, and no faith in what I would hear from anybody else. The notebooks of those days are filled with question marks: the large funny, sad questions of the very young.

The troubles of Aunt Lily were not spoken about and my mother, as far as I know, did not return to the house. But I did, every few days, circling it, standing down the street, seeing nothing, not even Honey. But after two weeks that was unbearable and so I decided to take some pickles to Caroline Ducky. As I turned in the back entrance, Uncle Willy came out the side entrance to load his car with fishing rods and a shotgun. He looked fine and easy in old tweed clothes and good boots.

When he saw me he said, "I'm going fishing and maybe a bird or two."

"Oh," I said, "I wish I were going. I do. I do."

"I'd like to have you," he said.

It's been too many years for me to remember how long we drove on the river road, but it was a long way and I was happier—exalted was the word I used when I thought about it afterward—than I had ever been before. It was as if I had changed my life and was proud of myself for the courage of the change. The wilder the country grew, the more we bumped along on the oyster shell roads, the wilder grew my fantasies: I was a rebel leader going to Africa to arouse my defeated tribe; I was a nun on my way to a leper colony; and when a copperhead crossed the road I was one of those crazy lady dancers who wound snakes around their bodies and seduced all men. Willy and I did not speak for a very long time, not one sentence, and then he said, "Oh, Lord, what about your mama, a toothbrush, all that stuff?"

There are many ways of falling in love and one seldom is more interesting or valid than another unless, of course, one of them lasts so long that it becomes something else, like your arm or leg about which you neither judge nor protest. I was not ever to fall in love very often, but certainly this was the first time and I would like to think that I learned from it. But the mixture of ecstacy as it clashed with criticism of myself and the man was to be repeated all my life, and the only thing that made the feeling for Uncle Willy different was the pain of that first recognition: not of love, but of the struggles caused by love; the blindness of a young girl trying to make simple sexual desire into something more complex, more poetic, more unreachable.

Somewhere, after that silent time, we stopped at a small store where Uncle Willy seemed to know the old lady who was sitting on the porch. He telephoned my mother from a back room and came out to say that all was O.K. He bought me a toothbrush and a comb, a pair of boots, heavy socks, a heavy woolen shirt, and twenty-four handkerchiefs. Maybe it was the extravagance of twenty-four that made me cry.

The bayou country has changed now, and if I hadn't seen it again a few months ago I would have forgotten what it looked like, which is the measure of the strangeness of that day because I remember best what things look like and forget what it has been like to be with them. But even now I could walk the route that Willy took that day so long ago as we left the car and began to move north, sometimes on a rough path, more often through undergrowth of strange and tangled roots. Swamp oak, cypress, sent out roots above ground and small plants and fern pushed against the wild high dark green leaves of a plant I had never seen before. There was constant movement along the ground and I was sweating with fear of snakes. Once Uncle Willy, ahead of me, called out and waved me away. I saw that the swamp had come in suddenly and that he was deep in the mush, pulling himself up and out by throwing his arms around a black gum tree. He was telling me to move to my left but I didn't understand what he meant until I sank into the mud, my feet, my ankles going in as if underground giants were pulling at them. I liked it, it was soft and comfortable, and I learned down to watch the things moving around me: crawfish, flat small things the shape of salamanders, then the brownness of something the size of my hand with a tail twice as long. I don't know how long I stood there, but I know Willy had called to me several times before I saw him. Above me now he had tied a branch to his pants belt and was throwing it a foot from me. It could not have been easy for him to pull me out as he stood on uncertain ground with my dead weight at the other end. I watched the power of the shoulders and the arms with the sleepy admiration of a woman in love. I think he was puzzled by my slowness, my lack of excitement or fear, because he kept asking me if something had happened and said he had been a fool to try a shortcut to the house.

I don't know where I thought we were going, or if I thought about it at all, but the house was the meanest I had ever seen and, over the next two days, more crowded with people. There was a room with three beds, and two others of Spanish moss on the floor, a kitchen of ells and wandering corners, dirty with coal smoke, filled with half-broken chairs and odd forgotten things against the walls. Willy was as gay as my father had always said he was, embracing people who came and went, throwing a small child in the air, and cooing at a baby who lay in an old box. He was at home here, this man who was accustomed to the most immaculate of houses, the imitated eighteenth-century elegance of Aunt Lily's house. The dirt and mess pleased him and so did the people. I could not sort them out, the old from the young, the relations of the men to the women, what child belonged to whom, but they were all noisy with pleasure at Willy's arrival, and bowls of hot water were brought from the stove and an old woman and a young woman cleaned his boots and washed his feet. A young girl of about my age took my shoes to dry on the stove and gave me a bowl and a dirty rag to wash with. I must have drawn back from the rag—obsessive cleanliness now seems to me less embarrassing than it seemed that day, New Orleans being a dirty city when I was young, with open sewers and epidemics—because Willy said something in Cajun French and the rag was taken out of my hand.

It was a good night, the best I had ever had up to then. The dinner was wonderful: jambalaya, raccoon stew, and wild duck with bitter pickles, all hot with red pepper that made the barrel-wine necessary after each bite. The talk was loud and everybody spoke together except when Willy spoke, but we were deep in Cajun country and my school French needed adjustment to the omitted sounds and dropped syllables. My pleasure in food and wine was, of course, my pleasure in Willy as he chased wine with whiskey, wolfed the food, and boomed and laughed and was amused, and pleased with me. I remember that a very tall man came into the room, a man in city clothes, and that my uncle left with him to sit on the porch, and everybody else disappeared. But after that I don't remember much because I was drunk and woke up in the bedroom that smelled of other people and saw two women on beds and one on the floor. I have never known whether I heard that night or the next night three quarrelsome voices outside the house, and my uncle's voice saying, "If it goes wrong, and the last one did, I'll get the blame. Nobody else. And that will be curtains." A man kept saying, "You got no choice." I had heard that voice before but I was too sleepy to think about it. Certainly by the time Willy shook me awake at dawn he was in a fine humor, laughing down in my face, saying I must never tell my mother he had got me drunk and to get ready now for the ducks.

I have been duck shooting many times since that early morning, but I have never liked it again because it never again had to do with the pleasure of crouching near Willy in the duck blind. I was then, was always to be, a bad shot and once Willy was angry with me because I ruined the flight overhead, but later he did so well and the dogs made such fine recoveries that we came back with fourteen ducks by nine o'clock. The house was empty and Willy made us giant sandwiches of many meats and peppers and said we were going to the store. We walked around to where we had left the car and drove down the bayou road to a settlement of twenty or thirty houses and a store that seemed to have everything—barrels of coffee, boots, bolts of cloth, guns, sausages, cheeses and ropes of red peppers, fur hats, oars, fish traps and dried fish.

I was standing on the porch when I heard Willy say to somebody inside, "Wait a minute, please, I'm on the phone. Certainly you can see that." Then a young man passed me carrying to our car a case of liquor, three or four giant bolts of cloth, a box of ladies' shoes with fancy buckles, a carton of coffee beans and a sewing machine. Inside, Willy said, "Hatchey, Hatchey? Ask them to hold off. No, it's not too late. Send a cable to the boat." (I don't know if I knew then the name Hatchey belonged to the man I had met on Willy's boat, and who had been outside on the porch the night before, or if I recognized it a long time later when my father told my mother about the troubles.) Then Willy came out and got in the car. The owner of th store called out about a check for last month's stuff and now all this, but Willy waved him away and said his office would send it. The owner said that would be fine, he just hoped Mr. Willy understood he needed the money, and the car drove off without me. A few minutes later it made a circle in the road and came back to the store. Willy opened the door for me and said, "Forgive me, kid. It's not a good day."

When we reached the house, Willy got out of the car and strode off. I didn't see him again until supper and then, as people thanked him for the gifts, he was bad-tempered and drank a lot. There had been plans for treeing raccoons that night, but Willy wouldn't go and wouldn't let me go. He and I sat on the porch for a long time while he drank whiskey and one of the old ladies brought pitchers of water for him. I think he had forgotten I was there because suddenly he began to whistle, as short call, then a long call. A young woman came down a side path as if she had been waiting there. She sat on the porch steps, at his feet. The second time he touched her hair I made a sound I had never heard myself make before, but neither of them noticed. A long time later, he threw an empty whiskey bottle into space, got up from his chair, toppled it as the girl rose to help him. She moved in back of him, put both arms under his, and they moved down the road. I followed them, not caring that I could almost certainly be heard as the oyster shell path crunched under me. They didn't go very far. There was another house, hidden by the trees, and then I knew I had seen the girl several times before; a big, handsome, heavy girl with fine dark hair.

I went back to the porch and sat there all night in a state that I could not describe with any truth because I believe that what I felt that night was what I was to feel about myself and other people years later: the humiliation of vanity, the irrational feeling of rejection from a man who, of course, paid me no mind, and had no reason to do so. It is possible to feel many conflicts and not know they are conflicts when you are young: I was at one minute less than nothing and, at another, powerful enough to revenge myself with the murder of Willy. My head and body seemed not to belong together, unable to carry the burden of me. Then, as later, I revenged myself on myself: when the sun came up I left the porch, no longer fearing the swamps. On the way down the road I, who many years later was to get sick at the sight of one in a zoo, stumbled on a snake and didn't care. A few hours after that, a truck gave me a ride into New Orleans. I had been walking in the wrong direction. I did not see Willy again for five years, and if he worried about my disappearance that night, I was never to hear about it.

One July day, three or four years later, on a beach, my father said to my mother, "What's the verdict on Willy?" He was asking what my mother's family was saying.

She said, "I'm sorry for him."

"Yes," said my father, "I am sure you are, but that's not what I'm asking."

"What can they do." she said, as she always did when my father attacked her family. "It isn't their fault that he lost everything."

"Have they forbidden you to see him?"

"Now, now," said my mother.

"So they have forbidden you."

"I'll see him as my conscience dictates," said my mother, "forbid or not, but I don't want fights."

I was old enough, grown by now, to say, "What happened?"

My father said, "He sent down a shipload of guns with Hatchey More intended for Christmas to use. They stopped the ship. There was a scandal."

"Guns to put down the natives?"

"Yes."

"You forgive that?" I asked.

"It's always been a disgrace," said my father who, to the end of his life, was a kind of left liberal who had admiration for the capitalist victors. "But it wasn't all Willy himself. He was just acting for the company. He happened to get caught. So they fired him. That old shooting-up stuff isn't liked by the new boys. Too raw. So Willy took the rap."

"And you feel sorry for him?"

"Yes I do," said my father, "he's stone dead broke. He was good to me."

I said, "He's a murderer."

"Oh, my! Oh, my!" said my mother. "We're all weak vessels."

During those years, because I had started to go to college, we went less often to New Orleans, three of four times, perhaps, for a month. On each visit, my mother went to see Aunt Lily, but I never again went in the front door of the house. I would go to the kitchen entrance to call on Caroline Ducky, the last time a few months before she died. She looked fine, that hot June day, more vigorous than ever. We spoke of Uncle Willy. She took for granted that I knew what everybody else knew: he had been thrown out of "the big company," had started his own fruit import company and was, according to New Orleans gossip, having a hard time. Somehow, somewhere, my aunt's money was again involved, but that made no sense to me because I couldn't see why she gave it or why he once again took it from her. But then I was a young eighteen and so little of what older people did made any sense to me that I had stopped worrying about it, finding it easier and more rewarding to understand people in books.

On one of the visits to Caroline Ducky, she said, "You ever see your Uncle Willy?"

"No."

"Me neither, much. He come around this house maybe once a month, pick up something, sleep in his office."

"Or with the Cajun girl."

"What Cajun girl? The part nigger Cajun girl?"

"I don't know," I said. "It doesn't make any difference to me if she's part nigger."

"Well," said Caroline Ducky's loud voice, "it makes a difference to me, you little white Yankee know-nothing."

I had already come half distance up the slippery mountain dangers of liberalism. "I think maybe it's the only solution in the end. Whites and blacks ..."

Caroline Ducky's large sewing basket went by my head. The old lady had remarkable strength, because when she saw the basket had missed me she rose and pulled me from the chair. "Get you down and pick up the mess you made."

As I was crawling around for needles and spools, fitting thimbles back into the pretty old box, she said, "That a nice box. Your mama gave it to me. I leave it to you when I go to die."

"I don't want it. I don't like people to throw things at me."

"You got a hard road to go," she said. "Part what you born from is good, part a mess of shit. Like your Aunt Lily. She made the shit and now she sit in it and poke around."

I was old enough to know what passed for wisdom among ladies: "I guess she's not had an easy time, Aunt Lily. Uncle Willy wanting her money, and his girls and all. That's what many people say."

"Many people is full a shit." With the years Caroline Ducky said shit more often than anybody I ever met except the head carpenter at the old Lyceum Theatre in Rochester, New York.

"Willy's got his side," said the old lady. "Where and why you think the morphine come here?"

I was so excited that I dropped the thread I was rewinding and tried not to shout. "The morphine the doctor gives Aunt Lily for her headaches?"

"He don't give her no morphine 'cause she don't have no headaches. Getting bad now, she won't last long." And Caroline Ducky giggled. (She was wrong. Aunt Lily lived another twenty-three years.) I guess Caroline Ducky was savoring Aunt Lily's death because she kept giggling for a while. Then she said, "That Peters ain't all nigger. His grandpa had a Wop store on Rampart Street. Wops know about stuff like that."

"Stuff like what?"

"Morphine," she screamed. "You wearing me out. And Wops make good fancy men. Peters been with your Aunt Lily long time now, but Mona Simpson down the road had him before that."

Over thirty years later, when *Toys in the Attic* had been produced and published, I had a letter from Honey. I guess he was out of the Mobile loony bin, at least for a while, because the letter had a San Diego postmark. He wanted to know if I ever came San Diego way, were my aunts still living and did I ever visit New Orleans; he himself never went there anymore although he still owned the St. Charles Avenue house, and, by the way, had I meant Mrs. Prine in my play to be his mother and her fancy man to be Peters? If I had, he didn't mind a bit, he'd just like to know. I had not realized until Honey's letter that the seeds of Mrs. Prine had, indeed, flown from Aunt Lily's famous gardenias to another kind of garden, but I thought it wise to deny even that to anybody as nutty as Honey. I showed my denial to Hammett, who talked me out of mailing it, saying that the less I had to do with Honey the better.

And that was because years before the letter, and years after that last time I ever saw Caroline Ducky, Aunt Lily and Honey, on her yearly New York buying sprees for jewelry and clothes and furniture, came twice to visit us on the farm in Pleasantville. I don't know why I invited them, some old hangover of curiosity, I guess, wanting to fill in missing parts of myself.

The first visit was O.K., although Honey seemed even more odd than I remembered and there was some mention of his nervous troubles. After they left, the cook reported that she had seen him kick our largest poodle and put a half-eaten piece of chocolate cake in his pocket.

A few years later Aunt Lily and Honey drove out with my father on a Sunday morning. Honey and I went swimming and I showed him the stables, where he teased a bad-tempered pony who kicked him. At lunch the conversation was disjointed. My aunt, as usual, ate almost nothing, but Honey went four times to the buffet table.

My father said, "You have a good capacity, Honey. The fish is pretty good, but how can you eat that other junk?"

"That other junk," I said, "is sauerbraten. I cooked it for the first time, to please you. It's German and I thought you'd like it."

"It can't be German," said my father, "it's Jewish. I don't know where you learned to make bad Jewish food."

When Dash laughed I was about to say something about loyalty, but was interrupted by Aunt Lily, who said to Honey, "Go vomit, dear."

Honey said, "I don't want to."

Aunt Lily sighed. Then she turned to my father. "You still see my husband, so called?"

"I'd like to see Willy, but I don't get home much anymore, and Willy doesn't come to New York."

"Oh, yes, he does," said Aunt Lily, "he comes all the time. He just doesn't want to see you anymore. He has no loyalty to anybody."

My father's face was angry. "He doesn't come North and you know it, because he doesn't have any money. None."

"That's right," said Honey through a mouthful of something. "Mama took it all. It's for me, she says, but she gives a lot to Peters."

Aunt Lily seemed to be dozing, so Honey said it again. When he got no answer he said it the third time and added, "That's because of fucking."

My father laughed. "Remember, Honey, my daughter is in the room." Then he said to Dash, "Some nuts." And he got up from the table to get himself a piece of sauerbraten.

Dash said to me, "Your father who hates the stuff has now eaten four pieces of it."

"You have to try everything to know you don't like it," said my father.

Aunt Lily turned to Honey. "I don't like your talk. Shut your face."

My father said to Aunt Lily, "Never punish a child for telling the truth. Haven't I lived by that, Lillian?"

"And by much else," I said.

My father turned to Dash. "Lillian's got the disposition of her mother's family. My family were good-natured. Look what's happening to Honey."

Honey had gone out into the hallway and was standing on his head. Aunt Lily said, "It's his way of adjusting his stomach. The doctor told me Willy has syphilis."

I said to Aunt Lily, "I don't believe you. Uncle Willy is a fine man. I admire him very much."

Dash said, "Watch it, you're not going to like what you're saying."

Soon after lunch, Aunt Lily said she wanted "a lie-down," was there a room to rest in. I took her upstairs, Dash went to his room, my father and I sat reading, and once in a while I watched from the window to see that Honey was doing nothing more than dozing on the lawn. Toward four o'clock their car arrived and I went to tell Aunt Lily. There was no answer to my knocks, but when I opened the door Aunt Lily was not asleep: she was sitting in a chair, staring out the window at the top of a tree. I spoke to her several times, moved in front of her, leaned over her. There was no sign of recognition, no answer. I went to get Honey. He was sitting in the car. Before I spoke he said, "She gets like that."

"What's the matter with her?"

"Peters takes care of it, not me. I'll send him back tomorrow."

"Where are you going?"

"To New York. I got a date."

I said to the chauffeur, "Wait here, please. This gentleman can't pay for the car without his mother," and went off to find Hammett. He put down his book and went with me to the room where Aunt Lily was sitting. He pulled a chair up next to her.

"You're a very handsome man," she said. "Handsome people have an easier time in this vale of tears."

"Your car is waiting," he said.

"I hope you are good to my niece. Are you good to ..." and faltered over my name.

"Better than she deserves," said Dash. "Please get up. I will help you to the car."

"In our South," she said, "it is a mark of woman's trust when she allows the use of her first name. Call me Lily."

"No," he said, "one is enough," and reaching down for her arms he brought her to her feet. But he had not correctly gauged her humor, because she pulled sharply away from him, moved to the bureau, and held tight to its sides.

I think she saw me for the first time. She said, "What are you doing here? You like Willy. You're no good."

"We'll talk about that another day," Dash said and moved quickly to take away the alligator pocketbook that had been her reason for the move to the bureau.

"Give me my bag immediately," she said, "there's a great deal of jewelry in that bag."

Dash laughed. "More than jewelry. Come along."

I followed them down the stairs and stood on the porch as Dash moved her down the driveway to the car. Once she stumbled and, as he caught her, she threw off his arm and moved away with the overdignified motions of a drunk. As Dash shut the door of the car, I heard Honey laugh and he waved to me as they drove past the porch.

"Well," said Dash, "that will be enough of them, I hope."

"What was that about her pocketbook?"

"She wanted a fix. I don't know what kind and don't want to. A bad pair. Why don't you leave them alone?"

"What did you mean when I said Uncle Willy was a fine man and you said I wasn't going to like what I was saying?"

"You told me that even as a child you hated what his company was doing, the murders, and what it meant to you."

"I never told you Willy did the murders. He's a good man. He just went where life took him, I guess."

"Oh, sure. Now let's leave that talk for another day or forever."

"Why should we leave it? You always say that when ..."

"Because I want to leave it," he said, "maybe in the hope you'll find out for yourself."

I thought about that for a few days, sulked with it, then left it and forgot about it.

A year later Dash and I moved to Hollywood for four or five months, each of us to write a movie. Soon after we got there, we had one of our many partings: Hammett was drinking heavily, dangerously. I was sick of him and myself and so one weekend I took off to see my aunts in New Orleans. I would not have liked to live with them for very long, but for a few days I always liked their modest, disciplined life in the shabby little house that was all they could afford since each had stopped working. It was nice, after the plush of Hollywood, to sleep on a cot in the ugly living room, crowded with stuff that poor people can't bring themselves to throw away, nice to talk about what we would have for the good dinner to which one of many old ladies would be invited to show off my aunts' quiet pride in me. Nicest of all was to take a small piece of all the Hollywood money and buy them new winter coats and dresses at Maison Blanche, to be delivered after I left for fear that they'd make me return them if I were there, and then to go along to Solari's, the fine grocers, and load a taxi with delicacies they liked and would never buy, hear Jenny protest over the calves'-foot jelly she liked so much and watch Hannah's lovely, greedy eyes deny the words she made over the cans of giant Belgian asparagus.

The taxi driver and I were piling in the Solari cartons when I saw Willy staring at me from across the street. He was much older: the large body hung now with loose flesh, the hair was tumbled, the heavy face lined and colored sick. I crossed the street and kissed him. He put an arm around me and pressed my head to his shoulder.

He said very softly, "So you turned into a writer? Come and have lunch with me."

He paid the taxi driver to take the stuff to my aunts' house and we walked a few blocks to Decatur Street and turned into an old building facing the river that had a large sign saying, "Guacosta Fruit Import Company." As we went up the steps he said, "This is my company, I am rich again. Do you need anything money can buy?"

Directly opposite the stair landing was an enormous room entirely filled by a dining room table. Along the table, at intervals of ten or twelve chairs, were printed signs, "French," "Mexican," "German," "Creole," "Plain steaks, chops," and seated at the table, sometimes in groups of four or five, occasionally alone, were perhaps twenty men who looked like, and maybe were, the men I had seen at Willy's house on the Sundays so many years before.

Willy put his arm around me, "What kind of food, kid? There's a different good chef for each kind." When I chose Creole, he whispered to the two men who were sitting in that section and they rose and moved down the table. We must have had a lot of wine because our lunch lasted long after everybody left and I didn't get back to my aunts until six that evening, and then I was so rocky that I had a hard time convincing them not to send for a doctor and during the night, through the thin walls, I heard them talking, and twice Hannah came to turn on the light and look down at me.

I was in the shower the next morning when there was a knock on the bathroom door and Willy said, "Come along. We're going to the country."

Going down the steps, I saw my aunts in the garden. I called out and Hannah waved, but Jenny turned her back, and Hannah dropped her hand.

Toward midday we went through the town of Hammond and Willy said, "In a few minutes." The long driveway, lined with moss oak, ended at a galleried plantation house. "We're home," he said. It was a beautiful, half empty house of oval rooms and delicate colors. Beyond the great lawns were strawberry fields and, in the distance, ten or twelve horses moved slowly in a field.

I said, "I like my farm in Pleasantville. But there's nothing like the look of Southern land, or there's no way for me to get over thinking so. It's home for me still."

"I'll give you this place," he said. "I'd like you to have it."

Late in the afternoon, after a long walk in the strawberry acres, I said my aunts would be hurt if I didn't have dinner with them. We had an argument about that, and then we started back to New Orleans. Willy's driving was erratic and I realized that he had had a great deal to drink during the day. When we took a swerve I saw that he had been dozing at the wheel. He stopped the car, said he thought I should drive, and he slept all the way to the outskirts of New Orleans.

I hadn't expected the voice, nor the soberness with which he said, "Pull over for a minute."

We stopped in the flat land that was beginning then to be as ugly as it is now.

"When are you going to Los Angeles?"

"Tomorrow morning."

"Do you have to?"

"No. I don't have to do anything," believing, as I had done all my life that was true, or believing it for the minute I said it.

"I've been faking. I'm broke, more than I've ever been. Stone broke. That lovely house will have to go this week, I guess, and I haven't got the stuff to pay a month's rent on the office. I owe everybody from here to Memphis to Costa Rica."

"I have some money now," I said.

"Don't do that," he said sharply, "don't say it again." He got out of the car, walked around it and came to my window. His face was gay and he was grinning now. "I am going to Central America on Friday. I'll move the way I first went as a boy, on mules. I'm the best banana buyer in the world. I'll get all the credit I want when I get there, San José, Cartago. Three or four months. I can't tell you how I want to go the way I did when I was young. It's rough country and wonderful. Come with me. You'll see with me what you could never see without me. A mule hurts, at first, but if I were your age ..." He touched my hand. "Anyway it's time you and I finished what we have already started. Come on."

That night, at dinner, I told my aunts I would not be leaving them until Friday. Hannah was pleased but Jenny said nothing. The next morning when I went into the dining room, Jenny pointed to a large florist box and watched me unwrap a dozen orchid sprays. She said Willy had phoned and left the name of a man who made fine riding boots, he had ordered me two pairs and I was to go down immediately, fit them, and come to his office for lunch. I was uneasy at the expression on Jenny's face and went to get dressed. When I came back she was sitting in the hall opposite my door, Hannah standing next to her. She raised her hand and Hannah disappeared.

"You're going riding on a horse?"

"Yes," I said.

"As I remember your riding, you don't need made-to-order boots."

"I'm going to Central America for a few months."

Jenny had rheumatism and always moved with difficulty. Now she got out of the chair, holding to a table. When I moved to help her she pulled her arm away from me.

"In that case," she said, "you can't stay here. You have been our child, maybe more, but you can't stay here."

I said, "Jenny! Jenny!" But she pushed passed me and slammed the door of the kitchen.

I lay on the bed for a long time but after a while I packed my bags and went to find a taxicab. It was raining a little and they were scarce that day and by the time I reached St. Charles Avenue there was a sudden, frightening curtain of rain, so common in New Orleans. I went into a restaurant and had a drink.

I phoned the Beverly Hills house from the restaurant. I said to Hammett, "I'm in New Orleans. I'm not coming back to Hollywood for a while and I didn't want you to worry."

"How are you?" he said.

"O.K. and you?"

"I'm O.K. I miss you."

"I miss you, too. Is there a lady in my bedroom?"

He laughed. "I don't think so, but they come and go. Except you. You just go."

"I had good reason," I said.

"Yes," he said, "you did."

"Anyway," I said, "I'll be back in a few months. Take care of yourself and I'll call you when I come back. Maybe then we won't have to talk about reasons and can just have a nice dinner."

"No," he said, "I don't think so. I'm not crazy about women who sleep with murderers."

"I haven't slept with him. And he's never killed anybody."

"No," he said, "he just hired people to do it for him. I was in that racket for a lot of years and I don't like it." He sighed. "Do what you want. Have a nice time but don't call me."

I flew to Los Angeles that night. I didn't telephone Dash but somebody must have told him I was there because after about ten days he called me, said he was on the wagon, and we had a nice dinner together. I never saw Willy again and never had an answer to the letter I had mailed from New Orleans.

On my birthday that year my aunts sent a hand-knitted sweater and the usual box of pralines with a note saying all the usual affectionate things and adding, as a postscript, that Willy had gone into bankruptcy and barely avoided jail for reasons they couldn't figure out. And not many months after that I had a telephone call from a man I knew who worked on a New Orleans newspaper. He said that Willy, driving up the road to Hammond and the strawberry plantation, with two men, had had an automobile accident that killed everybody in the car, and did I want to comment for the obit.

Years later, Caroline Ducky's grandchild, who had worked for Willy as a cleaning woman, said it hadn't been any mystery, that accident, because he had started out dead drunk from a one-room, cockroach apartment he had rented on Bourbon Street.

165

Two Other Southern Cities: Birmingham and Mobile

CARL CARMER

Carl Carmer first published *Stars Fell on Alabama* in 1934. In the "Foreword", he describes Alabama as "a land with a spell on it", and a "strange country in which I once lived". Amongst his other works are *Deep South* (poems), *America Sings* and *Hurricane's Children.*

Birmingham

There is a spot on the pike that enters Birmingham from the north where, a dozen miles away, one may catch his first glimpse of a city residence. To a man who has been traveling through wooded hills and valleys all day, passing little villages whose general stores and post offices bear the unmistakable imprint of American Southern life, the sight of a Roman temple at the summit of a mountain comes as something of a shock. Many a motorist has gazed upon that circular colonnade and driven on wondering about mirages and the tricks the sun's rays play on a man's vision. It is a far cry from the Tiber to Shades Mountain. Nevertheless, there on the topmost ridge outlined against the changing Alabama skies stands the lovely temple of Vesta, in exterior at least an exact replica of that jewel of stone that sleeps in the lowlands beside the yellow flood in distant Italy.

The fact that the temple belongs to a rich man who, having taken a fancy to its prototype while on a tour of Europe, ordered it built as his private residence only emphasizes the grotesquerie of its being where it is. This classic glory with a garage in its base is a symbol of the big town's quality, ever amazing the visitor though not always palpable to the blasé resident.

Birmingham is the *nouveau riche* of Alabama cities. With an arrogant gesture she builds her most luxurious homes on a mountain of ore yet unmined. Hardly a half-century ago she was the little crossroads town of Jones Valley. Now she numbers her population in hundreds of thousands. She has no traditions. She is the New

Source: Carl Carmer, "Birmingham" and "Mobile" from *Stars Fell on Alabama*, 1934.

South. On one side of her rises a mountain of iron. On another a mountain of coal. She lies in the valley between, breathing flame. The dark shafts of her smokestacks mock the beauty of the temple columns in the sky above her.

There is nothing of vanished glory about Birmingham. It is like no other American town. Only the mushroom cities of the West, springing up miraculously, like Tulsa or Oklahoma City, offer fit similes. The rhythm of living is quick. The air is alive with the catch-phrases of industrialism. Rotary and Kiwanis flourish. The kings of industry are the city's idols. Even religion is keyed to a swift advertising pace. Once a great banner hung across the busiest street announcing that Birmingham had more Sunday-school students per thousand population than any other city of America. And no one saw fit to comment on the incongruity in the fact that in the same week three citizens were illegally and outrageously flogged by members of the Ku Klux Klan, doubtless all duly accredited members of Sunday schools.

Birmingham is a muddle of similar contradictions. Her rich capitalists, many of them Yankees, rule the state politically. Yet she is the one city in Alabama where the Socialist party has enough converts to wield strong influence. Frequently the processes by which her corporations or her influential citizens attain their ends are, to say the least, open to a debate on ethics. Yet no city has a braver, more idealistic public press with which to combat them. Clubs devoted to the study of literature are surprisingly numerous and probably the best-known citizen is a writer, Octavus Roy Cohen (whose pictures of negro life on 18th Street never seemed truthful observation until the last year or so when 18th Street began to imitate them). But book publishers state that few Birmingham people buy books. With characteristic enthusiasm residents spend big sums on art but always for ultra-conservative work and usually for the second-rate. Itinerant art dealers on occasional pilgrimages from New York display only academic conventional landscapes before prospective Birmingham buyers whose fortunes were obtained by unconventional and daring methods.

The valley of the furnaces is an inferno. Molten steel, pouring from seething vats, lights the night skies with a spreading red flare. Negroes, sweating, bared to the waist, are moving silhouettes. On the top of a big mold they tamp the sand in rhythmic unison—a shambling frieze. Steel cranes, cars of the juggernaut, screech above the simmering red pools of spitting, rippling metal. And in the gardens that circle the temple on the quiet mountain the irises stand straight and cool in the moonshadows.

Such a catalogue of incongruities might be continued at length. But these few serve to show that Birmingham is not like the rest of the state. It is an industrial monster sprung up in the midst of a slow-moving pastoral. It does not belong—and yet it is one of the many proofs that Alabama is an amazing country, heterogeneous, grotesque, full of incredible contrasts. Birmingham is a new city in an old land.

Mobile

Mobile stays in the heart, loveliest of cities. I have made many journeys down the

Black Warrior and I have always found happiness at its mouth. And so I summarize my impressions rather than tell the story of a visit.

Few travelers "pass through" Mobile. The old city rests apart, remembering the five flags that have flown over her. Spain and France and England and the Old South, grown harmonious through the mellowing of time, are echoes in the streets. But since only people who "are going to Mobile" are her visitors, her charms have been less exploited than those of any of the other sea cities of the South.

Whether you come by train or by boat you arrive in the same part of town. There is a smell of hemp and tar about it. Long low two-story buildings, their intricate iron balconies interrupted here and there by signs—"Sailors' Supplies", "The Army and Navy Store," line the narrow streets. Sometimes the balcony overhangs the sidewalk and makes a roofed passage for pedestrians, ornate iron pillars supporting it at the street's edge. These buildings once housed a roistering assembly. The crews of ocean windjammers found liquor here in gilded saloons. They lined up at the mirrored bar with the bully-boys of North Alabama—keel-boatmen on the Black Warrior, planters' sons arrived by side-wheel steam packet from the wide estates on the Tombigbee, badman gamblers in extravagant apparel. One of these squalid doorways was the entrance to Madame Valerie's, where in chandeliered brilliance a soft-voiced Creole dowager conducted her salon of culture and lechery, her ladies advertised as educated, refined, charming; all sisters in profession, however, of the sloe-eyed ivory-colored quadroons in the "houses" nearer the water. The waterfront itself is no longer as picturesque as it was in the days of the clipper ships or the river packets. The gay welter of colorful types has disappeared. Where it once reveled you may sometimes meet a strange woman, ragged and unkempt—a small hat set on the top of her wide profusion of yellow hair. "Floating Island" the Mobilians call her and they will tell you she waits for a sailor lover who embarked fifty years ago and was drowned. Each day she looks out over the tossing horizon for signs of his returning boat—mumbling to herself.

Or, tottering along the cobbles on a sunny morning, Cudjo may greet you—a wizened black man who must be treated with respect. The boat that brought Cudjo to America was the last of the slavers to run the Federal Blockade. Hardly had he and his companions been delivered to the slave-dealers when the end of the war made them free men in an alien country. Huddling in a terrified group, they built their cabins close together—cabins that are now all empty save one—and in their little community they continued to use their native tongue. Cudjo is very old now. But he haunts the shores of the ocean over which he was brought, a frightened prisoner, so many years ago. He says he was the son of a king in Africa. Only a few words of the strange primitive language he once spoke so fluently remain in his memory. He repeats them slowly, knowing there is a reward. Where he stands all is businesslike that was once picturesque. The bustle of the quai has been supplanted by the silence of great warehouses. Above their dark massive screen white gulls circle and dip out of sight toward the waters of Mobile Bay.

It seems that almost any street of downtown Mobile will lead to Bienville Square—most revealing symbol of the city's quality. With modern business buildings completely surrounding it, the gnarled old oaks spread grotesquely, making sharp patterns of sunlight and shadow on this dreaming acre.

Business may be briskly American on one side of the street, but the Mobilian need only look to the other to feel the serene influence of time's passing over land and trees, in wind and sun and rain. The events that Bienville Square has seen, moreover, emanate a magic—a distilled essence of history which even the ignorant cannot help but feel. De Soto was here, Bienville and Iberville, General Andrew Jackson, Admiral Farragut.

It was near this square, the legend goes, that a German colony settled a little over two hundred years ago. Among them was a Russian woman whose beauty and prideful bearing were such that all Mobile wondered. The town's curiosity was soon satisfied. For with eyes flashing more brilliantly even than the gorgeous jewels she wore, the lady stated that she was wife of Alexis, son of Peter the Great. Her husband, she said, had been so cruel to her that she had fled from him to the refuge of a new world, and his pride had been so great that he had announced that she was dead. The story aroused such a storm of emotion in the breast of an aristocratic young French officer that he offered his name to her, and there was a wedding full of pomp and ceremony as befitted a princess and her noble consort. They sailed for France soon and lived happily ever after—so the story is told—even though it was later discovered that she was only a servant to the princess she impersonated, and had stolen the jewels. So Mobile provided America with a mystery of a Russian princess long before the days of Anastasia.

The air is soft in Mobile—filled with sea moisture. The tropics reach toward the town from the south. Palms raise straight trunks to the greening tufts that cap them. Fig trees and oleanders, magnolias and Cape jasmine, Cherokee roses and azaleas make the breezes heavy with sweet odor through the long warm season. It is a gentle air. Like the atmosphere that the people of Mobile create among themselves, it is friendly and easy-going. It folds with equal warmth about the white pillars lifted by a retired Black Belt planter and the wrought-iron patterns of a façade conceived by a French immigrant. Unlike the New Orleans Creoles, with their enclosed patios, Mobile's Latin colonists chose to build homes that looked out on the world. The lawns on which the French and Spanish houses rest have been green for almost two centuries. Outside the commercial streets down by the waterfront Mobile is a city of leisured space. The old part of the town is a honeycomb of exquisite design. Fleurs des lys in formal grace adorn a balcony that faces a wild profusion of grape clusters across the street. The bees of Napoleon, were they to take flight from their iron frame, might light upon the roses of Provence that clamber over the railings of both upper and lower galleries next door. At the city market, once the Spanish government buildings, the iron curves have a cleaner, freer sweep and they turn more delicately against the white stone.

Mobile has not always been a city on a byway. In the days of her glory the big-hatted, bright-waistcoated planter brought his wife and daughters down the Black Warrior for the theater, the horse racing, the shopping. Perhaps they embarked at Wetumpka on the famous *St. Nicholas*, its calliope tooting out *Life on the Ocean*

Wave to the panic of negroes along the shore. Or they may have come from Gainesville down the Tombigbee on that gorgeous packet *Eliza Battle*, fated to be consumed in flame with a loss of forty lives. In a bayou up the Warrior, a few miles from Mobile, lie many of the sisters of these ships. In that graveyard of the steamboats few names are discernible now. Perhaps the *Southern Belle* rests there, and the *Orline St. John*, the *Ben Lee*, stern-wheeler, the *Allen Glover* (named for her planter owner). An old riverman who knew them all might be able to tell which is the shell of that glory, *The Sunny South*, which the *Octavia, The Forest Monarch, Cherokee, Magnolia, Antoinette Douglas, Mary Clifton, A Fusilier, Empress, Selma, Eighth of January, Cremona, Fashion, Czar, Messenger.*

Paris gowns went back up the river. So did memories of Charlotte Cushman as Rosalind and Chanfran Booth as Shylock, of Parisian ballet, of Jenny Lind, of the race between the famous horses, Louisiana's *Ricardo* owned by W. S. Minor and Alabama's *Brown Dick* who belonged to Colonel Goldsby.

Though these days are memories now, the city has not forgotten. With all its outward semblance of calm, Mobile is gayest of American cities. Its free spirit, less commercialized than that of New Orleans, has kept its Gallic love of the fantastic and amusing. Behind the ornate balconies and long French windows that sedately face the streets live a people to whom carnival is a natural heritage.

While Mobile waited the coming of the new year, 1833, candles burning in the windows, the horses of dandies clopping daintily along the cobblestones of Dauphin Street, a band of young men in whom the liquors of many a bar rioted, descended upon a hardware store–accoutered themselves with rakes and cowbells–and turned the night into a bedlam. Thus the society of *Cowbellian de Rakian* was born. For a hundred years thereafter Mobile has had its mad, bad time of Carnival. Until the War Between the States, New Year's Eve witnessed its revels. Now the Cowbellians are no more; only the Strikers, a similar carnival organization, celebrate the birth of the year with a ball, and all the other social groups make merry on Shrove Tuesday at the annual Mardi Gras festival.

It is difficult for most residents of America to understand the social processes of a Southern coast city. The rigid formality that was once natural to the aristocratic émigré has now become a game that must be played as strictly according to the rules as bridge or chess. The Strikers' Ball given annually in Mobile at the old Battle House is a revelatory example of the quality that makes the survivals of social rituals in American life so charming. The Strikers are the oldest mystic society in Mobile. It is a popular fiction that no one knows who its members are though there is hardly a distinguished gentleman in the city who can truthfully deny membership. The origin of the name is explained variously. Some say that the first Strikers were markers of cotton bales; others that they were a group which broke away from the Cowbellian Society.

As New Year's Eve approaches an atmosphere of tension and mystery settles over the homes on Government Street and its environs. Débutantes look anxious, though they know that they at least will be present and be danced with. The hearts of post-débutantes and wives grow lighter when an envelope bearing the cherished "call-out" card, a masker's request for the honor of a dance, appears. The men of the house disappear frequently to attend unexplained "conferences" over costumes, favors, procedure. The younger men and the male visitors in town importantly make engagements for the "black-coat" dances that maskers unselfishly allow them.

The lobby of the old Battle House, as nine o'clock of New Year's Eve approaches, is filled with an excited crowd in full evening dress. They enter the ballroom to discover that curtains have been hung from the balcony to shut off the dance floor and the stage at the far end. Four or five rows of chairs, close to the curtains, are occupied by ladies, happy ladies who carry big bouquets of flowers, débutantes, sweethearts, wives who have received the "call-out" cards. Behind them sit the other guests of the Strikers.

At nine o'clock the band strikes up a march and the curtains are drawn. On the stage, grouped in striking tableau, stand the maskers. They may be in the laces and knee breeches of the court of Louis XIV, in the regimentals of the American Revolution, in the buckskin and beads of Indians, in the attire of any one of countless picturesque periods. Suddenly from the back of the stage the Captain of the Ball, in more elaborate dress than any other, leads out to the center of the tableau the girl who has been chosen by the Strikers as the princess of the night's revel. She wears a white gown and her arms are filled with red roses. There is a burst of applause as the two bow and then the Captain leads the girl down the center of the floor. Spotlights play on the couple from the balcony, sequins sparkle from their costumes, the applause grows deafening, almost drowning the blare of the band. Marching in single file the maskers follow the couple. At the end of the hall, while the Captain and his lady wait, they find their partners for the grand march—the first call-out. The Strikers' Ball has begun.

In the old days the guests were entertained at eleven o'clock with a champagne supper in the main dining room of the Battle House. The maskers had their supper in another room—a secret chamber where they might unmask without fear of being recognized. But prohibition brought the abandonment of a custom that may yet be revived.

Mardi Gras in Mobile is the most formal and elaborate function in modern America. Felix, Emperor of Joy, rules over the revels of this day of days. His identity and that of his queen are made known at a dinner in the Battle House on the preceding Saturday. They sit at the head of the central table. On Monday morning Felix proceeds once more to the Battle House wherein occurs a ritual entitled the Dressing of the King during which he and his knights attain at least a slight degree of alcoholic stimulation while he is being invested with the royal robes of his office. Thence the royal party is spirited by devious route to a government revenue cutter down the bay. The royal vessel, pennants fluttering, then moves up to the wharf at the foot of Government Street. Here King Felix makes his formal entry to the city, mounts his throne, and is borne through the streets in a vast procession of colorful and elaborate floats. In her pavilion before the Athelstan Club in Bienville Square the Queen awaits his coming. The throne float stops at the pavilion and a cupbearer brings His Majesty a silver flagon brimming with champagne. The King lifts it high in honor of the Queen, drinks, and the procession moves on through the crowds of merrymakers that line its path.

That evening at the municipal wharf the coronation ceremony takes place. Thousands crowd the vast building to its doors as the King and his court enter along a raised platform, over a hundred yards long, that runs down the center. Each participant in the ritual walks beneath a battery of spotlights the full length of this passage to the stage at the other end, on which the throne is reared.

After the coronation is over King and Queen and entire court in full costume appear at the ball of the Infant Mystics, their entrance heralded by massed trumpeters. This ceremonial visit at an end, they move on to other festivities throughout the city, ending their royal progress at a ball at the Athelstan Club where, regal robes discarded, they join in the dancing.

On the morning of the next day, Mardi Gras itself, the entire city is given over to masked merrymaking. Noon sees the parade of the Knights of Revelry and the Comic Cowboys, and the high float of the King sways through the streets again. The monarch's last appearance before the populace is in the flare of countless torches borne by strutting negroes to light the parade of the Order of Myths. That organization, founded in 1868 for the express purpose of dispelling the gloom brought about by the War Between the States, chose as its emblem the figure of Folly belaboring Death with colored bladders. The first float in its parade is always a representation of this emblem, and its annual ball on Mardi Gras night is always prefaced by Death's wild dash across the ballroom floor pursued by Folly who mercilessly whacks him with the resounding bladders. This ball, similar to the Strikers' in formal ceremonies, brings the day's revels to a close and the city enters the solemn Lenten period fortified by gay memories.

Mobile is a city of intimacies that have stood the test of time. On Government Street the houses shaded by magnolias and Cape jasmines shelter families whose grandfathers and great-grandfathers were friends. Along the azalea-strewn road to Spring Hill, the old Episcopal college, today as a hundred years ago, a black cook bears a gift of wine and jelly from her white folks' kitchen to the white folks next door. Affections are strong in this place, for they have been long depended on.

Even the heat of summer drives but few of the people of Mobile northward. Point Clear "across the bay" or Biloxi on the Gulf Coast a few miles away are pleasant enough for vacations. Country houses on the picturesque Dog River are usually filled with gay parties on week-ends throughout the year. At midday the city's homes are cool refuges and streets are empty. In the evening thousands of automobiles line Mobile Bay while a breeze from the moonlit waters blows inland and little sailboats scud about silhouetted against the shining surface.

It is easy to become adapted to the rhythm of this city. Acquaintances gradually become friends. The processes of earning a living are slow and comparatively unimportant to the living itself. Dignity and charm and gayety permeate life there. Mobile is a city of the lotos—bringing forgetfulness of everything except the pleasant passing of the hours.

Into the Desert:
A Footnote on Las Vegas

166

Fear and Loathing in Las Vegas

HUNTER S. THOMPSON

Hunter S. Thompson, born in Louisville, Kentucky, is one of the leading American journalists who came to prominence in the 1960s. *Fear and Loathing in Las Vegas* (1971) is an appropriate epilogue to any consideration of the American city. Subtitled "A Savage Journey to the Heart of the American Dream", it reflects both Thompson's individual style, as well as suggesting its terms of reference. Las Vegas thus becomes the ultimate *icon* of an America based on material and surface values. It is the city in a desert which, effectively, exists only as a series of advertisements and signs. Note the parallel use made of the city in *The American Dream* by Norman Mailer where it is the final resting place of the hero in his search for a negative point of belief. Thompson's style is characteristic of his work for *Rolling Stone* and *The New York Times Magazine*. See also Mario Puzo, *Inside Las Vegas* (1976).

Back Door Beauty ... & Finally a Bit of Serious Drag Racing on the Strip

Sometime around midnight my attorney wanted coffee. He had been vomiting fairly regularly as we drove around the Strip, and the right flank of the Whale was badly streaked. We were idling at a stoplight in front of the Silver Slipper beside a big blue Ford with Oklahoma plates ... two hoggish-looking couples in the car, probably cops from Muskogee using the Drug Conference to give their wives a look at Vegas. They looked like they'd just beaten Caesar's Palace for about $33 at the blackjack tables, and now they were headed for the Circus-Circus to whoop it up. ...

... but suddenly, they found themselves next to a white Cadillac convertible all covered with vomit and a 300-pound Samoan in a yellow fishnet T-shirt yelling at them:

Source: Hunter S. Thompson, from "Fear and Loathing in Las Vegas", New York 1971, from *The Great Shark Hunt* New York, 1979, pp. 633–41,

"Hey there! You folks want to buy some heroin?"

No reply. No sign of recognition. They'd been warned about this kind of crap: Just ignore it. ...

"Hey, honkies!" my attorney screamed, "Goddamnit, I'm serious! I want to sell you some pure fuckin' *smack*!" He was leaning out of the car, very close to them. But still nobody answered. I glanced over, very briefly, and saw four middle-American faces frozen with shock, staring straight ahead.

We were in the middle lane. A quick left turn would be illegal. We would have to go straight ahead when the light changed, then escape at the next corner. I waited, tapping the accelerator nervously. ...

My attorney was losing control: "Cheap heroin!" he was shouting. "This is the real stuff! You won't get hooked! Goddamnit, I *know* what I have here!" He whacked on the side of the car, as if to get their attention ... but they wanted no part of us.

"You folks never talked to a *vet* before?" said my attorney. "I just got back from Veet Naam. This is *scag*, folks! Pure scag!"

Suddenly the light changed and the Ford bolted off like a rocket. I stomped on the accelerator and stayed right next to them for about two hundred yards, watching for cops in the mirror while my attorney kept screaming at them: "Shoot! Fuck! Scag! Blood! Heroin! Rape! Cheap! Communist! Jab it right into your fucking eyeballs?"

We were approaching the Circus-Circus at high speed and the Oklahoma car was veering left, trying to muscle into the turn lane. I stomped the Whale into passing gear and we ran fender to fender for a moment. He wasn't up to hitting me; there was horror in his eyes. ...

The man in the back seat lost control of himself ... lunging across his wife and snarling wildly: "You dirty bastards! Pull over and I'll kill you! God damn you! You bastards!" He seemed ready to leap out the window and into our car, crazy with rage. Luckily the Ford was a two-door. He couldn't get out.

We were coming up to the next stoplight and the Ford was still trying to move left. We were both running full bore. I glanced over my shoulder and saw that we'd left other traffic far behind; there was a big opening to the right. So I mashed on the brake, hurling my attorney against the dashboard, and in the instant the Ford surged ahead I cut across his tail and zoomed into a side-street. A sharp right turn across three lanes of traffic. But it worked. We left the Ford stalled in the middle of the intersection, hung in the middle of a screeching left turn. With a little luck, he'd be arrested for reckless driving.

My attorney was laughing as we careened in low gear, with the lights out, through a dusty tangle of back streets behind the Desert Inn. "Jesus Christ," he said. "Those Okies were getting excited. That guy in the back seat was trying to *bite* me! Shit, he was frothing at the mouth." He nodded solemnly. "I should have maced the fucker ... a criminal psychotic, total breakdown ... you never know when they're likely to explode."

I swung the Whale into a turn that seemed to lead out of the maze—but instead of skidding, the bastard almost rolled.

"Holy shit!" my attorney screamed. "Turn on the fucking lights!" He was clinging to the top of the windshield ... and suddenly he was doing the Big Spit again, leaning over the side.

I refused to slow down until I was sure nobody was following us—especially that Oklahoma Ford: those people were definitely dangerous, at least until they calmed down. Would they report that terrible quick encounter to the police? Probably not. It had happened too fast, with no witnesses, and the odds were pretty good that nobody would believe them anyway. The idea that two heroin pushers in a white Cadillac convertible would be dragging up and down the Strip, abusing total strangers at stoplights, was prima facie absurd. Not even Sonny Liston ever got that far out of control.

We made another turn and almost rolled again. The Coupe de Ville is not your ideal machine for high speed cornering in residential neighborhoods. The handling is very mushy ... unlike the Red Shark,, which had responded very nicely to situations requiring the quick four-wheel drift. But the Whale—instead of cutting loose at the critical moment—had a tendency to *dig in*, which accounted for that sickening "here we go" sensation.

At first I thought it was only because the tires were soft, so I took it into the Texaco station next to the Flamingo and had the tires pumped up to fifty pounds each—which alarmed the attendant, until I explained that these were "experimental" tires.

But fifty pounds each didn't help the cornering, so I went back a few hours later and told him I wanted to try seventy-five. He shook his head nervously. "Not me," he said, handing me the air hose. "Here. They're your tires. *You* do it."

"What's wrong?" I asked. "You think they can't *take* seventy-five?"

He nodded, moving away as I stooped to deal with the left front. "You're damn right," he said. "Those tires want twenty-eight in the front and thirty-two in the rear. Hell, fifty's *dangerous*, but seventy-five is *crazy*. They'll explode!"

I shook my head and kept filling the left front. "I told you," I said. "Sandoz laboratories designed these tires. They're special. I could load them up to a hundred.

"God almighty!" he groaned. "Don't do that here."

"Not today," I replied. "I want to see how they corner with seventy-five."

He chuckled. "You won't even *get* to the corner, Mister."

"We'll see," I said, moving around to the rear with the air hose. In truth, I was nervous. The two front ones were tighter than snare drums; they felt like teak wood when I tapped on them with the rod. But what the hell? I thought. If they explode, so what? It's not often that a man gets a chance to run terminal experiments on a virgin Cadillac and four brand-new $80 tires. For all I knew, the thing might start cornering like a Lotus Elan. If not, all I had to do was call the VIP agency and have another one delivered ... maybe threaten them with a lawsuit because all four tires had exploded on me, while driving in heavy traffic. Demand an Eldorado, next time, with four Michelin Xs. And put it all on the card ... charge it to the St. Louis Browns.

As it turned out, the Whale behaved very nicely with the altered tire pressures. The ride was a trifle rough; I could feel every pebble on the highway, like being on roller skates in a gravel pit ... but the thing began cornering in a very stylish manner, very much like driving a motorcycle at top speed in a hard rain: one slip and ZANG, over the high side, cartwheeling across the landscape with your head in your hands.

About thirty minutes after our brush with the Okies we pulled into an all-night diner on the Tonopah highway, on the outskirts of a mean/scag ghetto called "North Las Vegas." Which is actually outside the city limits of Vegas proper. North Vegas is where you go when you've fucked up once too often on the Strip, and when you're not even welcome in the cut-rate downtown places around Casino Center.

This is Nevada's answer to East St. Louis—a slum and a graveyard, last stop before permanent exile to Ely or Winnemuca. North Vegas is where you go if you're a hooker turning forty and the syndicate men on the Strip decide you're no longer much good for business out there with the high rollers ... or if you're a pimp with bad credit at the Sands ... or what they still call, in Vegas "a hophead." This can mean almost anything from a mean drunk to a junkie, but in terms of commercial acceptability, it means you're finished in all the right places.

The big hotels and casinos pay a lot of muscle to make sure the high rollers don't have even momentary hassles with "undesirables." Security in a place like Caesar's Palace is super tense and strict. Probably a third of the people on the floor at any given time are either shills or watchdogs. Public drunks and known pickpockets are dealt with instantly—hustled out to the parking lot by Secret Service-type thugs and given a quick, impersonal lecture about the cost of dental work and the difficulties of trying to make a living with two broken arms.

The "high side" of Vegas is probably the most closed society west of Sicily—and it makes no difference, in terms of the day to day life-style of the place, whether the Man at the Top is Lucky Luciano or Howard Hughes. In an economy where Tom Jones can make $75,000 a week for two shows a night at Caesar's, the palace guard is indispensable, and they don't care who signs their paychecks. A gold mine like Vegas breeds its own army, like any other gold mine. Hired muscle tends to accumulate in fast layers around money/power poles ... and big money, in Vegas, is synonymous with the Power to protect it.

So once you get blacklisted on the Strip, for any reason at all, you either get out of town or retire to nurse your act along, on the cheap, in the shoddy limbo of North Vegas ... out there with the gunsels, the hustlers, the drug cripples and all the other losers. North Vegas, for instance, is where you go if you need to score smack before midnight with no references.

But if you're looking for cocaine, and you're ready up front with some bills and the proper code words, you want to stay on the Strip and get next to a well-connected hooker, which will take at least one bill for starters.

And so much for all that. We didn't fit the mold. There is no formula for finding yourself in Vegas with a white Cadillac full of drugs and nothing to mix with properly. The Fillmore style never quite caught on here. People like Sinatra and Dean Martin are still considered "far out" in Vegas. The "underground newspaper" here—the Las Vegas *Free Press*—is a cautious echo of *The People's World*, or maybe the *National Guardian*.

A week in Vegas is like stumbling into a Time Warp, a regression to the late fifties. Which is wholly understandable when you see the people who come here, the big Spenders from places like Denver and Dallas. Along with National Elks Club conventions (no niggers allowed) and the All-West Volunteer Sheepherders' Rally. These are people who go absolutely crazy at the sight of an old hooker stripping down to her pasties and prancing out on the runway to the big-beat sound of a dozen 50-year-old junkies kicking out the jams on "September Song."

It was some time around three when we pulled into the parking lot of the North Vegas diner. I was looking for a copy of the Los Angeles *Times*, for news of the outside world, but a quick glance at the newspaper racks made a bad joke of the notion. They don't need the *Times* in North Vegas. No news is good news.

"Fuck newspapers," said my attorney. "What we need right now is coffee."

I agreed, but I stole a copy of the Vegas *Sun* anyway. It was yesterday's edition, but I didn't care. The idea of entering a coffee shop without a newspaper in my hands made me nervous. There was always the Sports Section; get wired on the baseball scores and pro-football rumors: "Bart Starr Beaten by Thugs in Chicago Tavern; Packers Seek Trade" ... "Namath Quits Jets to be Governor of Alabama" ... and a speculative piece on page 46 about a rookie sensation named Harrison Fire, out of Grambling: runs the hundred in nine flat, 344 pounds and still growing.

"This man Fire has definite promise," says the coach. "Yesterday, before practice, he destroyed a Greyhound Bus with his bare hands, and last night he killed a subway. He's a natural for color TV. I'm not one to play favorites, but it looks like we'll have to make room for him."

Indeed. There is always room on TV for a man who can beat people to jelly in nine flat ... But not many of these were gathered, on this night, in the North Star Coffee Lounge. We had the place to ourselves—which proved to be fortunate, because we'd eaten two more pellets of mescaline on the way over, and the effects were beginning to manifest.

My attorney was no longer vomiting, or even acting sick. He ordered coffee with the authority of a man long accustomed to quick service. The waitress had the appearance of a very old hooker who had finally found her place in life. She was definitely *in charge* here, and she eyed us with obvious disapproval as we settled onto our stools.

I wasn't paying much attention. The North Star Coffee Lounge seemed like a fairly safe haven from our storms. There are some you go into—in this line of work—that you know will be heavy. The details don't matter. All you know, for sure, is that your brain starts humming with brutal vibes as you approach the front door. Something wild and evil is about to happen; and it's going to involve *you*.

But there was nothing in the atmosphere of the North Star to put me on my guard. The waitress was passively hostile, but I was accustomed to that. She was a big woman. Not fat, but large in every way, long sinewy arms and a brawler's jawbone. A burned-out caricature of Jane Russell: big head of dark hair, face slashed with lipstick and a 48 Double-E chest that was probably spectacular about twenty years ago when she might have been a Mama for the Hell's Angels chapter in Berdoo ... but now she was strapped up in a giant pink elastic brassiere that showed like a bandage through the sweaty white rayon of her uniform.

Probably she was married to somebody, but I didn't feel like speculating. All I wanted from her, tonight, was a cup of black coffee and a 29¢ hamburger with pickles and onions. No hassles, no talk—just a place to rest and re-group. I wasn't even hungry.

My attorney had no newspaper or anything else to compel his attention. So he focused, out of boredom, on the waitress. She was taking our orders like a robot when he punched through her crust with a demand for "two glasses of ice water—with ice."

My attorney drank his in one long gulp, then asked for another. I noticed that the waitress seemed tense.

Fuck it, I thought. I was reading the funnies.

About ten minutes later, when she brought the hamburgers, I saw my attorney hand her a napkin with something printed on it. He did it very casually, with no expression at all on his face. But I knew, from the vibes, that our peace was about to be shattered.

"What was that?" I asked him.

He shrugged, smiling vaguely at the waitress who was standing about ten feet away, at the end of the counter, keeping her back to us while she pondered the napkin. Finally she turned and stared ... then she stepped resolutely forward and tossed the napkin at my attorney.

"What *is* this?" she snapped.

"A napkin," said my attorney.

There was a moment of nasty silence, then she began screaming: "Don't give me that bullshit! I *know* what it means! You goddamn fat pimp bastard!"

My attorney picked up the napkin, looked at what he'd written, then dropped it back on the counter. "That's the name of a horse I used to own," he said calmly. "What's *wrong* with you?"

"You sonofabitch!" she screamed. "I take a lot of shit in this space, but I sure as hell don't have to take it off a *spic pimp!*"

Jesus! I thought. What's happening? I was watching the woman's hands, hoping she wouldn't pick up anything sharp or heavy. I picked up the napkin and read what the bastard had printed on it, in careful red letters: "Back Door Beauty?" The Question mark was emphasized.

The woman was screaming again: "Pay your bill and get the hell out! You want me to call the cops?"

I reached for my wallet, but my attorney was already on his feet, never taking his eyes off the woman ... then he reached under his shirt, not into his pocket, coming up suddenly with the Gerber Mini-Magnum, a nasty silver blade which the waitress seemed to understand instantly.

She froze: her eyes fixed about six feet down the aisle and lifted the receiver off the hook of the pay phone. He sliced it off, then brought the receiver back to his stool and sat down.

The waitress didn't move. I was stupid with shock, not knowing whether to run or start laughing.

"How much is that lemon meringue pie?" my attorney asked. His voice was casual, as if he had just wandered into the place and was debating what to order.

"Thirty-five cents!" the woman blurted. Her eyes were turgid with fear, but her brain was apparently functioning on some basic motor survival level.

My attorney laughed. "I mean the *whole* pie," he said.

She moaned.

My attorney put a bill on the counter. "Let's say it's five dollars," he said. "OK?"

She nodded, still frozen, watching my attorney as he walked around the counter and got the pie out of the display case. I prepared to leave.

The waitress was clearly in shock. The sight of the blade, jerked out in the heat of an argument, had apparently triggered bad memories. The glazed look in her eyes said her throat had been cut. She was still in the grip of paralysis when we left.